R $150

Brand Library & Art Center
1601 West Mountain Street
Glendale, CA 91201
(818) 548-2051
www.brandlibrary.org

ART LAW

PRACTISING LAW INSTITUTE®

RALPH E. LERNER

JUDITH BRESLER

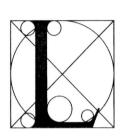 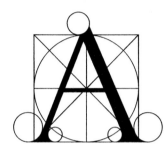 

The Guide for Collectors, Investors,
Dealers, & Artists

4th Edition

Volume II

Practising Law Institute
New York City

#38149

This work is designed to provide practical and useful information on the subject matter covered. However, it is sold with the understanding that neither the publisher nor the author is engaged in rendering legal, accounting or other professional services. If legal advice or other expert assistance is required, the services of a competent professional should be sought.

Cover Art:
VOLUME I: *The Dream* (detail) by Pablo Picasso, 1932 (oil on canvas)
Private Collection/Bridgeman Art Library
© 2012 Estate of Pablo Picasso/Artists Rights Society (ARS), New York
VOLUME II: *The Scream* (detail) by Edvard Munch, 1893 (oil, tempera, and pastel on cardboard)
Nasjonalgalleriet, Oslo, Norway/Bridgeman Art Library
© 2012 The Munch Museum/The Munch-Ellingsen Group/Artists Rights Society (ARS), New York

Slipcase Art:
Stepping Out (detail) by Roy Lichtenstein (1923–1997), 1978
Oil and Magna on canvas, 86 × 70 in. (218.4 × 177.8 cm).
© Estate of Roy Lichtenstein. Purchase, Lila Acheson Wallace Gift, Arthur Hoppock Hearn Fund, Arthur Lejwa Fund in honor of Jean Arp; and The Bernhill Fund, Joseph H. Hazen Foundation Inc., Samuel I. Newhouse Foundation Inc., Walter Bareiss, Marie Bannon McHenry, Louise Smith, and Stephen C. Swid Gifts, 1980 (1980.42). The Metropolitan Museum of Art, New York, NY, U.S.A. Image copyright © The Metropolitan Museum of Art. Image source: Art Resource, New York

Designed by Misha Beletsky

Practising Law Institute, New York 10019
© 1989, 1992 by Practising Law Institute
© 1998, 2005, 2012 by Practising Law Institute, Ralph E. Lerner, and Judith Bresler
All rights reserved.
Printed in the United States of America
Library of Congress Control Number: 2005907862
ISBN: 978-1-4024-1888-4
No part of this publication may be reproduced, stored in a retrieval system, or transmitted in any form by any means, electronic, mechanical, photocopying, recording, or otherwise, without the prior written permission of Practising Law Institute.

Table of Chapters

Table of Contents

VOLUME I

PART ONE ARTISTS AND DEALERS
CHAPTER 1   ARTIST-DEALER RELATIONS

PART TWO ARTWORK TRANSACTIONS
CHAPTER 2 PRIVATE SALES

CHAPTER 3   STATUTE OF LIMITATIONS FOR THEFT
AND BREACH OF WARRANTY

CHAPTER 5   PRINTS AND SCULPTURE MULTIPLES

VOLUME II
CHAPTER 11 COPYRIGHTS

PART FOUR COLLECTORS
CHAPTER 14 THE COLLECTION AS INVESTMENT PROPERTY

PART FIVE TAXES AND ESTATE PLANNING
CHAPTER 15 TAX AND ESTATE PLANNING FOR COLLECTORS

CHAPTER 18 ART LAW ONLINE AND DIGITAL ART

11

Copyrights

opyright law in visual art highlights the tension between, on the one hand, the stampedes of creative expression spurred by ever-evolving digital technology that has fostered a culture of mixing, matching, and recycling of images perfectly suited to the Pictures Generation and, on the other hand, the efforts of many creators of images to harness the global dissemination of such expression in order to reap the benefits of the exclusive rights accorded by copyright: the right to reproduce an artist's work, to distribute it, to display it publicly, and to create adaptations of it. The "Pictures Generation," the title of a 2009 exhibition at the Metropolitan Museum of Art in New York, refers to a group of artists who came of age, both artistically and chronologically, in a communications-saturated culture and who, working in an array of media, appropriate preexisting images for incorporation into their works of art.

Linked as it is to First Amendment rights (chapter 10), moral rights (chapter 12), and resale rights (chapter 13), the highly systemic body of copyright jurisprudence—involving also, as a result of the mounting exploitation of works beyond national boundaries, an array of international treaties promoting harmonization among nations of copyright protection (pages 981–993)—has a pivotal role in art law.

Although a treatise on copyright is far beyond the scope of this book, this chapter does present an overview of copyright law as it relates to artwork: a brief history of copyright; the basic elements of copyright law, including the Acts of both 1976 and 1909; the 1998 Copyright Term Extension Act; the exclusive rights that inhere in the copyright holder; joint ownership; works made for hire; copyright procedures; utilitarian objects; international perspectives; copyright infringement; and architectural works. Throughout this chapter, the terms "author" and "artist" and their derivatives are used interchangeably. Various forms issued by the United States Copyright Office that apply to the visual arts appear at the end of the chapter (Appendix 11-1).

While, as indicated later in this chapter, case law has refined the fair use analysis undertaken by federal courts in a copyright infringement action, we join those commentators who favor revising our copyright laws to accommodate a licensing arrangement that does away with permissions, that would yield payment to the author of the original image, and that would permit the author of the original image to opt out of any attribution in connection with a subsequent work based on the original image.

HISTORY

Historically, copyright has existed in two distinct forms: common-law copyright and statutory copyright. Common-law copyright evolved from court precedents, and statutory copyright has its origins in federal legislation. Common-law copyright afforded protection to works on creation without any copyright notice, and the protection lasted forever unless the work was published or registered. Statutory copyright afforded—at least until the United States acceded to the Berne Convention (discussed later in this chapter)—protection solely to works registered with the Copyright Office or published with copyright notice, and the protection extends for a fixed period of time.

The United States Constitution, article I, section 8, furnishes the basis for copyright protection in the United States. It provides that Congress shall have the power

> [t]o promote the Progress of Science and useful Arts, by securing for limited times to Authors and Inventors the exclusive Right to their respective Writings and Discoveries.

In 1791, Congress enacted the nation's first federal copyright statute, providing copyright protection for an initial term of fourteen years, plus a renewal term of fourteen years, and covering the making of copies of books, maps, and charts. The law was amended several times over the years to address successively broader categories of works of authorship and to provide increasingly longer periods of copyright protection. The Copyright Act of 1909 and the Copyright Act of 1976, as amended, constitute the present statutory basis for American copyright law, with the 1909 Act continuing to apply to works created before January 1, 1978. The Copyright Act of 1976 eliminates common-law copyright almost entirely, thereby simplifying the copyright system. All works created on or after January 1, 1978, are protected by statutory copyright from the time of creation in fixed tangible form, regardless of registration or publication with copyright notice.

ELEMENTS OF COPYRIGHT

Fixation

Copyright protection begins when an artist has fixed her work in a tangible medium of expression—that is, the artistic expression of the work must be placed in a material object, be it a block of alabaster, a sheet of paper, or a canvas. In addition, a copyrighted work must be fixed—that is, the work must be rendered in a sufficiently permanent and stable form. That requirement generally eliminates from eligibility for copyright protection such artworks as Christo and Jeanne-Claude's temporary installation pieces.[1]

Distinction Between the Work and the Copyright in the Work

A distinction must be made between ownership of the material object in which the copyrighted work is embodied, such as "a literary work printed on the pages of a book" or "pigment painted on a canvas,"[2] and that bundle of rights known as copyright that originally inheres in the author of a work. The transfer of copyright in a work is distinguished from the transfer of the work itself. Such transfers of copyright can be divided into three groups:

1. Transfers of copyright on or after January 1, 1978
2. Transfers of statutory copyright before January 1, 1978
3. Transfers of common-law copyright

TRANSFERS OF COPYRIGHT ON OR AFTER JANUARY 1, 1978

All transfers of copyright executed on or after January 1, 1978, require an instrument in writing signed by the owner of the rights to be transferred (or the owner's authorized agent).[3] The 1976 Act (effective January 1, 1978) specifically provides that the sale or other transfer of the ownership of a material object embodying a copyrighted work does not in and of itself constitute a transfer of the ownership in the copyright.[4] The converse also applies: Transfer of the ownership of a copyright does not, in the absence of an agreement to the contrary, convey property rights in the material object embodying the copyright.[5]

TRANSFERS OF STATUTORY COPYRIGHT BEFORE JANUARY 1, 1978

Similarly, the 1909 Act provided that a statutory copyright (generally, the copyright in published works) may be "assigned, granted, or mortgaged" but only "by an instrument in writing signed by the [copyright] proprietor."[6] And, like the 1976 Act, the 1909 Act specifically provided that ownership of a copyright is distinct from ownership of the material object embodying the copyright and that transfer of the material object does not constitute transfer of the copyright in the object.[7] Moreover, the 1909 Act provided, as did the 1976 Act, that transfer of ownership of a copyright does not, in the absence of an agreement to the contrary, convey property rights in the material object embodying the copyright.[8]

TRANSFERS OF COMMON-LAW COPYRIGHT[9]

It was recognized under common-law copyright (that is, generally, the copyright in and to unpublished works), no less than under the 1976 Act and the 1909 Act, that an author can convey ownership in a material object embodying the copyright while reserving the common-law copyright, but the statutory rules and the common-law rules then diverged. A number of courts in common-law copyright cases applied the rule (unlike the provisions in the Acts of 1976 and 1909) that an absolute and unconditional sale of the material object carries with it an implied assignment of the common-law copyright embodied therein.[10] As at least one major commentator noted,[11] that was an unfortunate rule, as it created a presumption of intent where such an intent generally did not exist. To avoid such a situation, New York[12] and California,[13] before the passage of the 1976 Act, enacted legislation generally providing that where an artist or the artist's heirs sold or otherwise transferred a work of art, the reproduction right was reserved to the transferor until the artwork passed into the public domain, unless the reproduction right was expressly transferred by a document in writing.

Idea and Expression

Copyright protects only the expression of ideas, not the ideas themselves.[14] For example, the creation of an elaborate theory of art or the construction of an ingenious method for installing an exhibition belongs to the realm of ideas and is, therefore, unprotectable under copyright law.[15] If, however, that theory or method is put in written form, it is then a protectable work of authorship and precludes the unlicensed copying of the expression of that theory or method, even though that theory or method is itself an unprotectable idea.[16] Although the idea-expression dichotomy was first recognized by statute in the 1976 Act, it has long been recognized by the courts[17] and was neither enlarged nor diminished by the 1976 Act.[18]

Accordingly, in the 2011 case of *Oldcaste Precast v. Granite Precasting & Concrete*,[19] a federal district court in the State of Washington denied the defendant manufacturer's motion to dismiss, on the issue of copyrightability, the plaintiff's copyright infringement suit. Both parties manufactured concrete utility vaults. The plaintiff claimed that the defendant had copied from plaintiff's catalog certain technical drawings of specific utility vaults manufactured by the plaintiff. The defendant unsuccessfully argued that the plaintiff's technical drawings were not copyrightable "because they all relate to 'unprotectable similarities in ideas, not in expression.'"[20] The federal district court disagreed, noting that the plaintiff was not seeking copyright protection for a concept such as a concrete vault but, rather, was seeking protection of a specific technical drawing that included particulars about various features of a vault it might later create. As the court observed, "technical drawings are expressly included as works covered by [the federal Copyright Act]. They are expressions of an idea: a utility vault, for example."[21]

An arrangement of artistic techniques that are not copyrightable element by element may, taken as a whole, be deemed a protected expression. In *Branch v. Ogilvy & Mather, Inc.*,[22] plaintiff Susan Branch, the author and illustrator of a cookbook entitled *Heart of the Home*, was asked in the fall of 1987 by defendant Ogilvy & Mather, an advertising agency, if she would be interested in preparing drawings, just like those in her cookbook, for the agency's print advertising campaign for a client, defendant Pepperidge Farm. The campaign sought to emphasize the old-fashioned image of Pepperidge Farm. Branch was interested and subsequently prepared preliminary drawings, called "comps," for the defendants, incorporating the arrangement of artistic elements found in her cookbook. Branch's cookbook was handwritten in script in black ink. Subject headings and recipe titles were painted in capital letters, using watercolors of varied shadings. The cookbook contained recipes, poems, pictures, quotations, and notes to the reader. Most of the recipes were enclosed in borders of lines, dots, flowers, and hearts in various combinations. Branch possessed a certificate of copyright registration for the cookbook's text and illustrations. Although Branch's comps were approved by Pepperidge Farms, Ogilvy & Mather ultimately hired a children's book illustrator to execute the advertisements for the campaign. Ogilvy sent the illustrator a copy of *Heart of the Home* and instructed her to base her handwriting on that found in the cookbook.

In April 1989, Branch brought suit for copyright infringement. The defendants, moving to dismiss the suit, argued that any similarities between the cookbook and the advertisements were that both works used the same ideas (handwritten text, borders, and the like) and that ideas are not subject to copyright protection. The court, however, found that in this case Branch's expression of ideas was distinguishable from the ideas themselves. For example, she expressed the idea of borders by creating unique borders for each recipe. As the court noted,

> [h]er use of lines, dots, flowers . . . distinguishes her borders from the otherwise infinite universe of borders which might have been created.[23]

In denying the defendants' motion to dismiss the suit, the court, referring to a previously cited case, stated:

> Although a plaintiff can protect neither his ideas nor his use of procedures and techniques to express these ideas, he can protect the creative arrangement and interaction of the techniques composing the expression. . . . [I]t is the combination of many different elements which may command copyright protection because of its particular subjective quality.[24]

It is settled law that the less divergence there is between expression and idea, the thinner the copyright.[25] As idea and expression converge in a work, progressively fewer aspects of the work embody unique expression. In such a case, the plaintiff must show near identity[26] between the works at issue in order to enforce copyright protection. When idea and expression coincide—that is, when the expression adds nothing additional to the idea—there is protection solely against identical copying of the work, rather than the broader protections against substantial similarity ordinarily afforded to works in which idea and expression diverge. (See discussion on infringement on pages 993–1027.) Accordingly, in *Gentieu v. Muller & Co.*,[27] a Missouri federal district court, in granting the defendant's motion to dismiss the suit on summary judgment, held that photographs of floating naked babies—that is, photographs of babies devoid of any background or props—were not copyrightable: A plaintiff cannot copyright either a photograph's subject matter or the poses used in a photograph.[28] Photographic elements that are copyrightable, according to the court, "include the photographer's selection of background, lights, shading, positioning and timing."[29] As the court further noted,

> the plaintiff, in using her copyrighted expression (lighting, choice of background, camera angle, etc.) has not expanded on the idea of a photograph of a naked baby . . . by utilizing her expression in such a way as to create a naked baby and nothing else, the plaintiff limits her copyright protection to the identical copying of the copyrightable elements of her work.[30]

Since the defendant previously used the idea and the technique present in the photographs at issue before he was arguably exposed to the plaintiff's photos, the case was properly dismissed.

Although a brass sculpture of five interlocking rings—the upper three having been modified to a lower case "a," "b," and "c"—was found to be copyrightable as the embodiment of an idea, the plaintiff-sculptor could not obtain a monopoly on the idea of the combination of the five rings, merely on his particular execution of the idea.[31] A glass sculpture composed of thirty-nine clear glass rectangles overlaying each other to form a spiral was found by an Illinois federal district court to be copyrightable. The placement, orientation, and dimensions of the glass panes and the degree of the spiral's arc were found to be a protectable artistic expression of an idea of a spiral sculpture composed of rectangular pieces of glass.[32] And although basic geometric shapes (such as squares, rectangles, circles, and ellipses) have long been in the public domain and, therefore, cannot be regulated by copyright,[33] the overall arrangement of such shapes on a page or canvas, for example, can be protectable.[34] A heart-shaped picture of the earth was found not to be copyrightable, as being an idea, not an expression.[35] In making such a determination, the federal Court of Claims noted that a court should neither draw the line so narrowly that . . . artists will have no incentive to produce original . . . artistic works, nor . . . draw it so broadly that future . . . artists will find a diminished store of ideas on which to build their works.[36]

In *Franklin Mint Corp. v. National Wildlife Art Exchange, Inc.,*[37] the Third Circuit affirmed a holding by a lower court that a wildlife artist did not infringe a copyright that he had once owned by painting another work, in his realistic style, portraying cardinals, the same general theme as the earlier work. In so holding, the Third Circuit observed that

in the world of fine art, the ease with which a copyright may be delineated may depend on the artist's style. A painter like Monet when dwelling upon impressions created by light on the facade of the Rouen Cathedral is apt to create a work which can make infringement attempts difficult. On the other hand, an artist who produces a rendition with photograph-like clarity and accuracy may be hard pressed to prove unlawful copying by another who uses the same subject matter and the same technique. A copyright in that circumstance may be termed "weak."[38]

Similarly, in *Concrete Machinery Co. v. Classic Lawn Ornaments, Inc.,*[39] plaintiff, a manufacturer and seller of molds to make decorative lawn animal statues, could not enjoin defendant, a manufacturer and seller of lawn statues, from making and selling similar animal statues, since the lifelike animals are common images admitting of only a limited number of expressions.

However, in *Maggio v. Liztech Jewelry,*[40] involving two manufacturers and sellers of decorative jewelry, a Louisiana federal district court, in denying Liztech's motion for a summary judgment on its copyright infringement claim, held that the parties' jewelry—composed of wire, beads, crystals, and other materials—permitted much variance of expression and that both the differences and the similarities of protected expression were issues of fact rendering summary judgment inappropriate.

In *Matthews v. Freedman,*[41] the First Circuit affirmed the district court's finding of no infringement in a case involving alleged infringement of T-shirts. The court held that the defendant's shirt, depicting the slogan "Someone Who Loves Me Went to Boston and Got Me This Shirt," surrounded by drawings of fish, a sailboat, lobster, a swan boat, ducklings, and a smiling sun, did not infringe the plaintiff's shirt. The latter bore the slogan "Someone Went to Boston and Got Me This Shirt Because They Love Me Very Much," amid drawings of fish, a sailboat, lobster, Faneuil Hall, and scattered hearts. In so holding, the court noted that the T-shirts reflected different expressions of unprotectable sentiment.

Originality

To receive copyright protection, a work of authorship must be original. That requirement was inferred by the courts from the 1909 Act[42] and expressly stated in the 1976 Act.[43] Generally, an original work of authorship is one that originates with the author and exhibits at least a minimal amount of creativity.[44] The work need not be novel; as long as the work is independently created and not copied from a prior existing work, it is granted copyright protection, even if it is substantially similar to or, in fact, identical with a prior work.[45] Moreover, artistic merit plays no role in determining what constitutes minimal creativity.[46]

A minimum standard of originality applies to the creation of a work of art: The artist need only show a "modicum of creativity" arising from independent effort to secure copyright protection.[47]

The foregoing principles apply not only to individual works of art but also to reproductions of such artwork.[48] Therefore, in *Alfred Bell & Co. v. Catalda Fine Arts*,[49] a British print producer and dealer who copyrighted in the United States eight mezzotint engravings of Old Master artworks that were in the public domain was able to sue successfully a lithograph dealer who produced and sold color lithographs of the eight mezzotints. The Second Circuit noted that federal copyright legislation explicitly provides for the copyrighting of "translations, or other versions of works in the public domain"[50] and that the mezzotints were such "versions." The court held that the mezzotints originated with those who made them and that the artistic effort and judgments required of the engraver working on the plates satisfied the originality requirement.

The minimum standard of originality was illustrated yet again in *Peter Pan Fabrics v. Rosstex Fabrics*,[51] involving the creation of a textile design. The plaintiff, Peter Pan Fabrics, purchased all right, title, and interest in an original design from Harmer Munro, an English design studio, and created a painting of a new design based on the Munro design. Peter Pan Fabrics then made printed fabric from the painting by "putting the design in repeat"—that is, altering the design's size and spacing to fit the screen or roller used to print the design on fabric, ensuring that one end of the design matched the other, enabling Peter Pan Fabrics to print a roll of fabric with a continuous design. The Munro design and the painting made from it were then destroyed by Peter Pan Fabrics to save storage space.

The fabric was first offered for sale in June 1985. After selling large quantities of the new design, Peter Pan Fabrics learned that the new design had been copied by the defendant company, Rosstex Fabrics, whereupon Peter Pan Fabrics registered the copyright and filed an action in infringement.

Rosstex Fabrics contended that Peter Pan Fabrics's copyright was invalid, since its version was neither original nor sufficiently distinguishable from the Munro design; moreover, the Munro design had been destroyed, so Peter Pan Fabrics could not prove which elements, if any, of the new design were original and hence protectable. In rejecting Rosstex's contention, the New York federal district court noted that "the law in this circuit with regard to textile designs is clear"[52] and, citing other cases, clarified the law as follows:

> The embellishment or expansion of the original design in repeat, so as to broaden the design and thereby cover a bolt of cloth, together with beginning the pattern

in a particular way so as to avoid showing an unsightly joint when the pattern is printed on textiles on a continual basis, constitutes modest but sufficient originality so as to support the copyright.[53]

In the 2010 case of *Universal Furniture v. Collezione*,[54] revisited later in this chapter, the Fourth Circuit, affirming rulings from a North Carolina federal district court, held that the plaintiff furniture company's compilation of decorative elements from different historical periods on its furniture met the originality test. Even though the component parts of the compilation were preexisting and not copyrightable, they were selected, modified, blended, and arranged on the furniture in ways sufficiently unique to satisfy the low threshold of the originality requirement. As the court elaborated, "[f]or compilations of preexisting elements, 'the principal focus should be on whether the selection, coordination, and arrangement are sufficiently original to merit protection.'"[55]

The Ninth Circuit's 2003 decision in the long-running case of *Ets-Hokin v. Skyy Spirits*[56] clarified minimum standards of originality for advertising photographs (also known as "product shots"). Plaintiff Joshua Ets-Hokin took a series of photographs in 1993 of defendant Skyy Spirits' blue vodka bottle for use in a marketing campaign. Skyy Spirits subsequently hired other photographers to photograph its vodka bottle and used those later photographs in its advertising and marketing materials. In 1996, Ets-Hokin sued Skyy Spirits, alleging infringement of his copyrights in the 1993 photographs. A California federal district court originally dismissed on summary judgment, holding that the photographs were not sufficiently original to merit copyright protection. On appeal, the Ninth Circuit in 2000 reversed, holding that the photographs met the requisite minimum standards of originality required for copyright protection. However, the court noted that such protection was limited here by the doctrines of merger and *scènes à faire* (explained below), because of the narrow range of artistic expression permitted within the strictures of a commercial shoot.[57] The Ninth Circuit then remanded the case to the federal district court with instructions to consider the two defensive doctrines. The district court once again dismissed the infringement suit on summary judgment and Ets-Hokin once again appealed. In now affirming the district court's dismissal, the Ninth Circuit commenced its reasoning as follows:

> Whether Ets-Hokin's photographs are subject to copyright protection is not before us.... We answered that question affirmatively in the previous iteration of this case. Rather, the question is the scope of Ets-Hokin's copyright within the limited landscape of commercial product shots.[58]

The Ninth Circuit went on to note that under the merger doctrine (that is, where a work's idea and expression merge), courts will not protect a copyrighted work from infringement, as that would grant a monopoly on the underlying idea. As to the related doctrine of *scènes à faire*, the Ninth Circuit observed that courts, likewise, will not protect a copyrighted work from infringement if the expressive elements of the work invariably flow from a commonplace idea. Acknowledging that the similarity between the Ets-Hokin photographs and the subsequent Skyy photographs is "inevitable,"[59] given that the photographs were for a product shoot of the Skyy bottle, the Ninth Circuit found that after applying the two limiting doctrines and subtracting the unoriginal elements, Ets-Hokin was left with only a thin copyright, which protects against copying which is virtually identical—nothing more. The court then noted that since the Ets-Hokin photographs and the later Skyy photographs were not virtually identical—it cited differences in lighting, camera angle, shadows, highlighting, reflections, and background—the Skyy photographs were not infringing.

The aforementioned cases should be contrasted with *Hearn v. Meyer*,[60] in which plaintiff, the author of a book entitled *The Annotated Wizard of Oz*, claimed that defendant, the author of a different book, infringed plaintiff's copyright in certain reproductions in plaintiff's book. The reproductions in question were *reproductions of reproductions* of three illustrations drawn by W. W. Denslow that originally appeared in the famous children's book, *The Wonderful World of Oz*. The plaintiff conceded that the reproductions of the original illustrations appearing in *The Wonderful World of Oz* were in the public domain, but he argued that his reproductions of those reproductions were entitled to their own copyright as reproductions of works of art. The New York federal district court disagreed. The court acknowledged that there were slight differences in coloration between the earlier reproductions and the plaintiff's reproductions but noted that the plaintiff never claimed that those insignificant variations were created intentionally or that they expressed the plaintiff's own artistic viewpoint. Accordingly, the court found that the plaintiff's reproductions were "mere slavish copies of W. W. Denslow's illustrations, as reproduced originally in *The Wonderful World of Oz*"[61] and, therefore, insufficiently original to be copyrightable.

Similarly, a Texas federal district court in *Simon v. Birraporetti's Restaurants*[62] dismissed a copyright infringement case on summary judgment when the plaintiff alleged that the defendant-restaurant infringed his copyright in a poster by creating an advertisement from it. In dismissing the case, the court noted that the plaintiff based the poster on his own photograph, which was in the public domain, and that the photograph and the poster were visually identical. Therefore, the court concluded that the poster failed to meet the requirement of originality necessary in a derivative work to entitle the work to a separate copyright. Thus, the copyright that the plaintiff had obtained in the poster was invalid, and, as a matter of law, the plaintiff could not support a claim of copyright infringement.

A work copied without distinguishable variation from a prior work—even though the duplication may require special skill, training, knowledge, and independent judgment on the part of the copyist—is not in itself sufficiently original to qualify for a copyright.[63] Thus, in *L. Batlin & Son v. Snyder*,[64] the Second Circuit held that the physical skill and special training required to convert a cast-iron Uncle Sam bank into plastic form did not display originality sufficient to support a claim of copyright. However, in *Alva Studios v. Winninger*,[65] a New York federal district court found that plaintiff's accurate three-dimensional half-scale reproduction of a Rodin sculpture, *Hand of God*, then in the public domain, together with plaintiff's distinct treatment of the rear side of the reproduction's base, was sufficient to qualify for copyright protection.

In *Gracen v. Bradford Exchange*,[66] the Seventh Circuit noted that a work derived from a copyrighted work must be substantially different from the underlying work in order to qualify for copyright protection. Accordingly, the plaintiff's painting of Judy Garland as Dorothy in *The Wizard of Oz*, based on the plaintiff's independent recollection of the movie and on the still photographs from the movie supplied to her by the Bradford Exchange, was not sufficiently original to qualify for copyright protection as a derivative work.

However, as the Seventh Circuit clarified in the 2009 case of *Schrock Photography v. Learning Curve International*,[67] there is no heightened standard of originality for copyright in a derivative work. The only "'originality' required for a new work to be copyrightable is enough expressive variation from public-domain or other existing works to enable the new work to be readily distinguishable from its predecessors."[68]

However, in *Mirage Editions v. Albuquerque A.R.T.*,[69] the defendant's removal from a book of artworks by the artist Patrick Nagel of pictures that the defendant then mounted individually onto ceramic tiles and sold at retail was deemed by the Ninth Circuit in 1988 to be a derivative work of the Patrick Nagel art book; that is, the defendant was found to have "recast or transformed the original images sufficiently" to so qualify. The court, quoting from Melville Nimmer's treatise on copyright, stated that

> [a] work will be considered a derivative work only if it would be considered an infringing work if the material which it has derived from a preexisting work had been taken without the consent of a copyright proprietor of such preexisting work.[70]

The court found that by appropriating and mounting the preexisting copyrighted art images without the consent of the copyright proprietors, the defendant prepared another version of Nagel's artworks—that is, a derivative work—and thereby infringed the copyrights.

Similarly, in the 1993 Ninth Circuit case of *Munoz v. Albuquerque A.R.T.*,[71] involving the same defendant and the same ceramic-tile-mounting process (defendant purchased an artist's note cards, mounted them, and distributed the resulting ceramic tiles), a federal district court in Alaska, citing *Mirage*, found that the defendant's actions constituted copyright infringement.[72]

Both *Mirage* and *Munoz* in the Ninth Circuit should be contrasted with *Lee v. Deck the Walls, Inc.*[73] (discussed on pages 934–936), a 1996 case involving yet again the same defendant and the ceramic-tile-mounting procedure with a fact pattern analogous to *Munoz*. However, an Illinois federal district court, in dismissing the copyright infringement case on summary judgment, found support in the Second Circuit for its determination that a purported infringing derivative work "must contain sufficient . . . originality to deem it a copyright infringement."[74] As the court further noted,

[t]here remains a narrow category of works in which the creative spark is utterly lacking or so trivial as to be virtually nonexistent. The mundane act of placing notecards onto a ceramic tile falls into [this] narrow category of works.[75]

In 1999, a New York federal district court held that a work that involves merely a photographic transfer from paper to fabric medium falls within this "narrow category," and is excluded from copyright protection unless the work involves nontrivial, original contributions to the derivative work.[76] Also in 1999, in *Cantor v. NYP Holdings, Inc.*,[77] a New York federal district court granted summary judgment in favor of the defendant newspaper publisher where the plaintiff's work lacked the minimal degree of creativity. The plaintiff, editor of a book entitled *The Graduates: They Came Out of New York's Public Schools*, alleged that the defendant infringed on his copyright interest when it published a newspaper article including photographs and their captions from the book. The court stated that the plaintiff's selections were "routine and obvious."

In the 1999 case of *Bridgeman Art Library, Ltd. v. Corel Corp.*,[78] after considering whether U.K. or U.S. law applied, a New York federal district court ultimately applied U.S. law to resolve whether the plaintiff's transparencies satisfied the minimum standard of originality to warrant copyright protection. The plaintiff, Bridgeman Art Library, was a British company that marketed reproductions of public domain works of art. After it acquired the rights to works of art owned by collectors and museums, it reproduced the artwork in large-format color transparencies and digital files.[79] Then it licensed high-resolution copies on transparencies to clients and provided them, free of charge, with low-resolution CD-ROM images as a digital catalog of available transparencies. The defendant, Corel Corporation, sold a similar CD-ROM in the United States and abroad.

The basis for Bridgeman's infringement claim was the following:

(1) the owners of the underlying artworks strictly limited access to those works;
(2) Bridgeman's transparencies of these works, from which it prepared its digital images, constituted the only authorized transparencies of some of these artworks; and
(3) by inference and conclusion, the images in Corel's CD-ROMs must be copies of Bridgeman's transparencies.

Bridgeman claimed a copyright in the allegedly infringed transparencies because it registered with the U.S. Copyright Office, and received a certificate of copyright registration for, a derivative work entitled *Old World Masters I*, a CD-ROM of images of substantially all of the reproductions allegedly infringed by Corel. Moreover, Bridgeman asserted that its works enjoyed copyright protection under U.K. and Canadian laws, as well as under the Berne Convention for the Protection of Literary and Artistic Works (Berne is discussed on pages 981–984).

In 1998, the New York federal district court, applying U.K. law, dismissed Bridgeman's infringement claim,[80] determining that the color transparencies were not original works and therefore not copyrightable. Bridgeman had argued unsuccessfully that its works were original for two reasons: the variation in medium from the underlying works was sufficient to support originality, and the images were original because they had color correction bars attached to them.[81] However, the court was unpersuaded by the variation in medium. As it noted, "[t]he mere reproduction of a work of art in a different medium should not constitute the required originality for the reason that no one can claim to have independently evolved any particular medium."[82] As to the color correction bars, plaintiff testified that they were employed to ensure that "the transparency is a genuine reflection of the colors"[83] of the underlying works of art, with the objective of creating transparencies as nearly identical to the original works as possible. In holding that the transparencies were not original works, the court also noted that the outcome would have been the same had U.S. copyright law been applied.[84]

On a motion for reconsideration and reargument, the New York federal district court, this time applying U.S. law, once again held that the color transparencies were not original and therefore not copyrightable.[85]

In revisiting the issue of choice of law, the court reasoned as follows. First, it noted that choice of law issues generally do not arise under the Berne Convention because Berne adopts a rule of national treatment: That is, authors receive in other Berne countries the same copyright protection for their works as those nations accord their own authors. Therefore, as the court noted, the holder of a U.K. copyright (the United Kingdom being a member of Berne) is entitled, if she sues for copyright infringement in a U.S. court, to the same rights and remedies that apply under U.S. law to holders of U.S. copyrights. However, as the court went on to ask, while the rule of national treatment clearly applies to the level of protection given to holders of foreign copyrights in Berne member nations, does the rule of national treatment extend to the copyrightability of subject matter? Continuing in this vein, the court raised the issue of whether Berne required the United States to enforce a foreign copyright—even if that copyright would not be valid under U.S. law. Raising an even more basic question, the court queried whether U.S. courts may even "give effect"[86] to any provisions of Berne that provide that the existence of copyright be determined under another nation's law. While it noted that the U.S. Supreme Court did not rule on this issue, the court went on to observe that Berne was not self-executing, that is, immediately effective without the necessity of ancillary legislation. The court then observed that the Berne Convention Implementation Act of 1988—the U.S. enabling legislation—provided that Berne shall be given effect under U.S. copyright law and shall not be enforceable in any action brought under the provisions of Berne itself.[87] Finally, in looking to the 1976 Act, the court cited section 104(c) of the act, which states in pertinent part that

> no right or interest in a work eligible for protection under this title may be claimed by virtue of . . . the provisions of the Berne Convention or the adherence of the United States thereto.[88]

Accordingly, the court determined that U.S. Copyright law is the sole determinant of what is entitled to copyright protection in the United States.

As to copyrightability, in applying U.S. law, the New York federal district court noted that since 1884, when the U.S. Supreme Court held in *Burrow-Giles Lithographic Co.* that photographs were "writings" under the Constitution's Copyright Clause, the courts have generally accorded photographs broad latitude for copyright protection due to U.S. copyright law's modest originality requirements.[89] However, the court also observed that there are certain instances—such as here—where photographs should be denied copyright protection for lack of originality: In this case, Bridgeman labored to make its transparencies "slavish copies" of the works of art, and while this may have involved some labor and technical skill, those qualities do not, in themselves, comprise the creative spark necessary to make the transparencies copyrightable.[90] The court also noted that while a certificate of copyright registration constitutes prima facie evidence of the validity of copyright, including the originality of a work (Bridgeman, as noted earlier, had obtained a certificate of copyright registration from the U.S. Copyright Office for its CD-ROM of images), the presumption is not irrebuttable.[91]

In the 2003 case of *Satava v. Lowry*,[92] the plaintiff Richard Satava, a glass artist from California, began creating and selling glass-in-glass jellyfish sculptures in 1990. By 2002, Satava's sculptures—selling for hundreds or thousands of dollars, depending on size—were offered in galleries and gift shops in forty states, including Hawaii. In the mid 1990s, the defendant Christopher Lowry, a glass artist from Hawaii, also began making glass-in-glass jellyfish sculptures. Lowry admitted that he saw a photograph of Satava's jellyfish sculptures in *American Craft* magazine in 1996, and that he examined a Satava jellyfish sculpture that a customer brought to him for repair in 1997. Lowry's sculptures resembled Satava's, and the latter sued Lowry in copyright infringement. A California federal district court granted Satava a preliminary injunction enjoining Lowry from making sculptures that resembled those of Satava. On appeal, the Ninth Circuit reversed, holding that the district court applied an erroneous standard of originality. The court, noting that ideas are not copyrightable, held that the idea of producing glass-in-glass jellyfish sculpture and elements of expression that follow from that idea are not protectable. While acknowledging that under certain circumstances a combination of unprotectable elements may qualify for copyright protection, the court found that such was not the case here: The plaintiff's selection of clear glass and the sculptures' shape, colors, proportion, and stereotypical jellyfish form were, taken together, too commonplace in glass-in-glass sculpture to be sufficiently original. While the court recognized that Satava's jellyfish sculptures had certain distinctive details, such as the curl of certain tendrils and the unique shape of the jellyfishes' bells, the copyright was so thin as to protect solely against virtually identical copying.

In the 2005 case of *Berry v. Taylor Gifts*,[93] the Third Circuit determined that a particular decorative, cement-cast outdoor sculpture, *Sculpture No. 646*, designed, manufactured, and sold by plaintiff Kay Berry, was sufficiently original to merit copyright protection. One of Berry's line of Garden Accent Rocks, the sculpture was a rectangular object having a stone-like appearance with a five-line verse from the public domain inscribed on its face. The verse appeared in a right-leaning font with the first letter of each word capitalized. In reversing a dismissal by a Pennsylvania federal district court of plaintiff's copyright infringement suit, the Third Circuit noted that

> [a] sculptural work's creativity derives from the combination of texture, color, size, and shape, as well as the particular verse inscribed and the way the verse is presented. It means nothing that these elements may not be individually entitled to protection . . . . When an author combines these elements and adds his or her own imaginative spark, creation occurs, and the author is entitled to protection as a result. This is true even when the author contributes only a minimal amount of creativity.[94]

ORIGINALITY AND SCÈNES À FAIRE

To elaborate further on the doctrine of *scènes à faire* (a French phrase literally translated as "scenes that must be done"), there are certain elements that must necessarily follow from a common theme or setting or that, for a particular topic, are so standard, stock, or common that they are denied copyright protection. For example, in a story about witches, one expects to find broomsticks, spells, and cauldrons; in a story about cowboys, one expects sheriffs, horses, and guns. Such elements are treated like unprotectable ideas, although the expression of such elements is protectable.

The 2006 case of *Reece v. Island Treasures Art Gallery*[95] centered on a dispute involving two artworks portraying a woman performing a hula movement on the beach: one work was a photograph, the other a stained glass artwork. The plaintiff Kim Reece, a professional fine art photographer, created and registered his photograph, *Makanani*, in 1988. The stained glass artwork, *Nohe*, was created in 1998 and was on display—but not for sale—at defendant Island Treasures Art Gallery.

At first glance, the works appear to be images of the same likeness: each depicts a woman performing a hula movement on the beach, kneeling in the sand with the right arm outstretched and an open left hand against the face. In each case, the woman is adorned in traditional hula kahiko fashion (kahiko being an ancient style of hula), wearing a maile lei and with long dark hair flowing behind her. Moreover, each image presents the woman from a perspective facing the left side of her body in profile and from the same angle and orientation.

Plaintiff Reece first became aware of *Nohe* when it was on display at the Island Treasures Art Gallery in May 2006 and ultimately sued both the gallery and the creator of *Nohe* in a copyright infringement suit, seeking to preliminarily enjoin the defendants from displaying or selling *Nohe* pending a final resolution of the case.

In denying Reece a preliminary injunction, the Hawaii federal district court observed that aside from the earlier-noted similarities between the two works, it "cannot say that these two images are 'substantially similar' under established legal principle."[96]

Applying first an extrinsic test, the court performed an "analytic dissection,"[97] which filters and isolates each of the constituent elements of the two works. In doing so, the court noted that any of the allegedly similar features of the two works must be protectable expression in order to sustain an actionable infringement. Here, the court found that the protected elements of *Makanani* are those that derive from Reece's expression of the idea of a hula dancer performing a particular movement: that is, the angle, timing, and lighting of the photograph, along with the expression of the hula performance and dress. Once the court separated the protectable elements, it applied the limiting doctrine of *scènes à faire*, which, the court noted, included in this case elements particular to the hula kahiko tradition and the dancer's hula kahiko dress. The court noted that when the protected elements of Reece's photograph, viewed in isolation, were compared to *Nohe*, the differences were clear: among such difference were the position of the dancer relative to her setting (one kneeling in the shorebreak with waves splashing her knees, facing the ocean, the other kneeling on the beach with her back to the ocean); slight differences in the alignment of the dancers' outstretched arms; the angle and thickness of the dancers' bent arms; the striking contrast between the dark and light and the shading of the sepia in the *Makanani* (all absent in *Nohe*); *Makanani's* expression of the traditional hula kahiko dress, which included leaves on the lei and on the wrists and ankles that were dark, full, and less clearly delineated in contrast to the bright, clearly marked green leaves of *Nohe*; and the serious, contemplative facial expression of the dancer in *Makanani* in contrast to the dancer's featureless face in *Nohe*.

The parties had agreed that Reece's photograph was entitled to "thin" protection, that is, protection against virtually identical copying, and the court concluded that in the context of "thin" protection, the two works were not virtually identical.

The court then applied the intrinsic test, a "subjective comparison that focuses on whether the ordinary reasonable audience would find the works substantially similar in the total concept and feel of the works."[98] The court noted that the different mediums in which each artist chose to work contributed to a different feel and concept of the works as a whole. That is, the court found that the sepia photograph's stark contrasts of darkness and light evoked a different feeling from that summoned by the brightly colored stained glass collage, the limitations of that medium rendering the latter work devoid of contours, shading, and depth. Moreover, as the court noted, the dancer's blank face in *Nohe*, rendering her anonymous, contrasts significantly with the model in *Makanani*, who is clearly a specific person, all of which contributed to a different response by the viewer to the two works of art.

Publication

THE COPYRIGHT ACT OF 1909

Under the Copyright Act of 1909, which is applicable to works created before January 1, 1978, publication was an event of critical importance: It marked the end of state common-law copyright protection of a work and the beginning of federal copyright protection. If a work was not published, it could theoretically endure forever under state common-law copyright. An author had to affix proper notice to all copies of a work when published, or else the work would be injected into the public domain.

An Illinois state court in 1948 held in *Morton v. Raphael*[99] that there was a publication of the murals that the plaintiff was commissioned to paint on the walls of a room in a Chicago hotel. On completion of her work, the plaintiff failed to secure a copyright, and the defendants, interior decorators engaged to redecorate that room, placed an advertisement in a national magazine showing several photographs of the newly decorated room, including the plaintiff's murals. The artist's suit for copyright infringement was unsuccessful, for, as the court noted, "it is universally held that where the work is made available to the public . . . without restriction, there has been a publication."[100] Since the murals were available to the public when they were painted on the hotel room walls and were open to the inspection of anyone who visited the hotel, that constituted a publication, causing the plaintiff to lose her common-law right in the murals.[101]

Although a number of other cases decided before the 1976 Act became law held that mere public exhibition of a work of art constitutes its publication,[102] the principle was qualified by the United States Supreme Court. In *American Tobacco Co. v. Werckmeister*,[103] the Court held under prior law that even though a work of art is publicly exhibited, a general publication of the work of art does not occur if the public is admitted to view the art with the understanding that no copying take place and with measures taken to enforce that restriction.

Following the *American Tobacco* rule, an Illinois federal district court held in *Letter Edged in Black Press v. Public Building Commission*[104] in 1970 that a public exhibition of a Pablo Picasso statue constituted a divestment of common-law copyright. The court noted that there had been no restrictions on copying and no guards to prevent copying. The court also found that there had been an unrestricted distribution of photographs of the statue bearing no copyright notice.

The 1909 Act contained no statutory definition of what constitutes publication. However, a definition did evolve through case law, indicating the following:

[P]ublication occurred when, by consent of the copyright owner, the original or tangible copies of a work are sold, leased, loaned, given away, or otherwise made available to the general public, or when an authorized offer is made to dispose of the work in any such manner, even if a sale or other such disposition does not in fact occur.[105]

In 1991, in *Schatt v. Curtis Management Group*,[106] a question arose as to whether under the 1909 Act the plaintiff either abandoned or forfeited his copyright in his photographic works as a consequence of extensive dissemination of copies of them. A New York federal district court ultimately ruled that although there was no abandonment of copyright, the plaintiff did forfeit his copyright in a single photograph published in the October 1956 issue of *Movie Life* magazine.

The plaintiff, Roy Schatt, is a well-known New York photographer whose photographs are often widely recognized. *James Dean: A Portrait*, a book of his photographs of the late actor, was published in 1982. (The photographs were taken during a nine-month period beginning in 1954, when Dean was a photography student under Schatt; an assemblage of those pictures later became known as the torn-sweater collection.) In August 1982, Schatt secured copyright protection for the book and for all the illustrations in it.

The defendant James Dean Foundation Trust was created by Dean's heirs to protect and market Dean's name, voice, signature, photographs, and likeness throughout the world. The foundation operated through its agent, the defendant Curtis Management Group, Inc.

Sometime after 1985, the foundation, through Curtis, entered into licensing arrangements with a number of third parties to market its alleged right of publicity in Dean. Among the defendant licensees were a poster manufacturer, a calendar distributor, and a manufacturer of wall magnets. Those licensees made products incorporating reproductions of one or more of the plaintiff's photographs of Dean, at times incorporating altered copies of the plaintiff's original work. In no case was the plaintiff acknowledged as the originator of the photographs; however, substantially all the reproductions bore a notice of copyright in the foundation's name and acknowledged Curtis as the licensing agent. The plaintiff claimed that in the summer of 1990 he noticed that many of his photographs of Dean were reproduced and incorporated, without his permission and without attribution to him, in posters, calendars, magnets, and the like that bore the copyright notice and the acknowledgment described above. Shortly thereafter, the plaintiff brought suit against the defendants, alleging, among other claims, copyright infringement of his common-law copyright.

In their motion to dismiss and in various cross-claims, the defendants asserted that the plaintiff, by his acquiescence and his inaction in the face of the wide circulation of copies of his photographs, evinced his intent to abandon any claim to copyright.[107] To support their assertion, the defendants asked the court to find that the plaintiff had constructive, if not actual, knowledge of the widespread dissemination of his pictures in various fan magazines and other publications and that his failure to defend his alleged copyright amounted to abandonment. However, because Schatt provided the court with evidence of actions inconsistent with an intention to abandon copyright, the court viewed the question of abandonment as a triable issue of fact.

The defendants next argued that even if Schatt did not abandon his copyright in the photographs, his failure to renew his statutory copyright constituted a forfeiture. They then offered several scenarios for the court to fix a date of investitive publication, that is, the date from which statutory copyright protection begins to run, and to thereby determine the date of public divestiture of copyright protection. As the court noted:

> The year of "publication" is dispositive here because if plaintiff published his photographs prior to 1962, any statutory copyrights pertaining thereto would have lapsed due to his failure to file for a renewal of the original twenty-eight year term as is required by 17 U.S.C. § 304(a).[108]

The court applied the 1909 Act because the alleged publication of Schatt's work occurred before January 1, 1978. Under the 1909 Act, once an artist chose to make her work available for general publication, all common-law copyright protection was lost, and her work could be protected only if the artist complied with the requirements of the act: publication with notice, registration, and prompt renewal.

Some of the factual predicates cited by the defendants for fixing a date of investitive publication include

(1) Schatt's dealings with *Life* magazine,
(2) *Movie Life*'s acquisition of the right to publish one or more of Schatt's James Dean photographs,
(3) *Modern Screen*'s publication of some of Schatt's works, and
(4) Schatt's sale of his photographs to fans of Dean before January 1, 1962.[109]

1. *Life* magazine acquisition. The defendants claimed that Schatt's offer to make his photographs available to *Life* magazine constituted a publication in 1954. The court, citing Nimmer, disagreed, as follows:

> If an author grants to another the right to publish his work, the grant does not in and of itself constitute a publication unless and until the grantee exercises that right. Furthermore, publication does not result from mere delivery of the manuscript of a work to a publisher, even if delivery is made for the purpose of having the work printed so that it may become available to the public.[110]

Therefore, the court concluded that Schatt's delivery of his photographs to *Life*, whether in the course of a commission or to offer *Life* a first look, did not constitute a general investitive publication that would start the running of the twenty-eight-year renewal period in the absence of *Life*'s publication of the pictures.

2. *Movie Life* acquisition. The defendants next contended that December 28, 1955, commenced the twenty-eight-year renewal period for a photograph of Dean, as that was the date Schatt made the photograph available to *Movie Life* magazine for publication in its March 1956 issue. The photograph was, in fact, used but not until the October 1956 issue. The court concluded that the defendants are entitled to a summary judgment on Schatt's claim of copyright in-

fringement as it relates to the one photograph of Dean published in the October 1956 issue of *Movie Life* magazine. As the court noted:

> As a matter of law, such publication divested plaintiff of any residual common-law copyright in that photograph and constituted an investitive publication thereby providing plaintiff with statutory protection of his copyright for the ensuing term of twenty-eight years. When such proprietary right was not renewed at the appropriate time, the photograph passed into the public domain.[111]

3. *Modern Screen* publication. As to Schatt's photographs appearing in *Modern Screen* magazine, Schatt claimed that because that publication of his photographs was unauthorized, it does not constitute a publication date on which to compute the statutory renewal period. As acknowledged by the court, section 26 of the Copyright Act of 1909 provides, in pertinent part, that

> "the date of publication" shall . . . be held to be the earliest date when copies of the first authorized edition were placed on sale, sold, or publicly distributed by the proprietor of the copyright or under his authority.[112]

As the defendants did not challenge Schatt's contention of lack of authorization, the court did not impute any publication date on the basis of the photographs' appearing in *Modern Screen*.

4. Schatt's sale of his photographs to fans of Dean. The defendants claimed that Schatt's distribution of "hundreds" of his Dean photographs to fans who visited Schatt's studio after Dean's death amounted to a general investitive publication of his work in 1955 and 1956. Schatt replied that between 1955 and 1962 only thirty-five to fifty people visited his studio to view his Dean photographs and that the sale of only one print through 1962, albeit that print bore a copyright notice, constituted a limited distribution, not permitting the fixation of an investitive date of publication.

The court disagreed. It reasoned that because Schatt chose to make a sale of a photograph with a copyright notice, his claim to copyright must be measured from the year stated in the notice; accordingly, Schatt's claim of any common-law copyright was divested as of the date of the publication with the copyright notice. However, as the defendants failed to provide the court with evidence as to which photographs, assuming at least one, were distributed with a copyright notice before 1962, the court denied that portion of the defendants' motion.

In the 2011 case of *Warner Bros. v. A.V.E.L.A., Inc.*[113] the Eighth Circuit determined, *inter alia*, that certain images extracted from publicity materials for the films *Gone with the Wind* and *The Wizard of Oz*, among other short film pieces, had been subject to a "general publication" and accordingly injected into the public domain. Here, Warner Bros. asserted ownership of registered copyrights to the 1939 MGM films. Before the two films were completed, publicity materials featuring images of the actors in costume posed on the film sets were distributed to theaters and published in newspapers and magazines. These images were not drawn from the film footage: rather, they were created independently by still photographers and artists before or during production of the films. The publicity materials—movie posters, lobby cards, still photographs, and press books—were distributed by MGM's parent company and did not comply with the notice requirements of the 1909 Act. Accordingly, Warner Bros. conceded that it had no registered federal copyrights in the actual publicity materials. Defendant AVELA had acquired restored versions of the publicity materials; from them, it extracted the images of famous characters from the films and licensed the extracted images for use on shirts, lunch boxes, playing cards, action figures, and the like. Warner Bros. sued AVELA, claiming that such use of the extracted images infringed the copyrights for the films. AVELA contended that the distribution of the publicity materials without copyright notice had injected them into the public domain, thus precluding restrictions of their use. Warner Bros. contended that the distribution of the publicity materials constituted a "limited publication" rather than a "general publication," so that the materials were not injected into the public domain. The basis for the Warner Bros. contention was that the publicity materials were not distributed directly to the general public but rather were leased solely to theaters under an agreement that required the materials to be returned or destroyed after the theater stopped running the applicable film.

In determining whether there was a limited or general publication of the publicity materials, the court looked to a framework developed by the Ninth Circuit "and adopted by several other circuits,"[114] that is, a limited publication is a distribution (1) to a definitely selected class of persons, (2) for a limited purpose, (3) without the right of reproduction, distribution, or sale. In working with this framework, the Eighth Circuit noted that the "return or destroy" provisions in the agreements with the theaters did not effectively preclude the theaters from buying such materials by the thousands to disseminate to the general public. Moreover, the court noted that the evidence indicated that the publicity materials were widely published in newspapers and magazines. Accordingly, the court found that MGM's parent company intended to abandon the right to control reproduction and dissemination of the publicity materials, with the intention of having them reach as much of the public as possible. As the court explained,

> [c]ourts have hesitated to find general publication if to do so would divest the common law right to profit from one's work but here it appears that [the MGM parent company] viewed the publicity materials as a tool to maximize profit from the copyrighted films, not as an independent source of revenue.[115]

Therefore, the court determined that the publicity materials were injected into the public domain.

On a closing note, any party acquiring copyright to a work of art created in the United States before 1978 must determine the circumstances relating to its publication. Although doing so may be difficult without the proper records, it is worth the effort. Otherwise, the acquiring party—be it a museum or some other institution, a private collector, or a gallery—may be unhappily surprised to find that the work has been injected into the public domain.

THE COPYRIGHT ACT OF 1976

Although publication is of diminished significance under current law, the event still holds some import. For one thing, notice is required on all copies of a work published before March 1, 1989, and notice confers certain procedural and substantive rights. For example, the registration certificate of a work registered within five years of its first publication can constitute prima facie evidence of the validity of that work's copyright. Registration certificate errors including failure to identify works as derivative works or copies of original artwork will not invalidate copyrights where they are not committed "knowingly with an intent to defraud or prejudice."[116] Moreover, if registration is effected within three months of a work's first publication, the copyright holder can avail herself of statutory damages and attorney's fees when appropriate.[117]

Unlike the provisions of the 1909 Act, copyright protection of a work created under the Copyright Act of 1976 and published before March 1, 1989, is not forfeited if proper notice is not affixed to each and every copy of the work. However, the work can be injected into the public domain if notice is omitted from a substantial number of its copies.[118] Moreover, any work under the 1976 Act can be injected into the public domain if registration of the work is not made within five years following its publication. In addition to registration, a reasonable effort to add notice to copies of works published without notice before March 1, 1989, is required to save the copyright on such works.[119] In most cases, there are no multiple copies of a work of art; there is only the original. (See the discussion on pages 959–962 concerning changes in the notice requirement for works of art published on or after March 1, 1989.)

The 1976 Act defines publication as the

> distribution of copies . . . of a work to the public by sale or other transfer of ownership, or by rental, lease, or lending. The offering to distribute copies . . . to a group of persons for purposes of further distribution, public performance, or public display, constitutes publication. A public performance or display of a work does not of itself constitute publication.[120]

At times, the 1976 Act's definition of "publication" has been somewhat narrowly construed by the courts. In *Vane v. Fair, Inc.*,[121] for example, the plaintiff-photographer, under an oral agreement with the defendant retail store chain, produced and delivered photographic slides to the defendant for use in the defendant's advertising mailers. The slides were devoid of the plaintiff's copyright notice, so a Texas federal district court held that such delivery by the plaintiff did not constitute a publication of the slides; rather, they were first published by the defendant in the form of mailers. In 2002, in *Epcon Group, Inc. v. Danburry Farms, Inc.*,[122] the Third Circuit upheld the copyright of the plaintiff's drawings where the plaintiff distributed architectural plans to municipal agencies prior to March 1, 1989. The court held that the distribution constituted a limited publication where the agencies were necessary parties without whose participation the plans could not be given practical effect.

Duration

The United States Constitution, to ensure the public's eventual access to the fruits of an author's labor, mandates that the federal term of copyright protection be for a limited time only.[123] Once the term of copyright protection for a work of authorship has expired, that work is said to have been injected into the public domain. Once a work is in the public domain, it is available to the public at large for the purposes of reproduction, distribution, adaptation, public performance, and public display—that is, all the uses that were once the exclusive rights of the copyright holder in the work.

WORKS CREATED ON OR AFTER JANUARY 1, 1978

Works created by individual authors that are not anonymous, pseudonymous, or made for hire (see discussion of each category later in this chapter) receive copyright protection from the time of creation, and that protection lasts for the life of the artist plus seventy years after the artist's death (life plus seventy).[124] Joint works receive copyright protection for life plus seventy of the last surviving artist.[125]

In October 1998, Congress enacted the Sonny Bono Copyright Term Extension Act (CTEA) into law, adding an additional twenty years to the then-current copyright term of life of the author plus fifty years.[126] The longer term harmonizes U.S. duration laws with those of the European Union (EU).[127] Such harmonization is essential in view of the United States's accession, effective March 1, 1989, to the Berne Convention,[128] the highest internationally recognized standard for the protection of works of authorship. As Berne prescribes certain minimum standards of protection—including copyright duration laws—for the United States, the EU, and its other member nations,[129] enactment of the CTEA undoubtedly has served to forestall infringement of a considerable number of copyrights held by U.S. authors and authors of works first published in the United States.[130]

The constitutionality of the CTEA was unsuccessfully challenged in the U.S. Supreme Court in *Eldred v. Ashcroft.*[131] In affirming the D.C. Circuit's decision, the Court, in January 2003, held that the CTEA did not violate the constitutional requirement that copyrights endure only for "limited times" and that the CTEA did not violate the petitioners' First Amendment rights.[132] The petitioners were corporations, associations, and individuals who alleged that they had prepared to use works in the public domain and that but for the CTEA they could have legally copied, distributed, or performed these works, which would have been injected into the public domain.[133] They maintained that "Congress went awry," not as to newly created works, but in enlarging the term for published works with existing copyrights.[134]

The Court granted certiorari to address two questions: whether the CTEA's extension of existing copyrights exceeds Congress's power under the "limited times" provision of the Copyright Clause; and whether the CTEA's extension of existing and future copyrights violates the First Amendment.[135] Addressing the first issue, the Court stated that in the Copyright Acts of 1831, 1909, and 1976, Congress provided for application of the enlarged terms to existing and future copyrights alike.[136] Further, the Court quoted a representative from the time of the 1831 Act who stated that "'Justice, policy, and equity alike forbid' that an 'author who had sold his [work] a week ago, be placed in a worse situation than the author who should sell his work the day after the passing of [the] act.'"[137] The Court also explained that the CTEA reflects judgments that Congress typically makes and that it "[seeks] to ensure that American authors would receive the same copyright protection in Europe as their European counterparts."[138] Further, the CTEA provides greater incentive for American and other authors to create and disseminate their works in the United States.[139] In resolving the first issue, the Court stated that

> the CTEA is a rational enactment; we are not at liberty to second-guess congressional determinations and policy judgments of this order, however debatable or arguably unwise they may be. Accordingly, we cannot conclude that the CTEA—which continues the unbroken congressional practice of treating future and existing copyrights in parity for term extension purposes—is an impermissible exercise of Congress' power under the Copyright Clause.[140]

The Court also disagreed with the petitioners' argument that the CTEA is a content-neutral regulation of speech that fails heightened judicial scrutiny under the First Amendment.[141] The Court stated that the Copyright Clause and the First Amendment were adopted close in time and that this proximity indicates that in the framers' view copyright's limited monopolies are compatible with free speech principles.[142] Further, the Court explained that copyright law has built-in First Amendment accommodations such as its protection solely of expression, and not of ideas, and its recognition of the fair use defense. The Court explained that "[t]he First Amendment securely protects the freedom to make—or decline to make—one's own speech; it bears less heavily when speakers assert the right to make other people's speeches."[143]

In summation, the Court stated that

> [t]he wisdom of Congress' action . . . is not within our province to second guess. Satisfied that the legislation before us remains inside the domain the Constitution assigns to the First Branch, we affirm the judgement of the Court of Appeals.[144]

Works Created Before January 1, 1978, with Subsisting Copyrights

Works under term of copyright—that is, works published with proper copyright notice or unpublished but registered—as of January 1, 1978, are protected for ninety years after the date of their publication.[145]

Works Created but Not Published or Registered Before January 1, 1978

These works receive copyright protection for the life of the artist plus seventy years.[146] In addition, the term cannot have expired before December 31, 2002. If the work was published on or before January 1, 1978, the term of copyright shall not expire before December 31, 2047.[147]

EXCLUSIVE RIGHTS

Under the Copyright Act of 1976, when a work of authorship is created, its copyright is born. The copyright vests in the creator of the work and consists of a bundle of several exclusive rights:

1. The right to reproduce
2. The right to adapt
3. The right to distribute
4. The right to perform
5. The right to display[148]

Each of these rights is subject to restrictions. Moreover, copyright infringement does not occur unless an unauthorized use of the copyrighted work falls within the scope of one of the five enumerated rights. The performance right applies not to pictorial, graphic, or sculptural works but, rather, to literary, musical, dramatic, and choreographic works, along with pantomimes, motion pictures, and other audiovisual works.[149] A discussion of the four exclusive rights that do apply to works of art follows, along with the relevant restrictions attached to those rights.

The Right to Reproduce

Perhaps the most basic of the exclusive rights consists of the right to reproduce the copyrighted work—that is, material objects in which the work of authorship is fixed[150]—in copies.[151] For a work to be fixed, its embodiment in a copy must be sufficiently permanent to permit it to be perceived, reproduced, or otherwise communicated for a period of more than transitory duration.[152] Thus, the duplication of a pictorial image on the sand or its projection on a television screen—

although perhaps violative of, for example, the display right—does not violate the reproduction right. Similarly, as indicated in *Amsinck v. Columbia Pictures Industries*,[153] exposure of the plaintiff-artist's *Baby Bears* artwork at various times in the defendant's motion picture *Immediate Family* for a total of ninety-six seconds was found by a New York federal district court to be "fleeting and impermanent" and, therefore, not a copy for purposes of a copyright infringement action. By requiring some permanence of a work's embodiment before copying can be found, the 1976 Act makes explicit what was usually[154] but not always[155] the law under the 1909 Act.

Infringement may occur even if the work is reproduced in a different medium or dimension, such as a sketch copied from a photograph[156] or a doll copied from a cartoon.[157] Moreover, for an infringement to arise, the copy need not be exact, as long as it is substantially similar to the copyrighted work.[158]

RESTRICTIONS

With respect to artwork, a few restrictions are imposed on the exclusive right of reproduction. For example, a library, under certain circumstances, has a limited right to reproduce an illustration where the illustration accompanies explanatory text.[159] For another example, if artwork is lawfully reproduced in useful articles that have been offered for sale or other distribution to the public, it is not a copyright infringement under the 1976 Act to make, distribute, or display photographs of those articles in connection with advertisements or commentaries related to the distribution or display of the articles or in connection with news reports.[160]

The Right to Adapt

The copyright holder has the exclusive right to make derivative works based on the underlying work of authorship.[161] If the derivative work is not itself an infringing work and if it meets the requirements of originality—that is, at least a variation "that is sufficient to render the derivative work distinguishable from its prior work in any meaningful manner"[162]—it is separately copyrightable. While the failure to note a work as a derivative on a registration application to the Copyright Office may rebut the presumption of its validity, such failure will not render the issued copyright invalid.[163]

In the earlier-noted case of *Lee v. Deck the Walls, Inc.*,[164] the mounting of 430 note cards of fifteen separate artworks onto individual ceramic tiles was found by an Illinois federal district court not to be a derivative work and, therefore, not copyrightable. By the same reasoning, neither was such a work an infringement. It was undisputed that the graphic artist Annie Lee held valid copyrights to the fifteen artworks in question and, therefore, had the exclusive right to create derivative works based on the artworks. A "derivative work," said the court in that case, is a work based upon one or more preexisting works, such as a translation, musical arrangement, dramatization, fictionalization, motion picture version, sound recording, art reproduction, abridgement, condensation, or any other form in which a work may be recast, transformed, or adapted.[165]

In addition, said the court, a "derivative work" consists of

editorial revisions, annotations, elaborations, or other modifications which, as a whole, represent an original work of authorship.[166]

The artist Annie Lee contended that the ceramic tiles were derivative works in that they were either art reproductions or the result of "recasting, transforming or adapting the original work,"[167] and she cited the earlier-noted *Mirage* and *Munoz* cases as persuasive authority. *Munoz*, in rejecting the defendant's contention that ceramic tile is a method of display, made a distinction between the mere framing of art and the mounting of a work onto a ceramic tile. According to *Munoz*, framing a work "does not recast or transform"[168] it; therefore, framing amounts merely to a form of display, whereas permanently affixing a work to a ceramic tile that can also be used, for example, as a trivet or a wall hanging transforms the work and renders it derivative.

The Illinois federal district court in the *Lee* case, however, rejected the distinction drawn by *Munoz* as being artificial:

The court chooses to focus on the artwork itself, not on the material on which the work was mounted or the ultimate use to which the tiles "lend themselves." The mode of affixation of the artwork onto the mat or tile is insignificant. In addition, the eventual manner of display and "use" of a product is not dispositive of the instant inquiry.[169]

Moving to the heart of the matter, the court noted that copyright protection

"has never accorded the copyright owner complete control over all possible uses of his work".... [A] person does not infringe a copyright by using the work in an unauthorized manner which occurs outside the scope of the copyright holder's exclusive rights.[170]

The plaintiff argued, in keeping with Ninth Circuit decisions,[171] that an originality requirement is inappropriate for copyright-infringement claims, but the Illinois court disagreed, looking to the Second Circuit to support its finding that "an alleged infringing 'derivative work' must contain sufficient creativity and originality to deem it a copyright infringement."[172] The court then noted that

the mundane act of placing notecards onto a ceramic tile falls into the narrow category of works in which no creative spark exists.... [Defendant] ART did not display any creativity in gluing Annie Lee's work onto the separate surface. ART did not reproduce the images ... and did not make any alteration to the drawings themselves.[173]

Accordingly, the court found that the tiles did not meet the definition of a derivative work and, therefore, could not sustain a claim of copyright infringement.

What constitutes a derivative work continues to vary among the circuit courts. In 1996, a California federal district court in the Ninth Circuit in *Greenwich Workshop v. Timber Creations*[174] held that the defendant's removal of copyrighted bookplates from the plaintiff's copyrighted book of artwork and the defendant's transposing of such bookplates onto matting and then framing and selling them constituted unauthorized derivative works and, accordingly, infringement of the plaintiff's copyrights in both the artwork and the book.

As in any copyright case, the standard for infringement is one of substantial similarity.[175] Copyright in a derivative work covers only those elements in the derivative work that are original to that work.[176] If the underlying work is protected by copyright, then copyright in the derivative work does not affect the protection accorded the underlying work.[177] If the underlying work is in the public domain, a copyright in the derivative work does not render the underlying work protectable.[178] Despite a line of earlier cases in conflict with the above principles,[179] the 1909 Act contained statutory language similar to that enunciated in this paragraph.[180]

Courts will adhere to specific provisions of a contract when the right to create derivative works is an issue in dispute. In 2001, in *Flack v. Friends of Queen Catherine, Inc.*,[181] a New York federal district court held that the specific provision of a contract controls where there is inconsistency between general and specific provisions with respect to the right to create derivative works. The defendant nonprofit organization commissioned the plaintiff artist to design and supervise the fabrication and installation of a thirty-five-foot bronze sculpture of Queen Catherine on a site in Queens, New York. Working at the defendant foundry, the artist was to sculpt in clay, from which wax molds would be made in order to cast the figure in bronze. In 1996, the artist began work on the thirty-five-foot sculpture, completing the head in clay. In 1998, in light of doubts that the nonprofit would be able to take delivery of the sculpture, the foundry terminated work on the project and terminated its agreement with the nonprofit. From that point on, the artist was excluded from further work on the sculpture. The nonprofit and the foundry later settled their differences and entered into a new agreement to complete the work. They discovered, however, that the waxes and molds drawn from the clay head had been damaged and new molds were required; but the clay head itself had also been damaged, so the defendants had someone rebuild it.

When the artist learned about these developments in 1999, she commenced an action, alleging a violation of her copyright interest. She argued that the rebuilding of the clay face, by using pictures of the original, constituted the infringing creation of a derivative work or reproduction. The nonprofit conceded to copying, but contended

> that (1) if the copying [were] a reproduction, then it was authorized under a provision of the Agreement [between the nonprofit and the artist] that designates both [the artist and the foundry] as the entities "responsible" for creating the 35' "en-

largement"; and (2) if the copying was so imprecise as to constitute the creation of a derivative work, then it was authorized under another provision of the . . . Agreement that grant[ed] [the nonprofit] an "exclusive, irrevocable license . . . to use the Art Work in furtherance of its not for profit purposes, including . . . the creation of derivative works and the reproduction . . . of the Art Work into souvenir . . . items such as . . . small replicas and models in mediums such as plastic, plaster or bonded bronze (excluding brass or bronze and not exceeding 15″ in height, including the dome)."[182]

The court held that the defendants infringed the plaintiff's right to make derivative works. The court explained that despite the nonprofit defendant's contractual right to create derivative works, the contract's express language controlled, and that language excluded brass and bronze models exceeding fifteen inches in height.

The Right to Distribute

The third exclusive right enumerated by the 1976 Act, the right of distribution, accords to the copyright owner the exclusive right to distribute copies of the copyrighted work to the public by sale or other transfer of ownership or by rental, lease, or lending.[183] Thus, the distribution right, in essence, is the right to control the publication of a work. Although the copyright holder's rights of public distribution cease with respect to a particular copy once she has parted with copyright ownership, such rights do not cease if the copyright holder has parted with mere possession of that copy.[184] Infringement of the distribution right can occur, for example, when a museum or bookstore sells posters or postcards duplicated without authorization from the copyright holder. Infringement occurs even if the objects were bought from a third party and were innocently sold by a museum or a bookstore without knowledge of the circumstances of duplication.

RESTRICTIONS

Under the 1976 Act, the restriction on the distribution right applicable to works of art is known as the first-sale doctrine. That doctrine provides that the owner of a particular lawfully made copy or any person authorized by the owner may, without the authority of the copyright owner, sell or otherwise dispose of the possession of that copy.[185] The 1909 Act contained a similar provision:

[N]othing in this title shall be deemed to forbid, prevent, or restrict the transfer of any copy of a copyrighted work, the possession of which has been lawfully obtained.[186]

For example, a museum, a private collector, or a gallery that owns a work of art may sell it to another, as long as the artwork was acquired from a party who had lawful ownership. The first-sale doctrine applies only to the right to resell a copy of the work; it does not permit any other exploitation of it except, under certain circumstances, to display that copy publicly to viewers present at the place where the copy is located.[187]

Under the first-sale doctrine, the copyright owner may make a profit on the first sale of her work but not on a further resale or rental of the work. However, influenced by such European nations as France, Germany, and Belgium, which recognize continuing resale rights for artists, California enacted a Resale Royalties Act in 1976, enabling artists under certain limited circumstances to recover a portion of the profit from the work as it passes through successive owners.[188] Responsive to California's initiative and to the European experience and influenced by pressure from artists' rights groups, the United States Register of Copyrights, in consultation with the Chair of the National Endowment for the Arts, conducted a study in the early 1990s on the feasibility of implementing resale-royalty rights for fine artists on a federal level. The study was mandated by the Visual Artists Rights Act of 1990, discussed in chapter 12 (Moral Rights). In December 1992, the Copyright Office published its report in a two-volume tome entitled *Droit de Suite: The Artist's Resale Royalty*. The report recommended against implementing such royalty-rights legislation, largely because of the questionable success of such legislation in most European countries and the problems associated with its enforcement. In addition, the report was critical of California's legislation, deeming it underused and underenforced. Further, the report questioned the compatibility of such resale-royalty legislation with United States copyright law, which addresses the public dissemination and commercial use of copies of works of authorship. The copyright report is discussed further in chapter 13 on resale rights.

As of this writing and as further explored in chapter 13, California's resale royalty rights legislation was struck down by a California federal district court, pending appeal, as being unconstitutional. In addition and as of this writing, a bill was pending in Congress providing for certain federal resale royalty rights to artists under limited circumstances. The bill is also addressed in chapter 13.

Courts often assess whether or not infringing distribution of copyrighted works has occurred in order to determine whether defendant's actions sufficiently establish venue and jurisdiction. In states such as New York, "it is . . . well established that offering even one copy of an offending work for sale . . . constitutes tortious conduct sufficient to trigger long-arm jurisdiction."[189] In 1998, a California federal district court held that a nonresident defendant's in-state distribution of a catalog featuring allegedly infringing photographs was sufficient to confer personal jurisdiction where the distribution resulted in actual sales being made in the state.[190] Where the defendant was not incorporated in California, did not maintain an office in California, did not conduct corporate activities in California, and did not make an effort to market or sell its products in California, the court held that defendant's contacts with California were not "substantial" enough for the court to exercise general jurisdiction.

The Right to Display

The final exclusive right applicable to works of art and codified for the first time in the Copyright Act of 1976 is the right to display the work publicly.[191] To display a work is to show a copy of it either directly or by a device or process. A motion picture, for example, is displayed when its frames are shown nonsequentially; when shown in sequence, however, the motion picture is considered performed.[192] To display "publicly," notes the 1976 Act, means to display a work

> at a place open to the public or at any place where a substantial number of persons outside of a normal circle of a family and its social acquaintances is gathered; or to transmit or otherwise communicate a . . . display of the work to [such] place . . . by means of any device or process, whether the members of the public capable of receiving the . . . display receive it in the same place or in separate places and at the same time or at different times.[193]

RESTRICTIONS

One restriction on the display right applicable to works of art permits the owner of a lawfully made copy of a work to display it directly or by projection of no more than one image at a time to viewers present at the place where the copy is located.[194] If, for example, a museum or a gallery owns a piece of sculpture but is not the copyright holder in that work, it may show the sculpture to the public directly or by projection, as long as the display takes place on museum grounds or on gallery premises and is not further projected to distant sites.

In the 2010 case of *Massachusetts Museum of Contemporary Art Foundation v. Buchel*[195] addressed as well in chapter 12, the First Circuit, in affirming in part and vacating in part the Massachusetts federal district court's grant of summary judgment in favor of the museum (known as MASS MoCA), held that there was a genuine issue of material fact as to whether MASS MoCA violated the artist Christoph Buchel's exclusive right of public display. In 2006, Buchel and MASS MoCA agreed that Buchel would build a large-scale installation piece, to be entitled *Training Ground for Democracy,* on the museum's premises. The installation was to include a number of integrated architectural and structural elements through which a visitor could walk and climb. The parties never formalized their relationship in a written agreement, and in the months following, conflicts arose involving both financial misunderstandings and Buchel's dissatisfaction with the way in which the museum was implementing his instructions and procuring the items necessary for the installation. Much of the time, the artist was off site during work on the installation. As negotiations over the project's completion stalled and it became clear that Buchel would not complete the installation, MASS MoCA in May 2007 announced the cancellation of *Training Ground* and contemporaneously publicized the opening of a new exhibit entitled *Made at MASS MoCA* consisting of a documentary project exploring the issues of col-

laboration between artists and institutions and exhibiting—albeit with yellow
tarpaulins covering the unfinished work—the materials and unfinished fabrications that were to have comprised elements of the installation.

That same month, the museum sued Buchel, seeking a declaration that it was
"entitled to present to the public the materials and partial constructions assembled in connection with an exhibit planned with the Swiss artist Buchel."[196] Buchel responded by asserting five counterclaims against the museum, including an
alleged violation of his exclusive right to publicly display his work. Although the
Massachusetts federal district court granted summary judgment in favor of the
museum, the First Circuit vacated and remanded the case for further proceedings
on some of Buchel's claims, including violation of his exclusive right to publicly
display his work. The appellate court found that there was significant evidence
that the work was repeatedly and deliberately exhibited to numerous individuals, including journalists, thereby creating a material issue of fact as to the museum's violation of Buchel's right. In so finding, the court noted that

> the moral rights granted to specific artists under VARA [(the Visual Artists Rights
> Act)] are separate and independent from the economic rights guaranteed by [other
> provisions of the federal Copyright Act]....Thus, the inadequacy of claims under
> VARA does not, on its own, signify the inadequacy of more traditional copyright
> claims.[197]

Moreover, as to the museum's assertion that the owner of a particular lawfully
made copy is entitled, without the authority of the copyright holder, to display
that copy publicly, and that the museum owned the physical copy of *Training
Ground*, the First Circuit observed that the evidence indicated that it was a material issue of fact as to whether the museum's copy was "lawfully made," as it may
have been created in violation of Buchel's rights under VARA, and additionally,
there was evidence that the museum understood that Buchel owned the physical
copy of *Training Ground*.

DIVISIBILITY OF COPYRIGHT

The Copyright Act of 1909

The Copyright Act of 1909 was based on the premise of a single copyright with
a single legal title held by the copyright proprietor.[198] Accordingly, the courts
inferred that the bundle of rights accruing to a copyright owner were indivis-
ible,[199] and a transfer of anything less than such a totality was deemed a license,
rather than an assignment.[200] Since only the copyright proprietor could bring an
infringement action,[201] the doctrine of indivisibility protected alleged infringers
from the harassment of successive lawsuits. It took the evolution of the communications media—that is, the development of motion pictures, television,
phonograph records, and legitimate stage productions—and the emergence of

performing-rights societies such as ASCAP, BMI, and SESAC to redefine commercial reality. Today, "copyright" is a label for a collection of diverse, separately marketable property rights.[202]

The Copyright Act of 1976

By recognizing the principle of divisibility, the Copyright Act of 1976 acknowledges the ever-expanding commercial possibilities inherent in copyright ownership. For example, the original copyright holder (or her transferee) of a painting can now sell the right of reproduction to Company *X*, sell the right of distribution to Company *Y*, retain the right of adaptation for herself, and grant a university a two-year exclusive license for the display of the work. Each one of those transferees now becomes an owner of a copyright interest in the painting. "Copyright owner" is defined as referring to the owner of any one or more of the exclusive rights in a copyright,[203] and the copyright owner has standing to sue for infringement of that right.[204] Also, a "transfer of copyright ownership" is defined as an assignment, exclusive license, or any other grant except a nonexclusive license.[205]

Licenses and Assignments

Under the 1976 Act, a copyright holder may exercise ownership prerogatives in a number of ways. He may assign the entire copyright interest to another, who then becomes the copyright holder, or may assign only one or more of the exclusive rights. In addition, the copyright holder may convey a license in and to a work. A license is a right amounting to a less-than-complete ownership interest in a work. If the grantor agrees not to convey that right to anyone else, it is an exclusive license; if the grantor also conveys the same right to a third party, it is a nonexclusive license. As noted above, assignments and exclusive licenses are considered transfers of copyright. To be effective under the 1976 Act, they must be accompanied by a signed writing.[206] The writing should clearly denote the principal terms of the conveyance, such as the royalty provisions, its duration, the name to be carried on the copyright notice (where copyright notice is mandatory), any termination provisions, and the responsibilities for maintaining an infringement suit against third parties.[207] Licensees should also be mindful that in the event their use of an artwork or photo exceeds the scope of a license, the artist may rightfully state a claim for infringement.[208]

The section of the 1976 Act mandating a signed writing for assignments and exclusive licenses, section 204(a),[209] has been found to be analogous to the statute of frauds.[210] That is, like the statute of frauds, section 204(a) was intended to resolve disputes between owners and alleged transferees and was not intended to operate for the benefit of a third-party infringer in the absence of a dispute between the owner and the transferee. Therefore, in *Kenbrooke Fabrics v. Soho Fashions*,[211] the plaintiff, an alleged copyright transferee, brought an infringement action against a third party, and the third party moved for dismissal on the grounds that the transfer was not memorialized in writing, but the New York federal district court, citing the Second Circuit decision in *Eden Toys v. Florelee Undergarment Co.*,[212] denied the motion. Established case law also holds that a subsequent memorialization of a prior oral transfer does relate back ab initio and does render the transfer valid.[213] Such decisional law is rooted in section 204(a), which provides that as an alternative to an "instrument of conveyance" there may be "a note or memorandum of the transfer."[214]

Is an exclusive licensee entitled to share in the settlement proceeds paid to the licensor by an infringer? That issue was decided in the affirmative—at least in theory—in the Eleventh Circuit case of *Original Appalachian Artworks v. S. Diamond Associates*.[215] Thus, the court held in 1995 that the licensee could not recover any portion of the settlement proceeds because the licensee (1) did not show that the infringer appropriated the licensee's exclusive license and (2) failed to demonstrate injuries sustained as a result of the infringer's sales, even absent such appropriation.[216] In that case, in 1983, the plaintiff-licensor, the owner of the copyright and the trademark for Cabbage Patch Kids, granted the defendant-licensee an exclusive license to use the "name, character, symbol, design, likeness and visual representation" of Cabbage Patch Kids solely in connection with the manufacture, distribution, and sale of a puffy-sticker product. In return, the defendant was to pay the plaintiff $45,000 and 10% of the sales revenues. The plaintiff retained the right to any goodwill associated with the Cabbage Patch name and the sole right to determine whether to sue for infringement.

In 1985, Topps Chewing Gum, Inc., began to market a product called Garbage Pail Kids, which consisted of a package containing sticker cards with images of characters very similar to Cabbage Patch Kids but depicted in unflattering situations. In March 1986, the plaintiff sued Topps for copyright and trademark infringement and unfair competition. In August 1986, Topps was preliminarily enjoined from selling its stickers, and in February 1987, the two parties settled for $7 million payable to the plaintiff, who agreed not to sue Topps and not to authorize any of its licensees to do so.

Two days later, on learning of the settlement, the defendant-licensee, claiming it had suffered injury as a result of Topps' infringement, unsuccessfully sought to intervene in the case and requested an accounting to determine how much of the settlement it was owed.

The plaintiff then sued the defendant-licensee for a declaratory judgment that the licensee had no interest in the proceeds of the settlement agreement. The defendant-licensee counterclaimed for a constructive trust or an equitable lien on those proceeds. The federal district court found in the plaintiff's favor, but the Eleventh Circuit reversed in 1990, noting that a copyright licensor

> was under an implied good faith obligation not to do anything that would impair or destroy the value of an exclusive licensee's [that is, the defendant's] rights.[217]

Therefore, as the court continued, if the defendant-licensee was injured by Topps' infringing conduct, even if that conduct did not infringe the defendant's exclusive rights under the license, the defendant was entitled to a portion of the settlement representing that injury.

Subsequent to the Eleventh Circuit's holding in 1990, it remanded to the district court to determine "whether and to what extent, [the defendant] suffered injury as a result of Topps' conduct."[218] On remand, the district court conducted a bench trial and concluded that the defendant had "only a limited item license"[219] that did not cover the bubble gum trading-card stickers marketed by Topps and that, therefore, Topps did not appropriate the defendant's exclusive license. Next, in analyzing whether the defendant had been damaged by Topps' conduct, even though it did not amount to an appropriation of the defendant's license, the district court determined that the defendant failed to sustain its burden of proof and that the evidence demonstrated no direct competition between Topps' Garbage Pail Kids stickers and the defendant's Cabbage Patch Kids stickers. Finally, the court noted that even if the defendant had proved injury, the defendant "offered no method to quantify [it] or to determine what proportion of the settlement was attributable to that injury."[220] The district court's holding was affirmed by the Eleventh Circuit in 1995.

Nonexclusive Licenses

Nonexclusive licenses, as distinct from assignments and exclusive licenses, may be granted orally[221] or may be implied from conduct. Where the existence of a license is in dispute, the defendant has the burden of showing that there was a license.[222] On the other hand, where it is undisputed that there was a license but its scope is disputed, the plaintiff has the burden to show that the defendant's use exceeded the license.[223] A licensee who exceeds the scope of an implied license commits copyright infringement.[224] Although in the 2012 case of *Psihoyos v. Pearson Education, Inc.*[225] a New York federal district court noted that "the Second Circuit has not yet ruled on the precise circumstances under which an implied non-exclusive license will be found,"[226] it observed that whichever of the differing tests for such a license followed in other circuits is applied, the paramount question is "whether there was a 'meeting of the minds' between the parties to permit the particular usage at issue."[227] That being said, the Second Circuit has generally followed the lead of other circuits in finding that implied nonexclusive licenses exist only in narrow circumstances where one party created a work at the request of the licensee with the intention that the latter exploit it.

In the 2010 Eleventh Circuit case of *Latimer v. Roaring Toyz, Inc.*,[228] an implied license was said to be created when one party (1) creates a work at another person's request; (2) delivers the work to that person; and (3) intends that the person copy and distribute the work. That case held that a photographer granted an implied license to one of the defendants to use his copyrighted photographs but that there remained a factual issue as to the scope of the implied license. Here, in January 2006, the defendant Kawasaki Motors Corp. engaged the defendant Roaring Toyz, Inc. to customize two of its new ZX-14 motorcycles that Kawasaki wished to introduce to the public. The customized motorcycles were to be displayed along with the standard production model during Daytona Bike Week in Florida.

Plaintiff Todd Latimer, a professional photographer, was retained by the magazine 2 *Wheel Tuner* to capture in photographs the progress of Roaring Toyz customization of the ZX-14 motorcycle. The photographs were to be included in the magazine, accompanying an article about the customization.

By late February 2006, Kawasaki was assembling a press kit for the ZX-14's World Press Introduction to be held in Las Vegas on February 26-28, 2006, and requested that Roaring Toyz provide it with photographs of the customized bikes. Roaring Toyz ultimately contacted Latimer to do the photo shoot, and Latimer agreed to photograph the bikes that night to meet Kawasaki's February 24 deadline. Latimer alleged that he understood that his photographs would be used on a placard to be displayed beside the motorcycles at Daytona Bike Week. However, the defendants insisted that they told Latimer that the photographs would be used for the press release in Las Vegas. In any event, Latimer also alleged that he made it clear to the defendants that the photographs could not be leaked before the publication of his article in 2 *Wheel Tuner*. The morning of February 24, Latimer emailed Roaring Toyz a selection of digitally edited photos of the customized ZX-14 motorcycles, each image containing a metadata file that included a copyright notice for the image. Roaring Toyz immediately emailed the images to Kawasaki. At the press launch on February 26, Kawasaki distributed a press kit to approximately thirty members of the media, including a representative of the magazine *Cycle World*, that included a compact disc that held five of Latimer's photographs with the metadata attached. In conjunction with an article about the launch of the ZX-14, *Cycle World* in its June 2006 issue published three of Latimer's photographs: two accompanying an article about the launch and a third placed on the table of contents page. Latimer learned of the allegedly infringing uses of his photographs when he read the June 2006 issue of *Cycle World*, and in October 2006 he brought suit in a Florida federal district court against Kawasaki and others, alleging, among other claims, copyright infringement. The Eleventh Circuit, in affirming the finding of the district court, found that Latimer had granted an implied license to Kawasaki to use his copyrighted photographs.[229]

> Latimer's conduct satisfies all three prongs of the implied license test. Kawasaki requested that Roaring Toyz provide it with photographs of the customized ZX-14s, and Roaring Toyz in turn asked Latimer to create those photographs. Latimer thus created the photos at Kawasaki's request. Latimer's . . . testimony indicates that he knew Roaring Toyz would send the photographs to Kawasaki to create the placard. Thus, when Latimer delivered the photographs to [the manager of Roaring Toyz websites and its marketing advisor], he constructively delivered them to Kawasaki. . . . Thus, Latimer granted Kawasaki an implied license to use his photographs.

The Eleventh Circuit, however, also found that there was a factual issue as to whether Kawasaki's use might have exceeded the scope of the implied license.[230]

It would seem clear that the prudent course is to memorialize nonexclusive licenses as well as exclusive licenses in writing.

Joint Ownership

The 1976 Act defines a "joint work" as one

> prepared by two or more authors with the intention that their contributions be merged into inseparable or interdependent parts of a unitary whole.[231]

The intention at the time of creation controls.[232] Case law under the 1909 Act stressed "fusion of effort," rather than the intent at the time of creation.[233]

Although the 1976 Act defines neither "inseparable" nor "interdependent," the courts have adopted relatively standard definitions of each term.[234] Parts of a unitary whole are deemed inseparable where they have little or no meaning when each stands alone, such as where two artists, Andy Warhol and Jean-Michel Basquiat, collaborated to produce sculptural works.[235] Parts of a unitary whole are deemed interdependent where "they have some meaning standing alone but achieve their primary significance because of their combined effect."[236] Similarly, where parts of a whole are neither interdependent nor inseparable, and where no express agreement to create a joint work exists, the court will not construe a joint work scenario.

In addition, a Texas federal district court in 1996, in holding the defendant, the American Academy of Orthopedic Surgeons, to be the sole copyright proprietor of the fourth edition of an instructional text and slide set, noted that the parties' intent regarding joint authorship was also key. In the Second Circuit's decision in *Thomson v. Larson*,[237] in 1998, the court held that beyond statutory intent to "merge" their contributions, parties must also have an intent that there be a sharing of the indicia of ownership and authorship.[238] Such indicia include "how a collaborator regarded herself in relation to the work in terms of billing and credit, decisionmaking, and the right to enter into contracts."[239] Citing a Second Circuit case, the Texas court in *Clogston v. American Academy of Orthopedic Surgeons* noted that

> [c]are must be taken to ensure that true collaborators in the creative process are accorded the perquisites of co-authorship and to guard against the risk that a sole author is denied exclusive authorship status simply because another person rendered some form of assistance.[240]

Thus, in *Johannsen v. Brown*,[241] an Oregon federal district court granted the plaintiff-artist's motion for summary judgment, declaring that his copyright in the illustration *American Relix*, a spoof on the Grant Wood painting *American Gothic*, was valid and enforceable. In rejecting the defendant-publisher's contention that it was a joint author, the court noted as follows:

[A]n author is a "party who actually creates the work, that is . . . who translates an idea into a fixed, tangible expression entitled to copyright protection." For the purposes of joint authorship, each author must "make an independently copyrightable contribution."[242]

The court went on to assess the defendant's contributions to *American Relix*: suggesting to the plaintiff-artist how the work should appear and creating the work's title. The court then concluded that

"a person who merely describes to an author what the commissioned work should look like is not a joint author for the purposes of the Copyright Act." [The defendant's] conception of the idea behind "American Relix" is insufficient, as a matter of law, to make him a joint author of the work.[243]

In another case rejecting joint authorship, *Brown v. McCormick*,[244] the plaintiff, a well-known professional quilter, contracted with Universal City Studios Inc., Amblin Entertainment, Inc., and a technical consultant, the defendants, to create a quilt to be used as a prop in the film *How to Make an American Quilt*. The plaintiff was to design the patterns for fifteen panels of the quilt and would retain the copyright in her designs. After she completed the patterns, the defendants made the quilt; but they also made a second quilt, which borrowed the basic design of one of the plaintiff's patterns, and they used both quilts in the film as well as in promotional material. Upon the plaintiff's infringement suit, the defendants argued that they were joint authors. For the first quilt, the Maryland federal district court, in 2000, held that a finding of joint authorship would have nullified the contract that granted the defendants the right to use the plaintiff's copyrighted work in one quilt. For the second quilt, which the plaintiff did not know that the defendants were making, the court held that it was "impossible that [the plaintiff] intended her work to be merged into a greater composition and she cannot be considered a joint author."[245]

In the 2001 case of *Gillespie v. AST Sportswear, Inc.*,[246] a New York federal district court denied the plaintiffs' motion for summary judgment where the defendants raised joint authorship as a defense to an infringement claim. The plaintiffs, a freelance art director/ graphic artist and a freelance photographer, sued the defendants, a sportswear distribution company and a fashion designer (Miles), alleging copyright infringement. The defendants had invited the plaintiffs to assist in the production of certain marketing materials, including photographs and design layouts. The parties disputed the extent to which the defendant Miles contributed to the overall photographic effort. As the court noted, there is little case law on joint authorship of photographs. But the court stated that where the trier of fact could potentially conclude that there was intention on the part of both parties to be joint authors and that Miles exercised sufficient control over the photo shoot, the court could not say as a matter of law that Miles's contributions were not sufficient to make him a joint author of the photographs and promotional materials.

Decisional law dating from the 1909 Act provides that in the absence of specific agreement to the contrary all joint authors share equally in the ownership of the joint work, even if their respective contributions to the work are not equal,[247] and that on the death of each joint owner, her heirs or legatees acquire her respective share of the joint work.[248] This principle was enunciated in *DeBitetto v. Alpha Books*,[249] where the plaintiff James DeBitetto and the defendant Sarah Hodgson were joint authors of a puppy care book. When Hodgson later published another book on dogs, the plaintiff sued her, alleging that her later book incorporated her work from their collaborative book effort. In granting defendants' motion to dismiss and for summary judgment in the infringement action, the court instructed that where a joint copyright exists, a joint holder has an undivided copyright interest in the work, and can use it without securing the other copyright owner's permission.

Under the 1976 Act, the duration of copyright of a joint work consists of the life of the last surviving author plus seventy years.[250] Under both the 1976 Act and the 1909 Act, a joint owner may grant a nonexclusive license in the work without obtaining the consent of the other joint owners.[251] Moreover, in the absence of an agreement to the contrary, one joint owner may always transfer her interest in a joint work to a third party but cannot transfer the interest of another joint owner without that joint owner's consent.[252]

A joint owner is limited in the claims that she can assert against her co-owner. In 2001, a New York federal district court in *Estate of Davis v. Trojer* held that "a joint copyright owner cannot assert a claim of infringement against her co-owner because an individual cannot infringe his own copyright."[253]

ANONYMOUS AND PSEUDONYMOUS WORKS

An anonymous work is a work on whose copies no natural person is identified as the author.[254] A pseudonymous work is a work on whose copies the author is identified under a fictitious name.[255] For all such works created on or after January 1, 1978, the copyright endures for a term of ninety-five years from the year of first publication of the work or a term of 120 years from the year of its creation, whichever expires first.[256] For works created before January 1, 1978, the provisions noted earlier in this chapter apply (see page 933).

COMPILATIONS AND COLLECTIVE WORKS

Under the Copyright Act of 1976, a compilation is a work formed by the collection and assemblage of preexisting materials or of data that are selected, coordinated, or arranged in such a way that the resulting work as a whole constitutes an original work of authorship.[257] An artwork analogous to a compilation may be a collage consisting, for example, of pieces of tinfoil, colored tissue, bits of newsprint, cotton balls, and cutouts of colored construction paper, arranged and mounted on a canvas in such a way as to create a work of artistic authorship. Another example is found in *Runstadler Studios v. MCM Ltd. Partnership*,[258] in which a glass sculpture, entitled *Spiral Motion* and composed of thirty-nine clear-glass rectangles and hexahedrons forming a twenty-four-inch spiral, was held to be copyrightable as a work of art, even though the thirty-nine elements were in and of themselves unprotectable. Copyright protection in a compilation

> extends only to the material contributed by the author of such work, as distin-guished from the preexisting material employed in the work and does not imply any exclusive right in the preexisting material.[259]

A collective work is a type of compilation, such as an anthology or an encyclo-pedia, in which a number of contributions, themselves separate and independent works, are assembled into a collective whole.[260] The contributions to the collec-tive work may emanate from the same or from different authors. As with other compilations, such a work qualifies for copyright protection by reason of the original effort expended in the process of compilation, even if no new matter is added.[261] For example, a calendar illustrated by copies of twelve separate works of art by disparate artists but having a common theme may well be copyrightable. In addition, a catalog, including photographs by various photographers, is a com-pilation, and protection may extend to selection, coordination, and arrangement of components as well as to individual works of authorship within the catalog.[262] As with derivative works, discussed earlier in this chapter (see pages 934–937), the amount of originality generally required to render a collective work pro-tectable is at least "some substantial variation from the underlying work, not merely a trivial variation."[263] As with a derivative work, a collective-work copy-right does not of itself make the preexisting works on which the later work is based copyrightable, nor does the collective-work copyright affect any copyright protection or lack of protection accorded the preexisting works.[264] Generally, the above principles relating to compilations and collective works under the 1976 Act also applied under the 1909 Act because of the earlier act's similar statutory language.[265]

WORKS MADE FOR HIRE

Under the Copyright Act of 1976, a work made for hire is either (1) a specially commissioned work in one of nine statutorily prescribed categories where both parties expressly agree in a signed written instrument that the work shall be con-sidered a work made for hire or (2) a work prepared by an employee within the scope of employment.[266]

Specially Commissioned Works

Specially commissioned works are works made for hire only if the parties expressly agree to that effect in a signed writing and the works fall into one of the following nine categories:

- Contributions to collective works
- Parts of motion pictures or other audiovisual works
- Translations
- Supplementary works
- Compilations
- Instructional texts
- Tests
- Answer materials for tests
- Atlases[267]

Thus, a specially commissioned portrait, for example, is not a work made for hire, because it does not fit any of the above categories. Nevertheless, to avoid any confusion, the artist should not sign anything indicating that such a commissioned work is a work made for hire.

The requirements of a signed writing and of what constitutes "specially commissioned" have received judicial attention in recent years. For example, in *Playboy Enterprises v. Dumas*,[268] Playboy sought a declaratory judgment that it was the sole copyright owner of certain works of art created by freelance artist Patrick Nagel that appeared in *Playboy* magazine from 1974 to 1984. The Second Circuit held in 1995 that those works created by Nagel before January 1977 were works for hire under the 1909 Act with the copyrights initially vested in *Playboy* magazine. The Second Circuit remanded the case to a New York federal district court to determine (1) whether the artworks created by Nagel between January 1977 and January 1, 1978 were made at *Playboy* magazine's "instance," thereby rendering them works for hire with the copyrights vested in *Playboy*, and (2) whether the artworks created by Nagel during the period of July 1979 through 1984 were works for hire with the copyrights vested in *Playboy*. The artist, Patrick Nagel, produced approximately 285 artworks that were published in *Playboy* magazine; from August 1975 until July 1984, at least one Nagel painting appeared in every issue. At first, *Playboy* furnished Nagel with specific instructions as to the content of the paintings, most of which were illustrations to accompany specific articles. The relationship, however, gradually evolved into one of greater freedom for the artist, so that sometime in 1977 or 1978, the parties established a course of conduct in which, without being provided specific instructions, Nagel would routinely submit his paintings and *Playboy* would generally publish his work. *Playboy* paid Nagel for each of the published paintings by check after Nagel delivered the work. Each check bore a legend endorsement, the wording of which changed over the years. The first legend, on checks issued between 1974 and July 1979, bore the following wording:

Any alteration of this legend agreement voids this check. By endorsement of this check, payee acknowledges payment in full for the assignment to Playboy Enterprises, Inc. of all right, title, and interest in and to the following items: [a description of a painting followed].[269]

The next sixty checks, issued between September 1979 and March 1981, bore the following legend:

Any alteration of this legend agreement voids this check. BY ENDORSEMENT, PAYEE: acknowledges payment in full for services rendered on a work-made-for-hire basis in connection with the Work named on the face of this check and confirms ownership by Playboy Enterprises Inc. of all right, title and interest (except physical possession), including all right of copyright . . . in and to the Work.[270]

The last ninety-four checks, issued between March 1981 and May 1984, were stamped with "essentially identical language,"[271] confirming that Nagel's services were rendered on a work-for-hire basis.

In examining the check legends, the Second Circuit held that those works that Nagel created on or after January 1, 1978, and that were paid for by checks bearing the earliest legend were not works made for hire; in the wording, the work-for-hire relationship was not mentioned, let alone acknowledged. However, the court held that works paid for by checks bearing the later legends satisfied the writing requirement of the 1976 Act. The court noted that although the parties must intend and agree before a work's creation that it will be a work made for hire, the written memorialization of the parties' precreation intent need not precede the work's creation. Therefore, as the court noted,

[w]hile Nagel's endorsement of Playboy's first check bearing [the second legend] may not evidence his pre-creation consent to a work-for-hire relationship, Nagel's subsequent pre-creation consent to such a relationship may be inferred from his continued endorsements.[272]

The Second Circuit found that beginning with the second check containing the second legend, Nagel's endorsement of *Playboy's* checks constituted sufficient evidence of a precreation work-for-hire agreement.

As to whether the works were specially ordered or commissioned, the Second Circuit, guided by Nimmer's treatise on copyright, held that the key element

would appear to be whether the "motivating factor in producing the work was the [person requesting preparation of the work] who induced [its] creation."[273]

On remand, the New York federal district court in 1997[274] held that the works created by Nagel from January 1977 to January 1, 1978 were made at *Playboy's* instance and were therefore works for hire, with *Playboy* as their author. However, the court held that many of the works created by Nagel after July 1979 were not works for hire. Although the court found that those works were also made at *Playboy*'s instance, the court noted that the payment checks for a number of those works were not actually signed by Nagel and that the signatories lacked authority to enter into work-for-hire agreements on Nagel's behalf. Therefore, since those works covered by the payment checks devoid of Nagel's signature failed to meet the writing requirement of the work-for-hire provision in the 1976 Act, the copyrights to such works were owned by Jennifer Dumas, Nagel's widow.

Works Prepared by an Employee

The Copyright Act of 1976 defines neither "employee" nor "scope of employment," but the United States Supreme Court in *Community for Creative Non-Violence (CCNV) v. Reid*[275] has provided guidance in ascertaining whether a work is for hire under the terms of the act:

> To determine whether a work is for hire under the [Copyright] Act, a court should first ascertain, *using principles of general common law of agency* [italics ours], whether the work was prepared by an employee or an independent contractor. After making this determination, the court can apply the appropriate subsection of [the work-made-for-hire provision].[276]

In *Reid*, the Court further held that in applying the principles of general common law of agency, each case must use a multifactor balancing test to determine if the work was produced by an employee or by an independent contractor. The Court then enumerated the thirteen specific factors to be weighed:

- The hiring party's right to control the manner and the means by which the product is accomplished
- The skill required of the hired party
- The source of the tools
- The location of the work
- The duration of the parties' relationship
- Whether the hiring party may assign additional projects to the hired party
- The extent of the hired party's discretion over the work schedule
- The method of payment
- The hired party's role in employing and paying assistants
- Whether the work is part of the hiring party's regular business
- Whether the hiring party is in business
- The provision of employee benefits
- The tax treatment of the hired party[277]

In *Reid*, plaintiff Mitch Snyder was a member and trustee of plaintiff CCNV, a Washington D.C. nonprofit association dedicated to eliminating homelessness in America. Synder retained the Baltimore artist James Earl Reid in the fall of 1985 to create a sculptured Nativity scene dramatizing the plight of the homeless; the sculptured scene was to be exhibited in the annual Christmastime Pageant of Peace in Washington. The agreement was made orally with little more than a handshake. The parties agreed that CCNV would pay Reid a total of $15,000 including materials but not including Reid's services, which he offered to donate. Neither party mentioned copyright.[278]

CCNV conceived the idea for the display: a modern Nativity scene of a black family (two life-sized adults and an infant) huddled on a streetside steam grate, positioned atop a pedestal, with steam being emitted from the grate. CCNV entitled the sculpture *Third World America* and devised the legend for the pedestal: "and still there is no room at the inn."[279] For a number of weeks, Reid worked exclusively on the statue, assisted at various times by people who were paid with funds provided in installments by CCNV. During that time, CCNV members visited Reid on a number of occasions to monitor his progress and to coordinate CCNV's construction of the base. On December 24, 1985, Reid delivered the completed statue to CCNV in Washington, and CCNV paid Reid the final installment of the $15,000 promised. The statue was joined to the steam grate and pedestal prepared by CCNV and was placed on display near the site of the pageant. In late January 1986, CCNV returned *Third World America* to Reid's studio in Baltimore for minor repairs. CCNV then planned to take the statue on an extensive tour to raise money for the homeless. Reid objected that the statue could not withstand the rigorous itinerary. In March 1986, CCNV asked Reid to return *Third World America*. Reid refused and made plans to take the statue on a modest tour. Both Reid and Snyder, the latter acting in his capacity as a CCNV trustee, filed competing certificates of copyright registration; then Snyder and CCNV commenced an action against Reid, seeking a return of *Third World America* and a declaration of copyright ownership.

CCNV alleged that CCNV members supervised and directed every step of the creation of the sculpture[280] and, therefore, that the sculpture was a work made for hire, with the copyright vesting in CCNV. Reid claimed that he, as the artist, created the sculpture, that under the 1976 Act it was not a work made for hire, and, accordingly, that he owned the copyright. The legal question presented was whether *Third World America* was a work made for hire under the terms of the 1976 Act.

Reasoning that Reid had been an employee of CCNV within the meaning of the 1976 Act's work-made-for-hire provision, because CCNV was the motivating force in the statue's production, the federal district court in Washington, D.C., held that CCNV was the exclusive owner of the copyright in the sculpture.[281] The District of Columbia Circuit reversed the district court's decision; it reasoned that under agency law Reid was an independent contractor and, therefore, that the work was not prepared by an employee under the 1976 Act's work-made-for-hire provision. The appellate court further noted that the sculpture was not a work made for hire under the provision's second section: The sculpture did not fall within one of the nine categories of works enumerated under that section, nor did the parties agree in writing that the sculpture be a work made for hire. Accordingly, the appellate court held that Reid owned the copyright but remanded the case to the district court for a determination of whether the sculpture was a joint work under the Copyright Act of 1976.[282]

The United States Supreme Court affirmed the holding that *Third World America* was not a work made for hire, noting that, under the principles of general common law of agency and in applying the earlier-noted thirteen factors, Reid was an independent contractor. As to the second section of the work-made-for-hire provision, CCNV conceded that the sculpture could not fall within that category. However, the Supreme Court did note, as did the appellate court, that the sculpture might be a joint work if, on remand, the district court determined that

CCNV and Reid prepared the work "with the intention that their contributions be merged into inseparable or interdependent parts of a unitary whole."[283]

On remand, in accordance with a motion by both parties for a consent judgment, the district court issued an order including the following provisions: Reid was the sole author of *Third World America*; CCNV was the sole owner of the original copy of *Third World America*; Reid was the sole copyright holder with respect to three-dimensional reproductions of *Third World America*; and Reid and CCNV were joint copyright holders with respect to two-dimensional reproductions of *Third World America*.[284]

Still applicable today, the *Reid* factors used to determine whether an artist is considered an independent contractor or, instead, the creator of a work for hire were applied in *Armento v. Laser Image, Inc.*[285] Gregory Armento was commissioned by the defendant, Laser Image, Inc., a graphic design company, to illustrate a series of maps of Asheville, North Carolina. In 1987, the defendant and plaintiff entered into one contract, and later a second. While some terms of the two contracts differed, the ownership provision at the heart of the controversy remained constant, stating that the illustrated maps would remain the sole property of Laser Image, and could not be reproduced by Armento without written consent. When the plaintiff later filed an infringement suit against the defendant, the main question before the court was whether the plaintiff created the illustrations for the defendant under the work-for-hire doctrine.

Using the factors set forth in *Community for Creative Non-Violence v. Reid*,[286] a North Carolina federal district court determined that the maps were a work for hire. The court concluded that Armento's work was a "specially commissioned" and "collective work." Although neither contract expressly contained the words "work for hire," the court noted that this "omission is not fatal,"[287] and stated that the language in the contracts was clear and definite enough to fulfill the writing requirement set forth in the statute, conferring ownership of the work on Laser Image.

The thirteen factors enumerated in *Reid* for assessing the employment status of the hired party were refined in the 1992 Second Circuit case of *Aymes v. Bonelli*,[288] which noted that no one of those factors is determinative and that they should not be tallied but, rather, should be weighed according to their significance in the case at hand. *Aymes* enumerated five such factors that are nearly always relevant:

- The hiring party's right to control the manner and the means by which the product is accomplished
- The skill required
- Whether the hiring party has the right to assign additional projects to the hired party
- The provision of employee benefits
- The tax treatment of the hired party[289]

However, the application—or misapplication—of the *Aymes* factors by the Second Circuit in 1995 led to a reversal and a paradoxical decision in *Carter v. Helmsley-Spear*,[290] a case of first impression, that is, presenting a novel question of law, regarding the federal Visual Artists Rights Act (VARA). *Carter* is discussed in connection with VARA in chapter 12. However, some comments on *Carter* are in order on the issue of works for hire.

In *Carter*, the manager of the lessee of a commercial building in Queens, New York, in December 1991 hired the plaintiffs, a group of three artists sometimes known as "Three-Js," to design, create, and install artwork in various parts of the building, primarily the lobby. Under the agreement, the plaintiffs had full authority as to design, color, and style, and the manager retained the authority to direct the location and the installation of the artwork within the building. The plaintiffs were to retain the copyrights to their works, and the manager was to receive 50% of any proceeds from their exploitation. The agreement, originally for a one-year period, was extended for several additional one-year terms.

In March 1994, the lessee's lease was terminated. In April, the lessee filed for bankruptcy, and the property was surrendered to the defendant, Helmsley-Spear. The defendant informed the plaintiffs that they could no longer continue to install artwork on the premises and had to vacate the building. The defendants also made statements indicating that they intended to remove the artwork already in place in the building's lobby; the plaintiff-artists then sued the defendants under the recently enacted and untested VARA. A New York federal district court issued a preliminary injunction, enjoining the defendant from removing the artwork pending resolution of the litigation. A bench trial was held in June and July 1994. Subsequently, the trial court granted the plaintiff-artists a permanent injunction, to remain in effect for the three plaintiffs' lifetimes. The defendant appealed, and the Second Circuit, holding that the plaintiffs' artwork in the building was a work for hire and thereby excluded by definition from VARA protection, reversed and vacated the injunction.

According to the Second Circuit, the federal district court, in determining that the artwork was not a work for hire (and thereby eligible for protection under VARA), correctly stated the legal test: an analysis of the facts under the *Reid* factors, with special emphasis on the five *Aymes* factors (see above). However, the Second Circuit found that the district court's factual findings were "clearly erroneous"[291] and so reviewed de novo the issue of whether or not the artwork was a work for hire.

In applying the five *Aymes* factors, the Second Circuit agreed with the district court that (1) the plaintiffs had the right to control the manner and the means of production and (2) a high level of skill was required by the plaintiffs to produce the sculptures. Those two factors favored the plaintiffs' contention that they were independent contractors. However, in contrast to the district court, the Second Circuit found that under the plaintiffs' employment agreement the defendant and its predecessors could and did assign the artists additional projects (the third *Aymes* factor), lending credence to the defendant's contention that the plaintiffs were employees working within the scope of their employment. The Second Circuit agreed with the district court that two other factors pointed strongly to employee status: the provision of employee benefits to the plaintiffs, such as health, life, and liability insurance and paid vacations (the fourth *Aymes* factor), and the tax treatment of the plaintiffs, whereby the defendant paid the plaintiffs' payroll and Social Security taxes (the fifth *Aymes* factor).

In addition, the Second Circuit found that several of the *Reid* factors (which the district court determined to be neutral or inconclusive) bolstered the defendant's contention that the artists were employees: The artists were furnished many of the supplies used to create the artwork; they were employed for a substantial period of time, with no set date of termination other than the completion of the artwork; and they could not hire paid assistants without the defendant's approval. In sum, the Second Circuit found that the *Aymes* and *Reid* factors weighed in favor of finding that the artists were employees, thereby rendering the artwork a work for hire and beyond the protection of VARA.

As noted in at least one scholarly comment,[292] peculiarities with the Second Circuit decision abound. The court virtually disregarded the agreement's provision that the artists retained the copyrights in the artwork. That factor is a crucial indicator of how the parties perceived themselves. For example, if an artwork, after installation, was reproduced without authorization, the artists, under the agreement, were the parties who had the right to bring suit. Further, by emphasizing, among the *Aymes* factors, the commercial aspects of the relationship between the parties, the Second Circuit was ignoring its own admonition in *Aymes* that the factors "should be weighed according to their significance in the case."[293] That being so, why emphasize employee benefits and the tax treatment of the artists where the rights at issue—moral rights—were distinctly nonmaterial rights aimed at preserving the artists' personalities, as expressed through their work, and the artists' honor? In addition, two of the *Reid* factors cited by the Second Circuit to bolster its position should be de-emphasized, if not totally disregarded.[294] First, since the artwork included such costly items as a used satellite dish, parts of an old bus, and nearly a million pieces of colored glass, it was natural for the wealthier lessee, not the artists, to furnish much of the materials. Second, because of the highly complex nature of the artwork, it was reasonable for the artists to be engaged for a lengthy period of time in its design, construction, and installation.

An analysis of an artist's employment status for work-made-for-hire purposes by considering the factors noted in *Reid* appears to be procedurally sound if the factors are analyzed correctly. A case in point is the 1998 case of *Oklahoma Natural Gas Co. v. LaRue*.[295] Here, the plaintiff, a natural gas utility company, had employed the defendant Lester LaRue as the safety coordinator for its Oklahoma City district. It was part of LaRue's job to investigate explosions and take photographs of the scene. At the site of the 1995 Oklahoma City bombing, LaRue took photographs of the overall scene and assisted company crews by locating and shutting off gas lines. One of the photographs taken by LaRue was of a firefighter cradling an injured infant, which became the well-publicized "firefighter and baby" photograph at the heart of the lawsuit. LaRue contracted with *Newsweek* magazine for publication of the photograph, which appeared on the cover of the magazine's May 1, 1995 issue.[296] LaRue also contracted with another company to produce bronze-like statues depicting the firefighter holding the baby, and approximately 700 of these were sold or otherwise distributed. LaRue then filed for copyright registration of his photograph. Determining that LaRue might have a conflict of interest in exploiting the photograph for personal gain, the gas company filed a competing application for copyright registration of the photograph, and subsequently brought suit for a determination of, among other issues, copyright ownership. Affirming an Oklahoma federal district court's grant of partial summary judgment for the company, the Tenth Circuit noted that "overwhelming evidence"[297] indicated that LaRue took the photograph within the scope of his employment. The court then cited the factors upon which it based its determination: Taking photographs was part of LaRue's job; it was during work hours; he used a company camera and film; the company paid to develop the film; he reported to the company throughout the day; and he never informed anyone that he was taking personal time.[298]

The Second Circuit's 1998 decision in *Langman Fabrics v. Graff Californiawear, Inc.*[299] relied on the *Aymes* factors to reverse its grant of summary judgment in favor of the defendant and to determine that an artist's work was arguably a work made for hire. Here, the plaintiff fabric finisher produced a feather-patterned printed fabric. The plaintiff sued the defendant for copyright infringement where the defendant's catalog offered a similar printed fabric. The defendant argued that the plaintiff did not own the copyright in the displayed fabric because it was created by an artist who was an independent contractor. The court explained that the design could be a work made for hire under the *Aymes* factors despite the fact that the artist's level of skill weighed in favor of independent contractor status, because there was a tax withholding, the work was regularly assigned, and fabric design was the plaintiff's regular business.

In 2000, in *SHL Imaging, Inc. v. Artisan House, Inc.*,[300] a New York federal district court relied on the five *Aymes* factors to conclude that photographs taken by a photographer were not works for hire where all of the factors weighed heavily in favor of the plaintiff photographer. The defendant, a manufacturer of mirrored picture frames, hired the plaintiff to produce photographs of the frames for use by the defendant's salespeople. The plaintiff later discovered that the defendant had used sixty-four of the photographs in a catalog, made 3,000 additional copies of the photographs for undisclosed purposes, reproduced them in 5,000 brochures, scanned eighty-three of them into a computer, and used them as magazine "comps" publicity releases, all without the plaintiff's permission. The court stated that the defendant's control over the creation was minimal and its instructions were so general that they "[fell] within the realm of unprotectable ideas."[301] Further, the plaintiff had twenty-five years of experience as a professional photographer while the defendant had no technical photographic skills. In addition, the defendant had no right to assign additional projects to the plaintiff, did not provide employee benefits for the plaintiff, and did not claim that it withheld any taxes or that it made any tax payments on behalf of the plaintiff. The term of a work made for hire under the 1976 Act is ninety-five years from the year of its first publication or 120 years from creation, whichever expires first.[302] It should also be noted that the author of a work made for hire, unlike the author of other works, does not have the right to terminate the copyright holder's ownership of copyright after thirty-five years.[303] Termination of copyright in general is discussed later in this chapter (see pages 969–970).

THE COPYRIGHT ACT OF 1909

Under the Copyright Act of 1909, the legal presumption was that employers owned the copyright to works created by their employees by virtue of the employment relationship.[304] Moreover, through case law, the for-hire rule was often presumed to exist for specifically commissioned works. Whether the copyright was initially vested in the commissioning party or in the independent contractor depended on the parties' intention, where cognizable.[305] When that intention was not expressly stated, most case law generally held that the copyright in the work was vested in the party commissioning the work.[306]

Thus, the 1909 Act granted broader rights to the commissioning party than does the 1976 Act in two respects: First, the copyright could be vested in the commissioning party, despite the absence of a written agreement to that effect, and, second, a commissioning party could claim the copyright as against the independent contractor whether or not the work belonged to one of the nine prescribed categories previously cited.[307]

The contours of the work-made-for-hire doctrine under the 1909 Act were examined by a New York federal district court in the 2011 case of *Marvel Worldwide, Inc. v. Kirby*.[308] The defendants were the heirs of Jack Kirby, a freelance artist who worked with Marvel Comics to create drawings for comic book series such as *The Mighty Thor*.[309] In 1972, Kirby assigned to Marvel Comics' predecessor all his right, title, and interest in any of the copyrights that he "may have or control" in any of the works that he created for Marvel. In that assignment document, Kirby explicitly acknowledged that he "created the works as an employee for hire" of Marvel's owners.[310] Kirby died in 1994, and in 2009 his heirs requested that the plaintiffs terminate Kirby's assignment with respect to his artwork published by Marvel Comics between 1958 and 1963.[311]

As noted above, under the works-made-for-hire doctrine articulated in the 1909 Act, if an employee creates a work in the regular course of employment, the employer owns the copyright in it, and it is considered a work made for hire. Courts interpreting this provision of the 1909 Act have extended such copyright ownership to those who commission the creation of a work and also to those who hire independent contractors to create works of art.[312]

The Second Circuit utilizes a two-part "instance and expense" test to analyze the works for hire doctrine under the 1909 Act. The instance prong of this test has two elements: (1) whether the hiring party "induces the creation of the work," and (2) whether the hiring party "has the right to direct and supervise the manner in which the work is carried out."[313] For purposes of this test, the hiring party need not have complete control over the artist's work; rather, the courts examine the degree to which the hiring party can accept, reject, edit, or generally control the creation of the work.[314] In addition, the instance prong examines whether the hiring party could have controlled the creation of the work; it does not matter whether the hiring party actually did exercise such control.[315] The expense prong examines which party bears the financial risk of a loss in profitability and is satisfied in favor of the hiring party if such party pays the artist a sum certain instead of royalties for his work.[316] If a hiring party can establish both prongs of the instance and expense test, it raises a rebuttable presumption that the work was made for hire and therefore that the hiring party owns the copyright in such work.

The *Marvel* court determined that Kirby's artworks were works made for hire, and as such Marvel Comics owned the copyright in those works. First, it was clear that the works were made at the instance of Marvel Comics.[317] After all, Kirby's assignments always came directly from the editor at Marvel Comics, Stan Lee; Kirby did not begin creating the works until Lee directed him to begin drawing. In addition, Lee had complete supervisory power over the creation of these works. He created the plots from which the artists created their drawings. He also reviewed all work before publication, and he had the ability (which he frequently exercised) to ask that artists edit their work prior to publication. If Lee did not approve of a certain work, it would not be published. Defendants testified that Lee would require Kirby to edit his works, and if Lee was not completely satisfied with Kirby's works, he did not publish them. Therefore, Marvel Comics clearly both induced the creation of Kirby's works and had the power to direct and control the creation of Kirby's works. The court thus held that the instance prong pointed in favor of Marvel Comics.

As to the expense prong, the court first noted that Kirby received a fixed fee for each page of his artwork that Marvel Comics published. This amount was a sum certain, not royalties, which weighed in favor of finding that the works were made for hire.[318] Defendants argued that Kirby, not Marvel Comics, bore the risk of profitability since Marvel Comics was not required to accept Kirby's works and had never paid Kirby a "turn-down fee" for any required revisions of his works. However, the court rejected this argument, reasoning that Marvel Comics alone bore the risk of the entire enterprise's failure.[319] That type of risk was the essence of the expense prong, and therefore the court held that Marvel bore the expense of the creation of the works. Since both the instance and expense prongs were satisfied, the court held that a rebuttable presumption was established in favor of Marvel Comics that the works were made for hire and that Marvel Comics owned the copyright in these works. Accordingly, the New York federal district court granted summary judgment in favor of Marvel Comics.

COPYRIGHT PROCEDURES

Unlike most nations, the United States historically required adherence to certain formalities to preserve both the copyright and remedies under the copyright. With the passage by Congress of the Berne Convention Implementation Act of 1988 (BCIA),[320] which amended the Copyright Act of 1976 and made the United States an adherent to the Berne Convention, such formalities have been relaxed. They have not, however, been altogether abolished. The BCIA became effective March 1, 1989. As it has no retroactive effect, the requirements of the law as it existed before March 1, 1989, continue to apply to preexisting issues and, therefore, remain relevant.

Notice

Notice requirements for works and copies of works publicly distributed on or after March 1, 1989, by authority of the copyright holder are permissive, rather than mandatory.[321] Nevertheless, we strongly recommend that all artists and others in whom copyright initially vests continue to affix a copyright notice to created works: Such affixation serves to defeat an infringer's defense of innocent infringement that may be raised in mitigation of actual or statutory damages.[322]

Works or copies of works publicly distributed by authority of the copyright holder under the 1976 Act before March 1, 1989, require a copyright notice. For such works, it is established law[323] that a single copyright notice applicable to a collective work as a whole also fulfills the notice requirements for those individual contributions created by the author of the collective work. The New York federal district court case of *Heyman v. Salle*[324] involved the professional photographer Kenneth Heyman, who, with co-plaintiff John Rublowsky, collaborated in 1964 on a book entitled *Pop Art*. The book contains both text and photographs, including a photograph, referred to as the Scull photo, on page 162 of the book that was the basis for the suit. The Scull photo depicts the Robert Scull family (with a maid in attendance) at the dinner table, with a pop art painting by James Rosenquist partially visible on the wall behind the table. The book was published in 1965, and a copyright for the book was immediately acquired. However, Heyman never registered his claim to copyright in the Scull photo. In 1982, David Salle, a well-known artist, designed all the costumes and the scenery, including huge stage backdrops, for an opera entitled *Birth of a Poet*, which was staged by some nonprofit organizations abroad and at the Brooklyn Academy of Music. Salle admitted that he ripped the Scull photograph out of the pop art book and made the scene it depicted into a backdrop. Salle indicated, however, that he merely wanted to "capture the imagery conveyed by the Scull Photo,"[325] rather than create an exact duplicate. The photograph is approximately 5½ inches by 7¼ inches, and the backdrop is approximately 50 feet by 30 feet.

At Salle's request, a friend, the photographer Jean Kallina, photographed portions of the Brooklyn Academy of Music performance; at least one photograph included the backdrop. Kallina presented Salle with the contact prints of the photographs. In 1987, Salle agreed to an interview that would be the basis for a monograph entitled *Salle*, published by Vintage Books. The monograph contained one of Kallina's photographs of the stage, including the backdrop. Kallina was compensated by Vintage Books for its use of the photograph. Later that year, Heyman saw the Salle monograph, including the Kallina photograph, and sued both Salle and Kallina on a variety of claims, including copyright infringement.

Salle asserted, among other defenses, that the plaintiffs never obtained a copyright for the Scull photo itself and that a copyright in a compilation or a collective work "does not extend copyright protection to the separate component parts of the compilation or collective work."[326]

The court disagreed. First, it noted that a compilation is

> a work formed by the collection and assembling of preexisting materials . . . that are selected, coordinated, or arranged in such a way that the resulting work as a whole constitutes an original work of authorship,[327]

and that those compilations composed of copyrightable contributions are known as "collective works."

The court then referred to section 103(b) of the Copyright Act of 1976, which states in pertinent part that "the copyright in a compilation or derivative work extends only to the material contributed by the author of such work."[328] The court then concluded that since Heyman took the Scull photo, itself an original work, the copyright of *Pop Art* extends to the Scull photo "as a component part that the author himself contributed."[329]

In the 2000 case of *Eastern America Trio Products, Inc. v. Tang Electronic Corp.*,[330] a New York federal district court held that although copyright protection for compilations may extend to the selection, coordination, and arrangement of the components of the compilations, even if such components are in the public domain, protection also extends to components that are individual original works by the authors of the compilations. In this case, since the plaintiff company affixed a copyright notice on each page of its catalog, the court held that it placed the defendant on notice that each individual work was protected by copyright.

FORM AND PLACEMENT OF NOTICE

THE COPYRIGHT ACT OF 1976

For copies of works publicly distributed by authority of the copyright owner on or after January 1, 1978, but before March 1, 1989, the prescribed copyright notice must be affixed to all "visually" perceptible copies of a work "publicly distributed" anywhere "by authority of the copyright owner."[331] The required form of notice consists of three elements:

1. "Copyright," "Copr.," or "©"
2. The year of the work's first publication
3. The name of the owner of the copyright in the work or an abbreviation by which the name can be recognized or a generally known alternative designation of the owner[332]

However, on a pictorial, graphic, or sculptural work that accompanies textual matter or that is reproduced on greeting cards, postcards, stationery, jewelry, dolls, toys, or any useful articles, the date may be omitted.[333]

As to its placement, "the notice shall be affixed to the copies in such manner and location as to give reasonable notice of the claim of copyright."[334] The notice for a two-dimensional work must be affixed directly or by a label to the front or the back of the work or to another material to which the copy is permanently attached. The same requirement applies to a three-dimensional work except that the notice must be affixed on a visible portion of the work.[335]

For copies of works publicly distributed by authority of the copyright owner on or after March 1, 1989 (when Berne became effective in the United States), the codified requirements as to the placement and the correct form of copyright notice are permissive, rather than mandatory.[336]

THE COPYRIGHT ACT OF 1909

Under the Copyright Act of 1909, the prescribed copyright notice was required to be affixed on each copy of a work "published or offered for sale in the United States by authority of the copyright proprietor."[337] The required form of notice for works of art was identical to the 1976 Act except that the year of the work's first publication was not required.[338] Moreover, for works of art, an alternative short-form notice was available, consisting of "©" plus the mark or symbol of the copyright proprietor, provided that the proprietor's name appeared on some accessible portion of the copy of the work.[339]

As to placement of the notice, the 1909 Act, unlike the 1976 Act, had no statutory requirement. Case law, however, dictated that the notice be placed on an integral part of the artwork that provided the public, on inspection, with notice of the proprietor's claim of copyright.[340] Such a placement was certainly not present in *Sherr v. Universal Match Corporation*.[341] In that case, the copyright claimant affixed a notice on the back of a tall statue depicting a charging infantryman. The notice was placed approximately twenty-two feet from the ground and was not visible to anyone inspecting the statue. The court held that the notice was inadequate and that exhibition of the statue injected it into the public domain.[342]

OMISSION OF NOTICE

For authorized public distribution of copies of works before March 1, 1989, the 1976 Act excused an omission of the required copyright notice "from no more than a relatively small number of copies ... distributed to the public,"[343] regardless of whether the omission was by accident[344] and regardless of whether the copyright owner had sought to comply with the 1976 Act.[345] In the Second Circuit, at any rate, deliberate omissions of copyright notice under the 1976 Act prior to March 1, 1989 are curable under the statute.[346] Under the 1909 Act, an omission of copyright notice from a "particular copy or copies" invalidated the copyright unless the copyright proprietor could demonstrate attempted compliance with the copyright notice provisions of the act.[347] Thus, an omission by accident or oversight (which is contrary to demonstrating attempted compliance) was not excused under the 1909 Act. Moreover, where notice is required, the 1976 Act offers the copyright owner increased protection in the event of failure to apply the notice to copies of a published work in two additional respects: The work is protected (1) if the copyright owner registers the work before or within five years after the publication without the notice and makes a reasonable effort to add the notice to all copies publicly distributed in the United States[348] and (2) if the notice was omitted by a third person in violation of the express written requirement of the copyright owner.[349]

Where an author consents to the inclusion of her work in a derivative work, the publication of the derivative work, to the extent that it discloses the original work, also constitutes publication of the underlying work, unless the underlying work is already protected by statutory copyright.[350]

DEFECTIVE NOTICE

For authorized public distribution of copies of works before March 1, 1989, the 1976 Act provides that where such copies omit the copyright owner's name or the date, when required, in the copyright notice, the work is deemed to have been published without any notice and is governed by the provisions discussed in the above section on omission of notice.[351] In the case of an error in name, the ownership and the validity of the copyright are not affected, but an innocent infringer may have a complete defense if that party can prove that she was misled by the notice.[352] The 1909 Act contained no provisions expressly addressing defective notice.

Registration

Berne made the placement of notice permissive, but the U.S. accession to Berne did not make registration permissive, at least for works originating in the United

States. In fact, under the 1976 Copyright Act, federal courts may adjudicate infringement claims involving unregistered works solely under the following circumstances:

- where the work is not a U.S. work;[353]
- where the infringement claim concerns rights of attribution and integrity[354] (that is, moral rights, addressed in chapter 12);
- where the holder attempted to register the work and registration was refused;[355] and
- where, with respect to certain types of unregistered works, the author "declare[s] an intention to secure copyright in the work" and "makes registration for the work, if required by [section 411(a) of the 1976 Act], within three months after [the work's] first transmission."[356]

It should be noted, as clarified by the 2010 United States Supreme Court case of *Reed Elsevier v. Muchnick*,[357] that registration of a work under the 1976 Act is a precondition to filing a claim and, notwithstanding prior jurisdictional treatment by the courts,[358] does not restrict a federal court's subject-matter jurisdiction over copyright infringement actions.

Registration under the 1976 Act is not a condition of copyright protection,[359] but failure to register can have deleterious effects on the copyright. Registration can be obtained at any time during the life of the copyright in any published or unpublished work, whether the copyright was obtained before or after January 1, 1978. The owner of the copyright or (for works created on or after January 1, 1978) of any exclusive right in a work of art—including pictorial, graphic, and sculptural works—may register by delivering to the Copyright Office

(1) the application form VA for copyright registration,[360]
(2) the fee for registration and issuance of a certificate of registration, and
(3) one deposit copy of an unpublished work or, for a published work, two deposit copies of the work's "best edition."[361]

(See discussion of deposit copies on page 966.) Form VA and related materials from the Copyright Office are reprinted at the end of this chapter (Appendix 11-1).

The certificate of registration is issued once the material deposited in the Copyright Office is found to be copyrightable and the other legal and formal requirements of the law have been met.[362] The certificate includes the information given in the application, along with the number and the effective date of the registration.[363] If registration is refused, the applicant receives written notification of the reasons for the refusal.[364]

Various provisions of the law encourage prompt registration. If, for example, registration is made before publication or within five years after publication without a required copyright notice, the registration can prevent invalidation of the copyright.[365] Moreover, with respect to published works, a certificate of registration from the Copyright Office obtained within five years following a work's first publication "constitutes prima facie evidence of the validity of the copyright and of the facts stated in the certificate."[366] While a registration made more than five years following a work's first publication is still valid, it is subject to whatever weight a court in its discretion deems appropriate. For example, in the 2008 case of *Sportsmans Warehouse v. Fair*,[367] where the defendant filed his copyright registration with respect to his elk sculpture *Royal Entrance* eleven years after his purported first publication of that work and nine years after the first proven publication of that work, the Colorado federal district court declined to extend the presumption of validity to the copyright. Registration is also required for the filing of a renewal claim.[368] Moreover, whether or not a work is published, the holder of the copyright, except for Berne Convention works whose country of origin is not the United States, cannot bring an infringement suit unless the work has first been registered.[369] The owner of a copyright or of any exclusive right in a work may register her copyright interest with the United States Copyright Office.[370] Although a single registration of copyright is permitted for a group of related works,[371] that procedure should not be abused, as noted in the case of *Tabra, Inc. v. Treasures de Paradise Designs, Inc.*[372] The plaintiff company designed, manufactured, and sold primitive jewelry made of beads, seashells, stones, horn, bones, and the like. In early 1989, the plaintiff registered six copyrights covering more than 250 designs of jewelry. Later in 1989, the defendants, importers and wholesalers of jewelry, brought back from Thailand examples of the "Juliet" line, a variety of primitive jewelry, and subsequently advertised the line in *Accessories* magazine. After the defendants disregarded the plaintiff's numerous cease-and-desist-from-infringement letters, the plaintiff brought an infringement action against the defendants and simultaneously sought a preliminary injunction against further sales and distribution of several styles of the defendants' jewelry.

The defendants asserted that primitive-look jewelry was on the market long before the plaintiff registered its alleged copyright and that at least thirty to forty manufacturers of primitive jewelry used the same material. The defendants argued, among other points, that the plaintiff's copyright was invalid because it was an attempt to copyright an idea, rather than its expression, and the jewelry lacked originality.

In denying the plaintiff injunctive relief, the court noted that the plaintiff's six copyright registrations covered more than 250 designs that were grouped by design year only and not by any distinguishing characteristics. As the court observed:

> Given the sheer number of arrangements that [the plaintiff] claims to have under its copyright protection, there is a tremendous likelihood that any arrangement of bone, shell, stone and bead findings will have a certain resemblance, and will perhaps even be substantially similar, to at least one of plaintiff's over 250 copyrighted articles. . . . [T]o hold that defendants' pieces infringe a valid copyright absent a

showing of direct copying would be tantamount to conferring on plaintiff a monopoly on the idea of primitive look jewelry.[373]

It is important to note that a single registration of a collective work registers the constituent parts of such a work only where the registration application identifies the authors and the titles of the constituent parts. In 2001, in *Morris v. Business Concepts, Inc.*,[374] the Second Circuit held that a freelancer's articles in *Allure* magazine were not automatically and independently registered by virtue of the publisher's registration of entire magazine issues as collective works. The court further explained that in order to have secured a copyright in the articles alone, the application must have included the name of the author and the title of the work. Since the magazine's registration did not specify this information, the magazine's application for registration applied only to its registration of the issue of the magazine as a collective work.

Registration may also be abused by furnishing erroneous information in an application for copyright.[375] Immaterial inadvertent errors in such an application do not jeopardize a registration's validity,[376] but a material error may well do so. However, where the work being registered is of a derivative nature and the registrant fails to indicate such on the application, copyright protection will be denied where the court finds that this failure to inform was motivated by a deliberate misrepresentation.[377] In one case, registrations of portrait photographs as unpublished collections were invalidated because the photographs were considered published by being delivered to customers.[378] Invalidation may also result from knowingly furnishing incomplete information on an application when the complete information might have occasioned rejection of the application, as illustrated in the case of *Whimsicality, Inc. v. Rubie's Costume Co.*[379]

The plaintiff, a small but thriving Vermont corporation founded in 1978, designed, manufactured, and sold various home-craft items, such as quilts, children's apparel, adult toys, and novelties. In 1985, it began distributing a line of items described to the United States Copyright Office (and for which it received copyright registrations) as "soft sculptures," although they were used primarily as costumes. In the ensuing years, the plaintiff enjoyed substantial success with that line of items, which grew to include at least sixty-six varieties, and the company received substantial publicity from the mass media for the quality of its designs.

In 1989, at the National Halloween Show, the plaintiff discovered that the defendant—a manufacturer and distributor of masquerade and theater-related items, including Halloween costumes—was displaying knockoff Halloween costumes of the plaintiff's soft sculptures for sale in the upcoming Halloween season. The plaintiff accordingly sued for infringement and moved for injunctive relief, whereupon the defendant, arguing that the plaintiff's copyright registrations were invalid because the soft sculptures were nothing more than uncopyrightable costumes, sought dismissal of the plaintiff's infringement claim.

In granting the defendant's motion to dismiss the lawsuit, the New York federal district court noted that although the plaintiff's possession of a registration certificate for each of the designs at issue created a rebuttable presumption that the works in question were copyrightable, that presumption could be successfully overcome if the copyright claimant knowingly failed to fully disclose the nature of its work to the Copyright Office. As the court observed:

> [T]he knowing failure to advise the Copyright Office of facts which might have occasioned a rejection of the application constitutes reason for holding the registration invalid and thus incapable of supporting an infringement action.[380]

As the court further noted:

> [I]t is uncontested that in every single piece of promotional literature [the plaintiff] describes these very same items only and always as costumes. . . . Thus it is clear . . . that [the plaintiff] considers the items to be costumes, promotes them as costumes, and profits principally because consumers purchase them as costumes.[381]

Moreover, the court observed that the Copyright Office rejected the defendant's applications for copyright for various costumes in part on the grounds that costumes are wearing apparel and thus not copyrightable.

In affirming the district court's dismissal of the copyright claim and the denial of injunctive relief, the Second Circuit took a dim view of what it termed the plaintiff's "misconduct" and "willful misrepresentation"[382] to the Copyright Office.

Deposit

Aside from being required as part of registration, copies of published works, whether or not the works bear a notice of copyright, must be deposited in the Copyright Office for the use of the Library of Congress.[383] The owner of the copyright or of the exclusive right of publication of a work published in the United States must deposit two complete copies of the work's best edition within three months after the date of its publication.[384] The Copyright Act permits the deposit of bona fide copies of the original work and reconstructions made from memory of the original fail to prove the content of the original drawing.[385] Failure to make a timely deposit results in the imposition of fines.[386] The deposit may simultaneously fulfill the deposit requirements of registration.

For copyright holders of pictorial, graphic, and sculptural works, the Register of Copyrights is empowered to exempt a work from the deposit requirement altogether, to require the deposit of only one copy, or to devise an alternate form of deposit for the purpose of easing any practical or financial hardship on the depositor when fewer than five copies of the work have been published or when the work has been published in a limited edition.[387] Artists frequently fulfill the requirement of deposit by filing color transparencies of their work.[388]

Recordation

Under the Copyright Act of 1976, any signed transfer of copyright ownership or other signed documents pertaining to a copyright may, if they meet certain conditions, be recorded in the Copyright Office.[389] Although permissive, rather than mandatory, prompt recordation is desirable for several reasons. First, recordation provides constructive notice of the facts stated in the recorded document.[390] Even if a third party did not have actual notice of the document, she is presumed to have had that information. However, for the constructive notice to be effective, the underlying work must have been registered.[391] Second, recordation, along with registration, is a prerequisite in infringement suits regarding transfers before March 1, 1989.[392] Third, recordation establishes the priority between conflicting transfers.[393] If an artist, for example, conveys a copyright in a piece of sculpture to a university in December 2003 and conveys the copyright in the same work to Collector X in January 2004, the university, as the first transferee, has, if it is located in the United States, a grace period of one month to record the copyright conveyance of the sculpture in the Copyright Office. If the university is not located in the United States, the grace period for recording the conveyance is two months. The expiration of the one-month or two-month grace period marks the beginning of a race between the two transferees. If the university is the last to record, it forfeits its right of copyright.[394] Recordation also determines the priority between a conflicting transfer of ownership and a nonexclusive license.[395]

Like the 1976 Act, the 1909 Act required a written instrument of assignment for the transfer of statutory copyright.[396] Although the Copyright Office did not have explicit authority to record the assignment of any rights less than the full copyright interest,[397] the Copyright Office did accept such partial assignments for recordation. Recordation under the 1909 Act did not necessarily serve as constructive notice to all persons of the contents of the recorded document,[398] and the grace period for recording documents was somewhat longer than it is in the 1976 Act.[399]

Renewals

The concept of copyright renewal was codified in the 1909 Act.[400] The rationale for the renewal provision was to provide authors, who frequently sold their copyrights outright to publishers for a relatively small sum, with a second chance to exploit their work. The provision was particularly pertinent to authors who initially sold the copyrights in their works to publishers for a pittance and later witnessed large profits made from their works by those publishers.[401] As the Supreme Court noted, the "basic consideration of public policy underlying the renewal provision" was the author's right to "sell his 'copyright' without losing his renewal interest."[402]

Although the concept of copyright renewal was abolished by the 1976 Act and was replaced by the idea of termination, a multitude of copyrighted works published before 1978 are now in their first or second term of statutory copyright. For works in their first term of statutory copyright as of January 1, 1978, the renewal provisions of the 1909 Act have been retained, with the renewal term extended from twenty-eight years to sixty-seven years.[403]

The 1976 Act distinguishes between those works securing statutory copyright protection from January 1, 1950, through December 31, 1963, and those works securing such protection from January 1, 1964, through December 31, 1977.[404] For works securing statutory copyright protection from January 1, 1950, through December 31, 1963, the renewal provisions of the 1909 Act have been retained, with the renewal term extended from twenty-eight years to December 31 of the sixty-seventh year.[405] If renewal was not made in a timely fashion, such copyrights expired on December 31 of the twenty-eighth year after statutory copyright was originally secured.[406] To secure the benefit of the sixty-seven-year renewal term, an application for renewal had to be made during the last calendar year of the first term of statutory copyright. If the renewal was not effective by December 31 of the twenty-eighth calendar year, the work was injected into the public domain.[407] If the work was

(1) a posthumous work;
(2) a composite—that is, a collective work; or
(3) a work made for hire,

the copyright proprietor in whom the renewal would vest, as opposed to the author, was required to make the renewal application.[408]

For all other works, the author, if still living, was required to make the renewal application.[409] If the author was dead, the renewal was to be made by the author's surviving spouse or children or, absent those, by her executor or the author's next of kin in the absence of a will.[410]

For works securing statutory copyright protection from January 1, 1964, through December 31, 1977, the claimants who are entitled to the renewal of various categories of work are virtually identical to those mentioned in the paragraph above. However, even if no renewal application is made, the 1976 Act accords a complete sixty-seven year renewal term (expiring December 31 of the sixty-seventh year) to the party who would have been entitled to file for renewal.[411] That is, instead of forfeiture of copyright, the 1976 Act prescribes automatic renewal of copyright.[412]

For works in their renewal term of statutory copyright as of January 1, 1978, the 1976 Act adds thirty-nine years to the original twenty-eight-year renewal term by extending the duration of any copyright in its renewal term or registered for renewal between December 31, 1976, and December 31, 1977, to a period of ninety-five years from the date the copyright was originally secured.[413] For example, if a painting was properly published with notice on September 1, 1942, and copyright in the painting was renewed effective September 1, 1970, its term of copyright expires on December 31, 2037.

Termination of Transfers

For works in their renewal term of copyright as of January 1, 1978, and for works created on or after that date, the concept of copyright renewal does not apply. Instead, the 1976 Act introduces the concept of termination of transfers—that is, a nonwaivable right given to authors (in this case, artists) and their statutory successors to terminate grants of copyright after the lapse of a prescribed period.[414] The rationale for including that reversion of rights in the 1976 Act was to protect authors against unprofitable transfers of copyright arising from the authors' unequal bargaining positions, due, in part, to the impossibility of determining a work's value until it has been exploited.[415] By making the termination a nonwaivable right, the 1976 Act departs from decisional law under the 1909 Act, which permitted an author to waive her rights to the renewal term even before the renewal rights vested in the author.[416]

Generally, the termination provisions apply not only to assignments of copyright but also to exclusive licenses, nonexclusive licenses, and any other conveyances of one or more of the rights "comprised in a copyright."[417] The termination right vests upon the service of a termination notice on the transferee of the interest in the work. If the artist of the work serves notice but dies before the termination takes place, the reversion of the copyright interests in the work goes to the artist's estate, not her statutory successors. If, however, the artist dies before the rights subject to termination have been vested in her, or survives to a date where she could serve the notice but then dies without serving the notice, her statutory successors, rather than her estate, have the right to serve a termination notice on the transferee and are the recipients of the reversion of the copyright interests.[418]

GRANTS EXECUTED BY THE ARTIST ON OR AFTER JANUARY 1, 1978

The artist (or, if the artist is dead, her statutory successors) may reclaim future copyright ownership of the work by terminating a transfer or license of copyright between the thirty-fifth and the fortieth years after the date of its grant.[419]

However, no provision of the 1976 Act prevents the parties to a grant from agreeing that the artist may terminate the grant at an earlier time. The right to terminate applies to all works except works made for hire, and the right cannot be bargained away.[420]

Moreover, the right to terminate a transfer or license applies solely to grants executed by a living artist on or after January 1, 1978; grants by will are not subject to termination.[421] Notice of termination specifying the termination date, which must be within the appropriate five-year period (see next paragraph), must be given in writing by the artist or by her heirs. The notice must be given between two and ten years before the termination date. If the termination rights are not exercised in a timely manner, the grantee of the copyright interest will benefit for the entire duration of copyright.[422] The estate-planning issues that result from the right of termination are discussed in chapter 16.

GRANTS EXECUTED BY THE ARTIST
BEFORE JANUARY 1, 1978

Termination of transfer also applies to the renewal term of a work's copyright,[423] which has been extended from twenty-eight to sixty-seven years. The termination right addresses those additional thirty-nine years of protection only. Thus, an artist (or, if the artist is dead, her statutory successors) may terminate any transfer of a copyright interest and recover all or part of the additional thirty-nine years of the renewal term. The termination right, which does not apply to works made for hire or to grants made by will, may take effect at any time during the five-year period beginning either fifty-six years after the date that copyright in the work was originally secured or on January 1, 1978, whichever date is later.[424] However, no provision of the 1976 Act prevents the parties to a grant from agreeing that the artist may terminate the grant at an earlier time. The terminating party must give written notice of the termination between two and ten years before its effective date and, in doing so, must comply with regulations prescribed by the Register of Copyrights.[425]

Statute of Limitations

Section 507 of the 1976 Act provides that the limitations period for a civil copyright action is three years.[426] Criminal copyright actions are governed by a five-year statute of limitations.[427] The statutory limitations period for civil actions may be modified by contract.[428] In actions for common law copyright infringement, reference must be made to the applicable state tort statute of limitations—for example, three years in New York and two years in California.[429]

The civil statute of limitations is measured from the time "the claim accrued," which by statute is the time that the infringement upon which suit is based occurred.[430] If such infringement occurred within three years prior to filing, the action will not be barred even if prior infringements by the same party as to the same work are barred because they occurred more than three years previously.[431] Where a series of infringements has occurred beginning more than three years before the commencement of the action, most courts allow the infringement suit to proceed based on acts of infringement that occurred within the statutory period, but bar recovery for any acts that occurred more than three years before the commencement of the action.[432] However, one commentator notes that once a defendant establishes a statute of limitations defense in a copyright infringement action, it is incumbent upon the plaintiff to come forward and demonstrate equitable reasons for tolling the statute.[433] Each infringement is deemed to be a separate act that resets the statutory period.[434]

Orphan Works

An orphan work is a work that has been copyrighted but whose copyright owner cannot be identified or located.[435] A work can become orphaned in a number of situations. For instance, the author may never have registered the work as copyrighted since registration with the Copyright Office is no longer a condition of copyright protection.[436] In addition, the artist may have died and the potential user may be unable to find the artist's heirs. Alternatively, the artist may have transferred the copyright to the work and never recorded this transfer. The inability to locate or identify the copyright owner of an orphan work poses a problem for those who wish to use the work, as this means that they cannot obtain the necessary permission from the copyright owner before using the work. If potential users then begin to utilize the work without the permission of the copyright owner, they may face an infringement suit and damages if the copyright owner surfaces in the future. While the possibility of an infringement suit disappears once the work's copyright term has expired, it sometimes is nearly impossible for potential users to determine if the work has been released to the public.[437] Problems created by orphan works have raised concerns that subsequent artists will be reticent to create new works incorporating them.[438] In addition, some worry that museums, educational institutions, libraries, and other nonprofit organizations will hesitate to provide orphan works for public enjoyment.[439] As a result, many orphan works have remained unused, regardless of their importance and value.

Congress has recognized the problems caused by orphan works, and as a result bills have been proposed that address these works. In 2006, bills were introduced in both houses, but both versions failed in committee. Then, in 2008, new bills were introduced to both houses.[440] The Senate version of the bill, entitled the Shawn Bentley Orphan Works Act of 2008, passed the Senate on September 26, 2008. This legislation was introduced to the House of Representatives the following day, but it died in committee at the end of the 110th Congressional session.

While the 2008 legislation was never approved by the House, an examination of the key provisions of this legislation may provide helpful insight into the content of any future proposals. The 2008 legislation enabled potential users to use copyrighted orphan works so long as they engaged in a good-faith diligent search for the copyright owner and filed a notice with the Copyright Office before using such orphan works.[441] The House's version of the bill provided that the user must file a notice with the Register of Copyrights prior to using an orphan work, and that this notice must (i) identify the work, its author, and any other identifying information and provide a description of the work, (ii) describe the intended uses of the work, (iii) describe the user's efforts to identify and locate the copyright owner, (iv) certify that a good-faith diligent search was made, (v) state the name of the user, and (vi) include any other information discovered during the search.[442] The user was required to include a copyright symbol or other notice approved by the Copyright Office when actually using the orphan work.[443] If the copyright owner was later revealed, he or she could not seek the usual penalties for infringement so long as the user engaged in a good-faith diligent search and filed the requisite notice with the Copyright Office. Instead, the user was liable to pay only "reasonable compensation" to the copyright owner, which the parties were required to negotiate in good faith based on a willing-buyer-willing-seller standard.[444] The copyright owner was permitted to seek an injunction, but if the user had integrated or adapted the orphan work into a new work that contained a significant degree of the user's own original expression, the injunction could not limit such original expression.[445] Finally, the proposed legislation required that the Copyright Office certify search databases to enable potential users to more easily find the missing copyright owners.[446]

The 2008 proposed legislation also established a safe harbor for nonprofit institutions, such as educational institutions, museums, libraries, and archives. The use of orphan works by these institutions would not create any liability so long as (1) the institution had no intention of commercial advantage with respect to its use of the work; (2) the intention of the use was primarily for educational, religious, or charitable purposes; and (3) once the copyright owner was discovered, the institution ceased any use of the orphan work.[447] As long as these requirements were satisfied, nonprofit institutions were not obligated to pay reasonable compensation to copyright owners.

Orphan works legislation has received much support from those wishing to facilitate greater access to copyrighted works. For instance, nonprofit institutions support such legislation, as it will allow them to provide the public with greater access to orphan works.[448] The American Association of Museums supports the introduction of such legislation since it will greatly diminish the time and expense of searching for copyright owners of orphan works. Oftentimes museums keep these works in storage until they are released into the public domain, as it is too difficult for them to search for the copyright owner. This is not ideal, because "[b]y the time such works are in the public domain, it is quite possible there will be little or no interest in them at all. Without a change in the law, [the public] may never know these orphans."[449]

The nonprofit safe harbor contained in the 2008 bills would further enable these institutions to provide orphan works to the public, as they generally will face no liability for using the works without the copyright owners' permission. Illustrators, compilers, and artists who adapt and transform the works of other artists also support the introduction of orphan works legislation, since it will enable them to incorporate orphan works into their own works without an overwhelmingly time-intensive and expensive search and without fear of facing an infringement lawsuit.

On the other hand, artists and organizations representing artists have opposed the orphan works legislation. For instance, shortly after the 2008 legislation was introduced to Congress, artist Frank Stella wrote an editorial criticizing many aspects of the proposed legislation.[450] First, artists are concerned that there is no clear guidance on what constitutes a good-faith diligent search. Under the 2008 bills, for instance, the only way for a copyright owner of an orphan work to truly determine whether a search has been adequately performed is to bring suit in federal court, and the costs of such a suit will likely vastly outweigh the licensing fee the artist receives for the work. In addition, artists are concerned that any orphan works legislation passed by Congress will hamper the artist's ability to make a living. This is especially true for paintings and other works of visual art, as they often do not have "universally accepted titles" that make it easy to search for them. In addition, the Internet has made it very "easy for an illustration, drawing or image of a painting to become separated from any publication in which it has been reproduced and which may have identified the artist."[451] While this problem may be alleviated in part by the creation of online visual search databases, artists are concerned about the expense, complexity, and time that will be required of them to create digital images of their works and place them onto such databases. Many artists have produced thousands of artworks, and the burdens imposed on them could be overwhelming, especially in light of the fact that many artists have limited administrative and financial support. Artists also are concerned that "reasonable compensation" is inadequate, since it may be prohibitively expensive for them to go to court if needed to recover the compensation.

At the time of the publication of this treatise, there is no pending orphan works legislation before Congress. Nonetheless, the issue continues to be of concern to members of the art community, and it is possible that future bills will be introduced. Artists and anyone who is interested in potentially using an orphan work should pay close attention to the status of any future orphan works legislation, since passage of such legislation will bring important changes to the treatment of orphan works in the art industry.

UTILITARIAN OBJECTS AND COPYRIGHT

In a sense, the above heading is oxymoronic: A property with the status of art is entitled to copyright protection under the Copyright Act of 1976, but an article having "an intrinsic utilitarian function that is not merely to portray the appearance of the article"[452] is not entitled to copyright protection. The act denies copyright protection to utilitarian elements of a property on the rationale that such elements, if they are to be protected at all, must satisfy the stringent requirements of utility patent law. That distinction does not mean that protectable art cannot be composed of utilitarian elements: The readymades by dada artist Marcel Duchamp, such as the object entitled *Hat Rack* and the "sculpture" entitled *Bicycle Wheel*, and *Brillo Boxes* by Andy Warhol can all be seen in museums and are recognized as art. The question of what constitutes "art" has for many centuries been the focus of aesthetic theory; perceptions range from the metaphysical ruminations of Plato in *The Republic* that art is merely an imitation of a greater reality to the eighteenth-century romantic view of art as an enlargement of nature to the current theory that searches for common elements that make certain properties "art."[453] Of necessity, the theoretical dimensions of the definition of "art" are beyond the scope of this book. They are also beyond the scope of United States copyright laws, which do not intend for judges or the Copyright Office to apply aesthetic judgments in determining what rises to the level of "art" and is, therefore, copyrightable.[454]

Section 102 of the 1976 Act, in delineating what is protectable, states, in pertinent part, that

[c]opyright protection subsists . . . in original works of authorship fixed in any tangible medium of expression . . . from which they can be perceived[455]

and that works of authorship include "pictorial, graphic, and sculptural works."[456]

Section 101 of the 1976 Act defines "pictorial, graphic, and sculptural works" to include

two-dimensional and three-dimensional works of fine, graphic, and applied art, photographs, prints and art reproductions, maps, globes, charts, diagrams, models, and technical drawings, including architectural plans. Such works shall include works of artistic craftsmanship insofar as their form but not their mechanic or utilitarian aspects are concerned; *the design of a useful article . . . shall be considered a pictorial, graphic, or sculptural work only if, and only to the extent that, such design incorporates pictorial, graphic, or sculptural features that can be identified separately from, and are capable of existing independently of, the utilitarian aspects of the article.* [italics ours][457]

Section 101 defines a "useful article" as one

having an intrinsic utilitarian function that is not merely to portray the appearance of the article or to convey information. An article that is normally part of a useful article is considered a "useful article."[458]

In attempting to clarify which materials having both aesthetic and utilitarian qualities are copyrightable and to what extent, the 1976 Act built on principles established in case law. In *Mazer v. Stein*,[459] a 1954 case, the United States Supreme Court addressed the issue of the validity of copyrights obtained for statuettes of male and female dancing figures made of semivitreous china whose intended use, as lamp bases to be made and sold in quantity, was utilitarian. The Court, in determining that the objects could be copyrighted, reviewed the development of copyright legislation. It noted that the Copyright Act of 1870 defined copyrightable subject matter as

any book, map, chart, dramatic or musical composition, engraving, cut, print, or photograph or negative thereof, or of a painting, drawing, chromo, statue, statuary, and of models or designs intended to be perfected as works of the fine arts.[460]

The Court then observed that in the Copyright Act of 1909, the fine-arts clause of the 1870 Act had been deleted and that the Copyright Office furnished sixty examples of registrations between 1912 and 1952 of "works of art possessing utilitarian aspects."[461] The Court then concluded that the legislative history of the 1909 Act and the practice of the Copyright Office unite to show that "works of art" . . . are terms that were intended by Congress to include the authority to copyright these statuettes.[462]

The Court also observed that it does not consider an object published as an element in a manufactured article and subsequently registered as an artwork to be an abuse of copyright. Therefore, although *Mazer v. Stein* extended copyright protection to applied art, the Copyright Office was impelled to develop distinctions between objects that have utilitarian functions but are works of art and, therefore, copyrightable and those utilitarian articles for which a patent would be appropriate, provided they meet the rigorous standards of patent protection.

The distinction is often delicate, and courts vary in their line-drawing approach. Courts inclined to maintain unmistakably separate domains of copyright and patent protection, the position adopted by the Copyright Office,[463] give broad construction to the statutory term "useful article," defining it to include both functional items, such as belt buckles, and nonfunctional items, such as toys.[464] In addition, such courts require that any copyrightable elements in the useful article be "physically separable" from it: That is, to qualify for protection, such elements must be able to be "physically separated from the article without impairing the article's utility" and, once separated, must stand alone as an artwork.[465] And so in *Esquire v. Ringer*,[466] a 1978 case applying the 1909 Act, the District of Columbia Circuit, in reversing a district court finding, held that the overall shape of certain outdoor lighting fixtures is not copyrightable as a work of art and that the Copyright Office properly denied copyright registration of the lighting designs. In so holding, the court noted that the Copyright Office's denial of registration found further support in the legislative history of the 1976 Act. Quoting from the House Report, the court observed that

> [e]ven if the appearance of an article is determined by aesthetic (as opposed to functional) considerations, only elements, if any, which can be identified separately from the useful article as such are copyrightable. And even if the three dimensional design contains some such element (for example, a carving on the back of a chair or a floral relief design on silver flatware), Copyright protection would extend only to that element, and would not cover the over-all configuration of the utilitarian article as such.[467]

One may wonder how the *Esquire* court would have dealt with the sculptures of the recently deceased late-twentieth-century artist Dan Flavin, whose arrangements of fluorescent lights have been exhibited in major museums, such as the Guggenheim Museum in New York City, as important art.

Contrary to the court in *Esquire*, other courts tolerate a narrow zone between copyrightable works of art and uncopyrightable works of industrial design, limit the application of the statutory term "useful article" to genuinely functional objects, and require only that the protectable elements of such objects be conceptually separable from the useful article.[468]

Conceptual Separability

To date, courts and commentators have been unable to agree on a definitive meaning of "conceptual separability,"[469] partly because the subjective nature of art itself eludes conclusive definition. As noted by the Seventh Circuit in *Galiano v. Harrah's Operating Co.*[470] "courts 'have twisted themselves into knots trying to create a test to effectively ascertain whether the artistic aspects of a useful article can be identified separately from and exist independently of the article's utilitarian function.'" What follows, then, are some of the formulations devised by courts and commentators in grappling with what is perhaps an unanswerable question.

For example, in the 1980 case of *Kieselstein-Cord v. Accessories by Pearl, Inc.*,[471] the Second Circuit, in reversing the finding of a lower court, upheld the copyrightability of two belt buckles that were solid sculptural designs cast in precious metals. In so holding, the Second Circuit referred to the legislative intent of the 1976 Act as expressed in the House Report, which indicates that copyright can inhere in the conceptual and the physical separation of an artistic element "from the utilitarian aspects of a useful article."[472] The court noted that it recognized "conceptually separable sculptural elements" in the belt buckles and observed that wearers of the buckles have used them to adorn "parts of the body other than the waist."[473] As the court stated,

> [t]he primary ornamental aspect of the . . . buckles is conceptually separable from their subsidiary utilitarian function. This conclusion is not at variance with the expressed congressional intent to distinguish copyrightable applied art and uncopyrightable industrial design. . . . Pieces of applied art, these buckles may be considered jewelry, the form of which is subject to copyright protection. . . . [T]he buckles rise to the level of creative art.[474]

Kieselstein-Cord's formulation of "conceptual separability" appears to require mere identification of artistic elements separate from the utilitarian function of the work, but the 1985 case of *Carol Barnhart, Inc. v. Economy Cover Corp.*[475] adopted a more stringent standard. Here, the Second Circuit denied copyrightability to mannequins of partial human torsos that were used to display articles of clothing. The objects in question were four life-size human upper-torso forms, two male and two female, that were designed by the plaintiff. Each torso, made of expandable white styrene, was without a neck, arms, and a back. One each of the male and female torsos was nude for the display of shirts and sweaters; the other two torsos were sculpted with shirts for the display of sweaters and jackets. In denying copyrightability, the court found that the aesthetic features of the forms—that is, the configuration of the breasts and the width of the shoulders—were inseparable from the forms' function as utilitarian objects.[476] In arriving at such a finding, the court observed that whatever the forms' aesthetically pleasing features, those features, even when "considered in the aggregate," cannot be envisioned as "existing independently of their utilitarian function."[477] The court distinguished between *Barnhart* and *Kieselstein-Cord* by noting that the ornamented surfaces of the [*Kieselstein-Cord*] buckles were not in any respect required by their utilitarian functions; the artistic and aesthetic features could thus be conceived of as having been added to, or superimposed upon, an otherwise utilitarian article. The unique article design was wholly unnecessary to performance of the utilitarian function.[478]

In drawing such a distinction, the court invoked a formulation of "conceptual separability" that demanded not only that the aesthetic elements of an article be separately identified from the article's utilitarian function but that such elements not be governed by the article's purpose.

The Second Circuit in *Barnhart* did not unilaterally stand behind its formulation of conceptual separability. In Judge Jon O. Newman's dissent, he essayed five other standards of conceptual separability, the last of which he adopted as his own. Under the five standards he proposed, conceptual separability exists or does not exist as follows:

1. It does not exist where an article is "used primarily to serve its utilitarian function," even though the article's "design elements [render] it usable secondarily solely as an artwork."[479]
2. It exists "whenever the decorative or aesthetically pleasing aspect of the article can be said to be 'primary' and the utilitarian function can be said to be 'subsidiary.'"[480]
3. It exists "where there is any substantial likelihood that even if the article had no utilitarian use it would still be marketable to some significant segment of the community simply because of its aesthetic qualities."[481]
4. It exists "whenever the design of a form has sufficient aesthetic appeal to be appreciated for its artistic qualities."[482]
5. It exists where the article stimulates "in the mind of the beholder a concept that is separate from the concept evoked by its utilitarian function."[483]

At least one of the above-noted standards has found resonance in subsequent case law. In the 1987 case of *Brandir International, Inc. v. Cascade Pacific Lumber Co.*,[484] the Second Circuit commented favorably on the standard of conceptual separability adopted by Judge Newman in his dissent in *Barnhart*. However, it did not adhere to that standard in affirming a lower-court denial of copyright protection to Ribbon Rack, a bicycle rack made of bent tubing, purportedly originating from a wire sculpture. Instead, the Second Circuit adopted still another approach to determining the existence of conceptual separability:

If design elements reflect a merger of aesthetic and functional considerations, the artistic aspects of a work cannot be said to be conceptually separable from the utilitarian elements. Conversely, where design elements can be identified as reflecting the designer's artistic judgment exercised independently of functional influences, conceptual separability exists.[485]

The Second Circuit case of *Hart v. Dan Chase Taxidermy Supply Co.*[486] also merits consideration. The parties to the action produced fish "mannequins," forms used for displaying fish skins. Appellants challenged the 1995 holding[487] of a New York federal district court that appellants' fish forms were not protectable under copyright law because the differences between their forms and all other fish forms were too slight. In 1996, on appeal,[488] the Second Circuit distinguished between the noncopyrightability of mannequins of human torsos as sculptural works and the protectibility of taxidermy forms designed to hold up fish skins. In differentiating the *Barnhart* torsos from the fish mannequins, the Second Circuit noted that in *Barnhart*

> the headless, armless, backless styrene torsos were little more than glorified coat-racks used to display clothing in stores. The torsos were designed to present the clothing, not their own forms. In taxidermy, by contrast, people . . . wish to see a complete "fish." The . . . shape, volume, and movement of the animal are depicted by the underlying mannequin. . . .
>
> [T]he fish mannequin is designed to be looked at. . . . The function of the fish form is to portray its own appearance, and that fact is enough to bring it within the scope of the Copyright Act.[489]

However, the Second Circuit at the same time noted that appellants' fish mannequins might not be protectable under the copyright laws because of the merger doctrine, that is, that the difference between appellants' works and all other fish forms may be so slight that any copy of the idea would invariably duplicate appellants' work.[490] On remand in 1997, the New York federal district court held[491] that this was precisely the case: that is, that apart from minor differences in, for example, the cant of the tails, all of the fish forms examined by the federal district court were materially the same; therefore the merger doctrine applied. This served to render appellants' fish forms uncopyrightable. On appeal, the Second Circuit in 1998 affirmed the district court's holding.[492]

The Seventh Circuit, in its 2004 holding in *Pivot Point v. Charlene Products*[493] that Pivot Point's mannequin head sculpture was subject to copyright protection, attempted to fashion a coherent approach to conceptual separability on the basis of past cases. Pivot Point, a company that developed and marketed educational techniques and tools for the hair design industry, engaged a German artist to create an original sculpture of a female human head to be marketed to cutting-edge hairstylists. Although Pivot Point advised the artist that it wanted a head that would imitate the "hungry" look of high fashion, it did not give the artist any specific dimensional requirements. The artist duly created a sculpture in plaster entitled *Mara*, a female human head with no makeup or hair. Pivot Point manufactured the sculpture, obtained a copyright registration for the design of *Mara*, and enjoyed great success with its new mannequin. Subsequently, at a trade show in 1989, the defendant Charlene, a wholesaler of beauty products, displayed its *Liza* mannequin, which had facial features strikingly similar to those of *Mara*. Later that year, Pivot Point filed an action for copyright infringement.

An Illinois federal district court, finding that *Mara* was an intrinsically useful article with no sculptural elements existing independently of its utilitarian aspects, and therefore not copyrightable, dismissed the case on summary judgment.

On appeal, the Seventh Circuit reversed. In forging its own theory of conceptual separability and holding that *Mara* was indeed subject to copyright protection, the court reasoned as follows. It examined, among others, the earlier-discussed cases of *Kieselstein-Cord, Barnhart,* and *Brandir,* and determined that

> [a] process-oriented approach for conceptual separability—focusing on the process of creating the object to determine whether it is entitled to copyright protection . . . reconciles the earlier case law pertaining to conceptual separability.[494]

The Seventh Circuit went on to note that

> In *Kieselstein-Cord* . . . the artistic aspects of the belt buckles reflected purely aesthetic choices, independent of the buckles' function, while in [*Barnhart*] the distinctive features of the torsos . . . showed clearly the influence of functional concerns. . . . [I]t was evident the designer incorporated [the torsos' artistic] features to further the usefulness of the torsos as mannequins.[495]

Moreover, the court observed that *Brandir* is consistent in that

> [i]n creating the Ribbon Rack, the designer clearly adapted the original aesthetic elements to accommodate and further a utilitarian purpose.[496]

Continuing to cite *Brandir,* the Seventh Circuit, in distilling its approach to conceptual separability, observed that

> [i]f the elements . . . reflect the independent artistic judgment of the designer, conceptual separability exists. Conversely, when the design of a useful article is 'as much the result of utilitarian pressures as aesthetic choices,' the useful and aesthetic elements are not conceptually separable.[497]

Finally, the court alluded to the 2004 case of *Mattel v. Goldberger Doll Manufacturing Company,*[498] in which the Second Circuit rejected the idea that a particular expression of facial features on a doll was not entitled to copyright protection.

Mindful of *Mattel,* and in applying its distilled concept of conceptual separability to the *Mara* mannequin, the Seventh Circuit concluded that

> The Mara face is subject to copyright protection . . . Mara can be conceptualized as existing independent from its use in hair display . . . because it is the product of [the German artist's] artistic judgment. . . . [T]here is no evidence that [the artist's] artistic judgment was constrained by functional considerations.[499]

And finally,

[j]ust as Mattel is entitled to protection for 'its own particularized expression' of
an 'upturned nose, bow lips, and widely spaced eyes,' . . . so too is . . . Pivot Point
. . . entitled to have [its] expression of the 'hungry look' protected from copying.[500]

More recently the Fourth Circuit, in the 2010 case of *Universal Furniture
International v. Collezione Europa USA*,[501] in finding that the decorative elements on certain furniture lines were conceptually separable from the utilitarian
aspects of the furniture, incorporated as part of its determination the "process-
oriented" approach cited in *Pivot Point*.[502] The parties were two competing furniture companies. The plaintiff, Universal, based in North Carolina, designed,
imported, and distributed furniture manufactured outside of the United States.
Its furniture lines in issue, the Grand Inheritance Collection (GIC) and the English Manor Collection (EMC), became available to the public in, respectively,
2001 and 2003. The design process for each line included the consultation of public domain sources such as furniture books and antiques magazines; collecting,
sorting, and synthesizing the various decorative elements; and conceptual hand
sketches inspired by but modifying the public domain sources, to combine and
blend the decorative elements from different historical periods to create a different look. In 2003, the decorative sculptural designs on each of the two lines were
registered with the U.S. Copyright office.

In 2004, defendant Collezione agreed to design, for a furniture purchasing
company, a cheaper alternative to Universal's GIC and EMC lines. Although Collezione was unaware that Universal had obtained copyright registrations for the
two furniture lines, it nevertheless believed that the GIC and EMC designs were
not entitled to copyright protection and that Collezione had the right to mimic
them. Accordingly, in 2004, Collezione introduced to the marketplace two furniture lines mimicking Universal's GIC and EMC lines. In 2005, Universal sued
Collezione in a North Carolina federal district court, seeking a preliminary injunction barring Collezione's promotion and sale of its two allegedly infringing
lines of furniture. The federal district court denied the preliminary injunction
and the denial was affirmed by the Fourth Circuit,[503] which, however, emphasized that the record was sparse and that it was not its intention to "categorically
exclude Universal's and other comparable design compilations from copyright
protection."[504] In 2007, Universal's lawsuit against Collezione proceeded to a
five-day bench trial in the North Carolina federal district court which ruled,
among other points, that Universal's GIC and EMC designs were copyrightable,
that is, that they were sufficiently unique in the compilation of the design elements so as to meet the originality requirement and that the decorative elements were conceptually separable from the furniture.[505] The court accordingly
awarded Universal a permanent injunction prohibiting Collezione from marketing or selling any of its furniture.

In affirming the permanent injunction, the Fourth Circuit, in terms of concep-
tual separability, and with a nod to the "process-oriented" approach taken by the
Seventh Circuit, noted, with respect to the decorative elements on the GIC and
EMC lines of furniture, that the process taken by Universal's designer

reflects an "artistic judgment exercised independently of functional influences." . . . [The designer's] objective in compiling these decorative elements onto the basic shapes of the furniture was not to improve the furniture's utility but to "give [the pieces] a pretty face." . . . For many of the decorative elements on the furniture, such as carved shells and leaves, [the designer's] purpose was entirely aesthetic. . . . Aesthetic choices were the dominant force at work in [the designer's] design process.[506]

However, the Fourth Circuit also noted that the test for conceptual separability is conjunctive:

[T]he decorative elements adorning the GIC and EMC lines must be capable of separate identification from the utilitarian aspects of the furniture, and they must be capable of "existing independently of, the utilitarian aspects of the [furniture]." . . . The elements serve no purpose divorced from the furniture—they become designs in space. . . . [T]he decorative elements adorning the GIC and EMC lines are . . . "artistic and aesthetic features" that can "be conceived of as having been added to, or superimposed upon, an otherwise utilitarian article," and they are therefore capable of existing independently of the furniture.[507]

INTERNATIONAL PERSPECTIVES

With the recent inclusion of intellectual property considerations in treaties governing international trade, no discussion of United States copyright law is thinkable without addressing its international context. An in-depth examination of international copyright is well beyond the scope this book, but a description of the international copyright conventions and relevant trade treaties to which the United States has acceded in recent years and a mention of some of the economic forces impelling such accession are not only appropriate but mandatory.

The Berne Convention

Effective March 1, 1989, the United States acceded to the Berne Convention[508] through the enactment of the BCIA.[509] Established in 1886[510] by ten nations who sought reciprocal copyright protection, Berne's membership totals 165 nations as of this writing,[511] and, with the accession of China in 1992 and the Russian Federation's in 1995, includes all the world's important nations.[512] Berne today is recognized as the most widely respected international copyright treaty, and it is designed to afford all authors who are citizens of a Berne member nation a basic level of protection within all member nations.

BERNE DOCTRINES

Berne achieves its objective of a basic level of protection for all nationals of member nations by adhering to two doctrines: the doctrine of national treatment and the doctrine of minimum standards.[513] The doctrine of national treatment provides that authors receive in other countries the same copyright protection for their works "as those countries accord their own authors."[514] Therefore, when the copyright owner of an artwork painted by a United States national sues for acts of infringement occurring in France, French law with all of its rights and remedies, not United States law, governs the lawsuit. The doctrine of minimum standards provides a baseline level of rights that all member nations must accord to foreign, not domestic, nationals of Berne member nations.[515] For example, Berne requires that all member nations grant copyright protection free of such formalities as copyright notice to works originating in other member nations. The United States could have acceded to Berne and still kept intact all United States requisite copyright formalities as codified in its domestic copyright law, but such formalities would have applied solely to United States nationals, resulting in politically injudicious treatment favoring foreign nationals over its own citizens.[516]

One notable exception to the doctrines of national treatment and of minimum standards is known as the rule of the shorter term. Where adopted, that rule allows a Berne member nation to cease copyright protection in, for example, a painting originating in another member nation when the copyright term in the latter nation has expired.[517] The rule also provides that when the latter nation's copyright term exceeds the term in the nation where protection for the painting is sought, the nation with the shorter term may apply to the painting its own term of protection.[518]

That exception was—and remains—of consequence to the United States. The rule of the shorter term was certainly an impetus for the enactment of the CTEA[519] which served to harmonize United States copyright duration laws with those of the EU. Nevertheless, Berne only requires its member nations to provide a term of copyright protection of life plus fifty, and this lesser period remains the term of copyright duration for a number of Berne nations.[520] This means that the United States, which, to date, has not adopted the rule of the shorter term, may well find itself, to its detriment, in a trade imbalance with those Berne nations which have adopted the rule of the shorter term and offer a lesser period of copyright protection to their domestic nationals.

For many years, the United States resisted joining Berne because at least two of Berne's principles are contrary to the tenets of United States copyright law: Berne's authorcentric focus and its antipathy to copyright formalities.[521]

DROIT MORAL

As to the first principle, article *6bis* of the Berne Convention mandates that member nations recognize and protect *droit moral*, a constellation of rights that inhere in the author of a work and are distinct from the author's pecuniary rights in the work. Those rights of *droit moral* mandated by Berne include the rights of attribution and of integrity.[522] The core of the attribution right, which encompasses an array of related rights,[523] recognizes that an author may be associated by name to her work and may remove her name from works created by another. The integrity right recognizes that an author may object to any modification or distortion of her work that may adversely affect the author's honor or reputation.[524] (*Droit moral* is examined in some detail in chapter 12.)

Berne's requirement that member nations recognize some form of *droit moral* epitomizes Berne's author-centered conception, shared by civil law countries, of copyright law: that the author is the primary beneficiary of copyright. That conception lies in stark contrast to the economically driven ideals of copyright law embraced by the United States and other common-law nations—that is, the provision of economic incentives to an author to create for the benefit of society at the least cost to consumers.[525] As discussed in chapter 12, accession by the United States to Berne in the late 1980s did not constitute a shedding of its ingrained antipathy to *droit moral*. In acceding to Berne, the BCIA basically declared that existing state *droit moral*, combined with then-current federal copyright law and trademark laws, enabled the United States to achieve minimum compliance with Berne, thereby making unnecessary any further amendment of United States copyright law to accommodate 6 *bis*.[526]

COPYRIGHT FORMALITIES

The Berne Convention provides that "the enjoyment and the exercise of [copyright] shall not be subject to any formality"[527] in any member nations other than the country of origin. That nonformalistic approach to copyright protection is antithetical to the elaborate copyright procedures (such as notice, registration, recordation, and deposit) that have evolved and been codified in United States copyright laws over the past two hundred or more years.[528] Berne does not purport to regulate the formalities that a member nation's domestic laws may impose on its own nationals in order to secure copyright protection, but Berne's adherence to the principle of minimum standards would, as noted above, obligate such a member nation to provide copyright protection free of formalities to works originating in other member nations. As the United States was neither willing to give an advantage to foreigners at the expense of its own nationals nor willing to amend its domestic copyright law to do away with notice requirements, it was for many years disinclined to accede to Berne. However, on finally joining Berne, the United States did permit foreign nationals of Berne member nations one advantage over its domestic claimants: Although Congress amended the 1976 Act to make the copyright-notice requirements for its nationals permissive, rather than mandatory, it eliminated, solely for foreign nationals of Berne member countries, the requirement of registration as a prerequisite to filing infringement suits.[529] Domestic claimants are still required to register.

The United States eventually joined Berne because of economic imperatives.

International markets, particularly Asian nations with which the United States had no copyright relations, were committing mass piracy of the products of its copyright-based industries, such as audiovisual works, computer software, sound recordings, and books. By the mid 1980s, such international piracy had cost United States copyright proprietors billions of dollars in revenue.[530] The United States had acceded to an international copyright treaty in 1955, the Universal Copyright Convention,[531] in order to gain a foothold in international copyright markets without having to substantially alter its domestic laws, but the Universal Copyright Convention, which has been called a "junior Berne Convention,"[532] was not protection enough.[533] In acceding to Berne, the United States immediately achieved copyright relations with an additional twenty-four nations.[534] Moreover, as a member of the Berne Convention, the United States, as noted below, has positioned itself to help shape the future of copyright protection in the international markets.

BERNE'S ENFORCEMENT INADEQUACIES

Although Berne is the preeminent international copyright treaty, membership in Berne does not suffice to protect a nation from ongoing mass piracy of the products of its copyright-protected industries; Berne's instrument of enforcement, one member country's suing another in the International Court of Justice in The Hague, is slow, cumbersome, and costly. Consequently, that instrument has never been invoked.[535] To remedy the lack of an effective enforcement mechanism for Berne nations, which have lost billions of dollars from piracy in the international markets,[536] copyright in the mid 1990s joined the multitude of industries covered by treaties governing international trade. A signatory nation whose copyright-protected products are pirated internationally should be able to obtain recourse by availing itself of the treaty's or treaties' enforcement mechanisms.

The World Trade Organization

In the wake of World War II, eighteen nations set into provisional operation[537] a draft treaty that evolved into the General Agreement on Tariffs and Trade (GATT). The objective of GATT was to surmount the edifice of national laws to promote commercialism and enhance free trade. To help achieve its objective, GATT was built on the overriding principle of most-favored nation[538]—that is, each signatory nation to GATT agreed to accord another signatory nation the same treatment it accorded to all other signatory nations. Although the number of signatory nations to GATT has fluctuated over the years, it ultimately achieved a membership of 117 nations.[539] Since 1947, a dozen negotiating rounds have been held to amend GATT, with the latest convocation commencing in 1986 at the ministerial meeting at Punta del Este, Uruguay (the Uruguay Round).[540] The Uruguay Round introduced into GATT's mechanisms for regulating trade in products the concept of developing mechanisms for regulating trade in services.[541] By that time government leaders throughout the world had developed an enhanced appreciation for products of copyright-protected industries as being crucial to their economies, so they added to the matrix of trade in services a trade structure for intellectual property.[542] From the perspective of the United States, negotiations of the Uruguay Round culminated seven years later, on December 15, 1993, when then-President Bill Clinton notified Congress that he intended to enter into the Uruguay Round trade agreements.[543] On April 15, 1994, the United States, along with 110 other nations, signed the Final Act Embodying the Results of the Uruguay Round of Multilateral Trade Negotiations (called the Final Act), in Marrakech, Morocco.[544]

Among the array of agreements encompassed by the Final Act is the Marrakech Agreement Establishing the World Trade Organization, April 15, 1994 (called the WTO Agreement) and the Agreement on Trade-Related Aspects of Intellectual Property Rights (called the TRIPs protocol).[545] On December 8, 1994, Congress passed the Uruguay Round Agreements Act (URAA),[546] the implementing legislation for the Final Act. The WTO Agreement—which established the World Trade Organization, an institution comparable in stature to the World Bank and to the International Monetary Fund[547]—took effect as did the URAA, January 1, 1995.[548] As of that date, the WTO replaced GATT. That is, the preeminent world trade structure is no longer known as GATT but is known as the WTO. Nations that adhere to the Uruguay Round Agreements are called Members.[549] Members are obligated to apply TRIPs one year after the WTO Agreement takes effect. TRIPs was implemented in the United States on January 1, 1996.[550] (Developing nations have a four-year grace period after the 1996 deadline, and least-developed nations have a ten-year grace period after the 1996 deadline to implement TRIPs.)[551]

Before discussing TRIPs, we should mention United States trade objectives that are articulated in other recent legislation fundamental to the eventual enactment of TRIPs.

THE OMNIBUS TRADE AND COMPETITIVENESS ACT OF 1988

In the international markets, the Omnibus Trade and Competitiveness Act (OTCA) of 1988[552] empowers the President to negotiate trade agreements in a variety of fields, including intellectual property.[553] A provision of the act colloquially known as "Super 301" empowered the United States trade representative to identify countries engaging in trade practices inimical to United States interests and the president to take retaliatory measures against those nations.[554] Although an extension of Super 301 was codified in the URAA, the extension has now expired.[555] OTCA seeks for the United States

(1) more open, equitable, and reciprocal market access; (2) the reduction or elimination of barriers and other trade-distorting practices; and (3) a more effective system of international trading disciplines and procedures.[556]

In addition to citing a number of other principal trade negotiating objectives, OTCA, specifically with respect to intellectual property, sought to supplement and strengthen the protection and enforcement mechanisms of Berne and the Universal Copyright Convention, and it proposed that GATT be amended to mandate protection of intellectual property.[557]

TRIPs

TRIPs incorporates the Berne Convention, the Rome Convention, and the Washington Treaty regarding semiconductor chips.[558] Of the three, the United States adheres solely to the Berne Convention, so the others are not discussed here. As with Berne, TRIPs adheres to the principle of minimum standards, which is applicable not to domestic claimants but to nationals of other member nations.[559] Nationals of other member nations are "those natural or legal persons that would meet the criteria for eligibility for protection provided for" in the Berne and Rome conventions and the Washington Treaty.[560] Also, like Berne, TRIPs adopts the principle of national treatment with one pertinent exception, the rule of the shorter term.[561] In addition and unlike Berne, TRIPs, with certain exceptions, adheres to a most-favored-nation principle.[562] TRIPs's six copyright provisions are largely harmonious with United States copyright law. Those provisions pertinent to art-related matters are noted below:

- TRIPs requires that all members comply with Berne, except for Berne's moral rights provisions, which are not incorporated into TRIPs.[563]
- TRIPs mandates protection for computer programs as literary works under Berne. Databases (which can include depictions of artworks) must also be protected, as the selection and the arrangement of their contents are intellectual creations.[564]
- TRIPs establishes minimum copyright duration for works other than photographic works and works of applied art. If copyright protection is predicated on a term other than a natural person's life, the term must be at least fifty years from the end of the calendar year of the authorized publication or, if there is no authorized publication within fifty years after the creation of the work, fifty years after the end of the calendar year of the creation of the work.[565]

In addition to the enforcement procedures encompassed in the Final Act, TRIPs sets forth a comprehensive array of remedial features, which include requiring the domestic laws of member nations to provide "expeditious remedies to prevent infringements and remedies which constitute a deterrent to further infringements."[566] Moreover, among other procedures available, aggrieved litigants may file a complaint with a WTO panel.[567]

AMENDMENT TO UNITED STATES LAW: COPYRIGHT RESTORATION

On December 8, 1994, with the enactment of the URAA, four of its provisions constituted amendments to the 1976 Copyright Act.[568] The one amendment relevant to art law is section 104A[569] the mechanism to resurrect copyrights for works of foreign origin that the United States is obligated by Berne to recognize. In so amending the 1976 Act, the United States, in adopting TRIPs, belatedly placed itself in compliance with Berne's article 18, which mandates a restoration to copyright in a member nation of works from other member nations that were in that nation's public domain because of a "lack of national eligibility."[570]

Under the URAA, the 1976 Act, as amended, conferred copyright protection, automatically effective January 1, 1996,[571] on restored works of foreign origin from an eligible[572] country. To qualify as a "restored work" under the 1976 Act, the work

(1) may not be in the source country's public domain through expiration of copyright term,
(2) must be in United States public domain because of either lack of national eligibility or noncompliance with copyright formalities imposed at any time by United States law, and
(3) had to have been created by "a national or domiciliary of an eligible country."[573]

Moreover, if published, the work had to have been first published in an eligible country and not in the United States within thirty days after its first publication. An "eligible country" is any nation other than the United States that becomes a member of the WTO, adheres to Berne, adheres to the WIPO copyright treaty, and adheres to the WIPO Performances and Phonograms Treaty.[574]

Once copyright is restored, the term runs

for the remainder of the term of copyright that the work would have otherwise been granted in the United States if the work never entered the public domain in the United States.[575]

Copyright ownership in a restored work initially vests "in the author or initial rightholder of the work as determined by the law of the source country of the work."[576] A party who exploits a restored work—a painting, for example—by mass-producing and distributing posters of it while that painting is in the public domain is termed and defined in the amended 1976 Act as a "reliance party."[577]

The 1976 Act provides that a copyright owner of a restored work may file with the Copyright Office a notice of intent, signed by the copyright owner, to enforce her restored copyright. The notice must include, among other data, the title or, if the work has no title, an identifying description of the restored work and an address and telephone number where the owner may be contacted.[578] To take advantage of the maximum remedies against the reliance party, the copyright owner should file such a notice within two years after the date of restoration, that is, by December 31, 1997.[579] The Register of Copyrights must publish lists of restored works in the *Federal Register*, along with each such work's owner if that owner has filed a notice of intent to enforce a restored copyright.[580]

Alternatively to the time-limited filing, an owner of a restored copyright may serve on a reliance party such a notice of intent to enforce, signed by the copyright owner, "at any time after the date of restoration of the restored copyright."[581] As in the former case, the notice must include, among the requisite data, information identifying the restored work and an address and telephone number where the owner may be contacted.[582] Such a service on a reliance party is effective as to that party and "any other reliance parties with actual knowledge of such service and the contents of that notice."[583] Owners of restored copyrights may avail themselves against reliance parties of all the statutory remedies for copyright infringement, provided a number of conditions are satisfied.[584]

As of the date of enforceability and for a year thereafter, a reliance party has a twelve-month sell-off period, during which she may sell existing copies of the work in which the copyright has been restored but may not manufacture new copies.[585] A reliance party's full-scale liability ripens only after the passage of the one-year sell-off period.[586]

In 2002, a New York federal district court, in *Cordon Holding B.V. v. Northwest Publishing Corp.*,[587] held that works qualified as restored works where they were first published in the Netherlands and had fallen into the public domain as a result of publication without notice under the 1909 Act. The plaintiffs owned the worldwide copyrights in the works of Dutch artist M.C. Escher. Escher, who died in 1972, made original drawings and then made master blocks from which he created "Art Reproductions." The defendants produced and sold over 35,000 copies of Escher's works in poster form. The plaintiffs alleged copyright infringement and the defendants admitted to copying, but argued that the works were in the public domain because they had been published without copyright notice. The plaintiffs argued that the drawings and master blocks remained unpublished, and thus that the art reproductions, as derivative works, were also unpublished. The court held that the publication of the art reproductions effectively published the original drawings and master blocks, and the works at issue fell into the public domain in the United States when they were published without copyright notice. However, since Escher's works were first published in the Netherlands, he was a domiciliary of the Netherlands, and since the reason why the work fell into the public domain in the United States was noncompliance with the notice requirement, Escher's works qualify as restored works under 17 U.S.C. § 104A(h)(6)(C)(i). However, the court noted that in light of the legal complexities of the case, it would deny the plaintiff's request for attorney's fees.[588]

An unsuccessful effort to claim "reliance party" status in an infringement suit is illustrated by *Troll Co. A/S v. Uneeda Doll Co.*[589] Here, the famous fuzzy-haired Troll doll was created in the late 1950s by Danish woodcarver Thomas Dam, who, in 1962, founded the Danish company Dam Things Establishment, through which he continued to market his Troll dolls. A year or two later, the Danish company licensed defendant Uneeda Doll Co's predecessor company to produce and distribute a specific line of troll dolls under the name "Wish-niks." Plaintiff Troll Company obtained a U.S. copyright for the Troll dolls in 1965. The application for the copyright specified Dam Things Establishment as the copyright owner, and the date and place of publication as November 1, 1961, in Denmark. That same year, however, the dolls were sold in the United States without a copyright notice, therefore invalidating the copyright and injecting the dolls into the public domain.

Notwithstanding, Dam's heirs after his death in 1989 granted the Troll Company the exclusive right to exploit and license the Troll doll. When the United States copyright to the Troll doll was automatically restored by virtue of the URAA, the Troll Company reapplied for registration of the restored copyright and was granted a registration number.

After the defendant Uneeda was expressly apprised in the early 2000s of the Troll Company's restored rights, the defendant represented to the plaintiff both in 2001 and 2004 that all production and distribution of the Wish-niks had ceased and that it had no intention of resuming such activities in the future. Then, in August 2005, on the eve of its long-planned launch of a marketing campaign from the Troll doll, the Troll Company learned that Uneeda was marketing and selling newly produced copies of the Troll doll, again dubbed "Wish-niks," but now bearing copyright notices in Uneeda's own name.

The Troll Company sued Uneeda in a New York federal district court for copyright infringement, seeking injunctive relief. Uneeda argued that it was exempted from suit at that time because it was a reliance party under section 104A of the 1976 Act. The court disagreed, however: Uneeda had ceased manufacturing, selling, and distributing its dolls prior to the copyright restoration and now, nearly ten years later, sought to reenter the market by manufacturing a new round of now-infringing dolls. The court noted that the continuing infringement doctrine is incorporated into the requirements of section 104A, that is, "the defendant must have engaged in an ongoing series of acts. Cessation of that activity for an appreciable period of time will deprive one of reliance party status."[590] Although both parties acknowledged that the Troll dolls were part of a cyclical market, the court noted that the defendant had not produced any evidence of manufacture or distribution of the "Wish-nik" dolls beyond 1995—that is, prior to January 1, 1996, the date the federal district court erroneously deemed to be the date of the restoration of the U.S. copyright in the Troll dolls. The court found that as the defendant had assured the Troll Company that it had ceased all production and distribution of its Troll dolls, the Troll Company had no reason to believe that the defendant possessed any reliance-party status; consequently, Troll Company's issuing defendant official notice in October 2005 of its intent to enforce its restored copyright in the Troll dolls was all it was required to do under the statute.[591] Accordingly, the court granted a preliminary injunction barring the defendant company from manufacturing, distributing, or selling its Wish-nik dolls pending resolution of the matter.

Uneeda appealed the preliminary injunction, arguing that the Troll Company was unlikely to succeed on its infringement claim because, among other points, Uneeda was a reliance party within the meaning of section 104A of the 1976 Act, entitling it to sell off its inventory of Wish-niks for one year following Troll Company's service of a notice on intent to enforce its restored copyright.

In affirming the preliminary injunction, the Second Circuit noted that section 104A creates three categories of reliance parties—and that in two of the three categories, the status of a reliance party turns on whether a person committed infringing acts with respect to a work before the source country of that work became an eligible country.[592]

Moreover, the Second Circuit observed that a source country that was a member of the Berne Convention when the URAA was enacted—such as Denmark— became an eligible country on the date of the URAA's enactment: December 8, 1994.[593] Therefore, the court noted,

[t]he District Court mistakenly looked to *the date of copyright restoration* [italics the courts], January 1, 1966, rather than the date of the URAA's enactment, to determine the date when Denmark became an eligible country and hence whether [defendant] or its predecessor was a reliance party by reason of having acted with respect to the Troll dolls prior to that date.[594]

A provision of section 104A[595] gives reliance party status to a person who "continues" to engage in infringing acts after December 8, 1994. The parties differed as to what constitutes "continues" and the Second Circuit was required to construe the term, evidently for the first time. Troll Company argued that the provision contained a "continuing acts requirement" and that Uneeda's resumption of sales nearly a decade later did not satisfy this requirement. Uneeda responded that the language does not require the infringing activity to be uninterrupted and the periodic renewal of cyclical exploitation "continues" such exploitation. Looking to the legislative history of section 104A, the Second Circuit construed the provision to require ongoing infringement without more than trivial interruption.

The parties construed a second provision of section 104A differently.[596] Uneeda claimed that it qualified as a reliance party under this provision because it made or acquired at least one copy of the Troll doll before the URAA's enactment to manufacture additional copies after the restoration of copyright. Troll Company argued more narrowly that parties who previously acquired copies of a work before the URAA's enactment were only permitted to dispose of those particular copies.

Finding Uneeda's interpretation of that provision to be overbroad, the Second Circuit concluded that Congress meant to limit the reliance party's benefit under that provision of section 104A[597] to copies already made or acquired before the URAA's enactment.

COPYRIGHT RESTORATION AS CONSTITUTIONAL

The constitutionality of section 104A was challenged by an array of orchestra conductors, musicians, educators, and publishers (petitioners) who formerly enjoyed free access and unfettered use of works of foreign classical music that had fallen into the public domain but were restored to copyright under section 104A. The petitioners asserted that section 104A exceeded Congress's authority under the Copyright Clause of the Constitution and violated the First Amendment. In January 2012, the U.S. Supreme Court, in *Golan v. Holder*,[598] affirming an opinion by the Tenth Circuit,[599] held section 104A to be constitutional.

Congress's Authority under the Copyright Clause. Petitioners argued that the Copyright Clause's confinement of a lifespan of a copyright to a "limited Tim[e]" prevented the removal of works from the public domain. However, the Court, comparing its upholding of the CTEA in *Eldred* (discussed on pages 931–932), noted in *Golan* that

> the terms afforded works restored by [section 104A] are no less "limited" than those the CETA lengthened.[600]

Moreover, as the Court observed, "the text of the Copyright Clause does not exclude application of copyright protection to works in the public domain."[601] The petitioners also argued that as section 104A affects only works already created, it cannot meet the objective of the Copyright Clause of promoting "the Progress of Science." Again the Court disagreed, noting that the creation of new works does not constitute the sole way in which Congress may promote knowledge and learning.[602] The Court further observed that Congressional practice, historical evidence, and its own earlier decisions suggested that providing incentives for the dissemination of existing works is an appropriate manner in which to promote science. Accordingly, the Court found that section 104A "falls comfortably within Congress' authority under the Copyright Clause."[603] Moreover, the Court observed that Congress determined that "full compliance with Berne . . . would expand the foreign markets available to U.S. authors and invigorate protection against piracy of U.S. work abroad."[604] Therefore, the Court declined to "reject the rational judgment Congress made."[605]

First Amendment. As it did in *Eldred*, with the CTEA, the Court here observed that the traditional perimeters of copyright expression, that is, the idea/expression dichotomy and the fair use defense, "both . . . recognized in our jurisprudence as 'built-in First Amendment accommodations,'"[606] are left undisturbed by section 104A. Moreover, as the Court noted, in cushioning the impact of restoration on "reliance parties" by deferring the date from which enforcement runs, "Congress adopted measures to ease the transition from a national scheme to an international copyright regime."[607] As to petitioners' claim that they had enjoyed "vested rights" in works that had already entered the public domain and that the limited rights accorded them by the built-in First Amendment accommodations were a poor substitute for the unfettered access to and usage of the works they enjoyed prior to section 104A's enactment, the Court noted that nothing in the historical record, congressional practice, or the Court's own jurisprudence warranted exceptional First Amendment solicitude for copyrighted works that were once in the public domain.[608]

Observing that Congress in the past has amended copyright law to accord protection to new categories of works as well as those previously in the public domain, the Court framed the issue as whether the prospective users of certain foreign works would pay for the right to use the author's protected expression in the manner they desired, or would content themselves with making a "fair use" of such a work. As the Court concluded, "[b]y fully implementing Berne, Congress ensured that most works, whether foreign or domestic, would be governed by the same legal regime."[609]

The WIPO Copyright Treaty

On December 20, 1996, the United States and 159 other nations, under the aegis of the World Intellectual Property Organization (WIPO), an agency of the United Nations, adopted two international treaties that enhance the standards of protection for copyrighted literary and musical works on the Internet.[610] The WIPO Performances and Phonograms Treaty, which focuses on the rights of producers and performers in sound recordings, is not pertinent to a treatise on art law and is, therefore, not addressed here. The WIPO Copyright Treaty (see Appendix 11-2 at the end of this chapter), which concerns literary and artistic works, grants protection for any original use of such a work on the Internet. Article 4 of the treaty protects computer programs as literary works, "whatever may be the mode or form of their expression." In article 5, the treaty also protects databases "which by reason of the selection or arrangement of their contents constitute intellectual creations." The copyright protection, however, does not extend to the material itself in the database and does not affect any copyright protection subsisting in such material. Other salient provisions of the WIPO Copyright Treaty follow:

- Articles 6 and 7 provide that authors of literary and artistic works have the exclusive right to distribute, sell, and rent such works electronically.
- Article 8 empowers authors to authorize "any communication to the public of their works, by wire or wireless means, including the making available to the public of their works in such a way that members of the public may access these works from a place and at a time individually chosen by them."
- Article 3 mandates that the exclusive rights of authors under each signatory nation's domestic law be broad enough to retain for its authors the article 8 right.
- Article 11 requires signatory nations to provide "effective legal remedies against the circumvention of effective technological measures" that authors may use to protect their copyrights.
- Article 12 requires that signatory nations make sure that their domestic

laws provide effective legal remedies against the knowing and unauthorized removal of electronic rights-management information from works or copies of works or that they distribute or communicate publicly such works or copies when such information has been removed or altered.

- Article 14 requires that signatory nations provide enforcement mechanisms under their domestic laws.

U.S. compliance with the WIPO Copyright Treaty (as well as with the WIPO Performance and Phonograms Treaty) required implementing legislation. Accordingly, in October 1998, Congress passed the Digital Millennium Copyright Act (DMCA), a massive piece of legislation that added a new chapter (chapter 12) to Title 17 of the United States Code and enhanced the viability of the 1976 Act to address circumstances arising in the world of the Internet. The DMCA is discussed at length, as it relates to art law, in chapter 18.

COPYRIGHT INFRINGEMENT

Duplicating a work without the consent of the copyright holder (usually, the artist or, occasionally, the collector) constitutes a form of copyright infringement. Infringement of copyright is defined as the violation of any one or more of the exclusive rights of the copyright holder:[611] the rights of reproduction, distribution, adaptation, performance, and display.[612] With the advent of the digital age, each of the exclusive rights involves, in different ways, the copyright holder's authority to keep others from copying the work without consent. In *Playboy Enterprises, Inc. v. Starware Publishing Corp.*,[613] for example, a Florida federal district court held in 1995 that the defendant's manufacture and distribution of 10,000 copies of its CD-ROM disc entitled *Private Pictures I*, composed of digitized photographs that are "virtual copies" of the plaintiff's copyrighted photographs in *Playboy* magazine, violated the plaintiff's exclusive rights of reproduction and distribution under the Copyright Act of 1976.

Infringement Tests

To bring an action in copyright infringement, a plaintiff must establish (1) ownership of copyright and (2) unauthorized copying by the defendant.[614] The first requirement can be satisfied with a certificate of copyright registration, which constitutes prima facie evidence in favor of the plaintiff.[615] As to the second requirement, if the plaintiff can establish direct evidence of copying with, for example, eyewitness testimony or an admission of copying, the court need only determine if such copying amounts to an improper appropriation of the plaintiff's protected expression.[616] In the absence of direct evidence of copying, a plaintiff can establish copying by showing (1) access by the defendant to the plaintiff's work and (2) substantial similarity between the two works.[617]

ACCESS

"Access" is defined by case law to mean that the defendant had an opportunity to view the plaintiff's work.[618] Although generally there must be some showing of access to sustain an infringement action, access may be inferred if the defendant's work is strikingly similar to the copyrighted work.[619] However, even with such a finding of striking similarity, the plaintiff should be able to demonstrate at least a bare possibility that the defendant had access to the plaintiff's work.[620] It is sufficient to show access through third parties connected to both a plaintiff and defendant.[621] Accordingly, in the 2008 case of *Lugosch v. Avery*,[622] where both parties designed and sold jewelry, the federal district court of Maine found that the copyright holder whose business was in Maine produced sufficient evidence on the issue of access so as to deny the accused infringer's motion for summary judgment. At issue were two of plaintiff's jewelry designs allegedly infringed by the defendant Texas jewelry company. The court found that the requirement of access was satisfied based on plaintiff's allegation that she sent direct mail advertisements to a former employee of the defendant while she worked for the defendant. As the court noted, while defendant provided case law for the proposition that "mere receipt of an unsolicited mailing of the allegedly copied material cannot establish the access element of an infringement claim,"[623] it noted that plaintiff provided a First Circuit case holding that the mailing of the material does create an inference that it was received and therefore creates a genuine issue of material fact on the issue of access.[624] Accordingly, the court concluded that plaintiff produced sufficient evidence to satisfy access. "Strikingly similar" is similarity that can only be explained by copying.[625]

SUBSTANTIAL SIMILARITY

Misuse of the term "substantial similarity" in the various federal circuit courts raises the following question: What elements of a work need to be substantially similar for infringement to inhere—all the work's elements or solely the copyrightable elements or some mixture of both? In 1946, *Arnstein v. Porter*,[626] the leading case on copyright infringement,[627] established a two-pronged test for infringement. It provided that if there is evidence of access and similarities between the two works, the trier of fact must ask the following two questions:

1. Are the similarities sufficient to prove that the defendant copied the plaintiff's work?
2. If so, is such copying an improper appropriation of plaintiff's protected expression?

Subsequent to *Arnstein*, courts began to apply the term "substantial similarity" (which did not appear in the *Arnstein* test) without deciding whether the term applied to the first or the second prong in *Arnstein*. However, following a scholarly observation[628] that "substantial similarity" is misapplied to *Arnstein's* first prong, which restricts its inquiry into whether the works' similarities are sufficient to establish copying of the plaintiff's work, the Second Circuit in 1992 rephrased the *Arnstein* test as follows:

> [First, c]opying [of the plaintiff's work] may be established . . . by . . . evidence of similarities that are probative of copying between the works. . . . If copying is established, a plaintiff must then show that the copying amounts to an improper appropriation by demonstrating that substantial similarity to protected material exists between the two works.[629]

Despite differences in terminology and temporary variances of approach,[630] circuit courts generally adhere to the *Arnstein* two-prong inquiry.[631] In addressing the first prong of *Arnstein*—that is, whether similarities between two works are sufficient to establish that the defendant copied the plaintiff's work—courts analyze the two works in toto, comparing their protected expression and their unprotectable underlying ideas. Expert testimony may be used to determine if copying has taken place.[632] If the defendant's work does not contain probative similarities, copying is not established, and the *Arnstein* test is dropped. If, on the other hand, the defendant's work does contain probative similarities, *Arnstein's* second prong, the issue of whether there was improper appropriation, must be addressed.

In determining the issue of improper appropriation, a court must be able to distinguish the protectable elements from the unprotectable elements in the plaintiff's work. As such a determination is not, as a rule, readily forthcoming, the courts, since 1930, have developed a number of tests to apply in conducting such an analysis. The four tests noted below are among the tests pertinent to artworks.

1. Abstractions test. In any work, as more and more of the elements are left out, patterns of increasing generality can be superimposed on the work. At some point on the spectrum of patterns or abstractions, the elements are no longer protected as they enter the realm of ideas, rather than expression. The abstractions test was first articulated in 1930 in *Nichols v. Universal Pictures Corp.*,[633] a Second Circuit case. Unfortunately, the test cannot pinpoint the line of demarcation between protectable expression and unprotectable ideas.

2. Total concept and feel. Originating in a 1970 Ninth Circuit copyright-infringement case[634] involving artworks on greeting cards, this test was devised for comparing elements of the two works, including characters depicted in the artworks, portrayal of mood, conveyance of mood with a particular message, and arrangement of visual elements on the greeting cards.[635]

The test has been used extensively in the Ninth Circuit[636] and in other circuits, such as in the 1996 case of *Singer v. Citibank*,[637] in which a New York federal district court in the Second Circuit held that the defendant's painting of the Times Square-Broadway area of New York City that was incorporated into a calendar disseminated by defendant, Citibank, did not infringe the plaintiff-artist's graphic artwork entitled *Times Square*. A New York federal district court relied on this test in *Kerr v. New Yorker Magazine*.[638] The court held that although both the plaintiff's and the defendant's images included a male figure with a skyline Mohawk, the "different feels [were] sufficient support for a finding that the two images [were] not substantially similar."[639] The court explained the significant differences: One was in color and the other black and white; one was pen and ink with crosshatching while the other had smooth lines and rounded contours; one showed the image from a three-quarter profile while the other was a true profile and the defendant displayed the buildings in the skyline in a different order.

However, this test been criticized by at least one major commentator on, among other grounds, being posited to "subvert the very essence of copyright."[640] That is, since concepts are codified under the 1976 Act[641] as being ineligible for copyright protection, how can the appropriation of a work's total concept be used as a basis for infringement?

3. *Aesthetic appeal.* In 1994, the Seventh Circuit—in comparing soft sculptured bear, duck, and elephant duffel bags of the plaintiff and the defendant manufacturers—examined the works both in their entirety and disassembled, element by element, and concluded that the ordinary lay observer would regard their aesthetic appeal as the same.[642] That test was also used in the Second Circuit in 1991[643] in a holding of no infringement in which the court determined that printed rose-pattern fabric sold by the defendant to women's clothing manufacturers would not be found by the average lay observer to have the same aesthetic appeal as the printed rose-pattern fabric sold to such manufacturers by the plaintiff.

Various courts have relied on the "aesthetic appeal" approach to determine substantial similarity. In 1998, in *Gibson Tex, Inc. v. Sears Roebuck & Co.*,[644] a New York federal district court applied this test to determine whether the defendants, a department store and a clothing manufacturer, infringed a designer's fabric design, which was based on a public domain design. Denying the plaintiff's motion for summary judgment, the court stated "where a plaintiff closely models its work after a design in the public domain, the showing of imitation must be stronger than usual and even small variations may protect a subsequent designer."[645]

The Eleventh Circuit's 2000 decision in *Leigh v. Warner Brothers, Inc.*[646] relied on the "aesthetic appeal" approach and reversed the lower court's grant of summary judgment for the defendant, declaring that substantial similarity is a question of fact for the jury. The controversy centered on the image of a statue used both on the cover of the novel *Midnight in the Garden of Good and Evil* and in the film version of the novel. The novel's cover photographer alleged that the filmmaker's film sequences, using the same statue, were substantially similar to the cover photograph. The court explained that the artistic and protectable elements of the photograph included the plaintiff's choice of lighting, shading, timing, angle, and film and that these elements would have to be substantially similar for the court to find infringement of the plaintiff's image. The court further stated that "'substantial similarity' is a question of fact and summary judgment is only appropriate if no reasonable jury could differ in weighing the evidence."[647]

A New York federal district court, in the 2000 decision of *Peker v. Masters Collection*,[648] held that a retailer's oil painting replicas of an artist's oil paintings established the necessary degree of similarity because "an average lay observer would recognize the alleged copy as having been appropriated from the copyrighted work." In *Peker*, the defendant purchased posters of the plaintiff's paintings, then treated each poster with a coat of acrylic paint that separated the ink from the poster and allowed the image to be transferred to canvases, which were further painted to match the color and style of the original painting. The resulting paintings were then framed and sold. The court stated that "the copying is blatant, and no average attentive lay observer would fail to recognize defendant's appropriation of [the plaintiff's work]."

In *Yankee Candle Co. v. Bridgewater Candle Co., LLC*,[649] a Massachusetts federal district court in 2000 held that where photographs depict common, ordinary subjects, such as the natural sources of candle scents, the copyrighted photograph and the infringing photograph must be almost perfectly identical to find infringement. Evaluating the plaintiff's photographs depicting the sources of the candle scents, the court stated that although there "is really only one way to convey the notion of Eucalyptus, Cranberry, Gardenia, Mulberry, Peach and Raspberry," the plaintiff's photographs could be protected if the defendant's photographs were identical in lighting, focus, positioning, and content.[650] The court held that no reasonable factfinder applying the ordinary observer test could possibly conclude that the parties' photographs were nearly identical where the various factors of composition were all distinctive.

In *Brown v. McCormick*,[651] referred to earlier in this chapter on page 946, a Maryland federal district court relied on the ordinary observer test and stated that the "test focuses on the overall similarities, rather than the minute differences between the two works, and exact reproduction or near identity is not required to establish infringement."[652] Of course, the works in question here were quilts and quilt patterns, which permit a wider range of expression than the candle scents of *Yankee Candle*. Accordingly, the court held that the plaintiff established substantial similarity through the ordinary observer test where the works were essentially identical and defendant's reversed alignment of one image and one new detail were the only differences between the parties' respective works

4. Successive filtering approach. In 1991, in *Feist Publications v. Rural Telephone Service Co.*,[653] the United States Supreme Court took a copyrighted work and distilled from it a core of protectable elements. A subsequent comparison of the two works enabled the Court to determine that the defendant copied only unprotectable material, thereby denying a finding of infringement. Such an approach, earlier labeled "successive filtering" by a leading commentator,[654] has subsequently received some support by other commentators[655] and by a number of courts.[656]

The Tenth Circuit has adopted the abstraction-filtration-comparison test. In 2000, the Tenth Circuit affirmed the lower court's decision in *Fisher v. United Feature Syndicate, Inc.*,[657] holding that the plaintiff illustrator failed to establish substantial similarity between his "Chipper" cartoon dog and the defendant copyright holder's "Snoopy" cartoon character, where the portrayal of both characters as cowardly detective dogs and the use of misspellings in the texts were their only similarities. The court further explained that the idea of a detective dog falls under the *scènes à faire* doctrine as an unprotectable element. After comparing the remaining protected elements, the court found that the alleged similarities failed to satisfy the reasonable ordinary observer standard and, therefore, the defendant did not infringe plaintiff's copyright.

Continuing with *Arnstein's* second prong, we note that once the core of protected expression in a plaintiff's work is identified, the fact finder assesses the defendant's copying of the plaintiff's protected expression to see if it rises to the level of improper appropriation—that is, infringement. The test traditionally applied by the fact finder in determining if copying rises to the level of improper appropriation is the ordinary-lay-observer test. Generally, both the Second Circuit[658] and the Ninth Circuit[659] disallow analysis, dissection, and expert testimony in determining the existence of improper appropriation. When such testimony is allowed in other circuits, the analysis, dissection, and expert testimony are usually present in cases addressing computer programs, not artworks.[660]

For an infringement to occur, the work need not be copied in the same medium in which it was originally produced. In *Woods v. Universal City Studios*,[661] for example, the artist obtained a preliminary injunction in 1996 against a movie company that built a chair for the film *12 Monkeys* based, without permission, on the artist's drawing. In *Rogers v. Koons*,[662] (discussed below at pages 1001–1004) the Second Circuit in 1992 held that the artist Jeff Koons committed a copyright infringement by creating a wooden sculpture depicting a couple seated on a bench and holding a litter of eight German shepherd puppies, based on a photograph by the photographer Art Rogers.

Further, unintentional copying is no defense against a charge of copyright infringement. In *Ciner Manufacturing Co. v. Plastic Craft Novelty Company*,[663] for example, a New York federal district court rejected a defense of innocent infringement where the plaintiff-designer and manufacturer of costume jewelry brought an infringement suit against the defendant-catalog company, which advertised and sold an item that, without the catalog company's knowledge, was a knockoff of the plaintiff's bracelet.

Common Source

The copying of a common source should be distinguished from actionable infringement. Actionable infringement does not occur where a third party has independently duplicated a work,[664] as when a photographer has taken a picture of the same scene from the same perspective as that in a prior copyrighted photograph. When the source is not protected by copyright, as stated by Justice Oliver

Wendell Holmes, "[o]thers are free to copy the original. They are not free to copy the copy."[665] However, indirect copying, through the creation or the assemblage of a common source, is prohibited. For example, an artist infringes on another's copyrighted painting of a still life if the later artist assembles the items used in the earlier still-life painting and arranges them in substantially the same manner as the objects in the copyrighted painting.[666]

Prerequisites to an Infringement Suit

To maintain an action charging infringement, the copyright holder of a work must have satisfied the statutory requirement of registration. As a benefit to copyright owners, the federal Copyright Office issues brief and self-explanatory forms specific to the type of work being registered. The registration form must be accompanied by one or two deposit copies of the work and a registration fee.[667] Copyright registration is deemed effective as of the date the Copyright Office receives the application, the deposit copy or copies, and the fee.[668]

Before the U.S. accession to the Berne Convention, transfers of copyright before March 1, 1989, had to satisfy another statutory prerequisite to an infringement suit: recordation. The plaintiff had to first record in the Copyright Office the instrument of transfer under which the plaintiff asserted ownership of the rights allegedly infringed. The 1976 Copyright Act permits the recordation for a nominal fee not only of the transfer instrument but also of all the documents relating to copyright ownership, including exclusive licenses and nonexclusive licenses.[669] Recordation gives constructive notice to the world of all the facts set forth in the documents recorded.[670] However, post-Berne, recordation of transfer instruments are now permissive, rather than a prerequisite to an infringement suit.

Fair Use

Described as the primary defense against an action of copyright infringement,[671] the fair-use defense creates a privilege to use the work of another in a reasonable manner, even though that use may technically constitute an infringement. The 1976 Copyright Act provides that the "fair use" of a copyrighted work by a third party does not constitute an infringement of copyright.[672] In determining whether a given use of a copyrighted work is a fair one for purposes of the exception, the courts balance four nonexclusive factors codified by the 1976 Act:

1. The purpose and the character of the use, including whether that use is of a commercial nature or is for nonprofit educational purposes
2. The nature of the copyrighted work
3. The amount and the substantiality of the portion used in relation to the work as a whole
4. The effect of the use upon the potential market for or value of the copyrighted work[673]

Generally, fair use occurs where one is using another's creation in the context of a new work, usually for purposes of criticism, comment, teaching, news reporting, scholarship, or research.[674] Examples include the taking of a photograph of a painting loaned by a collector to a university or some other institution for a review of the exhibition or for a reproduction to be put into the institution's documentary files.

However, appropriation in a less lofty context can also pass muster. In *Haberman v. Hustler Magazine, Inc.*,[675] a Massachusetts federal district court held that the defendant's unauthorized inclusion in two issues of *Hustler* of a small-scale depiction of an artwork by the plaintiff, accompanied by *Hustler's* comments on the artwork, constituted a fair use. Moreover, incidental appropriation of a plaintiff's work, if the appropriation is fleeting and reasonable, may also be deemed a fair use. But, in *Ringgold v. Black Entertainment Television, Inc.*,[676] the Second Circuit, in reversing the federal district court in 1997, held that when a poster created by the plaintiff-artist was exhibited on television as part of the background set in an episodic scene, even though the poster or a portion of it appeared in nine separate shots totaling only 26.75 seconds, the exhibition of the poster was not a fair use. The court held that summary judgment was not appropriate and remanded the case to the district court for further development of the fair use factors as they apply to the facts of the case. In particular, the Second Circuit observed that the poster was used for precisely a central purpose for which it was created—to be decorative—and as such, was generally not entitled to fair use protection. However, the Second Circuit's 1998 decision in *Sandoval v. New Line Cinema Corp.*[677] distinguished *Ringgold* and held that the defendant producer's use of the plaintiff photographer's transparencies in the film *Seven* constituted a *de minimis* use of the copyrighted material and, therefore, was not an actionable infringement claim. The factors the court evaluated, to determine that the allegedly infringing work fell below the quantitative threshold of substantial similarity, were the amount of the copyrighted work that was copied and the observability of the copyrighted work in the allegedly infringing work. The court stated that since the "photographs appear fleetingly and are obscured, severely out of focus, and virtually unidentifiable,"[678] the use was *de minimis*.

As noted above, the 1976 Act codifies four factors to be considered in each case,[679] along with other factors pertinent in a given situation, in determining if a use is fair. Over the years, however, the questions addressed by some of those factors and the relative weights accorded the factors have shifted. Largely because of the 1994 watershed decision of the United States Supreme Court in *Campbell v. Acuff-Rose Music, Inc.*,[680] a fair-use analysis today differs somewhat in emphasis and focus from a fair-use analysis conducted twenty years ago. The contrast to *Campbell* is illustrated in the Second Circuit case of *Rogers v. Koons*,[681] whose 1992 pre-*Campbell* fair-use analysis might well yield a different determination today.

ROGERS V. KOONS

In the early 1990s, both the art world and the copyright legal community were transfixed by a copyright-infringement suit brought against the well-known American artist and sculptor Jeff Koons by a professional photographer, Art Rogers. While a handful of photographers had sued artists in preceding years, this is the first such case which did not settle out of court, and as such, it stands as a landmark.[682] The finding of copyright infringement by the Second Circuit, affirming a New York federal district court decision,[683] included, along with a cogent analysis summarized below of the then-current matrix of factors in fair use, a condemnatory speculation about the defendant's motives in committing the infringement:

> The key to this copyright infringement suit . . . is defendants' borrowing of plaintiff's expression of a typical American scene. . . . The copying was so deliberate as to suggest that defendants resolved so long as they were significant players in the art business, and the copies they produced bettered the price of the copied work by a thousand to one, their piracy of a less well-known artist's work would escape being sullied by an accusation of plagiarism.[684]

The facts surrounding the infringement are as follows: In 1980, Rogers—a resident of California whose photographic works have been exhibited in various regions of the United States and have been described in French, British, and American publications—was commissioned by Jim Scanlon, another California resident who was familiar with Rogers's work, to make a photographic portrait of the Scanlons' new litter of eight German shepherd puppies. At the photographic session and later in his laboratory, Rogers drew on his creative judgment in selecting, for example, the light, the location, and the seating arrangement of the human subjects and the grouping of the puppies. The result was a charming photograph entitled *Puppies*, which depicted Scanlon and his wife, Mary, seated on a bench and holding the litter of puppies. Later that year, the picture was published in Rogers's photography column in a local newspaper. In 1982, it was exhibited, along with other works by Rogers, at the San Francisco Museum of Modern Art. In 1984, Rogers licensed the picture, along with other works, to Museum Graphics, a company that produces and distributes note cards and postcards with fine reproductions of photographs by well-respected American photographers, including Ansel Adams. The first printing of *Puppies* by Museum Graphics was of 5,000 copies, and a second printing was of a similar size. In 1989, Rogers licensed the photograph for use in an anthology entitled *Dog Days*.

In 1986, defendant Jeff Koons, a prominent and controversial artist living in New York City, began to create sculptures for what was eventually termed his "Banality Show"—that is, banality was the subject for an exhibition that was a "critical commentary on conspicuous consumption, greed and self-indulgence."[685] All the works in the exhibition were sculptures in various mediums.

Several copies of each work were produced: three copies to be purchased by the public and a fourth and final copy to be retained by the artist.

During the latter part of 1986 and throughout 1987, Koons collected material for possible sculptures and then contracted with various studios to craft the materials in accordance with his instructions. At some point in 1987, Koons purchased in a commercial card shop the Museum Graphics note card of *Puppies* imprinted with Rogers's copyright. Koons removed that portion of the card showing Rogers's copyright notice and forwarded the photograph to an art studio in Italy with instructions to make a polychromed wood sculptural version of the photograph that "must be just like photo."[686]

Koons perceived certain qualities in the note card that would make it a workable source for his art. He believed the notecard to be "commonplace" and "familiar," one that resonated with the mass culture and "resting in the collective sub-consciousness of people regardless of whether the card had actually ever been seen by such people."[687] While the sculpture was being carved, Koons communicated extensively with the studio and visited the studio once a week. To paint the polychromed wood sculpture, he provided a chart with an enlarged photograph of "Puppies" in the center, along with instructions to paint the sculpture "realistic as per photo, but in blues."[688]

The result was a blue polychromed wood sculpture 42 inches by 62 inches by 37 inches that depicted the Scanlons garishly dressed, with bulbous noses and daisies arranged in their hair, seated on a bench and holding the puppies. Koons entitled the work *String of Puppies* and displayed it at the Sonnabend Gallery in New York City, which opened the "Banality Show" in November 1988. After the exhibition of the sculpture, Koons sold three sculptures of *String of Puppies* to collectors for a total of $367,000 and retained an artist's-proof sculpture at his storage facility.

Rogers, who learned of the sculpture's existence through Scanlon, subsequently registered his photograph *Puppies* with the United States Copyright Office and then brought an action against Koons and Sonnabend Gallery in a New York federal district court in October 1989 for, among other claims, copyright infringement. In December 1990, Rogers obtained a ruling that Koons had, in fact, committed an infringement.[689] However, the parties had sought a ruling, rather than a trial, so the judge did not decide if Rogers should receive damages—that is, part of the $367,000 paid for the three sculptures. In February 1991, the federal district court concluded that both Sonnabend Gallery and Koons were liable for infringing profits, and the next month the court permanently enjoined both Koons and the gallery from making, lending, selling, or displaying any copies of *Puppies* or any derivative works based on *Puppies*. Koons and the gallery appealed to the Second Circuit both the lower court's injunction and its finding of copyright infringement; Rogers cross-appealed on the basis of the lower court's denial of an award of profits before trial. The Second Circuit affirmed the lower court's holdings.

The case is significant for the manner in which it addressed certain issues, notably those of originality and the fair-use doctrine. As to the originality of *Pup-*

pies, Koons asserted that the portion of Rogers's work allegedly infringed "was not an original work of authorship protected under the 1976 Copyright Act."[690] However, as the Second Circuit noted, "the quantity of originality that need be shown is modest—only a dash of it will do."[691] The court went on to observe that original elements in a picture may include the lighting, the selection of the camera and the film, the posing of the subjects, the angle, and almost any other variant concerned. In conclusion, the court stated the following:

> To the extent that these factors are involved, "Puppies" is the product of plaintiff's artistic creation. Rogers' inventive efforts in posing the group for the photograph, taking the picture, and printing "Puppies" suffices to meet the original work of art criteria.[692]

On the issue of fair use, the Second Circuit affirmed the lower court's determination that Koons's appropriation of Rogers's work was not protected under the fair-use privilege. In addressing each of the four codified fair-use elements noted on page 999 under the then-current analysis, the Second Circuit made a number of observations.

As to the purpose and the character of the use, the court asked "whether the original was copied in good faith to benefit the public or primarily for the commercial interests of the infringer."[693] The court noted that Koons's conduct in removing the copyright notice from a Rogers note card before sending it to the Italian artisans evinced bad faith on Koons's part and militated against a finding of fair use, as did his substantial profit from his deliberately exploitative use of Rogers's work. Koons contended that the primary purpose of the use was for social comment on modern society.

As to the nature of the copyrighted work, the court noted that the scope of fair use is broader for factual works than for fictional work, since public policy favors the dissemination of information, but the court analogized *Puppies* to a fictional work. Moreover, the court noted that *Puppies* represented an investment of time by the plaintiff "in anticipation of a financial return,"[694] another consideration that argued against fair use.

As to the amount and the substantiality of the work used, the court noted:

> [T]he essence of Rogers's photograph was copied nearly in toto. . . . In short, it is not really the parody flag that [the defendants] are sailing under, but rather the flag of piracy.[695]

This factor also weighed against fair use.

As to the effect of the use on the potential market for the original work, the court, noting that it was the most important fair-use factor, once more made a determination against a finding of fair use. The court observed that Koons's work was primarily commercial in nature—that is, Koons and the gallery expected to profit from their use of *Puppies* without making any payment to Rogers. The court further noted that with respect to this last factor a copyright proprietor need only demonstrate that if an unauthorized use becomes flagrant, it would prejudice the potential market for the original artist's work, a situation that, the court concluded, was presumed in the *Rogers* case.

Moreover, the court noted that Koons's sculpture may well have harmed the market for derivative works stemming from Rogers's photograph. The court observed that another artist might have been willing to purchase from Rogers the right to make a sculpture based on his photograph and that, conversely, Koons could make and sell photographs of his sculpture that would injure Rogers's potential market for his original photograph.

On the issue of infringing profits, Rogers's point on appeal, the Second Circuit refused to grant an award of profits, leaving the ascertainment of damages to the district court on remand. However, the Second Circuit did suggest that a reasonable license fee for the use of the photograph would best approximate the market injury sustained by Rogers arising from Koons's misappropriation. The Second Circuit also posed the alternative that Rogers elect statutory damages: "In fact, given Koons' willful and egregious behavior, we think Rogers may be a good candidate for enhanced statutory damages.[696]

CAMPBELL V. ACUFF-ROSE

The Second Circuit adhered to the then-current fair-use guidelines in *Rogers*, but the decision was controversial partly because the court did not recognize Koons's sculpture as being a parody of Rogers's photograph. Parody had been recognized in the Second Circuit, among other circuits,[697] as a form of comment or criticism that can pass muster under the fair-use defense in an infringement suit, but at that time the Supreme Court had yet to address the issue directly. The Court did address the issue in 1994 in the watershed case of *Campbell v. Acuff-Rose Music, Inc.*,[698] where it held that the defendant's commercial song parody may be a fair use within the meaning of the 1976 Act. The plaintiff-copyright holder of the Roy Orbison rock ballad "Oh Pretty Woman" sued a rap music group for copyright infringement when the group wrote and released on records, tapes, and CDs a song entitled "Pretty Woman" with the intention, "through comical lyrics, to satirize the original work."[699] In holding that "Pretty Woman" may be a fair use, the Supreme Court observed that the 1976 Act, like the doctrine of fair use, does not rely on bright-line rules; rather, the Court noted, the 1976 Act mandates a case-by-case analysis, with the four statutory factors to be explored and weighed together, in determining whether the use in a given instance is fair. In reaching its holding, the Supreme Court broke new ground, as summarized below.

In examining the purpose and the character of the use, the Court stated that the central issue posed is the following: Does the new work merely supersede the original work or does it contribute something new with a further purpose or different character—that is, is the new work *transformative*?[700] The Court further noted that the more transformative the new work, the less significant are other factors, such as commercialism, that may militate against a finding of fair use.[701]

The Court noted that parody may have transformative value, and it held, for the first time, that "parody, like other comment or criticism, may claim fair use."[702] The Court then went on to distinguish parody from satire. It noted that since satire criticizes merely the subject matter of the original work, it can stand alone and, therefore, has to justify any borrowing from the original work. Parody, on the other hand, targets another creative work; therefore, it must mimic the original work in order to make its point. The Court observed, moreover, that a parody that targets the original more loosely than does the parody in the case at hand may still pass muster under the fair-use defense, provided all other factors are satisfied.[703]

The Court insisted that the commercial purpose of an appropriating work never carries a presumption of unfair use and that if there were such a presumption, it would

> swallow nearly all of the illustrative uses listed in the [fair-use provision of the 1976 Act], including news reporting, comment, criticism, teaching, scholarship, and research, since these activities "are generally conducted for profit in this country."[704]

The Court, in referring to the effect of the use on the potential market for the original work, noted that a parodic work is unlikely to affect the market for the original work, since "the parody and the original usually serve different market functions."[705]

POST-CAMPBELL

In the 2001 decision of *Suntrust Bank v. Houghton Mifflin*,[706] the Eleventh Circuit, in reversing a lower court decision, relied heavily on *Campbell* to determine that defendant's commercial fiction novel was a parody of plaintiff's novel and thereby entitled to a fair use defense. The defendant published *The Wind Done Gone*, a critique and parody of *Gone with the Wind*. Plaintiff, which owned the copyright interest in *Gone with the Wind*, sued for copyright infringement. The circuit court agreed with the lower court that *The Wind Done Gone* was largely "an encapsulation of *Gone with the Wind* that exploits its copyrighted characters, story lines, and settings as the palette for the new story."[707] The court explained that the defendant used

> fifteen fictional characters from *Gone With the Wind*, incorporating their physical attributes, mannerisms, and the distinct features that [the original author] used to describe them, as well as their complex relationships with each other. Moreover, the various [fictional] locales, . . . settings, characters, themes, and plot of *The Wind Done Gone* closely mirror those contained in *Gone With the Wind*.[708]

Nevertheless, in evaluating the factors, the court emphasized that *The Wind Done Gone*'s highly transformative use of the copyrighted elements of *Gone with the Wind* strongly overshadowed and outweighed its commercial use. In addition, the court observed that it was unlikely that the parody would serve as a market substitute for the original.

In addition to cases involving a parody, *Campbell's* fair use analysis, including the transformative factor, has been applied to cases where the allegedly infringing work, because of its "further purpose or different character,"[709] has been found to pass fair use muster. For example, in *Kelly v. Arriba Soft Corp.,*[710] discussed in chapter 18, the Ninth Circuit in 2003, affirming in pertinent part a California federal district court decision, held that defendant's thumbnail, lower-resolution images of the plaintiff photographer's photographs constituted a "fair use" despite their exact replication of the photographs, because the thumbnails' function, unlike the artistic purpose of the originals, was to serve as a tool to help index and improve access to images on the Internet. Similarly, in the 2000 case of *Baraban v. Time Warner, Inc.,*[711] the plaintiff's photograph was originally used in an advertisement promoting nuclear energy; he sued an author and a book publisher in infringement for including the photograph in a book criticizing the efforts of the power industry to promote a positive view of nuclear energy. A New York federal district court, in granting defendant's motion for summary judgment, found that the use of the photograph was fair. In reaching its conclusion, the court noted that the photograph was used by the defendant for purposes of criticism and comment and that in reproducing it in black-and-white at less than one-quarter of its original size defendants did not harm the market for plaintiff's photograph.

KOONS REVISITED AFTER CAMPBELL

Campbell, with its revisions of fair use analysis, provided the courts with a more highly nuanced template for determining if a use is fair use in image appropriation. For example, note the following two 2006 cases in which a fair use was found.

In *Blanch v. Koons,*[712] Andrea Blanch, an established professional fashion and portrait photographer, created a photographic work in 2000 entitled *Silk Sandals by Gucci* at a "shoot" organized by the Condé Nast company for *Allure* magazine, one of its publications. *Silk Sandals* depicts a woman's lower legs and feet, adorned with bronze nail polish and dressy Gucci sandals, resting on a man's lap in, apparently, a first-class airplane cabin. According to the evidence, *Allure*, with the participation of Blanch, suggested the model, sandals, and nail polish for the advertisement and Blanch retained control over the camera, film, lighting, and composition of the photograph. In addition, and with the objective of achieving an erotic sensibility to the photograph, Blanch suggested the setting of the airplane cabin interior and the placement of the model's feet on the gentleman's lap. Blanch was subsequently paid $750 for *Silk Sandals*, which was published in the August 2000 issue of *Allure* as part of a six-page feature on metallic cosmetics. Blanch retained the copyright to *Silk Sandals* but neither published nor licensed it subsequent to its publication in *Allure*.

That same year, Deutsche Bank in collaboration with the Guggenheim Foundation commissioned artist Jeff Koons to create a series of paintings for exhibition, first at Deutsche Guggenheim Berlin, an art exhibition space housed in a Deutsche Bank building in Berlin, and then at the Guggenheim Museum in New York. For the commission, Deutsche Bank paid Koons $2 million. Accordingly, Koons created a series of seven paintings which he entitled *Easyfun-Ethereal*. To produce the paintings, he culled images from advertisements and from his own photographs, scanned them into a computer, digitally superimposed the scanned images against backgrounds of pastoral landscapes, and then printed color images of the resulting collages. These printed images constituted the templates that were used by his assistants in applying paints to billboard-sized ten-by-fourteen-foot canvasses. The *Easyfun-Ethereal* series was exhibited at the Deutsche Guggenheim Berlin from October 2000 through January 2001. Among the paintings in this series was *Niagara*, the subject of Blanch's infringement suit. *Niagara* depicts four pair of women's feet and lower legs dangling prominently over images of ice cream and pastries with a grassy field and Niagara Falls in the background. Koons stated that he was inspired to create *Niagara* by a billboard he saw in Rome depicting several sets of women's lower legs: that is, by juxtaposing woman's legs against a background of food and landscape his intention was to "comment on the ways in which some of our most basic appetites—for food, play and sex—are mediated by popular images."[713] In creating *Niagara*, Koons plucked images from fashion magazines and advertisements, including Blanch's *Silk Sandals*. When Blanch saw *Niagara* on display at the Guggenheim Museum in New York, she brought suit against Koons for copyright infringement.

In affirming a New York federal district court's dismissal of the suit on summary judgment, the Second Circuit noted, first, that

> [t]he ultimate test of fair use . . . is whether the copyright law's goal of "promoting the Progress of Science and useful Arts" "would be better served by allowing the use than by preventing it."[714]

The court then examined the four fair use factors.

Under the first factor, the purpose and character of the use, the court noted that Koons and Blanch each had sharply different objectives: Koons used Blanch's image in commenting on the social and aesthetic consequences of the mass media, whereas Blanch had sought to depict some sort of eroticism. Accordingly, the court found that the parties' different objectives confirmed the transformative nature of Koons's use of *Silk Sandals*. Moreover, as the court observed, "[a]although such transformative use is not absolutely necessary for a finding of fair use . . . transformative works lie at the heart of the fair use doctrine's guarantee of breathing space."[715] As to the commercialism of his use, the court noted that while Koons made a substantial profit from the sale of the *Niagara* image on postcards and catalog sales—approximately $127,000—commercial benefit does not render a use presumptively unfair and, in any event, is not as significant an issue as the transformative nature of the second work. In this case, the court noted that although Koons realized some economic gains, *Niagara*'s public exhibition in a museum worked a benefit to the public. Therefore, the commercialism under the first factor could properly be discounted. As to the issue under the first factor addressing justification for copying, the court found that *Niagara* was satire—not parody—since it targeted the genre of Blanch's photograph rather than the photograph itself, and accordingly required justification for the copying. However, Koons's assertion that *Silk Sandals* was typical of a certain style of mass communication and that by using a fragment of it he was commenting on the culture embodied in *Allure* magazine was accepted by the Second Circuit as justification for his use of *Silk Sandals*. As to the issue of bad faith under the first factor, the Second Circuit observed that, while Koons used Blanch's photograph without permission, failure to seek permission for copying does not amount to bad faith per se: that is, if the use is otherwise fair, no permission need be sought or granted.

Under the second factor, the nature of the copyrighted work, the court noted that two distinctions must be considered. First, is the copyrighted work factual, or is it, on the other hand, creative/fictional? Although the court noted that more leeway is given to the appropriation of factual works and that *Silk Sandals* is a fictional work, the court found that this distinction has limited implications here, as Koons used the work in a transformative way. The second distinction is whether the copyrighted work, when appropriated, was published or unpublished. The court observed that there is greater leeway to appropriate from published works, and since *Silk Sandals* had been published, this distinction favored Koons.

As to the third fair use factor, the amount and substantiality of what was used in relation to the work as a whole, the question, according to the Second Circuit, was whether there was excessive copying beyond Koons's justified purpose for doing so in the first place. The court found that the amount of copying by Koons was reasonable.

Finally, under the fourth factor, the effect of the use on the potential market or value of the original work, the court noted that the inquiry here was whether the secondary use usurped the market for the original work. Observing that Blanch acknowledged that she had made no further use of *Silk Sandals* after it was published in *Allure*, that the use of it by Koons brought no harm to her career or upset any plans she had for the photograph, and that the use did not damage the photograph's value, the Second Circuit found that this factor as well favored Koons.

Having found that each of the four fair use factors favored the artist Jeff Koons, the Second Circuit affirmed the New York federal district court's dismissal of the suit.

In *Bill Graham Archives v. Dorling Kindersley Ltd.*,[716] the Second Circuit, affirming a New York federal district court's decision, held that inclusion of seven images, to which plaintiff held the copyrights, in defendant's coffee table book constituted a fair use. Defendant Dorling Kindersley (DK) published *Grateful Dead: The Illustrated Trip*, intended as a cultural history of the musical group, in 2003. It was a 480-page chronological history of the Grateful Dead combining over 2000 images representing dates in the group's history with explanatory text. Plaintiff's seven images originally appeared on Grateful Dead event posters and tickets and were displayed in *Illustrated Trip* in significantly reduced form, accompanied by captions describing the concerts with which they were associated. Although DK at first sought permission to reproduce the seven images, the parties could not agree on an appropriate license fee. DK nevertheless proceeded with publication of *Illustrated Trip,* including the seven images without having entered into a license fee arrangement with plaintiff. When DK refused to meet plaintiff's post-publication demands for a license fee, the plaintiff sued for copyright infringement and DK moved for dismissal on summary judgment, asserting that its reproduction of the seven images in *Illustrated Trip* constituted a fair use.

In affirming the district court's holding that DK's use was fair, the Second Circuit, in addressing the first fair use factor preliminarily recognized, as did the lower court, that courts frequently accord fair use protection to the use of copyrighted material in biographies, viewing such works as forms of historic scholarship.[717] Additionally, the Second Circuit noted that DK's purpose in using the images in the biography as historical artifacts to document the Grateful Dead concerts was different from the images' original purpose: artistic expression and promotion of upcoming Grateful Dead concert events. The court also noted the manner by which DK displayed the images: they were significantly reduced in size and their expressive value was minimized by combining them with a timeline, text, and original graphic artwork in a collage-like effect. Moreover, as the court noted, the images constituted an inconsequential portion of *Illustrated Trip.* Finally, under the first fair use factor, the court observed that while *Illustrated Trip* was a commercial venture, none of the seven images was used to advertise or promote the sale of the book Accordingly, the Second Circuit found that the first fair use factor favored DK, in that the latter used the seven images transformatively and did not seek to exploit the images' expressive qualities for commercial gain.

As to the second factor, the court observed that, as the seven images were creative artworks (as opposed to factual material), the second factor weighed against DK. Nevertheless, the court accorded this factor little weight, since the creative works were used for the transformative purpose of contributing to the biographical history provided by the book.

In considering the third factor, the court noted that even though the seven images were reproduced in toto, "the visual impact of their artistic expression is significantly limited because of their reduced size ... [and] such use by DK is tailored to further its transformative purpose."[718] Accordingly, the court found that the third factor did not militate against a finding of fair use.

In addressing the fourth factor, the court held that the use DK made of plaintiff's images was transformatively different from their original expressive purpose and that a copyright holder cannot bar others from entering fair use markets merely by creating or licensing a market for transformative uses of its own creative work.

Accordingly, in weighing the four factors, the Second Circuit concluded that DK's use of the seven images in its book *Illustrated Trip* was fair.

However, a more-nuanced framework for fair use analysis does not always lead to a finding of fair use, as evidenced in the 2009 case of *Reyes v. Wyeth Pharmaceuticals*.[719] In that case, plaintiff Martha Reyes, an artist, created a glass sculpture, *Watcher of the Fire*, in 2001, as part of a series entitled *Guardians of the Four Elements*. Around February 2003, Reyes loaned *Watcher*, which she valued at $2,500, to defendant Felix Cordero for the purpose of photographing it. Codero offered *Watcher* to defendant Wyeth Pharmaceuticals for use in a publicity campaign called "Salud Wyeth" (meaning Wyeth Health). The campaign's objective was to educate the public about the importance of healthy living and to raise public awareness about health risks associated with various ailments. The campaign, which did not mention any Wyeth pharmaceutical products, was launched in May 2003 and was promoted through newspapers, magazines, billboard advertisements, and commercials in movie theaters and on television. In a sub-campaign of "Salud Wyeth" related to raising awareness about rheumatoid arthritis (RA), Wyeth created an advertisement containing a picture of a woman holding a rectangularly shaped stained glass sculpture, with the bottom of both the sculpture and the woman's body (from mid-torso downward) cropped from the picture. The top of the advertisement bore the caption "Wyeth Health," and the photo was overlaid with text indicating that the woman was an artist born to create, but unable to do so because of a diagnosis of RA. Below the cropped picture was text advising the viewer to consult a rheumatologist about treatments for RA, along with a website address for an RA organization, a symbol for the Rheumatologists of Puerto Rico Association, and the Wyeth logo. The advertisement was published on two separate occasions in a Puerto Rican newspaper.

Reyes, recognizing the sculpture in the advertisement as *Watcher*, filed criminal charges against Cordero in 2004 for misappropriating the sculpture. The charges were later dismissed after Cordero agreed to pay Reyes $2,500 for *Watcher*, which he claimed to have destroyed. Reyes continued to create and exhibit artworks. Among the works she exhibited and sold in 2006 was a second set of four sculptures again called *Guardians of the Four Elements*, which included one sculpture called the *Watcher of Fire* (rather than "Watcher of *the* Fire"). This second set measured about 24 by 12 inches, whereas the first set measured about 36 by 24 inches. Reyes explained that she designed the second set of watchers from a different angle because the original set had been exposed to the media. The second group of four sculptures sold for $6,000 as a set or $1,500 apiece.

Reyes brought a suit of copyright infringement against the defendants in the federal district court of Puerto Rico, and the defendants moved to dismiss on the grounds that they made a fair use of Reyes's sculpture.

In addressing whether the defendants' use of *Watcher* was fair, the court first noted that while the four statutorily provided factors guide fair use analysis, they do not control the analysis. As the court stated,

[t]he ultimate determination of fair use requires that the four factors be weighed together in light of the purpose of copyright: promoting the Progress of Science and useful Arts.[720]

The court then looked at the first fair use factor, the purpose and character of the use. In questioning, first, whether the advertisement's use of the *Watcher* was transformative, the court noted that Reyes produced the sculpture as a work of display art to be appreciated visually, and that in the defendants' advertisement, the sculpture was not altered in any way, nor did any of the text in the advertisement include any comments about the sculpture. The defendants did, however, incorporate the image of the sculpture in an advertisement intended to raise awareness about RA, a message which differs from the purpose of the sculpture itself, which has nothing to do with RA. However, this additional message did not entirely alter the character of the sculpture in the advertisement, where it was still presented to the viewer as a creative work of art. Accordingly, the court found the defendants' use of the *Watcher* to be "somewhat transformative (but not overwhelmingly so)."[721] Another issue under the first factor was whether the use of the copyrighted work was for profit. The defendants argued that the advertisement was part of a public service educational campaign that was not commercial: it did not promote any particular product or treatment, it was supported by the Rheumatologists Association of Puerto Rico, and it was not aimed at increasing revenue for the defendants. The court noted, however that the

crux of the profit/nonprofit distinction is not whether the sole motive of the use is monetary gain but whether the user stands to profit from exploitation of the copyrighted material without paying the customary price.[722]

Because the advertisement included Wyeth's logo, and served to build goodwill toward the defendants, and because they did not compensate Reyes for the use of her sculpture, the court found that this issue under the first factor, although not carrying much weight, favored Reyes. Still another issue to be considered under the first fair use factor was the defendants' good faith or lack of same. As the court noted, although it is possible that many people involved in the advertising campaign had no idea that *Watcher* was a copyrighted work of art and the defendants had not obtained the rights to use the sculpture, Cordero knew that *Watcher* belonged to Reyes and yet he utilized it in the campaign without seeking her permission, he subsequently destroyed the sculpture, and he did not make amends until after she instituted criminal proceedings against him. The court found that those actions did not constitute good faith and saw no reason why Cordero's actions should not be attributed to his fellow defendants. Accordingly, the court found that because the profit/nonprofit distinction and the good faith factors carried relatively little weight and the defendants' use of the sculpture was somewhat transformative, the final balance under the first factor favored neither party.

Addressing the second fair use factor, the nature of the copyrighted work, the court noted that it was undisputed that *Watcher* was a creative work of art and that traditionally such works are the core of intended copyright protection. Although the defendants argued that the weight of this factor should be mitigated because they did not seek to profit directly from Reyes's creativity, the court disagreed with their characterization of their use of the sculpture. The court noted, among other points, that the advertisement, albeit with text, clearly displayed two things only: *Watcher* and the woman holding it. Therefore, the court found that the second factor weighed against a finding of fair use.

In looking at the third fair use factor, the amount and substantiality of the portion of the work used, the court noted that the question under this factor was whether "the quantity and value of the materials used are reasonable in relation to the purpose of the copying."[723] The court went on to observe that, on occasion, the copying of an entire work may be consistent with fair use: for example, where the entire image may be necessary for the use as well as where the reproduced image comprises only a small portion of the challenged work. The court noted that while in the case at hand, the advertisement contained a photograph of *Watcher* with only a small portion of the top and the bottom of the image cropped, given that the image was of an artist exhibiting art, the advertisement's message could not have been as effectively communicated by including only a portion of the sculpture. Accordingly, the court found that the appropriation under the third factor was not excessive and that the factor militated neither for nor against a finding of fair use.

In considering the fourth factor, the effect of the use upon the market for or value of the copyrighted work, the court stated that this factor "must take account not only of harm to the original but also of harm to the market for derivative works."[724] The court noted that because fair use is an affirmative defense, it was up to the defendants to demonstrate that there was no harm to Reyes's interest in markets for derivative works for *Watcher* that she would either develop or license to others to develop. The court further noted the paucity of evidence in the record as to any derivative use market for Reyes's sculptures in general and *Watcher* in particular, but stated that the lack of evidence in the record was not determinative: rather, the court had to inquire whether wide-scale use of artwork, particularly sculpture, in advertisements or other visual media would affect the market for such art. In any event, the court determined that widespread use of artwork in advertisements without the copyright holder's permission would destroy the market for selling the artwork for use in advertisements. Accordingly, the court found that this fourth factor did not favor a finding of fair use.

Ultimately, in weighing together the four fair use factors, the federal district court of Puerto Rico found that the scale tilted against a finding of fair use.

The fair use doctrine was the central argument of artist Shepard Fairey in his 2009 lawsuit, *Fairey v. Associated Press*. Fairey created the iconic "Obama Hope" poster during the 2008 presidential campaign, which contained an image of Barack Obama pensively looking upward with the caption "HOPE." The image was in shades of red, white, and blue. During the presidential campaign,

Fairey gave away 300,000 free "Obama Hope" posters and sold approximately 4,000 posters. Additionally, he sold merchandise ranging from coffee mugs to T-shirts.[725]

In January 2009, the Associated Press contacted Fairey, claiming that his poster was based on its photograph and demanding that he pay them for the use of this photograph. Following these accusations, Fairey brought suit, requesting that the court issue a declaratory judgment that he was protected from any claims of copyright infringement based on the fair use doctrine. The AP countersued, claiming ownership of the copyright and "garden variety copyright infringement."[726] Additionally, the AP claimed that Fairey could not argue fair use because he used the photograph for his own commercial benefit. Mannie Garcia, the freelance photographer who took the photograph while on assignment for the AP, also asserted that he, not the AP, owned the copyright to the photograph. Garcia joined as a defendant and sought damages for copyright infringement.[727]

Fairey originally claimed that the inspiration for his poster was a photograph of Barack Obama and George Clooney taken by Garcia at a panel discussion at the National Press Club in 2006. Fairey argued that the Obama-Clooney photograph and the image on his poster were distinct, since he had cropped out Clooney and made adjustments to Obama's eyes and head.[728] However, he later admitted that the Obama-Clooney photograph was not the basis for the poster.[729] Rather, he acknowledged that he had used a close-up shot of Obama alone, taken by Garcia at the same panel. He also admitted that he had deleted files with the Obama close-up photograph and had manufactured other documents that made it appear he used the Obama-Clooney photograph instead.[730] Fairey ultimately pleaded guilty to criminal contempt due to his lies and fabrications regarding the source of the "Obama Hope" poster.[731]

In 2011, Fairey and the AP reached a settlement in the copyright case. The terms of the settlement included Fairey's agreement to request permission to license AP photographs going forward. Additionally, Fairey and the AP agreed to share in the profits for "Hope" merchandise.[732]

CARIOU V. PRINCE

A case which has transfixed the art world, in part because it may further refine the matrix of factors comprising fair use, is *Cariou v. Prince*.[733]

Plaintiff Patrick Cariou was a respected professional French photographer who had published a number of photography books, including *Yes Rasta*, published with a copyright notice in 2000 by Powerhouse Books, Inc. The photographs in *Yes Rasta* were the result of Cariou's having spent parts of six years in the mountains of Jamaica gaining the trust of his photographic subjects, the Rastafarians, an insular, spiritual group living apart from mainstream society. The book contained approximately 100 "strikingly original black-and-white photographs, mostly close-up portraits of stern, mystical-looking men within a distinctive tropical landscape . . . [and] an essay by Perry Henzell, . . . producer and director of the . . . Jamaican film, *The Harder They Come*."[734] The photographs in *Yes Rasta* were registered with the U.S. Copyright Office in November of 2001, with Cariou listed as the sole copyright holder in the photographs. Cariou testified that, in creating the photographs, he had made creative determinations in his choice of equipment, his staging, and his composition of each of the photographs, and in his choice of techniques and processes used in developing the photographs. Cariou also testified that he was "heavily involved in the layout, editing, and printing"[735] of *Yes Rasta*.

Richard Prince, a celebrated and successful appropriation artist whose style is informed by, among other elements, repetition, groupings, and his love for music,[736] began writing a screenplay in 2007 entitled *Eden Rock*, a fantasy account of survivors of a nuclear attack whose cruise ships end up in St. Barts, the survivors forming gangs and occupying the island's hotels and forming their own post-apocalyptic society. Around that time, Prince heard his stepson playing the alternative music of the *Easy Star All-Stars* band in the album *Radiodread* and the following day found a copy of *Yes Rasta* in a bookstore on St. Bart's and took an interest in the photographs. Inspired by his birthplace, the Panama Canal Zone, which he had visited recently, and by his *Eden Rock* screenplay, "Prince imagined a make-believe, post-apocalyptic enclave, the Canal Zone, in which bands and music are the only things to survive."[737]

To express his message, Prince created a series of paintings entitled *Canal Zone*, ultimately completing twenty-nine paintings in the series—of which twenty-eight included images taken from *Yes Rasta*. His first work in the series, *Canal Zone (2007)*, consisted of a board on which were tacked in a reordered fashion all or portions of thirty-five photographs torn from pages in *Yes Rasta*, some of the Rastafarians' faces bearing facemasks drawn or painted by Prince. Prince intended that *Canal Zone (2007)* serve as an introduction to the subsequent paintings in the series as well as to characters he intended to use in a screenplay. In the subsequent paintings in the *Canal Zone* series, Prince made varying use of the photographs, digitally scanning and enlarging the photograph images, and then "applying some directly to the canvas as a backdrop for collaging, and others as cut-out collage elements."[738] In some of the works in the series, collage elements of the photograph images were attached with scotch tape to other images for further scanning; in other works, the collage elements were affixed directly to the canvas with paint. Some paintings in the series consisted almost entirely of images from *Yes Rasta*, along with collaging, cropping, and overpainting; others used smaller portions of the *Yes Rasta* images.

From December 2007 through February 2008, Prince showed some of his artwork at the Eden Rock hotel in St. Barts, including *Canal Zone (2007)*. Although the work was not sold, portions of it were reproduced in a magazine article about Prince's *Canal Zone* show at the Gagosian Gallery. Gagosian, which had represented Prince since approximately 2005, held an exhibition of twenty-two of the twenty-nine paintings in the series from November 8, 2008 to December 20, 2008 at one of its Manhattan locations. The Gagosian Gallery also published and sold an exhibition catalog accompanying the show, similarly entitled *Canal Zone*, which included reproductions of many of the paintings in the show, some paintings in the series that were not in the show, and photographs of the photographs of *Yes Rasta* as they appeared in Prince's studio.

Other than by private sale to individuals he knew and liked, Cariou had never made commercial use of the photographs other than for inclusion in *Yes Rasta*. However, he had negotiated a show of the photographs through gallery owner Christiane Celle, who had planned to exhibit between thirty and forty of the photographs at her gallery with multiple prints of each to be sold at prices ranging between $3,000 and $20,000, depending on size. She also planned to have *Yes Rasta* reprinted for a book signing to be held during the gallery exhibition, and Cariou asserted that he had intended to issue and offer for sale artists' editions of the photographs.

The dispute arose when Cariou learned that Celle had cancelled his upcoming show because she did not want to appear to be riding on the coattails of Prince's success and because "she did not want to exhibit work which had been 'already done' at another gallery."[739] In December 2008, Cariou sued, among others, Richard Prince and Gagosian Gallery for copyright infringement in a New York federal district court, and both sides eventually moved for summary judgment.

To prevail in a copyright infringement case, as noted earlier, the plaintiff must establish two elements: ownership of a valid copyright, and unauthorized copying of elements of the plaintiff's work that are protectable. No party disputed Cariou's ownership of a valid copyright in the photographs. However, the defendants asserted at first that the photographs were not protectable as a matter of law, characterizing them as mere compilations of facts. The court dismissed that assertion, noting that under settled law for over a hundred years, "creative photographs are worthy of copyright protection even when they depict real people and natural environments,"[740] even without consideration of Cariou's creative choices in making the photographs, to which he testified. As to the second element, the court found that such copying was admitted by Prince[741] and, accordingly, was not in dispute.

The primary defense raised by the defendants in the lawsuit was fair use, and the New York federal district court duly applied the four-factor fair use analysis, noting that all of the four factors "are to be explored, and the results weighed together in light of the purposes of copyright."[742]

PURPOSE AND CHARACTER OF PRINCE'S USE OF THE PHOTOGRAPHS

Transformative Use. As the court noted, this primary consideration under the first fair use factor asks whether "the new work merely supersedes the objects of the original creation or instead adds something new, with a further purpose or different character."[743] The court noted that the more transformative the new work, the less significance is given to the other factors like commercialism that may militate against a finding of fair use. Here, the court declined defendants' invitation to find that the genre of appropriation was per se a fair use, regardless of whether the new artwork comments on the original works appropriated. It also found that Prince's use of Cariou's photographs, which did not comment on the photographs, was not transformative, as his paintings "merely recast, transform, or adapt the Photos [making them instead] infringing derivative works."[744] As the court noted, Prince testified that he had no interest in the original meaning of the photographs he used and did not have a message to communicate when creating art. As to the photographs, the court found that based on Prince's testimony, he did not, in creating the *Canal Zone* series, intend to comment on the photographs, on Cariou, or on the popular culture closely associated with Cariou, although, as the court acknowledged, "Prince intended his overall work to be creative and new."[745] Rather, Prince testified that he chose the photographs he appropriated for what he perceived to be their truth, which suggested to the court that his purpose for using Cariou's photographs was the same as Cariou's original purpose in taking them: to communicate to the viewer core truths about Rastafarians and their culture. Accordingly, while the court acknowledged that "there may be some minimal transformative element intended in Prince's use of the Photos, the overall transformativeness varies from work to work depending on the amount of the copying,"[746] and the transformative content is "minimal at best" and "not consistent" throughout the twenty-eight paintings in which Prince used the photographs. Therefore, the court found that the transformative prong of the first fair use factor "weighs heavily"[747] against a finding of fair use.

Commerciality. The second prong of the first fair use factor asks whether the otherwise infringing work "serves a commercial purpose or nonprofit educational purpose,"[748] and the court noted that the less transformative a work, the greater the importance of commerciality in determining fair use under the first factor. Here, the court found that there was substantial commercial exploitation of the photographs: the *Canal Zone* show at the Gagosian Gallery was advertised in seven newspapers, of which five included reproductions of photographs altered by Prince; the gallery issued some 7,500 exhibition invitation cards to its clients featuring a reproduction of a Prince work containing a photograph, with leftover invitations sold to a poster company; the gallery sold eight of the *Canal Zone* paintings for a total of nearly $10.5 million, split 60/40 between Prince and the gallery; seven other *Canal Zone* paintings were exchanged for art with an estimated value between $6 and $8 million; and the gallery sold $6,784.00 worth of *Canal Zone* exhibition catalogs. While the court recognized "the inherent public interest and cultural value of public exhibition of art and of an overall increase in public access to artwork,"[749] it found that, given the "overall low transformative content"[750] of Prince's works, the commerciality prong of the first fair use factor weighed against a fair use finding.

Bad Faith. This prong under the first fair use factor asks the court to consider the propriety of a defendant's conduct, which is integral to analyzing the character of the use. Here, Prince testified that he made no distinction between appropriating works in the public domain and works by a disclosed author; rather, he asked himself whether he likes the image.[751] The case in point was that Prince's employee contacted the publisher of *Yes Rasta* to publish additional copies of the book but never asked the publisher about a license to use the photographs or otherwise sought permission for their use. Accordingly, the court found that

Prince acted in bad faith, militating against a finding of fair use under the first factor. Moreover, noting that the Gagosian Gallery was aware that Prince was an appropriation artist but neither inquired as to whether Prince had obtained permission to use the photographs nor ceased its commercial exploitation of Prince's *Canal Zone* paintings after being notified that Prince was using the photographs without permission, the court found that the bad faith on the part of the gallery was equally clear. Accordingly, the first fair use factor weighed heavily in favor of Cariou and against Prince.

Nature of the Copyrighted Work

Here the court distinguishes between works that are expressive or creative, such as a work of fiction, and works that are more factual or informational, the latter category being accorded greater leeway for a fair use claim. The court found the photographs "highly original and creative artistic works" that thereby fell within "the core of the copyright's protective purposes."[752] Therefore, the second factor weighed against a fair use finding.

Amount and Substantiality of the Portion Used

The court noted that the question here was whether the extent of the copying was consistent with, or more than necessary to further, the purpose and character of the use. The court observed that if an entire work is reproduced, whatever the use, generally it may not constitute a fair use. The court also observed that where the portion used was essentially the heart of the copyrighted work, the third fair use factor weighs in favor of the copyright holder. Additionally, citing a Supreme Court case, the court noted that "a taking may not be excused merely because it is insubstantial with respect to the *infringing work*." [emphasis in original][753] Accordingly, the court found that in view of the slight transformative value of Prince's use, the amount of Prince's taking was greater than necessary and the third factor weighed against a fair use finding.

Market Harm

The fourth factor requires courts to consider the extent of market harm caused by the alleged infringer's actions, as well as whether such conduct, if widespread, would result in a substantially adverse impact on the potential market for the original and market harm for derivative works based on the original. The court noted that it was not significant that Cariou did not market his photographs more aggressively: the potential market for the original work and its derivatives must be examined even where the plaintiff has disavowed any intention to exploit them, given that he has the right to change his mind, and is entitled to preserve the opportunity to monetize his works. Here the court found market harm to the photographs in that, as a result of the *Canal Zone* exhibition and sale at the Gagosian Gallery, Celle cancelled her plans to exhibit and sell the *Yes Rasta* photographs and prints. Moreover, as artists might generally wish to engage in licensing original works for secondary uses by other artists, the court also found that Prince's use of the photographs unfairly damaged the potential markets for derivative use licenses for the photographs. Accordingly, the court found that the fourth factor, like the other three, weighed against a finding of fair use.

AGGREGATE ANALYSIS AND CONCLUSIONS AS TO LIABILITY

In weighing the four factors together, the New York federal district court found that the defendants were not entitled to the defense of fair use.

In addition, the court found that the Gagosian Gallery was directly liable for copyright infringement in copying constituent elements of the photographs when it published the *Canal Zone* exhibition catalog, created and distributed the invitation cards, and otherwise distributed reproductions of the photographs as appropriated by Prince, and by exhibiting and selling Prince's unauthorized works. Moreover, the court found the gallery liable as a vicarious infringer, in that, as the representative of Prince and the marketer of his *Canal Zone* paintings, it had the right and ability to supervise Prince's work, or at the very least the right and ability to ensure that Prince obtained the requisite licenses to use the photographs prior to his paintings being made available for sale. Further, the court found that the gallery was liable as a contributory infringer, in that it was well aware of, and capitalized on, Prince's reputation as an appropriation artist but never inquired into the propriety of his use of the photographs at the time that it reproduced, advertised, promoted, and sold the *Canal Zone* series paintings.

As of this writing, *Cariou* has been appealed to the Second Circuit[754] Whatever the ultimate determination of that court, it will not address the larger issue of how copyright law, in this age of digital art and the recycling and remixing of images, should evolve. A number of commentators, including the authors, believe that ultimately copyright law should adopt for its art images a pervasive system of licensing and elective attribution, in lieu of the case-by-case, fact-intensive subjectivity of fair use evaluation.

ART REPRODUCTIONS IN AUCTION AND GALLERY CATALOGS: A FAIR USE?

It is normal practice for auction houses and art galleries to create catalogs depicting high-quality images of the works of art that they are offering for sale.[755]

Often such catalogs are sold to the public, as in the case of auction catalogs. Where the depicted artwork is under subsisting copyright, an image of the artwork will generally be obtained either from the living artist or from the artist's estate. On certain occasions, however, the gallery or auction house will need to create its own transparency of the artwork for inclusion in the catalog. If a gallery or auction house is unable to secure permission from the copyright holder of the artwork to take a photograph of the work, may it nevertheless do so under the 1976 Act?

The fair use doctrine, codified in the 1976 Act as section 107, provides in pertinent part:

[T]he fair use of a copyrighted work, including such use by reproduction in copies
. . . for purposes *such as* [italics ours] criticism, comment, news reporting, teaching (including multiple copies for classroom use), scholarship, or research, is not an
infringement of copyright. In determining whether the use made in any particular
case is a fair use, the factors to be considered shall include [the four fair use factors
enumerated on p. 999 of this treatise].

While inclusion of images of artworks in auction and gallery catalogs does not
on first glance fall within the permitted uses enumerated in section 107, the words
"such as" allow room for other uses not specifically enumerated, provided that the
four codified factors weighed together lean toward a finding of fair use. Moreover,
a failure to deem the inclusion of art images in gallery and auction catalogs a fair
use would seem to undercut two exceptions that make possible auctions and gallery exhibitions and sales without running afoul of the 1976 Act: (1) the restriction on the exclusive right of public display (discussed on pages 939–940), which
permits the owner of a lawfully made copy of a work to display it to the public
under particular circumstances, and (2) the restriction on the exclusive right to
distribute (the first-sale doctrine, addressed on page 937–938), which permits the
owner of a lawfully made copy of a work to sell or otherwise dispose of it.
    Nevertheless, to avoid unnecessary complications—and possible copyright vi-
olation—it is the practice of the major auction houses and a number of the major
galleries to secure permission to display such images on, at least, the covers of
their auction catalogs and on attendant advertising and promotional literature.

Remedies for Copyright Infringement

The 1976 Copyright Act codifies the remedies available to the prevailing copyright holder in an infringement suit. In a civil suit such remedies include

(1) injunctive relief,
(2) impoundment and disposition,
(3) damages and profits, and
(4) costs and attorneys' fees.

INJUNCTIVE RELIEF

Under section 502 of the 1976 Copyright Act,[756] a court may grant temporary
and final injunctions to prevent or restrain copyright infringement. In *Reproducta Co. v. Kellmark Corp.*,[757] for example, a New York federal district court
in 1994 permanently enjoined the defendant company from reproducing a certain artist's work on any items other than calendars. However, where a plaintiff's claim for injunctive relief relies on cases where a showing of copyright
infringement creates a presumption of irreparable harm, and the plaintiff's claim
involves solely past infringements, a court will not find that a presumption of
irreparable harm exists, and will not grant an injunction on that basis alone. Ac-

cordingly, in the 2001 case of *Flack v. Queen Catherine, Inc.*,[758] discussed earlier in this chapter and in chapter 12, where the plaintiff sought a preliminary injunction enjoining the defendant from infringing her copyright in her sculpture by rebuilding its clay face and using pictures of the original to do so, plaintiff's motion was denied by a New York federal district court.

IMPOUNDMENT AND DISPOSITION

Section 503 of the 1976 Copyright Act[759] empowers a court at any time during an infringement action to impound all allegedly infringing copies of a work and all plates, molds, matrices, masters, and other implements by which such copies can be reproduced. As part of a final judgment or decree, a court may order the destruction (or other reasonable disposition) of all infringing copies of a work and all implements from which such copies can be reproduced.

DAMAGES

Section 504 of the 1976 Copyright Act[760] provides that the prevailing copyright holder in an infringement suit can elect to recover either (1) actual damages and profits or (2) statutory damages.

ACTUAL DAMAGES AND PROFITS

"Actual damages and profits" include the damages suffered by the copyright owner as a result of the infringement and any profits made by the infringer that are attributable to the infringement and that are not taken into account in computing the damages[761]—in other words, plaintiff's loss plus defendant's gain.[762] Determining the infringer's profits is a two-step process: First, the copyright owner establishes the infringer's gross revenue; second, the infringer must prove her deductible expenses and those elements of profit attributable to factors other than the copyrighted work. As noted in *Walker v. Forbes, Inc.*,[763] where the Fourth Circuit in 1994 awarded actual damages and infringer's profits to plaintiff because defendant magazine used plaintiff's photograph of a textile-machinery magnate to accompany an article without plaintiff's permission:

> This approach to damages . . . makes the infringer realize that it is cheaper to buy than to steal. . . . By stripping the infringer not only of the licensing fee but also of the profit generated as a result of the use of the infringed item, the law makes clear that there is no gain to be made from taking someone else's intellectual property without their consent.[764]

Although the 1976 Act does not define "actual damages," some general approaches for their computation have emerged through case law, based on the premise that such damages "be broadly construed to favor victims of infringement."[765] Accordingly, where an infringer of a work under copyright could have bargained with the copyright owner to pay for the right to use the work, courts have held that the actual damages are "what a willing buyer would have been reasonably required to pay to a willing seller for plaintiffs' work."[766] In addition, courts have permitted recovery of actual damages based on a calculation of a copyright owner's lost sales.[767] Moreover, while a court may be required to engage in some degree of speculation due to the nature of actual damages, the amount of damages may not be based on excessive speculation.[768] Similarly, a copyright holder may seek compensation for indirect losses such as market recognition, enhanced good will, and reputation, provided such claims are supported by the evidence and are not unduly speculative, but courts may not consider general claims of injured feelings.[769]

Going a step further, a New York federal district court affirmed a magistrate's ruling that permitted a copyright owner to expand the scope of its damage request against a competitor's infringement of its copyrighted floor lamp to include lost sales on noninfringed works that were sold as part of the same line of goods as the floor lamp.[770] The plaintiff and the defendant compete in the manufacture and the distribution of table and floor lamps. In May 1987, the plaintiff secured copyrights for table and floor lamps ornamented with a banana-leaf design. In May 1988, according to the plaintiff, the defendant manufactured and distributed lamps that infringed both the table and the floor models of the banana-leaf lamp and that bore a false copyright notice in the defendant's name. The plaintiff brought an infringement action. At trial, the plaintiff's copyright on the table lamp was declared invalid because of the omission of the requisite copyright notice on more than a few table lamps and the subsequent failure to make a reasonable effort to add notice to all copies of that table lamp publicly distributed in the United States.

As to damages, plaintiff contended that it was entitled to recover lost sales on its entire line of merchandise, since the lost sales resulted from the defendant's infringement of the floor lamp; that is, plaintiff's banana-leaf floor lamp was part of a new line intended to enable the company to sell its entire product line through major department store chains, a feat it had previously not achieved. The plaintiff further claimed that it is common in the lamp business for department stores to purchase a manufacturer's entire line and that the defendant's sale of an infringing floor lamp at a lower price disrupted plaintiff's plans to penetrate that market. Claiming it had therefore lost a major market advantage, plaintiff sought to establish its damages on the basis of those accounts in which it successfully sold its entire line. That theory was permitted by the magistrate and affirmed by a New York federal district court, subject to proof at trial.

In *Johnson v. Jones*,[771] although the Sixth Circuit found infringement and granted the plaintiff's request for the full amount of the defendant's gross revenue under section 504(b), the court denied the plaintiff's request for statutory damages and attorneys fees under sections 504(c) and 505. The court stated that section 504(b) requires the copyright owner "to present proof only of the infringer's gross revenue, and then the infringer is required to prove her deductible expenses."[772] Here, since the plaintiff met the burden of establishing the defendant's gross revenue and the defendant failed to provide any evidence of deductible expenses, the court awarded the plaintiff the entire value of the defendant's gross revenue. However, the court denied statutory damages and attorney's fees because the infringement commenced prior to the registration date. The court defined infringement as a continuing process from the date that it begins rather than a distinct and independent infringement for each separate act.

Where the Government Is the Infringer

Where a copyright owner's work is infringed by the government, the applicable statute, 28 U.S.C. § 1498(b), provides that the owner may recover "his reasonable and entire compensation as damages for such infringement, including the minimum statutory damages as set forth in section 504(c) of [the 1976 Copyright Act]."

In the 2012 case of *Gaylord v. United States*,[773] the federal circuit court determined that where "the government takes what is essentially a compulsory, nonexclusive license on the plaintiff's copyright,"[774] the copyright owner is entitled to compensatory damages (including the minimum statutory damages) but not to noncompensatory damages. The court also concluded that the methods used to ascertain "actual damages" under section 504 are appropriate for determining the copyright owner's loss. Moreover, the court determined that where a plaintiff cannot show lost sales, lost opportunities to license, or reduction in value of the copyright, actual damages should be based on "the fair market value of a license covering the defendant's use"[775] and the of the license should be calculated on what, hypothetically, a willing buyer would have reasonably been required to pay a willing seller for the copyright owner's work.[776]

In the instant case, the plaintiff Frank Gaylord, a nationally recognized sculptor, was selected to sculpt the statues for the Korean War Veterans Memorial (KWVM), which was authorized by federal legislation. The final design featured nineteen stainless steel statues representing a platoon of foot soldiers in formation, referred to as "The Column." Gaylord worked on "The Column" from 1990 to 1995, at which time the completed version was installed at the site of the memorial on the National Mall in Washington, D.C. From 1990 to 1995, Gaylord received five copyright registrations relating to the soldier sculptures, each copyright certificate listing Gaylord as the sole author. In January 1996, John Alli, an amateur photographer, took a photograph of the KWVM during a snowstorm and entitled it *Real Life*. In 2002, the U.S. Postal Service authorized a thirty-seven-cent postage stamp commemorating the Korean War, incorporating *Real Life* into the image on the stamp. The Postal Service paid Alli $1,500 for the use of his photograph but did not seek Gaylord's permission to depict "The Column" on the stamp, nor did Gaylord consent to such a use. From the time the Postal Service issued the stamp (July 27, 2003) until the stamp was retired (March 31, 2005), the Postal Service produced approximately 86.8 million of these stamps as well as other retail goods featuring images of the stamp. In July 2006, Gaylord sued the federal government in the Court of Federal Claims, alleging that the Postal Service infringed his copyright. On appeal, the Federal Circuit held that the Postal Service infringed Gaylord's copyrights and that there was no fair use, and remanded to the CFC for a determination of damages.

In determining Gaylord's actual damages, the CFC, endorsing a "zone of reasonableness" approach,[777] noted that the photographer Alli was paid $1,500 for the use of his photograph and that the highest amount the Postal Service had ever paid for use of an existing image on a stamp was $5,000. Accordingly, the CFC determined that the "zone of reasonableness" for the value of a work used on a stamp ranged from $1,500 to $5,000 and awarded Gaylord a one-time fee of $5000. Gaylord appealed the $5,000 award and the Court of Appeals for the Federal Circuit vacated the award and remanded to the CFC for a determination of the market value of the Postal Service's infringing use and an award of prejudgment interest. In so ruling, federal circuit court noted that

> [t]he trial court legally erred in this case. . . . In applying the so-called "zone of reasonableness" test, the court improperly limited its inquiry to the Postal Service's past licenses and . . . erroneously capped Mr. Gaylord's maximum damages without considering other evidence supporting a higher award. . . . On remand, the trial court must consider *all* [italics the court's] evidence relevant to a hypothetical negotiation rather than limiting its analysis to the Postal Service's past licenses . . . or . . . internal policies.[778]

STATUTORY DAMAGES AND ATTORNEY'S FEES

Before final judgment in an infringement suit, a copyright owner may elect, instead of actual damages and profits, to recover statutory damages.[779] Such damages cover all infringements involved in the action with respect to any one work. In each such action the court has the discretion to award the prevailing copyright holder damages in the amount of $750 or more but not to exceed $30,000. When the court finds willful infringement, the amount awarded may not exceed $150,000 per copyright infringed. Where a New York federal district court found willful infringement but the defendant had low net sales, it awarded the plaintiff as little as $20,000 per infringement.[780] If a court finds that an infringement is innocent, it may award the prevailing party as little as $200.

Section 412(2) of the 1976 Copyright Act provides that

> no award of statutory damages or of attorneys fees, as provided by sections 504 and 505, shall be made for...any infringement of copyright commenced after first publication of the work and before the effective date of its registration, unless such registration is made within three months after the first publication of the work.[781]

Accordingly, in the 2009 case of *Amador v. McDonald's*,[782] the plaintiff photographer was not entitled to receive statutory damages because he did not satisfy the prompt registration requirement. Here, the photographer Antonio Amador, who specialized in photographing the Puerto Rican landscape, saw for the first time in 2006 that blown-up versions of two of his photographs, *Cruise Ships in Old San Juan Bay* and *Plaza Las Delicia, Ponce,* were being publicly exhibited without his authorization at a McDonald's restaurant located in Luis Munoz Marin International Airport (LMMIA). In fact, the photographs had been displayed there from 2001 through October 2006. Thereafter, Amador brought suit alleging, among other claims, copyright infringement, and seeking, among other recourse, statutory damages and attorney's fees. In December 2008, the magistrate judge's report recommended that the defendant be found liable for copyright infringement and while the magistrate judge did not recommend the dismissal of Amador's claim for statutory damages and attorney's fees, she failed to determine whether Amador was entitled to such damages and fees as a matter of law.[783] Subsequently, the Puerto Rico federal district court held that Amador was not entitled to statutory damages and attorney's fees under sections 504 and 505.

In so holding, the court first noted that

> Section 412 was designed to promote two things. First, "by denying an award of statutory damages and attorney's fees where infringement takes place before registration, Congress sought to provide copyright owners with an incentive to register their copyrights promptly." Second, section 412 encourages the potential infringer to check the Copyright Office's database . . . to ensure that statutory damages and attorney's fees are reserved for infringers who had constructive notice that the work was covered by a valid copyright.[784]

The court noted that *Plaza Las Delicia, Ponce* was first published on January 1, 2003, and was registered on November 15, 2004; *Cruise Ships in Old San Juan Bay* was first published on January 1, 1999, and was registered on August 30, 2006. Therefore, as the court observed, as registration as to each of the photographs was not made within three months after the respective photograph's first publication, Amador could be entitled to statutory damages only if the photographs were registered prior to the commencement of the infringement. Amador argued—unsuccessfully—that since the two photographs were visible only when the restaurant was open, a new infringement occurred each day the restaurant opened. In disagreeing, the Puerto Rico federal district court held that the defendant "engaged in ongoing infringement which commenced in 2001 when [Amador's] two (2) color photos were first published in the McDonald's at LMMIA. . . . The fact that the photos were not visible when the restaurant was closed does not create a separate and distinct infringement every time the restaurant opens."[785] That is, as the court noted, a plaintiff may not receive statutory damages and attorney's fees for infringements commenced after registration if the same party commenced an infringement of the same work prior to registration.[786]

In 1999, in *Gerig v. Krause Publications, Inc.*,[787] a Kansas federal district court rejected the plaintiff's claim for statutory damages on the grounds that the infringing works were published in October 1997, but the registrations did not become effective until December 1997 and January 1998. Further, the court held that the plaintiff was not entitled to the three-month grace period provided under section 412 because the works were not registered within three months of their being first published. The court stated that section 412 "leaves no room for discretion, mandating that no attorney's fees or statutory damages be awarded so long as the infringement commenced before registration of the copyright."[788]

COSTS AND ATTORNEY'S FEES

Under section 505 of the 1976 Copyright Act,[789] a court in its discretion may allow the recovery of full costs by or against any party other than the United States government. The court may also award the prevailing party a reasonable attorney's fee as part of the costs.

CRIMINAL REMEDIES

Section 506 of the 1976 Copyright Act empowers a court to administer the criminal sanctions of fines and imprisonment[790] to anyone held to have infringed a copyright willfully either for "commercial advantage or private financial gain"[791] or by reproduction or distribution of one or more copies which have a total retail value of more than $1,000. When a party is so convicted, the court must order the forfeiture and the destruction or other disposition of all infringing copies of the work and all implements from which such copies can be manufactured.

TRADEMARK REMEDIES UNDER THE LANHAM ACT

Not normally looked to for recourse by copyright holders of visual art, section 43(a) of the Lanham Act,[792] the federal statute that protects trademarks, has been used by plaintiffs to obtain injunctive relief against infringements, as illustrated in the 1992 case of *Romm Art Creations Ltd. v. Simcha International, Inc.*[793] As noted by a New York federal district court, the case represents "a rarely visited area of the law—the interaction of the Lanham Act with the marketing and sale of limited editions and fine art posters."[794]

The plaintiff, a publisher and wholesale distributor of fine art posters and limited-edition paintings and sculptures, was granted the exclusive worldwide distribution rights in and to posters by Itzchak Tarkay, an Israeli artist of international renown. The posters at issue are reproductions of original works from the artist's collection of acrylic paintings known as "Women and Cafes." According to the plaintiff, the paintings, as a result of widespread distribution and advertising, have become known by the trade and by consumers as "Tarkays." Tarkay posters use distinctive border arrangements—a single margin on either the side or the bottom of the image, rather than the standard two-inch borders all around—and they feature women wearing bright clothing against vividly patterned backgrounds. Tarkay's original paintings sell for as much as $30,000 each; limited-edition prints of his work sell at prices from $1,200 to $2,500, and his posters are priced at $30 a piece.

The defendant buys and sells original art, limited editions, and posters and is the distributor of the Patricia Govezensky assemblage of limited editions and posters known as the "Patricia" line.

In October 1991, the plaintiff, in a New York federal district court, sought to enjoin the defendant from manufacturing, advertising, or selling particular posters, silk screens, and limited editions of reproductions of certain paintings bearing the signature "Patricia." Among its claims were trade-dress infringement under the Lanham Act, unfair competition, and dilution of the Tarkay trade dress in violation of the New York General Business Law and New York common law. ("Trade dress" is the total appearance and image of a product, including such features as size, texture, shape, color, color combinations, and graphics.) The plaintiff alleged, among other points, that the "Patricia" paintings "are slavishly similar and entirely derivative of the works of . . . Tarkay's 'Women and Cafes' collection"[795] and were prepared with the intention of causing widespread consumer confusion. In March 1992, the court granted the plaintiff a preliminary injunction, pending trial, thereby preventing the defendant from promoting, marketing, selling, or distributing the "Patricia" limited editions and posters that the court determined were too similar to the Tarkays.

In granting relief to the plaintiff under the Lanham Act, the court noted that the act provides civil redress to a party injured by unfair competition through false or misleading advertising or trademark or trade-dress infringement. In *Romm Art Creations*, the plaintiff was required to show that

(1) the trade dress was nonfunctional,
(2) the Tarkay trade dress acquired a second meaning, and
(3) there was a likelihood of confusion as to the source of the product.

As the court observed,

> [it has long been] recognized that recovery under [the Lanham Act] is not restricted to federally registered trademarks, but extends to "words, *symbols, collections of colors and designs,* or advertising materials or techniques" that the purchasing public has come to associate with a single source. [italics ours][796]

In finding that the Tarkay posters and limited editions were entitled to protection under the Lanham Act, the court relied in part on *Hartford House, Ltd. v. Hallmark Cards, Inc.,*[797] a Tenth Circuit case in which the plaintiff, Hartford House, a small commercial manufacturer of non-occasion greeting cards that conveyed emotional messages about personal relationships, brought an action against Hallmark Cards, alleging that Hallmark's "Personal Touch" line of cards infringed on the plaintiff's product. The Tenth Circuit affirmed the federal district court's holding that the combination of elements constituting the trade dress (in *Hartford House,* the overall look of Blue Mountain's "Airbrush Feelings" and "Watercolor Feelings" cards) was not functional and was, therefore, protectable under the Lanham Act. Indeed, as the federal district court in *Hartford House* stated,

[o]ne salutary purpose of the Lanham Act in this context is to protect a creative artists' [*sic*] rights in his or her creation and thus provide incentive to be creative. By protecting and fostering creativity, a product with [different] features . . . may well be developed. Offering consumers a choice in the non-occasion greeting card market stimulates, rather than stifles competition.[798]

In *Romm Art Creations*, the New York federal district court found that the plaintiff presented sufficient documentation to support its claim that Tarkay's works entered the market before those of "Patricia." Moreover, the court found that the Tarkay mark met the criteria for an arbitrary or fanciful mark and noted that "[a]n inherently distinctive trade dress is proof of secondary meaning."[799] Further, the court observed that once the plaintiff had established that the trade dress had acquired secondary meaning in the marketplace, the defendant had the burden to show that the trade dress in question was functional and, therefore, not protectable under the Lanham Act. The court found that the Tarkay trade dress was not functional and was, therefore, protectable under the Lanham Act. The court also found that the sufficient (indeed, striking) similarity between the Tarkay and the "Patricia" patterns could give rise to confusion on the part of the consumer.

Tarkay's unique artistic style enabled the plaintiff to obtain trade-dress protection in the form of injunctive relief. If, however, the principles of *Romm Art Creations* were adhered to in the area of visual arts, apparently only the first practitioner could use a given artistic style. For example, the late nineteenth-century postimpressionist technique of pointillism, which is characterized by the application of paint in small dots and brush strokes, was used by a number of master artists, including Georges Seurat and Camille Pisarro. Under *Romm Art Creations*, one of those artists committed a trade-dress violation and his works would be enjoined. The same reasoning applies to Cubism, the creators of which are generally credited to be Pablo Picasso and Georges Braque.[800] Would only one of those modern masters be permitted under *Romm Art Creations* to use that style? In the words of one commentator,

> society loses if artistic style is so guarded that artistic trends cannot emerge. . . . To follow the reasoning of *Romm Art* and allow only the originator of each artistic style to work in that style would defeat the very spirit of the Copyright Act and . . . deprive society of a dynamic creative process.[801]

ARCHITECTURAL WORKS

A full discussion of architectural works is beyond the scope of this book, but brief mention is made here of the 1990 Architectural Works Copyright Protection Act (here called the Architectural Act),[802] which amends the Copyright Act of 1976 to include protection for all architectural works created on or after December 1, 1990. An "architectural work" is defined as

> the design of a building as embodied in any tangible medium of expression, including a building, architectural plans, or drawings. The work includes the overall form as well as the arrangement and composition of spaces and elements in the design, but does not include individual standard features.[803]

Implementation of the Architectural Act has created two distinct copyrights capable of sustaining separate infringement: one in the architectural plans or drawings (already protected by the 1976 Copyright Act) and one in the architectural work itself—that is, the design of the constructed building. The term "building" is confined to habitable structures that are used but ordinarily not lived in, such as schools and places of worship. Copyright protection extends to an unconstructed architectural work embodied in plans or drawings.[804] Not covered under the Architectural Act are canals, bridges, pedestrian walkways, "structure-within-a-structure" spaces, and other nonhabitable three-dimensional constructions. Also not covered are unprotectable elements, such as windows, doors, and other standard building components.[805]

In the 1999 decision *Attia v. Society of the New York Hospital*,[806] the Second Circuit affirmed the lower court's decision that substantial similarity cannot be found where the plaintiff's drawings of an architectural work are "highly preliminary and generalized."[807] Here, the plaintiff architect and one of the defendants, an architectural firm, initially worked together on the development of plans for the expansion of a hospital facility, and the plaintiff prepared a series of architectural drawings and sketches. Eventually, the plaintiff's involvement was terminated. He filed suit claiming copyright infringement when the defendant's plans to erect the structure were illustrated in a newspaper article. The court stated that although "without doubt there are similarities between plaintiff's drawings and defendant's architectural plans . . . there was no infringement because the similarities do not go beyond the concepts and ideas contained in plaintiff's drawings."[808]

In *Richard J. Zitz, Inc. v. Pereira*,[809] the Second Circuit denied relief for copyright infringement of architectural works, holding that the copyright was invalid where the work was "substantially under construction" as of December 1, 1990. Apparently, submission of plans to obtain a building permit, the acquisition of the building permit, and commencement of construction prior to December 1, 1990 were, taken together, sufficient to render the copyright in the architectural work invalid.

In the post-9/11 case of *Shine v. Childs*,[810] the plaintiff Thomas Shine, a student in the Yale School of Architecture's master's program, developed as a course requirement a design proposal for a monumental skyscraper to be built in Manhattan and used by the media during the 2012 Olympic Games. During the first half of October 1999, Shine developed a preliminary model for his design, a tower whose top is in the shape of a parallelogram, referred to as *Shine '99*. By the end of the fall 1999 semester, Shine had developed a more sophisticated model of his design with a greater number of elements of design detail, entitled *Olympic Tower*. In December 1999, Shine presented his designs for *Olympic Tower* to a jury of experts invited by the Yale School of Architecture to evaluate and critique its students' work. Defendant architect David Childs was on the panel and he praised *Olympic Tower*, as did other luminaries of architecture. Childs's favorable reaction was also documented in *Retrospecta*, an annual alumni magazine published by the Yale School of Architecture, which included a photographic rendering of *Olympic Tower*.

Four years later, Childs's design for the Freedom Tower at the World Trade Center site was unveiled and Shine alleged that it was an infringement of both *Shine 99* and *Olympic Tower*. In 2004, Shine registered each of *Shine' 99* and *Olympic Tower* as an architectural work with the U.S. Copyright Office and sued David Childs and his architectural firm in a New York federal district court for copyright infringement. The defendants moved to dismiss the complaint or, alternatively, sought summary judgment, claiming Shine's works were not original and not worthy of protection, and further arguing that there was no substantial similarity between either work and the Freedom Tower. In 2005, after law enforcement authorities and others objected to the Freedom Tower's original design, the defendants unveiled a substantially redesigned version and scrapped the allegedly infringing design. But the court noted that because the defendants' original design for the Freedom Tower remained in the public domain, Shine's infringement claim as to the allegedly infringing original design stood.

The court first noted that Shine's certificates of copyright registration constituted prima facie evidence of the validity of both their copyrights and of the originality of the works.[811] Moreover, the court noted that "our Circuit [the Second Circuit] has held that 'a work may be copyrightable even though it is entirely a compilation of unprotectable elements.'"[812] Here, the court found both *Shine '99* and *Olympic Tower* worthy of copyright protection under the Architectural Act, and concluded that they were arguably protectable and original. However, in order to prevail in an infringement action, a plaintiff must prove actual copying and substantial similarity. The court did not find any evidence that the defendants copied *Shine '99* in form and shape, and therefore granted their motion for summary judgment on *Shine '99*. The court did conclude, however, that "reasonable ordinary observers could disagree on whether substantial similarity exists between the Freedom Tower and *Olympic Tower*."[813]

In the 2011 case of *Home Design Services v. Stewart*[814] the plaintiff residential design firm (HDS) sued Keith and Christine Stewart for one count of copyright infringement in a Florida federal district court for building two houses based on its architectural work, a house plan known as HDS-2089 and created in 1991. Plaintiff registered the house plan with the U.S. Copyright Office as a technical drawing in 2000 and filed a supplementary registration of it in 2004 as an architectural work. While plaintiff admitted that the individual components of that plan were not copyrightable, he claimed copyright protection in the particular arrangement of the floor plan as a whole and the front elevation. HDS apparently published artist concepts of the plan in an array of magazines and catalogs prior to 1995, attempting to solicit customers to buy the detailed plans; HDS asserted that the artist concepts published in the magazines and catalogs lacked the construction details necessary to build a home, though one could fill in the dimensions on the plan and then build a house without authorization.

The Stewarts stated that they collected ideas for the home they wanted to build by viewing various home designs and visiting houses. After compiling many ideas, Keith Stewart sketched a basic floor plan and hired a draftsman to draw up plans and working construction documents for the home. The draftsman drew up the documents and sold them to the Stewarts for $469. The Stewarts then built their first home in 1995, subsequently sold that home, and built a second, larger house based on the same plan. The Stewarts claimed that they never reviewed HDS's publications prior to the lawsuit and did not copy the HDS-2089 house plan. Plaintiff discovered the Stewarts' two homes after receiving reports from various sources that they had seen homes that might be infringing on plaintiff's copyrights. Plaintiff had no record that the Stewarts had purchased the HDS-2089 design plan and accordingly brought suit in 2009 in a Florida federal district court, moving for summary judgment.

In denying summary judgment on the issue of liability, the court found numerous disputes of material fact. Among the factual issues was whether there was a showing that the Stewarts copied constituent elements of the HDS-2089 house plan that are original. HDS asserted that there was "indirect evidence of copying, through 'proof of access to the copyrighted work and probative similarity,' from which factual copying may be inferred."[815] HDS asserted that the Stewarts had "reasonable opportunity to view"[816] its protected work because its artist conceptual drawing was widely available in magazines disseminated in the area where the Stewarts resided. However, the Florida federal court noted that

[w]hile the Eleventh Circuit regards a "reasonable opportunity to view" a protected work as access, it also stresses that a finding of access cannot be based on speculation or conjecture.[817]

The court noted that the evidence did not include an admission by the Stewarts that they looked at plans published in magazines. Moreover, the court observed that in the event access could be inferred, the question would then be "whether a reasonable jury could find the competing designs substantially similar at the level of protected expression."[818] The court noted that there were both similarities and several small differences between the two plans in the area of protectable expression, and that how those elements compare was a question of fact for a jury. Moreover, as the court observed, proof of access and substantial similarity raises only a presumption of copying—a presumption that may be rebutted with evidence of independent creation. Accordingly, the court denied a grant of summary judgment on the issue of liability.

Unlike the exclusive prerogatives attached to the copyright proprietor of other works under the 1976 Copyright Act, the copyright holder in a constructed architectural work cannot prevent others from making, distributing, or displaying paintings, photographs, or other pictorial representations of the work "if the building in which the work is embodied is located in or ordinarily visible from a public place."[819] Moreover, neither the author nor the copyright owner of such an architectural work may prevent the owner of the building from altering or destroying it.[820] It is probably difficult to reconcile the apparent inconsistencies in the 1976 Act, which now permits anyone to take a picture of a copyrighted constructed architectural work (a school, for example) located in a public place, but which prohibits the same person from taking a picture without authorization of a copyrighted mural on an outer wall of the architectural work. A common public misperception is that outdoor murals, because they can be seen free of charge, are in the public domain. In an incident in the early 1990s in San Francisco,[821] Susan Cervantes, a mural artist, sought a cash settlement from a film production company for the unauthorized reproduction of her work. Apparently, neighbors alerted Cervantes that a New York film crew was shooting a commercial in a school yard where she and others had painted two murals. The production company, which was using the murals as backdrops in the commercial, had secured permission from school officials but not from the artists who owned the copyrights.

Murals are often splashed across the outdoor walls of schools, museums, and other buildings accessible to the public. San Francisco has more than 400 murals, an art form evocative of the work of the Mexican muralist Diego Rivera, who applied his art to a wall of the San Francisco Art Institute in the 1930s.[822]

Since the enactment of the Architectural Act, it has become imperative for artists to register their murals with the United States Copyright Office in order to protect their copyrighted works and enable the artists to bring actions for infringement.

Note, however, that as to separability of artistic elements of architectural works themselves, the Ninth Circuit, at least, seems not to recognize the doctrine; in *Leicester v. Warner Brothers*,[823] it declined to treat a sculptural work that may have been conceptually separable from a building as being exempt from the limited protections accorded by the Architectural Act. Here, the plaintiff artist was commissioned in 1989 to create a "streetwall" for an office building under construction. The streetwall consisted of five towers and gates along a street to form a wall and entrance to a courtyard and the office building. It included brass metalwork design and grillwork and concentric rings that symbolized 1930s-era radio waves and modern telecommunications signals. When the streetwall appeared in the defendant's *Batman Forever* film, the plaintiff sued. The Ninth Circuit held that the towers were an integral part of the building because they were in alignment with the building to give the visual effect of a wall and they visually matched design features on the building. Applying the statute, the court held that Congress had exempted acts such as public photography of buildings, including integral parts like the streetwall, from prosecution. The Ninth Circuit concluded that if the streetwall was part of the building, it was not conceptually separate and entitled to individual protection.

The duration of copyright of architectural works is governed by sections 302 and 303 of the 1976 Act.[824] To illustrate with a few examples:

- If the author of a protected constructed architectural work died in 1990, copyright protection will expire December 31, 2060 (that is, the life of the author plus seventy years, ending on the last day of the seventieth year).
- If the author of a protected (that is, unpublished) unconstructed architectural work died in 1945, copyright protection will have expired December 31, 2002, if the work is not constructed by then (that is, the life of the author plus seventy years, but in no case shall the term of copyright in such a work have expired before December 31, 2002, according to section 303 of the 1976 Act). If the work was constructed by December 31, 2002, protection will continue through December 31, 2047 (that is, the date specified in section 303 of the 1976 Act that affords the minimum term of protection to such works published or constructed on or before December 31, 2002).
- If the architectural work was made for hire, the general rule is that copyright protection expires ninety-five years after its first publication or 120 years after the year of creation, whichever occurs first. If, therefore, a protected unconstructed architectural work made for hire was created in 1902, copyright protection expires December 31, 2022 (that is, the last day of the hundred-twentieth year after the year of creation, the work not having been published).
- If, however, such a work made for hire in 1902 was constructed before December 31, 2002, copyright protection expires December 31, 2047 (that is, the date specified in section 303 of the 1976 Act that affords the minimum term of protection to such works published or constructed on or before December 31, 2002).

NOTES TO CHAPTER 11

1. See discussion of site-specific art in chapter 10.
2. Berkowitz & Leaffer, *Copyright and the Art Museum*, 8 ART & L. 249, 258 (1984).
3. 17 U.S.C. § 204(a).
4. 17 U.S.C. § 202.
5. *Id.*
6. 17 U.S.C. § 28 (1909) (superseded 1976).
7. 17 U.S.C. § 27 (1909) (superseded 1976).
8. *Id.*
9. It is understood that the transfers of these unpublished works occur prior to January 1, 1978, as the transfer of copyright of all works on or after January 1, 1978, comes under the aegis of the 1976 Act.
10. 3 MELVILLE B. NIMMER & DAVID NIMMER, NIMMER ON COPYRIGHT § 10.09[B] (2011).
11. *Id.*
12. *Id.* at n.18.
13. *Id.* at n.19.
14. 17 U.S.C. § 102(b).
15. *See* Berkowitz & Leaffer, *supra* note 2, at 260.
16. *See* 1 NIMMER, *supra* note 10, § 2.03[D].
17. *See, e.g.,* Mazer v. Stein, 347 U.S. 201 (1954).
18. *See* 1 NIMMER, *supra* note 10, § 2.03[D].
19. Oldcaste Precast, Inc. v. Granite Precasting & Concrete, Inc., 2011 U.S. Dist. LEXIS 20977 (W.D. Wash.).
20. *Id.*, 2011 U.S. Dist. LEXIS 20977, at *15.
21. *Id.* at *14.
22. Branch v. Ogilvy & Mather, Inc., 16 U.S.P.Q.2d (BNA) 1179 (S.D.N.Y. 1990), 772 F. Supp. 1359 (1991).
23. *Id.* at 1185.
24. *Id.*
25. *See, e.g.,* Feist Publ'ns, Inc. v. Rural Tel. Serv. Co., 499 U.S. 340 (1991); Beaudin v. Ben & Jerry's Homemade, Inc., 95 F.3d 1 (2d Cir. 1996).
26. *See, e.g.,* Concrete Mach. Co. v. Classic Lawn Ornaments, Inc., 843 F.2d 600, 606 (1st Cir. 1988).
27. Gentieu v. Muller & Co., 712 F. Supp. 740 (W.D. Mo. 1989).
28. *Id.* at 742.
29. *Id.* (citing Burrow-Giles Lithographic Co. v. Sarony, 111 U.S. 53 (1884)).
30. *Id.* at 744.
31. Arthur v. ABC, 633 F. Supp. 146 (S.D.N.Y. 1985).
32. Runstadler Studios, Inc. v. MCM Ltd. P'ship, 768 F. Supp. 1292 (N.D. Ill. 1991).
33. Tompkins Graphics, Inc. v. Zipatone, Inc., 222 U.S.P.Q. (BNA) 49 (E.D. Pa., Aug. 15, 1983).
34. *See, e.g.,* Branch v. Ogilvy & Mather, Inc., 16 U.S.P.Q.2d (BNA) 1179 (S.D.N.Y. 1990), 772 F. Supp. 1359 (S.D.N.Y. 1991). *See also* Vickery Design, Inc. v. Aspen Bay Co., 185 F.3d 876 (10th Cir. 1999), which held that a "candle design is protectable but only to the extent of the creative and artistic modifications . . . not as to the overall size and configuration of the [candle]. . . ." (internal quotations omitted). 185 F.3d at 876.
35. Meade v. United States, 27 Fed. Cl. 367 (Fed. Cl. 1992), *aff'd*, 5 F.3d 1503 (Fed. Cir. 1993), *reh'g denied*, 1994 U.S. App. LEXIS 6186 (1994).
36. *Meade*, 27 Fed. Cl. at 372 (quoting PAUL GOLDSTEIN, COPYRIGHT: PRINCIPLES, LAW, AND PRACTICE § 2.3.1.2 (1989).
37. Franklin Mint Corp. v. Nat'l Wildlife Art Exch., Inc., 575 F.2d 62 (3d Cir.), *cert. denied*, 439 U.S. 880 (1978).
38. *Id.*, 575 F.2d at 65.

39. Concrete Mach. Co. v. Classic Lawn Ornaments, Inc., 843 F.2d 600 (1st Cir. 1988).
40. Maggio v. Liztech Jewelry, 912 F. Supp. 216 (E.D. La. 1996).
41. Matthews v. Freedman, 157 F.3d 25 (1st Cir. 1998).
42. *See* 1 NIMMER, *supra* note 10, § 2.01.
43. 17 U.S.C. § 102(a).
44. *See* Berkowitz & Leaffer, *supra* note 2, at 261.
45. *See* 1 NIMMER, *supra* note 10, § 2.01[A]. *See, e.g.*, Scholastic, Inc. v. Speirs, 28 F. Supp. 2d 862 (S.D.N.Y. 1998), which held that although images were similar, uncontested evidence revealed that the defendant's image was created independently and not copied.
46. Bleistein v. Donaldson Lithographing Co., 188 U.S. 239 (1903).
47. *See* Feist Publ'ns, Inc. v. Rural Tel. Serv. Co., 499 U.S. 340, 346 (1991).
48. 1 NIMMER, *supra* note 10, § 2.01[A].
49. Alfred Bell & Co. v. Catalda Fine Arts, Inc., 191 F.2d 99 (2d Cir. 1951), *aff'g* 74 F. Supp. 973 (S.D.N.Y. 1947).
50. *Id.*, 191 F.2d at 104.
51. Peter Pan Fabrics, Inc. v. Rosstex Fabrics, Inc., 733 F. Supp. 174 (S.D.N.Y. 1990).
52. *Id.* at 176.
53. *Id.*
54. Universal Furniture Int'l Inc. v. Collezione Europa USA, Inc., 618 F.3d 417 (4th Cir. 2010).
55. *Id.* at 430.
56. Ets-Hokin v. Skyy Spirits, Inc., 323 F.3d 763, *aff'g* (unpublished decision—docket number 3:96CV03690), *rev'g* 225 F.3d 1068 (9th Cir. 2000), *rev'g* 1998 WL 690856, 1998 U.S. Dist. LEXIS 15528 (N.D. Cal. 1998).
57. *Id.*, 225 F.3d at 1083.
58. Ets-Hokin v. Skyy Spirits, Inc., 323 F.3d 763 at 765.
59. *Id.* at 766.
60. Hearn v. Meyer, 664 F. Supp. 832 (S.D.N.Y. 1987).
61. *Id.* at 836.
62. Simon v. Birraporetti's Rests., Inc., 720 F. Supp. 85 (S.D. Tex. 1989).
63. In 2000, the Fourth Circuit affirmed the lower court's reliance on the jury instruction which stated "each of the separate works in the collective work must itself be copyrightable" and that a derivative work must be a "substantial variation from any preexisting work. The court held that a jury could reasonably conclude that a collective work failed to meet the minimal creativity requirement on the basis of the plaintiff's trial testimony. O'Well Novelty Comp., Ltd. v. Offenbacher, Inc., 55 U.S.P.Q.2d (BNA) 1828 (4th Cir. 2000)
64. L. Batlin & Son, Inc. v. Snyder, 536 F.2d 486 (2d Cir. 1976), *cert. denied*, 429 U.S. 857 (1976).
65. Alva Studios, Inc. v. Winninger, 177 F. Supp. 265 (S.D.N.Y. 1959).
66. Gracen v. Bradford Exch., 698 F.2d 300 (7th Cir. 1983).
67. Dan Schrock Photography v. Learning Curve Int'l, Inc., 586 F.3d 513 (7th Cir. 2009), 2009 U.S. App. LEXIS 24253, *on remand at, motion denied by, partial summary judgment denied by*, Schrock v. Learning Curve Int'l, Inc., 2010 U.S. Dist. LEXIS 103959 (N.D. Ill., Sept. 29, 2010).
68. *Id.*, 586 F.3d at 516.
69. Mirage Editions, Inc. v. Albuquerque A.R.T. Co., 856 F.2d 1341 (9th Cir. 1988), *cert. denied*, 489 U.S. 1018 (1989).
70. *Id.*, 856 F.2d at 1343.
71. Munoz v. Albuquerque A.R.T. Co., 829 F. Supp. 309 (D. Alaska 1993), *aff'd*, 38 F.3d 1218 (9th Cir. 1994).
72. In a relatively recent Second Circuit decision, where a jewelry artist used preexisting material in his own jewelry designs, the court applied a deferential standard of review concluding that the jewelry pieces were derivative works, satisfying the "actual copying" element of a copyright infringement claim. Yurman Design, Inc. v. PAJ, Inc., 262 F.3d 101 (2d Cir. 2001).
73. Lee v. Deck the Walls, Inc., 925 F. Supp. 576 (N.D. Ill. 1996), *aff'd*, 125 F.3d 580 (7th Cir. 1997).
74. *Id.*, 925 F. Supp. at 580 (citing Woods v. Bourne Co., 60 F.3d 978, 993 (2d Cir. 1995)); *see infra* note 231.

75. *Id.* at 581.
76. Earth Flag Ltd. v. Alamo Flag Co., 154 F. Supp. 2d 663 (S.D.N.Y. 2001).
77. Cantor v. NYP Holdings, Inc., 51 F. Supp. 2d 309 (S.D.N.Y. 1999).
78. Bridgeman Art Library, Ltd. v. Corel Corp., 36 F. Supp. 2d 191 (S.D.N.Y. 1999).
79. Bridgeman Art Library, Ltd. v. Corel Corp., 25 F. Supp. 2d 421 (S.D.N.Y. 1998), 1998 U.S. Dist. LEXIS 17920.
80. *Id.* at 426–27.
81. *Id.* at 427, 1998 U.S. Dist. LEXIS 17920, at *17.
82. *Id.* at 427, 1998 U.S. Dist. Lexis 17920, at *15.
83. *Bridgeman*, 36 F.Supp.2d at 199.
84. *Bridgeman*, 25 F. Supp. at 427, n.17.
85. Bridgeman Art Library, Ltd. V. Corel Corp., 36 F. Supp. 2d 191, 200 (S.D.N.Y. 1999).
86. *Id.* at 194.
87. *Id.* at 195.
88. *Id.* (citing 17 U.S.C. § 104(c)).
89. *Id.* at 195–96 (citing Burrow-Giles Lithographic Co. v. Sarony, 111 U.S. 53 (1884)).
90. *Id.* at 197.
91. Bridgeman Art Library, Ltd. V. Corel Corp., 36 F. Supp. 2d 191, 200 (S.D.N.Y. 1999).
92. Satava v. Lowry, 323 F.3d 805 (9th Cir. 2003), *cert. denied*, 540 U.S. 983 (2003).
93. Kay Berry, Inc. v. Taylor Gifts, Inc., 421 F.3d 199 (3d Cir. 2005).
94. *Id.* at 207 (citations omitted).
95. Reece v. Island Treasures Art Gallery, Inc., 468 F. Supp. 2d 1197 (D. Haw. 2006); *see also* Broughel v. Battery Conservancy, 2010 U.S. Dist. LEXIS 25496 (S.D.N.Y., March 16, 2010) *denying motion to file a second amended complaint*, 2009 U.S. Dist. LEXIS 35048 (S.D.N.Y. March 30, 2009).
96. *Reece*, 468 F. Supp. 2d at 1204.
97. *Id.*
98. *Id.* at 1208 (citations omitted).
99. Morton v. Raphael, 334 Ill. App. 399, 79 N.E.2d 522 (IIL. App. Ct. 1948).
100. *Id.*, 334 Ill. App. at 402, 79 N.E.2d at 523.
101. *Id.*, 334 Ill. App. at 403, 79 N.E.2d at 524.
102. *See, e.g.*, William A. Meier Glass Co. v. Anchor Hocking Glass Corp., 95 F. Supp. 264 (W.D. Pa. 1951); Pierce & Bushnel Mfg. Co. v. Werckmeister, 72 F. 54 (1st Cir. 1896).
103. Am. Tobacco Co. v. Werckmeister, 207 U.S. 284 (1907).
104. Letter Edged in Black Press, Inc. v. Pub. Bldg. Comm'n, 320 F. Supp. 1303 (N.D. Ill. 1970).
105. *See* 1 NIMMER, *supra* note 10, § 4.03[A].
106. Schatt v. Curtis Mgmt. Group, Inc., 764 F. Supp. 902 (S.D.N.Y. 1991).
107. *Id.* at 907.
108. *Id.* at 908.
109. *Id.* Other "factual predicates" cited by defendants for fixing a date of investitive publication were (1) the alleged testimony of plaintiff's agent that plaintiff had told her that he had "published" his works in 1954, and (2) the use of "1955" as the date of publication by plaintiff's licensees on postcards allegedly published in 1987 to 1989.
110. *Id.*
111. *Id.* at 909.
112. Schatt v. Curtis Mgmt. Group, Inc., 764 F. Supp. 902, 909 (S.D.N.Y. 1991)
113. Warner Bros. Entm't, Inc., v. A.V.E.L.A., Inc., 644 F.3d 584 (8th Cir. 2011).
114. *Id.* at 593.
115. *Id.* at 595 (citations omitted).
116. Arthur A. Kaplan Co. v. Panaria Int'l Inc., 48 U.S.P.Q.2d (BNA) 1315 (S.D.N.Y. 1998), *aff'd*, 205 F.3d 1321 (2d Cir. 2000).
117. *See* Berkowitz & Leaffer, *supra* note 2, at 271.
118. 17 U.S.C. § 405(a)(1).
119. 17 U.S.C. § 405(a)(2).

120. 17 U.S.C. § 101.

121. Vane v. Fair, Inc., 676 F. Supp. 133 (E.D. Tex. 1987), aff'd, 849 F.2d 186 (5th Cir. 1988), cert. denied, 488 U.S. 1008 (1989).

122. Epcon Group, Inc. v. Danburry Farms, Inc., 28 Fed. Appx. 127 (3d Cir. 2002).

123. U.S. Const. art. I, § 8.

124. 17 U.S.C. § 302(a).

125. 17 U.S.C. § 302(b).

126. Copyright Term Extension Act of 1998 (CTEA), Pub. L. No. 105-298, § 102(b) and (d), 112 Stat. 2827–28, (amending 17 U.S.C. §§ 302, 304).

127. L.M. Brownlee, *Recent Changes in the Duration of Copyright in the United States and European Union: Procedure and Policy*, 6 FORDHAM INTELL. PROP. MEDIA & ENT. L.J. 579 (Spring 1996). This article includes an excellent analysis of the issues involved in the need for international harmonization of copyright duration laws.

128. Berne Convention for the Protection of Literary and Artistic Works of September 9, 1896, completed at Paris on May 4, 1896, revised at Berlin on November 13, 1908, completed at Berne on March 20, 1914, revised at Rome on June 2, 1928, revised at Brussels on June 26, 1948, and revised at Stockholm on July 14, 1967 (with Protocol regarding developing countries), completed at Stockholm on July 14, 1967 (hereinafter Berne Convention or Berne) art. 7(1), 828 U.N.T.S. 221.

129. *See* Brownlee, *supra* note 127, at 585.

130. *Id.*

131. Eldred v. Ashcroft, 537 U.S. 186 (2003).

132. *Id.* at 193–94.

133. Eldred v. Reno, 74 F. Supp. 2d 1 (D.D.C. 1999).

134. *See Eldred*, 537 U.S. at 192.

135. *Id.* at 198.

136. *Id.* at 200–01.

137. Eldred v. Ashcroft, 537 U.S. 186, 204 (2003) (citing Miller, *Constitutionality of Copyright Term Extension*, 18 CARDOZO ARTS & ENT. L.J. 651, 694 (2000)).

138. *Id.* at 205–06.

139. *Id.* at 206.

140. *Id.* at 208.

141. *Id.* at 218–19.

142. *Id.* at 219.

143. *Id.* at 221.

144. *Id.* at 222.

145. 17 U.S.C. § 304(a). The current version of § 304(a) became effective October 27, 1998. For works within this category achieving statutory copyright protection prior to 1964, registration of the renewal term is requisite for full seventy-five-year protection. *See* discussion at pages 967–968.

146. 17 U.S.C. § 303. Under § 303 copyright in such work subsists from January 1, 1978.

147. *Id.*

148. 17 U.S.C. § 106.

149. 17 U.S.C. § 106(4).

150. 17 U.S.C. § 101.

151. 17 U.S.C. § 106(1).

152. 17 U.S.C. § 101.

153. Amsinck v. Columbia Pictures Indus., 862 F. Supp. 1044 (S.D.N.Y. 1994).

154. *See, e.g.,* MGM Distrib. Corp. v. Wyatt, 21 Copyright Office Bull. 203 (D. Md. 1932); Tiffany Prods., Inc. v. Dewing, 50 F.2d 911 (D. Md. 1931); Mura v. Columbia Broad. Sys., Inc., 245 F. Supp. 587 (S.D.N.Y. 1965).

155. Patterson v. Century Prods., Inc., 93 F.2d 489 (2d Cir. 1937); *see also* Pathe Exch. v. Int'l Alliance T.S.E., 3 F. Supp. 63 (S.D.N.Y. 1932).

156. Habersham Plantation Corp. v. Country Concepts, 209 U.S.P.Q. (BNA) 711 (N.D. Ga. 1980).

157. *See, e.g.,* Ideal Toy Corp. v. Kenner Prods. Div. of Gen. Mills Fun Group, Inc., 443 F. Supp. 291 (S.D.N.Y. 1977); King Features Syndicate v. Fleischer, 299 F. 533 (2d Cir. 1924).

158. *See* 2 NIMMER, *supra* note 10, § 8.01[G].

159. 17 U.S.C. § 108(i). *See also* Berkowitz & Leaffer, *supra* note 2, at 289 n.176.

160. 17 U.S.C. § 113(c).

161. 17 U.S.C. § 106(2).

162. *See* 1 NIMMER, *supra* note 10, § 3.03[A].

163. Gibson Tex, Inc. v. Sears Roebuck & Co., 11 F. Supp. 2d. 439 (S.D.N.Y. 1998).

164. *See* Lee v. Deck the Walls, Inc., 925 F. Supp. 576 (N.D. Ill. 1996), *aff'd,* 125 F.3d 580 (7th Cir. 1997).

165. *Id.,* 925 F. Supp. at 578–79 (quoting 17 U.S.C. § 101).

166. *Id.*

167. *Id.* at 579.

168. *Id.*

169. *Id.* at 580 (quoting Sony Corp. of Am. v. Universal City Studios, Inc., 464 U.S. 417, 432 (1984)). *See also* White-Smith Music Publ'g Co. v. Apollo Co., 209 U.S. 1, 19 (1908); Twentieth-Century Music Corp. v. Aiken, 422 U.S. 151, 155 (1975).

170. Lee v. Deck the Walls, Inc., 925 F. Supp. 576, 580 (N.D. Ill. 1996).

171. *Id.*

172. *Id.* (citing Woods v. Bourne Co., 60 F.3d 978, 993 (2d Cir. 1995)); *see infra* note 263.

173. *Id.* at 581.

174. Greenwich Workshop, Inc. v. Timber Creations, Inc., 932 F. Supp. 1210 (C.D. Cal. 1996).

175. *See* Berkowitz & Leaffer, *supra* note 2, at 290.

176. 17 U.S.C. § 103(b). *See also* 1 NIMMER, *supra* note 10, § 3.04.

177. 17 U.S.C. § 103(b); *see also* Cordon Holding B.V. v. Northwest Publ'g Corp., 63 U.S.P.Q.2d (BNA) 1013 (S.D.N.Y. 2002) (quoting Shoptalk, Ltd. v. Concorde-New Horizons Corp., 168 F.3d 586 (2d Cir.), *cert. denied,* 527 U.S. 1038 (1999)).

178. *Id.*

179. *See, e.g.,* Hartfield v. Peterson, 91 F.2d 998 (2d Cir. 1937); Leon v. Pac. Tel. & Tel. Co., 91 F.2d 484 (9th Cir. 1937); Amplex Mfg. Co. v. ABC Plastic Fabricators, Inc., 184 F. Supp. 285 (E.D. Pa. 1960); Yale Univ. Press v. Row, Peterson & Co., 40 F.2d 290 (S.D.N.Y. 1930).

180. Section 7 of the 1909 Act read, in pertinent part: "but the publication of any such new works shall not affect the force or validity of any subsisting copyright upon the matter employed or any part thereof, or be construed to imply an exclusive right to such use of the original works, or to secure or extend copyright in such original works."

181. Flack v. Friends of Queen Catherine, Inc., 139 F. Supp. 2d 526 (S.D.N.Y. 2001).

182. *Id.* at 536.

183. 17 U.S.C. § 106(3).

184. 2 NIMMER, *supra* note 10, § 8.12.

185. 17 U.S.C. § 109(a).

186. 17 U.S.C. § 27 (1909) (superseded 1976).

187. 17 U.S.C. § 109(c). *See also* Lee v. Deck the Walls, Inc., 925 F. Supp. 576 (N.D. Ill. 1996), *aff'd,* 125 F.3d 580 (7th Cir. 1997), *supra* note 73.

188. CAL. CIV. CODE § 986. *See* discussion of resale rights *infra* chapter 13.

189. Cordon Holding B.V. v. Northwest Publ'g Corp., 49 U.S.P.Q.2d (BNA) 1697 (S.D.N.Y. 1998).

190. Smith v. S. Jersey Vinyl, Inc., 47 U.S.P.Q.2d (BNA) 1944 (C.D. Cal. 1998).

191. 17 U.S.C. § 106(5).

192. 17 U.S.C. § 101.

193. *Id.*

194. 17 U.S.C. § 109(c).

195. Mass. Museum of Contemporary Art Found., Inc. v. Buchel, 593 F.3d 39 (1st Cir. 2010).

196. *Id.* at 46.

197. *Id.* at 63.

198. *See* 3 NIMMER, *supra* note 10, § 10.01[A].

199. *See, e.g.,* Goldwyn Pictures Corp. v. Howells Sales Co., 282 F. 9 (2d Cir. 1922); M. Witmark & Sons v. Pastime Amusement Co., 298 F. 470 (E.D.S.C. 1924), *aff'd,* 2 F.2d 1020 (4th Cir. 1924); New Fiction Publ'g Co. v. Star Co., 220 F. 994 (S.D.N.Y. 1915); Ed Brawley, Inc. v. Gaffney, 399 F. Supp. 115 (N.D. Cal. 1975).

200. *See* 3 Nimmer, *supra* note 10, § 10.01[A] (citing such cases as Hirshon v. United Artists Corp., 243 F.2d 640 (D.C. Cir. 1957); Goldwyn Pictures Corp. v. Howells Sales Co., 282 F. 9 (2d Cir. 1922); Hiawatha Card Co. v. Colourpicture Publishers, Inc., 255 F. Supp. 1015 (E.D. Mich. 1966)).

201. *See* 3 Nimmer, *supra* note 10, § 10.01[A].

202. 3 NIMMER, supra note 10, § 10.02.

203. 17 U.S.C. § 101.

204. 17 U.S.C. § 501(b).

205. 17 U.S.C. § 101.

206. 17 U.S.C. § 204(a).

207. *See* Berkowitz & Leaffer, *supra* note 2, at 301. *See also* Kaplan v. Panaria Int'l, Inc., 48 U.S.P.Q.2d (BNA) 1315 (S.D.N.Y. 1998) (holding that an author's confirmation of a copyright assignment, written after the commencement of a lawsuit, created a valid assignment).

208. Marvullo v. Gruner, 2001 WL 40772, 2001 U.S. Dist. LEXIS 266 (S.D.N.Y. Jan. 16, 2001).

209. 17 U.S.C. § 204(a).

210. *See, e.g.,* Werbungs und Commerz Union Austalt v. Le Shufy, 6 U.S.P.Q.2d (BNA) 1153 (S.D.N.Y. 1987).

211. Kenbrooke Fabrics, Inc. v. Soho Fashions, Inc., 690 F. Supp. 298 (S.D.N.Y. 1988).

212. *Id.* at 301 (citing Eden Toys, Inc. v. Florelee Undergarment Co., 697 F.2d 27 (2d Cir. 1982)).

213. 3 Nimmer, *supra* note 10, § 10.03[A][i].

214. In 2002, the Ninth Circuit held that an exclusive licensee cannot assign rights without consent of the original licensor. The court stated that 17 U.S.C. § 201(d)(2) limits the rights of an exclusive licensee to those "protections and remedies" afforded in the 1976 Act and the right to freely assign is not protection or remedy. Gardner v. Nike, Inc., 279 F.3d 774 (9th Cir. 2002).

215. Original Appalachian Artworks v. S. Diamond Assocs., 44 F.3d 925 (11th Cir. 1995), *cert. denied,* 516 U.S. 1045 (1996).

216. *Id.,* 44 F.3d at 930.

217. Original Appalachian Artworks v. S. Diamond Assocs., 911 F.2d 1548, 1550 (11th Cir. 1990).

218. *See Original Appalachian Artworks,* 44 F.3d at 928.

219. *Id.*

220. *Id.* at 929.

221. In 2002, the Ninth Circuit held that an exclusive licensee cannot assign rights without consent of the original licensor. The court stated that 17 U.S.C. Sec. 201(d)(2) limits the rights of an exclusive licensee to those "protections and remedies" afforded in the 1976 Act and the right to freely assign is not protection or remedy. Gardner v. Nike., Inc. 279 F.3d 774 (9th Cir. 2002).

222. Bourne v. Walt Disney Co., 68 F.3d 621, 631 (2d Cir. 1995).

223. *Id.*

224. *Atkins v. Fischer,* 331 F.3d 988, 992, 356 U.S. App. D.C. 403 (D.C. Cir. 2003).

225. Psihoyos v. Pearson Education, Inc., 2012 U.S. Dist. LEXIS 27265 (S.D.N.Y. Feb. 29, 2012).

226. *Id.* at *44-45.

227. *Id.* at *57 (citations omitted).

228. Latimer v. Roaring Toyz, Inc., 601 F.3d 1224 (11th Cir. 2010), *partial summary judgment granted in part and denied in part on remand,* 2010 U.S. Dist. LEXIS 98702 (M.D. Fla. Sept. 21, 2010).

229. *Id.,* 601 F.3d at 1236.

230. *Id.*

231. 17 U.S.C. § 101.

232. 1 Nimmer, *supra* note 10, at § 6.01

233 *Id.* at 1 NIMMER *supra* note 10, at §6.03.

234. Clogston v. Am. Acad. of Orthopedic Surgeons, 930 F. Supp. 1156, 1158 (W.D. Tex. 1996).

235. B. Adams, *Industrial-strength Warhol; Andy Warhol Museum, Pittsburgh, Pennsylvania,* ART IN AMERICA, Sept. 1994, at 9.

236. Childress v. Taylor, 945 F.2d 500, 505 (2d Cir. 1991).

237. Thomson v. Larson, 147 F.3d 195 (2d Cir. 1998).

238. *Id.* at 201.

239. *Id.* (citing *Childress,* 945 F.2d at 508–09).

240. *See Clogston v. Am. Acad. Of Orthopedic Surgeons,*, 930 F. Supp. 1156, 1158–59 (W.D. Tex. 1996) (citing *Childress,* 945 F.2d at 504).

241. Johannsen v. Brown, 797 F. Supp. 835 (D. Or. 1992).

242. *Id.* at 842 (quoting Cmty. for Creative Non-Violence (CCNV) v. Reid, 490 U.S. 730, 737 (1989)); *see infra* note 243; Ashton-Tate Corp. v. Ross, 916 F.2d 516, 521 (9th Cir. 1990).

243. *Ashton-Tate,* 916 F.2d at 521 (quoting S.O.S., Inc. v. Payday, Inc., 886 F.2d 1081, 1087 (9th Cir. 1989)).

244. Brown v. McCormick, 87 F. Supp. 2d 467 (D. Md. 2000).

245. *Id.* at 481.

246. Gillespie v. AST Sportswear, Inc., 58 U.S.P.Q.2d (BNA) 1134 (S.D.N.Y. 2001).

247. Sweet Music, Inc. v. Melrose Music Corp., 189 F. Supp. 655 (S.D. Cal. 1960); Eliscu v. T.B. Harms Co., 151 U.S.P.Q. (BNA) 603 (N.Y. Sup. Ct. 1966).

248. Edward B. Marks Music Corp. v. Wonnell, 61 F. Supp. 722 (S.D.N.Y. 1945).

249. DeBitetto v. Alpha Books, 7 F. Supp. 2d 330 (S.D.N.Y. 1998).

250. 17 U.S.C. § 302(b).

251. *See, e.g.,* Meredith v. Smith, 145 F.2d 620 (9th Cir. 1944); Noble v. D. Van Nostrand Co., 63 N.J. Super. 534, 164 A.2d 834 (N.J. Ch. 1960); *see also* Estate of Davis v. Trojer, 60 U.S.P.Q.2d (BNA) 1062, 2001 WL 829872 (S.D.N.Y., July 20, 2001).

252. *See* 1 NIMMER, *supra* note 10, § 6.11.

253. *See Estate of Davis,* 2001 WL 829872, at *2 (citing Weissmann v. Freeman, 868 F.2d 1313, 1318 (2d Cir. 1989)); Lennon v. Seaman, 63 F. Supp. 2d 428, 443 (S.D.N.Y. 1999).

254. 17 U.S.C. § 101.

255. *Id.*

256. 17 U.S.C. § 302(c).

257. 17 U.S.C. § 101.

258. *See* Runstadler Studios, Inc. v. MCM Ltd. P'ship, 768 F. Supp. 1292 (N.D. Ill. 1991); *see supra* note 29.

259. 17 U.S.C. §§ 101, 103(b). *See also* Mount v. Ormond, 1991 WL 191228, 1991 U.S. Dist. LEXIS 12941 (S.D.N.Y., Sept. 13, 1991).

260. 17 U.S.C. § 101.

261. *See* 1 NIMMER, *supra* note 10, § 3.03.

262. E. Am. Trio Prods., Inc. v. Tang Elec. Corp., 97 F. Supp. 2d 395 (S.D.N.Y. 2000), which held that plaintiff's registration of the catalog as a compilation gave the plaintiff the right to sue for infringement of individual photographs within the catalog.

263. Woods v. Bourne Co., 60 F.3d 978, 990 (2d Cir. 1995) (citing L. Batlin & Son, Inc. v. Snyder, 536 F.2d 486, at 491 (2d Cir. 1976) (en banc)).

264. *See* 1 NIMMER, *supra* note 10, § 3.04[A].

265. *See* 1 NIMMER, *supra* note 10, § 3.04[B][1], and referring to nn.13-14 therein. But note, also, a line of cases decided under the earlier Act in conflict with the Act's statutory language. Those cases, however, were criticized by Nimmer, who asserts that these cases were incorrect since "those courts fail to apply the standard of originality as it is understood in the law of copyright." *Id.*

266. 17 U.S.C. § 101.

267. *Id.*

268. Playboy Enters., Inc. v. Dumas, 53 F.3d 549 (2d Cir. 1995), *cert denied,* 516 U.S. 1010 (1995).

269. *Id.,* 53 F.3d at 552.

270. *Id.*

271. *Id.* at 560.

272. *Id.*

273. Playboy Enters., Inc. v. Dumas, 53 F.3d 549, 562 (2d Cir. 1995) (quoting Siegel v. Nat'l Periodical Publ'ns, Inc., 508 F.2d 909, 914 (2d Cir. 1974)).

274. Playboy Enters., Inc. v. Dumas, 960 F. Supp. 710 (S.D.N.Y 1997).

275. Cmty. for Creative Non-Violence (CCNV) v. Reid, 490 U.S. 730 (1989), *aff'g and remanding* 846 F.2d 1485 (D.C. Cir. 1988).

276. *Id.*, 490 U.S. at 751.

277. *Id.* at 751–52.

278. In the event that a contract does not mention copyright, under the "work-for-hire" doctrine, where one person employs another to produce work of an artistic nature, in the absence of a contractual reservation of the copyright in the artist, the presumption arises that title to the copyright is in the employer." However, if an employer materially breaches the employment contract, the employee may rescind the contract, and recapture the copyrights. Brown v. Cosby, 433 F. Supp. 1331, 1343 (E.D. Pa. 1977).

279. *See CCNV*, 490 U.S. at 733.

280. Cmty. for Creative Non-Violence (CCNV) v. Reid, 652 F. Supp. 1453, 1456 (D.C. 1987).

281. *Id.* at 1457.

282. *See* Cmty. for Creative Non-Violence (CCNV) v. Reid, 652 F.Supp. 1453, 1499 (D.C. 1987).

283. *See* Cmty. for Creative Non-Violence (CCNV) v. Reid, 490 U.S. 730, 753 (1989).

284. Cmty. for Creative Non-Violence (CCNV) v. Reid, 1991 WL 415523, 1991 U.S. Dist. LEXIS 21020 (D.D.C. Jan. 7, 1991).

285. Armento v. Laser Image, Inc., 950 F. Supp. 719 (W.D.N.C. 1996).

286. *See CCNV*, 490 U.S. at 730.

287. *See Armento*, 950 F. Supp. at 730.

288. Aymes v. Bonelli, 980 F.2d 857 (2d Cir. 1992), *remanded*, 30 U.S.P.Q.2d (BNA) 1718 (2d Cir. 1994), *aff'd*, 47 F.3d 23 (1995).

289. *Id.* at 861. *See also* Natkin v. Winfrey, 111 F. Supp. 2d 1003 (N.D. Ill. 2000), which held that photographers hired to take still photographs for the "Oprah Winfrey Show" were independent contractors and the photographs were not works made for hire. Here, the employer did not withhold income taxes, reported payments as nonemployee compensation on IRS 1099 forms, and never provided health or life insurance, pension benefits or paid vacation.

290. Carter v. Helmsley-Spear, Inc., 71 F.3d 77 (2d Cir. 1995), *cert. denied*, 517 U.S. 1208 (1996).

291. *Id.*, 71 F.3d at 85.

292. Note, 109 HARV. L. REV. 2110 (June 1996).

293. *Id.* at 2112.

294. *Id.* at 2113.

295. Okla. Natural Gas Co. v. LaRue, 156 F.3d 1244, 1998 WL 568321, 1998 U.S. App. LEXIS 30502 (10th Cir. 1998).

296. *Id.*, 1998 WL 568321, at *2.

297. *Id.* at *3.

298. *Id.*

299. Langman Fabrics v. Graff Californiawear, Inc., 160 F.3d 106 (2d Cir. 1998).

300. SHL Imaging, Inc. v. Artisan House, Inc., 117 F. Supp. 2d 301 (S.D.N.Y. 2000).

301. *Id.* at 314.

302. 17 U.S.C. § 302(c).

303. 17 U.S.C. § 203(a).

304. 17 U.S.C. § 26 (1909) (superseded 1976). *See also* 1 NIMMER, *supra* note 10, § 5.03[B][1][a].

305. *See* 1 NIMMER, *supra* note 10, § 5.03[B][2][c].

306. *Id.*

307. *Id.*

308. Marvel Worldwide, Inc. v. Kirby, 777 F. Supp. 2d 720, (S.D.N.Y. 2011).

309. *Id.* at 732-33.

310. *Id.* at 745.

311. *Id.* at 724.

312. *Id.*

313. *Id.* at 738 (citing Martha Graham Sch. & Dance Found., Inc. v. Martha Graham Ctr. of Contemporary Dance, Inc., 380 F.3d 624, 634-35 (2d Cir. 2004)).

314. *Id.* at 738-39.

315. *Id.* at 741.

316. *Id.* at 743-44.

317. *Id.* at 739-41.

318. *Id.* at 741-42.

319. *Id.* at 743.

320. Berne Convention Implementation Act of 1988, Pub. L. No. 100-568, 102 Stat. 2853 (1988) (hereinafter BCIA), § 7(a)(4).

321. 17 U.S.C. § 401(a).

322. 17 U.S.C. §§ 401(d), 504(c)(2).

323. Szabo v. Errisson, 68 F.3d 940 (5th Cir. 1995); Sylvestre v. Oswald, 91 Civ. 5060, 1993 WL 179101, 1993 U.S. Dist. LEXIS 7002 (S.D.N.Y., May 21, 1993).

324. Heyman v. Salle, 743 F. Supp. 190 (S.D.N.Y. 1989). In the somewhat related case of Morris v. Bus. Concepts, Inc., 283 F.3d 502 (2d Cir. 2002), the Second Circuit, in denying a petition for rehearing, held that in a suit for infringement of magazine articles written by a freelancer, where Conde Nast was the exclusive licensee of the articles, the fact that Conde Nast registered the issues of *Allure* magazines in which the freelancer's articles appeared does not confer registration on the freelancer's articles for purposes of § 411(a), since Conde Nast owned only some of the rights to the freelancer's articles at the time it registered the relevant issues of *Allure*.

325. *Heyman*, 743 F. Supp. at 191.

326. *Id.* at 193.

327. *Id.* at 192 (citing 17 U.S.C. § 101).

328. 17 U.S.C. § 103(b).

329. *See Heyman*, 743 F. Supp. at 193.

330. E. Am. Trio Prods., Inc. v. Tang Elec. Corp., 97 F. Supp. 2d 395 (S.D.N.Y. 2000).

331. 17 U.S.C. § 401(a); *see* BCIA, *supra* note 276.

332. 17 U.S.C. § 401(b); *see* BCIA, *supra* note 276.

333. *Id.*

334. 17 U.S.C. § 401(c); *see* BCIA, *supra* note 276.

335. *See* Berkowitz & Leaffer, *supra* note 2, at 277.

336. 17 U.S.C. § 401(a).

337. 17 U.S.C. § 10 (1909) (superseded 1976).

338. 17 U.S.C. § 19 (1909) (superseded 1976).

339. *Id.*

340. Coventry Ware, Inc. v. Reliance Picture Frame Co., 288 F.2d 193 (2d Cir. 1961), *rev'g* 186 F. Supp. 798 (S.D.N.Y. 1960), *cert. denied*, 368 U.S. 818 (1961); Sherr v. Universal Match Corp., 297 F. Supp. 107 (S.D.N.Y. 1967).

341. *See* Sherr v. Universal Match Corp., 297 F. Supp. 107 (S.D.N.Y. 1967), *aff'd*, 417 F.2d 497 (2d Cir. 1969), *cert. denied*, 397 U.S. 936 (1970).

342. *Id.*, 297 F. Supp. at 112.

343. 17 U.S.C. § 405(a)(1); *see* BCIA, *supra* note 276, § 13(b).

344. Beacon Looms, Inc. v. S. Lichtenberg & Co., 552 F. Supp. 1305 (S.D.N.Y. 1982).

345. *See* 2 NIMMER, *supra* note 10, § 7.13[A][1].

346. Neimark v. Ronai & Ronai, LLP, 500 F. Supp. 2d 338, 342 (S.D.N.Y. 2007) (citing an array of case law authority).

347. 17 U.S.C. § 21 (1909) (superseded 1976).

348. 17 U.S.C. § 405(a)(2); *see* BCIA, *supra* note 276, § 13(b).

349. 17 U.S.C. § 405(a)(3); *see* BCIA, *supra* note 276, § 13(b).

350. *See* Shoptalk, Ltd. v. Concorde-New Horizons Corp., 168 F.3d 586 (2d Cir.), *cert. denied,* 527 U.S. 1038 (1999), *supra note.*

351. 17 U.S.C. § 406(c); *see* BCIA, *supra note* 276, § 13(b).

352. 17 U.S.C. § 406(a); *see* BCIA, *supra note* 276, § 13(b).

353. 17 U.S.C. § 411(a).

354. *Id.*

355. *Id.*

356. 17 U.S.C. §§ 411(c)(1)-(2).

357. Reed Elsevier, Inc. v. Muchnick, 130 S. Ct. 1237 (2010).

358. *See, e.g.,* Lennon v. Seaman, 2002 WL 109525, 2002 U.S. Dist. LEXIS 1237 (S.D.N.Y., Jan. 28, 2002), where in 2002 a New York federal district court dismissed a copyright infringement counterclaim based on the alleged unauthorized use of photographs and writings made during the course of defendant's employment with Yoko Ono. The court ruled that the claim should be dismissed because defendant did not have either copyright registration or a pending application in the Copyright Office, "a jurisdictional prerequisite to filing federal action."

359. 17 U.S.C. § 408(a).

360. Sefton v. Webworld, Inc., 2001 WL 1512058, 2001 U.S. Dist. LEXIS 19286 (N.D. Tex., Nov. 21, 2001) (the effective date of copyright registration is the day on which application, deposit and fee have been received in the Copyright Office); Samara Bros., Inc. v. Wal-Mart Stores, 165 F.3d 120 (2d Cir. 1998), *rev'd and remanded,* 529 U.S. 205 (2002); Modtech, Inc. v. Designed Facilities Constr., Inc., 48 U.S.P.Q.2d (BNA) 1209 (C.D. Cal. 1998).

361. 17 U.S.C. §§ 408(a)–(b), 708(a); 37 C.F.R. §§ 201.3(c), 202.3(a), 202.3(b)(1)(iii), 202.3(b)(2), 202.3(c)(1), 202.3(c)(2); *see also* 37 C.F.R. § 202.10(a). "Best edition" means the edition of the work "published in the United States at any time before the date of deposit that the Library of Congress determines to be most suitable for its purposes." 17 U.S.C. § 101.

362. 17 U.S.C. § 410(a).

363. *Id.*

364. 17 U.S.C. § 410(b).

365. 17 U.S.C. § 405(a)(2); *see* BCIA, *supra note* 276, § 13(b).

366. 17 U.S.C. §410 (c).

367. Sportsmans Warehouse, Inc. v. Steven Fair, 576 F. Supp. 2d 1175 (D. Colo. 2008).

368. 3 NIMMER, *supra note* 10, § 9.05[B].

369. 17 U.S.C. § 411(a).

370. 17 U.S.C. § 408(a).

371. 17 U.S.C. § 408(c)(1).

372. Tabra, Inc. v. Treasures de Paradise Designs, Inc., 15 U.S.P.Q.2d (BNA) 1234, 1990 WL 126187, 1990 U.S. Dist. LEXIS 11384 (N.D. Cal., Apr. 24, 1990).

373. *Id.,* 15 U.S.P.Q.2d at 1237, 1990 WL 126187, at *3, 1990 U.S. Dist. LEXIS 11384, at *8.

374. Morris v. Bus. Concepts, Inc., 259 F.3d 65 (2d Cir. 2001).

375. *See* Yurman Design, Inc. v. Chaindom Enters., Inc., 2002 WL 31358991, 2002 U.S. Dist. LEXIS 18329 (S.D.N.Y., Sept. 30, 2002) (defendants must plead their affirmative defenses alleging fraudulent obtainment of copyright registration with the particularity required by the FED. R. CIV. P. 9(b)).

376. Data Gen. Corp. v. Grumman Sys. Support Corp., 36 F.3d 1147 (1st Cir. 1994). *See also* Kaplan v. Panaria Int'l, Inc., 51 U.S.P.Q.2d (BNA) 1216 (S.D.N.Y. 1999), which held that error in registering the wrong works did not invalidate plaintiff's copyright in the correct work.

377. Gibson Tex, Inc. v. Sears Roebuck & Co., 11 F. Supp. 2d 439 (S.D.N.Y. 1998)

378. Granse v. Brown Photo Co., 1985 WL 26033, 1985 U.S. Dist. LEXIS 18318 (D. Minn., July 1, 1985).

379. Whimsicality, Inc. v. Rubie's Costume Co., 891 F.2d 452 (2d Cir. 1989), *modifying* 721 F. Supp. 1566 (E.D.N.Y. 1989). *See also* Fonar Corp. v. Domenick, 105 F.3d 99 (2d Cir. 1997).

380. *See Whimsicality,* 721 F. Supp. at 1570.

381. *Id.*

382. *See Whimsicality,* 891 F.2d at 457.

383. 17 U.S.C. § 407.
384. *Id.*
385. 17 U.S.C. § 408. *See also* Kodadek v. MTV Networks, Inc., 152 F.3d 1209 (9th Cir. 1998).
386. Kodadek v. MTV Networks, Inc., 152 F.3d 1209 (9th Cir. 1998).
387. *Id.*
388. From a conversation in May 1997 with two examiners in the United States Copyright Office.
389. 17 U.S.C. § 205(a).
390. 17 U.S.C. § 205(c).
391. 17 U.S.C. § 205(c)(2).
392. 17 U.S.C. § 205(d); *see* BCIA, *supra* note 276, § 13(b).
393. 17 U.S.C. § 205(d).
394. *See* Berkowitz & Leaffer, *supra* note 2, at 302.
395. 17 U.S.C. § 205(e).
396. 17 U.S.C. § 30 (1909) (superseded 1976).
397. *Id.*
398. 3 NIMMER, *supra* note 10, § 10.07[B].
399. 17 U.S.C. § 30 (1909) (superseded 1976).
400. 17 U.S.C. § 24 (1909) (superseded 1976).
401. 3 NIMMER, *supra* note 10, § 9.02.
402. Fred Fisher Music Co. v. M. Witmark & Sons, 318 U.S. 643, 653–54 (1943).
403. 17 U.S.C. § 304(a).
404. *Id.*, effective June 26, 1992. Works achieving statutory copyright protection between January 1, 1950, through December 31, 1963, are governed by the original version of 304(a), Pub. L. No. 102-307, § 102(g)(2).
405. *Id.*
406. *See* Barris v. Hamilton, 51 U.S.P.Q.2d (BNA) 1191 (S.D.N.Y. 1999), which held that a series of Marilyn Monroe photographs first published in a U.K. newspaper in 1962 had the same effect as domestic publication and failure to file renewal in 1990 caused the copyright to lapse and the works to fall into the public domain.
407. Pub. L. No. 102-307 § 102(g)(2).
408. *Id.*
409. *Id.*
410. *Id.*
411. 17 U.S.C. § 304(a)(2)(A). For automatic renewal, the Act makes a distinction between general copyrighted works and works for hire, posthumous works, and composite works. For the latter three categories, the sixty-seven-year renewal term vests in the proprietor of the copyright as of the last day of the original term of copyright.
412. 17 U.S.C. § 304(a)(2).
413. 17 U.S.C. § 304(b). *See* Walthal v. Rusk, 172 F.3d 481 (7th Cir. 1999).
414. 17 U.S.C. §§ 304(c) and 203.
415. 3 NIMMER, *supra* note 10, § 11.01.
416. *Id.*
417. Classic Media, Inc. v. Mewborn, 532 F.3d 978, 986 n.5 (9th Cir. 2008); 3 NIMMER, *supra* note 10, §11.02[A].
418. 3 NIMMER, *supra* note 10, §§11.03 [A] [1], §11.03[A][2][a].
419. 17 U.S.C. § 203(a).
420. *Id.*
421. 3 NIMMER, *supra* note 10, § 11.07[B].
422. *See* Berkowitz & Leaffer, *supra* note 2, at 285.
423. 17 U.S.C. § 304(c).
424. *Id.*
425. *Id.*
426. 17 U.S.C. § 507(b).
427. 17 U.S.C. § 507(a).

428. 3 NIMMER, *supra* note 10, § 12.05[A].

429. *See* 3 NIMMER, *supra* note 10, § 12.05[A].

430. *Id.*

431. *Id.*

432. 3 NIMMER, *supra* note 10, § 12.05[B][1][b].

433. *See* 3 NIMMER, *supra* note 10, § 12.05[B][3].

434. Stone v. Williams, 970 F.2d 1043, 1049–50 (2d Cir. 1992), *cert. denied,* 508 U.S. 906 (1993).

435. Joel L. Hecker, *Orphan Works Relief—Pending Copyright Legislation,* 19 ENT., ARTS & SPORTS L.J. 9, 10 (Summer 2008) (N.Y. St. B. Ass'n, Albany, N.Y.).

436. 17 U.S.C. § 408(a).

437. *See, e.g.,* Sarah Zenewick, *Don't Want Your Work Orphaned? Time to Consider a Visual Registry,* PUB. KNOWLEDGE (June 20, 2006), http://publicknowledge.org/node/473.

438. The Importance of Orphan Works Legislation, U.S. COPYRIGHT OFFICE, www.copyright. gov/orphan/ (last visited May 21, 2012).

439. *Id.*

440. Orphan Works Act of 2008, H.R. 5889, 110th Congress (2008); Shawn Bentley Orphan Works Act of 2008, S. 2913, 110th Congress (2008).

441. Orphan Works Act of 2008, H.R. 5889, 110th Congress §§2(b)(1)(A), (b)(2) (2008); Shawn Bentley Orphan Works Act of 2008, S. 2913, 110th Congress §§2(b)(1)(A), (b)(2) (2008).

442. Orphan Works Act of 2008, H.R. 5889, 110th Congress §2(b)(3) (2008).

443. Orphan Works Act of 2008, H.R. 5889, 110th Congress §2(b)(1)(A)(iv) (2008); Shawn Bentley Orphan Works Act of 2008, S. 2913, 110th Congress §2(b)(1)(iii) (2008).

444. Orphan Works Act of 2008, H.R. 5889, 110th Congress §§2(a)(4), (b)(1)(B), (c) (2008); Shawn Bentley Orphan Works Act of 2008, S. 2913, 110th Congress §§2(a)(3), (b)(1)(B), (c) (2008).

445. Orphan Works Act of 2008, H.R. 5889, 110th Congress §2(c)(2) (2008); Shawn Bentley Orphan Works Act of 2008, S. 2913, 110th Congress §2(c)(2) (2008).

446. Orphan Works Act of 2008, H.R. 5889, 110th Congress §3 (2008); Shawn Bentley Orphan Works Act of 2008, S. 2913, 110th Congress §3 (2008). Some writers have suggested that such databases be visual. *See, e.g.,* Zenewick, *supra* note 437.

447. Orphan Works Act of 2008, H.R. 5889, 110th Congress §2(c)(1)(B) (2008); Shawn Bentley Orphan Works Act of 2008, S. 2913, 110th Congress §2(c)(1)(B) (2008).

448. *See, e.g.,* Maureen Whalen, *Marooned in Storage: Rescuing Orphan Works,* AM. ASS'N OF MUSEUMS, www.aam-us.org/pubs/mn/MN_SO06_orphan-works.cfm (last visited May 21, 2012). *See also Key Issues: Orphan Works,* PUB. KNOWLEDGE, http://www.publicknowledge. org/issues/ow (last visited May 21, 2012).

449. Whalen, *supra* note 448.

450. Frank Stella & Theodore Feder, *The Proposed New Law Is a Nightmare for Artists,* THE ART NEWSPAPER (June 1, 2008), www.theartnewspaper.com/articles/ The-proposed-new-law-is-a-nightmare-for-artists/8580.

451. *Id.*

452. 17 U.S.C. § 101.

453. Cynthia D. Mann, *The Aesthetic Side of Life: The Applied Art/ Industrial Design Dichotomy,* Apr. 9, 1990 (unpublished paper on file with the authors).

454. 1976 U.S.C.C.A.N., at 5667.

455. 17 U.S.C. § 102(a).

456. *Id.*

457. 17 U.S.C. § 101.

458. *Id.*

459. *See* Mazer v. Stein, 347 U.S. 201 (1954).

460. *Id.* at 209.

461. *Id.* at 212.

462. *Id.* at 213–14.

463. *See* 1 NIMMER, *supra* note 10, § 2.19

464. Whimsicality Inc. v. Battat, 27 F. Supp. 2d 456 (S.D.N.Y. 1998).

465. *Id.*

466. Esquire, Inc. v. Ringer, 591 F.2d 796 (D.C. Cir. 1978), *cert. denied*, 440 U.S. 908 (1979).

467. *Id.* at 803 (quoting from H.R. Rep. No. 94-1476 at 55 (1976)).

468. 1 Paul Goldstein, Goldstein on Copyright § 2.5.3 (3d ed. 2012).

469. *See, e.g.,* Carol Barnhart, Inc. v. Econ. Cover Corp., 594 F. Supp. 364 (E.D.N.Y. 1984), *aff'd,* 773 F.2d 411 (2d Cir. 1985); OddzOn Prods., Inc. v. Oman, 924 F.2d 346 (D.C. Ct. App. 1991); Custom Chrome, Inc. v. Ringer, 35 U.S.P.Q.2d (BNA) 1714 (D.D.C. June 29, 1995); Beehive Kitchenware v. R.S.V.P. Int'l, Inc., 353 F. Supp. 2d 218 (D. R.I. 2005).

470. Galiano v. Harrah's Operating Co., 416 F.3d 411, 417 (5th Cir. 2005) (quoting Masquerade Novelty, Inc. v. Unique Indus., Inc., 912 F.2d 663, 670 (3d Cir. 1990)).

471. Kieselstein-Cord v. Accessories by Pearl, Inc., 632 F.2d 989 (2d Cir. 1980).

472. *Id.* at 993 (citing H.R. Rep. No. 94-1476 at 55 (1976)).

473. *Id.*

474. *Id.* at 993–94.

475. *See* Carol Barnhart, Inc. v. Econ. Cover Corp., 594 F. Supp. 364 (E.D.N.Y. 1984).

476. *Id.* at 418.

477. *Id.*

478. *Id.* at 419.

479. *Id.* at 421.

480. Carol Barnhart, Inc. v. Econ. Cover Corp., 594 F. Supp. 364, 421 (E.D.N.Y. 1984).

481. *Id.*

482. *Id.* at 422.

483. *Id.*

484. Brandir Int'l, Inc. v. Cascade Pac. Lumber Co., 834 F.2d 1142 (2d Cir. 1987).

485. *Id.* at 1145 (quoting from Denicola, *Applied Art and Industrial Design: A Suggested Approach to Copyright in Useful Articles,* 67 Minn. L. Rev. 707 (1983)).

486. Hart v. Dan Chase Taxidermy Supply Co., 152 F.3d 918 (2d Cir. 1998) (unpublished) (opinion available at 1998 U.S. App. LEXIS 15219).

487. Hart v. Dan Chase Taxidermy Supply Co., 884 F. Supp. 71 (N.D.N.Y. 1995).

488. Hart v. Dan Chase Taxidermy Supply Co., 86 F.3d 320 (2d Cir. 1996).

489. *Id.* at 323.

490. *Id.* at 322.

491. Hart v. Dan Chase Taxidermy Supply Co., 967 F. Supp. 70 (N.D.N.Y. 1997).

492. *Hart,* 152 F.3d 918 (2d Cir. 1998), *aff'g* 967 F. Supp. 70 (N.D.N.Y. 1997)

493. Pivot Point Int'l, Inc. v. Charlene Prods., Inc., 372 F.3d 913 (7th Cir. 2004), *rev'g* 170 F. Supp. 2d 828 (N.D. Ill. 2001).

494. *Id.,* 372 F.3d at 930.

495. *Id.* at 931.

496. *Id.* at 927.

497. *Id.* at 931 (citing *Brandir,* 834 F.2d at 1147).

498. Mattel, Inc. v. Goldberger Doll Mfg. Co., 365 F.3d 133 (2d Cir. 2004).

499. Pivot Point Int'l, Inc. v. Charlene Prods. Inc., 372 F.3d 913, 931 (7th Cir. 2004).

500. *Id.*

501. Universal Furniture Int'l, Inc. v. Collezione Europa USA, Inc. 618 F. 3d 417 (4th Cir. 2010).

502. *Id.* at 432.

503. Universal Furniture Int'l, Inc. v. Collezione Europa USA, Inc., 196 F. App'x 166 (4th Cir. 2006).

504. *Id.* at 171.

505. *Universal Furniture,* 618 F.3d at 426.

506. *Id.* at 434 (citations omitted).

507. *Id.* (citation omitted).

508. *See* Berne Convention, *supra* note 128.

509. *See* BCIA, *supra* note 320.

510. 4 Nimmer, *supra* note 10, § 17.01[B][1].

511. World Copyright Center, *The Berne Convention Signatories, available at* www.worldcopyrightcenter.com/signatories-berne-convention.html.

512. 4 NIMMER, *supra* note 10, § 17.01[B][1][a].

513. *Id.*

514. *Id.* (citing at n.25 Berne (Paris text), *supra* note 128, art. 5(1)).

515. *Id.*

516. *Id.*

517. *See* Brownlee, *supra* note 127, at 588.

518. *Id.* at 589.

519. *See, e.g.,* M. Jackson, *Harmony or Discord? The Pressure Toward Conformity in International Copyright,* 43 Idea 607, 622 (2003).

520. For example, Australia, Chile, China, Egypt, Japan, and Singapore.

521. Robert J. Sherman, Note, *The Visual Artists Rights Act of 1522: American Artists Burned Again,* 17 CARDOZO L. REV. 373, 374 n.11 (1995).

522. Two other principal moral rights, the right of disclosure and the right of withdrawal, discussed in the chapter on moral rights (chapter 12) were not incorporated in article *6bis* of Berne.

523. *See* Sherman, *supra* note 521, at 381 n.48.

524. *Id.* at n.47.

525. *Id.* at 389.

526. *Id.* at 405.

527. Berne (Paris text), *supra* note 128, art. 5(2).

528. 4 NIMMER, *supra* note 10, § 17.01[B][1][a].

529. 2 NIMMER, *supra* note 10, § 7.16[B][1][b].

530. *See* Sherman, *supra* note 521, at 399.

531. 4 NIMMER, *supra* note 10, § 17.01[B][2].

532. *See* Sherman, *supra* note 521, at 400 and n.158 (citing P. Jaszi, *A Garland of Reflections on Three International Copyright Topics,* 8 CARDOZO ARTS & ENT. J. 47 (1989)) (citations omitted).

533. *Id. See also* 4 NIMMER, *supra* note 10, § 17.01[B][3], which notes that while the United States also adheres to the Buenos Aires Copyright Convention of 1910, given that all Buenos Aires signatories have subsequently joined the U.C.C., which takes precedence, the B.A. Copyright Convention only has current application to copyright relations with Honduras.

534. 4 NIMMER, *supra* note 10, § 17.01[C][2][a].

535. 4 NIMMER, *supra* note 10, § 18.05[A][2].

536. E.H. Smith, *Worldwide Copyright Protection Under the TRIPs Agreement,* 29 VAND. J. TRANSNAT'L L. 559, 562–71 (1996).

537. 3 NIMMER, *supra* note 10, § 18.05[A][1].

538. *Id.*

539. *Id.*

540. *Id.*

541. *Id.*

542. *Id.; see also* D. Nimmer, *GATT's Entertainment: Before and NAFTA,* 15 LOY. L.A. ENT. L.J. 135, 137 (1995).

543. 4 NIMMER, *supra* note 10, § 18.06; D. Nimmer, *supra* note 542, at 138.

544. 4 NIMMER, *supra* note 10, § 18.06 and n.11 (citing S. REP. NO. 103-412, at 5 (1994)).

545. *Id.,* and § 18.06[A].

546. Pub. L. No. 103-465, §§ 101–03, 108 Stat. 4809 (1994) (amending 17 U.S.C. § 104A).

547. 4 NIMMER, *supra* note 10, § 18.06[B][1].

548. *Id.* § 18.06[A][1]; *see also* Area summary: *International Trade Decisions of the Federal Circuit: Three Years of Rigorous Review,* 52 AM. U. L. REV. 1027, at 1110 (Apr. 2003).

549. 4 NIMMER, *supra* note 10, § 18.06[A][1].

550. *See id.*

551. *Id.*

552. Pub. L. No. 100-418, 102 Stat. 1121 (Aug. 23, 1988).
553. *See* D. Nimmer, *supra* note 542, at 138.
554. 4 NIMMER, *supra* note 10, § 18.04[C].
555. *Id.*
556. 19 U.S.C. § 2901(a)(1), (2), (3).
557. *See* D. Nimmer, *supra* note 542, at 139.
558. 4 NIMMER, *supra* note 10, § 18.06[A][1][a].
559. *Id.*
560. *Id.*
561. *Id.*
562. *Id.* § 18.06[A][1][b], with exceptions listed therein.
563. *Id.* § 18.06[A][2] (citing TRIPs art. 9(1)).
564. *Id.* (citing TRIPs art. 10(1), (2)).
565. *Id.* (citing TRIPs art. 12).
566. *Id.* § 18.06 [B][2] (citing TRIPs art. 41(1)).
567. *Id.*
568. *Id.* § 18.06[C][1].
569. 17 U.S.C. § 104A.
570. 3 NIMMER, *supra* note 10, § 9A.06[A].
571. *Id.* § 9A.03[C]
572. 17 U.S.C. § 104A.
573. 17 U.S.C. § 104A(h)(6).
574. 17 U.S.C. § 104A(h)(3).
575. 17 U.S.C. § 104A(a)(1)(B).
576. 17 U.S.C. § 104A(b).
577. *See* 17 U.S.C. § 104A(h)(4)(A).
578. 17 U.S.C. § 104A(e).
579. 17 U.S.C. § 104A(d)(2)(A)(i).
580. 17 U.S.C. § 104A(e)(1)(B).
581. 17 U.S.C. § 104A(e)(2)(A).
582. 17 U.S.C. § 104A(e)(2)(B).
583. 17 U.S.C. § 104A(c).
584. 17 U.S.C. § 104A(d)(2).
585. 17 U.S.C. § 104A(d)(2). Derivative works are governed by (d)(3).
586. *Id.*
587. Cordon Holding B.V. v. Northwest Publ'g Corp., 63 U.S.P.Q.2d (BNA) 1013, 2002 WL
     530991, 2002 U.S. Dist. LEXIS 6111 (S.D.N.Y. 2002).
588. *Id.*, 2002 WL 530991, at *11, 2002 U.S. Dist. LEXIS 6111, at *35.
589. Troll Co. A/S v. Uneeda Doll Co., 400 F. Supp. 2d 601 (S.D.N.Y. 2005), *aff'd*, 483 F.3d 150 (2d
     Cir. 2007).
590. *Id.*, 400 F. Supp. 2d at 603.
591. 17 U.S.C. § 104A(d).
592. Troll Co. A/S v. Uneeda Doll Co. Ltd., 483 F.3d 150, 157 (2d Cir. 2007), 2007 U.S. App. LEXIS
     8611, at *15.
593. *Id.*
594. *Id.*, 2007 U.S. App. LEXIS 8611, at *15-16.
595. 17 U.S.C. § 104A(h)(4)(A).
596. 17 U.S.C. § 104A(h)(4)(B).
597. *Id.*
598. Golan v. Holder, 132 S. Ct. 873, (2012).
599. Golan v. Holder, 609 F.3d 1076 (10th Cir. 2010).
600. Golan v. Holder, No. 10-545, Slip op. at p. 14 (U.S., Jan. 18, 2012).
601. Golan v. Holder, No. 10-545, Slip op. at p. 13 (U.S., Jan. 18, 2012).
602. Golan v. Holder, No. 10-545, Slip op. at p. 20 (U.S., Jan. 18, 2012).

603. Golan v. Holder, No. 10-545, Slip op. at p. 22 (U.S., Jan. 18, 2012).

604. *Id.*

605. Golan v. Holder, No. 10-545, Slip op. at p. 23 (U.S., Jan. 18, 2012).

606. Golan v. Holder, No. 10-545, Slip op. at p. 24 (U.S., Jan. 18, 2012).

607. Golan v. Holder, No. 10-545, Slip op. at p. 25 (U.S., Jan. 18, 2012).

608. Golan v. Holder, No. 10-545, Slip op. at pp. 26-27 (U.S., Jan. 18, 2012).

609. Golan v. Holder, No. 10-545, Slip op. at p. 30 (U.S., Jan. 18, 2012).

610. *Copyright Rules for Net Adopted by 160 Nations; WIPO Copyright Treaty; WIPO Performances and Phonegrams Treaty,* COMPUTER DEALER NEWS 2, vol. 13, at 10 (Jan. 27, 1997).

611. 17 U.S.C. § 501(a).

612. 17 U.S.C. § 106.

613. Playboy Enters., Inc. v. Starware Publ'g Corp., 900 F. Supp. 433 (S.D. Fla. 1995).

614. *See, e.g.,* Folio Impressions, Inc. v. Byer Cal., 937 F.2d 759, 763 (2d Cir. 1991), *aff'g* 752 F. Supp. 583 (S.D.N.Y. 1990); Keeler Brass Co. v. Cont'l Brass Co., 862 F.2d 1063 (4th Cir. 1988); Hustler Magazine, Inc. v. Moral Majority, Inc., 796 F.2d 1148 (9th Cir. 1986).

615. 17 U.S.C. § 410(c).

616. *See, e.g.,* Laureyssens v. Idea Group, Inc., 964 F.2d 131, 140 (2d Cir. 1992); Castle Rock Entm't v. Carol Publ'g Group, 955 F. Supp. 260 (S.D.N.Y. 1997), *aff'd,* 150 F.3d 132 (2d Cir. 1998).

617. *See, e.g.,* Grubb v. KMS Patriots, L.P., 88 F.3d 1, 5 (1st Cir. 1996); Williams v. Crichton, 84 F.3d 581, 587 (2d Cir. 1996); Towler v. Sayles, 76 F.3d 579, 581 (4th Cir. 1996); Norma Ribbon & Trimming, Inc. v. Little, 51 F.3d 45, 47 (5th Cir. 1995); Modtech, Inc. v. Designed Facilities Constr., Inc., 51 U.S.P.Q.2d (BNA) 1206 (C.D. Cal. 1999).

618. *See, e.g.,* Fisher v. United Feature Syndicate, Inc., 203 F.3d 834 (10th Cir. 2000); Sid & Marty Krofft Television Prods., Inc. v. McDonald's Corp., 562 F.2d 1157, 1172 (9th Cir. 1977); Judith Ripka Designs v. Preville, 935 F. Supp. 237, 246 (S.D.N.Y. 1996); Ganz Bros. Toys v. Midwest Imps., 834 F. Supp. 896, 901 (E.D. Va. 1993); Kebodeaux v. Schwegmann Giant Super Mkts., 1993 WL 114526, 1993 U.S. Dist. LEXIS 4532 (E.D. La., Apr. 8, 1993).

619. A.M. Broaddus, *Eliminating the Confusion: A Restatement of the Test for Copyright Infringement,* 5 DEPAUL-LCA J. ART & ENT. L. 43, 47 (1995). This article includes an excellent analysis of copyright infringement issues, focusing on a new proposal to extract protected expression from unprotectable material.

620. *See, e.g.,* Cranston Print Works Co. v. J. Mason Prods., 49 U.S.P.Q.2d (BNA) 1661 (S.D.N.Y. 1998), which held that even though defendant's fabric was purchased in the Far East, access could be inferred where, in light of the "global marketplace," the Rhode Island–based plaintiff had fabric that was in circulation for five years prior to the suit and where the works were strikingly similar.

621. Kerr v. New Yorker Magazine, Inc., 63 F. Supp. 2d 320 (S.D.N.Y. 1999) which stated that the defendant had access to the plaintiff's work on a number of different occasions including when (1) plaintiff mailed a postcard to an office where the defendant had visited, (2) postcard was displayed at a store or in a catalog, (3) postcard was given to a mutual friend and (4) plaintiff wore a T-shirt displaying the image to the defendant's exhibition opening.

622. Ronna Lugosch v. James Avery Craftsman, Inc., 2008 U.S. Dist. LEXIS; 58238 (D. Me., July 31, 2008), aff'd by, s.j. denied by, motion denied by, 2008 U.S. Dist. LEXIS 76788 (D. Me., September 30, 2008).

623. *Id.,* 2008 U.S. Dist. LEXIS 58238, at *18.

624. *Id.*

625. *Kerr,* 63 F. Supp. 2d at 324.

626. Arnstein v. Porter, 154 F.2d 464 (2d Cir. 1946).

627. *See* Broaddus, *supra* note 619, at 46.

628. A. Latman, *"Probative Similarity" As Proof of Copying: Toward Dispelling Some Myths in Copyright Infringement,* 90 COLUM. L. REV. 1187 (1990).

629. *See* Laureyssens v. Idea Group, Inc., 964 F.2d 131, 140 (2d Cir. 1992).

630. *See, e.g.,* Sid & Marty Krofft Television Prods., Inc. v. McDonald's Corp., 562 F.2d 1157, 1172 (9th Cir. 1977).

631. *See* Broaddus, *supra* note 619, at 52.
632. *Id.*
633. Nichols v. Universal Pictures Corp., 45 F.2d 119 (2d Cir. 1930), *cert. denied*, 282 U.S. 902 (1931).
634. Roth Greeting Cards v. United Card Co., 429 F.2d 1106 (9th Cir. 1970).
635. *Id.* at 1110.
636. *See, e.g.,* Sid & Marty Krofft Television Prods., Inc. v. McDonald's Corp., 562 F.2d 1157, 1172 (9th Cir. 1977).
637. Singer v. Citibank, N.A., 39 U.S.P.Q.2d (BNA) 1110 (S.D.N.Y. 1996). *See also* Reyher v. Children's Television Workshop, 533 F.2d 87 (2d Cir. 1976), *cert. denied*, 429 U.S. 980 (1976); Wildlife Express Corp. v. Carol Wright Sales, Inc., 18 F.3d 502 (7th Cir. 1994); Maggio v. Liztech Jewelry, 912 F. Supp. 216 (E.D. La. 1996); Le Moine v. Combined Communications Corp., 1996 WL 332688, 1996 U.S. Dist. LEXIS 8328 (N.D. Ill. June 13, 1996).
638. *See* Kerr v. New Yorker Magazine, Inc., 63 F. Supp. 2d 320 (S.D.N.Y. 1999).
639. *Id.* at 325–26.
640. *See, e.g.,* 4 NIMMER, *supra* note 10, § 13.03[A][1][c].
641. 17 U.S.C. § 102(b).
642. *See* Wildlife Express Corp. v. Carol Wright Sales, Inc., 18 F.3d 502 (7th Cir. 1994).
643. *See* Folio Impressions, Inc. v. Byer Cal., 937 F.2d 759, 763 (2d Cir. 1991)
644. Gibson Tex, Inc. v. Sears Roebuck & Co., 11 F. Supp. 2d 439 (S.D.N.Y. 1998).
645. *Id.* at 444.
646. Leigh v. Warner Bros., 212 F.3d 1210 (11th Cir. 2000).
647. *Id.* at 1216 (citing Beal v. Paramount Pictures Corp., 20 F.3d 454, 459 (11th Cir. 1994)).
648. Peker v. Masters Collection, 96 F. Supp. 2d 216 (E.D.N.Y. 2000).
649. Yankee Candle Co. v. Bridgewater Candle Co., LLC, 99 F. Supp. 2d 140 (D. Mass. 2000).
650. *Id.* at 147–48.
651. *See* Brown v. McCormick, 87 F. Supp. 2d 467 (D. Md. 2000); *see also supra* note 244.
652. *Id.* at 479 (citing Atari, Inc. v. N. Am. Philips Consumer Elec. Corp., 672 F.2d 607, 618 (7th Cir. 1982), *cert. denied*, 459 U.S. 880 (1982)).
653. *See* Feist Publ'ns, Inc. v. Rural Tel. Serv. Co., 499 U.S. 340 (1991); *see also supra* note 22.
654. Nimmer, Bernacchi & Frischling, *A Structured Approach to Analyzing the Substantial Similarity of Computer Software in Copyright Infringement Cases*, 20 ARIZ. ST. L. J. 625, 655–56 (1988); 4 NIMMER, *supra* note 10, § 13.03[E][1][b].
655. *See* Broaddus, *supra* note 619, at 59, which seeks to combine this with the abstractions test.
656. Novak v. Nat'l Broad. Co., 716 F. Supp. 745, 752 (S.D.N.Y. 1989), *later opinion*, 724 F. Supp. 141 (S.D.N.Y. 1989); *See* Laureyssens v. Idea Group, Inc., 964 F.2d 131, 153-55 (2d Cir. 1992); Autoskill, Inc. v. Nat'l Educ. Support Sys., Inc., 793 F. Supp. 1557 (D.N.M. 1992), *aff'd*, 994 F.2d 1476 (10th Cir. 1993), *cert denied*, 510 U.S. 916 (1993). *See also* Kaplan v. Stock Market Photo Agency, Inc., 133 F. Supp. 2d 317 (S.D.N.Y. 2001) (granting summary judgment to a defendant photo agency and photographer dismissing an infringement claim where photographs were similar only in unprotectable elements that flowed from the idea).
657. Fisher v. United Feature Syndicate, Inc., 203 F.3d 834 (10th Cir. 2000), *aff'g* 37 F. Supp. 2d 1213 (D. Colo. 1999).
658. *See* Arnstein v. Porter, 154 F.2d 464 (2d Cir. 1946).
659. *See* Sid & Marty Krofft Television Prods., Inc. v. McDonald's Corp., 562 F.2d 1157, 1172 (9th Cir. 1977); *see also supra* note 618.
660. *See* Broaddus, *supra* note 619, at 63.
661. Woods v. Universal City Studios, 920 F. Supp. 62 (S.D.N.Y. 1996).
662. Rogers v. Koons, 960 F.2d 301 (2d Cir.), *cert. denied*, 506 U.S. 934 (1992).
663. Ciner Mfg. Co. v. Plastic Craft Novelty Co., 1993 U.S. Dist. LEXIS 7463 (S.D.N.Y., Mar. 19, 1993).
664. *See* Berkowitz & Leaffer, *supra* note 2, at 310.
665. *See* Bleistein v. Donaldson Lithographing Co., 188 U.S. 239, 249 (1903).
666. Gross v. Seligman, 212 F. 930 (2d Cir. 1914).

667. 17 U.S.C. §§ 408(b), 708(a).

668. 17 U.S.C. § 410(d).

669. 17 U.S.C. § 205.

670. *Id.*

671. *See* Berkowitz & Leaffer, *supra* note 2, at 313.

672. 17 U.S.C. § 107.

673. *Id.*

674. *Id.*

675. Haberman v. Hustler Magazine, Inc., 626 F. Supp. 201 (D. Mass. 1986).

676. Ringgold v. Black Entm't Television, Inc., 40 U.S.P.Q.2d (BNA) 1299 (S.D.N.Y. 1996), *rev'd*, 126 F.3d 70 (2d Cir. 1997); *see* Begos, *"Ringgold": Visual Art Hollywood and Cyberspace*, N.Y.L.J., Oct. 6, 1997, at 1, col. 1.

677. Sandoval v. New Line Cinema Corp., 147 F.3d 215 (2d Cir. 1998).

678. *Id.* at 218.

679. 17 U.S.C. § 107.

680. Campbell v. Acuff-Rose Music, Inc., 510 U.S. 569 (1994).

681. *See* Rogers v. Koons, 960 F.2d 301 (2d Cir. 1992), *cert. denied*, 506 U.S. 934 (1992).

682. Lynne A. Greenberg, *The Art of Appreciation: Puppies, Piracy and Post-Modernism*, 11 CARDOZO ARTS & ENT. L. J. 1, 24 (1992).

683. Rogers v. Koons, 751 F. Supp. 474 (S.D.N.Y. 1990).

684. *See Rogers*, 960 F.2d at 303.

685. *See Rogers*, 751 F. Supp. at 476.

686. *Id.; see also* N.Y. TIMES, Sept. 19, 1991, at B2 col. 1.

687. *See* Rogers v. Koons, 960 F.2d 301, 305 (2d Cir.), *cert. denied*, 506 U.S. 934 (1992).

688. *Id.*

689. *See* Rogers v. Koons, 751 F. Supp. 474 (S.D.N.Y. 1990).

690. *See Rogers*, 960 F.2d at 306.

691. *Id.* at 307 (citing *Feist Publications*, 499 U.S. at 345).

692. *Id.*

693. Rogers v. Koons, 960 F.2d 301, 309 (2d Cir. 1992), *cert. denied*, 506 U.S. 934 (1992).

694. *Id.* at 310.

695. *Id.* at 311.

696. *Id.* at 313.

697. *See, e.g.*, Hustler Magazine, Inc. v. Moral Majority, Inc., 796 F.2d 1148 (9th Cir. 1986); Cardtoons, L.C. v. Major League Baseball Players Ass'n, 838 F. Supp. 1501 (N.D. Okla. 1993); New Line Cinema Corp. v. Bertlesman Music Group, 693 F. Supp. 1517 (S.D.N.Y. 1988).

698. *See* Campbell v. Acuff-Rose Music, Inc., 510 U.S. 569 (1994).

699. *Id.*, 510 U.S. at 572.

700. *See* Pierre N. Leval, *Toward A Fair Use Standard*, 103 HARV. L. REV. 1105 (1990).

701. *See Campbell*, 510 U.S. at 579.

702. *Id.*

703. Campbell v. Acuff-Rose Music, Inc., 510 U.S. 569, 581 (1994).

704. *Id.* at 584 (quoting Harper & Row Publishers, Inc. v. Nation Enters., 471 U.S. 539, 592 (1985)).

705. *Id.* at 591.

706. Suntrust Bank v. Houghton Mifflin Co., 268 F.3d 1257 (11th Cir. 2001).

707. *Id.* at 1267.

708. *Id.*

709. Campbell v. Acuff-Rose Music, Inc., 510 U.S. 569, 579 (1994)

710. Kelly v. Arriba Soft Corp., 336 F.3d 811 (9th Cir. 2003), *aff'g in part and rev'g in part* 77 F. Supp. 2d 1116 (C.D. Cal. 1999).

711. Baraban v. Time Warner, Inc., 54 U.S.P.Q.2d (BNA) 1759 (S.D.N.Y. 2000).

712. Blanch v. Koons, 467 F.3d 244 (2d Cir. 2006), *aff'g* 396 F. Supp. 2d 476 (S.D.N.Y. 2005).

713. *Id.*, 467 F.3d at 247.

714. *Id.* at 251 (citations omitted).

715. *Id.*

716. Bill Graham Archives v. Dorling Kindersley Ltd. 448 F.3d 605 (2nd Cir. 2006), *aff'g* 386 F. Supp. 2d 324 (S.D.N.Y. 2005).

717. *Id.*, 448 F.3d at 609.

718. *Id.* at 613.

719. Reves v. Wyeth Pharmaceuticals, 603 F. Supp. 2d 289 (D. P.R. 2009).

720. *Id.* at 296 (citations omitted).

721. *Id.* at 297.

722. *Id.*

723. *Id.*

724. *Id.* at 299.

725. Hiro Sendra, *Hope or Nope—Is "Obama Hope" Protected by Idea/Expression Dichotomy, Fair Use Doctrine and First Amendment?*, 10 Chi-Kent J. Intell. Prop. 65, 67 (2010).

726. Larry Neumeister, *Shepard Fairey vs. AP Lawsuit Dropped*, HUFFINGTON POST (Jan. 11, 2011), www.huffingtonpost.com/2011/01/12/shepard-fairey-ap-suit-dropped_n_807800.html .

727. Sendra, *supra* note 725, at 69-70.

728. *Id.* at 69.

729. David Ng, *Shepard Fairey Admits to Wrongdoing in Associated Press Lawsuit*, L. A. TIMES. Oct. 16, 2009, *available at* www.latimesblogs.latimes.com/culturemonster/2009/10/shepard-fairey-admits-to-wrongdoing-in-Associated-Press-lawsuit.html.

730. Bebeto Matthews, *Obama "HOPE" Poster Artist Pleads Guilty to Contempt*, U.S.A. Today, Feb. 24, 2012, www.usatoday.com/news/nation/story/2012-02-24/Obama-poster-artist/53237558/1.

731. *Id.*

732. Randy Kennedy, *Shepard Fairey and the A.P. Settle Legal Dispute*, N. Y. TIMES, Jan. 12, 2011, available at www.nytimes.com/20`11/01/13/arts/design/13fairey.html.

733. Cariou v. Prince, 784 F. Supp. 2d 337 (S.D.N.Y. 2011).

734. *Cariou*, Amended Complaint, Demand for Jury Trial, Case No. 08 CIV 11327 (DAB), pt. 16 (Jan. 14, 2009).

735. *Cariou*, 784 F. Supp. 2d at 343.

736. Memorandum of Law in Support of Defendants' Joint Motion for Summary Judgment, 08 CIV 11327 (DAB) pp. 3-4.

737. *Id.* at p. 5.

738. *Id.*

739. *Cariou*, 784 F. Supp. 2d at 343.

740. *Id.* at 346.

741. *Cariou*, Affidavit of Defendant Richard Prince in Support of Defendants' Motion for Summary Judgment, 08 CIV 11327 (DAB) (May 13, 2010).

742. *Cariou*, 784 F. Supp. 2d at 347.

743. *Id.*

744. *Id.* at 349.

745. *Id.*

746. *Id.*

747. *Id.*

748. *Id.*

749. *Id.* at 351.

750. *Id.*

751. *Id.*

752. *Id.* at 352.

753. *Id.* (citing Harper & Row v. Nation Enters., 471 U.S. 539, 565 (1985)).

754. *Cariou v. Prince*, Brief for Plaintiff-Appellee, 11-1197-cv, 2d. Cir., Jan. 25, 2012; Joint Reply Brief for Defendants-Appellants, 11-1197-cv (2d Cir. Feb. 22, 2012).

755. For an excellent article on the topic, see Barry Werbin, *Use of Art Images in Gallery and Auc-*

tion Catalogues: Copyright Minefield and Practical Advice, 23 NYSBA Entm't, Arts & Sports L. J. 35 (Spring 2012).

756. 17 U.S.C. § 502(a).

757. Reproducta Co. v. Kellmark Corp., 1994 WL 719705, 1994 U.S. Dist. LEXIS 18423 (S.D.N.Y. Dec. 27, 1994).

758. Flack v. Friends of Queen Catherine, Inc., 139 F. Supp. 2d 526 (S.D.N.Y. 2001)

759. 17 U.S.C. § 503.

760. 17 U.S.C. § 504.

761. *Id. But see* Raishevich v. Foster, 247 F.3d 337 (2d. Cir. 2001), which held that in a 42 U.S.C. § 1983 civil rights action, after police had destroyed the plaintiff's photographic transparencies the plaintiff was entitled to receive $12,000 in damages. The amount was based on the expected value of the work, the amount of images sold per year and the assumed period of time when the plaintiff would have derived such income.

762. Jenkins v. O'Brien, 367 F. App'x 439, 441 (4th Cir. 2010).

763. Walker v. Forbes, Inc., 28 F.3d 409 (4th Cir. 1994).

764. *Id.* at 412.

765. On Davis v. The Gap, Inc., 246 F.3d 152, 164 (2d Cir. 2001).

766. *See, e.g.,* Frank Music Corp. v. Metro-Goldwyn-Mayer, Inc., 772 F.2d 505, 512 (9th Cir. 1985); Jarvis v. K2 Inc., 486 F.3d 526, 533 (9th Cir. 2007).

767. *Jenkins,* 367 F. App'x at 442 (citations omitted).

768. *Id.*

769. *Id.* at 443.

770. Sunset Lamp Corp. v. Alsy Corp., 698 F. Supp. 1146 (S.D.N.Y. 1988).

771. Johnson v. Jones, 149 F.3d 494 (6th Cir. 1998).

772. *Id.* at 506 (citing 17 U.S.C. § 504(b)).

773. Gaylord v. United States, 678 F. 3d 1339 (Fed. Cir. 2012), *vacating and remanding* 98 Fed. Cl. 389 (2011), *on remand from* 595 F.3d 1364 (Fed. Cir. 2012).

774. *Id.,* 678 F.3d at 1343.

775. *Id.*

776. *Id.*

777. *Id.,* 98 Fed. Cl. at 391.

778. *Id.,* 678 F.3d at 1344.

779. 17 U.S.C. § 504(c).

780. Blue Ribbon Pet Prods., Inc. v. Rolf C. Hagen Corp., 66 F. Supp. 2d 454 (E.D.N.Y. 1999).

781. 17 U.S.C. § 412(2).

782. Amador v. McDonald's Corp., 601 F. Supp. 2d 403 (D. P.R. 2009).

783. Amador v. McDonald's Corp., 2008 U.S. Dist. LEXIS 107753 (D.P.R. Dec. 5, 2008).

784. *Amador,* 601 F. Supp. 2d at 409 (citations omitted).

785. *Id.* at 410.

786. *Id.*

787. Gerig v. Krause Publ'ns, Inc., 58 F. Supp. 2d 1261 (D. Kan. 1999).

788. *Id.* at 1268 (quoting Johnson v. Jones, 149 F.3d 494, 505 (6th Cir. 1998)).

789. 17 U.S.C. § 505.

790. *See* 18 U.S.C. § 2319.

791. 17 U.S.C. § 506(a).

792. 15 U.S.C. § 1125(a).

793. Romm Art Creations Ltd. v. Simcha Int'l, Inc., 786 F. Supp. 1126 (E.D.N.Y. 1992).

794. *Id.* at 1129.

795. *Id.* at 1131.

796. *Id.* at 1134.

797. Hartford House, Ltd. v. Hallmark Cards, Inc., 647 F. Supp. 1533 (D. Colo. 1986), *aff'd,* 846 F.2d 1268 (10th Cir.), *cert. denied,* 488 U.S. 908 (1988).

798. *Id.,* 647 F. Supp. at 1540.

799. *See* Romm Art Creations Ltd. v. Simcha Int'l, Inc., 786 F. Supp. 1126, 1136 (E.D.N.Y. 1992).

800. H.H. Arnason, *History of Modern Art/Painting Sculpture Architecture Photography* (3d ed., Harry N. Abrams 1986), at 142 .

801. Judith B. Prowda, *Application of Copyright and Trademark Law in the Protection of Style in the Visual Arts*, 19 COLUM.-VLA J. L. & ARTS, 269, 299 (1995).

802. Pub. L. No. 101-650, tit. VII, 104 Stat. 5133 (1991).

803. 17 U.S.C. § 101.

804. Hunt v. Paskernack, 192 F.3d 877 (9th Cir. 1999). *See also* 1 NIMMER, *supra* note 10, § 2.20.

805. Yankee Candle Co. v. New England Candle Co., 14 F. Supp. 2d 154 (D. Mass. 1998).

806. Attia v. Soc'y of the N.Y. Hosp., 201 F.3d 50 (2d Cir. 1999), *cert. denied*, 531 U.S. 843 (2000).

807. *Id.*, 201 F.3d at 55.

808. *Id.*

809. Richard J. Zitz, Inc. v. Pereira, 2000 WL 1239830, 2000 U.S. App. LEXIS 22418 (2d Cir., Aug. 31, 2000).

810. Shine v. Childs, 382 F. Supp. 2d 602 (S.D.N.Y. 2005).

811. *Id.* at 610 (citations omitted.)

812. *Id.*

813. *Id.* at 616.

814. Home Design Servs., Inc. v. Stewart, 2011 U.S. Dist. LEXIS 19913 (N.D. Fla. Feb. 28, 2011).

815. *Id.* at *9.

816. *Id.*

817. *Id.* at *10 (citations omitted).

818. *Id.* at *13.

819. 17 U.S.C. § 120(a).

820. 17 U.S.C. § 120(b).

821. Pressman, *Up Against the Wall*, 11 CAL. LAW, Sept. 1991, at 25.

822. *Id.*

823. Leicester v. Warner Bros., 232 F.3d 1212 (9th Cir. 2000).

824. 17 U.S.C. §§ 302, 303.

APPENDIX 11-1

Copyright Office Form VA

 Form VA

Detach and read these instructions before completing this form.
Make sure all applicable spaces have been filled in before you return this form.

BASIC INFORMATION

When to Use This Form: Use Form VA for copyright registration of published or unpublished works of the visual arts. This category consists of "pictorial, graphic, or sculptural works," including two-dimensional and three-dimensional works of fine, graphic, and applied art, photographs, prints and art reproductions, maps, globes, charts, technical drawings, diagrams, and models.

What Does Copyright Protect? Copyright in a work of the visual arts protects those pictorial, graphic, or sculptural elements that, either alone or in combination, represent an "original work of authorship." The statute declares: "In no case does copyright protection for an original work of authorship extend to any idea, procedure, process, system, method of operation, concept, principle, or discovery, regardless of the form in which it is described, explained, illustrated, or embodied in such work."

Works of Artistic Craftsmanship and Designs: "Works of artistic craftsmanship" are registrable on Form VA, but the statute makes clear that protection extends to "their form" and not to "their mechanical or utilitarian aspects." The "design of a useful article" is considered copyrightable "only if, and only to the extent that, such design incorporates pictorial, graphic, or sculptural features that can be identified separately from, and are capable of existing independently of, the utilitarian aspects of the article."

Labels and Advertisements: Works prepared for use in connection with the sale or advertisement of goods and services are registrable if they contain "original work of authorship." Use Form VA if the copyrightable material in the work you are registering is mainly pictorial or graphic; use Form TX if it consists mainly of text. **Note:** Words and short phrases such as names, titles, and slogans cannot be protected by copyright, and the same is true of standard symbols, emblems, and other commonly used graphic designs that are in the public domain. When used commercially, material of that sort can sometimes be protected under state laws of unfair competition or under the federal trademark laws. For information about trademark registration, write to the U.S. Patent and Trademark Office, PO Box 1450, Alexandria, VA 22313-1450.

Architectural Works: Copyright protection extends to the design of buildings created for the use of human beings. Architectural works created on or after December 1, 1990, or that on December 1, 1990, were unconstructed and embodied only in unpublished plans or drawings are eligible. Request Circular 41, *Copyright Claims in Architectural Works*, for more information. Architectural works and technical drawings cannot be registered on the same application.

Deposit to Accompany Application: An application for copyright registration must be accompanied by a deposit consisting of copies representing the entire work for which registration is to be made.

Unpublished Work: Deposit one complete copy.

Published Work: Deposit two complete copies of the best edition.

Work First Published Outside the United States: Deposit one complete copy of the first foreign edition.

Contribution to a Collective Work: Deposit one complete copy of the best edition of the collective work.

The Copyright Notice: Before March 1, 1989, the use of copyright notice was mandatory on all published works, and any work first published before that date should have carried a notice. For works first published on and after March 1, 1989, use of the copyright notice is optional. For more information about copyright notice, see Circular 3, *Copyright Notice*.

For Further Information: To speak to a Copyright Office staff member, call (202) 707-3000. Recorded information is available 24 hours a day. Order forms and other publications from the address in space 9 or call the Forms and Publications Hotline at (202) 707-9100. Access and download circulars, forms, and other information from the Copyright Office website at *www.copyright.gov.*

LINE-BY-LINE INSTRUCTIONS

Please type or print using black ink. The form is used to produce the certificate.

 SPACE 1: Title

Title of This Work: Every work submitted for copyright registration must be given a title to identify that particular work. If the copies of the work bear a title (or an identifying phrase that could serve as a title), transcribe that wording *completely* and *exactly* on the application. Indexing of the registration and future identification of the work will depend on the information you give here. For an architectural work that has been constructed, add the date of construction after the title; if unconstructed at this time, add "not yet constructed."

Publication as a Contribution: If the work being registered is a contribution to a periodical, serial, or collection, give the title of the contribution in the "Title of This Work" space. Then, in the line headed "Publication as a Contribution," give information about the collective work in which the contribution appeared.

Nature of This Work: Briefly describe the general nature or character of the pictorial, graphic, or sculptural work being registered for copyright. Examples: "Oil Painting"; "Charcoal Drawing"; "Etching"; "Sculpture"; "Map"; "Photograph"; "Scale Model"; "Lithographic Print"; "Jewelry Design"; "Fabric Design."

Previous or Alternative Titles: Complete this space if there are any additional titles for the work under which someone searching for the registration might be likely to look, or under which a document pertaining to the work might be recorded.

 SPACE 1: Author(s)

General Instruction: After reading these instructions, decide who are the "authors" of this work for copyright purposes. Then, unless the work is a "collective work," give the requested information about every "author" who contributed any appreciable amount of copyrightable matter to this version of the work. If you need further space, request Continuation Sheets. In the case of a collective work, such as a catalog of paintings or collection of cartoons by various authors, give information about the author of the collective work as a whole.

Name of Author: The fullest form of the author's name should be given. Unless the work was "made for hire," the individual who actually created the work is its "author." In the case of a work made for hire, the statute provides that "the employer or other person for whom the work was prepared is considered the author."

What Is a "Work Made for Hire"? A "work made for hire" is defined as: (1) "a work prepared by an employee within the scope of his or her employment"; or (2) "a work specially ordered or commissioned for use as a contribution to a collective work, as a part of a motion picture or other audiovisual work, as a translation, as a supplementary work, as a compilation, as an instructional text, as a test, as answer material for a test, or as an atlas, if the parties expressly agree in a written instrument signed by them that the work shall be considered a work made for hire." If you have checked "Yes" to indicate that the work was "made for hire," you must give the full legal name of the employer (or other person for whom the work was prepared). You may also include the name of the employee along with the name of the employer (for example: "Elster Publishing Co., employer for hire of John Ferguson").

"Anonymous" or "Pseudonymous" Work: An author's contribution to a work is "anonymous" if that author is not identified on the copies or phonorecords of the work. An author's contribution to a work is "pseudonymous" if that author is identified on the copies or phonorecords under a fictitious name. If the work is "anonymous" you may: (1) leave the line blank; or (2) state "anonymous" on the line; or (3) reveal the author's identity. If the work is "pseudonymous" you may: (1) leave the line blank; or (2) give the pseudonym and identify it as such (for example: "Huntley Haverstock, pseudonym"); or (3) reveal the author's name, making clear which is the real name and which is the pseudonym (for example: "Henry Leek, whose pseudonym is Priam Farrel"). However, the citizenship or domicile of the author *must* be given in all cases.

Dates of Birth and Death: If the author is dead, the statute requires that the year of death be included in the application unless the work is anonymous or pseudonymous. The author's birth date is optional but is useful as a form of identification. Leave this space blank if the author's contribution was a "work made for hire."

Author's Nationality or Domicile: Give the country of which the author is a citizen or the country in which the author is domiciled. Nationality or domicile *must* be given in all cases.

Nature of Authorship: Categories of pictorial, graphic, and sculptural authorship are listed below. Check the box(es) that best describe(s) each author's contribution to the work.

3-Dimensional sculptures: Fine art sculptures, toys, dolls, scale models, and sculptural designs applied to useful articles.

2-Dimensional artwork: Watercolor and oil paintings; pen and ink drawings; logo illustrations; greeting cards; collages; stencils; patterns; computer graphics; graphics appearing in screen displays; artwork appearing on posters, calendars, games, commercial prints and labels, and packaging, as well as 2-dimensional artwork applied to useful articles, and designs reproduced on textiles, lace, and other fabrics; on wallpaper, carpeting, floor tile, wrapping paper, and clothing.

Reproductions of works of art: Reproductions of preexisting artwork made by, for example, lithography, photoengraving, or etching.

Maps: Cartographic representations of an area, such as state and county maps, atlases, marine charts, relief maps, and globes.

Photographs: Pictorial photographic prints and slides and holograms.

Jewelry designs: 3-dimensional designs applied to rings, pendants, earrings, necklaces, and the like.

Technical drawings: Diagrams illustrating scientific or technical information in linear form, such as architectural blueprints or mechanical drawings.

Text: Textual material that accompanies pictorial, graphic, or sculptural works, such as comic strips, greeting cards, games rules, commercial prints or labels, and maps.

Architectural works: Designs of buildings, including the overall form as well as the arrangement and composition of spaces and elements of the design.

NOTE: Any registration for the underlying architectural plans must be applied for on a separate Form VA. Check the box "Technical drawing."

SPACE 3: Creation and Publication

General Instructions: Do not confuse "creation" with "publication." Every application for copyright registration must state "the year in which creation of the work was completed." Give the date and nation of first publication only if the work has been published.

Creation: Under the statute, a work is "created" when it is fixed in a copy or phonorecord for the first time. Where a work has been prepared over a period of time, the part of the work existing in fixed form on a particular date constitutes the created work on that date. The date you give here should be the year in which the author completed the particular version for which registration is now being sought, even if other versions exist or if further changes or additions are planned.

Publication: The statute defines "publication" as "the distribution of copies or phonorecords of a work to the public by sale or other transfer of ownership, or by rental, lease, or lending"; a work is also "published" if there has been an "offering to distribute copies or phonorecords to a group of persons for purposes of further distribution, public performance, or public display." Give the full date (month, day, year) when, and the country where, publication first occurred. If first publication took place simultaneously in the United States and other countries, it is sufficient to state "U.S.A."

SPACE 4: Claimant(s)

Name(s) and Address(es) of Copyright Claimant(s): Give the name(s) and address(es) of the copyright claimant(s) in this work even if the claimant is the same as the author. Copyright in a work belongs initially to the author of the work, including, in the case of a work made for hire, the employer or other person for whom the work was prepared. The copyright claimant is either the author of the work or a person or organization to whom the copyright initially belonging to the author has been transferred.

Transfer: The statute provides that, if the copyright claimant is not the author, the application for registration must contain "a brief statement of how the claimant obtained ownership of the copyright." If any copyright claimant named in space 4 is not an author named in space 2, give a brief statement explaining how the claimant(s) obtained ownership of the copyright. Examples: "By written contract"; "Transfer of all rights by author"; "Assignment"; "By will." Do not attach transfer documents or other attachments or riders.

SPACE 5: Previous Registration

General Instructions: The questions in space 5 are intended to find out whether an earlier registration has been made for this work and, if so, whether there is any basis for a new registration. As a rule, only one basic copyright registration can be made for the same version of a particular work.

Same Version: If this version is substantially the same as the work covered by a previous registration, a second registration is not generally possible unless: (1) the work has been registered in unpublished form and a second registration is now being sought to cover this first published edition; or (2) someone other than the author is identified as a copyright claimant in the earlier registration, and the author is now seeking registration in his or her own name. If either of these two exceptions applies, check the appropriate box and give the earlier registration number and date. Otherwise, do not submit Form VA. Instead, write the Copyright Office for information about supplementary registration or recordation of transfers of copyright ownership.

Changed Version: If the work has been changed and you are now seeking registration to cover the additions or revisions, check the last box in space 5, give the earlier registration number and date, and complete both parts of space 6 in accordance with the instruction below.

Previous Registration Number and Date: If more than one previous registration has been made for the work, give the number and date of the latest registration.

SPACE 6: Derivative Work or Compilation

General Instructions: Complete space 6 if this work is a "changed version," "compilation," or "derivative work," and if it incorporates one or more earlier works that have already been published or registered for copyright, or that have fallen into the public domain. A "compilation" is defined as "a work formed by the collection and assembling of preexisting materials or of data that are selected, coordinated, or arranged in such a way that the resulting work as a whole constitutes an original work of authorship." A "derivative work" is "a work based on one or more preexisting works." Examples of derivative works include reproductions of works of art, sculptures based on drawings, lithographs based on paintings, maps based on previously published sources, or "any other form in which a work may be recast, transformed, or adapted." Derivative works also include works "consisting of editorial revisions, annotations, or other modifications" if these changes, as a whole, represent an original work of authorship.

Preexisting Material (space 6a): Complete this space *and* space 6b for derivative works. In this space identify the preexisting work that has been recast, transformed, or adapted. Examples of preexisting material might be "Grunewald Altarpiece" or "19th century quilt design." Do not complete this space for compilations.

Material Added to This Work (space 6b): Give a brief, general statement of the *additional* new material covered by the copyright claim for which registration is sought. In the case of a derivative work, identify this new material. Examples: "Adaptation of design and additional artistic work"; "Reproduction of painting by photolithography"; "Additional cartographic material"; "Compilation of photographs." If the work is a compilation, give a brief, general statement describing both the material that has been compiled *and* the compilation itself. Example: "Compilation of 19th century political cartoons."

SPACE 7, 8, 9: Fee, Correspondence, Certification, Return Address

Deposit Account: If you maintain a Deposit Account in the Copyright Office, identify it in space 7a. Otherwise, leave the space blank and send the fee with your application and deposit.

Correspondence (space 7b): Give the name, address, area code, telephone number, email address, and fax number (if available) of the person to be consulted if correspondence about this application becomes necessary.

Certification (space 8): The application cannot be accepted unless it bears the date and the *handwritten signature* of the author or other copyright claimant, or of the owner of exclusive right(s), or of the duly authorized agent of the author, claimant, or owner of exclusive right(s).

Address for Return of Certificate (space 9): The address box must be completed legibly since the certificate will be returned in a window envelope.

○c Form VA
For a Work of the Visual Arts
UNITED STATES COPYRIGHT OFFICE

REGISTRATION NUMBER

VA   VAU

EFFECTIVE DATE OF REGISTRATION

Month   Day   Year

Privacy Act Notice: Sections 408-410 of title 17 of the *United States Code* authorize the Copyright Office to collect the personally identifying information requested on this form in order to process the application for copyright registration. By providing this information you are agreeing to routine uses of the information that include publication to give legal notice of your copyright claim as required by 17 U.S.C. §705. It will appear in the Office's online catalog. If you do not provide the information requested, registration may be refused or delayed, and you may not be entitled to certain relief, remedies, and benefits under the copyright law.

DO NOT WRITE ABOVE THIS LINE. IF YOU NEED MORE SPACE, USE A SEPARATE CONTINUATION SHEET.

1

TITLE OF THIS WORK ▼   NATURE OF THIS WORK ▼ See instructions

PREVIOUS OR ALTERNATIVE TITLES ▼

PUBLICATION AS A CONTRIBUTION If this work was published as a contribution to a periodical, serial, or collection, give information about the collective work in which the contribution appeared. **Title of Collective Work ▼**

If published in a periodical or serial give: **Volume ▼**   **Number ▼**   **Issue Date ▼**   **On Pages ▼**

2 a

NAME OF AUTHOR ▼   DATES OF BIRTH AND DEATH
Year Born ▼   Year Died ▼

WAS THIS CONTRIBUTION TO THE WORK A "WORK MADE FOR HIRE"?
☐ Yes
☐ No

AUTHOR'S NATIONALITY OR DOMICILE
Name of Country
OR { Citizen of _____
Domiciled in _____

WAS THIS AUTHOR'S CONTRIBUTION TO THE WORK
Anonymous? ☐ Yes ☐ No
Pseudonymous? ☐ Yes ☐ No
If the answer to either of these questions is "Yes," see detailed instructions.

NATURE OF AUTHORSHIP Check appropriate box(es). **See instructions**
☐ 3-Dimensional sculpture
☐ 2-Dimensional artwork
☐ Reproduction of work of art
☐ Map
☐ Photograph
☐ Jewelry design
☐ Technical drawing
☐ Text
☐ Architectural work

NOTE
Under the law, the "author" of a "work made for hire" is generally the employer, not the employee (see instructions). For any part of this work that was "made for hire" check "Yes" in the space provided, give the employer (or other person for whom the work was prepared) as "Author" of that part, and leave the space for dates of birth and death blank.

b

NAME OF AUTHOR ▼   DATES OF BIRTH AND DEATH
Year Born ▼   Year Died ▼

WAS THIS CONTRIBUTION TO THE WORK A "WORK MADE FOR HIRE"?
☐ Yes
☐ No

AUTHOR'S NATIONALITY OR DOMICILE
Name of Country
OR { Citizen of _____
Domiciled in _____

WAS THIS AUTHOR'S CONTRIBUTION TO THE WORK
Anonymous? ☐ Yes ☐ No
Pseudonymous? ☐ Yes ☐ No
If the answer to either of these questions is "Yes," see detailed instructions.

NATURE OF AUTHORSHIP Check appropriate box(es). **See instructions**
☐ 3-Dimensional sculpture
☐ 2-Dimensional artwork
☐ Reproduction of work of art
☐ Map
☐ Photograph
☐ Jewelry design
☐ Technical drawing
☐ Text
☐ Architectural work

3 a

YEAR IN WHICH CREATION OF THIS WORK WAS COMPLETED
This information must be given in all cases.
Year

b DATE AND NATION OF FIRST PUBLICATION OF THIS PARTICULAR WORK
Complete this information ONLY if this work has been published.
Month   Day   Year   Nation

4

COPYRIGHT CLAIMANT(S) Name and address must be given even if the claimant is the same as the author given in space 2. ▼

TRANSFER If the claimant(s) named here in space 4 is (are) different from the author(s) named in space 2, give a brief statement of how the claimant(s) obtained ownership of the copyright. ▼

See instructions before completing this space.

DO NOT WRITE HERE
OFFICE USE ONLY

APPLICATION RECEIVED

ONE DEPOSIT RECEIVED

TWO DEPOSITS RECEIVED

FUNDS RECEIVED

MORE ON BACK ▶
• Complete all applicable spaces (numbers 5-9) on the reverse side of this page
• See detailed instructions   • Sign the form at line 8

DO NOT WRITE HERE
Page 1 of _____ pages

EXAMINED BY	FORM VA
CHECKED BY	
CORRESPONDENCE ☐ Yes	FOR COPYRIGHT OFFICE USE ONLY

DO NOT WRITE ABOVE THIS LINE. IF YOU NEED MORE SPACE, USE A SEPARATE CONTINUATION SHEET.

PREVIOUS REGISTRATION Has registration for this work, or for an earlier version of this work, already been made in the Copyright Office?

☐ Yes ☐ No If your answer is "Yes," why is another registration being sought? (Check appropriate box.) ▼

a. ☐ This is the first published edition of a work previously registered in unpublished form.

b. ☐ This is the first application submitted by this author as copyright claimant.

c. ☐ This is a changed version of the work, as shown by space 6 on this application.

If your answer is "Yes," give: **Previous Registration Number ▼**   **Year of Registration ▼**

5

DERIVATIVE WORK OR COMPILATION Complete both space 6a and 6b for a derivative work; complete only 6b for a compilation.

a. Preexisting Material Identify any preexisting work or works that this work is based on or incorporates. ▼

6

a

See instructions before completing this space.

b. Material Added to This Work Give a brief, general statement of the material that has been added to this work and in which copyright is claimed. ▼

b

DEPOSIT ACCOUNT If the registration fee is to be charged to a Deposit Account established in the Copyright Office, give name and number of Account.

Name ▼   **Account Number ▼**

7

a

CORRESPONDENCE Give name and address to which correspondence about this application should be sent. Name/Address/Apt/City/State/Zip ▼

b

Area code and daytime telephone number (   )   Fax number (   )

Email

CERTIFICATION* I, the undersigned, hereby certify that I am the

check only one ▶ {

☐ author

☐ other copyright claimant

☐ owner of exclusive right(s)

☐ authorized agent of _____

Name of author or other copyright claimant, or owner of exclusive right(s) ▲

of the work identified in this application and that the statements made by me in this application are correct to the best of my knowledge.

8

Typed or printed name and date ▼ If this application gives a date of publication in space 3, do not sign and submit it before that date.

_____   **Date** _____

Handwritten signature (X) ▼

X _____

Certificate will be mailed in window envelope to this address:	Name ▼	YOU MUST: • Complete all necessary spaces • Sign your application in space 8
	Number/Street/Apt ▼	SEND ALL 3 ELEMENTS IN THE SAME PACKAGE: 1. Application form 2. Nonrefundable filing fee in check or money order payable to Register of Copyrights 3. Deposit material
	City/State/Zip ▼	MAIL TO: Library of Congress Copyright Office-VA 101 Independence Avenue SE Washington, DC 20559-6211

9

*17 U.S.C. §506(e): Any person who knowingly makes a false representation of a material fact in the application for copyright registration provided for by section 409, or in any written statement filed in connection with the application, shall be fined not more than $2,500.

Form VA-Full Rev 12/2008 Print 12/2008—20,000 Printed on recycled paper   U.S. Government Printing Office 2009-349-387 80,021

APPENDIX 11-2

WIPO Copyright Treaty

PREAMBLE

The Contracting Parties,

Desiring to develop and maintain the protection of the rights of authors in their literary and artistic works in a manner as effective and uniform as possible,

Recognizing the need to introduce new international rules and clarify the interpretation of certain existing rules in order to provide adequate solutions to the questions raised by new economic, social, cultural and technological developments,

Recognizing the profound impact of the development and convergence of information and communication technologies on the creation and use of literary and artistic works,

Emphasizing the outstanding significance of copyright protection as an incentive for literary and artistic creation,

Recognizing the need to maintain a balance between the rights of authors and the larger public interest, particularly education, research and access to information, as reflected in the Berne Convention,

Have agreed as follows:

ARTICLE 1
RELATION TO THE BERNE CONVENTION

(1) This Treaty is a special agreement within the meaning of Article 20 of the Berne Convention for the Protection of Literary and Artistic Works, as regards Contracting Parties that are countries of the Union established by that Convention. This Treaty shall not have any connection with treaties other than the Berne Convention, nor shall it prejudice any rights and obligations under any other treaties.

(2) Nothing in this Treaty shall derogate from existing obligations that Contracting Parties have to each other under the Berne Convention for the Protection of Literary and Artistic Works.

(3) Hereinafter, "Berne Convention" shall refer to the Paris Act of July 24, 1971 of the Berne Convention for the Protection of Literary and Artistic Works.

(4) Contracting Parties shall comply with Articles 1 to 21 and the Appendix of the Berne Convention.[2]

ARTICLE 2
SCOPE OF COPYRIGHT PROTECTION

Copyright protection extends to expressions and not to ideas, procedures, methods of operation or mathematical concepts as such.

ARTICLE 3
APPLICATION OF ARTICLES 2 TO 6
OF THE BERNE CONVENTION

Contracting Parties shall apply mutatis mutandis the provisions of Articles 2 to 6 of the Berne Convention in respect of the protection provided for in this Treaty.[3]

ARTICLE 4
COMPUTER PROGRAMS

Computer programs are protected as literary works within the meaning of Article 2 of the Berne Convention. Such protection applies to computer programs, whatever may be the mode or form of their expression.[4]

ARTICLE 5
COMPILATIONS OF DATA (DATABASES)

Compilations of data or other material, in any form, which by reason of the selection or arrangement of their contents constitute intellectual creations, are protected as such. This protection does not extend to the data or the material itself and is without prejudice to any copyright subsisting in the data or material contained in the compilation.[5]

ARTICLE 6
RIGHT OF DISTRIBUTION

(1) Authors of literary and artistic works shall enjoy the exclusive right of authorizing the making available to the public of the original and copies of their works through sale or other transfer of ownership.

(2) Nothing in this Treaty shall affect the freedom of Contracting Parties to determine the conditions, if any, under which the exhaustion of the right in paragraph (1) applies after the first sale or other transfer of ownership of the original or a copy of the work with the authorization of the author.[6]

ARTICLE 7
RIGHT OF RENTAL

(1) Authors of

(i)   computer programs;
(ii) cinematographic works; and
(iii) works embodied in phonograms, as determined in the national law of
      Contracting Parties,

shall enjoy the exclusive right of authorizing commercial rental to the public of
the originals or copies of their works.

(2) Paragraph (1) shall not apply

(i)   in the case of computer programs, where the program itself is not the
      essential object of the rental; and
(ii) in the case of cinematographic works, unless such commercial rental
      has led to widespread copying of such works materially impairing the
      exclusive right of reproduction.

(3) Notwithstanding the provisions of paragraph (1), a Contracting Party that,
on April 15, 1994, had and continues to have in force a system of equitable remuneration of authors for the rental of copies of their works embodied in phonograms may maintain that system provided that the commercial rental of works
embodied in phonograms is not giving rise to the material impairment of the
exclusive right of reproduction of authors.[7, 8]

ARTICLE 8
RIGHT OF COMMUNICATION TO THE PUBLIC

Without prejudice to the provisions of Articles 11(1)(ii), 11bis(1)(i) and (ii),
11ter(1)(ii), 14(1)(ii) and 14bis(1) of the Berne Convention, authors of literary
and artistic works shall enjoy the exclusive right of authorizing any communication to the public of their works, by wire or wireless means, including the making
available to the public of their works in such a way that members of the public
may access these works from a place and at a time individually chosen by them.[9]

ARTICLE 9
DURATION OF THE PROTECTION
OF PHOTOGRAPHIC WORKS

In respect of photographic works, the Contracting Parties shall not apply the provisions of Article 7(4) of the Berne Convention.

ARTICLE 10
LIMITATIONS AND EXCEPTIONS

(1) Contracting Parties may, in their national legislation, provide for limitations

of or exceptions to the rights granted to authors of literary and artistic works under this Treaty in certain special cases that do not conflict with a normal exploitation of the work and do not unreasonably prejudice the legitimate interests of the author.

(2) Contracting Parties shall, when applying the Berne Convention, confine any limitations of or exceptions to rights provided for therein to certain special cases that do not conflict with a normal exploitation of the work and do not unreasonably prejudice the legitimate interests of the author.[10]

ARTICLE 11
OBLIGATIONS CONCERNING
TECHNOLOGICAL MEASURES

Contracting Parties shall provide adequate legal protection and effective legal remedies against the circumvention of effective technological measures that are used by authors in connection with the exercise of their rights under this Treaty or the Berne Convention and that restrict acts, in respect of their works, which are not authorized by the authors concerned or permitted by law.

ARTICLE 12
OBLIGATIONS CONCERNING
RIGHTS MANAGEMENT INFORMATION

(1) Contracting Parties shall provide adequate and effective legal remedies against any person knowingly performing any of the following acts knowing, or with respect to civil remedies having reasonable grounds to know, that it will induce, enable, facilitate or conceal an infringement of any right covered by this Treaty or the Berne Convention:

  (i) to remove or alter any electronic rights management information without authority;
  (ii) to distribute, import for distribution, broadcast or communicate to the public, without authority, works or copies of works knowing that electronic rights management information has been removed or altered without authority.

(2) As used in this Article, "rights management information" means information which identifies the work, the author of the work, the owner of any right in the work, or information about the terms and conditions of use of the work, and any numbers or codes that represent such information, when any of these items of information is attached to a copy of a work or appears in connection with the communication of a work to the public.[11]

ARTICLE 13
APPLICATION IN TIME

Contracting Parties shall apply the provisions of Article 18 of the Berne Convention to all protection provided for in this Treaty.

ARTICLE 14
PROVISIONS ON ENFORCEMENT OF RIGHTS

(1) Contracting Parties undertake to adopt, in accordance with their legal systems, the measures necessary to ensure the application of this Treaty.

(2) Contracting Parties shall ensure that enforcement procedures are available under their law so as to permit effective action against any act of infringement of rights covered by this Treaty, including expeditious remedies to prevent infringements and remedies which constitute a deterrent to further infringements.

ARTICLE 15
ASSEMBLY

(1)

(a) The Contracting Parties shall have an Assembly.
(b) Each Contracting Party shall be represented by one delegate who may be assisted by alternate delegates, advisors and experts.
(c) The expenses of each delegation shall be borne by the Contracting Party that has appointed the delegation. The Assembly may ask the World Intellectual Property Organization (hereinafter referred to as "WIPO") to grant financial assistance to facilitate the participation of delegations of Contracting Parties that are regarded as developing countries in conformity with the established practice of the General Assembly of the United Nations or that are countries in transition to a market economy.

(2)

(a) The Assembly shall deal with matters concerning the maintenance and development of this Treaty and the application and operation of this Treaty.
(b) The Assembly shall perform the function allocated to it under Article 17(2) in respect of the admission of certain intergovernmental organizations to become party to this Treaty.
(c) The Assembly shall decide the convocation of any diplomatic conference for the revision of this Treaty and give the necessary instructions to the Director General of WIPO for the preparation of such diplomatic conference.

(3)

(a) Each Contracting Party that is a State shall have one vote and shall vote only in its own name.

(b) Any Contracting Party that is an intergovernmental organization may participate in the vote, in place of its Member States, with a number of votes equal to the number of its Member States which are party to this Treaty. No such intergovernmental organization shall participate in the vote if any one of its Member States exercises its right to vote and vice versa.

(4) The Assembly shall meet in ordinary session once every two years upon convocation by the Director General of WIPO.

(5) The Assembly shall establish its own rules of procedure, including the convocation of extraordinary sessions, the requirements of a quorum and, subject to the provisions of this Treaty, the required majority for various kinds of decisions.

ARTICLE 16
INTERNATIONAL BUREAU

The International Bureau of WIPO shall perform the administrative tasks concerning the Treaty.

ARTICLE 17
ELIGIBILITY FOR BECOMING PARTY TO THE TREATY

(1) Any Member State of WIPO may become party to this Treaty.

(2) The Assembly may decide to admit any intergovernmental organization to become party to this Treaty which declares that it is competent in respect of, and has its own legislation binding on all its Member States on, matters covered by this Treaty and that it has been duly authorized, in accordance with its internal procedures, to become party to this Treaty.

(3) The European Community, having made the declaration referred to in the preceding paragraph in the Diplomatic Conference that has adopted this Treaty, may become party to this Treaty.

ARTICLE 18
RIGHTS AND OBLIGATIONS UNDER THE TREATY

Subject to any specific provisions to the contrary in this Treaty, each Contracting Party shall enjoy all of the rights and assume all of the obligations under this Treaty.

ARTICLE 19
SIGNATURE OF THE TREATY

This Treaty shall be open for signature until December 31, 1997, by any Member State of WIPO and by the European Community.

ARTICLE 20
ENTRY INTO FORCE OF THE TREATY

This Treaty shall enter into force three months after 30 instruments of ratification or accession by States have been deposited with the Director General of WIPO.

ARTICLE 21
EFFECTIVE DATE OF BECOMING PARTY TO THE TREATY

This Treaty shall bind:

(i)   the 30 States referred to in Article 20, from the date on which this Treaty has entered into force;

(ii)   each other State from the expiration of three months from the date on which the State has deposited its instrument with the Director General of WIPO;

(iii) the European Community, from the expiration of three months after the deposit of its instrument of ratification or accession if such instrument has been deposited after the entry into force of this Treaty according to Article 20, or, three months after the entry into force of this Treaty if such instrument has been deposited before the entry into force of this Treaty;

(iv) any other intergovernmental organization that is admitted to become party to this Treaty, from the expiration of three months after the deposit of its instrument of accession.

ARTICLE 22
NO RESERVATIONS TO THE TREATY

No reservation to this Treaty shall be admitted.

ARTICLE 23
DENUNCIATION OF THE TREATY

This Treaty may be denounced by any Contracting Party by notification addressed to the Director General of WIPO. Any denunciation shall take effect one year from the date on which the Director General of WIPO received the notification.

ARTICLE 24
LANGUAGES OF THE TREATY

(1) This Treaty is signed in a single original in English, Arabic, Chinese, French, Russian and Spanish languages, the versions in all these languages being equally authentic.

(2) An official text in any language other than those referred to in paragraph (1) shall be established by the Director General of WIPO on the request of an interested party, after consultation with all the interested parties. For the purposes of this paragraph, "interested party" means any Member State of WIPO whose official language, or one of whose official languages, is involved and the European Community, and any other intergovernmental organization that may become party to this Treaty, if one of its official languages is involved.

ARTICLE 25
DEPOSITARY

The Director General of WIPO is the depositary of this Treaty.

---

1. *Entry into force*: March 6, 2002. *Source*: International Bureau of WIPO. *Note:* The agreed statements of the Diplomatic Conference that adopted the Treaty (WIPO Diplomatic Conference on Certain Copyright and Neighboring Rights Questions) concerning certain provisions of the WCT are reproduced in endnotes below.

2. *Agreed statements concerning Article 1(4)*: The reproduction right, as set out in Article 9 of the Berne Convention, and the exceptions permitted thereunder, fully apply in the digital environment, in particular to the use of works in digital form. It is understood that the storage of a protected work in digital form in an electronic medium constitutes a reproduction within the meaning of Article 9 of the Berne Convention.

3. *Agreed statements concerning Article 3*: It is understood that in applying Article 3 of this Treaty, the expression "country of the Union" in Articles 2 to 6 of the Berne Convention will be read as if it were a reference to a Contracting Party to this Treaty, in the application of those Berne Articles in respect of protection provided for in this Treaty. It is also understood that the expression "country outside the Union" in those Articles in the Berne Convention will, in the same circumstances, be read as if it were a reference to a country that is not a Contracting Party to this Treaty, and that "this Convention" in Articles 2(8), 2*bis*(2), 3, 4 and 5 of the Berne Convention will be read as if it were a reference to the Berne Convention and this Treaty. Finally, it is understood that a reference in Articles 3 to 6 of the Berne Convention to a "national of one of the countries of the Union" will, when these Articles are applied to this Treaty, mean, in regard to an intergovernmental organization that is a Contracting Party to this Treaty, a national of one of the countries that is member of that organization.

4. *Agreed statements concerning Article 4*: The scope of protection for computer programs under Article 4 of this Treaty, read with Article 2, is consistent with Article 2 of the Berne Convention and on a par with the relevant provisions of the TRIPS Agreement.

5. *Agreed statements concerning Article 5*: The scope of protection for compilations of data (databases) under Article 5 of this Treaty, read with Article 2, is consistent with Article 2 of the Berne Convention and on a par with the relevant provisions of the TRIPS Agreement.

6. *Agreed statements concerning Articles 6 and 7*: As used in these Articles, the expressions "copies" and "original and copies," being subject to the right of distribution and the right of rental under the said Articles, refer exclusively to fixed copies that can be put into circulation as tangible objects.

7. *Agreed statements concerning Articles 6 and 7*: As used in these Articles, the expressions "copies" and "original and copies," being subject to the right of distribution and the right of rental under the said Articles, refer exclusively to fixed copies that can be put into circulation as tangible objects.

8. *Agreed statements concerning Article 7*: It is understood that the obligation under Article 7(1) does not require a Contracting Party to provide an exclusive right of commercial rental to authors who, under that Contracting Party's law, are not granted rights in respect of phonograms. It is understood that this obligation is consistent with Article 14(4) of the TRIPS Agreement.

9. *Agreed statements concerning Article 8*: It is understood that the mere provision of physical facilities for enabling or making a communication does not in itself amount to communication within the meaning of this Treaty or the Berne Convention. It is further understood that nothing in Article 8 precludes a Contracting Party from applying Article 11*bis*(2) .

10. *Agreed statement concerning Article 10*: It is understood that the provisions of Article 10 permit Contracting Parties to carry forward and appropriately extend into the digital environment limitations and exceptions in their national laws which have been considered acceptable under the Berne Convention. Similarly, these provisions should be understood to permit Contracting Parties to devise new exceptions and limitations that are appropriate in the digital network environment. It is also understood that Article 10(2) neither reduces nor extends the scope of applicability of the limitations and exceptions permitted by the Berne Convention.

11. *Agreed statements concerning Article 12*: It is understood that the reference to "infringement of any right covered by this Treaty or the Berne Convention" includes both exclusive rights and rights of remuneration.

It is further understood that Contracting Parties will not rely on this Article to devise or implement rights management systems that would have the effect of imposing formalities which are not permitted under the Berne Convention or this Treaty, prohibiting the free movement of goods or impeding the enjoyment of rights under this Treaty.

APPENDIX 11-3

Fine Art License

DRAFT

FINE ART LICENSE

I. PLEASE PROVIDE THE FOLLOWING INFORMATION

- Title of Protected Work:
- Copyright registration number of Protected Work:
- Copyright Proprietor of Protected Work:
- Author of Protected Work (if different from directly above):
- Prospective title of your Work:
- Your Work shall be (check one):
  - ____ a single piece of fine art (*e.g.,* painting, sculpture, drawing, photograph)
  - ____ a signed and numbered limited edition fine print or sculpture multiple of 100 or fewer
  - ____ same as directly above in an edition size of 500 or fewer (but over 100)

II. TERMS AND CONDITIONS:

1. The Fine Art License Fee includes:

(a) a "Floor Amount" of
   - (i) $1,000 if your Work is to be a single piece of fine art;
   - (ii) $5,000 if your Work is to be a signed and numbered limited edition fine print or sculpture multiple or 100 or fewer; or
   - (iii) $10,000 if your Work is to be a signed and numbered limited edition fine print or sculpture multiple of 500 or fewer but over 100; plus

(b) Eight (8%) Percent of all revenues, if any, earned on the sale or lease of your Work, in excess of your recoupment of the Floor Amount ("Overage").

2. By forwarding this document to ARS along with payment to ARS of the applicable Floor Amount, you are hereby granted the right to (i) incorporate the Protected Work, in whole or in part, into your Work; (ii) publicly display your Work; (iii) advertise and promote your Work in all media; and (iv) sell or lease your Work. Your expression of your Work is hereby limited to one of the three (3) categories set forth in Paragraph I (a) above. All rights in and to, and all uses

of, the Protected Work not granted to you in this document are, as between you and the copyright proprietor, reserved to the copyright proprietor.

3. You hereby waive the right to and agree not to: (i) create any derivative works based on your Work; and (ii) initiate any lawsuit for copyright infringement of your Work, it being understood that such right vests solely in the copyright proprietor of the Protected Work.

4. You hereby agree to make timely payment(s) and applicable payments of any Overage through ARS to the copyright proprietor of the Protected Work. ARS or its agent may examine all portions of your books and records from time to time and at various times that relate to the sale or lease of your Work, in order to ensure your compliance with this Fine Art License. Failure by you to pay the full Fine Art License Fee shall result in liquidated damages of triple the amount found to be due and owing to the copyright proprietor of the Protected Work, plus all costs and expenses of the audit.

5. You agree to accord credit by name to the author of the Protected Work in the title of your Work (such as for example, "[Title of your Work], based on a painting by [name of author of the protected Work]," unless such author has elected not to receive such credit by checking the space provided in Paragraph 6 below.

6. By placing a check in the following space _____ I elect not to receive credit in connection with your Work.

ACCEPTED AND AGREED TO:

_____
Your signature

_____
Print your name and address and
phone number

_____
Author of Protected Work

12

Moral Rights

he enactment of the federal Visual Artists Rights Act (VARA)[1] on December 1, 1990, seemed to represent a victory for artistic principle, particularly when viewed in the historical context of U.S. copyright doctrine, which has consistently subordinated the sensibilities of the artist to the advancement of commerce.

However, the flurry of VARA cases since its enactment has only served to highlight its exceedingly narrow scope, its failure to comport with the moral rights requirements of the Berne Convention, and a general reluctance on the part of U.S. courts to interpret the statute so as to accord visual artists the full protections of what meager rights VARA does provide.

Before exploring VARA's substantial limitations, however, it seems appropriate to place moral rights in historical context.

ORIGINS

Most European nations and some Latin American nations have long recognized a cluster of rights unique and personal to the author of a work of art that are unrelated to the artist's pecuniary interests. These rights arise from the belief that an artist, in the process of creation, injects some of his spirit into the art and that, consequently, the artist's personality, as well as the integrity of the work, should be protected and preserved.[2] Known as moral rights or the *droit moral* and subscribed to by the member nations of the Berne Convention,[3] including the United States, that cluster of rights is the focus of this chapter.

Some commentators trace some of the beginnings of the *droit moral* to the philosophy of individualism that accompanied the French Revolution and to doctrines in civil-law nations that developed slowly in the nineteenth century and more rapidly in the twentieth century.[4] As the *droit moral* is considered to have originated in France and as that country remains its foremost champion,[5] the following discussion enumerating the categories of the *droit moral* focuses primarily, though not exclusively, on the French conception of those rights.

CATEGORIES OF MORAL RIGHTS

The following cluster of rights is, under French law, retained by the author of a work even after the work has entered the stream of public commerce.

*Right of Disclosure (*Droit de Divulgation*)*

The recognition that public disclosure of a work affects an artist's reputation provided a basis for the *droit de divulgation* (the right of disclosure)—that is, the artist has the sole prerogative to determine when and how to make his work public.[6] That right—found not only in France but in Germany, Japan, Spain, and Switzerland, among other countries as well[7]—received its most famous judicial endorsement at the turn of the twentieth century. In the case of *Whistler v. Eden,* the Paris Court of Appeals excused the artist James Abbott McNeill Whistler, who had been commissioned to paint a portrait of the wife of Lord Eden, from specific performance. Apparently, a dispute had arisen as to payment, whereupon Whistler, claiming to be dissatisfied with the work, painted out Lady Eden's head, painted in another head, and refused to deliver the portrait. When Lord Eden sued for breach of contract, Whistler, although required to pay damages for nonperformance, was not compelled to deliver the portrait. The decision reflects the French view that even where the right of disclosure may impair contractual obligations, an artist retains the absolute right to determine when to disclose his work to the public.

In addition to the aforementioned countries, Brazil recognizes an author's right to withhold publication of his work.[8]

*Right to Withdraw from Publication or to Make Modifications (*Droit de Retrait ou de Repentir*)*

Recognized in, among other countries, Germany, Spain, Belgium, Italy and Brazil,[9] as well in France, the *droit de retrait ou de repentir* permits an artist to withdraw a work's circulation *(droit de retrait)* or to modify a work *(droit de repentir),* even if exploitation rights in the work have been transferred to a third party, provided certain conditions are fulfilled. Under French law, the artist may exercise this right only if he indemnifies the third-party transferee beforehand for any damages the modification or withdrawal of the work would cause the transferee. Furthermore, if, after having exercised his right to modify the work or withdraw it from publication, the artist again elects to have it published, he must first offer his rights of exploitation to the original third-party transferee—and under the terms as originally agreed upon.[10] Moreover, French case law, which is stringent, provides that the artist's motive in exercising this particular right must be purely artistic, intellectual, or moral.[11]

*Right of Authorship (*Droit à la Paternité*)*

Over the course of time, the *droit à la paternité* has expanded into three rights.[12] The first of those rights permits an artist to be recognized by name as the author of his work or, if the artist wishes, to publish anonymously or pseudonymously. In France, the right has been broadly interpreted, so that an artist's name must appear on all copies of a work, as well as on the original piece, and on all publicity materials preceding or accompanying its sale, even if the author has contracted otherwise. A reproduction of a painting, sculpture, or architectural model must bear the name of the original artist. In addition, all publicity materials preceding or accompanying the sale of a work of art—be it an original, a copy, or a reproduction—must bear the name of the original artist, regardless of any contractual arrangements to the contrary. The second of the rights of authorship confers on the artist the right to prevent his work from being attributed to someone else. With the third right of authorship, the artist may prevent the use of his name on works that he did not, in fact, create. That right has been applied in at least two types of instances: First, an artist (or an heir) may remove the artist's name from distorted editions of the work, and, second, the artist may protest the use without permission of his name in advertisements.

According to at least one commentator,[13] *droit à la paternité* may be the least problematic of the moral rights to enforce. Perhaps for that reason, the right of paternity is one of the two moral rights reflected in the Berne Convention and one of the two such rights primarily protected by most of the legal systems acknowledging the *droit moral* today, the other being the right of integrity.

*Right of Integrity (*Droit au Respect de l'Oeuvre*)*

Considered by all scholars to be the most essential prerogative among moral rights,[14] the right of integrity empowers the artist, even after title to a work is transferred, affirmatively to prevent any tampering with it. Recognized in France as early as 1874, the right evolved rapidly during the twentieth century and, along with the right of paternity, is the moral right most frequently protected in those nations recognizing the doctrine of *droit moral*. As with the right of paternity, the right of integrity is mandated by the Berne Convention.[15]

The right to protect a work against tampering does not necessarily include protection against its complete destruction. The right against destruction, for example, "is neither expressly mentioned in [the Berne Convention] nor in the official comments."[16] In the United States under VARA, however, an author of a work of visual art may "prevent any destruction of a work of a recognized stature."[17]

CHARACTERISTICS OF MORAL RIGHTS ABROAD

To varying degrees, depending on the laws of a particular jurisdiction, moral rights abroad may be characterized as

(1) personal,
(2) perpetual, and
(3) inviolable and unassignable.[18]

The Personal Right

French law acknowledges that the *droit moral* attaches to the author of a work, rather than to the work itself, and, therefore, remains vested in the artist even after the work is transferred.[19] To claim moral rights in France, the author of a work must be a natural person, as opposed to a legal entity.[20] Similarly, in Japan[21] and Mexico,[22] the moral rights of the author are exclusively personal to the author. That proviso, however, is not uniform. Portuguese law, for example, provides that the moral right to a work that is injected into the public domain attaches to the state, which, in turn, exercises the right through cultural institutions.[23]

The Perpetual Right

French law,[24] Mexican law,[25] and Nigerian law[26] clearly provide that the *droit moral* is perpetual. Although that right may contradict the tenet that the *droit moral* vests solely in the person of the creator of the work, such laws distinguish between the moral right itself and the right to exercise it. Thus, the artist's heirs inherit only the right to exercise the prerogative, not the prerogative itself. Moreover, certain moral rights do, indeed, expire at the author's death. Such rights include (in France) the right to withdraw a work from publication and the right to make modifications in it. Generally, the rights of authorship and of integrity survive the author. More problematical is the right of disclosure. Although French law provides that the right is inheritable, a troublesome reality is that the heirs may misuse the right. Thus, French law further provides that in a case of serious misuse the courts can mandate appropriate measures, including administering the right themselves.

The Inviolable and Unassignable Right

French law pronounces the *droit moral* to be inviolable.[27] Not only may an artist not waive the prerogative, but the artist may not transfer the right to a third party, even when that party has become the owner of the material object and the transferee of exploitative rights in it. In reality, however, contractual clauses requiring a transfer of the *droit moral* as a condition of employment are often enforced by the French courts, and the statutory pronouncement of inviolability is checkered with exceptions. The Berne Convention, in mandating recognition by member nations of certain moral rights,[28] disregards the principle of assignability and does not prohibit waivability,[29] so the 165 member nations have developed various approaches to the two principles. For example, in the United Kingdom,[30] Canada,[31] and the Netherlands,[32] moral rights are not assignable, but they are waivable under certain circumstances. In Mexico,[33] such rights are neither waivable nor assignable. In Australia[34] and Germany,[35] moral rights are waivable to some extent. In Singapore,[36] they are assignable by written instrument, whereas in Japan,[37] Morocco,[38] and Nigeria,[39] they are not assignable at all.

DROIT MORAL AND THE UNITED STATES

As noted in chapter 11, the United States on March 1, 1989, acceded to the Berne Convention and accepted, in principle, the convention's concept of moral rights as embodied and reproduced in pertinent part in its article 6*bis*:

> Independently of the author's economic rights, and even after the transfer of said rights, the author shall have the right to claim authorship of the work and to object to any distortion, mutilation, or other modification of, or other derogatory action in relation to, the said work, which shall be prejudicial to his honor or reputation.[40]

Not until December 1, 1990, however, did American copyright law see the enactment of VARA,[41] legislation that amended the Copyright Act of 1976 to provide visual artists with the moral rights of attribution and integrity. (The act is reproduced in the statutory appendix at the end of volume 3.)

The enactment of VARA, which took effect on June 1, 1991, while a step in the right direction, falls grievously short, as will become apparent, of the protections for the artist that are envisioned in the Berne Convention's article 6*bis*.

Early Attitudes

Congress passed the first American copyright act in 1790. The principles of that law were derived from England's Statute of Anne, which was viewed as a three-way compromise[42] among the interests of publishers, authors, and censors. Historically, in the common-law countries of both the United States and Britain, statutory copyright protection was restricted to property interests conferred by the statute on the copyright owner, who is not necessarily the author.

That protection is in contrast to many civil-law nations whose statutes, in addition to recognizing property rights of copyright holders, protected rights of personality (moral rights) that initially vested in the works' authors. The recognition of an author's moral rights highlighted a fundamental distinction between civil-law nations and common-law nations in their perception of copyright. Civil-law nations view the author as the beneficiary of copyright, whereas common-law nations view society as the ultimate beneficiary, with copyright protection constituting a bundle of economic inducements to encourage the author to create for the benefit of the public.[43] Moral rights did exist in the United States before their federal codification in VARA. The courts, recognizing that the lack of statutory protection gave rise to injustice in particular situations, sought to acknowledge the existence of at least certain moral rights under various theories of copyright, unfair competition, breach of contract, defamation, and invasion of privacy. Eventually, a handful of states enacted limited moral rights statutes. A discussion of early attitudes in the United States toward moral rights as reflected by judicial law, state statute, and alternative approaches to preserve the rights of injured parties follows.

For most of the twentieth century, the judicial climate was not particularly hospitable to moral rights. In the New York case of *Crimi v. Rutgers Presby-terian Church*,[44] for example, the plaintiff, the artist Alfred Crimi, had in 1937 won a competition sponsored by the defendant to design and execute a mural to be placed on a rear wall of the church. A contract was drawn by the parties' attorneys, and, as per the contract, the work was completed on time, the agreed-on price was paid in full, the work was copyrighted, and the copyright was assigned to the church. As the years passed, a number of parishioners objected to some of the content of the mural, and in 1946, when the church was redecorated, the mural was painted over without first giving notice to the artist. When he learned of the overpainting, the artist brought an action for equitable relief, seeking to compel the church to remove the paint covering the mural or to permit him to remove the mural at the church's expense or to pay money damages to the artist. He alleged that the "artist has a continued limited proprietary interest in his work after its sale, to the extent reasonably necessary to the protection of his honor and reputation as an artist"[45] and that within that protection is the right of the work's continued existence without destruction, alteration, mutilation, or obliteration.[46]

The court noted that the Berne Convention upheld the doctrine of *droit moral* for its member nations but held that the United States was not a signatory to the Berne Convention. To further bolster its holding that no rights in the mural were reserved by the artist and that all right, title, and interest in the mural were sold and transferred to the church, the court cited both treatise and case law affirming that the concept of moral rights, although recognized and developed in the civil-law countries, has not yet received acceptance in the laws of the United States.[47]

Backdoor Recognition of Moral Rights

Despite the general hostility on the part of U.S. courts with regard to moral rights through most of the twentieth century, such rights did not go totally unrecognized by the courts. For example, in the 1952 case of *Granz v. Harris*,[48] both a right of attribution and a right of integrity, by way of breach of contract, were fashioned on behalf of an aggrieved concert-promoter with respect to two seventy-eight-RPM master records.

In the 1976 case of *Gilliam v. American Broadcasting Cos.*[49] an author's right of integrity was recognized on theories of copyright infringement and a violation of section 43(a) of the Lanham Act. ABC was enjoined at the direction of the Second Circuit from broadcasting edited versions of three separate programs of a comedy series, *Monty Python's Flying Circus*, originally written and performed by the plaintiffs—a group of mainly British writers and performers known as Monty Python—for broadcast by the British Broadcasting Corporation. (It should be noted, however, that more than thirty years later, and subsequent to U.S. enactment of federal moral rights legislation, the U.S. Supreme Court's *Dastar Corp. v. Twentieth Century Fox Film Corp.*[50] clarified that once a work under copyright protection has passed into the public domain, anyone can make any use of such a work, with or without attribution to the author. *Dastar* is touched upon at the close of this chapter.)

A few years subsequent to *Gilliam*, the Seventh Circuit, in *WGN Continental Broadcasting Co. v. United Video, Inc.*,[51] recognized a right of integrity, again by way of finding copyright infringement, where United Video, the cable television distributor of superstation WGN's evening news show, deleted WGN's teletext of news stories and replaced it with a Dow Jones teletext of business news.

In *Fisher v. Star Co.*,[52] a theory of unfair competition enabled the creator of the famous "Mutt and Jeff" cartoon characters to restrain a publisher from publishing, without his consent, other cartoons designated as "Mutt and Jeff" that were drawn by another cartoonist. The theory was that unauthorized and perhaps inferior depictions of the cartoon characters would deceive the public and reduce the characters' financial value to the creator.

In *Clevenger v. Baker Voorhis & Co.*,[53] an author who was both a lawyer and a writer prevailed on a claim of defamation when he alleged that a publisher had impaired his reputation by publishing a revised, error-ridden edition of his book bearing his name on the title page without indicating that he had not done the revision.

By bringing suit under a privacy statute, a marine painter, in *Neyland v. Home Pattern Co.*,[54] was able to prevent a magazine publisher from selling a crude reproduction of one of his paintings as a pattern for embroidered sofa and pillow cushions. The suit was for the unauthorized use of the artist's name for purposes of trade.

No Legislation Yields No Protection

In most circumstances, however, the aggrieved artist was left without relief. One notable incident occurred in 1980. In 1975, the Bank of Tokyo Trust Company in New York City commissioned the renowned artist Isamu Noguchi to create a sculpture for its United States headquarters near Wall Street. Designed particularly for the space, the sculpture was a seventeen-foot-long rhomboid suspended point downward from the ceiling of the lobby. Five years later, the bank decided to remove the massive sculpture from the lobby and, without notifying the artist, ordered the work to be cut up, removed,[55] and banished to storage, thus effectively destroying the work. Noguchi viewed that as an act of "vandalism and very reactionary." Others in the New York arts community were similarly outraged. However, since Noguchi had transferred all his rights in the sculpture to the bank, then-current law provided him with no relief. The bank, after all, was simply exercising a traditional property right, the right to destroy.[56]

Noguchi's plight was not an isolated case. In 1979, a change of ownership at the Samoset Resort in Rockport, Maine, brought about the dismantling of a twenty-five-foot-high sculpture by the artist Bernard Langlais that had been installed at the resort's entrance five years earlier. The dismantling, done by means of a chain saw, was accomplished without informing Langlais's widow in advance. Adding insult to injury, the resort left the fragments of the dismantled sculpture uncovered in a heap throughout a summer and an autumn at the rear of the resort's main entrance.[57]

In still another instance, two stone Art Deco sculptures, embedded in the facade of the Bonwit Teller building in New York City since the building's construction in 1928, were smashed by jackhammers in 1980 in the course of razing the building to make way for Trump Tower. The Metropolitan Museum of Art had been interested in acquiring the pieces, and the developer was willing to donate them to the museum if the removal costs were not unreasonable. In the end, although the removal costs were not prohibitive, the developer calculated that the costs in terms of delay would be too great. Accordingly, the pieces were destroyed, much to the surprise and dismay of the museum and others who had sought the sculptures' safekeeping.[58]

The publicity generated by those instances and others stoked the fires of public awareness of and sympathy for the plight of the artist. Thus, in 1979, the state of California pioneered moral rights legislation in the United States with the enactment of the California Art Preservation Act (discussed later in this chapter). However, even in 1982, an artist in New York could not seek redress for violation of a moral right by looking to New York legislation; rather, the artist was compelled to consider other theories.

For example, in *Stella v. Mazoh*,[59] the artist Frank Stella had to resort to a stolen-property theory to recover two rain-damaged canvases he had intended to discard but that had disappeared from the landing outside his studio, only to turn up for sale in the defendant's art gallery. Stella's purpose in bringing suit was to prevent the damaged paintings from being represented as his work, thereby harming his reputation as an artist. The parties ultimately settled the case out of court, and Stella recovered and destroyed the paintings. The next year, 1983, New York enacted a moral rights statute that would have been responsive to Stella's plight.

State Moral Rights Legislation

Starting with California in 1979 and up to 1990, several states enacted limited moral rights legislation generally restricted to versions of paternity and integrity rights. Understandably, no state adopted the moral right of withdrawal or modification by an artist once the artist's work entered the stream of commerce. To permit such a right to exist in the United States would wreak havoc with established courses of trade and with such bodies of law as the Uniform Commercial Code. The following is a state-by-state survey of the moral rights legislation enacted before the passage of the Visual Artists Rights Act of 1990, which amended the Copyright Act of 1976 and is discussed later in this chapter.

California's Moral Rights Legislation

California was the first state in the nation to enact moral rights legislation. Adopted in 1979, the California Art Preservation Act[60] secures rights of paternity and integrity for the artist. It prohibits intentional "defacement, mutilation, alteration, or destruction"[61] of "fine art" and empowers the artist to claim authorship or "for just and valid reason"[62] (which is not defined) to disclaim authorship. "Fine art" includes original paintings, sculpture, drawings, and works of art in glass "of recognized quality."[63] The quality is determined by the trier of fact. Remedies include injunctive relief, actual damages, punitive damages, and reasonable attorney and expert witness fees. Rights exist for the life of the artist plus fifty years and may be exercised by the artist's heir, legatee, or personal representative. The rights may be waived only by an express, signed, written instrument. The artist must enforce his rights within one year of the discovery of the act complained of or three years after the act, whichever is later. A building owner seeking to remove a work of fine art that can be removed without being mutilated is subject to liability unless the owner attempts to notify the artist of his intention and furnishes the artist an opportunity to remove the work. If a work cannot be removed without being damaged or destroyed, moral rights are waived unless the artist has reserved them in writing.

In addition, the California Cultural and Artistic Creations Preservation Act,[64] enacted in 1982, permits certain public and charitable institutions to enforce some of the rights granted to artists under the Art Preservation Act if the works of fine art are "of recognized quality and of substantial public interest."[65]

California's approach to *droit moral* legislation is to protect both the artist's reputation and the public interest in preserving the integrity of cultural and artistic creations. Moreover, California's legislation declares that fine art is an expression of the artist's personality; accordingly, its destruction or alteration is prohibited, whether the art is in the public eye or not; the art need only be "of recognized quality."

New York's Artists Authorship Rights Act[66]

New York was the second state in the nation to adopt moral rights legislation. Like the California statute, New York's law, enacted in 1983, grants artists the right of paternity—that is, the artist may claim authorship or "for just and valid reason"[67] disclaim authorship. "Just and valid reason" includes unauthorized alteration, defacement, mutilation, or other modification when damage to the artist's reputation has resulted or is reasonably likely to result. However, unlike the California statute, New York's legislation grants a right of integrity that merely prevents public display of a work of fine art that is "altered, defaced, mutilated or modified"[68] if the artwork is displayed as being the work of the artist and damage to the artist's reputation is reasonably likely to result.

The thrust of the New York statute is the preservation of the artist's reputation. Accordingly, the statute applies solely to works on public display on the assumption that an artist's reputation cannot be damaged by acts occurring in private. Moreover, New York's law does not forbid the total destruction of a work; apparently, an artist's reputation cannot be demeaned by a work that has ceased to exist. Works of fine art include, without limitation, paintings, sculpture, drawings, works of graphic art, prints, and, for purposes of the *droit moral* statute only, limited-edition multiples of not more than 300 copies. Remedies include legal and injunctive relief. The artist must enforce his rights within one year following discovery of the act complained of or three years after, whichever is later.

MASSACHUSETTS' MORAL RIGHTS STATUTE[69]

Enacted in 1984, the Massachusetts Moral Rights Statute is based on the California legislation, granting the rights of paternity and integrity. However, the Massachusetts statute differs from California's law in a number of details, including the following: In Massachusetts, the forbidden intentional defacement also includes defacement by gross negligence. "Fine art" is broadly defined to include, without limitation, paintings, prints, drawings, sculpture, craft objects, photographs, audiotapes and videotapes, films, and holograms "of recognized quality"[70] as determined by the court (not by the trier of fact). Remedies available to artists and certain artists' organizations include injunctive and declaratory relief, actual damages, and attorney and expert witness fees. Rights are for the artist's life plus fifty years and are exercisable by the artist's heir, legatee, or personal representative or by the state attorney general if the artist is deceased and the work of art is in public view. Rights may be waived by an express, signed, written instrument referring to the specific work concerned. Rights must be enforced within one year of the discovery of the act complained of or two years after, whichever is later. If a work of fine art can be removed from a building without being mutilated, the statute's prohibitions against defacement apply unless the building owner notifies the artist of his intention and provides the artist with an opportunity to remove the work. If a work cannot be removed without sustaining substantial damage, the statute's prohibitions against defacement are suspended unless the building owner has signed and recorded a written obligation.

MAINE'S MORAL RIGHTS STATUTE[71]

In 1985, Maine enacted a moral rights statute based on the New York model. The paternity right and the right of integrity are substantially similar to those of New York's statute. Works of "fine art" include, without limitation, paintings, drawings, prints, photographic prints, or limited-edition sculpture of no more than 300 copies. Both remedies and the time frame within which an action must be brought are modeled on the New York statute.

LOUISIANA'S ARTISTS' AUTHORSHIP RIGHTS ACT[72]

Signed into law in 1986, the Louisiana statute, although modeled on New York's legislation, has at least one noteworthy difference. As under New York law, the artist retains the right to claim authorship of his work of fine art and to disclaim authorship for just and valid reason. Louisiana's definition of "just and valid reason" is similar to New York's definition. However, unlike New York's law, Louisiana's right of integrity prohibits the unauthorized, knowing, public display of a work of fine art or its reproduction in an "altered, defaced, mutilated, or modified form"[73] or the unauthorized public display of a work attributed to the artist under circumstances reasonably likely to result in damage to the artist's reputation. Under the Louisiana statute, it is unclear whether the artist has to prove damage to his reputation if a work is subjected to unauthorized public display in a changed form; if the artist does not have to prove damage to his reputation, the burden of sustaining a claim under the statute is considerably lighter than if the artist does have to prove damage to his reputation. Works of "fine art" include, without limitation, paintings, drawings, prints, photographic prints, and limited-edition sculpture of no more than 300 copies. Both remedies and the time frame within which an action must be brought are modeled on the New York statute.

NEW JERSEY'S ARTISTS' RIGHTS ACT[74]

In 1986, New Jersey enacted moral rights legislation similar to that enacted in Maine and New York.

PENNSYLVANIA'S FINE ARTS PRESERVATION ACT[75]

Enacted late in 1986, Pennsylvania's statute is based on the California legislation, with its grant of paternity and integrity rights, but the Pennsylvania law applies only to works "displayed in a place . . . accessible to the public."[76] Artists' remedies include injunctive relief, actual damages, punitive damages (payable to a charitable or educational organization), and attorney and expert witness fees. Rights exist for fifty years after the artist's death and are exercisable by the artist's heir, legatee, or personal representative. Rights may be waived by an express, signed, written instrument. The artist must enforce his rights within one year after the discovery of the violation complained of or three years after the violation, whichever is later. In addition to specifically addressing the removal of works of fine art from buildings, the statute exempts from liability those building owners who alter or destroy works in the course of removing them from a building in "emergency situations."[77]

New Mexico's Act Relating to Fine Art in Public Buildings[78]

Effective June 19, 1987, the New Mexico act follows the California approach and uses language similar to that in the Massachusetts law but limits certain coverage to art in "public buildings." Paternity and integrity rights are granted. The forbidden intentional defacement also includes defacement by gross negligence. To be protected under the statute, the art must be "fine art" in "public view."[79] "Fine art" includes paintings, prints, drawings, sculpture, crafts objects, photographs, audiotapes and videotapes, films, and holograms "of recognized quality." "Public view" means on the exterior or the interior of a "public building"—that is, a building owned by the state or a political subdivision. The artist may claim "credit" or "for just and valid reason"[80] may disclaim authorship. Rights may be waived by an express, signed, written instrument referring to the particular work involved. No specific period of limitation is included in the act.

Rhode Island's Artists' Rights Act[81]

Enacted in 1987, Rhode Island's legislation follows the statutory approach of Maine, New Jersey, and New York. It prohibits the unauthorized knowing display in a public place of a work of "fine art" in an altered, defaced, mutilated, or modified form under circumstances in which it would reasonably be regarded as being the work of the artist. However, the New York requirement that damage to the artist's reputation be reasonably likely to result from the display is not included in the Rhode Island act. "Fine art" includes, without limitation, paintings, drawings, prints, photographic prints, and limited-edition sculpture of no more than 300 copies. The artist may claim authorship or "for just and valid reason"[82] disclaim authorship. "Just and valid reason" is defined as it is in the New York law. Provisions regarding remedies and time periods during which rights must be enforced are substantially similar to those in the New York law. As in the New York law, no provision forbids the destruction of a work.

Connecticut's Art Preservation and Artists' Rights Statute

In 1988, Connecticut enacted moral rights legislation modeled after the Pennsylvania act. The statute provides a more detailed definition of what qualifies as a "work of fine art" than that contained in the Pennsylvania act, and specifically limits claims in the case of molds or photographic negatives to those with a value of at least $2,500.[83] With regard to the right of integrity, the statute explicitly limits the right to cases of "intentional" acts of "physical defacement or alteration." Negligent alteration is not covered, nor is destruction.[84] Punitive damages are left within the courts' discretion and do not require payment to a charitable or educational organization. The Connecticut statute purports to recognize these rights in addition to those under VARA, stating that these rights "shall exist in addition to any other rights . . . applicable on or after October 1, 1988."[85] Unlike the Pennsylvania statute, the Connecticut statute does not address removal of art from a building in "emergency situations"; rather, it states that where a work of fine art cannot be removed from a building without "substantial physical deface- ment or alteration," the statutory rights and duties shall be deemed waived un- less expressly reserved in a writing signed by the building owner.[86]

NEVADA'S STATUTE

In 1989, as part of its statute governing Miscellaneous Trade Regulations and Prohibited Acts,[87] Nevada, like New York, enacted moral rights legislation lim- ited to works of art existing in not more than 300 copies.[88] The right of paternity is similar to other state statutes,[89] but the right of integrity applies only to work published or publicly displayed in a defaced, mutilated, or altered form where damage to the artist's reputation is reasonably foreseeable. However, the right of integrity applies to a reproduction of an artist's work as well as to the original work itself. Excluded from "alteration" are changes arising either from the pas- sage of time or from the nature of the materials themselves, unless the alteration is the result of negligent conservation.[90] There is a waiver provision similar to that found in the New York statute.

MORAL RIGHTS STATUTES FOR PUBLIC ART COMMISSIONS

UTAH
Adopted in 1985, the Utah Percent-for-Art statute[91] grants a full right of pater- nity for works created by artists working on commission in the state's public art program. The statute also grants such artists a right of first refusal if the state decides to sell the commissioned work.

GEORGIA
Georgia's statute[92] pertains to artists who have been commissioned to create art for state buildings. The statute grants the artist the right to claim authorship, the right to reproduce the work of art unless limited by the commissioning contract, and, if provided by the written contract, the right to receive a resale royalty if the work of art is subsequently sold by the state to a third party other than as part of the sale of the building in which the work of art is located.

MONTANA
Montana's statute[93] contains a provision that grants the artist the right to claim authorship for works of art created for state office buildings.

SOUTH DAKOTA
South Dakota's statute[94] accords to artists rights of attribution and rights of in- tegrity with respect to works acquired by the state for state buildings, as well as,

under certain circumstances, post-mortem moral rights for twenty years and the right to a resale royalty.

PUERTO RICO

The moral rights statute of Puerto Rico[95] accords moral rights of paternity and integrity (including post-mortem rights for fifty years) to the author of a literary, scientific and/or musical work, as well as to the author of an artistic work.

Judicial Scrutiny of State Legislation

WOJNAROWICZ V. AMERICAN FAMILY ASSOCIATION

During the 1980s and the early 1990s, a small number of state moral rights statutes were tested by case law. The 1990 case of *Wojnarowicz v. American Family Association*,[96] for one, subjected New York's legislation to particularly rigid scrutiny. The plaintiff was the late David Wojnarowicz, a controversial multimedia artist who frequently depicted, by means of sexually explicit works, the failure of both the federal government and the public to confront the AIDS epidemic in a constructive way. Wojnarowicz's artwork has received a measure of critical acclaim and has been featured in a number of museums and gallery exhibitions. His works have also been the focus of public debate concerning government funding of nontraditional art.

From January 23, 1990, through March 4, 1990, the University Galleries at Illinois State University presented a comprehensive exhibition of Wojnarowicz's's work entitled "Tongues of Flame" and published a 128-page catalog containing, among other items, more than sixty reproductions of his work. The National Endowment for the Arts awarded the University Galleries $15,000 to help fund the exhibit and the catalog. The artist owned the copyrights to all the works displayed in the exhibit and to all the reproductions of his work in the catalog.

On or about April 12, 1990, the American Family Association—a nonprofit Mississippi corporation with more than 60,000 members and about 500 local chapters nationwide, including several in the state of New York—and its executive director, Donald Wildmon, published and distributed a pamphlet to members of Congress, Christian leaders, Christian radio stations, and newspapers throughout the United States in an effort to halt the public funding by the National Endowment for the Arts of artworks such as those by Wojnarowicz.

Without the artist's authorization, Wildmon photographically copied fourteen fragments of the artist's work believed to be most offensive to the public and reproduced those fragments in the American Family Association pamphlet; eleven of the images depicted explicit sexual acts; the other three images portrayed Christ with a hypodermic needle inserted in his arm, an African purification ritual, and two men dancing together.

Wildmon wrote the text of the pamphlet, entitled *Your Tax Dollars Helped Pay for These "Works of Art."* The pamphlet said the photographs appearing in it "were part of the David Wajnarowicz [sic] 'Tongues of Flame' exhibit catalog."[97]

The pamphlet's envelope, which also indicated that the photographs inside were taken from the catalog of the "Tongues of Flame" exhibit, was marked "Caution—Contains Extremely Offensive Material."[98]

Wojnarowicz filed suit, alleging, among other claims, violation of the New York Artists Authorship Rights Act. In reply, the defendants mounted a battery of attacks against the New York statute. The New York federal district court found that the statute withstood the defendants' massive assault, thus rendering the case a key element in any moral rights discussion.

The defendants first argued that the state claim was preempted by federal copyright law. The court disagreed, stating the following:

> If the state law provides different rights than are available under the federal law, it is not preempted. . . . [T]he prevailing test may be referred to as the "extra element" test. That extra element must change not merely the scope of the action but its nature, so that the state law claim is qualitatively different from a copyright infringement claim.[99]

As the court concluded, the state law violation is predicated on an act incorporating elements significantly beyond copying, and there was, therefore, no preemption. Moreover, as the court noted, the state act strives to protect an artist's reputation from the attribution to him of altered or mutilated works of art; that is, unlike the economic objectives of United States copyright law, the state statute's intention to protect the artist's reputation is "a species of tort law traditionally reserved to the states."[100] Therefore, the New York Artists Authorship Rights Act is distinguishable from federal copyright law in its objective, as well as in its elements, and preemption does not obtain.

The defendants next asserted that the distribution of a copy of cropped images taken from the plaintiff's work was not a violation of the statute because it did not alter, deface, mutilate, or modify the original work. Again, the court did not agree; as it noted,[101] the statute plainly guards against alterations of reproductions, as well as of the original works, and, moreover,

> section 14.03(3)(b) of the Act confirms its applicability to altered reproductions of artworks in which no physical change has been made in the original work.[102]

As the court further noted, because the intent of the legislation was to protect the reputation of the artist and the integrity of the artwork, the

> spirit of the statute is best served by prohibiting the attribution to an artist of a published or publicly displayed altered reproduction of his original artwork.[103]

The court went on to observe that from a photographic reproduction it could not be determined whether it was the original or the copy that was altered but that both may cause the same harm to an artist's reputation when the altered version is published with attribution to the artist.[104]

In addition, the court rejected the defendants' claim that reproduction and publication out of context of minor segments of works did not constitute an alteration, defacement, mutilation, or modification of the plaintiff's artworks. As the court noted, extracting fragmentary images from complex collages certainly altered and modified the plaintiff's work.[105]

Moreover, the court found disingenuous the defendants' contention that their pamphlet had not been published. By mailing more than 200 pamphlets into the state of New York, thereby transferring ownership to entities that clearly intended to disseminate the pamphlet further, the defendants published their reproductions within the meaning of the 1976 Copyright Act.[106]

The defendants next claimed that the plaintiff failed to demonstrate that the alteration, modification, defacement, or mutilation would reasonably result in damage to the plaintiff's reputation under the New York Artists Authorship Rights Act. Again, the court disagreed; it was persuaded by the testimony of a contemporary art expert employed by the Museum of Modern Art. The expert explained that because the pamphlet's details implied that the plaintiff's work consists primarily of explicit images of homosexual sex activity, museums, believing the pamphlet to be representative of the artist's work, might fail to review his work and might be reluctant to exhibit his work because of its perceived association with pornography. That reluctance would have an adverse effect on the value of the plaintiff's work, as the public would be less likely to purchase his art, lacking, as it would, the pedigree of museum shows and accompanying reviews.[107]

The defendants next charged that when speech involves matters of public concern allegedly injuring the reputation of a public figure, actual malice must be proved in order to defeat First Amendment protection. Again the court disagreed, stating the following:

> The public display of an altered artwork, falsely attributed to the original artist . . . is not the type of speech or activity that demands protection, because such deception serves no socially useful purpose. The New York Statute does not impede truthful speech, but rather prevents false attribution, requiring only accurate labeling to permit dissemination of the desired message.[108]

The defendants also charged that the New York statute is unconstitutional, overbroad, and impermissibly vague. Still again, the court disagreed. It observed that the statute does not address a category of speech that is presumptively protected under the First Amendment; that is, the First Amendment does not protect the public display of altered artwork falsely attributed to the original artist. The court then distinguished between that situation and an example of protected speech: public display of an altered reproduction to express a grievance against the government in which there is no reasonably implied attribution to the original artist.[109] Moreover, as the court noted, narrowly tailored injunctive relief preventing solely the false attribution to the plaintiff of altered reproductions of his work does not constitute an unlawful prior restraint of protected speech.[110]

Nor, as the court observed, is the statute impermissibly vague merely because it requires a determination as to whether damage to an artist's reputation is reasonably likely to result from an alteration and attribution. The test is clearly whether a reasonable person would conclude that damage to the artist's reputation is likely.[111] As the court concluded, the statute is not overbroad:

> [B]ecause the statute proscribes only the false attribution to an artist of an altered original, limited edition or reproduction of his work, it does not sweep within its ban speech which is protected by the First Amendment.[112]

Morita v. Omni Publications International

In the case of *Morita v. Omni Publications International*,[113] the plaintiff-artist was not so successful in filing suit under the New York Artists Authorship Rights Act. The plaintiff, a graphic artist, designed an award-winning peace poster commemorating the fortieth anniversary of the bombing of Hiroshima. The poster is part of the permanent collection of the Hiroshima Museum of Modern Art. Subsequently, the defendant-photographer of the poster authorized the codefendant, *Omni* magazine, to use as the cover photograph of its May 1988 issue an outtake—that is, one of the photographs not used in the plaintiff's poster. The photograph was so used, along with the headline "Nuclear Renaissance: Reactors Are Back and the Reactions Are Good." The plaintiff filed suit, claiming, among other assertions, that the defendants' conduct violated the New York statute in that

> the placement of [his work] which was created solely to depict an anti-nuclear message together with a pro-nuclear text is an alteration, defacement, mutilation and modification of [his work] by defendants, without his consent and is reasonably likely to result in damage to his reputation.[114]

In granting the defendants' motion to dismiss the claim, the New York federal district court stated that the picture on the *Omni* magazine cover

> is not a mutilation or alteration of [the artist's] work at all. Nothing about it was changed between its creation and the use about which [the artist] is complaining. Juxtaposition with a magazine headline is not an alteration, defacement, mutilation or modification.[115]

Other Cases

In *Botello v. Shell Oil Co.*,[116] a California state appellate court determined in May 1991 that a mural is a painting entitled to protection under the state's Art Preservation Act. A few years earlier, in another California state appellate court case,[117] the court held that architectural plans were not among the works protected by California's act.

In the 1996 case of *Moakley v. Eastwick*,[118] the Massachusetts Supreme Judi-

cial Court determined that Massachusetts's moral rights statute did not have retroactive effect. The plaintiff, an established sculptor, was commissioned in 1971
by a Unitarian church to create and install a work of art on the church property.
The commission resulted in a sixty-eight-foot-long concrete block wall to which
the plaintiff affixed a 600-tile mural of a time line of social trends in the local
community, dating from the community's founding to the time of the commission. The most recent portions of the mural depicted drug use, nuclear war, and
civil unrest. Because of its construction, the mural could not be removed from
the church site without being damaged. In 1989, the property on which the mural was located was acquired by the defendant church, which found the mural to
be objectionable on religious grounds. In the process of attempting to remove
the mural in its entirety, the church damaged a portion of it during a congre-
gational clean-up day. In denying relief to the sculptor under Massachusetts's
moral rights statute, the Massachusetts Supreme Judicial Court agreed with the
defendant's contention that the statute "was not intended to apply retrospec-
tively to works created before its enactment and owned by someone other than
the artist."[119]

Federal Moral Rights Legislation: VARA

As discussed in chapter 11 , the United States, in acceding to the Berne Convention in March 1989, adopted a minimalist approach by determining that its then-
existing legislation—a patchwork of copyright law, common-law defamation,
unfair-competition laws, contract law, and a few moral rights state statutes—sufficed to place the United States in compliance with article 6*bis*, the moral rights
requirements, of Berne. The domestic and foreign skepticism that greeted that
pronouncement[120] was more than justified by *Serra*, the first post-Berne major
artists' rights case, discussed on pages 461–464 and reviewed briefly here.

In *Serra v. United States General Services Administration*,[121] the sculptor
Richard Serra, under a commission agreement with the federal government, created and installed a sculpture, *Tilted Arc*, on the Federal Plaza at Foley Square in
Manhattan in 1981. The artwork, a 120-foot-long-by-12-foot-high slab of Cor-
Ten steel that bisected the plaza, was conceived and designed specifically for its
location. When *Tilted Arc* was greeted with hostility by workers and residents in
the community, who raised aesthetic and practical objections to the sculpture in
a series of public hearings in 1985, it was ultimately removed from Federal Plaza
with saws and torches[122] and carted away by court order—only days after the
United States acceded to the Berne Convention.

In the wake of *Serra*, the United States determined that it had better revisit
the issue of moral rights. Therefore, in December 1990, VARA, a limited piece
of moral rights federal legislation amending the Copyright Act of 1976, was enacted into law. VARA amends the 1976 Act to grant to an author of a "work of
visual art" the rights of attribution and integrity.[123] Such rights are granted independently of and in addition to the exclusive rights of copyright granted to
authors under the 1976 Act.

Covered Works

VARA grants protections to authors of a "work of visual art."[124] A "work of visual art" is more narrowly defined than "pictorial, graphic, or sculptural works"[125] and includes paintings, drawings, prints, sculpture, and still photographic images produced for exhibition purposes. Each of those works must exist in a single copy or in a limited edition of no more than 200 copies that are signed and consecutively numbered by the artist or, in the case of a sculpture, that bear an identifying mark. Specifically excluded from coverage are posters, maps, globes, charts, technical drawings, diagrams, models, applied art, motion pictures and other audiovisual works, books, magazines, newspapers, periodicals, databases, electronic information services, electronic and similar publications, advertising, merchandising, promotional and packaging materials, and any works made for hire.

The constricted scope of works protected by VARA may well serve to reaffirm the significance of state moral rights statutes.

Limitations to Covered Works

Subject Matter

Puppets, costumes, and stage sets do not qualify as work of visual art under VARA. In *Gegenhuber v. Hystopolis Productions, Inc.*,[126] the two plaintiffs—professional performers, artists, and puppeteers—joined the defendant puppet theater in the late 1980s and produced *The Adding Machine*, an adult puppet show based on Elmer Rice's play of the same name. The plaintiffs participated in the creation, design, and construction of the puppets, sets, and costumes as well as the adaptation of the play, and it was agreed that they would each receive appropriate credit for their contributions to the production. After the puppet show's initial six-month run, the plaintiffs left the theater to pursue other opportunities, and subsequently learned that the defendant produced additional runs of the show in 1990, 1991, and 1992 in substantially the same form, either without appropriately crediting the plaintiffs or without giving them any credit at all. The plaintiffs filed suit in a state court alleging breach of agreement, among other claims. The defendant removed the case to federal court, asserting that the plaintiffs' claims were preempted by federal law including VARA. The Illinois federal district court, in remanding the case to state court, held that plaintiffs' claims were not preempted by VARA. In so holding, the court noted that the definition of "work of visual art"

> is silent as to a whole slew of copyrightable works . . . . By its terms, VARA does not include puppets, costumes or sets which arguably might be considered "visual art." We will not read into VARA that which Congress has evidently chosen to leave out.[127]

Similarly, an architectural work embodied in a building does not qualify as a "work of visual art" protected by VARA;[128] a sculpture—the façade of a Spanish galleon wrapped around an old school bus—was applied art, because it retained the bus's innate function of movement and transport and therefore, by definition, did not qualify as a "work of visual art" under VARA;[129] and a specially designed computer table did not qualify as a "work of visual art" under VARA.[130] Design images for a new NASCAR trophy did not qualify for protection under VARA since, by definition, technical drawings, diagrams, and models are excluded from the definition of "a work of visual art."[131] No ceramic goods or housewares designed by the plaintiffs constituted a "work of visual art" under VARA;[132] and no still photographic images produced for use as studies for paintings (rather than for exhibition purposes only) qualified as a "work of visual art" under VARA.[133]

The 2011 Seventh Circuit case of *Kelley v. Chicago Park District*[134] held that *Wildflower Works*, a wildflower display planted in a Chicago park and promoted as "living art," was not a "work of visual art" under VARA and, in fact, may not even be copyrightable. Here, Chapman Kelley, an artist nationally recognized for his representational paintings of landscapes and flowers, received permission in 1984 from the Chicago Park District to install an ambitious wildflower display consisting of two enormous oval flower beds featuring a variety of native wildflowers and edged with borders of gravel and steel at the north end of Grant Park, a prominent public space in downtown Chicago. By 2004, *Wildflower Works* had deteriorated and Chicago's goals for Grant Park had changed, so the Park District substantially reduced the size of *Wildflower Works*, reconfigured the oval flower beds into rectangles, and changed some of the planting material. Kelley subsequently sued the Park District for, among other claims, violating his right of integrity under VARA. The Illinois federal district court rejected Kelley's moral rights claims: it held that although *Wildflower Works* could be classified as both a painting and a sculpture and therefore a work of visual art under VARA, it "lacked sufficient originality to be eligible for copyright, a foundational requirement in the statute."[135] Additionally, the federal district court, following the First Circuit case of *Phillips v. Pembroke* (discussed below) concluded that site-specific art like *Wildflower Works* is categorically excluded from protection under VARA.[136]

The Seventh Circuit affirmed the lower court's holding that *Wildflower Works* was not entitled to protection under VARA—but for different reasons. First, it found (as did the lower court) that *Wildflower Works* was not entitled to copyright protection and that "to qualify for moral rights under VARA, a work must first satisfy basic copyright standards."[137] The Seventh Circuit (correctly) found that *Wildflower Works* was not copyrightable not because it failed the test for originality but rather because "a living garden lacks the kind of authorship and stable fixation normally required to support copyright."[138] As the court further noted:

> gardens are planted and cultivated, not authored. A garden's constituent elements are alive and inherently changeable, not fixed. Most of what we see and experience in a garden—the colors, shapes, textures, and scents of the plants—originates in nature, not the mind of the gardener….even though it was designed and planted by an artist.[139]

Having found that *Wildflower Works* was not copyrightable, the Seventh Circuit took issue with the lower court's finding that *Wildflower Works* was a "work of visual art" under VARA. As the Seventh Circuit observed:

> VARA supplements general copyright protection; to qualify for moral rights under VARA, a work must first satisfy basic copyright standards.[140]

The court continued:

> To qualify for moral rights protection under VARA, *Wildflower Works* cannot just be "pictorial" or "sculptural" in some aspect or effect, it must actually *be* a "painting" or a "sculpture." Not metaphorically or by analogy, but *really*. [italics the court's][141]

The Seventh Circuit also took issue with the First Circuit's holding in *Phillips* that site-specific art is categorically excluded from VARA, but noted that since it was resolving the VARA claim on other grounds, it need not address whether VARA is inapplicable to site-specific art.[142]

QUANTITY

The requirement that a "work of visual art" must exist as either a single copy or limited edition of no more than 200 copies signed and consecutively number by the artist was illustrated in the 1997 case of *Hart v. Warner Brothers*,[143] which, at the time, received some attention in the press. Here, the noted artist Frederick Hart created a sculpture in 1982 commissioned by the Washington National Cathedral depicting the creation of mankind, with hands and faces and bodies emerging out of a swirling void. The work, entitled *Ex Nihilo*, has since adorned the main entrance to the cathedral to great acclaim and has been seen by millions of visitors. In 1997,[144] Warner Brothers released a film entitled *Devil's Advocate* about a small-town lawyer seduced by the rich and powerful trappings of a New York law firm whose managing partner, John Milton, turns out to be Satan. In the film, occupying an entire wall of Milton's penthouse and serving as the central image in a number of scenes, is a bas-relief strikingly similar to *Ex Nihilo*. Moreover, in a scene near the end of the film, the human forms of the bas-relief—many being mirror images of the *Ex Nihilo* figures—become animated and begin to engage in sexual acts while Satan encourages his children to commit incest. The film makes clear to the audience that the bas-relief is meant to be an embodiment of all things demonic—in stark contrast to the sacred connotations of *Ex Nihilo*. Shortly after the film's release, Frederick Hart and other rightsholders sued Warner Brothers on a variety of theories including violation of Hart's moral rights under VARA. Unfortunately, as one of the authors of this treatise advised the *New York Times*, "the law limits its protection to the actual work. Mr. Hart's *Ex Nihilo* remains intact, and the allegedly distorted depictions of it do not fall within the [statute's] reach."[145] The case was ultimately settled.[146]

In the 2003 case of *Silberman v. Innovation Luggage*,[147] the plaintiff Silberman, a professional photographer, created a black-and-white photograph of the lower Manhattan skyline and Brooklyn Bridge in 1982. He subsequently created 200 high-quality signed and numbered prints, some of which were sold as art. In 1989, he gave a company an exclusive license to reproduce, publish, and sell the skyline photograph as posters. The photograph was reproduced in the company's poster catalog, which, in the course of business, found its way to defendant Innovation Luggage, Inc. The defendant scanned the catalog reproduction of the poster, copied a central portion of it, and then enlarged the scan to create its own posters, which were then displayed in its retail stores. Silberman filed suit alleging a violation of his moral rights under VARA. In dismissing his claim on summary judgment, the New York federal district court, looking to the plain meaning of the statute, held that Silberman did not state a claim because Innovation's posters "were not signed originals of Silberman's 'photographic image,' but rather were reproductions of reproductions of the original artwork."[148] As the court noted, only Silberman's signed and numbered prints fall within VARA's protective scope as works of visual art. First and second generation reproductions of the skyline photograph were clearly not protectable under VARA.

Similarly, images on notecards and lithographs were found not to be works of visual art under VARA, and so the author of those images did not sustain damage to her reputation that was cognizable under VARA when the defendant art company mounted the notecards and lithographs onto ceramic tiles and resold them.[149] Likewise, posters have been held not to be works of visual art under VARA, so an artist had no recourse under the statute when a company lifted the image from a poster reproducing the artist's painting, mounted the image on a canvas, and painted over the image to create a painted reproduction of the original painting.[150]

ADVERTISEMENT OR PROMOTION
Even a single, original painting, drawing, print, or sculpture may not qualify as a "work of visual art" under VARA's protective ambit if the work is deemed to be "any merchandising item or advertising, promotional, descriptive, covering, or packaging material or container"[151]—a limitation that can be rather broadly construed by the courts, as evidenced in the 2003 Second Circuit case of *Pollara v. Seymour*.[152] Pollara, a professional artist, was engaged in 1999 by a nonprofit group rendering legal services to the poor to paint a banner approximately ten feet high and thirty feet long. The banner was to serve as a backdrop to an information table set up by the nonprofit in a public plaza in Albany, New York, as part of a one-day effort to solicit donations. Pollara was paid $1,800 and worked for more than a hundred hours to create the multicolored banner: a tableau of two dozen people of different ethnicities and ages, and both sexes, standing on line in front of several shut doors labeled "PUBLIC DEFENDER," "LEGAL AID," and "PRISONERS LEGAL SERVICES." They appeared to be waiting to enter an open door marked "LAWYER." Inside the open door sat a person in a jacket and tie behind a desk, beside which was a trash can. Many of the people on line held pieces of paper, evidently indicating various matters to be addressed. Large lettering

across the top and left of the banner read: "EXECUTIVE BUDGET THREATENS RIGHT TO COUNSEL" and "PRESERVE THE RIGHT TO COUNSEL—NOW MORE THAN EVER!"

The banner, installed the evening before the fund-raising day, was left unattended. As the nonprofit group had failed to acquire the requisite permit for it, state employees removed it that evening and tore it in three pieces. When the nonprofit sued the state officials under VARA,[153] the New York federal district court noted that the banner was "visually appealing and demonstrated a great deal of artistic ability and creativity."[154] However, the court dismissed the suit on summary judgment, ruling that the banner was not a "work of visual art" under VARA because it constituted advertising or promotional material, both categories expressly excluded from protection under VARA. On appeal, the Second Circuit affirmed that Pollara's banner was not a "work of visual art" under VARA, observing that

> Congress chose to protect in VARA only a narrow subset of the many different forms and types of what can be called art, and expressly left unprotected works created for the primary purpose of promoting or advertising.[155]

For the same reason, in *Berrios Nogueras v. Home Depot*,[156] a federal district court in Puerto Rico dismissed the plaintiff-artist's suit under VARA, which was brought when Home Depot stores throughout Puerto Rico posted plaintiff's work of art, entitled *La Silla de Los Reyes Magos*, by means of promotional brochures or "shoppers" advertising paint—but failed to attribute authorship of the work to the artist. In dismissing the case, the federal district court noted that the right of attribution (one of the moral rights granted under VARA) does not apply to "reproduction, depiction, portrayal, or other uses of the otherwise protected work when used in connection with those works specifically excluded from the definition of 'works of visual art'"[157] under VARA.

In *Teter v. Glass Onion, Inc.*,[158] a Missouri federal district court dismissed an artist's VARA claim where the defendant art gallery displayed on its website electronic images of the artist's work for sale at the gallery, with the images bearing the gallery's watermark. While the artist asserted that the watermarks distorted his artwork in violation of his right of integrity under VARA, the court noted that the gallery's sole purpose for displaying the images on its website was to advertise to potential customers the particular works of the artist that were available at the gallery. The court noted that the gallery's

> electronic images are used for advertising purposes and fall comfortably within the works that are excluded from liability under VARA . . . . Because [the gallery's] digital images are not within the definition of a "work of visual art" under VARA, there is no basis for [the artist's] cause of action and summary judgment is granted.[159]

In *Kleinman v. City of San Marcos*,[160] the operator of a chain of novelty stores turned a smashed car into a cactus planter for the opening of a new store in San

Marcos, Texas, positioned the car-planter in front of his store as an advertising device, and commissioned certain artists to paint scenes of life in San Marcos on the car-planter and to include the phrase "make love not war." Subsequently, the City of San Marcos ticketed the store under an ordinance banning junked vehicles as a public nuisance. The operator and the artists contended, among other claims, that the car-planter was an expressive artwork and that interference with the display violated their rights under VARA. The Fifth Circuit, affirming a Texas federal district court holding, found that the car planter was promotional material and, therefore, outside the scope of VARA's protection.[161]

SITE-SPECIFIC WORKS

As VARA has been interpreted to date, it does not apply to site-specific art.[162] In the First Circuit case of *Phillips v. Pembroke Real Estate*,[163] the plaintiff David Phillips, a nationally recognized sculptor who worked primarily in stone and bronze forms that he integrated into local surroundings, was commissioned in 1999 by the defendant Pembroke Real Estate company, along with three other artists, to create art in Eastport Park, located in the South Boston Waterfront District. The defendant leased the land on which the park is built from the Massachusetts Port Authority. Phillips duly created approximately twenty-seven sculptures for the park in bronze and granite. He was also responsible for the design and installation of stone walls, granite stones inlaid into the park's walkways, and other landscape design elements. The park, as completed in 2000, was a public sculpture park with a nautical theme. In 2001, Pembroke decided to alter the park and retained a landscape artist whose design plan ultimately called for the removal of one of Phillips's sculptures and the relocation of some of the granite paving and the alteration of several walkways and finished granite objects. Objecting to this revised plan, Phillips filed suit in the Massachusetts federal district court, seeking injunctive relief under VARA among other statutes. The federal district court found (1) that Phillips had established the likelihood of showing that most, but not all, of his work in the park constituted "one 'integrated work of visual art,'" (2) that an artist has no right to the placement or public presentation of his sculpture under the public placement exception of VARA, and (3) that Pembroke could move Phillips's freestanding works and could disassemble and move the multi-element, integrated work of art piecemeal, so long as individual pieces comprising this integrated work were not altered, modified, or destroyed.[164] However, under the broader protections of the Massachusetts Art Preservation Act (MAPA) for site-specific art, the court granted a preliminary injunction preventing Pembroke from altering the park.[165]

Both Phillips and Pembroke appealed to the First Circuit. In the interim, the federal district court certified to the Massachusetts Supreme Judicial Court the question of whether Phillips's work in the park was protected under MAPA. The state court concluded that MAPA did not protect site-specific art.[166]

On appeal to the First Circuit, neither party disputed the federal district court's finding that certain of Phillips's work in the park was both integrated and site-specific art. "Site-specific art" is a type of "integrated art." In the words of the First Circuit,

> [a] work of "integrated art" is comprised of two or more physical objects that must be presented together as the artist intended for the work to retain its meaning and integrity. In a work of "site-specific art," one of the component physical objects is the location of the art. To remove a work of site-specific art is to destroy it.[167]

On appeal, Phillips challenged only the federal district court's conclusion that Pembroke was permitted, under the public presentation exception of VARA, to remove from the park Phillips's large, multi-element work of art which the district court found was both integrated and site-specific.

In reviewing the federal district court's decision de novo, the First Circuit disagreed with the district court's conclusion that VARA recognized site-specific art as a type of integrated art and that VARA treats site-specific art in the same manner that it treats other integrated art. As the First Circuit noted, a work of integrated art is not destroyed by removal from its location—unless it happens to be an integrated artwork that is site-specific.

> A simple example of a work of integrated art that is *not* [italics the court's] site-specific is Marcel Duchamp's work 'Bicycle Wheel', a sculpture integrating a bicycle fork, a bicycle wheel, and a stool in a particular arrangement….this sculpture does not integrate its location and could be part of a traveling exhibition of Duchamp's work without losing its artistic meaning or being destroyed.[168]

As the court continued, the conclusion that VARA applies to site-specific art but that such art may be removed (that is, destroyed) under the public presentation exception of VARA is "not a sensible reading of VARA's plain meaning. Either VARA recognizes site-specific art and protects it, or it does not recognize site-specific art at all."[169] The First Circuit held that "the plain language of VARA does not protect site-specific art."[170]

MORAL RIGHTS GRANTED

As noted earlier, VARA grants rights of attribution and integrity to the author of a work of visual art. Although those two rights are independent of the exclusive rights of copyright granted by the 1976 Copyright Act, they are, like the rights of copyright, subject to the 1976 Act's fair-use provisions.

ATTRIBUTION
The right of attribution encompasses three author's rights:

1. The right to be identified as the work's author
2. The right to prevent the use of the author's name as the author of a work that he did not create

3. The right to prevent the use of the author's name as the author of the
    work if it has been distorted, mutilated, or modified so as to be prejudicial
    to the author's honor or reputation

In the 2002 case of *Grauer v. Deutsch*,[171] a New York federal district court
refused to dismiss on summary judgment the claim of the plaintiff, a photographer's assistant, that the defendant, a prominent artist and photographer,
violated the assistant's moral right of attribution under VARA when, having
collaborated on two series of photographs that received critical acclaim, the two
parties had a falling out and the defendant exhibited the photographs without at-
tributing proper authorship to the plaintiff.

In the 2010 case of *Sherry Martin Photography v. Walt Disney Internet
Group*,[172] a California federal district court dismissed the VARA claims of Sherry
Martin, a professional freelance photographer, who asserted that the defendants
violated her moral rights of attribution and integrity by, among other actions,
publishing one of her photographs in a magazine without proper attribution to
her and by altering, modifying, and distorting the published photograph. Although the court acknowledged that the plaintiff adequately alleged that her
photograph met the definition of a work of visual art so as to qualify for protection under VARA, it noted that the reproduction of her photograph in defendants' magazine did not implicate plaintiff's attribution and integrity rights.
The court, citing from VARA, observed that attribution and integrity rights do
not apply to any reproduction or other depiction or use of a work of visual art in
a magazine, or other mass media, or in connection with advertising or promotion.[173] As the court stated,

> this exclusion exists "because such actions do not affect the single or limited edition
> copy, imposing liability in these situations would not further the paramount goal
> of the legislation: to preserve and protect certain categories of original works of art
> . . . . It is the original or limited edition still photographic image, whether in print or
> negative form, that garners the rights VARA bestows."[174]

INTEGRITY

The right of integrity encompasses two author's rights:

1. The right to prevent any intentional distortion, mutilation, or modifica-
    tion of a work of visual art that is prejudicial to the author's honor or
    reputation
2. The right to prevent any intentional or grossly negligent destruction of a
    work of recognized stature

The right of integrity granted by VARA is subject to certain limitations delineated by the act. For example, the right does not apply to a work of visual art
incorporated into a building in such a way that removing the work from the
building would cause the work's destruction, distortion, or mutilation where the

author consented to such work's installation either before June 1, 1991, or in a written instrument signed on or after June 1, 1991, by the owner of the building and the author that specifies that installation of the work may subject the work to destruction, distortion, or mutilation by reason of its removal.[175] In addition, the right of integrity does not apply to a work of visual art that *can* be removed from a building without causing harm, provided the building owner either makes a good-faith attempt without success to notify the author of the work's intended removal or does notify the author, who then fails to remove the work or to pay for its removal.[176]

However, case law has held that VARA protects the moral rights of an artist who creates an unfinished work that, if completed, would qualify for protection under the statute. In *Massachusetts Museum of Contemporary Art Foundation, Inc. v. Buchel*,[177] the artist Christoph Büchel, a Swiss visual artist known for building large-scale politically provocative environments for viewers to wander through, entered into discussions in late 2005 with the Massachusetts Museum of Contemporary Art (MASS MoCA) to build an installation piece on the museum premises. In 2006, Büchel proposed, and the museum agreed to, a project entitled *Training Ground for Democracy*, basically a village that would include a number of integrated architectural and structural elements through which a visitor could walk and climb. The parties never formalized the contours of their relationship in a written agreement and, accordingly, Büchel never signed a document waiving any of his moral rights under VARA. Over the course of 2006, conflicts developed about budgetary issues and about artistic vision: The museum was concerned about keeping its costs for the massive project under control, while Büchel was dissatisfied with how the museum was implementing his instructions and procuring the items necessary for the installation. Vitriolic exchanges between the parties continued into 2007, the installation languished in its unfinished state, and when it became clear that Büchel would not complete the installation, MASS MoCA sued Büchel in May 2007 in the Massachusetts federal district court, seeking a declaratory judgment that it was "entitled to present to the public the materials and partial constructions assembled in connection with and exhibit planned with . . . Büchel."[178] The following day, MASS MoCA issued a press release announcing the cancellation of *Training Ground* and contemporaneously publicized the opening of a new exhibit entitled "Made at MASS MoCA," a documentary project exploring issues raised in complex, collaborative projects between institutions and artists. The press release explained that due to space constraints imposed by the unfinished fabrications that were to have comprised elements of *Training Ground*, the documentary project would have to be exhibited in the only remaining gallery space—which would require visitors to pass through the space housing the unfinished elements of the cancelled installation. However, the press release also noted that reasonable measures, pending a court ruling, had been taken to restrict the public's view of these materials, and when the documentary exhibit opened, the public saw that the museum had placed yellow tarpaulins over the unfinished installation.

Büchel responded to MASS MoCA's suit by asserting five counterclaims, including seeking recourse under VARA preventing the museum from showing the incomplete installation. From the bench, the federal district court ruled in favor of the museum, holding that MASS MoCA was "entitled to present"[179] the unfinished installation to the public, provided it posted a disclaimer informing the public that the partial constructions and other materials constituted an unfinished project that did not "carry out the installation's original intent."[180] Although the museum subsequently changed course and began removing the elements of the unfinished installation and would not permit the public to enter it, the Massachusetts federal district court in 2008, realizing that some of the issues presented in the suit were now moot, nevertheless issued a written opinion, granting MASS MoCA's motion for summary judgment and denying Büchel relief on all five of his counterclaims.

On appeal the First Circuit, which reviewed the federal district court's interpretation of VARA de novo, held that VARA applies to a "work of visual art" even if that work is unfinished. The rationale for that holding was that while VARA does not, in itself, state when an artistic work becomes a "work of visual art" subject to VARA's protections, VARA is part of the Copyright Act, and the general definitions section of the Copyright Act provides that a work is created when it "is fixed in a copy for the first time . . . [and that] where a work is prepared over a period of time, the portion of it that has been fixed at any particular time constitutes the work as of that time."[181] As the First Circuit concluded,

> [r]eading VARA in accordance with the definitions in *section 101* [italics the court's], it too must be read to protect unfinished, but 'fixed,' works of art that, if completed, would qualify for protection under the statute.[182]

As the First Circuit further stated, given that Büchel had a right to protection under VARA for his artistic efforts in a partially completed work of art, the Massachusetts federal district court improperly granted summary judgment to MASS MoCA because, among other reasons, material disputes of fact exist as to whether the museum violated Büchel's integrity rights by continuing to work on and modify *Training Ground* over Büchel's objects and to his detriment.[183]

Thus, VARA protects an unfinished work that, if it had been finished, would be considered to be a "work of visual art," provided it has been "created" within the meaning of the Copyright Act. However, there is no moral right under VARA to *complete* a work of art.[184]

DISTORTION, MUTILATION, MODIFICATION, OR DESTRUCTION

In the 1997 New York federal district court case of *English v. BFC&R East 11th St. LLC*,[185] six artists sought to enjoin a developer from doing construction on a community garden lot where the plaintiffs had created five sculptures and had painted five murals on adjacent buildings. Drawing upon the notion of a "single work of art" developed in *Carter*,[186] the plaintiffs argued that the garden itself was an "environmental sculpture" with each mural and sculpture being an "integral component of the Mural Garden."[187] The court, however, did not rule on this issue, having determined from the evidence that all of the art except for one mural was placed on the property without the owner's consent. Citing a California case that refused to apply that state's moral rights statute to illegally placed art such as graffiti, the court held that VARA does not apply to artwork illegally placed on another's property where the artwork cannot be removed from the particular site. As to the individual sculptures, which the defendants had offered to remove before commencement of construction, the court observed that "[r]emoving the individual sculptures does not in and of itself constitute mutilation or destruction."[188] Supporting that conclusion by quoting the statute,[189] the court noted that

> [t]he modification of a work of art which is the result of . . . public presentation, including lighting and placement, of the work is not destruction, distortion, mutilation or other modification.[190]

The court then looked to VARA's legislative history, which provided, in pertinent part, that

> removal of a work from a specific location comes within [this] exclusion . . . because the location is a matter of presentation.[191]

Accordingly, the court held that removal of the plaintiffs' sculptures would not violate VARA. As to the murals, the court noted that while the construction would obstruct the view of all but one of them, the murals themselves would not be physically altered in any way; to equate obstruction with mutilation or obliteration, the court said, would enable building owners to discourage the development of adjoining lots simply by painting a mural on a building's façade. Finally, the court suggested that had the artwork been legally placed, the artists' claim would still have failed because neither the artists themselves nor the artwork was of a recognized stature.

The Second Circuit refused to hear an appeal that routine maintenance on the proposed construction project would likely destroy or mutilate the single mural painted with the defendants' permission, on the grounds that the issue had not been raised in the district court.[192]

DESTRUCTION AND STATE OF MIND

The issue of the requisite state of mind needed to incur liability for the destruction of artwork was addressed in the 1996 case of *Lubner v. Los Angeles*.[193] Here, two artists, Martin Lubner and Lorraine Lubner, lost much of their lifework after a parked city trash truck rolled down a hill and crashed into their house, damaging the house, their two cars, and their artwork. The Lubners recovered

$309,000 from their homeowners insurance carrier, of which $260,000 was paid as property damages for the artwork. They sued the city of Los Angeles for property damages exceeding their insurance policy limits and, among other injuries, for loss of reputation. Regarding loss of reputation, they sought relief under a provision of the California Art Preservation Act, which states in pertinent part that

> physical alteration or destruction of fine art, which is an expression of the artist's personality, is detrimental to the artist's reputation, and artists therefore have an interest in protecting their works of fine art against any alteration or destruction . . .[194]

The California state appellate court, affirming the trial court decision, held that established law does not recognize damages for loss of reputation under those circumstances. Noting the legislature's statements in the statute, the court held that the statute did not permit a cause of action for damages for the destruction of fine art due to simple negligence. The court then noted that the statute may have been preempted by VARA, which provides in pertinent part that the author of a work of visual art may

> prevent any destruction of a work of recognized stature, and any intentional or grossly negligent destruction of that work is a violation of that right.[195]

The court accepted the Lubners' arguments that they were recognized artists who have created and exhibited their artwork for more than forty years and that their art included works of recognized stature under VARA,[196] but the court noted that VARA's

> clear language limits recovery for destruction of visual arts to intentional or grossly negligent destruction. Thus, though it is not certain whether the California statute and the federal legislation are equal in scope . . . if [the California statute] is preempted by [VARA], the Lubners' action for damages resulting from simple negligence is not permitted.[197]

"RECOGNIZED STATURE"

THE CARTER CASE

There has been some case law illuminating the "recognized stature" requirement of VARA. The first such case, the New York federal district court decision (and Second Circuit reversal) of *Carter v. Helmsley-Spear, Inc.*[198] is treated at some length here as it is virtually the first case to flesh out the skeletal statute with some interpretive muscle. In *Carter*, discussed from the perspective of works made for hire in chapter 11, the manager of the lessee of a commercial building in Queens, New York, hired the "Three-Js," a trio of artists, to design, create, and install sculpture in various parts of the building, primarily the lobby, in December 1991. The agreement provided that the plaintiffs had full discretion as to the design, color, and style of their sculptural installations; would retain copyright in the installations and receive design credit for them; would receive $3,000 a week ($1,000 a week for each sculptor) to create the sculptural installations; and would share on a fifty-fifty basis with the lessee's manager any proceeds earned from exploiting the copyright. The agreement granted the manager the right to direct the location of the sculptural installations. The agreement, originally for one year, was extended for several additional one-year terms.

When the lessee filed for bankruptcy and the property was surrendered to the defendant, Helmsley-Spear, in April 1994, the defendant informed the artists that they could no longer install artwork on the premises and demanded that they vacate the building. The defendant also made statements indicating an intention either to alter or to remove the sculptural installations already in place in the lobby. The artists sued under VARA. After granting the plaintiffs a preliminary injunction, a New York federal district court held a bench trial in June and July 1994 that resulted in a permanent injunction to remain in effect throughout the life of the last surviving plaintiff and that barred the defendant from removing the plaintiffs' sculptural installations from the building.

In arriving at its decision, the federal district court had to resolve a number of preliminary issues discussed below.

Was the Plaintiffs' Artwork in the Lobby a Single Work of Art or Several Pieces That Must Be Treated Separately Under VARA?

The court found that the artwork in question consisted of "several sculptural and other elements that appear to form an integrated whole."[199] The floor and the walls were studded with a vast mosaic of recycled glass tiles containing words and phrases relating to sculptural elements on the ceiling and walls. Most of the sculptural elements were built from discarded objects, such as the headlights from a bus and portions of a satellite dish. The court found that a pervasive motif throughout the artwork was one of recycling and that a statement incorporated in the floor mosaic, "DO YOU REMEMBER WATER," flowing from a depiction of a huge mouth encompassing an elevator, attempted to portray the negative effect on society of the failure to recycle. The court's own inspection of the artwork, coupled with expert testimony, persuaded the court that the lobby artwork was a single work of art.

Was the Plaintiffs' Artwork Applied Art?

The defendant asserted that the artwork incorporated elements of "applied art," which are not "works of visual art" as defined by VARA and, therefore, not protectable under VARA. The term "applied art," observed the court, "describes two- and three-dimensional ornamentation or decoration that is affixed to otherwise utilitarian objects."[200] The court noted that even when one examined most of the artwork's sculptural elements individually, the vast majority were not applied art.

Sculptural elements affixed to the ceiling, for example, serve absolutely no utilitarian purpose. These elements do not automatically become applied art merely because the ceiling to which they are attached is a utilitarian object.[201]

Moreover, the court observed that a work of visual art under VARA can be defined as such even if it incorporates elements of applied art and that no provision in VARA prohibits the protection of works "that incorporate elements of, rather than constitute, applied art."[202]

Was the Plaintiffs' Artwork a Work Made for Hire?

As discussed in chapter 11, the court concluded that, contrary to the defendant's allegation that the artwork was a work made for hire (created by the plaintiff-employees in the scope of their employment) and thereby excluded from the definition of a work of visual art, the artwork was created by artists who were independent contractors. In addition, the court determined that the contract, which provided that the plaintiffs retain copyright in the artwork, supported a finding that the plaintiffs were independent contractors, rather than employees. Accordingly, the court found that the artwork was not a work made for hire.

Was the Plaintiffs' Artwork a Work of Visual Art Under VARA?

The court observed that the artwork was a single, copyrightable sculpture existing without a copy in a building lobby and was neither a work made for hire nor applied art. The court further noted that the artwork was created and installed in the lobby after June 1, 1991, the date VARA came into effect. Accordingly, the court found that the artwork was a "work of visual art" entitled to treatment under VARA.

Would Intentional Distortion, Mutilation, or Modification of the Artwork Be Prejudicial to the Plaintiffs' Honor or Reputation?

In construing the terms "prejudicial," "honor," and "reputation," the court applied dictionary definitions to this case of first impression, "convinced that these definitions were intended by VARA's drafters to be applied in interpreting the statute."[203] In so doing, the court noted that less-well-known artists "also have honor and reputations worthy of protection"[204] and that the legislative history of VARA suggests focusing "on the artistic or professional honor or reputation of the individual as embodied in the work that is protected."[205] On the basis of those determinations, together with supporting expert testimony, the court found that the plaintiffs' reputations would be damaged by intentional distortion, mutilation, or modification of the artwork.

Is the Artwork a Work of Recognized Stature?

Under VARA, the author of a work of visual art of recognized stature may prevent its destruction. As the court observed, VARA's legislative history indicates that the provision is preservative in nature: It seeks to preserve art for society's benefit. In the light of the provision's preservative purpose, the court determined that for a work of visual art to be protected under the provision a plaintiff must demonstrate (1) that the work of visual art has stature—that is, is perceived as meritorious, and (2) that the stature is recognized by art experts, other members of the art world, or some cross-section of society. The court noted that such a showing usually requires expert testimony. In addition, to secure injunctive relief under the provision, the plaintiff must demonstrate that the defendant has begun destruction of the artwork or intends to destroy it. On the basis of the evidence presented, the court determined that the plaintiffs' artwork was a work of recognized stature entitled to protection under VARA.

Does VARA Violate the Fifth Amendment?

The defendant contended, unsuccessfully, that if VARA was construed so as to protect the artwork, VARA is unconstitutional in that it "violates the Fifth Amendment by giving a third party the right to control the use of [the defendant's] property."[206] In disagreeing with the defendant's contention, the federal district court quoted from a 1922 Supreme Court decision, which articulated the basis of modern takings jurisprudence ("takings" referring to excessive regulation that, in effect, deprives the plaintiff of the use and benefits of his property without compensation). That decision noted that "while property may be regulated to a certain extent, if regulation goes too far it will be recognized as a taking."[207] As to what constitutes excessive regulation, the federal district court, noting that existing jurisprudence provides guidance in resolving that issue,[208] held that VARA does not effect an impermissible taking based on the following:

(1) VARA creates a comprehensive scheme designed to further the public interest by ensuring the preservation of certain types of artwork;
(2) VARA does not unduly burden the defendant or other property owners since it applies only to works installed after its effective date and it permits artists to contractually waive VARA protection;
(3) VARA does not diminish property value on its face, nor does it deprive the defendant of the property's primary commercial use; as the court noted, the evidence indicated that the property has been regularly leased to paying tenants; and
(4) VARA provides reciprocal benefits in that artists have their works preserved, and building owners, as members of society, benefit from the preservation of those cultural resources.[209]

Moreover, the court noted that as VARA's protection subsists only for the life of the last surviving author of a covered artwork, any effect it has on the defendant's property is temporary.[210]

The defendant further contended, again unsuccessfully, that VARA as applied would permit a third-party lessee to occupy the defendant's building permanently. The district court rejected that assertion, reiterating that "VARA's rights subsist for a limited period of time and are by no means permanent,"[211] that VARA's protection extends solely to covered works installed after the statute's effective date, and that here the defendant's agents were aware of the work's installation and did not object.

Accordingly, the federal district court granted the plaintiffs an injunction prohibiting the defendant from distorting, mutilating, or modifying their sculptural installation. The court also granted the plaintiffs an injunction prohibiting the defendant from destroying their sculptural installation. Because the plaintiffs demonstrated that elements of the installation cannot be removed without being destroyed, the court also ruled that the sculptural installation cannot be removed from the building's lobby. However, the court did not require the defendant to permit the plaintiffs to continue to work on the sculptural installation. As the court observed,

> VARA mandates preservation of protected art work and the protection of artists' moral rights. It does not mandate creation. Nothing in the statute compels defendants to allow plaintiffs to engage in further creation.[212]

As addressed in the work-made-for-hire discussion in chapter 11, the Second Circuit in 1995 vacated the injunction, holding that the sculptural installation fell within the statutory work-made-for-hire exception to VARA—that is, the plaintiff-artists were not entitled to injunctive relief prohibiting the building owners from removing, modifying, or destroying the work. The Second Circuit acknowledged that the lower court correctly identified the legal test for undertaking work-made-for-hire analysis, but it held that the lower court committed substantial factual errors; in conducting the analysis *de novo*, it determined that the key factors favored a finding that the artists were employees creating the sculptural installation within the scope of employment. (See the discussion of the Second Circuit's analysis on pages 954–956.)

In arriving at its holding (which, as discussed in chapter 11, we believe to be misguided), the Second Circuit necessarily did not comment on other issues addressed by the lower court. Therefore, the lower court's constructions of the statutory terms "prejudicial," "honor," "reputation," and "recognized stature"; its determination that VARA does not amount to a taking in violation of the Fifth Amendment; and its holding that VARA mandates preservation but not creation—all remain good law.

"RECOGNIZED STATURE" IN LATER CASE LAW

The test for "recognized stature" devised in *Carter* was followed in the 1999 Seventh Circuit case of *Martin v. Indianapolis*.[213] In 1984, plaintiff Jan Randolph Martin, an artist with some degree of commercial success who was employed as a production coordinator for a metal company, received permission from the Indianapolis Metropolitan Development Commission to erect a twenty-by-forty-foot stainless steel sculpture on a site owned by the chairman of the metal company. The company also agreed to furnish the materials. The resulting agreement between the city and the company included language providing that in the event the city had to acquire the land, the owner of the land and the owner of the sculpture would receive ninety days' notice to remove the sculpture. Martin completed the sculpture, entitled *Symphony #1*, in approximately two years, constructing it so that it might be disassembled and later reassembled. In the years following, *Symphony #1* received favorable notice in the press as well as in the art community and among the public at large. In 1992, the city decided to acquire the *Symphony #1* site as part of an urban renewal plan. Despite repeated notice to the city that the company would be willing to donate the sculpture to the city provided that the city would bear the costs of removal to a new site and consult with Martin as to the site's location, the city caused *Symphony #1* to be demolished without prior notice either to Martin or to the company.

Martin sued the city for violation of his rights under VARA. The Indiana federal district court in 1997 found that Martin's sculpture was a work of art protected by VARA and that the city violated VARA when it demolished the sculpture.[214] The court subsequently awarded Martin statutory damages in the maximum amount allowed for nonwillful VARA violation (that is, $20,000) along with costs and reasonable attorney's fees.[215] Both parties appealed. Martin argued that the city's violation was willful and requested enhanced statutory damages. The city argued that evidence admitted to establish *Symphony #1*'s recognized stature under VARA was inadmissible hearsay. The Seventh Circuit, in affirming the federal district court's decision, held that the destruction was the result of bureaucratic failure rather than willfulness. As to "recognized stature," the Seventh Circuit noted that "the only case found undertaking to define and apply 'recognized stature' is *Carter . . .*"[216] and then set forth *Carter's* twofold test: (1) the work must have stature in the sense of being viewed as "meritorious" and (2) that stature must be "recognized" by art experts, other members of the artistic community, or by some cross-section of society. As to the city's argument that the stature evidence was inadmissible hearsay, the Seventh Circuit, once again upholding the district court, noted that while, unlike in *Carter*, Martin offered no evidence of *Symphony #1*'s merits through experts or others by deposition, testimony, or affidavits, the various letters and newspaper and magazine articles offered by Martin about the work were admissible to show the newsworthiness of the work and that the declarants made such comments. Therefore, such comments were not hearsay because they were not being offered to prove the truth of the matter asserted. Accordingly, the comments were admissible.

In 2004, a New York federal district in *Scott v. Dixon*[217] addressed the issue of "recognized stature" under VARA. Plaintiff Linda Scott, a professional artist best known for her fifty-two-foot-tall roadside deer sculpture, *Stargazer Deer*, in eastern Long Island, claimed the dismantling and subsequent deterioration in a storage lot of a sculpture she had created for the defendant violated her right to prevent destruction of her work. The sculpture, a forty-foot-by-ten-foot steel swan commissioned by defendant in 1991, was located in defendant's private backyard until the property was sold, at which point, at the buyer's request, it was removed. Unlike *Stargazer Deer*, which was clearly accessible to public view, the swan, surrounded by twelve-foot hedges on defendant's property, was never clearly visible from a public street.

Through expert testimony, Scott established that after three years in storage, the swan sculpture had rusted, buckled, and corroded to such a point that it could not "be restored to its former condition as a work of art."[218]

In holding that the swan was not of recognized stature, the court determined that although the sculpture "may have had artistic merit" and that Scott had "achieved some level of local notoriety," those factors were not enough to achieve recognition under the *Carter* standard: that is, a work of artistic merit that has been "recognized" by members of the artistic community and/or the general public.[219] The court also held that

> [w]hen determining whether a work of art is of recognized stature under VARA, it is not enough that works of art authored by the plaintiff, other than the work sought to be protected, have achieved such stature. Instead, it is the artwork that is the subject of the litigation that must have achieved this stature.[220]

The same requirements, the court noted, would not be true of "a newly discovered Picasso."[221]

Scott alternatively argued that even if the swan were not of recognized stature, it was part of the artist's "Stargazer Series," which was recognized. While a *Newsday* newspaper article bolstered plaintiff's argument, the article's erroneous description of Scott's work as "renditions of human heads gazing skyward" and its failure to review the artistic merits of the swan served to undermine plaintiff's argument to the court.

PERSONS COVERED

Since the rights of attribution and integrity are personal and separate from the economic rights of copyright, VARA provides that the two moral rights are exercisable by the author of the work of visual art, whether or not the author is the copyright proprietor.[222] Moreover, the transfer of ownership of any copy of a work of visual art or the transfer of a copyright (or any exclusive right under copyright) shall not constitute a waiver on the part of the author of the rights of attribution and integrity.[223] As earlier noted, VARA excludes works made for hire from moral rights protection. Although that denial of moral rights is in conflict with moral rights theory, it is permissible under the Berne Convention, which deliberately does not define "author" in an attempt to accommodate the work-made-for-hire concept.[224] VARA also recognizes that a work of visual art may be created by two or more authors (a joint work), in which case the rights of attribution and integrity inhere in each author as a co-owner of the work.[225]

DURATION

VARA took effect June 1, 1991. Nevertheless, it applies to a work of visual art created before June 1, 1991, if the author still holds title to the artwork on that date. (VARA, however, does not apply to any destruction, distortion, or mutilation of a work that occurred before the effective date.) The duration of VARA for works created before June 1, 1991, is the life of the author plus seventy years.[226] Moral rights to works of visual art created on or after June 1, 1991, endure for the life of the author.[227] In the case of a joint work prepared by two or more authors, the moral rights endure for the life of the last surviving author.[228]

REGISTRATION

Copyright registration is not a prerequisite to legal actions for violations of moral rights or for the securing of all available remedies or for attorneys' fees.[229]

REMEDIES

With the exception of criminal penalties, VARA generally adopts for moral rights the same remedies as those provided in the 1976 Copyright Act[230]—that is, injunctions, impoundment of infringing articles, damages and profits, and costs and attorneys' fees. That provision is harmonious with article 6*bis* of the Berne Convention, which states that remedies for moral rights violations "shall be governed by the legislation of the country where protection is claimed."[231]

However, even where an artist raises a sufficient claim under VARA, an injunction to prevent infringement may not be forthcoming, as seen in the 2001 case of *Flack v. Friends of Queen Catherine*,[232] mentioned in chapter 11. Here, noted sculptor Audrey Flack won a commission to create a thirty-five-foot bronze sculpture of seventeenth-century Queen Catherine of Braganza to be placed in Queens, N.Y., overlooking the East River. The competition for the commission was organized by the defendant association, Friends of Queen Catherine (FQC), in 1992. By late 1997, Flack completed a clay version that met with FQC's approval. However, subsequent controversy surrounding the Queen as a historical figure caused the East River site to no longer be available for the statue. This prompted defendant Tallix, the foundry with whom FQC had contracted to fabricate the statue, to terminate its agreement with FQC over concerns that FQC would not take delivery.

In January 1999, FQC and Tallix executed a second agreement, this one excluding Flack and giving FQC sole authority and approval over casting and finishing the statue. Shortly thereafter, Flack discovered that the waxes and molds (intermediate stages between the clay form and the final bronze) had been damaged and that the statue's head had been stored outside the foundry where exposure to the elements had deteriorated parts of its face. Instead of contracting with Flack to reconstruct the clay face, Tallix and FQC hired one of Flack's assistants.

Following a temporary restraining order prohibiting Tallix from casting the altered head, Flack sought, in a New York federal district court, to enjoin the defendants from modifying or destroying the statue by asserting three different VARA claims.[233] The first claim alleged that Tallix had partially destroyed a work

of "recognized stature" by exposing the sculpture to outdoor elements, constituting a "grossly negligent" or "intentional" modification within the meaning
of VARA. The court noted, however, that VARA does not provide relief where
modification results from "the passage of time or the inherent nature of the material," even where gross negligence causes the modification.[234] Secondly, Flack
claimed that FQC's authorization to cast in bronze the modified version of the
statue without Flack's approval violated an integrity right granted to artists to
require the commissioning party to complete an unfinished work in accordance
with the artist's wishes. The court, citing the *Carter* case discussed earlier in this
chapter, disagreed with Flack, noting that "VARA most decidedly does not cover
works that do not yet exist."[235] Flack's third claim alleged that the decision to hire
her assistant to resculpt the face, which resulted in its distortion or mutilation,
was a "grossly negligent" or "intentional" modification within the meaning of
VARA. The defendants argued that Flack's assistant was hired merely to repair—
not modify—the clay face and that therefore the work on the clay face constituted efforts at "conservation," a process which is specifically exempted from
modifications giving rise to VARA liability. The court, while agreeing that the
assistant's work was an effort at conservation, noted that modification through
conservation that is grossly negligent may give rise to liability under VARA.[236]
As such, the court concluded that Flack's allegations of her assistant's lack of
competence to undertake the conservation, if proven, could support an inference
of grossly negligent hiring resulting in distortion of the model. Despite the validity of Flack's claim, the court refused to preliminarily enjoin modification or
destruction of the model where the alleged VARA violation is solely for past acts
and not prospective acts.

  While—at least in theory—application of the remedies of injunction and impoundment to violations of moral rights should not be a problem, the same cannot
be said for the damages and profits provisions of the 1976 Copyright Act. It has
been observed[237] that compensation for moral rights violations is directed to injuries of the personality, whereas the actual damages and profits provisions of the
1976 Copyright Act are intended to compensate for injuries to economic rights.
In addition, the suitability of the 1976 Copyright Act's provision for statutory
damages as it applies to moral rights violations has been questioned.[238] Although
on first glance the statutory-damages provision may seem ideal for situations in
which actual damages and profits are difficult to establish, the $150,000 ceiling
for monetary recovery may seem scarcely appropriate compensation for, say, the
mutilation of a fine painting by a noted artist.

PREEMPTION

VARA's preemption clause provides, in pertinent part:

> Nothing in paragraph (1) [of the preemption clause] annuls or limits any rights or
> remedies under the common law or statutes of any State with respect to—

(A) any cause of action from undertakings commenced before the effective date ... of [VARA];

(B) activities violating legal or equitable rights that are not equivalent to any of the rights conferred by [VARA] with respect to works of visual art or;

(C) activities violating legal or equitable rights which extend beyond the life of the author.[239]

Although the inclusion of a preemption clause in VARA makes it easier to discern the limits of Congressional intent in preempting state action in the moral rights arena, preemption issues were not resolved in the 1995 case of *Pavia v. 1120 Avenue of the Americas Associates*,[240] the first published decision in which such issues were raised. Here, the sculptor Philip Pavia was commissioned by the Hilton Hotels Corporation in 1963 to create an artwork to be placed in the lobby of the Hilton Hotel on Avenue of the Americas in New York City. Although Pavia was paid for his services, he retained title to the work, a large bronze sculpture entitled *The Ides of March*. The sculpture consisted of three large, diamond-shaped upright forms and one smaller form lying on its side. Although Pavia believed his work would be displayed "permanently and properly" in the hotel lobby, it was moved in 1988 to a parking garage accessible to the public, where it was displayed in a disassembled state with two of the four forms removed. From 1992 to 1994, Pavia asked the Hilton Hotels Corporation to display the sculpture properly, but the corporation was unable to retrieve the artwork from the garage. Pavia registered the sculpture for copyright protection in January 1995, and the following month he filed an action in a New York federal district court, alleging, among other claims, that the improper display of the sculpture injured his honor and reputation as an artist under New York's Artists' Authorship Rights Act and that the distortion and the mutilation of his sculpture harmed his artistic honor and reputation, in violation of VARA. Among the issues raised in *Pavia* was whether New York's state statute was preempted by the enactment of VARA. The federal district court, however, declined to confront the issue at that time, noting that

[w]hether the rights conferred by VARA are equivalent to those of [New York's moral rights statute] will occupy courts for years to come.[241]

Since *Pavia*, other courts have grappled more conclusively with preemption. For example, in *Board of Managers v. City of New York*,[242] a New York federal district court in 2003 held that VARA preempted the New York Artists' Authorship Rights Act (AARA), as the state statute grants rights "equivalent" to those granted under VARA. The issue was whether the board of a condominium building could permanently remove a sculpture installed on the building's façade by an artist in 1973 under the authorization of a previous owner and ultimately replace it with commercial signage.

In arriving at its conclusion regarding preemption, the court first looked to the preemption clause in VARA, then noted that VARA's legislative history provides that VARA preempts a state statute if (1) the work in question addressed by the state statute falls within the "subject matter" of copyright as defined under the federal copyright law and (2) the rights granted in the state statute are the same or "equivalent" to those granted by VARA.[243] Here, the court observed that the sculpture in the instant case was clearly included within the definition of copyrightable material as defined in the 1976 Act and that AARA grants artists rights equivalent to those found in VARA. The court then stated that "Congress has . . . unequivocably stated that preemption occurs" even where the rights granted by the state statute are more protective in scope "than [those found in] the federal statute."[244] Therefore, as the court reasoned, any state statute enacted to protect an artist's moral rights of attribution or integrity—and even those which would afford broader protections to an artist—would be preempted by VARA.

In 2004, the New York federal district court upheld the Landmarks Preservation Commission's order to the condominium board to restore the sculpture to the building's façade, finding that the commission's approval of the sculpture's historic and artistic value is content neutral and not violative of the First Amendment.[245] However, the 2004 decision did not resolve whether the reinstallation of the sculpture on the condominium's wall would amount to an unlawful taking in violation of the Fifth Amendment, as applied to the states by the Fourteenth Amendment, requiring compensation. On further hearing, the court found that the artist never owned title to the sculpture and, therefore, VARA did not apply.[246] In addition, should the sculpture be reinstalled, it would be a permanent physical occupation, since the condominium did not own the sculpture—and hence an unconstitutional physical taking of the condominium's property without compensation.[247]

On still further hearing in 2005, the New York federal district court ruled on the two issues before it: (1) ownership of the sculpture for purposes of an unlawful taking in violation of the Fifth and Fourteenth Amendments and (2) whether removal of the sculpture constituted destruction for purposes of VARA. As to ownership, the court found that the condominium was not the owner, as the work was never conveyed to the condominium by the entity that had title to the sculpture from the time it was first installed on the wall; however, the court found that any future reinstallation of the sculpture on the condominium's building would be a taking in violation of the Fifth and Fourteenth Amendments, requiring just compensation to the condominium. As to the removal of the sculpture, the court found that such removal in this case constituted "destruction" of the sculpture under VARA. As the court noted:

> The Work has undergone two substantial changes since it was first erected in 1973. In 1981, [the artist] repainted the Work with a new color scheme. In 1997 [there was an approved] removal of the easternmost row of braces [of the sculpture]. . . . The Work has metamorphosed from its original form as visualized by [the artist] . . . so that it would not be the original Work if it were to be put back on the wall of any building.[248]

VARA AND INSURANCE

In the 1993 case of *Moncada v. Rubin-Spangle Gallery*,[249] involving a VARA claim for an artwork created with a tenant's permission, Rene Moncada, a visual artist who paints his signature wall murals ("I am the best artist, Rene") on buildings in New York City, sued the Rubin-Spangle Gallery for, among other points, an alleged violation of VARA and malicious assault. In June 1991, Moncada had obtained permission from a tenant in a building in the Soho area of Manhattan to paint a mural on the building's exterior wall. One day after the mural was completed, the Rubin-Spangle Gallery, located directly opposite the mural wall, directed an employee to paint over the mural. When Moncada discovered what was about to happen, he tried to videotape the act on a camcorder. As Moncada looked through the viewfinder, the gallery owner placed her hand over the lens to keep Moncada from videotaping the paint-over and, in so doing, allegedly injured Moncada's eye. When he sued the gallery, the owner filed a third-party complaint against Aetna Casualty and Surety Company on the assumption that the gallery's commercial general liability policy with Aetna covered the cause of action for malicious assault. In granting Aetna's motion to dismiss the third-party complaint against it, the New York federal district court noted that injuries that flow directly and materially from an intended act are not considered accidental and ruled that Aetna had no duty to defend.

In *Cort v. St. Paul Fire & Marine Insurance Cos.*,[250] under circumstances analogous to *Moncada*, the Ninth Circuit in 2002 similarly held that the insurer of a commercial building owner was not required to defend claims brought against the owner under VARA. Here the plaintiff, owner of a factory building, purchased a general liability insurance policy from the defendant insurer in 1998. That same year, the owner found a tenant and began repairing the building, including covering an exterior wall with an opaque white sealant to eliminate leaks. The sealant covered a mural which had been lawfully painted on the wall and which, during the twelve years of its existence, had become a familiar neighborhood sight. When the mural's creator and other rightsholders ("the artists") sued the owner under VARA, the owner asked the insurer to provide a defense pursuant to the insurance policy, arguing that the artists' claim was included in the policy's coverage for, among other harms, personal injury. When the insurer refused to defend the artists' action, the owner sued the insurer. (Meanwhile, the owner and the artists reached a settlement whereby the artists ceded control of the mural to the owner in return for payment to them of $200,000.)

In affirming the California federal district court's dismissal on summary judgment, the Ninth Circuit found that the artists' complaints of intentional alteration and mutilation of the mural without attempting to notify the artists, and the "irreparable damage to the artists' reputation and prestige in the community" arising from loss of the "masterpiece,"[251] did not fall within the scope of the policy's coverage.

WAIVER AND TRANSFER OF RIGHTS

VARA provides that the author of a work of visual art may waive the moral rights granted by the statute but may not transfer them.[252] Regarding waivers, VARA includes two separate provisions: a waiver for movable works of visual art[253] and a waiver for works of visual art incorporated into buildings.[254]

WAIVER FOR MOVABLE WORKS OF VISUAL ART

For the waiver to be effective, it must be in writing signed by the author and must specify both the identity of the work and the uses to which the waiver applies. Moreover, the waiver applies only to the work and the uses so identified. For a joint work, a waiver of rights by one of the authors constitutes a waiver on behalf of all the authors of that work.[255] The waiver provision regarding joint works has been criticized by a number of commentators.[256] In the words of (the late) Melville and of David Nimmer:

> It makes limited sense to apply this provision to waivers of the integrity right—if co-artists F, G and H create a mural, and F consents to a specified modification, that waiver is rendered a nullity if G or H can file suit for the very same modification. But it makes little sense to apply this provision to waivers of the attribution right— even if F waives the right to be identified as the mural's creator, that is no reason to omit credit for G and H.[257]

WAIVER FOR WORKS OF VISUAL ART INCORPORATED INTO BUILDINGS

Where a work of visual art incorporated into a building cannot be removed from that building without causing its destruction, distortion, mutilation or other modification, and where the author consented to its installation in the building either before June 1, 1991, or in a written instrument executed on or after June 1, 1991, signed by the author and the building owner that specifies that such installation of the work may subject it to destruction, distortion, mutilation, or other modification by reason of its removal, then the moral rights conferred by VARA do not apply.

Where a work of visual art incorporated into a building *can* be removed from that building without causing its destruction, distortion, mutilation, or other modification, the moral rights conferred by VARA do apply unless the building owner made a diligent, good-faith effort without success to notify the author of the building owner's intended removal or the building owner provided such written notice to the author, and the author failed, within ninety days after receipt of such notice, either to remove the work or pay for its removal.

QUESTIONING THE WISDOM OF WAIVERS

VARA itself questioned the inclusion of any waiver prerogatives in the act by requiring the Register of Copyrights to conduct a study of the use of waivers under the act and to submit its findings to Congress, along with any resultant recommendations, in a final report due not later than June 1, 1996.[258] The final report was submitted to Congress in March 1996, but the findings, by the report's own admission, are "somewhat inconclusive."[259] The report did show that waivers are used relatively infrequently,[260] because most sales of works of visual art are unaccompanied by a written agreement, and VARA requires that waivers be in the form of signed written agreements. Moreover, the report revealed that many artists and purchasers of art are still unaware of federal moral rights legislation and, in particular, of VARA's waiver provisions.[261] When advised of the possibility of waiving moral rights, a consensus developed that distinguished between movable works of visual art and those that are incorporated into buildings.[262]

As to works incorporated into buildings, artists, representatives of art trade associations, and property owners alike maintained that the option of waiver is necessary. Each of those groups asserted that to repeal the waiver provision for works incorporated into buildings would have a chilling effect on artistic production,[263] since a property owner would be unwilling to commission a permanent art installation if he could not secure a waiver of the artist's moral rights. The Copyright Office endorses that view and asserts that the waiver provisions for artworks incorporated into buildings should be retained.

As to movable works of visual art, a near-consensus of artists and their representatives argued that because the concept of waiver is an anathema to the principle of moral rights, artists should enjoy such rights not subject to waiver.[264] The report goes on to note, however, that since most sales of movable works of visual art are not currently accompanied by a written contract and, therefore, valid waivers in such cases do not obtain, perhaps no legislative alteration of waivers is warranted at this time. Nevertheless, the report goes on to suggest that if the waiver provision for movable works is retained, it be amended to include a waiting period "parallel to" the waiver applicable to nonmovable works.[265] Such an amendment would furnish the author of any work of visual art the opportunity to remove his work before it is mutilated or destroyed.

DOES VARA MEET THE REQUIREMENTS OF BERNE?

As noted on page 981–982, when the United States acceded to the Berne Convention in the late 1980s, its antipathy to the concept of moral rights caused it to adopt a minimalist approach in amending its copyright laws to be in compliance with the demands of Berne. At the outset, Congress took the position that our then-current federal copyright and trademark laws, along with various state laws, rendered unnecessary any further amendment to the copyright laws to accommodate the moral rights requirements of Berne Article 6*bis*.[266] Then, some fourteen years later, subsequent to the enactment of VARA—the narrowness of VARA's scope having been tolerable, in part, because of the legal protections availing in the then-current copyright and trademark laws[267]—the U.S. Supreme Court in *Dastar*[268] illuminated the basic Procrustean imposition of moral rights on the economic underpinnings of U.S. intellectual property law. Briefly, in *Dastar*, Twentieth Century Fox owned the rights to a television series composed of twenty-six episodes and based on General Dwight D. Eisenhower's book, *Cru-*

sade in Europe, which recounted his experiences during World War II. The television series was first broadcast in 1949 but Fox failed to renew its copyright in the series and so it was injected into the public domain under then-current copyright law. Presumably aware that it had lost its copyright in the series, Fox relicensed the television rights to the Eisenhower book in 1988. In 1995, Dastar issued an inexpensive video set that it entitled *World War II Campaigns in Europe*, made by cutting and splicing the now-public-domain television series, removing all earlier attributions and inserting its own name and credits. When Fox sued Dastar under section 43(a) of the Lanham Act, which governs United States trademark law and prohibits, among other deceptive practices, the creation of a false designation of origin of goods that is likely to cause confusion,[269] the Supreme Court, relying on dictionary definitions of "origin" and "goods," held that the Lanham Act did not extend protection against false attribution to the originator of ideas or communications.[270]

VARA itself is rife with exceptions and limitations. As to covered works: Article 6*bis* of the Berne Convention mandates moral rights protection for all literary and artistic works, whereas VARA limits coverage to "works of visual art," as defined on page 1089. In addition, the right against destruction, as part of the right of integrity, is limited in VARA to works of "recognized stature."[271] As at least one commentator has observed, "limiting the right against destruction to works of recognized stature" is contradictory to moral rights theory, the Berne Convention, and the tradition in United States copyright law of refraining from judgments regarding quality.[272] However, as that commentator also observed,

> in recognizing a right against destruction at all, the Act arguably exceeds the scope of moral rights protection contemplated by article 6*bis* because the right against destruction is neither expressly mentioned in article 6*bis* nor in the official comments.[273]

Moreover, the right of attribution is narrower than that envisioned by Berne. Article 6*bis* permits the author the right of anonymity and the right to use a pseudonym,[274] whereas neither of those two rights is addressed by VARA.

In addition, and as alluded to earlier in this chapter, the rights of attribution and integrity that are accorded to an author of a "work of visual art" include a number of exceptions: for example, any modification of such a work resulting from the passage of time or the inherent nature of the materials, or resulting from conservation (in the absence of gross negligence) or resulting from the work's public presentation, including lighting and placement of the work (in the absence of gross negligence), does not constitute a "distortion, mutilation or other modification" legally cognizable under VARA.[275]

Further, VARA's protections, enduring for the life of the author, last for a shorter period than that mandated by Berne—that is, moral rights protection "at least until the expiry of the economic rights."[276] If a country at the time of accession does not protect both rights after an artist's death, Berne permits that country to continue to terminate one right at death on acceding to Berne.

With respect to the author of a covered work, Berne deliberately does not define "author" in an attempt to accommodate the work-made-for-hire concept.[277] Under VARA, a work-made-for-hire is automatically excluded from the definition of a "work of visual art" and is thereby denied moral rights protection.[278]

The waiver provisions in VARA are not clearly prohibited by article *6bis* of Berne, but the official comments to the Berne Convention approve a policy of nonwaiver, as shown by the following comment:

> [T]he moral right exists "independently of the author's economic rights" and even after transfer of the said rights. This protects the author against himself or herself, and stops entrepreneurs from turning the moral right into an immoral one.[279]

Berne does not address the transferability of moral rights,[280] whereas under VARA, the transferability of rights by the author is strictly prohibited,[281] thereby depriving the author of a work of visual art of an invaluable negotiating asset.

A number of commentators, as well as the drafters of VARA, assert that only the extremely limited scope of the legislation enabled VARA to be enacted into law.[282] Unfortunately, while according more moral rights protection than if there were no such legislation, VARA, as drafted and as judicially interpreted to date, is fraught with so many exclusions that, for practical purposes, it provides little more than a chimerical cloak of protection for the hapless visual artist.

NOTES TO CHAPTER 12

1.   Visual Artists Rights Act of 1990, Pub. L. No. 101-650, *104 Stat. 5089* (codified as amended in scattered sections of 17 U.S.C).

2.   *See, e.g.,* 1 Belgium Law Digest 1601; 1 Bulgaria Law Digest 1901; 1 Finland Law Digest 1901; 1 Greece Law Digest 17.01; 1 Hungary Law Digest 1801; 1 Ireland Law Digest 1802; 1 Italy Law Digest 1701; 1 Republic of Latvia law Digest 16.01; 1 Luxembourg Law Digest 16.01; 1 Spain Law Digest 18.01; 1 Sweden Law Digest 18.01; 1 Switzerland Law Digest 18.01; 1 Dominican Republic law Digest 17.01; Brazil Law Digest 17.01; Paraguay Law Digest 15.01; 1 Israel Law Digest 19.01; Turkey, Law. No. 56846, December 1951, on Intellectual and Artistic Works, *as last amended on* 7 June 1995 by Law No. 4110. *See also* www.wipo.int/wipolex/en/text.jsp?file_id=129903 (last accessed Feb. 24, 2011); Indian Copyright Act, 1957, http://bit.ly/eKKeaj (last accessed Feb. 24, 2011).

3.   International Union for the Protection of Literary and Artistic Works, signed at Berne, Sept. 9, 1886; Additional Act and Declaration, signed at Paris, May 4, 1896; revised at Berlin, Nov. 13, 1908; Additional Protocol, signed at Berne, Mar. 20, 1914; revised at Rome, June 2, 1928; revised at Brussels, June 26, 1948; revised at Stockholm, July 14, 1967 (but not ratified by a sufficient number of member states to bring the Stockholm Act into force); revised at Paris, July 24, 1971.

4.   For a thoughtful and comprehensive article on the origins of moral rights, see DaSilva, *Droit Moral and the Amoral Copyright: A Comparison of Artists' Rights in France and the United States*, 28 BULL. COPYRIGHT SOC'Y 1, 9 (1980). *See also* Davidson, *Lost in Translation: Distinguishing Between French and Anglo-American natural Rights in Literary property, and How Dastar Proves that the Difference Still Matters*, 38 CORNELL INT'L L.J. 583 (2005).

5.   Damich, *The New York Artists' Authorship Rights Act: A Comparative Critique*, 84 COLUM. L. REV. 1733, 1734 (1984).

6.   *See* DaSilva, *supra* note 4, at 17.

7.   Dietz, *the Moral Right of the Author: Moral Rights and the Civil Law Countries*, 19 Colum-VLA J.L. & Arts 199 (1995).

8.   *Waiver of Moral Rights in Visual Artworks*, Mar. 1, 1996, final report of the Register of Copyrights, at 32, 35–38, 41–42, 47 [hereinafter Final Report].

9.   *Id.* at 32–33, 38–41, 47; DaSilva, *supra* note 4, at 23–24.

10. *Code de la propriété intellectuelle*, Article L121-4. Note that since August 1, 2006, a new provision in the above-noted *Code*, that is, L.121-7-1, deprives the author of an otherwise qualified work, if the author is a civil servant, from exercising this right unless the author obtains the consent of his/her governmental authority.

11. *See, e.g., Court of Appeal of Poitiers*, July 29, 2010, Document 35 de 42; *Court of Appeal of Paris*, January 13, 1993, Document 92/0015663.

12. *See* DaSilva, *supra* note 4, at 26 for an in-depth discussion of *droit à la paternité*.

13. *Id.* at 28.

14. *Id.* at 31.

15. Damich, *Moral Rights Protection and Resale Royalties for Visual Art in the United States: Development and Current Status*, 12 CARDOZO ARTS & ENT. L.J. 387, 389 (1994).

16. Damich, *The Visual Artists Rights Act of 1990: Toward a Federal System of Moral Rights Protection for Visual Art*, 39 CATH. U. L. REV. 945, 963 (Summer 1990).

17. *Id.* at 962.

18. *See* DaSilva, *supra* note 4, at 11; Final Report, *supra* note 8, at 32–51.

19. *See* Final Report, *supra* note 8, at 39.

20. *Id.*

21. *Id.* at 42.

22. *Id.*

23. *See* DaSilva, *supra* note 4, at n.92.

24. *See* Final Report, *supra* note 8, at 39.

25. *Id.* at 42.
26. *Id.* at 46.
27. *Id.* at 39.
28. *Id.* at 26.
29. *Id.* at 52.
30. *Id.* at 48.
31. *Id.* at 34.
32. *Id.* at 44.
33. *Id.* at 42.
34. *Id.* at 31.
35. *Id.* at 38.
36. *Id.* at 46.
37. *Id.* at 42.
38. *Id.* at 43.
39. *Id.* at 46.
40. Berne Convention for the Protection of Literary and Artistic Works (last revised July 1971), *reprinted in* World Intellectual Property Organization, Guide to the Berne Convention for the Protection of Literary and Artistic Works (Paris Act, 1971) (1978), art 6*bis*, ¶ 1, at 41 ("Berne Convention").
41. Pub. L. No. 101-650, tit. VI, 104 Stat. 5128 (1990), codified at 17 U.S.C. §§ 101, 106A, 107, 113, 301, 411, 412, 501, 506 (2011).
42. *See* DaSilva, *supra* note 4, at 38.
43. For an informative discussion of the development of moral rights in the United States, *see* R.J. Sherman, *The Visual Artists Rights Act of 1990: American Artists Burned Again*, 17 Cardozo L.Rev. 373, 389 (1995). *See also*, Holland, *Moral Rights Protection in the United States and the Effect of the Family Entertainment and Copyright Act of 2005 on U.S. International Obligations*, 39 Vand. J. Transnat'l L. 217 (January 2006).
44. Crimi v. Rutgers Presbyterian Church, 194 Misc. 570, 89 N.Y.S.2d 813 (Sup. Ct. 1949). *See also* Vargas v. Esquire, Inc., 164 F.2d 522 (7th Cir. 1947) (artist Antonio Vargas did not have a legally cognizable right of attribution where *Esquire* magazine published a number of the artist's illustrations without attribution of authorship to the artist).
45. *Crimi*, 194 Misc. at 573, 89 N.Y.S.2d at 816.
46. *Id.*
47. *Id.*, 194 Misc. at 574–75, 89 N.Y.S.2d at 817–18.
48. Granz v. Harris, 198 F.2d 585 (2d Cir. 1952).
49. Gilliam v. Am. Broad. Cos., Inc., 538 F.2d 14 (2d Cir. 1976).
50. Dastar Corp. v. Twentieth Century Fox Film Corp., 539 U.S. 23 (2003).
51. WGN Cont'l Broad. Co. v. United Video, Inc., 693 F.2d 622 (7th Cir. 1982).
52. Fisher v. Star Co., 231 N.Y. 414, 132 N.E. 133 (1921).
53. Clevenger v. Baker Voorhis & Co., 8 N.Y.2d 187, 168 N.E.2d 643, 203 N.Y.S.2d 812 (1933).
54. Neyland v. Home Pattern Co., 65 F.2d 363 (2d Cir.), *cert. denied*, 290 U.S. 667 (1993).
55. Glueck, *Bank Cuts Up a Noguchi Sculpture and Stores It*, N.Y. Times, Apr. 19, 1980, at 1.
56. *See* Note, *Sculptures Vandalized*, 68 Art in Am. 202 (1980).
57. *See* Artnews, Dec. 1979, at 12.
58. *See* McFadden, *Bonwit Art Deco Sculptures Ruined*, N.Y. Times, June 6, 1980.
59. Stella v. Mazoh, No. 07585-82 (N.Y. Sup. Ct. Apr. 1, 1982).
60. Cal. Civ. Code § 987.
61. *Id.* § 987(c).
62. *Id.* § 987(d).
63. *Id.* § 987(f).
64. *Id.* § 989.
65. *Id.* § 989(d).
66. N.Y. Arts & Cult. Aff. Law § 14.03.
67. *Id.* § 14.03.2(a).

68. *Id.* § 14.03.1.
69. Mass. Ann. Laws ch. 231, § 85S.
70. *Id.* § 85S(b).
71. Me. Rev. Stat. Ann. tit. 27, § 303.
72. La. Rev. Stat. Ann. § 51:2151 to :2156.
73. *Id.* § 51:2153(1).
74. N.J. Stat. Ann. § 2A:24A-1 to -8.
75. 73 Pa. Cons. Stat. §§ 2101–10.
76. *Id.* § 2110.
77. *Id.* § 2108(d).
78. N.M. Stat. Ann. § 13-4B-1 to -3.
79. *Id.* § 13-4B-3A.
80. *Id.* § 13-4B-3B.
81. R.I. Gen. Laws § 5-62-2 to -6.
82. *Id.* § 5-62-4.
83. Conn. Gen. Stat. Ann. § 42-116s(2).
84. *Id.* § 42-116t(a).
85. *Id.* § 42-116t(d)(2).
86. *Id.* § 42-116t(e).
87. Nev. Rev. Stat. Ann. § 597.720 to .750.
88. *Id.* § 597.720(3).
89. *Id.* § 597.730.
90. *Id.* § 597.740.
91. Utah Code § 9-6-401 to -409.
92. Ga. Code Ann. § 8-5-1 to -9.
93. Mont. Code Ann. § 22-2-401 to -408.
94. S.D. Codified Laws §§ 1-22-9 to 1-22-17.
95. 31 L.P.R.A. §1401 *et seq.*
96. Wojnarowicz v. Am. Family Ass'n, 745 F. Supp. 130 (S.D.N.Y. 1990).
97. *Id.* at 134.
98. *Id.*
99. *Id.* at 135.
100. *Id.*
101 *Id.* at 136.
102. *Id.* at 137.
103. *Id.*
104. *Id.*
105. *Id.* at 138.
106. *Id.*
107. *Id.* at 139.
108. *Id.* at 140.
109. *Id.*
110. *Id.*
111. *Id.*
112. *Id.* at 141.
113. Morita v. Omni Publ'ns Int'l, Ltd., 741 F. Supp. 1107 (S.D.N.Y. 1990), 760 F. Supp. 45 (S.D.N.Y. 1991). *See also* Newmann v. Delmar Realty Co., N.Y.L.J., June 11, 1984, at 1. In *Delmar*, the plaintiff, the established fine artist Robert Newmann, secured a court order enabling him to complete his mural, pending the result of further litigation. In February 1982, Newmann signed an agreement with the defendant, Delmar Realty, owner of the building known as the Palladium, and with its tenant, Ron Delsener, a rock-music promoter, whereby Newmann would create a mural by May 1983 to be displayed on the rear wall of the Palladium until March 1988. The agreement also provided that should Delmar sell or lease the Palladium, it would notify Newmann and use its best efforts to persuade the new tenant to

agree to the project. In March 1983, Delmar entered into a fifteen-year lease with Muidallap, also a named defendant, and was apparently unsuccessful in its efforts to persuade Muidallap to continue with the mural project. In April 1983, Muidallap stopped Newmann's work, despite the artist's claim that he could complete the project in a matter of days. Apparently, Muidallap planned to install a new entrance in the rear wall and intended to paint the wall black. Newmann, seeking to enjoin the defendants Delmar Realty and Muidallap from interfering with the completion and the integrity of the mural in progress, maintained, among other points, that he was protected by the recently enacted New York moral rights statute. The court, although noting that denial of access to the uncompleted mural resulted in the mural's display in an unfinished form to the probable detriment of the artist, held in favor of the artist on a contractual basis. Thus, the court was relieved from determining whether the display of an uncompleted work was within the protective scope of a statute that addressed itself to the display of a work in "altered, defaced, mutilated or modified form." Newmann, accordingly, was permitted to finish his mural if he chose to do so, understanding that when the case was finally decided, Muidallap might be entitled to destroy it. In a later development in the case, Newmann sought an order of contempt of court against Muidallap for punching two holes in the wall near the artwork. The artist was unsuccessful in that effort. ARTNEWSLETTER, Nov. 27, 1984, at 5.

114. *See Morita*, 741 F. Supp. at 1114.
115. *Id.* at 1115.
116. Botello v. Shell Oil Co., 280 Cal. Rptr. 535 (Cal. Ct. App. 2d Dist.), *respondents' petition for review denied*, Cal. LEXIS 3348 (Cal. Sup. Ct. July 24, 1991).
117. Robert H. Jacobs, Inc. v. Westoaks Realtors, Inc., 205 Cal. Rptr. 620 (Cal. Ct. App. 2d Dist. 1984).
118. Moakley v. Eastwick, 423 Mass. 52, 666 N.E.2d 505 (Mass. 1996).
119. *Id.*, 666 N.E.2d at 508.
120. *See* Sherman, *supra* note 43, at 406.
121. Serra v. United States Gen. Servs. Admin., 847 F.2d 1045 (2d Cir. 1988), *aff'g* 667 F. Supp. 1042 (S.D.N.Y. 1987).
122. *See* Sherman, *supra* note 43, at 395.
123. 17 U.S.C. § 106A.
124. 17 U.S.C. § 101.
125. *Id.*
126. Gegenhuber v. Hystopolis Prods., Inc., No. 92-C1055, 1992 WL 168836, U.S. Dist. LEXIS 10156 (N.D. Ill. Jul. 10, 1992).
127. *Id.*, 1992 WL 168836, at *3–4, U.S. Dist. LEXIS 10156, at *11. *See also* Pepe Ltd. v. Grupo Pepe, Ltd., 24 U.S.P.Q.2d (BNA) 1354 (S.D. Fla.1992) (distribution in South Florida of counterfeit jeans did not constitute a violation under VARA as plaintiff's jeans were not a work of visual art" and thereby not protected under VARA).
128. Landrau v. Betancourt, 554 F. Supp.2d 102 (D.P.R. 2007).
129. Cheffins v. Stewart, 2011 U.S. Dist. LEXIS 5947 (D. Nev. Jan. 20, 2011).
130. Bretford Mf. v. Smith Sys. Mfg. Corp., 419 F.3d 576 (7th Cir. 2005).
131. NASCAR v. Scharle, 184 F. App'x 270 (3d Cir. 2007).
132. Mackenzie-Child, LLC v Mackenzie-Childs, 2010 U.S. Dist. LEXIS 8087 (W.D.N.Y. Jan.30, 2010).
133. Lilley v. Stout, 384 F. Supp.2d 83 (D.D.C. 2005).
134. Kelley v. Chicago Park District, LEXIS 2915 (7th Cir. Feb. 15, 2011), *aff'g in part, rev'g in part, and remanding with instructions to enter judgment for the Park District*, 2008 U.S. Dist. LEXIS 75791 (N.D. Ill. Sept. 29, 2008), *cert. denied*, No. 11-101 (U.S. Oct. 3, 2011).
135. *Kelley*, 2008 U.S. Dist. LEXIS 75791 (N.D. Ill. Sept. 29, 2008).
136. *Id.*
137. *Kelley*, LEXIS 2915, at *23.
138. *Id.* at *35.
139. *Id.* at *39.

140. *Id.* at *22.

141. *Id.* at *27.

142. *Id.* at *48.

143. Complaint of Frederick E. Hart v. Warner Bros., Inc., Civ. No. 97-1956-A (E.D. Va. 1997).

144. *Id.* at 7.

145. J. Bresler, *Letter to the Editor*, N.Y. TIMES, Feb. 17, 1998, at A-18.

146. The Virginia federal district court ultimately issued a preliminary injunction prohibiting the release of the film on cassette and Warner Brothers agreed to a settlement which included placement of a disclaimer on already-produced video cassettes disowning any connection with *Ex Nihilo*, and implementing graphic changes to subsequent printings of the film to be made to the plaintiffs' satisfaction. *Devil's Advocate Makers Settle Suit Brought by Noted Sculptor*, ANDREWS SPORTS & ENT. LITIG. REP. 11 (Feb. 28, 1998).

147. Silberman v. Innovation Luggage, Inc., 2003 WL 1787123, 2003 U.S. Dist. LEXIS 5420 (S.D.N.Y. Apr. 3, 2003).

148. *Id.*, 2003 WL 1787123, at *5, 2003 U.S. Dist. LEXIS 5420, at *14.

149. Lee. v. A.R.T. Co., 125 F.3d 580 (7th Cir. Ill. 1997).

150. Peker v. Masters Collection, 96 F. Supp.2d 216 (E.D.N.Y. 2000).

151. 17 U.S.C. §101.

152. Pollara v. Seymour, 344 F.3d 265, 68 U.S.P.Q.2d (BNA) 1145 (2d Cir. 2003).

153. *Id.* at 266 (citing Pollara v. Seymour [*Pollara II*], 206 F. Supp. 2d 333, 337–38 (N.D.N.Y. 2002)).

154. *Pollara II*, 206 F. Supp. 2d at 335.

155. *Pollara*, 344 F.3d at 271.

156. Berrios Nogueras v. Home Depot, 330 F. Supp. 2d 48 (D.P.R. 2004).

157. *Id.* at 51.

158. Teter v. Glass Onion, Inc., 723 F. Supp. 2d 1138 (W.D. Mo. 2010).

159. *Id.*

160. Kleinman v. City of San Marcos, 597 F. 3d 323 (5th Cir. 2010), *cert. denied*, 131 S. Ct. 159 (2010).

161. *Id.*, *aff'g* 2008 U.S. Dist. LEXIS 106739 (W.D. Tex. July 31, 2008).

162. Phillips v. Pembroke Real Estate, Inc., 459 F.3d 128 (1st Cir. 2006), *aff'g* 288 F. Supp. 2d 89 (D. Mass. 2003); Phillips v. Pembroke Real Estate, Inc., 443 Mass. 110 (2004); *but cf.* Chapman Kelley v. Chicago Park District, LEXIS 2915 (7th Cir. Feb. 15, 2011).

163. Phillips, 459 F.3d 128.

164. *Id.* at 131.

165. *Id.* at 132.

166. *Id.*

167. *Id.* at 129.

168. *Id.* at 140.

169. *Id.*

170. *Id.* at 143.

171. Grauer v. Deutsch, 2002 U.S. Dist. LEXIS 19233, 64 U.S.P.Q.2d (BNA) 1636 (S.D.N.Y. Oct. 11, 2002), *motion for reconsideration denied*, 2002 U.S. Dist. LEXIS 22209 (S.D.N.Y. Nov. 19, 2002).

172. Sherry Martin Photography v. Walt Disney Internet Grp., 2010 U.S. Dist. LEXIS 65036, 96 U.S.P.Q.2d (BNA) 1389.

173. *Id.*, 2010 U.S. Dist. LEXIS 65036, at *16 (citing 17 U.S.C. § 106A(c)(3) and 17 U.S.C. § 101).

174. *Id.* at *17 (citing H.R. Rep. No. 101-514, at 18 (1990)).

175. 17 U.S.C. §113(d).

176. *Id.*

177. Mass. Museum of Contemporary Art Found., Inc. v. Büchel, 593 F.3d 38 (1st Cir. 2010), *aff'g in part, vacat'g in part and remanding for further proceedings*, 565 F. Supp. 2d 245 (D. Mass. 2008).

178. *Id.*, 593 F.3d at 46.

179. *Id.*

180. *Id.* at 47.

181. *Id.* at 51 (citing 17 U.S.C. §101).

182. *Id.*

183. *Id.* at 57.

184. Broughel v. Battery Conservancy, 2009 U.S. Dist. LEXIS 35048 (S.D.N.Y. Mar. 30, 2009), *with plaintiff's leave to file a second amended complaint denied,* 2010 U.S. Dist. LEXIS 25496 (S.D.N.Y. Mar. 16, 2010); Carter v. Helmsley-Spear, Inc. 861 F. Supp. 303, 329 (S.D.N.Y. 1994), *aff'd in relevant part,* 71 F.3d 77 (2d Cir. 1995), *cert. denied,* 517 U.S. 1208 (1996).

185. English v. BFC&R E. 11th St. LLC, 1997 WL 746444, 1997 U.S. Dist. LEXIS 19137 (S.D.N.Y. Dec. 3, 1997).

186. *Carter,* 861 F. Supp. 303.

187. *English,* 1997 WL 746444, at *3, 1997 U.S. Dist. LEXIS 19137, at *9.

188. *Id.,* 1997 WL 746444, at *5, 1997 U.S. Dist. LEXIS 19137, at *15.

189. 17 U.S.C. § 106A(c)(2).

190. *English,* 1997 WL 746444, at *5, 1997 U.S. Dist. LEXIS 19137, at *15.

191. *Id.* (citing H.R. Rep. No. 101-514 (1990)).

192. English v. BFC Partners, 198 F.3d 233 (2d Cir. 1999) (unpublished disposition).

193. Lubner v. Los Angeles, 45 Cal. App. 4th 525, 53 Cal. Rptr. 2d 24 (2d Dist. 1996), *review denied,* 1996 Cal. LEXIS 4985 (Aug. 28, 1996).

194. Cal. Civ. Code § 987.

195. 17 U.S.C. § 106A(a)(3)(B).

196. *See Lubner,* 45 Cal. App. 4th at 531, 53 Cal. Rptr. 2d at 29 (citing the two-tiered test established in *Carter*).

197. *Id.*

198. Carter v. Helmsley-Spear, Inc. 861 F. Supp. 303, 329 (S.D.N.Y. 1994), *aff'd in relevant part,* 71 F.3d 77 (2d Cir. 1995), *cert. denied,* 517 U.S. 1208 (1996). The plaintiffs were John Carter, John Swing, and John Veronis.

199. *Id.,* 861 F. Supp. at 314.

200. *Id.* at 315.

201. *Id.*

202. *Id.*

203. *Id.* at 323.

204. *Id.*

205. *Id.*

206. *Id.* at 326.

207. *Id.* at 327 (citing Pa. Coal Co. v. Mahon, 260 U.S. 393, 415 (1922)).

208. *Id.* (citing Penn Cent. Transp. Co. v. New York City, 438 U.S. 104 (1978)).

209. *Id.* at 328.

210. *Id.*

211. *Id.*

212. *Id.* at 329.

213. Martin v. City of Indianapolis, 192 F.3d 608 (7th Cir. 1999), *aff'g* 28 F. Supp. 2d 1098 (S.D. Ind. 1998).

214. Martin v. City of Indianapolis, 982 F. Supp. 625 (S.D. Ind. 1997).

215. Martin v. City of Indianapolis, 4 F. Supp. 2d 808 (S.D. Ind. 1998).

216. *Martin,* 192 F.3d at 612.

217. Scott v. Dixon, 309 F. Supp. 2d 395 (E.D.N.Y. 2004).

218. *Id.* at 399.

219. *Id.* at 400 (citing Carter v. Helmsley-Spear, Inc., 861 F. Supp. 303 (S.D.N.Y. 1994)).

220. *Id.* (citing *Martin,* 982 F. Supp. at 631).

221. *Id.*

222. 17 U.S.C. § 106A(b).

223. 17 U.S.C. § 106A(e)(2).

224. *See* Damich, *supra* note 16, at 965.
225. 17 U.S.C. § 106A(b).
226. 17 U.S.C. § 106A(d)(2).
227. 17 U.S.C. § 106A(d)(1).
228. 17 U.S.C. § 106A(d)(3).
229. 17 U.S.C. §§ 411(a), 412.
230. 17 U.S.C. §§ 501(a), 506.
231. *See* Damich, *supra* note 16, at 970 (citing Berne Convention, art. 6*bis*, para. 2, at 43).
232. Flack v. Friends of Queen Catherine, Inc., 139 F. Supp. 2d 526 (S.D.N.Y. 2001).
233. Before addressing the merits of each claim, the court determined that the clay sculpture, although a model, qualified as a "work of visual art" under VARA. *Id.* at 532–34.
234. *Id.* at 534.
235. *Id.* at 535.
236. *Id.* (citing 17 U.S.C. § 106A(c)(2)).
237. Damich, *supra* note 16, at 971.
238. *Id.*
239. *Id.* at 627 (citing 17 U.S.C. § 301(f)).
240. Pavia v. 1120 Ave. of the Ams. Assocs., 901 F. Supp. 620 (S.D.N.Y. 1995).
241. *Id.* at 626.
242. Bd. of Mgrs. of Soho Int'l Arts Condo. v. City of New York, 2003 WL 21403333, 2003 U.S. Dist. LEXIS 10221 (S.D.N.Y. June 17, 2003).
243. *Id.*, 2003 WL 21403333, at *12, 2003 U.S. Dist. LEXIS 10221, at *41–42 (citing H.R. Rep. 101-514 at 21 (1990)).
244. *Id.*, 2003 WL 21403333, at *14, 2003 U.S. Dist. LEXIS 10221, at *45.
245. N.Y.L.J., Sept. 4, 2004 at 17; Bd. of Mgrs. of Soho Int'l Arts Condo. v. City of New York, 2004 WL 1982529, 2004 U.S. Dist. LEXIS 17807 (S.D.N.Y. Sept. 8, 2004).
246. N.Y.L.J., May 16, 2005, at 1; Bd. of Mgrs. of Soho Int'l Arts Condo. v. City of New York, 2005 WL 1153752, 2005 U.S. Dist. LEXIS 9139 (S.D.N.Y. May 13, 2005).
247. *Id.*
248. *Id.*, 2005 U.S. Dist. LEXIS 9139, at *12.
249. Moncada v. Rubin-Spangle Gallery, Inc., 835 F. Supp. 747 (S.D.N.Y. 1993).
250. Cort v. St. Paul Fire & Marine Ins. Cos., 311 F.3d 979 (9th Cir. 2002).
251. *Id.* at 982, 989.
252. 17 U.S.C. § 106A(e)(1).
253. 17 U.S.C. § 106A(e).
254. 17 U.S.C. § 113(d).
255. 17 U.S.C. § 106A(e)(1).
256. *See* Final Report, *supra* note 8, at 162.
257. 3-8D Melville B. Nimmer & David Nimmer, Nimmer on Copyright § 8D.06[D].
258. Act of December 1, 1990, Pub. L. No. 101-650, tit. VI, § 608, 104 Stat. 5132.
259. *See* Final Report, *supra* note 8, letter, dated March 1, 1996, from Register of Copyrights to President of the Senate.
260. *See* Final Report, *supra* note 8, at 134.
261. *Id.* at 132, 157.
262. *Id.* at 158.
263. *Id.* at 160.
264. *Id.* at 158.
265. *Id.*
266. *See* S. Rep. No. 100-352, at 9 (1988) ("[T]his existing U.S. law includes various provisions of the Copyright Act and Lanham Act, various state statutes, and common law principles such as libel, defamation, misrepresentation, and unfair competition, which have been applied by courts to redress authors' invocation of the right to claim authorship or the right to object to distortion."); *see also* 134 Cong. Rec. S14553 (daily ed. Oct. 5, 1988) (statement of Sen. DeConcini); *see also* H.R. Rep. No. 100-609, 2d Sess. at 32-34 (1988). There is a composite of

laws in this country that provides the kind of protection envisioned by Article 6*bis*. Federal laws include 17 U.S.C. § 106, relating to derivative works; 17 U.S.C. § 115(a)(2), relating to distortions of musical works used under the compulsory license respecting sound recording; 17 U.S.C. § 203, relating to termination of transfers and licenses; and section 43(a) of the Lanham Act, relating to false designations of origin and false descriptions. State and local laws include those relating to publicity, contractual violations, fraud and misrepresentation, unfair competition, defamation, and invasion of privacy. In addition, eight states have recently enacted specific statutes protecting the right of integrity and paternity in certain works of art. Finally, some courts have recognized the equivalent of such rights.

267. *See* Karen A. Skretkowicz, *Symposium: at the Intersection of Antitrust and Intellectual Property Law: Looking Both Ways to Avoid a Collision: Comment: Unauthorized Annexing of an Artist's World: An Argument for Creator-Assignee Standing to Sue for Copyright Infringement*, 30 SEATTLE UNIV. L. REV. 437 (Winter 2007).

268. Dastar Corp. v. Twentieth Century Fox Film Corp., 539 U.S. 23 (2003).

269. 15 U.S.C. § 1125(a) (1).

270. *See* Skretkowicz, *supra* note 267, at 450.

271. 17 U.S.C. § 106A(a)(3)(B).

272. *See* Damich, *supra* note 16, at 962.

273. *Id.* at 963.

274. Berne Convention, *supra* note 3, art. 6*bis*, para.1, comment 6*bis* 3, at 41.

275. 17 U.S.C. §106A(c).

276. Berne Convention, *supra* note 3, art. 6*bis*.

277. Guide to the Berne Convention for the Protection of Literary and Artistic Works (Paris Act, 1971) (World Intellectual Property Organization, 1978), art. 1, comment 16, at 11.

278. 17 U.S.C. §101.

279. Berne Convention, *supra* note 3, art 6*bis*, comment 6, at 42.

280. *Id.*.

281. 17 U.S.C. § 106A(e)(1).

282. *See* Sherman, *supra* note 43 at 408 and nn.200, 201.

13

Resale Rights (Droit de Suite)

WHAT IS *DROIT DE SUITE?*

Unlike an author of a book or a composer of a song, who is able to realize significant profit from the reproduction and further dissemination of the book or song, the visual artist's main source of revenue stems from the sale of the original work of art itself. Although U.S. copyright laws provide the same basic protections to authors, composers, and visual artists, the latter, despite any reproduction and distribution of their images on merchandise such as posters, note cards, T-shirts and the like, derives their primary source of income from the sale of the original work in which the image is embodied.

The artist's *droit de suite*—the right of an artist to participate in the proceeds realized from the resale of her work of art—is an attempt to rectify this disparity.

To date, at least fifty-nine nations worldwide (see pages 1129–1133) have adopted some form of *droit de suite* legislation. In general, and with variations among nations, *droit de suite* provides a visual artist or her estate with a royalty amounting to between 3% and 5% of the resale price of her work (not the original or first sale), with individual payments generally made on behalf of the artist to a copyright collecting society organized in the artist's home country. The royalty is implicated by sales involving at least one art professional (an auction house or dealer) as a party or intermediary to the transaction and is triggered only by works above a specific (relatively modest) value. In some nations, *droit de suite* legislation provides for a royalty based on the seller's profit, rather than the resale price. Some resale royalty schemes require art-professional sellers to allocate a small percentage of their sales proceeds to a special fund for the artists' benefit,[1] and others, such as the California Resale Royalties Act—found unconstitutional in May 2012 by a California federal district court, pending appeal—require the vendor to pay the royalty directly to the artist within ninety days following the sale. (The California statue is discussed on pages 1135–1140 of this chapter.)

While rooted in French law, the movement to introduce *droit de suite* legislation into the United States was born, according to any number of commentators,[2] at the now famous auction at Sotheby's, New York in 1973 when New York taxi company mogul Robert Scull auctioned off a portion of his collection of Pop art. Auction records were set that evening for, among other artists, Cy Twombly, Andy Warhol, and James Rosenquist. The artist Robert Rauschenberg, present at the memorable auction, watched as his painting *Thaw*, which Scull had purchased in 1958 for $900, fetched $85,000 and his painting *Double Feature*, which Scull had bought the following year for $2,300, was sold for $90,000. At the close of the auction, Rauschenberg approached Scull and hollered, "I've been working my ass off just for you to make that profit," and, according to Ethel Scull, took a swing at her husband. The artist and the mogul never spoke again.[3]

The Scull auction was a harbinger of the big business that art would become in the later twentieth century and that continues today. In the absence of federal resale royalty legislation and—in part—because of the potential upside to art sales in the secondary market, artists on occasion struggle to control the resale of their works, as evidenced in the 2010 case of *Robins v. Zwirner*.[4] In what the federal district judge called "an unflattering portrait of the art world,"[5] the plaintiff Craig Robins, an art collector owning a substantial collection of paintings by the noted South African contemporary artist Marlene Dumas, sought assistance from New York gallerist Jack Tilton, who then represented Dumas, in selling a Dumas painting entitled *Reinhardt's Daughter*. Tilton contacted David Zwirner, a New York dealer in contemporary art, to ascertain whether Zwirner could sell the painting on consignment. When Zwirner subsequently advised Tilton that he had found a buyer for the work, Tilton told Zwirner repeatedly that Robins wanted the transaction to be kept confidential (so that Dumas would never learn that Robins sold the painting) and allegedly Zwirner orally agreed to do so. According to Robins, Dumas did not sell to collectors who "churned" her work in the secondary market.[6]

In 2005, while collaborating with Dumas on a catalog, Zwirner informed the artist that Robins had sold *Reinhardt's Daughter*. Dumas "became so incensed that she literally blacklisted Robins from purchasing any other work of hers"[7] in the primary market. When Robins discovered that Zwirner had revealed his sale to Dumas of *Reinhardt's Daughter*, he became so furious that he sought to sue Zwirner. Robins alleged that he entered into an oral settlement agreement with Zwirner whereby he would receive first choice, after museums, to buy one or more Dumas works whenever the artist had an exhibition at Zwirner's gallery, and that Zwirner would remove Robins's name from the Dumas blacklist.

In March 2010, Zwirner, who had begun representing Dumas in 2008, opened an exhibition of the artist's work entitled *Against the Wall*. Robins emailed Zwirner stating his intention, pursuant to their earlier agreement, to buy three particular works from the Dumas exhibition. Instead, Zwirner offered Robins a Dumas painting entitled *The Grapes of Plenty*, which Robins called "a glaring, sarcastic insult."[8] Robins then sued Zwirner, seeking a preliminary injunction that would require Zwirner to comply with their 2005 settlement agreement and sell to Robins the three Dumas paintings he requested.

Ultimately, the New York federal district court, though noting that "some in the art world would desire a market that is neither open nor honest,"[9] denied Robins's application for a preliminary injunction on the grounds of the statute of frauds: (1) the oral service agreement, whereby Zwirner agreed to keep secret forever the sale of *Reinhardt's Daughter*, was within the statute because it could not be completed within one year, and (2) the oral right of first refusal and agreement to buy Dumas paintings was within the statute because it was an agreement for the sale of goods priced over $500. Absent something in writing, both agreements were unenforceable in a court of law.[10]

It should be stressed that the main objective of *droit de suite* legislation is not market transparency but rather the distribution to artists of some revenue generated from the resale of their works. And it should also be noted that artists may have legitimate reasons for attempting to control the resale of their works: for example, an artist may not wish to risk jeopardizing the market value of her work if one or more of her pieces are consigned to public auction and fail to sell. Without in any way advocating for it, the authors assert that if the United States had *droit de suite* legislation in place, artists would, in any event, be less likely to resent the sizable profits that could be realized by the sellers of their works because the artists, too, would be sharing in the abundance.

To date, many nations, including all of Europe except for Switzerland,[11] have adopted the *droit de suite* in some form. However, the United States, at this writing, is undergoing upheaval regarding *droit de suite* legislation: While there is limited *droit de suite* legislation in Georgia, as noted earlier, California's Resale Royalty Act (discussed on pages 1135–1140) has been found by a California federal district court to be unconstitutional, pending appeal; at the same time, federal resale royalty rights legislation, the Equity for Visual Artists Act of 2011 (discussed on pages 337 and 1135), is pending in Congress. The question of whether an artist should be entitled to resale rights has generated enormous controversy, particularly in nations such as the United States with a jurisprudence based on common, rather than civil, law.

EUROPEAN PERSPECTIVES

While it is beyond the scope of this treatise to provide an up-to-the-minute treatment of either the status or provisions of the *droit de suite* in other jurisdictions, the survey that follows should provide the reader with a general understanding of the origins of the *droit de suite*, current trends in the enactment of such legislation, and elements of the controversy underlying its enactment.

Origins

The first codification of *droit de suite* was under French law in the 1920s: it was established to assist the widows of artists killed in the 1914-1918 war.[12] Based on the premise that the artist's current body of work and reputation continue to be reflected in the value of an earlier work of that same artist,[13] the *droit de suite* enables an artist to reap financial benefit whenever the work is resold. There is some question as to whether *droit de suite*, as an artist's right, should be characterized as an additional moral right stemming from the right of attribution, or, like copyright, a property right of the artist, as it protects, primarily, an economic interest of the artist.[14] At least one commentator notes that the *droit de suite* could be characterized as a hybrid in that the "resale royalty builds the right to participate in the future economic exploitation of a work into the right of attribution by allowing the artist to profit from his increased reputation."[15] In any event, were there to be enacted federal resale rights legislation in the United States, it would undoubtedly, as with moral rights, be as amendments to U.S. copyright law.

European Union: Harmonization of Droit de Suite

With an objective of eradicating the distortions of free competition in the contemporary and modern art market involving the shifting potential sales of art from EU member nations having some form of *droit de suite* legislation (such as France and Italy[16]) to other EU member nations lacking any such laws (such as the United Kingdom and the Netherlands), the Council of the European Union, on September 27, 2001, adopted Directive 2001/84/EC (included at the end of this chapter as Appendix 13-4). The Directive requires each member nation to implement or, if already implemented, to conform *droit de suite* legislation on the resale of art, in accordance with the following:

- An inalienable resale royalty right vested in the artist and attached to the artist's works of art;[17]
- Artworks include works of graphic or plastic art such as pictures, collages, paintings, drawings, engravings, prints, lithographs, sculptures, tapestries, ceramics, glassware, and photographs, provided they are made by the artist himself or are copies that are limited in number and are numbered and signed or otherwise duly authorized by the artist;[18]
- For the royalty to be payable, the seller, buyer, or intermediary must be an art market professional such as a salesroom, art gallery, or art dealer;[19]
- The royalty does not apply to private sales between individuals or sales involving museums, provided that the museum is nonprofit and open to the public;[20]
- The term of the royalty is for the artist's life and seventy years thereafter;[21]
- The royalty is set at the following rates: 4% for the portion of the sale price up to EUR 50,000; 3% for the portion of the sale price from EUR 50,000.01 to EUR 200,000; 1% for the portion of the sale price from EUR 200,000.01 to EUR 350,000; 0.5% for the portion of the sale price from EUR 350,000.01 to EUR 500,000; and 0.25% of the portion of the sales price in excess of 500,000 EUR, with a maximum royalty of EUR 12,500;[22]
- It is up to the member nations to set a minimum sale price at which the royalty will be applied, provided such minimum price will not exceed EUR 3,000;[23]

- The royalty is payable by the seller;[24]
- For member nations having *droit de suite* legislation at the time the Directive was passed, the deadline for implementation of these terms is January 1, 2006;[25]
- For member nations not having *droit de suite* legislation at the time the Directive was passed, the deadline for implementation of these terms is January 1, 2010.[26]

Under the Directive, the *droit de suite* applies not only to EU nationals but also to foreign nationals whose home nation accords such rights to EU nationals.[27] The Directive further gives member nations the option to accord artists who are not nationals of a member state but have their habitual residence in that member state the same resale royalty rights and protection as that member state accords its own nationals.[28]

WORLD LEGISLATION

As of this writing, fifty-nine countries (plus the states of California, whose statute was struck down in May 2012, pending appeal, and, to a limited extent, Georgia) have adopted some form of *droit de suite* legislation:[29]

ALGERIA	Copyright Ordinance of April 3, 1973, articles 41, 60–67, 69, 70
AUSTRALIA	http://bit.ly/kGaX5d; *See also* http://www.aph.gov.au/house/committee/ccwea/resaleroyalty/index.htm
AUSTRIA†	
BELGIUM	Law of June 25, 1921 Royal Decree of September 23, 1921 Regulation of October 1, 1921 Regulation of September 5, 1923 Law of 1994—Copyright and Related Rights
BOLIVIA	Title IX the Resale Rights of Artists (April 2, 1992)
BRAZIL	Law of December 14, 1973, article 39
BULGARIA	Right of Compensation at Resale of Work of Art (title amend.—SG 99/05, in force from 10.01.2006)

BURKINA FASO	Law No. 032-99/AN of 22 December 1999 on the Protection of Literary and Artistic Property
CHILE	Law of August 28, 1970, article 36
CONGO (FORMERLY ZAIRE)	Law of July 7, 1982, articles 28, 30, 61
COSTA RICA	Law of October 14, 1982, as amended by law of February 9, 1984, article 151
CROATIA	Copyright and Related Rights Act, § 3.3.2, Resale Right (October 2003)
CYPRUS	In accordance with Cyprus Constitution, national treaties supersede the domestic legislation. New York embassy: 212-686-6016
CZECH REPUBLIC	Copyright Act no. 121/2001 Coll.
DENMARK	Law of 1989 Reform of the Copyright Act
ECUADOR	Law of July 30, 1976, articles 86–87
ESTONIA	COPYRIGHT ACT § 15.11 November 1992 as last amended on September 27, 2000
FINLAND	Law of 1995
FRANCE	Law of May 20, 1920 Decree of December 17, 1920 Ministerial order of December 17, 1920 Ministerial order of February 21, 1921 Law of October 27, 1922 Decree of May 31, 1924 Decree of December 24, 1924 Decree of September 15, 1956 Order of January 21, 1957 Copyright statute (law of March 11, 1957, as amended by law of July 3, 1985), articles 42 and 76 Circular number 1817 of February 14, 1958, of the National Chamber of Auctioneers (extract) Decree of June 10, 1967

GERMANY	Law of September 9, 1965, article 26 Law of November 10, 1972, article 26
GREECE	1993 Greek Copyright Act
GUINEA	Law of August 9, 1980, articles 24, 42
HUNGARY	Decree-law number 27 of 1978, article 46A Decree of December 7, 1978, article 35A Decree of August 24, 1988
ICELAND*	Copyright Act No. 73, May 29, 1972, last portion went into effect June 2008
IRAQ	As part of: Multilateral Convention for the Avoidance of Double Taxation of Copyright Royalties, with model bilateral agreement and additional Protocol. 1979. Madrid, 13 December 1979.* http://bit.ly/gmW4QV ← WIPO website stated that this nation's laws are not yet complete.
IRELAND	S.I. No. 312 of 2006, came into effect on 13 June 2006.
ITALY / HOLY SEE (VATICAN CITY)	Copyright statute (law of April 22, 1941), articles 144–55 Decree of May 18, 1942, articles 44–48
IVORY COAST	Law of July 28, 1978, articles 24, 25, 42, 43
LAOS	(Lao People's Democratic Republic): http://bit.ly/dGXWkR ← last updated 2006
LATVIA	Copyright Law § 17; entered April 27, 2010, into force of original text: May 11, 2000
LIECHTENSTEIN*	Law on Copyright and Neighboring Rights (Copyright Law) (of 19 May 1999); into force July 23, 1999.
LITHUANIA	Article 17. Law on Copyright and Related Rights No. VIII-1185 of May 18, 1999 (as amended on 19 January 2010 – by Law No XI-656); into force June 9, 1999
LUXEMBOURG	Copyright law of March 29, 1972, article 22

MADAGASCAR	Application of French law of March 11, 1957
MALI	Ordinance of July 12, 1977, articles 75, 82
MALTA	L.N. 174 of 2006 COPYRIGHT ACT
MONACO	
MONGOLIA	http://www.wipo.int/wipolex/en/text.jsp?file id=204032 Article 12, Sec.2
MOROCCO	Act of July 29, 1970, articles 28, 53
NETHERLANDS†	In 2006 incorporated European Directive. Translation from Dutch to English: http://bit.ly/idpRxq
NORWAY*	L.N. 174 of 2006 COPYRIGHT ACT; Resale Right Directive was implemented into the Norwegian Copyright Act on December 22, 2006, effective January 1, 2007
PARAGUAY	http://www.wipo.int/wipolex/en/text.jsp?file id=129426#P241 36196 Ch. 2, Sec. 47 Term
PERU	Copyright statute law of 1961, articles 92, 93
PHILIPPINES	Decree of November 14, 1972, articles 31–33
POLAND	Law of March 22, 1935, article 29
PORTUGAL	Decree-law of April 27, 1966, articles 59, 60
ROMANIA	Article 21, Law on Copyright and Neighboring Rights (No. 8 of March 14, 1996)
RUSSIAN FEDERATION	Article 17, Law on Copyright and Neighboring Rights, July 9, 1993
SENEGAL	Law of December 4, 1973, articles 19, 40
SERBIA AND MONTENEGRO	4.3.2. Droit de Suite Article, Law on Copyright and Related Rights, Enacted: December 22, 2009, into force: December 24, 2009

SLOVAK REPUBLIC	Sec. 19, Copyright Act No. 618/2003, Enacted: December 4, 2004, enforced January 1, 2004.
SLOVENIA	Article 35, COPYRIGHT AND RELATED RIGHTS ACTS 1 of 30 March 1995 as last amended on 15 December 2006, enforced: 13 January 2007
SPAIN	Law of November 11, 1987, articles 24, 26, 27 Royal decree of April 25, 1988
SWEDEN	Act of December 7, 1995
TUNISIA	Law of February 14, 1966, article 17
TURKEY	Law of December 10, 1951, articles 2–4, 45
UNITED KINGDOM†	Directive 2001/84/EC of the European Parliament adopted September 27, 2001, implemented in U.K. from 14 February 2006 by Statutory Instrument 2006 No. 346. As of January 1, 2012, the U.K. regulation included protection for the heirs or estates of artists deceased within seventy years.
URUGUAY	Law of December 15–17, 1937, as amended by law of February 15–25, 1938, article 9

† Artist's Resale Right will not apply in these countries on sales of works by deceased artists until 2012 at the earliest.
* These countries are in the EEA, but are not members of the European Union.

THE UNITED STATES CONCEPT

Federal Legislation

Many efforts have been made to introduce the *droit de suite* concept into federal legislation. Senator Jacob K. Javits of New York was a strong advocate for artists' resale rights, and the cause was subsequently taken up by Senator Edward M. Kennedy of Massachusetts. A brief examination of the most recent legislative attempts helps to illustrate the current state of potential federal *droit de suite* legislation.

The Visual Artists Rights Act of 1987,[30] as introduced but not passed, contained a resale-royalty provision patterned on the Italian concept. The 1987 bill would have established a system for the payment of royalties on the resale of works of art. The royalty payment was to be made by the seller at the rate of 7% of the difference between the seller's purchase price and the amount the seller receives in exchange for the work. The royalty would not have applied to resale prices of less than $1,000 or if the seller made less than a 50% gain on the sale. The administration of the law was to be by the Copyright Office, and the artist would be required to register to be eligible to receive royalties.

The proposed Visual Artists Rights Act of 1988[31] took a dramatic turn. The 1988 bill had no resale-royalty provision. Instead, the bill obligated the National Endowment for the Arts to conduct a one-year study to analyze the economic effects and the means of implementing new initiatives to enable artists to participate in the commercial exploitation of their work after the first sale of a work, including but not limited to a resale-royalty right for artists. Although the bill did not pass, it laid the groundwork for the 1990 legislation. The elimination of a federal *droit de suite* enhanced the possibility of the bill's future passage into law, since the main opposition to the bill was generated by the resale-royalty provision.

The Visual Artists Rights Act of 1990[32] became effective June 1, 1991, and contained no resale-royalty provision. However, because of the wide debate in the art community as to whether the concept of *droit de suite* should or should not apply, the law required that a study be conducted by the Register of Copyrights, in consultation with the chair of the National Endowment for the Arts, on the feasibility of implementing the following:

- A requirement that after the first sale of a work of art a royalty on any resale of the work, consisting of a percentage of the price, be paid to the author of the work
- Other possible requirements that would achieve the objective of allowing an author of a work of art to share monetarily in the enhanced value of that work[33]

In conducting the study, the Register of Copyrights was required to consult with appropriate departments and agencies of the United States, foreign governments, and groups involved with the creation, exhibition, dissemination, and preservation of works of art, including artists, art dealers, collectors of fine art, and curators of art museums. In December 1992, the Register of Copyrights issued to Congress a report ("Copyright Office Report") summarizing the findings.[34] In ultimately recommending against adoption of any such *droit de suite* legislation, the Copyright Office Report noted that the imposition of an encumbrance (that is, payment of a resale royalty by remote purchasers) attaching to a work that has been freely purchased could constitute a restraint against the free alienability of property that is a tradition of common law.[35] Moreover, as the Copyright Report also noted,[36] the costs of administering such a royalty could be unduly burdensome, could interfere with the traditional privacy concerns that are the hallmark, certainly in the United States, of most art transactions, and could divert resources that could otherwise be used in purchasing the works of emerging artists and otherwise promoting such artists. Perhaps most importantly, such a royalty would only serve the *resale* market, which would exclude most artists;[37] that is, only the wealthiest artists (or their estates) would benefit from such a royalty. The report concluded as follows: "The Copyright Office is not persuaded that there are legitimate economic interests of visual artists that would be helped by a resale royalty."[38] The report further concluded as follows:

> In summary, based on its analysis of the foreign and California experience with *droit de suite*, the administrative record of the hearings and written comments, and independent research, the Copyright Office is not persuaded that sufficient economic and copyright policy justification exists to establish *droit de suite* in the United States. The international community is now focusing on improving artists' rights, including the possibility of harmonization of *droit de suite* within the European Community. Should the European Community harmonize existing *droit de suite* laws, Congress may want to take another look at the resale royalty, particularly if the Community decides to extend the royalty to all its member States.[39]

Largely as a result of both the legislative initiatives abroad and of lobbying in the United States by artists and artists' rights societies,[40] a bill was introduced in December 2011 by Representative Jerrold Nadler in the House of Representatives[41] and Senator Herb Kohl in the Senate[42] that would require major auction houses such as Sotheby's, Christie's, and Phillips de Pury to set aside 7% of the price for works resold for more than $10,000, to be paid to a visual artists' collecting society. The collecting society would distribute 50% of the net royalty to the artist of the work sold, and deposit the remaining 50% of the net royalty into an escrow account to be established by the collecting society. The purpose of the account would be to fund acquisitions by U.S. nonprofit art museums of works of art authored by living artists domiciled in the United States. As it stands, the legislation applies solely to resales by public auction houses with more than $25 million in sales of visual art in the prior year. Resales of such art by art dealers, whether galleries or individual proprietors, are excluded under the bills, as are auction houses that operate only online.

At the same time that federal resale royalty rights legislation is pending, California's resale royalty rights statute has been found to be unconstitutional, pending appeal, in the May 2012 decision of *Estate of Graham v. Sotheby's*.[43] The decision is addressed on pages 1139–1140.

California Resale Royalties Act

California is the only state, to date, that has adopted *droit de suite* legislation[44] —Georgia's provisions (as seen below) notwithstanding. The law was enacted in 1976 and became effective on January 1, 1977. The California Resale Royalties Act (CRRA) is reproduced, as amended in 1982, at the end of this chapter (see Appendix 13-2). It attracted little attention before its passage, and it was enacted without consulting the art community beyond a limited number of artists who strongly supported the legislation.[45] Some of the important features of the statute are described below, as is the May 2012 decision finding it unconstitutional, pending appeal.

SUBJECT MATTER

The statute applies to the sale of a work of fine art,[46] which is defined as an original painting, sculpture, or drawing or an original work of art in glass.[47]

FIRST-SALE EXCLUSION

The statute does not apply to the initial sale of a work of art where legal title to the work is vested in the artist.[48] The statute is designed to apply only to the resale of works of art, and it contains various other special exclusions from the payment of royalties.[49]

REQUIRED SITUS

For the statute to apply, either the seller must be a resident of California at the time of the sale or the sale must take place in California.[50] In addition, the artist must be either a citizen of the United States or a resident of California for a minimum of two years.[51]

ROYALTY AMOUNT

When a work of fine art that is subject to the statute is sold, the artist is entitled to be paid by the seller or the seller's agent a royalty equal to 5% of the gross amount of the sales price.[52] The statute requires a gallery representative, dealer, broker, museum official, or other person acting as the agent for the seller to withhold 5% of the amount of the sale, locate the artist, and pay the artist.[53] If the seller or agent is unable to locate and pay the artist within ninety days, an amount equal to 5% of the amount of the sale is to be transferred to the Arts Council.[54] The Arts Council then has seven years following the date of sale to locate and pay the artist the amount of royalty due her on the sale. If the artist cannot be located during this time period, her right to receive payment terminates and the money is transferred to the Arts Council for use in acquiring fine art pursuant to California's Art in Public Buildings program.[55]

LIMITATION AND TERMINATION

If the artist does not receive the royalty, she may bring an action for damages, but that action must be taken within three years after the date of sale or one year after the discovery of the sale, whichever is later.[56] No royalty is due for any re-sale occurring after the artist's death,[57] except that if the artist dies after January 1, 1983, her rights under the statute continue and inure to her heirs or estate for twenty years after the artist's death.[58]

WAIVER OF RIGHTS

Under the statute, an artist's royalty rights are not transferable and may not be waived unless the artist is compensated in an amount in excess of 5% of the amount of the sale as consideration for the waiver.[59] The statute was amended in 1983 to provide that an artist may assign the right to collect the royalty payment to another person or entity. Presumably, that was done to allow an entity similar to ASCAP to operate for artists.

CASE LAW UNDER THE CALIFORNIA STATUTE

Prior to *Estate of Graham v. Sotheby's,* the CRRA withstood a couple of judicial challenges. *Morseburg v. Balyon*[60] was brought after an intentional violation of the California statute in order to challenge its validity. Howard Morseburg, an art dealer, sold two paintings that required the payment of royalties and then challenged the constitutionality of the California Resale Royalties Act. Morse-burg claimed that the act was unconstitutional because it was preempted by the 1909 Copyright Act[61] and that it violated the due process and contracts clauses of the U.S. Constitution.

The court first discussed the preemption issue and twice emphasized that its holding applied only to the 1909 Copyright Act. A preemption issue is raised when federal law and state law conflict, in which case federal law occupies the field.[62] In other words, are the rights created under state law (the California stat-ute) equivalent to one or more rights contained in federal law (the Copyright Act)? If there are equivalent federal and state rights, the federal rights preempt the state rights.

The court in *Morseburg* held that there was no federal preemption by the 1909 Copyright Act. The court based its conclusion on *Goldstein v. California,*[63] in which the United States Supreme Court held valid a California statute making it a criminal offense to pirate recordings produced by others, an activity against which the copyright holder at that time had no protection. In *Goldstein,* the Court refused to interpret the copyright clause of the Constitution as foreclos-ing the existence of all state power to grant to authors the exclusive right to their writings. In *Morseburg,* the court reasoned that the California statute in no way impaired any right created under the 1909 Copyright Act and that, therefore, the federal law did not preempt the CRRA.

The court was concerned with the word "vend" in section 1 of the 1909 Copy-right Act and whether that provision preempted any state law that may limit the right of the artist to vend. The court held the following:

Prior to the initial sale he [the artist] holds title to the work and, assuming proper steps have been taken, all rights given to him by reason of his copyright. None of these provide the right afforded to him by the California Resale Royalties Act. This is an additional right similar to the additional protection afforded by California's antipirating statute upheld in *Goldstein*. It is true that under the California Act the right it bestows cannot be waived or transferred. This limits the right created by state law but not any right created by the copyright law.[64]

That conclusion would properly be branded sophistry if it were true that the right to vend provided by section 1 of the 1909 Copyright Act meant a right to transfer the works at all times and at all places free and clear of all claims of others. That is not its meaning. It merely means that the artist has "the exclusive right to transfer the title for a consideration to others."[65] The CRRA does not impair that right; it merely creates a right in personam (an action seeking judgment against a person involving her personal rights and based on jurisdiction of her person, as distinguished from a judgment against property) against a seller of a "work of fine art."[66]

The court also concluded that the California statute does not violate the contracts clause or the due process provisions of the United States Constitution.

However, the court in *Morseburg* emphasized in its holding that it was applicable only under the 1909 Copyright Act, which left the California statute open to challenge as preempted under the 1976 Copyright Act.

In the 2011 case of *Baby Moose Drawings v. Valentine*,[67] Baby Moose Drawings, plaintiff-assignee of the artist Mark Grotjahn, sued Dean Valentine, an art collector and early buyer of Grotjhan's works, in a California federal district court for failing to pay the artist royalties as provided under the CRRA on his resale of three of the artist's works. Valentine argued, among other points, that the CRRA was preempted by the Copyright Act of 1976. The California federal court disagreed, finding that as the CRRA provides a right qualitatively different from the rights delineated in the Copyright Act of 1976, preemption did not lie.

In any event, aside from *Morseburg and Baby Moose*, each of which was decided on preemption grounds, there appear to be only two other decided cases: *Jacobs v. Westoaks Realtors*,[68] holding that architectural plans did not fall within the statute's definition of "fine art," and *Simons v. Horowitz*.[69] The latter case was a class action against art dealers, museums, and other art professionals brought by two individuals claiming to be fine artists seeking an accounting and payment to each member of the plaintiff class of commissions due on sales of fine art in California during a specified period of time. In directing the dismissal of the case, the California Court of Appeal noted that the defendant class was not certified and that the plaintiffs lacked standing to represent the plaintiff class, since there was no allegation, let alone evidence, that the named plaintiffs had any claim against any of the unnamed individual members of the presumed defendant class.

CRRA Struck Down Pending Appeal

In May 2012, a California federal district court in *Estate of Graham v. Sotheby's*[70] struck down the CRRA as being unconstitutional in that it violated the Commerce Clause of the U.S. Constitution. In October 2011, the plaintiffs, a collection of artists and their heirs, had brought class action complaints alleging, respectively, that Sotheby's and Christie's, acting as agents for California sellers, sold works of fine art at auction but failed to pay the appropriate resale royalty as set forth under the CRRA. In January 2012, Sotheby's and Christie's filed a joint motion to dismiss the complaints, arguing that the CRRA should be struck down as it (1) violates the Commerce Clause of the U.S. Constitution; (2) effects a taking of private property in violation of the United States and California constitutions; and (3) is preempted by the 1976 Copyright Act. The court found that the CRRA violated the Commerce Clause and, accordingly, did not address the preemption and Takings Clause arguments.

In holding that the CRRA violated the Commerce Clause, the California federal district court reasoned as follows: It first noted that although the Commerce Clause, which gives Congress the power to regulate commerce among the states, is phrased as an affirmative grant of power, that "the Supreme Court has long interpreted the Clause to have a 'negative aspect,' referred to as the dormant Commerce Clause."[71] That is, the dormant Commerce Clause curtails a state's power to discriminate against or burden, without justification, the flow of interstate commerce. Here, the court found the CRRA implicates the dormant Commerce Clause because the activity it regulates could, likewise, be regulated by Congress. That is, first the court found that a work of fine art sold from one state into another constitutes an article in interstate commerce, and accordingly, Congress may regulate such transactions under the Commerce Clause.[72] Second, the court found that the CRRA "substantially affects"[73] interstate commerce. In its words,

> [w]hen the number of art sale transactions throughout the United States that the CRRA purports to regulate are considered in the aggregate, the Court finds little doubt that the CRRA has a "substantial effect" on interstate commerce such that Congress could regulate the activity.[74]

The CRRA having been found to implicate the dormant Commerce Clause, the next issue addressed was whether the CRRA actually violates the Commerce Clause. The court noted that the Supreme Court devised a two-tiered approach to analyzing state economic regulations under the dormant Commerce Clause: (1) where a statute directly regulates or discriminates against interstate commerce, or when its effect favors in-state economic interests over out-of-state interests, the statute is generally struck down; (2) where a statute affects interstate commerce only indirectly, and regulates evenhandedly, a court should examine whether the state's interest is legitimate and whether the burden on interstate commerce clearly exceeds the local benefits.[75]

The California federal district court found that the CRRA violates the Commerce Clause per se and that the offending provisions could not be severed without creating a law that the California state legislature never intended to create. Accordingly, the court found that the CRRA must be struck down.

In so holding, the court noted that the Supreme Court has determined that a state statute directly controlling commerce occurring entirely outside the state's boundaries "exceeds the inherent limits of the enacting State's authority and is invalid regardless of whether the statute's extraterritorial reach was intended by the legislature."[76] Here, the California federal district court gave an example under the statute's reach: a California resident selling a painting by a New York artist at auction in a New York auction house, where it is purchased by a New York resident. Despite the transaction occurring wholly in New York—and despite both the artist and purchaser being New York residents—the CRRA requires the auction house to withhold a fixed percentage of the auction sale price, locate the artist, and remit the monies to the artist or, if the artist cannot be located, to send the monies withheld to the California Arts Council. Moreover, if the New York artist can be located and the New York auction house fails to comply in remitting the royalties due under the CRRA, the artist may sue the auction house under the California statute to recover the royalty. The court noted that the foregoing example of the CRRA's reach indicates that the CRRA has the "practical effect" of controlling commerce "occurring wholly outside the boundaries" of California even though it may have some "effects within the State."[77]

Although the CRRA has a severability provision, the court found that the offending provisions could not be severed. Looking again to the Supreme Court for guidance, the federal district court noted that "the relevant inquiry in evaluating severability" is whether the statute will function in a manner consistent with the intent of the legislature.[78] Here, the California federal district court noted that the legislative history of the CRRA indicated that the intent was that the statute apply to sales taking place outside California so long as the seller resided in California. Accordingly, the court struck down the statute in its entirety.

Georgia's Droit de Suite Statute[79]

In 1987, the state of Georgia enacted resale royalty rights legislation for artists, as part of its Art in State Buildings Program. The legislation is limited to works of visual art acquired by the state through the Georgia Council for the Arts by lease, purchase, or commission from an artist (with preference given to artists who are Georgia residents) for installation and display in state buildings in Georgia. A "work of visual art" is defined as

> any work of visual art, including, but not limited to, a drawing, painting, mural, fresco, sculpture, mosaic, or photograph; a work of calligraphy; a work of graphic art, including an etching, lithograph, offset print, silk screen, or a work of graphic art of like nature; crafts, including crafts in clay, textile, fiber, wood, metal, plastic,

glass, or like materials; or mixed media, including a collage, assemblage, or any other combination of the foregoing art media.[80]

While the statute accords Georgia sole physical ownership of each work of visual art acquired under the statute, it provides that the artist retains certain intangible rights, among which is the following:

> *If provided by written contract* [italics ours], the right to receive a specified percentage of the proceeds if the work of art is subsequently sold by the state to a third party other than as part of the sale of the building in which the work of art is located.[81]

The statute also provides that this right "may be extended to such artist's heirs, assigns, or personal representatives" for a period of twenty years following the artist's death *if so provided in a written contract*.[82] In short, if the resale right is not negotiated and agreed to in a written contract signed by the Georgia Council for the Arts and by the artist, it is not forthcoming.

NOTES TO CHAPTER 13

1. Caslon Analytics Profile: *Droit de Suite*, www.caslon.com.au/droitprofile.htm (version of April, 2010).

2. *Id. See, e.g.*, ANTHONY HADEN-GUEST, TRUE COLORS: THE REAL LIFE OF THE ART WORLD 16 (Grove/Atlantic 1996); Jennifer J. Wirsching, *Comment: The Time Is Now: The Need for Federal Resale Royalty Legislation in Light of the European Union Directive*, 35 Sw. U. L. REV. 431, 431 (2006).

3. HADEN-GUEST, *supra* note 2, at 16.

4. Robins v. Zwirner, 713 F. Supp. 2d 367 (S.D.N.Y. 2010).

5. *Id.* at 370.

6. *Id.* at 371.

7. *Id.*

8. *Id.* at 373.

9. *Id.* at 377.

10. *Id.* at 376.

11. Caslon Analytics, *supra* note 1; *see also* http://art-zurich.com/en/zurich-museums.html.

12. Caslon Analytics, *supra* note 1.

13. 16 COLUM.-VLA J.L. & ARTS 185,382 (1991-1992)(reprinting U.S. Copyright Office, Library of Congress, *Droit de Suite: The Artist's Resale Royalty*, Copyright Office Report Executive Summary (1992)).

14. For an informative wide-ranging discussion on *droit de suite*, see Channah Farber, *Note and Comment: Advancing the Arts Community in New Mexico Through Moral Rights and Droit de Suite: The International Impetus and Implications of Preemption Analysis*, 36 N.M. L. REV. 713 (Summer 2006).

15. *Id.* at 718.

16. *Id.* at 728 (citing Pierre Valentin, *Keeping Up with Art and Cultural Assets*, Withers Newsl. (Withers, London, United Kingdom, Summer 2005)).

17. Directive 2001/84/EC, Ch. I Art.1(1).

18. *Id.* Ch. I Art.2 (1) and (2).

19. *Id.* Ch. I Art.1(2).

20. *Id.* Whereas clause 18.

21. *Id.* Ch. II Art.8(1).

22. *Id.* Ch. II Art.4(1).

23. *Id.* Ch. II Art.1 and 2.

24. *Id.* Ch. I Art.1(4).

25. *Id.* Ch. III Art.12(1).

26. *Id.* Ch. II Art.8(2). For reasons presented to and approved by the European Commission, the deadline was not later than January 1,2012. *Id.* Ch. II Art 8(3).

27. *Id.* Ch. II Art.7(1).

28. *Id.* Ch. II Art.7(3).

29. *See, e.g.*, www.theglobeandmail.com/news/arts/visual-artists-seek-s-percentage-of-resale-riches/article1778386/; www.entertainm,entmedialawsignal.com/promo/about/; www.cinoa.org/index.pl?iid=2317&isa=Category ; (EU nations: www.cinoa.org/index.pl?iid=2316&isa=Categor).

30. Visual Artists Rights Act of 1987, S. 1619, H.R. 3221 (1987).

31. Visual Artists Rights Act of 1988, S. 1619, H.R. 3221 (1988).

32. Visual Artists Rights Act of 1990, Pub. L. No. 101-650, tit. VI, 104 Stat. 5089 (1990).

33. *Id.* § 608(b).

34. LIBRARY OF CONGRESS COPYRIGHT OFFICE GENERAL COUNSEL, DROIT DE SUITE: THE ARTIST'S RESALE ROYALTY: A REPORT OF THE REGISTER OF COPYRIGHTS (Dec. 1992).

35. *Id.* at 240.

36. *Id.* at 239.

37. *Id.* at 243-44. *See, e.g.*, Bernhard Berger, *Why Resale Rights for Artists Are a Bad Idea*, Selected Problems in Art Law, March 6, 2001 at www.law.harvard.edu/faculty/.../why_resale_rights_for_artists.htm.
38. *Id.* at 143.
39. *Id.* at 149.
40. *See, e.g.*, Andrew Russel, *VAGA Will Lobby for Federal Resale Royalties Bill*, Gallerist NY, *available at* http://galleristny.com/2011/11/vaga-plans-federal-resale-royalties-bill-as-artists-and-auction-houses-battle/.
41. H.R. 3688, 112th Cong., 1st Sess.
42. S. 2000, 112th Cong., 1st Sess.
43. Estate of Graham v. Sotheby's Inc., No. 2:11-cv-08604-JNH-FFM, 2012 WL 1765445 (C.D. Cal. May 17, 2012).
44. CAL. CIV. CODE § 986.
45. Emley, *The Resale Royalties Act: Paintings, Preemption and Profit*, 8 GOLDEN GATE U. L. REV. 239 (1978); Bolch, Damon & Hinshaw, *An Economic Analysis of the California Art Royalty Statute*, 10 CONN. L. REV. 689 (1978); Damich, *Moral Rights Protection and Resale Royalties for Visual Arts in the United States: Development and Current Status*, 12 CARDOZO ARTS & ENT. L.J. 387 (1994).
46. CAL. CIV. CODE § 986(a).
47. *Id.* § 986(c)(2).
48. *Id.* § 986(b)(1).
49. *Id.* § 986(b).
50. *Id.* § 986(a).
51. *Id.* § 986(c)(1).
52. *Id.* § 986(a).
53. *Id.* § 986(a)(1).
54. *Id.* § 986(a)(2).
55. *Id.* § 986(a)(5).
56. *Id.* § 986(a)(3).
57. *Id.* § 986(b)(3).
58. *Id.* § 986(a)(7).
59. *Id.* § 986(a).
60. Morseburg v. Balyon, 621 F.2d 972 (9th Cir.), *cert. denied*, 449 U.S. 983 (1980).
61. The 1976 Copyright Act became effective after the sales in question.
62. *See* Note, *The Preemption Doctrine: Shifting Perspectives on Federalism and the Burger Court*, 75 COLUM. L. REV. 623 (1975).
63. Goldstein v. California, 412 U.S. 546 (1973).
64. *See Morseburg*, 621 F.2d at 977.
65. *See* Bauer v. O'Donnell, 229 U.S. 1, 11 (1912).
66. *See Morseburg*, 621 F.2d at 977.
67. Baby Moose Drawings, Inc. v. Valentine, No. 11-00697, 2011 WL 1258529 (C.D. Cal. Apr. 1, 2011).
68. Robert H. Jacobs, Inc. v. Westoaks Realtors, Inc., 159 Cal. App. 3d 637, 205 Cal. Rptr. 620 (2d Dist. 1984).
69. Simons v. Horowitz, 151 Cal. App. 3d 834, 199 Cal. Rptr. 134 (1st Dist. 1984).
70. Estate of Graham v. Sotheby's Inc., Case No. 2:11-cv-08604-JNH-FFM, 2012 WL 1765445 (C.D. Cal. May 17, 2012).
71. *Id.*, 2012 WL 1765445, at *3.
72. *Id.* at *4.
73. *Id.*
74. *Id.*
75. *Id.* at *5.
76. *Id.*
77. *Id.* at *6.

78. *Id.*
79. Ga. Code Ann. §§ 8-5-1 to 8-5-9.
80. *Id.* § 8-5-3(4).
81. *Id.* § 8-5-7(a)(3).
82. *Id.* § 8-5-7(b).

APPENDIX 13-1

Model Droit de Suite *System**

Should Congress determine that federal *droit de suite* legislation is the best way to help artists, the Copyright Office suggests consideration for the following model system.

1. Oversight of the *Droit de Suite*: Collection and Enforcement

The Copyright Office suggests the Congress consider collective management of the *droit de suite* through a private authors' rights collecting society. The collection of art resale royalties would be handled on a direct or contractual basis, similar to collection of musical performance royalties by ASCAP and BMI.

The *droit de suite* has been effectively implemented only in those countries with active and efficient national authors' societies, such as SPADEM in France and Bild-Kunst in Germany. In the United States, the Artists' Rights Society (ARS) or the Visual Artists and Galleries Association, Inc. (VAGA), would be equipped to handle the practical collection of the *droit de suite*, since these organizations already have an effective collection and distribution system for reproduction rights. The royalty is collected by the society, which takes a percentage for administrative costs and distributes the remainder to the artist.

Individual management, as seen in California, places a nearly insurmountable burden on the artist to obtain information and to assert claims, often against valued clients or gallery owners. Likewise, the bureaucratic approach has proven far less successful than collective, private management.

The Office could serve a record-keeping function similar to the arts registry proposed in the Kennedy-Markey bills. Copyright Office records would be available to the artists' rights societies for purposes of collection, enforcement, and distribution. If a resale royalty were adopted in the United States, and particularly if it were extended to include dealer sales, the Office anticipates that a collection system with elements similar to the French or German systems would have the best chance of success.

2. Types of Sales

The Copyright Office suggests that, if a resale royalty is enacted in the United States, it should apply initially only to public auction sales. Auction sales are easiest to monitor. Including dealer sales—or even private sales, as proposed in the Waxman and Kennedy-Markey bills—increases the administrative and enforcement challenge.

The resale royalty could apply initially to auction houses and then in about five years, Congress could determine whether it should be extended.

The French law originally applied only to sales at auction, and Belgium has preserved this limitation. In 1957, France extended its law to sales "through a dealer" but implementing rules were never issued and the law still applies in practice only to auction. The French galleries do, however, make payments to an artists' social security. The German law requires a royalty on both auction and dealer sales, but in reality, Bild-Kunst collects a flat percentage of gallery revenue paid partly to artists qualifying for *droit de suite* and partly to an artists' social security fund.

As the collection mechanism matures, the artists' societies such as VAGA and ARS could develop a system to collect art resale royalties from galleries in this country that might be similar to the collection of performance royalties from radio stations by ASCAP, BMI and SESAC. Further, if the European Community adopts a position including dealers within a *droit de suite* requirement, that might be a justification for extending coverage to dealers in this country.

3. Measuring the Royalty

Based on the California and European experiences, a flat royalty of between three and five percent on the total gross sales price of the work seems more appropriate. There would be no need initially to set a threshold price to trigger the royalty mechanism if the royalty were applied initially only to auction sales, because auction sales usually deal in works with a minimum floor price. Similarly, there may be no practical need to legislate a floor price for dealer sales: Although one arts organization recommended a threshold resale price of as high as $5,000 to trigger the *droit de suite*, and Kennedy-Markey called for a threshold of $1,000, other groups called for figures as low as $250 or $500. Again, most art dealers trade only in works of at least that value, particularly in the resale market.

In those countries that have most successfully implemented the *droit de suite*, including France, Germany and Belgium, the resale royalty is measured on the total resale price. Measuring the royalty by the resale price departs from the rationale of allowing artists to participate in an increase in value, but is considered simpler and more practical. The difficulty in administering a royalty based on the difference between the purchase price and resale price may explain the law's disuse in countries such as Italy and Czechoslovakia.

Any resale royalty legislation could contain a rebuttable presumption that a work has increased in value between the time of purchase and resale. The purchaser/reseller would have the burden of proving to the collecting society that a work has not appreciated in value and therefore a royalty is not due.

4. Term

A term for the *droit de suite* coextensive with copyright seems appropriate. Under the current copyright law, this is life of the author plus 50 years. Should the European Community adopt a term for the *droit de suite* of life plus 70 years, there would be justification for similarly extending the term here.

The *droit de suite* would be descendible in a manner analogous to copyright.

5. Foreign Artists

The resale royalty would be applied to foreign artists on the basis of reciprocity. This is consistent with the Berne Convention and the general consensus.

6. Alienability

The Berne Convention recognizes an inalienable right to the resale royalty. The Office concludes that if a resale royalty is enacted in the United States it should be inalienable, but transferable for purposes of assigning collection rights. The Office also suggests that the *droit de suite* be non-waivable. However, this latter suggestion may be subject to the ultimate resolution of the waivability of moral rights in the United States.

7. Types of Works

The Copyright Office suggests that any *droit de suite* legislation apply to works of visual art as defined in 17 U.S.C. § 101 and in the Visual Artists Rights Act of 1990, with the following exception: For works in limited edition, the Copyright Office would suggest that the statute should fix the number of copies to which the resale royalty would apply at 10 or fewer. In France, for example, the royalty applies to eight copies of a limited edition sculptural work, which must be numbered, signed, and executed or controlled (*e.g.*, cast) by the artist.

8. Retroactivity

The Office suggests that, if Congress adopts a *droit de suite*, it should make the law prospective only, *i.e.*, effective only as to the resale of eligible works created on or after the date the law becomes effective.

* Reproduced from: *Droit De Suite*: The Artist's Resale Royalty, A Report of the Register of Copyrights, December 1992.

APPENDIX 13-2

California Resale Royalties Act

CALIFORNIA RESALE ROYALTIES ACT
CAL. CIV. CODE
SEC. 986. SALE OF FINE ART.

(a) Whenever a work of fine art is sold and the seller resides in California or the sale takes place in California, the seller or the seller's agent shall pay to the artist of such work of fine art or to such artist's agent 5 percent of the amount of such sale. The right of the artist to receive an amount equal to 5 percent of the amount of such sale may be waived only by a contract in writing providing for an amount in excess of 5 percent of the amount of such sale. An artist may assign the right to collect the royalty payment provided by this section to another individual or entity. However, the assignment shall not have the effect of creating a waiver prohibited by this subdivision.

(1) When a work of fine art is sold at an auction or by a gallery, dealer, broker, museum, or other person acting as the agent for the seller the agent shall withhold 5 percent of the amount of the sale, locate the artist and pay the artist.

(2) If the seller or agent is unable to locate and pay the artist within 90 days, an amount equal to 5 percent of the amount of the sale shall be tranferred to the Arts Council.

(3) If a seller or the seller's agent fails to pay an artist the amount equal to 5 percent of the sale of a work of fine art by the artist or fails to transfer such amount to the Arts Council, the artist may bring an action for damages within three years after the date of sale or one year after the discovery of the sale, whichever is longer. The prevailing party in any action brought under this paragraph shall be entitled to reasonable attorney fees, in an amount as determined by the court.

(4) Moneys received by the council pursuant to this section shall be deposited in an account in the Special Deposit Fund in the State Treasury.

(5) The Arts Council shall attempt to locate any artist for whom money is received pursuant to this section. If the council is unable to locate the artist and the artist does not file a written claim for the money received by the council within seven years of the date of sale of the work of fine art, the right of the artist terminates and such money shall be transferred to the council for use in acquiring fine art pursuant to the Art in Public Buildings program set

forth in Chapter 2.1 (commencing with *Section 15813*) *of Part 10b of Division 3 of Title 2, of the Government Code.*

(6) Any amounts of money held by any seller or agent for the payment of artists pursuant to this section shall be exempt from enforcement of a money judgment by the creditors of the seller or agent.

(7) Upon the death of an artist, the rights and duties created under this section shall inure to his or her heirs, legatees, or personal representative, until the 20th anniversary of the death of the artist. The provisions of this paragraph shall be applicable only with respect to an artist who dies after January 1, 1983.

(b) Subdivision (a) shall not apply to any of the following:

(1) To the initial sale of a work of fine art where legal title to such work at the time of such initial sale is vested in the artist thereof.

(2) To the resale of a work of fine art for a gross sales price of less than one thousand dollars ($1,000).

(3) Except as provided in paragraph (7) of subdivision (a), to a resale after the death of such artist.

(4) To the resale of the work of fine art for a gross sales price less than the purchase price paid by the seller.

(5) To a transfer of a work of fine art which is exchanged for one or more works of fine art or for a combination of cash, other property, and one or more works of fine art where the fair market value of the property exchanged is less than one thousand dollars ($1,000).

(6) To the resale of a work of fine art by an art dealer to a purchaser within 10 years of the initial sale of the work of fine art by the artist to an art dealer, provided all intervening resales are between art dealers.

(7) To a sale of a work of stained glass artistry where the work has been permanently attached to real property and is sold as part of the sale of the real property to which it is attached.

(c) For purposes of this section, the following terms have the following meanings:

(1) "Artist" means the person who creates a work of fine art and who, at the time of resale, is a citizen of the United States, or a resident of the state who has resided in the state for a minimum of two years.

(2) "Fine art" means an original painting, sculpture, or drawing, or an original work of art in glass.

(3) "Art dealer" means a person who is actively and principally engaged in or conducting the business of selling works of fine art for which business such person validly holds a sales tax permit.

(d) This section shall become operative on January 1, 1977, and shall apply to works of fine art created before and after its operative date.

(e) If any provision of this section or the application thereof to any person or circumstance is held invalid for any reason, such invalidity shall not affect any other provisions or applications of this section which can be effected, without the invalid provision or application, and to this end the provisions of this section are severable.

(f) The amendments to this section enacted during the 1981-82 Regular Session of the Legislature shall apply to transfers of works of fine art, when created before or after January 1, 1983, that occur on or after that date.

APPENDIX 13-3

Jurist Contract Form

SALE AND PURCHASE AGREEMENT

THIS AGREEMENT, made this ____ day of _____, 20__, between _____, residing at _____ ("Artist"), and _____, residing at _____ ("Collector").

WITNESSETH:

WHEREAS, Artist has created a certain work of art (the "Work"), which is fully described in Paragraph 1 below; and

WHEREAS, Collector desires to purchase the Work from Artist and Artist is willing to sell the Work to Collector upon the terms set forth in this Agreement.

NOW, THEREFORE, in consideration of the mutual promises set forth in this Agreement, as well as other good and valuable consideration, the receipt of which is hereby mutually acknowledged, the parties do hereby covenant and agree as follows:

1. The Transaction. The Artist hereby sells to the Collector, and the Collector hereby purchases from the Artist, for a total price of $_____ (the "Purchase Price"), the Work, which is described and identified as follows:

Title:
Medium:
Dimensions:
Date (or approximate period of creation):
Edition _____ of _____

2. Edition and Provenance. (a) Unless otherwise indicated in the space "Edition" in Paragraph 1 of this Agreement, the Work is unique. If the Work is unique, Artist hereby covenants that Artist shall not produce any exact duplicate of the Work; if the Work is one of an edition, Artist hereby covenants that the size of the edition shall not be increased after the date of execution of this Agreement.

(b) Upon receipt of a written request from Collector, Artist shall provide Collector with a written statement attesting to the authenticity of the Work and setting forth the size of the edition, if any.

3. Care of Work. (a) So long as the Work remains in Collector's possession, Col-

lector covenants to exercise reasonable care in maintaining the Work and further covenants not to alter or destroy the Work intentionally.

(b) If the Work is damaged in any manner, Collector shall notify Artist of the occurrence and the nature of the damage and shall afford Artist a reasonable opportunity to conduct, or to supervise, the restoration of the Work.

(c) If Artist does not take steps to commence the restoration of the Work within thirty (30) days after receipt of notice of damage from Collector, Collector shall be free to make whatever arrangements Collector deems appropriate for the restoration of the Work.

(d) Nothing contained in this Paragraph 3 shall be construed to require that Collector cause or permit the Work to be moved from the place where it is usually kept in order to allow Artist to conduct, or to supervise, its restoration.

4. Artist's Right to Borrow. (a) Artist reserves the right, upon giving Collector reasonable notice, to borrow the Work from Collector in order to include it in a public exhibition of Artist's works. Collector shall have the right, before permitting Artist to borrow the Work, to demand the submission, by Artist or by the exhibiting institution, of documents evidencing adequate insurance coverage on the Work and prepayment of shipping charges to and from the exhibiting institution.

(b) Artist shall not be entitled to borrow the Work more than once in any twelve-month period or for any single period longer than six (6) weeks, unless otherwise agreed to in writing by Collector.

(c) If Artist borrows the Work for inclusion in a public exhibition, it shall be Artist's responsibility to ensure that the exhibiting institution identifies the Work as belonging to Collector.

5. Notices to Be Supplied by Collector. (a) If Collector moves from the address set forth at the opening of this Agreement, Collector shall promptly notify Artist of the new address. Collector shall also promptly notify Artist of any subsequent changes of address.

(b) Collector shall notify Artist if Collector intends to lend the Work to any museum, gallery or other institution for purposes of exhibition or otherwise. If the Work is to be publicly exhibited, such notice shall include the name of the exhibiting institution, the title of the exhibition, the dates of the exhibition, and the name of the curator or other person, if any, in charge of the exhibition.

6. Reproduction. (a) Collector shall be entitled to permit the reproduction of the Work in books, art magazines and exhibition catalogues, as Collector shall see fit.

(b) Except as provided in subparagraph 6(a) above, Artist hereby reserves all rights whatsoever to copy or reproduce the Work, and Collector agrees not to permit such reproduction without first securing the written consent of the Artist.

(c) Nothing contained in this Paragraph 6 shall be construed as requiring that the Collector afford access to the Work for purposes of its being photographed, copied, or reproduced.

(d) *There may be inserted here a subparagraph governing the division between Artist and Collector of any fees received for a reproduction of the Work which Artist authorizes pursuant to subparagraph 6(b) above.*

7. Transfer of the Work. (a) If Collector, at any time after the execution of this Agreement, sells the Work, Collector shall pay to Artist a sum equal to fifteen percent (15%) of the excess of the gross amount realized from the sale of the Work over the Purchase Price.

(b) If Collector, at any time after the execution of this Agreement, exchanges, barters or trades the Work for another work of art, Collector shall pay to Artist a sum equal to fifteen percent (15%) of the excess of the fair market value of the work of art which Collector receives over the Purchase Price.

(c) Collector may, at any time, donate the Work to a museum and, in the event of such donation, no payment shall be required to be made to Artist. If, however, at any time after the execution of this Agreement, Collector donates the Work to any institution other than a museum and takes a tax deduction with respect of such donation, Collector shall pay Artist a sum equal to fifteen percent (15%) of the excess of the tax deduction so taken over the Purchase Price.

(d) If Collector, at any time after the execution of this Agreement, gives or transfers the Work to any person in any manner other than those enumerated in subparagraphs (a) through (c) of this Paragraph 7, Collector shall pay to Artist a sum equal to fifteen percent (15%) of the excess of the fair market value of the Work at the time of such transfer over the Purchase Price.

8. Duration and Effect. This Agreement shall remain in full force and effect until five (5) years after the death of Artist and shall operate to bind the parties as well as their heirs, legatees, executors, and administrators. However, the obligations imposed upon Collector by Paragraphs 3(b) and 4 of this Agreement shall terminate immediately upon the death of Artist.

9. Construction. This Agreement shall inure to the benefit of, and shall be binding upon, the successors, heirs, executors and administrators of the parties hereto. Any dispute arising hereunder shall be resolved in the _____ state court or in the United States District Court for the _____, and the parties hereto consent to the personal jurisdiction of these courts and agree that these venues are convenient and not to seek a change of venue or to seek to dismiss the action on the ground of forum non conveniens, not to remove any litigation from either of these courts to another federal court, not to assert any defense based on lack of jurisdiction of this court, and not to bring any action arising under, in connection with, or incidental to this Agreement in any other court.

10. Headings. Paragraph headings have been included in this Agreement solely for purposes of convenience and such headings shall not have legal effect or in any way affect the extent or interpretation of any of the terms of this Agreement.

IN WITNESS WHEREOF the parties have signed this Agreement as of the date first above written.

ARTIST

_____

[Name of Artist]

COLLECTOR

_____

[Name of Collector]

APPENDIX 13-4

European Union Directive on Resale Rights

SCOPE

DIRECTIVE 2001 / 84 / EC
OF THE EUROPEAN PARLIAMENT
AND OF THE COUNCIL
OF 27 SEPTEMBER 2001
ON THE RESALE FOR THE BENEFIT
OF THE AUTHOR OF
AN ORIGINAL WORK OF ART

THE EUROPEAN PARLIAMENT AND THE COUNCIL OF THE EURO-
PEAN UNION,

Having regard to the Treaty establishing the European Community, and in particular Article 95 thereof,

Having regard to the proposal from the Commission(1),

Having regard to the opinion of the Economic and Social Committee(2),

Acting in accordance with the procedure laid down in Article 251 of the Treaty(3),
and in the light of the joint text approved by the Conciliation Committee on 6
June 2001,

WHEREAS:

(1) In the field of copyright, the resale right is an unassignable and inalienable
right, enjoyed by the author of an original work of graphic or plastic art, to an
economic interest in successive sales of the work concerned.

(2) The resale right is a right of a productive character which enables the au-
thor/artist to receive consideration for successive transfers of the work. The subject-matter of the resale right is the physical work, namely the medium in which
the protected work is incorporated.

(3) The resale right is intended to ensure that authors of graphic and plastic
works of art share in the economic success of their original works of art. It helps
to redress the balance between the economic situation of authors of graphic and
plastic works of art and that of other creators who benefit from successive exploi-
tations of their works.

(4) The resale right forms an integral part of copyright and is an essential pre-rogative for authors. The imposition of such a right in all Member States meets the need for providing creators with an adequate and standard level of protection.

(5) Under Article 151(4) of the Treaty the Community is to take cultural aspects into account in its action under other provisions of the Treaty.

(6) The Berne Convention for the Protection of Literary and Artistic Works pro-vides that the resale right is available only if legislation in the country to which the author belongs so permits. The right is therefore optional and subject to the rule of reciprocity. It follows from the case-law of the Court of Justice of the Eu-ropean Communities on the application of the principle of non-discrimination laid down in Article 12 of the Treaty, as shown in the judgment of 20 October 1993 in Joined Cases C-92/92 and C-326/92 Phil Collins and Others (4), that do-mestic provisions containing reciprocity clauses cannot be relied upon in order to deny nationals of other Member States rights conferred on national authors. The application of such clauses in the Community context runs counter to the principle of equal treatment resulting from the prohibition of any discrimination on grounds of nationality.

(7) The process of internationalisation of the Community market in modern and contemporary art, which is now being speeded up by the effects of the new economy, in a regulatory context in which few States outside the EU recognise the resale right, makes it essential for the European Community, in the external sphere, to open negotiations with a view to making Article 14b of the Berne Con-vention compulsory.

(8) The fact that this international market exists, combined with the lack of a re-sale right in several Member States and the current disparity as regards national systems which recognise that right, make it essential to lay down transitional provisions as regards both entry into force and the substantive regulation of the right, which will preserve the competitiveness of the European market.

(9) The resale right is currently provided for by the domestic legislation of a majority of Member States. Such laws, where they exist, display certain differ-ences, notably as regards the works covered, those entitled to receive royalties, the rate applied, the transactions subject to payment of a royalty, and the basis on which these are calculated. The' application or non-application of such a right has a significant impact on the competitive environment within the internal market, since the existence or absence of an obligation to pay on the basis of the resale right is an element which must be taken into account by each individual wish-ing to sell a work of art. This right is therefore a factor which contributes to the creation of distortions of competition as well as displacement of sales within the Community.

(10) Such disparities with regard to the existence of the resale right and its application by the Member States have a direct negative impact on the proper functioning of the internal market in works of art as provided for by Article 14 of the Treaty. In such a situation Article 95 of the Treaty constitutes the appropriate legal basis.

(11) The objectives of the Community as set out in the Treaty include laying the foundations of an ever closer union among the peoples of Europe, promoting closer relations between the Member States belonging to the Community, and ensuring their economic and social progress by common action to eliminate the barriers which divide Europe. To that end the Treaty provides for the establishment of an internal market which presupposes the abolition of obstacles to the free movement of goods, freedom to provide services and freedom of establishment, and for the introduction of a system ensuring that competition in the common market is not distorted. Harmonisation of Member States' laws on the resale right contributes to the attainment of these objectives.

(12) The Sixth Council Directive (77/388/EEC) of 17 May 1977 on the harmonisation of the laws of the Member States relating to turnover taxes – common system of value added tax: uniform basis of assessment(5), progressively introduces a Community system of taxation applicable inter alia to works of art. Measures confined to the tax field are not sufficient to guarantee the harmonious functioning of the art market. This objective cannot be attained without harmonisation in the field of the resale right.

(13) Existing differences between laws should be eliminated where they have a distorting effect on the functioning of the internal market, and the emergence of any new differences of that kind should be prevented. There is no need to eliminate, or prevent the emergence of, differences which cannot be expected to affect the functioning of the internal market.

(14) A precondition of the proper functioning of the internal market is the existence of conditions of competition which are not distorted. The existence of differences between national provisions on the resale right creates distortions of competition and displacement of sales within the Community and leads to unequal treatment between artists depending on where their works are sold. The issue under consideration has therefore transnational aspects which cannot be satisfactorily regulated by action by Member States. A lack of Community action would conflict with the requirement of the Treaty to correct distortions of competition and unequal treatment.

(15) In view of the scale of divergences between national provisions it is therefore necessary to adopt harmonising measures to deal with disparities between the laws of the Member States in areas where such disparities are liable to create or maintain distorted conditions of competition. It is not however necessary to

harmonise every provision of the Member States' laws on the resale right and, in order to leave as much scope for national decision as possible, it is sufficient to limit the harmonisation exercise to those domestic provisions that have the most direct impact on the functioning of the internal market.

(16) This Directive complies therefore, in its entirety, with the principles of subsidiarity and proportionality as laid down in Article 5 of the Treaty.

(17) Pursuant to Council Directive 93/98/EEC of 29 October 1993 harmonising the term of protection of copyright and certain related rights(6), the term of copyright runs for 70 years after the author's death. The same period should be laid down for the resale right: Consequently, only the originals of works of modern and contemporary art may fall within the scope of the resale right. However, in order to allow the legal systems of Member States which do not, at the time of the adoption of this Directive, apply a resale right for the benefit of artists to incorporate this right into their respective legal systems and, moreover, to enable the economic operators in those Member States to adapt gradually to the aforementioned right whilst maintaining their economic viability, the Member States concerned should be allowed a limited transitional period during which they may choose not to apply the resale right for the benefit of those entitled under the artist after his death.

(18) The scope of the resale right should be extended to all acts of resale, with the exception of those effected directly between persons acting in their private capacity without the participation of an art market professional. This right should not extend to acts of resale by persons acting in their private capacity to museums which are not for profit and which are open to the public. With regard to the particular situation of art galleries which acquire works directly from the author, Member States should be allowed the option of exempting from the resale right acts of resale of those works which take place within three years of that acquisition. The interests of the artist should also be taken into account by limiting this exemption to such acts of resale where the resale price does not exceed EUR 10000.

(19) It should be made clear that the harmonisation brought about by this Directive does not apply to original manuscripts of writers and composers.

(20) Effective rules should be laid down based on experience already gained at national level with the resale right. It is appropriate to calculate the royalty as a percentage of the sale price and not of the increase in value of works whose original value has increased.

(21) The categories of works of art subject to the resale right should be harmonised.

(22) The non-application of royalties below the minimum threshold may help to avoid disproportionately high collection and administration costs compared with the profit for the artist. However, in accordance with the principle of subsidiarity, the Member States should be allowed to establish national thresholds lower than the Community threshold, so as to promote the interests of new artists. Given the small amounts involved, this derogation is not likely to have a significant effect on the proper functioning of the internal market.

(23) The rates set by the different Member States for the application of the resale right vary considerably at present. The effective functioning of the internal market in works of modern and contemporary art requires the fixing of uniform rates to the widest possible extent.

(24) It is desirable to establish, with the intention of reconciling the various interests involved in the market for original works of art, a system consisting of a tapering scale of rates for several price bands. It is important to reduce the risk of sales relocating and of the circumvention of the Community rules on the resale right.

(25) The person by whom the royalty is payable should, in principle, be the seller. Member States should be given the option to provide for derogations from this principle in respect of liability for payment. The seller is the person or undertaking on whose behalf the sale is concluded.

(26) Provision should be made for the possibility of periodic adjustment of the threshold and rates. To this end, it is appropriate to entrust to the Commission the task of drawing up periodic reports on the actual application of the resale right in the Member States and on the impact on the art market in the Community and, where appropriate, of making proposals relating to the amendment of this Directive.

(27) The persons entitled to receive royalties must be specified, due regard being had to the principle of subsidiarity. It is not appropriate to take action through this Directive in relation to Member States' laws of succession. However, those entitled under the author must be able to benefit fully from the resale right after his death, at least following the expiry of the transitional period referred to above.

(28) The Member States are responsible for regulating the exercise of the resale right, particularly with regard to the way this is managed. In this respect management by a collecting society is one possibility. Member States should ensure that collecting societies operate in a transparent and efficient manner. Member States must also ensure that amounts intended for authors who are nationals of other Member States are in fact collected and distributed. This Directive is without prejudice to arrangements in Member States for collection and distribution.

(29) Enjoyment of the resale right should be restricted to Community nationals as well as to foreign authors whose countries afford such protection to authors who are nationals of Member States. A Member State should have the option of extending enjoyment of this right to foreign authors who have their habitual residence in that Member State.

(30) Appropriate procedures for monitoring transactions should be introduced so as to ensure by practical means that the resale right is effectively applied by Member States. This implies also a right on the part of the author or his authorised representative to obtain any necessary information from the natural or legal person liable for payment of royalties. Member States which provide for collective management of the resale right may also provide that the bodies responsible for that collective management should alone be entitled to obtain information,

HAVE ADOPTED THIS DIRECTIVE:

CHAPTER I

SCOPE

ARTICLE 1
SUBJECT MATTER OF THE RESALE RIGHT

1. Member States shall provide, for the benefit of the author of an original work of art, a resale right, to be defined as an inalienable right, which cannot be waived, even in advance, to receive a royalty based on the sale price obtained for any resale of the work, subsequent to the first transfer of the work by the author.

2. The right referred to in paragraph 1 shall apply to all acts of resale involving as sellers, buyers or intermediaries art market professionals, such as salesrooms, art galleries and, in general, any dealers in works of art.

3. Member States may provide that the right referred to in paragraph 1 shall not apply to acts of resale where the seller has acquired the work directly from the author less than three years before that resale and where the resale price does not exceed EUR 10000.

4. The royalty shall be payable by the seller. Member States may provide that one of the natural or legal persons referred to in paragraph 2 other than the seller shall alone be liable or shall share liability with the seller for payment of the royalty.

ARTICLE 2
WORKS OF ART TO WHICH THE RESALE RIGHT RELATES

1. For the purposes of this Directive, "original work of art" means works of graphic or plastic art such as pictures, collages, paintings, drawings, engravings, prints, lithographs, sculptures, tapestries, ceramics, glassware and photographs, provided they are made by the artist himself or are copies considered to be original works of art.

2. Copies of works of art covered by this Directive, which have been made in limited numbers by the artist himself or under his authority, shall be considered to be original works of art for the purposes of this Directive. Such copies will normally have been numbered, signed or otherwise duly authorised by the artist.

CHAPTER II

PARTICULAR PROVISIONS

ARTICLE 3
THRESHOLD

1. It shall be for the Member States to set a minimum sale price from which the sales referred to in Article 1 shall be subject to resale right.

2. This minimum sale price may not under any circumstances exceed EUR 3000.

ARTICLE 4
RATES

1. The royalty provided for in Article 1 shall be set at the following rates:

    (a) 4% for the portion of the sale price up to EUR 50000;
    (b) 3% for the portion of the sale price from EUR 50000,01 to EUR 200000;
    (c) 1% for the portion of the sale price from EUR 200000,01 to EUR 350000;
    (d) 0,5% for the portion of the sale price from EUR 350000,01 to EUR 500000;
    (e) 0,25% for the portion of the sale price exceeding EUR 500000.

However, the total amount of the royalty may not exceed EUR 12500.

2. By way of derogation from paragraph 1, Member States may apply a rate of 5% for the portion of the sale price referred to in paragraph 1(a).

3. If the minimum sale price set should be lower than EUR 3000, the Member

State shall also determine the rate applicable to the portion of the sale price up to EUR 3000; this rate may not be lower than 4%.

ARTICLE 5
CALCULATION BASIS

The sale prices referred to in Articles 3 and 4 are net of tax.

ARTICLE 6
PERSONS ENTITLED TO RECEIVE ROYALTIES

1. The royalty provided for under Article 1 shall be payable to the author of the work and, subject to Article 8(2), after his death to those entitled under him/her.

2. Member States may provide for compulsory or optional collective management of the royalty provided for under Article 1.

ARTICLE 7
THIRD-COUNTRY NATIONALS ENTITLED TO RECEIVE ROYALTIES

1. Member States shall provide that authors who are nationals of third countries and, subject to Article 8(2), their successors in title shall enjoy the resale right in accordance with this Directive and the legislation of the Member State concerned only if legislation in the country of which the author or his/her successor in title is a national permits resale right protection in that country for authors from the Member States and their successors in title.

2. On the basis of information provided by the Member States, the Commission shall publish as soon as possible an indicative list of those third countries which fulfil the condition set out in paragraph 1. This list shall be kept up to date.

3. Any Member State may treat authors who are not nationals of a Member State but who have their habitual residence in that Member State in the same way as its own nationals for the purpose of resale right protection.

ARTICLE 8
TERM OF PROTECTION OF THE RESALE RIGHT

1. The term of protection of the resale right shall correspond to that laid down in Article 1 of Directive 93/98/EEC.

2. By way of derogation from paragraph 1, those Member States which do not apply the resale right on (the entry into force date referred to in Article 13), shall not be required, for a period expiring not later than 1 January 2010, to apply the resale right for the benefit of those entitled under the artist after his/her death.

3. A Member State to which paragraph 2 applies may have up to two more years, if necessary to enable the economic operators in that Member State to adapt gradually to the resale right system while maintaining their economic viability, before it is required to apply the resale right for the benefit of those entitled under the artist after his/her death. At least 12 months before the end of the period referred to in paragraph 2, the Member State concerned shall inform the Commission giving its reasons, so that the Commission can give an opinion, after appropriate consultations, within three months following the receipt of such information. If the Member State does not follow the opinion of the Commission, it shall within one month inform the Commission and justify its decision. The notification and justification of the Member State and the opinion of the Commission shall be published in the Official Journal of the European Communities and forwarded to the European Parliament.

4. In the event of the successful conclusion, within the periods referred to in Article 8(2) and (3), of international negotiations aimed at extending the resale right at international level, the Commission shall submit appropriate proposals.

ARTICLE 9
RIGHT TO OBTAIN INFORMATION

The Member States shall provide that for a period of three years after the resale, the persons entitled under Article 6 may require from any art market professional mentioned in Article 1 (2) to furnish any information that may be necessary in order to secure payment of royalties in respect of the resale.

CHAPTER III

FINAL PROVISIONS

ARTICLE 10
APPLICATION IN TIME

This Directive shall apply in respect of all original works of art as defined in Article 2 which, on 1 January 2006, are still protected by the legislation of the Member States in the field of copyright or meet the criteria for protection under the provisions of this Directive at that date.

ARTICLE 11
REVISION CLAUSE

1. The Commission shall submit to the European Parliament, the Council and the Economic and Social Committee not later than 1 January 2009 and every four years thereafter a report on the implementation and the effect of this Directive, paying particular attention to the competitiveness of the market in modern

and contemporary art in the Community, especially as regards the position of the Community in relation to relevant markets that do not apply the resale right and the fostering of artistic creativity and the management procedures in the Member States. It shall examine in particular its impact on the internal market and the effect of the introduction of the resale right in those Member States that did not apply the right in national law prior to the entry into force of this Directive. Where appropriate, the Commission shall submit proposals for adapting the minimum threshold and the rates of royalty to take account of changes in the sector, proposals relating to the maximum amount laid down in Article 4(1) and any other proposal it may deem necessary in order to enhance the effectiveness of this Directive.

2. A Contact Committee is hereby established. It shall be composed of representatives of the competent authorities of the Member States. It shall be chaired by a representative of the Commission and shall meet either on the initiative of the Chairman or at the request of the delegation of a Member State.

3. The task of the Committee shall be as follows:

- to organise consultations on all questions deriving from application of this Directive,
- to facilitate the exchange of information between the Commission and the Member States on relevant developments in the art market in the Community.

ARTICLE 12
IMPLEMENTATION

1. Member States shall bring into force the laws, regulations and administrative provisions necessary to comply with this Directive before 1 January 2006. They shall forthwith inform the Commission thereof.

When Member States adopt these measures, they shall contain a reference to this Directive or shall be accompanied by such reference on the occasion of their official publication. The methods of making such a reference shall be laid down by the Member States.

2. Member States shall communicate to the Commission the provisions of national law which they adopt in the field covered by this Directive.

ARTICLE 13
ENTRY INTO FORCE

This Directive shall enter into force on the day of its publication in the Official Journal of the European Communities.

ARTICLE 14
ADDRESSEES

This Directive is addressed to the Member States.

Done at Brussels, 27 September 2001.

For the European Parliament

The President
N. Fontaine C. Picquee

For the Council

_____

_____

The President

(1) 03 C 178, 21.6.1996, p.16 and 01 C 125, 23.4.1998, p.8.
(2) OJ C 75, 10.3.1997, p.17.
(3) Opinion of the European Parliament of 9 April 1997 (OJ C 132, 28.4.1997, p.88), confirmed on 27 October 1999, Council Common Position of 19 June 2000 (OJ C 300, 20.10.2000, p.1) and Decision of the European Parliament of 13 December 2000 (OJ C 232, 17.8.2001, p.173). Decision of the European Parliament of 3 July 2001 and Decision of the Council of 19 July 2001.
(4) [1993] ECR 1-5145.
(5) OJ L 145, 13.6.1977, p.1. Directive as last amended by Directive 1999/85/EC (OJ L 277, 28.10.1999, p.34).
(6) 03 L 290, 24.11.1993, p.9.

PART FOUR

COLLECTORS

14

The Collection As Investment Property

Maintaining a collection in good condition is expensive; the expenses may include framing, reframing, lighting, air conditioning and humidity controls, cleaning and other maintenance, security devices, publications, and insurance. The collector may incur travel and other buying expenses and fees when he adds to a collection. Those costs have increased substantially in recent years.

This chapter focuses on the deductibility of the expenses of maintaining a collection, the tax treatment of gains and losses realized on sale of a collection, certain problems of insurance, and sales tax issues. Identification as a dealer, an investor, or a collector and the tax ramifications of each are discussed.

May an art owner deduct all, some, or a portion of such collection-related expenses and losses incurred in holding the collection as an investment, or are all those expenses nondeductible personal expenses incurred in a hobby for personal use and enjoyment?[1] Before that question can be answered, it is necessary to determine whether the individual in question is a dealer, an investor, or a collector and to examine the general statutory provisions.

DEFINITIONS

Dealer

A dealer is someone engaged in the trade or business of selling works of art, primarily to customers. Although the term "trade or business" is not specifically defined in the Internal Revenue Code, court cases indicate that it is the pursuit or occupation to which one contributes a major or substantial part of one's time for the purpose of livelihood or profit.[2]

In December 1983, the United States Court of Appeals for the Second Circuit held that the determination of whether a taxpayer is engaged in a trade or business is not based on all the facts and circumstances.[3] Instead, the Second Circuit ruled that the following three specific conditions must exist for a trade or business status to be recognized:

1. The taxpayer must be regularly engaged in the activity.
2. The activity must be undertaken with the expectation of making a profit.
3. The taxpayer must hold himself out to others as engaged in the selling of goods and services.

Then, in 1987, in *Commissioner v. Groetzinger*,[4] the United States Supreme Court reaffirmed a facts-and-circumstances test and rejected the Second Circuit's condition that the taxpayer must hold himself out to others as engaged in the selling of goods and services. The Court stated that a judicial attempt to formulate and impose a test for all situations would be counterproductive, unhelpful, and even somewhat precarious for the overall integrity of the Internal Revenue Code.

The Court stated that in order to be engaged in a trade or business the taxpayer must be involved in the activity with continuity and regularity, and the taxpayer's primary purpose for engaging in the activity must be for income or profit. A sporadic activity, a hobby, or an amusement diversion does not qualify. Moreover, mere investment activities do not constitute a trade or business.[5]

Investor

An investor is someone who buys and sells works of art primarily for investment, rather than for personal use and enjoyment or as a trade or business. The cases in the securities area that distinguish a dealer from an investor should be equally applicable to the art world.[6] The word "primarily" means "of first importance."[7] The key is whether the taxpayer is engaged in the investment activity with the primary objective of making a profit.

In *Thomas B. Drummond*,[8] the taxpayer was a psychologist who devoted an average of fifty-eight hours a week to his psychology practice. During the 1970s, the taxpayer, who had an interest in and enjoyed art, purchased a number of drawings at auction or from private galleries. Having conducted research about the drawings throughout the 1970s and 1980s, he concluded that one of them (*Three Famous Heads* by Michelangelo Anselmi), which he had purchased for $1,300, could be sold for about $100,000. The taxpayer sold the drawings to a museum for $115,000 in 1989. He made no other sales of drawings during the 1980s and through 1994. The taxpayer reported the gain from the sale as ordinary business income on income tax Form 1040, schedule C, not as long-term capital gain on schedule D, since the schedule C business income enabled him to obtain a larger deduction for a contribution to his retirement plan.[9] The court had to decide whether the gain from the sale of the drawings was gain from property held by the taxpayer "primarily for sale to customers in the ordinary course of his trade or business" within the meaning of section 1221(a)(1). If it was, the gain at issue was ordinary income; otherwise, it was long-term capital gain. As used in section 1221(a)(1), the word "primarily" means "of first importance" or "principally."[10] The court concluded that the taxpayer was not engaged in a trade or business with respect to his art activities and that the gain on the sale of the drawings was long-term capital gain.

The case contains an excellent summary of the relevant principles, pointing out that the purpose of section 1221(a)(1) is to differentiate between the profits and losses arising from the everyday operation of a business and the realization of appreciation in value accrued over a substantial period of time from an investment. In determining whether a transaction is primarily from the operation of a business or from investment, the courts have examined various factors, including the following:

(1) the purpose for which the property was acquired;
(2) the purpose for which it was held;
(3) the frequency, continuity, and substantiality of sales;
(4) the duration of ownership;
(5) the use of the proceeds from the sale of the property;
(6) the business of the taxpayer; and
(7) the time and effort that the taxpayer devoted to sales activities relating to the asset in question by developing or improving that asset, soliciting customers, and advertising.

No single factor or combination of factors is necessarily controlling, and objective factors carry more weight than the taxpayer's subjective statement of his intent.[11]

Collector

A collector is someone who buys and sells works of art primarily for personal pleasure and is neither a dealer nor an investor and, ordinarily, may not deduct expenses and losses.

Statutory Provisions

The statutory framework involves the interaction of sections 67, 68, 162, 212, 165, 183, and 262 of the Internal Revenue Code of 1986, as amended.

- Section 67 generally limits miscellaneous deductions to those that exceed 2% of adjusted gross income.
- Section 68 generally limits an individual taxpayer's ability to claim itemized deductions if the taxpayer's adjusted gross income exceeds a specified statutory amount.
- Under section 162, a taxpayer may deduct from gross income all ordinary and necessary expenses incurred in a trade or business.
- Under section 212(1) and (2), a taxpayer may deduct expenses incurred in the production or the collection of income.

- Section 165 permits the deduction of losses sustained in a trade or business or in a transaction entered into for profit.
- Section 183 qualifies the foregoing provisions by specifically disallowing, with certain exceptions, deductions attributable to activities not engaged in for profit.
- Section 262 denies a deduction or loss for expenses that are personal in nature.

Therefore, a taxpayer claiming a deduction for an expense under section 162 or section 212 or for a loss under section 165 must be able to demonstrate an associated profit motive in order to avoid the ban of section 183 or section 262.

EXPENSES

Prior Law

Before the Tax Reform Act of 1969 added section 183 to the Internal Revenue Code, collection-related expenses were deductible only by someone who is a dealer (that is, someone engaged in a trade or business) or an investor (that is, someone who holds the collection for the production of income).[12] The Court of Claims dealt with the issue of the deductibility of collection-related expenses in the *Wrightsman* case.[13]

Charles Wrightsman was an art collector, not a dealer, and he conceded that he had originally purchased some works of art as a hobby and that he did derive pleasure and satisfaction from keeping his collection in his residence. However, he claimed that the property was held primarily for investment and, therefore, that the expenses related to the investment were deductible. The court disallowed the deductions, ruling that the test to be applied is whether, as a factual matter from an objective view of the operative facts and circumstances, the taxpayer acquired and held the works of art primarily for investment, rather than for personal use and enjoyment.

In *Wrightsman*, the Court of Claims also established the following guidelines and criteria:

1. The collector must establish that the investment purpose for acquiring and holding the items in the collection was "principal" or "of first importance."[14]
2. Artworks or other items that make up a collection can be the subject matter of investment. (A number of investment funds have been started with the intention of investing only in artworks, including Sovereign American Arts, Collectors Funding, Art Fund, and Fine Arts Fund.)[15]
3. The collector must intend to hold the property for investment. That intent can be shown by an analysis of the art collector's financial position, the collector's investment history, whether the collector believes that

works of art are a hedge against inflation, and whether the collector has made personal declarations of investment purpose and intention that are supported by circumstances and conduct evidencing that intention. Other indications of investment intent include the following:

    a. Consulting with experts on purchases
    b. Reading pertinent publications
    c. Participating in collection-related activities
    d. Devoting time to the collection
    e. Making an effort to display the collection publicly, so as to enhance its value
    f. Developing expertise about the collection
    g. Keeping businesslike records and using a businesslike method of accounting for the collection[16]

4. The retention of a collection, without any profitable sales, is not a bar to a showing that the property is held for investment.[17]
5. Even though the collector uses part of the collection to fulfill personal needs, that use does not make the collector's overall activity a hobby.
6. The fact that pleasure is derived from investment property does not preclude deductions.[18]
7. The fact that there is no substantial relationship between the collector's principal occupation and his collection activities is of little significance.
8. The proportion of the collection-related expenses that is attributable to the personal use of the collection is not deductible. The proportion attributable to personal use is a close approximation based on all the facts and circumstances.[19]

On the basis of the facts presented in *Wrightsman*, the report of the trial commissioner of the Court of Claims recommended that the deduction for the art-related expenses be allowed.[20] However, the court did not adopt the trial commissioner's report and disallowed all the art-related expenses. A dissenting opinion to the decision of the court adopted the conclusion of the trial commissioner and, we believe, should have been the conclusion reached by the court.

Conclusions Under *Wrightsman*

Under section 162, the dealer who buys and sells works of art can deduct the ordinary and necessary business expenses incurred in the trade or business of being a dealer.

Under section 212(1) or section 212(2), the investor who buys and holds works of art primarily for investment can deduct the ordinary and necessary expenses incurred in connection with property held for the production of income.

Under section 262, the collector cannot deduct art-related expenses in connection with collecting activities, since those expenses are nondeductible personal expenses.

Still, the opinion in *Wrightsman* indicates that the collector faces an extremely difficult, although not impossible, task to prove that he is an investor. In the past not many collectors were able to show that they acquired and held the works of art primarily for investment, rather than for personal use and enjoyment. Currently, with ever-increasing prices for top-quality works of art, the drop in interest rates, and the inherent risk in the stock market, more collectors are acquiring works of art as investment property and should be able to carry the burden of proof that they are, in fact, investors in works of art.[21]

Section 183

The Tax Reform Act of 1969 introduced section 183 to the Internal Revenue Code, effective January 1, 1970.[22] Although the section is known as the hobby-loss provision, because it disallows deductions and losses from activities not engaged in for profit, it does permit the deduction of certain collection-related expenses that were not previously deductible. Section 183(a) provides the following:

> In the case of an activity engaged in by an individual or an S corporation, if such activity is not engaged in for profit, no deduction attributable to such activity shall be allowed under this chapter except as provided in this section.

Section 183(c) defines the term "activity not engaged in for profit" to mean

> any activity other than one with respect to which deductions are allowable for the taxable year under section 162 or under paragraph (1) or (2) of section 212.

Therefore, for a collector to avoid the application of section 183, a collection-related expense has to be from an activity engaged in for profit and the expense must be deductible under section 162 or section 212(1) or (2). As previously discussed, the *Wrightsman* case makes the deduction of collection-related expenses under such sections extremely difficult because of the onerous burden of proof the taxpayer has in proving to the Internal Revenue Service (IRS) that he incurred the expenses in connection with works of art held primarily for investment. A collector can avoid section 183 only if he can prove that the intent to make a profit was the main motivation for the activity. The question of a collector's intent is by its nature a subjective inquiry that can be determined only by examining a variety of objective facts.[23] As summarized by the Senate Finance Committee,

> the facts and circumstances (without regard to the taxpayer's subjective intent) would have to indicate that the taxpayer entered upon the activity, or continued the activity with the objective of making a profit.[24]

Regulation section 1.183-2 sets forth a number of factors similar to the indications of investment activity listed in *Wrightsman* to be considered in determining whether or not an activity is engaged in for profit. The factors were promulgated in an effort "to comply with the congressional purpose of establish-ing objective tests to determine subjective intentions."[25] While the focus on the determination of profit motive is on the subjective intention of the taxpayer, the objective criteria set forth in Regulation section 1.183-2(b) may be cited to estab-lish the taxpayer's true intent.[26] The IRS instructs its examiners that in order to properly develop a section 183 issue, they must address each of the nine factors in the section 183 regulation. Those factors are the following:

1. The manner in which the taxpayer carries on the activity. A business-like manner with complete and accurate books and records is more likely than not to be profit-motivated.[27] The businesslike operation of the activ-ity is probably the most important factor in indicating a profit motive. It is likewise important to be able to show that the taxpayer changed methods in response to a period of losses or pursuant to professional advice.[28] In *Churchman*,[29] the court found that an artist carried on her artistic activities in a businesslike manner for profit since her work did not stop at the creative stage but went into the marketing phase of the art business, where the recreational element is minimal. For the taxpayer with a collection, the maintenance of businesslike records is essential.[30] A collector who maintains good books and records for his activity is more likely to have the profit intent required to escape section 183. These re-cords should include the purchase or sale details from an art transaction. It would be helpful in proving profit intent if, prior to the purchase of a work of art, the collector had a written analysis of comparable prices for similar works by the same artist and other relevant financial data. In ad-dition, having a separate bank account for art purchases and expenses would be helpful. Failure to maintain adequate financial books and re-cords may be viewed as indicating a lack of the necessary profit intent.[31]

2. The expertise of the taxpayer or the taxpayer's advisers. Preparation for the activity by an extensive study of accepted business, economic, and scientific practices or by consultations with experts may indicate a profit motive.[32] For the taxpayer with a collection, consultation with art experts and subscriptions to auction catalogs and collection magazines indicate a profit motive. Obtaining from time to time a fair market value appraisal by an independent art appraiser for the taxpayer's collection would be in-dicative of a profit intent.[33]

3. The time and effort expended by the taxpayer in carrying on the activity. Spending a great deal of time and effort is more likely than not to indicate a profit motive.[34] Although it would be burdensome and inconvenient, a collector who kept a diary of the time devoted to visiting museums, art shows, art fairs, and galleries, reading art magazines, and consulting with auction houses, art dealers, and art experts would have an easier time showing a profit intent than a collector without such records.

4. The expectation that assets used in the activity may appreciate in value. The term "profit" does encompass appreciation in value of the assets, but

unrealized appreciation alone may not be sufficient.[35] The taxpayer must show that his primary purpose is ultimately to realize a gain from the appreciation in value of the asset.[36] Since the mere owning of a collection produces no income, a profit can be realized only from future appreciation of the collection. But the expectation of appreciation may be insufficient in and of itself to escape the provisions of section 183.[37] There must be a "good-faith expectation" that the collection will increase in value, not just a hope.[38]

5. The success of the taxpayer in carrying on other similar or dissimilar activities for a profit. The fact that the taxpayer has engaged in similar activities in the past and converted them from unprofitable to profitable may indicate that he is engaged in the present activity for profit, even though the activity is presently unprofitable.[39]

6. The taxpayer's history of income or losses with respect to the activity. A series of realizations of income may indicate a profit motive.[40] But the realization of income must be reasonable in light of the activity. For example, a collector who spent $5,000 traveling throughout Europe in pursuit of travel photography, but sold only $30 worth of pictures, did not have a profit motive.[41] In *Churchman*,[42] a twenty-year history of losses was not fatal for an artist since the court believed that an artist may require a long time to achieve success before a profit is realized.

7. The amount of occasional profits, if any, that are earned. A taxpayer who generates only infrequent and small profits is not likely to have a profit motive.[43] A sale of an item in a collection at a large gain is clear evidence of a profit motive.

8. The financial status of the taxpayer. The fact that the taxpayer does not have substantial income or capital from sources other than the activity in question may indicate that the activity is engaged in for profit.[44] On the other hand, a taxpayer with substantial income from sources other than the activity in question may not have a profit objective, especially if personal or recreational elements are involved.[45] For the collector of valuable items of property, the presence of other sources of income is a difficult element to overcome. Obviously, this is a catch-22 provision and should be given less weight for the collector, since valuable items cannot be purchased by someone who does not have other sources of income and substantial liquid assets. A taxpayer's wealth, or lack thereof, should not be a major factor in determining a profit motive from a collecting activity. What should be considered is whether, based on all the facts and circumstances, the activity was carried on with an honest intent to make a profit.

9. Elements of personal pleasure or recreation. The regulations indicate that the greater the pleasure, the less likely it is that the collector has a profit motive.[46] Although not required by the Internal Revenue Code or *Wrightsman*, a physical segregation of the art investment property from the taxpayer's personal residence or office generally helps the taxpayer

prove his profit motive. Since a collecting activity generally has strong elements of personal pleasure, it can be expected that the IRS will cast a doubtful eye on anyone claiming that the activity is primarily profit-motivated.[47] However, the regulations indicate that a taxpayer with both profit and nonprofit objectives may satisfy the profit intent requirement. The regulation states: "[T]he fact that the taxpayer derives personal pleasure from engaging in the activity is not sufficient to cause the activity to be classified as not engaged in for profit if the activity is in fact engaged in for profit as evidenced by other factors whether or not listed in this paragraph."[48]

No one of the above factors is determinative, and the determination of a profit motive is not limited to the above factors. The test is this: Based on all the facts and circumstances, is a profit motive present? While the IRS focuses on the nine factors enumerated in the regulations, cases involving individuals who collect art are not easy to resolve. None of the examples in the regulation presents the common, but difficult, situation of a wealthy taxpayer with losses from a pleasurable collecting activity that is conducted in a businesslike manner.

The main objective of section 183 is to disallow deductions attributable to an activity not engaged in for profit. The nine factors listed above present an almost insurmountable barrier for a collector. Therefore, section 183(a) is an effort by the IRS to disallow deductions for all collectors who are not dealers or investors.

Section 183(b)

Section 183(b) does offer some help to the collector. The section allows the collector to claim deductions for expenses attributable to an activity not engaged in for profit up to the amount of the gross income derived from the activity, after first deducting those items, such as certain items of interest and taxes, that are allowable without regard to whether an activity is engaged in for profit.[49]

As discussed above, if the taxpayer can satisfy section 212(1) or (2), the collection-related expenses are deductible whether or not the taxpayer had any gross income from collection activities since he is classified as an investor. If the taxpayer (as in *Wrightsman*) cannot satisfy the test of section 212(1) or (2), the taxpayer can claim a deduction for collection-related expenses under section 183(b) up to the amount of his gross income from collection activities, so long as the collector is carrying on an activity within the meaning of section 183 and after first subtracting such items as interest and taxes that are deductible without regard to section 183. The collection-related expenses that are then deductible under section 183(b) are subject to the 2% rule of section 67(a) for deductions claimed on or after January 1, 1987.[50] The deductible expenses may be further limited under the provisions of section 68(a), effective January 1, 1991.[51]

For example, if in *Wrightsman* there had been gross income derived from the taxpayer's collection activities, the expenses at issue in that case would have been deductible under section 183(b) up to the amount of that gross income. Under prior law, if the expenses were not deductible under section 212(1) or (2), they could not be offset against any gross income from the activity not engaged in for profit.

The regulations contain detailed provisions on how to calculate the gross income from an activity for purposes of determining the amount available to offset deduction items.[52] For example, the regulations require that capital gains and losses from the collection activity be merged with all other capital gains and losses of the collector from noncollection activity.[53] Therefore, capital gains realized from sales of items in the collection are not available to offset collection expense deductions if the collector had losses on securities transactions that reduce the gains on collection sales to zero. For example, for capital transactions before January 1, 1987, the regulations require that the 60% long-term capital gains deduction of section 1202(a) be taken before arriving at the amount of capital gains gross income from collection activities that is available to offset deductions from the collection activities.[54] The Taxpayer Relief Act of 1997 lowered the long-term capital gains tax on the sale of securities to 20% and extended the holding period to eighteen months for long-term treatment. However, for the sale of collectibles the long-term capital gains tax rate was kept at 28% and the holding period was kept at more than one year. The Jobs and Growth Tax Relief Reconciliation Act of 2003 (effective May 6, 2003) further reduced the long-term capital gain rate to 15% for sales of securities and other capital assets and reduced the long-term holding period to more than twelve months but once again maintained the 28% rate on gain from the sale of collectibles held for more than one year. The term "collectible gain" is defined in Code section 1(h)(5)(A) to mean "gain from the sale or exchange of a collectible (as defined in section 408(m) without regard to paragraph (3) thereof) which is a capital asset held for more than one year but only to the extent such gain is taken into account in computing taxable income." It appears as if all long-term capital transactions (securities and collectibles) have to be netted to see if there is any net collectibles gain before any section 183(b) deduction is allowable.

CASES UNDER SECTION 183

Leonard L. Barcus[55] and *Mary L. Stanley*[56] illustrate the difficulty that a collector has in showing that he was engaged in an activity for profit. In *Barcus,* the court found that a married couple who bought and sold antiques were not profit-motivated; the court recognized that the expectation of profit need not be a reasonable one but ruled that the expectation must be a bona fide one. The court noted that the antiques that were purchased were used as furnishings in the taxpayers' residence before they were sold. In holding that, on the basis of all the facts, the taxpayers' purchase and sale of antiques did not constitute a trade or business or a transaction entered into for profit, the court took into consideration the testimony of the taxpayers that the antiques might some day greatly increase in value and be sold at a large profit. The court stated:

In reaching our conclusion we have not overlooked petitioners' statements that they owned antiques which they expected in the years to come would greatly increase in value and then could be sold at a very large profit. In our view this speculative hope of a profit at some time in the future is not persuasive that petitioners' intent in the purchase and sale of antiques was to make a profit.[57]

In *Stanley*, the court found that a collector of antique glass novelties and marbles had not carried the burden of proving that her collection activities were primarily for the production of income. The taxpayer in *Stanley* did not claim that she was engaged in a trade or business but only that she acquired glass novelties for investment purposes and that she published her book *A Century of Glass Toys* to enhance the marketability of her glass novelty collection. The court succinctly summarized the relevant legal principles:

> The test for determining whether an activity is engaged in for profit is whether the individual engaged in the activity with the primary purpose and intention of making a profit. The taxpayer must have a bona fide expectation of realizing a profit, although such expectation need not be reasonable. Whether petitioners had the requisite intention is a question of fact to be determined on the basis of all the facts and circumstances. The burden of proof is on the petitioners, with greater weight given to objective facts than to the petitioners' mere statement of their intent. No one factor is conclusive and thus we do not reach our decision herein by merely counting the factors enumerated in section 1.183-2(b), which support each party's position.[58] (citations omitted)

The court observed that there was no doubt that the taxpayer hoped or expected that her glass novelties would appreciate in value over time. However, a potential for appreciation is inherent in many, if not most, of the items that have traditionally been collected as a hobby—stamps, coins, works of art—for the pleasure afforded by the acquisition and possession of the collection itself. The mere fact that a collector is aware that the value of his collection may increase does not mean that he is primarily motivated by an expectation of profit, rather than by the personal satisfaction derived from pursuing a hobby, and a hobby is not thereby converted into an activity engaged in for profit.[59]

The court then commented on the *Wrightsman* case,[60] observing that in that case the taxpayer could not deduct expenses connected with his art collection under section 212, although he had an investment motive in acquiring it, since his primary purpose in collecting works of art was not investment but personal pleasure. Although *Wrightsman* was decided before the enactment of section 183, the court stated that the same standard of primary purpose is relevant under section 183.[61] Therefore, the court concluded that Stanley did not establish that investment was the most prominent purpose for her acquisition and holding of the glass novelties.

However, even though the court found in *Stanley* that there was no activity for profit, it did permit the deduction of collection-related expenses to the extent of the gross income derived from the collection activities as provided by section 183(b)(2). Under the law before the passage of section 183, those deductions would have been disallowed under section 262.

Maurice C. Dreicer[62] illustrates the application of section 183 and the test a taxpayer must meet to have losses allowed in an amount greater than the income received from an activity. In *Dreicer* the taxpayer, who received a substantial income from a family trust, had traveled extensively throughout the world for many years. Twenty years before the tax years in question, his book on international dining had been published, but, because it was a commercial failure, he had received only meager royalties. Although he had written a rough draft of a book on a similar topic during the tax years in question, he had abandoned his efforts to have it published after the manuscript had been rejected by two publishers. During the twenty years between the books, he had lectured before various travel organizations, written for a travel magazine, and participated in radio and television programs—all without compensation. The taxpayer claimed his travel and other related expenses as business expenses during the tax years in question, but the IRS disallowed the deduction on the ground that it was a hobby loss.

The Tax Court held that the taxpayer was not entitled to deduct his expenses because he did not have a bona fide expectation of profit from the pursuit of his career as a writer-lecturer. However, the appellate court ruled that although a taxpayer's expectation of profit is a factor to be considered in determining whether losses are deductible,[63] the legal standard is whether the taxpayer has engaged in the activity with the objective of making a profit. Consequently, the court remanded the case to the Tax Court for reconsideration under the profit-objective standard.

On rehearing, the Tax Court agreed with the appellate court that the correct legal standard to be applied was whether the taxpayer engaged in the activity with the objective of making a profit, not whether he had a reasonable expectation of making a profit. The Tax Court stated:

> The purpose of the standard adopted by the Court of Appeals is to allow deductions where the evidence indicates that the activity is actually engaged in for profit even though it might be argued that there is not a reasonable expectation of profit. See S. Rept. 91-552 (1969), 1969-3 C.B. 423, 489-490. We are in total agreement with the Court of Appeals that this is the proper legal standard under section 183. However, a taxpayer's declaration of his motive to make a profit is not controlling. His motive is the ultimate question; yet, it must be determined by a careful analysis of all the surrounding objective facts, and greater weight is given to such facts than to his mere statement of intent. Sec. 1.183-2(a) and (b), Income Tax Regs. Thus, although a reasonable expectation of profit is not required, the facts and circumstances must indicate that the taxpayer entered into the activity, or continued the activity, with the actual and honest objective of making a profit.[64]

In *Marie L. Johnson*,[65] the Tax Court seems to say that the profit requirement of section 183 is not to be applied with the same vigor in a sale-leaseback transaction as it is in a hobby-loss case.

In *Dailey*,[66] the United States Court of Appeals for the Eighth Circuit affirmed a Tax Court opinion holding that a mere floating expectation of realizing a profit was not sufficient to satisfy section 183. The taxpayers in *Dailey* intended to purchase and maintain appreciating art and antiques to provide a nest egg for their retirement. However, the court held that they could not deduct as investment expenses the costs of art and antiques magazine subscriptions, a magazine-sponsored trip to Europe, or travel within the United States, since they never took any active steps to sell any items in their collection and their expectations of realizing a profit were vague and uncertain.

In *H.D. Mandelbaum*,[67] the taxpayer Mandelbaum purchased an art-master package in 1979, consisting of copyrights and reproduction rights to *Water Carrier* by Chaim Goldberg from Jackie Fine Arts for approximately $190,000. Mandelbaum gave Jackie Fine Arts $7,500 in cash and executed three nonnegotiable nonrecourse notes; most of the debt on those notes was not due until January 1991. Mandelbaum knew that the values claimed by Jackie Fine Arts were, in his own words, "vastly overblown" and that the investment was "a dog." He received two appraisals valuing *Water Carrier* at between $190,000 and $195,000, but neither appraisal justified its figures or explained how they were determined.

Between 1979 and 1983, Mandelbaum claimed more than $115,000 in depreciation expense. In 1979, he also claimed a $17,000 investment tax credit. By 1989, Jackie Fine Arts was out of business and had forgotten about the notes that were due in 1991. The Tax Court, relying on previous opinions, concluded that Mandelbaum's acquisition of the art-master package was primarily, if not exclusively, motivated by tax considerations. Therefore, the court sustained the IRS's determination of deficiencies, additions to tax, and additional interest for tax-motivated transactions. The deduction for depreciation and the investment tax credits claimed were disallowed by the court because the art-master package transaction lacked economic substance. Noting Mandelbaum's failure to comply with orders issued by the court that were intended to facilitate closing the art-master cases, his failure to offer evidence or present a meritorious case, and his belated concession of other issues, the court awarded the government $10,000 in penalties under section 6673.[68]

In *S.P. Barr*,[69] an attorney engaged in an art-publishing enterprise, but the court found that he had no intention of making a profit. No documentary evidence was provided to corroborate his testimony that he carried on the activity in a businesslike manner. There was no evidence that he received qualified advice, and his attempts at the mail-order marketing of prints were minimal.

In *J.F. Moore*,[70] the court allowed an attorney to deduct the ordinary and necessary expenses incurred in connection with certain bona fide sales of gemstones, but he could not deduct certain distributorship fees purportedly paid or incurred to acquire an exclusive territorial franchise for the sale of the gemstones.

In *J.A. Harmon*,[71] expenses from the taxpayers' ceramics and quilting activities were allowable only to the extent of the gross income earned from those activities.

Full-time schoolteachers in *L.W. Paxton*[72] were not permitted to deduct expenses related to the sales of their homemade craft items at craft shows in an amount exceeding the gross income derived from the activity, because they failed to demonstrate that their work was an activity engaged in for profit. The schoolteachers had net losses for the five years in question and failed to take any steps to limit the losses.

Deductions were disallowed in *M. Reali*,[73] in which a surgeon and the owner of a private sanitation company were found not to have the requisite profit motive, under the criteria of regulation section 1.183-2(b), in connection with their lithograph-purchasing activities.

In *Stella Waitzkin*,[74] a painter was allowed to deduct expenses as an artist engaged in artistic activities, since, on the basis of all the facts and circumstances, she had the requisite objective of making a profit, notwithstanding ten years of net losses from her artistic activities. The court recognized the personal satisfaction achieved by the taxpayer through her artistic endeavors and national gallery showings. It also recognized that the taxpayer was well-off financially and had used the long history of tax losses to offset income from other sources. Yet the taxpayer was able to dispel the characterization of her artistic activity as a hobby by showing a businesslike approach to the activity, by demonstrating her full-time commitment to it, and by convincing the court that she had achieved some commercial success and acceptance. She demonstrated a history of sales of her paintings, adequate business records, an impressive resumé of gallery showings nationwide, growing commercial recognition, and a potential for appreciation in value of a large existing inventory of her artwork. Therefore, in a case involving an activity that could be primarily characterized as, and is commonly thought of as, providing the taxpayer with personal pleasure or satisfaction, the taxpayer nevertheless overcame a profit-motive challenge.[75]

In *Richard A. Stasewich*,[76] an accountant claimed he was also an artist and entitled to deduct the losses from his artistic activities. Stasewich claimed that he was conducting his accounting practice only to enable him to establish himself as an artist. The question for the court was whether the artist activity was "not engaged in for profit" within the meaning of section 183(c). Whether the required profit objective exists is to be determined on the basis of all the facts and circumstances of each case. The court recited the nine factors of regulation section 1.183-2 and found particularly significant the fact that Stasewich failed to keep adequate books and records and failed to implement a business plan to reverse his continued losses. In denying the losses, the court concluded that Stasewich was motivated more by satisfaction, pride, and prestige than by the objective of earning a profit. However, the court did allow Stasewich to offset any artist-activity-related expenses to the extent of the gross income from the activity.[77]

In *Deborah Joyce Windisch*,[78] an account clerk who worked full-time at a health services agency was denied loss deductions from her photographic activities. The taxpayer maintained meticulous records, but that was not in and of itself enough to overcome the unbusinesslike manner in which she carried on her photography activities. Most of her clients were family members or office-related friends, she set her prices too low to make a profit, she failed to pursue people who owed her money, and she had, the court thought, strong elements of personal pleasure and recreation in her photographic activities.

In *Wilbur Kenneth Griesmer*,[79] a retired factory worker was denied any deductions related to his meteorite and pyrite collection activities. The taxpayer combed the beaches of Lake Erie searching for what he considered to be meteorites, and in particular Martian meteorites, which he believed were quite valuable. The court looked at the factors under section 183 and found that none of the factors indicated that the taxpayer carried on his meteorite collecting activity with the requisite profit objective. In particular, the court noted that the collecting activity was not carried on in a businesslike manner, there were no books and records of income and expenses, and no part of the collection was ever offered for sale.

In *Tony L. Zidar*,[80] an individual spent more than $100,000 to build a stock car for the American Speed Association's 1992 racing season. To make a profit from his stock car activity, Zidar needed to obtain large sponsors. He could not rely on prize winnings to make a profit because he needed to hire drivers, and drivers take a significant portion of any prize winnings. He had no business plan for his stock car activity, nor did he speak with any consultants about how to operate a profitable stock car business. In 1992, Zidar was able to obtain only $5,571 in sponsorships. Unfortunately, while the stock car was being driven around the speedway between qualifying runs for a race, it collided with another race car and was destroyed. Zidar had no insurance on the stock car. The Tax Court disallowed all of Zidar's deductions relative to his stock car activity in excess of the $5,571 of income generated by the sponsorships, finding that he failed to demonstrate that he entered into the stock car activity with a good faith expectation of making a profit.[81] The case contains a detailed analysis of the nine nonexclusive factors to be considered in determining whether an activity is engaged in for profit.[82] In reaching its conclusion, the Tax Court placed the greatest weight on the manner of carrying on the activity, noting that the taxpayer had no separate bank account for his stock car activity, retained no business and financial advisor to aid him with his racing activities, participated in no special exhibitions to attract financial sponsorship of large companies, and never actually raced his vehicle (except in the ill-fated qualifying round).[83]

Section 68

If a taxpayer can carry the burden of proof that his art activities are engaged in for profit, the art-related expenses are deductible under section 212(1) or (2). Those expenses, if deductible, can be claimed as a miscellaneous expense on IRS Form 1040, schedule A. Section 67(a) limits the deduction for such expenses to amounts that exceed 2% of the taxpayer's adjusted gross income.[84] The amount of the deduction for such expenses can be further limited by section 68(a).

For tax years beginning after 1990, an individual whose adjusted gross income exceeds a specified threshold amount is required to reduce the amount allowable for itemized deductions by the smaller of (1) 3% of the excess of adjusted gross income over the threshold amount or (2) 80% of the total amount of the otherwise allowable itemized deductions.[85] The provision was phased out over a five-year period beginning in 2006. The overall limitation on itemized deductions imposed by section 68(a) was reduced by one-third in tax years 2006 and 2007 and by two-thirds in tax years beginning in 2008 and 2009.[86] The 3% limitation is completely repealed for tax years beginning after December 31, 2009,[87] but is reinstated for tax years beginning in 2013.[88] The 3% overall limitation on itemized deductions applies only after applying other limitations on itemized deductions, such as the 2% floor on miscellaneous itemized deductions.[89] That provision may have the effect of further limiting the amount of deductible art-activities expenses.

LOSSES

Losses on Sales

An individual can deduct a loss on a sale incurred in a trade or business[90] or in a transaction that is not connected with a trade or business but that is entered into for profit.[91] Generally, unless a collector can come within the requirements of section 183(b), as discussed above, a loss by a collector on the sale of a collection is not deductible.

A collector is someone who is not an investor and is not engaged in a trade or business under section 165(c)(1).[92] An individual in the trade or business of buying and selling works of art is a dealer and realizes ordinary income on sales that realize a gain and has ordinary losses under section 165(c)(1) on sales that realize a loss.

The United States Supreme Court has held that investment activities do not constitute a trade or business.[93] Therefore, a collector can buy and sell items and not be considered a dealer engaged in a trade or business. It must then be decided if the collector is an investor to determine whether the loss can be deducted under section 165(c)(2).

The test for deductibility under section 165(c)(2) of a loss incurred in any "transaction entered into for profit, though not connected with a trade or business," is a stricter test than that required for the deduction of expenses under section 212, under which the requirement is that an expenditure must be on property "held for the production of income."[94] Therefore, satisfying section 212 does not guarantee that a loss on a sale of a collection will be deductible under section 165(c)(2). The taxpayer-collector bears the burden of proving that the transaction was entered into for profit; what is necessary is evidence that at the time of purchase the taxpayer acquired the collection with a profit motive.

In *George F. Tyler*,[95] the taxpayer showed that from the outset he undertook stamp collecting as an investment; all purchases were made in consultation with a stamp expert. The court held that the purchase of the stamps was a transaction entered into for profit, and the loss incurred on the sale of the stamps was deductible under what is now section 165(c)(2). The case is unusual in the clarity of the fact that the taxpayer was able to offer convincing evidence of investment procedures from the outset.

Reacting to the *Tyler* case, the IRS issued Revenue Ruling 54-268,[96] which held that a loss sustained from the sale of a collection of stamps accumulated as a hobby does not represent a loss incurred in a trade or business or in a transaction entered into for profit within the meaning of section 165(c)(1) or (2). Accordingly, the ruling holds that such a loss is not deductible for federal income tax purposes.

In *Eugene G. Feistman*,[97] the issue was whether the losses from the taxpayer's activity known as "Feistman Stamps, Coins and Accessories" were incurred in an activity engaged in for profit. The losses resulted from expenses exceeding income and the court had to decide if the expenses were deductible under sections 162(a) or 212(1) or were nondeductible as mere hobby expenses. The taxpayer had litigated the issue in prior years and the tax court had held that the taxpayer's activities were a hobby and he did not have a bona fide profit motive.[98] The court examined the current activities of the taxpayer and found that what may have started as a hobby had changed into a profit-motivated activity and that the taxpayer had an "actual and honest objective of making a profit."[99]

An individual collector can deduct losses on sales as capital losses if it is proved that the collector is, in fact, an investor.[100] However, the allowance of such a loss is extremely rare, since the taxpayer has the burden of proving that the loss-generating activity was a transaction entered into for profit and not merely a hobby.[101]

Section 183(b) once again offers help to the collector who cannot meet the requirement of section 165(c)(2) that he entered into a transaction for profit. If the collector can prove that the collection is an "activity" within the meaning of section 183, capital losses are deductible under section 183(b) up to the amount of the gross income derived from the collection during the taxable year, after first subtracting such items as interest and taxes that are otherwise deductible without regard to section 183. Therefore, capital losses from the collection activity can be used to offset capital gains from the collection activity under section 183(b). Before the passage of section 183, the gains would have been taxable, but the losses would have been nondeductible personal losses if section 165(c)(2) was not satisfied.[102]

The burden of proving that the collector is engaged in a trade or business or that purchases made by the collector were made in transactions entered into for profit or in the production or the collection of income is extremely difficult. The collector should try to satisfy as many of the factual elements of regulation section 1.183-2(b) as possible. Even if the collector cannot prove a profit motive, the collector should keep adequate records to show that he is engaged in an activity for purposes of section 183, so that losses up to the amount of the gross income from that activity can be claimed as a deduction.

Losses on Inherited Property

If a collection is inherited and is immediately offered for sale and is sold at a loss, the loss is capital in nature and may be deductible under section 165(c)(2).[103] However, the collection must not first be converted to personal use and thereafter offered for sale. In that situation, it becomes more difficult to show that the transaction was entered into for profit.

Casualty Losses

A collector may want to become a self-insurer because of the high cost of insurance for the collection. The idea behind self-insuring is that the deduction allowed for a loss from fire, theft, or other casualty may save a high-bracket taxpayer more in taxes than the cost of insurance.[104] However, the Tax Equity and Fiscal Responsibility Act (TEFRA) of 1982 raised the stakes for the self-insurer by limiting the allowable casualty-loss deduction to the amount that exceeds 10% of the taxpayer's adjusted gross income.[105]

Before applying the limitation, the collector must first determine the amount of the loss. The amount of the loss from a casualty is the lower of (1) the fair market value of the property immediately before the casualty, reduced by the fair market value of the property immediately after the casualty (zero in the case of a theft), or (2) the property's adjusted basis.[106]

From that lower amount, the collector must subtract $100 for each casualty[107] and then subtract 10% of his adjusted gross income.[108] Only the amount of loss that exceeds the above limitations can be claimed as a casualty loss. The 10% limitation introduced by TEFRA became effective January 1, 1983.

For example, a collector purchased a painting for $100,000. Ten years later, when it had a fair market value of $500,000, it was stolen. There was no insurance, the taxpayer's adjusted gross income in the year of the theft was $300,000, and the theft took place during the year 2012. The casualty loss deduction is calculated as follows:

Amount of loss (lower of fair market cost value or basis)	$100,000
Limitations	$100
—Less: $100 per casualty Less: 10% of adjusted gross income (10% × 300,000)	$30,000
	<30,100>
Amount deductible	$69,900

If an item in a collection is purchased and later discovered to be a forgery and hence, almost worthless, it produces a deductible loss if the transaction amounted to a "theft" as defined by local law.[109] For it to constitute a theft, the taxpayer must bear the burden of proving that the item was sold to him with an intent to defraud.

Involuntary Conversions

Any amount of casualty loss is further reduced by any insurance recovery. If the collector receives insurance proceeds greater than the cost basis, the collector has a taxable gain[110] unless he can come within the exception of section 1033(a)(2). Under section 1033(a)(2), a gain from an involuntary conversion of property into money is not recognized if the insurance proceeds were used to purchase similar property (similar to the items collected) within two years after the close of the first taxable year in which any part of the gain on conversion was realized.[111]

In the above casualty-loss example, if the collector has a $50,000 insurance recovery on the painting, he has a realized taxable gain of $40,000, unless he reinvests the insurance proceeds in similar property within the applicable time period of section 1033(a)(2).

The question of what is similar property for a collector was dealt with in Private Letter Ruling 81-27-089. A fire had caused extensive damage to a collector's lithographs and other art items. The collector had difficulty in replacing the lithographs and wanted to use part of the insurance proceeds to purchase artwork in other artistic media. The IRS ruled that artwork in one medium that is destroyed in whole or in part and that is replaced with artwork in another medium will not be considered property similar or related in service or use. The Private Letter Ruling appears to be unduly narrow in its interpretation of the statute.

EXCHANGES

It is a common practice for collectors to exchange items, each intending to improve his collection. Dealers often encourage collectors to trade in works of art purchased from them in exchange for other works of art. Section 1031(a) allows certain "like-kind" exchanges to be made tax-free. The statute limits such exchanges to property held for productive use in a trade or business or for investment that is exchanged solely for property of a like kind to be held for productive use in a trade or business or for investment.[112] Accordingly, there are four requirements for a like-kind exchange to be tax-free under section 1031(a):

(1) there must be an exchange;
(2) the exchange must be of property of a type that qualifies under section 1031(a);[113]
(3) the replacement property must be of "like kind" to the property relinquished; and
(4) both the relinquished property and the replacement property must be held for productive use in a trade or business or for investment.

The general rule of section 1031(a) requires that qualifying property must be exchanged solely for other qualifying property. If an exchange would otherwise be eligible for tax-free treatment under section 1031(a) but for the receipt of cash (boot), any gain realized on the exchange is recognized to the extent of the boot received.[114]

In the usual case, a collector is engaged in a hobby, not a business. The collector may argue that he is an investor and held the property for investment. The term "investment" is not defined in section 1031.[115] In light of *Wrightsman* and sections 162, 165, 212, and 183, the term most likely means property held primarily for profit. The burden of proof for the collector who wants to be an investor may be difficult because of the lack of authorities and because of differences in terminology.[116] With the increases in values for top-quality works of art and dissatisfaction with the stock market, many individuals are investing substantial sums in works of art. When a collector pays $1 million, $5 million, or $10 million for a work of art, it is only logical to assume that there is some investment objective when the acquisition is made and that the work of art is being held for investment. Regulation section 1.1031(a)-1(b) indicates that unproductive real estate that is held by a nondealer for future use or future realization of the increase in value is property held for investment. The test is applied at the time of the exchange without regard to the taxpayer's motive before the exchange.[117] With the present long-term capital gain rate at 28% for gain from the sale of collectibles, there is increased motivation for collectors to come within the tax-free exchange provisions of section 1031(a). For the collector, the difference between the fair market value of the property received and the basis of the property given up results in a taxable gain. The investor, however, may be able to avoid any taxable gain under the umbrella of section 1031(a).

Even if a taxpayer can carry the difficult burden of proof of being an investor, the exchange may still have the problem of what constitutes like-kind property. The IRS has ruled, for purposes of section 1033 (the provision pertaining to involuntary conversions), that lithographs may not be replaced with artworks in "other artistic media" such as oil paintings, watercolors, sculpture, or other graphic forms of art.[118] The ruling seems unduly narrow and there is no indication whether the same result would apply under section 1031(a).[119] Under section 1031(a) the words "like-kind" refer to the nature or character of the property and not to its grade or quality. One work of art should be able to be exchanged for another work of art, even in a different medium, since the nature or character of the properties as "works of art" is the same.[120]

Initially, section 1031 was designed to apply to simultaneous transfers of like-kind property between two persons. The rules have evolved to allow multiparty exchanges and deferred exchanges. In a multiparty exchange, an exchange agent facilitates the exchange. For example, Collector *A* owns painting *X* and wants to acquire painting *Y* owned by Collector *B*. Collector *B* does not want painting *X*; Collector *B* wants cash. So Collector *A* transfers title to painting *X* (the relinquished property) to exchange agent *C*. Exchange agent *C* sells painting *X* and uses the proceeds to buy painting *Y* (the replacement property) from Collector

B and then transfers title to painting *Y* to Collector *A* in payment for painting *X*. This type of exchange is sometimes referred to as a Starker transaction after *Starker v. United States*,[121] where the court sanctioned the taxpayer's transfer of property in exchange for a promise by the recipient to convey like-kind property chosen by the taxpayer at a later date. Following the decision in *Starker*, Congress enacted section 1031(a)(3), which allows the transferor of the relinquished property up to forty-five days to identify the replacement property and 180 days to close on the acquisition of the replacement property. The taxpayer may identify as replacement property any three properties or multiple properties with a fair market value not in excess of 200% of the fair market value of the relinquished property.[122]

The regulations[123] under section 1031(a)(3) set forth detailed guidance concerning how a taxpayer can comply with the tax-free like-kind deferred exchange requirements, including four "safe harbors" that taxpayers can rely on to avoid constructive receipt of the proceeds from the sale of the relinquished property.[124] Each of the safe harbor regulations[125] contains highly technical and complex provisions, made more so since they were promulgated in anticipation of the exchange of real property and not collectibles. For example, under the third safe harbor, the taxpayer's transferee must be a "qualified intermediary."[126] A qualified intermediary is a person who is not the taxpayer or a "disqualified person" and who enters into an exchange agreement with the taxpayer and, as required by the exchange agreement, acquires the relinquished property from the taxpayer, transfers the relinquished property, acquires the replacement property, and transfers the replacement property to the taxpayer.[127]

A "disqualified person" is

(1) a person who is the agent of the taxpayer at the time of the transaction,[128]
(2) a person who is related to the taxpayer as described in either section 267(b) or section 707(b),[129] or
(3) a person who is related to the person described in (1) by the relationship described in (2) of this sentence.[130]

Persons who acted as the taxpayer's employee, attorney, accountant, investment banker or broker, or real estate agent or broker during the two-year period immediately preceding the taxpayer's transfer of the relinquished property are treated as agents of the taxpayer at the time of the transaction.[131] Again, the regulations and rulings are complex and technical as to who is or is not an agent of the taxpayer under the safe harbor provision. Although there is no specific authority, it appears that an art dealer can act as a qualified intermediary and not be a disqualified person. Because of the uncertainty involved, it is important that title to the relinquished property be transferred to the art dealer at a specific stated value and that the art dealer have the freedom to sell the relinquished property in order to use the proceeds to acquire the replacement property. Any amount received by the art dealer on the sale of the relinquished property in excess of the stated value should belong to the art dealer. It is preferable to use an art dealer who has not acted as the taxpayer's agent through a consignment of a collectible during the two years prior to the contemplated exchange transaction.

No recent cases or IRS rulings have shed light on the meaning of the terms in section 1031(a).[132] Generally, a collector has some difficulty in carrying the burden of proof under section 1031, since he must prove that a painting, say, was held for investment and was exchanged for a painting that was held for investment. Accordingly, many exchanges of appreciated works of art are taxable. However, if the investment objective can be satisfied, there is no reason why the collector cannot take advantage of a section 1031(a) tax-free exchange. The technical requirements and potential pitfalls are numerous and a full description is well beyond the scope of this book.[133] A very simple, straightforward intermediary exchange form is attached at the end of this chapter (Appendix 14-1 and Appendix 14-2). One important development is the requirement that a taxpayer who enters into a like-kind exchange as of January 1, 1990, must file IRS Form 8824. The form reveals to the IRS all the details about the exchange and calls attention to exchanges that heretofore may have gone unnoticed by the IRS. A copy of the form appears at the end of this chapter (Appendix 14-3).

Whether an exchange is a taxable or nontaxable transaction for federal income tax purposes, it is treated as a sale for sales tax purposes, and a sales tax may be payable on the exchange.[134] Generally, if the exchange is between two collectors, each of them should collect and pay over the sales tax. If the exchange is between a dealer and a collector, the dealer should collect and pay over the sales tax to the extent of the cash required from the collector to complete the exchange.[135] The sales tax provisions are explained in more detail later in this chapter.

RECORD KEEPING

In planning a collector's estate, an attorney must have the collector maintain adequate records. If both a husband and a wife participate in the collecting activity, careful records should indicate who is the owner of each item, and any insurance policies should be consistent with those ownership records. If any lifetime charitable contributions are contemplated, the record-keeping requirements of the Tax Reform Act of 1984 and the Tax Reform Act of 1986 make good records imperative. Those provisions are discussed in detail in chapter 15. Further, the date of purchase and the cost of each purchase are necessary to determine the gain or loss on the sale of the collection.[136]

SELF-DIRECTED RETIREMENT PLANS

Before January 1, 1982, an individual could purchase artworks or other collectibles in an individual retirement account (IRA) or a qualified retirement plan. After discovering that people were purchasing collectibles in their retirement plans and making personal use of those items, the IRS urged Congress to change the law. Section 408(m) was added to the Internal Revenue Code by the Economic Recovery Tax Act (ERTA) of 1981. That section penalizes an individual who directs his IRA or any self-directed retirement plan to invest in collectibles. The term "collectibles" includes works of art.[137]

Section 408(m) treats any acquisition of a collectible by an IRA or a self-directed retirement plan as a distribution of the value of that collectible from the IRA or retirement plan to the participant. That treatment means that the participant has taxable ordinary income equal to the value of the amount treated as a distribution. That interpretation has the practical effect of making it prohibitive for an IRA or a self-directed retirement plan to acquire collectibles.

The statute provides that section 408(m) is effective for property acquired in taxable years ending after December 31, 1981. The IRS explained, in part, the section 408(m) rules pertaining to collectibles as follows:

Q. What is the effect of the new requirement on collectibles that were acquired on or before December 31, 1981?
A. Since the new provision is not applicable to collectibles that were acquired on or before December 31, 1981, the retention of a collectible acquired prior to January 1, 1982, by an IRA or an individually-directed account is not treated as a distribution.[138]

A question remains, however, as to whether a transfer or rollover after December 31, 1981, of works of art acquired before January 1, 1982, is considered an acquisition by the IRA after December 31, 1981, and would now be treated as a distribution.[139]

A rollover is a transfer of assets from one retirement plan to another. Generally, such a transfer is not regarded as a distribution from the plan from which the assets are transferred and is not regarded as a contribution to the plan to which the assets are transferred. That is, the distribution is tax-free, and the contribution is not deductible or subject to any of the various limitations imposed on contributions to retirement plans. A rollover is merely the shifting of the pension assets from one holding vehicle to another and, as long as the requirements of section 402(a)(5) are met, the Internal Revenue Code provides that such transfers are tax-free.

On January 23, 1984, the IRS issued proposed regulations (still not finally adopted) under section 408(m) dealing with investments in collectibles. Proposed regulation section 1.408-10(d) defines the term "acquisition" for the purpose of section 408(m) as follows:

For purposes of this section, the term acquisition includes purchase, exchange, contribution, or any method by which an individual retirement account or individually-directed account may directly or indirectly acquire a collectible.

That is an extremely broad definition and appears to include any method by which an IRA acquired a collectible after December 31, 1981. The IRS could take the position that such a broad definition includes a rollover of a collectible acquired before January 1, 1982. However, notwithstanding the language of the proposed regulation, IRS Notice 82-3 indicates that collectibles acquired before January 1, 1982, may be retained in an IRA. Therefore, the broad language of the proposed regulation was probably intended to encompass in the broadest terms all acquisitions of collectibles if the collectibles were, in fact, purchased after December 31, 1981. Since a rollover is a mere shifting of assets from one retirement vehicle to another, such a transfer should not constitute an "acquisition of a collectible" after December 31, 1981, as long as the collectibles were, in fact, acquired before that date. However, there is no specific authority for the foregoing interpretation, and the IRS could take the position that a rollover is a taxable distribution.

The Tax Reform Act of 1986 amended section 408(m) to allow the purchases, after January 1, 1987, of gold and silver coins minted in the United States after October 1, 1986, as long as the coins were held in an IRA in the name of a trustee.[140] The Taxpayer Relief Act of 1997 further amended section 408(m) to include in the exception from the definition of "collectible" a platinum coin and certain gold, silver, platinum, or palladium bullion transactions. The definition under section 408(m) has taken on increased importance under the act since the long-term capital gain rate on the sale of a collectible (not in an IRA account) is currently taxed at a 28% rate rather than the 15% rate on the long-term sale of a security. However, an investment by an IRA in a coin that has been made into jewelry is still considered an investment in a collectible and is treated as a distribution.[141]

INSURANCE

Insurance is a significant consideration for collectors, artists, and dealers. It is the insurance policy that covers the risk of loss that may result from any number of causes. If, for example, the collector maintains a collection in his home, the collection should be insured against fire, theft, flood, earthquake, and all other risks attendant to the maintenance of artwork in the home.

As with any other contract, the insurance policy should be examined in detail to make sure that all risks that the collector wants covered are, in fact, covered. The examination should include a thorough review of the policy's exclusions. For instance, the policy may not cover mysterious disappearances or theft by dishonest employees who have been admitted to the residence.

In addition, the policy should cover appreciation in value. Therefore, a new appraisal for insurance purposes is needed from time to time in order to update the policy. The collector should maintain precise inventory records, appraisals, photographs, invoices, and other documentation so that the existence and the ownership of the insured items can be proved.

Further, the insurance policy should cover what happens if the collector suffers a loss, such as the theft of a painting, and the insurance company pays the collector for the then-insured value. If the painting is recovered years later, when it has greatly appreciated in value, what happens? If the collector is able to reclaim title and is not barred by the statute of limitations, he still has a problem because technically, the insurance company is the true owner of the painting, having taken the collector's rights by subrogation when it paid the collector after the theft of the painting. To cover such a situation, the collector should require the insurance policy to give him the option to acquire title to the painting from the insurance company for the amount paid to the collector by the insurance company at the time of the loss. Such a provision is crucial, because the current fair market value of the painting may be many times the amount of the insurance payment that was received by the collector. The insurance company sometimes requires that an interest factor be added before agreeing to such a provision.

If the collector is selling artwork on consignment through a dealer, the collector should require the dealer to insure that artwork from the time it leaves the collector's premises. The collector should make sure that the dealer's policy covers all risks and provides that the collector-consignor will be paid in full, regardless of the loss that may occur. The collector should always require that the dealer furnish a copy of the insurance policy proving such coverage to the collector.

Like the collector, the artist also wants to make sure that works of art consigned for sale are fully covered by the dealer's policy. The artist should also have his own insurance policy covering the works of art when they are on the artist's premises. Insurance policies can be intimidating since they consist of numerous pages of fine print. An artist must engage an insurance agent who can explain the policy, the risks involved, and precisely what is being insured.

SALES AND USE TAXES

Dealers—those individuals who, on the basis of all the facts and circumstances, are engaged in the trade or business of buying and selling works of art[142]—must register with the state sales tax department and obtain a resale certificate and number from the state in which the dealer is doing business. With a resale number, the dealer is not required to pay a sales tax on works of art purchased in any state, since the works purchased are being bought for resale. When the dealer sells the works purchased, the dealer then collects the sales tax from his customer—that is, the sales tax is paid by the ultimate consumer, who is usually the investor or the collector. The sales tax is a transaction tax, liability for which occurs when the transaction takes place.

A use tax is designed to complement the sales tax, and imposes a tax on the use within a state of works of art (or other items of tangible personal property) that would have been subject to the sales tax if they were purchased within the state. This means that an investor or collector who resides in one state, and buys an artwork in another state for delivery in the state where he resides, will owe a use tax to the state in which he is a resident. In this situation, a sales tax would not be due in the state where the purchase was made.

Sometimes the investor or the collector of artworks who may buy and sell a work from time to time attempts to avoid paying the sales or use tax by registering for a resale certificate and number, either in his own name or in the name of a corporation set up for that purpose. Doing so is usually a big mistake since, at best, the artworks purchased will be ordinary-income property that will produce ordinary income and not capital gain if sold, and a deduction will be limited to the artwork's cost if donated to charity. At worst, the investor or collector could face possible criminal charges.

Although an analysis of the sales tax law in every state is beyond the scope of this chapter, a review of the law as it applies in New York State can serve as a guide for dealers, investors, and collectors in all states. The references below are to the New York State sales tax statute and regulations thereunder.

Sale of Art

The New York State sales tax must be paid by the buyer and collected by the seller on the sale of tangible personal property in the state unless (1) the property is sold to a buyer for delivery out of the state of New York or (2) it is purchased by a dealer exclusively for resale.[143]

DELIVERY OUT OF STATE

The New York State sales tax law does not provide any specific exemption from the New York State sales tax for sales of tangible personal property delivered to purchasers outside New York State. However, such transactions are exempt from the sales tax for constitutional reasons pursuant to the commerce clause of the United States Constitution,[144] provided that the out-of-state purchaser does not take delivery in the state of New York.

The sales tax is a transactional tax that is based on the situs where a delivery is made or possession is transferred from the seller to the purchaser. Section 525.2(a)(3) of the sales tax regulation provides:

> . . . the sales tax is a "destination tax." The point of delivery or point at which possession is transferred by the vendor to the purchaser, or the purchaser's designee, controls both the tax incidence and the tax rate.[145]

Thus, the sales tax applies only to sales in which delivery takes place within New York State.

Section 526.7(e)(1) provides the following:

> . . . a sale is taxable at the place where the tangible personal property or service is delivered, or the point at which possession is transferred by the vendor to the purchaser or his designee.[146]

If the selling art dealer ships a work of art by common carrier to the purchaser, the sale (the taxable event) occurs where delivery is made to the purchaser. In Advisory Opinion TSB-A-89, the seller of audio-video equipment shipped its merchandise by common carrier from the seller's location directly to the customer in Florida. The customer was billed for the equipment and, presumably, for the shipping cost. The opinion holds that the New York sales tax does not apply.[147] In *Matter of the Petition of Richard L. Feigen & Co., Inc.,*[148] there are five examples of sales of art that were not subject to the New York State sales tax. The decision specifically covers works of art that were delivered by common carrier to an out-of-state purchaser that were not, under various fact situations, subject to the New York sales tax. The decision is not completely clear as to whether it is necessary for the dealer to be the person who hires and pays the common-carrier fees.

In order to avoid collecting the New York State sales tax, an art gallery is required to deliver the work of art to the purchaser out of New York State. The clearest case is one in which the art gallery delivers the work by a common carrier hired by the gallery and the common-carrier invoice is rendered to the gallery. The art gallery can seek reimbursement from the out-of-state purchaser. It also appears that the New York State sales tax should not apply, even if the purchaser selects the common carrier and is invoiced directly for the costs, so long as it is the art gallery that delivers the work to the common carrier. In the latter case, the art gallery is still required to have documented proof that it shipped the work by common carrier to the out-of-state purchaser. Therefore, if the purchaser wants to select the common carrier, it is always best if the art gallery is the entity that retains the common carrier at the request of the purchaser, even if the cost is to be paid by the purchaser.

Art galleries, among other entities, have been targeted by the New York State sales tax department for specific investigation for sales taxes due.[149] In the course of a sales tax audit, the agents check invoices and points of delivery, look to see if the bill of lading includes the weight of the item delivered, and take other steps to verify the interstate elements of the transaction.

If a purchaser has an item shipped to an out-of-state location, that individual may have a use tax liability in the state of delivery. Under certain circumstances, if that individual later brings the item back into New York State, it is possible that New York State could impose a use tax.[150] Those situations do not involve the responsibility of the art gallery unless it can be shown that the art gallery conspired in some way to assist the purchaser in avoiding the New York State sales tax.

Purchase Exclusively for Resale

Robert Guccione, well-known as the publisher of *Penthouse* magazine, found out how stringently the sales tax provisions can be applied in the case of *P-H Fine Arts, Ltd.*[151] Guccione pursued his interest in art with the purchase of works by Pablo Picasso, Edgar Degas, Marc Chagall, Amedeo Modigliani, Pierre-Auguste Renoir, Chaim Soutine, Salvador Dalí, and other great artists. He incorporated

P-H Fine Arts, Ltd. as a wholly owned subsidiary of *Penthouse* magazine for the purpose of buying and selling fine art. The works of art were hung in Guccione's town house for the purpose of creating a certain image in the eyes of corporate clients until the paintings could be sold. The town house was not open to the public, there was no price list, and Guccione never told anyone that the artwork was for sale. Furthermore, he kept no general ledger or sales journal, since the accountants for Guccione said that such records were unnecessary, because there were so few transactions. Therefore, after an audit the New York State Tax Commission took the position that the art was not purchased for resale. The unique defense put forth by Guccione was that by not telling anyone that the paintings were for sale, a great desire to own the paintings was created in the persons who had the opportunity to see them. Guccione testified as follows:

> He wants it [a painting] more now that he knows it is not for sale, and now, knowing how good it is and hearing from Ron who is an expert as well—he is really interested.[152]

Surprisingly, the court found that P-H Fine Arts proved that the artwork was purchased for resale. However, the court said that was not the end of the analysis. The court's interpretation of the sales tax law was that P-H Fine Arts had to prove that the intention of reselling the artworks was the only purpose for which the artworks were acquired. Therefore, the court concluded that P-H Fine Arts intended to use the artwork for a purpose other than resale: to allow the artwork to be displayed in a setting where it served the business interests of *Penthouse* and Guccione. At the time the artworks were purchased, Guccione had at least two purposes for the acquisition: resale and use by him and *Penthouse*; therefore, the artworks were not purchased *exclusively* for resale.[153] As a result, Guccione was required to pay more than $500,000 in sales tax.

TRADE-IN CREDIT

The federal income tax provisions related to tax-free like-kind exchanges under section 1031(a) were discussed earlier in this chapter. Even if a collector fails to satisfy the technical provisions of section 1031(a) so that the gain on the exchange is taxable, there will be a savings on the sales tax payable if the collector exchanges the artwork with a dealer. The New York State sales tax law provides that any allowance or credit for tangible personal property accepted in part payment by a vendor on the purchase of tangible personal property or services and intended for resale by the vendor is to be excluded when arriving at the receipt subject to the sales tax.[154] For example, a collector owns painting A that cost $10,000 and is now worth $50,000. The collector goes to an art dealer in New York City who is willing to allow the collector a $50,000 trade-in credit against the collector's purchase of painting B worth $100,000. The art dealer agrees to accept painting A as a trade-in and intends to resell painting A at a future date. The sales tax is calculated as follows:

Painting B sold to collector	$100,000.00
less trade-in credit for painting A	<$50,000.00>
Net amount due art dealer	$50,000.00
New York City tax (8.875%) on $50,000	× 0.08875
Sales Tax:	$4,437.50

If there were no trade-in credit, the sales tax would be based on $100,000 and would be $8,875—the New York City sales tax rate being 8.875%, effective August 2009. The sales tax rate will vary from county to county in New York State, and the applicable tax rate should always be checked, since it changes from time to time. If the trade-in qualified as an exchange under section 1031(a), there would be no federal income tax on the difference between the collector's cost of painting A ($10,000) and the trade-in credit or current value of painting A ($50,000). If the trade-in failed to qualify under section 1031(a), the collector would owe an income tax on the difference between his cost for painting A of $10,000 and the trade-in credit for painting A of $50,000. The ideal situation for the collector is to satisfy both the section 1031(a) provisions for federal income tax purposes and the trade-in credit rule for New York State sales tax purposes. The availability of the state trade-in credit should always be checked since it is not available in every state. For example, there is no trade-in credit in California.[155]

The above result does not work if two collectors exchange paintings, since only a vendor who accepts property as a trade-in with the intent to resell it can allow a trade-in credit free of the New York sales tax.[156]

Advice on Purchase or Sale

Interior decorating and design services are subject to the New York sales tax,[157] but an art advisor's service of consulting with a client solely for the purpose of recommending whether the client should purchase certain works of art from an investment-potential perspective is not a taxable interior decorating and design service.[158] It is not always clear where the line is drawn between art-advisory services that are subject to the sales tax and those that are not taxable.

When the art adviser advises a private collector within New York regarding quality and investment potential of art acquisitions with respect to specific artists and artworks, the art adviser is considered to be performing a consulting service. When the art adviser advises the client on the proper framing of an artwork and on the restoration procedure for such artwork without performing or arranging for the actual framing or restoration service, the art adviser is also considered to be performing a consulting service. The receipts from charges billed to the client for such consulting services are not subject to New York sales tax.[159]

However, when the art adviser supervises the installation of the artwork within the client's home, the art adviser is considered to be performing interior decorating and design services, and the total charges to the client, including charges for the above-noted consulting services, are subject to the New York sales tax.[160]

Purchase at Auction

When a work of art is purchased at Sotheby's or Christie's or most other auction houses, the buyer pays a fee over and above the hammer price known as the buyer's premium.[161] Publishing mogul Samuel D. Newhouse, Jr., argued that the 10% buyer's premium ($1,550,000) on his purchase at auction of Jasper Johns's *False Start* for $15.5 million was not subject to the New York sales tax, since it was not part of the purchase price but a fee paid for a separate service. In *In re Newhouse*[162] the court decided otherwise, holding that the buyer's premium was an integral aspect of Newhouse's purchase of the painting. The court agreed with the position of the New York sales tax department that at the auction all charges actually paid by the purchaser as a result of the sale of tangible personal property or the rendition of a service are subject to tax.[163] The court stated:

> There can be little doubt that [Newhouse's] purchase of *False Start* at a Sotheby's auction lends his purchase a special distinction given Sotheby's history, founded in 1744, and well-known name in fine arts. Therefore, the 10 percent "buyer's premium" may reasonably be viewed as the cost incurred by petitioner to purchase the painting at Sotheby's ... which added luster and value to the transaction. Therefore, the "buyer's premium" is an *integral* aspect of petitioner's purchase of the painting and was not a separate service arising from a different transaction.[164]

SITUS OF PROPERTY—STATE-SOURCE INCOME

Although an analysis of the state source rules in every state is beyond the scope of this chapter, a review of one recent case as it applies in New York State can serve as a guide for dealers, investors, and collectors in all states.

In *Henry A. and Marianne Ittleson*,[165] the issue was whether New York City and New York State can collect capital gain tax on the sale for $8.5 million of an Amedeo Modigliani painting that the taxpayers left in their New York City apartment when they moved to South Carolina. The Ittlesons had changed their domicile from New York to South Carolina prior to December 31, 1996, and moved to South Carolina prior to December 31, 1996. While they were renovating their South Carolina home, they left the Modigliani painting in their New York City apartment for nine weeks before it was sent to Sotheby's for sale. New York source income includes gain attributable to the ownership of tangible personal property in New York.[166] The New York State Division of Tax Appeals found that the facts indicated that the painting lacked sufficient nexus with New York to support the tax. According to the administrative law judge, the painting was in New York temporarily, solely for the purpose of being sold. He also noted that after the painting was consigned to Sotheby's it was exhibited in a number of foreign countries and therefore it became disassociated from New York and on its return to the auction house was in New York merely temporarily. The judge also found important that the New York State tax manual provides that a sale of artwork generates New York source income if the artwork is "located in the nonresident's New York apartment for an extended period of time."[167] The nine-week period following the Ittlesons' change of domicile, during which the paint-ing was stored in their New York apartment pending a transfer to the auction house, did not, according to the judge, amount to "an extended period of time" sufficient to trigger New York income tax liability on the gain.[168] In addition, the judge found that taxing the gain would violate the constitutional principles of due process, since the income the state and city sought to tax was not rationally related to the benefits provided by the state and city to the Ittlesons as nonresi-dents. On appeal, the decision was reversed by the New York State Tax Appeals Tribunal. Since the painting was in New York State for an extended period of time before the taxpayers changed their domicile, that period of time had to be considered in determining if the sale generated New York source income.[169]

Although the *Ittleson* case is peculiar to its facts, it serves as a warning to a nonresident of New York who has a residence in New York State and who sells artwork at a New York auction house. That may result in New York source in-come. The case also makes it clear, however, that nonresident sellers without a New York residence will not be subject to New York tax on art work brought to New York for sale.

DEPRECIATION

The allowance for depreciation permits taxpayers to recover the cost of purchas-ing an asset by offsetting deductions against income over a number of years. De-preciation is generally defined as a reasonable allowance for the exhaustion, wear and tear, and obsolescence of property used in a trade or business or for the pro-duction of income.[170] Several depreciation systems are currently in use for tax purposes: the modified accelerated cost recovery system (MACRS), the acceler-ated cost recovery system (ACRS), and the asset depreciation range (ADR) sys-tem. The proper one to apply depends on when the property at issue was placed in service. Property is placed in service when it is ready and available for use, not when it is actually put to use.

MACRS applies to most tangible depreciable property placed in service after 1986. ACRS applies to most tangible depreciable property placed in service after 1980 and before 1987. ADR applies to most assets placed in service after 1970 but not if ACRS or MACRS applies to them.

Generally, works of art and other collectibles are not subject to depreciation, even if they are used in the taxpayer's trade or business (such as a restaurant), since it has long been the rule that such property must have a determinable useful life.[171] Works of art and other collectibles that are not mere decorations do not have a determinable useful life.[172]

Two cases (*Liddle* and *Simon*) decided under ACRS permitted professional musicians to depreciate antique musical instruments that they used professionally, even though the instruments' values increased while the musicians owned them.[173] The cases turned on a technical interpretation of the ACRS rules in effect from 1981 through 1986, when it was not clear whether there was a useful-life requirement. To be able to claim a depreciation deduction for tangible personal property without a determinable useful life, the taxpayer must show that the property satisfies a four-part test:

(1) tangible property,
(2) placed in service between 1981 and 1986,
(3) subject to wear and tear, and
(4) used in the taxpayer's trade or business.[174]

In *Liddle*, the Tax Court could not agree with the IRS that a bass violin was a work of art and, thus, not depreciable.[175] According to the court, a work of art is a passive object—such as a painting, a sculpture, or a carving—that is displayed for the admiration of its aesthetic qualities, whereas the bass violin in question was used actively, regularly, and routinely by a musician to produce income in his full-time trade or business.[176]

The decisions in *Liddle* and *Simon* have limited application since they apply only to property depreciable under ACRS—that is, property placed in service between 1981 and 1986. Further, the IRS published a nonacquiescence with respect to the *Liddle* and *Simon* decisions, explaining that ACRS merely shortened the period over which assets are depreciated in order to stimulate economic growth, but did not convert nondepreciable assets into depreciable ones, compelling the IRS to pursue the issue in other circuits because of its position that the two cases were wrongly decided.[177]

Under current law, MACRS applies to property placed in service after 1986, and property that is depreciable if it wears out, has a determinable life of more than one year, and is used in a trade or business.[178] Therefore, since a form of the useful-life requirement is specifically retained under MACRS, a musician purchasing and using a rare and valuable instrument after 1986 (something that may appreciate in value over time) may not claim a depreciation deduction.

NOTES TO CHAPTER 14

1. I.R.C. §§ 162, 212(1), 212(2), 262, 183; Treas. Reg. § 1.212-1(c); *see* Anthoine, *The Collector of Taxes v. The Collector of Objects*, 59 TAXES 917 (1981).
2. *See* general definition in IRS Publication 334, Tax Guide For Small Business (1981). This definition has been dropped from later editions. Rev. Rul. 63-145, 1963-2 C.B. 86; *see* Boyle, *What Is a Trade or Business?*, 39 TAX LAW. 737 (1986); Weihrich & Christensen, *What Determines That An Activity Is A Trade or Business?*, 50 TAX'N FOR ACCOUNTANTS 346 (1993).
3. Gajewski v. Comm'r, 723 F.2d 1062 (2d Cir. 1983), *cert. denied*, 459 U.S. 818 (1984), *rev'g* 45 T.C.M. (CCH) 967 (1983) (rejecting the facts and circumstances test in Ditunno v. Comm'r, 80 T.C. 362 (1983)). *See also* Snyder v. Comm'r, 295 U.S. 134 (1935).
4. Comm'r v. Groetzinger, 480 U.S. 23 (1987). The *Groetzinger* case dealt with the question of whether a gambler was engaged in a "trade or business" as used in Code sections 162(a) and 62(1). The Supreme Court did limit its findings to the Code sections at issue in the case.
5. Whipple v. Comm'r, 373 U.S. 193 (1963); Higgins v. Comm'r, 312 U.S. 212 (1941); Moller v. United States, 721 F.2d 810 (Fed. Cir. 1983), *rev'g* 553 F. Supp. 1071 (Cl. Ct. 1982), *cert. denied*, 467 U.S. 1251 (1984); Yeager Estate v. Comm'r, 55 T.C.M. (CCH) 1101 (1988), *aff'd* 89-2 U.S. Tax. Cas. (CCH) ¶ 9633 (2d Cir. 1989).
6. Wood v. Comm'r, 16 T.C. 213 (1951); Kemon v. Comm'r, 16 T.C. 1026 (1951); *see* Hollis v. United States, 121 F. Supp. 191 (N.D. Ohio 1954); Seeley v. Helvering, 77 F.2d 321 (2d Cir. 1953); Nehring v. Comm'r, 16 T.C.M. (CCH) 224 (1957); Priv. Ltr. Rul. 81-40-015.
7. Malat v. Riddell, 383 U.S. 569 (1968); Treas. Reg. § 1.2121(c); Hayden v. Comm'r, 889 F.2d 1548 (6th Cir. 1989).
8. Drummond v. Comm'r, 73 T.C.M. (CCH) 1959 (1997).
9. In calendar year 1989, long-term capital gains were taxed at 28% and ordinary income was taxed at a maximum of 33%. *See* note 137 in chapter 15.
10. *Drummond*, 73 T.C.M. 1959 (citing *Malat*, 383 U.S. at 572). *See* Pasqualini v. Comm'r, 103 T.C. 1, 6 (1994).
11. *Drummond*, 73 T.C.M. at 1967; *see* Graves v. Comm'r, 867 F.2d 199, 202 (4th Cir. 1989).
12. I.R.C. § 262; Treas. Reg. § 1.212-1(c); Rev. Rul. 68-232, 1968-1 C.B. 79.
13. Wrightsman v. United States, 428 F.2d 1316 (Ct. Cl. 1970).
14. *See Malat*, 383 U.S. at 572; Treas. Reg. § 1.212-1(c).
15. *Shorting Rembrandt*, FORBES, Mar. 15, 1970, at 78; *see* Note, *Why Think of Your Estate As a Collection?*, 117 TR. & EST. 662 (1978); *infra* note 21. Low interest rates in 2012 have encouraged the creation of other art investment funds.
16. Tatt v. Comm'r, 166 F.2d 697 (5th Cir. 1948).
17. Higgins v. United States, 75 F. Supp. 252 (Ct. Cl. 1948); Churchman v. Comm'r, 68 T.C. 696 (1977), *acq.*, 1979-2 C.B. 1.
18. Tyler v. Comm'r, 6 T.C.M. (CCH) 275 (1947); Dember v. Comm'r, 25 T.C.M. (CCH) 620 (1966).
19. Cohan v. Comm'r, 39 F.2d 540 (2d Cir. 1930).
20. Wrightsman, Ct. Cl. Comm'r's Rep. No. 364-66, 69-7 Fed. Tax Rep. (CCH) ¶ 7910 (1969).
21. *See* ART & AUCTION, (each year's August issue devoted entirely to "investing in art"); N.Y. TIMES, July 23, 2004, section E page 2 (announcing the establishment of an art investment fund that intends to raise millions of dollars for investment in works of art).
22. Lee, *A Blend of Old Wines in a New Wineskin: Section 183 and Beyond*, 29 TAX L. REV. 347 (1974); Burns & Groomer, *Effects of Section 183 on the Business/Hobby Controversy*, 58 TAXES 195 (1980); Khorsandi, *Does Your Client Have a Profit Motive? An Analysis of Tax Court Criteria Used To Evaluate a Taxpayer's Profit Motive Under Section 183*, 47 TAX LAW. 291 (1993); Lewicki, *Home Office, Vacation Home and Home Rental Deductions*, 547-2nd Tax Mgmt. Section VIII (BNA); Campbell, *Hobby Activities Can Increase Tax Liability*, 53 TAX'N FOR ACCOUNTANTS 78 (1994); Note, *Racing Without A Profit Objective and Crash-*

ing Into Section 183: Zidar v. Comm'r, 55 Tax Law. No. 3 (2001–02); IRS Audit Guide: IRC § 183: Activities Not Engaged in for Profit, 2009 (available on IRS website).

23. Treas. Reg. § 1.183-2(a); Edge v. Comm'r, 32 T.C.M. (CCH) 1291, 1298 (1973); Churchman v. Comm'r, 68 T.C. 696 (1977), *acq.*, 1979-2 C.B. 1; Jasienski v. Comm'r, 64 T.C.M. (CCH) 1369 (1992); Westphal v. Comm'r, 68 T.C.M. (CCH) 1038 (1994); Hayden v. Comm'r, 889 F.2d 1548 (6th Cir. 1989).

24. S. Rep. No. 552, 91st Cong. 1st Sess. 104 (1969).

25. Jasionowski v. Comm'r, 66 T.C. 312 (1976).

26. *Westphal*, 68 T.C.M. 1038.

27. Ellis v. Comm'r, 47 T.C.M. (CCH) 991 (1984).

28. McLarney v. Comm'r, 44 T.C.M. (CCH) 752 (1982); Treas. Reg. § 1.183-2(b)(1).

29. Churchman v. Comm'r, 68 T.C. 696 (1977), *acq.*, 1979-2 C.B. 1.

30. Krebs v. Comm'r, 63 T.C.M. 2413 (1992) (promotion of wife's music career conducted in businesslike manner); Peacock v. Comm'r, 83 T.C.M. (CCH) 1662 (2002) (taxpayers never studied tournament fishing from a business person's point of view); Lewis v. Comm'r, 64 T.C.M. (CCH) 269 (1992) (taxpayers engaged in sailboat charter activity did not conduct it in businesslike fashion because books and records were incomplete, boat was docked at marina that prohibited commercial use, and taxpayers bought insurance for personal use only); Sloan v. Comm'r, 55 T.C.M. (CCH) 1238 (1988), *aff'd in unpublished opinion* (4th Cir. 1990) (federal employee had no profit motive for his weekend legal practice where it was not conducted in a businesslike way: he billed only a few of his clients, did not keep timesheets or carry malpractice insurance); Hires v. Comm'r, 40 T.C.M. 342 (CCH) (1980) (publishing and writing activities related to the taxpayer's botanical research were not carried on in a businesslike way); Schwartz v. Comm'r, T.C.M. 2003-86; Zarins v. Comm'r, 2002-1 U.S. Tax. Cas. (CCH) ¶ 50,471; Peacock v. Comm'r, T.C. Memo 2001-122 (deep-sea fishing activity not carried on in a businesslike manner); Doxtator v. Comm'r, T.C. Memo 2005-113 (taxpayer's Native American finance activity not conducted in a businesslike manner).

31. Zidar v. Comm'r, 82 T.C.M. (CCH) 357 (2001).

32. Treas. Reg. § 1.183-2(b)(2). The employment of professional advisors helps support a profit motive. Mills v. Comm'r, 699 F. Supp. 1245 (E.D. Ohio 1983); Dwyer v. Comm'r, 61 T.C.M. (CCH) 2187 (1991).

33. Kretschmer v. Comm'r, 57 T.C.M. (CCH) 441 (1989); Roach v. Comm'r, 58 T.C.M. (CCH) 545 (1989); Rogghianti v. Comm'r, 55 T.C.M. (CCH) 446 (1988).

34. Treas. Reg. § 1.183-2(b)(3); Christensen v. Comm'r, 56 T.C.M. (CCH) 425 (1988).

35. Treas. Reg. § 1.183-2(b)(4); Capodice v. Comm'r, 56 T.C.M. (CCH) 829 (1988) (holding property solely with expectation that it will eventually increase in value does not establish profit motive).

36. Jasienski v. Comm'r, 64 T.C.M. (CCH) 1369 (1992) (unrealized appreciation in limousines relevant in determining profit objective).

37. Antonides v. Comm'r, 91 T.C. 686 (1988), *aff'd*, 893 F.2d 656 (4th Cir. 1990) (yacht appreciation with yacht income, still not profit motivated).

38. Engdahl v. Comm'r, 72 T.C. 659 (1979); Allen v. Comm'r, 72 T.C. 28 (1979).

39. Treas. Reg. § 1.183-2(b)(5).

40. Treas. Reg. § 1.183-2(b)(6).

41. Bentley v. Comm'r, 56 T.C.M. (CCH) 216 (1988), *aff'd in unpublished opinion* (9th Cir. 1990).

42. Churchman v. Comm'r, 68 T.C. 696 (1977), *acq.*, 1979-2 C.B. 1.

43. Treas. Reg. § 1.183-2(b)(7). *Compare* Dwyer v. Comm'r, 61 T.C.M. (CCH) 2187 (1991) (the large auto purses sought by the taxpayer supported his profit motive), *with* Plunkett v. Comm'r, 47 T.C.M. (CCH) 1439 (1984) (taxpayer could not cover his expenses even if he won every mud race he entered).

44. Treas. Reg. § 1.183-2(b)(8).

45. *Id. See* Apple v. Comm'r, 748 F.2d 890 (4th Cir. 1984); Frazier v. Comm'r, T.C. Memo 1985-61.

46. Treas. Reg. § 1.183-2(b)(9).

47. *See* Wrightsman v. United States, 428 F.2d 1316 (Ct. Cl. 1970); Stanley v. Comm'r, 40 T.C.M. (CCH) 516 (1980); Barcus v. Comm'r, 32 T.C.M. (CCH) 660 (1973), *aff'd per curiam*, 492 F.2d 1237 (2d Cir. 1974); Samansky, *Hobby Loss or Deductible Loss: An Intractable Problem*, 34 U. Fla. L. Rev. 46 (1981).

48. Treas. Reg. § 1.183-2(b)(9). *But see* Treas. Reg. § 1.183-2(a); Treas. Reg. § 1.183-1(d)(3) Ex. (i).

49. Treas. Reg. § 1.183-1(b).

50. I.R.C. § 67(a) limits the deduction for such expenses to amounts that exceed 2% of adjusted gross income. *See* Treas. Reg. § 1.67-1T(a)(1)(iv).

51. I.R.C. § 68(a). The section limits an individual taxpayer's ability to claim itemized deductions if the taxpayer's adjusted gross income exceeds a specified statutory amount. Under section 68, all otherwise allowable itemized deductions are reduced by the lesser of (1) 3% of the amount by which the taxpayer's adjusted gross income exceeds the statutory amount; or (2) 80% of the itemized deductions. The effect of section 68 was lessened for years beginning after 2005 and before 2010. Section 68 does not apply to taxable years beginning after 2009 and before 2013. I.R.C. §.68(g). For taxable years beginning after 2012, the section 68 limitation applies.

52. Treas. Reg. § 1.183-1(b).

53. Treas. Reg. § 1.183-1(b)(4).

54. *Id.*

55. Barcus v. Comm'r, 32 T.C.M. (CCH) 660 (1973), *aff'd per curiam*, 492 F.2d 1237 (2d Cir. 1974).

56. Stanley v. Comm'r, 40 T.C.M. (CCH) 516 (1980); *see also* Eastman v. United States, 80-2 U.S. Tax Cas. (CCH) ¶ 9742 (Ct. Cl. 1980) (No. 538-78); Allen v. Comm'r, 72 T.C. 28 (1979); Feistman v. Comm'r, 44 T.C.M. (CCH) 30 (1982) (stamp collector showed he was profit-motivated); *compare* Feistman v. Comm'r, 41 T.C.M. (CCH) 1057 (1981); Dailey v. Comm'r, 44 T.C.M. (CCH) 1352 (1982); Wilson v. Comm'r, 42 T.C.M. (CCH) 787 (1981) (foot massaging activity of the taxpayer was not profit–motivated); Steele v. Comm'r, 41 T.C.M. (CCH) 1092 (1981); Burleson v. Comm'r, 46 T.C.M. (CCH) 1394 (1983) (dog breeding expenses were profit-motivated); Estate of Elizabeth Powers v. Comm'r, 84-2 U.S. Tax Cas. (CCH) ¶ 9590 (1st Cir. June 21, 1984), *aff'g* 46 T.C.M. (CCH) 1333 (1983) (horse breeding expenses were not profit-motivated); Salzman v. Comm'r, 55 T.C.M. (CCH) 278 (1988) (licensing of ultrasonic toothbrush was not for profit); Krivitsky v. Comm'r, 54 T.C.M. (CCH) 493 (1987) (mining activities were not conducted with a profit motive); Hawkins v. Comm'r, 54 T.C.M. (CCH) 1529 (1988) (exotic animal farm was not profit-motivated); Barr v. Comm'r, 56 T.C.M. (CCH) 1255 (1989) (art publishing enterprise did not have profit intention).

57. *See Barcus*, 32 T.C.M. at 673.

58. *See Stanley*, 40 T.C.M. at 516. *See* Dunn v. Comm'r, 70 T.C. 715 (1978), *aff'd without published opinion*, 607 F.2d 995 (2d Cir. 1979); Phillips v. Comm'r, 73 T.C.M. (CCH) 2297 (1997) (Arabian horse breeding activities was profit–motivated even though there was a lengthy five-to-ten-year startup loss period, and unforeseen circumstances can help a taxpayer explain profit motive in spite of low-level of activity).

59. *Id.*

60. *See Wrightsman*, 428 F.2d 1316.

61. *See Stanley*, 40 T.C.M. at 516.

62. Dreicer v. Comm'r, 39 T.C.M. (CCH) 233 (1979), *rev'd and remanded*, 665 F.2d 1292 (D.C. Cir 1981), *on remand*, 78 T.C. 642 (1982), *aff'd in unpublished opinion*, (D.C. Cir. 1983). *See* McGuire v. Comm'r, 64 T.C.M. (CCH) 739 (1992).

63. *See* Treas. Reg. § 1.183-2(b) (listing factors to be considered by court in determining whether activity is engaged in for profit). *See* Khorsandi, *Does Your Client Have a Profit Motive? An Analysis of Tax Court Criteria Used To Evaluate a Taxpayer's Profit Motive Under Section 183*, 47 Tax Law. 291 (1993); Jasienski v. Comm'r, 64 T.C.M. (CCH) 1369 (1992).

64. Dreicer v. Comm'r, 78 T.C. 642, 644–45 (1982), *aff'd in unpublished opinion* (D.C. Cir. 1983).

65. Johnson v. United States, 86-2 U.S. Tax Cas. (CCH) ¶ 9705 (Ct. Cl. 1986).

66. Dailey v. Comm'r, (8th Cir. 1982) (unpublished), *aff'g* 44 T.C.M. (CCH) 1352 (1982).

67. H.D. Mandelbaum v. Comm'r, 59 T.C.M. (CCH) 516 (1990).

68. For similar lithograph tax-shelter cases, see Rose v. Comm'r, 88 T.C. 386 (1987), aff'd, 868 F.2d 851 (6th Cir. 1989); Ballard v. Comm'r, 56 T.C.M. (CCH) 153 (1988).

69. S.P. Barr v. Comm'r, 56 T.C.M. (CCH) 1255 (1989).

70. J.F. Moore v. Comm'r, 85 T.C. 72 (1986).

71. J.A. Harmon v. Comm'r, 51 T.C.M. (CCH) 1491 (1986).

72. L.W. Paxton v. Comm'r, 61 T.C.M. (CCH) 2630 (1991).

73. M. Reali v. Comm'r, 48 T.C.M. (CCH) 826 (1984). See D.C. Harrington v. Comm'r, 48 T.C.M. (CCH) 837 (1984); S.A. Miller v. Comm'r, 52 T.C.M. (CCH) 239 (1986).

74. Stella Waitzkin v. Comm'r, 63 T.C.M. (CCH) 2740 (1992). The case is also discussed in chapter 16.

75. See Khorsandi, supra note 63. In contrast to the result reached by the court in Waitzkin, in William James Courville v. Comm'r, 71 T.C.M. (CCH) 2496 (1996), the court found that an individual who spent significant time and effort in golfing activities but who failed to earn any income from those activities did not have an actual and honest objective of making a profit. Factors indicating that the taxpayer lacked a profit motive were that he took personal pleasure in playing the game, he never worked in any capacity as a professional golfer, and he failed to qualify to participate in any Professional Golf Association tournament.

76. Richard A. Stasewich v. Comm'r, 72 T.C.M. (CCH) 1 (1996).

77. Id. at 5 (citing I.R.C. § 183(b)).

78. Deborah Joyce Windisch v. Comm'r, 72 T.C.M. (CCH) 361 (1996). See Klapper v. Comm'r, 60 T.C.M. (CCH) 182 (1990) (where a lawyer failed to prove that his writing, photography, and law activities were engaged in for profit); Callahan v. Comm'r, 71 T.C.M. (CCH) 2103 (1996) (writing activities were not carried on in a businesslike manner).

79. Wilbur Kenneth Griesmer v. Comm'r, 77 T.C.M. (CCH) 1948 (1999).

80. Zidar v. Comm'r, 82 T.C.M. (CCH) 357 (2001).

81. Id.

82. Treas. Reg. § 1.183-2(b); Golanty v. Comm'r, 72 T.C. 411 (1979), aff'd without published opinion, 647 F.2d 170 (9th Cir. 1981).

83. See and compare Mills v. United States, 699 F. Supp. 1245 (N.D. Ohio 1988), which held that a taxpayer's motorcycle racing activity was engaged in with an actual and honest profit objective. Although Mills never sustained a profit from his motorcycle racing, he had opened a separate bank account for the activity, secured a financial and business advisor, and generally conducted the activity in a businesslike manner. See Note, Racing Without a Profit Objective and Crashing Into Section 183: Zidar v. Comm'r, 55 TAX LAW. 871 (2001/02).

84. I.R.C. § 67(a); Treas. Reg. § 1.67-1T(a)(1)(iv).

85. I.R.C. § 68(a).

86. I.R.C. § 68(f), added by 2001 Tax Relief Act § 103, effective beginning in 2006.

87. I.R.C. § 68(g), added by 2001 Tax Relief Act § 103.

88. I.R.C. § 68(g), as amended by the Tax Relief, Unemployment Insurance Reauthorization and Job Creation Act of 2010.

89. I.R.C. § 68(d).

90. I.R.C. § 165(c)(1).

91. I.R.C. § 165(c)(2).

92. See supra notes 2 and 6.

93. See Higgins v. Comm'r, 312 U.S. 212 (1941).

94. Horrman v. Comm'r, 17 T.C. 903 (1951); McAuley v. Comm'r, 35 T.C.M. (CCH) 1236 (1976).

95. Tyler v. Comm'r, 6 T.C.M. (CCH) 275 (1947).

96. Rev. Rul. 54-268, 1954-2 C.B. 88.

97. Feistman v. Comm'r, 44 T.C.M. (CCH) 30, 1982 Tax Ct. Memo LEXIS 440 (1982).

98. Feistman v. Comm'r, 41 T.C.M. (CCH) 1060 (1981).

99. Feistman, 1982 Tax Ct. Memo LEXIS 440, at *18.

100. See Wrightsman v. United States, 428 F.2d at 1316 n.2; see supra note 13. The loss, however, was not allowed in Wrightsman.

101. *See* Lee, *A Blend of Old Wines in a New Wineskin: Section 183 and Beyond*, 29 TAX L. REV. 347 (1974); Anthoine, *The Collector of Taxes vs. The Collector of Objects*, 59 TAXES 917 (1981).
102. I.R.C. § 262.
103. Reynolds v. Comm'r, 4 T.C.M. (CCH) 837 (1945), *aff'd*, 155 F.2d 620 (1st Cir. 1946) (sale of inherited jewelry); Marx v. Comm'r, 5 T.C. 173 (1945) (sale of inherited yacht); M. Assmann Estate v. Comm'r, 16 T.C. 632 (1951) (sale of inherited house); Watkins v. Comm'r, 32 T.C.M. (CCH) 809 (1973) (sale of inherited house).
104. I.R.C. § 165(c)(3), (a), (h) (effective Jan. 1, 1983); Treas. Reg. § 1.165-8.
105. I.R.C. § 165(h)(1)(B). Section 67(a)'s 2% limitation does not apply; *see* I.R.C. § 67(b)(3).
106. Treas. Reg. § 1.165-7(b).
107. I.R.C. § 165(h)(1)(A).
108. I.R.C. § 165(h)(1)(B).
109. I.R.C. § 165(c)(3); Treas. Reg. § 1.165-8; Gevstell v. Comm'r, 46 T.C. 161 (1966); Krahmer v. United States, 810 F.2d 1145 (Fed. Cir. 1987), *aff'g in part and rev'g in part* 85-2 U.S. Tax Cas. (CCH) ¶ 9970 (Cl. Ct. 1985).
110. I.R.C. § 1231(a); Treas. Reg. § 1.1033(c)-1(a).
111. I.R.C. § 1033(a)(2).
112. I.R.C. § 1031(a); Treas. Reg. § 1.1031(a)-1(b); *see* Cal. Fed. Life Ins. Co. v. Comm'r, 680 F.2d 85 (9th Cir. 1982), *aff'g* 76 T.C. 107 (1981); Rev. Rul. 76214, 1976-1 C.B. 218; Rev. Rul. 79-143, 1979-1 C.B. 264; Rev. Rul. 82-96, 1982-1 C.B. 113; Rev. Rul. 82-166, 1982-2 C.B. 190.
113. I.R.C. § 1031(a)(2) provides that the properties involved in a like-kind exchange may not be stock in trade or other property held primarily for sale (inventory), stocks, bonds or notes, other securities or evidence of indebtedness or interest, interests in a partnership, certificate of trust, or beneficial interests or choses in action. Therefore, an exchange between an art dealer and a collector, if all requirements are satisfied, may be tax-free to the collector but will be taxable to the art dealer. *See* Rev. Rul. 75-292, 1975-2 C.B. 333.
114. I.R.C. § 1031(b); Coleman v. Comm'r, 180 F.2d 758 (8th Cir. 1950).
115. *See supra* notes 6–11 and the accompanying text.
116. *Compare* I.R.C. §§ 162, 165, 212, 183 *with* I.R.C. § 1031(a).
117. Rev. Rul. 57-244, 1957-1 C.B. 247, where the IRS ruled that unimproved real estate qualified for a like-kind exchange where the taxpayer abandoned his original intention to construct a personal residence on it and, thereafter, held it only for investment.
118. Priv. Ltr. Rul. 81-27-089.
119. In a 1992 Field Service Advice, the IRS National Office stated they will not rule on the issue unless forced to do so on audit. FSA from Branch 5 of Office of Chief Counsel, Income Tax and Accounting, dated Nov. 25, 1992.
120. *Id.*; Rev. Rul. 76-214, 1976-1 C.B. 218 (exchange of noncurrency bullion-type gold coins of one country for noncurrency bullion-type gold coins of a second country is "like-kind" because it is the exchange of bullion-type coins for bullion-type coins). *See also* Rev. Rul. 79-143, 1979-1 C.B. 264; Priv. Ltr. Rul. 81-17-053. In Rev. Rul. 82-166, 1982-2 C.B. 190, the IRS ruled that gold bullion held for investment and silver bullion held for investment are not of "like-kind" because silver and gold are intrinsically different metals and primarily used in different ways.
121. Starker v. United States, 602 F.2d 1341 (9th Cir. 1979).
122. Treas. Reg. § 1.1031(k)-1(c)(4).
123. Treas. Reg. § 1.1031(k)-1.
124. The regulations are based on typical deferred exchange transactions pertaining to exchanges of real estate. Treas. Reg. § 1.1031(k)-1 provides four safe harbors, which state that certain issues, such as agency and constructive receipt will, in effect, be ignored for purposes of determining whether the taxpayer is in actual or constructive receipt of money or other property before the taxpayer actually receives like-kind replacement property. These safe harbors have resulted in the creation of an entire industry of "qualified intermediaries" willing to act (for a fee) to assist taxpayers in completing deferred exchanges that are nontaxable under I.R.C. § 1031.

125. Treas. Reg. § 1.1031(k)-1.

126. Treas. Reg. § 1.1031(k)-1(g)(6); Treas. Reg. § 1.1031(k)-1(g)(4)(i), (ii).

127. Treas. Reg. § 1.1031(k)-1(g)(4)(iii).

128. Treas. Reg. § 1.1031(k)-1(k)(2).

129. Treas. Reg. § 1.1031(k)-1(k)(3).

130. Treas. Reg. § 1.1031(k)-1(k)(4).

131. Treas. Reg. § 1.1031(k)-1(k)(2).

132. *See* Handler, *Planning Deferred Like-Kind Exchanges Under the New Final Regulations,* 75 J. TAX'N 10 (1991); Griffith, *Section 1031 Exchanges of Personal Property And Multiple Assets,* 47 TAX LAW. 53 (1993); Lipton, *The "State of The Art" in Like-Kind Exchanges,* 91 J. TAX'N 78 (1999); Levine, 567-3rd T.M., *Taxfree Exchanges Under Section 1031;* Kove & Kosakow, *Estate Planning Benefits of Deferred Like-Kind Exchanges of Real Estate,* 28 EST. PLAN. 372 (2001); Dukes, *Tax Deferred Exchanges of Property-Mistakes and Misconceptions,* 79 TAXES 31 (2001); Lipton, *The "State of the Art" in Like-Kind Exchanges Revisited,* 98 J. TAX'N 334 (2003); Wagner, *Ruling Paves the Way for Professionals to Operate As Section 1031 Exchange Intermediaries,* 99 J. TAX'N 349 (2003).

133. *Id.*

134. *See, e.g.,* N.Y. COMP. CODES R. & REGS. tit. 20, §§ 526.5(f), 526.7(d).

135. *See* discussion of sales tax at pages 1193–1198.

136. Franklin v. Comm'r, 77-2 U.S. Tax Cas. (CCH) ¶ 9574 (W.D.N.C. 1977); Herrald, Inc. v. Comm'r, 35 T.C.M. (CCH) 1134 (1976).

137. Treas. Reg. § 1.408-10(b)(1).

138. I.R.S. Notice 82-3, 1982-1 C.B. 353 (pt. III.A., Q.3).

139. I.R.C. § 402(a)(5) covers rollovers from a qualified retirement plan to an IRA account. I.R.C. § 402(a)(7) covers spousal rollovers of amounts paid to a surviving spouse from a qualified retirement plan on the death of the covered employee.

140. I.R.C. § 408(m)(3).

141. I.R.S. Notice 87-16, 1987-1 C.B. 446.

142. *See supra* note 4.

143. N.Y. TAX LAW § 1105(a).

144. U.S. CONST., art. 1, § 8; *see* Miller Bros. v. Maryland, 347 U.S. 340, 344–45 (1954).

145. N.Y. COMP. CODES R. & REGS. tit. 20, § 525.2(a)(3).

146. N.Y. COMP. CODES R. & REGS. tit. 20, § 526.7(e)(1).

147. State of New York—Commissioner of Taxation and Finance, Advisory Opinion-TSB-A-89(42)S; 1989 N.Y. Tax LEXIS 493 (Nov. 14, 1989).

148. Matter of the Petition of Richard L. Feigen & Co., Inc., Decision of the State Tax Commission, June 19, 1981 (TSBH81143S) Sales Tax, July 22, 1981.

149. The Manhattan District Attorney's office has been conducting an intense investigation of art dealers and collectors who may be in violation of New York State's Sales and Compensating Use Tax Law. For information on those art dealers who have pled guilty to a violation see the website www.manhattanda.org/whatsnew/index.htm. The continuing investigation has raised millions of dollars for New York State. *See A Tax That's Often Ignored Suddenly Attracts Attention,* N.Y. TIMES, June 5, 2002.

150. N.Y. TAX LAW § 1110; *see In re* Helga Marston, State of New York—Tax Appeals Tribunal, DTA No. 813105; 1996 N.Y. Tax LEXIS 114 (Feb. 29, 1996); N.Y.S. Advisory Opinion TSB-A-08 (7) S (Petition No. S061220C) (Feb. 14, 2008) (a peculiar advisory opinion involving the loan of a work of art from a nonresident of New York to a museum located in New York; the opinion raised the issue that if the nonresident lender of the art work was engaged in business in New York, the loan of the art work might be considered a "use" that could be subject to New York use tax).

151. P-H Fine Arts, Ltd., State of New York—Tax Appeals Tribunal, DTA No. 807866; 1994 N.Y. Tax LEXIS 605 (Oct. 13, 1994).

152. *Id.* at *19.

153. *Id.* at *33.

154. N.Y. COMP. CODES R. & REGS. tit. 20, § 526.5(f).

155. CAL. REV. & TAX. CODE § 6012.

156. N.Y. COMP. CODES R. & REGS. tit. 20, § 526.7(d). Example 1 of this Regulation provides: *A* and *B* exchange automobiles. The exchange is a sale under the Tax Law and each party is liable for the payment of the tax measured by the current market value of the automobiles received.

157. N.Y. TAX LAW § 1105(c)(7). The New York City sales tax on such services was repealed effective December 1, 1995.

158. State of New York—Commissioner of Taxation and Finance, Advisory Opinion—TSB-A-91(47)S (July 5, 1991).

159. *Id.*

160. *Id.* N.Y. TAX LAW § 1105(c)(7).

161. See discussion in chapter 4, page 318.

162. *In re* Newhouse, State of New York—Tax Appeals Tribunal, DTA No. 809455, 1993 N.Y. Tax LEXIS 193 (May 6, 1993).

163. *Id.* (citing *In re* Penfold v. State Tax Comm'n, 494 N.Y.S.2d 552 (1985), involving a refuse company that had a dumping charge that claimed the charge was a separate, nontaxable service; there the court said: "The record is clear that the petitioner's customers purchased but one service, the removal of refuse. Disposal of that refuse is, in our view, an integral aspect of that service and cannot reasonably be reckoned a separate service arising from a different transaction.").

164. *Id.*

165. *In re* Henry A. & Marianne Ittleson, DTA No. 819283, 2004 WL 1523317 (N.Y. Div. Tax. App. July 1, 2004), *rev'd*, DTA No. 819283, 2005 WL 2108132 (N.Y. Tax App. Tribunal, Aug. 25, 2005).

166. N.Y. TAX LAW § 631(b)(1)(A).

167. Ittleson, 2004 WL 1523317. The N.Y. Income Tax District Office Audit Manual notes that where a nonresident (who is not an art dealer) consigns a piece of art to a New York auction house for sale, such sale is not treated as New York source income.

168. *Id.*

169. Ittleson, 2005 WL 2108132.

170. I.R.C. § 167; Treas. Reg. § 1.167(a)-1.

171. Judge v. Comm'r, 35 T.C.M. (CCH) 1264 (1976); Rev. Rul. 68-232, 1968-1 C.B. 79 (which states: "A valuable and treasured art piece does not have a determinable useful life. While the actual physical condition of the property may influence the value placed on the object, it will not ordinarily limit or determine the useful life. Accordingly, depreciation of works of art generally is not allowable."); Associated Obstetricians & Gynecologists v. Comm'r, 46 T.C.M. (CCH) 613 (1983), *aff'd*, 762 F.2d 38 (6th Cir. 1985); Clinger v. Comm'r, 60 T.C.M. (CCH) 598 (1990); Tech. Adv. Mem. 86-41-006.

172. *Id.*

173. Simon v. Comm'r, 68 F.3d 41, 95-2 U.S. Tax Cas. (CCH) ¶ 50,552 (2d Cir. 1995), *aff'g* 103 T.C. 247 (1994); Liddle v. Comm'r, 65 F.3d 329, 95-2 U.S. Tax. Cas. (CCH) ¶ 50,488 (3d Cir. 1995), *aff'g* 103 T.C. 285 (1994). *See* Goetzl, *Depreciation of Antique Musical Instruments: Liddle v. Commissioner and Simon v. Commissioner*, 49 TAX LAW. 759 (1996). *Compare* Browning v. Comm'r, 890 F.2d 1084, 89-2 U.S. Tax. Cas. (CCH) ¶ 9666 (9th Cir. 1989).

174. *See* Goetzl, *supra* note 173, at 767.

175. *See* Liddle, 65 F.3d 329.

176. *Id.*

177. Action on Decision 1996-009, *nonacq.*, 1996-29 I.R.B. 4.

178. I.R.C. § 168.

APPENDIX 14-1

*Agreement for Exchange of Property**

AGREEMENT FOR EXCHANGE OF PROPERTY

This Agreement for Exchange of Property ("Agreement") is entered into as of this _____ day of _____, 20__ by and between _____ ("Investor"), residing at _____, and Art Dealer (the "Company"), having an office at _____, and is made with reference to the following facts:

    A. Investor is the owner of the following work of art (the "Relinquished Work"):

Artist:
Title:
Medium:
Size:
Date:

    B. Investor desires to exchange the Relinquished Work for the Exchange Works, defined below, pursuant to the provisions of Section 1031 of the Internal Revenue Code of 1986, as amended (the "IRC"), upon the terms and conditions set forth in this Agreement.

    C. The Company is willing to acquire the Exchange Works and exchange the Exchange Works for the Relinquished Work upon the terms and conditions set forth in this Agreement.

NOW, THEREFORE, in consideration of the foregoing, and the mutual covenants and conditions contained in this Agreement, the parties agree as follows:

1. 1031 Exchange.

    A. *Transfer of the Relinquished Work.* On _____, 20__ (the "Transfer Date"), Investor shall transfer to the Company and the Company shall accept and acquire from Investor, legal title in and to the Relinquished Work. Investor shall deliver to the Company a bill of sale in the form of attached Exhibit A (the "Relinquished Work Bill of Sale"). The Relinquished Work will be in the physical possession of the Company or its Art Dealer as of the Transfer Date, having been shipped to the Company by common carrier.

    B. *Relinquished Work Exchange Value.* The parties agree that on the Transfer Date and for all purposes of this Agreement, the fair market value for

the Relinquished Work (the "Relinquished Work Exchange Value") shall be
_____ Dollars ($_____).

C. *Exchange of Exchange Works.* The Company shall purchase such other
works of art as identified by, and on the terms and conditions specified in
writing by, Investor that Investor believes will satisfy the requirements of
"like kind property" for purposes of Section 1031 of the IRC (the "Exchange
Works"). The Company agrees to convey title to the Exchange Works to Investor in exchange and as consideration for the transfer of the Relinquished
Work to the Company and to deliver to Investor a bill of sale in the form of
attached Exhibit C for the Exchange Works (the "Exchange Works Bill of
Sale"). The Company shall transfer title to the Exchange Works to Investor
and this exchange of property shall be completed and Investor shall receive
the Exchange Works on or before the earlier of (i) one hundred eighty (180)
days after the Transfer Date, or (ii) the due date (including extensions) for
Investor's federal income tax return for Investor's taxable year during which
the Transfer Date occurs (the "Exchange Date").

D. *Identification of Exchange Works.* Investor shall specifically identify
the Exchange Works in a writing delivered to the Company within forty-
five (45) days after the Transfer Date (the "Identification Period"). The
Exchange Works identified by Investor shall be described on written identification statements in the form of attached Exhibit B (the "Identification
Statements") and shall be delivered to the Company within the Identification Period. The date of the identification of each Exchange Work and the fair
market value for each Exchange Work (collectively, the "Exchange Works
Exchange Value") for all purposes of this Agreement shall be stated by Investor on the Identification Statements.

E. *Failure to Identify Exchange Works.* If Investor does not identify any
Exchange Works within the Identification Period, then an amount equal to
the Relinquished Work Exchange Value shall be paid by the Company to Investor within ten (10) days thereafter.

F. *Excess Cash Requirements.* To the extent that the Exchange Works Exchange Value exceeds the Relinquished Work Exchange Value, Investor shall
pay to the Company the full amount of such excess cash and the Company
shall use such cash to acquire the Exchange Works.

G. *Relinquished Work Sales Proceeds.* If the Relinquished Work is sold by
the Company prior to the Exchange Date, the proceeds of any such sale shall
be held by the Company in a separate interest bearing account, in escrow,
designated for and to be used exclusively by the Company to acquire title to
the Exchange Works identified by Investor. Investor shall have no right to

receive, pledge, borrow or otherwise obtain the benefit of the cash proceeds of any sale prior to the Exchange Date.

H. *Satisfaction of Obligations*. In the event Exchange Works are purchased by the Company and the Relinquished Work Exchange Value exceeds the Exchange Works Exchange Value, then the Company shall pay to Investor an amount equal to the difference between the Relinquished Works Exchange Value and the Exchange Works Exchange Value on the earlier of (i) the Exchange Date, or (ii) the day after Investor receives title to all of the Exchange Works from the Company, provided, however, that in no event shall the Company pay any such amount to Investor prior to the forty-sixth (46th) day after the Transfer Date. Investor shall have no right to receive, pledge, borrow or otherwise obtain the benefits of any such amount or related property prior to such time. The Company may offset any damages from Investor it may have against the unexpended Relinquished Work Exchange Value.

I.   Form 8824. Investor represents that he will prepare and file IRS Form 8824, Like-Kind Exchanges, with his tax return for the year during which the Transfer Date occurred and upon request will furnish the Company with a copy of the completed IRS Form 8824.

2. *Representations and Warranties of, and Indemnities by, Investor*. Investor does hereby represent and warrant to the Company that:

A.   The Relinquished Work is an authentic work of art created by the artist indicated on the first page of this Agreement and the Relinquished Work Bill of Sale.

B.   Investor has full legal authority to enter into this Agreement, to make the representations and warranties contained herein, to deliver the Relinquished Work Bill of Sale and to complete the transaction contemplated herein.

C.   Investor is the sole and absolute owner of the Relinquished Work, has the full right to sell and transfer title to the Relinquished Work, and the Relinquished Work, at the time of transfer of title, will be free and clear of any and all rights, claims, liens, mortgages, security interests or other encumbrances held by any person.

D.   Other than as specifically represented and warranted by Investor as set forth in this Agreement, Investor makes no representations or warranties, express or implied, with respect to the Relinquished Work, including without limitation, representations or warranties as to value or condition.

E.   Investor does hereby agree to indemnify, defend and hold the Company free and harmless from any and all demands, claims, suits, judgments, obligations, damages, losses or other liability, including reasonable attorney or other professional fees and other costs, fees and expenses, suffered or incurred by, or asserted or alleged against the Company arising by reason of, or in connection with, the breach, falsity or inaccuracy of any of Investor's representations or warranties contained in this Agreement. Such indemnification shall survive the termination of this Agreement.

3. *Representations and Warranties of, and Indemnities by, the Company.* The Company does hereby represent and warrant to Investor that:

A. The Company has full legal authority to enter into this Agreement, to make the representations and warranties contained herein, and to complete the transaction contemplated herein.

B. The Exchange Works are authentic works of art created by the artists indicated on the Identification Statements and the Exchange Works Bill of Sale.

C. At the time the Company transfers title of the Exchange Works to Investor, the Company will be the sole and absolute owner of the Exchange Works, have the full right to sell and transfer title to the Exchange Works, and the Exchange Works will be free and clear of any and all rights, claims, liens, mortgages, security interests or other encumbrances held by any person.

D. Other than as specifically represented and warranted by the Company as set forth in this Agreement, the Company makes no representations or warranties, express or implied, with respect to the Exchange Works, including without limitation, representations or warranties as to value or condition.

E. The Company does hereby agree to indemnify, defend and hold Investor free and harmless from any and all demands, claims, suits, judgments, obligations, damages, losses or other liability, including reasonable attorney or other professional fees and other costs, fees and expenses, suffered or incurred by, or asserted or alleged against Investor arising by reason of, or in connection with, the breach by the Company, falsity or inaccuracy of any of the Company's representations or warranties contained in this Agreement. Such indemnification shall survive the termination of this Agreement.

4. Sales Tax.

A. The Company represents that it is an art dealer and is acquiring the Relinquished Work for resale and agrees to furnish Investor with a New York resale certificate.

B. Investor agrees to pay any and all applicable state sales or use tax due

on the acquisition of the Exchange Works by Investor and agrees to indemnify and hold the Company (in any capacity) harmless from any and all
demands, claims, suits, judgments or other liability (including reasonable
attorney fees and other expenses incurred by the Company in connection
therewith) awarded to any person or entity arising by reason of Investor's
breach of this Agreement to pay such taxes. Such indemnification shall survive the termination of this Agreement. If no sales or use tax is applicable on
the acquisition of the Exchange Works by Investor, then Investor will have
no obligation under this Paragraph.

5. *Additional Obligations and Indemnities.* The Exchange Works shall only be
acquired by the Company pursuant to the written directions of Investor. Investor agrees to reimburse the Company for any costs or expenses (exclusive of the
purchase price of the Exchange Works) incurred by the Company in acquiring
the Exchange Works at the direction of Investor and not otherwise properly paid
for out of the Relinquished Work sales proceeds. Except as otherwise provided in
writing, the Company shall have no liability to Investor in connection with the
physical condition, value, acquisition costs or terms, sales or use taxes payable
with respect to the Exchange Works, or investment potential of the Exchange
Works. Further, the Company is making no representation or warranty of any
kind or nature that the transaction contemplated by this Agreement qualifies as
a tax-free exchange under Section 1031 of the IRC. Further, Investor agrees to
indemnify the Company and hold the Company harmless from any and all demands, claims, suits, judgments or other liability (including attorney fees and
other expenses incurred by the Company in connection therewith) which the
Company incurs by reason of good-faith compliance with Investor's directions,
including, without limitation, any liability with respect to sales or use taxes payable in connection with the Exchange Works. Investor hereby releases the Company from any responsibility for the failure of the seller of the Exchange Works
to comply with their obligations. These indemnifications and releases shall survive the termination of this Agreement.

6. *Fee.* Investor shall pay the Company a fee for acting as qualified intermediary
in the amount of $_____ (_____ Dollars).

7. *General Provisions.*

A. *Successors and Assigns.* The rights and obligations under this Agreement shall be binding upon and inure to the benefit of the parties to this
Agreement and their respective heirs, successors, representatives and permissible assigns.

B. *Counterparts.* This Agreement may be executed in two or more counterparts, including by facsimile or PDF, each of which shall be an original, and all
of which shall constitute one and the same instrument.

C. *Interpretation.* No provision of this Agreement is to be interpreted for or against either party because that party or that party's legal representative drafted such provision.

D. *Disputes.* Any dispute arising hereunder shall be resolved in the courts of the State of New York or in the appropriate United States District Court for the State of New York and the parties hereby consent to the personal jurisdiction of those courts, provided, however, that the parties hereto agree that they will make concerted efforts to settle any dispute between them in an amicable manner without the necessity of litigation.

E. *Survival of Representation, Warranties and Indemnification.* The benefits of the representations, warranties, covenants and indemnities contained in this Agreement shall survive completion of the transactions contemplated by this Agreement.

F. *Confidentiality.* Neither party will disclose to any person or entity, except to either party's attorneys and advisors, and as may be required by law, regulation or in response to process, or in order to carry out the terms of this Agreement, (i) the identity of the parties and (ii) the terms of this Agreement or the negotiations with respect thereto.

G. *Notice.* Every notice, and other communication, which any party is required or desires to make or communicate upon or to the other with regard to this Agreement shall be in writing and shall be deemed to have been delivered or communicated at the time that such notice or other communication shall have been either personally delivered or upon actual receipt after being deposited, registered or certified, properly addressed to the address of the party as contained in this Agreement, first class postage and fees prepaid, return receipt requested, in the United States mail.

H. *Additional Documents and Acts.* In addition to the documents and instruments to be delivered as provided in this Agreement, each of the parties shall, from time to time at the request of the other party, execute and deliver to the other party such other instruments and documents, and shall take such other action as may be required to more effectively carry out the terms of this Agreement.

I. *Incorporation of Exhibits.* All exhibits attached to this Agreement are by such reference incorporated in this Agreement and made a part of this Agreement.

J. *Validity–Waiver.* No breach of any provision shall be waived unless in writing. Waiver of any one breach of any provision of this Agreement shall not be deemed to be a waiver of any other breach of the same or any other provision of this Agreement. This Agreement may be amended only by a written agreement executed by the parties in interest at the time of the modification.

K. *Headings–Gender–New York Law.* Paragraph titles or captions contained in this Agreement are inserted as a matter of convenience and for reference, and in no way define, limit, extend or describe the scope of this Agreement or any provision of this Agreement. Any word in this Agreement used in the singular or plural, and in the masculine, feminine or neuter, shall be either singular or plural, and masculine, feminine or neuter, as the context may indicate. The word "person" shall include corporation, firm, partnership, joint venture, trust or estate. This Agreement and all matters relating to it shall be governed by the laws of the State of New York, without regard to conflict of laws principles.

IN WITNESS WHEREOF, the parties have executed this Agreement effective on the date first above set forth.

_____

[Name of Investor]

ART DEALER

_____

[Name of Art Dealer]
By:
Its:

Exhibit A

BILL OF SALE

Dated: _____

Sold by: [Name and Address of Dealer] ("Seller")
Sold to: [Name and Address of Collector] ("Buyer")
Work Sold: Title: (the "Work")
Artist:
Medium:
Size:
Date:

Purchase Price: $_____ (_____Dollars) — Trade-in Credit

FOR VALUE RECEIVED, Seller hereby irrevocably and without condition or reservation of any kind sells, transfers and conveys to Buyer the Work, and all right to possession and all legal and equitable ownership of the Work, to have and to hold the Work unto Buyer, its successors and assigns, forever.

Seller represents and warrants to Buyer that upon delivery by Seller to Buyer of the Work and this Bill of Sale, good, valid and marketable title and exclusive and unrestricted right to possession of the Work, free of all Claims (as defined below) will pass from Seller to Buyer.

Seller represents and warrants that: (i) the Work is an authentic work of art created by the artist indicated above in this Bill of Sale; (ii) Seller is the sole and absolute owner of the Work and has full legal authority to sell and transfer good, valid and marketable title to the Work to Buyer; and (iii) Seller will transfer to Buyer good, valid and marketable title and exclusive and unrestricted right to possession of the Work, free and clear of any and all rights or interests of others, claims, liens, security interests, restrictions, conditions, options or other encumbrances of any kind held by any person. The representations and warranties contained in this Bill of Sale and all other terms hereof shall survive the delivery of this Bill of Sale and the transfer of the Work to Buyer.

Seller does hereby agree to indemnify and hold Buyer free and harmless from any and all demands, claims, suits, judgments, damages, losses and other liability (including but not limited to reasonable attorneys' fees and other reasonable expenses incurred by Buyer in connection with the matters so indemnified) asserted by or awarded to any person or entity against Buyer arising by reason of the breach, falsity or inaccuracy of any of Seller's representations or warranties contained in this Bill of Sale.

The terms and provisions of this Bill of Sale shall be binding upon Seller and his successors, assigns and legal representatives and shall inure to the benefit of Buyer and its successors, assigns and legal representatives. This Bill of Sale may be executed by facsimile or PDF, each of which shall be an original.

IN WITNESS WHEREOF, Seller has executed this Bill of Sale, effective _____, 2012.

_____

[Name of Investor]

Exhibit B

IDENTIFICATION OF EXCHANGE WORKS

Pursuant to Paragraph 1.D. of the Agreement for Exchange of Property between Investor and Art Dealer dated the _____ day of _____, 20__, Investor hereby identifies the following Exchange Works for purchase. This Identification Statement may be executed in two or more counterparts, including by facsimile or PDF, each of which shall be an original, and all of which shall constitute one and the same instrument.

_____
[Name of Investor]

Date: _____, 2012

			Fair Market Value
1.	Artist:		$_____
	Title:		
	Medium:		
	Size:		
	Date:		
2.	Artist:		$_____
	Title:		
	Medium:		
	Size:		
	Date:		

Identification of Exchange Works acknowledged this ___ day of _____,
2012 by Art Dealer.

ART DEALER

_____
[Name of Art Dealer]
By:
Its:

Exhibit C

BILL OF SALE

Dated: _____

Sold by: [Name and Address of Dealer] ("Seller")
Sold to: [Name and Address of Collector] ("Buyer")
Work Sold: Title: (the "Work")
Artist:
Medium:
Size:
Date:
Provenance: See Schedule A

Purchase Price: $_____ (_____ Dollars) - Trade-in Credit

FOR VALUE RECEIVED, Seller hereby irrevocably and without condition or reservation of any kind sells, transfers and conveys to Buyer the Works, and all right to possession and all legal and equitable ownership of the Works, to have and to hold the Works unto Buyer, his successors and assigns, forever.

Seller represents and warrants to Buyer that upon delivery by Seller to Buyer of the Works and this Bill of Sale, good, valid and marketable title and exclusive and unrestricted right to possession of the Works, free of all Claims (as defined below), will pass from Seller to Buyer.

Seller hereby represents and warrants to Buyer that: (i) the Works are authentic, that is, the Works were created by the artists indicated above in this Bill of Sale, and the attribution, provenance and description of the Works made in this Bill of Sale and Schedule A attached hereto are accurate and complete; (ii) Seller is the sole and absolute owner of the Works, has full legal authority to sell and transfer good, valid and marketable title to the Works, and the Works are free and clear of any and all rights or interests of others, claims, liens, security interests, restrictions, conditions, options or other encumbrances of any kind held or claimed by any person (collectively, "Claims"); (iii) Seller has informed Buyer of all facts and information within Seller's knowledge about the Works, including, without limitation, facts and information pertaining to the authenticity, provenance and title to the Works; and (iv) Seller has not restored or repaired any part of the Works, nor consented thereto, and to the best of Seller's knowledge no other party has performed any major restoration or repair. The benefits of the representations and warranties contained in this Bill of Sale shall survive the delivery of this Bill of Sale and transfer of the Works to Buyer.

Seller agrees to indemnify and holds Buyer harmless from any and all demands, claims, suits, judgments, losses and other liabilities (including but not limited to reasonable attorneys' fees and other reasonable expenses incurred by Buyer in connection with the matters so indemnified) asserted by or awarded to any person or entity against Buyer arising by reason of the breach, alleged breach, falsity or inaccuracy of any of Seller's representations or warranties contained in this Bill of Sale.

Seller agrees to deliver the Works by common carrier to Buyer at _____, or such other location as directed by Buyer. Buyer agrees to timely reimburse Seller for reasonable third party costs and expenses approved in advance by Buyer and paid by Seller relating to the packing, transporting, shipping and insuring the Works for delivery by common carrier, which shall be experienced art handlers, to Buyer pursuant to this Bill of Sale.

The terms and provisions of this Bill of Sale shall be binding upon Seller and its successors, assigns and legal representatives and shall inure to the benefit of Buyer and his successors, assigns and legal representatives. This Bill of Sale may be executed by facsimile or PDF, each of which shall be an original.

IN WITNESS WHEREOF, Seller has executed this Bill of Sale, effective _____, 2012.

ART DEALER

_____
[Name of Art Dealer]
By:
Its:

---

*   CAUTION: This form reflects a very simple, straightforward qualified intermediary exchange which may not be covered under the safe harbor provisions. The form should not be used without obtaining legal advice. Each transaction is different and the form may or may not be appropriate for a particular transaction or client, or only after significant revisions. The form also assumes that the Investor is comfortable with the financial ability and trustworthiness of the art dealer as an exchanger.

APPENDIX 14-2

Sample Invoice—Exchange and Trade-In Credit

Art Dealer Gallery, Inc.
[Art dealer address]

_____, 20__

[Name of Investor]

[Address of Investor]

INVOICE

Artist: [the Exchange Work]
Title:
Medium:
Size:
Date:

Purchase Price:	$1,200,000.00		
LESS:	<1,000,000.00>		Trade-In Credit for [Relinquished Work]
	200,000.00		
PLUS Sales Tax:	17,750.00		New York City 8.875% sales tax
TOTAL DUE:	$217,750.00		
_____, 20___			

PAYMENT MAY BE WIRED TO:
Bank Name:
Bank Address:
ABA Number:
Account Number:
Account Name:

APPENDIX 14-3

IRS Form 8824–Like-Kind Exchanges

Form **8824**	**Like-Kind Exchanges**	OMB No. 1545-1190
Department of the Treasury Internal Revenue Service	**(and section 1043 conflict-of-interest sales)** ▶ **Attach to your tax return.**	**20**12 Attachment Sequence No. **109**

Name(s) shown on tax return	Identifying number

Part I   **Information on the Like-Kind Exchange**

Note: *If the property described on line 1 or line 2 is real or personal property located outside the United States, indicate the country.*

1 Description of like-kind property given up:

2 Description of like-kind property received:

3 Date like-kind property given up was originally acquired (month, day, year)	**3**	MM/DD/YYYY
4 Date you actually transferred your property to other party (month, day, year)	**4**	MM/DD/YYYY
5 Date like-kind property you received was identified by written notice to another party (month, day, year). See instructions for 45-day written identification requirement	**5**	MM/DD/YYYY
6 Date you actually received the like-kind property from other party (month, day, year). See instructions	**6**	MM/DD/YYYY

7 Was the exchange of the property given up or received made with a related party, either directly or indirectly (such as through an intermediary)? See instructions. If "Yes," complete Part II. If "No," go to Part III   . .   ☐ **Yes** ☐ **No**

Part II   **Related Party Exchange Information**

8 Name of related party	Relationship to you	Related party's identifying number
Address (no., street, and apt., room, or suite no., city or town, state, and ZIP code)		

9 During this tax year (and before the date that is 2 years after the last transfer of property that was part of the exchange), did the related party sell or dispose of any part of the like-kind property received from you (or an intermediary) in the exchange or transfer property into the exchange, directly or indirectly (such as through an intermediary), that became your replacement property? . . . .   ☐ Yes ☐ No

10 During this tax year (and before the date that is 2 years after the last transfer of property that was part of the exchange), did you sell or dispose of any part of the like-kind property you received?   . . . . . .   ☐ Yes ☐ No

*If both lines 9 and 10 are "No" and this is the year of the exchange, go to Part III. If both lines 9 and 10 are "No" and this is **not** the year of the exchange, stop here. If either line 9 or line 10 is "Yes," complete Part III and report on this year's tax return the deferred gain or (loss) from line 24 **unless** one of the exceptions on line 11 applies.*

11 If one of the exceptions below applies to the disposition, check the applicable box:

a ☐ The disposition was after the death of either of the related parties.

b ☐ The disposition was an involuntary conversion, and the threat of conversion occurred after the exchange.

c ☐ You can establish to the satisfaction of the IRS that neither the exchange nor the disposition had tax avoidance as one of its principal purposes. If this box is checked, attach an explanation (see instructions).

For Paperwork Reduction Act Notice, see the instructions.   Cat. No. 12311A   Form **8824** (2012)

Form 8824 (2012)   Page **2**

Name(s) shown on tax return. Do not enter name and social security number if shown on other side.	Your social security number

Part III   **Realized Gain or (Loss), Recognized Gain, and Basis of Like-Kind Property Received**

Caution: *If you transferred and received (a) more than one group of like-kind properties or (b) cash or other (not like-kind) property, see* **Reporting of multi-asset exchanges** *in the instructions.*

Note: *Complete lines 12 through 14 only if you gave up property that was not like-kind. Otherwise, go to line 15.*

12   Fair market value (FMV) of other property given up   **12**

13   Adjusted basis of other property given up   **13**

14   Gain or (loss) recognized on other property given up. Subtract line 13 from line 12. Report the gain or (loss) in the same manner as if the exchange had been a sale   **14**

     Caution: *If the property given up was used previously or partly as a home, see* **Property used as home** *in the instructions.*

15   Cash received, FMV of other property received, plus net liabilities assumed by other party, reduced (but not below zero) by any exchange expenses you incurred (see instructions)   **15**

16   FMV of like-kind property you received   **16**

17   Add lines 15 and 16   **17**

18   Adjusted basis of like-kind property you gave up, net amounts paid to other party, plus any exchange expenses **not** used on line 15 (see instructions)   **18**

19   **Realized gain or (loss).** Subtract line 18 from line 17   **19**

20   Enter the smaller of line 15 or line 19, but not less than zero   **20**

21   Ordinary income under recapture rules. Enter here and on Form 4797, line 16 (see instructions)   **21**

22   Subtract line 21 from line 20. If zero or less, enter -0-. If more than zero, enter here and on Schedule D or Form 4797, unless the installment method applies (see instructions)   **22**

23   **Recognized gain.** Add lines 21 and 22   **23**

24   Deferred gain or (loss). Subtract line 23 from line 19. If a related party exchange, see instructions   **24**

25   **Basis of like-kind property received.** Subtract line 15 from the sum of lines 18 and 23   **25**

Part IV   **Deferral of Gain From Section 1043 Conflict-of-Interest Sales**

Note: *This part is to be used* **only** *by officers or employees of the executive branch of the Federal Government or judicial officers of the Federal Government (including certain spouses, minor or dependent children, and trustees as described in section 1043) for reporting nonrecognition of gain under section 1043 on the sale of property to comply with the conflict-of-interest requirements. This part can be used* **only** *if the cost of the replacement property is more than the basis of the divested property.*

26   Enter the number from the upper right corner of your certificate of divestiture. (**Do not** attach a copy of your certificate. Keep the certificate with your records.)   ▶ _____

27   Description of divested property ▶ --

28   Description of replacement property ▶ --

     ----

29   Date divested property was sold (month, day, year)   **29**   MM/DD/YYYY

30   Sales price of divested property (see instructions)   **30**

31   Basis of divested property   **31**

32   **Realized gain.** Subtract line 31 from line 30   **32**

33   Cost of replacement property purchased within 60 days after date of sale   **33**

34   Subtract line 33 from line 30. If zero or less, enter -0-   **34**

35   Ordinary income under recapture rules. Enter here and on Form 4797, line 10 (see instructions)   **35**

36   Subtract line 35 from line 34. If zero or less, enter -0-. If more than zero, enter here and on Schedule D or Form 4797 (see instructions)   **36**

37   **Deferred gain.** Subtract the sum of lines 35 and 36 from line 32   **37**

38   **Basis of replacement property.** Subtract line 37 from line 33   **38**

Form **8824** (2012)

PART FIVE

TAXES AND

ESTATE

PLANNING

15

Tax and Estate Planning for Collectors

ost people are collectors of one thing or another, and the number of people who are serious collectors with valuable collections is growing rapidly.[1] In fact, paintings, stamps, coins, and other items of tangible personal property have increased in value at a much greater rate than have most stocks and bonds. As those collectibles increase in value, the estate planner must give them greater attention. Planning for the collector's lifetime and testamentary disposition of tangible personal property to charitable organizations was made increasingly complicated as a result of numerous changes in the tax law, beginning with the Tax Reform Act of 1969, continuing through the Economic Growth and Tax Relief Reconciliation Act of 2001, the Jobs and Growth Tax Relief Reconciliation Act of 2003, the Pension Protection Act of 2006, the Tax Relief, Unemployment Insurance Reauthorization, and Job Creation Act of 2010, and forward, with each year's tax act containing new and complex provisions. It seems that hardly a year goes by without some new and arcane legislation to confuse collectors. The problems are complicated by the fact that in most cases items of collectible tangible personal property (hereinafter called "the collection") are unique and difficult to value. Not knowing the value of the collection complicates the planning for its disposition.

Perhaps the most difficult problem in planning the collector's estate is knowing what she really wants. Most collectors have an emotional involvement to some extent with the items that make up their collections; for example, a painting may have been in the collector's family for generations. Collectors may own items that they consider very valuable but that are, in fact, almost worthless, or the reverse may be true. They may be secretive about what they have and about the true worth of the collection. One moment they may want their children to have the collection, and the next moment their desires may shift to their favorite museums. The care and maintenance of the collection may be the most important part of the collector's life, taking up the greatest amount of her time and energy. Any encroachment or even suggestion of less involvement with the collection may be threatening to the collector. Making a decision with respect to the collection's eventual disposition may also be something that the collector wishes to avoid.

In planning a collector's estate, an attorney must know the client's particular personality traits. Gaining that knowledge requires more than a one-hour conference. It is important for the attorney to acquaint the client slowly with all the available possibilities and to give the client time to consider the alternatives. That time is crucial; the client who is devoted to and involved with her collection may never have thought about its disposition and may have shied away from considering the problems. Therefore, knowing the client, knowing her desires and needs, working together over a period of time, and developing a sense of trust are absolutely necessary in planning any collector's estate.

VALUATION

Knowing the value or approximate value of a collector's estate is of utmost importance for many purposes:

- For income tax purposes if the collection is transferred during life to a charitable donee[2]
- For gift tax purposes if the property is transferred during life to a noncharitable donee[3]
- For estate tax purposes if the property is owned at death[4]
- For insurance purposes if the property is maintained during life (since insurance companies require an appraisal in order to determine the premiums for coverage)

As important as the concept of value is, there is no simple rule or answer. Although the Internal Revenue Service (IRS) has by regulation attempted to create rules of valuation, those rules are not workable in all situations and are most difficult to apply when it comes to unique items of tangible personal property.[5]

In his treatise on federal estate and gift taxation, Randolph Paul stated that value is essentially and peculiarly a difficult question of fact, with the burden of proof falling on the taxpayer.[6] The treatise pointed out, however, that valuation is more than a question of fact; it is a prophecy, a matter of opinion and judgment. In the valuation process, it is unsafe to neglect any apparent factor; the composite of all the factors involved in a single case should lead to a conclusion. Paul stated that it is wrong to assign to any particular factor a precise weight and noted that individualized treatment of each problem is essential. Paul pointed out that the courts have observed that

> [m]arket value is so dependent on times, places, conditions, and people that that which is a good rule in one case may be no rule under other circumstances.[7]

IRS Valuation Regulations

The IRS regulations for estate tax, gift tax, and income tax contain certain parallel provisions, although they are not consistent in every respect.[8]

The estate tax regulation defines fair market value as the price at which the property would change hands between a willing buyer and a willing seller, "neither being under any compulsion to buy or to sell and both having reasonable knowledge of relevant facts."[9]

The gift tax and income tax regulations contain identical language.[10] The hypothetical sale must be in the market in which such property is most commonly sold to the public. When trying to place a value on a unique collection, those guidelines do not offer much help. The regulations contemplate a retail market that, when one is dealing with collectibles, may not exist. Regulation section 20.2031-1(b) gives the example of a used car to illustrate which market is to be considered retail. The regulation states that the market value is the market price at which the general public can buy the car, not the wholesale price the dealer can pay for the car. When dealing with an average automobile, there is no problem, since a market exists for its sale. However, if the automobile is a rare antique, such a market may not exist. The contemplated retail-market rule of regulation section 20.2031-1(b) is an attempt by the IRS to formulate a simple rule where one does not fit. (The rule was injected into the estate tax regulations by T.D. 6826, 1965-2 C.B. 367. Similar language was inserted into the gift tax regulations by the same T.D. 6826 and is also contained in income tax regulation section 1.170A-1(c)(2).)

Neither the rule that value is the price at which an item can be sold at retail to the public nor the rule that value is the price that a member of the public can obtain on the sale of the item is appropriate in every estate, gift, and income tax situation.

The following examples[11] show the importance of various factors, including the nature of the tax (estate tax vis-à-vis gift tax) involved, and how some of the mechanical rules of the IRS regulations, observed to the exclusion of relevant factors, produce an erroneous substitute for true value.

Example 1: A father buys an automobile from a dealer in order to give it to his son. Barring some unusual circumstances, the value for gift tax purposes should be the amount paid for the automobile, not the amount for which the father could sell it back to the dealer. The value for gift tax purposes should ordinarily be the same whether the father gives the cost of the automobile in cash to his son (who, in turn, buys the automobile for himself) or buys the automobile and gives that to his son.

Example 2: In a variation of the facts in example 1, the father buys the same automobile at the same price for the same purpose but dies before consummating the gift. The father was heavily in debt; therefore, the executor of his estate decides that it is wise to sell the automobile, which has not been driven since its delivery to the father, in order to obtain cash with which to pay the father's debts and the estate's administration expenses. In that case, the automobile should be valued at the sale price for estate tax purposes.

Example 3: A husband buys an expensive emerald ring as a birthday gift for his wife. He gives her the ring, but she dies a few days later in an automobile accident and by her will leaves all her jewelry to her daughter. The value of the gift for gift tax purposes, as in example 1 above, should usually be the amount paid for the ring. However, the value of the ring in the determination of the estate tax liability of the donee wife may depend on several circumstances. If the deceased wife's estate was not complicated by obligations and lack of liquidity and if neither the executor nor the daughter needs or desires to sell the ring, the value for estate tax purposes may arguably be intermediate between the amount for which the executor could sell the ring and what the executor would have to pay to buy such a ring. Under other circumstances, the estate tax value would be the realizable sales price.

In example 1 above, the gift tax rule set out in regulation section 25.2512-1 is proper under normal circumstances, subject to one qualification. The regulation states that

> an item of property . . . which is generally obtained by the public in the retail market . . . [should be valued at] the price at which the item or a comparable item would be sold at retail.

It seems that in example 1, if the father bought the automobile, whether new or used, at somewhat less or more than the usual retail selling price, his actual cost should ordinarily be the value for gift tax purposes. Thus, to that extent the detailed mechanical rule set out in the regulation seems incorrect.

In example 2, the application of the mechanical estate tax rule of regulation section 20.2031-1(b) seems clearly wrong, although the general statement of valuation principles in that section is proper. The regulation states that

> the fair market value of an automobile . . . includable in the decedent's gross estate is the price for which an automobile of the same or approximately the same description, make, model, age, condition, etc., could be purchased by a member of the general public and not the price for which the particular automobile of the decedent would be purchased by a dealer in used automobiles.

But when the executor finds it advisable to sell a new car for whatever price the executor can get, as in example 2, the estate tax value should normally be the actual sale price in whatever market the executor makes the sale. The difficulty with that section of the regulations is in its use of mechanical rules that in many cases do not fit the facts.

In example 3, the application of the mechanical gift tax rule quoted above seems proper under most circumstances. But the application of the mechanical estate tax rule of regulation section 20.2031-1(b), which is analogous to the gift tax rule, is of questionable validity in most cases and clearly wrong in others. Again, the IRS error lies in promulgating rules that in many instances are too specific and mechanical for the determination of true value.

The presence of improper mechanical rules causes unfair valuations by the IRS. The above examples illustrate that there is no simple rule and that value cannot always be made to depend on a retail market. If a rule exists, it should be that fair market value depends on all the facts and circumstances in each case.

IRS Valuation Procedures

RULES BEFORE JANUARY 1, 1985

Two Revenue Procedures provide guidelines for the valuation of unique items of tangible personal property. Revenue Procedure 65-19, 1965-2 C.B. 1002, permits, under certain conditions, estate tax return values to be based on the bona fide sale of tangible personal property through newspaper classified advertisements or public auction. The Revenue Procedure equates such a sale to a retail sale at the retail price. The sale must be within a reasonable time, and there must not be any substantial change in market conditions. Therefore, if an item is sold at public auction, the IRS will generally accept the sale price as the retail fair market value.

Revenue Procedure 66-49, 1966-2 C.B. 1257, sets forth guidelines for an appraisal of tangible personal property. An appraisal of a collection, particularly in the fine arts, should include the following:

1. A complete description of the object, including the size, subject matter, medium, name or names of the artist or artists, approximate date created, and interest transferred
2. The cost, date, and manner of acquisition
3. A history of the item, including proof of its authenticity
4. A photograph of a size and quality sufficient to identify the subject matter fully, preferably a 10-inch-by-12-inch or larger print
5. A statement of the factors on which the appraisal was based, including the following:
   a. The facts about the sales of other works by the same artist or artists, particularly on or around the valuation date
   b. Quoted prices in dealers' catalogs of the works by the artist or artists or of other comparable artists
   c. The economic state of the art market at or around the time of valuation, particularly with respect to the specific property
   d. A record of any exhibitions at which the particular art object was displayed
   e. A statement as to the standing of the artist in the profession and in the particular school, time, or period

Choosing an Appraiser

Choosing the proper appraiser is the most important consideration.[12] Revenue Procedure 66-49 refers to an appraisal by a qualified person and requires the inclusion of a summary of the appraiser's qualifications. The weight given to the appraisal by the IRS depends largely on the appraiser's competence and knowledge about the property and the market for that property. In choosing the appraiser, the attorney or the executor should inquire as to whether the appraiser is familiar with the market and whether she has dealt with the subject matter. For example, an appraiser who is a world authority on sixteenth-century French art is probably not the best person to appraise a piece of late-twentieth-century sculpture.

Additional Information on Appraisers and Valuation

IRS Publication 561, *Determining the Value of Donated Property*, a copy of which appears at the end of this chapter (Appendix 15-13), sets forth additional information on preparing appraisals and choosing an appraiser. Publication 561 notes that there are many types of collections and that much written material is available to assist individuals in valuing collections. That material includes catalogs, dealers' price lists, bibliographies, textbooks, specialized hobby periodicals, and other materials that help in determining fair market value. Publication 561 also states that "these sources are not always reliable indicators of fair market value and should be supported by other evidence."

For example, a dealer may sell an item for considerably less than that shown on a price list after the item has remained unsold for a long period of time. That example is consistent with the IRS policy and its revenue procedures, which indicate that the best measure of value is an arm's-length sale in the market. Certainly, if a dealer puts an extremely high price on an object and is unable to sell it at that price, the list price of the item should not be the measure of its fair market value. The price that the item is sold for is the fair market value that the IRS will accept.

Publication 561 indicates that a signed copy of any appraisal should accompany the tax return. The more complete the information filed with the tax return, the more unlikely it is that the IRS will question items on it. The weight given an appraisal depends on both the qualifications of the appraiser and the completeness of the appraisal report. A satisfactory appraisal discusses all the facts on which an intelligent judgment of valuation should be based. The appraisal may not be given any weight in the presence of any of the following:

- Not all the applicable factors are considered
- The opinion is not supported with facts, such as purchase price and comparable sales
- Little more than a statement of opinion is given

- The opinion is not consistent with known factors
- The opinion is beyond reason and arbitrary

In evaluating the appraiser, Publication 561 states that the weight given an appraisal depends, in addition to the completeness of the report, on the appraiser's familiarity with the property, experience, background, and knowledge of the facts at the time of the contribution. Despite the appraiser's qualifications, however, her opinion will not be given weight if it is clearly opposed to common sense and the existing facts. The appraiser's opinion is never more valid than the facts on which it is based; without those facts (according to the IRS), it is simply a guess. An appraiser who is associated with the donor or the donee, whether the donee is an individual or an organization, may be given less weight than an appraisal by an unrelated party. In fact, as discussed below, certain related persons are now prohibited from preparing an appraisal for charitable contribution purposes.

The appraiser selected should be aware of the IRS guidelines and should be furnished a copy of Revenue Procedure 66-49, so that the appraisal will meet the guidelines contained therein.

Appraisal Rules Effective January 1, 1985, Prior to Changes Made by the Pension Protection Act of 2006

Section 170(a)(1) expressly declares that a charitable contribution is deductible only if it is verified in the manner required by IRS regulations. Prior law had no specific statutory requirement that donors obtain appraisals to verify the fair market value of their donations. Rather than amend Internal Revenue Code section 170(a)(1) to include the substantiation requirements, section 155(a) of the Tax Reform Act of 1984 requires that the Treasury Department issue regulations under section 170 that incorporate the charitable deduction substantiation requirements of section 155(a). Therefore, effective January 1, 1985, no income tax charitable deduction is allowed for any contribution of property for which an appraisal is required under the Tax Reform Act of 1984 unless the substantiation requirements of the regulations are met.

Final regulations encompassing the rules contained in section 155(1) of the Tax Reform Act of 1984 were issued on May 4, 1988.[13] Hearings were held on the proposed regulations in June 1985, and the final regulations were issued on May 4, 1988.

The rules apply to any charitable contribution made after December 31, 1984, by an individual, a closely held corporation, a personal service corporation, a partnership, or an S corporation of an item of property (other than money or publicly traded securities), the claimed value of which exceeds $5,000.[14] The $5,000 amount applies to a single item of property or to the aggregate of similar items of property donated during one calendar year, such as a set or a number of stamps, coins, lithographs, or books. According to *General Explanation of the Revenue Provisions of the Tax Reform Act of 1984*, similar items of donated property are aggregated, whether all the items are donated to one donee or the items are donated to two or more donees. For example, the substantiation requirements apply if the taxpayer claims a deduction in one year of $2,000 for rare books given to College *A*, $2,500 for rare books given to Museum *B*, and $900 for rare books given to Public Library *C*,[15] a total of $5,400, which is $400 over the approved limit.

If the $5,000 limit is reached, the taxpayer must meet the following substantiation requirements:

1. Obtain a qualified appraisal for the property contributed
2. Attach a fully completed appraisal summary to the tax return on which the donor first claims the deduction for the contribution
3. Maintain records containing certain specific information about the contribution

If a taxpayer does not conform strictly to the substantiation requirements, no deduction is allowed under section 170.[16]

In *D'Arcangelo v. Commissioner*,[17] the Tax Court found that a certified public accountant was not entitled to any charitable deduction for art supplies donated to a high school because he failed to obtain a qualified appraisal. The taxpayer had submitted a letter of appraisal from the principal of the high school but failed to show that the principal was a qualified appraiser because, among other factors, the appraiser (the principal) admitted that he had never appraised similar property, he was not certain what property was donated, and he did not view the donated property at the time of the donation. Further, the appraiser was an employee of the donee high school and is, therefore, expressly prohibited by regulation section 1.170A-13(c)(5)(iv)(D) from appraising the donated property. In that case, the taxpayer not only lost his deduction for the fair market value of the donated property but was not even entitled to a deduction for his cost. Since no qualified appraisal was made by a qualified appraiser, the taxpayer's deduction was zero.[18]

QUALIFIED APPRAISAL

The term "qualified appraisal" means an appraisal prepared by a qualified appraiser not more than sixty days before the date of the contribution of the appraised property.[19] The appraisal must be signed and dated by a qualified appraiser who charges an appraisal fee that is not based on a percentage of value and that contains the following information:

1. A detailed description of the property
2. The physical condition of the property
3. The date or expected date of the contribution
4. The terms of any agreement or understanding entered into or expected to be entered into by or on behalf of the donor that relates to the use, sale, or other disposition of the property contributed

5. The name, address, and taxpayer identification number of the appraiser
6. A detailed description of the appraiser's background and qualifications
7. A statement that the appraisal was prepared for income tax purposes
8. The date on which the property was valued
9. The appraised fair market value of the property
10. The method of valuation used to determine the fair market value
11. The specific basis for the valuation, such as any specific comparable sales transactions
12. A description of the fee arrangement between the donor and the appraiser

Obviously, the cost to the taxpayer of having a qualified appraisal prepared is going to be high because of the detailed information required. A separate qualified appraisal is required for each item of property that is not included in a group of similar items of property. If the appraisal is for a group of similar items, the detailed information is required for each individual item other than items worth less than $100, for which a group description is allowed.

The qualified appraisal must be received by the donor before the due date (including extensions) of the taxpayer's income tax return.[20] That deadline is important, since the entire charitable deduction is lost if the taxpayer does not comply with that provision.

Qualified Appraiser

The term "qualified appraiser" means an individual who holds herself out to the public as an appraiser who is an expert as to the particular type of property being appraised; who understands that if she makes a false or fraudulent over-statement of value, she may be subject to a civil penalty under section 6701; and who is completely independent of the donor.[21] To be independent of the donor, the qualified appraiser cannot be the donor or the donee, a party to the transaction in which the donor acquired the property,[22] a person employed by any of the foregoing, or a person related (within the meaning of section 267(b)) to any of the foregoing.

For example, if a person acquired a painting from an art dealer and later donated the painting to a museum, the donor, the dealer who sold the painting, the museum, any person employed by the donor or the dealer or the museum, or any person related to any of the foregoing is not a qualified appraiser. The regulations are so broad that they appear to disqualify an auction house from being a qualified appraiser if the donor had purchased the property at auction from that auction house.

The final regulations adopted on May 4, 1988, did retain the provision that disqualifies someone who regularly performs appraisals for a person who is not otherwise excluded from being a qualified appraiser and does not do a substantial number of appraisals for other persons[23]—for example, someone who performs appraisals for only one person. Also excluded as a qualified appraiser is any person who, if the donor had knowledge of the facts, would cause a reasonable person to expect that the appraiser would falsely overstate the value of the donated property. For example, the donor and the appraiser make an agreement concerning the amount at which the property will be valued, and the donor knows that the amount exceeds the fair market value of the property.

The appraiser selected must be a qualified appraiser because, if the donor chooses unwisely and the appraiser is later found not to be a qualified appraiser, the entire charitable deduction is lost, since it is then too late to correct the defect.[24] In order to obtain the income tax deduction, the taxpayer must attach to the income tax return a qualified appraisal prepared by a qualified appraiser.

APPRAISAL SUMMARY

Regulation section 1.170A-13(c)(4) sets forth the required information that must be on the appraisal summary attached to the donor's income tax return. In February 1985, the IRS issued Form 8283 ("Noncash Charitable Contributions—Appraisal Summary"); the latest version of Form 8283 was issued in December 2006, and a copy of it appears at the end of this chapter (Appendix 15-14). Completion of Form 8283 satisfies the appraisal-summary requirements. The form is required for all noncash gifts to a charitable donee of more than $500.

The instructions for Form 8283 now require that a signed copy of the full appraisal be attached to Form 8283 and filed with the individual taxpayer's federal income tax return. However, for individual objects valued at more than $20,000, the taxpayer need no longer attach a photograph to the tax return. The instructions do require that the taxpayer provide the IRS, on request, a photograph of a size and a quality to fully show the object, preferably an 8-inch-by-10-inch color photograph or a color transparency no smaller than 4 inches by 5 inches, for any individual art object valued at $20,000 or more. We recommend that a taxpayer obtain the photograph before making the charitable donation, so that it is readily available should the IRS request it.

Form 8283 must be signed and dated by both the appraiser and the donee-charitable organization. The person signing on behalf of the donee must be an official authorized to sign the tax returns of the donee organization or a person designated by the donee organization to sign Form 8283. The instructions also require that after June 6, 1988, the donor must provide the donee with a copy of the qualified appraisal. On February 1, 2011, the IRS changed the threshold value for works of art that are subject to review by the Art Panel from $20,000 to $50,000.[25] To date there has not been a corresponding change in Form 8283 or the accompanying instructions.

If the taxpayer fails to attach the required appraisal summary to her tax return, the IRS can disallow the entire charitable deduction. However, regulation section 1.170A-13(c)(4)(iv)(H) allows a taxpayer to submit the appraisal summary within ninety days after the IRS requests it, and the IRS will not disallow the charitable deduction if the taxpayer's failure to attach the appraisal summary was a good-faith omission.

The IRS has recently revised IRS Publication 561, entitled *Determining the Value of Donated Property*; a copy appears at the end of this chapter (Appendix

15-13). The publication is an excellent summary of what the IRS is looking for to support claimed values of tangible property for donation or estate tax purposes.

APPRAISAL FEE

The fee paid to the appraiser cannot be based on a percentage of the appraised value of the donated property.[26]

PENSION PROTECTION ACT OF 2006

The Pension Protection Act of 2006 (PPA) revised the definition of a "qualified appraisal"[27] to mean an appraisal of property which is

1. treated as a qualified appraisal under the regulations or other guidance prescribed by the IRS; and
2. conducted by a qualified appraiser in accordance with generally accepted appraisal standards and any regulations or other guidance prescribed by the IRS.

Qualified Appraisal

Effective for returns filed after February 16, 2007, the appraisal must contain a declaration that the appraiser understands that a substantial or gross valuation misstatement resulting from an appraisal of the value of property that the appraiser knows, or reasonably should have known, would be used in connection with a return or claim for refund may subject the appraiser to a civil penalty under section 6695A.[28] This statement is in addition to the requirement that the appraisal contain a statement that the appraiser understands that an intentionally false or fraudulent overstatement of the value of the appraised property may subject the appraiser to civil penalty under section 6701 for aiding and abetting an understatement of tax liability.

The existing IRC regulations still apply, requiring that the appraisal not be prepared more than sixty days before the date of the contribution of the appraised property and that the appraisal be signed and dated by a qualified appraiser who charges an appraisal fee that is not based on a percentage of the value of the appraised property.[29] The qualified appraisal must contain the following information:

1. A detailed description of the property
2. The physical condition of the property
3. The date or expected date of the contribution
4. The terms of any agreement or understanding entered into or expected to be entered into by or on behalf of the donor that relates to the use, sale, or other disposition of the property contributed
5. The name, address, and taxpayer identification number of the appraiser
6. A detailed description of the appraiser's background and qualifications
7. A statement that the appraisal was prepared for income tax purposes
8. The date on which the property was value

9. The appraised fair market value of the property
10. The method of valuation used to determine the fair market value
11. The specific basis for the valuation, such as any specific comparable sales transactions
12. A description of the fee arrangement between the donor and the appraiser

Obviously, the cost to the taxpayer of having a qualified appraisal prepared is going to be high because of the detailed information required. A separate qualified appraisal is required for each item of property that is not included in a group of similar items of property. If the appraisal is for a group of similar items, the detailed information is required for each individual item other than items worth less than $100, for which a group description is allowed.

The qualified appraisal must be received by the donor before the due date (including extensions) of the taxpayer's income tax return.[30] That deadline is important, since the entire charitable deduction is lost if the taxpayer does not comply with that provision.

QUALIFIED APPRAISER

The PPA now includes in the Internal Revenue Code a definition of a "qualified appraiser"[31] to mean an individual who

1. has earned an appraisal designation from a recognized professional appraiser organization, or has otherwise met minimum education and experience requirements set forth in regulations;
2. regularly performs appraisals for pay; and
3. meets other requirements that the IRS may prescribe in regulations or other guidance.

An individual cannot be a qualified appraiser with respect to any specific appraisal unless he or she

1. demonstrates verifiable education and experience in valuing the property type being appraised; and
2. has not been prohibited from practicing before the IRS at any time over the three-year period ending on the appraisal date.

It is now imperative that the donor check the credentials of the appraiser in order to ensure that the appraiser is an expert in the item being appraised. In other words, an expert appraiser for Dutch seventeenth-century drawing will not be the correct appraiser for a work of contemporary art.

Notice 2006-96

Notice 2006-96, issued by the IRS in October 2006, offers some guidance as to the new appraisal rules introduced by the PPA.[32] According to the Notice, an appraisal will be treated as a qualified appraisal under the new rules if the appraisal complies with all the requirements of the existing IRS regulations and is conducted by a qualified appraiser in accordance with generally accepted appraisal standards. An appraisal is treated as having been conducted in accordance with generally accepted appraisal standards if, according to the Notice, the appraisal is consistent with the substance and principles of the Uniform Standards of Professional Appraisal Practice (USPAP), as developed by the Appraisal Standards Board of the Appraisal Foundation.[33]

An appraiser will be treated as having demonstrated verifiable education and experience in valuing the type of property subject to the appraisal if the appraiser makes a declaration in the appraisal that, because of the appraiser's background, experience, education, and membership in a professional association, the appraiser is qualified to make appraisals of the type of property being valued. For appraisals for returns filed after February 16, 2007, the appraiser will be treated as having met the minimum education and experience requirements if the appraiser (1) has successfully completed college or professional-level coursework that is relevant to the property being valued, (2) has at least two years' experience in the trade or business of buying, selling, or valuing the type of property being valued, and (3) gives a full description of his or her educational background.[34]

APPRAISAL FOUNDATION

We discussed in chapter 7 at page 492 the establishment of the USPAP by the Appraisal Foundation. Those standards were previously not technically applicable to personal property appraisals, but the standards do offer an excellent guide to the well-prepared appraisal for tax purposes.[35] However, as discussed above, IRS Notice 2006-96 now recognizes the USPAP standards as consistent with a qualified appraisal for tax purposes. Any taxpayer submitting a qualified appraisal for a charitable deduction would be well advised to obtain the appraiser's assurances that he or she is USPAP-certified and that the appraisal will be prepared in accordance with USPAP guidelines.

GUIDING PRINCIPLE

The foregoing is only a brief summary of the valuation rules. In the future, the IRS may issue revenue rulings and other guidelines to clarify numerous unanswered questions. In the meantime, extreme care must be exercised in choosing the appraiser in order to make sure that she is an expert in the field and is not disqualified from preparing a qualified appraisal for the donor. It is also important to keep in mind that if the $5,000 claimed deduction amount is reached for a contribution of property, the new appraisal rules apply whether the donated property is capital-gain property or ordinary-income property, whether the property has appreciated or depreciated in value since its acquisition by the donor, and whether the donee is a public charity, a private foundation, or some other donee eligible to receive contributions that may qualify for deduction under section 170.[36] (See Appendix 15-11 at the end of this chapter.)

ADVANCE-VALUATION-RULING PROCEDURE

In what appeared to be an attempt to find a way to resolve charitable-deduction-valuation issues without litigation, the Revenue Reconciliation Act of 1993 contained a provision that required the IRS to prepare a report on the development of a procedure enabling a taxpayer to receive an advance ruling from the IRS as to the value of tangible personal property for income tax purposes before the transfer of the property to a qualifying charitable organization. With the above mandate, the IRS issued on December 28, 1995, Revenue Procedure 96-15, I.R.B. 1996-3, which contains the procedure for an advance valuation determination. Under Revenue Procedure 96-15, the IRS states that it will issue an advance ruling for income tax purposes on the valuation of property only

(1) *after* the transfer of the property to a qualifying charitable organization,
(2) if the taxpayer pays a user fee to the IRS of $2,500 for the first three items transferred and $250 for each additional item, and
(3) if the taxpayer has already obtained a qualified appraisal by a qualified appraiser of each item of property and at least one of the items of property has a value of $50,000 or more.

The procedure also requires that the taxpayer attach a completed Form 8283 and a copy of the qualified appraisal to the advance ruling request.

Once the IRS issues a determination under Revenue Procedure 96-15, it must be attached to the taxpayer's income tax return, and it is binding on the IRS. If the taxpayer disagrees with the IRS determination, the taxpayer may submit with her tax return additional information in support of a different valuation. The procedure should appeal to those taxpayers interested in a high degree of certainty when they file their income tax returns.

An interesting aspect of Revenue Procedure 96-15 is that it is also applicable to estate and gift tax returns, including items transferred to family members rather than charitable organizations. The same detailed appraisals must be prepared by the taxpayer and submitted to the IRS with a ruling request. The procedure may be useful to an estate containing valuable works of art in order to have an agreed-on value early in the administration of an estate.

IRS Record-Keeping Requirements

If a lifetime gift is made to a charitable organization, the income tax regulations require that the income tax return for the year in which the deduction is claimed include an attachment with information similar to that contained in Revenue Procedure 66-49. Regulation section 1.170A-13, adopted December 26, 1984, contains more detailed record-keeping requirements. The regulation retains the prior record-keeping requirements for contributions made before 1982 and applies new rules to contributions made on or after January 1, 1983. Even if the appraisal requirements do not apply (for example, in the case of gifts of $5,000 or less), the general rules pertaining to charitable contributions of property valued in excess of $500, other than money, do apply. The new rules contain more detailed requirements for noncash contributions than for cash contributions.[37] Donors must maintain records indicating the following:

1. The name of the donee-charitable organization
2. The date and the location of the contribution
3. A description of the property
4. The fair market value of the property, the method used in determining the fair market value, and a signed copy of any appraisal
5. Factual details on section 170(e)(1) property
6. Special rules for partial-interest contributions
7. The terms of any agreement or understanding entered into by or on behalf of the taxpayer that relates to the use, the sale, or the disposition of the property contributed

If the value of the tangible personal property is in excess of $500, the taxpayer must also maintain records indicating the following:

8. The manner and approximate date of the acquisition of the property
9. The cost or other basis of the property. In this regard, the regulation indicates that if the property was held for more than one year, records of cost or other basis are required only if available.

Item 7 above is particularly important and is aimed at proposed gifts that, because of certain retained rights, are not treated as completed charitable contributions eligible for the income tax charitable deduction.[38]

IRS Art Advisory Panel

A twenty-two-person advisory panel of art experts has been appointed to help the IRS determine whether realistic appraisals of fair market value have been placed on works of art.[39] The panel, which was set up in 1968, classifies the artwork valuation submitted by a taxpayer as clearly justified, questionable, or clearly unjustified. The panel also recommends appraisers to the IRS and reviews appraisals. Generally, if a particular item has a value of more than $50,000, it is sent by the local IRS audit office to the art panel in Washington, D.C., for consideration. The threshold amount was increased from $20,000 to $50,000 effective for donations made after February 1, 2011. The report issued by the art panel is supposed to be only advisory. However, for all practical purposes, the local IRS district offices have been considering the valuation reports to be mandatory and binding on them. The annual report of the Art Advisory Panel states that "the determinations of the Advisory Panel become the position of the Internal Revenue Service."

Unfortunately, it often takes from six months to a year to have a request processed through the national office, since the IRS in Washington, D.C., has a limited staff to process the huge volume of valuation cases referred. The art panel, which reviews the documentation prepared by the IRS, is also faced with an enormous volume of cases. Therefore, the taxpayer's documentation must be as complete as possible before the information is submitted to the national office. If an attorney feels that the art panel did not review the submitted items correctly, she can, at an appellate conference, request a resubmission to the art panel. Additional documentation should be submitted indicating why the art panel may have been in error. The art panel may change the value placed on a work of art.

The 2011 Annual Report of the Art Advisory Panel is included at the end of this chapter (Appendix 15-15).

Determining Fair Market Value

The question of the fair market value of a collection is difficult and must rest on expert appraisals. Resolving valuation disputes with the IRS, as demonstrated by the litigated cases, can be a time-consuming and expensive proposition.[40] The Tax Reform Act of 1976 recognized the plight of the taxpayer who is faced with a valuation issue and an IRS agent who supplies little or no information to support the IRS determination.

THE IRS DETERMINATION OF VALUE

Section 7517 provides that the IRS must, on written request by a donor or executor, furnish a written statement explaining the basis on which the IRS has determined or proposes to determine a valuation of property that is different from the valuation submitted by the donor or the executor. That section applies to all valuation issues, whether the donation involves a lifetime transfer or a testamentary transfer to a charitable transferee or a noncharitable transferee. The conference committee report explains that the reason for the change is to encourage the resolution of valuation issues at the earliest possible time, and that resolution can best be achieved if all the parties have full information as to how another party arrived at the valuation. The IRS must furnish its statement within forty-five days of the date of the request or the date of its determination (or proposed determination), whichever is later. The IRS statement must

(1) explain the basis on which the valuation was determined or proposed,
(2) set forth any computation used, and
(3) contain a copy of any expert appraisal made by or for the IRS.

The statute specifically provides that the IRS statement is not intended to be a final or binding representation of the IRS position. Section 7517 is effective for transfers made after December 31, 1976.

REVENUE RULINGS ON VALUATION

The IRS has given increased attention to valuation questions in a series of Revenue Rulings.

REVENUE RULING 79-256, 1979-2 C.B. 105

A taxpayer, who was not an art dealer, bought a substantial part of the total limited edition of a lithograph series and, after holding the prints for more than a year, contributed them to various art museums. The IRS ruled that the taxpayer's charitable deduction was limited to his cost under section 170(e)(1)(A) since the property was ordinary income property. The IRS viewed the taxpayer's activities, in terms of frequency and continuity, as equivalent to a trade or business for the purpose of section 170(e), even though he was not engaged in a trade or business for the purpose of any other section of the Internal Revenue Code. The IRS deemed the taxpayer's bulk acquisition and subsequent disposal of a substantial part of the total limited edition of the prints to be substantially equivalent to the activities of a commercial art dealer. The ruling also stated that the contributions had been made before a "period of accumulation and enjoyment" of the donated property by the donor. There does not appear to be any basis in the Internal Revenue Code to support the new tests that the IRS attempted to introduce (that is, a test of the frequency of the donor's activities and a test of the donor's period of accumulation and enjoyment) as tests to determine whether an individual is engaged in a trade or business in a way that would limit the deduction for the donated property to the taxpayer's cost. The Tax Court rejected the IRS dealer theory in *Kenneth Sandler*, discussed on page 1268.

REVENUE RULING 79-419, 1979-2 C.B. 107

A donor bought art books at wholesale; the seller held them for one year before delivery; the donor then contributed the books to various charitable organizations. The seller was in a country where the retail price of the books was legally fixed by law, and the donor imported them into the United States. The ruling held that the books could only have been offered at a discount to purchasers outside the country of the seller. The IRS ruled that the level of the donor's contribution activity was tantamount to the activity of a dealer selling property in the ordinary course of a trade or business. Accordingly, the donor's deduction was limited to the cost of the books or to their fair market value, whichever was less, since the books were ordinary income property under section 170(e)(1)(A). The ruling made no mention of the test of the donor's "period of accumulation and enjoyment" as stated in Revenue Ruling 79-256.

REVENUE RULING 79-432, 1979-2 C.B. 289

Revenue Ruling 79-432 specifically addressed the use of lithographs as a tax shelter. Essentially, the IRS held that the substance of the transaction did not present a situation in which the taxpayer had any property at risk and, therefore, denied the claimed deduction. In valuing the lithographs, the IRS returned to its longtime rule that fair market value is the value at which something changes hands between a willing buyer and a willing seller when neither is under any compulsion to act.

Revenue Ruling 80-69, 1980-1 C.B. 55

A taxpayer, who was not a dealer, purchased assorted valuable gems from a promoter at wholesale and then contributed them one year later to a charitable organization that satisfied the related use rule of section 170(e)(1)(B)(i). The IRS ruled that the fair market value of the gems was the price the donor paid for them one year earlier, relying on the "willing buyer and willing seller" language of regulation section 1.170A-1(c)(2). The ruling made no mention of the level of the donor's activities as being substantially equivalent to a dealer's activities under section 170(e); nor did the ruling mention a period of accumulation and enjoyment.

Revenue Ruling 80-233, 1980-2 C.B. 69

In a situation similar to the one presented in Revenue Ruling 80-69, a taxpayer purchased Bibles in bulk at wholesale, held them for one year, and then contributed them to various religious charities that made use of the Bibles. The IRS ruled that the fair market value was the wholesale price. In relying on the "willing buyer and willing seller" language of the regulation, the IRS said that in determining the fair market value, it referred to the most active and comparable marketplace at the time of the donor's contribution. The prices at which similar quantities of Bibles are sold in arm's-length transactions are the most probative evidence of fair market value. (See also Revenue Ruling 80-329, 1980-2 C.B. 70.)

Recent Rulings

The most recent Revenue Rulings indicate a shift of the IRS position on fair market value away from an attack on the character of the property contributed (ordinary income property versus capital gain property) through a test of frequency of activities and period of enjoyment and back to the "willing buyer and willing seller" test of fair market value that is in regulation section 1.170A-1(c) (2). Those rulings indicate that the IRS will challenge any contribution scheme that does not have economic reality.[41]

Litigation on Valuation

Retail Market, Tax Shelters, and the Blockage Discount

Evidence of IRS willingness to litigate charitable-contribution schemes that have no economic reality is found in *Anselmo v. Commissioner*,[42] which involved the valuation of gems donated to the Smithsonian Institution. In *Anselmo*, the taxpayer purchased colored gemstones and donated them nine months later, after the long-term capital gain holding period had been satisfied. The Tax Court found that members of the public did not generally purchase unset gems; rather, the usual consumers of unset gems were manufacturing and retail jewelers who used them to create jewelry. The Tax Court looked to the regulations and the definition of "retail market" to measure fair market value. The court found that the retail market in which to find comparable values for the donated gems was the market in which the jewelry stores made their purchases and not the market in which an individual member of the public made a purchase at a jewelry store. In effect, the Tax Court said there can be more than one retail market, and the market that is closest to the taxpayer's activities is the market the court looks to for comparable values.[43] The court further held that a separate fair market value should be determined for each unit of property donated.

In *Richard A. Skripak*,[44] the Tax Court upheld the validity of a book contribution program but substantially lowered the value of the books contributed. The taxpayer in *Skripak* participated in a charitable contribution tax reduction program promoted by Reprints, Inc. Reprints identified libraries to receive books and contributors who would contribute the books to the libraries. The contributors bought the books from Reprints at one-third of the normal price and, after holding them for longer than six months (the then applicable period to qualify for long-term capital gain property), contributed them to libraries at their retail price. The court held that the contributions were legitimately made and were not a sham as alleged by the IRS. However, the court further held that the books had a value of only 20% of the retail price, less than the amount the contributors actually paid for them.

In *Skripak*, the Tax Court allowed the taxpayer to participate in a tax reduction program that was motivated solely by the goal of obtaining a charitable deduction without having the deduction disregarded on the ground that the program was a sham. However, taxpayers entering into such shelters risk having the amounts of their deductions reduced if the donated properties are not properly valued, and the taxpayers could lose money, since the donated properties could be found to have a value of less than they paid for them. In *Skripak*, the court still looked to the retail market for the valuation of the books, but applied a blockage discount, since the simultaneous marketing of all the books would substantially depress the market for the books.[45] A "blockage discount" is a reduction in market value that is based on the theory that a large number of similar items offered for sale at one time distorts the market value and results in a reduced market value. The court in *Skripak* correctly pointed out that a determination of the fair market value of a group of items includes a consideration of how many of the items would be available for sale at any one time and the length of time necessary to liquidate the entire inventory.

The same blockage-discount theory was argued by the IRS in the *Rimmer*[46] case. In 1974, the taxpayer purchased approximately 85,000 pieces of Yiddish and Hebrew sheet music. In 1986, he contributed the sheet music to the National Yiddish Book Center. Although there were 85,000 items, there were only 650 titles in that total. The taxpayer valued the sheet music at $340,000, but the IRS said that its value was no more than $71,000. The court noted that the donation must be valued in the retail market and then went on to find for the IRS, applying a blockage discount that is based on the amount of time it would take to dispose of the entire collection and citing *Skripak*.[47]

The application of a blockage discount theory by the IRS in the case may not be correct, although the result appears to be correct. The court should have reached its result by examining the proper retail marketplace for a large number of items of sheet music in reaching its conclusion, rather than by applying blockage. The IRS in its *Valuation Guide for IRS Agents* notes that a blockage discount

> applies only to estate tax valuations and not to charitable contribution valuations, since the taxpayer (contributor) actually controls the market by how many items are contributed.[48]

In *Leibowitz*,[49] the taxpayer donated 7,378 items of movie memorabilia, including 546 duplicates of movie posters. Once again the court was faced with identifying the appropriate market in which to value the movie memorabilia. The court found that the retail marketplace was the correct marketplace, since these kinds of items were sold in retail stores. Furthermore, and most importantly, it was estimated that all of the movie memorabilia could be sold in a retail store within a year without affecting the prices obtained for each individual item. This made the IRS blockage discount argument moot. Rather than apply a blockage discount as the court did in *Rimmer*, the court correctly identified the retail marketplace (retail stores that sold movie memorabilia), valued each individual item based on comparable sales prices, and rejected the IRS's argument about applying a blockage discount.

More recently, in *Arbini*,[50] the court was faced with a valuation issue involving the charitable contribution of bound volumes of 33,710 Los Angeles and Chicago newspapers donated to a museum of comic art. The court had to decide the appropriate market to use for purposes of determining the fair market value of the donated newspapers. There were two possible markets for old newspapers: the retail market in which individual newspapers are sold to purchasers interested in obtaining a newspaper from a specific date, and the wholesale market where groups of newspapers are sold to collectors and newspaper dealers interested in purchasing a collection of newspapers. The court, relying in part on the reasoning in *Anselmo*,[51] correctly concluded that the ultimate consumers of the bound newspapers would be newspaper collectors, newspaper dealers, and others interested in obtaining a newspaper collection. Therefore, the appropriate market for purposes of determining the fair market value of the newspapers was the wholesale market. This analysis, in contrast to *Rimmer* discussed above, correctly identifies the appropriate marketplace for the donated property.

Chapter 16 contains a detailed discussion of the blockage discount for estate tax purposes, particularly as it applies to estates of artists.

The *Samuel E. Hunter*[52] case involved a taxpayer who purchased a group of high-quality prints by prominent artists and donated them to various charities. The story began when Marlborough Gallery sold the prints in bulk to a middleman, who was able to buy them at one-sixth of Marlborough's retail list price because Marlborough was disposing of excess inventory. The art was not unsalable and, in fact, Marlborough retained a number of the prints for sale to the public at its normal retail price. The middleman then resold the prints to the taxpayer at one-third to one-fourth of Marlborough's list price. The taxpayer claimed a charitable deduction for the Marlborough list price of each print.

The Tax Court held that the transaction was not a sham and that it was not relevant that the taxpayer never took possession of the prints. It further dismissed the IRS contention that the blockage discount applied, since the number of prints was small.

The court concluded, however, that the deduction for the taxpayer was limited to what he paid for the prints. The court reasoned that the relevant retail market was the market in which the middleman had sold the prints to the taxpayer—that is, the market in which the taxpayer had made his purchase. Perhaps a different result might have been arrived at if the taxpayer had made his purchases directly from Marlborough Gallery, rather than through a middleman. The case indicates that whenever a purchase and a donation are close in time, the IRS will give the charitable deduction careful examination.[53]

That does not mean that if someone finds a bargain, she cannot make a donation of the property. In *Bernard Lightman*,[54] the taxpayer made an advantageous bulk purchase of a number of works of art by one artist and donated the paintings to a museum a little more than one year after their purchase. The court recognized that the taxpayer had been given a price concession on the purchase and that their cost was not indicative of the values of the individual paintings. Instead, the court used auction prices of other paintings by that artist as the measure of market value for donation purposes. For a case involving the advantageous purchase of a gemstone followed by its contribution, see *James H. Rhoades*.[55]

Auction prices are not the absolute measure of fair market value. In *Raymond Biagiotti*,[56] which involved the valuation of pre-Columbian and Mayan art, the Tax Court observed that Sotheby's auction sales did not represent a significant portion of the sales of such art in the United States and did not accurately represent the average sale prices of that art. The court found that a better measure of value was what collectors paid private dealers, since collectors rely on dealers' guarantees of authenticity, and auction houses do not guarantee authenticity.

The common thread running through the opinions of the above cases is that the judges want valuation cases to be settled before litigation. If the taxpayer is careful in selecting the appraiser and if the appraisal includes the elements set forth in the regulations about a qualified appraisal—that is, if, among other requirements, there are comparable sales and the valuation methods of the appraiser are set forth—valuation cases can be settled with the IRS.

GIFFORD M. MAST, JR. CASE

The case of *Gifford M. Mast, Jr.*[57] involved determining the fair market value of glass stereoscopic negatives, a photographic viewing technique that was popular between the mid-nineteenth century and the mid-twentieth century. The technique involves a pair of photographs that, when viewed in a special device called a stereoscope or a stereoscopic viewer, produce a three-dimensional image. The taxpayer had a large collection of glass stereoscopic negatives and donated them to the University of California, claiming an income tax deduction of $1,544,000. The IRS initially said that the value was zero.

The taxpayer based his original claimed value on an appraisal by an expert who had many years' experience as a collector of photographic equipment but who was not a licensed appraiser. Apparently, the court did not realize that art appraisers are not licensed anywhere in the United States. In any event, the appraiser arrived at a per-unit value based on replacement costs and his knowledge of the market sales of comparable negatives and arrived at a price of $1,544,000. At trial the taxpayer called two additional experts, one a professional appraiser and a senior member of the Appraisers Association of America and of the American Society of Appraisers and the other expert a full-time dealer.

The professional appraiser did a thorough analysis of the collection and clearly stated in her testimony, as reiterated by the court, that there are

a number of distinct approaches to valuation; the income approach, the cost estimated approach, the revenue approach and the market data comparison approach.[58]

The appraiser estimated the value of the collection at $1,590,000, based on the market-data-comparison approach. That method of valuation is based on comparisons with reported sales, offers to sell by catalog, showroom and gallery pricing, and historic data. The court noted that the appraiser contacted leading galleries and received opinions about the collection's replacement value. The appraiser also contacted auction houses and obtained estimates of the collection's replacement value. The appraiser also used a careful review of other available data, background knowledge, and experience as indicators of value.

The dealer gave his opinion on the basis of what he thought the items in the collection could be sold for. He arrived at a value of $1,200,000.

The IRS used a full-time professional appraiser but retained her only shortly before trial, so her analysis was less thorough than was the analysis of the taxpayer's appraiser. The valuation approach used by the IRS appraiser was to compare the donated collection with allegedly comparable photographic collections that had been sold. She concluded that the collection had a value of $450,000.

The court, in reaching its conclusion, first reiterated that most commonly used phrase from the IRS regulations, that fair market value is

the price at which the Property would change hands between a willing buyer and a willing seller, neither being under any compulsion to buy or sell and both having reasonable knowledge of relevant facts.[59]

The court noted that fair market value is a question of fact to be determined by an examination of the entire record and that the market data comparison approach seems the most reasonable. The court stated that the IRS expert used a valuation method that differed substantially from that used by the taxpayer's experts. Rather than use a market-data-comparison approach, the IRS expert determined fair market value on the basis of the sales of five allegedly comparable collections. The court found that before that approach can be used, it must first be determined whether the five collections were, in fact, comparable.[60] The court decided that the IRS expert relied on collections that were not comparable, and the court gave little weight to the IRS expert's testimony.

In reaching its holding that the fair market value of the glass stereoscopic negatives was $1,250,000, the court pointed out that questions of fair market value are properly resolved through settlement negotiations, rather than litigation. The court went on to state the following:

> In the absence of settlement, we are left to adjudicate the validity of conflicting experts' opinions who are convinced that both their conclusions and methods are correct. The result is an over-zealous effort, during the course of the ensuing litigation, to infuse a talismanic precision into an issue which should frankly be recognized as inherently imprecise and capable of resolution only by a Solomon-like pronouncement. *Messing v. Commissioner* 48 T.C. 502, 512 (1967).[61]

The IRS in *Mast, Jr.* had originally held in its notice of deficiency that the value of the collection was zero. In a later appeal,[62] the taxpayer was successful in his position that the IRS had acted unreasonably; the court found the IRS liable for $25,000 in legal fees, as provided for by section 7430 prior to its amendment by the Tax Reform Act of 1986 and the Technical and Miscellaneous Revenue Act of 1988. The court found that it was unreasonable for the IRS to determine, without the advice of an expert, that the collection had a zero value and then to stick with that determination throughout a trial, despite the fact that the IRS had no evidence to support such a position and the fact that the taxpayer had provided the testimony of three qualified appraisers, each of whom valued the collection at nearly the same amount as the taxpayer claimed.

OTHER VALUATION CASES

In *Heriberto A. Ferrari*,[63] the issue involved the valuation of twenty-one pieces of pre-Columbian art donated to the Duke University Museum of Art and to the Mint Museum of Art. The case, which is similar to the *Biagiotti* case, discussed the proper marketplace for determining comparable sale prices of pre-Columbian art. The court correctly pointed out that the market to be looked at for comparable sales is the retail sales market at art galleries, not auction sales. When the time comes to purchase pre-Columbian art or antiquities, most buyers want to rely on the guarantee of authenticity and the connoisseurship of the art dealer; unless the buyers themselves are dealers or experts, they do not want to buy at auction where the purchased antiquity may not be covered by any warranty of authenticity. The *Heriberto A. Ferrari* opinion includes an excellent discussion of what to look for in determining value. The court succinctly stated that value is determined by the item's condition, its uniqueness or rarity, its authenticity, its size, and the market value of comparable objects.[64] In noting that retail gallery prices are the correct comparable marketplace to look at, the court found that different galleries price even the same or similar objects at different levels. Therefore, the court found that fair market value, as defined by the IRS regulations, is in this case not a single price but a range of prices, not necessarily the highest price at which an object would change hands between a willing buyer and a willing seller.[65] Any appraiser hired in a valuation case or for appraising property to be donated to charity must be fully familiar with the proper marketplace to be selected for finding comparable sale prices to support the valuation of the donated property.

In the case of *In re Stanley P. De Lisser, Debtor*,[66] the court, in totally denying a deduction for any increase in value over the taxpayer's cost of a donated graphics collection, noted the following:

> The appraisal lacks minimal information such as a summary of the appraiser's qualification, a statement of the value and the appraiser's definition of the value, the basis upon which his appraisal was made, and the cost, date and manner of acquisitions.[67]

The court found that absent any facts to the contrary, the artwork's purchase price is the best indication of its value when the date of acquisition and the date of physical delivery of the artwork are only twelve months apart.

The case of *Jack C. Chou*[68] involved the fair market value of a carved opal donated to a museum. In 1982, the taxpayer purchased a rough opal for $19,500. The taxpayer returned the opal to the seller to be carved and then donated it thirteen months later to a museum. The seller recommended two appraisers to the taxpayer; they appraised the donated, now carved, opal at an average value of $300,000. The court, in holding that the value was $30,000, noted that the opal was purchased only a little more than a year before it was donated and that cost is important evidence of value when no intervening factors explain a substantial or unusual appreciation.[69] In reaching its conclusion, the court stated that it must determine the appropriate market for purposes of valuation and that the determination is a question of fact. The court seems to have gotten off the track and to have been misled by the IRS's valuation expert. The court stated that in valuing gemstones the market may be retail, wholesale, or a "collector's market."[70] The court first dismissed the wholesale market because the taxpayer was not a dealer in gemstones. The IRS expert testified that the appropriate marketplace is the collector's market, because a knowledgeable buyer would not pay the higher retail prices, and, the IRS expert continued, the record indicated that the taxpayer was a knowledgeable, albeit amateur, collector. The court concluded that only values from the collector's market are appropriate.

It appears to us that the analysis in *Jack C. Chou* is incorrect to the extent that it relies on a so-called collector's market. The court's opinion seems to imply that a knowledgeable taxpayer would get a lower income tax deduction for a donation than would a less intelligent taxpayer who did not know what she was doing. We do not believe that there is a defined collector's market that should be used for comparable values. Whether a taxpayer is knowledgeable or not should not be a determining factor in the amount of the available deduction for the donation. The amount of the deduction should depend on the value of the item, based on comparable sales in the most appropriate marketplace in which the item is most commonly purchased and sold. Since the case was such an obvious abuse of the donation process, the court seems to have gone overboard in rationalizing its decision.

Differences of opinion in valuation cases are illustrated in the case of *Fuad S. Ashkar*,[71] which involved the valuation of ancient biblical fragments donated to a university. The expert for the IRS valued the items at $25,000, and the expert for the taxpayer valued the items at $700,000. The court, in not following either expert, noted that the experts were academic scholars, rather than professional appraisers of ancient documents. The court relied on the evidence of an offer that had been made for the collection; that offer of $337,500 was fairly close to the average of the prices given by the two experts. The court opinion also erroneously referred to a so-called collector's market.[72]

The *Thomas G. Murphy*[73] case involved the valuation of what was known as "the million-dollar rock," a sandstone rock sculpture that depicted the face of John Wayne. The rock was donated to Lubbock Christian College in Lubbock, Texas. The court correctly pointed out that the taxpayer's valuation of $500,000 was erroneously based on a faulty appraisal that failed to discuss the condition of the sculpture and failed to verify the accuracy of comparable prices. The IRS expert, who used the auction market for comparable prices, pointed out that when the sculpture was viewed from the left side, the left temple was missing, the left eyebrow was missing, a large wedge-shaped area was missing below the left eye, the left cheek was missing, and part of the left chin was missing. Because of its extremely poor condition, the court upheld the IRS expert and valued the sculpture at $30,000. The case is also instructive in that the gift was donated on the condition that it not be sold or otherwise disposed of for a period of two years after its receipt; that restriction, the court found, reduced the fair market value of the donated sculpture.[74] The court also upheld the negligence and overvaluation penalties imposed by the IRS. The taxpayer appealed the assessment of the penalties only, and the United States Court of Appeals for the Ninth Circuit reversed the penalties, finding that from the record viewed as a whole, Murphy's reliance on the appraisal report was reasonable and in good faith.[75]

In identifying the proper marketplace to find comparable sales, the case of *Joseph M. Isaacs*[76] is instructive. The case involved a bulk purchase of Alexander Calder-designed tapestries that were handwoven by Guatemalan Indians. The tapestries were purchased for $900 each and were donated at a value of $10,000 each. The IRS argued that in the most common marketplace in which a group of the tapestries would sell, the price would be deeply discounted below the wholesale price. That was the same theory argued in the *Samuel E. Hunter* case (see page 1246), which involved a donation in bulk of a group of lithographs. In *Isaacs*, the court held that the tapestries were worth $3,000 each, based on the court's own determination of fair market value and comparable sale prices from the testimony of various experts.

In *Engel v. Commissioner*,[77] the court was faced with valuing wild-game-trophy mounts donated to a museum when there was not an active sales market for the donated property. The court noted that

> [b]ased upon the record in this case, there is not a sufficient showing of an active market and comparable sales to warrant exclusive reliance upon that method of valuation as respondent [the IRS] would have us do. On the other hand, there also is not such a total lack of market as to require the use of replacement cost alone, as Perry [the donor's expert] advocates.[78]

Recognizing that determining fair market value is extremely difficult when only a thin market for the donated items exists, the court reached a compromise figure for the donated property.

Frank P. Perdue, best known for his chickens, was successful when the IRS challenged his donation of gold artifacts to the National Museum of American History.[79] The court pointed out that when the artifacts were valued, a premium could be added for the excitement and the glamour associated with the fact that the items were recovered from a sunken Spanish ship. The court stated correctly that "neither section 170 nor the Treasury regulations thereunder specifies which market a taxpayer should use in calculating fair market value." The regulations that refer to a "retail market" are in the estate tax regulations[80] and technically do not apply to the income tax donation sections of the Internal Revenue Code, although it is our understanding that it is the policy of the IRS to treat the estate tax regulations as though they applied equally for estate tax and donation purposes. In determining the proper marketplace, the IRS expert said that the numismatic or precious metals market should be used and not the retail museum or gift shop market. The IRS expert also stated "that he has yet to meet a knowledgeable buyer in the glamour market." The IRS expert went on to state that the comparable auction prices that the taxpayer's expert used were not valid, since auctions attract only wealthy people without a lot of knowledge. That statement is an example of how an overzealous IRS expert can ruin a case for the IRS with a clearly erroneous conclusion. The expert's testimony was discredited when the expert remarked that auction prices were not relevant, since only people without knowledge purchase in that market.

The *Perdue* case should be compared with the *James L. Ferman, Jr.*[81] case, which dealt with the valuation of donated gold and silver artifacts recovered from the same sunken Spanish ship as in *Perdue*. Ferman's appraiser relied on what is known as the "glamour market," in which a premium is paid for the excitement and romantic appeal of the artifact. The appraiser for the IRS relied on the numismatic market, because he believed that market best meets the requirements for determining fair market value. The court reached a different result than in *Perdue*, noting that the *Perdue* case arose before the mother lode was found and involved largely distinctive pieces. In finding for the IRS in *Ferman*, the court based its determination on the facts that market conditions had changed, supply had changed, and the appraiser for the IRS was more knowledgeable and persuasive.

The *George O. Doherty*[82] case pitted against each other the two foremost authorities on the paintings of Charles M. Russell. The taxpayer donated a painting to the Charles M. Russell Museum and valued it at $200,000. The IRS said that the painting was a forgery and was worth only $100. The court noted that the credentials of the two experts were beyond question, yet they reached different conclusions. The court declined to rule on the authenticity of the painting in the light of the fact that the two experts could not agree on its authenticity. In reaching its conclusion that the painting had a value of $30,000, the court recognized that a dispute over the authenticity of a painting acts as a depressant on its value.

The case of *James J. Mitchell*[83] is an example of how important it is to pick the correct appraiser. The case involved the valuation of two American Western paintings, one by Frederic Remington and one by Charles Marion Russell. The taxpayer's expert had years of experience and expertise in American Western art, and her report exhaustively researched all comparable sales and presented the material in an understandable manner. The IRS expert, on the other hand, had little or no personal experience with American Western art and his comparables were not comparable. The IRS expert attempted to use private sales, rather than only public auction records, but was unable to provide the court with exact sale prices, exact sale dates, identities of buyers or sellers, information on the condition of the paintings, or discussions on provenance. The court found that the taxpayer's report was more accurate and ruled, for the most part, for the taxpayer.

THE QUEDLINBURG TREASURES

An interesting twist to the identification of the proper market in which to value works of art was discussed in Private Letter Ruling 91-52-005. The ruling closely follows the facts in what became known in the newspapers as the story of the Quedlinburg Treasures. In 1945, the decedent's United States Army unit was placed in charge of guarding some rare medieval art objects in Quedlinburg, Germany. The decedent stole and shipped the art objects to his home in Texas. When he died in 1980, his Texas inheritance tax return did not list any of the art objects. No federal estate tax return was filed, even though the art objects had a value of many millions of dollars.

First, the IRS ruled that under section 2033 the stolen art property was includable in the decedent's gross estate. The IRS stated that

> the nature of ownership that is required for inclusion of property in a decedent's gross estate under section 2033 . . . [is] based upon a decedent's possession of the economic equivalent of ownership, rather than upon the decedent's possession of a technical legal title.[84]

The decedent had successfully sold a number of the stolen items during his lifetime and retained possession and enjoyment of the remaining objects until his death, at which time the items passed to his heirs. Therefore, at the time of his death, the decedent possessed the necessary degree of ownership for inclusion of the items in his gross estate under section 2033.

Next, the IRS had to decide how the art property should be valued. The decedent's attorney argued that the proper market to look at for valuation purposes was the illicit market in which stolen art objects are regularly sold and that since there was no market for stolen medieval art objects, the value of the property must be zero. The IRS rejected that argument, analogizing, in part, to income tax cases in which the IRS had placed a value on cocaine and marijuana by referring to its street-market price. The IRS noted that the art objects held by the decedent were of great historical, artistic, cultural, and religious significance and that there were individuals in the "discreet retail market" who were eager to purchase such otherwise unobtainable objects at premium prices. The IRS concluded that the fair market value of the art objects was "the highest price that would have been paid, at the time of the decedent's death, whether in the discreet retail market or in the legitimate art market."

The decedent's attorney then argued that if the objects were includable in the gross estate at their fair market value, the decedent should be entitled to claim a deduction under section 2053(a)(3) for claims against the estate by the legitimate owners of the art objects. The IRS rejected the deduction, noting that in order to be enforceable under Texas law, a claim had to be submitted within a certain period of time, which had passed, and that section 2053(a)(3) provides that claims against an estate are allowable only to the extent that they are allowable by the laws of the jurisdiction under which the estate is administered.

BUYER'S PREMIUM

When collectibles are purchased at most auction houses, a buyer's premium (currently 25% of the first $50,000, 20% on the next $950,000, and 12% on the amount above $1,000,000 at Christie's and Sotheby's) is added to the final auction bid price and is paid by the buyer. We believe that the buyer's premium should be viewed as one additional fact to be taken into consideration by the appraiser in the valuation process. The premium may have little or no relevance for an estate tax appraisal, since the estate can never receive the buyer's premium, but it may carry weight in an appraisal for charitable-contribution purposes. But it is the position of the IRS, as stated in a recent Private Letter Ruling,[85] that when an estate sells collectibles at auction, it must use the hammer price (the final auction bid price) plus the 12% buyer's premium as the federal estate tax value, even though the estate has no access to the buyer's premium, can never obtain it, and has no right to it.[86] We believe that it is not correct to include the buyer's premium in the valuation process when collectibles are sold by an estate and the estate uses the selling price as the measure of value. Because of the importance of the issue, a review of the applicable legal principles is called for.

The IRS based its ruling on *Publicker v. Commissioner*,[87] in which a donor purchased two items of jewelry and had to pay a federal excise tax on each item as part of the purchase price. The donor subsequently transferred the jewelry to her daughter. In determining the fair market value of the jewelry for gift tax purposes, the court concluded that the "price at which such property would change hands between a willing buyer and a willing seller" includes the excise tax paid by the purchaser of the property.[88]

The IRS's reliance on *Publicker* is misguided. *Publicker* is not relevant to estate sales of works of art at an auction because it involved an excise tax, not a buyer's premium, and it involved an issue of gift tax, not estate tax. Furthermore, the property in *Publicker* was not sold. The buyer's premium, therefore, should not be included in the valuation process where an estate sells works of art and uses the selling price as the measure of value on the federal estate tax return, rather than a date-of-death appraised value.

The determination of fair market value is defined in IRS regulation section 20.2031-1(b) as

> the price at which the property would change hands between a willing buyer and willing seller, neither being under any compulsion to buy or sell and both having reasonable knowledge of all relevant facts.

The regulation goes on to state the following:

> [N]or is the fair market value of an item of property to be determined by the sales price of the item in a market other than that in which such item is most commonly sold to the public, taking into account the location of the item wherever appropriate. Thus, in the case of an item of property includable in the decedent's gross estate, which is generally obtained by the public in the retail market, the fair market value of such an item of property is the price at which the item or a comparable item would be sold at retail.[89]

In valuing collectibles for estate tax purposes, the appraiser must identify the retail market in which the item is most commonly sold to the public. The IRS has emphasized—particularly in charitable contribution cases, as discussed above—that fair market value must be determined in the retail marketplace in which the item is most commonly sold in any given situation and that there may be more than one retail marketplace.[90]

Regulation section 20.2031-1(b) gives the example of a used car includable in a decedent's gross estate to illustrate which market is to be considered retail. The regulation states that the market price at which the general public could buy the car is the appropriate or most common marketplace, not the wholesale marketplace where a dealer would buy the car. That example, limited as it is, illustrates that the reality of a given situation controls the determination of the appropriate marketplace. The most common method of disposing of cars is at retail. The retail car market is easily accessible to the executor of the estate by advertisement, and the retail values of automobiles are published monthly and are generally known to the public. Hence, in the used-car situation, the IRS looked at the reality of the situation and reasonably chose the value available to the executor as the retail market value. Accordingly, the executor is able to ascertain the fair market value for the automobile.

More complex is the selection of the appropriate marketplace for collectibles for estate tax purposes. One guide available to facilitate such an inquiry is Revenue Procedure 65-19, which states that the price paid for an item in a decedent's gross estate at a public auction or in answer to a classified newspaper advertisement will be considered its retail price.[91] The sale must be within a reasonable time, and there must not be any substantial change in market conditions.

Although a retail dealer's market does exist in the art field (there are many retail art galleries), that market is generally not available to the executor and, unlike the executor in the used-car example in the regulations, an executor of an estate containing paintings cannot function as a dealer of fine art and dispose of the paintings in that market. An executor can place an advertisement in a newspaper and sell a used car, but it would not be prudent for an executor to sell a valuable painting in that manner. The art market is composed of highly specialized experts whose dealer-customer relationships are more analogous to a lawyer-client relationship than to a used-car dealer-customer relationship. Years of trust, experience, prestige, and warranties bind an art dealer to her customers. Thus, because of the fiduciary responsibilities that executors have to the beneficiaries to obtain a fair price for estate property and to avoid even the appearance of self-dealing, the most commonly used marketplace of artworks for an executor is public auction.[92] Accordingly, the auction value of collectibles is the fair market value for an estate, since the auction market is the marketplace that is available to the estate.

The selection of the appropriate marketplace by either the IRS or the taxpayer must be within the bounds of reasonability and reality. In discussing the choice of an appropriate marketplace to value mutual fund shares, Judge Theodore Tannewald stated in *Estate of Wells v. Commissioner*:

> I do not dispute the principle that [the Commissioner's] regulations should be sustained unless they are unreasonable. But it does not follow that, because [the Commissioner] has a choice of alternatives, his choice should be sustained where the alternative chosen is unrealistic. In such a situation the regulations embodying that choice should be held to be unreasonable.[93]

United States v. Cartwright[94] was an estate tax case involving the value of mutual fund shares for federal estate tax purposes. The taxpayer argued that the value should be the redemption value of the shares on the date of death not, as argued by the IRS, the asked price for the shares, which included the load charge for buyers.

The United States Supreme Court in *Cartwright* ended a conflict among several circuits in holding that IRS regulation section 20.2031-8(b), which outlined the procedure for the valuation of mutual funds for estate tax purposes, is invalid. The Court found the regulation unreasonable and void, although not technically inconsistent with the Internal Revenue Code. The Court agreed with Judge Tannewald's dissent in the case of *Estate of Wells v. Commissioner*[95] noted above.

Following Judge Tannewald's rationale, the Court found that regulation section 20.2031-8(b) purported to assign a value to mutual fund shares that the estate could not hope to obtain and that the mutual fund could not offer;[96] therefore, the regulation "imposes an unreasonable and unrealistic measure of value."[97] Hence, regulation section 20.2031-8(b) was held invalid, and mutual fund valuation for estate tax purposes is the redemption price.[98] The buyers' market that was hypothetically possible (the selling price that included the front-load charge) but realistically unavailable to the estate was held not to be the appropriate retail value in that situation. The Supreme Court concluded that the arbitrarily chosen asked price for mutual fund shares was not a realistic measure of their true value to the executor, since the estate could never receive the commission that went to the mutual fund.

The Court pointed out that, by analogy, in valuing shares of publicly traded stock in an estate, the executor is not required to value the shares above the mean price on the decedent's date of death, even though the buyer of those shares had to pay a commission to his stockbroker to buy the shares. Thus, the IRS was held in *Cartwright* to be acting beyond the scope of its discretionary powers by choosing a market valuation that was hypothetically possible but realistically not available to the taxpayer.

The amount that an estate can realize must now be determined and considered in the valuation process. The U.S. Court of Appeals for the Second Circuit in *Cartwright* decided the following:

> [I]f there is indeed a widely accepted principle of valuation contained within that [referring to 20.2031-1(b)] recently revised regulation, it is most certainly embodied in the sentence: "All relevant facts and elements of value as of the applicable valuation date shall be considered in every case." We would agree . . . that the retail sales price of a property unit may be an important factor in the determination of its fair market value; yet it is also clear that other factors can affect the price which a willing seller reasonably could expect to receive from a sale of that particular unit; and if these other factors cause the retail price to be an unreasonable or unrealistic value standard, the retail price has not always been followed in valuation disputes as the sole criterion of value.[99]

The decisions of the Supreme Court and the court of appeals appear to state that reasonability and reality must be considered in valuation disputes.

When an estate sells a collectible, the most common marketplace available to it is the auction market, which is, for all practical purposes, the only market available to the executor. If the selling price is to be the measure of value for estate tax purposes, the hammer price should be the measure of value without the 12% buyer's premium. As in *Cartwright*, the reality of the situation is that the executor has no access to the buyer's premium, can never obtain it, and has no right to it. If the executor chooses to sell at auction, only the hammer price is available.

To value a collectible at a figure that includes the buyer's premium is as unrealistic and unreasonable as it was to value mutual funds at an unobtainable price, which the United States Supreme Court held in *Cartwright* to be unreasonable and void. As Judge Tannewald stated in the *Wells* case:

> The touchstone of fair market value has always been the price which a willing seller could reasonably be expected to be able to obtain from a disposition of the property in question.[100]

That price should not include the buyer's expenses paid to a third party.

Unfortunately, the IRS continues to insist on including the auction house buyer's premium as part of the value when an estate uses the selling price of a collectible as the estate tax value. That position encourages executors to rely on the date-of-death appraised value for the collectibles, a subjective value that would, on audit, be argued with the IRS. That could lead to an increase in unagreed estate tax cases because the executor and the IRS are often unable to agree on the value of the collectibles. A position by the IRS that discourages agreed estate tax cases would be detrimental to the orderly administration of estates. We believe that most taxpayers would find it inherently unfair to be forced to pay an estate tax on amounts that could never be received.

Supporting the IRS theory is *Estate of Robert C. Scull, deceased v. Commissioner*,[101] in which the executors sold works of art owned by the decedent at public auction ten and one-half months after the decedent's death. The court, in disregarding the date of death appraisal, said that the auction results (evidence of actual sales) are the best measure of value. The executors argued that only the hammer price should be used and that a discount should be allowed for the appreciation in value since the date of death. The court, relying on *Publicker*,[102] held that the proper measure of value is what could be received on, not what is retained from, a hypothetical sale. Accordingly, the hammer price plus the buyer's premium was includable in the decedent's estate for federal estate tax purposes. The court did, however, allow a 15% discount from that total for post-death appreciation in value.

Fortunately, the IRS ruling[103] that requires the inclusion of the buyer's premium, as supported by the *Scull* case, may have little practical application in most estates, because the buyer's premium should be deductible by the estate as an administration expense under regulation 20.2053-3(d)(2). However, even though an estate's selling expenses in disposing of works of art may be deductible under state law, the IRS may disallow those expenses because they are not necessary to pay the decedent's debts, expenses of administration, or taxes; to preserve the estate; or to effect distributions.[104]

The various circuit courts have reached different conclusions as to whether state or federal law determines what is a deductible administrative expense for federal estate tax purposes. Some have held that state law controls.[105] Others have held that although state law is important, policy considerations require that federal regulations determine the issue.[106]

In most cases, the executors should be able to claim a deduction for the buyer's premium under regulation 20.2053-3(d).[107] The consignment contracts of Sotheby's and Christie's auction houses specifically provide that the seller authorizes the auction house to receive and retain the buyer's premium from the sale proceeds. Because the buyer's premium is, in effect, a selling cost of the estate paid by the buyer, it should be deductible to the extent that the requirements of regulation sections 20.2053-3(a) and 20.2053-3(d) are satisfied.

Works of art sold or disposed of among multiple beneficiaries under a residuary clause should satisfy the IRS requirement that the sale be necessary to effect distribution of the estate.[108] As a practical matter, executors cannot divide works of art among multiple beneficiaries because they cannot physically divide the works or precisely determine each work's respective value. Therefore, they are unable to fulfill their fiduciary duty of fairness to all beneficiaries.

In any event, a well-prepared appraisal of works of art should always state whether the comparable auction prices used for valuation include the buyer's premium and the amount of the premium.[109]

CURRENT TREND IN VALUATION CASES

The trend in valuation cases indicates that settlement is clearly the best course of action. Settlement is best achieved by being initially careful and thorough in the selection of the appraiser and by making sure that the appraisal complies with all the requirements of the IRS regulations. Most important, the appraisal should show comparable prices and identify the proper marketplace for valuing the donated property. Being thorough and complete at the time of a donation is most often the best course of action and best enables the taxpayer to sustain the value of the donated property and avoid expensive litigation.[110]

Penalties for Incorrect Valuations

PRIOR LAWS

The Tax Reform Act of 1984 amended Internal Revenue Code section 6659 by adding section 6659(f) to deal specifically with overvaluations of property contributed to charity. The penalty provision was applicable to returns filed after 1984 and for the tax years ending on or before December 31, 1989. As amended, the section imposed a graduated penalty between 10% and 30% of the tax liability underpayment. The 30% penalty applied if the reported value of the works of art, real estate, and similar assets exceeded the correct value by 250% or more. In 1989, section 6659 was repealed, effective January 1, 1990.

Section 6661 imposed a penalty for substantial underpayment of tax liability. The Tax Reform Act of 1986 amended section 6661, effective January 1, 1987, to increase the penalty from 10% to 20% on the amount of the underpayment of tax under certain conditions. The Omnibus Budget Reconciliation Act of 1986 increased the penalty to 25% of the underpayment. The Technical and Miscellaneous Revenue Act of 1988 clarified the matter: The 25% penalty rate was to apply to penalties asserted after October 21, 1986. Section 6661 was repealed, effective January 1, 1990.

The Tax Reform Act of 1984 added section 6660 to the Code; that section applied to gift and estate taxes. Section 6660 applied in cases of valuation understatement, not valuation overstatement, which were penalized under section 6659. Section 6660 was repealed, effective January 1, 1990.

New Penalty Rules

The Revenue Reconciliation Act of 1989[111] repealed the penalty provisions of sections 6659, 6660, and 6661 in an attempt to streamline rather complex provisions and to provide a fairer and more effective penalty system.[112] Currently, section 6662 consolidates the generally applicable penalties relating to the accuracy of tax returns into one accuracy-related penalty equal to 20% of the portion of the underpayment to which the penalty applies. This provision became effective January 1, 1990. The Pension Protection Act of 2006 (effective August 17, 2006) further modified the thresholds for the applicable penalties.

For income tax purposes under section 6662(e), there is a "substantial valuation misstatement" if the value of a work of art contributed to charity is 150% or more of the amount determined to be the correct amount of the valuation.[113] The 20% penalty is increased to 40% if the discrepancy is 200% or more, a "gross valuation misstatement."[114] Under section 6664(c)(2), no penalty is imposed for an underpayment of tax resulting from a substantial or gross overvaluation of a charitable deduction for a work of art if it is shown that there was reasonable cause for the underpayment and if the taxpayer acted in good faith with respect to the underpayment. However, that exception does not apply unless (1) the claimed value of the property was based on a qualified appraisal made by a qualified appraiser and (2) the taxpayer also made a good-faith investigation of the value of the contributed property.[115] To satisfy the second requirement, the taxpayer should keep a diary or a memorandum about her personal investigation of the value of the property. That is, there should be careful documentation of the taxpayer's investigation of the property's value. Under section 6662(e)(2), at least $5,000 of additional tax must be due for the penalty to apply.

The reasonable cause exception for underpayment due to "gross valuation missatements" on charitable deduction property was eliminated effective August 17, 2006. The reasonable cause exception remains, however, for a "substantial valuation misstatement."[116]

The willingness of the IRS to impose penalties in appropriate cases is illustrated by the *Jacobson*[117] case, which involved a stamp collector who had a collection of both postage stamps and postal stationery, that is, first-day-of-issue stamps that have passed through the mail. The taxpayer had acquired 60,484 first-day pages, which he owned for approximately twenty-five years. He never had any insurance on the contributive property, and he stored the property in boxes in his bakery warehouse. The court took note of the facts that the warehouse had a rodent problem, was very hot during the summer, and had almost no security. The taxpayer claimed a deduction for the donated stamp property in the amount of $949,030, but the tax court held that the correct value was $12,973. The question was then presented whether the section 6662(h)(2)(A) 40% penalty applies since there was a gross valuation misstatement, that is, the value of the property claimed on the tax return ($949,030) was 400% or more of the amount determined to be the correct value ($12,973). The taxpayer said he relied on his appraisal in claiming the $949,030 deduction and that he therefore acted reasonably even though the court found that the valuation was too high. The court pointed out that there is a two-part requirement to avoid the penalty: There must be reasonable cause for the taxpayer's position and the taxpayer must have acted in "good faith."[118] The good-faith exception applies only if (1) the claimed value of the property was based on a "qualified appraisal" made by a "qualified appraiser" and (2) in addition to obtaining such an appraisal, the taxpayer made a good-faith investigation of the value of the contributed property.[119] The court found that the taxpayer had not acted in good faith, because his conduct with respect to the contributed property was not consistent with a taxpayer's behavior if the property had substantial value: That is, there was no insurance; the property was inappropriately stored in a hot, rodent-infested warehouse; there was no security; and it was not treated like property that had a value of almost $1 million.[120] Accordingly, the court assessed the penalty.

For estate and gift tax purposes, section 6662(g)(1) imposes the 20% penalty if the value of any property claimed on an estate or gift tax return is 50% or less of the amount determined to be correct.[121] If the understatement is attributable to a gross valuation misstatement of 25% or less of the correct amount, the penalty amount is increased to 40% of the underpayment.[122] At least $5,000 of additional tax must be due for the penalty to apply.[123]

Unlike the income tax law, estate and gift tax laws do not require a qualified appraisal by a qualified appraiser. The IRS has discretionary authority to waive all or part of the section 6662 penalty if the taxpayer establishes that there was a reasonable basis for the valuation claimed and that the claim was made in good faith.[124]

The section 6662(g) penalty appears to apply for estate and gift tax purposes only to valuation understatements, not to overstatements.[125] Therefore, if a decedent bequeathed artwork to a museum and an estate tax charitable deduction is claimed, no section 6662 penalty is imposed if the IRS determines that the work had a smaller value than that claimed on the estate tax return. In most cases, the estate tax does not increase or decrease in the case of a valuation overstatement of a charitable bequest, since the size of the gross estate increases as the charitable deduction increases; the two cancel each other out, leaving only the remainder subject to the estate tax. Therefore, the section 6662 penalty should generally not apply to an estate charitable bequest that may be overstated in value. However, a valuation overstatement of a work of art could increase the executor's commission (which is deductible on the estate tax return) and have the net effect of decreasing the estate tax.

A section 6662 penalty could be applied in an estate tax situation for income tax purposes. For example, when the unlimited marital deduction[126] applies or when the estate is less than the estate tax exemption equivalent (that is, less than $5,120,000 in year 2012), there is no estate tax.[127] However, any artwork, as well as other tangible property of the estate, receives a step-up in basis equal to the estate tax value.[128] If the artwork that was overvalued for estate tax purposes is later sold at a loss, the estate or the heirs have a capital loss that may be deductible under section 165(c)(2), as discussed on page 1186. If the loss claimed to reduce the income tax results from the overvaluation, the IRS can invoke the penalty provisions of section 6662.[129]

New Disclosure Rules for Donee Charitable Organizations

The Tax Reform Act of 1984 requires a donee of any property for which an income tax charitable deduction of more than $5,000 was claimed to file an information report with the IRS if the contributed property is sold, exchanged, or otherwise disposed of within two years after the date of receipt of the contribution.[130] That provision became effective January 1, 1985. In February 1985, the IRS issued Form 8282 ("Donee Information Return") to be used by donees for the purpose of satisfying the filing requirement. The latest version of the form, dated April 2009, is reproduced at the end of chapter 17 (see Appendix 17-5). All exempt organizations have to keep records in sufficient detail to meet the filing requirement. Records are particularly important for charities that solicit contributions of property for the purpose of a fund-raising auction.

The regulations for Internal Revenue Code sections 6050L and 6050L(b), which were adopted on May 4, 1988, indicate that the information report (Form 8282) must be filed by an exempt organization that disposes of donated property if the aggregate value of similar items of property equals the $5,000 amount. The donee organization must supply the following information to the IRS:

- The name, address, and employer identification number of the donee
- A description of the property
- The name and social security number of the donor
- The date of the contribution to the donee
- The amount received by the donee on any disposition
- The date of the disposition by the donee
- Any other information that may be required by Form 8282

The conference committee report for section 6050L indicated that the regulations would require the donor to inform the donee of any donation of similar items made during the taxable year. At the present time, regulation sections 1.170A-13 and 1.6050L-1 do not contain such a requirement. Charities receiving property as a donation may want to consider requiring a statement from the donor that the donor will inform the charity of any contributions of similar property to other donees within the same taxable year.

REGULATION OF APPRAISERS

An appraiser may be subject to a $1,000 penalty under section 6701 if the appraiser (1) aids or assists in the preparation or presentation of an appraisal in connection with a tax return or document, (2) knew that the appraisal would be used in connection with the tax laws, and (3) knew that it would result in an understatement of the tax liability of another person.[131] If the IRS proves that the appraiser had such knowledge, the appraiser is subject to the civil penalty under section 6701.[132] In addition, the IRS can bar appraisers against whom the section 6701 penalty was assessed after July 18, 1984, from appearing before or presenting evidence to the IRS.[133] Under the IRS regulations, appraisals made before the effective date of the disqualification of the appraiser are not barred from being considered qualified appraisals.

There is a new penalty to be assessed against appraisers for certain types of valuation misstatements under section 6695A. A person who prepares an appraisal of property must pay a penalty if (1) he knows, or reasonably should have known, that the appraisal would be used in connection with a federal tax return or refund claim; and (2) the claimed value of the appraised property results in a substantial valuation misstatement or a gross valuation misstatement related to income tax. The penalty is the lesser of (1) the greater of $1,000 or 10% of the tax underpayment amount attributable to the misstatement; or (2) 125% of the gross income received by the appraiser for preparing the appraisal. However, under section 6695A(c), no penalty is imposed if the appraiser establishes that the appraised value of the property was more likely than not the proper value for the property.

APPRAISAL COSTS

The IRS has ruled that the cost of an appraisal of property that is contributed to a charitable organization is deductible for income tax purposes under section 212(3) as an expense paid in connection with the determination of income tax liability.[134] The breadth of that section is reflected in the language of the corresponding regulation, which states that those appraisal expenses are deductible "whether the taxing authority be Federal, State, or municipal, and whether the tax be income, estate, gift, property or any other tax."[135] Accordingly, when a gift is made to a noncharitable donee, the appraisal fee incurred for the gift tax valuation is similarly an income deduction. The cost of an appraisal of property is also deductible for estate tax purposes.[136]

CHARITABLE TRANSFERS

The lifetime transfer of a collection to a charitable organization saves the donor income taxes because of the allowable income tax deduction; at the same time, the lifetime transfer relieves the donor of the expense and the worry connected with the maintenance of a valuable collection. For example, a painting that cost the collector $1,000 some years ago may have a fair market value of $10,000 to-day. A contribution today of the painting to charity that meets all the requirements discussed below produces an allowable charitable deduction of $10,000. For someone in the 35% tax bracket, such a contribution saves $3,500 in federal income taxes. Since the donor's out-of-pocket cost was only $1,000, the taxpayer has made a $2,500 tax-free economic profit and has enjoyed the painting through her years of ownership.[137] The problem for the estate planner is to make sure the contribution is correctly made, so that the tax benefit described is achieved.[138]

A testamentary transfer of a collection to a charitable organization saves the decedent's estate a great amount in estate taxes, because of the allowable estate tax deduction and, at the same time, relieves the estate of the problem of raising the cash necessary to pay the estate tax on a potentially nonliquid asset.

Complete Inter Vivos Charitable Transfers

REQUIREMENTS FOR CLAIMING A CHARITABLE DEDUCTION

To claim a charitable deduction for the full fair market value of a donated collection, the taxpayer must generally comply with four specific requirements. Before donating a collection to a charitable organization, the donor must determine the following:

1. The status of the charitable organization: The collection must be contributed to a public charity, not a private foundation.
2. The type of property being contributed: The collection must be long-term capital gain type property and not ordinary income type property.
3. Whether the collection satisfies the related use rule: The use of the collection by the donee charity must be related to the tax-exempt purpose of the charity.
4. Whether there is a qualified appraisal prepared by a qualified appraiser

Each factor is considered below.

STATUS OF THE ORGANIZATION
Charitable organizations are characterized as either public or private.[139] Public charities generally receive part of their support from the general public. They include churches, schools, hospitals, museums, and other publicly supported organizations; private operating foundations (see page 1297); and certain organiza-

tions operated in connection with another public organization. They also include those private foundations that distribute all their receipts each year. Private charities include all other exempt organizations and include the usual kinds of private foundations.[140]

It is important to verify the status of the charitable organization as either a public or a private charity. There is a different result when a taxpayer makes a contribution to a public charity, as opposed to a private charity. Verification of a charity's status can be made by checking IRS Publication 78, *Cumulative List of Exempt Organizations* (now also available on the Internet), or by asking the charitable organization to provide copies of letters from the IRS stating its status. It is, however, preferable to obtain copies of the letters from the IRS stating the organization's status. There is a difference between the organization's exemption ruling under section 501(c)(3) and its ruling as a public organization under section 509(a). Generally, a taxpayer will only receive a deduction of her cost for a donation of an appreciated collection made to a private charity as opposed to the full fair market value for a donation made to a public charity.

TYPE OF PROPERTY
Capital Gain Property
In most cases, a collection is "capital gain property." The term includes any property the sale of which at its fair market value at the time of the contribution would have resulted in long-term capital gain.[141] Any appreciation in value, no matter how small, makes the property capital gain property. The property is capital gain property if all of the following factors are present:

- It is a capital asset under section 1221
- It has appreciated in value
- It has been held for more than one year for contributions made on or after January 1, 1988

Contribution of capital gain property receives favorable tax treatment. The distinction between ordinary income (including short-term capital gain) and long-term capital gain for tax rate purposes is that ordinary income is taxed as high as 35% and long-term capital gain on collectibles is taxed at a maximum of 28%. The Taxpayer Relief Act of 1997 reduced the long-term capital gain rate to 20% on the sale of securities, real estate and other capital assets (other than collectibles) held more than eighteen months (changed to "more than twelve months" by the IRS Restructuring and Reform Act of 1998), but maintained the 28% rate on gain from the sale of collectibles held for more than one year. The Jobs and Growth Tax Relief Reconciliation Act of 2003 (effective May 6, 2003) further reduced the long-term capital gain rate to 15% for sales of securities and other capital assets held for more than twelve months but once again maintained the 28% rate on gain from the sale of collectibles held for more than one year. The term "collectibles gain" is defined in section 1(h)(5)(A) to mean gain from the sale or exchange of a collectible (as defined in section 408(m) without regard to paragraph (3) thereof) which is a capital asset held for more than 1 year but only to the extent such gain is taken into account in computing gross income.

Section 1(h)(5)(B) (added by the Taxpayer Relief Act of 1997) is designed to prevent taxpayers from converting the 28% rate to the 15% rate by creating a partnership, corporation, or trust under rules similar to the rules of section 751.

The characterization of donated property as capital gain property or ordinary income property is particularly important with regard to charitable contributions, and the proper characterization of contributed property as long-term capital gain property is crucial if the donor is to receive the full charitable deduction for appreciated tangible personal property. Although the IRS Restructuring and Reform Act of 1998 reduced the holding period for long-term transactions on the sale of capital assets to more than twelve months (the same rule that applies to collectibles), it kept the 28% tax rate for long-term transactions as it applies to collectibles. Since the maximum ordinary income tax rate is currently 35%, there is now a smaller difference between ordinary income treatment and capital gains treatment on the sale of collectibles. This may serve as increased incentive for individuals to make donations of collectibles rather than sell them. Collectors should note that section 1(h)(5) now clearly provides that losses from the sale of collectibles can be used to offset gains from the sale of collectibles.

Generally, if the four requirements for making a charitable donation are satisfied, a taxpayer will receive a deduction for the full fair market value for a donation of long-term capital gain property but will be limited to her cost for ordinary income property.

Ordinary Income Property
The property is ordinary income property[142] if any of the following factors are present:

- The property was created by the donor
- It was received by the donor as a gift from the creator
- It is held in inventory by a dealer
- It would produce short-term capital gain if sold—that is, it is owned for one year or less before being contributed
- It would produce a capital loss if sold

All works of art created by the artist are ordinary income property since that property, by the definition contained in section 1221(a)(3), cannot be a capital asset. Hence, the artist may be surprised that contributions of her own work do not receive the favored capital gain property deduction treatment. Even more surprised may be the collector who accepted the artwork as a gift from the artist. Classification as ordinary income property greatly reduces any available charitable deduction.

A problem often encountered by a collector is the possibility of receiving a gift of a work of art from the artist who created it. In that connection, reference must be made to section 1221(a)(3) for the definition of the term "capital asset." Section 1221(a)(3)(C) states that the term "capital asset" "does not include property held by a taxpayer in whose hands the basis of such property is determined, for purposes of determining gain from a sale or exchange, in whole or in part by reference to the basis of such property in the hands" of the taxpayer whose personal efforts created the property. Under section 1015, which covers the determination of basis for gifts, the basis of the property in the hands of the donee is determined by its basis in the hands of the donor. Therefore, a collector who receives artwork as a gift from an artist has the same basis in the property as does the artist. Since artwork is ordinary income property in the artist's hands, it cannot be a capital asset in the donee-collector's hands. Therefore, a taxpayer should be aware that a gift of a work of art from the creator retains its character as ordinary income property in the hands of the donee. If the property is purchased by the collector, it is converted into capital gain property, which results in an increased charitable deduction since the collector can now claim a deduction for the fair market value of the artwork as opposed to only its basis, that is, its cost.

The Tax Reform Act of 1976 required that the basis of all property passing from a decedent be determined by reference to the basis of the property in the hands of the decedent.[143] That was required because all inherited property was to be subject to new carryover-basis rules, which were postponed until January 1, 1980, by the Revenue Act of 1978 and were eventually repealed by section 401 of the Crude Oil Windfall Profit Tax Act of 1980. The heirs of the artist would have suffered if the carryover-basis rules had been implemented. Under those rules, the artist's heirs or legatees would not have been able to realize long-term capital gain on the sale of inherited artwork since the property would not qualify as a capital asset because of section 1221(a)(3)(C). Before the Tax Reform Act of 1976 and under current law since the carryover-basis rules were repealed, the gain on property inherited from an artist is taxed as capital gain.[144]

One of the most important tax consequences of death is that property included in a decedent's gross estate for federal estate tax purposes, subject to certain exceptions, acquires a "step-up" in basis for income tax purposes equal to its federal estate tax value, pursuant to section 1014. In other words, if a collector purchased a painting for $10,000 and when she dies the painting is valued at $100,000 for federal estate tax purposes, for income tax purposes the painting acquires a step-up in basis equal to $100,000. The Economic Growth and Tax Relief Reconciliation Act of 2001[145] was to terminate this step-up in basis for property included in a decedent's estate for those decedents dying after December 31, 2009, which is when the federal estate tax was scheduled to be repealed. The repeal came into effect but only for decedents dying in calendar year 2010.[146] In such cases, the new modified carryover basis system applies under new section 1022. Under the new system, the basis for certain property treated as transferred on the death of a property owner in 2010 equals the lower of the asset's fair market value at the decedent's death or the decedent's adjusted basis in the asset. In other words, the basis for income tax purposes may remain at the original cost of the property purchased. There are a number of adjustments that allow some step-up in basis. For example, the executor may increase the basis of carryover basis property in the aggregate by up to $1.3 million. That is, the amount of $1.3 million may be added to the decedent's cost basis prior to her death. A full discussion of this new provision is beyond the scope of this chapter.[147] The modified carryover basis system is in effect only for decedents dying in calendar year 2010. The step-up-in-basis rule under section 1014 has been reinstated for decedents dying in calendar year 2011 and thereafter.

When advising a collector who is making a charitable contribution, an attorney should find out how the collector acquired the property and what she did with it in order to determine if ordinary income property is present. Keep in mind that IRS Form 8283 requires the taxpayer to state how the donated property was acquired. If the property was acquired by gift from the creator of the property (the artist), the taxpayer's deduction is limited to the artist's cost of materials. Revenue Ruling 79-256, 1979-2 C.B. 105, involved a man who grew plants as a hobby and contributed them to charity; the ruling also involved a collector who purchased a substantial part of the limited edition of a particular lithograph series and later contributed the prints to various charities. In each case, the IRS held that the donor's activities were substantially equivalent to the activities of a dealer selling property in the ordinary course of a trade or business; therefore, the IRS limited the charitable deduction to the donor's cost of the property since the property as inventory is ordinary income property. The ruling appears to be far-reaching, without any statutory or court precedent.

The IRS "dealer" theory was put to rest in the case of *Kenneth Sandler*.[148] The case involved a doctor who purchased grave sites in bulk and one year later donated them to a church. The IRS argued that the doctor's activities were substantially equivalent to those of a dealer, that the property should be deemed ordinary income property, and that the deduction should be limited to the doctor's cost. The Tax Court held that the doctor was not engaged in the trade or business of selling grave sites and, therefore, that the property donated was not ordinary income property. However, the court looked closely at the proper marketplace to value the grave sites, holding that the proper retail market in that case was the sale to the ultimate consumer who did not hold the item for subsequent resale. Therefore, the court concluded that the proper comparable marketplace was the market in which the taxpayer-donor made his purchase and limited the taxpayer's contribution to his cost.

Related Use Rule

The Pension Protection Act of 2006 (PPA)[149] added new section 170(e)(7)(A), which provides if a charitable organization receives appreciated tangible personal property as a charitable organization and disposes of the property within three years of receiving it, the donor may not derive any tax benefit beyond a deduction in the amount of the property's basis.[150] However, this rule will not apply if the donee provides a "certification" from the donee charity that the property was put to a use related to the donee's exempt purpose or was at least intended for such a use.[151]

The related use rule applies to capital gain property that is tangible personal property contributed to a public charity. The term "tangible personal property" includes paintings and art objects not produced by the donor. The related use rule requires that the use of the tangible personal property by the donee organization be related to the purpose or the function constituting the basis for the donee's exemption under section 501. If the use of the collection by the donee organization is unrelated to the purpose or the function constituting the basis for the donee's exemption, the amount of the charitable deduction must be reduced by 100% of the appreciation in value of the collection.[152] In that instance, after the 100% appreciation reduction, the remainder may be deducted up to 50% of the taxpayer's contribution base.[153]

One of the major changes made by the Tax Reform Act of 1986 was the amendment of section 170(e)(1) so that 100% of the appreciation in value is lost as a charitable deduction if the related use rule is not satisfied. The new rule is effective for contributions made on or after January 1, 1987. Under the law in effect before January 1, 1987, only 40% of the appreciation in value was lost as a charitable deduction. Therefore, a taxpayer must be careful to comply with the related use rule; otherwise, the charitable deduction for appreciated long-term capital gain property that is tangible personal property will be limited to her cost. As mentioned above but worth repeating, if the donee charity disposes of the donated property within three years of the gift, the donor's deduction will retroactively reduced to the property's cost.

The regulations[154] provide that a taxpayer may treat the contribution of a collection as meeting the related use rule if:

1. The taxpayer establishes that the collection is not in fact put to an unrelated use by the donee; or if,
2. At the time of the contribution, it is reasonable to anticipate that the collection will not be put to an unrelated use by the donee organization.

If a collector donates a collection to a museum and the collection is of a general type normally retained by museums for museum purposes, it is reasonable for the donor to anticipate, unless she has actual knowledge to the contrary, that the collection will not be put to an unrelated use by the donee, whether or not the collection is later sold or exchanged by the donee. However, if an item is donated for the purpose of sale at an art auction to be run by the charity, that is an unrelated use, and 100% of the appreciation in value is lost as a charitable deduction.

Example 1: A painting contributed to an art museum that is a public charity and that can and, in fact, does from time to time display the painting prominently and publicly satisfies the related use rule. The contribution is deductible to the extent of the fair market value of the property within the 30% limitation.

Example 2: If the same painting is contributed to the Red Cross, which is a public charity and which from the outset intends to sell the painting and, in fact, promptly does sell it, the deduction must be reduced by 100% of the appreciation in value, with the balance deductible within the 50% limitation.[155]

The regulations[156] also indicate that the related use rule is met even if the donee sells or otherwise disposes of only an "insubstantial" portion of the collection.

According to Representative Wilbur D. Mills, who was then the chairman of the House Ways and Means Committee:

> What we are trying to say is that we will allow you to give this appreciated property and take today's market value as a charitable deduction without any tax consequences to you whatsoever if you give it to a charitable organization that normally would use the property for its exempt purposes. Now, a clear case is a gift of a picture or work of sculpture, or anything of that sort, to a museum. The question does arise with respect to a college or university as to whether or not they are using this for their exempt purpose, whether it is used in their teaching. Of course, the college could have a course in art, and if the gift were to be used for that purpose it would probably qualify as such a gift.[157]

To date there have been few litigated cases on the subject of related use. However, a number of Private Letter Rulings in this area do shed some light on what the IRS considers a related use.

Private Letter Ruling 77-51-044
The IRS held that the related use rule was satisfied when lithographs were displayed in a camp and center devoted to handicapped and retarded children, since the lithographs were used in connection with an art appreciation program. (Private Letter Rulings 79-11-109 and 79-34-082 reach similar results in dealing with the exhibition of works of art.)

Private Letter Ruling 80-09-027
The IRS held that the related use rule was not satisfied when a donor gave an antique car to a university, since the university did not offer a course in antique car restoration.

Private Letter Ruling 81-43-029
The IRS held that the related use rule was satisfied when a donor gave his collection of porcelain art objects to a public charity operating a retirement center, since the display of the art was related to the charity's exempt purpose of creating a living environment for its residents.

Private Letter Ruling 82-08-059
The IRS held that the related use rule was satisfied when a donor gave his stamp collection to a college, since it would be exhibited and the college had, as part

of its curriculum, the teaching of engraving skills. In the ruling request the do-nor included letters from the college, explaining in detail how it would use the collection.

Private Letter Ruling 91-31-053
The IRS held that the related use rule was satisfied when a donor gave seeds, greenhouses, plants, livestock, animal semen, beds, desks, tilling equipment, and cafeteria equipment to a private school with exempt status under sections 501(c) (3) and 509(a)(1). The donated items of tangible personal property were to be used by the school in its plant science and animal science curriculum.

Private Letter Ruling 98-33-011
The IRS held that the related use rule was satisfied when a donor donated paint-ings to a Jewish community center that was not a museum but did have an arts wing and library. The community center proposed to solicit contribution of works of art that would be selected by a group of volunteers from the local community but would not be restricted to Jewish artists or to Jewish themes. The community center would accept only works of art that it expected to use in a manner related to the purpose or function constituting the basis for the community center's ex-emption under section 501(c)(3). The community center would display some of the works of art, and others would be put on loan with affiliated charitable or-ganizations. The community center represented that it did not intend to sell the donated works of art except on a limited and infrequent basis when the collection exceeded the space available for display or an item was no longer relevant or it became too costly to provide maintenance and security for the work of art. The Private Letter Ruling held that so long as any loans to other charitable organi-zations further the community center's exempt purpose or function, then such activities will not be unrelated to the exempt purpose of the community center. However, the IRS pointed out that the community center may not rely on the exempt purpose or function of the charitable organization to which the works of art are loaned. The purpose of the loan must be to further the exempt purpose of the community center.

It is important to make sure that a proper paper trail shows that it was reason-able for the taxpayer to anticipate that the property would not be put to an un-related use by the donee.[158]

Related Use Reporting
Prior to the PPA, the IRS required the donee charity to file IRS form 8282 if the donee charity disposes of the property within two years of receipt. Presumably this would give the IRS the opportunity to audit the donor-taxpayer's income tax return if the price the donated item was sold for was less than the deduction claimed by the donor. Under the PPA, the reporting requirement is increased to apply to dispositions made within three years after receipt by the donee char-ity.[159] Obviously, there is a new focus on the actual use the charity makes of the donated property. In addition, the information that must be reported now in-

cludes a description of the donee's use of the property and a statement indicating whether its use was related to its exempt purpose or function. If the donee charity indicates a related use, it must include with the disclosure form the certification discussed below. Form 8282 was revised as of April 2009.

Where there is no certification and a donee organization sells, exchanges, or otherwise disposes of the applicable property in the donor's tax year in which the contribution was made, the donor's deduction is limited to basis and not fair market value.[160] If the donated property is disposed of by the donee organization in a subsequent year within three years of the contribution, the donor must include as ordinary income for the year in which the disposition occurs an amount equal to the excess, if any, of (1) the amount of the deduction previously claimed by the donor as a charitable contribution with respect to such property over (2) the donor's basis in such property at the time of the contribution.[161]

The limitation on the deduction in the first tax year or the recapture of the tax benefit in a subsequent year does not apply if the donee organization makes a "certification"[162] to the IRS. A certification is a written statement signed under penalty of perjury by an officer of the donee organization which either

1. certifies that the property's use was related to the donee's exempt purpose or function and describes how the property was used and how such use furthered the exempt purpose of function; or
2. states the intended use of the property by the donee at the time of the contribution and certifies that such intended use became impossible or infeasible to implement.

In essence, the claim that donated property was put to an exempt use now triggers much more scrutiny if the donee organization does not retain that property at least until the end of the third year after the property was donated.

These new rules do not apply to any contribution of exempt use property with a claimed value of $5,000 or less.

Related Use Penalty

In conjunction with the new recapture rules discussed above, there is a new penalty for the fraudulent identification of exempt use property.[163] In addition to any criminal penalty, any person who identifies applicable property (as defined in section 170(e)(7)(C)) as having a use that is related to the donee's exempt purpose or function and who knows that the contributed property is not intended for such a use is subject to a $10,000 penalty.

QUALIFIED APPRAISAL BY A QUALIFIED APPRAISER

This requirement is discussed in detail earlier in this chapter on pages 1237–1239.

CHARITABLE DEDUCTION LIMITATIONS

GENERAL PERCENTAGE LIMITATION
For contributions of cash and ordinary income property to a public charity, the charitable deduction is limited to 50% of the taxpayer's contribution base.[164] For contributions to a private charity, the limit is the smaller of (1) 30% of the taxpayer's contribution base, or (2) the excess of 50% of the taxpayer's contribution base over the amount of charitable contributions allowable to public charities, determined without regard to the 30% limitation (discussed below).[165] The term "contribution base" means adjusted gross income computed without regard to any net operating loss carryback to the taxable year under section 172.[166]

ORDINARY INCOME PROPERTY PERCENTAGE LIMITATION
The amount of the charitable deduction for a contribution of ordinary income property is limited to the basis of the property in the hands of the donor (within the applicable general percentage limitation discussed above). That result is reached because the amount of the charitable deduction is determined by subtracting from the fair market value of the property the amount of gain that would not have been long-term capital gain if the property contributed had been sold by the taxpayer at its fair market value.[167] Before making a contribution, the donor must be sure the property is capital gain property and not ordinary income property, since the available income tax deduction is substantially reduced for a contribution of ordinary income property.[168]

Any excess amount over the 50% or 30% limitations for a contribution of ordinary income property to either a public or private charity may be carried forward for five years, retaining its character as ordinary income property.[169] The carryover provision was extended to contributions made to a private charity by the Tax Reform Act of 1984, effective for contributions made in taxable years ending after October 16, 1984.

CAPITAL GAIN PROPERTY PERCENTAGE LIMITATION
A contribution to a public charity of a collection that is capital gain property and that meets the related use rule (discussed above) is allowable as a charitable deduction to the extent of the full fair market value of the property on the date of the contribution but not in excess of 30% of the taxpayer's contribution base.[170] Any amount that exceeds the 30% limitation may be carried forward for five years, retaining its character as capital gain property.[171] If the contributed collection satisfies the related use rule, the taxpayer may elect to increase the 30% limitation to 50% of her contribution base. However, if that election is made, the amount of the deduction must be reduced by 100% of the appreciation in value of the collection;[172] in other words, the deduction is limited to the donor's cost.

Before December 31, 1986, the amount of reduction required if the election was made was only 40% of the appreciation in value. Section 301(b)(2) of the Tax Reform Act of 1986 amended Internal Revenue Code section 170(e)(1) so that

100% of the appreciation in value is lost as a charitable deduction if the taxpayer elects to increase the percentage limitation for the deduction from 30% to 50%. That change has had the effect of substantially reducing the use of the election.

A contribution to a private charity of a collection that is capital gain property is allowable as a charitable deduction to the extent of the fair market value of the collection on the date of the contribution, *reduced* (regardless of what use the charity makes of the collection) by 100% of the appreciation in value. After the reduction, the deduction is limited to the smaller of (1) 20% of the taxpayer's contribution base or (2) the excess of 30% of the taxpayer's contribution base over the amount of charitable contributions allowable to public charities, determined without regard to the 30% limitation.[173] The amount of the charitable deduction that exceeds the applicable percentage limitation may be carried forward for five years for contributions made in taxable years ending after July 18, 1984.[174] The percentage limitations on lifetime gifts to private foundations and the loss of 100% of any appreciation in value as a deduction make the use of a private foundation to hold a collection impractical, unless the foundation can qualify as a "private operating foundation"[175] (see page 1297).

EXAMPLES

The chart that appears at the end of this chapter (Appendix 15-12) and the following examples illustrate the foregoing rules.

Example 1: Ms. Collector received a painting as a gift from a little-known artist. At the time of the gift, the painting had a basis of $100, representing the artist's cost for paint, canvas, and brushes. Twenty years later, after the artist had become famous, the painting has a fair market value of $10,000. If Ms. Collector now contributes the painting to an art museum, her maximum charitable deduction is $100, because the property contributed is ordinary income property. The entire $9,900 of appreciation in value is lost as a charitable deduction.

Example 2: Mr. Collector has a contribution base of $100,000. He contributes capital gain property with a fair market value of $50,000, in which he has a basis of $10,000, to a public charity. If the contribution satisfies the related use rule and there is a qualified appraisal by a qualified appraiser, Mr. Collector is allowed a deduction of $30,000 (30% of $100,000) and a carryover of $20,000. If the contribution does not satisfy the related use rule, Mr. Collector is allowed a deduction of $10,000 ($50,000 minus $40,000 appreciation equals $10,000), and there is no carryover. If there is not a qualified appraisal by a qualified appraiser, Mr. Collector would not be allowed any deduction.

Example 3: Mr. Collector has a contribution base of $100,000. He contributes capital gain property with a fair market value of $60,000 in which he has a basis of $40,000 to a public charity. If the contribution satisfies the related use rule and there is a qualified appraisal by a qualified appraiser, Mr. Collector is allowed a deduction of $30,000 (30% of $100,000) and a carryover of $30,000. If the contribution does not satisfy the related use rule or the election to increase the deduction is made, Mr. Collector is allowed a deduction of $40,000 ($60,000 minus $20,000 appreciation equals $40,000), and there is no carryover.

THE SECTION 68 LIMITATION

As discussed above, if a donor of a collection complies with the four requirements (donation to a public charity; long-term capital gain property donated; compliance with the related use rule; and obtaining a qualified appraisal by a qualified appraiser), the donor is allowed a deduction for the full fair market value of the donated property up to 30% of the donor's contribution base.[176] However, the amount of the deduction that actually benefits the donor can be subject to a limitation that may result in the loss of part of the tax benefit of the charitable deduction.

For tax years beginning after 1990, an individual whose adjusted gross income exceeds a specified threshold amount is required by section 68 of the Internal Revenue Code to reduce the amount allowable for itemized deductions by the smaller of (1) 3% of the excess of adjusted gross income over the threshold amount or (2) 80% of the total amount of the otherwise allowable itemized deductions.[177] The provision was phased out over a five-year period beginning in 2006. The overall limitation on itemized deductions imposed by section 68(a) was reduced by one-third in tax years 2006 and 2007 and by two-thirds in tax years 2008 and 2009.[178] The limitation was completely repealed for tax years beginning after December 31, 2009,[179] but is reinstated for tax years beginning in 2013.[180] The section 68(a) limitation on itemized deductions applies only after applying other limitations on itemized deductions, such as the 2% floor on miscellaneous itemized deductions.[181] The section 68 limitation could have the effect of limiting the amount of tax benefit from the charitable deduction.

ALTERNATIVE MINIMUM TAX

The Tax Reform Act of 1986 added a further complication to the process of charitable giving. Beginning in 1987 and ending on December 31, 1990, any long-term appreciation in value of property donated to a charitable organization was considered a preference item for purposes of computing the alternative minimum tax (AMT).[182] The effect of that provision was gradually to eliminate the benefits of donating appreciated long-term capital gain property. In other words, being subject to the AMT can, depending on the taxpayer's mix of income and deductions, have the economic effect of limiting the contribution to the taxpayer's cost or adjusted basis in the property.[183]

The Revenue Reconciliation Act of 1990 opened a one-year window (calendar year 1991) for contributions of tangible personal property. On December 11, 1991, President George H.W. Bush signed the Tax Extension Act of 1991, which extended the one-year period for an additional six months through June 30, 1992. Accordingly, for calendar year 1991 and for the first six months of 1992, a contribution of appreciated tangible personal property to a public charity was not subject to the alternative minimum tax. Therefore, taxpayers were able to make contributions in the year 1991 and for the first six months of 1992 and not be concerned that the appreciation in value would be subject to the AMT, which had been increased from 21% to 24% beginning in 1991.

Revenue Ruling 90-111 issued on December 14, 1990,[184] made it clear that for contributions of tangible personal property made in 1991 any excess amount above the 30% limitation carried over would also be exempted from the application of the alternative minimum tax. That ruling opened the contribution window for even highly appreciated and valuable works of art, since there is a six-year period (the year of contribution plus the five-year carryover period) to use up the full value of the contributed property as a tax deduction. The holding of Revenue Ruling 90-111 was equally applicable to any contribution of tangible personal property that was made in the first six months of 1992.

The Revenue Reconciliation Act of 1993, which was signed by President Bill Clinton on August 10, 1993, repealed section 56(a)(6) and thereby eliminated any long-term appreciation in value of tangible personal property donated to a charitable organization as a preference item for purposes of computing the alternative minimum tax.[185] Thus, the difference between the fair market value of donated appreciated property and the basis of such property is no longer a tax preference item for alternative minimum tax purposes. The new provision is effective retroactive to July 1, 1992, for donations of appreciated tangible personal property. Under the new rule, if the related use rule and other requirements are complied with, there is no longer the risk of having a charitable donation limited to the cost of the property, rather than the full fair market value.

Notwithstanding the foregoing repeal of section 56(a)(6), a collector must still take into consideration the implication of the AMT before making any large charitable contribution in order to make sure that no tax benefit from the contribution is lost. The calculation of the AMT is based on alternative minimum taxable income that includes, among other requirements, adding back to taxable income deductions for miscellaneous itemized deductions, medical expenses, taxes, and interest. Therefore, an individual with large state income tax deductions may be subject to the AMT.[186] Further, in the calculation of alternative minimum taxable income, the allowable charitable deduction is based on a percentage of the taxpayer's adjusted gross income for regular tax purposes, not for AMT purposes.[187] The safest course of action before making any contribution is for the collector to have an accountant project the potential tax savings and the application of the AMT.

CHECKLIST FOR COLLECTORS

To maximize the charitable deduction, the donor should do the following:

- Make the contribution of appreciated tangible personal property to a public charity

- Be sure that the contribution satisfies the related use rule
- Make the contribution only with long-term capital gain property
- Be sure that there is a qualified appraisal by a qualified appraiser of the contributed property
- Make the contribution when the AMT does not apply

A deed of gift should be used, and formal acceptance by the charitable organization should be indicated on the deed, as set forth in Appendix 15-2 at the end of this chapter. In addition, the deed of gift should be drafted in such a manner that it supports the taxpayer's compliance with the related use rule, and it should also require the donee organization to sign IRS Form 8283. Before the gift is made, there should be discussion and correspondence with the charitable organization to make sure that the related use rule is met. The correspondence should establish the proof necessary to meet the related use rule. Consideration should be given to the special election to increase the charitable deduction from 30% to 50% when the appreciation in the value of the property is relatively small. After the donor dies, there is no carryover of any remaining contribution deduction to her estate. (See Appendixes 15-1, 15-2, and 15-3 at the end of the chapter.)

Before making the contribution, the donor should do the following:

1. Check the type of organization—public charity or private charity
2. Check the type of property—capital gain property or ordinary income property
3. Check compliance with the related use rule
4. Do the mathematical calculation for application of the section 68 limitation
5. Consider the special election to increase the deduction from 30% to 50%
6. Prepare the deed of gift, sign it, and have it signed by the donee organization
7. Obtain a qualified appraisal by a qualified appraiser
8. Make sure that IRS Form 8283 is completed by the donee organization and the appraiser and that it is attached to the taxpayer's income tax return
9. Obtain the necessary photographs for property in excess of $20,000
10. File the gift tax return if required—under the Taxpayer Relief Act of 1997 a gift tax return is no longer required for the outright charitable transfer of the donor's entire interest in the property transferred to a charitable organization
11. Maintain the documentation for the income tax return required by the income tax regulations

If the $5,000 claimed deduction amount is reached, the new appraisal rules apply whether

(1) the donated property is capital gain property or not,
(2) the property has appreciated or depreciated in value since its acquisition by the donor,
(3) the donee is a public charity or a private foundation, and
(4) the related use rule is or is not satisfied.

Partial Inter Vivos Charitable Transfers

Although a complete transfer of a collection to a charitable organization has many tax and estate-planning advantages, the donor must still give up possession of the collection in order to receive the benefits from its transfer. Is it possible to obtain the tax and estate-planning benefits of a complete transfer and still keep possession of the collection?

RETAINED LIFE ESTATE: THE FUTURE INTEREST RULE

Before 1964, a remainder interest was deductible; reserving a life interest in a collection while enjoying an immediate deduction for the present gift of the remainder to charity was a widespread practice.[188] However, the Revenue Act of 1964 added section 170(f), now section 170(a)(3), to the Internal Revenue Code, which postpones any income tax charitable deduction for a gift of a future interest in tangible personal property until there is no intervening interest in, right of possession of, or enjoyment of the property held by the donor, the donor's spouse, or any of the donor's brothers, sisters, ancestors, or lineal descendants. That amendment was generally applicable to contributions made after December 31, 1963, and the same rule currently applies.[189]

If an individual has made a gift of a future interest in property before January 1, 1964, and has taken a charitable deduction, she can now contribute her life interest and obtain a charitable deduction based on the gift's present value and calculated in accordance with the actuarial tables of the regulations under the Internal Revenue Code.[190] Prior to April 30, 1989, the 10% actuarial tables under regulation section 20.2031-7(f) were used to value such interests. Code section 7520, effective May 1, 1989, now sets forth the tables to be used.[191]

The term "future interest" includes situations in which a donor purports to give a collection to a charitable organization but has an understanding, arrangement, or agreement (whether written or oral) with the charitable organization that has the effect of reserving to or retaining in the donor a right to the use, possession, or enjoyment of the property.[192] In other words, no present deduction is allowed if a donor gives a collection away with some sort of understanding or agreement through which the donor can borrow it back when she desires.

The contribution of a future interest does not necessarily mean that the charitable deduction is lost; it may only be postponed. Regulation section 1.170A-5(a)(5) provides that the other provisions of section 170 are applicable to a contribution until the contribution is treated as made under section 170(a)(3).

Example 1: In 2012, Mr. Collector transferred a painting to an art museum by deed of gift but reserved to himself the right to the use, possession, and enjoyment of the painting during his lifetime. The value of the painting in 2012 was $90,000. Since the contribution consisted of a future interest, no deduction was allowed in 2012.

Example 2: The same facts as in example 1 apply except that in 2014 Mr. Collector relinquished all his rights to the use, possession, and enjoyment of the painting and delivered it to the museum. If the value was $100,000 in 2014, Mr. Collector was entitled to a deduction of $100,000 in 2014, subject to the applicable percentage limitations.

The above examples, which are similar to those in the regulations, can be a trap for the unwary. If a charitable transfer of a remainder interest in a collection is made, the donor, as indicated above, does not receive a current charitable deduction. The danger is that she may incur a current gift tax liability. Under section 2522(c)(2) and regulation section 25.2522(c)-3(c)(1), there is no gift tax charitable deduction for a transfer of the remainder interest in a collection. However, since a transfer of the remainder interest has taken place, there is a transfer subject to the gift tax.[193]

Under Revenue Ruling 77-225, 1977-2 C.B. 73, a taxpayer claimed a charitable-contribution deduction for a donation of a rare book collection. However, the taxpayer retained for his life the right of full access to the collection and the right to deny access to others. The IRS ruled that the taxpayer was not entitled to a charitable deduction, since the rights the taxpayer retained were equivalent to the retention of substantial rights to actual possession and enjoyment of the collection. Therefore, the gift was a donation of a future interest in tangible personal property, which is not deductible under section 170(a)(3). Although the ruling did not cover the gift tax question, we believe that a taxable gift was made.[194]

The future-interest rule of section 170(a)(3) must be read in conjunction with the partial-interest rule of section 170(f)(3)(A), which denies a deduction for a partial interest in property with certain exceptions not applicable to tangible personal property unless that interest is in the form of an annuity trust or unitrust, which gives the beneficiary a fixed annual percentage of the fair market value. However, if there is no intention to avoid the application of section 170(f)(3)(A) by the conveyance, it appears that the rule does not apply.[195]

Example 3: In 2012, Mr. Collector transferred to his sons a life interest in a painting and on the same date transferred the remainder interest to charity with the intention of avoiding section 170(f)(3)(A). No deduction was allowed to Mr. Collector for his remainder interest. If there had been no intention of avoiding section 170(f)(3)(A), section 170(a)(3) would still have prevented any current deduction, and there would have been a gift tax on the present interest and the remainder interest.

Therefore, for all practical purposes a remainder interest in a collection should never be transferred to a charitable organization.[196]

However, the foregoing discussion does not apply to transfers of a remainder interest in a collection made in trust. That type of transfer is governed by sections 170(f)(2) and 170(f)(3)(A), which denies any income tax charitable deduction for the value of a remainder interest in trust unless the trust is a charitable remainder annuity trust, a charitable remainder unitrust, or a pooled income fund as those terms are defined in sections 664 and 642(c)(5). With certain exceptions discussed below, the practical effect of sections 170(f)(2) and 170(f)(3)(A) is to deny any income tax charitable deduction for the value of a remainder interest in a collection transferred in trust because such non-income-producing property cannot be put in the form of a guaranteed annuity, nor can it pay out a fixed yearly percentage of its fair market value. (See discussion of charitable remainder trusts at pages 1289–1296.)

Fractional Gifts Before August 17, 2006

Prior to August 17, 2006, the collector who wanted to give away a collection and still enjoy its possession on a part-time basis could convey an undivided fractional interest in the property to a charity. The transfer of an undivided fractional interest was not a transfer of a future interest that ran afoul of section 170(a)(3) or section 170(f).[197] Therefore, an immediate charitable deduction was allowable for the value of the undivided fractional interest donated. In the case of James I. Winokur,[198] the court held that it is the right to entitlement or possession, not actual physical possession, that controls whether a purported present interest is to be regarded as a future interest.

For example, Ms. Collector transferred an undivided one-fourth present interest in a painting to an art museum by deed of gift. She was entitled to the possession of the painting for nine months each year, and the museum was entitled to possession for three months each year. Ms. Collector could deduct one-fourth of the fair market value of the painting as a charitable contribution on the date of the gift, subject to the permissible maximum.

The IRS position was to accept as the allowable charitable deduction the undivided percentage of the fair market value given to the charitable organization. Presumably, that position was based on Revenue Ruling 57-293,[199] which gives a specific example covering that situation. The part of that ruling dealing with a gift of a future interest is no longer applicable because of section 170(f).

Fractional Gifts After August 17, 2006

The Internal Revenue Service was concerned that there was abuse of the fractional gift technique: situations were discovered where a taxpayer claimed a deduction for a fractional interest in a work of art yet retained physical possession of the donated property for the full year. Under new section 170(o) introduced by the PPA, effective for contributions made after August 17, 2006, fractional gifts are no longer desirable.

Valuation Limitation

Under section 170(o), the collector's initial contribution of a fractional interest in a work of art is determined as under current law and described above (full fair market value times the fractional interest donated). For purposes of determining the deductible amount of each additional contribution in the same work of art, the fair market value of the donated item is now limited to the *lesser* of (1) the value used for purposes of determining the charitable deduction for the initial fractional contribution or (2) the fair market value of the item at the time of the subsequent contribution.[200] For example, the collector who gives away a 50% interest in a painting when it is worth $1,000,000 would still be able to claim a $500,000 deduction. However, when the collector donates the remaining 50% interest ten years later when the painting is worth $2,000,000, the collector's donation would be limited to 50% of the initial fair market value of $1,000,000— that is, $500,000—not 50% of the $2,000,000 current value.

Timing Limitation

The collector must complete the donation of his entire interest in the work of art before the earlier of (1) ten years from the initial fractional contribution or (2) the donor's death.[201] If the donee charity is no longer in existence, the collector's remaining interest may be contributed to another section 170(c) organization.

Use Limitation

Under the new provisions, the donee charity of a fractional interest in a work of art must (1) have substantial physical possession of the work of art during the donor-allowed possession period (maximum of ten years) and (2) use the work of art for an exempt use during such period—that is, satisfy the related-use rule.[202] The Joint Committee on Taxation Report[203] gives an example of an art museum described in section 501(c)(3) that is the donee of a fractional interest in a painting and that includes the painting in an art exhibit sponsored by the museum: such use generally will be treated as satisfying the related-use requirement. However, that report provides no example as to the meaning of "substantial physical possession." For example, if a collector donates a 10% fractional interest in a painting to a museum and plans on donating the remaining 90% ten years later, does the collector violate the substantial physical possession rule if the museum has physical possession over the ten-year period for only 10% of that period? The regulations will need to clarify this provision, but if the museum has physical possession for a period of time equal to the donated percentage interest, that should be sufficient to satisfy this requirement.

Recapture of Deduction

If the collector violates the ten-year timing limitation or the use limitation (the substantial possession or related-use requirement), then the collector's charitable income and gift tax deductions for all previous contributions of interests in the work of art are recaptured plus interest.[204] In any case in which there is a recapture of a deduction, the statute also imposes an additional tax in an amount equal to 10% of the amount recaptured.

DENIAL OF DEDUCTION

No income or gift tax deduction is allowed for a contribution of a fractional interest in a work of art unless immediately before such contribution all interests in the work of art are owned (1) by the collector or (2) by the collector and the donee organization.[205] The IRS is authorized to make exceptions to this rule in cases where all persons who hold an interest in the work of art make proportional contributions of undivided interests in their respective shares of the work to the donee organization. For example, if collector A owns an undivided 50% interest in a painting and his brother, collector B, owns the other undivided 50% interest in the same painting, the IRS may (under regulations to be issued) provide that A may take a deduction for a charitable contribution of less than the entire interest held by A, provided that both A and B make proportional contributions of undivided fractional interests in their respective shares of the painting to the same donee organization (for example, A contributes 25% of A's interest and B contributes 25% of B's interest).

DANGER OF FRACTIONAL GIFTS AND THE REPEAL

The PPA contained similar limitations as described above for gift and estate tax purposes.[206] Like the income tax provision, the estate tax provision limited the estate tax charitable deduction to the lesser of (1) the fair market value at the time of the initial fractional contribution or (2) the fair market value at the time of the subsequent contribution.[207] In order to avoid the recapture of the income tax deduction, the transfer to the donee charity must be completed by the earlier of (1) ten years from the initial contribution or (2) the donor's death. For example, the collector who gives away a 50% interest in a painting to a museum when it is worth $1,000,000 would receive a $500,000 income tax deduction. If the collector dies four years later when he still owns the remaining 50% interest and if the painting is then worth $2,000,000, his estate tax charitable deduction is limited to $500,000, that is, 50% of the initial value of $1,000,000 for the 50% interest. This would mean that the collector's estate would have a 50% interest in a painting going to a museum with a value of $1,000,000 (for the 50% interest) for which the estate was only entitled to a $500,000 deduction, resulting in the estate's having to pay an estate tax on the remaining $500,000. This is a trap for the uninformed and was not the result intended by the legislation. On December 29, 2007, President Bush signed the Tax Technical Corrections Act of 2007.[208] The Act repealed the changes made to the estate tax and the gift tax that resulted in the tax trap described above in this paragraph. The net effect of this change is as if the special valuation limitation (value at time of initial gift) never existed for estate and gift tax purposes.

PLANNING

If the valuation limitation described above is changed (which seems doubtful at the time of publication of this book), then fractional gifts may still be useful for a collector who owns a very valuable work of art and therefore needs to spread the deduction for the initial value over a twelve-year period (year of donation plus five-year carryover for two transfers). For example, assume a painting with a fair market value of $5,000,000 owned by an individual with an average yearly adjusted gross income (AGI) of $1,000,000. Since the maximum allowable charitable deduction is 30% of AGI, his maximum deduction if the entire painting was donated is $1,800,000 ($300,000 × 6; that is, 30% of AGI and a five-year carryover). If a one-half fractional interest in the painting is donated, the same $1,800,000 deduction over a six-year period is allowable (50% of $5,000,000 is $2,500,000). In year seven, the individual can donate the remaining 50% interest in the painting and receive another $1,800,000 deduction spread over the following six years. Since the initial value of the painting is high, the individual would not be concerned with loss of the appreciation in value of the painting as a deduction. However, until there is a change in the tax code, this type of fractional gift should not be made.

FRACTIONAL INTEREST—VALUATION ISSUES

When the collector dies, the value of the undivided fractional interest that was kept by the collector is included in her estate.[209] Because of Revenue Ruling 57-293, it is difficult to argue that if the retained undivided interest is bequeathed to a noncharitable beneficiary, there should be a discount for the minority undivided interest retained. The first case that bears on this issue is *Estate of Robert C. Scull v. Commissioner*,[210] in which the value of the decedent's 65% undivided interest in an art collection was reduced by 5% to reflect the uncertainties involved in any acquisition of the interest, which was the result of a divorce proceeding still being appealed. If the bequest is made to a person who does not own the other part of the interest, the taxpayer should have a fair chance of convincing the IRS to allow some discount for the fractional interest. If the bequest is made to a museum that already owns a partial interest in the artwork, the estate tax charitable deduction should be the percentage owned by the decedent multiplied by the full fair market value of the painting on the decedent's date of death. Generally, before a museum will accept a fractional gift, it wants assurances that it will receive the balance of the undivided interest when the collector dies. The museum does not want to be left owning a fractional interest in a work of art with the donor's heirs fighting over the remaining fractional interest. Therefore, the collector should always discuss such a gift with the museum before making it. The issue of the value of the noncharitable fractional interest owned at death is discussed below in some detail.

Private Letter Ruling 93-03-007 should be reviewed by anyone contemplating a donation of a fractional interest in a collection. The IRS ruled that the charitable deduction for the gift of an undivided fractional interest equals the product of (1) the fraction and (2) the fair market value (determined without regard to the existence of a certain loan agreement) of the entire work of art at the date of the gift of the fractional interest.[211] Under a gift-loan agreement, the taxpayer in that private letter ruling imposed conditions requiring continuous display of the collection and editorial control over publicity concerning the collection. If those conditions were not complied with, the collection would revert to the donor or his heirs. The IRS ruled that such conditions had no effect on the gift, since the chance that the work would revert to the estate of the donor is so remote as to be negligible.[212]

When a fractional interest in a collection is donated to a charitable organization, the organization usually requires the donor to promise to donate or bequeath the balance to the organization. Private Letter Ruling 93-03-007 also states that when one promises to transfer property in the future, the gift tax consequences of the promise are judged as of the time at which it is possible to determine that the transfer must be made and that the transfer will be of a determinable amount. Therefore, the mere execution of a promised-gift agreement does not constitute a taxable gift, because at that time it is not possible to determine that the future transfer must be made by the donor. The promised gift could be satisfied by the donor's estate.

More recently, Private Letter Ruling 200223013 dealt with fourteen separate rulings pertaining to the federal income, gift, and estate tax consequences of gifts of fractional interest in works of art to be made by a married couple to a tax-exempt museum. The proposed gift was subject to a detailed and comprehensive gift and loan agreement (GLA) that contained a number of restrictions and limitations. So long as the museum complied with the GLA, the donors were not permitted to transfer during their lifetimes (or at the death of the first of them to die) by gift or otherwise any item of artwork to any party other than to each other or the museum. If the museum complied with the GLA, then the donors (or their legal representative) were obligated at a date no later than the death of the last to die of the donors to transfer to the museum all of the donors' remaining ownership interests in the artworks. If the museum breached the GLA, the artwork was to be distributed to other charitable organizations. Under the GLA, the museum was required to hold and display the artwork subject to numerous conditions, including that the museum was required to obtain the donors' consent to any changes in the gallery or installation design. In addition, the museum was permitted to deaccession any artwork, but only to the extent such work was replaced with a similar item of artwork

(1) typified by the collection,
(2) that is consistent with the spirit of the collection, and
(3) that has a value substantially equal to the value of the deaccessioned artwork in the collection.

Upon the death of the donors, these approval rights transferred to their daughter.

For income tax purposes, the IRS held, following the formula in Private Letter Ruling 93-03-007, that the amount of the income tax deduction allowable for a fractional interest is equal to the percentage of the artwork donated multiplied by the fair market value of the entire artwork. No reduction in the amount of the income tax deduction is required because only a fractional interest was donated or because of the restrictions placed on the donee with regard to the artwork as described above.

For estate tax purposes, the IRS ruled that the approval rights retained by the donor that pass to her successors in interest have no value for federal estate tax purposes under sections 2031 and 2033. The IRS also ruled that because the artwork will pass to other charitable organizations if the museum breaches the GLA, there is no possibility that the items will pass for other than a charitable purpose as defined in section 2055(a) and, hence, the value of the bequest will qualify for the federal estate tax charitable deduction under section 2055. Moreover, the IRS determined that the amount includable in the donor's gross estate under sections 2031 and 2033 with respect to the retained undivided fractional interest is the fair market value of the item of artwork multiplied by the donor's fractional interest therein and that the amount deductible under section 2055 with respect to such item is the value included in the donor's gross estate.

Finally, the IRS ruled with respect to the federal estate tax that when the donor died the bequest to the donor's spouse of any retained fractional interest in the artwork will qualify for the federal estate tax marital deduction permitted under section 2056(b)(7) (assuming the required election is made). The ruling went on to confirm that the amount of the marital deduction is the fair market value of the artwork (determined without regard to the existence of the GLA) multiplied by the fraction of the artwork transferred to the surviving spouse. This avoids any potential problem that the estate inclusion amount under section 2031 may not be the same amount as either the charitable deduction under section 2044 or the marital deduction under section 2056.[213]

As discussed above, fractional gifts to a museum are no longer advisable. However, should the valuation rule change so that appreciation in value is allowable as a deduction, the donor should also be aware of the following questions that should be answered before making the donation.

1. Who will pay for packing and transportation each time the collection is moved?
2. Who will pay for insurance? Generally, the donor's insurance covers the collection when it is in the donor's possession, and the museum's insurance covers the collection when it is in the museum's possession. Insurance coverage during the packing and shipping period should be discussed.
3. In the future operation of the museum, what will be done with the collection, how will it be exhibited, and will the museum consult with the donor?
4. Does the museum have an endowment; if so, how are funds allocated to its operation? As the museum expands in size, its expenses will increase. Will there be a special curator for the collection, and how will the curator be selected and paid?

5. What, if any, involvement will the donor have with respect to the exhibition of the collection at the museum?

6. What will happen if the artwork is damaged? Every time art is moved, there is always the risk of some damage. There should be some procedure involving condition reports, and perhaps some works of art should not be moved every year. For example, some Calder mobiles are susceptible to damage every time they are packed and rehung.

A review of the IRS interpretation of fractional gifts beginning with Revenue Ruling 57-293 and then Private Letter Rulings 93-03-007, 200223013, and 200418002 shows that the IRS has been consistent in its interpretation for income tax, gift tax, and estate tax that the proper approach for determining the amount of the deduction, whether the work of art is donated during lifetime or is transferred at death, is to take the full fair market value of the work of art multiplied by the percentage transferred. The same methodology is true whether the work of art is transferred to charity or to a noncharitable beneficiary, that is, a member of the taxpayer's family. In other words, fractional interests in works of art seem to receive a different treatment than fractional interest in real estate or other assets for which it is fairly common to claim a discount for lack of control, minority ownership, or lack of 100% interest.[214]

Perhaps works of art are treated differently because one can still fully enjoy a work of art for a percentage of the time and, in fact, that percentage may have a market value equal to the percentage multiplied by the fair market value of the work of art. Accordingly, in light of the foregoing rulings, if one is thinking of transferring works of art to family members either during one's lifetime or on death, it should not be assumed that the discounts usually available for lack of a 100% ownership interest will be available.

LEASEBACK

A collector may donate a collection to a charity and then seek to lease it back at its fair rental value, but the rent paid is not a deductible charitable gift. In theory, that technique produces a charitable deduction for the property itself at the time of the gift, and the collection should not be included as part of the donor's estate. However, if the rent is too low, the IRS may claim that the taxpayer has retained a life estate under section 2036(a), which would make the collection includable in the gross estate. However, the fair rental value would probably be prohibitively high, and the charity would probably not participate in such an arrangement, since the rent paid might constitute unrelated business income. Furthermore, there is no independent method to determine the rental value of art and the taxpayer would be in a largely indefensible position in trying to set a rental value. Therefore, as a practical matter, the gift-leaseback technique is not workable except under unusual circumstances.[215]

LIMITED PRESENT INTEREST

Before January 1, 1970, a transfer of a present interest in a collection to a charity for an immediate, limited period, with the remainder interest going to a noncharitable donee other than the donor, resulted in a current charitable deduction. That type of transfer was used when the taxpayer desired an immediate income tax deduction and wanted to make a gift of the collection to a member of her family in the future.

The Tax Reform Act of 1969 changed that result by providing that a charitable deduction is not to be allowed for contributions to a charity of less than the taxpayer's entire interest in the property, except to the extent a deduction would be allowed under the act if the interest had been transferred in trust.[216] The effect of that amendment is to deny any charitable deduction for a contribution of the right to the present use of the collection for a period of time, since such non-income-producing property cannot be put in the form of a guaranteed annuity, nor can it pay out a fixed percentage yearly of its fair market value.[217] Therefore, the transfer of a limited present interest is an unacceptable form of contribution.

However, a deduction is allowed if the present interest is the taxpayer's entire interest and the partial interest in the collection was not created in order to avoid the restrictions under the Internal Revenue Code.[218] For example, if a taxpayer made a contribution of a remainder interest in a collection before 1964 and now wishes to contribute the present interest that she retained, the taxpayer may take a deduction for that interest.

GIFT ANNUITIES

Large charitable organizations have gift annuity plans that allow an individual to transfer a collection to charity in return for an annuity for life.[219] Briefly, a gift of a collection to a charitable organization in return for a lifetime annuity has the following features:

1. There is an income tax charitable deduction for the difference between the fair market value of the collection and the present value of the annuity.[220] All the rules discussed above that govern the amount of the deduction apply.
2. The present value of the annuity is determined by comparison with a comparable commercial contract, and the fair market value of the collection is determined by an appraisal.
3. The taxpayer has to recognize a capital gain, spread over the period of the annuity, on the difference between the basis for the collection and the present value of the annuity. The basis for the collection must be allocated between the value of the annuity and the fair market value of the collection in accordance with the bargain sale rules, discussed below.[221]

BARGAIN SALE

A bargain sale of a collection to a charitable organization occurs when the collection is sold to a charity for an amount less than its fair market value by an individual with donative intent. A bargain sale has elements of both a sale and a gift. The sale element is the sales price the collector charges. The gift element is the difference between the sales price paid by the charity and the fair market value of the collection sold to the charity.

A bargain sale[222] of a collection to a charitable organization has the following tax features:

1. The basis of the property must be allocated between the sale portion and the gift portion.
2. The sale portion is subject to taxation—capital gain or ordinary income.
3. The gift portion is allowed as a charitable deduction to the extent of its fair market value. All the rules discussed above that govern the amount of the deduction apply.

There is a greater than usual problem of proof of fair market value on a bargain sale to a charitable organization; therefore, it may be prudent to obtain two appraisals. In addition, the donor bears the burden of proof to show that she had the requisite donative intent that must be present for any gift to charity. When a donor makes an outright gift to a charity, the donative intent is usually presumed to exist. In the case of a bargain sale, the facts may suggest that there was no donative intent, in which case no charitable deduction is allowed. For example, negotiations between the charity and the donor may suggest that the seller sought a high price but agreed to a lower price simply because the charity would not pay the high price. An attempt by the donor to characterize the sale as a bargain-sale donation after the fact is likely to fail, even when a subsequent appraisal shows the fair market value to be greater than the sale price.[223] Therefore, from the outset of negotiations, the donor must make the donative intent clear (perhaps expressed as a fraction of the value of the collection) and must memorialize the donative element in the final bargain-sale agreement.

The bargain-sale donation is a useful planning technique for an individual with some charitable intention. For example, an elderly client with most of her assets tied up in a valuable collection who does not have enough income can first sell the collection to a charitable organization under the bargain-sale rules. Doing so gives her cash to invest to increase current income. The long-term capital gains tax rate of 28% (collectibles are taxed at a higher rate than the long-term capital gain rate of 15% that applies to the sale of securities) and the allowable charitable deductions, combined with the bargain-sale rules, satisfies the client's need to increase current income, leaves an estate to pass on to any heirs, and does so at little tax cost. There is no substitute for actually working out the mathematical calculations for each client.

LOANS TO CHARITIES

Before 1988, there was concern that the loan of a work of art to a charitable organization would be treated as a transfer subject in part to federal gift tax. Section 7872(a)(1) treats an interest-free loan as a transfer of the interest on the loan from the lender to the borrower. The "interest" is the value of the use of the work of art. No income tax charitable deduction is allowed for such a transfer since it is a split-interest transfer and not in the form for which a deduction is allowed. The Technical and Miscellaneous Revenue Act of 1988 amended section 2503 retroactively to July 31, 1969, by adding a new subsection 2503(g) to provide that a loan of a "qualified work of art" to a public charity or a private operating foundation for use in carrying on its charitable purpose will not be treated as a transfer for federal gift tax purposes.[224] For other transfer tax purposes, the work is valued as if the loan had not been made. Thus, the estate of a decedent-owner of a qualified work of art on loan at the time of her death includes the full value of the work of art in the decedent's estate for federal estate tax purposes. A "qualified work of art" is any archaeological, historic, or creative tangible personal property.[225] The provision is effective for transfers occurring after July 31, 1969. A loan of a work of art to a private foundation (other than a private operating foundation) is a taxable gift.

CHARITABLE REMAINDER TRUST: INTER VIVOS

Section 664 sets forth the requirements for a charitable remainder trust. Generally, a charitable remainder trust must provide for the distribution of a specific amount, at least annually, to one or more persons, at least one of whom is a noncharitable beneficiary.[226] The payment period must be for the life or lives of the individual beneficiaries or for a term of years, not in excess of twenty years. At the termination of the noncharitable interest, the remainder must be paid to one or more exempt organizations described in section 170(c). The charitable remainder trust is exempt from income tax, so the trustee can sell assets without the payment of capital gains tax and the grantor of the trust is entitled to an income tax deduction based on the present value of the remainder interest as calculated under the provisions of section 664.

There are two types of charitable remainder trusts: annuity trust and unitrust. A charitable remainder annuity trust is required to pay a fixed yearly sum to the noncharitable beneficiary equal to at least 5% but not more than 50% of the fair market value of the trust assets, valued as of the date the trust is created.[227] In other words, the annuity trust payment remains constant over the term of the trust. A charitable remainder unitrust is required to pay a fixed yearly sum to the noncharitable beneficiary equal to at least 5% but not more than 50% of the fair market value of the trust assets valued each year on the valuation date.[228] In other words, the unitrust payment changes each year, depending on the value of the trust assets on the valuation date. The Taxpayer Relief Act of 1997 added the 50% limitation referred to above and added a new requirement for both annuity trusts and unitrusts that the value (determined under the section 7520 valuation tables) of the remainder interest going to the charitable organization is at least 10% of the initial net fair market value of the property placed in the trust. The new provisions are effective for transfers in trust after July 28, 1997.

A detailed discussion of charitable remainder trusts is beyond the scope of this chapter. The following brief analysis focuses on issues relevant to the use of tangible personal property with a charitable remainder trust.

COLLECTION KEPT FOR TRUST TERM

A collector may use a charitable remainder unitrust or annuity trust to sell the collection during the first year of the trust. A collection may have a low cost and be worth a great deal of money. If a collector who is in need of income sells it at auction, she will have to pay approximately one-third of the gain in federal and state income taxes, leaving only the balance to be invested to produce income. Instead, if the collector contributes the collection to a charitable remainder unitrust or annuity trust and the trust is the seller, the collection may be sold tax-free, and the collector gets an income tax charitable deduction and the trust keeps the one-third of the gain that would have gone in income taxes for future investment to produce a greater amount of income for the collector. The trust instrument should direct the sale in the first year of any non-income-producing property to avoid any problem under sections 170(a)(3) or 170(f)(2)(A).

As previously discussed, section 170(a)(3) prevents any charitable deduction of a future interest in tangible personal property when there is an outright transfer to a charitable organization. If, however, the transfer of the collection is to be made in trust, that type of transfer must first be examined under section 170(a)(3) and then be governed by section 170(f)(2)(A). A split-interest transfer in trust is governed by section 170(f)(2)(A), which denies any income tax charitable deduction for the value of a remainder interest in trust unless the trust is a charitable remainder annuity trust, a charitable remainder unitrust, or a pooled income fund, as those terms are defined in sections 664 and 642(c)(5). With one possible exception, discussed below, the effect of section 170(f)(2)(A) is to make a transfer of that type impractical, since non-income-producing property, such as a work of art, cannot be put in the form of a guaranteed annuity, nor can it pay out a fixed yearly percentage of its fair market value.

A charitable remainder unitrust is permitted to pay out only its income if that income is less than the stated payout percentage—a so-called net income method charitable remainder unitrust (NIMCRUT). However, if from the outset it is clear that the property put in trust will never produce any income, the charitable deduction may be denied on the ground that a valid charitable remainder unitrust was not created, since the trust cannot make an annual payment. The regulations[229] issued under section 664 indicate that a charitable remainder unitrust must make an annual payment to the noncharitable beneficiary. The regulations make no mention of a remainder interest in non-income-producing property, such as a work of art. The only exceptions to the required unitrust form for a remainder interest in property given to a charity are contained in section

170(f)(3)(B)(i), which concerns a remainder interest in a personal residence or a farm.

In addition, a remainder trust created with a collection has to satisfy the future interest rule of section 170(a)(3), which postpones any income tax charitable deduction for a gift of a future interest in tangible personal property until there is no intervening interest in, right of possession of, or enjoyment of the property held by the donor, the donor's spouse, or any of the donor's brothers, sisters, ancestors, or lineal descendants.

The regulations state that a remainder trust does not qualify under section 664 if its governing instrument contains a

provision which restricts the trustee from investing the trust assets in a manner which could result in the annual realization of a reasonable amount of income or gain from the sale or disposition of trust assets.[230]

In Revenue Ruling 73-610, 1973-2 C.B. 213, the grantor of an irrevocable trust contributed a collection of antiques, in addition to income-producing assets, to a trust. The governing instrument of the trust provided that the grantor's wife, who was the sole income beneficiary of the trust for her life, should have the use of the antique collection for her life. At her death, the antique collection and all the remaining assets in the trust were to be distributed to a charitable tax-exempt organization. In all other respects, the trust complied with the provisions of section 664 defining charitable remainder trusts. The IRS held that the retention of a life estate in the antiques collection for the grantor's wife restricted the trustee from investing all the trust assets in a manner that could result in the annual realization of a reasonable amount of income or gain from the sale or disposition of the trust assets. Therefore, the trust did not qualify as a charitable remainder trust. Similarly, in Revenue Ruling 76-165, 1976-1 C.B. 279, the IRS held that a remainder interest in household furnishings that were bequeathed to a surviving spouse for life and then to a charitable organization did not qualify as a deductible remainder interest.[231]

Therefore, a work of art that is to be held for the trust term will probably disqualify the trust from being a charitable remainder unitrust or a charitable remainder annuity trust, and there will be no income tax charitable deduction.

COLLECTION SOLD WITHIN FIRST YEAR

One way to deal with Revenue Ruling 73-610 is to specifically direct and empower the trustee to sell any non-income-producing property (the work of art) at her discretion within the taxable year of its receipt by the trust. In such a case, the trustee is not *restricted* from investing the assets in a manner that could result in the annual realization of a reasonable amount of income or gain from the sale or the disposition of trust assets. A Private Letter Ruling[232] gives some support to that position.

In Private Letter Ruling 94-52-026 the taxpayer created an inter vivos charitable remainder annuity trust that was to be funded with publicly traded securities and an appreciated musical instrument. The taxpayer was not in the business of dealing in musical instruments, nor did he depreciate the instrument, since it did not have a determinable useful life. In other words, the instrument was a capital asset, and the exception contained in section 1221(a)(2) did not apply. The taxpayer requested a number of specific rulings, including the following:

1. That the trust qualifies as a charitable remainder annuity trust under section 664(d)(1)
2. That the charitable contribution of the musical instrument contributed to the trust is deductible to the extent of the charitable remainder interest
3. That in accordance with sections 170(b)(1)(C)(i), 2055(a)(2), and 2522(a)(2), provided there is no prearranged contract for the sale of the musical instrument, if the trust sells the musical instrument before the end of the calendar year in which the musical instrument is contributed to the trust, the charitable contribution is deductible up to 30% of the contribution base and, because the musical instrument has been sold, section 170(a)(3) does not apply
4. That provided there are no prearranged contracts for the sale of the property contributed to the trust, the taxpayer does not realize gain with respect to the property sold by the trust, and any gain is properly reportable by the trust, and the beneficiary includes in income only such amounts of income or gain distributed by the trust.

The IRS refused to rule on whether the trust qualifies as a charitable remainder annuity trust. The ruling relied on Revenue Procedure 94-3, 1994-1 I.R.B. 79, which sets forth sample provisions for charitable remainder trusts; the ruling also stated that taxpayers relying on such provisions can be assured that the IRS will recognize the trust as meeting all the requirements of a charitable remainder annuity trust.

The ruling then discussed section 170(a)(3) and noted that it provides that payment of a charitable contribution consisting of a future interest in tangible personal property shall be treated as made only when all intervening interests in and rights to the actual possession or enjoyment of the property have expired or are held by persons other than the taxpayer or by those related to the taxpayer, as described in section 267(b) or 707(b).[233] The ruling than went on to conclude that because the musical instrument is tangible personal property, section 170(a)(3) prevents any deduction for the remainder interest as long as the trust retains it, because the taxpayer as the annuity trust beneficiary has retained an income interest in the musical instrument. The ruling then added the following important statement:

> However, an income tax deduction would be allowed under section 170(a)(3) when the trustee sells the musical instrument. When the musical instrument is sold, the taxpayer no longer retains an intervening interest in the tangible personal prop-

erty as contemplated under section 170(a)(3), that is, the taxpayer is only holding an income interest in the sale proceeds from the musical instrument. Accordingly, the taxpayer's intervening interest in the musical instrument is treated as terminated upon its sale.

The ruling also concluded that the sale by the trust would be treated as putting the musical instrument to an unrelated use for section 170(e)(1)(B)(i) purposes—that is, the related use rule would not be satisfied.[234] Accordingly, the taxpayer's charitable deduction was reduced to the portion of the taxpayer's basis that was allocable to the remainder interest in the musical instrument.

In discussing the capital gain issue, the ruling relied on *Palmer v. Commissioner*.[235] The donor in *Palmer* had voting control of both a corporation and a tax-exempt private foundation. Pursuant to a single plan, the donor contributed shares of the corporation's stock to the foundation and then caused the corporation to redeem the stock from the foundation. The Tax Court held that the transfer of stock to the foundation was a valid gift and that the capital gain was not attributable to the donor since the foundation was not bound to go through with the redemption at the time it received title to the shares. In the case of the musical instrument, the ruling stated that since there was no prearranged sale contract whereby the trust was legally bound to sell the musical instrument, the taxpayer was not required to recognize any gain from the sale of the musical instrument.

Creating a charitable remainder unitrust or annuity trust to sell a work of art during the first year of the trust can be a useful planning technique. Private Letter Ruling 94-52-026 now gives some degree of comfort that the planning technique does work, even though a private letter ruling is binding only on the taxpayer who requested it. A work of art may have a low cost and be worth a great deal of money. If a collector in need of income sells it, she has to pay approximately one-third of the gain in federal and state income taxes, leaving only the balance to be invested to produce income. Instead, if the collector contributes the work of art to a charitable remainder unitrust and the trust is the seller, the work of art can be sold tax-free, and the trust keeps the one-third of the gain that would have been paid in income taxes.[236] Since the trust has more capital from the saved tax payment, it can produce more income for the collector. The collector can also claim a charitable deduction. However, the amount of the deduction is limited to the price the collector paid for the work of art (her cost), which is allocated to the remainder interest in the work of art since such a contribution does not satisfy the related use rule.

The trust instrument should direct the sale of any non-income-producing property in the year of receipt to avoid any problem under sections 170(a)(3) and 170(f)(2)(A). A direction in the trust instrument to sell any non-income-producing property should not run afoul of the Pomona College problem, in which appreciated securities were contributed to a tax-exempt organization with a promise that the securities would be sold and invested in tax-exempt securities and a tax-exempt annuity paid to the donor. In such a case, the IRS has held that the donor is taxable on the gain realized on the sale of the securities.[237] With respect to a charitable remainder unitrust, the trustee has no obligation to invest in tax-exempt securities, and the annual distributions out of the unitrust are characterized as either taxable ordinary income or taxable long-term capital gain, even if the trustee invests in tax-exempt securities.[238]

Subject to certain limitations, a grantor may serve as the trustee of her own charitable remainder trust.[239] If a collection is to be used to fund the charitable remainder trust, it is preferable to use an independent trustee, even if the collection will be sold in the first year of the trust. The House Ways and Means Committee stated the following in its report on unitrusts:

> It is contemplated that a charitable contribution deduction would be denied where assets which do not have an objective ascertainable market value, such as real estate or stock in a closely held corporation, are transferred in trust, unless an independent trustee is the sole party responsible for making the annual determination of value.[240]

That requirement was incorporated into the regulations on December 10, 1998, and it should serve as a warning for a grantor who wishes to be a trustee of her charitable remainder trust when it is funded with a collection.[241] The regulation requires a trustee who is the grantor of her own charitable remainder trust to rely on a yearly qualified appraisal by a qualified appraiser to value unmarketable assets, like an art collection.[242] An independent trustee would not need to use a qualified appraisal by a qualified appraiser to value unmarketable assets.[243]

Even if the trustee sells the collection in the first year of the trust, the amount of the allowable charitable deduction available for the collector is limited to that portion of the collector's cost which is allocable to the remainder interest of the work of art, since the transfer to the charitable remainder trust of a work of art that will be sold does not satisfy the related use rule of section 170(e)(1)(B)(i).[244] Regulation section 1.170A-4(b)(3)(i) provides as follows:

> The use by a trust of tangible personal property contributed to it for the benefit of a charitable organization is an unrelated use if the use by the trust is one which would have been unrelated if made by the charitable organization.

Although the regulation is not entirely clear, it causes a problem, because the trust is making no use of the property contributed to it; to qualify as a charitable remainder unitrust, the trust cannot hold non-income-producing property. An argument for the full charitable deduction (the key is to satisfy the related use rule) can be made as follows: If the property was contributed directly to the remainderman charity (the organization that will receive the principal of the trust after the death of the noncharitable income beneficiary) and if it was reasonable to anticipate that the remainderman charity would not have put the property to an unrelated use, the related use rule is satisfied, and the charitable deduction should be allowable in full. The problem is convincing the IRS that it was reasonable to anticipate such use. The argument may be enhanced if the contributed property is sold to the designated remainderman charity by the trustee. There is, however, no authority for that position, and without a specific IRS ruling we do not recommend it.

One commentator has made the following suggestion: If the charitable remainderman of the trust is a grant-making foundation, described in section 170(b)(1)(A)(iv), whose function is to receive, hold, invest, and administer property and make expenditures for the benefit of a college or university, then a sale by the trust of a work of art would satisfy the related use rule, since the sale would produce funds that would eventually allow the remainderman charity to make grants.[245] That appears to be a very aggressive position; although the trust may qualify as a charitable remainder unitrust, there would be no charitable deduction above the collector's cost of the contributed property.

As noted earlier in this chapter, and worth repeating here, the Taxpayer Relief Act of 1997 added two new provisions that must be considered in the creation of a charitable remainder annuity trust or unitrust. There is now a prohibition against a provision that allows a distribution from the trust of more than 50% of the trust assets to the noncharitable beneficiary in any one year,[246] and a new requirement for both annuity trusts and unitrusts that the value (determined under the section 7520 valuation tables) of the remainder interest going to the charitable organization must be at least 10% of the initial net fair market value of the property placed in the trust.[247] The new provisions are effective for transfers in trust after July 28, 1997.

COLLECTION SOLD AFTER FIRST YEAR

Although it is advisable to sell the work of art placed in the charitable remainder trust within the first year of the creation of the trust, this may not always be possible. A charitable remainder unitrust is permitted to pay out only its income if that income is less than the stated payout percentage—a so-called net income method charitable remainder unitrust (NIMCRUT).[248] The NIMCRUT may have what is called a "makeup" provision. Under such a provision, any amount by which the trust income falls short of the stated pay out percentage is to be paid in subsequent years to the extent the trust's income exceeds the fixed percentage in later years.[249] A charitable remainder trust may start as a NIMCRUT and later convert to a traditional charitable remainder trust—a so called "flip unitrust."[250] This type of unitrust is ideal for a work of art if there is doubt about its sale in the first year of the trust.

A NIMCRUT may convert to a straight unitrust using the same unitrust payout percentage if the governing instrument of the trust meets the following requirements:

1. The change from a net income unitrust to a straight unitrust must be triggered on a specific date or by a single event. The occurrence of that event (the "triggering event") may not be discretionary with, or within the control of, the trustee or any other person.[251] The regulations make

it clear that a specific date is a permissible triggering event. Permissible triggering events also include the marriage, divorce, death, or birth of a child with respect to any individual. The sale of unmarketable assets— such as a work of art, real estate, closely held stock, or restricted stock— also is a permissible triggering event. The sale of marketable securities is not a permissible triggering event, however, because the timing of the sale is considered to be within the control or discretion of the trustee. Lastly, a beneficiary's or other person's attaining a specific age is a permissible triggering event.[252]

2. The change from a net income unitrust to a straight unitrust must occur at the beginning of the tax year of the unitrust that immediately follow the tax year during which the triggering event occurs.[253] For example, under this rule, if the triggering event occurs on July 1, 2011, the conversion of the unitrust to a straight unitrust must occur on January 1, 2012.

3. In the case of a net income unitrust with a makeup provision, the unitrust's governing instrument must provide that any makeup amount not paid as of the conversion date is forfeited.[254]

As discussed above, in order to avoid the yearly requirement of a qualified appraisal by a qualified appraiser, the grantor should not be the trustee; an independent trustee should be used.

WHEN THE CHARITABLE DONATION IS COMPLETED

Section 170(a) provides that a deductible charitable contribution is a gift made during the taxable year to or for the use of an organization described in section 170(c). The taxpayer must comply with specific formalities, as discussed on page 61, in order to obtain the charitable deduction. The *Bennett* case[255] emphasizes the point that there must be a completed gift in order to obtain the charitable deduction.

In *Bennett*, the taxpayer wanted to make a donation of an antique piano to a college. The college accepted the piano but wanted to delay the transfer until it had a proper place for the piano. In 1982, the taxpayer executed a deed of gift, transferring his entire interest in the piano to the college. The college then issued a loan agreement, purportedly lending the piano back to the taxpayer. The piano was never delivered to the college. The taxpayer was required to keep the piano insured, and the insurance policy named both the taxpayer and the college as insured parties as their respective interests may appear. The college had the right to recall the piano on short notice.

When the taxpayer's gift to the college was being audited by the IRS, an IRS valuation expert went to the college in 1985 to inspect the piano and discovered that the piano was not there. That changed the case from one that was initially questioning the fair market value of the piano on the date of the donation to one questioning whether the donation was completed, allowing a deduction under section 170. The court found that state law is used to determine whether an item of personal property that is the subject of a charitable contribution has been delivered within the taxable year. Unfortunately for the taxpayer, he lived in Louisiana, where the state law governing inter vivos gifts of personal property requires actual delivery of the property or a written deed of gift signed (that is, executed) before a notary public and two witnesses. Since the taxpayer's deed of gift was signed by the taxpayer but was not notarized or witnessed, the gift was held to be invalid under Louisiana law.

If the taxpayer had complied with the Louisiana law on the deed of gift, the charitable donation would probably have been allowed. The court pointed out that although tangible personal property must normally be physically delivered to complete a gift, the delivery of a deed to the donee may substitute for delivery of the gift when actual delivery is inconvenient or impractical.[256]

PRIVATE OPERATING FOUNDATIONS

A private operating foundation falls somewhere between a private foundation and a public charity.[257] The major advantage of a private operating foundation is that, from the donor's point of view, she is treated in the same manner for tax purposes as if the contribution were made to a public charity. In other words, contributions of works of art to a private operating foundation can be deducted to the extent of their full fair market value so long as the specific donation requirements are satisfied.[258] Doing so includes satisfying the four requirements for obtaining the maximum charitable deduction: The property has been owned for more than one year and was not a gift from the artist, the property satisfies the related use rule (that is, the use of the art is related to the exempt purpose of the donee-charity), there is a qualified appraisal by a qualified appraiser, and the contribution is made to a public charity or a private operating foundation. If those requirements are met, the full fair market value donation of a collection is available for a donation to a private operating foundation.[259] Since the donor is the creator of the private operating foundation and can act as its president, the donor is afforded a degree of control over the collection and at the same time obtains a tax deduction for the full value of the donated property.

Private operating foundations are organizations that devote their assets or income to the active conduct of a charitable purpose, rather than making grants to other organizations. To qualify as a private operating foundation, the organization must satisfy the income test and either the asset test, the endowment test, or the support test.[260]

INCOME TEST
The income test, which must be satisfied by all private operating foundations, means that the foundation spends substantially all of the smaller of its adjusted net income or its minimum investment return (5% of its investment assets) directly for the active conduct of the activities constituting the purpose or function for which the foundation was organized and operated.[261] In other words, the income generated in the foundation and the expenditure of funds must be for

the direct activities of the foundation and not merely for the making of grants. Grants made to other organizations to assist them in conducting activities are considered an indirect, rather than a direct, means of carrying out activities constituting the charitable purpose of the foundation.[262] However, amounts paid to acquire or maintain assets that are used directly in the conduct of the foundation's exempt activities (the foundation's operating assets), such as works of art owned by a museum, are considered direct expenditures for the active conduct of the foundation's exempt activities. Those amounts also include administrative expenses. For example, if an individual was paid a fee to make sure that the foundation's works of art were properly insured, properly loaned to other organizations, properly stored when not on loan, and other related administrative activities, the fee would be an expenditure directly for an exempt purpose.[263]

In addition to meeting the income test, a private operating foundation must meet one of three alternative tests: the asset test, the endowment test, or the support test.

Asset Test

The asset test means that the foundation must have substantially more than half of its assets devoted directly to the active conduct of activities constituting the foundation's charitable, educational, or other similar exempt purpose.[264] The IRS regulations give an example of satisfying the asset test in order to qualify for private operating foundation status as follows:

> Example (4). Z, an exempt organization described in section 501(c)(3), is devoted to improving the public's understanding of Renaissance art. Z's principal assets are a number of paintings of this period which it circulates on an active and continuing basis to museums and schools for public display. These paintings constitute 80 percent of Z's assets. Under these circumstances, although Z does not have a building in which it displays these paintings, such paintings are devoted directly to the active conduct of activities constituting Z's exempt purpose. Therefore, Z has satisfied the assets test described in this paragraph.[265]

Revenue Ruling 74-498[266] specifically dealt with the qualification of a foundation that owns art as a private operating foundation. In that ruling, the foundation was formed to further the arts, it owned a collection of well-known paintings, and the foundation had an endowment of stocks and bonds that produced income. Part of the income was used in a program of grants intended to further the arts, and the balance was used in a program of loaning the paintings owned by the foundation for display in museums, universities, and similar institutions. At any given time, all but a few of the paintings were in the hands of exhibiting institutions. Generally, when they were not on loan, the foundation's paintings were in transit, being reconditioned or restored, or being stored pending a scheduled exhibit. In that ruling, the IRS held that the foundation's collection of paintings was being used in an active loan program and, therefore, it was being used directly to carry out its exempt purpose in the manner indicated in the IRS regulations.

A similar result was concluded by the Internal Revenue Service in Private Letter Ruling 93-38-042, dated June 29, 1993.[267] In that ruling, the IRS made it clear that the artwork that was placed on loan to other institutions was *excluded* in determining the foundation's minimum investment return. The minimum investment return is 5% of a foundation's investment assets and is the amount that a foundation must use or expend each year for exempt purposes.[268]

Therefore, a donor can create a private operating foundation that can use the donor's name or any other name and to which the donor can contribute appreciated works of art and claim a deduction for the full fair market value. The donor, as president of the foundation, has to arrange to lend the items to other public tax-exempt organizations, so that the foundation can satisfy the asset test described above. The donor can contribute a cash amount to cover operating expenses. The donor and any other individuals can be members of the board of directors. When the works of art are not on loan or exhibition, they should be placed in temporary storage. The objective is to be absolutely sure that the donor has created a private operating foundation retroactive to the date of formation— that is, the year in which the foundation is created—with the result that a deduction for the full fair market value of the donated art is allowable.

In making use of a private operating foundation, the donor-president of the foundation must be aware that its exempt status will be lost if any personal benefit inures to the donor.[269] Therefore, it is crucial to understand what use can be made of the collection when it is not on exhibition at other institutions. A donor often wants to know about the possibility of exhibiting the collection in her home or on real estate that she owns. The question is whether any of the art can be stored or exhibited in the donor's home during the times it is not on exhibition.

In Revenue Ruling 74-600,[270] the IRS was asked to rule on the question of whether the placing of paintings owned by a private foundation in the residence of a founder of the foundation constituted an act of self-dealing—that is, something that would disqualify the organization's tax-exempt status. The paintings were on exhibition in various museums for a number of years and then were returned to the residence of the founder, where they were displayed together with the founder's large private art collection in a part of his residence devoted to paintings and other works of art. Approximately 2,000 individuals visited the founder's private collection each year, and special tours were arranged for small groups and other individuals interested in the arts. The IRS ruled that the placement of the art in the founder's residence resulted in a direct use of the foundation's assets by or for the benefit of a private person, and, therefore, the foundation was not tax-exempt.

A similar result was reached in a 1987 technical advice memorandum[271] dealing with sculptures that were outside on a taxpayer's residential property, where the sculpture was open to exhibition to the public. The foregoing IRS position indicates how sensitive the government is to any personal use of art assets after the donation has been made.

If there is a separate structure on the donor's property, preferably a structure not attached to her residence, a ruling may be obtained that no personal use was made of the collection and that there was an exhibition space open to the public. Alternatively, the donor could build a storage space on her property and take the works of art out for conservation or for use in the storage space when scholars or other interested parties are in attendance.[272] The collection should never be used in the donor's personal residence. We strongly recommend that the items be placed in a storage facility, not on the donor's property, when the items are not on loan.

For a collector who wants the tax benefits of donating her art collection yet cannot cope with losing total control over the collection, the private operating foundation (by satisfying the income test and asset test) offers an alternative that should be given serious consideration.

ENDOWMENT TEST

The endowment test requires direct distributions of at least two-thirds of the foundation's minimum investment return—that is, 3 1/3% (2/3 times 5%) of its endowment.[273] The distributions must be made directly for the active conduct of the foundation's exempt purpose. Most foundations that satisfy the income test will, as a practical matter, satisfy the endowment test in order to qualify as a private operation foundation.

SUPPORT TEST

The support test requires that

(1) at least 85% of the foundation's support, other than gross investment income, be from a combination of the general public and five or more exempt organizations,

(2) not more than 25% of support, other than gross investment income, be from any one exempt organization, and

(3) not more than 50% of support be from gross investment income.[274]

The support test will rarely be used by a collector to qualify a foundation as a private operating foundation because of its fund raising aspects.

TECHNIQUES TO AVOID

Three cases illustrate what should not be done with works of art.

In *J.W. Kluge*,[275] the taxpayer sold valuable works of art to a closely held corporation wholly owned by him. However, he retained the works of art in his home after the sale. The Tax Court upheld the IRS in its holding that the taxpayer received a taxable dividend equivalent to the sale prices allocated to the works of art since he retained the beneficial use of the objects in his home. Therefore, the payment by the corporation was for his personal benefit, rather than for a valid business purpose.

In *S. Prestley Blake*,[276] the taxpayer contributed highly appreciated securities to a charity with an understanding that the charity would sell the securities and use the proceeds to buy the taxpayer's yacht. The Second Circuit affirmed the conclusion of the Tax Court, which was that the taxpayer, in substance, had himself sold the stock, retained the proceeds, and made a gift of the yacht to the charity. Therefore, the taxpayer had to recognize the gain on the sale of the stock by the charity. The Second Circuit based that conclusion on its finding that under state law the charitable donee was legally obligated by the terms of its understanding with the taxpayer to sell the donated stock and to buy his yacht. But the court went further and stated that it would have reached the same conclusion even if there had been no such binding legal obligation:

> [W]here there is an understanding that a contribution of appreciated property will be utilized by the donee charity for the purpose of purchasing an asset of the contributor, the transaction will be viewed as a matter of tax law as a contribution of the asset—at whatever its then value is—with the charity acting as a conduit of the proceeds from the sale of the stock.[277]

In *Ford*,[278] the taxpayer was a limited partner in a partnership that owned one asset, an underwater research vessel with a fair market value of $600,000. After fully depreciating the vessel, the partnership transferred it to a corporation wholly owned by the partnership. The stock of the corporation was then donated to a university, and the taxpayer took a charitable contribution deduction based on his share of the $600,000 value. The Tax Court held that the creation of the corporation was a sham since its sole purpose was to avoid taxes. Therefore, the corporation was disregarded, resulting in a reduction of the charitable contribution to zero under section 170(e)(1)(A), which requires the amount of the contribution to be reduced by the amount of ordinary income that would have been realized on a sale of the contributed property.

Complete Testamentary Charitable Transfers

An individual may wish to keep possession of a collection during life and bequeath it to a charitable organization on death. Doing so results in an estate tax charitable deduction to the extent of the fair market value of the property at the date of death.[279] In the case of a bequest at death, there is no distinction between a public charity and a private foundation. Moreover, in general, the related use rule does not apply to testamentary transfers.[280] However, section 2055(e), introduced by the Economic Recovery Tax Act (ERTA) of 1981 contains a new related use rule for a testamentary charitable transfer when there is a retained copyright interest. That provision is discussed in detail below.

Whenever a valuable collection constitutes a substantial portion of the assets that an individual wants to leave to charity at her death, consideration must be given to the extent of the charitable bequest. For example, a collection left to charity at the time a will is drafted may constitute only 40% of a testator's estate. However, by the time of the testator's death, the collection may have increased in value, and the testator's other assets may have decreased in value. That change could result in the charitable bequest constituting more than 50% of the testator's estate. If that situation causes a problem under local state law, provision must be made to avoid the problem by either drafting a clause with a percentage limitation or drafting the will so that it cannot be challenged.[281]

Generally, the full estate tax charitable deduction is allowable for a bequest to either a public charity or a private foundation. Private foundations include all tax-exempt organizations other than those described in section 509(a)(1), (2), (3), or (4). However, if the bequest is to a private foundation that has not complied with the requirement under the Tax Reform Act of 1969 of including certain amendments in its governing instrument or that has failed to notify the IRS of its status, the entire estate tax charitable deduction will be denied.[282]

If the testator wishes to bequeath a collection to a private foundation, the drafter of her will should obtain a copy of the foundation's governing instrument to ascertain whether the instrument meets the Tax Reform Act of 1969 requirement mentioned above and should also obtain a statement from the organization that it has notified the IRS of its status.

Changes Under ERTA

The Economic Recovery Tax Act (ERTA) of 1981 amended section 2056 to provide for an unlimited estate tax marital deduction. Before January 1, 1982, a taxpayer had to integrate the marital deduction and the charitable deduction to achieve the best result.[283] Individuals dying on or after January 1, 1982, have an unlimited marital deduction, so no charitable deduction is necessary to reduce the federal estate tax to zero if the decedent left her entire estate to the surviving spouse.

In fact, even if the testator wants the charitable organization to receive the collection at her death, the testator should not bequeath it to the charitable organization. Instead, the testator should leave the collection outright to the surviving spouse and have the surviving spouse make the donation to the charitable organization either during the surviving spouse's life or at death. The surviving spouse would receive an income tax charitable deduction under section 170, within the applicable percentage limitations previously discussed, for a lifetime transfer or a charitable deduction under section 2055 for a transfer at death. The surviving spouse would pay no federal estate tax on the estate of the deceased spouse because of the unlimited marital deduction.

Outright testamentary charitable transfers are still important for unmarried individuals. Such bequests allow the collection to be kept together as a unit and eliminate the problem of raising the money necessary to pay the estate taxes attributable to the inclusion of a valuable collection in the gross estate and eliminate any need for a forced sale of the collection in order to pay the estate taxes.

A testator who wishes to bequeath a collection to a charitable organization should make a specific bequest in her will. The bequest should be specific enough to identify clearly the property to be given. The testator should consider the possibility that a specific charitable organization may renounce the bequest. Therefore, the proposed gift and any conditions attached to it should be discussed with the charitable organization. (See Appendixes 15-6 and 15-9 at the end of the chapter.)

Under the current rules effective January 1, 2011, section 1014 provides that all property takes a basis equal to the value on the date of death or six months later. Under the Economic Growth and Tax Relief Reconciliation Act of 2001, new carryover basis rules were to apply for property included in a decedent's estate for persons dying after December 31, 2009, which is when the federal estate tax was scheduled to be repealed. However, the new modified carryover basis system will apply under new section 1022 only for individuals dying in calendar year 2010. Under the new system, the basis for certain property treated as transferred on the death of a property owner after 2009 will equal the lower of the asset's fair market value at the decedent's death or the decedent's adjusted basis in the asset. In other words, the basis for income tax purposes may remain at the original cost of the property purchased. There are a number of adjustments that allow some step-up in basis. A full discussion of this new provision is beyond the scope of this chapter.[284] In December 2010, the Tax Relief, Unemployment Insurance Reauthorization, and Job Creation Act of 2010 reinstated the estate tax as well as repealed the new carryover basis rules for individuals dying on or after January 1, 2011.[285]

Partial Testamentary Charitable Transfers

Before January 1, 1970, a collector was able to bequeath a collection to a member of her family for life and, on the family member's death, outright to a charitable organization, resulting in an estate tax charitable deduction for the value of the remainder interest. A similar deduction was obtainable for a present interest to a charitable organization with a remainder interest to a noncharitable legatee. The Tax Reform Act of 1969 eliminated those deductions.

CHARITABLE REMAINDER TRUST: TESTAMENTARY

The Tax Reform Act of 1969 denied the estate tax charitable deduction for a remainder interest in property (with certain exceptions not applicable here) unless the interest was in a trust that was a charitable remainder annuity trust, a charitable remainder unitrust, or a pooled income fund.[286] In the usual case, a charitable remainder trust is created during the lifetime of the donor to take advantage of the ability to sell the property transferred to the trust without paying any capital gains tax.

A testamentary charitable remainder trust initially appears impractical, since non-income-producing property, such as a collection, cannot be put in the form of a guaranteed annuity, nor can it pay out a fixed yearly percentage of its fair market value. A charitable remainder unitrust is permitted to pay out only its income if that income is less than the stated payout percentage—a so-called net income charitable remainder unitrust (NIMCRUT).[287] However, if it is clear from the outset that the property put in trust will never produce any income, the charitable deduction may be denied on the ground that a valid charitable remainder unitrust was not created since the trust cannot make an annual payment. The regulations[288] issued under section 664 indicate that a charitable remainder unitrust must make an annual payment to the noncharitable beneficiary. The regulations make no mention of a remainder interest in non-income-producing property, such as a collection. The only exceptions to the required unitrust form for a remainder interest in property given to a charity are contained in section 2055(e)(2), which concerns a remainder interest in a personal residence or farm.

Further, the regulations at 1.664-1(a)(3) state that a remainder trust does not qualify under section 664 if its governing instrument contains a

> provision which restricts the trustee from investing the trust assets in a manner which could result in the annual realization of a reasonable amount of income or gain from the sale or disposition of trust assets.[289]

The IRS has stated that the purpose of that regulation is "to prevent charitable remainder trusts from investing in non-productive assets or in assets that would produce no taxable income."[290]

In Revenue Ruling 73-610, 1973-2 C.B. 213, the grantor of an irrevocable trust contributed a collection of antiques, in addition to income-producing assets, to a trust. The governing instrument of the trust provided that the grantor's spouse, who was the sole income beneficiary of the trust for her life, should have the use of the antique collection for her life. At her death, the antique collection and all the remaining assets in the trust were to be distributed to a charitable tax-exempt organization. In all other respects, the trust complied with the provisions of section 664 defining charitable remainder trusts. The IRS held that the retention of a life estate in the collection of antiques for the grantor's spouse restricted the trustee from investing all the trust assets in a manner that could result in the annual realization of a reasonable amount of income or gain from the sale or disposition of the trust assets. Therefore, the trust did not qualify as a charitable remainder trust. Similarly, in Revenue Ruling 76-165, 1976-1 C.B. 279, the IRS held that a remainder interest in household furnishings that were bequeathed to a surviving spouse for life and then to a charitable organization did not qualify as a deductible remainder interest. If the beneficiary of a charitable trust has the use of a collection, the trust does not qualify as a unitrust or an annuity trust since the "use" is not a unitrust or annuity trust distribution.[291]

Notwithstanding the foregoing, a collection may still be used for the purpose of creating a testamentary charitable remainder trust that qualifies for the estate tax charitable deduction.[292] The deceased collector's estate would receive an estate tax deduction for the charitable remainder interest that is the value of the trust's assets less the present value of the stream of unitrust or annuity trust payments as computed under the IRS tables.

One way to deal with Revenue Ruling 73-610 is to empower the executor or the trustee to sell all or part of the collection at her discretion. In such a case, the trustee is not restricted from investing the assets. However, the problem of a yearly payout is still present unless all or substantially all of the collection is sold.

A testamentary charitable remainder trust is deemed created at the decedent's death, even though the actual funding of the trust may be deferred. The funding of a testamentary charitable remainder trust can be delayed until the end of a reasonable period of time for the administration of the decedent's estate.[293] The IRS requires that the governing instrument of a testamentary charitable remainder trust grant the trustee the authority to defer the payment of the annuity or unitrust amount until the end of the taxable year of the trust in which the trust is completely funded,[294] even though the obligation to pay the annuity or unitrust amount begins at the decedent's death.[295] If payment is deferred—and it will almost always be deferred in an estate administration—a correcting adjustment must be made within a reasonable period after the close of the trust's first fiscal year in which it is completely funded.[296] In the case of an underpayment, the trust must pay the excess to the annuity or unitrust recipient, and, in the case of an overpayment, the recipient must repay the difference to the trust.[297] Those rules give the executor of the estate ample time to sell the collection after the collector's death and then fund the charitable remainder trust.

Example: G transfers property to a trust over which she retains an inter vivos power of revocation. Upon G's death the trust is required to pay the debts and administration expenses of G's estate. When the expenses are paid, the trust terminates and distributes all of its remaining assets to a separate trust T, which meets the definition of a charitable remainder trust. Trust T will qualify as a charitable remainder trust from the date of G's death because it will function exclusively as a charitable remainder trust from its creation. For purposes of section 2055, trust T will be deemed to be created at G's death, provided the governing instrument requires that the obligation to pay the annuity or unitrust amount begins on the date of G's death, even though the same instrument provides payment shall be deferred until the end of the taxable year in which the trust is funded.[298]

As noted above, if payment is deferred, a correcting adjustment must be made within a reasonable period after the close of the trust's first taxable year in which it is completely funded.[299] In the event of an underpayment, the trust must pay the excess to the annuity or unitrust recipient, and in the case of an overpayment the recipient must repay the difference to the trust.[300] All payments must include interest. The applicable rate of interest depends on when the instrument was executed and whether it had been subsequently amended. The rate is the section 7520 rate for transfers made after April 30, 1989.

That technique is useful for a collector who wishes to benefit a family member after the collector's death but wants the collection to be located at a museum and wants to reduce the amount of the estate tax. The testamentary charitable remainder unitrust does not have to name a specific charity as the remainderman of the trust but can leave the designation up to the executor or trustee.[301] Such a provision improves the fiduciary's ability to sell the collection to a museum, since the museum, the buyer of the collection, can be designated by the fiduciary as the charitable remainderman of the trust. Since the museum will, in essence, be getting its money back after the death of the income beneficiary, the museum should be in a good position to make any such purchase.

But what if the executor of the collector's estate is unable to sell the collection so that the testamentary charitable remainder trust is funded with the collection? Even if there is no restriction on the trustee's ability to sell the collection, so that the Revenue Ruling 73-610 problem is avoided, the trustee must still make an annual payment from the trust to the noncharitable beneficiary. The regulations provide that the payment of the annuity or unitrust amount may be made in cash or other property.[302] In the case of a distribution made in other property, the amount paid, credited, or required to be distributed is considered as an amount realized by the trust from the sale of other disposition of the property.[303] The collection will have a new basis equal to its fair market value on the collector's date of death (or six months later),[304] so the realization of gain by the trust should be minimal. The basis of the property in the hands of the recipient is its fair market value at the time it was paid, credited, or required to be distributed.[305] Nothing in the regulations prevents the trustees from using a work of art to pay the required annuity or unitrust amount, but there is still the problem of a yearly valuation of the collection and all the inherent problems associated with valuing an asset that by its very nature does not have a precise value. In addition, even if the trustee is not restricted from selling the collection, so that regulation 1.664-1(a)(3) is not a problem, state law governing the investment decisions of the trustee may mandate the sale of all or a large portion of non-income-producing assets, such as a collection held in a charitable trust.[306]

The use of a testamentary charitable remainder trust can be a useful means to reduce the estate tax on a collection. However, it is advisable to sell the collection during the administration of the estate or shortly after the charitable remainder trust is funded to avoid a potential problem when calculating the annuity or unitrust trust amount or any other problem that may jeopardize the charitable deduction allowable to the estate.

CHARITABLE LEAD (INCOME) TRUST

A testamentary charitable lead trust is the reverse of a charitable remainder trust—that is, the charity receives its interest first for a term of years or for a period measured by the lives of one or more individuals and, at the end of the trust term, the remainder is paid to the decedent's heirs. The lead trust can be in the form of a lead unitrust or a lead annuity trust.[307]

The annual unitrust amount is a fixed percentage of the net fair market value of the trust's assets as revalued each year. Accordingly, the amount paid varies each year, depending on the value of the trust's assets that year on the valuation date. The annual annuity trust amount is a fixed annuity amount, often expressed as a percentage of the initial fair market value of the trust's assets. Once established, the annuity amount remains the same each year.

The principal benefit of a testamentary charitable lead trust is the estate tax savings as a result of the charitable deduction. The deceased collector's estate receives an estate tax deduction for the charitable income interest (which is the present value of the stream of unitrust or annuity trust payments as computed under the IRS tables),[308] and the collector's estate pays an estate tax on the value of the trust's remainder interest. Even though the estate tax is payable only on the value of the remainder interest, the property that forms the trust corpus receives a full stepped-up basis equal to the date-of-death value, since it is fully includable in the deceased collector's estate. Since section 2055 does not impose any percentage limitations on the amount of the estate tax charitable deduction, it is possible to establish a sufficiently long charitable income interest so that the estate tax charitable deduction will be large enough to almost eliminate the estate tax with respect to the property bequeathed to the charitable lead trust. However, this technique is best suited for an otherwise financially secure heir of the deceased collector, since the trust may not terminate for many years. If, on termination of the charitable lead trust, the remaining corpus of the trust will ultimately be paid to grandchildren of the deceased collector, the generation-skipping tax provisions must be taken into consideration.[309]

Like the testamentary charitable remainder trust, the testamentary charitable lead trust is not likely to be funded until some time after the death of the collector in order to allow for a period of administration of her estate. As discussed above under testamentary charitable remainder trusts, the regulations set forth extensive rules applicable to testamentary charitable remainder trusts.[310] Even though there is no comparable authority dealing with the funding of a testamentary charitable lead trust, we think that the same rules should be applicable to them. Therefore, the funding of the testamentary charitable lead trust can be delayed until the end of a reasonable period of time for the administration of the decedent's estate. If payment is deferred—and it will almost always be deferred in an estate administration—a correcting adjustment must be made within a reasonable period after the close of the trust's first fiscal year in which it is completely funded. Such an adjustment gives the executor or the trustee time to sell the collection before funding the trust and enhances the executor's ability to sell the collection to a museum if the museum can be named as the charitable income beneficiary by the executor. In essence, a museum may be willing to buy the collection since it would be getting a large part of its money back over the trust term.

Nothing in the regulations prevents the trustee from using a work of art to pay the required annuity or unitrust amount to the charitable organization.[311] However, as previously noted, there is still the problem of a yearly valuation of the collection and all the problems associated with valuing an asset that by its very nature does not have a precise value. Therefore, although the use of a testamentary charitable lead trust is useful in reducing the estate tax payable on a collection, the collection's sale during the administration of the estate is the safest course of action to assure the estate tax charitable deduction.

A testator can create a testamentary charitable lead annuity trust (CLAT) or a testamentary charitable lead unitrust (CLUT).[312] In a CLUT, both the lead beneficiary and the remainder beneficiary share in any appreciation in value of the trust, whereas the charitable lead interest in a CLAT remains fixed. This makes a CLAT more advantageous to the noncharitable beneficiary since all appreciation in excess of that which the actuarial tables assume will occur inures to the benefit of the noncharitable remainder beneficiary. The value of an annuity interest in a CLAT is determined under section 7520. This section requires the Treasury to prescribe valuation tables providing factors to value such an interest.[313] In conjunction with such factors, section 7520 also mandates the use of a defined interest rate.[314]

In valuing the interests in a testamentary CLAT, the appropriate valuation date in determining the annuity amount is the date of the decedent's death or the alternate valuation date.[315]

The key element in a testamentary charitable lead trust is whether or not over the trust term the trust assets grow at a greater rate than the section 7520 rate used to value the trust assets for estate tax purposes. If an estate is permitted to claim a low valuation for assets going into a charitable lead annuity trust, the annuity amount is fixed at that value and the post-death appreciation in value will pass estate-tax-free to the noncharitable beneficiary at the end of the trust term.

Questions exist relating to the date the trust is actually created and the date when payment of the charitable income interest must commence. The regulations set forth extensive rules applicable to testamentary charitable remainder trusts.[316] As noted above, even though there is no comparable authority concerning testamentary charitable lead trusts, it would seem that the same rules should be applied to testamentary charitable lead trusts. Accordingly, the lead interest should become payable as of the date of death even though it may not be paid until a later date.

The governing instrument of the testamentary charitable lead trust should mandate that within a reasonable time after the funding of the trust, final adjustments as to the exact amount of annuity or unitrust installments should be determined.

Because the estate is subject to tax on its net taxable income during the period of administration, consideration should be given to making a current distribution to the charitable lead beneficiary in order to be able to obtain an income tax charitable deduction.[317]

Although interest is required to be paid with respect to any underpayment of the annuity or unitrust amount during estate administration for a testamentary charitable remainder trust,[318] interest is not required to be paid in the case of a lead trust. However, to avoid any question with respect to the estate tax deduction in the case of a lead trust, consideration should be given to providing for the payment of interest. Local law in some jurisdictions may require payment of interest on legacies.

PLANNING FOR THE COLLECTOR—CHARITABLE LEAD AND CHARITABLE REMAINDER TRUSTS

As indicated above, both a testamentary charitable remainder trust and a testamentary charitable lead trust have a period of time after the decedent's death (a period of reasonable administration) before the trust must be fully funded and start acting as a charitable remainder or charitable lead trust.

It is not necessary to name the specific charitable organization in a testamentary charitable remainder or lead trust. The governing instrument of a testamentary charitable remainder trust may permit the income beneficiary or the trustee to designate the charitable remainderman.[319]

Similarly, a testamentary charitable lead trust may permit the remainderman or the trustee to designate the charitable lead beneficiary.[320]

For the collector who desires to have her collection remain as a unit after her death but does not want to make an outright bequest of her entire collection to charity, the use of a testamentary charitable lead trust coupled with a testamentary charitable remainder trust may be desirable. A charitable lead annuity trust for one-half of the collection and a charitable remainder unitrust for one-half of the collection would create an estate tax charitable deduction that would substantially reduce the estate taxes payable. Assume the entire collection is sold to a museum after the decedent's death as described below, there would be an annual cash flow (6% or 7% of the trust assets valued annually) from the charitable remainder unitrust to the decedent's child and an annual annuity payment from the charitable lead annuity trust to the museum with, at the end of the trust term, a substantial estate-tax-free payment to the decedent's child from the charitable remainder annuity trust of the post-death appreciation in the value of the assets. This might be accomplished by taking the following steps:

1. The collection would be valued for federal estate tax purposes pursuant to the advanced ruling request procedure under Revenue Procedure 96-15.[321] This would fix the value of the collection for federal estate tax purposes, and the determination is binding on the Internal Revenue Service.

2. The decedent's will would direct that the collection be divided one-half into a 6% charitable lead annuity trust, and one-half into a 6% charitable remainder unitrust, each trust for a twenty-year term.

3. The decedent's will would not name a charitable remainderman for the charitable remainder trust and would not name a charitable beneficiary of the charitable lead annuity trust.

4. The executor and trustee of the will would then discuss with various museums the sale of the collection. Efforts would be made to achieve a sales price for the collection to the museum in an amount in excess of the Revenue Procedure 96-15 amount by promising the purchasing museum

that it will be named as the charitable remainderman of the charitable remainder unitrust and as the charitable lead beneficiary of the charitable lead annuity trust. This should enable the museum to purchase the collection for an amount in excess of the federal estate tax fixed value, since the museum would be receiving back most of its money over the twenty-year term. In other words, in reality the museum would not be paying more than the fixed value as determined under Revenue Procedure 96-15; it would only be spreading out the payment over twenty years and, in fact, in present value terms the net cost to the museum will be substantially less than the purchase price. This should result in the charitable lead annuity trust being able to beat the section 7520 rate so that the noncharitable beneficiary would receive a substantial tax-free benefit at the end of the twenty-year term.[322]

5. The sale of one-half of the collection by the charitable remainder unitrust would be done immediately after that part of the collection is transferred to the trust.[323] Since a charitable remainder trust is a tax-exempt entity, there would be no capital gain on the sale. The noncharitable income beneficiary would be entitled to receive the unitrust amount calculated from the date of death plus interest at the section 7520 rate.

6. The sale of one-half of the collection by the charitable lead annuity trust would be done immediately after that part of the collection is transferred to the trust. Since a charitable lead annuity trust is not a tax-exempt entity,[324] a capital gains tax[325] would be payable on the sale on this part of the collection to the extent the sales price exceeds the Revenue Procedure 96-15 value. However, the annuity amount will be based on the Revenue Procedure 96-15 value and not on the sales price value. Although the annuity amount must be paid calculated from the date of death of the decedent, it appears that interest on that amount is not required to be paid.

This planning technique works best when there is a child of the taxpayer who has some assets of her own and the decedent, as well as the child, desires to keep the works of art together at one museum.

Spousal Use

As discussed above, a married collector should not, on death, leave her collection outright to a charitable organization but should leave it first to the surviving spouse, who can then contribute the collection to the charity and take an income tax charitable deduction for transfers made during the surviving spouse's life and an estate tax charitable deduction for transfers made under the spouse's will. However, the testator may want assurance that the surviving spouse will, in fact, transfer the collection to the charitable organization after her death.

Before January 1, 1982, if a testator created a trust for the surviving spouse and wanted it to qualify for the marital deduction, the surviving spouse had to have a general power of appointment over the corpus of the trust. Therefore, the first spouse to die could not be certain that the corpus of the trust would be received by the charitable organization. ERTA changed that situation in two ways.

First, ERTA added section 2056(b)(8), which provides that if the surviving spouse is the only noncharitable beneficiary of an otherwise qualified charitable remainder trust, the terminable interest rule of section 2056(b)(1) does not apply, and the life interest qualifies for the marital deduction. The remainder interest qualifies for the charitable deduction under section 2055(e)(2), so there is no tax on the estate of the first spouse to die. However, as discussed above, there is still the problem of the yearly payout and distributions in kind. Therefore, unless a specific ruling is obtained, section 2056(b)(8) is probably not much help to the collector.

Second, ERTA added the more helpful section 2056(b)(7).[326] That section allows a trust that is created for the sole benefit of the surviving spouse to qualify for the marital deduction, even though the surviving spouse does not have a general power of appointment. That type of trust is known as a qualified terminable interest property (QTIP) trust.

If a collection can be left in a QTIP trust with a designated charitable organization to take the remainder after the death of the surviving spouse, there is no estate tax on the death of the first spouse to die, since the QTIP trust qualifies 100% for the marital deduction under section 2056(b)(7); the testator is assured that the charitable organization will receive the collection after the death of the surviving spouse; and the estate of the surviving spouse receives a charitable deduction under section 2055(a) equal to 100% of the then fair market value of the collection.

To reach the above result, the estate planner must see that two requirements are met. First, the QTIP trust must qualify for the marital deduction. Section 2056(b)(7)(B)(ii)(I) provides the following:

> (ii) QUALIFYING INCOME INTEREST FOR LIFE.— The surviving spouse has a qualifying income interest for life if—
>   (I) the surviving spouse is entitled to all the income from the property, payable annually or at more frequent intervals, . . .

Since a collection generally does not produce any current income, is there a problem in placing a collection in a QTIP trust in the light of the requirement of section 2056(b)(7)(B)(ii)(I)? Currently, there is no definitive answer. However, we believe that a collection can be placed in a QTIP trust that qualifies for the marital deduction under section 2056(b)(7). Under regulation section 20.2056(b)-5(f)(4), the power to retain or invest in unproductive property is not fatal to the marital deduction under section 2056(b)(5) if the surviving spouse has the right to require that the property be productive or be converted within a reasonable time. In the case of *Estate of Robinson v. United States*,[327] the trustees were authorized to invest in non-income-producing assets, but the court found that the trust, when construed in the light of the overall intent of the decedent and with regard to local law, afforded the surviving spouse the degree of beneficial enjoyment necessary to satisfy the requirements of section 2056 and the applicable IRS regulations.

That conclusion is aided if the QTIP trust is funded not only with the collection but also with enough other income-producing assets to provide the surviving spouse with a reasonable amount of income to fund that spouse's life style. In addition, the trust should have a provision to this effect:

> My trustee shall have no power to invest in or to retain non-income-producing property without the consent of my said [husband or wife].

Second, the remainder (including the collection) of the QTIP trust that is transferred to the charitable organization after the death of the surviving spouse must qualify for the estate tax charitable deduction in the surviving spouse's estate.[328] The Technical Corrections Act of 1982 added section 2044(c) to make it clear that property in a QTIP trust that is includable in the gross estate of the surviving spouse under section 2044(a) is treated as property passing from the surviving spouse for purposes of the charitable deduction under section 2055.[329]

Therefore, it should now be possible to place a collection in trust for a surviving spouse, with the testator receiving a 100% marital deduction on death and the surviving spouse receiving a 100% charitable deduction on the surviving spouse's death without the necessity of giving the surviving spouse a general power of appointment.

IRS Private Letter Ruling 89-52-024 involved a taxpayer who proposed a codicil to his will that would bequeath to his wife a life estate (not in trust in this case) in a work of art. The wife was to have the exclusive and unrestricted right to use the property during her lifetime, including the right to sell, mortgage, or otherwise encumber or assign the life estate or to license or exploit any intellectual property right in the work during her life. The remainder interest was to pass to charity at her death. The IRS was asked to rule that the split-interest transfer would qualify for the marital deduction under section 2056(b)(7) but not for the charitable deduction under section 2055(a)(2).

The IRS ruled that no charitable deduction would be allowed since the transfer was not in the form of a charitable remainder unitrust or annuity trust. However, the transfer would qualify for the marital deduction since the wife's use of the work of art and the rights she had over it constituted a qualified income interest for life in the work of art. Although not dealt with in the ruling but concluded under the facts of the ruling, the work of art would be includable in the gross estate of the surviving spouse (the wife) under section 2044(a) but would qualify for the estate tax charitable deduction in her estate under section 2044(c).

DOUBLE DEDUCTION DENIED

The Technical Corrections Act of 1982 added subsection 2056(b)(9), which provides that the value of an interest in property cannot be deducted more than once in computing a single decedent's or donor's estate or gift tax liability.[330] Apparently, that provision is intended to prevent the double deduction that could result when a transfer of property qualifies for the marital deduction and the remainder interest in the same property qualifies for the charitable deduction. However, as noted above, a split-interest bequest of a collection qualifies for the charitable deduction only under limited circumstances.

FRACTIONAL INTEREST

A bequest of an undivided fractional interest in a collection to a charitable organization does qualify for an estate tax charitable deduction.[331] For example, if the testator gave an undivided three-quarters interest to the charitable organization during her life, the testator could give the remaining quarter under her will on death. The estate tax charitable deduction would be one-quarter of the fair market value as determined for estate tax purposes.

Private Letter Ruling 200223013 (discussed at page 1284) dealt with fourteen separate rulings pertaining to the federal income, gift, and estate tax consequences of gifts of fractional interest in works of art to be made by a married couple to a tax-exempt museum. The proposed gift was subject to numerous restrictions placed on the museum.

For estate tax purposes, the IRS ruled that the approval rights retained by the donor that pass to her successors in interest have no value for federal estate tax purposes under sections 2031 and 2033. The IRS also ruled that because the artwork will pass to other charitable organizations if the museum breaches the restrictions, there is no possibility that the items will pass for other than a charitable purpose as defined in section 2055(a) and, hence, the value of the bequest will qualify for the federal estate tax charitable deduction under section 2055. Moreover, the IRS determined that the amount includable in the donor's gross estate under sections 2031 and 2033 with respect to the retained undivided fractional interest is the fair market value of the item of artwork multiplied by the donor's fractional interest therein and that the amount deductible under section 2055 with respect to the item is the same value, that is, the amount included in the donor's gross estate.

Finally, the IRS ruled with respect to the federal estate tax that when the donor died the bequest to the donor's spouse of any retained fractional interest in the artwork will qualify for the federal estate tax marital deduction permitted under section 2056(b)(7) (assuming the required election is made). The ruling went on to confirm that the amount of the marital deduction is the fair market value of the artwork (determined without regard to the existence of the restrictions) multiplied by the fraction of the artwork transferred to the surviving spouse. This avoids any potential problem that the estate inclusion amount under section 2031 may not be the same amount as either the charitable deduction under section 2044 or the marital deduction under section 2056.

AMOUNT OF DEDUCTION

Private Letter Ruling 200418002 held that an estate would receive a full charitable estate tax deduction under section 2055 for a proposed bequest of a collection to a museum even though there were substantial restrictions imposed on the museum pursuant to an agreement that required the museum to display and care for the collection.

The taxpayers, husband and wife, entered into an agreement with a museum concerning the taxpayers' donation of the collection either during the lifetime of either or both of them or on the death of the survivor of them. The agreement provided that in the event the taxpayers elected, in their sole discretion, to make the donation, the museum would display and maintain the collection in accordance with the terms and conditions of the agreement.

The agreement further stated that it was the intention of the parties that the collection would at all times be located, housed, and permanently displayed, in perpetuity, at the museum; all works of art in the collection would be included within the museum's blanket insurance policy; and the museum would provide all conservation and curatorial services for each work of art in the collection. The museum was restricted from selling or otherwise disposing of any of the works of art in the collection. In the event of any attempted sale, trade, transfer, or disposition of any work of art in the collection in violation of the terms of the agreement, the ownership of that work of art would immediately and automatically vest in a foundation separate from the museum. The agreement provided that the museum would promote the use of the collection so as to make the public aware of the quality of the collection and the setting in which the collection was displayed, all to the end that the collection would become open and accessible to, and stimulate the interest of, the general public.

The taxpayers requested this ruling to ensure that the estate of the survivor of them would receive a charitable estate tax deduction if it made the bequest, and that the amount of the deduction would be equal to the full fair market value of the collection included in the survivor's gross estate under sections 2031 and 2033. The IRS ruled that the estate would be entitled to a charitable deduction equal to the full fair market value of the collection.

In general, the amount allowable as an estate tax charitable deduction under section 2055 is the fair market value of the property passing to charity. In certain instances, however, this value may not be the same as the value determined for estate tax inclusion purposes under section 2031.[332]

The ruling noted that under the terms of both wills, the collection would pass to the museum on the death of the survivor of the taxpayers. The museum was an organization described in section 501(c)(3), and if the museum did not accept the collection, the collection would pass to another organization also described in section 501(c)(3). Under the agreement, the museum could not sell any of the collection and could loan art in the collection only under defined circumstances. Under no circumstances would the collection revert to the taxpayers or inure to the benefit of other private individuals.

Accordingly, the IRS ruled that the value of the proposed bequest of the collection to the museum on the death of the survivor of the taxpayers would be deductible under section 2055. In addition, the amount of that deduction would be the full fair market value of the collection includable in the gross estate under sections 2031 and 2033. In essence, the IRS said the restrictions imposed on the museum had no effect on the fair market value of the collection.

RETAINED COPYRIGHT INTEREST

Section 423 of ERTA amended sections 2055(e) and 2522(c) to permit, under certain conditions, a charitable gift or estate tax deduction for the transfer by gift or bequest after December 31, 1981, of a work of art—but not its copyright—to a charitable organization.

On October 21, 1983, the IRS published proposed regulations pertaining to sections 2055(e) and 2522(c). On May 17, 1984, the final regulations were published in the Federal Register.[333] The final regulations clarify the statute in a number of ways, and they point out a potential trap for the unwary artist and collector.

TAX LAW BACKGROUND
If a decedent or a donor transfers an interest in a property to both a charitable donee and a noncharitable donee—that is, transfers to each a split interest that is less than the entire interest—no estate or gift tax charitable deduction is allowed unless the gift is made in certain specified forms.[334] No charitable deduction is allowed for a remainder interest unless the remainder interest qualifies as a charitable remainder annuity trust, a charitable remainder unitrust, a pooled income fund, a farm, or a personal residence. No charitable deduction is allowed for an income interest unless it is in the form of a guaranteed annuity interest or a unitrust interest.

A split-interest charitable transfer of non-income-producing property, such as a work of art, does not qualify for a charitable deduction, since it cannot be put in the form of a guaranteed annuity or pay out a fixed percentage of its fair market value yearly. To qualify as a unitrust, the trust must be able to make an annual income payment to the noncharitable beneficiary, and the trustee must not be restricted from investing the trust assets in a manner intended to realize an annual income.[335]

Under the existing IRS regulations, an original work of art and a copyright interest relating to that work of art are for tax purposes two interests in the same property.[336] Since a work of art cannot qualify for any of the specified forms of split-interest charitable transfers, no charitable deduction was allowable under pre-1982 law when a collector gave the original artwork to a charity and retained the copyright interest attributable to that work of art.

COPYRIGHT LAW BACKGROUND
The Copyright Act of 1976, which went into effect January 1, 1978, treats the original artwork and the intangible copyright as two separate items of property. Section 202 of the Copyright Act provides the following:

Ownership of a copyright, or any of the exclusive rights under a copyright, is distinct from ownership of any material object in which the work is embodied.

A brief explanation of the Copyright Act of 1976, as it applies to the visual arts, follows.[337] The 1976 Act almost entirely eliminates common-law copyrights. All works of art are now protected by statutory copyright as soon as they are created in tangible form. The copyright is completely separate from ownership of the physical work of art. The copyright can be transferred only in writing, and its owner or the owner's agent must sign that transfer. The term of copyright is the artist's life plus seventy years. Under prior copyright law, it was possible for copyright protection to be lost if publication took place without a proper copyright notice. "Publication" means public distribution. A copyright notice is no longer necessary under current law for a work of art.

The history of the 1976 Act indicates that Congress did not intend unique works of art to be considered as published when they are sold or offered for sale in such traditional ways as through an art dealer, a gallery, or an auction house. However, to be on the safe side, an artist should place the required copyright notice on a work of art before the artwork is sold or publicly displayed. The form of copyright notice is as follows: "©" or "Copr." or "Copyright" followed by the artist's name or an abbreviation by which she is recognized and the year of publication. The copyright notice can be placed on the front or the back of the work of art or on any backing, mounting, matting, framing, or other material to which the work is permanently attached or in which it is permanently housed.

INTERACTION OF TAX LAW AND COPYRIGHT LAW

The tax regulations have always treated a work of art and its copyright as two interests in the same property. The Copyright Act of 1976 treats a work of art and its copyright as two separate property interests. The inconsistency made it impossible to obtain a charitable deduction for a work of art transferred to a charity if the contributor retained the copyright interest. Section 2055(e)(4) is an attempt by Congress to allow some flexibility in that area.[338]

Section 2055(e) was amended by ERTA by adding subsection (4), which provides for estate tax purposes that a work of art and its copyright are treated as separate properties in certain cases. The statute applies only to a "qualified contribution of a work of art"[339] and defines the term "work of art" as any tangible personal property with respect to which there is a copyright under federal law.[340] As stated above, a federal statutory copyright for a work of art comes into existence at its creation. Therefore, all works of art created after January 1, 1978, meet the definition of the statute.

The term "qualified contribution" means

any transfer of property to a qualified organization if the use of the property by the organization is related to the purpose or function constituting the basis for its exemption under Section 501.[341]

That rule is similar to the related use rule under section 170(e)(1)(B)(i). Therefore, a contribution is a qualified contribution for purposes of the retained copyright provision only if the related use rule is satisfied. If the contribution is not a qualified contribution, the old split-interest rule applies; that is, the work of art and its copyright are treated as two interests in the same property, rather than as two separate property interests.

The statute applies only to qualified contributions made to a qualified organization.[342] The term "qualified organization" means any organization described in section 501(c)(3) other than a private foundation under section 509. For that purpose, a private operating foundation under section 4942(j)(3) is not treated as a private foundation.

Therefore, section 2055(e)(4) for the first time allows a decedent to make a transfer of a work of art to a charitable organization, with her estate retaining the copyright interest so long as the transfer is not made to a private foundation and the transfer satisfies the estate tax related use rule of section 2055(e)(4)(C).[343]

THE COLLECTOR

Under the Copyright Act of 1976, the artist retains the ownership of the copyright in a unique work of art created on or after January 1, 1978, unless the copyright is specifically transferred in writing. Accordingly, in most cases, when the collector purchases a work of art created on or after January 1, 1978, she is purchasing a work of art without the copyright.

The final regulations under section 2055(e)(4) make it clear that section 2055(e)(4) does not apply to a decedent who never had the copyright interest. Section 2055(e)(4)(A) states that the work of art and the copyright are treated as separate properties for purposes of section 2055(e)(2), which applies to split-interest transfers—that is, transfers in which separate property interests in the same property pass from one person to two separate persons at the same time. If the testator never had the copyright, she cannot make a split-interest transfer under section 2055(e)(2). Example (2) of regulation section 20.2055-2(e)(1)(ii) (e) reads as follows:

> B, a collector of art, purchased a work of art from an artist who retained the copyright interest. B died in 1983. Under the terms of B's will the work of art is given to Y charity. Since B did not own the copyright interest, paragraph (e)(1)(i) of this section does not apply to disallow a deduction under section 2055 for the value of the work of art, regardless of whether or not the contribution is a qualified contribution under paragraph (e)(1)(ii)(c) of this section.

Therefore, when the will of a collector transfers a work of art to a charitable organization, the collector need not worry about satisfying the related use rule of section 2055(e)(4)(C) if she has never owned the copyright interest. If she does own the copyright interest, the charitable bequest should contain specific language to the effect that the copyright is included in the transfer in order to avoid any possibility of running afoul of the related use rule of section 2055(e)(4)(C).

The Artist

The problem and the potential trap for the artist are best illustrated by a simple example: The will of an artist bequeaths a specific work of art that was created after January 1, 1978, to the artist's local church and the balance of the estate to the artist's son. The will reads as follows: "I give and bequeath my painting entitled 'xyz' to the A Church. All the rest of my property of any kind I give and bequeath to my son."

Since the artist owned the copyright at the time of death (federal statutory copyright comes into existence at creation) and since the A Church, although a public charity, probably cannot satisfy the related use rule of section 2055(e)(4)(C), will the artist's estate get the estate tax charitable deduction?

The quoted provision in the artist's will does not pass the copyright in the work of art to the charity since the copyright is a separate property interest and must be separately bequeathed.[344] The copyright interest was not included in the charitable transfer; it was transferred as part of the residuary clause. Therefore, the transfer was a split-interest transfer that, unless the provisions of section 2055(e)(4) were satisfied, results in the loss of the charitable deduction. If the transfer to the local church did not satisfy the related use rule of section 2055(e)(4)(C), the charitable deduction is lost.

The final regulations under section 2055(e)(4) also contain an example illustrating the potential trap for the artist.[345] The example makes it clear that the IRS looks to local state law to see if the purported transfer of the work of art to the charitable organization includes the copyright. We believe that the simple will clause quoted above does not include the copyright interest in any local jurisdiction in the United States. Such a clause allows the copyright interest to become a part of the residuary estate.[346]

To avoid the problem of an inadvertent split-interest transfer that fails to satisfy the related use rule of section 2055(e)(4)(C), estate planners should examine the artist's will to make sure that any charitable transfers of works of art created after January 1, 1978, are transfers that also specifically transfer the copyright interest to the same charitable organization. For example: "I give and bequeath to the A Charity my painting entitled 'ABC,' oil on canvas, measuring 30 inches by 50 inches and dated 1988, and my copyright interest, if any, in that painting." Under that provision, the copyright interest will not inadvertently fall into the residue, thereby causing a split-interest transfer that may not satisfy the related use rule. Although there is no definitive authority, a clause that merely transfers "all my right, title, and interest in and to 'ABC' painting" may not be sufficient to transfer the copyright in the work of art. The careful drafter of a will must specifically include the copyright interest. (See Appendixes 15-7, 15-8, and 15-9 at the end of the chapter.)

Additional Problems under Section 2055(e)(4)

The final regulations do not address the question of whether a decedent's estate receives a charitable deduction for the full fair market value of the property transferred to a charity if a copyright interest is specifically retained.

The House Committee Report on H.R. 4242 indicates that the retention of the copyright or the failure to transfer the copyright does not affect the fair market value determination.[347] The report states that the value of a work of art and of the copyright can be determined separately from the sales of similar properties. The report then states the following:

> Moreover, the use or exploitation of the artwork or copyright generally does not affect the value of the other property. Accordingly, the value of the artwork (determined from comparable sales) which is used to determine the amount of the charitable deduction should provide a high degree of correlation with the value of property received by charity.

On the basis of the foregoing, the retention of a copyright interest apparently does not reduce the fair market value of the work of art given to a charity.

Section 2055(e)(4) speaks of a qualified contribution of a work of art.[348] It does not cover a contribution of a copyright interest. If a decedent transfers the copyright to a charity and retains the work of art for her heirs, that is not a qualified contribution of a work of art, and section 2055(e)(4) does not apply. Since such a transfer is a split-interest transfer not in unitrust form, no charitable deduction is allowed for the transfer of the copyright interest.

If the testator transfers the work of art to a public charity, satisfies section 2055(e)(4), and retains the copyright for her heirs, it is not clear whether the heirs can later transfer the copyright in such a manner as to receive a charitable deduction. Even if they can obtain a charitable deduction, it is a contribution of ordinary income property since a copyright is not a capital asset under section 1221(a)(3). Therefore, the amount of their deduction is limited to their basis in the copyright.[349]

Conclusion

Section 2055(e)(4) is a benefit for the artist who wants to bequeath works of art to a charitable organization and retain the copyright for reproduction purposes for the artist's heirs. Before January 1, 1982, that could not be done. If the artist wants to bequeath a work of art to a charitable organization but does not intend to retain the copyright interest, care must be taken to make sure that both the work of art and the copyright are specifically transferred to the charity. Otherwise, the statute is a trap for the unwary artist, whose estate tax charitable deduction may fail because of the related use rule of section 2055(e)(4)(C).

For collectors, section 2055(e)(4) presents no problem as long as the collector does not own the copyright. However, in preparing a will for a collector, an attorney should take care to make sure that if the collector does own any copyright interest, it is transferred to the charitable organization, along with the work of art.

NONCHARITABLE TRANSFERS

Not all collectors want to leave their collections to charitable organizations. There may be a strong family tie to a particular item that the collector wishes to stay in the family, a young member of the family may have developed a particular interest in the collection, or the collection may constitute a substantial portion of the collector's estate. In such cases noncharitable transfers must be considered.

Inter Vivos Transfers

Before January 1, 1977, a lifetime gift of a collection to a noncharitable beneficiary resulted in saving a large amount in estate taxes, because gift tax rates were only three-fourths as large as the estate tax rates in the corresponding bracket. The Tax Reform Act of 1976 removed some of the advantages of and the incentives for making lifetime gifts to a noncharitable beneficiary, although some do remain.

For gifts made on or after January 1, 1977, only one tax rate schedule covers both gift tax and estate tax.[350] The value of all taxable gifts made on or after January 1, 1977, is added to the taxable estate for the purpose of determining the applicable estate tax bracket. In other words, a donor can no longer take advantage of the low starting point on two separate rate schedules. To the extent that taxable gifts are made, they push the donor's estate into a higher estate tax bracket.

ADVANTAGES OF LIFETIME GIFTS

There are still advantages in making lifetime gifts of a collection:

1. A married donor can take advantage of the unlimited gift tax marital deduction for gifts made to a U.S. citizen spouse, effective January 1, 1982, for gifts made on or after that date.[351] The shifting of assets to one's spouse can be an effective estate planning tool. For example, the gift can remove the value of the donated assets from the donor's estate at no cost and can increase the donee's estate to the point at which the spouse can take maximum advantage of the unified credit, so that there is no tax in the donee's estate if that spouse dies first and leaves the donee's estate to their children or in trust for the surviving spouse. However, the donee should not leave the donated property back to the donor outright.
2. The donor can reduce any gift tax on gifts made to someone other than the donor's spouse by having the spouse consent to those gifts and by taking advantage of the gift-splitting provisions,[352] which permit a donor to compute the gift tax as if one-half of the gifts had been made by the donor's spouse.

3. Property used to pay the gift tax is not included in the estate of the donor for estate tax purposes if the donor lives at least three years after the date of the gift.[353]

4. A gift tax is paid only on the actual amount passing to the donee. An estate tax, on the other hand, is paid not only on the amount passing to the beneficiary but also on the money used to pay the estate tax.

5. Any appreciation in value after the date of the gift is removed from the donor's gross estate.

6. The amount of the gift tax can be reduced by taking advantage of the $13,000 annual exclusion.[354] ERTA increased the annual exclusion from $3,000 to $10,000 for gifts made on or after January 1, 1982. The Taxpayer Relief Act of 1997 increased, effective January 1, 1999, the $10,000 annual exclusion by inflation rounded to the next lowest multiple of $1,000 (if the inflation adjusted amount is not a multiple of $1,000). The requirement that the inflation adjustment be made only in increments of $1,000 meant that the first adjustment increasing the annual exclusion to $11,000 was not made until the year beginning 2001. The current annual exclusion is $13,000. The Revenue Act of 1978 amended section 2035 to provide that even if a donor dies within three years of a gift, if the donor was not required to file a gift tax return under section 6019, the value of the gift is not included in the gross estate.[355] Except under certain limited circumstances, most of section 2035 was abolished under ERTA for decedents who die on or after January 1, 1982.[356] That change freed from estate tax any appreciation in value of the property between the date of the gift and the date of the decedent's death.

7. The amount of the gift tax can be reduced by taking advantage of the $5,120,000 exclusion (unified credit against gift tax) under section 2505(a) in 2012. The 2010 Tax Relief Act (TRA)[357] reunified the estate and gift tax exclusions after 2010 by increasing the section 2010(c) estate tax exclusion amount to $5 million for decedents dying in 2010-2012, increasing the section 2505(a) gift tax exclusion amount to $5 million for gifts made in 2011-2012 (the amount remains at $1 million for gifts made in 2010), and adjusting the $5 million amount for inflation in multiples of $10,000 in 2012. For year 2012, the exclusion amount is increased to $5,120,000. The 2010 TRA also provides for portability of the exclusion for spouses dying in 2011-2012 (the applicable exclusion amount is the sum of the basic exclusion amount plus, in the case of a surviving spouse, the deceased spousal unused exclusion amount)[358] After 2012, the applicable exclusion amounts return to their pre-EGTRRA amounts ($1 million with no inflation adjustments and no portability) if the 2010 TRA changes are not extended or made permanent. A complete analysis of the 2010 TRA is well beyond the scope of this chapter. Once again, estate and tax planning is handicapped by the uncertainty in the gift and estate tax law.

Disadvantages of Lifetime Gifts

A lifetime gift to a noncharitable beneficiary also has certain disadvantages:

1. The collector must part with dominion and control of the collection.
2. On a valuable collection, the gift tax for a transfer to someone other than a spouse may be so high as to make such a transfer impractical.
3. Since the gift tax is payable in the year of the gift, the present loss of the gift tax money and the loss of future income on that money may be more painful than the thought of a larger estate tax that is not due until nine months after death and then only to the extent that the estate has not decreased in value or been consumed.
4. A married collector who is planning to take advantage of the unlimited estate tax marital deduction on death should consider owning the collection on death, so that the surviving spouse can receive a step-up in basis for the collection under section 1014(a).[359] That technique enables the surviving spouse to sell the collection and avoid the capital gains tax on any appreciation in value. If lifetime gifts are made, the advantage of a step-up in basis is lost.

Intrafamily Transfers

The lifetime gift of a collection to a noncharitable beneficiary can be outright, in trust, or a gift of a legal life estate. An intrafamily transfer, particularly if it is made to a family member living in the same household, can cause the donor a difficult burden of proof on the question of completion of the gift. A transfer of a collection to a family member must be evidenced by a deed of gift with a signed acceptance, the filing of a gift tax return, and the changing of the insurance policy, if any, to the new owner. It is also advisable to effect delivery of the collection being transferred. The foregoing is important to avoid the argument that the donor retained a lifetime use of the collection, which would make it includable in the donor's estate under section 2036(a). The problem is more difficult if the donor made a lifetime gift of the collection to a family member who did not share the donor's household and the donor did not physically deliver the collection to the donee. The retention of the collection in the donor's household for the donor's lifetime probably makes it includable in the donor's estate under section 2036(a)(1), even if the donor paid a gift tax on its transfer.[360]

Basis on Transfer

As noted above, the estate of a decedent who owns a collection that has appreciated in value receives a step-up in the basis of the collection to its fair market value on the date of death or six months later. As a result of the unlimited gift tax marital deduction, transfers between spouses can be made at no gift tax cost. Therefore, one spouse can transfer a collection to the other shortly before the donee dies for the purpose of receiving a step-up in basis for the transferred collection. If the will of the donee spouse leaves the same collection to the surviving spouse, there is no estate tax, because of the unlimited estate tax marital deduction, and the surviving spouse regains the collection at a stepped up basis. To discourage such predeath transfers, section 1014(e) provides that there is no step-up in basis in the case of appreciated property acquired by a decedent by gift during the one-year period before the death if that property is then reacquired by the donor under the decedent's will. That provision is effective for individuals who die after December 31, 1981.

The value of a collection included in an individual's gross estate for federal estate tax purposes is generally the value on the date of the person's death. However, the executor may elect to value the collection on the alternative valuation date, which is generally six months after the decedent's death.[361] As noted above, the basis of a collection acquired from a decedent is the value of the collection on the date of death or six months later. As a result of the unlimited estate tax marital deduction, in most cases there is no estate tax on the estate of the first spouse to die. Therefore, it is advantageous to the surviving spouse to have the collection valued on the date when the value is the highest, rather than the lowest, for federal estate tax purposes. That advantage was never the intent of section 2032 when it was enacted. The Tax Reform Act of 1984 changed the rule to provide that the alternative valuation date may be used only when both the total value of all property in the gross estate and the federal estate tax liability of the estate are reduced.[362] Therefore, in a zero tax estate the alternative valuation date cannot be used to obtain a larger stepped-up basis for a collection in a decedent's estate.

GRANTOR RETAINED INCOME TRUSTS

The discussion of grantor retained income trusts (GRITs) has been substantially changed as a result of the introduction of chapter 14 into the Internal Revenue Code by the Revenue Reconciliation Act of 1990.[363] A grantor retained income trust (GRIT) is a technique for transferring tangible property, such as a painting, to a family member at a reduced value for gift tax purposes. For example, under the old rule, section 2036(c), a donor could transfer a painting with a value of $1,500,000 to a son, retaining the use of the painting for a term of years (say, nine years). The donor would keep the painting for nine years; after the expiration of that term, the painting would be delivered to the donor's son. The painting had to be physically delivered to the remainderman (the son) at the end of the term of nine years. Since the donor had retained the use of the painting for a period of time (the nine years), the value of the remainder interest in the painting given to the donor's son was determined under the IRS actuarial tables.[364] That retained use reduced the value of the gift to the son (the son was receiving only a remainder interest), since the son was receiving less than the whole interest in the painting. The value of the gift to the son might, therefore, be only $600,000, instead of $1,500,000, the value of the entire interest in the painting. At the end of the term of nine years, the painting was transferred to the son at no additional gift tax cost. The benefit of the technique was further enhanced if the painting appreciated in value during the term of years that the donor retained its use.

The Revenue Reconciliation Act of 1990 repealed section 2036(c) and added the new rules of chapter 14 (sections 2701–2704), effective October 8, 1990. Under the new provisions, the general rule—the one governing the transfer of property to a family member[365] when there is a retained interest for a term of years—is to value the retained interest in the property that is transferred to a family member at zero, rather than compute the value under the IRS actuarial tables.[366] That zero-value rule makes the value of the property for gift tax purposes equal to the full fair market value of the property on the date of the gift. That rule (save for the exception described below) effectively eliminates any leverage that had been available by the use of a GRIT to transfer property to the next generation. Under the new rules, the value of the use of the property for a term of years is zero, so the value of the property transferred is equal to its full fair market value and is not reduced by any retained interest, as was done under the prior law.

Section 2702(c)(4) offers an exception under certain conditions for a GRIT transfer of tangible property (for example, a painting).[367] Under the exception, the value of the retained interest in a painting for a term of years is not zero if the nonexercise of rights under that interest does not have a substantial effect on the valuation of the remainder interest in the property.[368] In such a case, the value of the term interest

> shall be the amount which the holder of the term interest establishes as the amount for which such interest could be sold to an unrelated third party.[369]

Works of art, including paintings, sculptures, antiques, rugs, and other collectibles, should fall within the exception since exercising ownership rights over the tangible property does not have a substantial effect on the value of the remainder interest if the tangible property is put to normal use. In other words, the failure to exercise an ownership right over a painting (the right to exhibit, loan, or store the painting) does not increase the value of the painting that passes to the donee at the end of the term of years.

Even if a painting falls within the exception for tangible property, establishing the value of the term interest retained by the donor is no easy task. The regulations adopted on January 28, 1992, provide that the donor bears the burden of proof in establishing the value of the retained term interest and that the value is the amount a willing buyer would pay a willing seller for the term interest, each having reasonable knowledge of the relevant facts and neither being under any compulsion to buy or sell.[370] If the donor cannot reasonably establish the value of the term interest, the interest is valued at zero. The regulations[371] go on to provide that the best evidence of the value of any term interest consists of actual sales or rentals that are comparable to the nature and the character of the property and the duration of the term interest. Little weight is accorded appraisals in the absence of such evidence. Amounts determined under the IRS actuarial tables are not evidence of what a willing buyer would pay a willing seller for the retained interest.

The regulations establish a difficult burden of proof for the donor. In appraising a painting, whether for gift or donation purposes, the art appraiser often has difficulty in finding another work of art that is exactly comparable. The test of the regulations is hard to satisfy since finding comparable evidence of the fair market value of a painting similar in its nature and character and in the duration of the term interest is usually impossible. To our knowledge, virtually no market exists for the rental of valuable works of art for a term of years; to the extent that such a transaction may exist, it is highly confidential, and the details would not be available to an art appraiser.[372] The example given in the regulations does not offer much help:

> Facts. *A* transfers a painting having a fair market value of $2,000,000 to *A*'s child, *B*, retaining the use of the painting for 10 years. The painting does not possess an ascertainable useful life. Assume that the painting would not be depreciable if it were used in a trade or business or held for the production of income. Assume that the value of *A*'s term interest, determined under section 7520, is $1,220,000, and that *A* establishes that a willing buyer of *A*'s interest would pay $500,000 for the interest.

> Example 9. Assume that the only evidence produced by *A* to establish the value of *A*'s 10-year term interest is the amount paid by a museum for the right to use a comparable painting for 1 year. *A* asserts that the value of the 10-year term is 10 times the value of the 1-year term. *A* has not established the value of the 10-year term interest because a series of short-term rentals the aggregate duration of which equals the duration of the actual term interest does not establish what a willing buyer would pay a willing seller for the 10-year term interest. However, the value of the 10-year term interest is not less than the value of the 1-year term because it can be assumed that a willing buyer would pay no less for a 10-year term interest than a 1-year term interest.[373]

Since it appears to be extremely difficult to establish the value of a retained interest in tangible property under the new IRS rules, the use of a GRIT for transferring a painting among family members is eliminated as an effective estate planning device. However, a GRIT is still useful for the transfer of a painting to nonfamily members.

The *Stone* Case

Stone v. United States[374] allowed a 5% discount to an estate that owned an undivided 50% interest in nineteen paintings that were left to family members. *Stone* is the first case to reflect on whether or not discounts based on lack of control, minority ownership, or lack of 100% interest with respect to ownership of works of art can lead to a discount for estate tax purposes as it does for real estate. In *Stone*, the estate claimed a 44% discount for the undivided 50% interest in the paintings owned by the decedent on the date of death. The IRS argued that there should be no discount at all (the court noted, however, that the IRS's own expert said 2% was appropriate, and eventually the IRS conceded a 5% discount). The federal district court in California concluded that a hypothetical willing seller of an undivided fractional interest in art would likely seek to sell the entire work of art and split the proceeds, rather than seek to sell his or her fractional interest at a discount. In other words, the court thought that a hypothetical willing seller who is under no compulsion to sell would seek the consent of the other co-owner or co-owners to sell the collection and divide the proceeds or, barring such consent, would bring a legal action to partition. Therefore, at a minimum, because an undivided interest holder has the right to partition, a hypothetical seller under no compulsion to sell would not accept any less for his or her undivided interest than could be obtained by splitting proceeds in this manner. Rather than reach its own conclusion, the court ordered the parties to meet and confer to see if they could agree on an appropriate discount, based on the cost of a hypothetical partition action. When the parties were unable to agree, the court was forced to make a decision.

The court in *Stone* then decided[375] that the taxpayer's appraisal methodology was flawed because (1) it failed to take into account that collectors of art are often drawn to the aesthetics of a particular work of art, rather than viewing art simply as an investment vehicle; and (2) the mathematical assumptions made by the appraiser as to the rate of return on investments in art and the appropriate net present value percentage were made without supporting evidence. The taxpayer could not meet his burden of persuading the court that a hypothetical buyer would demand, and a hypothetical seller would agree to, a discount greater than 5%.

The Ninth Circuit Court of Appeals affirmed the district court opinion in *Stone* on March 24, 2009.[376] In doing so, the Ninth Circuit pointed out that the regulations require valuation based on a hypothetical willing buyer and a hypothetical willing seller but it is the taxpayer who bears the burden of proof. The court found that the taxpayer's expert lacked experience with the art market and that there are dissimilar motives driving purchasers of art and purchasers of real estate or limited-partnership shares. Although there was very little market data on the sale of fractional interests in works of art, the IRS regulations required the assumption of a hypothetical market. In the assumed hypothetical market for the sale of the fractional interest, the district court did not "clearly err" in adopting the IRS position of a 5% discount.

A review of the IRS interpretation of fractional gifts beginning with Revenue Ruling 57-293 and then Private Letter Rulings 93-03-007, 200223013, and 200418002 shows that the IRS has been consistent in its interpretation for income tax, gift tax, and estate tax that the proper approach for determining the amount of the deduction, whether the work of art is donated during the donor's lifetime or is transferred at death, is to take the full fair market value of the work of art multiplied by the percentage transferred. The position of the IRS is that the same methodology is true whether the work of art is transferred to charity or to a noncharitable beneficiary, that is, a member of the taxpayer's family. In other words, fractional interests in works of art seem to receive a different treatment than fractional interests in real estate or other assets for which it is fairly common to claim a discount for lack of control, minority ownership, or lack of 100% interest.[377]

The case is a warning sign that art is treated differently from real estate or closely held businesses when it comes time to apply discounts. Accordingly, it should not be assumed that the discounts usually available for lack of 100% ownership interest will be available in the same manner as in real estate cases.

Perhaps works of art are treated differently because one can still fully enjoy a work of art for a percentage of the time and, in fact, that percentage may have a market value equal to the percentage multiplied by the fair market value of the work of art. With no market data available for the sale of an undivided fractional interest in art, it could just as easily be assumed as not that a hypothetical willing buyer would be willing to pay the full fair market value of a painting times a percentage times equal to his percentage of ownership, in order to own and have personal use of the painting, even if it is only for a percentage of each year. Such is the passion of art collectors. If a transfer is made to a person who does not own the other part of the interest, the taxpayer should have a fair chance of convincing the IRS to allow some small discount for a fractional interest in the painting. If the transfer is made to a transferee—for example, a museum—that already owns a partial interest in the painting, the charitable deduction should be the percentage transferred multiplied by the full fair market value of the painting on the date of transfer. However, in light of the foregoing rulings and the decision in the *Stone* case, if one is thinking of transferring works of art to family members either during one's lifetime or on death, one should not assume that the discounts usually available for lack of a 100% ownership interest will be available.

FAMILY LIMITED PARTNERSHIPS

In *Holman v. Commissioner*,[378] the issue was the value of units in a family limited partnership (FLP) that held only Dell, Inc. common stock. The taxpayer drafted the FLP with various stated purposes, including providing protection for family assets, maintaining control over family assets, and promoting the family's knowledge of and about family assets. The taxpayer then applied various discounts based on restrictions on the transfer of the FLP units to family members—the restrictions justified by the carrying out of the FLP purposes. The Tax Court concluded that there was no "bona fide business arrangement" and the restrictions were "merely a testamentary device such that the donors failed to satisfy § 2703(b)(2)."

The decision was affirmed by the Eighth Circuit,[379] which noted that in attempting to sort permissible and impermissible uses of such restrictions, "Congress repealed an earlier Code provision, I.R.C. § 2036(c) (1987), because 'the committee [was] concerned that the statute's complexity, breadth, and vagueness posed an unreasonable impediment to the transfer of family business.'"[380] In 1990, Congress enacted in its place a statute that broadly prohibits consideration of restrictions for valuation purposes, but allows taxpayers to prove eligibility for an exception that permits valuation based on such restrictions.[381]

To be eligible for the exception and gain the benefit of having such restrictions considered for valuation purposes, the taxpayer must satisfy a three-part test: (1) the restriction must be "a bona fide business arrangement," (2) it must not be "a device to transfer such property to members of the decedent's family for less than full and adequate consideration," and (3) its terms must be "comparable to similar arrangements entered into by persons in arms' length transaction." Because the Tax Court found that there was not a bona fide business arrangement, it addressed only the first test of section 2703(b). The Eighth Circuit affirmed the concept of section 2703(b)—that the "context matters" in which any restrictions are created—and found that the motivation of the taxpayers was primarily personal and aimed at wealth transfer rather than a bona fide business arrangement.

If, instead of Dell, Inc. stock, the FLP held works of art, the taxpayer would have to address all three parts of section 2703(b). Not only would there have to be a "bona fide business purpose," but the taxpayer would bear the burden of proof that (1) the transfer was not a device to transfer the works of art to family members for less than full and adequate consideration in money or money's worth and (2) the terms were comparable to similar arrangements entered into by persons in an arm's-length transaction. As discussed further below, it would be extremely difficult for a taxpayer to carry this burden of proof as it applies to works of art, since there is no similar business arrangement in the art world and there is no comparable similar arrangement entered into by persons in an arm's-length transaction. The only comparable arrangement is where two dealers jointly purchase a work of art and hold it for resale. In such a case, there are no discounts involved between the dealers and each wants to realize his percentage share of the value of the work of art.

Estate of James A. Elkins[382] involved an attempt by the taxpayer to use fractional interests and restrictions to reduce the value on the transfer of an art collection to family members. In *Elkins*, the decedent held an undivided interest in sixty-four pieces of art. In sixty-one of them, he held a 73% interest, with his three children owning the balance. The parties stipulated that the undiscounted value of the sixty-one pieces was $18,000,000. In the other three art works, the decedent held a 50% interest, with the balance held by his children, and the stipulated undiscounted value was $5,500,000.

Two of the works of art (a Jackson Pollock and a Pablo Picasso) were subject to an "Art Lease." The rest were subject to a "Cotenants Agreement." Each document contained a restriction on the use and assignment or sale of the art work.

The Cotenants Agreement provided in part:

7.   An item of the Property may only be sold with the unanimous consent of all of the Cotenants. Any net proceeds from the sale of such item shall

be payable to the Cotenants in accordance with their respective percentage interests in the Property.

8. This Agreement shall be binding on Cotenants and on their respective heirs, personal representatives, successors and assigns.

9. This Agreement shall be governed and construed under the laws of the State of Texas.

The Art Lease provided in part:

Section 10:

Lessors and Lessee each agrees not to sell his or her percentage interest in any item of the Property during the Initial Term or any Additional Term without the joinder [sic] of all of the Property Owners for the purpose of selling the item of Property in its entirety.

Section 13:

This Lease, and the respective rights, duties and obligations of Lessors and Lessee hereunder, may not be transferred or assigned by any or all of Lessors and Lessee without the consent of Lessors and Lessee. Subject to the preceding sentence, this Lease shall be binding upon and inure to the benefit of Lessors and Lessee and their respective heirs, representatives, successor or assigns.

The Estate claimed a 44% discount based on fractional discount, lack of control, and lack of marketability. The position of the IRS was that no discount should apply since the arrangement fails the tests of section 2703(b). In the taxpayer's plan, the decedent wanted to keep possession of the art collection during his lifetime so he leased back from the children the percentage of art he did not own. However, no rental payments were made and the lease agreement left blank the amount of rent due.

Although at this writing the case has not yet been decided by the Tax Court, when section 2703(b) is applied to the above facts, it appears to us that the taxpayer has little chance of success. The taxpayer may try to justify the arrangement as a "bona fide business arrangement" in that he wants to keep the art collection together as a whole. Even if the court so determines, there still seems to be no justification for the arrangement other than a device to transfer property to the decedent's children at less than fair market value. Further, there is no comparable similar arrangement in the art world that exists by persons in an arm's-length transaction. There is no determinable market for the rental value of fractional interests in works of art; in fact, there is no market for the rental of valuable works of art, whether a fractional interest or otherwise. At best, we believe the taxpayer would be entitled to some discount based on the cost of a partition action, under the *Stone* case, but the amount would not likely be very large.

The taxpayer countered the above argument by saying that section 2703(a) does not apply. Section 2703(a) provides that, for estate tax purposes "the value of the property must be determined without regard to . . . any restriction on the right to sell or use such property." The taxpayer argued that the cotenants agreement and the lease only restrict the sale and use of the works of art but do not restrict the sale and use of the "fractional interests" in the works of art.[383] The taxpayer argued that Paragraph 8 of the Cotenants Agreement (quoted above) expressly contemplates that a sale of a fractional interest would itself be unrestricted and that Paragraph 7 (also quoted above) restricts only the sale of the art as a whole and not a fractional interest. It remains to be seen what the Tax Court thinks of this distinction and whether or not the works of art are, in fact, treated differently from other property.

LIFETIME SALES

A lifetime sale of a collection generally results in a capital gain or a capital loss. A capital gain is taxable,[384] and a capital loss is nondeductible[385] unless it can be shown that the collection was held as an investment property, which is discussed in detail in chapter 14. If the collection is ordinary income property, the collector realizes ordinary income on its sale.[386]

Testamentary Transfers

A collector who has not made a lifetime transfer of the collection must provide for its disposition on her death. The fair market value of the collection, on the date of death or six months later, is included in the gross estate.[387] However, despite the potential tax disadvantage, the collector may prefer to enjoy possession of the collection throughout her lifetime.

OUTRIGHT TRANSFER

A specific bequest in the will should be used to bequeath a collection outright to a noncharitable beneficiary or beneficiaries. (See Appendixes 15-7 and 15-8 at the end of the chapter.) The attorney should make sure that the items are sufficiently identified so that there is no confusion after the testator's death. If the beneficiary and the testator live in different cities, the problem of the cost of shipping should be considered. The cost is borne by the beneficiary unless a special clause is used in the will. (See Appendix 15-10 at the end of the chapter.) In addition to amounts that qualify for the marital deduction, the amount that can be bequeathed estate-tax-free has been increased from $1 million to $5 million under the 2010 Tax Relief Act (TRA).[388] As note earlier, the TRA reunified the estate and gift tax exclusions after 2010 by increasing the section 2010(c) estate tax exclusion amount to $5 million for decedents dying in 2010-2012, increasing the section 2505(a) gift tax exclusion amount to $5 million for gifts made in 2011-2012 (the amount remains at $1 million for gifts made in 2010), and adjusting the $5 million amount for inflation in multiples of $10,000 in 2012. For year 2012, the exclusion amount is increased to $5,120,000. The 2010 TRA also provides for portability of the exclusion for spouses dying in 2011-2012 (the applicable exclusion amount is the sum of the basic exclusion amount plus, in the case of a surviving spouse, the deceased spousal unused exclusion amount). After 2012, the applicable exclusion amounts return to their pre-EGTRRA amounts ($1 million with no inflation adjustments and no portability) if the 2010 TRA changes are not extended or made permanent. A complete analysis of the 2010 TRA is well beyond the scope of this chapter. Once again, estate and tax planning is handicapped by the uncertainty in the gift and estate tax law.

In *Estate of Ludwig Neugass*,[389] the decedent had a valuable art collection, some of which he wished his wife to have outright. His will provided that his wife was to have a right to take any items she chose within six months of his death. The IRS disallowed the marital deduction for the items chosen, alleging that such a right was a terminable interest, which does not qualify for the marital deduction. The Tax Court upheld the IRS, but the court of appeals reversed and held for the taxpayer.

It is safest to decide before the testator's death which items should be left to the surviving spouse and to leave those items outright. As the court in *Neugass* pointed out, the factor that determines whether the marital deduction is allowed is whether or not the action required by the surviving spouse is a mere formality, as opposed to being subject to a condition that may never be met.[390]

TRANSFER IN TRUST

A testator may wish to give the surviving spouse a life estate in a collection, with the remainder to go to their children on the spouse's death. The basic idea is to make one transfer cover two estates, with only one estate tax imposed. Although a legal life estate can be used, it is preferable to create a trust, because of its greater flexibility. The terms of the trust should specify who should pay for insurance, storage, and any other expenses. The life tenant may be given a special power of appointment, either inter vivos or testamentary, as to all or one or more of the items in the collection. The trustee should be given the power to cause any of the items to be sold, in which event the trust should provide how the proceeds are to be held and applied. That clause is necessary so that in the event of a family misfortune the life tenant is not left with a valuable collection and no money with which to pay bills. As always, the estate planner must be careful with the selection of the trustee and the powers given to the beneficiary, or the trust will be included in the life tenant's estate. The trust can be drafted so that it qualifies for the estate tax marital deduction.[391]

SELLING THE COLLECTION AFTER DEATH

Deduction of Selling Expenses

Since a collection may constitute the bulk of a decedent's estate, the executor may have to sell all or a part of the collection in order to pay estate taxes and other administrative expenses. The sale may also be necessary to make sure that the decedent's spouse or children are financially secure and will receive income yearly. The commission expenses on the sale of a large collection can be large. Therefore, a will must be drafted so that such commissions can be claimed as deductions on the federal estate tax return.

Section 2053(a)(2) provides the following:

> [T]he value of the taxable estate shall be determined by deducting from the value of the gross estate such amounts . . . for administrative expenses . . . as are allowable by the laws of the jurisdiction, whether within or without the United States, under which the estate is being administered.

Regulation section 20.2053-3(d)(2) provides the following:

> Expenses for selling property of the estate are deductible if the sale is necessary in order to pay the decedent's debts, expenses of administration or taxes, to preserve the estate, or to effect distribution. The phrase "expenses for selling property" includes brokerage fees and other expenses attending the sale, such as the fees of an auctioneer if it is reasonably necessary to employ one.

That regulation has been in substantially similar form since 1919. The regulation imposes the requirement that the expenses be necessary for one of the stated purposes in order to be deductible, even though that requirement is not in the statute.

In *Sternberger's Estate*,[392] the Tax Court permitted a deduction for brokerage and legal fees incurred in connection with the sale of the decedent's residence, which the decedent's widow and daughter did not wish to occupy. The court stated that the expenses were properly allowable under New York law, and, even though the proceeds were not needed to pay the debts and expenses (and hence the residence automatically became a part of the residuary estate at the death of the decedent), a deduction was properly allowable under the predecessor of what is now section 2053(a)(2) since the executor was the one who actually made the sale.

In *Estate of Swayne*,[393] the Tax Court reversed itself and disallowed similar expenses for selling a Connecticut residence because the sale was not necessary, despite the fact that the sale was authorized by the local probate court. The court distinguished the case from *Sternberger* on the grounds that *Sternberger* involved New York law and did not raise the question of the necessity of the sale. Another distinction was that in *Swayne* the real property was specifically bequeathed, and in *Sternberger* it was part of the residue.

Estate of David Smith[394] involved a well-known artist who died owning 425 pieces of sculpture that he had created. At the time of his death, a contract with an art gallery was in existence that provided that the gallery had the exclusive right to sell the sculptures and receive commissions. That contract was renewed by Smith's executors. The decedent's will did not specifically direct his executors to sell the sculptures but provided for his estate to go in trust for his children. The estate did sell a substantial number of the sculptures, some to satisfy claims against the estate and others to fund the trusts for his daughters. The commissions paid to the gallery were allowed by the New York Surrogate's Court on an intermediate accounting.

The issue in the case involved the deduction for the commissions paid to the gallery. The IRS said that the deduction for the commissions paid is limited by the "necessary" requirement of regulation section 20.2053-3(d)(2). The executor initially argued that the commissions were deductible in full because the sales were made to preserve the estate or to effect the distribution of the estate or both. The executor contended that because of the volatile nature of the art market, it was necessary to sell the sculptures in order to preserve the estate.

The majority opinion of the Tax Court, relying on *Swayne*, held that the commissions on the sale of the decedent's sculptures were allowable as deductions on the estate tax return only to the extent that the sales were necessary to pay administrative expenses, debts, and taxes. The court specifically cited the "necessary" provision of the regulations and added that the provision of the statute that deductions are permitted for expenses allowable under the applicable state law "established a threshold and not an exclusive condition; the requirement of [the] regulations must also be satisfied."

Five judges dissented from the decision of the Tax Court on the grounds that the test of the statute depends on state law and that the "necessary" requirement of the regulations is invalid.

On appeal to the Second Circuit, the executors for the first time contested the validity of regulation section 20.2053-3(d)(2) and its "necessary" test. The Second Circuit did not pass on the legal issue of the validity of the regulation. Instead, the court said that the case turns on the question of fact as to whether the gallery fees were necessary under section 222 of the New York Surrogate's Court Procedure Act, which required such fees to be necessary in order to be allowable. The court found that the question of the necessity of the gallery fees was not contested in the lower court (although they were approved on the accounting); therefore, the federal court could make a de novo inquiry into the factual necessity of the gallery fees. The Second Circuit found the determination of the Tax Court in that regard was not clearly erroneous and affirmed the Tax Court decision.

One judge on the three-judge panel dissented and based his opinion on the dissent in the Tax Court and the Sixth Circuit opinion in *Estate of Park*, discussed below. The dissenting judge thought that the state surrogate's decision approving the gallery fees was binding on the federal courts and that the Tax Court had no authority to act as a surrogate Surrogate. Permission to appeal to the United States Supreme Court was denied.

The decision of the Second Circuit is questionable. Apparently, the court was saying that if the commissions were so outrageous that they were contested at the probate court level and were allowed in whole or in part, there would not be a de novo inquiry by the Tax Court. That reasoning is incorrect, since the laws of the state are interpreted and administered by the courts of the state and not by the Tax Court.

Further, the "necessary" requirement contained in the New York statute appears to have been misinterpreted by the Second Circuit. The "necessary" term has been replaced in a new statute by the term "reasonable and proper."[395] The revisers' note to the statute states that the new term is designed to incorporate the substance of its predecessor. Therefore, it is reasonable to conclude that the term "necessary" in the New York statute meant "reasonable and proper" and did not have the same meaning as the "necessary" requirement in regulation section 20.2053-3(d)(2).

In *Estate of Park*,[396] the Tax Court followed its decision in *Smith*, upholding the commissioner's refusal to allow a deduction for the expenses of selling a residence that passed to four residuary legatees. The legatees had asked the executor to sell the house, and its sale was not necessary to raise cash in order to pay administrative expenses. Therefore, the Tax Court disallowed the selling expenses as an estate tax deduction.

On appeal to the Sixth Circuit, the Tax Court was reversed on the ground that the literal language of the statute permitting a deduction for expenses allowable under local law leaves the issue of deductibility to state law. The expenses involved were paid out of probate assets, were admittedly allowable under Michigan law and, hence, the Sixth Circuit held, were deductible under section 2053(a)(2). In effect, the Sixth Circuit held that the "necessary" requirement of the regulations was invalid.

The *Smith* case was followed in *Hibernia Bank*,[397] but different reasoning was used in *Estate of Joseph Vatter*.[398] In *Vatter*, the decedent's will provided for the distribution of the residuary estate to a testamentary trust. Three parcels of rental properties, which were old and required maintenance, were part of the residuary estate. Because the trustee of the testamentary trust (a bank), would not accept the parcels as part of the trust, they were sold by the executor. The Tax Court upheld the deductibility of the sale expenses as being necessary to "effect distribution" of the residuary estate, finding them to be allowable administration expenses under both New York law and IRS regulations, even though the entire proceeds of the sale were not needed to pay the estate's obligations for debts, expenses, and taxes.

The *Vatter* case was decided by Judge Forrester, one of the dissenting Tax Court judges in *Smith*.

In Private Letter Ruling 78-02-006, the IRS followed *Park* in ruling that since the selling expenses under consideration in the ruling were allowable under local Ohio law, that was enough to qualify them as deductible under section 2053(a)(2), and there was no need to establish that the expenses were necessary, as required by the regulation. However, the ruling contained the following warning:

> The decision in the *Park* case will not be followed by the Service in disposing of similar cases outside the Sixth Circuit. In the Sixth Circuit, the Service is following *Park* for practical reasons only and may choose to litigate the issue again at some

more opportune time in the future. Thus, since Ohio is in the Sixth Circuit, the deductibility of the administration expenses is determined by reference to state law alone.[399]

In September 1997, the Sixth Circuit sitting en banc overruled *Park* in *Estate of Marguerite S. Millikin v. Commissioner*.[400] The Sixth Circuit had to examine the deductibility of expenses of maintaining and selling the decedent's residence after the removal of artworks from the residence and after the filing of the federal estate tax return. At death, the decedent was the beneficiary of a marital trust over which she had a general power of appointment. The trust held the decedent's house, which contained an extensive art collection, and the decedent's will gave a museum the right to select and retain any works of art in the house. The museum completed its selection by March 1990 and the estate filed its estate tax return on March 16, 1990. The trust paid all the expenses of maintaining the house after the decedent's death and until its sale in April 1994. The maintenance and selling expenses were $757,356.

Initially, the Sixth Circuit in *Millikin Estate*[401] affirmed the Tax Court, when it held that the decedent's estate was not entitled to deduct under section 2053 the expenses of maintaining and selling the house incurred after the filing of the estate tax return. The court based its decision on the Ohio statute that provides that the probate court must make "just and reasonable" allowances for "actual and necessary expenses."[402] Applying the Ohio statute, the court found that the expenses incurred with respect to the house after the filing of the estate tax return were not necessary expenses. The court reiterated the position stated in *Park* that it was the view of the Sixth Circuit that the deductibility of administration expenses is governed exclusively by state law and that the "necessary" requirement in regulation section 20.2053-3(d)(1) is not recognized.

The Sixth Circuit then reversed itself and overruled *Park*.[403] The court stated that it would no longer look only to state law in determining if an expense was an allowable deduction under section 2053(a)(2). Instead, the court held that it would follow a two-part test: First, the expense must meet the requirements of the Internal Revenue Code and Regulations so that it is deductible under section 2053(a)(2); and second, the expense must be allowable in the jurisdiction in which the estate is administered.[404] Because the Tax Court applied a different test for deductibility and because the facts were not sufficiently developed for the Sixth Circuit to apply the new test, the case was reversed and remanded for further proceedings.

The case of *Estate of Vera T. Posen*,[405] decided December 10, 1980, was reviewed by the full Tax Court and contains an excellent summary of many of the cases. The Tax Court held that a New York estate could not deduct expenses incurred in selling a decedent's cooperative apartment, even though those expenses were allowable administration expenses under applicable New York state law, because the sale was not necessary to pay estate taxes, effect estate distribution, or preserve the estate, as required by regulation section 20.2053-3(d)(2). In so holding, the Tax Court upheld the validity of the regulation and noted that under section 2053(a)(2) state law is not solely determinative of the deductibility of administrative expenses. The Tax Court distinguished *Vatter*, stating that in *Vatter* the sale of the real estate was necessary to effect distribution, since the residuary trustee would not otherwise accept the property, whereas in *Posen* the sale of the cooperative apartment was made solely for the benefit of the estate's heir.

One judge dissented on the ground that the regulation was invalid because state law controlled the deduction of estate expenses. A second dissent, in which three other judges joined, agreed that the regulation was invalid but noted that even if it were valid, the expenses were deductible because the sale was made in order to pay estate taxes and preserve the estate. Another dissenting judge thought that the regulation was valid but agreed with the second dissent as to the reasons for the sale.

The Tax Court's opinion illustrates the split of opinion in the federal courts about the effect of state law on the deductibility of administrative expenses. The Fifth, Sixth, and Ninth Circuits follow the Tax Court in concluding that state law provides merely a threshold test for determining deductibility under section 2053(a)(2) and that the requirements of the IRS regulations must also be satisfied. The Seventh Circuit has taken the position that the allowability of an expense under state law is itself determinative of deductibility as an administrative expense under section 2053(a)(2). The Second Circuit, to which *Posen* would be appealed, has not expressed an opinion as to the validity of the regulation.

In *Estate of Helen Ward DeWitt*,[406] decided in September 1987, the Tax Court once again refused to declare regulation section 20.2053-3(d)(2) and the "necessary" provision invalid. The case involved estate administration expenses that were approved by the New York state probate court as deductions for federal estate tax purposes. The IRS had denied the deductions for executor's commissions, legal fees, accounting fees, investment counsel fees, and disbursements made by those persons. The Tax Court noted that administration expenses approved by a state court are deductible for federal estate tax purposes only if the state court's ruling is based on facts demonstrating that the expenses were actually and necessarily incurred in the administration of the estate. The Tax Court held that such proof was established for the attorney's fees, accountant's fees, and executors' commissions but not for the fees paid to the investment adviser.

The final answer on the validity of regulation section 20.2053-3(d)(2) has not yet been given. It is clear that if the will contains a specific direction to sell, the expenses of the sale are deductible.[407] If the will contains no specific direction to sell, the expenses should be deductible if allowable by the local probate court, as is stated in section 2053(a). The "necessary" requirement of the regulations, which gives the Tax Court the power to question the local probate court, appears to us to be invalid.

The issue involved in *Estate of Streeter*[408] varies from the "necessary" requirement of regulation section 20.2053-3(d)(2). A collection was bequeathed in trust with a direction that it be sold by the trustees. The same persons were named as executors and trustees. The issue in the case concerned the deduction of sales commissions on the estate tax return. The executors transferred the collection to themselves in their capacity as trustees, and in that capacity they signed the sales agreement with the auction house. The Tax Court held that the expenses were incurred by the trust on the sale and, therefore, were properly deductible only by the trust, not by the executors.

On appeal to the Third Circuit (first hearing), the Tax Court was reversed, and the commissions were allowed as a deduction on the estate tax return under section 2053(a)(2). The Third Circuit did not have to consider the validity of regulation section 20.2053-3(d)(2) since it held that the expenses were deductible under the regulations as written. The court found that the sole purpose of the trust was to effect distribution of the decedent's estate, and the duties imposed by the decedent on the trustees were those normally performed by executors. A dissenting opinion held that a valid trust was created and that the expenses were the expenses of the trustees, not the executors.

On rehearing before the full bench of the Third Circuit, the dissenting opinion in the first hearing was adopted, upholding the Tax Court. The majority held that a valid trust was, in fact, created and that the expenses of the sale were the expenses of the trustees, not the executors. The Third Circuit noted that had the executors been empowered and directed by the will to sell the collection, the sale expenses would have been deductible under regulation section 20.2053-3(d)(2).

The taxpayer had relied on section 2053(b) and the regulations thereunder, which pertain to expenses incurred in connection with nonprobate property. There are two categories of estate tax deductions: (1) those payable out of property subject to claims that are allowable by the law of the probate jurisdiction[409] and (2) those incurred in administering property that is included in the gross estate but is not subject to claims.[410] Expenses of the first type are deductible under regulation section 20.2053-3(a), and expenses of the second type are deductible under regulation section 20.2053-8(a). The deductions in the second category do not include amounts pertaining to property passing through the probate estate, as was the case in *Streeter*.

The cases make it clear that if the executor is directed by the will to sell the collection, the expenses are allowed as a deduction under section 2053(a)(2) on the estate tax return. If no direction is included in the will and the sale is made by the executors, the sale must run the risk of the application of the "necessary" requirement in the regulations. The estate planner must not make the mistake made in *Streeter*: leaving the collection to a trust and directing the trustee to sell the collection. Under those circumstances, the expenses are not deductible, even if the "necessary" requirement of the regulation is finally held to be invalid.

The question of what is a deductible miscellaneous administration expense for federal estate tax purposes under regulation section 20.2053-3(d) is not clear. Estates incur selling expenses in disposing of works of art in an estate. Those expenses may be allowable expenses in the applicable state probate court, but the IRS may still attempt to disallow the expenses because of the additional requirement under regulation section 20.2053-3(d)(2) that the expenses be necessary in order to pay the decedent's debts, expenses of administration, or taxes; to preserve the estate; or to effect distribution. The various circuit courts of appeals have reached different conclusions as to whether state law or federal law controls the determination of what is a deductible administrative expense for federal estate tax purposes. The Seventh Circuit has held that state law controls the issue.[411] The Second, Fifth, Sixth, and Ninth Circuits have held that although the position of state law on the issue is important, policy considerations require that federal regulations also be applied to make the determination.[412] The Fourth Circuit, in *Estate of Margaret D. Love*,[413] joined the Second, Fifth, Sixth, and Ninth Circuits in holding that federal law is controlling in determining whether an estate is entitled to a claimed administration expense. Although the *Love* case did not involve a selling expense (the question was the deductibility of a foal-sharing expense), it does emphasize the point that the allowability of an expense by a state probate court is no guarantee that the expense will be deductible for federal estate tax purposes. If it is anticipated that large or unusual administrative expenses will be incurred in administering an estate, the deductibility of those expenses should be planned for in advance. That can be done by directing the executor to sell the works of art, thereby satisfying the requirement of the IRS regulation that the expense be necessary to effect the distribution of the estate.[414]

As discussed in detail on pages 1254–1255 of this chapter, the IRS has issued Private Letter Ruling 92-35-005, which requires an estate that sells works of art at auction to use the hammer price plus the auction house buyer's premium as the federal estate tax value. In most cases, the executors are able to claim a deduction for the buyer's premium under regulation section 20.2053-3(d). The consignment contracts of both Sotheby's and Christie's (and presumably other auction houses that have a buyer's premium) specifically provide that the seller (the consignor-estate) authorizes the auction house to receive and retain from the proceeds of sale the buyer's premium. Accordingly, under the IRS theory, the buyer's premium is, in effect, a cost of the estate incurred in selling the works of art, which cost is paid by the buyer. The cost is, therefore, deductible to the extent that the requirements of regulation sections 20.2053-3(a) and 20.2053-3(d) are satisfied. Works of art that are directed to be sold or that are disposed of under the residuary clause among multiple beneficiaries should satisfy the IRS requirement that the sale be necessary to effect distribution of the estate. As a practical matter, works of art cannot be divided among multiple beneficiaries, since the artworks cannot be broken up and their respective values cannot be determined with enough precision to enable the executors to fulfill their fiduciary duty of fairness to all beneficiaries.

Denial of Double Deduction

Before the Tax Reform Act of 1976, the allowability of sale expenses was important, not only for estate tax purposes but also for income tax purposes, because Revenue Ruling 71-173[415] held that expenses allowable under section 2053 as a deduction on the estate tax return can also be offset against the selling price in computing the estate's taxable income. That ruling resulted in the expenses being claimed as a deduction on the estate tax return and as a reduction of the selling price (which reduces the amount of taxable income) on the income tax return. The Tax Reform Act of 1976 changed that result by amending section 642(g) to limit the deduction for selling expenses to either the estate tax return or the income tax return. The new statute eliminates the double deduction by including "an offset against the sales price of property in determining gain or loss" as the equivalent of a deduction. Revenue Ruling 71-173 no longer has any validity.[416] The new rule became effective January 1, 1977.[417]

Example: Mr. Collector died with a collection having a fair market value of $1,200,000 on the date of his death. His will contained a direction to sell the collection, and selling expenses of $200,000 were incurred.

The gross value of the collection at $1,200,000 should be included on schedule F of Form 706 (the estate tax return). The executor has a choice with regard to the selling expenses. They can be claimed as a deduction on schedule J of Form 706, with the result that for estate tax purposes the net amount taxable is $1 million ($1,200,000 minus $200,000). For income tax purposes, the executor reports on the fiduciary income tax return (Form 1041) the difference between the amount realized ($1,200,000) and the basis of the collection ($1,200,000), which was stepped-up under section 1014(a).

Alternatively, the selling expenses can be claimed as an offset on the fiduciary income tax return. For income tax purposes, the executor reports the difference between the amount realized less the selling expenses ($1,200,000 minus $200,000 equals $1 million) and the basis of the collection ($1,200,000). That arithmetic results in a $200,000 long-term capital loss on the sale. For estate tax purposes, the estate is taxable on the full $1,200,000. There is no $200,000 deduction on schedule J of Form 706.

The executor must compare the tax under each alternative calculation in each case to see which calculation produces the best result. Consideration must now be given to the fact that many estates owe no federal estate tax, as a result of the unlimited marital deduction[418] introduced by ERTA.

Basis for Purposes of Sale

One of the most important tax consequences of death is that property included in a decedent's gross estate for federal estate tax purposes acquires a "step-up" in basis for income tax purposes equal to its federal estate tax value.[419] Section 1014 provides that the basis of property acquired from a decedent is the fair market value of the property at the date of the decedent's death or the alternate valuation date. In other words, if a collector purchased a painting for $10,000 and when she dies the painting is valued at $100,000 for federal estate tax purposes, her heirs will acquire the painting with a "step-up" in basis equal to $100,000. The fair market value of the property as of the date of the decedent's death or as of the alternate valuation date is deemed to be the value of the property "as appraised for purposes of the federal estate tax."[420]

Janis v. Commissioner[421] is an example of a taxpayer who wanted to have his cake and eat it too! Here the decedent, the well-known New York City art dealer Sidney Janis, died owning many works of art in the gallery that he ran as a sole proprietorship. The IRS Art Panel first determined the total value of the works of art owned at death to be $36,000,000 based on a per item appraisal submitted by the executors. The panel then allowed a $13,600,000 discount based on the following arguments made by the taxpayer:

(1) there were numerous works by individual artists;
(2) some of the art would be sold in the dealer market as opposed to the retail market;
(3) the executor's inability to sell the gallery in the retail market for the sum of the value of the individual works of art;
(4) the fact that a buyer of the gallery would not pay the full resale price of the underlying assets in a bulk sale; and
(5) any buyer would consider the cost of maintaining the business for a reasonable period of time.[422]

After accepting the taxpayer's arguments that reduced the value of the artworks by $13,600,000 the IRS Art Panel agreed to further apply a blockage discount (blockage is discussed in this chapter beginning at page 1244 and in chapter 16 as it applies to artist's estates). The panel first acknowledged that the blockage concept generally applies to a large number of works by one artist, usually in an artist's estate. It then went on to apply some of the general blockage discount principles to the gallery's inventory as follows:

> A number of factors have been considered in determining whether a blockage discount is appropriate and to what extent it should be applied to the subject properties. Consideration was given to the prominence of the artists; the types of works in the estate; the distribution of the items (for example, the number and types, and their quality and saleability); the number of similar items available in the marketplace; the market's response to such works around the valuation date; the number of sales and the prices at which sales were made during the period immediately preceding and following death; the annual sales of the gallery; length of time necessary to dispose of the items; the works that are saleable within a relatively short period of time; the works that can only be marketed over a long period; the demonstrated earning capacity of the business; the tangible and intangible assets, including goodwill; and the reputation of the gallery and provenance.
>
> In addition, consideration was given to the possible disbursement and handling of the gallery. One option would be the continuation of the gallery through Sidney Janis' surviving sons and the selling of the items in the course of business. Another option would be the sale of the gallery to a willing purchaser.
>
> Attention was given to the gallery's annual gross and net receipts of the inventory since 1985.[423]

This resulted in a further 37% reduction of the value of the gallery's inventory or a total combined discount of approximately 60.42%. This was a great success for the taxpayer—but it was not enough.

When the heirs of the estate sold some of the artworks, they used as their new stepped-up basis the original per item appraised value accepted by the IRS Art Panel before the application of the 60.42% discount. The heirs argued that the term "appraised value" in regulation section 1.1014-3(a) refers to the undiscounted fair market value since the discount determined by the IRS Art Panel was attributable to the collection as a whole and does not apply in determining the value of each work of art sold separately. In addition, the heirs argued that *Augustus v. Commissioner*,[424] a 1939 case dealing with the sale of stock, supported the use of the undiscounted value for income tax purposes. The court distinguished the *Augustus* case and found that because the substantive effect of the blockage discount was to establish a proportionate value for each work of art in the collection, it follows that the "appraised value" contemplated by section 1.1014-3(a) is a value that includes the blockage discount.[425] Accordingly, the taxpayer's step-up in basis was limited to the discounted per artwork value.[426]

THE MUSEUM AND RESTRICTED GIFTS

A museum's responsibility vis-à-vis its collection is different from the responsibility of the artist, the collector, or the dealer.[427] Museums are commonly viewed as charitable trust organizations. A trust is a fiduciary relationship in which a party known as a trustee (in this case, the museum) holds property that must be administered for the benefit of others, known as beneficiaries. In a charitable trust, the beneficiary is the public or a broad segment of the public and the property must be used to benefit the public.

At its core, a museum is an educational organization. Its primary purpose is to collect objects deemed worthy of preservation and to instruct the public through the presentation of exhibits and other activities generated by critical collecting. As an educational organization, a museum is obliged to promote the unfettered competition of ideas. As a charitable trust, a museum's first obligation in its collection activities is to benefit the public. Therefore, when objects are accepted for accession—that is, inclusion in a museum's collection— the acceptance should be based on a good-faith judgment that such objects are appropriate for the collection.

In the past, museums accepted restricted gifts as a matter of course, although not always happily. A restricted gift is one offered to a museum and accepted by it with legally binding conditions as to the gift's use or disposition. An example of such a gift is a painting donated with the proviso that it be exhibited or retained forever. Historically, it was relatively easy for a museum to accept restricted gifts: If the object in question was of great interest to the museum, it would be pleased to acquire it; if the museum's collection was modest, it had less bargaining power than more affluent museums and would readily accept such a gift; if it was a prestigious organization being offered a first-rate work of art, accepting restrictions on the gift was easy to rationalize.

Over the past twenty years, however, interest has increased in the role of museums and in their obligations to the public. Accordingly, the museum community, in rethinking its position on restricted gifts, has published an array of guidelines through its various interest groups, ranging from caution about restricted gifts to downright discouragement of the acceptance of restricted gifts. That discouragement is amply buffered by the principles of trust law—that is, as trustees, museums owe a strict duty of loyalty to their beneficiaries, the public. In the case of a restricted gift, the donor is requiring the trustee to honor the donor's wishes over and above the interests of the trustee's beneficiary. Because of the museum's role as educator, that requirement could give rise to a conflict of interest; for example, in accepting a restricted gift of a collection of art from a particular period, a museum may be obligated forever to display the collection, even if later scholarship does not consider the collection appropriate for exhibit and even if the museum could put its space to better use.

That the museum community is now taking a stern view of restricted gifts is notable, since in today's market few museums can afford to buy a major masterpiece. Philippe de Montebello, the director of the Metropolitan Museum of Art in New York City, noted that he could not buy one pastel by Edgar Degas with the museum's total acquisition fund for all departments.[428]

Although most donors are aware that museums are heavily dependent on their largess, a donor is well advised to discuss with the museum the nature of any restrictions she intends to impose on a prospective gift to that organization. Such a discussion may prevent the occurrence of a lawsuit along the lines of *Reed v. Whitney Museum of Art*,[429] in which the donor sued the museum for its failure to abide by certain conditions alleged to have been accepted. The action was withdrawn when the museum agreed to relinquish the gift to another museum.

Museums have also been subject to criticism for being willing, on occasion, to accept works of art with questionable value or provenance. Such actions by a museum are in violation of its responsibilities as a charitable trust organization. Moreover, both museums and prospective donors should be aware that, with respect to all gifts of artwork that leave a museum's collection (are deaccessioned) within three years of the date of their receipt, the IRS regulations require the filing of Form 8282. The latest version of the form, dated April 2009, is reproduced at the end of chapter 17 (see Appendix 17-5). That is, museums must report to the IRS the sale of any such artwork and the price at which it was sold. That requirement is of particular importance to the donor, as the IRS, cross-checking with computers, is now able to challenge the donor, on her individual income tax return in the event of an unseemly discrepancy between the price the museum sold the work of art for and the amount of the original deduction taken by the donor.

NOTES TO CHAPTER 15

1. Material in this chapter has appeared in part in the following: Lerner, *Estate Planning for the Art Collector, in* Successful Estate Planning Ideas and Methods (P-H 1988); Lerner, *Planning the Collector's Estate, in Representing Artists, Collectors, and Dealers* 19 (R. Lerner, ed. PLI 1985); Lerner, *Transferring Tangible Property to Charitable Organizations,* 114 Tr. & Est. 402 (1975); Lerner, *Transfers of Tangible Personal Property to Charity,* N.Y.L.J., June 21, 1976, at 1; Lerner, *New Carryover Basis Rules,* 4 Est. Plan. 72 (1977); Lerner, *Planning the Collector's Estate, in* Art Law 11 (R. Lerner, ed. PLI 1988); Lerner, *Tax and Estate Planning For Collectors, in* The Law and Business of Art 9 (R. Lerner, ed. PLI 1990); Lerner, *Valuing Works of Art for Tax Purposes,* 28 Real Prop., Prob. & Tr. J. 1 (1993); Lerner, *Works of Art and Other Items of Tangible Personal Property: Valuation-Taxation-Planning,* Part 1, 10 ALI-ABA Est. Plan. Course Mat. J. 27 (Feb. 2004), Part 2, ALI-ABA Est. Plan. Course Mat. J. 27 (Apr. 2004); Lerner, *Planning For Collectibles,* 37th Annual Heckerling Institute on Estate Planning (2003); Lerner, *Works of Art and Other Items of Tangible Personal Property,* in 33rd Annual Estate Planning Institute, at 599 (PLI Estate Planning & Admin. Course Handbook Series No. 319, 2002); Lerner, *Legal Aspects of Owning Art and Other Valuable Personal Property, in* Valuation, Taxation & Planning Techniques for Sophisticated Estates 2004, at 327 (PLI Course Handbook Series No. 111, 2004); Lerner, *Art and Other Collectibles, in* Estate Planning for Special Assets, CEB-California, ch. 7 (2011).
2. Treas. Reg. §§ 1.170A-1(a)(2)(ii), (c), 1.170A-13.
3. Treas. Reg. § 25.2512-1.
4. Treas. Reg. § 20.2031-6.
5. The discussion below encompasses the ideas presented in the proposed recommendation by the Washington subcommittee on valuation of tangible personal property of the ABA's Committee on Estate and Gift Taxes, dated June 19, 1975, and a letter from James H. Lewis, council director to the committee, dated January 4, 1975.
6. R. Paul, Federal Estate and Gift Taxation § 18.03 (1942).
7. Chi. Ry. Equip. Co. v. Blair, 20 F.2d 10 (7th Cir. 1927).
8. Treas. Reg. §§ 20.2031-6 (1958), 25.2512-1 (as amended in 1992), 1.170A-1(c)(2) (as amended in 1990).
9. Treas. Reg. § 20.2031-6.
10. Treas. Reg. §§ 25.2512-1, 1.170A-1(c)(2).
11. *See supra* note 5.
12. Clark, *Fine Art: Administering this Valuable Estate Asset,* 117 Tr. & Est. 132 (1978); Vencel & Whitman, *Giving Art to Museums: Special Considerations for the Estate Planner,* 122 Tr. & Est. 35 (1983); Weitman, Jr., *The Changing Collectibles Market,* 128 Tr. & Est. 10 (1989); Polisher & Peeler, *A Collector's Guide to Art, Taxes and Charitable Deductions,* 136 Tr. & Est. 26 (1997).
13. Treas. Reg. § 1.170A-13.
14. Tax Reform Act of 1984 § 155(a)(2); Treas. Reg. § 1.170A-13(c)(1).
15. Joint Committee on Taxation Staff, General Explanation of the Revenue Provisions of the Tax Reform Act of 1984, at 506 (1984).
16. Treas. Reg. § 1.170A-13(c)(1) (as amended in 1990).
17. D'Arcangelo v. Comm'r, 68 T.C.M. (CCH) 1223 (1994).
18. *Id. See also* Teitell, *No Qualified Appraisal, No Deduction,* 134 Tr. & Est. 84 (1995); John L. Louderback v. Comm'r, 69 T.C.M. (CCH) 1675 (1995); Bond v. Comm'r, 100 T.C. 32 (1993).
19. Tax Reform Act of 1984 § 155(a)(2); Treas. Reg. § 1.170A-13(c)(3)(i).
20. Treas. Reg. § 1.170A-13(c)(3)(iv)(B).
21. Tax Reform Act of 1984 § 155(a)(2); Treas. Reg. § 1.170A-13(c)(5)(i).
22. Treas. Reg. § 1.170A-13(c)(5)(iv)(B) does allow a party to the transaction to be a qualified appraiser if the property is donated within two months of the date of acquisition and its appraised value does not exceed its acquisition price. *See supra* notes 17 and 18.

23. Treas. Reg. § 1.170A-13(c)(5)(iv)(F).
24. If the appraiser is not a "qualified appraiser," she cannot prepare a "qualified appraisal," and, therefore, the donor cannot attach a qualified appraisal to her return when it is due. The question of who is a qualified appraiser is raised on audit, a time after the due date of the donor's tax return. *See* Treas. Reg. § 1.170A-13(c)(3)(i)(A). *See also supra* notes 17 and 18.
25. *See* IRS Int Rev Man 4.48.2.1 (SBSE-04-0111-008), effective January 27, 2011.
26. Treas. Reg. § 1.170A-13(c)(6)(i). There is one narrow exception for fees paid to an association that regulates appraisers.
27. I.R.C. § 170(f)(ll)(E)(i).
28. Notice 2006-96, 2006-46 IRB 902, § 3.04(2).
29. Treas. Reg. § 1.170A-13(c)(3).
30. Treas. Reg. § 1.170A-13(c)(3)(iv)(B).
31. I.R.C. § 170(f)(ll)(E)(ii),(iii).
32. Notice 2006-96, 2006-46 IRB 902, 10/19/2006
33. *Id.* at § 3.02(2).
34. *Id.* at § 3.03(3)(b).
35. *See* Excerpt from Uniform Standards of Professional Appraisal Practice (USPAP) 2011 reproduced at the end of chapter 7 (Appendix 7-1). *See also* Recommendations on Internal Revenue Service Valuation Policies & Procedures, I.R.S. Publication 3579 (2000), where it states: "The IRS strongly encourages utilizing methodologies or guidelines which will produce better quality appraisals. The IRS is not opposed to USPAP in itself and, as previously discussed, our requirements and procedures in many cases agree with USPAP. However, the IRS cannot endorse USPAP as the only means and standard." *But see supra*, note 25.
36. General Explanation, *supra* note 15, at 506.
37. Treas. Reg. §§ 1.170A-1(a)(2)(ii), 1.170A-13(b).
38. *See* Rev. Rul. 77-225, 1977-2 C.B. 73.
39. I.R.S. News Release IR-68 (Feb. 1, 1968); *See* O'Connell, *Defending Art Valuations for Tax Purposes*, 115 Tr. & Est. 604 (1976) (includes an excellent discussion of the workings of the IRS Art Panel). The Art Panel was expanded from twelve to twenty-two members in 1984 to provide expertise in pre-Columbian, Far Eastern, and Asian art. I.R.S. News Release IR-84-7 (Jan. 16, 1984).
40. Arbini v. Comm'r, 81 T.C.M. (CCH) 1753 (2001) (bound collections of newspapers); Leibowitz v. Comm'r, 73 T.C.M. (CCH) 2858 (1997) (movie memorabilia); Wehausen v. Comm'r, 56 T.C.M. (CCH) 299 (1988) (valuation of mathematical journals); Rhoades v. Comm'r, 55 T.C.M. (CCH) 1159 (1988) (opal); Williams v. Comm'r, 54 T.C.M. (CCH) 1471 (1988) (Indian artifacts); Goldstein v. Comm'r, 89 T.C. 535 (1987) (posters); Shein v. Comm'r, 53 T.C.M. (CCH) 1292 (1987) (paintings); Frates v. Comm'r, 53 T.C.M. (CCH) 96 (1987) (paintings and sculpture); Angell v. Comm'r, 52 T.C.M. (CCH) 939 (1986) (paintings; court upheld civil fraud penalties for gross overvaluation); Biagiotti v. Comm'r, 52 T.C.M. (CCH) 588 (1986) (pre-Columbian and Mayan art objects); Koftinow v. Comm'r, 52 T.C.M. (CCH) 261 (1986) (statue valued using French Grid system; see Action on Decision 87-023, in which IRS said it would resist such an approach); Neely v. Comm'r, 85 T.C. 934 (1985) (African art; see Teitell, *Deductions for African Art*, N.Y.L.J., Mar. 17, 1986, at 1); Johnson v. Comm'r, 85 T.C. 469 (1985) (Indian artifacts); Lio v. Comm'r, 85 T.C. 56 (1985) (lithographs); Harken v. Comm'r, 50 T.C.M. (CCH) 994 (1985) (paintings and sketches); Skala v. Comm'r, 49 T.C.M. (CCH) 419 (1985) (vintage aircraft); Krauskopf v. Comm'r, 48 T.C.M. (CCH) 620 (1984) (racing car); Glen v. Comm'r, 79 T.C. 208 (1982) (tape recordings of interviews with noted scientists and I.R.C. § 170(e)(1)); Isbell v. Comm'r, 44 T.C.M. (CCH) 1143 (1982) (Han Dynasty ceramic jar); Hawkins v. Comm'r, 44 T.C.M. (CCH) 715 (1982) (mosaic table purchased from Vatican Studio); Peterson v. Comm'r, 44 T.C.M. (CCH) 650 (1982) (ivory carvings); Monaghan v. Comm'r, 42 T.C.M. (CCH) 27 (1981) (portraits); Reynolds v. Comm'r, 43 T.C.M. (CCH) 115 (1981) (watercolors); Raznatovich v. Comm'r, 41 T.C.M. (CCH) 79 (1980) (unindexed negatives of aerial photography); Sylvester v. Comm'r, 37 T.C.M. (CCH) 1847 (1978) (photocopy of book manuscript); Vanderhook v. Comm'r, 36 T.C.M. (CCH) 1394 (1977) (paintings); Fur-

stenberg v. United States, 78-1 U.S. Tax Cas. (CCH) ¶ 9267 (Ct. Cl. 1978), 79-1 U.S. Tax Cas. (CCH) ¶ 9280 (Ct. Cl.) (rare paintings), 595 F.2d 603 (1979); Sevier v. Comm'r, 36 T.C.M. (CCH) 1392 (1977); Franklin v. Comm'r, 77-2 U.S. Tax Cas. (CCH) ¶ 9574 (W.D.N.C. 1977) (antiques); Peters v. Comm'r, 36 T.C.M. (CCH) 552 (1977) (paintings); Gordon v. Comm'r, 35 T.C.M. (CCH) 1227 (1976) (paintings); Posner v. Comm'r, 35 T.C.M. (CCH) 943 (1976) (paintings); Cupler v. Comm'r, 64 T.C. 946 (1975) (unique item of medical equipment); Jarre v. Comm'r, 64 T.C. 183 (1975) (original music manuscripts); Farber v. Comm'r, 33 T.C.M. (CCH) 673 (painting), aff'd, 76-1 U.S. Tax Cas. (CCH) ¶ 9118 (2d Cir. 1974); Lee v. United States, 75-1 U.S. Tax Cas. (CCH) ¶ 9165 (C.D. Cal. 1975) (theatrical material); Rupke v. Comm'r, 32 T.C.M. (CCH) 1098 (1973) (wooden cabinet and painting); Barcus v. Comm'r, 32 T.C.M. (CCH) 660 (1973) (antiques); Winokur v. Comm'r, 90 T.C. 733 (1988) (paintings); Sammons v. Comm'r, 838 F.2d 330 (9th Cir. 1988) (Indian artifacts—limited to cost); Mast, Jr., v. Comm'r, 56 T.C.M. (CCH) 1522 (1989) (glass stereoscopic negatives); Saltzman v. United States, 89-2 U.S. Tax Cas. (CCH) ¶ 9391, 750 F. Supp. 61 (E.D.N.Y. 1988) (videotape of Bolshoi Ballet valued at cost); Engel v. Comm'r, 66 T.C.M. (CCH) 378 (1993) (wild game trophy mounts).

41. *See supra* note 25.
42. Anselmo v. Comm'r, 80 T.C. 872 (1983), aff'd, 757 F.2d 1208 (11th Cir. 1985); see also cases cited *supra* note 40; Ford v. Comm'r, 46 T.C.M. (CCH) No. 556 (1983); Teitell, *Charitable Donations of Art Works: The Special Considerations Involved*, 51 J. Tax'n 326 (1979); Zobel & Shore, *The IRS Crackdown on Valuation Abuses: How Far Does It Go; What Does It Portend?*, 52 J. Tax'n 276 (1980); Melvin, *Valuation of Charitable Contributions of Works of Art*, 60 Taxes 756 (1982); Anthoine, *Charitable Contributions After the 1986 Tax Act and Problems in Valuation of Appreciated Property*, 11 Law & Arts 283 (1987).
43. Anthoine, *supra* note 42, contains an excellent discussion of valuation cases and the trend toward looking to the applicable retail market for comparables. *See* Dubin v. Comm'r, 52 T.C.M. (CCH) 456 (1986) (stating that the proper market for determining the value of donated property is a question of fact to be resolved by considering all the relevant evidence in the record).
44. Skripak v. Comm'r, 84 T.C. 285 (1985).
45. *See also* Calder v. Comm'r, 85 T.C. 713 (1985)
46. Rimmer v. Comm'r, 69 T.C.M. (CCH) 2620 (1995).
47. *Id.* (citing *Skripak*, 84 T.C. at 324–25).
48. *See* I.R.S. Valuation Guide for Income, Estate and Gift Taxes, Valuation Training for Appeals Officers, reproduced by Commerce Clearing House, at CCH No. 4 Extra Edition, Jan. 28, 1994, at 5–10. *See also* Leibowitz v. Comm'r, 73 T.C.M. (CCH) 2858 (1997) (blockage discount did not apply to a donation). For a detailed discussion of the blockage discount, particularly as it applies to the estates of artists, see chapter 16.
49. *Leibowitz*, 73 T.C.M. (CCH) 2858.
50. Arbini v. Comm'r, 81 T.C.M. (CCH) 1753 (2001).
51. Anselmo v. Comm'r, 80 T.C. 872 (1983), aff'd, 757 F.2d 1208 (11th Cir. 1985).
52. Hunter v. Comm'r, 51 T.C.M. (CCH) 1533 (1986). *See also* Sandler v. Comm'r, 52 T.C.M. (CCH) 563 (1986); Pasqualini v. Comm'r, 103 T.C. 1 (1994); Pasqualini v. Comm'r, 68 T.C.M. (CCH) 89 (1994).
53. *See also* Jennings v. Comm'r, 56 T.C.M. (CCH) 595 (1988).
54. Lightman v. Comm'r, 50 T.C.M. (CCH) 266 (1985).
55. Rhoades v. Comm'r, 55 T.C.M. (CCH) 1159 (1988).
56. Biagiotti v. Comm'r, 52 T.C.M. (CCH) 588 (1986).
57. Gifford M. Mast, Jr. v. Comm'r, 56 T.C.M. (CCH) 1522 (1989).
58. *Id.* at 1525.
59. Treas. Reg. § 1.170A-1(c)(1).
60. *See* Mast, Jr. v. Comm'r, 56 T.C.M. at 1529.
61. *Id.*
62. Gifford M. Mast, Jr. v. Comm'r, 57 T.C.M. (CCH) 1355 (1989).
63. Heriberto A. Ferrari v. Comm'r, 58 T.C.M. (CCH) 221 (1989).

64. *Id.* at 222.

65. *Id.* at 223. The court noted that it is astounding that these parties did not seek an arbitrated solution by an art expert rather than a litigation in the Tax Court.

66. *In re* Stanley P. De Lisser, Debtor, 90-2 U.S. Tax Cas. (CCH) ¶ 50,352 (Bankr. N.D. Tex. 1990).

67. *Id.* at 85,081.

68. Jack C. Chou v. Comm'r, 58 T.C.M. (CCH) 1496 (1990).

69. *Id.* at 1499.

70. *Id.* at 1498.

71. Fuad S. Ashkar v. Comm'r, 61 T.C.M. (CCH) 1657 (1991).

72. *Id.* at 1662.

73. Thomas G. Murphy v. Comm'r, 61 T.C.M. (CCH) 2935 (1991).

74. *Id.* at 2940. Tangible property (works of art) that are donated to a charity and disposed of by the charity within two years of receipt are required to be listed on IRS Form 8282 revealing the name, address, and Social Security number of the donor and the price at which the charity disposed of the property.

75. Thomas G. Murphy v. Comm'r, 1993 U.S. App. LEXIS 26485 (Oct. 5, 1993).

76. Joseph M. Isaacs v. Comm'r, 62 T.C.M. (CCH) 827 (1991); see discussion of identifying the correct marketplace *supra* notes 46–50.

77. George H. Engel v. Comm'r, 66 T.C.M. (CCH) 378 (1993).

78. *Id.* at 384.

79. Franklin P. Perdue v. Comm'r, 62 T.C.M. (CCH) 845 (1991).

80. Treas. Reg. § 20.2031-1(b).

81. James L. Ferman, Jr. v. Comm'r, 68 T.C.M. (CCH) 1063 (1994).

82. George O. Doherty v. Comm'r, 63 T.C.M. (CCH) 2112 (1992), *aff'd*, 16 F.3d 388, 94-1 U.S. Tax Cas. (CCH) 112 (1994).

83. Estate of James J. Mitchell v Comm'r, T.C. Memo 2011-94 (2011).

84. Priv. Ltr. Rul. 91-52-005.

85. Priv. Ltr. Rul. 92-35-005.

86. *Id.*

87. Publicker v. Comm'r, 206 F.2d 250 (3d Cir. 1953).

88. *Id.* at 256 (quoting Reg. 108, § 86.19).

89. Treas. Reg. § 20.2031-1(b). *See* I.R.S. Valuation Guide for Income, Estate and Gift Taxes, Fed. Est. & Gift Tax Rep. (CCH) No. 115 (Oct. 14, 1985); I.R.S. Valuation Guide for Income, Estate and Gift Taxes, Std. Fed. Tax Rep. (CCH) No. 4 (Jan. 28, 1994).

90. Cases exemplifying the diversity of retail markets include Leibowitz v. Comm'r, 73 T.C.M. (CCH) 2858, 2868 (1997) (the relevant market is the most common market, i.e., retail stores not memorabilia conventions); Engel v. Comm'r, 66 T.C.M. (CCH) 378 (1993) (market for sale of wild game trophy mounts not sufficiently active to warrant exclusive reliance); Issacs v. Comm'r, 62 T.C.M. (CCH) 827 (1991); Chou v. Comm'r, 58 T.C.M. (CCH) 1496 (1990) (market or valuing gemstones may be a retail, wholesale, or a collector's market, but determination depends on the facts of each case); Biagiotti v. Comm'r, 52 T.C.M. (CCH) 588 (1986) (better valuation of pre-Columbian and Mayan art was price collectors paid private dealers, not what they paid at an auction); Hunter v. Comm'r, 51 T.C.M. (CCH) 1533 (1986) (relevant retail market was one in which taxpayer bought prints from middleman, not one in which taxpayer ordinarily would have bought prints from gallery); Skripak v. Comm'r, 84 T.C. 285 (1985) (retail market for books with blockage discount was proper market for valuation, even though taxpayer participated in charitable contribution tax shelter and bought books at a discount); Anselmo v. Comm'r, 80 T.C. 872 (1983) (comparable retail market for donated gems was market in which jewelry stores and not members of the public made purchases), *aff'd*, 757 F.2d 1208 (11th Cir. 1985); Ferrari v. Comm'r, 58 T.C.M. (CCH) 221 (1989) (pre-Columbian art best valued on a range of prices in the retail gallery market, not auction sales); Priv. Ltr. Rul. 91-52-005 (Dec. 27, 1991) (fair market value of stolen art objects was highest price that purchaser would have paid whether in the illicit or legitimate art market).

91. Rev. Proc. 65-19, 1965-2 C.B. 1002.

92. Alan Halperin, *The IRS Rules That a Picture Is Worth 1,100 Words*, 132 Tr. & Est. 36, 38 (1993).

93. Estate of Wells v. Comm'r, 50 T.C. 871, 878 (1968), *aff'd sub nom.* Ruehlmann v. Comm'r, 418 F.2d 1302 (6th Cir. 1969) (Judge Tannewald's dissent discussing appropriate marketplace to value mutual fund shares), *cert. denied*, 398 U.S. 950 (1970).

94. United States v. Cartwright, 411 U.S. 546 (1973), *aff'g* 457 F.2d 567 (2d Cir. 1972), *aff'g* 323 F. Supp. 769 (W.D.N.Y. 1971).

95. *See Wells*, 50 T.C. 871.

96. *See Cartwright*, 411 U.S. at 553.

97. *See id.* at 557.

98. *Id.* at 552.

99. *See Cartwright*, 457 F.2d at 571.

100. *See Wells*, 50 T.C. at 878.

101. Estate of Robert C. Scull v. Comm'r, 67 T.C.M. (CCH) 2953 (1994).

102. *See* Publicker v. Comm'r, 206 F.2d 250 (3d Cir. 1953).

103. Priv. Ltr. Rul. 92-35-005.

104. Treas. Reg. § 20.2053-3(d)(2). See discussion at page 1331.

105. *See* Estate of Jenner v. Comm'r, 577 F.2d 1100 (7th Cir. 1978).

106. Estate of Love v. Comm'r, 57 T.C.M. (CCH) 1479 (1989), *aff'd*, 923 F.2d 335 (4th Cir. 1991); Hibernia Bank v. United States, 581 F.2d 741 (9th Cir. 1978); Estate of Smith v. Comm'r, 57 T.C. 650 (1972), *aff'd*, 510 F.2d 479 (2d Cir.), *cert. denied*, 423 U.S. 827 (1975); Pitner v. United States, 388 F.2d 651 (5th Cir. 1967). In these circuits, the allowing of an expense by a state probate court is no guarantee that the expense will be deductible for federal estate tax purposes. Therefore, if executors anticipate large or unusual administrative expenses, they can ensure deductibility by selling the works of art and satisfying the Service's requirement that the expenses be necessary to effect the distribution of the estate. *See* Priv. Ltr. Rul. 81-19-002 (Jan. 16, 1981) (auctioneer's commissions, incurred in selling the decedent's property, and allowable administrative expenses under state laws were necessary to effect distribution of the estate because decedent's will directed that his property be sold and that the proceeds be distributed to the estate's beneficiaries). See discussion *supra* at page 1331 discussing selling expenses.

107. See discussion at page 1338.

108. Priv. Ltr. Rul. 81-19-002.

109. For example, Mayer's International Auction Price Index, HISLOP-Art Sale Index, and ADEC-International Art Price Annual do not include the buyer's premium in their reported prices. On the other hand, Gorden's Print Price Annual does include it. The buyer's premium is 20% of the first $200,000 and 12% on amounts over $200,000 at Christie's and Sotheby's in the United States and England but is higher in other European countries.

110. For other recent valuation cases, see Robert A. Hall v. Comm'r, 59 T.C.M. (CCH) 80 (1990) (value of vintage football film collection); Thomas J. Baker v. Comm'r, 59 T.C.M. (CCH) 698 (1990) (value of videotapes of surgeons' operations); Harry D. Mandelbaum v. Comm'r, 59 T.C.M. (CCH) 516 (1990) (art-master tax shelter); Robert L. Sanz v. Comm'r, 60 T.C.M. (CCH) 1160 (1990) (value of foreign-language books); Daniel I. Rhode v. Comm'r, 60 T.C.M. (CCH) 1535 (1990), *aff'd sub nom.* Abrahams v. Comm'r, 961 F.2d 207 (3d Cir. 1992) (value of books); Alexander Weintrob v. Comm'r, 61 T.C.M. (CCH) 1947 (1991) (value of gravesites); William E. Straw v. Comm'r, 62 T.C.M. (CCH) 1056 (1991) (value of a horse); Dorian M. Bennett v. Comm'r, 62 T.C.M. (CCH) 1400 (1991) (value of piano and when gift is effective); Albert Victor Mills v. Comm'r, 62 T.C.M. (CCH) 1345 (1991) (value of vintage car); Estate of Darwin A. Miller v. Comm'r, 62 T.C.M. (CCH) 997 (1991), *aff'd*, 983 F.2d 232 (5th Cir. 1993) (value of animal hunting trophies); Chronicle Publ'g Co. & Subsidiaries v. Comm'r, 97 T.C. 445 (1991), *aff'd*, 63 T.C.M. (CCH) 1899 (1992) (value of newspaper clipping library, not a capital asset under § 170(e)(1)(A)); Robert E. Bronson v. Comm'r, 63 T.C.M. (CCH) 2225

(1992) (art-master tax shelter). *See* Karlen, *Appraiser's Responsibility for Determining Fair Market Value*, 13 COLUM.-VLA J.L. & ARTS 185 (1989); Lerner, *Valuing Works of Art For Tax Purposes*, 28 REAL PROP., PROB. & TR. J. 1 (1993).

111. Revenue Reconciliation Act of 1989, Pub. L. No. 101-239, 103 Stat. 2301.

112. Revenue Reconciliation Act § 7721(c).

113. I.R.C. § 6662(e)(1)(A).

114. I.R.C. § 6662(h)(1).

115. I.R.C. § 6664(c).

116. I.R.C. § 6664(c)(2).

117. Jacobson v. Comm'r, 78 T.C.M. (CCH) 930 (1999).

118. I.R.C. § 6664(c)(1).

119. I.R.C. § 6664(c)(2) and (3).

120. *Jacobson*, 78 T.C.M. 930.

121. I.R.C. § 6662(g)(1).

122. I.R.C. § 6662(h)(2).

123. I.R.C. § 6662(g)(2).

124. I.R.C. § 6664(c)(1).

125. I.R.C. §§ 6662(b)(5); 6662(g).

126. I.R.C. § 2056.

127. I.R.C. § 2010.

128. I.R.C. § 1014.

129. I.R.C. § 6662(e)(1)(A).

130. Tax Reform Act of 1984 § 155(b), adding I.R.C. § 6050L. *See* Treas. Reg. § 1.6050-1T.

131. I.R.C. § 6701. *See* CCA 200512016. As of 2012, there are no temporary, proposed, or final regulations issued under I.R.C. § 6701.

132. I.R.C. § 6703(a) (placing the burden of proof on the I.R.S.)

133. Tax Reform Act of 1984 § 156; 31 U.S.C. § 330(c); 31 C.F.R. §§ 10.77 to .97 (1989) (adopted at 50 Fed. Reg. 42,016 (Oct. 17, 1985)).

134. Rev. Rul. 67-461, 1967-2 C.B. 125.

135. Treas. Reg. § 1.212-1(l).

136. Treas. Reg. § 20.2053-3(d)(1).

137. The Tax Reform Act of 1986 lowered the maximum ordinary income tax rate from 50% to 38.5% for 1987 and 28% for 1988. The maximum tax rate on capital gains was increased from 20% for 1986 to 28% for 1987 and years thereafter. A 33% ordinary income tax rate applies in 1988, 1989, and 1990 to specified ranges of income, e.g., between $71,900 and $149,250 for married individuals filing joint returns and surviving spouses. The Revenue Reconciliation Act of 1990 eliminated the 33% bracket, and provided that all long-term capital gains are taxed at 28% and all other income is taxed at 31%. The Revenue Reconciliation Act of 1993 kept the capital gains rate at 28%, but added new brackets that effect higher income individuals. For married individuals, the new rates are 36% for taxable incomes above $140,000 and 39.6% for taxable incomes above $250,000. The rates are effective January 1, 1993. *See* Steinberg & Thompson, *Reassessing the Tax-Favored Status of the Charitable Deduction for Gifts of Appreciated Assets*, 49 NAT'L TAX J. 215 (1996). The Taxpayer Relief Act of 1997 reduced the long-term capital gain rate to 20% on the sale of securities held for more than eighteen months, but maintained the 28% rate on the sale of collectibles (as defined in section 408(m) without regard to paragraph (3) thereof) held for more than one year. The eighteen-month holding period was reduced to twelve months by the IRS Restructuring and Reform Act of 1998. The Jobs and Growth Tax Relief Reconciliation Act of 2003 (effective May 6, 2003) further reduced the long-term capital gain rate to 15% for sales of securities and other capital assets held for more than twelve months but once again maintained the 28% rate on gain from the sale of collectibles held for more than one year. The maximum ordinary income tax rate was reduced to 35%.

138. *See generally* Anthoine, *Deductions for Charitable Contributions of Appreciated Property— The Art World*, 35 TAX L. REV. 239 (1980); Speiler, *The Favored Tax Treatment of Purchasers*

of Art, 80 COLUM. L. REV. 214 (1980); Feld, *Artists, Art Collectors and Income Tax*, 60 B.U. L. REV. 625 (1980); Symposium, *Law and the Arts*, 85 DICK. L. REV. 182 (1981); Auten & Rudney, *Tax Reform and the Price of Donating Appreciated Property*, 33 TAX NOTES 285 (1986); Sanders & Toolson, *Planning for Charitable Giving After the Tax Reform Act of 1986*, TAXES (June 1987); Wittenbach & Milani, *A Flowchart Focusing on the Individual Charitable Contribution*, TAXES (Apr. 1988); Anthoine, *supra* note 42; *Charitable Contributions of Appreciated Art After the Tax Reform Act of 1986*, 53 TEX. B.J. 459 (1990).

139. I.R.C. §§ 170(b)(1)(A)(i)–(viii), (E)(i)–(iii), 509(a); Treas. Reg. § 1.170A-9.

140. I.R.C. §§ 170(b)(1)(B), 509(a).

141. I.R.C. §§ 170(b)(1)(C)(iv), 1221; Treas. Reg. §§ 1.170A-8(d)(3), 1.170A-4(b)(2). *See* Thomas B. Drummond v. Comm'r, 73 T.C.M. (CCH) 1959 (1997); Pasqualini v. Comm'r, 103 T.C. 1 (1994).

142. I.R.C. §§ 1221(a)(3), 170(e)(1)(A); Treas. Reg. §§ 1.170A-8(d)(3), 1.170A-4(b)(2).

143. I.R.C. § 1023(a) as it read prior to its repeal by Pub. L. No. 96-223, effective December 31, 1979.

144. Fullerton v. Comm'r, 22 T.C. 372 (1954); Feber v. Comm'r, 22 T.C. 261 (1954). That assumes that the artist's estate is not deemed to be carrying on a trade or business, but is merely conducting an orderly administration of the artist's estate. *See* Strasser v. Comm'r, 52 T.C.M. (CCH) 1140 (1986).

145. Pub. L. No. 107-16, June 7, 2001.

146. Pub. L. No. 111-312.

147. See Blattmachr & Detzel, *Estate Planning Changes in the 2001 Tax Act—More Than You Can Count*, 95 J. TAX'N 74 (2001), for a detailed discussion of these provisions.

148. Sandler v. Comm'r, 52 T.C.M. (CCH) 563 (1986); *see also* Lio v. Comm'r, 85 T.C. 61 (1986).

149. The Pension Protection Act of 2006, P.L.109-280, August 17, 2006.

150. I.R.C. § 170(e)(7)(C).

151. I.R.C. § 170(e)(7)(B).

152. I.R.C. § 170(e)(1)(B)(i); Treas. Reg. § 1.170A-4(b)(3).

153. I.R.C. §§ 170(b)(1)(A), (C)(i).

154. Treas. Reg. § 1.170A-4(b)(3)(ii), (i). *See* Anthoine, *supra* notes 42 and 138.

155. *See* Isbell v. Comm'r, 44 T.C.M. (CCH) 1143 (1982).

156. Treas. Reg. § 1.170A-4(b)(3)(ii).

157. 115 Cong. Rec. H40869 (bound ed. 1969); 115 Cong. Rec. H13038 (daily ed. Dec. 23, 1969).

158. *See also* Priv. Ltr. Rul. 85-36-022 (condominium to charity: unrelated use); Priv. Ltr. Rul. 84-39-005 (manuscripts to university: related use); Priv. Ltr. Rul. 83-33-019 (art collection to museum: related use); Priv. Ltr. Rul. 94-52-026 (musical instrument to be sold: unrelated use); Priv. Ltr. Rul. 93-03-007 (paintings to museum: related use); Priv. Ltr. Rul. 79-11-109 (lithographs to numerous schools: related use); Priv. Ltr. Rul. 79-34-082 (fractional interest in painting to museum: related use); Priv. Ltr. Rul. 93-03-007 (fractional interest in painting to museum: related use); Priv. Ltr. Rul. 94-52-026 (violin to charitable remainder trust: no related use); *see* Coleman v. Comm'r, 56 T.C.M. (CCH) 710 (1988) (horse to American Cancer Society: unrelated use); Jennings v. Comm'r, 56 T.C.M. (CCH) 595 (1988) (paintings to cancer society, hospital, and college: unrelated use); Priv. Ltr. Rul. 98-33-011 (paintings to Jewish Community Center: related use); Priv. Ltr. Rul. 91-47-049 (violin to school: related use).

159. I.R.C. § 6050 L(a)(1).

160. I.R.C. § 170(e)(7).

161. I.R.C. § 170(e)(7)(A); I.R.C. § 170(e)(1)(B)(i).

162. I.R.C. § 170(e)(7)(D).

163. I.R.C. § 6720B.

164. I.R.C. § 170(b)(1)(A).

165. I.R.C. § 170(b)(1)(B). The limitation was increased from 20% to 30% by the Tax Reform Act of 1984, effective for contributions made in taxable years ending after July 18, 1984.

166. I.R.C. § 170(b)(1)(F).

167. I.R.C. § 170(e)(1)(A); Treas. Reg. § 1.170A-4(a)(1); *See* Maniscalco v. Comm'r, 80-2 U.S. Tax

Cas. (CCH) ¶ 9717, 632 F.2d 6 (6th Cir. 1980), *aff'g* 37 T.C.M. (CCH) 1174 (1978); Beghe, *The Artist, the Art Market and the Income Tax*, 29 Tax L. Rev. 491 (1974); Anthoine, *supra* note 42; Bell, *Changing IRC 170(e)(1)(A): For Art's Sake*, 37 Case W. Res. L. Rev. 536 (1987).

168. *See* Orchard v. Comm'r, 34 T.C.M. (CCH) 205 (1975) (opera tapes held less than six months not capital gain property). *See also* Glen v. Comm'r, 79 T.C. 208 (1982) (valuation of tape recordings of interviews with noted scientists); Ford v. Comm'r, 46 T.C.M. (CCH) 1353 (1983).

169. I.R.C. § 170(d)(1)(A), (b)(1)(B) last sentence.

170. I.R.C. § 170(b)(1)(C)(i).

171. I.R.C. § 170(d)(1)(A), (b)(1)(C)(ii).

172. I.R.C. § 170(b)(1)(C)(iii), (e)(1).

173. I.R.C. § 170(b)(1)(C)(i), (e)(1)(B)(ii).

174. I.R.C. § 170(b)(1)(D)(ii).

175. I.R.C. § 4942(j)(3). Contributions to a private operating foundation are treated like contributions to a public charity. *See* Treas. Reg. § 53.4942(b)-1.

176. I.R.C. § 170(b)(1)(C)(i).

177. I.R.C. § 68(a).

178. I.R.C. § 68(f), added by 2001 Tax Relief Act § 103, effective beginning in 2006.

179. I.R.C. § 68(g), added by 2001 Tax Relief Act § 103.

180. Pub. L. 111-312, § 101(a)(1).

181. I.R.C. § 68(d).

182. I.R.C. § 57(a)(6) prior to its repeal effective June 30, 1992. A detailed description of the alternative minimum tax is beyond the scope of this chapter. *See generally* Kern, *The Alternative Minimum Tax for Individuals*, 65 Taxes 307 (1987); Khokhar, 228-4th BNA T.M. Portfolio, Alternative Minimum Tax.

183. *See* Joint Committee on Taxation Staff, General Explanation of the Revenue Provisions of the Tax Reform Act of 1984, at 444 (1984); Sanders & Toolson, *Planning for Charitable Giving After The Tax Reform Act of 1986*, Taxes (June 1987); Auten & Rudney, *Tax Reform and the Price of Donating Appreciated Property*, 33 Tax Notes 285 (1986); Brachtl & Peller, *The Chilling Effect of the AMT on Charitable Contributions*, 128 Tr. & Est. 24 (1989).

184. Rev. Rul. 90-111, 1990-2 C.B. 30; I.R.C. § 57(a)(6)(B). *See* von Eisner, *Moynihan, Art, and the AMT*, 49 Tax Notes 1579 (1991); Lozier, *New Incentives to Give*, 44 Tax Law. 885 (1991).

185. The Revenue Reconciliation Act of 1993 eliminated the tax preference for contributions of appreciated tangible personal property by deleting I.R.C. § 57(a)(6), effective June 30, 1992 (Revenue Reconciliation Act of 1993, Pub. L. No. 103-66, § 13171(a)).

186. I.R.C. §§ 56(b)(1)(A); 56(b)(1)(B); 56(b)(1)(C).

187. Treas. Reg. §§ 1.55-1(a); 1.55-1(b). Note that prior to the issuance of the regulations (effective Jan. 1, 1994) a separate calculation was required under section 170 for regular tax and AMT purposes, see Priv. Ltr. Rul. 93-21-063 and Rook, *The IRS Adds Another Level of Complexity to the AMT—With Some Unexpected Results*, 71 Taxes 596 (1993).

188. Rev. Rul. 57-293, 1957-2 C.B. 153; Rev. Rul. 58-455, 1958-2 C.B. 100.

189. I.R.C. § 170(f) was renumbered I.R.C. § 170(a)(3) by the Tax Reform Act of 1969, Pub. L. No. 91-172, § 201(a)(1), 83 Stat. 487, 562 (1969). *See* Treas. Reg. §§ 1.170-1(d)(2), 1.170A-5.

190. Treas. Reg. §§ 1.170A-5(b) ex. 5, 1.170A-7(a)(2)(i).

191. See I.R.S. Notice 89-24 (Feb. 17, 1989), which provides guidance to taxpayers in determining the present value of an annuity, an interest for life or for a term of years, or a remainder or reversionary interest pursuant to methods established under I.R.C. § 7520. The provision, added by the Technical and Miscellaneous Revenue Act of 1988, Pub. L. No. 100-647, applies to gifts made after April 30, 1989, and to the estates of decedents who die after that date.

192. Treas. Reg. § 1.170A-5(a)(4). *See also* Treas. Reg. § 1.170A-13(b)(2)(ii)(G), 1.170A-13(c)(2) (D).

193. Treas. Reg. § 25.2511-1(d). See also Rev. Rul. 77-300, 1977-2 C.B. 352, which deals with the gift tax question on split-interest gifts.

194. *Id.*

195. Treas. Reg. §§ 1.170A-5(b) ex. 1, 1.170A-5(b) ex. 2, 1.170A-7.

196. Tidd, *Charitable Remainder Trusts: Funding and Investment Considerations,* 57 TAXES 577 (1979) (discusses why tangible personal property should never be put in inter vivos charitable remainder trust).

197. Treas. Reg. §§ 1.170A-5(a)(2); 1.170A-7(b)(l)(i); I.R.C. § 170(f)(3)(B)(ii).

198. Winokur v. Comm'r, 90 T.C. 733 (1988). *See also* Priv. Ltr. Rul. 8333019; Priv. Ltr. Rul. 8535019.

199. Rev. Rul. 57-293, 1957-2 C.B. 153. *See also* Priv. Ltr. Rul. 7728046; Priv. Ltr. Rul. 7934082; Priv. Ltr. Rul. 9303007; Priv. Ltr. Rul. 200223013.

200. I.R.C. § 170(o)(2).

201. I.R.C. § 170(o)(3)(A)(i).

202. I.R.C. § 170(o)(3)(A)(ii).

203. Staff of the Joint Committee on Taxation, Technical Explanation of H.R.4, The Pension Protection Act of 2006.

204. I.R.C. § 170(o)(3)(A).

205. I.R.C. § 170(o)(l)(A).

206. I.R.C. § 2055(g); I.R.C. § 2522(e).

207. I.R.C. § 2055(g)(1).

208. Pub. L. No. 110-172.

209. I.R.C. § 2033.

210. Estate of Robert C. Scull v. Comm'r, 67 T.C.M. (CCH) 2953 (1994).

211. Priv. Ltr. Rul. 93-03-007.

212. *Id.* (citing United States v. Dean, 224 F.2d 26, 29 (1st Cir. 1955)); 855 Inv. Co. v. Comm'r, 95 T.C. 156 (1990); Briggs v. Comm'r, 72 T.C. 646 (1979).

213. *See* Ahmanson Found. v. United States, 674 F.2d 761 (9th Cir. 1981); DiSanto v. Comm'r, 78 T.C.M. (CCH) 1220 (1990); Estate of Schwan v. Comm'r, 82 T.C.M. (CCH) 168 (2001); Deukmejian v. Comm'r, 41 T.C.M. (CCH) 738 (981); *cf.* Cooley v. Comm'r, 33 T.C. 223 (1959), *aff'd per curiam,* 283 F.2d 945 (2d Cir. 1960); Priv. Ltr. Rul. 200418002.

214. Given the basic premises of valuation (the price a hypothetical willing buyer will pay to a hypothetical willing seller), the question arises whether there is a particular reason why a fractional interest in an item of property would make the property less appealing to the hypothetical willing buyer. Neither the Internal Revenue Code nor the regulations (except for the reference in Treas. Reg. § 20.2031-1) contain any specific provision on the issue of valuing fractional interests. *See* Hood, Jr., 830-2nd BNA T.M. Portfolio, Valuation: General and Real Estate, section II.H.4. The IRS usually takes the position that in the absence of evidence to the contrary the fact that the interest involved is a fractional interest does not warrant any discount, that is, the value of such interest is equivalent to the proportionate part of the value of the entire interest. However, when it comes to a fractional interest in real estate, some discount is generally allowed. Iacono v. Comm'r, 41 T.C.M. (CCH) 407 (1980); *In re* Gilberts Estate, 163 N.Y.S. 974 (1917); Stevens Estate v. Comm'r, 79 T.C.M. (CCH) 1519 (2000); Forbes Estate v. Comm'r, 81 T.C.M. (CCH) 1399 (2000); Baird Estate v. Comm'r, 82 T.C.M. (CCH) 666 (2001); Tech. Adv. Mem. 199943003 (where the National Office advised that if a discount is appropriate, one method of determining the fair market value of a decedent's undivided interests in tracts of real property is to subtract the partition sale costs from the fair market value of the undivided interests). The first case that addressed the issue with respect to works of art was Estate of Robert C. Scull v. Comm'r, 67 T.C.M. (CCH) 2953 (1994), where a 5% discount was allowed on a 65% interest because of uncertainties in a continuing divorce proceeding. This has been further clarified in Stone v. United States, 2007 U.S. Dist. LEXIS 38332 (N.D. Cal. May 25, 2007), *later opinion,* 2007 U.S. Dist. LEXIS 58611 (N.D. Cal. Aug. 10, 2007), *aff'd sub nom.* Stone *ex rel.* Stone Trust Agreement v. United States, 2009 U.S. App. LEXIS 6349 (9th Cir. Mar. 24, 2009) (unpublished). See discussion at page 1325.

215. *See* Rev. Rul. 67-246, 1967-2 C.B. 104; I.R.C.

216. I.R.C. § 170(f)(3)(A).

217. I.R.C. § 170(f)(2)(B); Treas. Reg. § 1.170A-6(c); *See* Note, *Denial or Charitable Deduction for the Use of Property,* 74 DICK. L. REV. 290 (1970).

218. Treas. Reg. §§ 1.170A-6(a)(2), 1.170A-7(a)(2)(i). *See* Priv. Ltr. Rul. 79-34-082.
219. *See* Garibaldi, *Gift Annuities*, 30 N.Y.U. Inst. Fed. Tax'n 117 (1972); Note, *Private Annuities*, 23 Vand. L. Rev. 675 (1970); Teitell, *Federal Tax Implications of Charitable Gift Annuities*, 113 Tr. & Est. 642 (1974); Teitell, *Charitable Gift Annuities*, N.Y.L.J., Oct. 21, 1985, at 1; Teitell, *Technical Corrections and Miscellaneous Revenue Act of 1988*, N.Y.L.J., Nov. 21, 1988, at 3; Friedman, *Charitable Gift Annuities Can Be the Best Way to Help Both Charities and Donors*, 7 J. of Tax'n of Exempt Orgs. 261 (1996); Friedman, *Donor Annuity Programs Require Careful Planning by Issuing Charity*, 8 J. of Tax'n of Exempt Orgs. 24 (1996); Priv. Ltr. Rul. 200449033.
220. Treas. Reg. § 1.170A-1(d).
221. Rev. Rul. 69-74, 1969-1 C.B. 43; Treas. Reg. § 1.1011-2(a)(4); Note, *Private Annuities, supra* note 219; Priv. Ltr. Rul. 200449033.
222. *See* I.R.C. § 1011(b); Treas. Reg. §§ 1.1011-2, 1.170A-4(c)(2); Priv. Ltr. Rul. 83-33-019; Whittaker, *Dealing with Outright Gifts to Charity in Kind*, 30 N.Y.U. Inst. Fed. Tax'n 45 (1972); Ginsburg, *Bargain Sales and Charitable Gift Annuities*, in Private Foundations Tax Exemption and Charitable Contributions Under the Tax Reform Act of 1969, at 49 (S. Weithorn ed. PLI 1970); Moore, *Outright Charitable Giving: Sophisticated Use of Old Techniques and Development of New Techniques*, 42 N.Y.U. I Inst. Fed. Tax'n 27 (1984); Weithorn & Leuhring, *Special Techniques for Charitable Giving: Making the Most of the Unusual*, 44 N.Y.U. Inst. Fed. Tax'n 37 (1986). *See also* Estate of Bullard v. Comm'r, 87 T.C. 261 (1986) (application of I.R.C. § 170(e)(1) to bargain sale).
223. Maier Brewing Co. v. Comm'r, 54 T.C.M. (CCH) 46 (1987); Connell v. Comm'r, 842 F.2d 285 (11th Cir. 1988); Waranch v. Comm'r, 58 T.C.M. (CCH) 584 (1989); Klauer v. Comm'r, T.C. Memo 2010-65.
224. I.R.C. § 2503(g)(1). Note that the section contains a "related use rule" similar to I.R.C. § 170(e)(1)(B)(i); see discussion at page 1268.
225. I.R.C. § 2503(g)(2)(A).
226. A detailed discussion of charitable remainder trusts is beyond the scope of this chapter. *See* Brier & Knauer, 435-2nd BNA T.M. Portfolio, Charitable Remainder Trusts and Pooled Income Funds; Schlesinger, *Split Interest Charitable Trusts*, 51 N.Y.U. Inst. Fed. Tax'n 17-1 (1992); Belcher, *Charitable Split-Interest Trusts*, 54 N.Y.U. Inst. Fed. Tax'n 21-1 (1996); McCoy, *Don't Forget the "T" in CRT*, U. Miami 30th Inst. on Est. Plan. ¶ 1400 (1996); Mering, *Charitable Remainder Trusts—Comeback Player of the Year*, U. Miami 26th Inst. on Est. Plan. ¶ 900 (1992); Soled, *The Versatile Use of Charitable Remainder Unitrusts*, 74 Taxes 308 (1996); Fooden, *Charitable Remainder Trusts*, 46 C.P.A. J. 44 (1996); Rev. Rul. 72-395, 1972- C.B. 340; Rev. Rul. 80-123, 1980-1 C.B. 205; Rev. Rul. 82-128, 1982-2 C.B. 71; Rev. Rul. 88-81, 1988-2 C.B. 127; Van Dolson, *The Need to Update IRS' Sample Charitable Remainder Trust Forms*, 27 Est. Planning 414 (2000); McKinnon, *Planning to Meet a Range of Donor Needs with "Flip" Charitable Remainder Trusts*, 12 J. of Tax'n of Exempt Orgs. 253 (2001); Kline, *Charitable Remainder Trusts: State of the Art?*, 28 Tax Mgmt. Estates, Gifts & Trusts J. 147 (2003); Fox, *New Prop. Regs. on Distributions from CRTs Provide Opportunity*, 31 Est. Planning 172 (2004); see Rev. Procs. 2005-52 through 2005-59, I.R.B. 2005-34, Aug. 22, 2005, for sample I.R.S. forms of CRUTs.
227. I.R.C. § 664(d)(1).
228. I.R.C. § 664(d)(2).
229. Treas. Reg. § 1.664-3(a)(1).
230. Treas. Reg. § 1.664-1(a)(3). *See also* Treas. Reg. § 1.170A-6(c)(3)(iii).
231. *See also* Estate of Sara C. Cassidy v. Comm'r, 49 T.C.M. (CCH) 580 (1985); Priv. Ltr. Rul. 78-02-016.
232. Priv. Ltr. Rul. 94-52-026.
233. The Ruling refers to Example (7) of Treas. Reg. § 1.170A-5(b) as an illustration of the application of § 170(a)(3).
234. See discussion of related use rule at page 1268.

235. Palmer v. Comm'r, 62 T.C. 684 (1974), *aff'd on another issue*, 523 F.2d 1308 (8th Cir. 1975), *acq.*, Rev. Rul. 78-197, 1978-1 C.B. 83; Priv. Ltr. Rul. 85-52-009; Priv. Ltr. Rul. 86-23-007; Priv. Ltr. Rul. 94-13-020.

236. I.R.C. § 664(c).

237. Rev. Rul. 60-370, 1960-2 C.B. 203. *See also* Palmer, 62 T.C. at 684; Rev. Rul. 78-197, 1978-1 C.B. 83.

238. I.R.C. § 664(b).

239. Priv. Ltr. Rul. 77-30-015. *But see* Priv. Ltr. Rul. 94-42-017.

240. H.R. Rep. No. 413 (Pt. 1), 91st Cong., 1st Sess., 50 (1969). *See also* Priv. Ltr. Rul. 91-38-024. Treas. Reg. § 1.664-1(a)(7) provides that if a charitable remainder trust holds unmarketable assets and if the trustee is either (a) the grantor of the trust, (b) a noncharitable beneficiary, or (c) a related or subordinate party to the grantor or noncharitable beneficiary (within the meaning of section 672(c) and regulations), then the trustee must use a current qualified appraisal from a qualified appraiser (as defined in Treas. Reg. § 1.170A-13(c)(3) and (c)(5), respectively) to value the unmarketable assets. A qualified appraisal from a qualified appraiser is not required if there is an independent trustee. The regulation was proposed on April 18, 1997, and is effective for trusts created on or after December 10, 1998. T.D. 8791, 63 Fed. Reg. 68,188 (Dec. 10, 1998).

241. Treas. Reg. § 1.664-1(a)(7).

242. Treas. Reg. § 1.664-1(a)(7); Teitell, *Charitable Remainder Trusts—Who Can and Should Be the Trustee*, 117 Tr. & Est. 320 (1978).

243. *See* Priv. Ltr. Rul. 200034019.

244. Treas. Reg. § 1.170A-4(b)(3)(i). See discussion in text at page 1268.

245. Tidd, *Charitable Remainder Trusts: Funding and Investment Considerations*, 57 Taxes 577 n.7 (1979).

246. I.R.C. §§ 664(d)(1)(A) and 664(d)(2)(A).

247. The 10% rule was added to the law by the Taxpayer Relief Act of 1997 (TRA 1997), Pub. L. No. 105-34.

248. I.R.C. § 664(d)(3)(A).

249. I.R.C. § 664(d)(3)(B).

250. Treas. Reg. § 1.664-3(a)(1)(i)(c). *See* Michele A.W. McKinnon, *Planning to Meet a Range of Donor Needs with "Flip" Charitable Remainder Unitrusts*, 12 J. of Tax'n of Exempt Orgs. 253 (2001).

251. Treas. Reg. § 1.664-3(a)(1)(i)(c)(1).

252. Treas. Reg. § 1.664-3(a)(1)(i)(d) and (e).

253. Treas. Reg. § 1.664-3(a)(1)(i)(c)(2).

254. Treas. Reg. § 1.664-3(a)(1)(i)(c)(3).

255. Dorian M. Bennett v. Comm'r, 62 T.C.M. (CCH) 1400 (1991).

256. *See* Goldstein v. Comm'r, 89 T.C. 533 (1987); Sandler v. Comm'r, 52 T.C.M. (CCH) 563 (1986); Winokur v. Comm'r, 90 T.C. 733 (1988) (distinguished since it stands for proposition that where an undivided fractional interest is the subject of a deed of gift, the right to possession is sufficient and delivery is not required); Murphy v. Comm'r, 61 T.C.M. (CCH) 2935 (1991). For a case as to when a gift of a painting is completed in a noncharitable context involving the widow of German expressionist painter Max Beckmann, see Keoseian v. von Kaulbach, 763 F. Supp. 1253 (S.D.N.Y. 1991), *aff'd mem.*, 956 F.2d 1160 (2d Cir. 1992); von Kaulbach v. Keoseian, 783 F. Supp. 170 (S.D.N.Y. 1992). See Priv. Ltr. Rul. 91-52-036, dealing with a donor who wanted some degree of control over artworks donated and to be donated to an art museum, and Priv. Ltr. Rul. 92-18-067, where a charitable donation was allowed on signing of the deed of gift even though delivery was not made because construction of the museum was not finished.

257. I.R.C. § 4942(j)(3).

258. I.R.C. §§ 170(b)(1)(A)(vi) and 170(b)(1)(E)(i).

259. *Id.*

260. Treas. Reg. § 53.4942(b)-1(a)(1). *See* Cesare, 296-3rd BNA T.M. Portfolio, Private Foundations and Public Charities—Definition and Classification.

261. I.R.C. § 4942(j)(3)(A); Treas. Reg. § 53.4942(b)-1(a)(1)(ii).

262. Treas. Reg. § 53.4942(b)-1(b)(1).

263. Treas. Reg. §§ 53.4942(b)-1(b)(1); 53.4942(b)-1(b)(2)(i); 53.4942(b)-1(d) ex. 1.

264. I.R.C. § 4942(j)(3)(B)(i); Treas. Reg. § 53.4942(b)-2(a).

265. Treas. Reg. § 53.4942(b)-2(a)(6) ex. 4.

266. Rev. Rul. 74-498, 1974-2 C.B. 387.

267. See Priv. Ltr. Rul. 88-45-059, where the IRS ruled that a railroad museum's collection was used in the active conduct of charitable activity, and Priv. Ltr. Rul. 92-36-035, where the IRS ruled that the planned loan of works of art is a direct exempt activity and that the foundation qualified as a private operating foundation.

268. I.R.C. §§ 4942(a)(1); 4942(e)(1); Treas. Reg. § 53.4942(a)-2(c)(1).

269. I.R.C. § 501(c)(3).

270. Rev. Rul. 74-600, 1974-2 C.B. 385.

271. Priv. Ltr. Rul. 88-24-001.

272. *See supra* notes 265 and 266.

273. I.R.C. § 4942(j)(3)(B)(ii); Treas. Reg. § 53.4942(b)-2(b)(1).

274. I.R.C. § 4942(j)(3)(B)(iii); Treas. Reg. § 53.4942(b)-2(c)(1).

275. Kluge v. Comm'r, 41 T.C.M. (CCH) 690 (1981).

276. Blake v. Comm'r, 42 T.C.M. (CCH) 1336 (1981), *aff'd*, 697 F.2d 473 (2d Cir. 1982). *See also* Rev. Rul. 78-197, 1978-1 C.B. 83; Priv. Ltr. Rul. 84-11-029; Priv. Ltr. Rul. 84-31-014; Priv. Ltr. Rul. 85-52-009; Priv. Ltr. Rul. 86-23-007.

277. *See Blake*, 697 F.2d at 480.

278. Ford v. Comm'r, 46 T.C.M. (CCH) 1353 (1983).

279. I.R.C. § 2055(a).

280. I.R.C. § 170(e)(1)(B)(i); Treas. Reg. § 20.2055-1(a)(4).

281. N.Y. Est. Powers & Trusts Law § 5-3.3; *In re* Estate of Cairo, 35 A.D.2d 76, 312 N.Y.S.2d 925 (2d Dep't 1970), *aff'd mem.*, 29 N.Y.2d 527, 272 N.E.2d 574, 324 N.Y.S.2d 81 (1971). Section 5-3.3 was repealed, effective July 7, 1981. The memorandum in support of repeal points out that New York was one of only eight American jurisdictions that imposed restrictions on testamentary dispositions to charity and that the New York provision could be easily circumvented.

282. I.R.C. §§ 508(d)(2), (a), (e), 2055(e)(1); Treas. Reg. § 20.2055-5(b).

283. Rudick, *Bounty Twice Blessed*, 16 Tax L. Rev. 273, 304 (1961). Before January 1, 1982, the marital deduction was the greater of $250,000 or one-half the adjusted gross estate. The charitable deduction was subtracted after determining the marital deduction.

284. *See* Blattmachr & Detzel, *Estate Planning Changes in the 2001 Tax Act—More Than You Can Count*, 95 J. Tax'n 74 (2001), for a detailed discussion of these provisions.

285. Pub. L. No. 111-312.

286. I.R.C. §§ 2055(e)(2)(A), 664(d); Treas. Reg. § 20.2055-2(e)(i).

287. I.R.C. § 664(d)(3).

288. Treas. Reg. § 1.664-3(a)(1).

289. Treas. Reg. § 1.664-1(a)(3); Pusey, *Investment Options of Charitable Remainder Trustees Are Hard to Limit*, 7 J. of Tax'n of Exempt Orgs. 168 (1996). *See also* Treas. Reg. § 1.170A-6(c)(3)(iii).

290. Gen. Couns. Mem. 36,606 (Mar. 4, 1976). In Gen. Couns. Mem. 37,645 (Aug. 22, 1978), the IRS expressed the view that investing in unproductive assets might force the trustee to invade corpus more quickly than was contemplated when the present value of the remainder interests was calculated thereby destroying the congressionally intended correlation between the amount allowable as a deduction and the amount that charity will ultimately receive.

291. Rev. Rul. 73-610, 1973-2 C.B. 213; Rev. Rul. 76-165, 1976-1 C.B. 279; Estate of Sara C. Cassidy v. Comm'r, 49 T.C.M. (CCH) 580 (1985); Priv. Ltr. Rul. 78-02-016; Priv. Ltr. Rul. 91-14-025 (where the IRS held that a valid charitable remainder trust is not created where a

fractional interest in real property is transferred to the trust and the grantor retains a fractional interest for his use); Horowitz, *Charitable Planned Giving*, 72 TAXES 685, 690 (1994).

292. Tidd, *Charitable Remainder Trusts: Funding and Investment Considerations*, 57 TAXES 577 (1979), in which Mr. Tidd expresses the opinion that while an individual is generally ill-advised to place tangible personal property in an inter vivos charitable remainder trust, there is no reason, generally speaking, why such property should not be placed in a testamentary charitable remainder trust. Contrary to our view expressed in the first edition of this book, we believe that a collection can be used to create a testamentary charitable remainder trust, with certain caveats as discussed in the text. *See* Priv. Ltr. Rul. 94-13-020. The Taxpayer Relief Act of 1997 added two new limitations that must be complied with in creating a charitable remainder annuity trust or a charitable remainder unitrust. Neither type of trust can contain a provision that would require an annual distribution of more than 50% of the fair market value of the trust assets, and the value (determined under the section 7520 valuation tables) of the remainder interest going to the charitable organization must be at least 10% of the initial fair market value of the property placed in the trust. The new provisions are effective for transfers in trust after July 28, 1997.

293. Treas. Reg. § 1.664-1(a)(6) ex. 5.

294. Rev. Rul. 80-123, 1980-1 C.B. 205.

295. Treas. Reg. § 1.664-1(a)(5)(i); 1.664-1(a)(6) ex. 4.

296. Treas. Reg. § 1.664-1(a)(5)(i).

297. *Id.* All payments must include interest.

298. Treas. Reg. § 1.664-1(a)(6) ex.(4).

299. Treas. Reg. § 1.664-1(a)(5)(i).

300. *Id.*

301. Rev. Rul. 76-7, 1976-1 C.B. 179; Rev. Rul. 76-8, 1976-1 C.B. 179; Priv. Ltr. Rul. 94-45-010; *See also* Priv. Ltr. Rul. 89-19-016 (trustee of charitable remainder unitrust may have the power to name a substitute charitable remainderman relying on Rev. Rul. 76-7); Priv. Ltr. Rul. 94-45-010 (income beneficiaries/trustees may have power to designate by majority vote which departments within a university will receive the remainder, relying on Rev. Rul. 76-8); Priv. Ltr. Rul. 200034019 (grantor may retain inter vivos and testamentary powers to name charitable beneficiaries without disqualifying trust as section 664 charitable remainder unitrust, relying on Rev. Rul. 76-8).

302. Treas. Reg. § 1.664-1(d)(5).

303. *Id.*

304. I.R.C. § 1014(a).

305. *See supra* note 267; Treas. Reg. § 1.664-1(d)(5) ex.; Priv. Ltr. Rul. 89-31-029; Priv. Ltr. Rul. 92-01-029.

306. A model Uniform Prudent Investors Act (UPIA) was promulgated by the National Conference of Commissions on Uniform State Laws in 1994 and recommended for enactment by the states. As of this publication, forty-five states have adopted the UPIA or substantial portions thereof. *See, e.g.*, CAL. PROB. CODE §§ 16045 to 16054 (2011); FLA. STAT. ANN. §§ 518.11 & 518.122 (2011); 760 ILL. COMP. STAT. ANN. 5/5 & 5/5-1 (2011); N.Y. EST. POWERS & TRUSTS LAW § 11-2.3 (2011).

307. A detailed discussion of charitable lead trusts is beyond the scope of this chapter. *See* Etheridge, Jr., 866 BNA T.M. Portfolio, Charitable Income Trusts; Blattmachr, *A Primer On Charitable Lead Trusts: Basic Rules and Uses*, 134 TR. & EST. 48 (1995); Robinson, *Using Charitable Lead Trusts Funded With Real Estate*, 21 EST. PLAN. 228 (1994); Wilfert, *Using Charitable Lead or Remainder Trusts for Noncharitable Purposes*, 23 EST. PLAN. 204 (1996); Schlesinger, *Split Interest Charitable Trusts*, 51 N.Y.U. INST. FED. TAX'N 17-1 (1992); Belcher, *Charitable Split-Interest Trusts*, 54 N.Y.U. INST. FED. TAX'N 21-1 (1996), Gopman & Mielnicki, *Planning with Testamentary Charitable Lead Annuity Trusts*, 138 TRS. & ESTS. 34 (1999); Gopman & Steinberg, *IRS Issues Final Regulations Relating to Charitable Lead Trusts*, 26 TAX MGMT. EST. GIFTS & TR. J. 109 (2001); Grumet, *Choosing the Best Charitable Lead Trust to Meet a Client's Needs*, 30 EST. PLAN. 86 (2003); Beckwith, *Charitable Lead*

Trusts Re-examined "The Dawning of a Golden Age?", 37TH ANNUAL HECKERLING INSTI-TUTE ON ESTATE PLANNING (2003); Steve R. Akers, *Estate Planning in 2010 and Beyond: Now What?*, 44th Annual Heckerling Institute on Estate Planning, January 2010.

308. I.R.C. § 2055(e)(2)(B); Treas. Reg. § 20.2055-2(e)(vi); Treas. Reg. § 20.2055-2(f).

309. See generally I.R.C. § 2642 and the regulations thereunder. The rules for determining the applicable "inclusion ratio" for a charitable lead annuity trust are more complex than for a charitable lead unitrust, I.R.C. § 2642(e). Therefore, a charitable lead unitrust may be the better option to utilize in a generation-skipping situation.

310. Treas. Reg. § 1.664-1(a)(5).

311. *See* Belcher, *supra* note 307, at 21–33.

312. I.R.C. § 2055(e)(2)(B). For an excellent discussion and background, see Etheridge, Jr., 866 BNA T.M. Portfolio, Charitable Income Trust, A-35.

313. I.R.C. § 7520(a)(1).

314. I.R.C. § 7520(a)(1). The defined interest rate must equal 120% of the federal midterm rate in effect under I.R.C. § 1274(d)(1) for the month in which the valuation date falls.

315. I.R.C. §§ 2033; 2032.

316. Treas. Reg. § 1.664-1(a)(5).

317. I.R.C. § 642(c).

318. Treas. Reg. § 1.664-1(a)(5). Under Treas. Reg. § 1.664-1(a)(5)(iv)(a), interest is payable at the section 7520 rate for transfers after April 30, 1989.

319. Rev. Rul. 76-7, 1976-1 C.B. 179 and Rev. Rul. 76-8, 1976-1 C.B. 179. *See also* Priv. Ltr. Rul. 89-19-016 (trustee of charitable remainder unitrust may have the power to name a substitute charitable remainderman relying on Rev. Rul. 76-7); Priv. Ltr. Rul. 94-45-010 (income beneficiaries/trustees may have power to designate by majority vote which departments within a university will receive the remainder, relying on Rev. Rul. 76-8); Priv. Ltr. Rul. 200034019 (grantor may retain inter vivos and testamentary powers to name charitable beneficiaries without disqualifying trust as section 664 charitable remainder unitrust, relying on Rev. Rul. 768).

320. Priv. Ltr. Rul. 200043029 (IRS ruled that annuity interest in charitable lead annuity trust and unitrust interest in charitable lead unitrust would qualify under section 2055(e)(2) where trusts were to be created at death of surviving spouse and no specific charities were named as charitable income beneficiaries; trustees would have power to designate and change charitable income beneficiaries).

321. Rev. Proc. 96-15, 1996-1 C.B. 627 contains the procedure for obtaining an advance valuation determination. Although designed for income tax charitable donations, it is equally applicable to noncharitable transfers. The IRS requires the payment of a user fee of $2,500 for the first three items to be valued and $250 for each additional item and generally applies only to items that have a value in excess of $50,000. The fees paid would be deductible on the federal estate tax return as an administrative expense.

322. For a discussion of an attempt to use tangible personal property in a testamentary charitable lead annuity trust, see Gopman, *The Formula CLAT and the Super Formula CLAT: Estate Planning With Charitable Lead Annuity Trusts Established at Death—Part I*, 23 TAX MGMT. EST., GIFTS & TR. J. 186, n.51 (July–Aug. 1998), discussing the CLAT under the will of Jacqueline Kennedy Onassis.

323. Palmer v. Comm'r, 62 T.C. 684 (1974), *aff'd on another issue*, 523 F.2d 1308 (8th Cir. 1975), *acq.*; Rev. Rul. 78-197, 1978-1 C.B. 83.

324. A testamentary charitable lead annuity trust is not a tax exempt entity and is taxed in accordance with the provisions of Subchapter J of the Code. However, the trust should be entitled to an income tax deduction for the amount of the annuity paid to the museum each year during the trust term. I.R.C. § 642(c)(1).

325. The Jobs and Growth Tax Relief Reconciliation Act of 2003 (effective May 6, 2003) reduced the long-term capital gain rate to 15% for sales of securities and other capital assets held for more than twelve months but maintained the 28% rate on gain from the sale of collectibles held for more than one year. The term "collectibles gain" is defined in section 1(h)(5)(A) to

mean gain from the sale or exchange of a collectible (as defined in section 408(m) without regard to paragraph (3) thereof) which is a capital asset held for more than one year but only to
the extent such gain is taken into account in computing taxable income.

326. A detailed analysis of section 2056(b)(7) is beyond the scope of this book. *See* Weiss, *New Estate Planning Focus,* 55 J. TAX'N 274 (1981); Garlock, *Estate Tax Unlimited Marital Deduction,* 56 J. TAX'N 236 (1982); Blattmachr, *The New Estate Tax Marital Deduction,* TR. & EST.,
Jan. 1982; Planning and Drafting for the Marital Deduction (L. Hirschson ed. PLI 1982); 27TH
ANNUAL ESTATE PLANNING INSTITUTE (C. Feldman & A. Parker ed. PLI 1996).

327. Estate of Robinson v. United States, 46 A.F.T.R.2d (P-H) ¶ 6185 (E.D. Tenn. 1980). *See* Priv.
Ltr. Rul. 87-42-001.

328. Under section 2044(a), the value of the QTIP trust is includable in the gross estate of the surviving spouse.

329. That was the congressional intent. *See* Staff of the Joint Committee on Taxation, General Explanation of the Economic Recovery Tax Act of 1981, at 236–37 n.4, 238 n.5 (1981).

330. *See id.* at 238 n.5.

331. Treas. Reg. § 20.2055-2(e)(2)(i). *See* Priv. Ltr. Rul. 93-03-007; Priv. Ltr. Rul. 200223013; Priv.
Ltr. Rul. 200418002.

332. *See* Ahmanson Found. v. United States, 674 F.2d 761 (9th Cir. 1981); Estate of Schwan v.
Comm'r, 82 T.C.M. (CCH) 168 (2001); DiSanto v. Comm'r, 78 T.C.M. (CCH) 1220 (1990);
(applying these principles in the case of the estate tax marital deduction); Deukmejian v.
Comm'r, 41 T.C.M. (CCH) 738 (1981); Priv. Ltr. Rul. 200223013.

333. Treas. Reg. §§ 20.2055-2(e)(1)(ii), 25.2522(c)-3(c)(1)(ii). *See generally* Lerner, *Final Regulations Under Section 2055(e)(4),* 62 J. TAX'N 300 (1985).

334. I.R.C. §§ 2055(e)(2), 2522(c)(2).

335. Treas. Reg. § 1.664-3(a)(1), (3); *see* Rev. Rul. 73-610, 1973-2 C.B. 213. See discussion at
page 1303 of charitable split-interest trusts.

336. Treas. Reg. §§ 1.170A-7(b)(1)(i), 20.2055-2(e)(2)(i), 25.2522(c)-3(c)(2)(i). *See generally* Ste-
phenson, *Tax Benefits of Gifts Increased as a Result of Several Provisions in New Tax Law,*
55 J. TAX'N 218 (1981).

337. *See* T. CRAWFORD, THE VISUAL ARTIST'S GUIDE TO THE NEW COPYRIGHT LAW (1978);
M. NIMMER & D. NIMMER, NIMMER ON COPYRIGHT (2011); P. GOLDSTEIN, COPYRIGHT
(2010); chapter 11 of this book.

338. The House Committee Report on H.R. 4242 (ERTA) points out at 184 the inconsistency between the copyright law and the tax law, but does not state specifically that the inconsistency
is the reason for the change in the tax law.

339. I.R.C. § 2055(e)(4)(A).

340. I.R.C. § 2055(e)(4)(B).

341. I.R.C. § 2055(e)(4)(C).

342. I.R.C. § 2055(e)(4)(D).

343. The House Committee Report on H.R. 4242 (ERTA) concluded that the rule allowing a deduction in such cases should apply only for estate and gift tax purposes and not for income
tax purposes.

344. *See* 3 NIMMER, *supra* note 337, § 10.09, and 1 GOLDSTEIN, *supra* note 337, § 4.4.2. Section
201(d)(1) of the Copyright Act of 1976 provides that ownership of copyright "may be bequeathed by will or pass as personal property by the applicable laws of intestate succession."
Section 204(a) of the Act provides that "a transfer of copyright ownership, other than by
operation of law, is not valid unless an instrument of conveyance, or a note or memorandum
of the transfer, is in writing and signed by the owner of the rights conveyed or such owner's
duly authorized agent." (West 2004).

345. *See* Treas. Reg. § 20.2055-2(e)(1)(ii)(e) ex. (1).

346. For a discussion of copyright interests in community property states, see Bauman & Hoffman, *Estate Planning for Individuals in the Entertainment Industry,* 31 U.S.C. L. CENTER
TAX INST. 875 (1979); Patry, *Copyright and Community Property: The Question of Preemption,* 28 BULL. COPYRIGHT SOC'Y 237 (1981).

347. That interpretation was confirmed in the ERTA General Explanation, *supra* note 329, at 259.

348. I.R.C. § 2055(e)(4)(A).

349. I.R.C. § 170(e)(1)(A).

350. I.R.C. §§ 2001(c), 2501(a).

351. I.R.C. § 2523

352. I.R.C. § 2513.

353. I.R.C. § 2035(c).

354. I.R.C. § 2503(b). The $10,000 annual exclusion was increased to $13,000 by the "cost of living adjustment" as provided in I.R.C. § 2503(b)(2).

355. I.R.C. § 2035(b)(2).

356. I.R.C. § 2035(d).

357. P.L. 111-312, §§ 301(b), (e); 302(a), (b), (f), 303.

358. P.L. 111-312, § 303.

359. *See also* I.R.C. § 1014(b)(10), added by the Technical Corrections Act of 1982.

360. *See* Roemer v. Comm'r, 46 T.C.M. (CCH) 1176 (1983); Neuwirth, *How to Protect Lifetime Transfers from Being Included in the Estate of the Transferor*, Tax'n for Law. (May–June 1982).

361. I.R.C. § 2032(a).

362. I.R.C. § 2032(c) (effective for decedents who die after July 18, 1984).

363. Pub. L. No. 101-508, enacted November 5, 1990, applicable to transfers after October 8, 1990.

364. I.R.C. § 7520.

365. The rules of I.R.C. §§ 2701–04 only apply to transfers to a member of the donor's family where the donor (or his spouse, an ancestor of the donor or his spouse, or the spouse of any such ancestor) retains an interest in the property. A family member is defined under I.R.C. § 2704(c)(2) as the donor's spouse, ancestors of the donor or his spouse, lineal descendants of the donor or his spouse, the donor's siblings, and the spouses of any such ancestor.

366. I.R.C. § 2702(a)(2)(A).

367. Note that under I.R.C. § 2702(c)(1) a transfer of property with respect to which there are one or more term interests is treated as a transfer in trust.

368. I.R.C. § 2702(c)(4). Note that Treas. Reg. § 25.2702-2(c)(2) adds the requirement that the tangible property must also be property for which no deduction for depreciation or depletion would be allowable if the property were used in a trade or business or held for the production of income. A work of art will generally satisfy this requirement because it lacks an ascertainable useful life within the meaning of the depreciation rules. *See* Judge v. Comm'r, 35 T.C.M. (CCH) 283 (1976).

369. I.R.C. § 2702(c)(4)(B).

370. Treas. Reg. § 25.2702-2(c)(1).

371. Treas. Reg. § 25.2702-2(c)(3).

372. A possible source of information on the rental value of works of art are companies that lease works of art such as LeasArt, based in Century City, California, and Art America, based in New York City. *See* Carol Vogel, *The Art Market*, N.Y. Times, Feb. 28, 1992, at C16. Most of these companies have ceased doing business since there is no rental market for works of art.

373. Treas. Reg. § 25.2702-2(d)(2) ex. 9.

374. Stone v. United States, 2007 U.S. Dist. LEXIS 38332 (N.D. Cal. May 25, 2007), *later opinion*, 2007 U.S. Dist. LEXIS 58611 (N.D. Cal. Aug. 10, 2007), *aff'd sub nom.* Stone *ex rel.* Stone Trust Agreement v. United States, 2009 U.S. App. LEXIS 6349 (9th Cir. Mar. 24, 2009) (unpublished).

375. *Id.,* 2007 U.S. Dist. LEXIS 58611.

376. Given the basic premises of valuation (the price a hypothetical willing buyer will pay to a hypothetical willing seller), the question arises whether there is a particular reason why a fractional interest in an item of property would make the property less appealing to the hypothetical willing buyer. Neither the Internal Revenue Code, nor the regulations (except for the reference in Treas. Reg. § 20.2031-1) contain any specific provisions on the issue of valuing fractional interests. *See* Hood, Jr., 830-2nd BNA T.M. Portfolio, Valuation: General and

Real Estate, section II.H.4. The IRS usually takes the position that in the absence of evidence to the contrary the fact that the interest involved is a fractional interest does not warrant any discount, that is, the value of such interest is equivalent to the proportionate part of the value of the entire interest. However, when it comes to a fractional interest in real estate, some discount is generally allowed. Iacono v. Comm'r, 41 T.C.M. (CCH) 407 (1980); *In re* Gilberts Estate, 163 N.Y.S. 974 (1917); Stevens Estate v. Comm'r, 79 T.C.M. (CCH) 1519 (2000); Forbes Estate v. Comm'r, 81 T.C.M. (CCH) 1399 (2000); Baird Estate v. Comm'r, 82 T.C.M. (CCH) 666 (2001); Tech. Adv. Mem. 199943003, where the National Office advised that if a discount is appropriate, one method of determining the fair market value of a decedent's undivided interests in tracts of real property is to subtract the partition sale costs from the fair market value of the undivided interests. The first case that addressed the issue with respect to works of art was Estate of Robert C. Scull v. Comm'r, 67 T.C.M. (CCH) 2953 (1994), where a 5% discount was allowed on a 65% interest because of uncertainties in a continuing divorce proceeding. This has been further clarified in Stone v. United States, 2007 U.S. Dist. LEXIS 38332 (N.D. Cal. May 25, 2007), *later opinion,* 2007 U.S. Dist. LEXIS 58611 (N.D. Cal. Aug. 10, 2007), *aff'd sub nom.* Stone *ex rel.* Stone Trust Agreement v. United States, 2009 U.S. App. LEXIS 6349 (9th Cir. Mar. 24, 2009) (unpublished).

377. Stone *ex rel.* Stone Trust Agreement v. United States, 2009 U.S. App. LEXIS 6349 (9th Cir. Mar. 24, 2009) (unpublished).

378. Holman v. Comm'r, 130 T.C. 170 (2008), *aff'd,* 601 F.3d 763 (8th Cir. 2010).

379. *Holman,* 601 F.3d 763. *See also* Fisher v. U.S., 2010 U.S. Dist. LEXIS 91423, 2010-2 U.S. Tax Cas. P60601; *Context Matters: Rules for Reducing Taxable Value,* 120 Yale L.J. Online 141 (2010).

380. *Holman,* 601 F.3d at 768 (quoting Finance Committee Report, 136 Cong. Rec. S15680).

381. I.R.C. § 2703(b).

382. Elkins v. Comm'r, Dkt. 16597-10, _____ T.C. _____ (2012).

383. The taxpayer's argument relies on Estate of Strangi v. Comm'r, 115 T.C. 478, 488-89 (2000), *aff'd on this point,* 293 F.3d 279, 282 (5th Cir. 2002), where there was an intervening partnership interest.

384. I.R.C. §§ 1001, 1002.

385. I.R.C. § 262.

386. I.R.C. § 1221(a)(3).

387. I.R.C. § 2033.

388. Pub. L. No. 111-312, § 303.

389. Estate of Ludwig Neugass v. Comm'r, 77-1 U.S. Tax Cas. (CCH) ¶ 13,192 (2d Cir. 1977), *rev'g and remanding* 65 T.C. 188 (1976).

390. *See* Rev. Rul. 82-184, 1982-2 C.B. 215.

391. *See* I.R.C. § 2056(b)(7). See also the discussion of QTIP trusts below.

392. Sternberger's Estate v. Comm'r, 18 T.C. 836 (1952), *aff'd,* 207 F.2d 600 (2d Cir. 1953), *rev'd on other issue,* 348 U.S. 187 (1955).

393. Estate of Swayne v. Comm'r, 43 T.C. 190 (1964); *See* Estate of Carson v. Comm'r, 35 T.C.M. (CCH) 330 (1976).

394. Estate of David Smith v. Comm'r, 57 T.C. 650 (1972), *aff'd,* 510 F.2d 479 (2d Cir.), *cert. denied,* 423 U.S. 827 (1975).

395. New York Surrogate's Court Procedure Act section 222 was in effect in the *Smith* case. That section was succeeded as of September 1, 1967 by what is now N.Y. Est. Powers & Trusts Law § 11-1.1(b)(22) (McKinney 2004).

396. Estate of Park v. Comm'r, 475 F.2d 673 (6th Cir. 1973), *rev'g* 57 T.C. 705 (1972), *overruled, see infra* note 400. *See* Estate of Joslyn v. Comm'r, 78-1 U.S. Tax Cas. (CCH) ¶ 13,227 (9th Cir. 1978).

397. Hibernia Bank v. Comm'r, 75-2 U.S. Tax Cas. (CCH) ¶ 13,102 (N.D. Cal. 1975), *aff'd,* 78-2 U.S. Tax Cas. (CCH) ¶ 13,261 (9th Cir. 1978).

398. Estate of Joseph Vatter v. Comm'r, 65 T.C. 633 (1975), *aff'd,* 77-1 U.S. Tax Cas. (CCH) ¶ 13,169 (2d Cir. 1977); *see* Spragens, *Current Appellate Cases Create Conflict in Deductibility*

of Selling Costs as Administration Expenses Under Section 2053(a)(2), TAXES, July 1976; Englebrecht & Carnes, *Standards for Deducting Administrative Fees from an Estate Vary in the Circuits*, 18 TAX'N FOR LAW. 210 (1990); Caron, *Must a Administration Expense Allowed by State Law Also Meet a Federal Necessity Test?*, 70 J. TAX'N 352 (1989).

399. Priv. Ltr. Rul. 78-02-006. *See* Priv. Ltr. Rul. 79-12-006.

400. Estate of Marguerite S. Millikin v. Comm'r, 106 F.3d 1263 (6th Cir. 1997), *aff'g* 69 T.C.M. (CCH) 3032 (1995), *rev'd*, 125 F.3d 339 (6th Cir. 1997).

401. *See id.*, 106 F.3d at 1263.

402. OHIO REV. CODE ANN. § 2113.36.

403. *Millikin*, 106 F.3d at 1263.

404. *Millikin*, 125 F.3d at 345.

405. Estate of Vera T. Posen v. Comm'r, 75 T.C. 355 (1980). *See also* Marcus v. United States, 83-1 U.S. Tax Cas. (CCH) ¶ 13,521 (11th Cir. 1983), *rev'g and remanding* 81-2 U.S. Tax Cas. (CCH) ¶ 13,431 (D. Fla. 1981); Ferguson v. United States, 81-1 U.S. Tax Cas. (CCH) ¶ 13,409 (D. Ariz. 1981).

406. Estate of DeWitt v. Comm'r, 54 T.C.M. (CCH) 759 (1987).

407. See Priv. Ltr. Rul. 81-19-002, in which an auctioneer's commissions that were incurred in selling the decedent's property, and that were allowable administrative expenses under applicable (New York) state law, were deductible by the estate because the decedent's will directed that his property be sold and the proceeds distributed to the estate's beneficiaries. The commissions were, therefore, necessary "to effect distribution" of the estate.

408. Estate of Streeter v. Comm'r, 74-1 U.S. Tax Cas. (CCH) ¶ 12,970 (3d Cir. 1974), *aff'g* 30 T.C.M. (CCH) 1118 (1971).

409. Treas. Reg. § 20.2053-1(a)(1).

410. Treas. Reg. § 20.2053-1(a)(2).

411. Estate of Jenner v. Comm'r, 577 F.2d 1100 (7th Cir. 1978).

412. Pitner v. United States, 388 F.2d 651 (5th Cir. 1967); Hibernia Bank v. United States, 581 F.2d 741 (9th Cir. 1978); Estate of David Smith v. Comm'r, 57 T.C. 650 (1972), *aff'd*, 510 F.2d 479 (2d Cir.), *cert. denied*, 423 U.S. 827 (1975). *See* Note, *The Estate Tax Deduction for Administration Expenses: Reformulating Complementary Roles for Federal and State Law Under I.R.C. § 2053(a)(2)*, 67 CORNELL L. REV. 981 (1982); Estate of Marguerite S. Millikin v. Comm'r, 106 F.3d 1263 (6th Cir. 1997), *aff'g* 69 T.C.M. (CCH) 3032 (1995), *rev'd*, 125 F.3d 339 (6th Cir. 1997).

413. Estate of Margaret D. Love v. Comm'r, 57 T.C.M. (CCH) 1479 (1989), *aff'd*, 923 F.2d 335 (4th Cir. 1991); *see* Tow, *Estate of Love and Sec. 2053(a)(2): Why State Law Should Control the Determination of Deductible Administration Expenses*, 12 VA. TAX REV. 283 (1993); Priv. Ltr. Rul. 93-42-002.

414. Priv. Ltr. Rul. 81-19-002 (Jan. 16, 1981).

415. Rev. Rul. 71-173, 1971-1 C.B. 204.

416. The statute also changes the holding in Estate of Bray v. Comm'r, 46 T.C. 557 (1966), *aff'd*, 396 F.2d 452 (6th Cir. 1968).

417. I.R.C. § 642(g).

418. I.R.C. § 2056(a).

419. I.R.C. § 1014(a); Treas. Reg. § 1.1014-1(a). Note that the section 1014 step-up in basis was repealed for decedents dying in calendar year 2010 and reinstated for decedents dying in calendar year 2011 and thereafter.

420. Treas. Reg. § 1.1014-3(a).

421. Conrad Janis v. Comm'r, 87 T.C.M. (CCH) 1322 (2004).

422. *Id.*

423. *Id.*

424. Augustus v. Comm'r, 40 B.T.A. 1201 (1939), *aff'd*, 118 F.2d 38 (6th Cir. 1941).

425. *Janis*, 87 T.C.M. 1322.

426. The court in *Janis* also found that the taxpayers violated the "duty of consistency." A taxpayer's duty of consistency applies if (i) the taxpayer made a representation of fact or reported

an item for tax purposes in one year; (ii) the IRS acquiesced in or relied on that fact for that year; and (iii) the taxpayer desires to change the representation previously made in a later tax year after the earlier year has been closed by the statute of limitations. The court noted that all three elements were present in this case, in particular, that the taxpayer used the undiscounted basis on the sale of artworks after the statute of limitations on assessments had expired against the Janis estate. See cases cited in *Janis*.

427. For an excellent, in-depth treatment of the subject, see Malaro, *Restricted Gifts and Museum Responsibilities*, 18 J. ARTS MGMT. & L. 41 (1986); Sare, *Art for Whose Sake? An Analysis of Restricted Gifts to Museums*, 13 COLUM.-VLA J.L. & ARTS 377 (1989); chapter 17 of this book.

428. COSMOPOLITAN 144 (Mar. 1989).

429. *See* ARTNEWS, vol. 84, no. 6, at 23–24 (1985).

APPENDIX 15-1

Information Required Before Contribution

Gentlemen:

I am considering making a contribution to you of a work of art [described briefly]. Before doing so, I wish to have your counsel's opinion as to: (1) Whether your operations qualify you as an organization described in Section 170(b)(1)(A)(i) through (viii) of the Internal Revenue Code; and (2) whether the work of art would be used by your organization for a purpose or function related to the basis for your exemption under Section 501 of the Internal Revenue Code. I would also like to know the grounds for your counsel's opinion.

Very truly yours,

_____

Art Collector Donor

APPENDIX 15-2

Deed of Gift of Entire Interest to Museum

DEED OF GIFT

WHEREAS, _____, having an address at _____, is the sole owner ("Owner") of the work of art listed on Schedule A attached hereto and made a part hereof (the "Work"); and

WHEREAS, Owner desires to give the Work to the _____ Museum, having an office at _____ ("Museum"), upon the terms and conditions herein set forth;

NOW, THEREFORE, the undersigned hereby gives, grants, conveys, assigns and transfers to the Museum all of Owner's right, title and interest in and to the Work, including any copyright interest therein, if any, (the "Gift") upon the condition that the Work be made generally available by the Museum for study and inspection by the general public at such times and under such regulations and upon such conditions as the Museum may reasonably impose and that the Work be utilized by the Museum for its educational and cultural purposes, including without limitation, the lending of the Work to other museums open to the general public. Nothing herein shall be deemed to limit the unrestricted discretion of the Museum to use the Work in furtherance of its exempt purposes.

IN WITNESS WHEREOF, the undersigned has hereunto set [his/her] hand and seals this _____ day of _____, 20__.

_____

[Name of Owner]

ACCEPTANCE OF DEED OF GIFT

The above described Gift is accepted by the undersigned on behalf of the _____ Museum, having an office at _____, on this ____ day of _____, 20__.

_____ MUSEUM

_____

By:
Its:

SCHEDULE A

THE WORK

Title:
Artist:
Medium:
Size:
Date:

APPENDIX 15-3

Deed of Gift of Entire Interest from Foundation to Museum

DEED OF GIFT

WHEREAS, the _____ Foundation, having an address at _____ (the "Foundation"), is the sole owner of the work of art listed on Schedule A attached hereto and made a part hereof (the "Work"); and

WHEREAS, the Foundation is desirous of giving the Work to the _____ Museum, having an office at _____ ("Museum"), upon the terms and conditions hereinafter set forth;

NOW, THEREFORE, the undersigned does irrevocably and without condition or reservation give, grant, convey, confirm and transfer unto the Museum all of its right, title and interest in and to the Work, upon the condition that the Work be made generally available by the Museum for study and inspection by the general public at such times and under such regulations and upon such conditions as the Museum may reasonably impose and that the Work be utilized by the Museum for its educational and cultural purposes, including without limitation, the lending of the Work to museums open to the general public. Nothing herein shall be deemed to limit the unrestricted discretion of the Museum to use the Work in furtherance of its exempt purposes.

The Foundation affirms that a) it has good and complete right, title, and interest in and to the Work; b) it has full authority to give, transfer and assign its right, title and interest in and to the Work; c) the Work is free and clear of all encumbrances and restrictions; and d) to the best of the Foundation's knowledge, the Work has not been imported or exported into or from any country contrary to its laws.

In addition, the Foundation agrees to transfer to the Museum copies of all documentation, and share with the Museum all information, it has, if any, relating to the Work, including the ownership, display and restoration of the Work prior to the date of this gift.

This Deed of Gift and all matters relating to it shall be governed by the laws of the County and State of _____. This Deed of Gift shall inure to the benefit of, and shall be binding upon, the successors, heirs, executors and administrators of the parties hereto. Any dispute arising hereunder shall be resolved in the courts of the County and State of _____.

IN WITNESS WHEREOF, the undersigned has hereunto set his hand and seal this _____ day of _____, 20__.

[Name of Foundation]

_____
By:
Its:

ACCEPTANCE OF DEED OF GIFT

The above described Gift is accepted by the undersigned on behalf of the _____ Museum, having an office at _____, on this ___ day of _____, 20__.

[Name of Museum]

_____
By:
Its:

SCHEDULE A

THE WORK

Title:
Artist:
Medium:
Size:
Date:

PROVENANCE

EXHIBITED

LITERATURE AND REFERENCES

APPENDIX 15-4

Deed of Gift of One-Fourth Interest to a Museum

DEED OF GIFT

WHEREAS,_____,havinganaddressat_____,
is the sole owner ("Owner") of the work of art listed on Schedule A attached
hereto and made a part hereof (the "Work"); and

WHEREAS, Owner desires to give to the _____ Museum, having an office at
_____ ("Museum"), an undivided one-fourth (¼) interest in the
Work upon the terms and conditions herein set forth;

NOW, THEREFORE, the undersigned hereby gives, grants, conveys, assigns
and transfers to the Museum an undivided one-fourth (¼) interest in the Work,
including any copyright interest therein, if any (the "Gift") it being understood
that the Museum shall have rights of possession, dominion and control of the
Work for one-fourth (¼) of the time during any twelve-month period after the
date hereof. The Museum to have the sole discretion to decide the months during
which it will exercise such rights.

IN WITNESS WHEREOF, the undersigned has hereunto set [his/her] hand
and seal this _____ day of _____, 20__.

_____
[Name of Owner]

ACCEPTANCE OF DEED OF GIFT

The above described Gift is accepted by the undersigned on behalf of the
_____ Museum, having an office at _____, on
this ___ day of _____, 20__.

_____ Museum

_____
By:
Its:

SCHEDULE A

THE WORK

Title:
Artist:
Medium:
Size:
Date:

APPENDIX 15-5

Deed of Gift of One-Fourth Interest with Promised Gift Agreement

DEED OF GIFT

WHEREAS,_____, having an address at_____ ("Owner"), is the sole owner of the work of art listed on Schedule A attached hereto and made a part hereof (the "Work"); and

WHEREAS, Owner desires to give to the _____ Museum, having an office at _____ ("Museum"), an undivided one-fourth (1/4) interest in the Work upon the terms and conditions herein set forth;

NOW, THEREFORE, in consideration of the mutual promises contained herein, the parties hereto agree as follows:

1. *Gift of Interest.*

Owner hereby gives, grants, conveys, assigns and transfers to the Museum all of his right, title and interest in and to an undivided one-fourth (¼) interest in the Work, including any copyright interest therein, if any (the "Gift"). The Museum hereby accepts title to the Gift.

It is Owner's intention to vest in the Museum the absolute ownership of the Gift at this time, and hereby granting The Museum the rights of possession, dominion and control of the Work for one-fourth (¼) of the time during any twelve-month period after the date hereof ("Museum's Time," the other thee-fourths (¾) of the time shall be referred to hereinafter as "Owner's Time"). The Museum to have the sole discretion to decide the months during which it will exercise such rights.

2. *Exhibition*

In keeping with the Museum's rights of possession, dominion and control of the Work as described in Paragraph 1 above, it is expressly understood and agreed that the Museum may exhibit the Work at its premises during the months during which the Museum chooses to exercise such rights. The Work shall not be loaned to any entity without the written consent of Owner. For display purposes for the Work, the credit line for the Work shall refer to Owner as "Anonymous."

3. *Care of Work*

While the Work is in the possession of the Museum, the Museum will give to the Work the same care it gives comparable property of its own. The Museum will take precautions to protect the Work from fire, theft, mishandling, dirt, and insects, and from extremes of light, temperature, and humidity while in the Museum's custody.

4. *Insurance.*

A. Owner will be responsible for insuring the entire Work during the Owner's Time. The Museum will be responsible for insuring the entire Work during the Museum's Time.

B. The Museum agrees to provide at its cost all risk, wall-to-wall insurance coverage using standard fine arts commercial insurance from a company rated by A.M. Best's A- or better and/or United States Government Indemnity for the safekeeping and preservation of the Work during the Museum's Time. The Work to be insured for the value stated on Schedule A attached hereto (the "Insurance Value"); provided, however, that if the fair market value for the Work shall increase after the date of the signing of this Agreement, then the Museum shall insure the Work for the increased fair market value, consistent with the Museum's insurance policy. The Museum shall insure the Work at the Museum's cost from the time the Work is first located at its premises and until the Work is transferred to Owner. The Museum agrees that the insurance coverage it will obtain for the Insurance Value for the Work as indicated on Schedule A is the stated value for the Work and all claims, whether for full or partial damage, will be based on an amount no less than this value. The Museum agrees to provide Owner with a Certificate of Insurance evidencing such insurance coverage, and naming Owner as loss payee and additional insured. The Museum agrees to accept the obligation of caring for the Work during the time when the Work is located at its premises and when the Work is shipped to the Owner. The Museum agrees to accept responsibility for the Work and liability for any deficiencies and/or exclusions in insurance coverage and excluding solely the negligence or other wrongful acts of Owner or his servants or agents, or pre-existing condition flaws in the Work when the Work is first located at the Museum's premises. In the case of any loss or damage, Owner agrees to use reasonable efforts as required to enable the Museum to submit and pursue a claim for insurance coverage. The Museum shall pay all costs (both Owner's and the Museum's costs) in connection with the Museum submitting and pursuing a claim for insurance coverage. In the case of partial loss or damage to the Work, Owner and the Museum shall agree upon the reasonable cost of repair of the Work and the amount of any reduction in the fair market value of the Work after repair, or in the absence of agreement, these amounts will be determined by an appraiser mutually acceptable to Owner and the Museum. If the parties are unable to agree upon an appraiser, then each party will appoint an appraiser and those two appraisers will attempt to agree on the amount of loss in value or if they are also unable to agree, the two appraisers will select a third appraiser to determine the loss in value. The Museum shall pay all costs in connection with the appraiser's valuation. The insurance policies provided by the Museum shall expressly state that they provide primary coverage, which shall not be diminished by reason of any insurance coverage obtained by Owner.

5. *Shipping.*

The Museum, after consulting with and obtaining the approval of Owner, agrees to arrange and pay for the packing and shipping of the Work from Owner's premises to the Museum for the Museum's Time, and from the Museum back to Owner's premises when the Work is not at the end of the Museum's Time. The method of shipment must be agreed upon by both parties.

6. *Pledge.*

Owner does hereby pledge (the "Pledge") to transfer all of his undivided three-fourth ¾ interest in and to the Work (the "Interest") to the Museum either by way of gift during Owner's lifetime or by bequest under Owner's Last Will and Testament; provided, however, that Owner has complied with the terms and conditions of this Agreement at all times.

Owner agrees that this Pledge shall extend to and be binding upon Owner's executors, administrators, heirs, assigns, and other estate fiduciaries, and upon the trustees of any lifetime trust which becomes irrevocable upon Owner's death and which has title to the Work. Should this Pledge not be completed during the lifetime of Owner, then the failure to include a specific bequest of the Interest in the Last Will and Testament of Owner shall not release Owner's heirs, executors, administrators or other estate fiduciaries, or the trustees of any lifetime trust which becomes irrevocable upon his death and which has title to the Interest, from the binding obligation of delivering and transferring title in and to the Interest to the Museum in accordance with this Agreement.

If the Work is stolen or destroyed in any party's possession before fulfillment of the Pledge, the amount of the Pledge with respect to the Work shall be limited to the insurance proceeds payable as a result, if any, and such proceeds shall be payable to the Museum no later than the death of Owner.

This Pledge is a definite commitment and Owner understands that the Museum is relying and may continue to rely on this Pledge in a variety of ways, including without limitation, (a) the Museum's decision not to acquire other works of art based on its expectation of receiving the Interest; (b) the Museum's ability to make this Pledge (but not the identity of Owner) known to others in order to encourage them to make similar commitments; and (c) the Museum's taking or failing to take other actions in reliance upon this Pledge.

7. *Miscellaneous.*

This Agreement represents the entire understanding of all the parties hereto, supersedes any and all other and prior agreements between the parties and declares all such prior agreements between the parties null and void. The terms of this Agreement may not be modified or amended, except in a writing signed by the party to be charged. This Agreement and all matters relating to it shall be governed by the laws of the State of _____ without regard to conflict of laws principles. This Agreement shall inure to the benefit of, and shall be binding upon, the successors, heirs, assigns, executors and administrators of the parties hereto. Any dispute arising hereunder shall be resolved in the _____ State Supreme Court, _____ County or in the United States District Court for the _____, and the parties hereto consent to the personal jurisdiction of those courts. This agreement may be executed in two or more counterparts, including facsimile or PDF, each of which shall be Deemed an original and all of which together shall constitute one and the same instrument.

IN WITNESS WHEREOF, Owner and the Museum have hereunto set their hands and seals this _____ day of _____, 20__.

_____
[Name of Owner]
The _____ Museum

_____
By:
Its:

SCHEDULE A

THE WORK

Artist:
Title:
Medium:
Size:
Date:

APPENDIX 15-6

Specific Bequest of a Work of Art

I give and bequeath to the .... Museum in the City of
........................., and the State of ...., the items described below, including any copyright interest therein, if any:

1. Oil painting entitled "............................." by .... dated
    ....

2. Etc.

PROVIDED, HOWEVER, if at the time of my death the ....
Museum is not an organization described in Section 2055(a) of the Internal Revenue Code of 1986, or corresponding provisions of any subsequent Federal tax
laws, I give and bequeath said items to such other organization as is described in
said Section 2055(a) and is designated by my Executor.

APPENDIX 15-7

Specific Items to Named Individuals

I give and bequeath the following articles of tangible personal property, including any copyright interest therein, if any, to such of the following persons as shall survive me:

(a) To my son, ..., the oil painting entitled "......................" by .... dated ....

(b) To my friend, ..., the sculpture entitled "................" by .... dated ....

(c) Etc.

(d) I give and bequeath all of my tangible personal property not hereinbefore effectually disposed of in subdivisions (a) through (c) of this Clause to ....

APPENDIX 15-8

Items to a Class of Individuals

To my children, ..., ..., and
......................., or such of them as shall survive me, I give and bequeath all
paintings and sculpture, including any copyright interest therein, if any, that are
not in the preceding paragraphs of my Will otherwise specifically disposed of. In
the event my children who survive me cannot agree among themselves as to the
division of such property, my son, ..., shall have the right of first
selection, my daughter, ..., shall have the right of second selection, and my daughter, ..., shall have the right of third
selection, and so on thereafter, my said son and daughters in such order each having the right of further selection until all articles of tangible personal property
covered by this Clause have been selected.

APPENDIX 15-9

Specific Items to Unnamed Charities

I give and bequeath the following described items:

1. Oil painting entitled "...................." by .... dated
...................., including any copyright interest therein, if any;

2. [Etc.] to such organization or organizations as my Executors, in their sole
and absolute discretion, shall select, designate and appoint. The words "organization or organizations" as hereinabove used in this Clause shall be deemed to
mean and include only such organization or organizations to which a transfer is
deductible for federal estate tax purposes and is described in Section 2055(a) of
the Internal Revenue Code of 1986, or corresponding provisions of any subsequent federal tax laws.

APPENDIX 15-10

Expenses for Tangibles

I direct that all expenses of insuring, storing, transporting, and otherwise caring for any property bequeathed in this [Subdivision No. _____, Clause No. _____] shall be paid by my Executor as an expense of administration of my estate until actual delivery of each article of property to the beneficiary at the location designated by such beneficiary.

APPENDIX 15-11

*Information Required to Be Contained in an
Appraisal of Tangible Personal Property Being
Contributed to Charity for Which a Deduction Will
Be Claimed for Federal Income Tax Purposes*

QUALIFIED APPRAISAL

The following information is required pursuant to Treas. Reg. Section 1.170A-13(c)(3)(ii). Donors of tangible personal property to charity should require the appraiser to include the following information in the appraisal.

1. DESCRIPTION OF THE PROPERTY—in sufficient detail for a person who is not generally familiar with the type of property to ascertain that the property that was appraised is the property that was (or will be) contributed. Description should include dimensions, color, materials used, and, if known, date of creation, maker, location of origin and whatever other factual details would be helpful.

2. PHYSICAL CONDITION of the property—the appraisal should note any repairs, defects, worn elements, fading, etc.

3. DATE (OR EXPECTED DATE)—OF CONTRIBUTION TO Charity.

4. DATE OR DATES ON WHICH THE PROPERTY WAS VALUED by the appraiser—note that the appraisal can not be prepared more than 60 days prior to the actual date of contribution of the appraised property.

5. METHOD OF VALUATION used to determine the fair market value - such as comparable sales approach or replacement cost-less-depreciation approach.

6. SPECIFIC BASIS FOR VALUATION, if any, such as specific comparable sales transactions.

7. TERMS OF ANY AGREEMENT—or understanding between the donor and the donee charity relating to the use, sale or other disposition of the property. If none, the appraisal should so state, or if there are, the appraisal should explain.

8. FEE ARRANGEMENT between donor and appraiser - fees based on a percentage of the value will render the appraisal invalid for income tax contribution purposes.

9. QUALIFICATIONS of the APPRAISER including background, experience, education and membership, if any, in professional appraiser associations. There should be included, in addition, specific examples of qualifications by way of experience or background to appraise the particular items which are the subject of the appraisal.

10. FAIR MARKET VALUE—the appraised value of the property which is the subject of the appraisal as of the date (or expected date) of contribution.

11. PURPOSE OF APPRAISAL—a statement that the appraisal was prepared for federal income tax purposes.

12. SIGNATURE of appraiser on the appraisal. The name, address and taxpayer identification number of the appraiser must be on the appraisal.

APPENDIX 15-12

Charitable Contributions Chart

	TYPE OF PROPERTY	PUBLIC CHARITY 50%	PRIVATE FOUNDATION 30%
1.	Cash	deductible up to 50% of AGI; 5-year carryover for excess	deductible up to 30% of AGI; 5-year carryover for excess
2.	Long-term capital gain property which is *not* tangible personal property	deductible for full FMV[4] up to 30% of AGI; 5-year carryover for excess	deductible for full FMV minus 100% of increase in value up to 20% of AGI, *i.e.*, limited to cost; 5-year carryover for excess; special rule for "Qualified Appreciated Stock"[1]
3.	Long-term capital gain property which *is* tangible personal property	deductible for full FMV[4] up to 30% of AGI *if* satisfy the related use rule[2];[3] if RUR is not satisfy, must subtract 100% of increase in value from FMV with balance deductible up to 50% of AGI; 5-year carryover for excess	deductible for full FMV minus 100% of increase in value up to 20% of AGI, *i.e.*, limited to cost; 5-year carryover for excess
4.	Short-term capital gain property	deductible up to 50% of AGI but limited to cost of property, not FMV; 5-year carryover for excess	deductible up to 20% of AGI but limited to cost of property, not FMV; 5-year carryover for excess
5.	Property that has decreased in value	deductible up to 50% of AGI but limited to *lesser* of FMV or cost; 5-year carryover for excess	deductible up to 30% AGI but limited to *lesser* of FMV or cost; 5-year carryover for excess

1. For contributions of Qualified Appreciated Stock made from 7/1/96 through 6/30/98, no subtraction for the increase in value is required, i.e., a deduction for full FMV is allowed.

2. *Related use rule* means the property contributed is related to the exempt purpose of the donee charitable organization.

3. For contributions of tangible personal property a qualified appraisal by a qualified appraiser is required along with Form 8283.

4. The amount of the increase in value is not a preference item and is not subject to the alternative minimum tax. The AMT as it applied to the increase in value was repealed effective 1/1/93 for property in (2) above and effective 7/1/92 for property in (3) above.

APPENDIX 15-13

IRS Publication 561—Determining the Value of Donated Property

Publication 561
(Rev. April 2007)
Cat. No. 15109Q

Department
of the
Treasury

**Internal
Revenue
Service**

Determining the Value of Donated Property

Get forms and other information faster and easier by:

Internet • www.irs.gov

Contents

Introduction

This publication is designed to help donors and appraisers determine the value of property (other than cash) that is given to qualified organizations. It also explains what kind of information you must have to support the charitable contribution deduction you claim on your return.

This publication does not discuss how to figure the amount of your deduction for charitable contributions or written records and substantiation required. See Publication 526, Charitable Contributions, for this information.

Comments and suggestions. We welcome your comments about this publication and your suggestions for future editions.

You can write to us at the following address:

Internal Revenue Service
Individual Forms and Publications Branch
SE:W:CAR:MP:T:I
1111 Constitution Ave. NW, IR-6406
Washington, DC 20224

The type and rule above prints on all proofs including departmental reproduction proofs. MUST be removed before printing.

We respond to many letters by telephone. Therefore, it would be helpful if you would include your daytime phone number, including the area code, in your correspondence.

You can email us at *taxforms@irs.gov*. (The asterisk must be included in the address.) Please put "Publications Comment" on the subject line. Although we cannot respond individually to each email, we do appreciate your feedback and will consider your comments as we revise our tax products.

Ordering forms and publications. Visit *www.irs.gov/formspubs* to download forms and publications, call 1-800-829-3676, or write to the address below and receive a response within 10 business days after your request is received.

National Distribution Center
P.O. Box 8903
Bloomington, IL 61702–8903

Tax questions. If you have a tax question, visit *www.irs.gov* or call 1-800-829-1040. We cannot answer tax questions sent to either of the above addresses.

Useful Items
You may want to see:

Publication

❑ 526   Charitable Contributions

Form (and Instructions)

❑ 8282   Donee Information Return
❑ 8283   Noncash Charitable Contributions
❑ 8283-V   Payment Voucher for Filing Fee
     Under Section 170(f)(13)
See *How To Get Tax Help*, near the end of this publication, for information about getting these publications and forms.

What Is Fair Market Value (FMV)?

To figure how much you may deduct for property that you contribute, you must first determine its fair market value on the date of the contribution.

Fair market value. Fair market value (FMV) is the price that property would sell for on the open market. It is the price that would be agreed on between a willing buyer and a willing seller, with neither being required to act, and both having reasonable knowledge of the relevant facts. If you put a restriction on the use of property you donate, the FMV must reflect that restriction.

Example 1. If you give used clothing to the Salvation Army, the FMV would be the price that typical buyers actually pay for clothing of this age, condition, style, and use. Usually, such items are worth far less than what you paid for them.

Example 2. If you donate land and restrict its use to agricultural purposes, you must value the land at its value for agricultural purposes, even though it would have a higher FMV if it were not restricted.

Factors. In making and supporting the valuation of property, all factors affecting value are relevant and must be considered. These include:

- The cost or selling price of the item,
- Sales of comparable properties,
- Replacement cost, and
- Opinions of experts.

These factors are discussed later. Also, see *Table 1* for a summary of questions to ask as you consider each factor.

Date of contribution. Ordinarily, the date of a contribution is the date that the transfer of the property takes place.

Stock. If you deliver, without any conditions, a properly endorsed stock certificate to a qualified organization or to an agent of the organization, the date of the contribution is the date of delivery. If the certificate is mailed and received through the regular mail, it is the date of mailing. If you deliver the certificate to a bank or broker acting as your agent or to the issuing corporation or its agent, for transfer into the name of the organization, the date of the contribution is the date the stock is transferred on the books of the corporation.

Options. If you grant an option to a qualified organization to buy real property, you have not made a charitable contribution until the organization exercises the option. The amount of the contribution is the FMV of the property on the date the option is exercised minus the exercise price.

Example. You grant an option to a local university, which is a qualified organization, to buy real property. Under the option, the university could buy the property at any time during a 2-year period for $40,000. The FMV of the property on the date the option is granted is $50,000. In the following tax year, the university exercises the option. The FMV of the property on the date the option is exercised is $55,000. Therefore, you have made a charitable contribution of $15,000 ($55,000, the FMV, minus $40,000, the exercise price) in the tax year the option is exercised.

Determining Fair Market Value

Determining the value of donated property would be a simple matter if you could rely only on fixed formulas, rules, or methods. Usually it is not that simple. Using such formulas, etc., seldom results in an acceptable determination of FMV. There is no single formula that always applies when determining the value of property.

This is not to say that a valuation is only guesswork. You must consider all the facts and circumstances connected with the property, such as its desirability, use, and scarcity.

For example, donated furniture should not be evaluated at some fixed rate such as 15% of the cost of new replacement furniture. When the furniture is contributed, it may be out of style or in poor condition, therefore having little or no market value. On the other hand, it may be an antique, the value of which could not be determined by using any formula.

Cost or Selling Price of the Donated Property

The cost of the property to you or the actual selling price received by the qualified organization may be the best indication of its FMV. However, because conditions in the market change, the cost or selling price of property may have less weight if the property was not bought or sold reasonably close to the date of contribution.

The cost or selling price is a good indication of the property's value if:

- The purchase or sale took place close to the valuation date in an open market,
- The purchase or sale was at "arm's-length,"
- The buyer and seller knew all relevant facts,
- The buyer and seller did not have to act, and
- The market did not change between the date of purchase or sale and the valuation date.

Example. Tom Morgan, who is not a dealer in gems, bought an assortment of gems for $5,000 from a promoter. The promoter claimed that the price was "wholesale" even though he and other dealers made similar sales at similar prices to other persons who were not dealers. The promoter said that if Tom kept the gems for more than 1 year and then gave them to charity, Tom could claim a charitable deduction of $15,000, which, according to the promoter, would be the value of the gems at the time of contribution. Tom gave the gems to a qualified charity 13 months after buying them.

The selling price for these gems had not changed from the date of purchase to the date he donated them to charity. The best evidence of FMV depends on actual transactions and not on some artificial estimate. The $5,000 charged Tom and others is, therefore, the best evidence of the maximum FMV of the gems.

Terms of the purchase or sale. The terms of the purchase or sale should be considered in determining FMV if they influenced the price. These terms include any restrictions, understandings, or covenants limiting the use or disposition of the property.

Rate of increase or decrease in value. Unless you can show that there were unusual circumstances, it is assumed that the increase or decrease in the value of your donated property from your cost has been at a reasonable rate. For time adjustments, an appraiser may consider published price indexes for information on general price trends, building costs, commodity costs, securities, and works of art sold at auction in arm's-length sales.

Example. Bill Brown bought a painting for $10,000. Thirteen months later he gave it to an art museum, claiming a charitable deduction of $15,000 on his tax return. The appraisal of the painting should include information showing that there were unusual circumstances that justify a 50% increase in value for the 13 months Bill held the property.

Table 1. **Factors That Affect FMV**

IF the factor you are considering is...	THEN you should ask these questions...
cost or selling price	Was the purchase or sale of the property reasonably close to the date of contribution? Was any increase or decrease in value, as compared to your cost, at a reasonable rate? Do the terms of purchase or sale limit what can be done with the property? Was there an arm's-length offer to buy the property close to the valuation date?
sales of comparable properties	How similar is the property sold to the property donated? How close is the date of sale to the valuation date? Was the sale at arm's-length? What was the condition of the market at the time of sale?
replacement cost	What would it cost to replace the donated property? Is there a reasonable relationship between replacement cost and FMV? Is the supply of the donated property more or less than the demand for it?
opinions of experts	Is the expert knowledgeable and competent? Is the opinion thorough and supported by facts and experience?

Arm's-length offer. An arm's-length offer to buy the property close to the valuation date may help to prove its value if the person making the offer was willing and able to complete the transaction. To rely on an offer, you should be able to show proof of the offer and the specific amount to be paid. Offers to buy property other than the donated item will help to determine value if the other property is reasonably similar to the donated property.

Sales of Comparable Properties

The sales prices of properties similar to the donated property are often important in determining the FMV. The weight to be given to each sale depends on the following.

- The degree of similarity between the property sold and the donated property.

- The time of the sale — whether it was close to the valuation date.

- The circumstances of the sale — whether it was at arm's-length with a knowledgeable buyer and seller, with neither having to act.

- The conditions of the market in which the sale was made — whether unusually inflated or deflated.

The comparable sales method of valuing real estate is explained later under *Valuation of Various Kinds of Property.*

Example 1. Mary Black, who is not a book dealer, paid a promoter $10,000 for 500 copies of a single edition of a modern translation of the Bible. The promoter had claimed that the price was considerably less than the "retail" price, and gave her a statement that the books had a total retail value of $30,000. The promoter advised

her that if she kept the Bibles for more than 1 year and then gave them to a qualified organization, she could claim a charitable deduction for the "retail" price of $30,000. Thirteen months later she gave all the Bibles to a church that she selected from a list provided by the promoter. At the time of her donation, wholesale dealers were selling similar quantities of Bibles to the general public for $10,000.

The FMV of the Bibles is $10,000, the price at which similar quantities of Bibles were being sold to others at the time of the contribution.

Example 2. The facts are the same as in Example 1, except that the promoter gave Mary Black a second option. The promoter said that if Mary wanted a charitable deduction within 1 year of the purchase, she could buy the 500 Bibles at the "retail" price of $30,000, paying only $10,000 in cash and giving a promissory note for the remaining $20,000. The principal and interest on the note would not be due for 12 years. According to the promoter, Mary could then, within 1 year of the purchase, give the Bibles to a qualified organization and claim the full $30,000 retail price as a charitable contribution. She purchased the Bibles under the second option and, 3 months later, gave them to a church, which will use the books for church purposes.

At the time of the gift, the promoter was selling similar lots of Bibles for either $10,000 or $30,000. The difference between the two prices was solely at the discretion of the buyer. The promoter was a willing seller for $10,000. Therefore, the value of Mary's contribution of the Bibles is $10,000, the amount at which similar lots of Bibles could be purchased from the promoter by members of the general public.

Replacement Cost

The cost of buying, building, or manufacturing property similar to the donated item should be considered in determining FMV. However, there must be a reasonable relationship between the replacement cost and the FMV.

The replacement cost is the amount it would cost to replace the donated item on the valuation date. Often there is no relationship between the replacement cost and the FMV. If the supply of the donated property is more or less than the demand for it, the replacement cost becomes less important.

To determine the replacement cost of the donated property, find the "estimated replacement cost new." Then subtract from this figure an amount for depreciation due to the physical condition and obsolescence of the donated property. You should be able to show the relationship between the depreciated replacement cost and the FMV, as well as how you arrived at the "estimated replacement cost new."

Opinions of Experts

Generally, the weight given to an expert's opinion on matters such as the authenticity of a coin or a work of art, or the most profitable and best use of a piece of real estate, depends on the knowledge and competence of the expert and the thoroughness with which the opinion is supported by experience and facts. For an expert's opinion to deserve much weight, the facts must support the opinion. For additional information, see *Appraisals*, later.

Problems in Determining Fair Market Value

There are a number of problems in determining the FMV of donated property.

Unusual Market Conditions

The sale price of the property itself in an arm's-length transaction in an open market is often the best evidence of its value. When you rely on sales of comparable property, the sales must have been made in an open market. If those sales were made in a market that was artificially supported or stimulated so as not to be truly representative, the prices at which the sales were made will not indicate the FMV.

For example, liquidation sale prices usually do not indicate the FMV. Also, sales of stock under unusual circumstances, such as sales of small lots, forced sales, and sales in a restricted market, may not represent the FMV.

Selection of Comparable Sales

Using sales of comparable property is an important method for determining the FMV of donated property. However, the amount of weight given to a sale depends on the degree of similarity between the comparable and the donated properties. The degree of similarity must be close enough so that this selling price would

The type and rule above prints on all proofs including departmental reproduction proofs. MUST be removed before printing.

have been given consideration by reasonably well-informed buyers or sellers of the property.

Example. You give a rare, old book to your former college. The book is a third edition and is in poor condition because of a missing back cover. You discover that there was a sale for $300, near the valuation date, of a first edition of the book that was in good condition. Although the contents are the same, the books are not at all similar because of the different editions and their physical condition. Little consideration would be given to the selling price of the $300 property by knowledgeable buyers or sellers.

Future Events

You may not consider unexpected events happening after your donation of property in making the valuation. You may consider only the facts known at the time of the gift, and those that could be reasonably expected at the time of the gift.

Example. You give farmland to a qualified charity. The transfer provides that your mother will have the right to all income and full use of the property for her life. Even though your mother dies 1 week after the transfer, the value of the property on the date it is given is its present value, subject to the life interest as estimated from actuarial tables. You may not take a higher deduction because the charity received full use and possession of the land only 1 week after the transfer.

Using Past Events to Predict the Future

A common error is to rely too much on past events that do not fairly reflect the probable future earnings and FMV.

Example. You give all your rights in a successful patent to your favorite charity. Your records show that before the valuation date there were three stages in the patent's history of earnings. First, there was rapid growth in earnings when the invention was introduced. Then, there was a period of high earnings when the invention was being exploited. Finally, there was a decline in earnings when competing inventions were introduced. The entire history of earnings may be relevant in estimating the future earnings. However, the appraiser must not rely too much on the stage of rapid growth in earnings, or of high earnings. The market conditions at those times do not represent the condition of the market at the valuation date. What is most significant is the trend of decline in earnings up to the valuation date. For more information about donations of patents, see *Patents*, later.

Valuation of Various Kinds of Property

This section contains information on determining the FMV of ordinary kinds of donated property. For information on appraisals, see *Appraisals*, later.

Household Goods

The FMV of used household goods, such as furniture, appliances, and linens, is usually much lower than the price paid when new. Such used property may have little or no market value because of its worn condition. It may be out of style or no longer useful.

You cannot take a deduction for household goods donated after August 17, 2006, unless they are in good used condition or better. A household good that is not in good used condition or better for which you take a deduction of more than $500 requires a qualified appraisal. See *Deduction over $500 for certain clothing or household items*, later.

If the property is valuable because it is old or unique, see the discussion under *Paintings, Antiques, and Other Objects of Art*.

Used Clothing

Used clothing and other personal items are usually worth far less than the price you paid for them. Valuation of items of clothing does not lend itself to fixed formulas or methods.

The price that buyers of used items actually pay in used clothing stores, such as consignment or thrift shops, is an indication of the value.

You cannot take a deduction for clothing donated after August 17, 2006, unless it is in good used condition or better. An item of clothing that is not in good used condition or better for which you take a deduction of more than $500 requires a qualified appraisal. See *Deduction over $500 for certain clothing or household items*, later.

For valuable furs or very expensive gowns, a Form 8283 may have to be sent with your tax return.

Jewelry and Gems

Jewelry and gems are of such a specialized nature that it is almost always necessary to get an appraisal by a specialized jewelry appraiser. The appraisal should describe, among other things, the style of the jewelry, the cut and setting of the gem, and whether it is now in fashion. If not in fashion, the possibility of having the property redesigned, recut, or reset should be reported in the appraisal. The stone's coloring, weight, cut, brilliance, and flaws should be reported and analyzed. Sentimental personal value has no effect on FMV. But if the jewelry was owned by a famous person, its value might increase.

Paintings, Antiques, and Other Objects of Art

Your deduction for contributions of paintings, antiques, and other objects of art, should be supported by a written appraisal from a qualified and reputable source, unless the deduction is $5,000 or less. Examples of information that should be included in appraisals of art objects— paintings in particular—are found later under *Qualified Appraisal*.

Art valued at $20,000 or more. If you claim a deduction of $20,000 or more for donations of art, you must attach a complete copy of the signed appraisal to your return. For individual objects valued at $20,000 or more, a photograph of a size and quality fully showing the object, preferably an 8 x 10 inch color photograph or a color transparency no smaller than 4 x 5 inches, must be provided upon request.

Art valued at $50,000 or more. If you donate an item of art that has been appraised at $50,000 or more, you can request a Statement of Value for that item from the IRS. You must request the statement before filing the tax return that reports the donation. Your request must include the following.

- A copy of a qualified appraisal of the item. See *Qualified Appraisal*, later.

- A $2,500 check or money order payable to the Internal Revenue Service for the user fee that applies to your request regarding one, two, or three items of art. Add $250 for each item in excess of three.

- A completed Form 8283, Section B.

- The location of the IRS territory that has examination responsibility for your return.

If your request lacks essential information, you will be notified and given 30 days to provide the missing information.

Send your request to:

Internal Revenue Service
Attention: Art Appraisal (C:AP:ART)
P.O. Box 27720
McPherson Station
Washington, DC 20038

Refunds. You can withdraw your request for a Statement of Value at any time before it is issued. However, the IRS will not refund the user fee if you do.

If the IRS declines to issue a Statement of Value in the interest of efficient tax administration, the IRS will refund the user fee.

Authenticity. The authenticity of the donated art must be determined by the appraiser.

Physical condition. Important items in the valuation of antiques and art are physical condition and extent of restoration. These have a significant effect on the value and must be fully reported in an appraisal. An antique in damaged condition, or lacking the "original brasses," may be worth much less than a similar piece in excellent condition.

Art appraisers. More weight will usually be given to an appraisal prepared by an individual specializing in the kind and price range of the art being appraised. Certain art dealers or appraisers specialize, for example, in old masters, modern art, bronze sculpture, etc. Their opinions on the authenticity and desirability of such art would usually be given more weight than the opinions of more generalized art dealers or appraisers. They can report more recent comparable sales to support their opinion.

To identify and locate experts on unique, specialized items or collections, you may wish to use the current Official Museum Directory of the American Association of Museums. It lists museums both by state and by category.

To help you locate a qualified appraiser for your donation, you may wish to ask an art historian at a nearby college or the director or curator of a local museum. The Yellow Pages often list specialized art and antique dealers, auction-eers, and art appraisers. You may be able to find a qualified appraiser on the Internet. You may also contact associations of dealers for gui-dance.

Collections

Since many kinds of hobby collections may be the subject of a charitable donation, it is not possible to discuss all of the possible col-lectibles in this publication. Most common are rare books, autographs, sports memorabilia, dolls, manuscripts, stamps, coins, guns, phono-graph records, and natural history items. Many of the elements of valuation that apply to paint-ings and other objects of art, discussed earlier, also apply to miscellaneous collections.

Reference material. Publications available to help you determine the value of many kinds of collections include catalogs, dealers' price lists, and specialized hobby periodicals. When using one of these price guides, you must use the current edition at the date of contribution. How-ever, these sources are not always reliable in-dicators of FMV and should be supported by other evidence.

For example, a dealer may sell an item for much less than is shown on a price list, particu-larly after the item has remained unsold for a long time. The price an item sold for in an auc-tion may have been the result of a rigged sale or a mere bidding duel. The appraiser must ana-lyze the reference material, and recognize and make adjustments for misleading entries. If you are donating a valuable collection, you should get an appraisal. If your donation appears to be of little value, you may be able to make a satis-factory valuation using reference materials available at a state, city, college, or museum library.

Stamp collections. Most libraries have cata-logs or other books that report the publisher's estimate of values. Generally, two price levels are shown for each stamp: the price postmarked and the price not postmarked. Stamp dealers generally know the value of their merchandise and are able to prepare satisfactory appraisals of valuable collections.

Coin collections. Many catalogs and other reference materials show the writer's or pub-lisher's opinion of the value of coins on or near the date of the publication. Like many other collectors' items, the value of a coin depends on the demand for it, its age, and its rarity. Another important factor is the coin's condition. For ex-ample, there is a great difference in the value of a coin that is in mint condition and a similar coin that is only in good condition.

Catalogs usually establish a category for coins, based on their physical condition—mint or uncirculated, extremely fine, very fine, fine, very good, good, fair, or poor—with a different valuation for each category.

Books. The value of books is usually deter-mined by selecting comparable sales and ad-justing the prices according to the differences between the comparable sales and the item being evaluated. This is difficult to do and, ex-cept for a collection of little value, should be done by a specialized appraiser. Within the gen-eral category of literary property, there are deal-ers who specialize in certain areas, such as

Americana, foreign imports, Bibles, and scien-tific books.

Modest value of collection. If the collec-tion you are donating is of modest value, not requiring a written appraisal, the following infor-mation may help you in determining the FMV.

A book that is very old, or very rare, is not necessarily valuable. There are many books that are very old or rare, but that have little or no market value.

Condition of book. The condition of a book may have a great influence on its value. Collec-tors are interested in items that are in fine, or at least good, condition. When a book has a miss-ing page, a loose binding, tears, stains, or is otherwise in poor condition, its value is greatly lowered.

Other factors. Some other factors in the valuation of a book are the kind of binding (leather, cloth, paper), page edges, and illustra-tions (drawings and photographs). Collectors usually want first editions of books. However, because of changes or additions, other editions are sometimes worth as much as, or more than, the first edition.

Manuscripts, autographs, diaries, and simi-lar items. When these items are handwritten, or at least signed by famous people, they are often in demand and are valuable. The writings of unknowns also may be of value if they are of unusual historical or literary importance. Deter-mining the value of such material is difficult. For example, there may be a great difference in value between two diaries that were kept by a famous person—one kept during childhood and the other during a later period in his or her life. The appraiser determines a value in these cases by applying knowledge and judgment to such factors as comparable sales and condi-tions.

Signatures. Signatures, or sets of signatures, that were cut from letters or other papers usually have little or no value. But complete sets of the signatures of U.S. presidents are in demand.

Cars, Boats, and Aircraft

If you donate a car, a boat, or an aircraft to a charitable organization, its FMV must be deter-mined.

Certain commercial firms and trade organi-zations publish monthly or seasonal guides for different regions of the country, containing com-plete dealer sale prices or dealer average prices for recent model years. Prices are reported for each make, model, and year. These guides also provide estimates for adjusting for unusual equipment, unusual mileage, and physical con-dition. The prices are not "official," and these publications are not considered an appraisal of any specific donated property. But they do pro-vide clues for making an appraisal and suggest relative prices for comparison with current sales and offerings in your area.

These publications are sometimes available from public libraries or at a bank, credit union, or finance company. You can also find pricing in-formation about used cars on the Internet.

An acceptable measure of the FMV of a donated car, boat, or airplane is an amount not in excess of the price listed in a used vehicle pricing guide for a private party sale, not the

dealer retail value, of a similar vehicle. However, the FMV may be less than that amount if the vehicle has engine trouble, body damage, high mileage, or any type of excessive wear. The FMV of a donated vehicle is the same as the price listed in a used vehicle pricing guide for a private party sale only if the guide lists a sales price for a vehicle that is the same make, model, and year, sold in the same area, in the same condition, with the same or similar options or accessories, and with the same or similar war-ranties as the donated vehicle.

Example. You donate a used car in poor condition to a local high school for use by stu-dents studying car repair. A used car guide shows the dealer retail value for this type of car in poor condition is $1,600. However, the guide shows the price for a private party sale of the car is only $750. The FMV of the car is considered to be no more than $750.

Boats. Except for inexpensive small boats, the valuation of boats should be based on an appraisal by a marine surveyor because the physical condition is so critical to the value.

More information. Your deduction for a donated car, boat, or airplane generally is lim-ited to the gross proceeds from its sale by the qualified organization. This rule applies if the claimed value of the donated vehicle is more than $500. In certain cases, you can deduct the vehicle's FMV. For details, see Publication 526.

Inventory

If you donate any inventory item to a charitable organization, the amount of your deductible con-tribution generally is the FMV of the item, minus any gain you would have realized if you had sold the item at its FMV on the date of the gift. For more information, see Publication 526.

Patents

To determine the FMV of a patent, you must take into account, among other factors:

- Whether the patented technology has been made obsolete by other technology;

- Any restrictions on the donee's use of, or ability to transfer, the patented technology; and

- The length of time remaining before the patent expires.

However, your deduction for a donation of a patent or other intellectual property is its FMV, minus any gain you would have realized if you had sold the property at its FMV on the date of the gift. Generally, this means your deduction is the lesser of the property's FMV or its basis. For details, see Publication 526.

Stocks and Bonds

The value of stocks and bonds is the FMV of a share or bond on the valuation date. See *Date of contribution,* earlier, under *What Is Fair Market Value (FMV).*

Selling prices on valuation date. If there is an active market for the contributed stocks or bonds on a stock exchange, in an over-the-counter market, or elsewhere, the FMV of each share or bond is the average price between the highest and lowest quoted selling prices on the valuation date. For example, if the highest selling price for a share was $11, and the lowest $9, the average price is $10. You get the average price by adding $11 and $9 and dividing the sum by 2.

No sales on valuation date. If there were no sales on the valuation date, but there were sales within a reasonable period before and after the valuation date, you determine FMV by taking the average price between the highest and lowest sales prices on the nearest date before and on the nearest date after the valuation date. Then you weight these averages in inverse order by the respective number of trading days between the selling dates and the valuation date.

Example. On the day you gave stock to a qualified organization, there were no sales of the stock. Sales of the stock nearest the valuation date took place two trading days before the valuation date at an average selling price of $10 and three trading days after the valuation date at an average selling price of $15. The FMV on the valuation date was $12, figured as follows:

$$[(3 \times \$10) + (2 \times \$15)] \div 5 = \$12$$

Listings on more than one stock exchange. Stocks or bonds listed on more than one stock exchange are valued based on the prices of the exchange on which they are principally dealt. This applies if these prices are published in a generally available listing or publication of general circulation. If this is not applicable, and the stocks or bonds are reported on a composite listing of combined exchanges in a publication of general circulation, use the composite list. See also *Unavailable prices or closely held corporation*, later.

Bid and asked prices on valuation date. If there were no sales within a reasonable period before and after the valuation date, the FMV is the average price between the bona fide bid and asked prices on the valuation date.

Example. Although there were no sales of Blue Corporation stock on the valuation date, bona fide bid and asked prices were available on that date of $14 and $16, respectively. The FMV is $15, the average price between the bid and asked prices.

No prices on valuation date. If there were no prices available on the valuation date, you determine FMV by taking the average prices between the bona fide bid and asked prices on the closest trading date before and after the valuation date. Both dates must be within a reasonable period. Then you weight these averages in inverse order by the respective number of trading days between the bid and asked dates and the valuation date.

Example. On the day you gave stock to a qualified organization, no prices were available. Bona fide bid and asked prices 3 days before the valuation date were $10 and 2 days after the valuation date were $15. The FMV on the valuation date is $13, figured as follows:

$$[(2 \times \$10) + (3 \times \$15)] \div 5 = \$13$$

Prices only before or after valuation date, but not both. If no selling prices or bona fide bid and asked prices are available on a date within a reasonable period before the valuation date, but are available on a date within a reasonable period after the valuation date, or vice versa, then the average price between the highest and lowest of such available prices may be treated as the value.

Large blocks of stock. When a large block of stock is put on the market, it may lower the selling price of the stock if the supply is greater than the demand. On the other hand, market forces may exist that will afford higher prices for large blocks of stock. Because of the many factors to be considered, determining the value of large blocks of stock usually requires the help of experts specializing in underwriting large quantities of securities, or in trading in the securities of the industry of which the particular company is a part.

Unavailable prices or closely held corporation. If selling prices or bid and asked prices are not available, or if securities of a closely held corporation are involved, determine the FMV by considering the following factors.

- For bonds, the soundness of the security, the interest yield, the date of maturity, and other relevant factors.

- For shares of stock, the company's net worth, prospective earning power and dividend-paying capacity, and other relevant factors.

Other factors. Other relevant factors include:

- The nature and history of the business, especially its recent history,

- The goodwill of the business,

- The economic outlook in the particular industry,

- The company's position in the industry, its competitors, and its management, and

- The value of securities of corporations engaged in the same or similar business.

For preferred stock, the most important factors are its yield, dividend coverage, and protection of its liquidation preference.

You should keep complete financial and other information on which the valuation is based. This includes copies of reports of examinations of the company made by accountants, engineers, or any technical experts on or close to the valuation date.

Restricted securities. Some classes of stock cannot be traded publicly because of restrictions imposed by the Securities and Exchange Commission, or by the corporate charter or a trust agreement. These restricted securities usually trade at a discount in relation to freely traded securities.

To arrive at the FMV of restricted securities, factors that you must consider include the resale provisions found in the restriction agreements, the relative negotiating strengths of the buyer and seller, and the market experience of freely traded securities of the same class as the restricted securities.

Real Estate

Because each piece of real estate is unique and its valuation is complicated, a detailed appraisal by a professional appraiser is necessary.

The appraiser must be thoroughly trained in the application of appraisal principles and theory. In some instances the opinions of equally qualified appraisers may carry unequal weight, such as when one appraiser has a better knowledge of local conditions.

The appraisal report must contain a complete description of the property, such as street address, legal description, and lot and block number, as well as physical features, condition, and dimensions. The use to which the property is put, zoning and permitted uses, and its potential use for other higher and better uses are also relevant.

In general, there are three main approaches to the valuation of real estate. An appraisal may require the combined use of two or three methods rather than one method only.

1. Comparable Sales

The comparable sales method compares the donated property with several similar properties that have been sold. The selling prices, after adjustments for differences in date of sale, size, condition, and location, would then indicate the estimated FMV of the donated property.

If the comparable sales method is used to determine the value of unimproved real property (land without significant buildings, structures, or any other improvements that add to its value), the appraiser should consider the following factors when comparing the potential comparable property and the donated property:

- Location, size, and zoning or use restrictions,

- Accessibility and road frontage, and available utilities and water rights,

- Riparian rights (right of access to and use of the water by owners of land on the bank of a river) and existing easements, rights-of-way, leases, etc.,

- Soil characteristics, vegetative cover, and status of mineral rights, and

- Other factors affecting value.

For each comparable sale, the appraisal must include the names of the buyer and seller, the deed book and page number, the date of sale and selling price, a property description, the amount and terms of mortgages, property surveys, the assessed value, the tax rate, and the assessor's appraised FMV.

The comparable selling prices must be adjusted to account for differences between the sale property and the donated property. Because differences of opinion may arise between appraisers as to the degree of comparability and the amount of the adjustment considered necessary for comparison purposes, an appraiser should document each item of adjustment.

Only comparable sales having the least adjustments in terms of items and/or total dollar adjustments should be considered as comparable to the donated property.

The type and rule above prints on all proofs including departmental reproduction proofs. MUST be removed before printing.

2. Capitalization of Income

This method capitalizes the net income from the property at a rate that represents a fair return on the particular investment at the particular time, considering the risks involved. The key elements are the determination of the income to be capitalized and the rate of capitalization.

3. Replacement Cost New or Reproduction Cost Minus Observed Depreciation

This method, used alone, usually does not result in a determination of FMV. Instead, it generally tends to set the upper limit of value, particularly in periods of rising costs, because it is reasonable to assume that an informed buyer will not pay more for the real estate than it would cost to reproduce a similar property. Of course, this reasoning does not apply if a similar property cannot be created because of location, unusual construction, or some other reason. Generally, this method serves to support the value determined from other methods. When the replacement cost method is applied to improved realty, the land and improvements are valued separately.

The replacement cost of a building is figured by considering the materials, the quality of workmanship, and the number of square feet or cubic feet in the building. This cost represents the total cost of labor and material, overhead, and profit. After the replacement cost has been figured, consideration must be given to the following factors:

- Physical deterioration—the wear and tear on the building itself,

- Functional obsolescence—usually in older buildings with, for example, inadequate lighting, plumbing, or heating, small rooms, or a poor floor plan, and

- Economic obsolescence—outside forces causing the whole area to become less desirable.

Interest in a Business

The FMV of any interest in a business, whether a sole proprietorship or a partnership, is the amount that a willing buyer would pay for the interest to a willing seller after consideration of all relevant factors. The relevant factors to be considered in valuing the business are:

- The FMV of the assets of the business,

- The demonstrated earnings capacity of the business, based on a review of past and current earnings, and

- The other factors used in evaluating corporate stock, if they apply.

The value of the goodwill of the business should also be taken into consideration. You should keep complete financial and other information on which you base the valuation. This includes copies of reports of examinations of the business made by accountants, engineers, or any technical experts on or close to the valuation date.

Annuities, Interests for Life or Terms of Years, Remainders, and Reversions

The value of these kinds of property is their present value, except in the case of annuities under contracts issued by companies regularly engaged in their sale. The valuation of these commercial annuity contracts and of insurance policies is discussed later under *Certain Life Insurance and Annuity Contracts.*

To determine present value, you must know the applicable interest rate and use actuarial tables.

Interest rate. The applicable interest rate varies. It is announced monthly in a news release and published in the Internal Revenue Bulletin as a Revenue Ruling. The interest rate to use is under the heading "Rate Under Section 7520" for a given month and year. You can call the IRS office at 1-800-829-1040 to obtain this rate.

Actuarial tables. You need to refer to actuarial tables to determine a qualified interest in the form of an annuity, any interest for life or a term of years, or any remainder interest to a charitable organization.

Use the valuation tables set forth in IRS Publications 1457, Actuarial Values (Book Aleph), and 1458, Actuarial Values (Book Beth). Both of these publications provide tables containing actuarial factors to be used in determining the present value of an annuity, an interest for life or for a term of years, or a remainder or reversionary interest. For qualified charitable transfers, you can use the factor for the month in which you made the contribution or for either of the 2 months preceding that month.

Publication 1457 also contains actuarial factors for computing the value of a remainder interest in a charitable remainder annuity trust and a pooled income fund. Publication 1458 contains the factors for valuing the remainder interest in a charitable remainder unitrust. You can download Publications 1457 and 1458 from *www.irs.gov.* In addition, they are available for purchase via the website of the U. S. Government Printing Office, by phone at (202) 512-1800, or by mail from the:

Superintendent of Documents
P.O. Box 371954
Pittsburgh, PA 15250-7954

Tables containing actuarial factors for transfers to pooled income funds may also be found in Income Tax Regulation 1.642(c)-6(e)(6), transfers to charitable remainder unitrusts in Regulation 1.664-4(e), and other transfers in Regulation 20.2031-7(d)(6).

Special factors. If you need a special factor for an actual transaction, you can request a letter ruling. Be sure to include the date of birth of each person the duration of whose life may affect the value of the interest. Also include copies of the relevant instruments. IRS charges a user fee for providing special factors.

For more information about requesting a ruling, see Revenue Procedure 2006-1 (or annual update), 2006-1 I.R.B. 1. Revenue Procedure 2006-1 is available at *www.irs.gov/irb/2006-01_IRB/ar06.html.*

For information on the circumstances under which a charitable deduction may be allowed for the donation of a partial interest in property not in trust, see *Partial Interest in Property Not in Trust,* later.

Certain Life Insurance and Annuity Contracts

The value of an annuity contract or a life insurance policy issued by a company regularly engaged in the sale of such contracts or policies is the amount that company would charge for a comparable contract.

But if the donee of a life insurance policy may reasonably be expected to cash the policy rather than hold it as an investment, then the FMV is the cash surrender value rather than the replacement cost.

If an annuity is payable under a combination annuity contract and life insurance policy (for example, a retirement income policy with a death benefit) and there was no insurance element when it was transferred to the charity, the policy is treated as an annuity contract.

Partial Interest in Property Not in Trust

Generally, no deduction is allowed for a charitable contribution, not made in trust, of less than your entire interest in property. However, this does not apply to a transfer of less than your entire interest if it is a transfer of:

- A remainder interest in your personal residence or farm,

- An undivided part of your entire interest in property, or

- A qualified conservation contribution.

Remainder Interest in Real Property

The amount of the deduction for a donation of a remainder interest in real property is the FMV of the remainder interest at the time of the contribution. To determine this value, you must know the FMV of the property on the date of the contribution. Multiply this value by the appropriate factor. Publications 1457 and 1458 contain these factors.

You must make an adjustment for depreciation or depletion using the factors shown in Publication 1459, Actuarial Values (Book Gimel). You can use the factors for the month in which you made the contribution or for either of the two months preceding that month. See the earlier discussion on *Annuities, Interests for Life or Terms of Years, Remainders, and Reversions.* You can download Publication 1459 from *www.irs.gov.*

For this purpose, the term "depreciable property" means any property subject to wear and tear or obsolescence, even if not used in a trade or business or for the production of income.

If the remainder interest includes both depreciable and nondepreciable property, for example a house and land, the FMV must be allocated between each kind of property at the time of the contribution. This rule also applies to a gift of a remainder interest that includes property that is part depletable and part not depletable. Take into account depreciation or depletion only for the property that is subject to depreciation or depletion.

For more information, see section 1.170A-12 of the Income Tax Regulations.

Undivided Part of Your Entire Interest

A contribution of an undivided part of your entire interest in property must consist of a part of each and every substantial interest or right you own in the property. It must extend over the entire term of your interest in the property. For example, you are entitled to the income from certain property for your life (life estate) and you contribute 20% of that life estate to a qualified organization. You can claim a deduction for the contribution if you do not have any other interest in the property. To figure the value of a contribution involving a partial interest, see Publication 1457.

If the only interest you own in real property is a remainder interest and you transfer part of that interest to a qualified organization, see the previous discussion on valuation of a remainder interest in real property.

Qualified Conservation Contribution

A qualified conservation contribution is a contribution of a qualified real property interest to a qualified organization to be used only for conservation purposes.

Qualified organization. For purposes of a qualified conservation contribution, a qualified organization is:

- A governmental unit,

- A publicly supported charitable, religious, scientific, literary, educational, etc., organization, or

- An organization that is controlled by, and operated for the exclusive benefit of, a governmental unit or a publicly supported charity.

The organization also must have a commitment to protect the conservation purposes of the donation and must have the resources to enforce the restrictions.

Conservation purposes. Your contribution must be made only for one of the following conservation purposes.

- Preserving land areas for outdoor recreation by, or for the education of, the general public.

- Protecting a relatively natural habitat of fish, wildlife, or plants, or a similar ecosystem.

- Preserving open space, including farmland and forest land, if it yields a significant public benefit. It must be either for the scenic enjoyment of the general public or under a clearly defined federal, state, or local governmental conservation policy.

- Preserving a historically important land area or a certified historic structure. There

must be some visual public access to the property. Factors used in determining the type and amount of public access required include the historical significance of the property, the remoteness or accessibility of the site, and the extent to which intrusions on the privacy of individuals living on the property would be unreasonable.

Building in registered historic district. A contribution after July 25, 2006, of a qualified real property interest that is an easement or other restriction on the exterior of a building in a registered historic district is deductible only if it meets all of the following three conditions.

1. The restriction must preserve the entire exterior of the building and must prohibit any change to the exterior of the building that is inconsistent with its historical character.

2. You and the organization receiving the contribution must enter into a written agreement certifying, that the organization is a qualified organization and that it has the resources and commitment to maintain the property as donated.

3. If you make the contribution in a tax year beginning after August 17, 2006, you must include with your return:

   a. A qualified appraisal,

   b. Photographs of the building's entire exterior, and

   c. A description of all restrictions on development of the building, such as zoning laws and restrictive covenants.

If you make this type of contribution after February 12, 2007, and claim a deduction of more than $10,000, your deduction will not be allowed unless you pay a $500 filing fee. See Form 8283-V, Payment Voucher for Filing Fee Under Section 170(f)(13), and its instructions.

Qualified real property interest. This is any of the following interests in real property.

1. Your entire interest in real estate other than a mineral interest (subsurface oil, gas, or other minerals, and the right of access to these minerals).

2. A remainder interest.

3. A restriction (granted in perpetuity) on the use that may be made of the real property.

Valuation. A qualified real property interest described in (1) should be valued in a manner that is consistent with the type of interest transferred. If you transferred all the interest in the property, the FMV of the property is the amount of the contribution. If you do not transfer the mineral interest, the FMV of the surface rights in the property is the amount of the contribution.

If you owned only a remainder interest or an income interest (life estate), see *Undivided Part of Your Entire Interest*, earlier. If you owned the entire property but transferred only a remainder interest (item (2)), see *Remainder Interest in Real Property*, earlier.

In determining the value of restrictions, you should take into account the selling price in arm's-length transactions of other properties

that have comparable restrictions. If there are no comparable sales, the restrictions are valued indirectly as the difference between the FMVs of the property involved before and after the grant of the restriction.

The FMV of the property before contribution of the restriction should take into account not only current use but the likelihood that the property, without the restriction, would be developed. You should also consider any zoning, conservation, or historical preservation laws that would restrict development. Granting an easement may increase, rather than reduce, the value of property, and in such a situation no deduction would be allowed.

Example. You own 10 acres of farmland. Similar land in the area has an FMV of $2,000 an acre. However, land in the general area that is restricted solely to farm use has an FMV of $1,500 an acre. Your county wants to preserve open space and prevent further development in your area.

You grant to the county an enforceable open space easement in perpetuity on 8 of the 10 acres, restricting its use to farmland. The value of this easement is $4,000, determined as follows:

FMV of the property before granting easement:		
$2,000 × 10 acres		$20,000
FMV of the property after granting easement:		
$1,500 × 8 acres	$12,000	
$2,000 × 2 acres	4,000	16,000
Value of easement		$4,000

If you later transfer in fee your remaining interest in the 8 acres to another qualified organization, the FMV of your remaining interest is the FMV of the 8 acres reduced by the FMV of the easement granted to the first organization.

More information. For more information about qualified conservation contributions, see Publication 526.

Appraisals

Appraisals are not necessary for items of property for which you claim a deduction of $5,000 or less. (There is one exception, described next, for certain clothing and household items.) However, you generally will need an appraisal for donated property for which you claim a deduction of more than $5,000. There are exceptions. See *Deductions of More Than $5,000*, later.

The weight given an appraisal depends on the completeness of the report, the qualifications of the appraiser, and the appraiser's demonstrated knowledge of the donated property. An appraisal must give all the facts on which to base an intelligent judgment of the value of the property.

The appraisal will not be given much weight if:

- All the factors that apply are not considered,

- The opinion is not supported with facts, such as purchase price and comparable sales, or

- The opinion is not consistent with known facts.

The appraiser's opinion is never more valid than the facts on which it is based; without these facts it is simply a guess.

The opinion of a person claiming to be an expert is not binding on the Internal Revenue Service. All facts associated with the donation must be considered.

Deduction over $500 for certain clothing or household items. You must include with your return a qualified appraisal of any single item of clothing or any household item that is not in good condition or better, that you donated after August 17, 2006, and for which you deduct more than $500. See *Household Goods* and *Used Clothing*, earlier.

Cost of appraisals. You may not take a charitable contribution deduction for fees you pay for appraisals of your donated property. However, these fees may qualify as a miscellaneous deduction, subject to the 2% limit, on Schedule A (Form 1040) if paid to determine the amount allowable as a charitable contribution.

Deductions of More Than $5,000

Generally, if the claimed deduction for an item or group of similar items of donated property is more than $5,000, you must get a qualified appraisal made by a qualified appraiser, and you must attach Section B of Form 8283 to your tax return. There are exceptions, discussed later. You should keep the appraiser's report with your written records. Records are discussed in Publication 526.

The phrase "similar items" means property of the same generic category or type (whether or not donated to the same donee), such as stamp collections, coin collections, lithographs, paintings, photographs, books, nonpublicly traded stock, nonpublicly traded securities other than nonpublicly traded stock, land, buildings, clothing, jewelry, furniture, electronic equipment, household appliances, toys, everyday kitchenware, china, crystal, or silver. For example, if you give books to three schools and you deduct $2,000, $2,500, and $900, respectively, your claimed deduction is more than $5,000 for these books. You must get a qualified appraisal of the books and for each school you must attach a fully completed Form 8283, Section B, to your tax return.

Exceptions. You do not need an appraisal if the property is:

- Nonpublicly traded stock of $10,000 or less,
- A vehicle (including a car, boat, or airplane) for which your deduction is limited to the gross proceeds from its sale,
- Qualified intellectual property, such as a patent,
- Certain publicly traded securities described next.
- Inventory and other property donated by a corporation that are "qualified contributions" for the care of the ill, the needy, or infants, within the meaning of section

170(e)(3)(A) of the Internal Revenue Code, or

- Stock in trade, inventory, or property held primarily for sale to customers in the ordinary course of your trade or business.

Although an appraisal is not required for the types of property just listed, you must provide certain information about a donation of any of these types of property on Form 8283.

Publicly traded securities. Even if your claimed deduction is more than $5,000, neither a qualified appraisal nor Section B of Form 8283 is required for publicly traded securities that are:

- Listed on a stock exchange in which quotations are published on a daily basis,
- Regularly traded in a national or regional over-the-counter market for which published quotations are available, or
- Shares of an open-end investment company (mutual fund) for which quotations are published on a daily basis in a newspaper of general circulation throughout the United States.

Publicly traded securities that meet these requirements must be reported on Form 8283, Section A.

A qualified appraisal is not required, but Form 8283, Section B, Parts I and IV, must be completed, for an issue of a security that does not meet the requirements just listed but does meet these requirements:

1. The issue is regularly traded during the computation period (defined later) in a market for which there is an "interdealer quotation system" (defined later).

2. The issuer or agent computes the "average trading price" (defined later) for the same issue for the computation period,

3. The average trading price and total volume of the issue during the computation period are published in a newspaper of general circulation throughout the United States, not later than the last day of the month following the end of the calendar quarter in which the computation period ends,

4. The issuer or agent keeps books and records that list for each transaction during the computation period the date of settlement of the transaction, the name and address of the broker or dealer making the market in which the transaction occurred, and the trading price and volume, and

5. The issuer or agent permits the Internal Revenue Service to review the books and records described in item (4) with respect to transactions during the computation period upon receiving reasonable notice.

An interdealer quotation system is any system of general circulation to brokers and dealers that regularly disseminates quotations of obligations by two or more identified brokers or dealers who are not related to either the issuer or agent who computes the average trading price of the security. A quotation sheet prepared and distributed by a broker or dealer in the regular course of business and containing only quotations of

that broker or dealer is not an interdealer quotation system.

The average trading price is the average price of all transactions (weighted by volume), other than original issue or redemption transactions, conducted through a United States office of a broker or dealer who maintains a market in the issue of the security during the computation period. Bid and asked quotations are not taken into account.

The computation period is weekly during October through December and monthly during January through September. The weekly computation periods during October through December begin with the first Monday in October and end with the first Sunday following the last Monday in December.

Nonpublicly traded stock. If you contribute nonpublicly traded stock, for which you claim a deduction of $10,000 or less, a qualified appraisal is not required. However, you must attach Form 8283 to your tax return, with Section B, Parts I and IV, completed.

Deductions of More Than $500,000

If you claim a deduction of more than $500,000 for a donation of property, you must attach a qualified appraisal of the property to your return. This does not apply to contributions of cash, inventory, publicly traded stock, or intellectual property.

If you do not attach the appraisal, you cannot deduct your contribution, unless your failure to attach the appraisal is due to reasonable cause and not to willful neglect.

Qualified Appraisal

Generally, if the claimed deduction for an item or group of similar items of donated property is more than $5,000, you must get a qualified appraisal made by a qualified appraiser. You must also complete Form 8283, Section B, and attach it to your tax return. See *Deductions of More Than $5,000*, earlier.

A qualified appraisal is an appraisal document that:

- Is made, signed, and dated by a qualified appraiser (defined later) in accordance with generally accepted appraisal standards,
- Meets the relevant requirements of Regulations section 1.170A-13(c)(3) and Notice 2006-96, 2006-46 I.R.B. 902 (available at *www.irs.gov/irb/2006-46_IRB/ar13.html*),
- Relates to an appraisal made not earlier than 60 days before the date of contribution of the appraised property,
- Does not involve a prohibited appraisal fee, and
- Includes certain information (covered later).

You must receive the qualified appraisal before the due date, including extensions, of the return on which a charitable contribution deduction is first claimed for the donated property. If the deduction is first claimed on an amended return, the qualified appraisal must be received

The type and rule above prints on all proofs including departmental reproduction proofs. MUST be removed before printing.

before the date on which the amended return is filed.

Form 8283, Section B, must be attached to your tax return. Generally, you do not need to attach the qualified appraisal itself, but you should keep a copy as long as it may be relevant under the tax law. There are four exceptions.

- If you claim a deduction of $20,000 or more for donations of art, you must attach a complete copy of the appraisal. See *Paintings, Antiques, and Other Objects of Art*, earlier.

- If you claim a deduction of more than $500,000 for a donation of property, you must attach the appraisal. See *Deductions of More Than $500,000*, earlier.

- If you claim a deduction of more than $500 for an article of clothing, or a household item, that is not in good used condition or better, that you donated after August 17, 2006, you must attach the appraisal. See *Deduction over $500 for certain clothing or household items*, earlier.

- If you claim a deduction in a tax year beginning after August 17, 2006, for an easement or other restriction on the exterior of a building in a historic district, you must attach the appraisal. See *Building in registered historic district*, earlier.

Prohibited appraisal fee. Generally, no part of the fee arrangement for a qualified appraisal can be based on a percentage of the appraised value of the property. If a fee arrangement is based on what is allowed as a deduction, after Internal Revenue Service examination or otherwise, it is treated as a fee based on a percentage of appraised value. However, appraisals are not disqualified when an otherwise prohibited fee is paid to a generally recognized association that regulates appraisers if:

- The association is not organized for profit and no part of its net earnings benefits any private shareholder or individual,

- The appraiser does not receive any compensation from the association or any other persons for making the appraisal, and

- The fee arrangement is not based in whole or in part on the amount of the appraised value that is allowed as a deduction after an Internal Revenue Service examination or otherwise.

Information included in qualified appraisal. A qualified appraisal must include the following information:

1. A description of the property in sufficient detail for a person who is not generally familiar with the type of property to determine that the property appraised is the property that was (or will be) contributed,

2. The physical condition of any tangible property,

3. The date (or expected date) of contribution,

4. The terms of any agreement or understanding entered into (or expected to be entered into) by or on behalf of the donor that relates to the use, sale, or other disposition of the donated property, including, for example, the terms of any agreement or understanding that:

    a. Temporarily or permanently restricts a donee's right to use or dispose of the donated property,

    b. Earmarks donated property for a particular use, or

    c. Reserves to, or confers upon, anyone (other than a donee organization or an organization participating with a donee organization in cooperative fundraising) any right to the income from the donated property or to the possession of the property, including the right to vote donated securities, to acquire the property by purchase or otherwise, or to designate the person having the income, possession, or right to acquire the property,

5. The name, address, and taxpayer identification number of the qualified appraiser and, if the appraiser is a partner, an employee, or an independent contractor engaged by a person other than the donor, the name, address, and taxpayer identification number of the partnership or the person who employs or engages the appraiser,

6. The qualifications of the qualified appraiser who signs the appraisal, including the appraiser's background, experience, education, and any membership in professional appraisal associations,

7. A statement that the appraisal was prepared for income tax purposes,

8. The date (or dates) on which the property was valued,

9. The appraised FMV on the date (or expected date) of contribution,

10. The method of valuation used to determine FMV, such as the income approach, the comparable sales or market data approach, or the replacement cost less depreciation approach, and

11. The specific basis for the valuation, such as any specific comparable sales transaction.

Art objects. The following are examples of information that should be included in a description of donated property. These examples are for art objects. A similar detailed breakdown should be given for other property. Appraisals of art objects—paintings in particular—should include all of the following.

1. A complete description of the object, indicating the:

    a. Size,

    b. Subject matter,

    c. Medium,

    d. Name of the artist (or culture), and

    e. Approximate date created.

2. The cost, date, and manner of acquisition.

3. A history of the item, including proof of authenticity.

4. A professional quality image of the object.

5. The facts on which the appraisal was based, such as:

    a. Sales or analyses of similar works by the artist, particularly on or around the valuation date.

    b. Quoted prices in dealer's catalogs of the artist's works or works of other artists of comparable stature.

    c. A record of any exhibitions at which the specific art object had been displayed.

    d. The economic state of the art market at the time of valuation, particularly with respect to the specific property.

    e. The standing of the artist in his profession and in the particular school or time period.

Number of qualified appraisals. A separate qualified appraisal is required for each item of property that is not included in a group of similar items of property. You need only one qualified appraisal for a group of similar items of property contributed in the same tax year, but you may get separate appraisals for each item. A qualified appraisal for a group of similar items must provide all of the required information for each item of similar property. The appraiser, however, may provide a group description for selected items the total value of which is not more than $100.

Qualified appraiser. A qualified appraiser is an individual who meets all the following requirements.

1. The individual either:

    a. Has earned an appraisal designation from a recognized professional appraiser organization for demonstrated competency in valuing the type of property being appraised, or

    b. Has met certain minimum education and experience requirements. For real property, the appraiser must be licensed or certified for the type of property being appraised in the state in which the property is located. For property other than real property, the appraiser must have successfully completed college or professional-level coursework relevant to the property being valued, must have at least 2 years of experience in the trade or business of buying, selling, or valuing the type of property being valued, and must fully describe in the appraisal his or her qualifying education and experience.

2. The individual regularly prepares appraisals for which he or she is paid.

3. The individual demonstrates verifiable education and experience in valuing the type of property being valued. To do this, the appraiser can make a declaration in the

The type and rule above prints on all proofs including departmental reproduction proofs. MUST be removed before printing.

appraisal that, because of his or her background, experience, education, and membership in professional associations, he or she is qualified to make appraisals of the type of property being valued.

4. The individual has not been prohibited from practicing before the IRS under section 330(c) of title 31 of the United States Code at any time during the 3-year period ending on the date of the appraisal.

5. The individual is not an excluded individual.

In addition, the appraiser must complete Form 8283, Section B, Part III. More than one appraiser may appraise the property, provided that each complies with the requirements, including signing the qualified appraisal and Form 8283, Section B, Part III.

Excluded individuals. The following persons cannot be qualified appraisers with respect to particular property.

1. The donor of the property, or the taxpayer who claims the deduction.

2. The donee of the property.

3. A party to the transaction in which the donor acquired the property being appraised, unless the property is donated within 2 months of the date of acquisition and its appraised value is not more than its acquisition price. This applies to the person who sold, exchanged, or gave the property to the donor, or any person who acted as an agent for the transferor or donor in the transaction.

4. Any person employed by any of the above persons. For example, if the donor acquired a painting from an art dealer, neither the dealer nor persons employed by the dealer can be qualified appraisers for that painting.

5. Any person related under section 267(b) of the Internal Revenue Code to any of the above persons or married to a person related under section 267(b) to any of the above persons.

6. An appraiser who appraises regularly for a person in (1), (2), or (3), and who does not perform a majority of his or her appraisals made during his or her tax year for other persons.

In addition, a person is not a qualified appraiser for a particular donation if the donor had knowledge of facts that would cause a reasonable person to expect the appraiser to falsely overstate the value of the donated property. For example, if the donor and the appraiser make an agreement concerning the amount at which the property will be valued, and the donor knows that amount is more than the FMV of the property, the appraiser is not a qualified appraiser for the donation.

Appraiser penalties. An appraiser who prepares an incorrect appraisal may have to pay a penalty if:

1. The appraiser knows or should have known the appraisal would be used in connection with a return or claim for refund, and

2. The appraisal results in the 20% or 40% penalty for a valuation misstatement described later under *Penalty*.

The penalty imposed on the appraiser is the smaller of:

1. The greater of:

   a. 10% of the underpayment due to the misstatement, or

   b. $1,000, or

2. 125% of the gross income received for the appraisal.

In addition, any appraiser who falsely or fraudulently overstates the value of property described in a qualified appraisal of a Form 8283 that the appraiser has signed may be subject to a civil penalty for aiding and abetting as understatement of tax liability, and may have his or her appraisal disregarded.

Form 8283

Generally, if the claimed deduction for an item of donated property is more than $5,000, you must attach Form 8283 to your tax return and complete Section B.

If you do not attach Form 8283 to your return and complete Section B, the deduction will not be allowed unless your failure was due to reasonable cause, and not willful neglect, or was due to a good faith omission. If the IRS requests that you submit the form because you did not attach it to your return, you must comply within 90 days of the request or the deduction will be disallowed.

You must attach a separate Form 8283 for each item of contributed property that is not part of a group of similar items. If you contribute similar items of property to the same donee organization, you need attach only one Form 8283 for those items. If you contribute similar items of property to more than one donee organization, you must attach a separate form for each donee.

Internal Revenue Service Review of Appraisals

In reviewing an income tax return, the Service may accept the claimed value of the donated property, based on information or appraisals sent with the return, or may make its own determination of FMV. In either case, the Service may:

- Contact the taxpayer to get more information,

- Refer the valuation problem to a Service appraiser or valuation specialist,

- Refer the issue to the Commissioner's Art Advisory Panel (a group of dealers and museum directors who review and recommend acceptance or adjustment of taxpayers' claimed values for major paintings, sculptures, decorative arts, and antiques), or

- Contract with an independent dealer, scholar, or appraiser to appraise the property when the objects require appraisers of highly specialized experience and knowledge.

Responsibility of the Service. The Service is responsible for reviewing appraisals, but it is not responsible for making them. Supporting the FMV listed on your return is your responsibility.

The Service does not accept appraisals without question. Nor does the Service recognize any particular appraiser or organization of appraisers.

Timing of Service action. The Service generally does not approve valuations or appraisals before the actual filing of the tax return to which the appraisal applies. In addition, the Service generally does not issue advance rulings approving or disapproving such appraisals.

Exception. For a request submitted as described earlier under *Art valued at $50,000 or more*, the Service will issue a Statement of Value that can be relied on by the donor of the item of art.

Penalty

You may be liable for a penalty if you overstate the value or adjusted basis of donated property.

20% penalty. The penalty is 20% of the underpayment of tax related to the overstatement if:

- The value or adjusted basis claimed on the return is 200% (150% for returns filed after August 17, 2006) or more of the correct amount, and

- You underpaid your tax by more than $5,000 because of the overstatement.

40% penalty. The penalty is 40%, rather than 20%, if:

- The value or adjusted basis claimed on the return is 400% (200% for returns filed after August 17, 2006) or more of the correct amount, and

- You underpaid your tax by more than $5,000 because of the overstatement.

How To Get Tax Help

You can get help with unresolved tax issues, order free publications and forms, ask tax questions, and get information from the IRS in several ways. By selecting the method that is best for you, you will have quick and easy access to tax help.

Contacting your Taxpayer Advocate. The Taxpayer Advocate Service is an independent organization within the IRS whose employees assist taxpayers who are experiencing economic harm, who are seeking help in resolving tax problems that have not been resolved through normal channels, or who believe that an IRS system or procedure is not working as it should.

You can contact the Taxpayer Advocate Service by calling toll-free 1-877-777-4778 or TTY/TDD 1-800-829-4059 to see if you are eligible for assistance. You can also call or write to your local taxpayer advocate, whose phone number and address are listed in your local telephone directory and in Publication 1546, The Taxpayer Advocate Service of the IRS - How To Get Help With Unresolved Tax Problems. You can file Form 911, Application for Taxpayer Assistance Order, or ask an IRS employee to complete it on your behalf. For more information, go to *www.irs.gov/advocate*.

Low income tax clinics (LITCs). LITCs are independent organizations that provide low income taxpayers with representation in federal tax controversies with the IRS for free or for a nominal charge. The clinics also provide tax education and outreach for taxpayers with limited English proficiency or who speak English as a second language. Publication 4134, Low Income Taxpayer Clinic List, provides information on clinics in your area. It is available at *www.irs.gov* or at your local IRS office.

Free tax services. To find out what services are available, get Publication 910, IRS Guide to Free Tax Services. It contains a list of free tax publications and describes other free tax information services, including tax education and assistance programs and a list of TeleTax topics.

 Internet. You can access the IRS website at *www.irs.gov* 24 hours a day, 7 days a week to:

- *E-file* your return. Find out about commercial tax preparation and *e-file* services available free to eligible taxpayers.
- Check the status of your 2006 refund. Click on *Where's My Refund*. Wait at least 6 weeks from the date you filed your return (3 weeks if you filed electronically). Have your 2006 tax return available because you will need to know your social security number, your filing status, and the exact whole dollar amount of your refund.
- Download forms, instructions, and publications.
- Order IRS products online.
- Research your tax questions online.
- Search publications online by topic or keyword.

- View Internal Revenue Bulletins (IRBs) published in the last few years.
- Figure your withholding allowances using our withholding calculator.
- Sign up to receive local and national tax news by email.
- Get information on starting and operating a small business.

 Phone. Many services are available by phone.

- *Ordering forms, instructions, and publications.* Call 1-800-829-3676 to order current-year forms, instructions, and publications, and prior-year forms and instructions. You should receive your order within 10 days.
- *Asking tax questions.* Call the IRS with your tax questions at 1-800-829-1040.
- *Solving problems.* You can get face-to-face help solving tax problems every business day in IRS Taxpayer Assistance Centers. An employee can explain IRS letters, request adjustments to your account, or help you set up a payment plan. Call your local Taxpayer Assistance Center for an appointment. To find the number, go to *www.irs.gov/localcontacts* or look in the phone book under *United States Government, Internal Revenue Service.*
- *TTY/TDD equipment.* If you have access to TTY/TDD equipment, call 1-800-829-4059 to ask tax questions or to order forms and publications.
- *TeleTax topics.* Call 1-800-829-4477 to listen to pre-recorded messages covering various tax topics.
- *Refund information.* To check the status of your 2006 refund, call 1-800-829-4477 and press 1 for automated refund information or call 1-800-829-1954. Be sure to wait at least 6 weeks from the date you filed your return (3 weeks if you filed electronically). Have your 2006 tax return available because you will need to know your social security number, your filing status, and the exact whole dollar amount of your refund.

Evaluating the quality of our telephone services. To ensure IRS representatives give accurate, courteous, and professional answers, we use several methods to evaluate the quality of our telephone services. One method is for a second IRS representative to listen in on or record random telephone calls. Another is to ask some callers to complete a short survey at the end of the call.

 Walk-in. Many products and services are available on a walk-in basis.

- *Products.* You can walk in to many post offices, libraries, and IRS offices to pick up certain forms, instructions, and publications. Some IRS offices, libraries, grocery stores, copy centers, city and county government offices, credit unions, and office supply stores have a collection of products available to print from a CD or photocopy from reproducible proofs. Also, some IRS offices and libraries have the Internal Revenue Code, regulations, Internal Revenue Bulletins, and Cumulative Bulletins available for research purposes.

- *Services.* You can walk in to your local Taxpayer Assistance Center every business day for personal, face-to-face tax help. An employee can explain IRS letters, request adjustments to your tax account, or help you set up a payment plan. If you need to resolve a tax problem, have questions about how the tax law applies to your individual tax return, or you're more comfortable talking with someone in person, visit your local Taxpayer Assistance Center where you can spread out your records and talk with an IRS representative face-to-face. No appointment is necessary, but if you prefer, you can call your local Center and leave a message requesting an appointment to resolve a tax account issue. A representative will call you back within 2 business days to schedule an in-person appointment at your convenience. To find the number, go to *www.irs.gov/localcontacts* or look in the phone book under *United States Government, Internal Revenue Service.*

 Mail. You can send your order for forms, instructions, and publications to the address below. You should receive a response within 10 business days after your request is received.

National Distribution Center
P.O. Box 8903
Bloomington, IL 61702-8903

 CD for tax products. You can order Publication 1796, IRS Tax Products CD, and obtain:

- A CD that is released twice so you have the latest products. The first release ships in January and the final release ships in March.
- Current-year forms, instructions, and publications.
- Prior-year forms, instructions, and publications.
- Bonus: Historical Tax Products DVD - Ships with the final release.
- Tax Map: an electronic research tool and finding aid.
- Tax law frequently asked questions.
- Tax Topics from the IRS telephone response system.
- Fill-in, print, and save features for most tax forms.
- Internal Revenue Bulletins.
- Toll-free and email technical support.

Buy the CD from National Technical Information Service (NTIS) at *www.irs.gov/cdorders* for

1396   ART LAW

The type and rule above prints on all proofs including departmental reproduction proofs. MUST be removed before printing.

$25 (no handling fee) or call 1-877-CDFORMS (1-877-233-6767) toll free to buy the CD for $25 (plus a $5 handling fee). Price is subject to change.

 CD for small businesses. Publication 3207, The Small Business Resource Guide CD for 2006, is a must for every small business owner or any taxpayer about to start a business. This year's CD includes:

- Helpful information, such as how to prepare a business plan, find financing for your business, and much more.

- All the business tax forms, instructions, and publications needed to successfully manage a business.

- Tax law changes for 2006.

- Tax Map: an electronic research tool and finding aid.

- Web links to various government agencies, business associations, and IRS organizations.

- "Rate the Product" survey—your opportunity to suggest changes for future editions.

- A site map of the CD to help you navigate the pages of the CD with ease.

- An interactive "Teens in Biz" module that gives practical tips for teens about starting their own business, creating a business plan, and filing taxes.

An updated version of this CD is available each year in early April. You can get a free copy by calling 1-800-829-3676 or by visiting *www.irs.gov/smallbiz.*

Index

To help us develop a more useful index, please let us know if you have ideas for index entries. See "Comments and Suggestions" in the "Introduction" for the ways you can reach us.

1398   A R T   L A W

The type and rule above prints on all proofs including departmental reproduction proofs. MUST be removed before printing.

Tax Publications for Individual Taxpayers

See *How To Get Tax Help* for a variety of ways to get publications, including by computer, phone, and mail.

General Guides

- 1 Your Rights as a Taxpayer
- 17 Your Federal Income Tax (For Individuals)
- 334 Tax Guide for Small Business (For Individuals Who Use Schedule C or C-EZ)
- 509 Tax Calendars for 2007
- 553 Highlights of 2006 Tax Changes
- 910 IRS Guide to Free Tax Services

Specialized Publications

- 3 Armed Forces' Tax Guide
- 54 Tax Guide for U.S. Citizens and Resident Aliens Abroad
- 225 Farmer's Tax Guide
- 463 Travel, Entertainment, Gift, and Car Expenses
- 501 Exemptions, Standard Deduction, and Filing Information
- 502 Medical and Dental Expenses (Including the Health Coverage Tax Credit)
- 503 Child and Dependent Care Expenses
- 504 Divorced or Separated Individuals
- 505 Tax Withholding and Estimated Tax
- 514 Foreign Tax Credit for Individuals
- 516 U.S. Government Civilian Employees Stationed Abroad
- 517 Social Security and Other Information for Members of the Clergy and Religious Workers
- 519 U.S. Tax Guide for Aliens
- 521 Moving Expenses
- 523 Selling Your Home
- 524 Credit for the Elderly or the Disabled
- 525 Taxable and Nontaxable Income
- 526 Charitable Contributions
- 527 Residential Rental Property
- 529 Miscellaneous Deductions
- 530 Tax Information for First-Time Homeowners

- 531 Reporting Tip Income
- 536 Net Operating Losses (NOLs) for Individuals, Estates, and Trusts
- 537 Installment Sales
- 541 Partnerships
- 544 Sales and Other Dispositions of Assets
- 547 Casualties, Disasters, and Thefts
- 550 Investment Income and Expenses
- 551 Basis of Assets
- 552 Recordkeeping for Individuals
- 554 Older Americans' Tax Guide
- 555 Community Property
- 556 Examination of Returns, Appeal Rights, and Claims for Refund
- 559 Survivors, Executors, and Administrators
- 561 Determining the Value of Donated Property
- 564 Mutual Fund Distributions
- 570 Tax Guide for Individuals With Income From U.S. Possessions
- 571 Tax-Sheltered Annuity Plans (403(b) Plans)
- 575 Pension and Annuity Income
- 584 Casualty, Disaster, and Theft Loss Workbook (Personal-Use Property)
- 587 Business Use of Your Home (Including Use by Daycare Providers)
- 590 Individual Retirement Arrangements (IRAs)
- 593 Tax Highlights for U.S. Citizens and Residents Going Abroad
- 594 What You Should Know About the IRS Collection Process
- 596 Earned Income Credit (EIC)
- 721 Tax Guide to U.S. Civil Service Retirement Benefits
- 901 U.S. Tax Treaties
- 907 Tax Highlights for Persons with Disabilities

- 908 Bankruptcy Tax Guide
- 915 Social Security and Equivalent Railroad Retirement Benefits
- 919 How Do I Adjust My Tax Withholding?
- 925 Passive Activity and At-Risk Rules
- 926 Household Employer's Tax Guide
- 929 Tax Rules for Children and Dependents
- 936 Home Mortgage Interest Deduction
- 946 How To Depreciate Property
- 947 Practice Before the IRS and Power of Attorney
- 950 Introduction to Estate and Gift Taxes
- 967 The IRS Will Figure Your Tax
- 969 Health Savings Accounts and Other Tax-Favored Health Plans
- 970 Tax Benefits for Education
- 971 Innocent Spouse Relief
- 972 Child Tax Credit
- 1542 Per Diem Rates
- 1544 Reporting Cash Payments of Over $10,000 (Received in a Trade or Business)
- 1546 The Taxpayer Advocate Service of the IRS – How to Get Help With Unresolved Tax Problems

Spanish Language Publications

- 1SP Derechos del Contribuyente
- 579SP Cómo Preparar la Declaración de Impuesto Federal
- 594SP Que es lo que Debemos Saber sobre el Proceso de Cobro del IRS
- 596SP Crédito por Ingreso del Trabajo
- 850 English-Spanish Glossary of Words and Phrases Used in Publications Issued by the Internal Revenue Service
- 1544SP Informe de Pagos en Efectivo en Exceso de $10,000 (Recibidos en una Ocupación o Negocio)

Commonly Used Tax Forms

See *How To Get Tax Help* for a variety of ways to get forms, including by computer, phone, and mail.

Form Number and Title

- 1040 U.S. Individual Income Tax Return
  - Sch A&B Itemized Deductions & Interest and Ordinary Dividends
  - Sch C Profit or Loss From Business
  - Sch C-EZ Net Profit From Business
  - Sch D Capital Gains and Losses
  - Sch D-1 Continuation Sheet for Schedule D
  - Sch E Supplemental Income and Loss
  - Sch EIC Earned Income Credit
  - Sch F Profit or Loss From Farming
  - Sch H Household Employment Taxes
  - Sch J Income Averaging for Farmers and Fishermen
  - Sch R Credit for the Elderly or the Disabled
  - Sch SE Self-Employment Tax
- 1040A U.S. Individual Income Tax Return
  - Sch 1 Interest and Ordinary Dividends for Form 1040A Filers
  - Sch 2 Child and Dependent Care Expenses for Form 1040A Filers
  - Sch 3 Credit for the Elderly or the Disabled for Form 1040A Filers
- 1040EZ Income Tax Return for Single and Joint Filers With No Dependents
- 1040-ES Estimated Tax for Individuals
- 1040X Amended U.S. Individual Income Tax Return

Form Number and Title

- 2106 Employee Business Expenses
- 2106-EZ Unreimbursed Employee Business Expenses
- 2210 Underpayment of Estimated Tax by Individuals, Estates, and Trusts
- 2441 Child and Dependent Care Expenses
- 2848 Power of Attorney and Declaration of Representative
- 3903 Moving Expenses
- 4562 Depreciation and Amortization
- 4868 Application for Automatic Extension of Time To File U.S. Individual Income Tax Return
- 4952 Investment Interest Expense Deduction
- 5329 Additional Taxes on Qualified Plans (Including IRAs) and Other Tax-Favored Accounts
- 6251 Alternative Minimum Tax—Individuals
- 8283 Noncash Charitable Contributions
- 8582 Passive Activity Loss Limitations
- 8606 Nondeductible IRAs
- 8812 Additional Child Tax Credit
- 8822 Change of Address
- 8829 Expenses for Business Use of Your Home
- 8863 Education Credits
- 9465 Installment Agreement Request

APPENDIX 15-14

IRS Form 8283—Noncash Charitable Contributions

Form **8283** (Rev. December 2006) Department of the Treasury Internal Revenue Service	**Noncash Charitable Contributions** ▶ Attach to your tax return if you claimed a total deduction of over $500 for all contributed property. ▶ See separate instructions.	OMB No. 1545-0908 Attachment Sequence No. **155**
Name(s) shown on your income tax return		Identifying number

Note. Figure the amount of your contribution deduction before completing this form. See your tax return instructions.

Section A. Donated Property of $5,000 or Less and Certain Publicly Traded Securities—List in this section **only** items (or groups of similar items) for which you claimed a deduction of $5,000 or less. Also, list certain publicly traded securities even if the deduction is more than $5,000 (see instructions).

Part I   **Information on Donated Property**—If you need more space, attach a statement.

1	(a) Name and address of the donee organization	(b) Description of donated property (For a donated vehicle, enter the year, make, model, condition, and mileage, and attach Form 1098-C if required.)
A		
B		
C		
D		
E		

Note. If the amount you claimed as a deduction for an item is $500 or less, you do not have to complete columns (d), (e), and (f).

	(c) Date of the contribution	(d) Date acquired by donor (mo., yr.)	(e) How acquired by donor	(f) Donor's cost or adjusted basis	(g) Fair market value (see instructions)	(h) Method used to determine the fair market value
A						
B						
C						
D						
E						

Part II   **Partial Interests and Restricted Use Property**—Complete lines 2a through 2e if you gave less than an entire interest in a property listed in Part I. Complete lines 3a through 3c if conditions were placed on a contribution listed in Part I; also attach the required statement (see instructions).

2a Enter the letter from Part I that identifies the property for which you gave less than an entire interest ▶_____ .
If Part II applies to more than one property, attach a separate statement.

  b Total amount claimed as a deduction for the property listed in Part I: **(1)** For this tax year   ▶ _____ .
                                                    (2) For any prior tax years   ▶ _____ .

  c Name and address of each organization to which any such contribution was made in a prior year (complete only if different from the donee organization above):

Name of charitable organization (donee)

Address (number, street, and room or suite no.)

City or town, state, and ZIP code

  d For tangible property, enter the place where the property is located or kept ▶ _____

  e Name of any person, other than the donee organization, having actual possession of the property ▶ _____

		Yes	No
3a	Is there a restriction, either temporary or permanent, on the donee's right to use or dispose of the donated property?		
b	Did you give to anyone (other than the donee organization or another organization participating with the donee organization in cooperative fundraising) the right to the income from the donated property or to the possession of the property, including the right to vote donated securities, to acquire the property by purchase or otherwise, or to designate the person having such income, possession, or right to acquire?		
c	Is there a restriction limiting the donated property for a particular use?		

For Paperwork Reduction Act Notice, see separate instructions.   Cat. No. 62299J   Form **8283** (Rev. 12-2006)

Form 8283 (Rev. 12-2006)   Page **2**

Name(s) shown on your income tax return	Identifying number

Section B. Donated Property Over $5,000 (Except Certain Publicly Traded Securities)—List in this section only items (or groups of similar items) for which you claimed a deduction of more than $5,000 per item or group (except contributions of certain publicly traded securities reported in Section A). An appraisal is generally required for property listed in Section B (see instructions).

Part I   **Information on Donated Property**—To be completed by the taxpayer and/or the appraiser.

4   Check the box that describes the type of property donated:

☐ Art* (contribution of $20,000 or more)   ☐ Qualified Conservation Contribution   ☐ Equipment

☐ Art* (contribution of less than $20,000)   ☐ Other Real Estate   ☐ Securities

☐ Collectibles**   ☐ Intellectual Property   ☐ Other

*Art includes paintings, sculptures, watercolors, prints, drawings, ceramics, antiques, decorative arts, textiles, carpets, silver, rare manuscripts, historical memorabilia, and other similar objects.

**Collectibles include coins, stamps, books, gems, jewelry, sports memorabilia, dolls, etc., but not art as defined above.

Note. In certain cases, you must attach a qualified appraisal of the property. See instructions.

5	(a) Description of donated property (if you need more space, attach a separate statement)	(b) If tangible property was donated, give a brief summary of the overall physical condition of the property at the time of the gift	(c) Appraised fair market value
A			
B			
C			
D			

	(d) Date acquired by donor (mo., yr.)	(e) How acquired by donor	(f) Donor's cost or adjusted basis	(g) For bargain sales, enter amount received	See instructions	
					(h) Amount claimed as a deduction	(i) Average trading price of securities
A						
B						
C						
D						

Part II   **Taxpayer (Donor) Statement**—List each item included in Part I above that the appraisal identifies as having a value of $500 or less. See instructions.

I declare that the following item(s) included in Part I above has to the best of my knowledge and belief an appraised value of not more than $500 (per item). Enter identifying letter from Part I and describe the specific item. See instructions. ▶ _____

Signature of taxpayer (donor) ▶   Date ▶

Part III   **Declaration of Appraiser**

I declare that I am not the donor, the donee, a party to the transaction in which the donor acquired the property, employed by, or related to any of the foregoing persons, or married to any person who is related to any of the foregoing persons. And, if regularly used by the donor, donee, or party to the transaction, I performed the majority of my appraisals during my tax year for other persons.

Also, I declare that I hold myself out to the public as an appraiser or perform appraisals on a regular basis; and that because of my qualifications as described in the appraisal, I am qualified to make appraisals of the type of property being valued. I certify that the appraisal fees were not based on a percentage of the appraised property value. Furthermore, I understand that a false or fraudulent overstatement of the property value as described in the qualified appraisal or this Form 8283 may subject me to the penalty under section 6701(a) (aiding and abetting the understatement of tax liability). In addition, I understand that a substantial or gross valuation misstatement resulting from the appraisal of the value of the property that I know, or reasonably should know, would be used in connection with a return or claim for refund, may subject me to the penalty under section 6695A. I affirm that I have not been barred from presenting evidence or testimony by the Office of Professional Responsibility.

Sign Here   Signature ▶   Title ▶   Date ▶

Business address (including room or suite no.)	Identifying number

City or town, state, and ZIP code

Part IV   **Donee Acknowledgment**—To be completed by the charitable organization.

This charitable organization acknowledges that it is a qualified organization under section 170(c) and that it received the donated property as described in Section B, Part I, above on the following date ▶ _____

Furthermore, this organization affirms that in the event it sells, exchanges, or otherwise disposes of the property described in Section B, Part I (or any portion thereof) within 3 years after the date of receipt, it will file **Form 8282**, Donee Information Return, with the IRS and give the donor a copy of that form. This acknowledgment does not represent agreement with the claimed fair market value.

Does the organization intend to use the property for an unrelated use? . . . . ▶ ☐ Yes   ☐ No

Name of charitable organization (donee)	Employer identification number

Address (number, street, and room or suite no.)	City or town, state, and ZIP code	

Authorized signature	Title	Date

♻ Printed on Recycled Paper   Form **8283** (Rev. 12-2006)

APPENDIX 15-15

Art Advisory Panel 2011 Annual Report

The Art Advisory Panel
of the
Commissioner
of
Internal Revenue

Annual Summary Report for
Fiscal Year 2011
(Closed meeting activity)

2

Overview

Created in 1968, the Art Advisory Panel of the Commissioner of Internal Revenue (the Panel) provides advice and makes recommendations to the Art Appraisal Services (AAS) unit in the Office of Appeals for the Internal Revenue Service (IRS). Chartered under the Federal Advisory Committee Act (FACA), the Panel helps the IRS review and evaluate the acceptability of tangible personal property appraisals taxpayers submit in support of the fair market value claimed on the wide range of works of art involved in income, estate, and gift tax returns.

When a tax return which includes an appraisal of a single work of art or cultural property valued at $50,000 or more has been selected for audit, the IRS local office must refer the case to AAS and subsequent referral to the Panel when applicable. The AAS staff provides the support and coordination of the Panel and its appraisers independently review taxpayers' appraisals for art works not referred to the Panel.

The Panel provides essential information to help foster voluntary compliance. The information and recommendations play an important role in the IRS's efforts to cost-effectively address the potentially high abuse area of art valuation. The information, advice, and insight into the world of art the Panelists provide cannot be obtained effectively from within the IRS and does not duplicate the work performed in the IRS or elsewhere. The AAS appraisers review appraisals by researching public information; the Panel provides additional knowledge of private sales based on their personal experience as dealers, scholars, and museum curators, and from information obtained from other members of their relatively small industry. The panelists' knowledge is particularly beneficial in the authentication of works of art.

Art Appraisal Services takes steps to ensure objectivity and taxpayer privacy. Information provided to the Panelists does not include the tax consequences of any adjustments to the value or who did the appraisal. To minimize recognition by the Panelists of a taxpayer's entire collection, the art works are discussed in alphabetical order by artist or, in the case of decorative art, by object type. In the event of a conflict of interest involving a Panelist and a work of art under review, the Panelist does not participate in the discussion and is excused from the meeting.

Before Panel meetings, AAS appraisers send photographs and written materials to the panelists about the works of art under review. The materials include information from the taxpayer's appraisal, such as size, medium, physical condition, and provenance, and the AAS appraiser's own research, including available information on public and private sales of relevant art work.

During their meetings, the panelists review the information provided, along with the research and findings of both the Panelists and staff appraisers. After discussing each item individually, they reach a consensus on its value. Panel discussions are lively, but serious; despite the different perspectives of dealers, auction house experts and museum curators, disagreements are rare. When disagreements happen, they generally result from insufficient information. In these cases, the Panelists will indicate

3

that additional research, such as inspecting the property or consulting with additional experts, is necessary before making a recommendation as to value. Once the additional work is completed, the item may be brought up for review at a subsequent Panel meeting.

The Panel's recommendations are advisory. The AAS staff reviews all of the Panel's recommendations, which become the position of the IRS only with AAS concurrence. During FY 2011, AAS adopted 93% of the Panel's recommendations in full.

The AAS staff provides written reports or memos to the requesting IRS office, with a copy for the taxpayer, outlining the Panel's recommendations for adjustments to fair market value with all supporting evidence.

Taxpayers may request reconsideration of an adjusted claimed value only if they provide additional information or new probative evidence. The staff may submit such information, if deemed substantive, to the Panel for reconsideration at a subsequent meeting.

Panel Leadership

The Director, Art Appraisal Services serves as the Panel Chair and Designated Federal Officer (DFO) for purposes of the FACA.

Panel Sub-Committees

The DFO has the authority to create subcommittees or workgroups. Subcommittees may be established for any purpose consistent with the Panel's charter, and they are comprised of Panel members. There are currently two subcommittees: the Fine Arts Panel, which reviews paintings, sculpture, watercolors, prints, and drawings, etc; and the Decorative Arts Panel, which reviews antique furniture, decorative art, ceramics, textiles, carpets, and silver, etc.

Meetings

The Panel generally meets once or twice a year in each specialty area, usually in Washington, DC. Panel meetings are closed to the public since all portions of the meetings concern matters that are exempted from disclosure under the provisions of section 552b(c)(3), (4), (6) and (7) of Title 5 of the U.S. Code. This determination, which is consistent with section 10(d) of the Federal Advisory Committee Act, as amended (5 U.S.C. App.2), is necessary to protect the confidentiality of tax returns and return information as required by Internal Revenue Code § 6103.

4

The meetings held during this reporting period included:

Type	Date
Decorative Arts	December 8, 2010
Fine Arts	May 25, 2011
Decorative Arts	June 1, 2011
Fine Arts	September 22, 2011

Summary of Panel Recommendations

During FY11, the Panel completed its review of 344 items with an aggregate taxpayer valuation of $111,185,250 on 52 taxpayer cases under audit. The average claimed value of a charitable contribution item was $1,008,500; the average claimed value for an estate and gift item was $409,070.

The Panel recommended accepting 43% and adjustments to 56% of the appraisals it reviewed. One percent of the appraisals reviewed required additional staff development before the Panel could make a value recommendation. The Panel recommended total net adjustments of $26,096,240 on the reviews AAS has finalized for these meetings. On the adjusted items, the Panel recommended a 46% reduction on the charitable contribution appraisals and a 51% increase on items in estate and gift appraisals.

The Panel also reconsidered 3 items in 3 taxpayer cases originally valued at $360,000 by the taxpayers and $1,000,000 by the Panel. After reviewing the additional information, which included a subsequent sale, the Panel revised their recommendation to $592,500. These items are not included in the information above or that follows.

Comprehensive Recommendations Report

Panel Type	# of items	Total T/P Claimed Value	Total Panel Recommended Value
Fine Art	238	$98,849,750	$120,017,490
Decorative Art	106	$12,335,500	$17,264,000
Total	344	$111,185,250	$137,281,490

5

Type of Tax	# of items adjusted	T/P Claimed Value	Type of Adjustment	Panel Recommended Value
Estate	118	$33,298,000	Increase	$58,986,000
	17	$4,025,000	Decrease	$2,433,000
Gift	31	$12,065,000	Increase	$18,145,000
	21	$7,325,000	Decrease	$4,545,240
Charitable Cont.	5	$2,825,000	Decrease	$1,525,000
Totals	196	$59,538,000	Net Increase	$85,544,240

6

Art Advisory Panel of the Commissioner of Internal Revenue 2011

Ms. Stephanie Barron

Senior Curator
Twentieth Century Art
Los Angeles County Museum of Art
Los Angeles, CA

Mr. Douglas Baxter

President
PaceWildenstein
New York, NY

Mr. Leon Dalva

Dalva Brothers, Inc.
New York, NY

Mr. Michael Findlay

Director
Acquavella Galleries, Inc.
New York, NY

Mr. Brock Jobe

Deputy Director
Winterthur Museum
Winterthur, DE

Mr. Christian Jussel

Unaffiliated Scholar/Art Adviser
New York

Mr. Ian Kennedy

Curator of European Paintings &
Sculpture to 1900
The Nelson-Atkins Museum of Art
Kansas City, MO

Mr. Leigh Keno

Leigh Keno American Antiques
New York, NY

Ms. Rebecca Lawton

Curator of Paintings and Sculpture
Amon Carter Museum
Fort Worth, TX 9

Ms. Barbara Mathes

Barbara Mathes Gallery
New York, NY

7

Ms. Nancy McClelland	McClelland + Rachen New York, NY
Ms. Susan Menconi	Partner Menconi & Schoelkopf Fine Art New York, NY
Mr. Howard Rehs	Director Rehs Galleries, Inc. New York, NY
Mr. James L. Reinish	Martha Parrish & James Reinish, Inc. New York, NY
Mr. Joseph Rishel	Curator European Painting before 1900 & John G. Johnson Collection Philadelphia Museum of Art Philadelphia, PA
Dr. Andrew Robison	Mellon Senior Curator National Gallery of Art Washington, DC
Mr. Louis Stern	Louis Stern Fine Arts Inc. Los Angeles, CA
Dr. Scott Schaefer	Senior Curator of Paintings J. Paul Getty Museum Los Angeles, CA
Mr. David Tunick	David Tunick, Inc. New York, NY

16

Tax and Estate Planning for Artists

Taxes and estate planning for an artist involve many unique problems. For one, often the artist is not accustomed to coping with sophisticated tax problems and is more concerned with the present state of his art and career than with what may happen in the future. Moreover, making decisions with respect to the eventual disposition of the art may be something the artist wishes to avoid; the artist may be emotionally involved with the work and unsure of how he wants to dispose of it. The artist may also believe that his art is very valuable when in reality it is not; or the reverse may be true. In addition, the value of the art may vary radically between the time an artist's estate plan is drawn up and the time of death.

Constant changes in the tax law, beginning with the Tax Reform Act of 1969 and continuing almost yearly to date, have radically altered the tax treatment of artists' estates over the years. The tax laws treat charitable contributions by artists, as the artist may see it, unfairly. All those problems are further complicated when the artist is distrustful of lawyers and accountants. Obviously, the first and most important function in planning an artist's estate is to gain the artist's confidence and learn what he really wants. Knowing and working with the artist over a period of time and developing a sense of trust is essential in planning any artist's estate.

VALUATION

Knowing the value or the approximate value of an artist's estate is necessary for estate planning. Determining the value of an artist's works is difficult because of the unique qualities inherent in each piece of art, the uncertainties of the art market, variations in quality, and the effect when a large number of items by the same artist are put on the market for sale. In fact, the death of the artist may influence the value of the art. Surprisingly and contrary to popular belief, the death of an artist generally decreases the value of the artist's art, because the artist is no longer alive to prompt and assist in the sale of the art. Collectors love meeting and talking with artists, and doing so is no longer possible after an artist's death.

As important as the concept of value is, no simple rule covers value. The estate tax regulation[1] defines fair market value as

> the price at which the property would change hands between a willing buyer and a willing seller, neither being under any compulsion to buy or sell and both having reasonable knowledge of relevant facts.

The gift tax and income tax regulations contain identical language.[2]

For estate tax purposes, an item's fair market value should be based on the market in which the item is "most commonly sold to the public."[3] Further, the fair market valuation must be made on the date of death[4] or six months later.[5]

The general concept and basic rules regarding valuation are discussed in chapter 15 at pages 1228–1263 and are not repeated here. Those concepts and rules are equally applicable to artists. The following discussion emphasizes the valuation problems unique to artists' estates.[6]

As is the case in planning the collector's estate, an important consideration is the choice of the proper appraiser. The appraiser must be someone who is familiar with the market for the particular artist and someone who has dealt with the artist's works in the past.[7] It is also a good idea in a large estate to have a second appraisal. Appraisals that are unrealistic cause problems in the long run.[8]

Appraisals of artists' estates are difficult. It is not simply a matter of determining the price at which the last pieces sold and multiplying that amount by the number of pieces left in the artist's estate. Sometimes artwork has a greater value when the artist is alive than when the artist is dead. Sometimes the price of an artist's work is adversely affected after death because of the great number of pieces that come on the market at one time. Marketing and selling artwork often involves a great deal of patience and selective selling, with intermittent shows. In other words, there may be a limited market for an artist's work at a certain price and, once that market is exhausted, there may be no willing buyers. The regulations specifically state that "all relevant facts and elements of value as of the applicable valuation date shall be considered in every case."[9] The appraiser must be familiar with all those factors and try to document them to the extent possi-ble.

Blockage Discount

A blockage discount is appropriate when a decedent's estate contains a substantial block of the same general type of property. The concept is derived from block sales of securities when

> the size of the block of stock to be valued in relation to the number of shares changing hands in sales may be relevant in determining whether selling prices reflect the fair market value of the block of stock to be valued.[10]

When the size of the block would overtax the market, thereby depressing the selling price, courts routinely discount the value of the securities to take that effect into account.[11]

The blockage discount had its genesis in stock-valuation cases, but it is also appropriately applied in valuing other types of property, including works of art. The Internal Revenue Service (IRS) has acknowledged the relevance of blockage discounts in the context of artwork valuation.

> The concept of blockage is essentially one of timing. A discount may be allowed where a large quantity of any one type of art is offered on the market at one time and would substantially depress its value. The amount of discount would be determined, in part, on a reasonable estimate of the time it would take to sell the entire quantity in smaller lots. Some of the factors to be considered in determining whether a blockage discount is available are the opportunity cost of holding the inventory, the carrying costs of the inventory, and the expected period of time it will take to dispose of the inventory.[12]

As indicated in the cases discussed below, the courts and the IRS concede a discount from the fair market value of an individual work of art when a large number of items must be absorbed by the market. No specific percentage is applicable in all cases. The amount of discount should be based on an art appraiser's opinion of the effect on the market of offering a large number of works by the same artist at the same time, with consideration given to the number of works on hand, the number previously sold, the size of the potential market, and the necessity of price reductions and concessions to make sales. The market for a seven-foot sculpture weighing five tons is smaller than the market for a 3-foot-by-2-foot oil painting. Relative price also enters into the determination; the market for oil paintings selling for more than $1 million is probably smaller than the market for those selling for $10,000.

DAVID SMITH

Estate of David Smith[13] is a landmark decision involving the application of a blockage discount to works of art in an artist's estate. The case illustrates many of the problems involved in valuing an artist's estate, although it does not provide all the answers. David Smith was a sculptor who died owning 425 pieces of his work. He had sold fewer than 100 pieces during the twenty-five years before his death. Although he had great artistic success, only in the last few years before his death did his works have great financial success. The pieces were unusual in that most were very large: Half were more than seven feet tall, and many weighed several tons. The pieces were located at his studio in Bolton Landing, New York. The executors valued the works at their highest hypothetical retail sale price— that is, the price each would bring if it were the only item offered for sale—then subtracted 75% for a blockage discount and 33% of the remainder for selling commissions that were contracted for, thus reaching a value of $714,000. The

IRS at first reached a figure of $5,250,418 and, before trial, reduced that figure to $4,284,000, which was the executors' figure for the highest value on an item-by-item basis. The court decided that the value was $2,700,000, which was not far from the midway point between the IRS value and the executors' value.[14]

In *Smith*, the court allowed a blockage discount in valuing the works of David Smith, recognizing the "impact of . . . simultaneous availability of an extremely large number of items of the same general category."[15] The estate argued that the fair market value of the works must be determined in the light of the effect that offering all 425 sculptures on the market at the same time would have.[16] The IRS argued that the fair market value of the pieces should be based on the price at which the pieces would have sold in the retail art market on a one-at-a-time basis.[17] In rejecting the IRS argument that no discount should be applied, the court held that the

> respondent should have given considerable weight to the fact that each item of sculpture would not be offered in isolation. We think that, at the very least, each willing buyer in the retail art market would take into account, in determining the price he would be willing to pay for any given item, the fact that 425 other items were being offered for sale at the same time. The impact of such simultaneous availability of an extremely large number of items of the same general category is a significant circumstance which should be taken into account.[18]

In affirming the court's decision, the Second Circuit stated the following:

> Had the large number of artistic works which he left at his death been generally known and had all of these works been immediately placed on the market they would have brought substantially less than could be received by feeding them slowly into the market over a period of time.[19]

On the basis of *Smith*, therefore, appraisers must consider whether to apply a blockage discount when valuing the works of art of a deceased artist for federal estate tax purposes. The amount of the blockage discount is a question of fact to be determined by the appraiser.[20] Furthermore, each artist's works of art must be considered in the light of that artist's particular facts and circumstances.[21]

Smith indicates that the following points should be considered in valuing an artist's estate:

1. The state of the artist's reputation at death (Has the artist's reputation fully blossomed?)
2. Marketplace acceptance of works of such size and character
3. The relationship of the works to all the artist's other works, including relative size, the period in the artist's life when they were created, and their quality when compared with other works by the artist
4. Whether the works are part of a complete series owned by the artist
5. The number and the prices of sales during the artist's life and the prices

at which sales were made during the period immediately before and after death (In *Smith*, the court noted that sales too far removed from the date of death should not be considered, and little weight was given to sales more than two years after the artist's death.)[22]

6. The accessibility of the works of art (Large transportation costs or other expenses involved in getting the works of art to the market may be taken into consideration in determining value.)[23]

Although the Tax Court in *Smith* considered the above factors, the case is inconclusive since it never discussed the weight and the importance of each factor. The decision is made more vague by the Tax Court's statement, in referring to the above factors, that "we do not mean to imply that we have set forth every consideration which has influenced our decision herein."[24] Therefore, we are left to guess as to what other factors influenced the court in reaching its Solomon-like pronouncement of value.

In addition to the above factors, a court should consider the following factors in the valuation of an artist's works at death:

1. The nature of the art market and how it functions, including the influence of art critics, museum shows, and gallery shows[25]

2. The possibility that the works on hand are unsold because they are the less desirable works by the artist and, therefore, not worth so much as those sold before the artist's death

3. The effect of the artist's death on the market value of his works

Regarding the third factor, note that the difficult question of that effect of the artist's death was not resolved by *Smith*. Obviously, once an artist dies, he can produce no more works. But that does not necessarily mean that the value of the artist's works will automatically increase. Often, after an artist dies, the executors must sell many of the works to raise cash for the administration of the estate, and many sales can have an adverse effect on prices. The fact of the artist's death should be one of many facts taken into consideration, but it should be given little weight. The IRS regulations require a valuation at the date of death, not two or three years after death.

The other major issue in *Smith* dealt with the deductibility of the selling commissions from the value of the works of art. That issue is discussed in detail in chapter 15 on pages 1332–1334. Generally, commission expenses are not a factor affecting value.[26] For such expenses to be deductible as administrative expense under section 2053, the will should direct the sale of the works. Such a direction prevents the IRS from raising the question of the "necessity" of the sale, which is the test required by the regulations but one on which the courts have reached differing opinions.[27] It is often difficult to determine at the time of the drafting of the artist's will which, if any, items he may want sold after death. One solution is to direct the executor to sell such items at such times and under such conditions as the executor in his discretion may determine to be necessary in order to raise sufficient funds for the payment of estate taxes and administrative expenses. The timing of such sales can stretch out over years, and an estimate of the net amount realized after the expenses of the sales have been subtracted is a factor in determining value.

LOUISA J. CALDER

The case of *Louisa J. Calder*,[28] which dealt with blockage discount in a gift-tax context, disclosed facts pertaining to the blockage discount in Alexander Calder's estate. Louisa J. Calder, the widow of Alexander Calder, inherited 1,226 Calder gouaches from the estate. At the audit of the federal estate tax return, the IRS agent valued the gouaches at a fair market value approximately three times greater than the value placed on the works by Calder's estate. However, the IRS did acknowledge that because of the large number of works of art by Calder in the estate, a blockage discount was appropriate. The IRS allowed a blockage discount of 60% of the separate retail values of the 1,226 items, and that discount made the value reported on the estate tax return acceptable to the IRS.

Less than two months after Alexander Calder's death, his widow made, through trusts, gifts of the 1,226 gouaches inherited from her husband to six separate persons. Mrs. Calder attempted to claim that the gifts of the works of art were subject to the same blockage discount (60%) that was allowed in her husband's estate. In other words, she argued that the discount should be applied on an aggregate basis to all the items gifted at one time, even if they were made to separate persons. The Tax Court held that the blockage discount must be applied against each separate gift, rather than against the combined total block (all the gifts combined) and that it was not realistic to apply the total sales figure for all the gouaches sold during the year to each gift separately in determining the liquidation period.[29]

The Tax Court characterized the IRS approach—that is, treating the gouaches as a large number of liquid assets whose worth could be realized only through liquidation over a period of time at a uniform rate that yielded an assumed amount of dollars each year over the period—as being valid only to the extent that the underlying assumptions regarding the number of paintings that could be liquidated each year were valid.[30] The IRS approach proved wrong in practice. Its prediction of the number of gouaches to be sold each year far exceeded the actual annual sales. The Tax Court, therefore, recalculated the blockage discount, using actual sales figures for each of the six gifts, rather than arbitrary estimates applied by the IRS. The result was that, in view of fewer sales made, the Tax Court determined that it would take a significantly longer period of time to liquidate each gift, resulting in a larger blockage discount and a gift tax value almost half that calculated by the IRS.

GEORGIA O'KEEFFE

Subsequently, the Tax Court dealt with the issue of the application of the block-age discount in an artist's estate in *Estate of Georgia O'Keeffe*.[31] At issue in the *O'Keeffe* case was the fair market value of approximately 400 works of art created by Georgia O'Keeffe. The works represented a spectrum of the artist's work, from early works on paper to canvases done in the early 1970s.

O'Keeffe died in 1986 at the age of ninety-eight. The executors of the O'Keeffe estate had the works of art appraised and then applied a 75% blockage discount based on the recommendation of the estate's appraiser.[32] On audit, the IRS agreed with the taxpayer on the per-canvas valuation total of $72,759,000 but applied a blockage discount much lower than the 75% sought by the estate. The IRS based its discount on a formula that was apparently developed by the art advisory panel of the IRS and not previously made public. In *O'Keeffe* the IRS adopted a three-tiered formula, allowing no blockage discount whatsoever for works valued at more than $500,000, a 20% discount on works valued at between $200,000 and $500,000, and a 50% discount on all other works. Apparently, that three-tier approach has been used in many other artists' estates, and it is a good indication of how the IRS approaches the valuation issue.[33] The amount of the discount in each tier is subject to question, and it appears to us that some discount should always apply at each tier.

An unusual aspect in *O'Keeffe* is the fact that the vast majority of the works of art were not subject to estate taxes, since they were either specifically bequeathed to various charitable organizations or went to the tax-exempt Georgia O'Keeffe Foundation as part of the residuary estate. The IRS and the executors had stipulated that the O'Keeffe artworks were valued at $72,759,000 before any applicable discount. Forty-two of the paintings, valued at $22,575,000, were left as specific bequests to eight museums; the New Mexico inheritance tax was to be paid in works of art; and a large portion of the remaining paintings were to go to the Georgia O'Keeffe Foundation. The tax issue involved the question of whether the blockage discount applied to the relatively small number of paintings that were specifically bequeathed to individual heirs.

The court concluded that the value of all the works of art was $36,400,000, a 50% discount from the agreed per-item value. That figure was reached by applying a 75% discount to half of the artworks and a 25% discount to the other half of the artworks.[34] Although the opinion is not clear as to how the court reached that conclusion, since the opinion is highly critical of both the IRS valuation expert and the executors' valuation expert, the court set down a number of guidelines that are helpful in valuing works of art in an artist's estate.

In reaching its conclusion, the court rejected the IRS approach of dividing the artworks into three tiers based on gross appraised value and applying no discount to the most valuable works and differing discounts to the other works. In *O'Keeffe* the court thought that the works should be segmented not by value but by quality, uniqueness, and salability:

There should be at least two categories, *i.e.*, works that are salable within a relatively short period of time at approximately their individual values and works that
can only be marketed over a long period of years with substantial effort.[35]

Thus, the court appeared to apply a 25% discount to the easily salable items and
a 75% discount to the difficult-to-sell items.

We believe that a better approach to use when determining the applicable
blockage discount in an artist's estate would be to segregate the works of art into
at least three categories, consisting of the following:

1. Major works: those of the highest quality that have significance or im-
    portance for the artist and with an indication of those that are readily sal-
    able and those that would be difficult to sell
2. Less important works: those that are ordinary and can be sold only over
    many years with substantial effort
3. Insignificant works: those that may have little or no value and are mere
    studies, models, exercises, or unfinished works and are not ordinarily sold

Each work of art in each category would then be valued, and a percentage
blockage discount would apply to each category, with the smallest discount applying to the major works that are readily salable. All works of art should be subject to some discount, regardless of the category.

Factors that the appraiser should consider in determining the amount of the
blockage discount include the following:

1. The artist's reputation at death, including the long-term prospects for
    market acceptance of the artist's works
2. Marketplace acceptance of similar works
3. The relationship of the works to the artist's other works, including size,
    date of creation, and quality
4. Whether the works are part of a complete series owned by the artist
5. The number of sales and the prices obtained during the artist's life and
    the sales and prices immediately before and after the artist's death
6. The accessibility of the works of art
7. The nature and the functions of the art market, including the influence of
    critics and of museum and gallery shows
8. The possibility that the unsold works are less desirable than those sold
    before the artist's death
9. The effect of the artist's death on the market value of the artist's work
10. The amount of time it would take the market to absorb the artist's works
    under normal circumstances
11. The costs involved in disposing of the artist's works, the opportunity and
    carrying costs of holding the art as inventory (see discussion of *Smith*
    above at page 1411), and the marketing costs[36]
12. The financial risks associated with owning a nonliquid asset

Even though in *O'Keeffe* the vast majority of the works of art had been bequeathed to charitable organizations, the blockage discount still applied. In arriving at the appropriate blockage discount, the court held that, as a matter of law, all the works of art created by Georgia O'Keeffe and owned by her at the time of her death, regardless of whether or not they were to go to charity, should be included in the blockage calculation.

> Determination of fair market value assumes that works are in the market and precludes consideration that works are "unavailable for sale." He [the IRS valuation expert] was not entitled to consider the actual disposition of the works of art of the estate any more than fair market value may be determined by assuming that particular purchasers will purchase works of art from the estate.[37]

O'Keeffe is particularly significant since many artists at their death bequeath some works of art to museums and other charitable organizations and other works of art to family members. The total number of works owned by the artist at his death is taken into consideration in determining the blockage discount, regardless of the recipient. This would include works that will be transferred pursuant to a promised gift agreement with a museum. See Appendix 16-3. Such a calculation reduces the value of the works of art going to family members for federal estate tax purposes.

The court in *O'Keeffe*, after criticizing both the taxpayer's valuation expert and the IRS valuation expert, went on to discuss the willing-buyer/willing-seller definition of fair market value in a confusing manner. The court found that the definition of fair market value does not necessarily require that the property change hands on the date of death if doing so would mean that one of the parties was acting under compulsion. The court went on to hold the following:

> Unlike the situation in Estate of Smith v. Commissioner, the evidence in this case shows that the amount that would be paid for individual purchases of O'Keeffe's works and the amount that would be paid by a hypothetical en bloc purchaser would not be the same.[38]

But if fair market value is to be determined as of the date of death and is defined as a sale between a willing buyer and a willing seller, the property must change hands, or else there is no sale. We note that both the IRS regulation and the *IRS Valuation Guide for Income, Estate and Gift Taxes*, in discussing fair market value, specifically refer to the "price at which property would change hands."[39] Further, the opinion in *O'Keeffe* seems to contradict itself when it refers to the basic premise of valuing property in an estate:

> Property includable in a decedent's gross estate is generally included at its fair market value *on the date of the decedent's death*. Sec. 2031(a). Fair market value is the price at which property *would change hands* between a willing buyer and a willing seller, neither being under any compulsion to buy or to sell and both having rea-

sonable knowledge of relevant facts. *United States v. Cartwright*, 411 U.S. 456, 551 (1973); sec. 20.2031-1(b), Estate Tax Regs.[40] [emphasis added]

The court seemed to be saying that the hypothetical sale between the willing buyer and the willing seller must not be a forced sale and that although the objective is to value the works of art on the date of death, the hypothetical sale contemplated is not necessarily on the date of death if it would mean a forced sale or that either party was acting under any compulsion to buy or sell.

The court in the *O'Keeffe* case also discussed the question of what part estimated expenses play in arriving at the appropriate blockage discount. The IRS argued that the expenses of any hypothetical sale have nothing to do with determining value, since expenses are determined under section 2053 and not under section 2031. The executors argued that the expenses are relevant in determining the appropriate discount, since any person purchasing the works of art in a hypothetical sale would have to calculate any costs involved—that is, the expenses necessarily incurred in the future disposal of the works of art. The court did not resolve the dispute but did find "that the works could not be sold simultaneously on the date of death and that carrying costs would be incurred."[41]

We believe that the taxpayer's argument is correct and that all estimated expenses, whether they are expenses of purchase or expenses of sale, are factors to be taken into consideration in arriving at the appropriate blockage discount. It is not correct simply to state that the blockage discount is automatically 50% if an art dealer would normally charge a 50% commission to sell the works of art.[42] The correct statement is that in the hypothetical willing-buyer/willing-seller transaction contemplated by regulation section 20.2031-1(b), an art dealer is a likely bulk purchaser of the works of art. It is unrealistic to expect an art dealer to purchase works of art unless he can resell them over time at a reasonable profit. It is equally unrealistic to think that an executor of an estate can market the works of art directly to the public. A work of art is vastly different from a used automobile that can be easily sold through a newspaper advertisement. In estimating at what point the bulk purchase of the works of art would become attractive to the art dealer, one must estimate the dealer's marketing costs, the time necessary for the market to absorb the art, the opportunity cost of holding the art as inventory (that is, the value of other potential profitable projects that cannot be entered into, since the purchaser's capital is tied up in ownership of the decedent's works of art), the carrying costs of the inventory, and the expected period of time it will take to dispose of the inventory.[43]

Although an art dealer is a likely bulk purchaser of works of art from an artist's estate, the court in *O'Keeffe* pointed out that the determination of the amount of the blockage discount is not necessarily the price that would be paid by a bulk purchaser who would purchase for resale. The court indicated that the hypothetical sale between the willing buyer and the willing seller could also involve sales to collectors, depending on the individual circumstances of an artist's estate. The court stated the following:

The parties have not reasonably quantified assumptions about the specific markets in which segments of the works in the estate would be salable. Petitioner has erroneously assumed that all of the art would initially be sold to a bulk purchaser, who would purchase for resale. Petitioner thus ignores the market of collectors who, while taking into account resale value, are not primarily interested in the rate of return on the investment.[44]

The court's conclusion, based on a lack of testimony by both the IRS and the estate as to the appropriate marketplace, seems unrealistic to us, since the executor of an estate, as a fiduciary, is not in a position to market works of art directly to collectors. The executor can dispose of the works in bulk to a potential purchaser or purchasers—most likely an art dealer or a group of dealers. The executor could conceivably sell some works at auction in an attempt to reach the collectors market, as indicated in *O'Keeffe*. However, the reality of the art world is that the executor would substantially hurt any chance of making a bulk sale of the works of art if some of the works were separately offered on the auction market. If the executor attempted to sell all the works of art created by the artist at auction, the marketplace would probably dictate a blockage discount at least as large as that estimated (and probably larger) in order to sell the works of art in bulk to an art dealer.

Although *O'Keeffe* is instructive about how an executor should approach the valuation problems inherent in an artist's estate, it also indicates that cases of that type are better settled than taken to trial since valuing art and applying the appropriate blockage discount are subjective and inexact sciences.

The application of the blockage discount to all works of art owned by the artist at death is also important for reasons other than estate taxes. For example, in a state like New York, where executors' commissions are based on the value of the gross estate, the correct calculation of the executors' commissions depends on the correct (after blockage discount) valuation of the artist's estate.[45] Section 2031(a) requires an executor to include the value of the decedent's property on the federal estate tax return. If the appraiser does not consider the application of any blockage discount in the valuation of the decedent's works of art, the gross estate will not include the correct value of the decedent's property as required by section 2031(a). Although a reduction in value may have no effect on the estate tax payable, the value finally determined on the federal estate tax return is relevant in determining the basis of the decedent's works of art in the hands of the distributee under section 1014(a)(1); the new basis is the fair market value of the property on the decedent's date of death or six months later.[46] In short, to comply with section 1014(a)(1), the appraiser must accurately determine the fair market value of the decedent's works of art for federal estate tax purposes.

ANDY WARHOL

Estates taxes were not at issue in the case *In re Determination of Legal Fees Payable by the Estate of Andy Warhol, Deceased*.[47] The last will and testament of the artist Andy Warhol left his artworks to the Andy Warhol Foundation for the Visual Arts, a tax-exempt organization, so no estate taxes were due. However, valuation of the works of art was important since the executor of the estate had signed a contract with the attorney for the estate, Edward Hayes, agreeing to pay Hayes a fee based on a percentage of the value of the estate's assets. The attorney for the estate sued the Foundation (which was the sole residuary beneficiary of the estate) for legal fees that he alleged were owed to him since the appraisals obtained by the Foundation and by Hayes reached different conclusions as to the value of the art created by Andy Warhol.[48]

Christie's was initially hired by the executor of the estate to appraise the art, which consisted of 4,118 paintings, 5,103 drawings, 19,086 prints, and 66,512 photographs. However, Christie's communicated primarily with the Foundation and submitted its appraisal to the Foundation. On the basis of Christie's appraisal, the estate valued all the art at $265 million, which was then discounted by applying a blockage discount to arrive at a total value of $103,353,000. The appraiser for Hayes valued the same works of art at $708 million and stated that no blockage discount was appropriate.

The court valued the art at $390,979,278, an amount not far from the midway point between the two appraisals. The court determined the unit value of each type of art and then applied a percentage discount to arrive at the fair market value for that category. The discounts were as follows:

Paintings	20%
Photographs	20%
Drawings	35%
Prints	35%

Unfortunately—because of the manner in which the case was presented to the court, the confusion resulting from the emotionally charged issues, or the court's skepticism as to Christie's independence (the court thought that a conflict of interest might exist because of Christie's interest in obtaining future business from the Foundation)—the court missed the opportunity for a well-reasoned opinion. Since the case was not a tax case, the Surrogate's Court was not bound by the willing-buyer/willing-seller definition of fair market value contained in the IRS regulations nor by the guidelines of *Smith*, *Calder*, and *O'Keeffe*. The court reached a conclusionary opinion that not only adds nothing to the knowledge in this area but in some respects appears to be contrary to the facts. In discussing the discount for the paintings, the opinion stated the following:

> In arriving at the discount rate, the Court has considered the *smaller number* of works in this category, the particular importance of the paintings as representing Warhol's finest creations, and the fact that sales will take place over a long period of time.[49] [emphasis added]

Smaller compared with what? It is correct that there were fewer paintings

(4,118) than photographs (66,512), but the number of paintings is huge compared with the number at issue in *Smith, Calder,* or *O'Keeffe* or, to our knowledge, in the estates of most artists.

More important, the court ignored the fact that not all works created by an artist are masterpieces or truly great works. That is why it is necessary, as discussed above, to divide each category of work (paintings, drawings, etc.) into at least three categories consisting of major works, less important works, and insignificant works. Instead, the court in *Warhol* applied an across-the-board 20% discount to all the paintings without regard to the fact that only a small number of them (particularly the rare 1950s and 1960s works) are truly "Warhol's finest creations." In *Warhol* there were 4,188 paintings, more than ten times the number in *O'Keeffe*. Yet in *O'Keeffe* the court recognized that half the value of the estate consisted of relatively undesirable works, which would take more than ten years to market and which required a discount of 75%. Likewise, in *Warhol* some paintings were not highly marketable, such as the many commissioned portraits of unknown persons, which were not even bought by the subjects themselves or their families. Christie's recognized that such works require a large discount; by contrast, the Surrogate assigned a 20% across-the-board discount that in our opinion cannot be reconciled with the facts or the law.[50]

The court's conclusion with respect to the photographs is even more egregious. Most artists work in a number of mediums, even though they earn the bulk of their income from sales of one type of art because there is little or no market demand for other types of art that they create. Andy Warhol was no exception; he worked in paintings, drawings, sculptures, prints, and photography, even though the market demand was for his paintings. The court did note the following:

> There is little in the way of comparable sales in this category. Apparently Warhol did not sell his photographs during his lifetime and there have been few sales, in relation to the size of the category by the Foundation since his death.[51]

Rather than recognizing the lack of sales as evidence that no market existed for the vast majority of the photographs, the court leaped to the conclusion that because the Foundation sold fifty-five out of the 66,512 photographs (less than one-tenth of 1%) over the six years after Warhol's death, there was a market for all 66,512 photographs. The court then accepted the appraisal by Hayes's expert and applied the same across-the-board 20% discount as was used with the paintings, which the Surrogate had recognized as "Warhol's finest creations" and for which an established market existed. That conclusion, in our view, is clearly wrong.

The court was critical of the appraisers used by both Hayes and the Foundation, finding that each concentrated only on the elements that helped its respective side and that neither of the appraisers addressed the blockage issue properly. Perhaps that is the reason for the court's conclusions that seem inconsistent with the facts. The court did correctly state that certain factors must be considered in determining the blockage discount:

The factors to be considered in arriving at the appropriate discount include the nature and number of the artworks involved, the marketability of the particular artist, the likelihood of future markets for the work, the stability or permanence of the reputation of the artist, the likelihood of appreciation or risk of depreciation in both the art market and the work of the particular artist, and the length of time necessary for the various markets to absorb all of the work.[52]

Ultimately, the Surrogate's Court awarded a legal fee to Hayes of $7,200,000, which was based on the complexity of the matter and on the court's determination of the value of the Warhol works of art.[53] Interestingly, the appellate division[54] reduced the fee awarded to Hayes to $3,500,000, approximately half of what was determined by the Surrogate's Court. Although the appellate division affirmed the Surrogate's determination of the value of the works of art (thereby avoiding the need to delve into the morass of fair market value), one can by analogy view the 50% reduction in Hayes's fee as equivalent to a doubling of the blockage discount applied by the Surrogate's Court. Under that analysis the discounts would range from 40% to 70%, amounts that are in keeping with prior decided case law, as in *Smith*, *Calder*, and *O'Keeffe*. In our view the analysis by the Surrogate's Court is flawed because each category of art was never subdivided into at least three categories consisting of major works, less important works, and insignificant works.[55]

Perhaps the Surrogate said it best when, at the outset of her opinion, she stated:

> The value of any art collection is "inherently imprecise and capable of resolution only by a Solomon-like pronouncement." Morris v. Messing, 48 T.C. 502, 512. It is difficult, if not foolhardy, to attempt an answer.[56]

BLOCKAGE BY ANOTHER NAME

The concept of a blockage discount as it applies to an artist's estate is really another way of valuing the artist's business. During his lifetime, the artist is in the business of creating art and selling it. In the vast majority of cases, such sales take place through an art dealer. On the artist's death, his estate must value the artist's business for estate tax purposes, with the works of art being the inventory left in the artist's business. The blockage discount is another way of reflecting the discounts available in valuing a privately owned business with all inherent business risks.[57]

Smith, *Calder*, *O'Keeffe*, and *Warhol* illustrate the vagaries of the application of the blockage discount. A well-prepared appraisal that takes into consideration all the factors discussed above is the best course of action to take in an artist's estate. The executor of an artist's estate must exercise care not to claim a discount that is unrealistic; otherwise, penalties can be imposed on the estate.

Penalties

The Tax Reform Act of 1984 added section 6660 to the Internal Revenue Code to apply to estate and gift taxes. Section 6660 sets forth penalties for a valuation understatement in the case of any underpayment of estate tax or gift tax. Section 6660 was repealed, effective January 1, 1990,[58] in an attempt to streamline complex provisions and to provide a fair and effective penalty system.[59]

Currently, section 6662 consolidates the generally applicable penalties related to the accuracy of tax returns into one accuracy-related penalty equal to 20% of the portion of the underpayment to which the penalty applies. The new provision became effective January 1, 1990. The Pension Protection Act (effective August 17, 2006) further modified the thresholds for the applicable penalties.

For estate and gift tax purposes, section 6662(g)(1) imposes a 20% penalty if the value of any property claimed on an estate or gift tax return is 50% or less of the amount determined to be correct.[60] If the understatement is attributable to a gross valuation misstatement of 25% or less of the correct amount, the penalty amount is increased to 40% of the underpayment.[61] At least $5,000 of additional tax must be due for the penalty to apply.[62]

Unlike the income tax law, estate and gift tax laws do not require a qualified appraisal by a qualified appraiser. Those technical terms apply to charitable contributions for income tax purposes. The IRS has discretionary authority to waive all or part of the section 6662 penalty if the taxpayer establishes that there was a reasonable basis for the valuation claimed and that the claim was made in good faith.[63]

The section 6662(g) penalty appears to apply for estate and gift tax purposes only to valuation understatements, not to overstatements.[64] Therefore, if a decedent bequeathed artwork to a museum and an estate tax charitable deduction is claimed, no section 6662 penalty is imposed if the IRS determines that the work had a smaller value than that claimed on the estate tax return. In most cases, the estate tax does not increase or decrease in the case of a valuation overstatement of a charitable bequest, since the amount of the gross estate increases as the charitable deduction increases; the two amounts cancel each other out, leaving only the remainder subject to the estate tax. Therefore, the section 6662 penalty should generally not apply to an estate charitable bequest that may be overstated in value. However, a valuation overstatement of a work of art can increase the executor's commission, which is deductible on the estate tax return, and have the net effect of decreasing the estate tax.

A section 6662 penalty can be applied in an estate tax situation for income tax purposes. For example, when the unlimited marital deduction[65] applies or when the estate is less than the applicable exclusion amount (for example, less than $5,120,000 in year 2012), there is no estate tax.[66] However, any artwork, as well as other tangible property in the estate, receives a step-up in basis equal to the estate tax value.[67] If the artwork that was overvalued for estate tax purposes is later sold at a loss, the estate or the heirs have a capital loss that may be deductible under section 165(c)(2), as discussed on page 1184. If the loss claimed to reduce the income tax results from the overvaluation, the IRS can invoke the penalty provisions of section 6662.[68] The same result may occur if the works of art are overvalued, resulting in a reduction of the applicable capital gains tax for the surviving spouse of the artist.

CHARITABLE TRANSFERS

Inter Vivos Transfers

Artists want to have their work owned and exhibited at museums, thus enhancing the artist's reputation and increasing the value of the work. Before the Tax Reform Act of 1969, museums found it easy to solicit contributions of artwork from artists. At that time, the artist realized no income on the contribution and received a charitable deduction from income equal to the market value of the artwork donated; any costs to produce the work that had been taken as deductions in previous years did not have to be recaptured and offset against the amount of the charitable deduction.[69]

Effective January 1, 1970, any artist who contributes his work to a charitable organization is entitled to a charitable deduction only to the extent of the cost of the materials used in the creation of the work of art, since, in the artist's hands, artwork is ordinary income property—that is, property whose sale would not result in long-term capital gain.[70] Works created by artists are not capital assets.[71]

The amount of a charitable deduction for a contribution of ordinary income property is limited to the basis of that property in the hands of the donor within the applicable percentage limitation. That result is reached because the amount of the charitable deduction is determined by subtracting from the property's fair market value the amount of gain that would not have been long-term capital gain if the donated property had been sold by the taxpayer at its fair market value.[72] In *Maniscalco*,[73] the court held that a professional artist was not entitled to a charitable contribution deduction for the market value of three portraits donated to charitable organizations, because the allowable charitable contributions deduction for an artist's own works is limited to the cost basis and no amount is allowable for the value of the artist's own labor. The artist's constitutional objection to section 170(e) was held to be without merit.

Example: An artist created a work that cost him $100 for paint and canvas. A number of years later he contributed the work to a museum when the work had a fair market value of $5,000. The artist is limited to a charitable deduction of $100: the artist's cost of materials.

PLANNING ADVICE

The artist owns both the work and the copyright to the work. In order for the artist to obtain an income tax charitable deduction for his cost of materials, the artist *must* donate *both* the work of art and the copyright.[74] Under the income tax regulations, a work of art and its copyright are not treated as two distinct property interests, as they are under federal copyright law, and for estate and gift tax purposes.[75] Failure of the artist to effect the donation of the copyright and the work of art will prevent any charitable deduction under the partial interest rule of section 170(f)(3).[76] An artist may make a lifetime gift to a museum because he wants the work of art as part of a museum collection in order to enhance the artist's reputation. Since the maximum income tax charitable deduction for the artist is limited to his cost,[77] the artist is generally better advised to forego any charitable deduction for the contribution and keep the copyright to the donated work of art.[78] Alternative and preferable advice for the artist who wants his work in a museum is to deliver the work to the museum under a "promised gift" agreement with title not passing until after the death of the artist or the artist and his spouse. This would allow the artist the freedom to retain the copyright on his death for his heirs and also reduce the value of noncharitable transfers of works of art under the blockage discount rules, as discussed earlier in this chapter pertaining to the *Estate of Georgia O'Keeffe*. See Appendix 16-3. It also enables the surviving nonartist spouse to receive an income tax deduction for the full fair market value of the donated work rather than the cost of materials.

If the artist gives the work as a gift to a collector and the collector contributes it to a museum, the collector's charitable deduction is the same as it was for the artist—that is, the cost of the materials used.[79] Therefore, an artist should sell the work to the collector if the collector ever intends to contribute it to a museum. If the work is purchased by the collector and then contributed to a public charitable organization, such as a museum supported by the public, the donor can claim the full fair market value of the donated work as a charitable deduction within the applicable percentage limitations, assuming that the "related use" rule is satisfied. The charitable contribution rules pertaining to the collector are discussed in detail in chapter 15.

ARTISTS EXCHANGING WORKS

Artists are sometimes misled into believing that they can avoid the rule that limits their charitable deduction for works created by them to the cost of the materials used by making an exchange. That is, one artist makes a gift of a work of art to another artist who is a friend and receives in exchange a gift of a work of art from that artist; then each makes a donation of the work of art that was received as a gift. That maneuver does not work. If an artist or any individual makes a donation of a work of art that was a gift from the creator of that work (the other artist), the work of art received as a gift is not a capital asset in the hands of the individual who received it as a gift.[80] As stated above, any charitable deduction of a work of art received as a gift from the creator of the work is limited to the artist's cost of materials used in the creation of that work. Although there may be other advantages when artists donate works of art to museums, receiving a tax deduction for the full value of the donation is not one of them.

If the artists who are exchanging works that each of them created take the position that the exchange is a trade, not two gifts, each of the artists realizes taxable ordinary income on the difference between the cost of the materials and the fair market value of the work of art received in the trade.[81] The trade or exchange cannot be made tax-free since the works of art created by the artists are their inventory or stock in trade held primarily for sale.[82]

The above limitations, which became effective January 1, 1970, drastically reduced the number of artworks donated by artists to museums.[83] Numerous bills have been introduced in Congress over the past thirty years to give artists some increased tax benefits on the contribution of artwork to museums.[84] To date, none has become law.

CHARITABLE REMAINDER TRUST: INTER VIVOS

Section 664 sets forth the requirements for a charitable remainder trust. Generally, a charitable remainder trust must provide for the distribution of a specific amount, at least annually, to one or more persons, at least one of whom is a noncharitable beneficiary.[85] The payment period must be for the life or lives of the individual beneficiaries or for a term of years, not in excess of twenty years. At the termination of the noncharitable interest, the remainder must be paid to one or more exempt organizations described in section 170(c). The charitable remainder trust is exempt from income tax, so the trustee can sell assets without the payment of capital gains tax and the grantor of the trust is entitled to an income tax deduction based on the present value of the remainder interest as calculated under the provisions of section 664.

There are two types of charitable remainder trusts: annuity trust and unitrust. A charitable remainder annuity trust is required to pay a fixed yearly sum to the noncharitable beneficiary equal to at least 5% but not more than 50% of the fair market value of the trust assets, valued as of the date the trust is created.[86] In other words, the annuity trust payment remains constant over the term of the trust. A charitable remainder unitrust is required to pay a fixed yearly sum to the noncharitable beneficiary equal to at least 5% but not more than 50% of the fair market value of the trust assets valued each year on the valuation date.[87] In other words, the unitrust payment changes each year, depending on the value of the trust assets on the valuation date. The Taxpayer Relief Act of 1997 added the 50% limitation referred to above and added a new requirement for both annuity trusts and unitrusts that the value (determined under the section 7520 valuation tables) of the remainder interest going to the charitable organization is at least 10% of the initial net fair market value of the property placed in the trust. The new provisions are effective for transfers in trust after July 28, 1997.

A detailed discussion of charitable remainder trusts is beyond the scope of this chapter. Chapter 15, on page 1289, discusses the use of an inter vivos charitable remainder trust funded with works of art owned by a collector, and that technical discussion is not repeated here. The discussion below focuses on the unique issues when a charitable remainder trust is funded with property created by an artist.

There does not appear to be any specific prohibition against an artist's funding a charitable remainder trust with works of art that he created, even though such property is ordinary income property.[88]

In Private Letter Ruling 94-13-020 an inter vivos charitable remainder unitrust was created by a sole proprietor, *A*, who was engaged in the business of cattle ranching and farming. The crops and slaughtered cattle (the "farm items") raised by *A* are sold to customers in the ordinary course of his business. In a step to wind up and retire from his ranching and farming operation, *A* created a charitable remainder unitrust and funded it with transfers of the farm items. The ruling states that *A* can claim no income tax charitable contribution for the transfer since he had deducted all the costs incurred in raising the cattle and the crops. The farm items can be sold by the trustee of the unitrust shortly after their receipt by the unitrust, although there was no prearranged sale. The ruling request specifically stated that the unitrust will not engage in regularly carried on sales of the farm items as a dealer and that the farm items to be sold are not held by the unitrust for sale to customers in the ordinary course of any unitrust business.

The IRS ruled that A would not recognize any gross income on the transfer of farm items to the unitrust[89] and that there would be no income tax charitable deduction since there was no basis for purposes of applying section 170(e)(1).[90] The creator of the unitrust, A, did not recognize any ordinary income since A was not legally bound to sell the farm items before their transfer to the unitrust.[91] Most significantly, the private letter ruling analyzed the unrelated trade or business income rules[92] and found that, under the facts and circumstances in the ruling request, the occasional or one-time sale of the farm items was not a sale from a business regularly carried on,[93] since such sales will be infrequent and intermittent. Therefore, there was no unrelated trade or business income. That finding is important because any unrelated trade or business income received by a charitable remainder unitrust would result in the unitrust becoming taxable.[94]

Private Letter Ruling 94-13-020 lends support for the use of a charitable remainder trust when an artist wants to avoid a large amount of taxable ordinary income on the occasional sale of a work of art (not in the normal course of business) and would like to fund a charitable foundation after the artist's death or the death of the artist and his spouse. However, as described below, the technical problems are numerous, and caution must be exercised, since there is no specific authority for such a plan.[95]

THE ARTWORK AND THE COPYRIGHT

Although Private Letter Ruling 94-13-020 contains no prohibition against funding a charitable remainder unitrust with ordinary income property, the analysis cannot stop there because the Ruling does not deal with property created by an artist. Under the income tax regulations, a work of art and its copyright are not treated as two distinct property interests.[96] Instead, the work of art and the copyright are treated as one property interest. This must be distinguished from the gift tax and estate tax IRC sections where the work of art and the copyright are treated as two separate property interests.[97] The section 664 regulations define a charitable remainder trust as a trust with respect to which a deduction is allowable under section 170, 2055, 2106, or 2522[98] and which meets the description of a charitable remainder annuity trust (as described in regulation 1.664-2) or a charitable remainder unitrust (as described in regulation 1.664-3). Sections 2055 and 2106 are inapplicable to inter vivos transfers since they involve the estate tax charitable deduction and a deceased individual. Section 2522 pertains to the gift tax charitable deduction. Under section 2522(c)(3), the gift tax charitable deduction is allowable for a transfer of a work of art when the donor retains the copyright only if the use of the property by the donee charitable organization is related to the purpose or function constituting the basis for its exemption under section 501.[99] Since the work of art transferred to the charitable remainder trust will be sold to raise the funds necessary to pay the unitrust distribution amount, the related-use rule will not be satisfied.[100] Therefore, in order for a gift tax charitable deduction to be allowable, the artist must transfer the work of art and the copyright, or the related-use rule of sections 2522(c)(3) and 2055(e)(4) will operate to prevent any gift tax charitable deduction.

That leaves section 170 pertaining to the income tax charitable deduction. As stated above, for income tax purposes the work of art and the copyright are treated as one property interest, so no income tax charitable deduction is available to the artist unless there is a transfer of the work of art and the copyright.[101] In order to transfer the copyright, there must be a specific writing effectuating the transfer.[102]

Therefore, the only way a deduction is allowable under either section 170 or section 2522 for an artist who creates an inter vivos charitable remainder trust is if the artist transfers the work of art and the copyright to the trust when the trust is created. A retention of the copyright by the artist will not only prevent any deduction under section 170 or section 2522, but also disqualify the trust as a charitable remainder trust so that the sale of the work of art transferred to the trust will be a taxable event to the artist.

The artist must also take into consideration the "future interest" rule of section 170(a)(3), which postpones any income tax charitable deduction for a gift of a future interest in tangible personal property until there is no intervening interest in, right of possession of, or enjoyment of the property held by the donor, the donor's spouse, or certain related individuals.[103] Regulation sections 1.664-2(d) and 1.664-3(d) respectively reference section 170(a)(3) and the regulations thereunder for the rules postponing the time for a deduction of a charitable contribution of a future interest in tangible personal property to a charitable remainder trust.

For example, if an artist transfers a painting and the copyright to a charitable remainder trust, and the artist is the unitrust beneficiary of the trust, any income tax charitable deduction is allowable but is postponed until the artist no longer holds an intervening interest in the property. The sale of the painting by the trust followed by the investment of the proceeds terminates the intervening interest of the artist in the painting as contemplated by section 170(a)(3).[104] The artist, as the unitrust beneficiary, would still have an interest in the sale proceeds, and an income tax charitable deduction would be allowable and deductible at that time since section 170(a)(3) only pertains to an interest in tangible personal property (the painting) and not the sale proceeds.[105] Since the character of the painting is ordinary income type property, the amount of the charitable deduction would be the value of the remainder interest in the artist's cost of materials for the painting.[106]

PLANNING WITH THE INTER VIVOS UNITRUST

The inter vivos charitable remainder trust has limited use for the artist. On occasion it may enable an established artist to sell a work of art that has appreciated greatly in value without paying a current income tax, since the trust is itself exempt from income tax unless it has unrelated business taxable income.[107] However, the technique works only if the artist transfers the work of art and the copyright to the charitable remainder trust, something the artist may be reluctant to do. As described above, any current charitable deduction would be limited to the value of the remainder interest in the artist's cost of materials. In order to avoid any issue with respect to unrelated trade or business income, the work of art used to fund the charitable remainder trust should be, to the extent possible, a work not currently offered for sale to customers and one that has been segregated for some time from other works produced for sale.[108] The independent trustee of the unitrust should not use the artist's regular art gallery to sell the work of art. It should be sold privately. The advantage, of course, is that more principal is retained by the trustee on the sale of the work of art (no income tax is paid on the sale) that can be used to generate the unitrust payout to the artist or the artist's spouse. This may be a real benefit to the artist, particularly if the work of art and the copyright are sold by the independent trustee to a museum where the artist would want the work of art to be.[109] The artist should be cautioned that there can be no prearranged sale contract obligating the trustee to sell the work of art to the museum, or the artist will be forced to recognize the taxable gain on the work's sale.

Although it is advisable to sell the work of art transferred to the charitable remainder trust within the first year of the creation of the trust, this may not always be possible. A charitable remainder unitrust is permitted to pay out only its income if that income is less than the stated payout percentage—a so-called net income method charitable remainder unitrust (NIMCRUT).[110] The NIMCRUT may have what is called a "makeup" provision. Under such a provision, any amount by which the trust income falls short of the stated payout percentage is to be paid in subsequent years to the extent the trust's income exceeds the fixed percentage in those years.[111] A charitable remainder trust may start as a NIMCRUT and later convert to a traditional charitable remainder trust—a so-called "flip unitrust."[112] This type of unitrust is ideal for a work of art if there is doubt about its sale in the first year of the trust.

A NIMCRUT may convert to a straight unitrust using the same unitrust pay-out percentage if the governing instrument of the trust meets the following requirements:

1. The change from a net income unitrust to a straight unitrust must be triggered on a specific date or by a single event. The occurrence of that event (the "triggering event") may not be discretionary with, or within the control of, the trustee or any other person.[113] The regulations make it clear that a specific date is a permissible triggering event. Permissible triggering events also include the marriage, divorce, death, or birth of a child with respect to any individual. The sale of unmarketable assets— such as a work of art, real estate, closely held stock, or restricted stock— also is a permissible triggering event. The sale of marketable securities is not a permissible triggering event, however, because the timing of the sale is considered to be within the control or discretion of the trustee. Lastly, a beneficiary's or other person's attaining a specific age is a permissible triggering event.[114]

2. The change from a net income unitrust to a straight unitrust must occur at the beginning of the tax year of the unitrust that immediately follow the tax year during which the triggering event occurs.[115] For example, if the triggering event occurs on July 1, 2004, the conversion of the unitrust to a straight unitrust must occur on January 1, 2005.

3. In the case of a net income unitrust with a makeup provision, the unitrust's governing instrument must provide that any makeup amount not paid as of the conversion date is forfeited.[116]

In order to avoid the yearly requirement of a qualified appraisal by a qualified appraiser, the artist/grantor should not be the trustee—an independent trustee should be used.[117]

Testamentary Transfers

At the present time, artists receive limited tax benefits from lifetime gifts to museums, so they make few contributions. However, on an artist's death, the income tax restrictions do not apply.

OUTRIGHT BEQUESTS

The estate of an artist may claim a deduction on its estate tax return for the full fair market value on the artist's date of death for the works of art bequeathed to charitable organizations.[118] The deduction is not limited to the artist's cost of materials, as it is for income tax purposes. The amount of the deduction is unlimited and is not subject to any percentage limitations. The full estate tax deduction is available, whether the bequest is to a public charity or a private foundation. Private foundations include all tax-exempt organizations other than those described in sections 590(a)(1), (2), (3), and (4). However, if the bequest is to a private foundation that has not complied with the requirement of the Internal Revenue Code to include certain amendments in its governing instrument or that has failed to notify the IRS of its status, the entire estate tax charitable deduction will be denied.[119]

If the artist wishes to bequeath his works to a private foundation, the drafter of the will should obtain a copy of the governing instrument of the private foundation to ascertain whether the instrument meets the IRS requirements mentioned above. The drafter should also obtain a statement from the organization that it has notified the IRS of its status.

The artist may wish to create a private foundation. If so, the foundation should be created during the life of the artist, rather than under the artist's will, with initial funding of $100. The foundation can then apply for tax-exempt status under section 501(c)(3), and the artist's will can bequeath the artist's work to the then existing IRS-approved foundation. The foundation should have powers broad enough to dispose of the artist's works to other charitable organizations and to sell artwork to meet expenses.

Whether works of art are bequeathed to a public charity or to a private foundation, the will should be prepared in a manner that clearly identifies the artworks. Doing so is often a problem in an artist's will because the works the artist wants to leave to a charitable organization may vary from the time the will is drafted to the time of the artist's death. The drafter of the will must be careful of incorporation by reference problems (such as a bequest that refers to "all works of art in my country house"), and should consider the possibility that a specific charitable organization may renounce the bequest. Any proposed gift and any conditions imposed should be discussed with the charitable organization before the artist signs the will.

RELATED USE

Generally, a testator making a testamentary charitable transfer under his will is not concerned with the "related use" rule (the artwork must be related to the exempt purpose of the charity) that applies to an income tax charitable transfer. However, section 2055(e)(4)(C) does contain a related use rule that applies to certain split-interest testamentary charitable transfers.

The problem and the potential trap for the artist are best illustrated by a simple example: The will of an artist bequeaths a specific work of art that he created after January 1, 1978, to his local church and the balance of his estate to his son with these words:

> I give and bequeath my painting entitled "XYZ" to the A Church. All the rest of my property of any kind I give and bequeath to my son.

Since the artist owned the copyright at the time of his death (federal statutory copyright comes into existence at creation) and since the A Church, although a public charity, probably cannot satisfy the related use rule of section 2055(e)(4)(C), does the artist's estate get the estate tax charitable deduction?[120]

The quoted provision in the artist's will does not pass the copyright in the work of art to the charity since the copyright is a separate property interest and must be separately bequeathed. Since the copyright interest was not included in the charitable transfer, it was transferred as part of the residuary clause. Therefore, the transfer is a split-interest transfer that unless the requirements of section 2055(e)(4) are satisfied, results in the loss of the charitable deduction. So, if the transfer to the A Church does not satisfy the related use rule of section 2055(e)(4)(C), the charitable deduction is lost.

Example (1) of the final regulations under section 2055(e)(4)[121] makes it clear that the IRS looks to local state law to see if the purported transfer of the work of art to the charitable organization includes the copyright. We believe that the will clause quoted above does not include the copyright interest in any local jurisdiction in the United States. Such a clause allows the copyright interest to become a part of the residuary estate.

To avoid the problem of an inadvertent split-interest transfer that fails to satisfy the related use rule of section 2055(e)(4)(C), estate planners should examine the wills of artists to make sure that any charitable transfers of works of art created after January 1, 1978, are transfers that also specifically transfer the copyright interest to the same charitable organization. For example:

> I give and bequeath to the XYZ Charity my painting entitled "ABC," oil on canvas, measuring 30 inches by 50 inches, and dated 1988, and my copyright interest, if any, in that painting.

Under that will provision, the copyright interest will not inadvertently fall into the residue, thereby causing a split-interest transfer that may not satisfy the related use rule. If the work of art and the copyright are transferred to a charitable organization then the related use rule of section 2055(e)(4)(C) does not apply and the artist's estate is entitled to a full fair market value deduction even if the charitable organization immediately sells the bequeathed work of art. Although there is no definitive authority, a clause that merely transfers "all my right, title, and interest in and to 'ABC' painting" may not be sufficient to transfer the copyright in the work of art. The careful drafter should specifically include the copyright interest.

If the copyright interest is to be retained by the artist's estate, the transfer of the work of art must be made to a qualified organization.[122] The term "qualified organization" means any organization described in section 501(c)(3) other than a private foundation, which is described in section 509. For that purpose, a private operating foundation under section 4942(j)(3) is not treated as a private foundation. See Appendix 16-4.

A testamentary charitable transfer by an artist is beneficial to the artist's estate. As described above, the value of the artwork is deductible in full, thereby reducing the taxable estate and, hence, the tax assessed against the estate. That disposition helps prevent a forced sale of the artist's works to raise the necessary cash to pay taxes and administrative expenses. Although a testamentary charitable transfer reduces the potential size of the allowable marital deduction (the marital deduction is now unlimited), a planned bequest to the proper museum may in the long run enhance the value of the remaining works of art for the artist's heirs.

CHARITABLE REMAINDER TRUST: TESTAMENTARY

Discussed in detail in chapter 15 on pages 1303–1306 is the use of a testamentary charitable remainder trust funded with works of art by a collector. An artist can create a charitable remainder trust under his will and can fund it with works of art so long as the will of the artist also transfers the copyright to those works of art.[123] The section 664 regulations define a charitable remainder trust as a trust with respect to which a deduction is allowable under sections 170, 2055, 2106, or 2522[124] and which meets the description of a charitable remainder annuity trust (as described in regulation 1.664-2) or a charitable remainder unitrust (as described in regulation 1.664-3). Sections 170 and 2522 are inapplicable to testamentary transfers since they involve the income tax and gift tax charitable deduction and a transfer by a living individual. Under sections 2055 and 2106, the estate tax charitable deduction is allowable for a transfer of a work of art when the donor retains the copyright only if the use of the property by the donee charitable organization is related to the purpose or function constituting the basis for its exemption under section 501.[125] Since the work of art transferred to the charitable remainder trust will be sold to raise the funds necessary to pay the unitrust distribution amount, the related-use rule will not be satisfied.[126] Therefore, in order for an estate tax charitable deduction to be allowable, the will of the artist must transfer the work of art and the copyright or the related-use rule of section 2055(e)(4) will disallow any estate tax charitable deduction.

A testamentary charitable remainder trust is deemed created at the decedent's death, even though the funding of the trust may be deferred. The funding of a testamentary charitable remainder trust can be delayed until the end of a reasonable period of time for the administration of the decedent's estate.[127] The IRS requires that the governing instrument of a testamentary charitable remainder trust grant the trustee the authority to defer the payment of the annuity or unitrust amount until the end of the trust's taxable year in which the trust is completely funded,[128] even though the obligation to pay the annuity or unitrust amount begins at the decedent's death.[129] If payment is deferred—and it will almost always be deferred in an estate administration—a correcting adjustment must be made within a reasonable period after the close of the trust's first fiscal year in which it is completely funded.[130] In the case of an underpayment, the trust must pay the excess to the annuity or unitrust recipient; in the case of an overpayment, the recipient must repay the difference to the trust.[131] Those rules give the executor of the estate ample time to sell works of art after the artist's death and then fund the charitable remainder trust.

That technique is useful for an artist who wishes to benefit a family member after the artist's death and wants to reduce the amount of the estate tax. But what if the executor of the artist's estate is unable to sell the works of art shortly after the artist's death so that the testamentary charitable remainder trust is funded with works of art created by the artist? Even if there is no restriction on the trustee's ability to sell the works of art,[132] the trustee must still make an annual payment from the trust to the noncharitable beneficiary. The regulations provide that the payment of the annuity or unitrust amount may be made in "cash or other property."[133] In the case of a distribution made in other property, the amount paid, credited, or required to be distributed is considered as an amount realized by the trust from the sale or other disposition of property.[134] The works of art then have a new basis equal to their fair market value on the artist's date of death (or six months later).[135] The basis of the property in the hands of the recipient is its fair market value at the time it was paid, credited, or required to be distributed.[136] Nothing in the regulations prevents the trustee from using a work of art to pay the required annuity or unitrust amount, but the trustee still has the problem of a yearly valuation of the works of art and all the inherent problems associated with valuing assets that by their very nature do not have a precise value. In addition, even if the trustee is not restricted in selling the collection, so that regulation 1.664-1(a)(3) is not a problem, state laws that govern investment decisions of trustees may mandate the sale of all or a large portion of non-income-producing assets, such as the works of art held in a charitable trust.[137]

A testamentary charitable remainder trust can be a useful means to reduce the estate tax on works of art created by an artist. However, it is preferable to sell the works of art during the period of administration of the estate or shortly after the charitable remainder trust is funded to avoid a potential problem in calculating the annuity or unitrust amount or any other problem that may jeopardize the charitable deduction allowable to the estate.

MARITAL BEQUEST

As an alternative, the artist can leave the works of art to his surviving spouse free of estate tax because of the unlimited marital deduction (for surviving spouses who are United States citizens). Then the surviving spouse can make a lifetime contribution of the works of art to charity. On the death of the artist, the character of the works of art is changed from ordinary income property to capital gain property, so the surviving spouse is able to obtain an income tax charitable deduction for the full fair market value of the artwork contributed, within the applicable percentage limitations.

SIZE OF BEQUEST

The drafter must also consider the size and the content of any charitable bequest. If the artist wishes to leave more than 50% of his estate to charity, there may be a problem. Local state law may require a clause with a percentage limitation or such a drafting of the will that cannot be challenged.[138]

DISCRETIONARY BEQUESTS

A basic principle of charitable tax planning is that charitable deductions are not allowable when there is any significant possibility that the transferred property will not be received by the donee charity. When a charitable bequest is made to charity, a deduction is not available if the bequest is made subject to a condition that can defeat the charitable transfer unless the occurrence of the event in question appears on the date of the gift to be so remote as to be negligible.[139] It is not unusual for an artist who wishes to bequeath a large portion of the works he created during his lifetime to a charitable foundation subject to the selection by various friends or relatives of a number of the works of art. The artist may not be able to identify which specific works of art he wants to leave to his friends or relatives and may want to give them the ability to choose works of art after the artist's death. The estate-planning problem arises if the IRS takes the position that the charitable bequest was not ascertainable on the date of the artist's death, since the friends or relatives could select many works of art and thereby defeat the charitable bequest.[140] The way to draft around that problem is to set a time limitation, requiring that the selection be made within six months of the artist's date of death. The regulations provide that the power to divert a bequest away from a charitable beneficiary will not defeat a charitable deduction, provided such power is not exercised and the power completely terminates before the due date for the decedent's federal estate tax return.[141] Providing for such a time limitation, an example of which appears at the end of this chapter as Appendix 16-2, prevents the loss of the entire charitable deduction.

NONCHARITABLE TRANSFERS

Most artists do not want to leave all their works to charitable organizations. Since the works of art often constitute the bulk of the assets in the artists' estate, they are the artists' means of providing financial security for their families.

Inter Vivos Transfers

Before January 1, 1977, a lifetime gift by an artist of his work to a noncharitable donee resulted in a saving in estate taxes, because gift tax rates were only three-fourths of estate tax rates in the corresponding bracket. For gifts on or after January 1, 1977, the same tax rate schedule covers both the gift tax and the estate tax.[142] The advantages and the disadvantages are summarized in general terms in chapter 15.

One important reason for an artist to make lifetime gifts is to remove his work from the estate at a low value and to avoid the tax on the appreciation in value over the years. If a gift is made to family members, the artist should adhere to certain formalities, such as these:

- Use a deed of gift with a signed acceptance
- File a gift tax return
- Change the physical location of the work
- Procure new insurance[143]

Following such formalities prevents questions after the artist's death about whether the property is includable in the artist's estate as a transfer with a retained life estate.[144]

ASSIGNMENT OF INCOME

The artist may want to make gifts of works of art in order to shift the income tax burden to family members in lower tax brackets.[145] The donee takes the artist's basis in the work, and any gain on its sale is ordinary income.[146] That result assumes that the artist realizes no income on the donative transfer[147] and that the income realized on the donee's subsequent sale of the work is attributed to the donee, rather than to the artist.[148] When the property is the product of the donor's personal efforts, rather than personal services rendered to another, the creator is not taxed on the income realized when the donee subsequently sells the property.[149]

Mark Tobey[150] is the most significant case bearing on the issue of whether the proceeds of sales of artwork constitute the artist's earned income. Mark Tobey, an artist, was a United States citizen living in Switzerland. During the years in question, he sold certain paintings through galleries in the United States and received the net proceeds. The issue in the case was whether the proceeds constituted foreign earned income within the meaning of section 911 and were thus eligible for the $25,000 exclusion from United States taxation.

The IRS took the view that the receipts could not be earned income since they were not receipts for Tobey's services but receipts from the sale of his paintings. The income resulted from the sale of personal property, so it was not earned income.[151] Tobey argued that the income from the sale of his paintings was compensation for personal services actually rendered.[152] The Tax Court held that since the paintings were the result of the taxpayer's personal efforts, the income derived from the sales of that property was properly categorized as "earned income." The court concluded as follows:

The concept of the artist as not "earning" his income for the purposes of section 911 would place him in an unfavorable light. For the most part, the present-day artist is a hard-working, trained, career-oriented individual. His education, whether acquired formally or through personal practice, growth and experience, is often costly and exacting. He has keen competition from many other artists who must create and sell their works to survive. To avoid discriminatory treatment, we perceive no sound reasons for treating income earned by the personal efforts, skill and creativity of a Tobey or a Picasso any differently from the income earned by a confidence man, a brain surgeon, a movie star or, for that matter, a tax attorney.[153]

The question raised by the *Tobey* case is this: If an artist makes a gift of his work to a family member, has the artist effectively shifted the income—that is, the proceeds of the sale—to the donee, or has the artist run afoul of the assignment-of-income rules?[154]

The decision in *Tobey* should not require that the artist's income be equated with personal service income for all tax purposes in which an issue may turn on the presence or the absence of property.[155] A gift of created property is unlike the assignment of the right to income from future services, in which the donor retains control, or of rights to income from past services, in which the donor's disposition of the right to receive the income is deemed to result in an economic benefit to the donor.[156] In the absence of any prearranged sale, the artist-donor does not have any definite right to income on the transfer of property that the donor created. By making the gift, the artist parts with the ability to control whether and when income from the sale of the artwork will be realized. The lack of the accrual of any "right to income" is the reason there should be no income taxation to the artist at the time of the gift and no income taxation to the artist at the time of sale by the donee. Therefore, gifts to family members are effective devices to shift income to members of the artist's family who are in lower tax brackets than the artist.

The later case of *Robert H. Cook*[157] followed *Tobey* in holding that an American sculptor living in Italy and selling noncommissioned sculptures made in Italy through his United States dealers did not have U.S.–source income. The court held that for section 911 purposes the artist is entitled to treat the sales as from his labor or personal services and sourced as earned abroad under sections 861(a)(3) and 862(a)(3) and not from the sale of personal property sourced in the United States under section 863. The amount of the foreign earned income exclusion under section 911 is $80,000 in years 2002 through 2007 and will be adjusted for inflation beginning in year 2008.

The Tax Reform Act of 1986 greatly reduced the ability of the artist-taxpayer to shift income to a minor child in a low tax bracket. For calendar year 2012, the net unearned income of a child under the age of eighteen in excess of $1,900 is subject to income tax at the parents' top marginal rate. In year 2012, the applicable standard deduction for unearned income of a child who is a dependent was the greater of $500 or $250 plus earned income, up to the maximum allowable standard deduction.[158]

Right of Termination Under the Copyright Act

The interaction of the tax law and the copyright law can produce odd results, as was shown in the discussion of section 2055(e)(4) on pages 1316-1319. In discussing inter vivos gifts by an artist, we must consider the right of termination under the copyright law and its possible effects on the gift tax and the estate tax.

The Copyright Act of 1976 created a right of termination that permits an artist to terminate any inter vivos (but not testamentary) transfer or license of a copyright or of any of the separate rights therein with respect to a work of art created on or after January 1, 1978.[159] Even if an artist transferred the copyright to a work of art, the artist can terminate the transfer and get back his copyright, so long as the right is exercised within certain narrow time periods. The right of termination is exercisable by the artist during his lifetime. After the artist's death, the right of termination is exercisable by a majority in interest of his spouse and children. The right of termination passes only by operation of law. Special timing rules govern the narrow time periods during which a right of termination may be exercised.[160]

Therefore, this tax issue arises: Can the donor-artist (the copyright owner) make a gift of a copyright, or does the right of termination make the gift incomplete for gift tax purposes? To make a completed gift, the donor must relinquish dominion and control over the property given.[161] If a gift is subject to a right of termination, the IRS may argue that the gift is incomplete—that is, that the donor-artist has not parted with complete dominion and control, even though the right of termination is conferred by statute and may never be exercisable. The better interpretation is that copyrights can be effectively transferred by gift and that the right of termination is, at best, a claim that may under certain circumstances be exercised against the transferred property. A transferred copyright may also be interpreted as a completed gift for a term of years.[162] In any event, the right of termination does not enable the artist's heirs to reclaim possession of the work of art transferred by gift. The property subject to the right of termination is the copyright interest and in most cases is of little or no value as it applies to a work of art. Although there is no authority, the right of termination should not make an otherwise validly transferred copyright includable in a deceased artist's estate under section 2038, since the right of termination was not retained by the artist but was reserved to the artist by statute. The right of termination applies only to works of art created on or after January 1, 1978.

Testamentary Transfers

An artist must provide for the disposition of his unsold works after death. The fair market value of the artwork on the date of death or six months later is included in the artist's gross estate, and the estate tax is calculated by including in the tax base the artist's taxable gifts made after December 31, 1976.[163]

A specific bequest in the will should be used to leave the artwork outright to the beneficiary. The bequest should include any copyright interest that may exist in the artwork. The item must be sufficiently identified to prevent confusion and lawsuits after the artist's death. When an artist leaves a great many works, identification often presents a problem, so identification should be as precise as possible. If the beneficiary lives in a different city from the testator, the cost of shipping must be considered. That cost is borne by the beneficiary unless a special clause in the will concerns shipping costs.

If the artist leaves artwork in trust, it is advisable to include a clause pertaining to unproductive property, especially when a credit shelter or nonmarital trust is part of the artist's estate plan. (See Appendix 16-1 at the end of this chapter.) If the trust is to qualify for the marital deduction, a provision giving the surviving spouse the power to make the trust productive of income must be included in the trust clause.

WILL-BUMPING

The interaction of the tax law and the copyright law can produce another unforeseen problem with regard to works of art created before January 1, 1978. For works of art created after January 1, 1978, the term of copyright protection is generally seventy years after the artist's death.[164] Under the old copyright law, the period of protection was unrelated to the artist's death. Instead, it was for a term of twenty-eight years, and that term could be renewed in the final year for another twenty-eight years.[165] The renewal right could be exercised by the artist or by his successors. For a work of art in its initial term when the artist died, the artist's will could dispose only of what was left of the initial term since the right to renew the copyright and, consequently, the copyright ownership during the renewal term were governed by the Copyright Act, which established priorities among family members with regard to the right to renew. Therefore, the artist may think he has disposed of the copyright in one manner under his will when, in fact, the will is "bumped" (the dispositive provision in the will becomes void) and the copyright is disposed of under the copyright law.[166] That is not a problem when the copyright is disposed of to family members in the same manner as the copyright law provides or when the copyright is of no value, but the careful estate planner must be aware of the potential problem.

For works created since the beginning of 1978 and, therefore, not subject to the renewal-term structure and for works created before 1978 that are in their renewal term when the creator dies, with one possible exception discussed below, there is no problem. Copyright ownership of the work after the creator's death is governed solely by the creator's will or by the state law of intestate succession.

For works created before 1978 that are in their *initial* twenty-eight year term when the creator dies, the creator's will or state succession law governs the disposition of copyright ownership *only* during what is left of the initial term. The right to renew the copyright and, consequently, the copyright ownership of the work during its renewal term are governed by the Copyright Act, which established priorities with regard to the right to renew.[167] If the creator dies before the time for renewal, next in priority is the class consisting of the surviving spouse and the children of the creator. That provision can wreak havoc in an estate plan if the artist wishes to dispose of his pre-1978 copyrighted property in a manner contrary to the statute. Fortunately, with one important exception noted below, the days of will-bumping have drawn to a close. The only works subject to will-bumping are those first copyrighted fewer than twenty-eight years ago but before 1978. As each year passes, fewer and fewer works are subject to the renewal term provisions. On December 31, 2005, the last day on which any copyright can conceivably be renewed, the threat of will-bumping has for the most part disappeared.[168]

The termination rights provisions are now found under sections 203 and 304(c) of the 1976 Copyright Act. Section 203 governs transfers made on or after January 1, 1978, while section 304(c) governs transfers before that date.[169] More specifically, for transfers executed on or after January 1, 1978, authors have an nonwaivable right to terminate the transfer and recover the interest during a five-year window of opportunity that begins thirty-five years from the execution of the transfer.[170] In other words, thirty-five years after a copyright assignment, an author can terminate that assignment and retake the interest. For transfers executed before January 1, 1978, authors have an nonwaivable right to terminate the transfer and recover any interest during a five-year window of opportunity that begins fifty-six years after the work was copyrighted.[171]

Termination rights attach to all assignments except those effectuated by an author's will.[172] Unlike renewal rights, termination rights are nonwaivable and nonassignable, which preserves the concept of will-bumping unless the copyright assignment was effectuated by an author's will.[173] The question remains whether a will substitute, like a revocable trust, created by the artist during his lifetime and to which he transferred the copyright to works he created, escapes any claim of termination after the artist's death because the copyright was disposed of by the trust and not by "the will." It appears from the legislative history that Congress was attempting to eliminate the concept of will-bumping and that a court could interpret the term "the will" to include a revocable trust.

SELLING EXPENSES

The deductibility of selling expenses is discussed in detail in chapter 15. If the artist's will directs the sale of his works, the gallery commissions and other selling expenses are allowable as estate tax deductions.[174] The rules governing the deduction of selling expenses from the artist's estate are the same as those with respect to the collector's estate and are discussed in detail in chapter 15 on pages 1331-1339.

POSTMORTEM SALES—BASIS ADJUSTMENT

Under current law, when an artist dies, his works of art receive a stepped-up basis equal to the fair market value at the date of death, for income tax purposes for sales after his death.[175] As a practical matter, the six-month alternative valuation is the same as the valuation on the date of death. The full amount of the predeath appreciation is not subject to income tax. Equally important, the character of the works of art for income tax purposes changes from ordinary income property to capital gain property, and any postmortem appreciation realized on sales by the estate or the heirs is treated as capital gain.[176] That treatment assumes that the artist's estate is not deemed to be in the trade or business of selling paintings. Ordinarily, if the executor merely conducts an orderly administration of the artist's estate in collecting and protecting assets and maximizing their value, even over a long period of time, the executor is not deemed to be carrying on a trade or business.

One of the most important tax consequences of death is that property included in a decedent's gross estate for federal estate tax purposes, subject to certain exceptions, acquires a "step-up" in basis for income tax purposes, pursuant to section 1014, equal to its federal estate tax value. In other words, if a collector purchased a painting for $10,000 and when he dies the painting is valued at $100,000 for federal estate tax purposes, for income tax purposes the painting acquires a step-up in basis equal to $100,000. The Economic Growth and Tax Relief Reconciliation Act of 2001[177] terminated this step-up in basis for property included in a decedent's estate for those persons dying in calendar year 2010, which is the one year when the federal estate tax was repealed. For decedents dying in 2010, a new modified carryover basis system will apply under new section 1022. Under the new system, the basis for certain property treated as transferred on the death of a property owner after 2009 will equal the lower of the asset's fair market value at the decedent's death or the decedent's adjusted basis in the asset. In other words, the basis for income tax purposes may remain at the original cost of the property purchased. There are a number of adjustments that allow some step-up in basis. For example, the executor may increase the basis of carryover basis property in the aggregate by up to $1.3 million. That is, the amount of $1.3 million may be added to the decedent's cost basis prior to his death. A full discussion of this new provision is beyond the scope of this chapter.[178] As with all other provisions of the 2001 Act, the modified carryover basis system expired on December 31, 2010, and the existing rule for step-up in basis under section 1014 has been reinstated. Therefore, unless there are additional Congressional changes to the Internal Revenue Code, the modified carryover basis rules will only apply to decedents dying in calendar year 2010. Although carryover basis no longer applies, it is impossible to predict what Congress may do in the future. The lesson is clear: Complete and detailed records as to the date of acquisition and the cost of acquisition of collectibles will be important if the carryover basis rules are ever in effect in any form. At the present time, there is no exception in new section 1022 for the creative person so that his heirs can realize capital gains on sales after the death of the artist. Under the new provision, for artists who died in calendar year 2010, all gains from sales by the artist's heirs will be ordinary income.

The distinction between ordinary income (including short-term capital gain) and long-term capital gain for tax rate purposes is that ordinary income is taxed as high as 35% and long-term capital gain on collectibles is taxed at a maximum of 28%. The Taxpayer Relief Act of 1997 reduced the long-term capital gain rate to 20% on the sale of securities, real estate, and other capital assets (other than collectibles) held more than eighteen months (changed to "more than twelve months" by the IRS Restructuring and Reform Act of 1998), but maintained the 28% rate on gain from the sale of collectibles held for more than one year. The Jobs and Growth Tax Relief Reconciliation Act of 2003 (effective May 6, 2003) further reduced the long-term capital gain rate to 15% for sales of securities and other capital assets held for more than twelve months but once again maintained the 28% rate on gain from the sale of collectibles held for more than one year. The term "collectibles gain" is defined in section 1(h)(5)(A) to mean:

> gain from the sale or exchange of a collectible (as defined in section 408(m) without regard to paragraph (3) thereof) which is a capital asset held for more than 1 year but only to the extent such gain is taken into account in computing gross income.

The heirs of the artist will generally inherit works of art that are characterized as "collectibles" for income tax purposes. Section 1(h)(5)(B) (added by the Tax-payer Relief Act of 1997) is designed to prevent taxpayers from converting the 28% rate to the 15% rate by creating a partnership, corporation, or trust under rules similar to the rules of section 751. Since the maximum ordinary income tax rate is currently 35%, there is now a smaller difference between ordinary income treatment and capital gains treatment on the sale of collectibles. However, if the long-term capital gain rate for collectibles ever receives parity with other capital assets, the difference will be significant.

The *Tobey* case, discussed on pages 1436-1437, held that an artist's income from the sale of his work was earned income for the purpose of the foreign income exclusion under section 911. That finding can cause problems if it is extended beyond its application to section 911. Income earned before death is characterized as "income in respect of a decedent" (as that term is defined in section 691) when it is received.[179] Therefore, the IRS may argue that under the *Tobey* rationale the proceeds of sales of the artist's work after death constitute income in respect of a decedent,[180] that there is no step-up in basis on the artist's death,[181] and that the sales proceeds are ordinary income.[182] Obviously, that result would not be nearly so favorable to the taxpayer as a step-up in basis and capital gain treatment.

Notwithstanding *Tobey*, postmortem sales should not be treated as income in respect of a decedent.[183] The proper test of whether an item is income in respect of a decedent is whether the decedent had a right to the proceeds at the time of death.[184] The courts have rejected the IRS economic activities test. Under that theory, postmortem income derived from a disposition of a creative person's works and copyrights was treated as income in respect of a decedent on the premise that such income was earned by the deceased artist during his lifetime and is tantamount to deferred compensation. The preferred test is this: If further negotiations or activities are necessary to realize the proceeds on sale, the postmortem proceeds are not income in respect of a decedent.[185]

Generally, four elements must be present for an item to be income in respect of a decedent:[186]

1. The decedent must have entered into a legally significant arrangement for the disposition of the property to elevate the legal right beyond a mere expectancy.
2. The decedent must have performed the substantive acts required as conditions to the sale, so that the property was in a deliverable state at the date of the decedent's death.
3. There must be no economically material contingencies in existence at the date of the decedent's death that may disrupt the sale.
4. The decedent would have eventually received the proceeds if he had lived.

Private Letter Ruling 90-43-068 now sheds some additional light on the issue. The Private Letter Ruling deals with the following facts: *B* was an artist who died and left a valid will. At death, *B* owned a number of paintings that he had created. Pursuant to *B*'s last will and testament, his paintings were left to his son, *A*. The will contained no instructions concerning the disposition of the paintings and no restrictions on *A*'s use of the paintings. None of the paintings left to *A* was subject to an agreement of sale or negotiations for sale at the time of *B*'s death. After *A* inherited the paintings, none of them was sold, and *A* has been holding them for his personal use. Citing the appropriate regulations under section 691, the ruling held that, on the basis of the information submitted, any income from the disposal of the paintings received by A pursuant to the will is not income in respect of the decedent under section 691(a)(1). Consequently, the character of any income in *A*'s hands from the disposition of the paintings is not governed by section 691(a)(3).

Although the ruling is limited to the specific individual who requested it, it does lend support to the conclusion reached on page 1442 that postmortem sales in an artist's estate are not treated as income in respect of a decedent.[187] Therefore, under current law the postmortem sales in an artist's estate are not treated as income in respect of a decedent.

As discussed earlier in this chapter, the result in Private Letter Ruling 90-43-068 would be different under the carryover basis rules that applied only for calendar year 2010. Under new section 1022, the basis of all "carryover basis property" that passes from a decedent is (with certain exceptions) to be determined by reference to the basis of the property in the hands of the decedent.[188] Section 1221(a)(3)(C) states that the term "capital asset" does not include property held by a taxpayer "in whose hands the basis of such property is determined, for purposes of determining gain from a sale or exchange, in whole or in part by reference to the basis of such property in the hands" of the taxpayer whose personal efforts created the property. Therefore, under the calendar year 2010 carryover basis rules, the creator could not leave artworks under a will to an individual who could realize capital gains on their sale, since the property could not qualify as a capital asset. If those provisions ever come back into effect under the Internal Revenue Code, the will drafter must check their impact on an artist's estate.

Paying the Estate Tax

Tax Deferral

The federal estate tax is due nine months after the artist's death.[189] If the assets in the artist's estate consist of valuable works of art, sufficient funds may not be available to pay the estate tax.

The executor of the artist's estate may elect to pay the estate tax in installments. Under section 6166, the estate tax may be paid in installments over a fourteen-year period, with the first four annual payments consisting of interest only. For the estate to be eligible for installment payments, the artist must have been actively engaged in the trade or business of being an artist and producing the works of art that are a part of the estate. The section 6166 election gives the estate time to gradually liquidate the works of art constituting the closely held business in order to pay the estate tax in installments over a fourteen-year period.

Although the term "trade or business" is not specifically defined, the United States Supreme Court in *Commissioner v. Groetzinger*[190] does offer some help. In *Groetzinger* the Court stated that in order to be engaged in a trade or business, the taxpayer must be involved in the activity with continuity and regularity, and the taxpayer's primary purpose for engaging in the activity must be for income or profit. A sporadic activity, a hobby, or an amusement diversion does not qualify. The Court reaffirmed the facts-and-circumstances test and thereby rejected the test that a trade or business involves holding oneself out to others as being engaged in the selling of goods and services. The Court stated that a judicial attempt to formulate and impose a test for all situations would be counterproductive, unhelpful, and even precarious for the overall integrity of the Internal Revenue Code.

To be eligible for installment payments, the artist's estate must consist of works of art created by the artist (the closely held business) whose value exceeds 35% of the artist's adjusted gross estate (the gross estate less all deductions other than marital and charitable deductions).[191] An interest in a business for section 6166 purposes includes an interest as a sole proprietor, an interest in a partnership, or shares in a corporation.[192]

If the estate of an artist dying after 1997 qualifies, interest is imposed at 2% on the estate tax attributable to the first $1 million (as indexed for inflation) in taxable value of the closely held business (that is, the first $1 million in value in excess of the section 2010(c) applicable exclusion provided by the unified credit and any other exclusions).[193] The interest rate imposed on the amount of deferred estate tax attributable to taxable value of the closely held business in excess of the indexed $1 million amount is payable at 45% of the section 6621 underpayment rate.[194] The interest paid on the deferred estate tax may not be deducted for either estate or income tax purposes.[195]

If more than 50% of the works of art attributable to the closely held business is distributed, sold, or otherwise disposed of, the extension of time to pay ceases and payment of the unpaid tax is accelerated upon notice and demand of the IRS.[196]

If deferral is not possible under section 6166, the IRS may, for reasonable cause under section 6161(a)(2), extend the time for payment of the estate tax for a reasonable period not in excess of ten years. Under this section, the IRS, in the case of inability to liquidate estate assets without a forced sale, often grants renewable extensions of one year. It is within the sole discretion of the IRS to grant an extension on the basis of reasonable cause, which may include the following:

1. Insufficient liquid assets to pay the tax
2. Substantial estate assets consisting of rights to receive payments in the future
3. Assets subject to litigation claims
4. Insufficient funds to pay family allowances and creditors' claims[197]

Example 2 of regulation section 20.6161-1(a)(1) states that reasonable cause for an extension exists if a substantial part of an estate's assets consists of rights to receive money in the future, such as annuities, copyright royalties, accounts receivable, etc., the estate's assets provide insufficient present cash with which to pay the estate tax, and the estate cannot borrow against these assets except on "terms that would inflict loss upon the estate." This example should provide ample grounds for an extension in the estate of an artist.

Example 3 of regulation section 20.6161-1(a)(1) additionally offers the illustration of assets tied up in litigation—a situation not unknown in the estates of successful artists.

QUALIFIED FAMILY-OWNED BUSINESS INTERESTS
The Taxpayer Relief Act of 1997 added new section 2033A to the Code providing for a special estate tax exclusion for a qualified family-owned business for decedents dying after December 31, 1997. However, section 2033A never became effective since it was replaced by section 2057.[198] Section 2057 provides an estate tax deduction for "qualified family-owned business interests." However, section 2057 will also not apply to decedents dying after 2003. The section 2057 deduction was drafted so that it was coordinated with the unified credit to correct inequities in the estate tax calculations that would develop as the unified credit increased. Under section 2057(a), the estate tax liability is calculated as if the estate were allowed a maximum qualified family-owned business interest deduction of $675,000 and an applicable exclusion under section 2010 of $625,000 (the applicable exclusion amount in 1998), regardless of the year of the decedent's death. The Economic Growth and Tax Relief Reconciliation Act of 2001[199] repealed section 2057 for estates of decedents dying after 2003 because, beginning in 2004, the section 2010 applicable exclusion amount will exceed the combined $1.3 million offset allowed by sections 2010 and 2057, thereby eliminating the

need for section 2057.[200] Even if section 2057 becomes applicable again in future years, it may not be beneficial to the heirs of a deceased artist. As previously discussed, if the heirs want to take the position that the character of the inherited works of art has changed from ordinary income property to capital gain property, it may not be possible to qualify under the provisions of section 2057 as a continuation of a family-owned business.

State Estate Tax

In addition to the federal estate tax, most states have some form of estate or inheritance tax. Two states have special provisions that should be noted. New Mexico allows the acceptance of works of art for display from the estates of artists in payment of death taxes.[201] In Connecticut, the commissioner of revenue services may grant an extension of up to five years for payment of the succession tax (with interest from six months after death) in the estate of an artist whose works constitute more than 50% of the estimated value of the net taxable estate where the actual market value of the works may not be ascertainable so as to allow the sale of the works necessary for payment of the taxes.[202]

FIDUCIARY RESPONSIBILITY

No discussion of an artist's estate is complete without mentioning *In re Rothko*.[203] Mark Rothko, an abstract expressionist painter, died on February 25, 1970. His will was admitted to probate on April 27, 1970, and letters testamentary were issued to his executors. On May 21, 1970, less than one month after their appointment, the executors signed contracts selling 798 works of art by Rothko to corporations controlled by one of the executors.

The executors of Rothko's estate were Bernard J. Reis, an officer and owner of Marlborough Gallery and Rothko's dealer; Theodoros Stamos, a friend and struggling artist; and Morton Levine, a friend and professor of anthropology at Fordham University. Reis also drafted Rothko's will, even though he was not licensed to practice law in New York. The case, because of Rothko's fame and the enormous dollar amounts involved, received a great deal of publicity but did no more than reaffirm existing New York law.

An executor must not be involved in self-dealing of any kind or nature, must avoid all conflicts of interest, and must not violate the duty of loyalty to the estate.[204] An executor must use the same diligence and prudence in the care and management of the estate assets and affairs as would prudent persons of discretion and intelligence, accented by "not honesty alone, but the punctilio of an honor the most sensitive."[205] Alleged good faith on the part of a fiduciary who is forgetful of his duty is not enough.

Reis and Stamos each had an obvious conflict of interest; Reis was selling to his Gallery and Stamos was offered a show of his work and representation by Marlborough Gallery. Both were fined and removed as executors. Levine had no conflict of interest, had objected orally to the proposed sales to the corporations controlled by Reis, and had sought independent legal counsel. That was not enough; in fining Levine more than $6 million and removing him as an executor, the court stated the following:

> [H]e could not close his eyes, remain passive or move with unconcern in the face of the obvious loss to be visited upon the estate by participation in those business arrangements and then shelter himself behind the claimed counsel of an attorney.[206]

Clearly, the selection of an executor of an artist's estate should be done with care and in such a manner as to avoid the problems that arose in the *Rothko* case. The *Rothko* decision should be read and reread each year by every attorney who represents artists.

INCOME TAXES
Deduction for Expenses of Creating Art

An artist completes schedule C of Form 1040, the federal income tax return, to report income from sales and to deduct the ordinary and necessary expenses of creating works of art. The Tax Reform Act of 1986 attempted to change the manner in which an artist claims deductions for expenses. Section 263A, which became effective January 1, 1987, provided uniform capitalization rules to govern the treatment of costs incurred in the production of property for resale. The section was enacted to prevent the inappropriate mismatching of income and expenses that results from allowing the current deduction of the costs of producing the property. Section 263A vastly complicated the record-keeping burden for artists by requiring them to capitalize expenses and allocate the expenses among the various works of art.

Partial relief from those rules was granted by Internal Revenue News Release IR-88-81 of May 13, 1988, which created a simplified method for deducting the business expenses of artists. Under the new method the artist can generally deduct 50% of his business expenses in the year in which they were incurred and 25% in each of the two succeeding years.

Further relief was granted by the Technical and Miscellaneous Revenue Act of 1988. That Act added new section 263A(h), which provides that the uniform capitalization rules of section 263A do not apply to any otherwise deductible expense (a "qualified creative expense") paid by an individual engaged in the business of being an artist. Section 263A(h) emphasizes the personal efforts of the creative individual. The legislative history explains:

> It is inequitable to apply the uniform capitalization rules to authors, photographers, and artists, while other taxpayers performing personal services are not subject to the same rules. For example, attorneys and consultants may produce a written product over a period of years and receive payment after the product is completed. The uniform capitalization rules do not apply to the costs of producing such written

product. In addition, the application of the uniform capitalization rules to authors, photographers, and artists is unduly burdensome for those authors, photographers, and artists who do not elect the simplified method provided by the Internal Revenue Service. The otherwise deductible expenses of these authors, photographers, and artists must be allocated among each project and generally are deductible over the period that income is estimated to be derived from the project.[207]

A "qualified creative expense" is defined as an expense incurred by an individual in the trade or business (other than as an employee) of being a "writer," "photographer," or "artist," which, except for the section 263A uniform capitalization rules, would be deductible for the taxable year. Section 263A(h)(2) provides that a qualified creative expense does not include "any expense related to printing, photographic plates, motion picture films, video tapes, or similar items."

An artist is defined as any individual whose personal efforts create or may reasonably be expected to create a picture, painting, sculpture, statue, etching, drawing, cartoon, graphic design, or original print edition.[208] Expenses paid or incurred by a personal service corporation that directly relate to the activities of a qualified employee-owner may also qualify for the exemption to the extent that the expenses would qualify if paid or incurred directly by the employee-owner (the artist).

In determining whether an expense is paid or incurred in the business of being an artist, the originality and the uniqueness of the item created (or to be created) and the predominance of the aesthetic value over the utilitarian value of the item created are to be taken into account. The House committee report gives this as an example: Any expense paid or incurred in producing jewelry, silverware, pottery, furniture, and similar household items is generally not considered as being paid or incurred in the business of being an artist.

Stella Waitzkin

The case of *Stella Waitzkin v. Commissioner*[209] illustrates the problems an artist can have with the Internal Revenue Service on his income tax return. First, the IRS questioned whether or not the taxpayer, Stella Waitzkin, was a legitimate artist engaged in artistic activities with the objective of making a profit. The IRS argued, that since Waitzkin had not made a profit from her artistic activities, her deductions relating to those activities must be disallowed.[210] In considering all the facts and circumstances, the court found that Waitzkin was engaged in her painting activities with the requisite profit motive. The court stated the following:

> The test to determine whether an activity is engaged in for profit is whether the individual is engaged in the activity with "the actual and honest objective of making a profit." *Dreicer v. Commissioner*, 78 T.C. 642 (1982). Although petitioner's expectation of profit need not be reasonable, she must continue the activity with the objective of making a profit.[211]

The court noted that throughout Waitzkin's career she improved her skills, devoted most of her time to producing artwork, obtained fellowships that were for artists, did not lead a lavish life style, promoted her work, had her work shown by art dealers, consistently sold art for a number of years, and had her art exhibited in numerous showings and exhibitions. Those factors point to a profit objective for an artist.[212]

The IRS next challenged various artist business expenses claimed by Waitzkin on schedule C of her 1984 income tax return. The court allowed as ordinary and necessary business expenses the deductions taken for insurance, materials, services, advertising, and rent paid on two rooms used solely as storage for her artwork.[213] She was not able to take investment credits for or deduct the costs of her computer, furniture, or humidifier, because she did not establish that they had any business use.

Business Use of Residence

Waitzkin had also claimed a deduction for part of the rent she paid on her studio-apartment. The court noted that section 280A strictly limits the deduction of expenses associated with an office in the home. The section provides that, as a general rule, no deduction for an office or work space shall be allowed if the taxpayer uses that space as a residence during the taxable year. An exception to the general rule of nondeductibility permits a deduction for the expenses of a home office if a portion of the residence is used exclusively and on a regular basis for the taxpayer's business.[214] On the basis of the facts in the case, the court found that Waitzkin had used 50% of her studio apartment exclusively and on a regular basis for her business and allowed a deduction for 50% of her rent.

The studio-apartment deduction allowed in *Waitzkin* that applied to her 1984 calendar year tax return would not have been allowed under current law because of a new deduction-limitation rule. The Internal Revenue Code strictly limits the deduction of expenses in connection with the business use of a personal residence.[215] For an artist to claim a deduction for a portion of the expenses of a studio-residence, he must prove that the studio (the business-use portion) is used

(1) exclusively
(2) on a regular basis
(3) as the principal place of business for the artist.[216]

In addition, effective January 1, 1987, the available deduction is limited to the excess of (1) the gross income from the use of the dwelling unit over (2) the deductions allocable to the unit that are allowable without regard to business use.[217] The effect of that limitation is to keep the artist from deducting a loss attributable to the business use of his studio-residence. Excess deductions may be taken into account in the succeeding year when computing the deduction for the allocable business use of the studio-residence for that tax year.[218] The amount carried forward to a succeeding tax year is allowable only up to the amount of income generated from the business in which it arose, whether or not the studio is used as a residence during that year.

The exclusive-use requirement is generally what causes the biggest problem for an artist who is claiming a deduction for expenses attributable to using part of his studio-residence for business. To meet the exclusive-use test, the portion of the residence used for business must be used solely for the purpose of carrying on a trade or business. The test is not satisfied when there is a mixed use of the portion in question. For example, the artist and members of his family should not watch television in, have parties in, or make use of the studio for any personal activities. The regulations[219] strictly interpret the exclusive-use rule. They state that the exclusive-use rule is met only if there is no use of the business portion of the residence at any time during the tax year other than for business purposes. Anything beyond a de minimis personal use violates the exclusive-use rule.

Should Artists Incorporate?

At one time, it was advantageous for an artist to incorporate. Before 1986, much larger retirement-plan deductions were available to employees of a corporation than to a self-employed individual. Because of changes in the Internal Revenue Code, the use of a corporate structure by an artist for the sole purpose of getting the benefits of a corporate retirement plan is unnecessary since parity has now been achieved between corporate-employee benefit plans and those for self-employed individuals.

An artist may have other sound reasons for not doing business in corporate form. As a corporation, the artist would have to maintain numerous corporate formalities, beginning with an employment contract between the corporation and the artist, keeping regular corporate minutes, providing for only reasonable compensation, and keeping various corporate books and records and tax returns. Artists are not generally known for meticulous record keeping, and long-term compliance with burdensome corporate formalities may prove to be unrealistic, with the result that the corporate entity would be ignored.

More important, with the amendment of section 336[220] and the repeal of the *General Utilities* doctrine,[221] the holding of works of art by an artist in a corporation and then liquidating the corporation after the artist's death can turn into a tax disaster for the artist's estate. Under the provisions of section 336, if the works of art are in the corporation and the corporation is liquidated in order to distribute the works to the artist's heirs, an income tax becomes payable by the corporation as a result of the distribution in liquidation.[222] If the works of art are sold by the corporation, an income tax is payable by the corporation. However, if there is no corporation and the artist owns the works of art in his name at death, the works of art receive a step-up in basis equal to their value for federal estate tax purposes. In that case no income tax is payable on the sale of the works of art after the artist's death unless they are sold for more than the estate tax value.

An even worse tax mishap was seen in *Estate of Louise Nevelson*.[223] Approximately six years before the death of the artist Louise Nevelson, her son created a corporation. All the shares of the corporation were owned by her son. The corporation then hired Louise Nevelson to create art, paying her approximately $40,000 a year plus some expenses, an amount far below the value of the works of art she created. When Louise Nevelson died, her executor (her son) took the position that none of the works of art were taxable in her estate, since she did not own any shares of the corporation that owned all the works of art. The matter was settled before trial; according to the settlement, the works of art created by Louise Nevelson that were unsold on the date of her death were not transferred by her to her son's corporation during her lifetime and were, therefore, includable in her gross estate.[224] That type of tax planning should be avoided.

MISCELLANEOUS ISSUES

Merchandising Rights

Artists who become well known to the public should be aware of the cluster of prerogatives known as merchandising rights. Generally, they include the right to authorize the use of the name, the likeness, or some other attribute of an artist or artistic work on or in connection with the products of another party.[225] The creator of a work of pop art, for example, may not be averse to licensing the right to reproduce his work on tote bags or coffee mugs and to receive royalties from their sale. The contract that gives merchandising rights to another party—that is, the licensee—should include, among other provisions, the grant, ownership, consideration, term, territory, quality control, indemnity, accounting, and copyright.

Grant

The artist would grant the licensee the exclusive rights to produce and distribute specified attributes of the artist or an artistic work on or in connection with the specified goods. The grant should include a reservation of all other rights to the artist. The goods in connection with the license should be as narrowly described as possible to permit the artist to license many different parties to manufacture and sell many different kinds of goods. For example, an artist may wish to license one party to reproduce and sell an artistic work on a poster and another party to reproduce and sell the same artistic work on paper plates. Therefore, neither license should be for "paper goods"; instead, each license should be for the specific category or categories of goods involved.

Ownership

The artist is the sole and exclusive owner of all merchandising rights in the artistic work, subject only to the specific rights granted to the licensee, and all permitted uses of the artistic work must inure to the benefit of the artist.

CONSIDERATION

The artist should be paid a percentage of all funds received by the licensee that arise from that party's exercise of any rights granted under the contract. Often, an up-front payment is made to the artist on the signing of the license agreement.

TERM

The duration of the license agreement should be specified. The licensee should generally be permitted a nonexclusive right to sell off inventory for a specific period of time, often six months.

TERRITORY

The territory covered by the grant of rights should be specified.

QUALITY CONTROL

A sample of each category of licensed goods and a sample of each item of packaging, advertising, and promotional material related to the goods should be submitted to the artist for written approval before distribution. The artist should not unreasonably withhold approval, but no item disapproved by the artist should be distributed.

INDEMNITY

The licensee should indemnify the artist and hold him harmless for any loss or liability incurred by the artist because of any defect or violation of third-party rights related to the licensed goods or any of the packaging, advertising, or promotional material related to the goods when the artist's work is used in connection with the merchandising agreement.

ACCOUNTING

The licensee should give the artist the right to review the licensee's books and records and should furnish quarterly financial reports to the artist.

COPYRIGHT

The agreement should clearly state that the artist owns the copyright and that the licensee acquires no rights through the use of the artwork.

Definition of Artist As It Applies to Real Estate

A few states, such as New York, have passed special legislation addressing the living and working space of artists. The laws give exceptions to zoning laws or special provisions for artists.

The question of who qualifies as an artist under such statutes has posed problems. A New York City ordinance defines "artist" to mean a person who is regularly engaged in the fine arts, such as painting and sculpture, or in the performing and creative arts, including choreography and filmmaking, or in the composition of music on a professional basis and who is certified by the New York City Department of Cultural Affairs or the New York State Council on the Arts or both.[226] Whether someone can be so certified raises complex questions that can easily lead to litigation.

Photography

The photograph as a work of art is increasingly important, and prices for old photographs have risen dramatically in recent years. The photographer as an artist has a number of problems. Most important, he must convince the buyer that the photograph is a unique, original work that exists in no other copy or in no more than a given number of copies. Obviously, an unlimited number of duplicates could be produced from a photographic negative, each of which would then be an original, lessening the value of the first copy.

One solution is to have the artist sign the back of the first photograph, indicating the number of copies made and warranting that no further copies will be made and perhaps indicating that the negative will be destroyed.

Computer technology has caused new problems for the photographer. Photographs can now be changed by deleting parts of the image, adding new parts, or simply moving the image around. Questions as to what is the original, who owns the copyright, and whether a new work of art is being created are new potential problems for the photographer.

Video Art

With the advent of digital cameras and the ability to make and modify digital images with extensive special effects, more artists have been experimenting with digital images as art. The artist who creates a work of art on a computer has unlimited access to images of all sorts. As readily as a digital or video work of art can be created, it can also be copied. The artist who creates a work of art on videotape may use multiple tapes or may create the tape in conjunction with other art forms. The video artist wants to make sure that when his work of art is exhibited, it is shown in the manner in which it was created. The most difficult problem for the video artist is the ease of video reproduction, which means that copyright protection for the video artist is most important. The artist selling a video artwork should use an agreement that protects the copyright; if the artist sells the video artwork through a gallery, the gallery should be required to protect the artist's copyright. The copyright can be protected by a written agreement requiring anyone who purchases or rents a video artwork not to make further copies, reproduce it in any manner, or show it in any manner not consistent with the manner in which it was created.[227]

Artistic Materials

Questions can arise concerning the durability of a work of art over a period of time. In other words, does an artist or his gallery make an implied warranty of fitness to a buyer with respect to the quality or the durability of the materials used in the work of art? A collector who purchases an expensive work would not be happy if it began to fade or fall apart after a period of time and might seek redress against the artist or the gallery or both. Although there may be an implied warranty of fitness for a particular purpose in an art transaction, the existence of the warranty is basically a question of fact to be determined by the circumstances of the contracting parties.[228]

Sales Tax

The discussion pertaining to sales tax as it applies to an art dealer in chapter 14 at page 1193 applies equally to the artist who sells directly to a collector a work of art he created. Any such in-state sale would constitute a retail sale of tangible personal property subject to the sales tax.[229]

However, when an artist purchases art materials (paints, canvas, varnishes, etc.) that are incorporated as physical components of the finished work of art that will be resold, the purchases of those art materials are not retail sales and the artist should not pay sales tax on them.[230] In New York, in order to avoid paying the sales tax on the purchase of the art materials, the artist must furnish the seller with a resale certificate confirming that the purchased art materials will be incorporated into a work of art to be sold.

If the artist grants a right to reproduce an original painting, illustration, photograph, sculpture, or similar work and the payment made for such right is in the nature of a royalty, then such payment is not subject to the sales tax since it is not a "license to use" or a retail sale.[231] Mere temporary possession or custody for the purposes of making the reproduction is not considered a transfer of possession that would convert the reproduction right into a "license to use."[232] However, where some use other than reproduction is made of the original work (such as retouching or exhibiting a photograph), the transaction is deemed to be a "license to use" and is, therefore, taxable.[233]

NOTES TO CHAPTER 16

1.   Treas. Reg. §§ 20.2031-1(b); 20.2031-6.
2.   Treas. Reg. §§ 25.2512-1; 1.170A-1(c)(2).
3.   Treas. Reg. § 20.2031-1(b).
4.   I.R.C. § 2031(a).
5.   I.R.C. § 2032(a).
6.   *See* Sloane, *Valuing Artists' Estates: What is Fair?*, Artnews, Apr. 1976, *reprinted in* 2 ART &
     L. No. 5 (Summer 1976); Echter, *Equitable Treatment for the Artist's Estate*, 114 TR. & EST.
     394 (1975); Cutrow, *Estate Planning for the Artist, in* ART LAW 413 (R. Lerner ed. PLI 1988);
     Cutrow, *Estate Planning for the Artist, in* THE LAW AND BUSINESS OF ART 311 (R. Lerner,
     ed. PLI 1990); Hoot, ed., *Estate Planning For Artists: Will Your Art Survive? A Symposium
     Sponsored by Volunteer Lawyers for the Arts*, 21 Colum. VLJ J.L. & ARTS 15 (1996); Craw-
     ford & Sare, 815-2nd BNA T.M. Portfolio, *Estate Planning for Authors and Artists*; Ralph Le-
     rner, *Valuing Works of Art for Tax Purposes*, 28 REAL PROP. PROB. & TR. J., No. 3, 593 (1993).
7.   Rev. Proc. 66-49, 1966-2 C.B. 1257.
8.   *Compare* Maudlin v. Comm'r, 60 T.C. 749 (1973), *with* Rebay v. Comm'r, 22 T.C.M. (CCH)
     181 (1963).
9.   Treas. Reg. § 20.2031-1(b).
10. Treas. Reg. § 20.2031-2(e).
11. Robinson v. Comm'r, 82 T.C. 467, 468–69 (1984); *see also* Maytag v. Comm'r, 187 F.2d 962
     (10th Cir. 1951) (noting that the effect of placing a block of securities on the market is one
     factor to take into account for valuation).
12. Valuation Guide for Income, Estate and Gift Taxes, Fed. Est. & Gift Tax Rep. (CCH) No. 115 at
     30 (Oct. 14, 1985). *See also* I.R.S. Valuation Guide for Income, Estate and Gift Taxes, Std. Fed.
     Tax Rep. (CCH) No. 4 (Jan. 28, 1994).
13. Estate of David Smith v. Comm'r, 57 T.C. 650 (1972), *aff'd*, 510 F.2d 479 (2d Cir.), *cert. denied*,
     523 U.S. 827 (1975). *See* further discussion of *Smith* in chapter 15 at page 1332.
14. *Id.* at 655; Hoffman, *Artists May Have Unexpectedly Large Estates*, CPA J., June, 1972.
15. *Estate of Smith*, 57 T.C. at 658 (citations omitted).
16. *Id.* at 657.
17. *Id.* at 656–57.
18. *Id.* at 658 (citations omitted).
19. Estate of Smith v. Comm'r, 510 F.2d 479, 480 (2d Cir.), *cert. denied*, 423 U.S. 827 (1975).
20. *See* Estate of Smith v. Comm'r, 57 T.C. 650, 656 (1972) (stating that determination of fair
     market value of the works of art at the time of the artist's death is a question of fact) (citing
     McGuire v. Comm'r, 44 T.C. 801, 812 (1965), *aff'd*, 510 F.2d 479 (2d Cir.), *cert. denied*, 423 U.S.
     827(1975)).
21. *See* McGuire v. Comm'r, 44 T.C. at 812 (stating that fair market value must be determined on
     the facts of each case).
22. *See* Estate of Smith, 57 T.C. at 659.
23. *Id.*; Treas. Reg. § 20.2031-1(b).
24. *See* Estate of Smith, 57 T.C. at 658.
25. *See* Echter, *Equitable Treatment for the Artist's Estate*, 114 TR. & EST. 394 (1975).
26. *See* Estate of Smith, 57 T.C. at 659; Publicker v. Comm'r, 206 F.2d 250 (3d Cir. 1953); Gould
     Est. v. Comm'r, 14 T.C. 414 (1950).
27. Treas. Reg. § 20.2053-3(d)(2). *See* discussion and cases in chapter 15 at pages 1331–1338.
28. Calder v. Comm'r, 85 T.C. 713 (1985).
29. *See* Treas. Reg. § 25.2512-2(e); Rushton v. Comm'r, 60 T.C. 272 (1973), *aff'd*, 498 F.2d 83
     (1974); *see Calder*, 85 T.C. 713.
30. The IRS attempted to guess how many works from each of the six gifts would be sold each
     year and multiplied the annual estimated sales by each of the six persons by the agreed-on

value of each work. The IRS then applied a present-value factor and treated the sale as if it were an annuity.

31. Estate of Georgia T. O'Keeffe v. Comm'r, 63 T.C.M. (CCH) 2699 (1992).

32. *Id.* at 2703.

33. *Id.* at 2704. *See* Joann Lewis, *O'Keeffe Heirs Tackle the Art of Tax Litigation*, WASH. POST, Dec. 1, 1991, at G1.

34. *See O'Keeffe*, 63 T.C.M. at 2707.

35. *Id.*

36. *See supra* note 12.

37. *See O'Keeffe*, 63 T.C.M. at 2703. *See* Estate of Bright v. United States, 658 F.2d 999 (5th Cir. 1981); Propstra v. United States, 680 F.2d 1248 (9th Cir. 1982); Minahan v. Comm'r, 88 T.C. 492 (1987).

38. *O'Keeffe*, 63 T.C.M. at 2706 (citation omitted).

39. I.R.S. Valuation Guide for Income, Estate and Gift Taxes, Fed. Est. & Gift Tax Rep. (CCH) No. 115, at 9 (Oct. 14, 1985); Treas. Reg. § 20.2031-1(b).

40. *O'Keeffe*, 63 T.C.M. at 2703.

41. *See id.* at 2706. *See* Covey, *Estate, Gift and Income Taxation— 1992 Developments*, U. MIAMI 27th INST. ON EST. PLAN. ¶ 114.4A (1993).

42. *See Estate of Smith*, 57 T.C. at 659.

43. *See Estate of Bright*, 658 F.2d 999; Estate of Joslyn v. Comm'r, 500 F.2d 382 (9th Cir. 1974), *rev'g* 57 T.C. 722 (1972), *on remand*, 63 T.C. 478 (1975), *rev'd*, 566 F.2d 677 (9th Cir. 1977); Estate of Jenner v. Comm'r, 577 F.2d 1100 (7th Cir. 1978); I.R.S. Valuation Guide, *supra* note 39, at 30.

44. *See O'Keeffe*, 63 T.C.M. at 2706.

45. Under New York law the compensation of executors is based in part on the value of property received and distributed by the executor, such value to be determined in such manner as the court may direct. N.Y. Surr. Ct. Proc. Act § 2307(2). Generally, it is the practice of the New York Surrogate's Court to accept the value as fixed in the estate tax proceeding as the basis for the computation of commissions. *In re* Fry's Trust, 214 N.Y.S.2d 54 (Sup. Ct. Nassau County 1961); *In re* Estate of Vera Sheinman, 275 N.Y.S.2d 197 (Sur. Ct. N.Y. County 1966); *In re* Coudert, 65 N.Y.S.2d 234 (Sur. Ct. N.Y. County 1945); *In re* Estate of Ellmers, 43 N.Y.S.2d 91 (Sur. Ct. N.Y. County 1943); *In re* Wagemaker, 38 N.Y.S.2d 951 (Sur. Ct. Wayne County 1942); *In re* Estate of Baldwin, 284 N.Y.S. 754 (Sur. Ct. Westchester County 1935), *aff'd,* 295 N.Y.S. 480 (Sup. Ct. 1937); 7 Warren's Heaton on Surrogates' Courts § 103.02[5][d] (ed. 2012).

46. I.R.C. §§ 1014(a); 2031(a); 2032(a).

47. *In re* Determination of Legal Fees Payable by the Estate of Andy Warhol, Deceased, N.Y.L.J., Apr. 18, 1994, at 29, col. 5; *In re* Warhol Estate, No. 824/87, *unpublished opinion*, N.Y. County Surrogate's Court, Apr. 14, 1994.

48. The issues in the case were separated with the first trial dealing with the valuation of the works of art and the second trial dealing with the legality and enforceability of the estate's contact with Hayes.

49. *See Warhol Estate, unpublished opinion,* at 22.

50. *See generally* "Commentary of Victoria Bjorklund on the Surrogate's Warhol Opinion," paper presented at National Conference of Appraisers Association of America (Nov. 18, 1994).

51. *See Warhol Estate, unpublished opinion,* at 17.

52. *See Warhol Estate, unpublished opinion,* at 12.

53. *In re* Warhol Estate, 165 Misc. 2d 725, 735, 629 N.Y.S.2d 621, 627 (1995). The legal fee would have been $10 million based strictly on the percentage arrangement.

54. *In re* Warhol Estate, 637 N.Y.S.2d 708 (App. Div. 1st Dep't. 1996).

55. *See* discussion of *Smith* and *O'Keeffe, supra* at pages 1411–1419. *See* Covey, *Estate, Gift and Income Taxation—1994 Developments*, U. Miami 29th Inst. on Est. Plan. ¶ 109.2A (1995), that is critical of the Surrogate's Court opinion in *Warhol* where in note 7 the Surrogate implied that inflation and present value may to some extent offset each other.

56. *See Warhol Estate, unpublished opinion,* at 1.
57. For an excellent analysis and commentary on this theory *see* Schaengold, *Valuation of Artist's Estates: David Smith, Georgia O'Keeffe and Andy Warhol—Have We Missed the Forest for the Trees?,* 20 TAX MGMT. EST., GIFTS & TR. J. 225 (Nov./Dec. 1995); Schaengold, *Artist's Artworks Valuation: Is "Blockage" the Issue? The Estate of Georgia O'Keeffe and an Alternative Approach,* 17 TAX MGM'T EST., GIFTS & TR. J. 167 (Nov./Dec. 1992). *See also* Bridges, *Portrait of the Artist As a Limited Partner,* 21 TAX MGMT. EST., GIFTS & TR. J. 83 (Mar./Apr. 1996), where the author states that the artworks in the artist's estate should be valued as a business under Treas. Reg. § 20.2031-3 rather than Treas. Reg. § 20.2031-6.
58. Revenue Reconciliation Act of 1989, Pub. L. No. 101-239, 103 Stat. 2301.
59. Revenue Reconciliation Act § 7721(c).
60. I.R.C. § 6662(g)(1).
61. I.R.C. § 6662(h)(2).
62. I.R.C. § 6662(g)(2).
63. I.R.C. § 6664(c)(1).
64. I.R.C. §§ 6662(b)(5); 6662(g).
65. I.R.C. § 2056.
66. The Economic Growth and Tax Relief Reconciliation Act of 2001 ("2001 Act") accelerated the increase in the amount of the available applicable exclusion amount. Beginning with decedents dying in 2002, the 2001 Act increased the applicable exclusion amount to $1 million in 2002 and 2003; to $1.5 million in 2004 and 2005; to $2 million in 2006, 2007 and 2008; and to $3.5 million in 2009. A complete analysis of the 2001 Act is well beyond the scope of this chapter. Under the 2001 Act the estate tax was repealed for decedents dying in 2010 but was reinstated in 2011. The exclusion amount is $5 million in 2011 and $5,120,000 in 2012. If the 2001 Act provisions are not again passed, the estate tax applicable exclusion amount will revert to $1 million in 2013. I.R.C. § 2010(c), as amended by 2001 Act.
67. I.R.C. § 1014. The Economic Growth and Tax Relief Reconciliation Act of 2001 reinstates new carryover basis rules for property included in a decedent's estate for persons dying in calendar year 2010, the federal estate tax was repealed. A new modified carryover basis system will apply under new section 1022 in year 2010. Under the new system, the basis for certain property treated as transferred on the death of a property owner after 2009 will equal the lower of the asset's fair market value at the decedent's death or the decedent's adjusted basis in the asset. In other words, the basis for income tax purposes may remain at the original cost of the property purchased. There are a number of adjustments that allow some step-up in basis. A full discussion of this new provision is beyond the scope of this chapter. As with all other provisions of the 2001 Act, the modified carryover basis system expires on January 1, 2011, and the existing step-up in basis rule under section 1014 was reinstated. See Blattmachr & Detzel, *Estate Planning Changes in the 2001 Tax Act—More Than You Can Count,* 95 J. TAX'N 74 (2001), for a detailed discussion of these provisions.
68. I.R.C. § 6662(e)(1)(A).
69. Berghe, *The Artist, the Art Market and the Income Tax,* 29 TAX L. REV. 491, 514 (1974); Feld, *Artists, Art Collectors and Income Tax,* 60 B.U. L. REV. 625 (1980).
70. I.R.C. § 170(e)(1)(A); Treas. Reg. § 1.170A-4(a)(1).
71. I.R.C. § 1221(a)(3)(C).
72. I.R.C. § 170(e)(1)(A); Treas. Reg. § 1.170A-4(a)(1).
73. Maniscalco v. Comm'r, 632 F.2d 6 (6th Cir. 1980), *aff'g* 37 T.C.M. (CCH) 1174 (1978).
74. I.R.C. § 170(f)(3).
75. Treas. Reg. § 1.170A-7(b)(1)(i). *See and compare* I.R.C. §§ 2055(e)(4), 2522(c)(3), which are discussed below.
76. Treas. Reg. § 1.170A-7(b)(1).
77. I.R.C. § 170(e)(1)(A); Treas. Reg. § 1.170A-4(a)(1).
78. I.R.C. § 2522(c)(3) would prevent any gift tax on the transfer (allowing a gift tax charitable deduction), but only if the provisions of that section are met, since for gift tax purposes the work of art and the copyright are treated as separate pieces of property.

79. I.R.C. §§ 1221(a)(3)(C), 1015.

80. *Id.*

81. I.R.C. § 1001.

82. I.R.C. § 1031(a)(2)(A); *see* discussion on exchanges in chapter 14.

83. R. Duffy, Art Law: Representing Artists, Dealers, and Collectors 234 (1977).

84. *See* Berghe, *supra* note 69.

85. A detailed discussion of charitable remainder trusts is beyond the scope of this chapter. *See* Brier & Knauer, 435-2nd BNA T.M. Portfolio, *Charitable Remainder Trusts and Pooled Income Funds;* Schlesinger, *Split Interest Charitable Trusts,* 51 N.Y.U. Inst. Fed. Tax'n 17-1 (1992); Belcher, *Charitable Split-Interest Trusts,* 54 N.Y.U. Inst. Fed. Tax'n 21-1 (1996); McCoy, *Don't Forget the "T" in CRT,* U. Miami 30th Inst. on Est. Plan. ¶ 1400 (1996); Horowitz, *The Trust About Charitable Remainder Trusts,* 45 Tax Law. 293 (1992); Horowitz, *Charitable Planned Giving,* 72 Taxes 685 (1994); Mering, *Charitable Remainder Trust—Comeback Player of the Year,* U. Miami 26th Inst. on Est. Plan. ¶ 900 (1992); Soled, *The Versatile Use of Charitable Remainder Unitrusts,* 74 Taxes 308 (1996); Fooden, *Charitable Remainder Trusts,* 46 C.P.A. J. 44 (1996); Rev. Rul. 72-395, 1972-C.B. 340; Rev. Rul. 80-123, 1980-1 C.B. 205; Rev. Rul. 82-128, 1982-2 C.B. 71; Rev. Rul. 88-81, 1988-2 C.B. 127.

86. I.R.C. § 664(d)(1).

87. I.R.C. § 664(d)(2).

88. Priv. Ltr. Rul. 94-13-020.

89. *Id.*; Rev. Rul. 55-531, 1955-2 C.B. 520; Rev. Rul. 55-138, 1955-1 C.B. 223; Farrier v. Comm'r, 15 T.C. 277 (1950); SoRelle v. Comm'r, 22 T.C. 459 (1954), *acq.*, 1955-1 C.B. 6.

90. Treas. Reg. §§ 1.170A-1(c)(4); 1.170A-1(c)(4) exs. 5 and 6.

91. Rev. Rul. 78-197, 1978-1 C.B. 83; Palmer v. Comm'r, 62 T.C. 684 (1974), *acq.*, 1978-2 C.B. 2.

92. I.R.C. §§ 511, 512, 513, and 514.

93. I.R.C. § 512(a)(1); Treas. Reg. § 1.513-1(a).

94. Treas Reg. § 1.664-1(c).

95. For example, to qualify as a charitable remainder trust, the trust must satisfy the definition of a charitable remainder trust and function exclusively as a charitable remainder trust from the date of creation. Treas. Reg. § 1.664-1(a)(4). Under I.R.C. § 512(b)(5) and Treas. Reg. § 1.512(b)-1(d), there is excluded from unrelated business taxable income all gains from the sale, exchange, or other disposition of property, unless the property is stock in trade or other property of a kind that would be properly includible in inventory if on hand at the close of the taxable year or unless the property is property held primarily for sale to customers in the ordinary course of the business. An artist desiring to create an inter vivos charitable remainder trust should not use his regular art gallery to sell the work of art. The trustee should sell it privately.

96. Treas. Reg. § 1.170A-7(b)(1)(i).

97. I.R.C. §§ 2055(e)(4), 2522(c)(3).

98. Treas. Reg. § 1.664-1(a)(1)(iii)(a).

99. I.R.C. § 2055(e)(4)(C); Treas. Reg. § 20.2055-2(e)(1)(ii). Sections 2055(e)(4) and 2522(c)(3) were enacted by Economic Recovery Tax Act of 1981, Pub. L. No. 97-34, § 423, applicable to estates of decedents dying and transfers made after December 31, 1981. Section 2055(e)(4) sets out the detailed rules. Section 2522(c)(3) simply states that rules similar to those of section 2055(e)(4) apply for purposes of the gift tax charitable deduction for partial interests in property.

100. *See* discussion *infra* at page 1431 and chapter 15 at page 1278; and accompanying text; Priv. Ltr. Rul. 94-52-026.

101. Treas. Reg. § 1.170A-7(b)(1)(i); I.R.C. § 170(f)(3).

102. 17 U.S.C. § 204; 17 U.S.C. § 28 (1909) (superseded 1976); *see generally supra* chapter 11.

103. I.R.C. § 170(a)(3). *See* discussion in chapter 15 at page 1278 and accompanying text.

104. Treas. Reg. § 1.170A-5(b) ex. 6.

105. I.R.C. § 170(a)(3). *See* Priv. Ltr. Rul. 94-52-026.

106. I.R.C. § 170(e)(1)(B)(ii).

107. I.R.C. § 664(c).
108. *Supra*, note 95. The Internal Revenue Service has not ruled on whether UBTI would be generated by a sale of a work of art created by an artist/grantor of a charitable remainder trust.
109. *See* Palmer v. Comm'r, 62 T.C. 684 (1974), *aff'd on other grounds*, 523 F.2d 1308 (8th Cir. 1975), *acq.*, Rev. Rul. 78-197, 1978-1 C.B. 83; Priv. Ltr. Rul. 94-52-026.
110. I.R.C. § 664(d)(3)(A).
111. I.R.C. § 664(d)(3)(B).
112. Treas. Reg. § 1.664-3(a)(1)(i)(c). *See* Michele A. W. McKinnon, *Planning to Meet a Range of Donor Needs with "Flip" Charitable Remainder Unitrusts*, 12 J. TAX'N EXEMPT ORG. 253 (2001).
113. Treas. Reg. § 1.664-3(a)(1)(i)(c)(1).
114. Treas. Reg. § 1.664-3(a)(1)(i)(d) and (e).
115. Treas. Reg. § 1.664-3(a)(1)(i)(c)(2).
116. Treas. Reg. § 1.664-3(a)(1)(i)(c)(3).
117. Treas. Reg. § 1.664-1(a)(7); Teitell, *Charitable Remainder Trusts—Who Can and Should Be the Trustee*, 117 TR. & EST. 320 (1978).
118. I.R.C. § 2055(a).
119. I.R.C. §§ 508(d)(2), (a), (e), 2055(e)(1); Treas. Reg. § 20.2055-5(b).
120. This provision is discussed in greater detail in chapter 15 at pages 1316–1319.
121. *See* Treas. Reg. § 20.2055-2(e)(1)(ii)(e) ex. (1).
122. I.R.C. § 2055(e)(4)(D).
123. *See supra* note 97 and accompanying text. I.R.C. §§ 2055(a); 2055(e)(2).
124. Treas. Reg. § 1.664-1(a)(1)(iii)(a).
125. I.R.C. § 2055(e)(4)(C); Treas. Reg. § 20.2055-2(e)(1)(ii).
126. *See* discussion, *supra* at page 1431 and chapter 15 at page 1291; Priv. Ltr. Rul. 94-52-026.
127. Treas. Reg. § 1.664-1(a)(6) ex. 5.
128. Rev. Rul. 80-123, 1980-1 C.B. 205.
129. Treas. Reg. §§ 1.664-1(a)(5)(i); 1.664-1(a)(6) ex. 4.
130. Treas. Reg. § 1.664-1(a)(5)(i).
131. *Id.* All payments must include interest.
132. *See* Rev. Rul. 73-610, 1973-2 C.B. 213.
133. Treas. Reg. § 1.664-1(d)(5).
134. *Id.*
135. I.R.C. § 1014(a).
136. *See supra* note 133. *See* Treas Reg. § 1.664-1(d)(5) ex.; Priv. Ltr. Rul. 89-31-029; Priv. Ltr. Rul. 92-01-029.
137. A model Uniform Prudent Investors Act (UPIA) was promulgated by the National Conference of Commissions on Uniform State Laws in 1994 and recommended for enactment by the states. As of this publication, forty-one states have adopted the UPIA or substantial portions thereof. *See, e.g.*, Cal. Prob. Code §§ 16,045 to 16,054; Fla. Stat. Ann. §§ 518.11 and 518.122; 760 Ill. Comp. Stat. Ann. 5/5 and 5/5-1; N.Y. Est. Powers & Trusts Law § 11-2.3.
138. N.Y. Est. Powers & Trusts Law § 5-3.3 (repealed 1981 N.Y. Laws ch. 461, effective July 7, 1981); *In re Estate of Cairo*, 35 A.D.2d 76, 321 N.Y.S.2d 925 (2d Dep't 1970), *aff'd without opinion*, 29 N.Y.2d 527, 272 N.E.2d 574, 324 N.Y.S.2d 81 (1971).
139. Treas. Reg. § 20.2055-2(b)(1).
140. *See* Estate of David N. Marine v. Comm'r, 97 T.C. 368 (1991), *aff'd*, 93-1 USTC ¶ 60,131, 990 F.2d 136 (4th Cir. 1993).
141. Treas. Reg. § 20.2055-2(c)(1)(ii); I.R.C. § 2055(a).
142. I.R.C. §§ 2001(c), 2502(a).
143. *See* Duffy, *supra* note 83, at 237; Cutrow, *supra* note 6.
144. I.R.C. § 2036; Treas. Reg. § 25.2511-2.
145. *See* Duffy, *supra* note 83, at 200; Berghe, *supra* note 69, at 505.

146. I.R.C. §§ 1221(a)(3)(C), 1015.

147. Estate of W.G. Farrier v. Comm'r, 15 T.C. 277 (1950) (*acq.*); SoRelle v. Comm'r, 22 T.C. 459 (1954).

148. S. Rep. No. 2375, 81st Cong., 2d Sess. 43–44 (1950); *see* Wodehouse v. Comm'r, 177 F.2d 881 (2d Cir. 1949); Wodehouse v. Comm'r, 178 F.2d 987 (4th Cir. 1949).

149. Heim v. Fitzpatrick, 262 F.2d 887 (2d Cir. 1959); Comm'r v. Reece, 233 F.2d 30 (1st Cir. 1956).

150. Tobey v. Comm'r, 60 T.C. 227 (1973). *See* Gen. Couns. Mem. 36,492 (Nov. 17, 1975).

151. *Id.* at 230.

152. *Id.* at 230.

153. *Id.* at 235.

154. Lucas v. Earl, 281 U.S. 111 (1930). The theory in the assignment of income cases is that the one who earns the right to income has retained sufficient control over that income so that it is not properly taxed to anyone else.

155. *See* Berghe, *supra* note 69, at 499; Duffy, *supra* note 83, at 202.

156. *See* Berghe, *supra* note 69, at 506.

157. Cook v. United States, 599 F.2d 400 (Ct. Cl. 1979). *See generally* Spellmann, *United States Tax Rules for Nonresident Authors, Artists, Musicians, and Other Creative Professionals*, 27 Vand. J. Transnat'l L. 219 (1994).

158. I.R.C. §§ 63(c)(5), 1(i).

159. 17 U.S.C. § 203(a) (1988), as amended by 1988 Act; *see generally* Fraiman & Jordan, 815 BNA T.M. Portfolio, *Estate Planning for Authors and Artists*.

160. *See* Fraiman & Jordan, *supra* note 159; Cutrow, *supra* note 6.

161. Treas. Reg. § 25.2511-2.

162. *See* Fraiman & Jordan, *supra* note 159.

163. I.R.C. §§ 2033, 2001(b)(1).

164. 17 U.S.C. § 302(a), as amended by the 1978 Act and by the 1998 Sonny Bono Copyright Term Extension Act (Pub. L. No. 105-298). *See* chapter 11.

165. Copyright Act of 1909 § 23, 35 Stat. 1075 (1909). *See* chapter 11.

166. For an excellent discussion of the problem, *see* Nevins, *The Magic Kingdom of Will-Bumping: Where Estates Law and Copyright Law Collide*, 35 J. Copyright Soc'y 77 (1988); Nevins, *Copyright Law vs. Testamentary Freedom: The Sound of a Collision Unheard*, 23 Real Prop., Prob. & Tr. J. 47 (1988).

167. *Id.*

168. *Id.* Year 2005 less twenty-eight years to year 1977. Works created on or after January 1, 1978, are not subject to a renewal term, *supra* note 164.

169. 17 U.S.C. §203; 17 U.S.C. §304. See Lee-ford Tritt, *Liberating Estates Law from the Constraints of Copyright*, 38 Rutgers L.J. 109 (2006) for a detailed and informative article on this topic.

170. 17 U.S.C. § 203(a)(3).

171. 17 U.S.C. § 304(c)(3).

172. 17 U.S.C. § 203(a).

173. *Id.*

174. I.R.C. § 2053(a)(2); Treas. Reg. § 20.2053-3(d)(2). *Compare* Estate of David Smith v. Comm'r, 57 T.C. 650 (1972).

175. I.R.C. § 1014.

176. Estate of Jacques Ferber v. Comm'r, 22 T.C. 261 (1954); Garrett v. United States, 120 F. Supp. 193 (Ct. Cl. 1954); Fullerton v. Comm'r, 22 T.C. 372 (1954).

177. Pub. L. No. 107-16 (June 7, 2001).

178. See Blattmachr & Detzel, *Estate Planning Changes in the 2001 Tax Act—More Than You Can Count*, 95 J. Tax'n 74 (2001), for a detailed discussion of these provisions.

179. I.R.C. § 691; *see* Ferguson, *Income and Deduction in Respect of Decedents and Related Problems*, 25 Tax L. Rev. 5 (1969).

180. I.R.C. § 691(a)(3).

181. I.R.C. § 1014(c).

182. I.R.C. §§ 691(a)(3), 1221(a)(3)(C).

183. *See* Berghe, *supra* note 69.

184. Trust Co. v. Ross, 392 F.2d 694 (5th Cir. 1967), *aff'g per curiam* 262 F. Supp. 900 (N.D. Ga. 1966).

185. Keck v. Comm'r, 415 F.2d 531 (6th Cir. 1969), *rev'g* 49 T.C. 313 (1968). *See* Treas. Reg. § 1.691(a)-2(b) ex. 5(2); Fraiman & Jordan, *supra* note 159; Biblin & Klinger, *Selected Problems in Estate Planning for Artists and Athletes*, 8 Ann. UCLA-CEB Est. Plan. Inst. 81 (May 1988).

186. Estate of Peterson v. Comm'r, 74 T.C. 630(1980); Note, *Tax Court Enunciates Four Requirements for Determining Whether a Decedent Possessed the Requisite Right to Sale Proceeds at the Time of Death for Purposes of Section 691*, 7 Est. Plan. 362 (1980).

187. *See* Priv. Ltr. Rul. 93-26-043.

188. *See supra* note 178.

189. I.R.C. §§ 6018, 6075.

190. Comm'r v. Groetzinger, 107 S. Ct. 980 (1987); *see* Boyle, *What Is a Trade or Business?*, 39 Tax Law. 737 (1986); Barcal, *IRS Active Trade or Business Requirement for Estate Tax Deferral: An Analysis*, 54 J. Tax'n 52 (Jan. 1981); *supra* note 57.

191. I.R.C. § 6166(a)(1); 6166(a)(6); 6166(b)(9).

192. I.R.C. § 6166(b)(1). Obviously, for an interest in a corporation to qualify it must be nonreadily tradable stock, *i.e.*, there is no market for the stock on a stock exchange or in an over-the-counter market.

193. I.R.C. § 6601(j). Thus, estates of decedents dying in later years will receive the benefit of the increases in the amount exempted by the unified credit. Under the 2001 Act, Pub. L. No. 107-16, § 521(a), the amount exempted by the unified credit increased to (1) $1 million for estates of decedents dying in 2002–2003; (2) $1,500,000 for estates of decedents dying in 2004–2005; (3) $2 million for estates of decedents dying in 2006–2008; (4) $3,500,000 for estates of decedents dying in 2009; (5) zero for decedents dying in 2010; (6) $5,000,000 for decedents dying in 2011; and (7) $5,120,000 for decedents dying in 2012. Section 6601(j)(3) indexed the $1 million amount subject to the 2% rate for inflation, rounded down to the nearest $10,000 starting in 1999. Before amendment by the Taxpayer Relief Act of 1997, Pub. L. No. 105-34, § 503, section 6601(j) provided that the lesser of the amount of tax deferred or $345,800 less the unified credit ($192,800 from 1987–1997) was subject to 4% interest and the balance of the tax deferred bore interest at the section 6621 underpayment rate.

194. I.R.C. § 6601(j)(l)(B).

195. I.R.C. §§ 2053(c)(1)(D), 163(k). For decedents dying before 1998, the interest paid was deductible on supplemental estate tax returns. Pub. L. No. 105-34, § 503(d)(2), allowed the estate of a decedent dying before 1998 for which a section 6166 election was made to elect to pay future installments under amended section 6601(j) and pay the reduced interest rate and forego the interest deduction. The election had to be made before January 1, 1999.

196. I.R.C. § 6166(g). The Conference Agreement accompanying the 2001 Act, Pub. L. No. 107-16, indicates that the rules accelerating the unpaid section 6166 installments if more than 50% of the closely held business is disposed of will continue to apply after 2009 to estates of decedents dying before January 1, 2010, because the termination of the estate tax is effective only for decedents dying after December 31, 2009.

197. Treas. Reg. § 20.6161-1(a).

198. The change from the exclusion to the deduction, incorporated into the IRS restructuring legislation as a technical correction, made the deduction available for estates of decedents dying after 1997 and repealed section 2033A retroactive to its effective date. Pub. L. No. 105-206, § 6007(b). For a detailed description of section 2057, *see* Harl & McEowen 829 BNA T.M. Portfolio, *The Family-Owned Business Deduction—Section 2057*.

199. Pub. L. No. 107-16 (June 7, 2001).

200. *Id.* § 521(d).

201. N.M. Stat. Ann. §§ 7-7-15 to -20.

202. Conn. Gen. Stat. Ann. § 12-376c.

203. *In re* Rothko, 84 Misc. 2d 830, 379 N.Y.S.2d 923 (Sur. Ct. 1975), *modified*, 56 A.D.2d 499, 392 N.Y.S.2d 870 (1st Dep't), *aff'd*, 43 N.Y.2d 305, 372 N.E.2d 291, 401 N.Y.S.2d 449 (1977).

204. *In re* Scarborough Props. Corp., 25 N.Y.2d 553, 255 N.E.2d 641, 307 N.Y.S.2d 641 (1969); Renz v. Beeman, 589 F.2d 735 (2d Cir. 1978), *cert. denied*, 444 U.S. 834 (1979); Restatement (Second) of Trusts § 170 (1959).

205. Meinhard v. Salmon, 249 N.Y. 458, 464, 164 N.E. 545, 550 (1928).

206. *See In re* Rothko, 43 N.Y.2d at 320, 372 N.E.2d at 297, 401 N.Y.S.2d at 455.

207. H.R. Rep. No. 4333, 100th Cong. 2d Sess. 531 (1988).

208. I.R.C. § 263A(h)(3)(C).

209. Stella Waitzkin v. Comm'r, 63 T.C.M. (CCH) 2740 (1992).

210. I.R.C. § 262(a).

211. *See Waitzkin*, 63 T.C.M. at 2744.

212. *Id.* at 2745.

213. I.R.C. § 162(a).

214. I.R.C. § 280A(c)(1).

215. I.R.C. § 280A(a).

216. I.R.C. § 280A(c)(1). *See* Wood, 547-2nd BNA T.M. Portfolio, *Home Office, Vacation Home and Home Rental Deductions*. The Taxpayer Relief Act of 1997 amended section 280A to expand the definition of "principal place of business" to cover situations where an office is used to conduct administrative activities of the taxpayer's trade or business and there is no other fixed location of the trade or business where the taxpayer conducts substantial administrative activities. The expanded definition will not be much help for the artist. *See* Diane Cameron Hutton v. Comm'r, 74 T.C.M. (CCH) 1480 (1997).

217. I.R.C. § 280A(c)(5).

218. I.R.C. § 280A(c)(5).

219. Prop. Treas. Reg. § 1.280A-2(g).

220. I.R.C. § 336 as amended by the Tax Reform Act of 1986, Pub. L. No. 99-514.

221. Under the tax codes (I.R.C. §§ 336 and 337) as it existed prior to July 31, 1986, a corporation recognized no gain or loss on a distribution of its assets to shareholders in liquidation or, if certain conditions were met, on a liquidation sale of its assets. The statutory provisions providing for nonrecognition were referred to as the General Utilities rules after the Supreme Court case said to be codified in the provision. Gen. Utils. & Operating Co. v. Helvering, 296 U.S. 200 (1935). The repeal of the *General Utilities* doctrine is designed to require the corporate level recognition of gain on a corporation's sale or distribution of appreciated property, irrespective of whether it occurs in a liquidating or nonliquidating context. The provision is generally effective for liquidation sales and distributions after July 31, 1986.

222. I.R.C. § 336.

223. Estate of Louise Nevelson v. Comm'r, 72 T.C.M. (CCH) 321 (1996).

224. *Id.* at 322.

225. For further reading on this topic, *see* Borchard & Hart, *Solving Common Problems Arising from Use of Trademarks in the Arts*, 10 Colum.-VLA J.L. & Arts 171 (1986); Kaufman, *Licensed Artwork Can Drive the Market*, Art Bus. News, Feb. 1997 at 1; Leland, Licensing Art and Design (1990); Ginsburg, *Exploiting the Artist's Commercial Identity: The Merchandizing of Art Images*, 19 Colum.-VLA J.L. & Arts 1 (1995).

226. N.Y. Mult. Dwell. Law § 276.

227. *See* T. Crawford, Legal Guide for the Visual Artist 142 (1986).

228. U.C.C. § 2-315 and cmt. 1. *See also* discussion in chapter 2.

229. N.Y. Tax Law § 1105(a). As in chapter 14 at page 1193, the references are to the New York State sales tax law. Similar provisions exist in most states and should be checked prior to proceeding.

230. N.Y. Tax Law § 1101(b)(4)(i).

231. N.Y. Comp. Codes R. & Regs. tit. 20, § 526.7(f)(1).

232. N.Y. Comp. Codes R. & Regs. tit. 20, § 526.7(f)(2).

233. N.Y. Comp. Codes R. & Regs. tit. 20, § 526.7(f)(3).

APPENDIX 16-1

Credit Shelter Nonmarital Trust for Artist's Works of Art

The property bequeathed to the Trustees of the Trust created under this Clause may consist substantially or entirely of works of art, and it is my intention in creating this trust that my Trustees retain such works of art as investment assets of the trust estate. Notwithstanding the provisions of this Clause requiring current distribution of the income of the trust, my Trustees shall be under no obligation to sell any work of art or any other non-income-producing asset of the trust estate or to make the trust estate productive of income, except as my Trustees shall in their absolute discretion determine, and, for that purpose, I expressly intend that any provisions of the laws of the State of _____ regarding underproductive property shall not apply to such trust. My Trustees shall not be subject to surcharge for any decline in value of any original assets of such trust.

My Trustees shall be authorized to payout of the income or out of the principal of the trust created by this Clause such sums as they shall in their sole discretion determine for insurance, storage, or other care or maintenance of any works of art and to retain out of the income of the trust such sums as they may consider necessary as a reserve for future expenditures for such care and maintenance. I direct that the determination of my Trustees to pay such sums or to retain such income and the determination of my Trustees as to what assets of such trust are properly included in the expression "works of art" shall be conclusive and binding upon all persons interested in such trust.

APPENDIX 16-2

Outright to Charity Subject to Selection Within Time Limitation

CLAUSE _____:

A. Except for those items disposed of under Clause _____ below, I give and bequeath to the _____ FOUNDATION, INC., now located in New York, New York, all works of art created by me, including any copyright interest therein, and all art property owned by me, including any copyright interest therein. The term "art property" shall mean and include all sketches, maquettes, artists' proofs, working drawings and other similar items that are generally not finished works of art for sale, materials and supplies used by me in the creation of paintings or other works of art, and all books, correspondence, research materials or other documents or materials used by me or written by me or received by me relating in any way to a work of art created by me or to any of my artistic endeavors. My Executors shall have the authority to determine what assets of my estate are properly included in the term "art property" and such determination shall be conclusive and binding upon all persons interested in my estate.

B. I give and bequeath to the _____ FOUNDATION, INC., now located in New York, New York, the sum of _____ Thousand Dollars ($_____,000) to be used for its general purposes.

C. Anything hereinabove to the contrary notwithstanding, if at the time of my death the _____ FOUNDATION, INC. does not qualify as an organization described in sections 501(c)(3) and 2055(a) of the Internal Revenue Code, then I give and bequeath the property described above in Paragraphs A and B of this Clause to such other organization or organizations that are described in sections 501(c)(3) and 2055(a) of the Internal Revenue Code and are designated by my Executors.

CLAUSE _____:

I give and bequeath to the following listed individuals that survive me, the works of art created by me as described below:

A. To my daughter _____, two paintings no larger than ten square feet each and four drawings on paper of any size, such items to be selected by my daughter within six months of my date of death.

B. To my friend _____, one painting no larger than six

square feet, such item to be selected by my friend within six months of my date of death.

C. To my friend _____, one drawing on paper of any size, such item to be selected by my friend within six months of my date of death.

My Executors shall arrange for the above named individuals to select the works of art in the order in which they are named. If an individual does not make his or her selection within six months of my death the bequest to such individual shall thereafter be null and void.

APPENDIX 16-3

Loan and Promised Gift Agreement

LOAN AND PROMISED GIFT AGREEMENT

THIS LOAN AND PROMISED GIFT AGREEMENT (this "Agreement") is made and entered into as of the _____ day of _____, 20__, by and among _____ ("Artist") and _____ ("Wife"), residing at _____, and _____, a tax-exempt organization having an office at _____ (the "Museum").

WITNESSETH:

WHEREAS, Artist is the creator and the owner of the work of art described on Schedule A attached hereto and incorporated herein by this reference (the "Work"); and

WHEREAS, Artist wishes to loan the Work to the Museum for exhibition and study;

WHEREAS, Artist and Wife promise to gift the Work to the Museum at a future date; and

WHEREAS, the Museum has agreed to exhibit the Work and to accept the gift for such purposes and on the terms and conditions hereinafter set forth.

NOW, THEREFORE, in consideration of the mutual promises contained herein, the parties hereto agree as follows:

1. Artist agrees to loan the Work to the Museum without charge so long as it is made available for exhibition and study by members of the general public and bears a suitable notice identifying the Work as a loan from Artist.

2. The Work will be exhibited at the premises of the Museum and at any other location that the Museum deems suitable for exhibition at all times that such locations are open for business. However, the Work may be temporarily unavailable for such periods of time as may be appropriate for preservation, conservation, building renovation, photograph or scholarly examination.

3. Artist and Wife agree to either gift the Work to the Museum during their joint lifetimes or to bequeath the Work to the Museum under the Last Will and Testament of the survivor of them. If for any reason there is no specific bequest of the Work to the Museum made in the Last Will and Testament of the survivor

of Artist and Wife, then this Agreement shall constitute a binding legal obligation of such survivor's estate to be fulfilled by such survivor's executors.

4. The Museum shall maintain the Work and shall insure it for its fair market value against loss or damage, naming Artist or Wife, as the case may be, as an additional insured and loss payee until title passes to the Museum.

5 The Museum shall pay all costs of packing, shipping, insurance, and any other cost in connection with exhibiting, caring for and maintaining the Work.

6. Artist owns the copyright in the Work. As such, the Museum shall not photograph or reproduce in any media the Work unless such reproduction is specifically authorized by Artist, or the subsequent owner of the copyright if Artist is not living. Nothing in this Agreement shall constitute a loan, transfer or promised gift of the copyright to the Work.

7 The Museum will give to the Work the same care it gives comparable property of its own. The Museum will take precautions to protect the Work from fire, theft, mishandling, direct, and insects, and from extremes of light, temperature, and humidity while in the Museum's custody.

8. Artist, or if Artist in not living Wife, may terminate this Loan on thirty (30) days' notice if the Museum fails to fulfill its obligations under this Agreement.

IN WITNESS WHEREOF, the parties hereto have hereunto signed their hands and seals as of the _____ day of _____, 20___.

_____
[Name of Artist]

_____
[Name of Wife]

[Name of Museum]

_____
By:
Its:

SCHEDULE A

The Work

Artist:
Title:
Medium:
Size:
Date:

APPENDIX 16-4

Bequest of Art—Retained Copyright

If my wife, _____ _____, shall not survive me, I hereby make the following bequests:

A. I give and bequeath to the _____ _____ FOUNDATION, INC., now located in New York, New York, the sum of _____Thousand Dollars ($_____,000.00) to be used for its general purposes.

B. I give and bequeath to the _____ _____ FOUNDATION, INC., now located in New York, New York, all signed paintings on canvas created by me and owned by me at the time of my death, including any copyright interest therein.

C. I give and bequeath to the _____ _____ FOUNDATION, INC., now located in New York, New York, all signed photographs created by me and owned by me at the time of my death, excluding any copyright interest therein.

D. I request that the _____ _____ FOUNDATION, INC. exhibit the works of art bequeath to it under this Clause at and/or distribute such works of art to such other organization or organizations that are described in Section 501(c)(3) of the Internal Revenue Code and that would in the judgment of the _____ _____ FOUNDATION, INC. benefit from owning such works of art. My Executor shall have the authority to determine which assets of my estate are properly included in Paragraphs B and C of this Clause and such determination shall be conclusive and binding upon all persons interested in my estate.

E. I give and bequeath to the _____ _____ FOUNDATION, INC. now located in New York, New York, all art property that I own at the time of my death and the copyright interest therein. The term "art property" shall mean and include all sketches, drawings, and unsigned paintings created by me, all unsigned photographs created by me, and other similar items that are generally not finished works of art for sale, all technical files, materials and supplies used by me in the creation of my paintings and photographs, correspondence, research materials or other documents or materials used by me or written by me or received by me relating in any way to a work of art created by me or to any of my artistic endeavors. My Executor shall have the authority to determine which assets of my estate are properly included in the term "art property" and such determination shall be conclusive and binding upon persons interested in my estate.

F.   Notwithstanding any other provision of this Clause to the contrary, if the
_____ _____ FOUNDATION, INC. shall not
qualify as an organization described in Sections 501(c)(3), 2055(a) and 170(b)
(1)(A) of the Internal Revenue Code, then I give and bequeath the property described above in Paragraphs A, B, C and E of this Clause to such other organization or organizations that are described in Sections 501(c)(3), 2055(a) and 170(b)
(1)(A) of the Internal Revenue Code and are designated by my Executor.

PART SIX

MUSEUMS

AND

MULTIMEDIA

17

Museums

In recent years, the issues facing art museums have garnered much public attention. For instance, the *New York Times* in March 2012 published a special section devoted entirely to art museums, focusing on issues such as the importance of an acquisition fund, the variation of photography policies among museums, and the impact of naming rights to a museum on fundraising.[1] This special section made evident that museums face a wide variety of issues, both legal and nonlegal. In this chapter, we clarify some of the more important topics of art museum law, an always-evolving area, highlighting important developments since the publication of the last edition of this treatise. We discuss issues faced by art museums when introducing new works of art to their collections, such as issues of title and copyright in accessioning works and the role of loan agreements. In addition, we examine issues surrounding a museum's removal of works, such as the legal, ethical, and public relations problems of deaccessioning works from permanent collections, as well as the difficulties posed by, and legislative responses to, indefinite loans to art museums. Additional issues that art museums face are dealt with more thoroughly in other chapters, including the chapters on taxes, copyrights, international trade, and expert opinions and liabilities. First and foremost, however, it is important to understand the basic structure of an art museum.

ORGANIZATIONAL STRUCTURE

An art museum is a

> permanent, nonprofit institution, essentially educational and aesthetic in purpose, with professional staff, which acquires or owns works of art, cares for them, interprets them, and exhibits them to the public on some regular schedule.[2]

The fact that an art museum is *nonprofit* does not preclude it from making a profit; it merely prohibits the museum from distributing any profits to anyone.

In the United States, art museums are either public or private.[3]

Public Museums

A public museum is one created by a government, be it county, city, state, or the federal government; it may also be part of a state or city university system. For example, the Smithsonian Institution is a creation of the federal government. Public museums are government-controlled and subject to statutory regulation, which varies from state to state, in both their organization and their operation. As governmental agencies, public museums are automatically exempt from federal income taxes; in addition, donations made solely for public purposes to public museums provide the donors with charitable contribution deductions from income tax.[4]

Private Museums

Private art museums generally qualify for tax-exempt status under section 501(c)(3) of the Internal Revenue Code, which describes tax-exempt organizations as those operated exclusively for religious, charitable, scientific, public safety testing, literary, or educational purposes, for fostering national or international sports competition, or for the prevention of cruelty to children or animals.[5] Private art museums may be tax-exempt as private foundations or public charities under section 509(a).[6]

Generally, a private art museum is organized either as a charitable trust or, commonly, as a nonprofit corporation.

CHARITABLE TRUST

A trust is a fiduciary relationship with respect to property in which the creator of the trust designates, in the trust instrument, a trustee to administer the trust property for the benefit of another, the beneficiary. The trustee holds legal title to the trust property but can use that property only for the good of the beneficiary. The beneficiary holds the equitable or beneficial title to the trust property and, as the beneficial owner "equitably entitled to its advantages,"[7] is empowered to enforce the trust.

A charitable trust is created with little formality: The enabling document—a correctly executed declaration of trust or testamentary instrument—is not, as is the case with a nonprofit corporation, filed with the secretary of state. The trust document need only include the following: the name of the grantor, the names of the original trustees, the trust's charitable purposes, the trust's period of duration, the manner of selection of successor trustees, and a provision that upon termination of the trust the assets will be distributed to charitable organizations.[8] The property transferred to the trust is described in a schedule attached to the trust document.

Unlike a private trust, a charitable trust, such as an art museum, must substantially redound to the social benefit of the public.[9] A private trust has a specific beneficiary who can enforce the trust. In contrast, the beneficiary of a charitable trust is the public or some segment of the public,[10] and the trust is enforceable by the attorney general of the state in which the trust is located.[11]

The art museum as a charitable trust is administered by a board of trustees. The trust relationship imposes on the board of trustees a high degree of responsibility[12] to protect, preserve, and increase the museum's assets—its trust funds and its collections. Among other affirmative duties to the beneficiary, the board of trustees is charged with the duties of loyalty[13] and care.[14] The duty of loyalty, the trustees' most fundamental duty,[15] requires each member of the board of trustees to administer the museum assets solely for the public's benefit. In many states that duty means that, as a rule, each trustee must refrain from any self-dealing.[16] In other words, the trustee may not engage in any transaction with the art museum or any transaction between the art museum and any enterprise in which the trustee has a substantial pecuniary interest, even if the transaction is fair. The duty of care requires each member of the board of trustees to manage the museum's assets with "such care and skill as a man of ordinary prudence would exercise in dealing with his own property."[17] Moreover, in certain transactions, such as in the investment of museum trust funds, each trustee is under an additional duty "to use the caution exercised by a prudent man in conserving the property."[18] That is, the trustee must not endanger the trust property through speculative transactions, and the law is quick to deem as negligent any deviation from a suitable investment.[19]

NONPROFIT CORPORATION

Most art museums are nonprofit corporations—that is, they are incorporated under the nonprofit statutes found in most states.[20] Articles of incorporation setting forth the corporation's purpose are filed with the secretary of state, and the commencement of corporate existence depends on the state's grant, usually in the form of a charter or certificate of incorporation, issued when that state accepts the articles of incorporation.[21] In accordance with its bylaws, a corporation is managed by a board of directors elected by the corporate members or appointed by the board if the nonprofit corporation lacks members.[22] Like a charitable trust, an art museum organized as a nonprofit corporation is barred from distributing any profits.[23] Moreover, such a museum, lacking beneficiaries other than the public at large or a segment of the public, falls under the aegis, as with the charitable trust, of the attorney general in the state where the museum is located.[24]

A museum in corporate form does have an advantage: Unlike trustees of a charitable trust, who may incur personal liability in contract, tort, and property actions, the directors of a corporation (whether nonprofit or for-profit) escape personal liability for such lawsuits entered against the museum unless the lawsuit involves a breach of the fiduciary relationship between a director and the museum.[25]

Because most state statutes regarding nonprofit corporations lack a codified standard of conduct for their corporate directors, courts are generally free to apply either the trustee standard of fiduciary conduct noted above or the standard of fiduciary conduct applicable to directors of for-profit corporations.[26] Although directors of nonprofit corporations, like trustees, incur fiduciary obligations to the public, including the duty of loyalty and the duty of care, trustees are generally bound to a higher standard of conduct than are directors of nonprofit corporations. To satisfy the duty of loyalty, a corporate director need only deal fairly with the museum corporation. Therefore, unlike a trustee of a museum that is a charitable trust, a director of a nonprofit corporation may engage in what might otherwise be considered self-dealing as long as she can establish that the transaction is intrinsically fair to the museum.[27] To satisfy the duty of care in managing museum assets, a director must simply avoid committing gross negligence.[28] The business-judgment rule gives directors latitude to use their own judgment and excuses any resulting simple negligence. Therefore, a director is able to take a certain amount of measured risk with museum assets, provided the risk is in the best interests of the museum corporation.[29]

At least one commentator has argued persuasively that a uniform standard of conduct—the trustee standard—should apply to issues of deaccessioning (that is, the disposal of objects) regardless of a museum's organizational structure.[30] After all, whether an art museum is a charitable trust or a nonprofit corporation, the museum's managers perform the same role, and the public in each case is the beneficiary. That position could be expanded: Despite a museum's organization, the trustee standard should be uniformly applied to any issue directly concerning a museum's collection policy, such as accessioning (that is, the acquisition of objects), care of collections, and access to collections. As noted by still another commentator,[31] some case law[32] does, in fact, exact from board members a higher than usual standard for issues directly concerning the museum's collection policy.

INCOMING WORKS

An art museum seeks or acquires artwork for a variety of purposes: for incorporation into one of its collections (accessioning); for exhibition or study as part of a loan arrangement; and, as a recipient of a temporary deposit, to render an authentication of the artwork as a favor to the depositor. The museum also acquires artwork in a variety of ways, such as purchase, gift, bequest, exchange, and loan. The legal considerations raised by a museum's acquisition of artwork depend on the purpose of the acquisition and its nature. Acquisition by both accessioning and loan is addressed below.

Accessioning

Accessioning is defined in museum parlance as the formal process of accepting an artwork, recording it, and incorporating it into one of the museum's collections

with the intention of retaining it for the foreseeable future.[33] An art museum ordinarily has several types of collections: a permanent collection, which usually includes its finest artwork; a study collection, which may include related art objects
that add insight and appreciation to the permanent collection; and an archival or
book collection that supplements the other collections. Once an artwork is accessioned, the museum incurs obligations to the public with respect to that artwork:
It must be properly documented, stored, maintained, conserved, and made available to the public. Because accessioning imposes such demands on a museum's
resources, an artwork's provenance, rarity, and condition should be considered, as
well as its ability to fill an appropriate niche in a given collection. The decision to
accession a work rests solely with the museum and specifically with the museum
personnel to whom such authority is delegated. If, therefore, a museum is notified that it is a beneficiary of a testamentary bequest of artwork or that it is the
potential recipient of an inter vivos (lifetime) gift of art, it is under no obligation
to accept all or even some of the artwork. Rather, the estate's executor, in the case
of a testamentary bequest, should furnish the museum with the pertinent portion of the will, so that the bequest may be verified, and the museum can consider
whether it is in its best interest to accept the bequest. Then the museum should
advise the executor of its decision to accept some, all, or none of the bequest.[34] In
the case of an inter vivos gift, the museum, if it chooses not to accept the gift, may
advise the potential benefactor of more suitable institutional recipients.

Once a museum has accessioned a work of art, it must be sure to create and
maintain proper records of the work and its accession. The importance for a museum of a proper curatorial record-keeping system is illustrated in *Denver Art
Museum v. de Menil*.[35] Adelaide de Menil was a good-faith purchaser of a Navajo blanket from an art dealer in November 1970. When de Menil consigned
the blanket for sale at Sotheby's in December 1997, the Denver Art Museum,
upon learning of the sale, claimed that it was the owner of the blanket, asserting
that it had purchased a Navajo blanket in 1950 and discovered a Navajo blanket
was missing in 1970. The court noted that the museum's record-keeping system
from the 1950s through the 1970s was far from perfect and it would be difficult
to determine if the Navajo blanket in question was the one claimed to have been
stolen from the museum in 1970. Because the museum's records were not accurate, it could not establish that the blanket was in fact stolen from it; therefore,
the court dismissed the museum's claim to possession.[36] The court also noted
that from 1970 to 1997, the museum

(1) did not contact anyone to find out any information about the blanket,
(2) never filed a police report,
(3) never filed an insurance claim,
(4) never notified the FBI, Interpol, or any other law enforcement agency,
(5) never contacted *Art Alert* (now called *Trace Magazine*) or any compa-
    rable association, claiming that the blanket was stolen or, in any event,
    illegally removed; and
(6) never circulated fliers to dealers about the allegedly stolen blanket.

Even though the court did not have to reach a final decision of possession, it noted that based on these factors it would have found for the defendant under Colorado's statute of limitations.[37]

Sometimes a museum may accession a work as the third-party beneficiary of a purchase agreement between two private individuals or organizations. Issues may arise if the purchaser ultimately decides not to donate the work to the museum, and the resolution of this problem may lie in the specific language of the purchase agreement. For instance, in *Michael Werner Gallery v. Rich*, the Michael Werner Gallery, as representative of artist Peter Doig, sold James H. Rich a painting by Doig entitled *Red Boat (Imaginary Boys)* at a fraction of the work's value.[38] Specifically, the July 2004 invoice of the sale between the parties stated that "the artwork, while purchased privately, is done so with the explicit agreement that the work is to be given as an eventual gift to the Carnegie Museum of Art" in Pittsburgh, Pennsylvania. However, Rich later decided to auction the work at Christie's.[39] The Gallery then sued on behalf of Doig in a New York state court, claiming that the condition in the purchase agreement prohibited Rich from arranging for the work to be sold at Christie's. The complaint stated that Doig ultimately wanted his art to be available for the enjoyment of the public, and that he was amenable to selling the work at the discounted price only on that condition.[40] The parties ultimately settled the case, and the Gallery permitted the work to be auctioned at Christie's, so long as if the work sold, Rich would provide a donation to the Carnegie Museum of Art that consisted of a substantial sum of money and a different Doig painting. Alternatively, the settlement provided that if *Red Boat* did not sell at auction, it would go to the Carnegie Museum of Art as originally planned.[41]

ISSUES OF TITLE

When an art museum seeks to acquire an artwork for accession, it must ascertain the accompanying quality of title: Is it obtaining free and clear possession of ownership, or is the title to the artwork in some way encumbered or restricted? Is the museum able to obtain adequate documentation of the ownership rights and restrictions it is acquiring? In the case of a gift, the museum should require the transferor of the artwork in question to sign a deed of gift that affirms that the transferor is the owner of the artwork or the owner's authorized agent for purposes of passing title.[42] (Model deeds of gift are found at the close of chapter 15; see Appendixes 15-2 and 15-3.) The museum should require the transferor of the artwork to supply a detailed provenance of the artwork, and the museum should independently check the accuracy of the provenance. If a museum purchases an artwork for accession and the title turns out to be faulty, the museum generally has a contractual cause of action based on a breach of warranty of title, which is covered by section 2-312 of the Uniform Commercial Code (U.C.C.). As noted in the discussion of the U.C.C. in chapter 2, in an action on a contract for breach of warranty of title, it is not necessary to establish either the transferor's negligence or the transferor's intent to make a false representation. It is sufficient to establish that the warranty of title existed and was not met.

If an art museum acquires, through gift or purchase, an artwork for accession and later determines that it is stolen property, the museum may lose the artwork to the true owner. As discussed in chapter 3, unless the statute of limitations in the state in which the museum is located has expired or the museum is successfully able to assert the defense of laches against the aggrieved original owner (that is, that the aggrieved original owner, with knowledge of the artwork's whereabouts, delayed unreasonably to the museum's detriment in seeking its return), or the museum has obtained title through adverse possession, which is difficult to establish in the case of personal property, title generally remains vested in the aggrieved original owner. On demand, that owner may reclaim possession of the artwork or its present value. As noted in chapter 3, neither a thief nor any purchaser from a thief, including an innocent purchaser who subsequently transfers art to a museum, can convey good title. If a museum is required either to return artwork purchased by it to the aggrieved original owner or to pay the aggrieved original owner its present value, the museum may generally seek recourse from the seller based on the sales contract.

In *Johnson v. Smithsonian Institution*, James Johnson in the late 1990s sued both the Smithsonian Institution and the Michael Rosenfeld Gallery to recover artwork created by his uncle, the African-American artist William Johnson, which was in their possession.[43] There were two categories of artwork in issue: the 1946 artwork and the 1956 artwork. From the mid 1920s until 1948 when he was declared incompetent by the New York State Supreme Court, Johnson created over 1,000 pieces of art in a variety of media and received recognition for his work from several organizations including the Harmon Foundation, a New York nonprofit organization that assisted African-American artists.[44] As the Harmon Foundation also served as a caretaker and agent for some of Johnson's artwork, the Foundation at various times had some of the artwork in its possession.

In 1946, Johnson informed the Foundation that he was relocating to Denmark and requested the return of all of his works then held by the Foundation. Unbeknownst to Johnson, the Foundation allegedly returned only some of his work and fraudulently retained the rest—the 1946 artwork.[45] When Johnson was declared incompetent, a court-appointed committee collected Johnson's artwork, stored it in a New York City warehouse, and had the artwork appraised. In 1956, the appraiser determined that the artwork was worthless and the committee, in preparing a final accounting of the estate, sought and obtained an order from the New York State Supreme Court authorizing the committee to abandon the property.[46] Approximately one month after the abandonment order was issued, the committee allegedly transferred, without consideration, much of the abandoned Johnson artwork (the 1956 artwork) to the Harmon Foundation. The Foundation restored the artwork and donated most of it to the Smithsonian in 1967 (where, today, it is recognized as having substantial value). In the 1980s or 1990s, the Rosenfeld Gallery acquired approximately thirty pieces of Johnson's work from undisclosed sources, rendering it impossible to tell if such works were from the 1946 artworks, the 1956 artworks, or another group of artworks entirely.

Over the years, Johnson's family made a number of demands to the Smithsonian, and subsequently to the Rosenfeld Gallery, for the return of the artist's work. Most of the demands were not met. On July 16, 1997, the present lawsuit was instituted against the Smithsonian and the Rosenfeld Gallery, without including the Harmon Foundation as a party.

The 1956 artwork. The Second Circuit, affirming a lower court decision,[47] held that under the Rooker-Feldman doctrine (where only the U.S. Supreme Court has subject matter jurisdiction to review state court judgments), the Johnson family was barred from bringing claims as to artwork subject to the 1956 state court order. Moreover, as the Second Circuit noted, this doctrine bars federal courts from considering claims which are "inextricably intertwined" with a prior state court determination.

The 1946 artwork. The Second Circuit affirmed the lower court's dismissal of claims against the Smithsonian, but on the grounds that the plaintiff failed to comply with the jurisdictional requirements of the Federal Tort Claims Act (FTCA) and that plaintiff's claims against the Smithsonian were time-barred under the FTCA.[48] The Second Circuit, however, noting that the claims against the Rosenfeld Gallery were not governed by the FTCA, held that the claims against the Gallery were improperly dismissed and remanded the case to the lower court for a decision on jurisdictional issues.[49] Upon remand, the lower court dismissed the case against Rosenfeld Gallery for lack of subject matter jurisdiction (specifically, a lack of diversity), and the Second Circuit affirmed that decision in 2001.[50]

In the 2000 case of *Schwartz v. Cincinnati Museum Association*, the descendants of the American impressionist artist Theodore Robinson claimed title to three paintings of which, at the time of the suit, two were in the possession of the Cincinnati Museum and one was in the possession of the Butler Museum of American Art.[51] In 1896, while he was still alive, Robinson loaned twenty-seven paintings, including the three in question, to the Central Art Association for an exhibition tour. When the artist died later that same year, his brother, Hamline Robinson, was appointed administrator of his estate. While Hamline was administering the estate, an agent for Central Art sold two of the three paintings in question, and when the tour was over, returned the other twenty-five paintings to the estate, explaining that he had sold two of them. While the agent did not specify which of the two paintings he had sold, he forwarded the administrator a Central Art catalog listing the two paintings by name as paintings exhibited in Central Art's 1897 tour. The third painting in question allegedly became part of the Robinson estate after the artist's death and was purportedly stolen or converted from the Robinson estate. The three paintings were ultimately acquired at different times during the 1900s by the two defendant museums, and each painting was displayed regularly for more than thirty years. The plaintiff in the instant suit was the ancillary administrator of the Robinson estate.

Here, the Sixth Circuit affirmed a lower court decision dismissing the complaint as barred by Ohio's four-year statute of limitations for the recovery of personal property. Under the Ohio statute, a cause of action for the wrongful taking of personal property accrues only when there is either actual or constructive knowledge of the wrongdoing.[52] The court found that Hamline had at least constructive knowledge of any alleged wrongdoing; that is, Hamline was under a fiduciary duty to carefully administer his brother's estate, and he had knowledge of such facts that "would lead a fair and prudent man, using ordinary care and thoughtfulness, to make a further inquiry" regarding the missing paintings.[53] Accordingly, the court found that the cause of action accrued over a century earlier and was barred by Ohio's four-year statute of limitations.

A federal district court in Ohio engaged in a similar anaylsis and reached a similar conclusion in a 2006 case, *Toledo Museum of Art v. Ullin.*[54] In this case (also discussed in chapter 9), the Toledo Museum of Art (TMA), had continuous ownership of Paul Gauguin's painting entitled *Street Scene in Tahiti* since 1939. After heirs of Martha Nathan asserted claims of ownership to the Gauguin, the museum brought suit against the heirs to quiet title to the work. The defendants counterclaimed for, among other things, conversion. The TMA moved to dismiss the defendants' claim as time-barred under Ohio's four-year statute of limitations for conversion of personal property.[55]

Martha Nathan inherited the painting in question upon her husband's death. She was a resident of Germany during the Nazi era, and in May 1938 she was forced to turn over some of her paintings to the Staedel Art Institute. However, since she had already moved the Gauguin painting to Basel, Switzerland, that piece was not confiscated by the Nazis. Instead, she sold the Gauguin painting, along with a number of other artworks that she had stored in Basel, to some European art dealers in December 1938.[56] TMA then purchased the Gauguin painting from those dealers in May 1939.[57]

Nathan, and later her estate, actively pursued restitution and damages for the losses she suffered as a result of the Nazi regime, and she was successful in those claims. However, she did not include a claim for the Gauguin work. The court found this fact to be of substantial importance and noted that she could have investigated and made a claim for this work at the same time she made claims for her other lost artwork.[58] Since she did not do so, the court determined that she did not believe she had a claim to the painting.[59] In addition, the court wrote that "[e]ven if, for some unexplained reason, she could not discover any wrongdoing at [the time of sale to the art dealers], once the chaos of World War II Europe subsided, a reasonable and prudent person would have made further inquiry into the terms of her sale to the art dealers."[60] The court noted that the defendants, as the heirs to Nathan's estate, were imputed with knowledge of her interest in the painting. Even if her knowledge was not imputed to them, however, the court held that the defendants too should have made an inquiry into the ownership of the Gauguin work. After all, upon her death in 1958, her executor made additional Holocaust-related claims upon the final accounting of her estate. In addition, there was a public debate surrounding Nazi looting of private assets, including a number of Congressional hearings. Based on this, the court found that a reasonably prudent person would have made an inquiry into the ownership of the Gauguin painting.[61] Instead, defendants did not contact TMA about the painting or assert a claim of ownership to it until 2004, and they did not file suit until 2006. The court granted TMA's motion to dismiss, since Ohio's four-year statute of limitation for conversion of personal property had run long before the defendants filed suit.[62]

Hope springs eternal when one is searching for buried treasure. In *Sanchez v. Trustees of the University of Pennsylvania*, the grandchildren of Pablo Isaias Sanchez sued the university to obtain a valuable collection of pre-Columbian gold art objects allegedly stolen from their grandfather more than eighty years earlier.[63] Around 1909, Sanchez discovered a collection of pre-Columbian gold art objects buried on his land in Tumaco, Colombia. At some point before 1920, the collection disappeared and was ultimately sold to the university for $5,000. In November 2002, the family retained an attorney to search for the collection, which was located at the university within a few months. However, this was one of the few efforts by the family, over an eighty-year period, to search for the objects.

The issue was the application of the laches defense made by the university in its motion for summary judgment.[64] In granting the university's motion and dismissing the complaint, the court found that no reasonable fact-finder could find that the plaintiffs' efforts were diligent.[65] The court noted that the only alleged search for which there was admissible evidence occurred when a grandchild walked into the Metropolitan Museum of Art and a few art galleries in New York looking for the collection. No one wrote any letters or placed telephone calls to any museum, hired any investigators, consulted any experts, reported the theft, or conducted any research of any kind. By contrast, the court pointed out, the long delay resulted in deceased witnesses, faded memories, lost documents, and hearsay testimony of questionable value, all of which was prejudicial to the university. Since the university established both prongs of the laches defense (unreasonable delay and resulting prejudice to the defendant), the court dismissed the complaint.[66]

In *Springfield Library & Museum v. Knoedler*, the museum sued Knoedler, the dealer, for breach of warranty of title for a Jacopo da Ponte painting it had purchased in 1955.[67] In 2001, the museum voluntarily returned the painting to the Italian government, which claimed that it had been stolen from its Polish embassy during World War II. Knoedler moved to dismiss the case, alleging that any cause of action accrued in 1955. In denying Knoedler's motion, the court relied on the doctrine of equitable estoppel—a judicially devised doctrine that precludes a party to a lawsuit, because of that party's improper conduct, from asserting a claim or defense, regardless of its substantive validity.[68] The court noted that when the Italian government first inquired about the painting in 1966, Knoedler encouraged the museum to challenge and put off the Italian government in the hope that the painting would never have to be returned. In fact, the challenge proved successful for thirty-four years until, based on further inquiries from the Italian government and the museum's investigation of the facts, the painting was voluntarily returned. The court held that Knoedler, having lulled the museum into a false sense of security about any claim against it, was now equitably estopped from claiming the benefit of any available defenses to a breach of warranty claim.[69]

In addition to claims of laches and breach of warranty, stolen artwork may also be subject to forfeiture statutes. In *United States v. Davis*, the Second Circuit examined the contours of forfeiture law with respect to stolen artwork.[70] In 1981, the Pissarro monotype *Le Marché* was stolen from the Musée Faure in France. The work ended up in an art gallery in San Antonio, Texas, which sold it to Davis for $8,500. Davis was unaware that the work had been stolen, until she attempted to auction the work at Sotheby's in 2003, at which time the French Police informed U.S. officials that the work had been stolen. The U.S. government then instituted civil forfeiture proceedings against Davis to return the work to the Musée Faure. The government claimed that the National Stolen Property Act (NSPA) had been violated, which "criminalizes, among other things, the possession or sale of stolen goods valued at $5,000 or more that have moved in interstate or international commerce, with the knowledge that the goods were stolen."[71] The district court entered a final judgment of forfeiture, which Davis appealed.

Davis made several claims on appeal, none of which were successful. First, she claimed that property is subject to forfeiture under 19 U.S.C. § 1595a(c) only if it enters the country "contrary to customs law."[72] This statute provides that property is subject to forfeiture if it is "introduced into the United States 'contrary to law.'"[73] The court did not reach a decision about whether the statute's language meant "contrary to any law," but it did determine that in this case, a violation of the NSPA sufficed.[74] Second, Davis argued that *Le Marché* did not satisfy the $5,000 threshold of the NSPA and that summary judgment should not have been granted for the government on this issue.[75] The court disagreed, noting that none of her evidence showed a genuine issue of material fact that the monotype was worth less than $5,000. After all, the court noted, she purchased it for $8,500.[76] Third, Davis argued that the language of 19 U.S.C. § 1595a(c) provides for forfeiture only if the property "is stolen" at the time of forfeiture.[77] The court also rejected this argument, holding that the plain language of the statute, which provides for forfeiture if the property "is stolen, smuggled, or clandestinely imported or introduced" into the United States, clearly means that the proper inquiry regarding the status of the property is to be made at the time the property enters the country.[78] Fourth, Davis claimed that the innocent-owner defense applies to actions under 19 U.S.C. § 1595a. The court noted, however, that no such defense legally exists under this statute and that subsequent amendments to the statute have included no reference to such a defense. Fifth, Davis argued that the forfeiture violated the Excessive Fines Clause of the Eighth Amendment. The court rejected this argument, finding that this civil forfeiture was remedial, not punitive, as (1) it was not part of a criminal prosecution and (2) it was brought under a customs statute, which is traditionally viewed as remedial.[79] Finally, Davis claimed that she was entitled to just compensation under the Takings Clause of the Fifth Amendment. However, the court noted that the Supreme Court had held on multiple occasions that the government need not provide compensation when the taking is exercised under a governmental power other than eminent domain. The Second Circuit concluded by affirming the forfeiture and denying Davis any compensation.

ISSUES OF ILLEGAL EXPORT

What if an art museum is offered artwork that is not stolen but is illegally exported from its country of origin? As noted in chapter 8, the United States does not enforce the export laws of other countries.[80] However, the retention by a United States museum of such objects today may be prohibited by international treaty and, even when not forbidden, often creates international ripples. There is increasing worldwide sympathy for the principle of repatriation of major cultural properties and for the halting of their improper export. To that end, article 7(a) of the United Nations Educational, Scientific, and Cultural Organization (UNESCO) Convention provides the following:

> The State parties to the Convention undertake: (a) to take the necessary measures, consistent with national legislation, to prevent *museums* and similar institutions within their territories from acquiring cultural property originating in another State Party which has been illegally exported after entry into force of this Convention, in the States concerned. (emphasis added)[81]

While that provision of UNESCO (unlike articles 7(b) and 9) has not been implemented in the United States, other treaties abound. As noted in chapter 8, the United States signed treaties with Mexico in 1970[82] and with Peru in 1981[83] that prohibit exportation of any pre-Columbian items from those countries. In 1972, the United States enacted a statute that prohibits entry into the United States of any architectural sculpture or mural or fragment from a pre- Columbian Indian culture that is not accompanied by a proper export license issued by the country of origin.[84] The art covered by that statute does not have to be stolen to be considered illegally exported under the export laws of the thirteen Latin American signatories.

Although the United States does not ordinarily enforce the export laws of foreign countries in the absence of a specific international treaty, the transporting in the United States of stolen foreign cultural property is a federal crime under the National Stolen Property Act (NSPA),[85] provided it can be established that the accused had knowledge that the property had been stolen. However, the distinction between property that has been stolen in or from a foreign nation and property merely illegally exported has been blurred by the *McClain* case, discussed on pages 629–630.[86] Under *McClain*, the problem incurred by a museum is determining whether to acquire or retain an object under a difficult-to-decipher foreign statute: Should the museum elect to acquire or retain the object, it may be sued by the foreign country in an American court. *McClain* was reinforced by the holding in the *Schultz*[87] case, which now makes it clear (at least in the Second

Circuit) that the NSPA applies to property that is stolen in violation of a foreign patrimony law.

A museum acquiring an artwork should carefully check the work's provenance and also ascertain if the artwork was reported as stolen property. Organizations maintaining a database on stolen artworks include

(1) the International Foundation for Art Research (IFAR), based in New York, and the Art Loss Register (ALR), based in London, which are connected;
(2) the Federal Bureau of Investigation (FBI); and
(3) the International Criminal Police Organization (Interpol).

For example, the Metropolitan Museum of Art in New York City has a formal policy of checking major acquisitions with the Art Loss Register. Numerous websites listing stolen works of art can also be checked.

ISSUES OF U.S. PROTECTED ARTIFACTS

United States historical sites and treasures are also protected, thereby affecting a museum's title to acquisitions. The Archaeological Resources Protection Act of 1979[88] prohibits the receipt, purchase, or sale of any archaeological resource removed from federal or Native American property without a permit after 1979. "Archaeological resource" is defined here as "any material remains of past human life or activities which are of archaeological interest" and which are "at least 100 years of age."[89] The act requires that all excavation on Indian lands be subject to a permit secured through the consent of the Native American tribe that owns the land. That requirement affords some protection to Native Americans, who perceive their culture as separate from the historical heritage of the United States and who have demanded repatriation of Native American artifacts through another statute, the American Indian Religious Freedom Act of 1978. That statute provides the following:

> [I]t shall be the policy of the United States to protect and preserve for American Indians their inherent right of freedom to believe, express, and exercise the traditional religions of the American Indian, Eskimo, Aleut, and Native Hawaiians, including but not limited to access to sites, use and possession of sacred objects and the freedom to worship through ceremonials and traditional rites.[90]

However, that act applies only to federal agencies and does not require museums to return religious artifacts belonging to Native American tribes. It is, therefore, not surprising, as noted by at least one commentator, that courts have determined that the act is merely a statement of federal government policy to recognize the religious beliefs of Native Americans and other peoples.[91]

The Native American Graves Protection and Repatriation Act (NAGPRA) was signed into law on November 16, 1990.[92] NAGPRA describes the rights of Native

American lineal descendants, Indian tribes, and native Hawaiian organizations with respect to human remains, funerary objects, sacred objects, and objects of cultural patrimony with which they can demonstrate lineal descent or cultural affiliation. NAGPRA's purpose is to require that federal agencies and museums receiving federal funds inventory holdings of such remains and objects and work with Indian tribes and native Hawaiian organizations to reach agreement on the repatriation or other disposition of those remains and objects.[93]

In *Bonnichsen v. United States*, the court was faced with the question of who had rights to a 9,300-year-old human skeleton discovered along the Columbia River in the state of Washington in 1996.[94] On one side were scientists who wanted to perform tests on the remains. On the other side, asserting rights under NAGPRA, were Native American groups (represented by the U.S. Department of the Interior) who wanted the remains for reburial in accordance with their religion, without any scientific testing. The district court found for the scientists, stating that the mere fact that the remains were very old was not, in itself, enough to trigger NAGPRA.[95] The Ninth Circuit affirmed, finding that under NAGPRA the definition of "Native American" is written in the present tense— "of, or relating to, a tribe, people or culture that is indigenous to the United States."[96] Since there was no evidence that the 9,300-year-old skeleton had any relationship to an existing tribe, NAGPRA did not apply.

The Omnibus Crime Act of 1994 includes a provision, 18 U.S.C. § 668, making the theft of an item of cultural heritage from a museum a federal crime punishable by up to ten years in prison.[97] Therefore, the FBI can immediately investigate thefts of objects of cultural heritage, which are defined as objects that (1) are worth $100,000 or more or (2) are more than 100 years old and worth more than $5,000.[98] The act also extends the statute of limitations to twenty years[99] and makes knowingly trafficking in such stolen objects an explicit federal crime.[100]

In *United States v. O'Higgins*, the court upheld the constitutionality of section 668.[101] O'Higgins was charged with stealing "objects of cultural heritage" from the Music Division of the New York Public Library for the Performing Arts in New York City in violation of the statute.[102] The two items allegedly stolen were a leaf from a copy of a piano minuet by Wolfgang Amadeus Mozart, signed by the composer, with an estimated value of $50,000, and an essay and three letters by Richard Wagner; each of the items was alleged to be over 100 years old and to have a value of over $5,000. O'Higgins moved to dismiss the charges on the grounds that section 668 is unconstitutional because Congress exceeded its power to legislate under the Commerce Clause.[103] He argued that his theft from the library had no impact on interstate commerce, so he could not be convicted under the statute.[104] The court found to the contrary, stating that common sense suggests that stealing objects of cultural heritage from a museum significantly impacts the institution's mission, and as the museum's activities affect interstate commerce, thefts from the museum do as well. The court mentioned two instances in which museums were victimized by art thieves and concluded that "there can be no doubt that the theft of a world famous Rembrandt would substantially affect interstate commerce through its impact on the value of other works of art and the cost of insurance."[105]

As noted earlier, section 668 applies only to museums. The issue of what is considered a "museum" for purposes of this statute was explored in *United States v. Pritchard*.[106] The defendant Pritchard was convicted of stealing a confederate uniform from a historic house in Memphis under section 668. On appeal, Pritchard argued that his conviction should be overturned since, to be considered a "museum" under the statute, an organization had to "own" the tangible objects that it exhibited to the public.[107] In this case, the confederate uniform (along with all of the other objects at the historic house) was on loan from an individual who had inherited it; therefore, argued Pritchard, the historic house could not be considered a museum because it displayed only borrowed objects, not objects that it owned. The court was unwilling to accept that argument. Although it was somewhat of a stretch, the court found that the historic house itself was "an object of great historical and aesthetic significance," and since the organization owned, utilized, and cared for the historic house, the court held it was a museum.[108] Pritchard's conviction was affirmed.

ISSUES OF COPYRIGHT

When an art museum acquires an artwork for accession, it must ascertain whether it is also acquiring one or more of that bundle of rights in and to the artwork known as copyright. The museum should also ascertain the identity of any copyright holders. As discussed in chapter 11, copyright is the legal recognition of certain exclusive property rights that a creator has in and to her work, such as:

(1) the right to reproduce or make copies of the work;
(2) the right to adapt or make derivative works based on the original work;
(3) the right to distribute—that is, sell, rent, or loan the work;
(4) the right to perform the work publicly (if applicable to the nature of the work); and
(5) the right to display the work publicly.[109]

Generally, the museum's inquiry is pertinent solely to works created within the past ninety-five years; any copyright attaching to works more than ninety-five years old has expired, thereby putting such works into the public domain. If the work acquired was created on or after January 1, 1978, it is governed by the Copyright Act of 1976, as amended,[110] and may be protected by copyright even if it bears no copyright notice. If the acquired work was created before January 1, 1978, and bears a copyright notice, the museum should ascertain whether the copyright has expired; if the copyright has not expired, the museum should obtain the identity of the copyright holder. If the acquired work was created before January 1, 1978, and does not bear a copyright notice, the chances are that the copyright has been forfeited and that the work is in the public domain. As noted in chapter 11, when a work is in the public domain, everyone is free to exercise the rights in and to the work that would inhere in the copyright holder if the work had copyright protection.

When an art museum acquires ownership of an artwork, is it also acquiring ownership of any existing copyright in and to the work? If ownership of the artwork has been conveyed to the museum on or after January 1, 1978, ownership of copyright in and to the artwork is *not* conveyed unless such a transfer is memorialized in a writing signed by the transferor or the transferor's authorized agent.[111] If ownership of a protected artwork has been conveyed to the museum before January 1, 1978, but subsequent to the date of its first publication, conveyance of the copyright in the work similarly requires a writing signed by the transferor or the transferor's authorized agent.[112] However, when ownership of a protected unpublished artwork has been conveyed to the museum before January 1, 1978, then, as a general rule, the conveyance of the artwork carried with it an implied assignment of the copyright embodied in it.[113] As a rule, a museum should note in its records the copyright status and the copyright holder, along with any limitations of rights, of each artwork accessioned for its collections.

Should an art museum attempt to obtain copyright interests in each protected artwork it accessions for its collections? Without copyright interests, a museum is limited in the use it can make of the protected artwork it owns. Under the copyright statutes, a museum, as owner of the physical artwork, may display it publicly (provided the display is not projected to distant sites) and lend it elsewhere for display at the place where the art is lent.[114] Under the fair-use doctrine, discussed on pages 999–1019, it can generally also photograph or copy a work for internal registration use or archival use or for internal teaching, scholarship, or research purposes without obtaining permission of the copyright holder.[115] However, a museum may wish to make other use of an accessioned artwork: It may wish to reproduce it for inclusion in art catalogs to be sold to the public or in salable slide collections of artwork, or it may wish to reproduce an artwork in poster form, on note cards, or even on mugs or T-shirts or as jewelry to be sold in the museum's gift shop.[116] To secure permission for such use, the museum should negotiate with the copyright owner an exclusive or nonexclusive license (the exclusive license must be in writing) (see discussion of copyright licenses on pages 941–945) with provisions to pay royalties to the copyright owner if there are significant commercial considerations. Since the copyright owner often stands to benefit from the increased exposure of the artwork afforded by a museum, she often agrees to grant a limited license to the museum. If, however, a museum is required to pay a significant sum of money to acquire such additional rights, it may not be worth the expenditure of the museum's limited resources.

RESTRICTED GIFTS

A gift is a voluntary transfer of property from one to another without consideration.[117] A valid gift must include

(1) an intention to make a gift;

(2) delivery—actual, constructive, or symbolic—of the property given that is complete and unconditional; and

(3) an acceptance by the donee.[118]

On occasion, property may be given to an art museum in the form of a charitable trust in which certain restrictions are placed on the use of the trust property. It has been suggested that museums, as a general policy, should not accept gifts of artwork for accession that have strings attached.[119] It has also been suggested that museums should have a procedure for considering exceptions to the above rule; for example, for the museum's own protection, a deed of gift for restricted gifts should be countersigned by the museum official authorized to approve such exceptions, and the terms of the restrictions should be noted in the accession records.[120]

Whether a museum should accept a restricted gift depends, in part, on the restriction. A requirement, for example, to display an artwork forever places the museum in conflict with its fiduciary role to the public; at some future time, the artwork may no longer be relevant to or a desirable example of a particular collection. Likewise, a promise to return an artwork to the donor if sometime in the future the museum decides to dispose of the artwork may be an unduly burdensome promise. What if the donor's heirs cannot be found? As a possible solution, at least one commentator has suggested that the deed of gift use precatory language, rather than mandatory language.[121] That is, the donor may state that it is her wish, but not command, that the artwork be administered in a certain manner. Although not imposing a legal obligation, which can be problematic for some museums, precatory language can be construed to impose a moral obligation on the museum to adhere in good faith to the donor's restriction, deviating only when so dictated by sound judgment in the particular circumstances.

When a legally restricted gift in the form of a charitable trust becomes impossible or impracticable to carry out, a museum may petition the court for relief from the restrictions by means of a *cy pres* action.[122] The *cy pres* doctrine requires that a charitable trust be executed with as close an approximation to the donor's original intent as is reasonably practicable, and the doctrine may be invoked only if the donor evinced a general charitable intention.[123] The purpose of *cy pres*, which may be invoked only by the courts and which may apply to a charitable corporation or a charitable trust, is to prevent the failure of a gift.[124] If the donor, when making the original gift, indicated a specific purpose for the gift without evincing a general charitable intention, the doctrine does not apply, and the gift will most likely fail.

Some states have set forth specific requirements for *cy pres* relief. For instance, New York courts engage in a two-step analysis to determine whether to grant *cy pres* relief.[125] The first element is that *cy pres* relief must be available. This requires a three-prong analysis: (1) the gift was charitable in nature, (2) the donor had a general, not specific, charitable intent, and (3) the circumstances have changed since the time of the gift in such a way as to make compliance with the restrictions in the gift impossible or impracticable. The second element of the analysis requires that the "proposed modification most closely approximates the donor's charitable intent."[126]

This analysis was applied in *In re Fisk University*, in which the Tennessee Supreme Court upheld lower court decisions granting *cy pres* relief to Fisk University, located in Nashville, Tennessee, with respect to a donation of 101 works of art from Georgia O'Keeffe.[127] O'Keeffe directly owned four of these works; the remainder was part of the estate of her husband, photographer and gallery owner Alfred Stieglitz, which she donated to Fisk in her capacity as executrix of his estate and/or as the owner of a life estate in the pieces. All of these works were gifted subject to a number of restrictions, including that the pieces would not be sold and that the works of art were to be displayed at Fisk as the Alfred Stieglitz Collection. About twenty years after Georgia O'Keeffe's death, Fisk was facing serious financial difficulties and sought to sell two of the paintings of the Alfred Stieglitz Collection in order to raise much needed revenue. However, the conditions placed upon the donation prohibited Fisk from doing so. As a result, Fisk filed suit, asking the court to grant *cy pres* relief from compliance with the restrictions included in O'Keeffe's donation. The trial court granted summary judgment for The O'Keeffe Museum (the residuary beneficiary of Georgia O'Keeffe's estate), reasoning that Fisk had not satisfied all of the requirements for *cy pres* relief."[128]

As to the first element of the *cy pres* analysis, The Tennessee Appellate Court, in two separate decisions, reversed the trial court and held that cy pres relief was available. First, the court noted that it was undisputed that the gifts to Fisk were charitable in nature, satisfying the first prong of the first element of the New York *cy pres* analysis.[129] Second, the court found that O'Keeffe had a general, rather than specific, charitable intent. To make this determination, the court noted that a donor will be found to have a general charitable intent if: the provisions of such gift so indicate, the donor made similar charitable gifts to other charities, and the gift lacks a divesting clause that is effective upon the breach of the conditions in the gift.[130] The court noted that it was clear in O'Keeffe's husband's will, as well as in her correspondence to Fisk regarding the gifts, that the purpose of the donation was to "make the Collection available to the public in *Nashville* and *the South* for the benefit of those who did not have access to comparable collections to promote the general study of art" (italics in the decision).[131] In addition, O'Keeffe made similar charitable gifts to other nonprofit institutions and the gift contained no divesting clause, which further showed that O'Keeffe had a general charitable intent. The court also held that the final prong of the first element of the *cy pres* analysis was satisfied, based on testimony by Fisk's President regarding the University's financial difficulties, in which she stated that Fisk was not viable in light of these difficulties.[132] These financial difficulties indicated that circumstances had changed in such a manner as to make compliance with the conditions in O'Keeffe's donation impracticable.

The specific *cy pres* relief which Fisk requested was an arrangement with the Crystal Bridges Museum of American Art, Inc. in Benton, Arkansas, which would permit the University to sell a 50% interest in the Collection for $30 million and under which both Fisk and Crystal Bridges would have the right to display the collection two out of every four years.[133] The Tennessee Attorney General submitted two alternative arrangements. First, the Attorney General proposed that the Frist Center for Visual Arts take control of and display the Collection until Fisk regained financial stability.[134] Second, the Attorney General suggested the establishment of an endowment at Fisk funded by private donations that would generate income sufficient to maintain and display the Collection at Fisk.[135]

In 2010, upon remand from the Tennessee Appellate Court, the trial court approved Fisk's proposal but required that Fisk would place $20 million of the proceeds into an endowment for the Collection.[136] The trial court held that Fisk's proposed arrangement with Crystal Bridges would closely approximate O'Keeffe's charitable intent, since Crystal Bridges had "superior resources . . . to provide this important Collection excellent support and access to the public," the arrangement would ensure that the "Collection retains a presence in Nashville," and "the proposal enhanced Ms. O'Keeffe's purpose of sharing the Collection with Nashville and the South."[137] On the other hand, the court found that both of the Attorney General's proposals would "frustrate the unique dispositional design of Ms. O'Keeffe's charitable gift," especially her intent that the Collection be located in Nashville.[138] The trial court required Fisk to establish a $20 million endowment for the benefit of the Collection in order to fund necessary expenses, ensure that Fisk did not default on its monetary obligations with Crystal Bridges, and separate the collection from Fisk in the possible event Fisk became bankrupt.[139]

The Appellate Court affirmed the trial court's decision that the arrangement with Crystal Bridges closely approximated O'Keeffe's charitable intent. However, the Appellate Court found that the trial court's requirement that Fisk establish a $20 million endowment was an abuse of its discretion. After all, O'Keeffe never required such an endowment to be created as part of her gift, and there was no indication that Fisk or O'Keeffe ever contemplated establishing such an endowment. The Appellate Court held that the trial court had "no authority under the statute and the facts of this case to effectively decree the manner by which the Collection would be used by Fisk in furtherance of its educational mission."[140]

The Tennessee Attorney General appealed the case to the Tennessee Supreme Court. In April 2012, the Tennessee Supreme Court refused the Tennessee Attorney General's appeal and, at the time of this writing, the case has been sent to Tennessee's Chancery Court to work out the final details of the arrangement.[141] At the time of this writing, Fisk plans to use the $30 million sale proceeds for improving academic programs, enhancing its endowment, increasing student scholarships, and refurbishing buildings.[142]

Related to *cy pres* is the "doctrine of deviation," which may be invoked in the case of private trusts and, particularly, charitable trusts.[143] A court may apply this doctrine to alter the prescribed method of accomplishing the purpose of the trust. Unlike *cy pres*, which is invoked to modify the purpose of a charitable trust, the doctrine of deviation is enforced to ease administrative restraints not anticipated by the donor, so that the original purpose of the charitable trust can be executed.[144]

The doctrine of deviation was relied on by the Court of Common Pleas in the *Barnes Foundation* case, where the foundation sought permission to increase the number of trustees on its governing board and to relocate the art collection in its Merion, Pennsylvania, gallery to a new facility in Philadelphia.[145] The removal of the art collection to Philadelphia was requested despite the fact that the trust indenture of Dr. Barnes, the founder, mandated that it be maintained in Merion in one gallery exactly as established by Dr. Barnes prior to his death. In its first decision, the court found that in the current sophisticated world of charitable fundraising, it was appropriate to expand the size of the board.[146] Moreover, the court found that since the foundation was on the brink of financial collapse, the provision in Dr. Barnes's indenture mandating that the gallery be maintained in Merion was not sacrosanct, and could yield under the doctrine of deviation. However, before the court would allow the move to Philadelphia (the deviation), it had to be convinced that the move was the least drastic modification of the indenture that would accomplish the donor's desired ends. In its second decision, rendered after extensive hearings which generated 1,200 pages of testimony, the court found that the foundation showed clearly and convincingly the need to deviate from the terms of Dr. Barnes's indenture.[147] The court relied on the doctrine of deviation and noted:

> As we have cited many times in the course of the litigation involving the foundation, section 381 of the Restatement (Second) of Trusts states: "[A] court will direct or permit the trustee of a charitable trust to deviate from a term of the trust if it appears to the court that compliance is impossible or illegal or that owing to circumstances not known to the settlor and not anticipated by him, compliance would defeat or substantially impair the accomplishment of the purposes of the trust." It is only the administrative provisions of a trust that are subject to deviation, *i.e.,* "the details of administration which the settlor has prescribed in order to secure the more important result of obtaining for the beneficiaries the advantages which the settlor stated he wished them to have."[148]

The Barnes collection moved to a new facility in Philadelphia that opened on May 19, 2012.[149]

TAXES

As noted earlier in this chapter, public art museums are automatically exempt from federal income taxes, and donors to such museums obtain charitable contribution deductions from income tax for donations made solely for public purposes. Likewise, private art museums that qualify under section 501(c)(3) have tax-exempt status and provide the donor with a charitable-contribution deduction. The subject of charitable giving from a tax perspective is dealt with in full in chapter 15 on taxes and estate planning for collectors.

Loans

When a person or other entity loans artwork to an art museum, the transaction—delivery, use, and return—is subject to the law of bailment. A bailment is the delivery of property by one person to another for a particular use upon a contract, express or implied, that after the purpose is completed the property is returned to the person who delivered it. The lender is the bailor, and the museum is the bailee.

STANDARD OF CARE

Under the common law, the standard of care to which a bailee was held depended on the nature of the bailment.[150] When the bailment was for the sole benefit of the bailee, the bailee was held to a high duty of care and was liable for even slight negligence; when the bailment was for the mutual benefit of the bailor and the bailee, an intermediate standard of ordinary care of the property was imposed, and the bailee was liable for ordinary negligence; and when the bailment was solely for the bailor's benefit, the bailee was required to exercise only slight care and was liable only for gross negligence. However, the distinction among degrees of negligence is often difficult to determine, so some case law appears to dispense with those distinctions in favor of an ordinary or reasonable standard of care appropriate to the particular circumstances.[151] That means, for example, that when a lender delivers a work of art to a museum for a particular purpose, such as an exhibition, with the understanding that the property will be returned in its same condition when the purpose is concluded, the museum need not under every circumstance return it in exactly the same condition in order to avoid liability. If something happens to the artwork while it is in the museum's custody (if it is damaged or stolen, for example), it may be sufficient for the museum to account for it by noting that the artwork was damaged or stolen. If the lender is subsequently able to prove that the artwork's damage or theft was due to the museum's negligence while the artwork was in its custody, the lender will be able to recover damages. However, if negligence by the museum cannot be established, the lender, under the law of bailment, as illustrated below, may have no basis of recovery for damage to the property.

In *Colburn v. Washington State Art Association*, the plaintiff, a lapidary and manufacturer of jewelry, was approached by a curator of a museum maintained in Seattle, the defendant, and was invited to put some of his goods on exhibition in the museum's rooms.[152] After some urging by the museum, the plaintiff agreed to do so, with the understanding that he could place his business card by the exhibit as a form of advertising, thus creating a bailment for the benefit of both parties. When the plaintiff went to examine the exhibit case in which his goods were to be put, he requested the use of a padlock on the case for further security. The museum refused to comply, not wanting to tamper with the cases, and advised the jeweler that all the cases, none of which had padlocks, were securely wired together and that, moreover, a watchman was on duty to enhance security. The plaintiff thereupon left his goods with the museum and visited his exhibit several times over the next few months. The plaintiff's goods had been placed there without any agreement as to their remaining any particular length of time, and he was free to remove them at any time.

About six months after the goods were placed on exhibition, some of them were stolen from the exhibit case. At the time, a museum officer was aware of suspicious behavior on the part of two youths in the museum, sought to apprehend them, failed, and went to the police. The plaintiff sued the museum, arguing that the goods were placed on exhibition under a contract amounting to a warranty for their return. The trial court agreed and found for the plaintiff for an amount equal to the value of the goods stolen and not recovered. However, the appeals court reversed, holding that the situation was nothing more than a

> bailment for the mutual benefit of both appellant and respondent. This being the nature of the relation between them . . . it seems plain . . . that appellant was bound to exercise ordinary diligence only.[153]

Moreover, the court found that the museum had exercised reasonable care under the circumstances. The court then noted the general rule in bailment law: When a bailor sues a bailee to recover damages for goods placed in the bailee's possession that are not accounted for in any manner and are not returned to the bailor on demand, there is a presumption of negligence against the bailee. However, in cases of loss by burglary, larceny, fire, and other causes that by themselves do not indicate negligence on the part of the bailee, the bailee has met the prima facie case of negligence against her, and the burden then shifts to the plaintiff, as in any other case of alleged negligence.[154]

Under bailment law, reckless indifference may be equivalent to negligence, thus giving rise to liability. In a case in which a defendant-museum borrowed a diamond brooch for exhibition with no pecuniary advantage accruing to the plaintiff, the museum's custody of the brooch was so casual that it did not know "when or how the brooch was lost, or if stolen by whom, when and in what circumstances."[155] When the loss was finally noticed, the museum refrained from informing the plaintiff for two months. Consequently, the museum did not overcome the prima facie case of negligence established by the plaintiff.[156]

THE LOAN AGREEMENT

If bailment law remained the sole underpinning for the loans of artwork to art museums and similar institutions, the chances are that most loans would founder, since the lender is generally afforded little protection against loss or damage to her artwork. That loans continue to flourish must be attributed to the practice of using loan agreements. The bailee's duty of care may be altered by contract, as parties to an agreement are free to contract as they choose, provided the agreement does not violate public policy. Moreover, the loan agreement can provide that certain risks taken by the lender are to be covered by insurance. Since the loan agreement and the related insurance policy should fit seamlessly and since insurance policies themselves are not uniform, the loan agreements will vary. Model loan agreements are found at the end of this chapter (see Appendixes 17-1, 17-2, 17-3, and 17-4). Nevertheless, certain provisions are common to virtually all loan arrangements between lenders and museums. Those provisions are discussed below.

DATES OF EXHIBITION
The agreement notes the dates or the period of time during which the artwork will be exhibited.

LENDER'S IDENTIFICATION
The lender indicates her name, address, telephone number, and the exact form of her name for the exhibition label and the catalog.

THE WORK BEING LOANED
The loan agreement generally includes a questionnaire seeking to ascertain basic facts about the work being loaned—for example, the name of the artist, the title of the work, the medium or materials used, the date of the work (if it appears at all), whether the work is signed, and its size. The questionnaire may also require known details on the provenance of the work.

INSURANCE
The museum undertakes to insure the borrowed work for an amount of money specified by the lender. The insurance normally covers all forms of risk except those arising from inherent vice, governmental action, war, invasion, hostilities, rebellion, insurrection, nuclear damage, and so on.[157] As a result of the attack on the World Trade Center in New York City on September 11, 2001, many collectors will not loan works of art unless they are assured that the museum has terrorism coverage as part of its insurance policy. However, a loss caused by one of those extended perils may still leave the museum liable as a bailee if the lender can prove either actual negligence or reckless indifference. If the lender chooses to rely on her own insurance, rather than the museum's insurance, the lender is generally required by the borrower to add the museum as an additional insured party or to provide a waiver of subrogation against the museum. That requirement protects the museum in the event of loss.

For example, suppose a collector, under her own insurance, lends a valuable work of art to a museum, and, because of negligence on the part of a museum employee, the artwork is damaged. The collector's insurance company reimburses the collector for the sizable restoration costs incurred by the collector plus loss in value; in so doing, the collector's rights arising from the incident are subrogated—that is, passed on—to her insurance company. The insurance company in turn can sue the museum for the restoration costs incurred and the loss in value resulting from the museum's negligence, leaving the museum unprotected. If the lender obtains from her insurance company a waiver of subrogation against the museum, that could not happen. And if the museum is listed as an additional insured party on the lender's policy, that could not happen, as an insurance company cannot seek reimbursement from the insured. However, under most loan agreements, even if the lender fails to obtain the waiver of subrogation against the museum or to list the museum as an additional insured party, the lender is deemed to release the museum from any liability in connection with the loan.

CATALOG AND PUBLICITY

The museum may want to obtain photographs of the work for catalog reproduction and publicity. It may also want to reproduce the work in its publications and for publicity purposes in connection with the exhibition. The museum may also seek permission to use the work for telecasts for publicity or educational purposes. In addition, it may wish to make and distribute slides for educational use.

FRAMING

The agreement addresses the condition of the work's framing, if any. The museum may also seek permission to reframe or remat the work for the exhibition.

SHIPPING

The agreement sets forth the pickup and delivery dates agreed to by the parties. It also details the shipping arrangements for the work of art and notes how the costs of crating, shipping, and transporting are to be borne.

ADDITIONAL CONDITIONS

The agreement generally includes a schedule of additional conditions governing the loan. Some common conditions include a statement as to the standard of care to which the museum will adhere (usually, care comparable to that given to its own property); a notice of any change of address on the part of the lender; the notices to be given if the ownership of the work changes during the term of the loan; and, in the absence of a specified term of duration, a ceiling on the length of the term of the loan.

UNRETURNABLE LOANS

To cover those situations in which the museum, through no fault of its own, is unable to return a work of art at the end of the term of the loan, a number of museums have added to their agreements a provision similar to the following:

> The Museum's right to return the work shall accrue absolutely at the termination date of the loan. If reasonable efforts to return the work fail, then the Museum shall have the right to place the work in storage at Lender's expense for storage fees and

the cost of insurance and to have and enforce a lien for such fees and costs. If the work is not claimed after three years from the date of commencement of this loan, Lender hereby gives all right, title, and interest in the work as an unrestricted and unredeemable absolute charitable gift to the Museum.[158]

INTERNATIONAL LOANS

The exchange of artworks among citizens of diverse nations by means of loans or traveling exhibitions adds a dimension of goodwill toward and knowledge of the culture of the participating nations. However, such exchanges raise heightened legal concerns regarding insurance, seizure, and force majeure.

INSURANCE

The cost of insuring international incoming loans of artistic treasures accounts for a major portion of an exhibition budget[159] and has historically caused a number of even well-endowed museums in the United States to forgo participation in international exchanges. To ensure a stream of funds to acquire international exhibitions on loan and thereby share in the world's cultural treasures, Congress enacted the Arts and Artifacts Indemnity Act[160] in 1975. Under the act, the federal government guarantees to pay loss or damage claims arising out of museum exhibitions of artworks, including tapestries, paintings, sculptures, folk art, graphics, craft arts, manuscripts, rare documents and books, photographs, motion pictures, audiotapes, and videotapes, provided such property is of educational, cultural, or scientific value and is certified by the secretary of state or a designee as being in the national interest.

FOREIGN LOANS: SEIZURE AND OTHER JUDICIAL PROCESS

If a foreign lender is involved in litigation, or there are provenance questions regarding a loaned object of cultural significance from a foreign lender, there is an ever-present risk that the object on loan in the United States will be seized by court order in conjunction with that litigation, or other judicial process will be brought against the object, the lender or the borrowing institution while it is on temporary exhibition in the United States, even if the litigation is unrelated to the loan. To overcome that deterrent to foreign incoming loans, the United States in 1965 enacted an immunity statute (referred to in chapter 2) that shields objects determined to be of cultural significance from court seizure or judicial process that may have the effect of depriving the borrowing institution of custody of the object.[161] The statute holds that objects imported into the United States by nonprofit organizations for temporary display are granted immunity from judicial process, including seizure, provided that, before the object enters the country, the U.S. Department of State, on application by the borrowing institution, determines that the object is of cultural significance and finds that the temporary exhibition of the object is in the national interest. The statute does not define cultural significance or national interest, so it is within the discretion of the Department of State to make these determinations. If all criteria are met, a notice of immunity, in accordance with the statute, is published in the *Federal Register*, and the U.S. Attorney General is empowered to intervene in any judicial proceeding to enforce the immunity protection. Immunity from seizure or judicial process for the applicable property then remains in effect for the time the property is in the United States for the temporary exhibition.

FORCE MAJEURE

The international aspects of a loan raise particular concerns about the occurrence of circumstances beyond the parties' control, such as: war, natural disaster, and political unrest. Because cultural property is unique, its security and preservation is of primary importance. Accordingly, loan arrangements between a museum and a foreign lending party tend to excuse performance of some elements of the loan agreement if events beyond the parties' control make such performance hazardous.[162] Therefore, a foreign loan agreement generally states that its provisions are subject to the doctrine of force majeure—that is, superior or irresistible force.

TAXATION

The Internal Revenue Code in section 2105(c) specifically exempts from United States estate tax works of art owned by a nonresident who is not a citizen of the United States when those artworks are on loan to a public gallery or museum in the United States at the time of the death of the owner of the works of art.

OUTGOING WORKS

Deaccessioning

Deaccessioning is the process by which an art museum removes and disposes permanently of works in its collection.[163] There are valid reasons for deaccession. For example, a museum may wish to prune a collection to define its areas of interest more clearly. Moreover, for a museum with limited financial resources (which describes most museums), the costs of properly storing and conserving artwork may not permit the retention of peripheral art objects. Since a museum exists to serve the public, it must preserve the public's confidence in it as a responsible institution. Accordingly, a museum's decision to dispose permanently of an art object or objects should not be taken without considering the legal, public relations, and ethical issues governing deaccessioning.

LEGAL ISSUES

Although deaccessioning artwork from an art museum is neither illegal nor unethical per se, a museum contemplating the procedure should first consult its own charter and the state statutes addressing the disposal of assets of charitable organizations to determine if there are any limitations in its disposition rights.[164]

Generally, an art museum may deaccession collection objects when its governing board decides to do so; the museum need not seek court approval. If, however, a museum wishes to sell collection objects acquired by gift when there are restrictions on the objects' disposition, court approval may be required. As noted earlier, the state attorneys general oversee museums (whether they are nonprofit corporations or charitable trusts) and may either initiate or participate in court proceedings that address the propriety of deaccessioning a museum's collection objects. When a deed of gift includes no restrictions but merely precatory language (a general nonbinding expression of the donor's intent) addressing the issue of deaccessioning, a museum need not seek court approval but should attempt to consult with the donor or the donor's estate before the disposition.[165]

Few court cases have dealt with deaccessioning. In Massachusetts, two judgments were issued authorizing museums to apply sales proceeds toward capital improvements and operating expenses.[166] In another case, the court granted an attorney general a preliminary injunction preventing the auction of paintings.[167] In still another case, a museum that relied heavily on public funding that was severely cut was permitted by the court to sell an Henri Matisse painting valued at more than $4 million.[168] The court's decision regarding the allocation of the proceeds was reserved for a later date, but, since the painting failed to sell, the decision and its supporting analysis never came to light. In the other cases noted, the judgments issued were not accompanied by opinions; therefore, any insights the courts may have had in reaching their decisions were never revealed.[169]

If there is little guidance to date on deaccessioning from state courts, there is even less from state legislation. In August 1996, New York enacted legislation setting forth guidelines for the objectives and procedures of museum deaccessioning. The statute—which covers only one museum, the New York State Museum in Albany—provides as follows:

> Proceeds derived from the deaccessioning of any property from the collection of the museum shall be used only for the acquisition of property for the collection or for the preservation, protection and care of the collection and shall not be used to defray ongoing operating expenses of the museum. The state comptroller shall establish a fund, separate from the general fund, for the proceeds of deaccessioning.[170]

In New York, there are further rules regarding deaccessioning that are applicable to New York museums chartered by the New York State Board of Regents. Specifically, effective June 8, 2011, the Board of Regents amended its Rule 3.27, relating to museum collections management policies.[171] In light of the fact that museums are facing "deficits that threaten the ownership or integrity of their collections," the amendment clarifies the Regents' Rules with respect to deaccessioning works. The amended rules set forth ten situations in which museums may deaccession items in their collections:

(i)   the item is inconsistent with the mission of the institution as set forth in its mission statement;

(ii)   the item has failed to retain its identity;

(iii)   the item is redundant;

(iv)   the item's preservation and conservation needs are beyond the capacity of the institution to provide;

(v)   the item is deaccessioned to accomplish refinement of collections;

(vi)   it has been established that the item is inauthentic;

(vii)   the institution is repatriating the item or returning the item to its rightful owner;

(viii) the institution is returning the item to the donor, or the donor's heirs or assigns, to fulfill donor restrictions relating to the item for which the institution is no longer able to meet;

(ix)   the item presents a hazard to people or to other collection items; and/or

(x)   the item has been lost or stolen and has not been recovered.[172]

The amended rules also provide that the proceeds from deaccessioning can be used only for the "acquisition of collections or the preservation, conversation or direct care of collections" and not for operational expenses, as collateral for a loan, or for any other purpose. In addition, the amended rules require museums to have a written collections management policy that is readily available to the public and that identifies clear standards for the institution to use when making decisions about collections. Finally, the rules require museums to annually report all works deaccessioned or disposed of in the previous year.[173]

Section 6050L of the Internal Revenue Code requires a donee-museum of any property for which an income tax charitable deduction of more than $5,000 was claimed to file an information report with the IRS if the contributed property is sold, exchanged, or otherwise disposed of within three years after the date of receipt of the contribution.[174] The IRS has issued Form 8282 ("Donee Information Return") to be used by donee-museums for the purpose of satisfying the filing requirement. The latest version of the form is dated April 2009, a copy of which appears at the end of this chapter (Appendix 17-5). All exempt organizations have to keep records in sufficient detail to meet the filing requirement.

PUBLIC RELATIONS ISSUES

When a museum decides to sell parts of its collections, it should advertise the upcoming sales at public auctions or in the public marketplace. Such advertising serves to inform the community about the upcoming deaccessioning, permits public witness to the disposition of the collection objects, encourages a broad market of potential purchasers, and affords the public an opportunity to protest the museum's intended action if anyone is so inclined. Moreover, in keeping with its responsibility to the public and its liability under a number of state statutes addressing the disposition of assets of a charitable organization, the museum should attempt to place the deaccessioned artwork with another museum or nonprofit public organization where the artwork will remain accessible to the public.[175]

Despite the controversy surrounding it, the practice of deaccessioning has gained acceptance throughout the art museum community and to a smaller extent with the public at large, provided the proceeds of the disposal are applied to the purchase of artwork that is either superior or more appropriate to the museum's collections.[176] Examples of such deaccessionings include the following:

- In 1989, the Minneapolis Walker Art Center sold twenty-five nineteenth-century paintings, including Frederic Church's *Home by the Lake*, in order to add to its collections of twentieth-century art.[177]
- In 1989, the Museum of Modern Art in New York City sold at auction and by private treaty seven of its masterpieces—a Giorgio de Chirico, two Pablo Picassos, a Wassily Kandinsky, a Claude Monet, a Pierre-Auguste Renoir, and a Piet Mondrian—for a reported total of $40 million. The proceeds were used to buy Vincent van Gogh's *Portrait of Joseph Rou-lin*.[178]
- In 1990, the Guggenheim Museum in New York City, amid great public outcry, auctioned at Sotheby's for more than $47 million three paintings at the heart of its stellar collection of early modernism: a 1914 Kandinsky, a 1918 Marc Chagall, and a 1923 Amedeo Modigliani. The sales proceeds were used to acquire 211 works of minimalist art from the late 1970s belonging to the Italian Count Giuseppe Panza di Biumo. The acquired Panza collection included fourteen stark sculptures by Richard Serra and a dozen fluorescent-light pieces by Dan Flavin.[179]
- In 1999, the Museum of Modern Art in New York City sold at auction George Bellows' *Polo Crowd* for $27.5 million. The painting had been owned by Mrs. John Hay Whitney for almost seventy years until her death in 1998, when it was bequeathed to MoMA. MoMA decided to sell the painting in order to raise funds for future acquisitions because it fell outside MoMA's traditional collecting mission.[180]
- In 2003, the Aldrich Museum of Contemporary Art in Ridgefield, Connecticut, sold its entire collection of paintings and sculpture in order to concentrate on the museum's mission of photography.[181]
- In 2004, the Museum of Modern Art in New York City sold at auction nine works from its permanent collection ostensibly to raise funds for new acquisitions. The works sold included works by Chagall, de Chirico, Léger, Magritte, Picasso, and Pollock.
- In 2009, the Los Angeles County Museum of Art sold at auction fourteen of its works by Old Masters for $5.8 million. The museum had shifted its focus to art made after 1950 and determined that such Old Master paintings were no longer appropriate[182] to include in its collections. The sale proceeds were used for new acquisitions.[183]
- In 2011, the Cleveland Museum of Art sold thirty-two Old Master paintings at auction. Most of them had been gifts, some had been downgraded in their attributions, and one had lost its value through "overzealous clean-

ing." Proceeds from the sale were used to revamp and improve the museum's Old Master collection.[184]

- In 2011, the Boston Museum of Fine Arts sold at auction eight works to fund the acquisition of Caillebotte's *Man at His Bath*, a rare Impressionist work which the museum described as "one of the greatest works by artist." The works sold included some of the museum's famous collection pieces by artists such as Monet, Gauguin, Pissarro, Renoir, Sisley, Vasily Vereshchagin, and Maxime Camille Louis Maufra. The Monet, Gauguin, and Pissarro works had been exhibited not only at the BMFA but also at other museums throughout the world.[185]
- In 2011, the Museum of Modern Art in New York City sold at auction Rufino Tamayo's *Watermelon Slices* for $2.2 million. The museum planned to use the funds to acquire new works.[186]
- In 2011, the Art Institute of Chicago offered at auction works by Picasso, Matisse, and Braque. The museum had long considered deaccessioning these works, noting that it had "better examples from the exact same period." The funds were put towards future acquisitions.[187]

However, the voice of the public has sometimes overridden such deaccessioning decisions. In the spring of 1990, for example, the Modern Art Museum of Fort Worth intended to sell at auction through Sotheby's the Thomas Eakins painting *The Swimming Hole*, one of the most famous nineteenth-century works by an American artist. The museum arranged for the sale in order to raise funds to acquire works of modern art, the focus of its collection. The public outcry to keep the painting in Texas was so furious that the museum withdrew the painting from auction and helped to raise $10 million to enable the Amon Carter Museum across the street from it to buy *The Swimming Hole*.[188] Similarly, in 2005, the Heckscher Museum of Art in Huntington, New York, applied to the New York State Board of Regents for permission to sell George Grosz's *Eclipse of the Sun* for $19 million to finance, in part, a construction project. The proposal drew intense criticism from people who raised doubts about the museum's priorities. The museum petitioned the Regents for an exception to its rule that prohibits organizations from using proceeds derived from the deaccessioning of property for "purposes other than the acquisition, preservation, protection or care of collections."[189] The Regents eventually acquiesced to the public's demands and voted to stop the sale of the work on March 21, 2005.[190] Further, in 2009, Brandeis University announced that, due to the recession and money constraints, it would close its Rose Art Museum and sell at auction its vast collection of contemporary art. The collection included masterpieces by Willem de Kooning, Jasper Johns, Roy Lichtenstein, and Andy Warhol. However, there was much public protest surrounding this proposal, which culminated in a lawsuit intended to prevent the museum from selling its collections. In 2011, the parties reached a settlement, and the university decided it would not sell the museum's artwork.[191]

Decisions by museums to deaccession artwork to meet operating expenses or capital expenditures will continue to meet with strong public criticism. The following are examples of such deaccessionings that were carried out despite public outcry:

- In 1991, the Brandeis's Rose Art Museum sold by public auction at Christie's, New York, eleven paintings by such artists as Renoir, Henri Toulouse-Lautrec, and Edouard Vuillard in order to raise $3.65 million for operating expenses.[192]
- In 1994, the University of California, Los Angeles (UCLA)/ Armand Hammer Museum of Art and Cultural Center sold through Christie's, New York, an illustrated manuscript by Leonardo da Vinci for $30.8 million to cover legal expenses arising from claims against Hammer's estate.[193]
- In 1995, the New York Historical Society, in a series of court-approved auctions at Sotheby's, New York, monitored by the New York State attorney general's office, sold Old Masters paintings, paperweights, and Americana and applied the $17.6 million in sales proceeds to operating expenditures. The sales conditions, negotiated by the attorney general's office, granted qualified New York museums the opportunity to submit preemptive bids for a period of one week after a buyer's purchase of an object.[194]
- In 1996, the Shelburne Museum in Vermont sold at auction through Sotheby's five impressionist masterpieces by Edgar Degas and Edouard Manet, and from the sale raised $31.2 million for capital improvements, for enhancement of the museum's security, and for climate control.[195]
- A highly publicized and controversial case occurred in 2007 with respect to the Maier Museum of Art at Randolph College in Virginia. The school's president arrived unannounced at the museum with support staff, police officers, and art handlers. They took four paintings from the museum's American art collection, which the college trustees had decided to sell at auction to raise funds for the college's general operating expenses. The public was outraged; there were lawsuits, campus debates, angry letters from academics, curators, and leading professional organizations, resignations from faculty and museum staff, and withdrawal of financial support by alumnae and other supporters of the college. One of the paintings, Tamayo's *Troubadour*, sold at auction for $7.2 million in 2008.[196]
- In 2008, the National Academy Museum and School in New York City sold two Hudson River School landscape paintings for $13.5 million. The museum had been facing financial difficulties and was operating at a deficit, and it used the proceeds of the sale to cover its expenses. This decision was highly criticized, and as a result the academy was sanctioned by the Association of Art Museum Directors, which nearly closed the academy's doors forever. The academy has since learned its lesson and has revamped its finances and management structure; nonetheless, the sanctions are in place until 2015.[197]
- In 2011, the Birger Sandzen Memorial Gallery on the campus of Bethany College in Lindsborg, Kansas, sold at auction Marsden Hartley's *Untitled (Still Life)* for $3.2 million. The gallery decided to sell this work when a

fundraising campaign for renovations was short of its target by $700,000. Sotheby's had estimated that the work would bring between $700,000 and $900,000 at sale, so the final sale price come as a surprise to many. This painting had been part of the gallery's collection since 1968, but the gallery's curator determined that it was no longer appropriate for the gallery, which focused on the works of former Bethany College professor Birger Sandzen. Much of the proceeds were put towards the planned $1.7 million renovation, and the excess was put towards future acquisitions.[198]

ETHICAL ISSUES

Deaccessioning collection objects to raise funds for a museum to make capital improvements or to meet operating expenses are different matters entirely. As noted earlier, the New York State Board of Regents has amended its rules regarding deaccessioning, which now prohibit museums chartered by the Board from using deaccessioning proceeds to pay operating expenses.[199] In addition, various codes of ethics promulgated by museum professional groups unequivocally proscribe the application of such sales proceeds to capital improvements or operating expenses. As a typical example, the American Association of Museums code of ethics provides the following:

> [D]isposal of collections through sale, trade, or research activities is solely for the advancement of the museum's mission. . . . [I]n no event shall they be used for anything other than acquisition or direct care of collections.[200]

Other museum professional organizations have similar provisions.[201] Codes of ethics, however, generally lack the force of law, and the courts to date have issued no clear guidelines as to whether and under what circumstances such a prohibition is enforced.

Outgoing Loans

LOAN RECIPIENTS

Art museums maintain their collections for the benefit of the public. Accordingly, a museum may not lend to its own officers and trustees, who are bound by a duty not to self-deal. Museums generally do not lend to private persons because such loans could jeopardize the museums' tax-exempt status; under the Internal Revenue Code no part of museums' net earnings can inure to the benefit of any private person. Therefore, most museums lend solely to institutional borrowers that are likely to make the museums' collection objects available to at least some segments of the public. In addition, with a security system and other facilities, an institution is presumably able to duplicate the level of care common to a museum environment. Some museums limit borrower eligibility to educational entities or nonprofit organizations in order to avoid the possibility of commercial ventures that may not be in consonance with the museum's mission or image.[202] General agreement provisions are discussed below.

Objects Loaned

When a museum approves an outgoing loan, it usually lends objects from its permanent collections. The museum should examine the accession records of the objects to be loaned to make sure that no restrictions hinder the anticipated transaction. Because a museum is obliged to preserve its trust assets, it generally should not lend objects of extreme frailty and should loan objects of extreme rarity only with the utmost caution.[203] And if a museum contemplates lending an object received on loan, it must first secure the owner's permission.

Insurance

All objects on outgoing loan should be covered by insurance. Generally, the borrower assumes the insurance costs either by providing insurance satisfactory to the lending museum and furnishing the lender with a certificate of insurance or a copy of the policy before shipment or by reimbursing the lending museum if that museum provides its own insurance. One commentator has wisely suggested that the lending museum's outgoing loan agreement provide that failure by the borrowing museum to secure the agreed-on coverage in no way releases the borrower from liability for loss of or damage to the objects loaned.[204] Such a provision rebuts any inference that the lending museum has waived its rights of coverage.

Traveling Exhibitions

If a museum houses in its permanent collections key works by a great artist, the strategic loan of those key pieces may empower the museum to serve as co-host for a national or international traveling exhibition of the artist's works. In recent years, for example, a few great Paul Cézanne masterpieces owned by the Philadelphia Museum of Art enabled that museum in 1996 to serve as the sole stop in the United States in a yearlong magnificent international exhibition on the works of Cézanne.[205] Similarly, the National Gallery in Washington, D.C., was able to secure its participation in the Vermeer show of 1996.[206] Other great museums in the United States were interested in co-hosting both exhibitions and loaned paintings to the exhibitions; New York's Metropolitan Museum of Art, for example, lent four Cézannes to the Philadelphia show. However, lenders are generally loath to part with their artworks for lengthy periods of time[207] because of the physical stress that travel imposes on artwork. That reluctance curtails the number of museums that participate in any traveling show. When a museum hosts or co-hosts a major exhibition, it derives significant benefits: enhanced stature in the museum world, improved credibility with the public, and sorely needed funds derived from ticket sales and the merchandising of ancillary items, such as postcards and T-shirts. However, if a museum generates the concept for an interesting show of an artist's work but lacks a critical mass in quality or quantity of examples of that artist's oeuvre, the exhibition may come to pass but minus that museum. For the 1995 James Abbott McNeill Whistler retrospective at the National Gallery, the idea was proposed by the St. Louis Art Museum, with the retrospective to be executed in conjunction with the National Gallery and subsequently exhibited in London. Instead, the St. Louis Art Museum, lacking the requisite masterpieces, was preempted from the show;[208] the ultimate participants were the National Gallery, the Tate Gallery in London, and the Musée d'Orsay in Paris, which contributed Whistler's portrait of his mother.[209]

Art exhibitions are not always joint efforts. Museums throughout the United States can and do conceive of art shows composed solely of works from their own permanent collections and send the shows on the road. However, such museums have reportedly met with difficulties in attempting to exhibit their shows in certain major museums in metropolitan areas such as New York City.[210] That is because most major museums prefer to hold shows curated by their own experts; after all, that is how a museum's stature is enhanced and scholarly reputations made.[211]

Indefinite Loans

Until quite recently, American museums followed the practice of accepting works of art on indefinite loan. Unfortunately, that procedure gave rise to an array of complications, such as cluttering the storerooms of museums with objects of doubtful title. Some of those long-stored objects may be infested with vermin, threatening the preservation of other stored works of perhaps greater value. The museum's staff may hesitate to treat those infested objects when they do not know if title has somehow attached to the museum. If the works are treated, the museum may have borne expenses for objects that (1) it probably does not own and (2) it certainly is not exhibiting. Moreover, even when the owner of an artwork does surface, the owner may have difficulty in reclaiming the work on demand if the museum does not keep accurate records. An example of that is dealt with in the case of *Redmond v. New Jersey Historical Society*, in which the New Jersey Historical Society, in asserting ownership through adverse possession, refused to turn over a Gilbert Stuart to the lender's heirs.[212]

At issue in the *Redmond* case was the question of who was entitled to the exclusive right of possession of a Gilbert Stuart portrait of Captain James Lawrence—Lawrence's only descendants or the New Jersey Historical Society? The portrait was in the possession of Mary Lawrence Redmond, the sole surviving grandchild of Captain Lawrence, at the time of her death in 1887. She was survived by her fourteen-year-old son, Preston Redmond. By her will she devised and bequeathed all her property to her son and his heirs, providing that if her son left no descendants, the Gilbert Stuart portrait was to go to the New Jersey Historical Society. A few months later, an executor of her estate delivered the portrait to the Historical Society, where it remained. In 1938, Preston Redmond died, survived by a widow and three children. By his will Preston Redmond devised and bequeathed all his property to his wife and, on her death, the remainder to his three children. His widow, individually and as the executor of his estate, assigned and transferred all her interest in and to the portrait to her three children.

Shortly after Preston Redmond's death his three children, the complainants in the action, demanded the portrait's return from the New Jersey Historical Society. The demand was refused, so in March 1939 the complainants commenced a suit to recover the portrait. Among the defenses asserted by the Historical Society were those of adverse possession and the statute of limitations. That is, the Historical Society claimed that by the time of the suit it had the exclusive right of possession of the portrait and that the complainants were time-barred from bringing suit. However, the court noted that to establish adverse possession, the party asserting the defense had to prove each element of the defense by a preponderance of the evidence: The Historical Society had to prove that its possession of the portrait was

> hostile as well as actual, visible, exclusive and continuous. . . . It must be "adversary," it "must begin, and continue for the whole term, in hostility."[213]

The Historical Society took the position that the delivery of the portrait by Mary Lawrence Redmond's executor, its receipt by the Historical Society, and the society's claim to it each constituted a conversion of the portrait and commenced the running of the statute of limitations. The court disagreed with the Historical Society's contentions and found that the society's records

> besp[o]ke no assertion of ownership. The first assertion of ownership by the Society was in 1938, when it refused to deliver the portrait to complainants, and the statute of limitations did not begin to run until that time.[214]

Moreover, the court noted that since the Historical Society made several announcements that the portrait was bequeathed to it under Mary Redmond's will and testament, the society failed to prove that its possession of the portrait was adversary or hostile.[215]

When Does the Statute of Limitations Begin to Run?

Although that question is discussed in some detail in chapter 3,[216] it is addressed here with respect to bailment situations. Case law holds that for bailments of an indefinite term the statute of limitations does not commence until an actual demand for the return of the goods is made, usually by way of a presentment of a receipt.[217] That does not mean that the bailor is permitted to postpone the demand indefinitely so as to defeat the policy of the statute of limitations. Rather, a duty rests with the bailor to make a demand within a reasonable time for the return of the property, the issue of reasonableness to be determined by the facts and the circumstances of each case.[218] In the 1980 case of *Houser v. Ohio Historical Society*,[219] the court observed the following:

> In Ohio, and in a majority of other jurisdictions, a reasonable time within which the demand must be made is ordinarily presumed to be the period of the statute of limitations applicable to the bailor's cause of action for return of the property.[220]

However, the court did recognize a well-known exception:

> [T]hat a demand will not be presumed if to do so would be contrary to the express terms of the agreement between the parties, or if the circumstances indicate that the parties contemplated a quick demand or an unusual delay in making the demand.[221]

In a situation involving an indefinite loan in which nothing occurs to begin the running of any statute of limitations—that is, no demand, actual or presumptive, for the return of the property has been made—the time for the return of the goods can seemingly be extended indefinitely, enabling distant heirs of the bailor to recover the bailed property.[222]

The Eighth Circuit examined the consequences of such an indefinite loan in a 2007 case, *Lackawanna Chapter of the Railway & Locomotive Historical Society, Inc. v. St. Louis County, Missouri*.[223] The parties disagreed over which had the right to possess the Delaware, Lackawanna & Western Railroad's historic steam engine No. 952, which first entered service in 1905. In April 1939, the railroad transferred ownership of the engine to the Railway and Locomotive Historical Society. Then, in 1953, the Historical Society offered the engine to the National Museum of Transportation in St. Louis, Missouri. The Historical Society and the National Museum of Transportation only engaged in correspondence and never entered into a formal, written loan agreement; nonetheless, in this correspondence, the parties referred to the transfer as a "permanent loan."[224] In 1984, St. Louis County acquired the National Museum of Transportation and all its property. Thereafter, around 1990, the Historical Society began attempts to possess the engine once more, in order to move the engine closer to its original home in Pennsylvania and also to ensure that it was receiving proper maintenance and care. In 1999, the Historical Society transferred ownership of the engine to its Lackawanna chapter, the plaintiff in the suit.

In the district court, St. Louis moved for summary judgment, claiming that the correspondence between the Historical Society and the National Museum of Transportation did not constitute a written, enforceable agreement.[225] The district court agreed and granted summary judgment for St. Louis, since the correspondence did not establish an enforceable agreement. In the absence of such an agreement, St. Louis's exclusive possession and control of the engine established a presumption that it owned that locomotive, which Lackawanna failed to rebut.[226]

On appeal, the Eighth Circuit found that the lower court had confused the issues, focusing on ownership of the artifact rather than the true issue of "how a museum might *continue* to possess an artifact that it *has* possessed in its capacity as an institution regularly dedicated to the public display of the property of others."[227] The court held that, when the period of exhibition is indefinite, possession and control alone are not enough to establish ownership of the artifact. Therefore, the court determined that there was, at the least, an implied indefinite bailment between the parties, since the engine was to be displayed at the National Museum of Transportation for an indefinite period.[228] This determination raised further issues, such as the effect of Missouri's statute of limitations and the effect of the transfer of the National Museum of Transportation's property to St. Louis. The court remanded the case to the district court to decide these further issues and to reexamine the case in light of the question of whether the indefinite bailment should allow Lackawanna to regain possession of the engine.[229]

LEGISLATIVE SOLUTIONS

In view of some of the problems engendered by old loans, museums in a number of states in recent years have urged the enactment of legislation to ameliorate the situation. Generally, the purposes of the old-loan legislation are to establish a method to determine the ownership of loaned cultural property that has been abandoned by the lender, to establish uniform procedures for the termination of loans of property to museums, to allow museums to conserve loaned property under certain conditions, and to limit actions to recover loaned property. The state of Washington adopted such a statute in 1975,[230] followed by a number of other states, including Alaska, Arizona, Arkansas, California, Colorado, Florida, Georgia, Illinois, Indiana, Iowa, Kansas, Kentucky, Louisiana, Maine, Minnesota, Mississippi, Michigan, Missouri, Montana, Nebraska, Nevada, New Hampshire, New Mexico, North Carolina, North Dakota, Ohio, Oklahoma, Oregon, South Carolina, South Dakota, Tennessee, Texas, Virginia, Washington, Wisconsin, and Wyoming.[231] New York's legislation originally covered only the New York State Museum in Albany, but it has since been amended to apply to a variety of institutions, such as museums, zoos, and historical societies.[232]

Southwest Museum v. Farquhar is a case brought under such a statutory scheme.[233] The museum sought a judgment declaring it to be the owner of a painting by Albert Bierstadt that had been in its possession since 1926. The museum stated that it had complied with the California old-loan statute and had given the required notice of intent to terminate the loan in 1982 and had received no claim in the next three-year period. The museum also claimed that the twenty-five-year period under the California statute had run.

The defendant in the lawsuit, John P. Farquhar, a grandson of the lender, brought a cross-complaint, seeking judgment establishing that he owned the painting. He claimed that the museum failed to comply with the provisions of the California old-loan statute and, further, that the statute violated the constitutions of the United States and of the state of California. He also claimed that the museum:

(1) breached its fiduciary duty to act honorably with regard to the loan status with which the museum obtained custody of the painting,
(2) wrongfully denied the loan contract governing its possession of the painting,
(3) converted the painting, and
(4) wrongfully concealed from him its intention to assert an ownership interest in the painting.

The case was settled on a confidential basis.

APPRAISALS AND AUTHENTICATIONS

The question arises on occasion as to whether the rendering of appraisals and authentications of artwork constitutes appropriate museum activity. Appraisal and authentication differ conceptually and legally. Accordingly, the question is analyzed separately for each activity.

Appraisals

To appraise an artwork is to evaluate and affix a monetary value to it. An artwork may be appraised for any number of purposes—for example, insurance, federal estate tax, or the making of a charitable donation. When a museum, as a donee or a prospective donee of a gift of artwork, is asked to appraise an artwork, the museum is an interested party. Appraisals for tax purposes by an interested party have long been viewed with suspicion by the Internal Revenue Service (IRS).[234] That suspicion was codified in the Tax Reform Act of 1984, which disqualifies a museum-donee from appraising for federal income tax purposes a gift in excess of $5,000.[235] Instead, the IRS requires each such charitable contribution to have had a "qualified appraisal" done by a "qualified appraiser."[236] Such an appraiser must sign a declaration stating the following:

> I declare that I am not the donor, the donee, a party to the transaction in which the donor acquired the property, employed by or related to any of the foregoing persons, or a person whose relationship to any of the foregoing persons would cause a reasonable person to question my independence as an appraiser.[237]

Even when artwork given to a museum as a gift is worth $5,000 or less, the museum is an interested party (the donee) and should properly refrain from rendering an appraisal of the art.[238]

Authentications

To authenticate an artwork is to evaluate it and to make a determination as to whether or not it is genuine. Unlike an appraisal, a pure authentication sets no monetary value, so the IRS is not directly involved. Since no body of law expressly proscribes the rendering of authentications by museums, the propriety of a museum's doing so becomes one of policy, not legality. If an art museum decides to render authentications as a public service, it should establish and adhere to a consistent policy with respect to which segments of the public it serves. Often, a museum's anticipated benefits of furthering scholarship are more than offset by the personnel and financial costs incurred.[239] In addition, the museum exposes itself vis-à-vis the commissioning party and possibly others to an array of liabilities in tort and contract, even when authentications are provided as a public service.

However, if the museum is committed to rendering authentications, a museum's contractual liabilities can be virtually eliminated by the drafting and execution of, and adherence to, a proper contract. Proper contracts for appraisals and authentications are explored in detail in chapter 7 on expert opinions and liabilities.

A museum's exposure in tort liability for rendering authentications includes, principally, various theories of negligence and the torts of disparagement and defamation. A good errors-and-omissions insurance policy can provide a museum with significant protection against some of those liabilities (primarily, negligence), but an understanding by the museum of all the underlying theories of exposure is crucial. Those theories are examined extensively in chapter 7.

INCOME-PRODUCING ACTIVITIES

As noted earlier, an art museum, either as a government-controlled entity or as a charitable organization, has tax-exempt status. A museum can engage in a certain amount of commercial activity without forfeiting that status, but neither Congress nor case law has established a bright-line rule defining "too much."[240] Nevertheless, the following question arises: Is income-producing activity by the tax-exempt museum also tax-exempt? The Internal Revenue Code provides that if and to the extent that a museum engages in income-producing activities unrelated to the museum's exempt purpose, that museum will be taxed in the same manner as a taxable organization.[241] According to the code, unrelated business income tax (UBIT) is imposed on a museum's net income from any trade or business that the museum regularly carries on and that is unrelated to the museum's charitable and educational purposes.[242] "Trade or business" refers to any museum activity conducted for the production of income from the sale of goods or the performance of services.[243] Whether such activity is regularly carried on depends on the frequency, the continuity, and the consistency with which it is conducted.[244] An activity is unrelated if it is not substantially related—that is, if it does not contribute importantly to the accomplishment of a museum's mission.[245]

With little government funding and insufficient subsidies from charitable donations (despite the federal income tax benefits that accrue to charitable donors), museums are compelled to generate additional streams of revenue. Accordingly, many museums operate snack bars, cafeterias, or restaurants. The IRS has determined that such activity is related to the museum's educational purpose if the eatery is operated for the convenience of the museum personnel and the visitors to the museum.[246] Another common source of revenue is through the management of museum gift shops. Understandably, museums have taken the position that the merchandise sold in museum gift shops is related to its educational mission. Clearly, reference books, historical texts, volumes of collected art criticism covering a museum's collections, audiotapes and videotapes, compact discs (CDs), and CD-ROMs on a museum's collection objects are related to a museum's educational purpose. Similarly, postcards, posters, and notepaper bearing reproductions from a museum's collection have been found to stimulate interest in the museum's art and, therefore, to be related to the museum's educational mission.[247] Indeed, the IRS has found the concept of relatedness to cut a broad swath; "relatedness" also includes, as a pair of commentators have recently noted, the following:

> Ties and scarves "inspired by" textile designs in the museum's collection, pitchers and candlesticks that are reproductions of items in the collection, money clips inspired by the marginalia in medieval manuscripts, reproductions of Bauhaus furniture.... Often these items are accompanied by a slip of paper explaining their art-historical sources—though buyers may be as baffled as they are enlightened when told only that a set of beads is derived from an "Eighth Century Visigothic" model.[248]

In any event, the determination of merchandise relatedness is made on an item-by-item basis.[249] The sales of items of merchandise that do not contribute importantly to the museum's exempt purposes are taxed, as in the case of scientific books and such office items as staplers and paper clips sold in the gift shop of an art museum.[250]

For a museum to secure related merchandise for its gift shop, it generally enters into a variety of licensing arrangements with manufacturers for the use of likenesses from its collections and, perhaps, for the use of museum logos. A discussion of the various conditions of such licensing arrangements is beyond the scope of this chapter, but all such licensing arrangements should be formalized in writing by an agreement.[251]

NOTES TO CHAPTER 17

1. Fred A. Bernstein, *At Galleries, Cameras Find a Mixed Welcome*, N.Y. TIMES, Mar. 15, 2012, at F8; Fred A. Bernstein, *Who Wants to Donate to a Billionaire's Museum?*, N.Y. TIMES, Mar. 15, 2012, at F4; Judith H. Dobrzynski, *How an Acquisition Fund Burnishes Reputations*, N.Y. TIMES, Mar. 15, 2012, at F4.
2. Association of Art Museum Directors, Professional Practices in Art Museums, Report of the Ethics and Standards Committee (1981).
3. *See* M.E. PHELAN, MUSEUM LAW 2 (1994), for general comments on the organizational structure of public and private museums.
4. *Id.* at 79.
5. *Id.*
6. *Id.* at 81.
7. J.L. White, *When It's OK to Sell the Monet: A Trustee-Fiduciary-Duty Framework for Analyzing the Deaccessioning of Art to Meet Museum Operating Expenses*, 94 MICH. L. REV. 1041, 1049 n.35 (1996).
8. *See* PHELAN, *supra* note 3, at 7.
9. RESTATEMENT (THIRD) OF TRUSTS § 28 (2003).
10. *Id. See also* M.C. MALARO, A LEGAL PRIMER ON MANAGING MUSEUM COLLECTIONS 8 (1985); SCOTT, LAW OF TRUSTS § 348 (4th ed.).
11. *See* SCOTT, *supra* note 10, § 348; MALARO, *supra* note 10, at 19.
12. *See* MALARO, *supra* note 10, at 8.
13. *See* SCOTT, *supra* note 10, § 170; RESTATEMENT, *supra* note 9, Appendix § 170.
14. SCOTT, *supra* note 10, § 174.
15. *Id.* § 170.
16. *Id.* § 170 n.3. If the trust is a private foundation for tax purposes, then § 4941 specifically prohibits certain acts of self-dealing. *See* PHELAN, *supra* note 3, at 134.
17. *See* SCOTT, *supra* note 10, § 174.
18. *Id.*
19. *See* White, *supra* note 7, at 1053.
20. *See* MALARO, *supra* note 10, at 4.
21. *See* PHELAN, *supra* note 3, at 9.
22. *Id.*
23. C.C. Clark & J. Sare, *Income-Producing Activities of U.S. Museums—Where Does Charity Stop and Commerce Begin?*, International Bar Association Conference—Museums in the Global Society, London, England, Feb. 1996.
24. *Id.* at 6.
25. *See* White, *supra* note 7, at 1050.
26. *Id.* at 1051.
27. *Id.* at 1052. However, if the nonprofit corporation is a private foundation for tax purposes, then § 4941 specifically prohibits certain acts of self-dealing. *See* PHELAN, *supra* note 3, at 134.
28. *Id.*
29. *Id.*
30. *See* White, *supra* note 7.
31. *See* MALARO, *supra* note 10.
32. Citing, *e.g.*, Lefkowitz v. Museum of the Am. Indian-Heye Found., Index No. 41416/75 (N.Y. Sup. Ct., N.Y. County, June 27, 1975); State of Washington v. Leppalvoto, No. 11781 (Wash. Super. Ct., Klickitat County, Apr. 1977); Harris v. Attorney Gen., 31 Conn. Supp. 93, 324 A. 2d 279 (Super. Ct. 1974).
33. *See* MALARO, *supra* note 10, at 53.
34. *Id.* at 55.
35. Denver Art Museum v. de Menil, 1999 U.S. Dist. LEXIS 23342 (S.D.N.Y. June 2, 1999).

36. *Id.* at *19.

37. *Id.* at *18. *See* COLO. REV. STAT. §§ 13-80-101(h) and 13-80-108(7).

38. Michael Werner Gallery v. Rich (N.Y. Sup. Ct., N.Y. County, filed 2011); *see* ALI-ABA, LE-GAL ISSUES IN MUSEUM ADMINISTRATION 248 (2012).

39. ALI-ABA, *supra* note 38.

40. *Id.*

41. *Id.*

42. *See* PHELAN, *supra* note 3, at 33 and 48.

43. Johnson v. Smithsonian Inst., 189 F.3d 180 (2d Cir. 1999), *on remand*, 80 F. Supp. 2d 197 (S.D.N.Y. 2000).

44. *Id.* at 183.

45. *Id.*

46. *Id.* at 184.

47. Johnson v. Smithsonian Inst., 9 F. Supp. 2d 347 (S.D.N.Y. 1998).

48. *Johnson*, 189 F.3d at 189-90. The lower court dismissed such claims on the grounds that the Harmon Foundation was a necessary party with respect to those claims, but the statute of limitations having run against it, it could not be made a defendant. *Johnson*, 9 F. Supp. 2d at 354.

49. *Johnson*, 189 F.3d at 190.

50. *Johnson*, 80 F. Supp. 2d at 201.

51. Schwartz v. Cincinnati Museum Ass'n, 35 F. App'x. 128, 2002 U.S. App. LEXIS 7139 (6th Cir. 2002).

52. OHIO REV. CODE ANN. § 2305.09.

53. *Schwartz*, 2002 U.S. App. LEXIS 7139.

54. Toledo Museum of Art v. Ullin, 477 F. Supp. 2d 802 (2006).

55. *Id.* at 803.

56. *Id.* at 804.

57. *Id.* at 805.

58. *Id.* at 807.

59. Toledo Museum of Art v. Ullin, 477 F. Supp. 2d 802, 807 (2006).

60. *Id.*

61. *Id.*

62. *Id.* at 809.

63. Sanchez v. Trs. of the Univ. of Pa., 2005 U.S. Dist. LEXIS 636 (S.D.N.Y. Jan. 18, 2005).

64. Under the doctrine of laches, a suit will be dismissed when a plaintiff has engaged in unreasonable delay in bringing suit and defendant has suffered prejudice as a result of the delay. *See* Robins Island Pres. Fund, Inc. v. Southold Dev. Corp., 959 F.2d 409, 423 (2d Cir. 1992), and discussion of laches in chapter 3 of this book.

65. *Sanchez*, 2005 U.S. Dist. LEXIS 636.

66. *Id.*

67. Springfield Library & Museum Ass'n, Inc. v. Knoedler Archivum, Inc., 341 F. Supp. 2d 32, 2004 U.S. Dist. LEXIS 20437 (D. Mass. 2004).

68. *Id.* at **15 (quoting FDIC v. Roldan Fonseca, 795 F.2d 1102, 1107 (1st Cir. 1986)).

69. *Id.* at **23.

70. United States v. Davis, 648 F.3d 84 (2d Cir. 2011).

71. *Id.* at 87. *See also* 18 U.S.C. §§ 2314, 2315.

72. *Id.* at 89.

73. *Id.* at 89.

74. *Id.* at 90.

75. United States v. Davis, 648 F.3d 84, 90 (2d Cir. 2011).

76. *Id.* at 90-91.

77. *Id.* at 91.

78. *Id.* at 90-91. *See also* 19 U.S.C. § 1595a(c)(1)(A).

79. *Id.* at 96-97.

80. Jeanneret v. Vichey, 693 F.2d 259 (2d Cir. 1982), *rev'g* 541 F. Supp. 80 (S.D.N.Y. 1992).

81. *See* UNESCO Convention art. 7(a).

82. Treaty of Cooperation for the Recovery and Return of Stolen Archaeological, Historical and Cultural Property, July 17, 1970, United States–Mexico, 22 U.S.T. 494, T.I.A.S. No. 7088.

83. Agreement with Peru for the Recovery and Return of Stolen Archaeological, Historical and Cultural Properties, Sept. 15, 1981, United States–Peru, T.I.A.S. No. 10136.

84. Importation of Pre-Columbian Monumental or Architectural Sculpture or Murals Act, 19 U.S.C. §§ 2091–95.

85. 18 U.S.C. § 2314.

86. United States v. McClain, 593 F.2d 658 (5th Cir.), *cert. denied*, 444 U.S. 918 (1979). In United States v. McClain, 545 F.2d 988 (5th Cir. 1977), the court had initially reversed the conviction of the defendants on the ground that Mexico did not declare ownership of all pre-Columbian art until 1972.

87. United States v. Schultz, 333 F.3d 393 (2d Cir. 2003), *aff'g* 178 F. Supp. 2d 445 (S.D.N.Y. 2002). *See* Martha Lufkin, *Criminal Liability For Receiving State-Claimed Antiquities in the United States: The* Schultz *Case*, 8 ART ANTIQUITY & L. 321 (2003).

88. 16 U.S.C. § 470ee.

89. 16 U.S.C. § 470bb(1).

90. 42 U.S.C. § 1996.

91. *See* PHELAN, *supra* note 3, at 294 (citing Lyng v. Northwest Indian Cemetery Protective Ass'n, 485 U.S. 439 (1988)); Wilson v. Block, 708 F.2d 735 (D.C. Cir.), *cert. denied*, 464 U.S. 956 (1983); United States v. Top Sky, 547 F.2d 483 (9th Cir. 1976); Crow v. Gullett, 541 F. Supp. 785 (D.S.D. 1982), *aff'd*, 706 F.2d 856 (8th Cir.), *cert. denied*, 464 U.S. 977 (1983).

92. 25 U.S.C. §§ 3001–13.

93. *See* Livesay, *The Impact of the Federal Repatriation Act on State-Operated Museums*, 24 ARIZ. ST. L.J. 293 (1992).

94. Bonnichsen v. United States, 357 F.3d 962 (9th Cir. 2004).

95. Bonnichsen v. United States, 217 F. Supp. 2d 1116 (D. Or. 2002).

96. *Bonnichsen*, 357 F.3d at 972.

97. 18 U.S.C. § 668 provides:

> (a) Definitions: In this section—(1) "museum" means an organized and permanent institution, the activities of which affect interstate commerce, that—(A) is situated in the United States; (B) is established for an essentially educational or aesthetic purpose; (C) has a professional staff; (D) owns, utilizes, and cares for tangible objects that are exhibited to the public on a regular schedule. (2) "object of cultural heritage" means an object that is—(A) over 100 years old and worth in excess of $5,000; or (B) worth at least $100,000.

> (b) Offenses: A person who—(1) steals or obtains by fraud from the care, custody, or control of a museum any object of cultural heritage; or (2) knowing that an object of cultural heritage has been stolen or obtained by fraud, if in fact the object was stolen or obtained from the care, custody, or control of a museum (whether or not that fact is known to the person), receives, conceals, exhibits, or disposes of the object, shall be fined under this title, imprisoned not more than 10 years, or both.

98. 18 U.S.C. § 668(a)(2).

99. 18 U.S.C. § 3294.

100. 18 U.S.C. § 668(b).

101. United States v. O'Higgins, 55 F. Supp. 2d 172 (S.D.N.Y. 1998).

102. 18 U.S.C. § 668(a).

103. *O'Higgins*, 55 F. Supp. 2d at 173–74. Article I, Section 8, of the Constitution provides: "The Congress shall have Power. . . . To regulate Commerce with foreign Nations, and among the

several States, and with the Indian Tribes."

104. *O'Higgins*, 55 F. Supp. 2d at 174.

105. *Id.* at 176.

106. United States v. Pritchard, 346 F.3d 469 (3d Cir. 2003).

107. 18 U.S.C. § 668(a)(1)(D).

108. *Pritchard*, 346 F.3d at 475–76.

109. 17 U.S.C. § 106.

110. 17 U.S.C. § 301.

111. 17 U.S.C. § 204(a).

112. 17 U.S.C. § 28 (1909) (superseded 1976).

113. 3 MELVILLE B. NIMMER & DAVID NIMMER, NIMMER ON COPYRIGHT § 10.09[B] (2004). But note that New York and California had enacted legislation that reversed this presumption. *See, respectively*, N.Y. GEN. BUS. LAW art. 12-E, § 223, repealed in 1983 subsequent to enactment of the Copyright Act of 1976, and CAL. CIV. CODE § 982(c) and (e).

114. 17 U.S.C. § 109(c).

115. 17 U.S.C. § 107.

116. *See* Butler, *Keeping the World Safe from Naked-Chicks-in-Art Refrigerator Magnets: The Plot to Control Art Images in the Public Domain through Copyrights in Photographic and Digital Reproductions*, 21 HASTINGS COMM. & ENT. L.J. 55 (1998).

117. BROWN, PERSONAL PROPERTY § 7.1 (3d ed. 1975). For gift tax purposes, *see* Treas. Reg. §§ 25.2511-1 and 25.2511-2.

118. BROWN, *supra* note 117.

119. *See* MALARO, *supra* note 10, at 104.

120. *Id.*

121. *Id.* at 105.

122. *See* SCOTT, *supra* note 10, §§ 348.1 and 399.

123. *Id.* § 399.2.

124. *Id.* § 399.

125. Georgia O'Keeffe Found. (Museum) v. Fisk Univ., 312 S.W.3d 1, 39 (Tenn. Ct. App. 2009).

126. *Id.*

127. The court applied New York substantive law and Tennessee procedural law. *In re* Fisk Univ., 2011 Tenn. App. LEXIS 641, at *7-8 (Tenn. Ct. App. 2011).

128. *Georgia O'Keeffe Found. (Museum)*, 312 S.W.3d at 18.

129. *Id.* at 40.

130. *Id.* at 41-42.

131. *Id.* at 42.

132. *In re Fisk Univ.*, 2011 Tenn. App. LEXIS 641, at *12-13.

133. *Georgia O'Keeffe Found. (Museum)*, 312 S.W.3d at 17.

134. *In re Fisk Univ.*, 2011 Tenn. App. LEXIS 641, at *21.

135. *Id.* at *22.

136. *Id.* at *7.

137. *Id.* at *23.

138. *Id.* at *22-23.

139. *Id.* at *37-38.

140. *Id.* at *38-39.

141. Daniel Grant, *Fisk Wins Lengthy Fight to Leverage Art Collection*, ARTNEWSLETTER (May 1, 2012), http://artnewsletter.artnews.com/Arti-cle.aspx?id=1602.

142. *Id.*

143. *See* SCOTT, *supra* note 10, § 381.

144. *Id.*

145. *In re* Barnes Found., 25 Fiduc. Rep. 2d 39, 69 Pa. D. & C. 4th 129 (2004). *See* Goldman, *Just What The Doctor Ordered? The Doctrine of Deviation, The Case of Doctor Barnes's Trust and The Future Location of the Barnes Foundation*, 39 REAL PROP., PROB. & TR. J. 711 (2005).

146. *In re* Barnes Found., 24 Fiduc. Rep. 2d 94 (Pa. C.P. Orphans' Ct. 2004).

147. *Barnes Found.*, 69 Pa. D. & C. 4th 129.

148. *Id.* at n.13 (citing BOGERT, THE LAW OF TRUSTS AND TRUSTEES § 561, at 27). For a contrary result where the court did not allow the application of the doctrine of reasonable deviation for the justification of a charitable trust selling seventeen paintings, *see* Museum of Fine Arts v. Beland, 432 Mass. 540, 735 N.E.2d 1248 (2000).

149. *Philadelphia*, BARNES FOUND. Barnesfoundation.org/about/campuses/philadelphia (last visited April 16, 2012).

150. *See, e.g.*, Breckinridge County v. Gannaway, 243 Ky. 49, 47 S.W.2d 934 (1932); Harlan State Bank v. Banner Fork Coal Corp., 261 S.W. 16 (Ky. 1924); Nuell v. Forty-North Corp., 358 S.W.2d 70 (St. Louis Ct. App. 1962).

151. *See, e.g.*, Mickey v. Sears, Roebuck & Co., 196 Md. 326, 76 A.2d 350 (1950); First Nat'l Bank v. Ocean Nat'l Bank, 60 N.Y. 278 (1875).

152. Colburn v. Wash. State Art Ass'n, 80 Wash. 662, 141 P. 1153 (1914).

153. *Id.* at 1155.

154. *Id.* at 1156.

155. Gardini v. Museum of City of N.Y., 173 Misc. 791, 792, 19 N.Y.S.2d 96, 97 (City Ct. 1940).

156. *Id.* at 98.

157. Some art insurance policies that will compensate a collector for the theft of an artwork will not, as a matter of public policy, compensate her for any ransom payments the collector may have to pay to recover the work, even if the sum is only a fraction of what the insurer will have to pay if the work is not recovered. That policy is not always the case, however, as in Kraut v. Morgan & Bros. Manhattan Storage Co., 38 N.Y.2d 445, 343 N.E.2d 744, 381 N.Y.S.2d 25 (1976). In that case, when the defendant storage company was concededly negligent in permitting rare Russian enamels to be stolen from its premises, the plaintiff, who was forced to make ransom payments to secure their return, sought to recover that sum, along with the value of the items not returned, and the New York State Court of Appeals held for the plaintiff, rejecting the defendant's public policy argument.

158. The Art Institute of Chicago Loan Agreement, Michigan Avenue at Adams Street, Chicago, Illinois 60603.

159. *See* MALARO, *supra* note 10, at 206 (citing Pfeffer, *Insuring Museum Exhibitions*, 27 HASTINGS L. REV. 1123 (May 1976)).

160. 20 U.S.C. §§ 971–77.

161. 22 U.S.C. § 2459. Institutions applying for immunity under the statute should contact the Department of State at (202) 619-6084 to receive an application and a list of the required supporting documentation.

162. *See* MALARO, *supra* note 10, at 209.

163. *See* PHELAN, *supra* note 3, at 302.

164. *Id.*

165. *See* MALARO, *supra* note 10, at 148.

166. *See* White, *supra* note 7, at 1046 (citing, in note 23, Holyoke Pub. Library Corp. v. Shawmut Bank, No. 93-002 (P. & Fam. Ct. Hampden County, Mass. Jan. 26, 1993); Hammond Museum, Inc. v. Harshbarger, No. 92E-0067-G1 (P. & Fam. Ct. Essex County, Mass. Oct. 5, 1992)).

167. *Id.* (citing, in n.23, Commonwealth v. Reading Pub. Museum & Art Gallery, No. 72430 (C.P. Orphans' Ct. Berks County, Pa. Aug. 15, 1991)).

168. *Id.* at 1044 (citing, in n.15, Trs. of Everhart Museum v. Commonwealth, No. 1043-92 (C.P. Orphans' Ct. Lackawanna County, Pa. Aug. 25, 1992)).

169. *Id.* at 1046–47.

170. N.Y. EDUC. LAW § 233-aa(5)(a)-(b) (Consol. 2012).

171. N.Y. State Bd. of Regents, *Amendment of Regents Rule. § 3.27 Relating to Museum Collections Management Policies*, http://www.regents.nysed.gov/meetings/2011Meetings/May2011/511brca3revised.pdf (last visited April 16, 2012).

172. *Id.*

173. *Id.*

174. 26 U.S.C. § 6050L.

175. T. Ambrose & C. Paine, Museum Basics (1993).

176. *See* White, *supra* note 7, at 1043.

177. USA TODAY, May 1, 1990, at 1D.

178. SEATTLE TIMES, June 16, 1991, at K2.

179. TIME, Jan. 20, 1992, at 36; *id.*

180. N.Y. LAW J., May 22, 2000 at S3. *See* Smith, *What's No Longer on Museum Walls*, N.Y. TIMES, May 31, 1999, at E1.

181. N.Y. TIMES, Oct. 31, 2003, at E40.

182. FORBES, Apr. 4, 2004.

183. Mike Boehm, *LACMA's Deaccessioned Old Masters; One Down, One to Go*, L.A. TIMES BLOGS (March 6, 2009, 11:15 a.m.), http://latimesblogs.latimes.com/culturemonster/2009/03/lacma-deaccessi.html.

184. Steven Litt, *Cleveland Museum of Art to Auction 32 Old Master Paintings at Sotheby's*, CLEVELAND.COM (Jan. 15, 2011, 2:00 p.m.), http://www.cleveland.com/arts/index.ssf/2011/01/cleveland_museum_ of_art_to_auc.html.

185. Lee Rosenbaum, *Boston MFA Purchases Caillebotte's Male Nude, Denudes its Permanent Collection*, ARTSJOURNAL.COM (Sept. 21, 2011), http://www.artsjournal.com/culture-grrl/2011/09/boston_mfa_ to_purchase_cailleb.html.

186. Walter Simon, *Tamayo Tops Latam Auction, Kinetic Art Sales Strong*, REUTERS.COM (Nov. 17, 2011), http://www.reuters.com/article/2011/11/17/us-art-auction-latam-idUSTRE7AG1K620111117.

187. Lauren Viera, *Art Institute Paintings to Fetch $10-$16 Million at Auction*, CHICAGOTRIBUNE.COM (Jan. 11, 2011), http://articles.chicagotribune.com/2011-01-11/entertainment/ct-live-0112-art-institute-developmen20110111_1_art-institute-paintings-institute-spokeswoman-erin-hogan-deaccession.

188. INDEP., Sept. 8, 1990, at 44.

189. B. Genocchio, *Trading a Masterpiece for a Dream*, N.Y. TIMES, Feb. 13, 2005.

190. Christina M. Wetherbee, *Critical Sales: Questioning Deaccession Ethics in American Museums Through the Heckscher Museum*, December 2006, http://domappo1.shu.edu/depts/uc/apps/libraryrepository.nsf/resourceid/9083B5F20B6C6C078525736F004A3125/$File/Wetherbee-Christina-M_Masters.pdf?Open. See also http://query.nytimes.com/gst/fullpage.html?res=9A06E2DB133EF93AA25751C0A9609C8B63

191. Armando Montaño, *Brandeis U. Agrees to Settlement in Dispute Over Rose Art Museum*, THE CHRONICLE OF HIGHER EDUCATION (June 30, 2011), http://chronicle.com/article/Brandeis-U-Agrees-to/128113/.

192. N.Y. TIMES, Oct. 9, 1992, at C30.

193. FACTS ON FILE WORLD NEWS DIGEST, Dec. 1, 1994, at 908 Cl.

194. N.Y. TIMES, Mar. 10, 1995, at C26.

195. PITTSBURGH POST-GAZETTE, Dec. 27, 1996, at 20; BOSTON GLOBE, Mar. 31, 1996, at 33.

196. Laura R. Katzman and Karol A. Lawson, *The (Im)permanent Collection: Lessons from a Deaccession*, AM. ASS'N. OF MUSEUMS, http://www.aam-us.org/pubs/mn/deaccession.cfm (last visited Apr. 16, 2012).

197. Robin Pogrebin, *A Chastised Museum Returns to Life*, N.Y. TIMES, Apr. 18, 2011, at C1.

198. http://acn.liveauctioneers.com/index.php/features/art-design/6096-criticism

199. www.regents.nysed.gov/meetings/2011Meetings/May2011/511brca3revised.pdf

200. AMERICAN ASSOCIATION OF MUSEUMS CODE OF ETHICS FOR MUSEUMS 8 (1994), adopted November 12, 1993.

201. *See, e.g.*, Association of Art Museum Directors, Professional Practices in Art Museums app. A (2011); International Council of Museums, Code of Professional Ethics 22 (1987); American Ass'n for State and Local History, Statement of Professional Ethics I (1992).

202. *See* MALARO, *supra* note 10, at 174.

203. *Id.* at 175.
204. *Id.* at 177.
205. N.Y. TIMES, Feb. 25, 1996, at B1.
206. *Id.*
207. *Id.*
208. *Id.*
209. TIME, July 24, 1995, at 60.
210. N.Y. TIMES, *supra* note 205.
211. *Id.*
212. Redmond v. N.J. Historical Soc'y, 132 N.J. Eq. 464, 28 A.2d 189 (1942).
213. *Id.* at 194.
214. *Id.* at 195.
215. *Id.*
216. *See* discussion in chapter 3 on statutes of limitations, addressing accrual, pages 253–254.
217. Houser v. Ohio Historical Soc'y, 62 Ohio St. 2d 77, 403 N.E.2d 965, 16 Ohio Op. 3d 67 (1980).
218. *Id.* at 967; Lowney v. Knott, 83 R.I. 505, 120 A.2d 552 (1956).
219. *See Houser*, 403 N.E.2d 965.
220. *Id.* at 968.
221. *Id.*
222. *In re* Estate of Therese Davis McCagg, 450 A.2d 414 (D.C. 1982).
223. Lackawanna Chapter of the Ry. & Locomotive Historical Soc'y, Inc. v. St. Louis County, Missouri, 497 F.3d 832 (8th Cir. 2007).
224. *Id.* at 834.
225. *Id.* at 835.
226. *Id.*
227. *Id.* at 836.
228. *Id.*
229. *Id.* at 838.
230. WASH. REV. CODE § 27.40.034 (the statute governs only the state museum at the University of Washington).
231. ALASKA STAT. §§ 15.57.200 to .290; ARIZ. REV. STAT. ANN. §§ 44-351 to -356; ARK. CODE ANN. §§ 13-5-1001 to -1013; CAL. CIV. CODE §§ 1899 to 1899.11; COLO. REV. STAT. ANN. §§ 38-14-101 to -112; FLA. STAT. § 265.565; GA. CODE ANN. §§ 10-1-529.1 to -529.7; 765 ILL. COMP. STAT. ANN. 1033/1 to /999; IND. CODE ANN. §§ 32-34-5-1 to -16; IOWA CODE ANN. §§ 305B.1 to .13; KAN. STAT. ANN. §§ 58-4002 to -4013; KY. REV. STAT. ANN. §§ 171.830 to .849; LA. REV. STAT. ANN. § 25:345 (the statute applies only to the State Museum); ME. REV. STAT. ANN. tit. 27, § 601; MICH. COMP. LAWS §§ 399.602 to .613; MINN. STAT. §§ 345.70 to .74; MISS. CODE ANN. §§ 39-19-1 to -21; MO. REV. STAT. §§ 184.104 to .122; MONT. CODE ANN. §§ 22-3-501 to -510, 22-3-521 to -523; NEB. REV. STAT. §§ 51-702 to -712; NEV. REV. STAT. ANN. §§ 381.001, .004, .009; N.H. REV. STAT. ANN. § 201-E:1 to -E:7; N.M. STAT. ANN. §§ 18-10-2 to -5; N.C. GEN. STAT. §§ 121-2 and 121-7; N.D. CENT. CODE § 47-07-14; OHIO REV. CODE ANN. §§ 3385.01 to .10; OR. REV. STAT. §§ 358.415 to .440; 60 OKLA STAT. § 683.2 (providing that museums are not subject to the provisions of the Uniform Unclaimed Property Act (60 OKLA STAT. § 651 to 688), but if they choose to comply with the requirements of the Act they will thereby be subject to the Act); S.C. CODE §§ 27-45-10 to -100; S.D. CODIFIED LAWS §§ 43-41C-1 to -4; TENN. CODE ANN. §§ 66-29-201 to -204; TEX. PROP. CODE ANN. §§ 80.001 to .008; VA. CODE ANN. §§ 55-210.31 to .38; WASH. REV. CODE. ANN. §§ 63.27.010 to .050; WIS. STAT. ANN. §§ 171.30 to .33; WYO. STAT. ANN. §§ 34-23-101 to -108.
232. N.Y. EDUC. LAW § 233-aa (Consol. 2012).
233. Southwest Museum v. Farquhar, No. C708347 (Cal. Super. Ct. L.A. County, Dec. 14, 1988); *see* Linden Havemeyer Wise, *Old Loans: A Collections Management Problem*, ALI-ABA COURSE OF STUDY, Mar. 1990, Houston, Texas.
234. *See* MALARO, *supra* note 10, at 251.

235. Treas. Reg. § 1.170A-13C.

236. Tax Reform Act of 1984, Pub. L. No. 98-369, § 155, 98 Stat. 494, 691–95 (1984).

237. See instructions to IRS Form 8283 required to be signed by the appraiser and attached to a taxpayer's income tax return.

238. Most museums require their curators to sign a statement by which they agree not to perform any appraisal of a work of art that may be donated to the museum.

239. See MALARO, supra note 10, at 258.

240. See Clark & Sare, supra note 23, at 8. See John W. Madden, Jr. v. Comm'r, 74 T.C.M. (CCH) 440 (1997), where an outdoor arts museum, which was a tax-exempt private foundation, did not receive unrelated business taxable income (UBTI) from the rental of office building spaces to the public. The museum was created to introduce people to the outdoor arts. By offering the building spaces for special events, the museum exposed the artwork to an audience that normally would not have seen it. Thus, the rental activity was substantially related to the museum's exempt purpose. However, the museum did realize UBTI with respect to its long-term lease agreements with a concert promoter for the use of its outdoor amphitheater because the activity constituted a trade or business. The lease provided for a six-year initial term, and it required the museum to make arrangements for security and parking. Further, individual seats were installed to prepare the amphitheater for the productions which included popular performers and commanded premium ticket prices. The substantial amount of money at stake indicated that the museum executed the leases to make a profit, not to further its exempt purpose.

241. I.R.C. § 511.

242. I.R.C. §§ 512, 513.

243. I.R.C. § 513(a).

244. See PHELAN, supra note 3, at 170.

245. See Clark & Sare, supra note 23, at 11.

246. Rev. Rul. 69-268, 1969-1 C.B. 160; Rev. Rul. 74-399, 1974-2 C.B. 172.

247. See Clark & Sare, supra note 23, at 11; Butler, supra note 116.

248. Id.

249. See PHELAN, supra note 3, at 172.

250. Rev. Rul. 73-105, 1973-1 C.B. 264.

251. S. Hodes & K. Gross, Museums in the Commercial Marketplace: The Need for Licensing Agreements, 10 CONN. L. REV. 620 (1978)

APPENDIX 17-1

*Loan Agreement
(for Lending Multiple Works
to Multiple Museums)*

LOAN AGREEMENT

THIS AGREEMENT made and entered into as of this _____ day of _____, 20__, by and between _____, residing at _____ _____("Lender"), and _____ _____ Museum, located at _____ ("Borrower   1"),   and   _____   Museum,   located   at _____ ("Borrower 2") (individually "Borrower" and collectively "Borrowers").

WITNESSETH:

WHEREAS, Lender is the owner of the works of art listed on Schedule A attached hereto ("Works");

WHEREAS, Borrowers wish to borrow the Works for exhibition; and

WHEREAS, Lender wishes to lend the Works to Borrowers for exhibition.

NOW THEREFORE, in consideration of the mutual promises contained herein, the parties hereto agree as follows:

1. *Period and Purpose of the Loan.*

The period of the loan for the Works shall commence upon the earliest of Borrower 1 packing and/or pick up and/or receipt of the Works from Lender, on or about _____, 20__, and end after the Works have been returned to Lender, unpacked and inspected on or before _____, 20__ ("Loan Period"). Unless otherwise agreed in writing, the loan terminates at the end of the Loan Period. The Works will be loaned for the purpose of an exhibition titled _____ ("Exhibition").

2. *Location of the Exhibition.*

The Exhibition will take place at the following locations for the indicated periods:

Borrower 1: _____, 20__ to _____, 20__

Borrower 2: _____, 20__ to _____, 20__

The Works will not travel to any other location and will be returned only to Lender or to a location as directed in writing by Lender ("Lender's Location"). Unless otherwise agreed in writing, the loan terminates at the end of the Loan Period.

3. *Credit Line.*

The credit line for exhibition, catalogue and publicity purposes shall read as follows: _____.

4. *Photography and Reproduction.*

a.   Lender does not own the copyright for the Works. As such, Lender lacks the authority to grant permission to Borrowers to photograph or otherwise reproduce the Works. Borrowers agree to observe and comply with all copyright, trademark and other intellectual property laws and regulations, all moral rights including, without limitation, attribution rights, and all rights of privacy and publicity (individually and collectively, "Intellectual Property Rights") relating to the Works, and not to infringe or violate any Intellectual Property Rights. Each Borrower is solely responsible for determining whether the Works are subject to any Intellectual Property Rights and for obtaining all approvals, waivers, licenses and consents as necessary or required in connection with any reproduction, display, distribution, creation of derivative works or other use (any "Use") that such Borrower desires to make relating to the Works. Borrowers acknowledge that Lender has not made any representations about the availability of any such approvals, waivers, consents or licenses, or ability to use any image or reproduction relating to the loan. Each Borrower agrees to and will release, indemnify and defend Lender and his trustees, officers, employees and agents ("Lender's Agents") from and against any Use of the Works by such Borrower or any director, officer, employee, agent, contractor, representative or invitee of such Borrower (such "Borrower's Agents").

b.   Provided the provisions of subparagraph 4.a. herein have been followed, Lender has no objection to Borrowers photographing the Works for reproduction in the Exhibition catalogue or for archival, educational and publicity purposes in connection with the Exhibition, such as for postcards and commercial merchandise sold during the Exhibition for the benefit of Borrowers. Any other reproduction of the Works by any person for any purpose must be approved in advance by Lender, and Borrowers agree to follow the provisions of subparagraph 4.a. herein after obtaining such approval from Lender. Borrowers agree to pay all costs of any such reproduction of the Works. Borrowers agree to use reasonable efforts to prevent the unauthorized reproduction of the Works. Each Borrower further agrees that it shall be solely responsible for defending such Borrower's Use of the Works, as well as for any costs or judgments resulting from such Use.

c. A digital file of the Works has been provided by Lender to Borrowers free-of-charge for use in connection with the Exhibition. The digital file is for reproduction in a catalogue only. Each Borrower agrees that any photography, video or reproduction of the Works not based on the digital file must be supervised by such Borrower's curatorial or conservation employees. Borrowers agree that any photography, video or reproduction of the Works not based on the digital file involving light levels which exceed forty (40) lux must be limited to a maximum of ten (10) minutes to limit exposure of the Works to excessive light levels.

d. Borrowers agree to provide Lender with two (2) copies of any publication produced by a Borrower illustrating or mentioning the Works at Lender's address set forth on the first page of this Agreement.

5. *Insurance.*

a. Borrowers agree to provide broad worldwide all-risk fine arts insurance on a wall-to-wall basis, including but not limited to the perils of flood, earthquake, inventory shortage, and full terrorism, under United States Government Indemnity and/or Borrowers' blanket fine arts policy at their own cost and expense for the periods as indicated in subparagraph 5.b. herein. Borrowers hereby confirm that the only exclusions in the United States Government Indemnity coverage provided under this Agreement are normal wear and tear, inherent vice and damage sustained due to or resulting from any repairing, restoration or retouching process. Borrowers hereby confirm that the only exclusions in each Borrower's fine arts insurance coverage provided under this Agreement are those set forth on Schedule B attached hereto without any deductible. All insurance obtained by each Borrower must be acceptable to Lender in form and content, complying with all of the following terms and conditions. Each Borrower agrees not to invalidate or prejudice, by its actions or inactions, its insurance policy. Each Borrower agrees to provide Lender with a Certificate of Insurance and/or a Certificate of Indemnity (both referred to as "COI") evidencing such insurance coverage and naming Lender as a loss payee and additional insured. The COIs shall be delivered to Lender no less than ten (10) days prior to the Loan Period commencing.

b. Borrower 1 shall insure the Works at its cost from the time the Works are released from Lender to Borrower 1 at the commencement of the Loan Period, through exhibition at Borrower 1's premises, and until the Condition Reports, as defined in subparagraph 8.b. herein, are updated and signed at the Works' arrival at Borrower 2's premises. Borrower 2 shall insure the Works at its cost from the time the Condition Reports are updated and signed at the Works' arrival at Borrower 2's premises, through exhibition at Borrower 2's premises, and until the Works are returned to Lender and accepted by Lender.

c.   Each Borrower agrees that its insurance coverage and/or United States Government Indemnity shall provide primary protection during the period indicated in subparagraph 5.b. above and that the coverage arranged by such Borrower shall not be diminished in any way by reason of any insurance coverage maintained or obtained by Lender. Each Borrower also agrees that all insurance and United States Government Indemnity policies hereunder provided by such Borrower shall expressly state the foregoing. Lender's coverage will in all events be secondary and non-contributory to Borrowers' policies and will not release, waive or diminish any of Borrowers' obligations in this Agreement.

d.   Borrowers agree to insure the Works for the periods as indicated in subparagraph 5.b. herein for the amounts which are stated on Schedule A attached hereto ("Insurance Values"). Borrowers agree that all claims will be based on the Insurance Values.

e.   Each Borrower shall maintain standard commercial general liability insurance during the period that such Borrower is responsible for the Works as indicated in subparagraph 5.b. herein for all claims alleging bodily injury, property damage liability and personal injury with a limit of not less than $_____ for each occurrence and in the aggregate. Lender shall be added as an additional insured to such insurance policy.

f.   Each Borrower agrees to maintain levels of commercial insurance and/or United States Government Indemnity at a minimum to cover an amount equal to all the works on loan to such Borrower during the period that such Borrower is responsible for the Works as indicated in subparagraph 5.b. herein. In the event of any loss or damage to the Works: (i) the insurance will include the costs and expense of restoration plus any diminution in value, including any appraisal fees to establish diminution in the value, and Borrower responsible for the Works at such time as indicated in subparagraph 5.b. herein or its insurer shall be responsible for reasonable expenses incurred for Lender's representative, if requested by Lender, to inspect and report on the damaged Works; (ii) Lender can have his choice of appraiser, conservator and/or restorer as required, so long as such choice is approved by the insurer; (iii) Lender agrees to use reasonable efforts as required to enable Borrowers to submit and pursue claims for insurance coverage; (iv) Borrowers or their insurers will not undertake any restoration or repair of the damaged Works without Lender's written approval; (v) Borrowers must take and pay the cost of reasonable actions Lender may require to secure and protect the Works from further damage or loss; and (vi) if there is any disagreement over the value of the Works or the amount of diminution in value such disagreement will be settled by a panel of three (3) competent and disinterested market experts to be selected as follows: Lender will select one, Borrower responsible for the Works at such time as indicated in subparagraph 5.b. herein or its insurer will select one and the two selected experts will select the third. Each expert will determine the amount of loss separately and, if failing to agree, they will jointly select then submit their opinions in writing to an umpire who will decide the amount of loss. In no event will a public auction be used as a method to establish the value. An insurance claim will be handled pursuant to the terms of such Borrower's insurance and/or United States Government Indemnity. Each Borrower agrees that Lender's recovery shall not be limited to the amount paid by such Borrower's insurance and/or United States Government Indemnity if such payment is determined to be inadequate in the opinion of Lender.

g. In the event of cancellation or default of a Borrower's insurance for any reason or non-compliance with the insurance required in this Paragraph 5, Lender may, at his discretion, purchase insurance for his own behalf for the Works. Such Borrower shall bear such costs for such insurance.

h. A Borrower's failure to provide the insurance required under this Agreement or comply with any of the provisions of this Paragraph 5, including, without limitation, receipt by Lender of any insurance policy endorsement or COI evidencing coverage that is less than required or any communication from such Borrower that it is not in compliance with any of the requirements, will not be deemed to be, or constitute, a waiver by Lender of any requirements of this Agreement or Borrowers' covenants, liabilities or obligations.

6. *Shipping.*

Borrowers, after consulting with Lender and obtaining the approval of Lender, agree to arrange for and pay for all costs in connection with packing and shipping the Works, from (i) their current locations to Borrower 1; (ii) from Borrower 1 to Borrower 2; and (iii) from Borrower 2 back to Lender at the end of the Loan Period. The Works will be shipped by a shipper acceptable to Lender, and each packing of the Works for shipment to Lender will be supervised by Lender or Lender's Agents. Lender reserves the right to designate the type of vehicle to be used to transport the Works to and back from the exhibition locations.

7. *Expenses.*

Borrowers, as they shall agree amongst themselves, will pay all costs of packing, shipping, courier, insurance, application of a shatterproof anti-reflective and removal of such shatterproof anti-reflective at the end of the Exhibition, and any other cost in connection with exhibiting the Works at the Exhibition.

8. *Care, Preservation and Exhibition.*

a. Each Borrower will give the Works the same care it gives comparable property of its own. Precautions will be taken to ensure that light levels for the Works shall not exceed forty (40) lux, unless approved and supervised by Lender in accordance with subparagraph 4.c. herein, and to protect the Works from fire, theft, mishandling, dirt and insects, and from extremes of light, temperature and humidity while in each Borrower's custody.

b. Prior to the packing of the Works at the commencement of the Loan Period, Borrower 1 shall arrange for condition reports to be prepared for the Works ("Condition Reports") by a conservator or other qualified employee acceptable to Lender ("Qualified Employee"). On arrival and unpacking of the Works at each exhibition location, a Qualified Employee shall update the Condition Reports indicating any change in the condition of the Works. During the Loan Period, any change in condition shall be noted on the Condition Reports. Any damage to the Works, regardless of who may be responsible, must be reported immediately to Lender. The Condition Reports shall be made available for review by Lender at any time during the Loan Period. A Qualified Employee shall oversee the repacking of the Works at each exhibition location and update the Condition Reports at such times. The Condition Reports will be updated again by a Qualified Employee when the Works are unpacked at Lender's Location. Borrowers, as they shall agree amongst themselves, shall pay any costs in connection with preparing and updating the Condition Reports.

c. Borrowers will not perform any conservation on the Works, or frame, unframe or reframe the Works, without the specific, prior written consent of Lender. The Works will be protected with a shatterproof anti-reflective at the expense of Borrowers for the duration of the Exhibition. Application of the shatterproof anti-reflective will be done at _____. The shatterproof anti-reflective will be removed after the duration of the Exhibition once the Works are returned to Lender.

9. *Works Not Being Offered for Sale.*

Borrowers understand and agree that Lender is lending the Works to Borrowers solely for purposes of the Exhibition and that BORROWERS HAVE NO AUTHORITY OR RIGHT TO SELL OR PASS TITLE TO THE WORKS OR TO OFFER THE WORKS FOR SALE UNDER ANY CIRCUMSTANCES.

10. *Miscellaneous.*

a. Each Borrower agrees to and will release, indemnify and defend Lender and Lender's Agents from and against all costs, losses, taxes, assessments, demands, fees and expenses (including attorneys' fees and costs), claims, damages, suits, actions and/or proceedings, threatened against or suffered by Lender or Lender's Agents relating to or arising out of any breach or failure of performance by such Borrower under this Agreement and any negligent, wrongful or intentional act or omission by or on behalf of such Borrower or such Borrower's Agents.

b. This Agreement represents the entire understanding of all the parties hereto, supersedes any and all other and prior agreements between the parties and declares all such prior agreements between the parties regarding the Works null and void. The terms of this Agreement may not be modified or amended, except in a writing signed by the party to be charged. If a Borrower violates any term of this Agreement, Lender may, in addition to pursuing other remedies he sees fit and is entitled to under the law, terminate this Agreement at his sole discretion with regard to any or all Borrowers, and Borrower responsible for the Works at such time as indicated in subparagraph 5.b. herein agrees to return the Works in accordance with Paragraph 6 herein within five (5) business days of receiving written notice of such termination. This Agreement and all matters relating to it shall be governed by the laws of the State of _____ without regard to conflict of laws principles.

c. This Agreement shall inure to the benefit of, and shall be binding upon, the successors, heirs, executors and administrators of the parties hereto. Any dispute arising hereunder shall be resolved in the _____ state court or in the United States District Court for the _____, and the parties hereto consent to the personal jurisdiction of these courts and agree that these venues are convenient and not to seek a change of venue or to seek to dismiss the action on the ground of forum non conveniens, not to remove any litigation from either of these courts to another federal court, not to assert any defense based on lack of jurisdiction of this court, and not to bring any action arising under, in connection with, or incidental to this Agreement in any other court.

d. This Agreement may be executed in two or more counterparts, including facsimile or PDF, each of which shall be deemed an original, and all of which together shall constitute one and the same instrument.

IN WITNESS WHEREOF, the parties hereto have hereunto signed their hands and seals the day and year first above written.

BORROWER 1
[Name of Borrower 1]

_____

By:
Its:

BORROWER 2
[Name of Borrower 2]

_____

By:
Its:

LENDER

_____

[Name of Lender]

SCHEDULE A

THE WORKS

		Insurance Value
1.	Artist:	
	Title:	
	Medium:	
	Size:	
	Date:	
2.	Artist:	
	Title:	
	Medium:	
	Size:	
	Date:	
3.	Artist:	
	Title:	
	Medium:	
	Size:	
	Date:	

SCHEDULE B

INSURANCE EXCLUSIONS

APPENDIX 17-2

Loan Agreement (for Lending One Work to a Museum)

LOAN AGREEMENT

THIS AGREEMENT made and entered into as of this _____ day of _____, 20___, by and between _____, residing at _____ _____ ("Lender"), and _____ _____ Museum, located at _____ _____ ("Borrower").

WITNESSETH:

WHEREAS, Lender is the owner of the work of art listed on Schedule A attached hereto ("Work");

WHEREAS, Borrower wishes to borrow the Work for exhibition; and

WHEREAS, Lender wishes to lend the Work to Borrower for exhibition.

NOW THEREFORE, in consideration of the mutual promises contained herein, the parties hereto agree as follows:

1. *Period and Purpose of the Loan.*

The period of the loan for the Work shall commence upon the earliest of Borrower packing and/or pick up and/or receipt of the Work from Lender, on or about _____, 20___, and end after the Work has been returned to Lender, unpacked and inspected, on or before _____, 20___ ("Loan Period"). Unless otherwise agreed in writing, the loan terminates at the end of the Loan Period. The Work will be loaned for the purpose of an exhibition titled _____ to be displayed at Borrower's premises from _____, 20___ through _____, 20___ ("Exhibition").

2. *Location of the Exhibition.*

The Exhibition will take place at Borrower's premises located at _____ ("Exhibition Location"). The Work will not travel to any other location.

3. *Credit Line.*

The credit line for exhibition, catalogue and publicity purposes shall read as follows: _____.

4. *Photography and Reproduction.*

a. Lender does not own the copyright for the Work. As such, Lender lacks
    the authority to grant permission to Borrower to photograph or other-
    wise reproduce the Work. Borrower agrees to observe and comply with all
    copyright, trademark and other intellectual property laws and regulations,
    all moral rights including, without limitation, attribution rights, and all
    rights of privacy and publicity (individually and collectively, "Intellectual
    Property Rights") relating to the Work, and not to infringe or violate any
    Intellectual Property Rights. Borrower is solely responsible for determin-
    ing whether the Work is subject to any Intellectual Property Rights and for
    obtaining all approvals, waivers, licenses and consents as necessary or re-
    quired in connection with any reproduction, display, distribution, creation
    of derivative works or other use (any "Use") that Borrower desires to make
    relating to the Work. Borrower acknowledges that Lender has not made
    any representations about the availability of any such approvals, waivers,
    consents or licenses, or ability to use any image or reproduction relating to
    the loan. Borrower agrees to and will release, indemnify and defend Lender
    and his trustees, officers, employees and agents ("Lender's Agents") from
    and against any Use of the Work by Borrower or any director, officer, em-
    ployee, agent, contractor, representative or invitee of Borrower (such "Bor-
    rower's Agents").

b. Provided the provisions of subparagraph 4.a. herein have been followed,
    Lender has no objection to Borrower photographing the Work for repro-
    duction in the Exhibition catalogue or for archival, educational and public-
    ity purposes in connection with the Exhibition, such as for postcards and
    commercial merchandise sold during the Exhibition for the benefit of Bor-
    rower. Any other reproduction of the Work by any person for any purpose
    must be approved in advance by Lender, and Borrower agrees to follow the
    provisions of subparagraph 4.a. herein after obtaining such approval from
    Lender. Borrower agrees to pay all costs of any such reproduction of the
    Work. Borrower agrees to use reasonable efforts to prevent the unauthor-
    ized reproduction of the Work. Borrower further agrees that it shall be
    solely responsible for defending Borrower's Use of the Work, as well as for
    any costs or judgments resulting from such Use.

c. A digital file of the Work has been provided by Lender to Borrower free-
    of-charge for use in connection with the Exhibition. The digital file is for
    reproduction in a catalogue only. Borrower agrees that any photography,
    video or reproduction of the Work not based on the digital file must be su-
    pervised by Borrower's curatorial or conservation employees. Borrower
    agrees that any photography, video or reproduction of the Work not based
    on the digital file involving light levels which exceed forty (40) lux must be
    limited to a maximum of ten (10) minutes to limit exposure of the Work to
    excessive light levels.

d. Borrower agrees to provide Lender with two (2) copies of any publication produced by Borrower illustrating or mentioning the Work at Lender's address set forth on the first page of this Agreement.

5. *Insurance.*

a. Borrower agrees to provide broad worldwide all-risk fine arts insurance on a wall-to-wall basis, including but not limited to the perils of flood, earthquake, inventory shortage, and full terrorism, under United States Government Indemnity and/or Borrower's blanket fine arts policy at its own cost and expense for the Loan Period. Borrower hereby confirms that the only exclusions in the United States Government Indemnity coverage provided under this Agreement are normal wear and tear, inherent vice and damage sustained due to or resulting from any repairing, restoration or retouching process. Borrower hereby confirms that the only exclusions in Borrower's fine arts insurance coverage provided under this Agreement are those set forth on Schedule B attached hereto without any deductible. All insurance obtained by Borrower must be acceptable to Lender in form and content, complying with all of the following terms and conditions. Borrower agrees not to invalidate or prejudice, by its actions or inactions, its insurance policy. Borrower agrees to provide Lender with a Certificate of Insurance and/or a Certificate of Indemnity (collectively "COI") evidencing such insurance coverage and naming Lender as a loss payee and additional insured. The COI shall be delivered to Lender no less than ten (10) days prior to the Loan Period commencing.

b. Borrower agrees that its insurance coverage and/or United States Government Indemnity shall provide primary protection and that the coverage arranged by Borrower shall not be diminished in any way by reason of any insurance coverage maintained or obtained by Lender. Borrower also agrees that all insurance and United States Government Indemnity policies hereunder provided by Borrower shall expressly state the foregoing. Lender's coverage will in all events be secondary and non-contributory to Borrower's policies and will not release, waive or diminish any of Borrower's obligations in this Agreement.

c. Borrower agrees to insure the Work for the amount which is stated on Schedule A attached hereto ("Insurance Value"). Borrower agrees that all claims will be based on the Insurance Value.

d. Borrower shall maintain standard commercial general liability insurance during the Loan Period for all claims alleging bodily injury, property damage liability and personal injury with a limit of not less than $_____ for each occurrence and in the aggregate. Lender shall be added as an additional insured to such insurance policy.

e. Borrower agrees to maintain levels of commercial insurance and/or United States Government Indemnity at a minimum to cover an amount equal to all the works on loan to Borrower during the Loan Period. In the event of any loss or damage to the Work: (i) the insurance will include the costs and expense of restoration plus any diminution in value including any appraisal fees to establish diminution in the value, and Borrower or its insurer shall be responsible for reasonable expenses incurred for Lender's representative, if requested by Lender, to inspect and report on the damaged Work; (ii) Lender can have his choice of appraiser, conservator and/or restorer as required, so long as such choice is approved by the insurer; (iii) Lender agrees to use reasonable efforts as required to enable Borrower to submit and pursue a claim for insurance coverage; (iv) Borrower or its insurer will not undertake any restoration or repair of the damaged Work without Lender's written approval; (v) Borrower must take and pay the cost of reasonable actions Lender may require to secure and protect the Work from further damage or loss; and (vi) if there is any disagreement over the value of the Work or the amount of diminution in value such disagreement will be settled by a panel of three (3) competent and disinterested market experts to be selected as follows: Lender will select one, Borrower or its insurer will select one and the two selected experts will select the third. Each expert will determine the amount of loss separately and, if failing to agree, they will jointly select then submit their opinions in writing to an umpire who will decide the amount of loss. In no event will a public auction be used as a method to establish the value. An insurance claim will be handled pursuant to the terms of Borrower's insurance and United States Government Indemnity. Borrower agrees that Lender's recovery shall not be limited to the amount paid by Borrower's insurance and/or United States Government Indemnity if such payment is determined to be inadequate in the opinion of Lender.

f.   In the event of cancellation or default of Borrower's insurance for any reason or non-compliance with the insurance required in this Paragraph 5, Lender may, at his discretion, purchase insurance on his own behalf for the Work. Borrower shall bear such costs for such insurance.

g.   Borrower's failure to provide the insurance required under this Agreement or comply with any of the provisions of this Paragraph 5, including, without limitation, receipt by Lender of any insurance policy endorsement or COI evidencing coverage that is less than required or any communication from Borrower that it is not in compliance with any of the requirements, will not be deemed to be, or constitute, a waiver by Lender of any requirements of this Agreement or Borrower's covenants, liabilities, or obligations.

6. *Shipping.*

Borrower, after consulting with Lender and obtaining the approval of Lender, agrees to arrange for and pay for all costs in connection with packing and shipping the Work, from the Work's location at the commencement of the Loan Period to the Exhibition Location, and packing and shipping the Work from the Exhibition Location back to Lender at the end of the Loan Period. The Work will be shipped by a shipper acceptable to Lender, and the packing of the Work for shipment to Lender at the end of the Loan Period will be supervised by Lender or Lender's Agents. Lender reserves the right to designate the type of vehicle to be used to transport the Work to and back from the Exhibition Location.

7. *Expenses.*

Borrower will pay all costs of packing, shipping, courier, insurance, application of a shatterproof anti-reflective and removal of such shatterproof anti-reflective at the end of the Exhibition, and any other cost in connection with exhibiting the Work at the Exhibition.

8. *Care, Preservation and Exhibition.*

a. Borrower will give the Work the same care it gives comparable property of its own. Precautions will be taken to ensure that light levels for the Work shall not exceed forty (40) lux, unless approved and supervised by Lender in accordance with subparagraph 4.c. herein, and to protect the Work from fire, theft, mishandling, dirt and insects, and from extremes of light, temperature and humidity while in Borrower's custody.

b. Prior to the packing of the Work at the commencement of the Loan Period, Borrower shall arrange for a condition report to be prepared for the Work ("Condition Report") by a conservator or other qualified employee acceptable to Lender ("Qualified Employee"). On arrival and unpacking of the Work at the Exhibition Location, the Qualified Employee shall update the Condition Report indicating any change in the condition of the Work. During the Loan Period, any change in condition shall be noted on the Condition Report and any damage to the Work, regardless of who may be responsible, must be reported immediately to Lender. The Condition Report shall be made available for review by Lender at any time during the Loan Period. At the end of the Exhibition, the Qualified Employee shall oversee the repacking of the Work and update the Condition Report. The Condition Report will be updated again by the Qualified Employee when the Work is unpacked at Lender's Location. Borrower shall pay any costs in connection with preparing and updating the Condition Report.

c. Borrower will not perform any conservation on the Work, or frame, unframe or reframe the Work, without the specific, prior written consent of Lender. The Work will be protected with a shatterproof anti-reflective at the expense of Borrower for the duration of the Exhibition. Application of the shatterproof anti-reflective will be done at _____. The shatterproof anti-reflective will be removed after the duration of the Exhibition once the Work are returned to Lender.

9. *Return of Loan.*

The Work will be returned only to Lender or to a location as directed in writing by Lender. Unless otherwise agreed in writing, the loan terminates at the end of the Loan Period.

10. *Work Not Being Offered for Sale.*

Borrower understands and agrees that Lender is lending the Work to Borrower solely for purposes of the Exhibition and that BORROWER HAS NO AUTHORITY OR RIGHT TO SELL OR PASS TITLE TO THE WORK OR TO OFFER THE WORK FOR SALE UNDER ANY CIRCUMSTANCES.

11. *Miscellaneous.*

a. Borrower agrees to and will release, indemnify and defend Lender and Lender's Agents from and against all costs, losses, taxes, assessments, demands, fees and expenses (including attorneys' fees and costs), claims, damages, suits, actions and/or proceedings, threatened against or suffered by Lender or Lender's Agents relating to or arising out of any breach or failure of performance by Borrower under this Agreement and any negligent, wrongful or intentional act or omission by or on behalf of Borrower or Borrower's Agents.

b. This Agreement represents the entire understanding of all the parties hereto, supersedes any and all other and prior agreements between the parties and declares all such prior agreements between the parties regarding the Work null and void. The terms of this Agreement may not be modified or amended, except in a writing signed by the party to be charged. If Borrower violates any term of this Agreement, Lender may, in addition to pursuing other remedies he sees fit and is entitled to under the law, terminate this Agreement at his sole discretion, and Borrower agrees to return the Work in accordance with Paragraph 6 herein within five (5) business days of receiving written notice of such termination. This Agreement and all matters relating to it shall be governed by the laws of the State of _____ without regard to conflict of laws principles.

c. This Agreement shall inure to the benefit of, and shall be binding upon, the successors, heirs, executors and administrators of the parties hereto. Any dispute arising hereunder shall be resolved in the _____ state court or in the United States District Court for the _____, and the parties hereto consent to the personal jurisdiction of these courts and that the venues are convenient and not to seek a change of venue or to seek to dismiss the action on the ground of forum non conveniens, not to remove any litigation from either of these courts to another federal court, not to assert any defense based on lack of jurisdiction of this court, and not to bring any action arising under, in connection with, or incidental to this Agreement in any other court.

d. This Agreement may be executed in two or more counterparts, including facsimile or PDF, each of which shall be deemed an original, and all of which together shall constitute one and the same instrument.

IN WITNESS WHEREOF, the parties hereto have hereunto signed their hands and seals the day and year first above written.

BORROWER
[Name of Borrower]

_____

By:
Its:

LENDER

_____

[Name of Lender]

SCHEDULE A

THE WORK

		Insurance Value
1.	Artist:	
	Title:	
	Medium:	
	Size:	
	Date:	

SCHEDULE B

INSURANCE EXCLUSIONS

APPENDIX 17-3

Loan Agreement (Loan to a Commercial Art Gallery)

LOAN AGREEMENT

THIS AGREEMENT made and entered into as of this _____ day of _____, 20__, by and between _____ residing at _____ ("Lender"), and _____ Gallery, Inc., with an office at _____ _____ ("Borrower").

WITNESSETH:

WHEREAS, Lender is the owner of the work of art listed on Schedule A attached hereto ("Work");

WHEREAS, Borrower wishes to borrow the Work for exhibition; and

WHEREAS, Lender wishes to lend the Work to Borrower for exhibition.

NOW THEREFORE, in consideration of the mutual promises contained herein, the parties hereto agree as follows:

1. *Period and Purpose of the Loan.*

The period of the loan shall commence upon the earliest of Borrower packing and/or pick up and/or receipt of the Work from Lender (on or about _____, 20__) and end after the Work has been returned to Lender, unpacked and inspected on or before _____, 20__ ("Loan Period"). Unless otherwise agreed in writing, the loan terminates at the end of the Loan Period. The Work will be loaned for the purpose of an exhibition entitled _____ ("Exhibition").

2. *Location of the Exhibition.*

The Exhibition will take place at one of Borrower's premises in New York ("Exhibition Location"). The Work will not travel to any other location and will be returned to Lender's premises at _____ or to any other location directed in writing by Lender ("Lender's Location") after the Exhibition. The Exhibition will be from _____, 20__ to _____, 20__ ("Exhibition Period").

3. *Credit Line.*

The credit line for exhibition, catalogue and publicity purposes shall read as follows: _____.

4. *Photography and Reproduction.*

a. Lender does not own the copyright for the Work. As such, Lender lacks the authority to grant permission to Borrower to photograph or otherwise reproduce the Work. Borrower agrees to observe and comply with all copyright, trademark and other intellectual property laws and regulations, all moral rights including, without limitation, attribution rights, and all rights of privacy and publicity (individually and collectively, "Intellectual Property Rights") relating to the Work, and not to infringe or violate any Intellectual Property Rights. Borrower is solely responsible for determining whether the Work is subject to any Intellectual Property Rights and for obtaining all approvals, waivers, licenses and consents as necessary or required in connection with any reproduction, display, distribution, creation of a derivative work or other use (any "Use") that Borrower desires to make relating to the Work. Borrower acknowledges Lender has not made any representations about the availability of any such approvals, waivers, consents or licenses, or ability to use any image or reproduction relating to the loan. Borrower agrees to and will release, indemnify and defend Lender and his trustees, officers, employees and agents ("Lender's Agents") from and against any Use of the Work by Borrower or any director, officer, employee, agent, contractor, representative or invitee of Borrower ("Borrower's Agents").

b. Provided the provisions of subparagraph 4.a. herein have been followed, Lender has no objection to Borrower photographing the Work for reproduction in a catalogue or for archival, educational and publicity purposes. Any other reproduction of the Work by any person for any purpose must be approved in advance by Lender. Borrower agrees that, after obtaining such approval from Lender, it will follow the provisions of subparagraph 4.a. herein. Borrower agrees to use reasonable efforts to prevent the unauthorized reproduction of the Work. Borrower further agrees that it shall be solely responsible for defending Borrower's Use of the Work, as well as for any costs or judgments resulting from such Use.

c. Borrower agrees to provide Lender with three (3) copies of any publication produced by Borrower illustrating or mentioning the Work.

5. *Insurance.*

a. Borrower agrees to provide broad worldwide all risk fine arts insurance on a wall-to-wall basis, including but not limited to the perils of flood, earthquake, and full terrorism, at its own cost and expense for the Loan Period. Borrower agrees that the only exclusions in Borrower's fine arts insurance coverage provided under this Agreement are those set forth on Schedule

B attached hereto without any deductible. All insurance obtained by Borrower must be acceptable to Lender in form and content and must comply with all of the following terms and conditions. Borrower agrees not to invalidate or prejudice, by its action or inactions, its insurance policy. Borrower agrees to provide Lender with a Certificate of Insurance (COI) evidencing such insurance coverage naming Lender as a loss payee and additional insured. The COI shall be delivered to Lender no less than ten (10) days prior to the Loan Period commencing. Notwithstanding the foregoing, Borrower agrees to indemnify Lender for any and all loss or damage to the Work (including all claim expenses) no matter how occurring during the Loan Period, irrespective of Borrower's insurance whether insured or not, the loss is under Borrower's deductible or excluded in Borrower's policy including any claim settlement from Borrower's insurance that is inadequate in the opinion of Lender, and such payments shall be paid by Borrower to Lender within one year of the damage, loss or expenses not covered by Borrower's insurance policy.

b.   Borrower agrees that its insurance coverage shall provide primary protection and that the coverage arranged by Borrower shall not be diminished in any way by reason of any insurance coverage maintained or obtained by Lender and all insurance policies hereunder provided by Borrower shall expressly state the foregoing. Lender's coverage will in all events be secondary and non contributory to Borrower's policies and will not release, waive or diminish any of Borrower's obligations in this Agreement.

c.   Borrower agrees to insure the Work for the amount which is stated on Schedule A attached hereto ("Insurance Value"). Borrower agrees that all claims will be based on the Insurance Value.

d.   Borrower shall maintain standard commercial general liability insurance during the Loan Period for all claims, alleging bodily injury, property damage liability and personal injury with a limit of not less than _____ for each occurrence and in the aggregate and Lender shall be added as an additional insured to such insurance policy.

e.   Borrower agrees to maintain levels of insurance at a minimum to cover an amount equal to all the works on loan to Borrower during the Loan Period. In the event of any loss or damage to the Work: (i) the insurance will include the costs and expense of restoration plus diminution in value including any appraisal fees to establish diminution in the value and Borrower or its insurer shall be responsible for reasonable expenses incurred for Lender's representative, if requested by Lender, to inspect and report on the damaged Work; (ii) in the event of any loss, Borrower and Lender agree that _____ shall serve as appraiser, and _____ shall serve as conservator and/or restorer as required; (iii) Borrower's insurance policy shall allow for negotiation and settlement of any claim with Lender at Lender's discretion; (iv) Borrower or its insurer will not undertake any restoration or repair of the damaged Work without Lender's written approval; (v) Borrower must take and pay the cost of reasonable actions

Lender may require to secure and protect the Work from further damage or loss; and (vi) if there is any disagreement over the value of the Work or the amount of diminution in value such disagreement will be settled by a panel of three (3) competent and disinterested market experts to be selected as follows: Lender will select one, Borrower or its insurer will select one and the two selected experts will select the third. Each will determine the amount of loss separately and failing to agree, they will jointly select then submit their opinions in writing to an umpire who will decide the amount of loss.

f. In the event of cancellation or default of Borrower's insurance for any reason or non compliance with the insurance required in this Paragraph 5, Lender may, at his discretion, purchase insurance for his own behalf for the Work. Borrower shall bear such costs for such insurance.

g. Borrower's failure to provide the insurance required under this agreement or comply with any of the provisions of this Paragraph 5, including without limitation, receipt by Lender of any insurance policy endorsement or COI evidencing coverage that is less than required or any communication from Borrower that it is not in compliance with any of the requirements, will not be deemed to be, or constitute, a waiver by Lender of any requirements of this Agreement or Borrower's covenants, liabilities or obligations.

6. *Shipping.*

a. Borrower, after consulting with Lender and obtaining the approval of Lender, agrees to arrange for and pay for all costs in connection with packing and shipping the Work, from the Work's location at the commencement of the Loan Period to the Exhibition Location, and packing and shipping the Work from the Exhibition Location back to the Lender's Location at the end of the Loan Period. The Work will be shipped by a shipper acceptable to Lender and the packing of the Work for shipment to the Lender's Location will be supervised by Lender or Lender's Agents. Lender reserves the right to designate the type of vehicle to be used to transport the Work to and back from the Exhibition Location.

b. Borrower agrees to arrange for and pay for all costs in connection with the following requirements:
    i.   Shipment must be approved and by FINE ART shippers only;
    ii.   Single shipment is required with no other cargo going to and from the Exhibition Location;
    iii. Two people must be on the vehicle;
    iv.   A background check must be performed on the driver and his or her partner prior shipment of the Work;
    v.   The driver and partner must each have a cell phone on vehicle at all times. One person is required to remain in the vehicle during rest stops. The driver and partner must alternate all times away from

vehicle. The vehicle must never be unattended during transit of the Work;

vi.   The vehicle is to be secured with modern security/tracing/locking system—i.e., LoJack (level III or IV) or equivalent—and must have air-suspension, shock proofing, climate control and lift gate;

vii. A vehicle equipped with cell phone and radio contact to the police must accompany the lead vehicle transporting the Work at all times;

viii. The Work must be crated by the selected/approved fine art shipper;

ix.   Double crating is required for the Work. The crated Work must be physically secured to the sides of the truck, as per museum standards;

x.   The shippers must allow the crated Work to remain crated for a period of twenty-four (24) hours upon arrival both at the Exhibition Location and upon return to Lender before unpacking to acclimatize;

xi.   The Condition Report must be prepared by a qualified conservator prior to crating. A minimum of 3 "close-up" detailed digital photos in front and 3 of the back of the canvas must be on file with Lender. All photos must be taken within the hour prior to packing of the Work. The Work must undergo the same procedure after unpacking;

xii. Borrower will provide Lender with confirmation as to where the Work will be held upon arrival and what security will be provided to secure the Work. The Work must not be stored in a basement;

xiii. A courier must accompany the shipment of the Work at all times;

xiv. A stationed guard must be located next to the Work for the duration of the Exhibition during hours open to the public.

7. *Expenses.*

Borrower will pay all costs of crating, packing, shipping, insurance and any other cost in connection with exhibiting the Work at the Exhibition.

8. *Care, Preservation, and Exhibition.*

a.   Borrower will give the Work the same care it gives comparable property of its own. Precautions will be taken to protect the Work from fire, theft, mishandling, dirt and insects, and from extremes of light, temperature and humidity while in Borrower's custody.

b.   Prior to the packing of the Work at the commencement of the Loan Period, Borrower shall arrange for a condition report to be prepared for the Work ("Condition Report") by a conservator or other qualified employee acceptable to Lender ("Qualified Employee"). On arrival and unpacking of the Work at the Exhibition Location, the Qualified Employee shall update the Condition Report indicating any change in the condition of the Work. During the Exhibition, any change in condition shall be noted on the Condition Report. Any damage to the Work, regardless of who may be responsible, must be reported immediately to Lender. At the end of the Loan Period, the

Qualified Employee shall oversee the repacking of the Work and update the Condition Report. The Condition Report will be updated again by the Qualified Employee when the Work is unpacked at Lender's Location. Borrower shall pay any costs in connection with preparing and updating of the Condition Report. Borrower shall provide the Condition Report to Lender within 48 hours of the Condition Report being prepared or updated.

c.   Borrower will not perform any conservation on the Work, or frame, unframe or reframe the Work, without the specific, prior written consent of Lender.

9. *Work Not Being Offered for Sale.*

Borrower understands and agrees that Lender is lending the Work to Borrower solely for purposes of the Exhibition and that BORROWER HAS NO AUTHORITY OR RIGHT TO SELL OR PASS TITLE TO THE WORK OR TO OFFER THE WORK FOR SALE UNDER ANY CIRCUMSTANCES.

10. *Miscellaneous.*

a.   Borrower agrees to and will release, indemnify and defend Lender and Lender's Agents from and against all costs, losses, taxes, assessments, demands, fees and expenses (including attorneys' fees and costs), claims, damages, suits, actions and/or proceeding, threatened against or suffered by Lender or Lender's Agents relating to or arising out of any breach or failure of performance by Borrower under this Agreement and any negligent, wrongful or intentional act or omission by or on behalf of Borrower or Borrower's Agents.

b.   This Agreement represents the entire understanding of all the parties hereto, supersedes any and all other and prior agreements between the parties and declares all such prior agreements between the parties null and void. The terms of this Agreement may not be modified or amended, except in a writing signed by the party to be charged. This Agreement and all matters relating to it shall be governed by the laws of the State of _____ without regard to conflict of law principles.

c.   This Agreement shall inure to the benefit of, and shall be binding upon, the successors, heirs, executors and administrators of the parties hereto. Any dispute arising hereunder, including any dispute involving insurance coverage or proceeds, shall be resolved in the _____ Court, _____ County or in the United States District Court for the _____ District, and the parties hereto consent to the personal jurisdiction of those courts and agree that these venues are convenient and not to seek a change of venue or to seek to dismiss the action on the ground of forum non conveniens, not to assert any defense based on lack of jurisdiction of this court, and not to bring any action arising under, in connection with, or incidental to this Agreement in any other court.

d. This Agreement may be executed in two or more counterparts, includ-
    ing facsimile or PDF, each of which shall be deemed an original, and all of
    which together shall constitute one and the same instrument.

IN WITNESS WHEREOF, the parties hereto have hereunto signed their hands
and seals the day and year first above written.

BORROWER

[Name of Borrower]

_____

By:
Its:

LENDER

_____

[Name of Lender

SCHEDULE A

	The Work	Insurance Value
1.	Artist:	$
	Title:	
	Medium:	
	Date:	
	Size:	

SCHEDULE B

INSURANCE EXCLUSIONS

APPENDIX 17-4

Loan and Conditional Gift Agreement

LOAN AND CONDITIONAL GIFT AGREEMENT

THIS LOAN AND CONDITIONAL GIFT AGREEMENT ("Agreement") is made and entered into as of the _____ day of _____, 20__, by and between _____ ("Wife") and _____ ("Husband"), residing at _____ (each individually during the period that he/she is the owner of the Work, as defined below, shall be referred to as "Lender"), and _____ Museum, having an office at _____ ("Borrower").

WITNESSETH:

WHEREAS, Wife and Husband are the owners of the work of art more fully described on Schedule A attached hereto and incorporated herein by this reference ("Work");

WHEREAS, Borrower wishes to borrow the Work for exhibition;

WHEREAS, Lender wishes to lend the Work to Borrower for exhibition;

WHEREAS, Wife and Husband wish to transfer ownership of the Work to Borrower either by way of gift during their lifetimes or by bequest under the Last Will and Testament of the last to die of Wife and Husband; and

WHEREAS, Borrower has agreed to exhibit the Work and to accept the gift or bequest for such purposes and on the terms and conditions hereinafter set forth.

NOW, THEREFORE, in consideration of the mutual promises contained herein, the parties hereto agree as follows:

1. *Period of The Loan.*

The period of the loan shall be from the date the Work is released to Borrower until the date which (i) the Work is transferred to Borrower in accordance with Paragraph 11 herein, or (ii) is ten (10) business days after written notice from Lender to Borrower terminating such loan (the "Loan Period").

2. *Location and Exhibition of the Work.*

The Work will be exhibited at the premises of Borrower and at any other location that Borrower deems suitable for exhibition at all times that such locations are open for business. However, the Work may be temporarily unavailable for such periods of time as may be appropriate for preservation, conservation, building renovation, photography or scholarly examination.

Lender agrees that during the Loan Period the Work may be relocated to any exhibition location for purposes of exhibition or study anywhere in the world for any duration of time as Borrower determines without prior notice to Lender. Borrower remains liable for all the terms and conditions of this Agreement regardless of the Work's location.

3. *Credit Line.*

The credit line for exhibition, catalogue and publicity purposes at any time that Lender has an ownership interest in the Work shall read as follows: courtesy of _____ and _____.

4. *Copyright, Photography and Reproduction.*

Lender does not own the copyright in the Work. Borrower agrees that any request to photograph the Work for reproduction in a catalogue or for educational and publicity purposes must be cleared, in advance, with the owner of the copyright for the Work, if the Work is not in the public domain. Borrower may not reproduce the image of the Work for postcards, slides and posters or other commercial purposes without permission from Wife and Husband and the copyright owner, if any.

5. *Insurance.*

Borrower agrees to provide at its cost all risk, wall-to-wall insurance coverage using standard fine arts commercial insurance from a company rated by A.M. Best's A- or better and/or United States Government Indemnity for the safekeeping and preservation of the Work, the Work to be insured for the value stated on Schedule A attached hereto (the "Insurance Value"); provided, however, that if the fair market value for the Work shall increase after the date of the signing of this Agreement, then Borrower shall insure the Work for the increased fair market value, consistent with Borrower's insurance policy. Borrower shall insure the Work at Borrower's cost from the time the Work leaves its current location and until the Work is (i) transferred to Borrower in accordance with Paragraph 11 herein or (ii) returned to Lender. Borrower agrees that the insurance coverage it will obtain for the Insurance Value for the Work as indicated on Schedule A is the stated value for the Work and all claims will be based on an amount no less than this value. Borrower agrees to provide Lender with a Certificate of Insurance evidencing such insurance coverage, and naming Lender as loss payee and additional insured. Borrower agrees to accept the obligation of caring for the Work during the Loan Period. Borrower agrees to accept responsibility for the

Work and liability for any deficiencies and/or exclusions in insurance coverage and excluding solely the negligence or other wrongful acts of Lender or their servants or agents, or pre-existing condition flaws in the Work at the beginning of the Loan Period. In the case of any loss or damage, Lender agrees to use reasonable efforts as required to enable Borrower to submit and pursue a claim for insurance coverage. Borrower shall pay all costs (both Lender's and Borrower's costs) in connection with Borrower submitting and pursuing a claim for insurance coverage. In the case of partial loss or damage to the Work, Lender and Borrower shall agree upon the reasonable cost of repair of the Work and the amount of any reduction in the fair market value of the Work after repair, or in the absence of agreement, these amounts will be determined by an appraiser mutually acceptable to Lender and Borrower. If the parties are unable to agree upon an appraiser, then each party will appoint an appraiser and those two appraisers will attempt to agree on the amount of loss in value or if they are also unable to agree, the two appraisers will select a third appraiser to determine the loss in value. Borrower shall pay all costs in connection with the appraiser's valuation. The insurance policies provided by Borrower shall expressly state that they provide primary coverage, which shall not be diminished by reason of any insurance coverage obtained by Lender.

6. *Shipping.*

Borrower, after consulting with and obtaining the approval of Lender, agrees to arrange for and pay for all costs in connection with packing and shipping the Work from its current location to Borrower and returning the Work to Lender at the end of the Loan Period if the Work is not transferred to Borrower in accordance with Paragraph 11 herein. The method of shipment must be agreed upon by both parties.

7. *Expenses.*

Borrower will pay all costs of packing, shipping, insurance and any other cost in connection with exhibiting and caring for the Work during the Loan Period. Borrower shall pay all costs in connection with preparing and updating the Condition Report, as defined in Paragraph 8.b. herein.

8. *Care, Preservation, and Exhibition.*

a.   Borrower will give to the Work the same care it gives comparable property of its own. Borrower will take precautions to protect the Work from fire, theft, mishandling, dirt, and insects, and from extremes of light, temperature, and humidity while in Borrower's custody.

b.   During the packing of the Work each time it changes location, a conservator or authorized representative of Borrower or Lender shall be present to oversee the packing of the Work and Borrower shall arrange for a condition report (the "Condition Report") to be prepared by a conservator or authorized representative of Borrower acceptable to Lender. On arrival and uncrating of the Work at any location, a conservator or other authorized representative of Borrower shall be present to update and revise the Condition Report indicating any change in the condition of the Work. During the Loan Period any change in condition shall be noted on the Condition Report and Lender shall receive a copy of the Condition Report within forty-eight (48) hours after it is updated.

c.   If the Work is returned to Lender at the end of the Loan Period, a conservator or authorized representative of Borrower or Lender shall be present to oversee the repacking of the Work and shall update the Condition Report, with any change in condition noted on the Condition Report. The Condition Report will again be updated by a conservator or authorized representative of Borrower or Lender who is present when the Work is unpacked at the location chosen by Lender.

d.   Borrower will not perform any conservation on the Work without the specific written consent of Lender, except in an emergency to prevent further damage.

9. *Return of Loan.*

Unless transferred in accordance with Paragraph 11 herein or otherwise agreed in writing, the loan terminates in accordance with Paragraph 1 herein. If this loan shall terminate in accordance with Paragraph 1 herein, the Work will be returned only to Lender or to a location as directed in writing by Lender.

10. *Warranty of Borrower.*

Borrower warrants that it has the authority to enter into this Agreement and that the person who has executed the Agreement below on behalf of Borrower has the authority to bind Borrower.

11. *Pledge.*

Lender hereby pledges (the "Pledge") to transfer all of Lender's right, title and interest in the Work to Borrower either by way of gift during their lifetimes (in whole or by fractional transfers) or by bequest under the Last Will and Testament or other testamentary instrument of the second to die of Wife or Husband; provided, however, that (i) Borrower has complied with the terms and conditions of this Agreement at all times, and (ii) the loan has not been terminated pursuant to Paragraph 1 herein prior to the death of the second to die of Wife or Husband. Lender agrees that this Pledge shall extend to and be binding upon their executors, administrators, heirs, assigns and other estate fiduciaries, and upon the trustees of any lifetime trust which becomes irrevocable upon the death of the second to die of Wife or Husband and which has title to the Work. Lender agrees that the failure of the second to die of Wife or Husband to include a specific bequest of all title and interest in the Work in his/her Last Will and Testament or other testamentary disposition shall not release his/her heirs, executors, administrators or other estate fiduciaries, or the trustees of any lifetime trust which becomes irrevocable upon the second to die of Wife or Husband, and which has title to the Work, from the binding obligation of delivering and transferring title in and to the Work to Borrower in accordance with this Paragraph if the conditions of this Paragraph have been satisfied.

If the Work is stolen or destroyed in any party's possession before fulfillment of the Pledge, the amount of the Pledge with respect to the Work shall be limited to the insurance proceeds payable as a result, if any, and such proceeds shall be payable to Borrower no later than the death of the second to die of Wife and Husband.

For purposes of this Agreement, the fair market value of the Work shall be the fair market value stated in the last appraisal obtained by Lender, provided the appraisal is as of a date not more than three (3) years before the date for which the determination of fair market value is required or, if there is no such appraisal, as determined by an appraiser chosen by Lender or Lender's executors at the time the determination is required.

12. *Miscellaneous.*

This Agreement represents the entire understanding of all the parties hereto, supersedes any and all other and prior agreements between the parties and declares all such prior agreements between the parties null and void. The terms of this Agreement may not be modified or amended, except in a writing signed by the party to be charged. This Agreement and all matters relating to it shall be governed by the laws of the State of _____. This Agreement shall inure to the benefit of, and shall be binding upon, the successors, heirs, assigns, executors and administrators of the parties hereto. Any dispute arising hereunder shall be resolved in the _____ State Supreme Court, _____ County or in the United States District Court for the _____, and the parties hereto consent to the personal jurisdiction of those courts. This agreement may be executed in two or more counterparts, including facsimile or PDF, each of which shall be deemed an original, and all of which together shall constitute one and the same instrument.

IN WITNESS WHEREOF, the parties hereto have hereunto signed their hands and seals the day and year first above written.

BORROWER

_____ Museum

_____

By:
Its:

LENDER

_____

[Wife's Name]

_____

[Husband's Name]

SCHEDULE A

	The Work	Insurance Value
1.	Artist:	$
	Title:	
	Medium:	
	Date:	
	Size:	

APPENDIX 17-5

IRS Form 8282—Donee Information Return

Form **8282**	**Donee Information Return**	OMB No. 1545-0908
(Rev. April 2009)	(Sale, Exchange, or Other Disposition of Donated Property)	
Department of the Treasury Internal Revenue Service	▶ See instructions.	**Give a Copy to Donor**

Parts To Complete

• If the organization is an **original donee,** complete *Identifying Information,* Part I (lines 1a–1d and, if applicable, lines 2a–2d), and Part III.

• If the organization is a **successor donee,** complete *Identifying Information,* Part I, Part II, and Part III.

Identifying Information

Print or Type	Name of charitable organization (donee)	**Employer identification number**
	Address (number, street, and room or suite no.) (or P.O. box no. if mail is not delivered to the street address)	
	City or town, state, and ZIP code	

Part I — Information on ORIGINAL DONOR and SUCCESSOR DONEE Receiving the Property

1a Name of original donor of the property	1b Identifying number(s)

1c   Address (number, street, and room or suite no.) (P.O. box no. if mail is not delivered to the street address)

1d   City or town, state, and ZIP code

Note. Complete lines 2a–2d only if the organization gave this property to another charitable organization (successor donee).

2a Name of charitable organization	2b Employer identification number

2c   Address (number, street, and room or suite no.) (or P.O. box no. if mail is not delivered to the street address)

2d   City or town, state, and ZIP code

Part II — Information on PREVIOUS DONEES. Complete this part only if the organization was not the first donee to receive the property. See the instructions before completing lines 3a through 4d.

3a Name of original donee	3b Employer identification number

3c   Address (number, street, and room or suite no.) (or P.O. box no. if mail is not delivered to the street address)

3d   City or town, state, and ZIP code

4a Name of preceding donee	4b Employer identification number

4c   Address (number, street, and room or suite no.) (or P.O. box no. if mail is not delivered to the street address)

4d   City or town, state, and ZIP code

For Paperwork Reduction Act Notice, see page 4.   Cat. No. 62307Y   Form **8282** (Rev. 4-2009)

| **Part III** | **Information on DONATED PROPERTY** |

1. Description of the donated property sold, exchanged, or otherwise disposed of and how the organization used the property. (If you need more space, attach a separate statement.)	**2.** Did the disposition involve the organization's entire interest in the property?		**3.** Was the use related to the organization's exempt purpose or function?		**4.** Information on use of property. • If you answered "Yes" to question 3 and the property was tangible personal property, describe how the organization's use of the property furthered its exempt purpose or function. Also complete Part IV below. • If you answered "No" to question 3 and the property was tangible personal property, describe the organization's intended use (if any) at the time of the contribution. Also complete Part IV below, if the intended use at the time of the contribution was related to the organization's exempt purpose or function and it became impossible or infeasible to implement.
	Yes	**No**	**Yes**	**No**	
A					
B					
C					
D					

		Donated Property			
		A	**B**	**C**	**D**
5	Date the organization received the donated property (MM/DD/YY)	/ /	/ /	/ /	/ /
6	Date the original donee received the property (MM/DD/YY)	/ /	/ /	/ /	/ /
7	Date the property was sold, exchanged, or otherwise disposed of (MM/DD/YY)	/ /	/ /	/ /	/ /
8	Amount received upon disposition	$	$	$	$

| **Part IV** | **Certification** |

You must sign the certification below if any property described in Part III above is tangible personal property and:
• You answered "Yes" to question 3 above, or
• You answered "No" to question 3 above and the intended use of the property became impossible or infeasible to implement.

Under penalties of perjury and the penalty under section 6720B, I certify that either: (1) the use of the property that meets the above requirements, and is described above in Part III, was substantial and related to the donee organization's exempt purpose or function; or (2) the donee organization intended to use the property for its exempt purpose or function, but the intended use has become impossible or infeasible to implement.

▶ _____ | _____
Signature of officer   Title   ▶ _____
     Date

Sign Here

Under penalties of perjury, I declare that I have examined this return, including accompanying schedules and statements, and to the best of my knowledge and belief, it is true, correct, and complete.

▶ _____ | _____
Signature of officer   Title   ▶ _____
     Date

_____
Type or print name

General Instructions

Section references are to the Internal Revenue Code.

Purpose of Form

Donee organizations use Form 8282 to report information to the IRS and donors about dispositions of certain charitable deduction property made within 3 years after the donor contributed the property.

Definitions

 For Form 8282 and these instructions, the term "donee" includes all donees, unless specific reference is made to "original" or "successor" donees.

Original donee. The first donee to or for which the donor gave the property. The original donee is required to sign Form 8283, Noncash Charitable Contributions, *Section B. Donated Property Over $5,000 (Except Certain Publicly Traded Securities)*, presented by the donor for charitable deduction property.

Successor donee. Any donee of property other than the original donee.

Charitable deduction property. Any donated property (other than money and publicly traded securities) if the claimed value exceeds $5,000 per item or group of similar items donated by the donor to one or more donee organizations. This is the property listed in Section B on Form 8283.

Who Must File

Original and successor donee organizations must file Form 8282 if they sell, exchange, consume, or otherwise dispose of (with or without consideration) charitable deduction property (or any portion) within 3 years after the date the original donee received the property. See *Charitable deduction property* above.

If the organization sold, exchanged, or otherwise disposed of motor vehicles, airplanes, or boats, see Pub. 526, Charitable Contributions.

Exceptions. There are two situations where Form 8282 does not have to be filed.

1. Items valued at $500 or less. The organization does not have to file Form 8282 if, at the time the original donee signed Section B of Form 8283, the donor had signed a statement on Form 8283 that the appraised value of the specific item was not more than $500. If Form 8283 contains more than one item, this exception applies only to those items that are clearly identified as having a value of $500 or less. However, for purposes of the donor's determination of whether the appraised value of the item exceeds $500, all shares of nonpublicly traded stock, or items that form a set, are considered one item. For example, a collection of books written by the same author, components of a stereo system, or six place settings of a pattern of silverware are considered one item.

2. Items consumed or distributed for charitable purpose. The organization does not have to file Form 8282 if an item is consumed or distributed, without consideration, in fulfilling your purpose or function as a tax-exempt organization. For example, no reporting is required for medical supplies consumed or distributed by a tax-exempt relief organization in aiding disaster victims.

When To File

If the organization disposes of charitable deduction property within 3 years of the date the original donee received it and the organization does not meet exception 1 or 2 above, the organization must file Form 8282 within 125 days after the date of disposition.

Exception. If the organization did not file because it had no reason to believe the substantiation requirements applied to the donor, but the organization later becomes aware that the substantiation requirements did apply, the organization must file Form 8282 within 60 days after the date it becomes aware it was liable. For example, this exception would apply where Section B of Form 8283 is furnished to a successor donee after the date that donee disposes of the charitable deduction property.

Missing information. If Form 8282 is filed by the due date, enter the organization's name, address, and employer identification number (EIN) and complete at least Part III, columns 1, 2, 3, and 4; and Part IV. The organization does not have to complete the remaining items if the information is not available. For example, the organization may not have the information necessary to complete all entries if the donor did not make Section B of Form 8283 available.

Where To File

Send Form 8282 to the Department of Treasury, Internal Revenue Service Center, Ogden, UT 84201-0027.

Other Requirements

Information the organization must give a successor donee. If the property is transferred to another charitable organization within the 3-year period discussed earlier, the organization must give the successor donee all of the following information.

1. The name, address, and EIN of the organization.

2. A copy of Section B of Form 8283 that the organization received from the donor or a preceding donee. The preceding donee is the one who gave the organization the property.

3. A copy of this Form 8282, within 15 days after the organization files it.

The organization must furnish items 1 and 2 above within 15 days after the latest of the date:

● The organization transferred the property,

● The original donee signed Section B of Form 8283, or

● The organization received a copy of Section B of Form 8283 from the preceding donee if the organization is also a successor donee.

Information the successor donee must give the organization. The successor donee organization to whom the organization transferred this property is required to give the organization its name, address, and EIN within 15 days after the later of:

● The date the organization transferred the property, or

● The date the successor donee received a copy of Section B of Form 8283.

Information the organization must give the donor. The organization must give a copy of Form 8282 to the original donor of the property.

Recordkeeping. The organization must keep a copy of Section B of Form 8283 in its records.

Penalties

Failure to file penalty. The organization may be subject to a penalty if it fails to file this form by the due date, fails to include all of the information required to be shown on the filed form, or includes incorrect information on the filed form. The penalty is generally $50 per form. For more details, see section 6721 and 6724.

Fraudulent identification of exempt use property. A $10,000 penalty may apply to any person who identifies in Part III tangible personal property the organization sold, exchanged, or otherwise disposed of, as having a use that is related to a purpose or function knowing that such property was not intended for such a use. For more details, see section 6720B.

Specific Instructions

Part I

Line 1a. Enter the name of the original donor.

Line 1b. The donor's identifying number may be either an employer identification number or a social security number, and should be the same number provided on page 2 of Form 8283.

Line 1c and 1d. Enter the last known address of the original donor.

Lines 2a–2d. Complete these lines if the organization gave the property to another charitable organization successor donee (defined earlier). If the organization is an original donee, skip Part II and go to Part III.

Part II

Complete Part II only if the organization is a successor donee. If the organization is the original donee, do not complete any lines in Part II; go directly to Part III.

If the organization is the **second donee,** complete lines 3a through 3d. If the organization is the **third or later donee,** complete lines 3a through 4d. On lines 4a through 4d, give information on the preceding donee.

Part III

Column 1. For charitable deduction property that the organization sold, exchanged, or otherwise disposed of within 3 years of the original contribution, describe each item in detail. For a motor vehicle, include the vehicle identification number. For a boat, include the hull identification number. For an airplane, include the aircraft identification number. Additionally, for the period of time the organization owned the property, explain how it was used. If additional space is needed, attach a statement.

Column 3. Check "Yes" if the organization's use of the charitable deduction property was related to its exempt purpose or function. Check "No" if the organization sold, exchanged, or otherwise disposed of the property without using it.

Signature

Form 8282 is not valid unless it is signed by an officer of the organization. Be sure to include the title of the person signing the form and the date the form was signed.

How To Get Tax Help

Internet

You can access the IRS website 24 hours a day, 7 days a week at *www.irs.gov/eo* to:

● Download forms, instructions, and publications;

● Order IRS products online;

● Research your tax questions online;

● Search publications online by topic or keyword;

● View Internal Revenue Bulletins (IRBs) published in the last few years; and

● Sign up to receive local and national tax news by email. To subscribe, visit *www.irs.gov/eo.*

DVD

You can order Publication 1796, IRS Tax Products DVD, and obtain:

● Current-year forms, instructions, and publications.

● Prior-year forms, instructions, and publications.

● Tax Map: an electronic research tool and finding aid.

● Tax law frequently asked questions.

● Tax topics from the IRS telephone response system.

● Fill-in, print, and save features for most tax forms.

● IRBs.

● Toll-free and email technical support.

● Two releases during the year.

Purchase the DVD from National Technical Information Service (NTIS) at *www.irs.gov/cdorders* for $30 (no handling fee) or call **1-877-CDFORMS** (1-877-233-6767) toll-free to buy the DVD for $30 (plus a $6 handling fee). Price is subject to change.

By Phone

You can order forms and publications by calling 1-800-TAX-FORM (1-800-829-3676). You can also get most forms and publications at your local IRS office. If you have questions and/or need help completing this form, please call 1-877-829-5500. This toll free telephone service is available Monday thru Friday.

Paperwork Reduction Act Notice. We ask for the information on this form to carry out the Internal Revenue laws of the United States. You are required to give us the information. We need it to ensure that you are complying with these laws and to allow us to figure and collect the right amount of tax.

You are not required to provide the information requested on a form that is subject to the Paperwork Reduction Act unless the form displays a valid OMB control number. Books or records relating to a form or its instructions must be retained as long as their contents may become material in the administration of any Internal Revenue law. Generally, tax returns and return information are confidential, as required by section 6103.

The time needed to complete this form will vary depending on individual circumstances. The estimated average time is:

Recordkeeping . . . . 3 hr., 35 min.
Learning about the law or the form . . . . 12 min.
Preparing and sending the form to the IRS . . . . 15 min.

If you have comments concerning the accuracy of these time estimates or suggestions for making this form simpler, we would be happy to hear from you. You can write to the Internal Revenue Service, Tax Products Coordinating Committee, SE:W:CAR:MP:T:T:SP, 1111 Constitution Ave. NW, IR-6526, Washington, DC 20224. Do not send the form to this address. Instead, see *Where To File* on page 3.

18

Art Law Online and Digital Art

INTRODUCTION

The backbone of digital art—which continues to grow in prominence in all segments of the art market—is electronically based technology that uses mathematical algorithms for the creation, "storage, processing, and presentation of information."[1] Digital art "encompasses digital video, sound art, digitally altered photographs, sculpture first sketched on a computer, and online audience-participation pieces," among other creative endeavors.[2] The success of Canadian-born artist Chris Levine, who is known for utilizing the latest digital technology, illustrates the steady demand for digital art. Having now developed the reputation as a highly skilled laser artist, Levine's rise to fame began in 2004 when he was commissioned by the Jersey Heritage Trust to create a hologram portrait of Queen Elizabeth II.[3] Using several high-tech cameras, including a digital camera that shot 200 images over eight seconds, as well as other equipment connected to his laptop computer, Levine proceeded to send the captured images from the digital cameras to his computer.[4] Several holographic 3-D lightbox images were produced; however, it was not until several years later, in 2007, that Levine released the photo-shoot's most notable work, *The Lightness of Being*.[5] In 2011, the celebrated portrait was eventually turned into a 3-D lightbox for display in a London gallery and priced at £75,000.[6]

Art created wholly on a computer has elevated the careers of many artists by presenting opportunities in areas other than the sale of their artwork. In 2009, Jorge Colombo began creating drawings using a phone application called "Brushes" on his smartphone.[7] His modern methods and digital works soon generated enough attention to afford Colombo the chance to have his digital drawings appear weekly in the *New Yorker* magazine, and to host several workshops at the Museum of Modern Art on how to create drawings using electronic equipment instead of conventional art materials.[8] It seems as if the art world's curiosity about the realm of digital art has only just begun. Presently, there is an influx of both solicitations for new works of digital art and concurrent offers to subsidize such new works.[9] For example, in 2012, the British Broadcasting Company and the Arts Council England in a partnership are set to launch "The Space," a multi-platform service specifically designed to promote and fund the creation of up to £2.5 million of digital art that can be displayed on computers, mobile phones, and tablets.[10]

The noncommercial, mass digitization of traditional works of art has also gained traction with the February 2011 launch of the Google Art Project (GAP).[11] GAP permits any member of the public with an Internet connection and the proper hardware to visit a one-stop virtual platform to view artwork from around the world at no cost. While still in its beginning stages, the growth in GAP has been remarkable. In one year, GAP acquired 151 art partners across forty countries to participate in Google's goal of creating a "unique online experience" for interested audiences desiring to view thousands of artwork in one virtual location.[12] On a basic level, the procedure for participating in GAP is simple. Museums and galleries select, without any curatorial direction from Google, those paintings, sculptures, and other works to be digitally recorded, processed, and integrated into GAP. Visitors of the site may view artwork in one of two ways. A visitor may click on an art image and view the artwork on a black backdrop apart from the museum or gallery it originates or, like a virtual tour, the artwork may be viewed through a feature that allows the user to travel through the digitally replicated museum or gallery space that hosts the work.[13] When using the virtual tour feature to travel through an art space, a visitor may see a work of art that is rendered unrecognizable, which indicates that the particular artwork has not been permitted to become part of GAP. Recently, Google was asked to remove several paintings from GAP by the Toldeo Museum of Art, citing copyright issues as the reason for the request.[14] As Google places the burden on the museums (which generally own the respective artworks but not the copyrights therein) to seek the proper copyright permissions for each work of art featured, relatively few artworks under subsisting copyright are included in GAP at this time.[15]

The ease of transmitting digital artwork to several different types of mediums within a few moments and the ability for digital art to have a potentially infinite number of replications has caused collectors to rethink traditional concepts of ownership.[16] Digitally created works of art can be created, accessed, and manipulated in a variety of formats. Increasingly, artists are appropriating and creating new digital visual images to reflect our evolving technology-based society.[17] While traditional rules applicable to traditional art forms have been tailored to apply in digital space, some believe that current copyright legislation is at times over-accommodating to the copyright holder at the expense of both fair use and an enriched public domain.[18]

Although digital art images are found in formats as wide-ranging as charitable organization websites to sexual-content sites, and masterful digital photography to popular electronic video games, we limit our discussion to the legal issues that apply to digitally created fine-art visual images, including the purchase and sale of fine art online. In particular, this chapter addresses the application of the Copyright Act, the Digital Millennium Copyright Act (DMCA), and other federal statutes pertinent to the production, use, and commercial sale of digital works of art.[19]

COPYRIGHTS IN THE DIGITAL AGE

Overview

As discussed in, respectively, chapter 11 (copyright) and chapter 12 (moral rights), section 106 and 106A of the Copyright Act grants the copyright owner of pictorial, graphic, and sculptural work the following exclusive rights:

1. to reproduce the copyrighted work in copies;
2. to prepare derivative works based upon the copyrighted work;
3. to distribute copies of the copyrighted work to the public by sale or other transfer of ownership, or by rental, lease, or lending;
4. to display the copyrighted work publicly;[20]
5. to prevent misattribution and distortion of that work.

Unlike the advancement of learning,[21] "the progress of useful [a]rts,"[22] or commercial growth,[23] the promotion of aesthetics is an aspect of human endeavor not specifically addressed by the Copyright Act. This omission becomes relevant when one considers that unlike the often more informational character of written text, art, including digital art, is not necessarily about advanced learning or economics. As one commentator asserts, "the application of the copyright laws is problematic [within the realm of digital arts], and any problems will be magnified in the digital age when reproduction, alteration, and publication of all the arts will be accelerated and commonplace."[24]

Although traditional principles of copyright law apply to pictorial, graphic, and sculptural works of art online, the Internet poses unique issues of how to apply the law. One of the threshold requirements of proving copyright infringement, namely proof of access, has been forever changed by the Internet.[25] The engines for publication were once controlled by few, yet now almost anyone can purchase a domain name, create a website, and market the site's contents to millions of Internet users. In different ways, demonstrating wide dissemination of publication and reasonable opportunity for the alleged infringer to have listened, seen, or touched the work that is the subject of a dispute will both be easier and harder for the plaintiff to establish.[26] For instance, if content is placed in a publicly accessible website for a particular audience, such as a site for ordinary artists to upload digital photographs of their paintings, and subsequently an artist accuses a fellow user of the site of creating and selling a painting that is substantially similar to a painting of the artist, there may be no trouble in showing that a defendant had access to her work, but much difficulty in distinguishing the elements of her work from all other submissions in the site. A singular aspect of digitally created and transmitted art is that text, sound, and visual information (including visual art, photographs, and animated images), unlike traditional works of art, can be presented and stored as art in a variety of digital and electronic forms. This means that an artwork can be generated, altered, and used by and on the same device, irrespective of whether the artwork is provided online or offline. Traditional means of art production and distribution carry high costs. In contrast, the Internet makes possible inexpensive worldwide distribution, reproduction, linking, framing, uploading, and downloading of visual art to computers and digital televisions,[27] or any suitably equipped electronic device. The lower costs and the ease and efficiency of transferring a traditional work of art into digital form and disseminating such an image also mean a copyright infringer can make hundreds or thousands of cheap copies. The price to the guilty infringer can add up quickly.[28]

Courts have had mixed success applying traditional copyright concepts to the Internet, sometimes arriving at conflicting results. What actually constitutes an act of infringement of artwork on the Internet therefore remains unclear. In fact, an overview of cases that have addressed the issue does not clarify behavior in such a way as to provide comfort and guidance to the copyright owner, the public, or even the putative infringer. Although few cases to date have specifically addressed issues pertinent to the creation, appropriation, and distribution of digital art under copyright protection, several cases have sought to establish certain electronic rights for copyright holders of photographic, text, musical, cinematic works, and the right to use the program and files that comprise a website.[29] Given the differing judicial approaches to the application of traditional copyright principles to issues created by the use of digital images, no bright-line rules have emerged to provide guidance. The following is an exploration of pertinent law available to date.

Exclusive Rights of Copyright Holders Within the Digital Medium

REPRODUCTION OF THE COPYRIGHTED WORK IN DIGITAL COPIES

In order for a visual work of art to be displayed on or transmitted over the Internet, it must first be reproduced in electronic form, that is, digitized. Generally, a digital reproduction is accomplished either by scanning the work of art or through digital photography. The result is not a reproduction in the traditional photomechanical sense; rather, the software in the sending hardware device, like a digital camera, interacts with the software in the receiving hardware device, such as a computer or mobile phone, to reproduce an exact replica of the original visual work of art. This copy materializes on the screen of the receiving device. The sending and receiving machines communicate with each other through machine language (object code), a combination of 1s and 0s. Still, it is a reproduction in an electronic form, and the right to digitize, and prevent others from doing so, is among the exclusive rights granted to copyright holders.

The right to digitize a visual work of art can be potentially lucrative to the copyright holder because web pages and websites are ordinarily composed of numerous digital images and virtually every online interaction causes a digital reproduction to be made. Courts have held, for example, that a digital reproduction occurs when a visual work of art is converted to electronic form,[30] uploaded and posted on a website,[31] viewed by users on the Internet,[32] downloaded from the Internet,[33] or transmitted to other users.

However, the notion that creation of a digital reproduction infringes the rights of a copyright holder can be troubling. For example, whenever an end-user accesses the Internet, a visual webpage is displayed and a copy of the websites viewed and the images contained therein is made in the temporary storage of the user's computer. Some courts have deemed these actions as a violation of a copyright holder's right to digitally reproduce her work.[34] It follows that the very act of using a computer to view visual art has, in the past, been held to be an infringement because a copy was made in the end-user's computer memory.[35] However, the subsequently enacted DMCA, discussed later in this chapter, has changed the law's treatment of intermediate and temporary storage and has imposed limitations of liability for such storage of material under certain circumstances.

THE CREATION OF DIGITAL DERIVATIVE WORKS

APPROPRIATION

While, as noted in chapter 11, artists have for centuries appropriated from earlier images in the creation of new images, the technological tools and software available to them in the digital environment provide a breeding ground for infringing derivative works. For example, in the 2011 California federal district court case of *Friedman v. Guetta*,[36] the defendant Thierry Guetta, known as Mr. Brainwash, incorporated plaintiff's copyrighted digital photograph of the band Run-DMC in several works of art, all of which were put on display and a few of which were sold before and during his 2008 Life is Beautiful show. On January 4, 2010, plaintiff filed suit, claiming that defendant had infringed his rights "by creating, reproducing, displaying, and selling" artwork containing his copyrighted photograph.[37] Defendant admitted that even though he obtained a digital copy of the photograph from the Internet and directly altered that copy for his artwork, his use of the photograph should be deemed fair under the fair use doctrine.[38] However, as the court observed, the defendant had downloaded an exact digital copy of the photograph and had used the substantial elements of the photograph in his works, altering only the background. Because the band members were readily identifiable and in the same pose, clothing, and facial expressions as in the photograph, the court held that the defendant had appropriated the heart of the photograph. Finding the plaintiff had satisfactorily proved infringement, the court added that to hold otherwise would "eviscerate any protection by the

Copyright Act" for all artists wishing to control the display and reproduction of their work.[39]

Courts have consistently held that uploading or downloading a copyrighted work is the equivalent of copying and, as noted earlier, the volume of works infringed can produce startling statutory damages.[40]

LICENSING DIGITAL ARTWORK

To avoid both direct and secondary liability (distinguished later in this chapter), it has become standard practice among digital platform owners to provide Terms of Service: that is, a commonly used Internet license, or a similarly behaving license on the digital platform, in the form of a link or a click-through agreement that sets forth the conditions a user must accept for use of the services provided on the digital platform. Often, users accept all terms within the license merely by visiting the website.[41] These licenses may shield a platform owner and its affiliates, but they may not extend a copyright liability shield to other users. This distinction has become of particular importance in the age of social media networks.

Licenses manifest as either an express contract, such as through a written document or clearly stated promises, or as an implied contract, which is a contract that is determined to be present though there is no physical document or clear exchange of promises.[42] The specific aspects of an implied license—and how a court determines that one exists—are outside the scope of this chapter. However, two cases show how a court may treat an express or implied license for purposes of disputes concerning digital art and the Internet.

AGENCE FRANCE PRESSE V. MOREL[43]

This 2011 case highlights some of the confusion an express license can cause copyright holders and parties interested in work available online. On January 12, 2010, Daniel Morel, a well-known photojournalist, photographed the aftereffects of the Haiti earthquake and uploaded his digital photographs to a social networking site, Twitter,[44] using the site's ancillary program called Twitpic. Twitter allows a user to input text up to 140 characters, while its application Twitpic allows users to upload pictures. However, Twitter and Twitpic are two separate entities, incorporated in different states, and containing different Terms of Service (TOS).[45] Twitpic's TOS provides that copyright for all pictures vests in the author, yet still cautions that the author concurrently surrenders a nonexclusive license to use and distribute the pictures to Twitpic and its affiliate sites in exchange for use of the social media platform.[46]

Soon after the photographs were posted on the site, news outlets contacted Morel for permission to feature his photographs in breaking stories on Haiti. Unbeknownst to Morel and within minutes of his posting, Lisandro Suero, a resident of the Dominican Republic, downloaded Morel's pictures, uploaded them to his own Twitter page without a single mention of Morel, and tweeted[47] that he had exclusive photographs of the aftermath in Haiti.[48] A photo editor acting on behalf of the plaintif, French news service Agence France Presse (AFP), contacted both Morel and Suero to acquire the photographs, yet before Morel could respond, AFP downloaded thirteen of Morel's photographs from Suero's Twitpic page,[49] and uploaded the photographs to AFP's online photo database. Getty Images, Inc., AFP's exclusive image licensing company in North America and the United Kingdom, then took the photographs from AFP's database, attached the credit line "AFP/Getty/Lisandro Suero" to Morel's images, and proceeded to license them to numerous news agencies.[50]

The New York federal district court noted that Twitpic's TOS, like Twitter's TOS, "'necessarily require[d]' Morel as promisor to confer certain rights of use on two classes—Twitter's partners and sublicensees."[51] AFP and other news outlets were not—nor were intended to be—affiliates of Twitter or Twitpic, but rather were users of the networks, and therefore did not qualify as third-party beneficiaries and did not have a license to use Morel's photographs.[52]

TETER V. GLASS ONION, INC.[53]

In contrast to the *Agence France Presse* case, a 2011 case, *Teter v. Glass Onion, Inc.*, demonstrates how a court may find an implied license of digital images. Lee Teter, an artist known for his depictions of early American life, maintained an agreement with Treasure Palace Ltd., doing business as the 83 Spring Street Gallery, governing the sale of a select number of Teter's artworks. By the terms of the agreement, Teter sold certain paintings and prints to the gallery, which then advertised his works on its website and displayed them for resale. Teter's family company, Summer Field Fine Art (SFFA), acted as Teter's authorized publisher and represented him on general business matters. In February 2007, defendant Glass Onion, Inc., interested in buying the 83 Spring Street Gallery, met with Teter and his family, and subsequently purchased the gallery and all of its accompanying assets.[54] Under the new management, Teter continued to sell various paintings and prints to the gallery. Upon receipt of each work, the gallery took photographs and posted the pictures on its website.

Subsequently, Glass Onion decided to remodel the gallery website, emailing SFFA to ask for permission to use the images of Teter's artwork on the new website. Sometime in late spring 2007, Teter's daughter, on behalf of SFFA, sent a reply to Glass Onion authorizing the use of images of the artwork in the gallery's possession for its revamped website.[55] In March 2008, following SFFA's shift of management to Teter's daughter and spouse, the SFFA sent a new dealership agreement to Glass Onion containing new terms and conditions for becoming an authorized SFFA dealer. Glass Onion rejected the new agreement.

In May 2008, SFFA sent a letter requesting Glass Onion to remove all images from the gallery's website and advertisements, as such privileges were reserved solely for authorized SFFA dealers. Against SFFA's wishes, Glass Onion retained the thumbnail images both on the gallery website and in advertisements, and agreed only to place watermarks over the images to deter infringement. As a result, Teter filed suit in a Missouri federal district court, alleging, among an array of claims,[56] copyright infringement. Glass Onion moved for dismissal on summary judgment on all of Teter's claims, and Teter moved for judgment as a matter of law on his copyright infringement claim and for dismissal of Glass Onion's counterclaims.

It was undisputed that Teter lawfully owned the copyright in all of his artwork, and that no written contract existed authorizing the reproduction and display of digital images of the artwork for Glass Onion's website. Therefore, the Missouri federal district court found clear copyright infringement of the exclusive rights of reproduction and display.[57] However, turning to Glass Onion's defenses, the court found that Teter, through his conduct,[58] had granted Glass Onion an implied license to use digital images of the artwork in advertising, in that the latter had inherited such broad permissions from the previous owner of the gallery, and Teter was plainly aware of Glass Onion's use of the digital images on the gallery's website.

However, having determined that an implied license existed, the court found that it was revocable: the court observed that there was no consideration given for the licensing right to display the digital images of the artwork on the gallery website,[59] and that with the May 2008 letter, Teter had explicitly revoked permission for use of the digital images on the website.

The revocation of the implied license created two timetables of copyright infringement for the case: (1) possible infringement that occurred during the time of the implied license, by exceeding the scope of the license, and (2) possible infringement that occurred after the license was revoked. Before the date of revocation, the court noted that despite Glass Onion's broad implied license, the fact that, among other things, the defendant took photographs of each work (instead of using photographs authorized or supplied by Teter), altered the resolution on the new photographs, and uploaded them to its website for public display[60] gave rise to issues of fact as to whether Glass Onion had created electronic copies and displayed such copies outside the scope of the implied license.[61]

For reasons discussed later in the chapter, the court deemed the rights of reproduction and display as falling outside the jurisdiction of the implied contract, and rejected all of Glass Onion's affirmative defenses.[62]

COLLECTIVE WORKS

In the art arena, digital collective works such as gallery brochures and museum and auction catalogs implicate copyright issues. For example, when artwork that is not part of a museum's permanent collection is exhibited, may the museum digitalize an exhibit catalog including that work? Although case law has not yet addressed this question from an art entity's perspective, several recent cases involving freelance employees provide some guidance on the issue of the right to prepare a derivative work in the context of collective works.

In the 2001 case of *Greenberg v. National Geographic* (*Greenberg I*),[63] a freelance photographer whose photographs had appeared in the *National Geographic* print magazine sued the publisher, claiming that the inclusion of his work in a CD-ROM edition of the *National Geographic* was unauthorized. The photographer was not an employee of the *National Geographic*, nor did he work under a contract. The alleged infringement occurred when the magazine created a thirty-disc CD-ROM library, *The Complete National Geographic* (CNG), containing every issue of its magazine since 1888, including, without additional permission, the freelance photographer's work. The CNG was composed of three parts:

(1) an animated, twenty-five-second introductory sequence of ten of the magazine's covers, which overlapped and faded into one another to musical accompaniment;
(2) exact scanned reproductions of each cover and page of the magazine, issue by issue; and
(3) a software program enabling users to select, view, navigate, and print the digital replicas.

One of plaintiff's photographs appeared in the sequence, and his contributions to four issues appeared in the CNG.

The Eleventh Circuit held that the CNG did not fall within the magazine's privilege to include "contributions to collective works" in a "revision" of that collective work and therefore infringed the photographer's right to create a derivative work.

However, a few weeks after *Greenberg I*, the Supreme Court in the 2001 decision *New York Times v. Tasini*[64] affirmed a Second Circuit judgment of copyright infringement, holding that the inclusion in electronic databases of articles that were written for newspapers and a magazine was not authorized under section 201(c) of the Copyright Act because the databases reproduced and distributed the articles as standalones rather than as part of the collective work to which the author contributed. To protect what rights a freelancer was presumed to give away in contributing to a collective work absent a contract specifying otherwise, Congress added section 201(c) to prevent publishers from "revis[ing] the contribution itself or includ[ing] it in a new anthology or an entirely different collective work."[65]

The Court determined in *Tasini* that under section 201(c) of the Copyright Act, the inclusion of articles in electronic databases, such as LexisNexis and CD-ROM storage devices, requires the author's consent.

Subsequent to *Tasini* and guided by the Supreme Court's holding, the Eleventh Circuit in the 2008 case of *Greenberg v. National Geographic (Greenberg II)*[66] held that the CNG fell within the magazine's privilege to include a "revision" of the original collective work under the second prong of section 201(c), and therefore, the publisher was "privileged to reproduce and distribute" the collective work.[67]

This en banc decision, in reversing the holding in *Greenberg I*, found that "the revision of a magazine by reproducing it in its original context in a new 'distinct form'—i.e., a digital version—is not a difference that would undo a publisher's privilege under § 201(c)."[68] In support of its holding, the court first noted that *Tasini* set forth two principles:

First, the concept of "revision" necessarily includes some element of novelty or "newness" as defined by the Court, and second, consideration of the context in which the contributions are presented is critical in determining whether that novelty is sufficient to defeat the publisher's § 201(c) privilege.[69]

The court pointed out that similar to microform—discussed at length in *Tasini*—CNG uses the same selection, navigation, and arrangement for individual contributions as used in the original collective work.[70] Here, upon accessing the CNG, the program displayed each digitized page in a magazine in the exact layout, arrangement, and position as its print version, departing from the original only in resolution and size of the images and text.[71] Moreover, a user of the CNG could not isolate a copyrightable article or image from the rest of its original collective work.[72] The court also reasoned that to decide that the addition of new elements to a collective work, such as a search function or zoom function, qualified the work as an entirely different collective work would render the "revision" prong of the 201(c) privilege useless.[73] Unlike the defendants in *Tasini*, National Geographic kept the periodicals and all corresponding text and images intact upon conversion from print to digital format for the CNG, the new elements added to the digitized magazines did not make the CNG ineligible for 201(c) privilege protection, and therefore, the CD-ROM library constituted a privileged revision under the Copyright Act.[74]

Other claims abounded against National Geographic's CNG product. A consolidation of those cases was the basis of the 2005 Second Circuit case of *Faulkner v. National Geographic*,[75] which affirmed[76] a grant of summary judgment by a New York federal district court that dismissed claims of copyright infringement connected to the National Geographic's CNG product. Here, the plaintiffs, a group of freelance photographers and writers, sought to foreclose the defendant's reliance on section 201(c) based on *Greenberg I*. The Second Circuit, however, noted that *Tasini* "represented an intervening (post-*Greenberg I*) change in law"[77] and that "the CNG is a revision for Section 201(c) purposes."[78] In support of its reasoning, the Second Circuit looked at the legislative history of the statute, which states:

> Under the language of this clause a publishing company could reprint a contribution from one issue in a later issue of its magazine, and could reprint an article from a 1980 edition of an encyclopedia in a 1990 revision of it; the . . . publisher could not revise the contribution itself or include it in a new anthology or an entirely different . . . magazine or other collective work.[79]

The Second Circuit then noted that the Supreme Court in *Tasini* "gave tacit approval to microfilm and microfiche as permissible Section 201(c) revisions"[80] in that they "represent a mere conversion of intact periodicals (or revisions of periodicals) from one medium to another."[81] Similar to the manner microfiche reproduced articles, the CNG databases maintained the original context of each magazine article in the collective works. The Second Circuit, following *Tasini*, concluded that "because the original context of the Magazines is omnipresent in the CNG and because it is a new version of the magazine, the CNG is a privileged version."[82]

In 2008, a New York federal district court ruled on the only remaining issue from the *Faulkner* cases, namely five photographs contained in the CNG.[83] As to the copyright claims, the court rejected the claim for punitive damages as it ran contrary to clear statutory language that established limitations on damages for copyright infringement to only actual damages. In addition, the court wholly debunked the plaintiff's expert testimony for basing his calculations for damages on unsupported punitively functioning multipliers.[84] The court stated that a reasonable license authorizing defendant's use of the images, the value of which is dependant on the value of the license at the time of infringement, would be a suitable form of actual damages.[85]

These decisions have not enabled authors in the electronic publishing market to negotiate higher prices. As to visual artists, *Faulkner* and *Greenberg II* make clear that the reproduction of magazine art in electronic form that maintains its original print context is within the print publisher's "revision" privilege.

DISTRIBUTION OF DIGITAL COPIES OF THE COPYRIGHTED WORK TO THE PUBLIC

Defendants have been found to have violated a copyright holder's distribution rights where a video has been seeded and transmitted over the Internet,[86] and where clip art from a compilation of public domain material has been made available for downloading from a publicly accessible website.[87]

Where violation of distribution rights is alleged, defendants traditionally assert the first sale doctrine, discussed in chapter 11, as a defense to the purported infringement. With respect to digital images, however, the doctrine is inapplicable:[88] in order for an owner of a copy of a copyrighted work to exercise his right to "sell or otherwise dispose of" it, the owner must first make an unauthorized digital reproduction, which results in a copyright infringement.

Defendants may be charged with direct copyright infringement or contributory copyright infringement, but plaintiffs in many recent cases have alleged both types.[89] Direct copyright infringement requires that the defendant take affirmative steps to cause the infringement, whether by scanning and uploading the copyrighted material to, for example, a server, storage device, or website, encouraging user downloading, or overseeing content distribution by selecting from user uploads.[90] Direct copyright infringement is a strict-liability offense that does not take into account a defendant's intent or knowledge.

In contrast to the direct infringement cases, other courts have under similar factual circumstances rejected claims of direct infringement, looking instead to impose liability for contributory infringement. Contributory infringement is a theory of liability under which "one who, with knowledge of the infringing activity, induces, causes or materially contributes to the infringing activity of another."[91] To succeed, a plaintiff must show direct infringement by a primary party, knowledge of the infringement by the defendant, and either contribution, causation, or inducement by the defendant.[92] Knowledge is measured under an objective standard and does not require the defendant to have actual awareness, so long as the defendant is in possession of facts that ought to have prompted investigation or appreciation of the infringement.

Contributory infringement should be distinguished, as a theory of liability, from vicarious infringement. To prove a defendant vicariously liable for copyright infringement, a plaintiff must show direct infringement by a primary party, a direct financial benefit to the defendant, and the right and ability to supervise the infringer.[93] In determining "the right and ability to supervise," reference is often made to the traditional "dance hall operator" and "landlord" defendants; that is, the dance hall operator is liable because he has the right and ability to supervise infringing conduct, whereas the landlord does not and, therefore, escapes liability. In other words, the "right and ability to supervise" describes a relationship between the defendant and the direct infringer.[94]

The secondary liability doctrines of contributory infringement and vicarious infringement, while not codified in the Copyright Act, are rooted in common-law principles and are well established in the law.[95]

The unceasing array of social media networks being developed and in practice today—with business models centered on the notion of sharing photographs, videos, writings, and any other creation that is capable of being uploaded to a server—have slowly welded the right of distribution to the right of reproduction.[96] Few cases to date involve claims exclusively focusing on a copyright holder's right to distribute over the Internet because most such claims also implicate the copyright holder's right of reproduction. Differences as to whether an author has forfeited her rights in her copyrighted work by virtue of uploading the work to a website dedicated to public dissemination has led to litigation. The *Morel* case (discussed earlier with respect to the license issue on page 1566) is rich with these issues and serves as a good introduction.[97]

As previously noted, in *Morel*, plaintiff's photographs of Haiti were downloaded, sold, and redistributed by several defendants. At the time the photographs were uploaded to Twitter, Morel did not have a copyright notice on his pictures, though his Twitter page did place the attributions "Morel" and "Photomorel"[98] beside the images.[99] However, there was no attribution to or mention of Morel by any of the three parties that subsequently downloaded his photographs: not by Suero, who initially downloaded Morel's photographs, nor the photo editor from Agence France Presse (AFP) who uploaded the photographs to AFP's image center, nor AFP's image distributor, Getty Images, Inc., which attached only the credit line "AFP/Getty/Lisandro Suero" to the photographs.[100]

In January 2010, an AFP employee contacted Morel on Twitter commending him for his photography. Based on this communication, Morel alleged that AFP knew Morel was the author of the photographs, which should have prompted an industry "kill," which is "an order removing the images from the Image Forum, deleting them from archives, and instructing AFP's licensees to delete the images."[101] Instead, the next day, after being contacted by Corbis, Morel's exclusive photo licensor, AFP issued a kill on only eight of the thirteen images and excluded any duplicate images credited to Suero.[102] That same day, the photo editor who initially downloaded the thirteen pictures from Suero's Twitter page sent an email to Getty admitting Morel was the original author of the photographs.[103]

Subsequently, AFP sought a declaratory judgment that AFP did not violate any of Morel's copyrights.[104] In response, Morel filed counterclaims against AFP and several other news agencies[105] alleging copyright infringement, contributory and vicarious infringement, and violations of the Digital Millennium Copyright Act (DMCA) (addressed on pages 1576–1586) and the Lanham Act.[106]

The New York federal district court found that neither AFP nor Getty had obtained a valid license to use Morel's photographs, and that there was sufficient evidence to demonstrate that AFP had knowledge that Morel was the true author of the photographs.[107] Therefore, the court denied AFP's motion to dismiss Morel's contributory infringement claim.

Importantly, sections 1202(a)[108] and 1202(c)[109] of the DMCA protect against the deliberate falsification of copyright management information (CMI). Email exchanges, specifically the email from AFP's photo editor to Morel inquiring about the photographs that was sent before downloading the photographs, and the email from the photo editor to Getty admitting Morel was the author, satisfied the knowledge and intent prongs under the DMCA credit line provisions.[110] Additionally, the court relied on several recent opinions to support the finding "that the notations 'Morel,' 'daniel morel,' and 'photomorel' fall within the scope of CMI under the plain language of the statute."[111]

The court discarded Morel's Lanham Act claims for false representation and false advertising. As established by the Supreme Court in *Dastar Corp. v. Twentieth Century Fox Film Corp.*,[112] Congress did not intend for trademark law to add an additional layer of protection to right of attribution claims that are traditionally shielded by copyright laws. In *Dastar*, the defendant Dastar reedited and sold a television series that was in the public domain, but without any mention of the copyrighted novel from which the series originated. The holder of the copyright in the novel sued the defendant for reverse passing off under section 43(a) of the Lanham Act, 17 U.S.C. § 1125(a).[113] The Supreme Court reasoned that the Lanham Act was not intended to protect creative works, and the "origin" of any "communicative product," such as a book or video, referred to the producer of the good, rather than the creator of the content or person who came up with the idea of the good.[114] Applying the Supreme Court's reasoning, the federal district court noted that "[b]ecause photographs are "communicative products" protected by copyright, false designation of their authorship is not cognizable under section 43(a)(1)(A) after *Dastar*."[115]

Because there were unresolved issues of material fact, the court granted the motion to dismiss for Morel's vicarious infringement claims against one news station and Lanham Act claims against AFP and Getty, but denied the motion with "respect to Morel's claims for direct copyright infringement against AFP and another news station; his claims for contributory infringement against AFP; and his claims for DMCA violations against AFP, Getty, and two news stations."[116]

COMPILATIONS

In the 2011 case of *Denny Manufacturing Co. v. Drops & Props, Inc.*,[117] an Alabama federal district court held the defendant in civil contempt for reproducing and distributing, in violation of an injunction, photographic backdrops to which the plaintiff held copyrights.[118] Plaintiff created artistic backdrops for photographers either by employing artists who hand-painted images on canvas, or by creating digital images scaled to large dimensions and then printed.[119] The backdrops and other products were marketed through plaintiff's website, catalog, and CD-ROM catalog. Initially, in 2008, the parties entered into a settlement agreement enjoining the defendant from "imitating, reproducing, distributing, or making any other infringing use of" of the copyrighted works, including in any online store, website, catalog, or social media.[120] With one exception, the defendant was also required to destroy all infringing material, such as the digital images on its websites, physical and online catalogs, and CD collections.[121] In July 2010, plaintiff requested that defendant remove a number of copyrighted images, including a prop and a backdrop called *Aladdin's Valley* that defendant used to market its own products, from defendant's websites, the physical and downloadable versions of its catalog, and third-party Internet sites.[122] While all physical copies were destroyed, a subsequent inspection of defendant's downloadable catalog and advertisements on a third-party social media website revealed that plaintiff's copyrighted images were still on display.[123]

The Alabama federal district court determined that the plaintiff established by clear and convincing evidence that the defendant was in violation of the injunction and had demonstrated a prima facie case of civil contempt.[124] The court first considered the online catalog and use of the *Aladdin's Valley* backdrop and a prop in advertising. It found that the defendant's actions of immediately destroying the physical copies containing the images, removing the backdrop and prop from defendant's website, and employing a computer program that prevented customers from purchasing any of plaintiff's backdrops still listed in the catalog demonstrated good faith effort and a simple, inadvertent failure to delete the online downloadable catalog.[125] However, the plaintiff also provided the court with a list of fifteen additional copyright-protected works, in a compilation of images, that the defendant allegedly infringed by creating substantially similar copies. By comparing plaintiff's backdrop images to defendant's images, the court determined the defendant had infringed the plaintiff's copyright in the compilation.[126]

PUBLIC DISPLAY OF THE DIGITAL COPYRIGHTED WORK

Copyright holders of digital visual works have the exclusive right to publicly display their works.[127] The right to publicly display and the right to distribute copies have often overlapped in the context of the Internet. In the past, courts have found that the appearance on users' computer screens of small-scale images of copyrighted works and the availability of full-scale replicas of copyrighted pictures available through publicly accessible websites constitute evidence sufficient to deny dismissal on summary judgment of claims of direct infringement of display rights.[128]

Courts, however, are not uniform in their treatment of the digital display right. For example, in *Perfect 10, Inc. v. Amazon.com, Inc.*,[129] Amazon's parent company, Google, provided links to third-party websites that displayed thumbnail-sized images of copyrighted photographs. Plaintiff alleged that this violated the display rights and distribution rights of its copyrighted images. Employing the analysis of the lower court, the Ninth Circuit found plaintiff was unlikely to succeed on its claims for the thumbnail images, because Google was likely to succeed on its fair use defense.[130]

Although few art-related cases involving the online violation of exclusive rights of copyright have been litigated, some instruction can be found in two disputes concerning notable artists and the display rights of digital works.

In the earlier-addressed *Teter v. Glass Onion*,[131] Teter alleged copyright infringement and sought dismissal of Glass Onion's affirmative defenses. A Missouri federal district court found that, in the absence of a contract authorizing the defendant to use the copyrighted images, Teter's right of reproduction and right of display in the images were violated.[132] The court, however, remanded this point, stating that issues of fact existed as to whether the electronic copies of the images were prohibited under the implied license before March 20, the date when plaintiff had officially revoked the license.[133]

The court then considered defendant's four affirmative defenses. As to the defense that under the U.C.C. Teter had sold his artwork to the defendant and therefore, the latter had the right to take pictures of the artwork, the court compared the conduct of both parties with the purpose of the exclusive rights as set forth in section 202 of the Copyright Act and concluded that ownership of the tangible object is not equivalent to ownership of the exclusive rights of copyright embedded in the object. Therefore, the exclusive rights of reproduction and display were not included within the implied contract or with the transfer of ownership of the artwork.[134] As to the second defense, estoppel, the court noted that it could not render a decision without discovering whether Teter knew that defendant had made electronic copies of the images, when the record showed only that Teter knew his display rights were being infringed. As to the third defense, the first sale doctrine, the court noted that the first sale rule applied solely to the sale and distribution of Teter's physical paintings and prints and was inapplicable to the exclusive intangible rights involved in this dispute.[135] Finally, in direct contrast to the findings in *Perfect 10*, the court decided an application of fair use was inappropriate, and subsequently denied defendant's motion for summary judgment concerning the same exclusive rights.[136]

Upon rejecting defendant's affirmative defenses, the court remanded for determination of whether defendant had violated plaintiff's exclusive rights of reproduction and display after the date plaintiff had revoked the implied license.[137]

Basing his work upon a collection housed at the Metropolitan Museum of Art in New York City, digital artist Michael Mandiberg in 2001 exhibited a project that featured his scanned reproductions of photographs taken by the respected-but-controversial appropriation artist Sherrie Levine. Mandiberg's reproductions of Levine's work were displayed on two websites designed for the project, and access was available to the general public.[138] The public was encouraged to download and print the images, to which was attached a "certificate of authenticity" stating that the image was a genuine Mandiberg.

The irony of Mandiberg's appropriation is that Levine's originals, shot in the late 1970s, are head-on black-and-white documentary images of Depression-era Alabama sharecroppers originally shot by legendary photographer Walker Evans in 1936. A downloaded print has the same resolution as Levine's prints and looks almost exactly like Evan's images. Although an artist's use of copyrighted images without permission solely to advance his own work constitutes infringement, Mandiberg may have escaped liability for two reasons. First, the two exhibition websites cast the project as an educational resource because the project was the only place outside the Metropolitan Museum of Art where an individual could learn certain particulars about some of Levine's photographs. But more importantly, the museum, in which the copyrights for both the Evans images and the Levine photographs resided, granted Mandiberg access and use.[139]

The threshold level of originality required of digital works of art is not yet clear, but it is unlikely to differ significantly from that of traditional works.[140] The Supreme Court opinion in *Tasini*[141] made clear that a mere change in medium is insufficient to satisfy the originality requirement. Moreover, as noted in *Bridgeman v. Corel*[142] (discussed in chapter 11), sufficient originality was not found to rise to the level of a copyrightable derivative work where, in addition to a change in medium, color correction bars were added to 120 digitally reproduced color transparencies of famous paintings in the public domain.

Digital Millennium Copyright Act (DMCA)[143]

OVERVIEW

One of the most significant federal laws applicable to the use of art in the digital realm is the DMCA.[144] Enacted in 1998,[145] the act implements the World Intellectual Property Organization (WIPO) treaties on copyright and on performers and phonograms, and also limits the copyright infringement liability of online service providers (OSPs) and Internet service providers (ISPs) under certain circumstances. In addition to creating substantial changes to the Copyright Act, as applied to art, the DMCA also provides protections for artists whose images may readily be used illegally on the Internet. Its most significant provisions create civil and criminal penalties[146] for anyone who:

- circumvents a technological measure that effectively controls access to copyrighted material,[147] such as descrambling a scrambled work, decrypting an encrypted work, or other efforts to avoid, bypass, remove, deactivate, or impair technological measures without the authority of the copyright owner;[148]

- manufacturers, imports, offers to the public, provides, or otherwise traffics in any technology, product, service, device, or component that is either designed or produced for the purpose of circumvention, has only a limited commercial purpose or use other than circumvention, or is marketed for the use of circumvention;[149]
- falsifies, removes, alters, or distributes false copyright management information, which is information that identifies or manages a copyrighted work and its author.[150]

A very narrow exception is provided for nonprofit libraries, archives and educational institutions,[151] law enforcement and other government activities,[152] reverse engineering,[153] and encryption research[154] under specific circumstances. As such, the DMCA can be used to secure criminal and civil sanctions against an unauthorized party who attempts to circumvent a technological device that encrypts a copyrighted pictoral, graphic, or sculptural image from a website and attempts to download or gain access to its contents. Critics of the DMCA (and there are many of us) note its lack of accommodation to the fair use defense, its violation of rights of free speech and privacy, and its negative impact on scientific research—indeed, on potentially any research.[155]

Though the DMCA broadly defines service providers[156] to include many types of Internet service providers and web entities that host a variety of online services, such as accessible web forums, social networking platforms, databases, and web pages involving digital or electronic art forms,[157] against which rights of copyright can be enforced,[158] the DMCA carves out an equally wide limitation to liability, or safe harbors, for ISPs who are unknowingly involved in infringing activity under certain circumstances. This is significant to artists and art handlers because an ISP is likely to avoid liability for monetary relief under circumstances where the ISP is engaged in:

- conduit activities that are largely automatic interactions of computers connected to the Internet and for which there is no explicit requirement to register an agent to obtain the law's protections;
- transmission or routing of material through a system or network controlled by or for the service provider;
- providing connections for material through such a system or network;
- intermediate and transient storage of that material in the course of transmitting, routing, or providing connections;
- intermediate and temporary storage of material on a system or network controlled or operated by or for the service provider ("system caching");
- long-term storage of information on the service provider's system or network, requiring agent registration to obtain the law's protections;

- storage at the direction of a user of material that resides on a system or network controlled or operated by or for the service provider;
- referring or linking users to online locations containing infringing material or infringing activity, by using information location tools, including a directory, index, reference, pointer, or hypertext link;
- removing material based on an allegation of infringement or knowledge of facts or circumstances from which infringement is apparent or putting it back up based on an assertion of misidentification or mistake on the complainant's part.[159]

If an ISP, however, does not fall within these safe harbor provisions, and copyright infringement is found, the DMCA provides for treble damages and even criminal sanctions for certain types of infringing activity.[160]

In essence what is required of an ISP is that it adopt a policy that provides for termination, in appropriate circumstances, of service access for repeat copyright infringers; implements that policy in a reasonable manner; and informs its clients of the policy.[161]

In applying the DMCA, courts have generally taken the position that Congress did not intend for the DMCA to simply rewrite copyright law for the online world.[162] Rather, it was Congress's intent that courts would continue to determine how to apply the Copyright Act to the Internet and that the DMCA would merely create a floor of protection for ISPs.[163] Interpretation and application of the DMCA has not always been uniform, however, especially with regard to its safe harbor provisions. As one court pointed out, the DMCA draws no distinction between direct and indirect liability for copyright infringement. Moreover, it does not address how to treat an ISP acting as a host server for users to post potentially infringing material that other users will request, nor does it address under what conditions the safe harbor provisions will absolve an ISP from direct liability.[164] In addition, it is important to note that presently there is a circuit split as to the knowledge requirement for ISPs that do not have actual knowledge or awareness of facts from which to infer infringing activity.[165] In the 2012 case of *Viacom Intern., Inc. v. YouTube, Inc.*,[166] the Second Circuit rejected the Ninth Circuit's specific knowledge requirement, and remanded for the district court to decide the standard.

DMCA Safe Harbor Provisions

Contributory Infringement

A number of courts have heard cases involving a multitude of online copyright claims. Often, a publisher or ISP is charged with violations of the DMCA on the basis of secondary liability. Two theories of secondary liability are contributory infringement and vicarious liability, and each is derived from "common law concepts of tort liability."[167] From traditional tort principles, "'[v]icarious liability' (grounded in the tort concept of *respondeat superior*) and 'contributory infringement' (founded on the tort concept of enterprise liability)," emerged through the courts.[168] A defendant may be liable of contributory infringement when "with knowledge of the infringing activity, [it] induces, causes, or materially contributes to the infringing conduct of another."[169] Courts differ as to whether a party guilty of secondary copyright infringement is per se ineligible for safe harbor protection.[170]

In the 2012 case of *Wolk v. Kodak Imaging Network, Inc.*,[171] a New York federal district court dismissed the plaintiff's claims of both direct and secondary copyright infringement against Kodak. Here, Sheila Wolk, an independent artist who sold and licensed digital photographs of her fantasy-themed paintings exclusively through an online store, sued defendants Photobucket and Kodak Imaging Network (Kodak), a subsidiary of Eastman Kodak, on various claims of direct liability infringement, contributory infringement, and vicarious infringement.[172] Photobucket was an Internet service provider that supplied a free online platform for photo sharing. The website was entirely user-generated, so a user could upload any picture or video to the site, which was then stored and accessible to the public. At the time the suit was brought, Photobucket had over nine billion images and videos.[173] Kodak operated an online photography service called KODAK Gallery, which allowed customers to upload their personal digital photographs to the online shop and share their photographs in a variety of ways.

In January 2009, Kodak and Photobucket entered into an agreement that allowed Photobucket users to print their digital images by submitting their photographs to the Gallery. The electronic bridge between the two businesses, Wolk complained, encouraged Photobucket users to upload Wolk's watermark-protected images to Photobucket, use the free software on the site to edit out the watermarks, then use the channel to send the manipulated images to the Gallery for printing and placement on all manner of products.[174]

Through a series of partially successful takedown notices between 2008 and 2010, a few of Wolk's works were removed from Photobucket; however, many of her takedown notices did not include the necessary URL links of the infringing content. Providing URLs was a vital step in the takedown process, because Photobucket did not have the technological means to search through over nine billion images and videos for infringing material. Nonetheless, in early July 2010, Wolk filed suit for copyright infringement of twenty-two different paintings, and supplied Photobucket with a 123 URLs linking to infringement of her paintings.[175] Photobucket removed 102 images, but requested Wolk to provide additional information necessary to locate the remaining twenty-one images.[176] Instead of responding to this request, Wolk, over the course of the next few months, listed over 700 URLs of alleged infringement, which Photobucket used to trace and remove all 700 images. By the end of her search, Wolk claimed she had unearthed approximately 3,000 infringements of her artwork.[177] Photobucket insisted it had never received notice of those extra infringements, and filed a motion for summary judgment dismissing Wolk's claims.

The court first considered Wolk's counts against Kodak, and rejected her claim that she was entitled to statutory damages per work of art infringed under the Copyright Act.[178] The court applied the Second Circuit's holdings in *Cartoon*

Network LP, LLLP v. CSC Holdings, Inc.[179] and *Twin Peaks Productions, Inc. v. Publications Intern., Ltd.*,[180] for the standard of "willful" infringement or "volitional conduct" for direct liability. Under *Cartoon Network*, defendant must actively participate in direct copyright infringement instead of being a passive provider of a space where infringement takes place, and under *Twin Peaks* the active participation must be willful. The court determined that the creation of products with the images and the display of the images on defendant's website through Kodak's automated service—which was performed entirely through electronic means—did not constitute volitional acts.[181] The failure of Wolk's claim of direct infringement caused all of her remaining claims against Kodak to collapse. Thus, Kodak's motion for summary judgment was granted.[182] Next, the court analyzed the claims against the other defendant, Photobucket, to see whether the ISP satisfied the notice and takedown requirements of the DMCA safe harbor provisions. That process is addressed in the next section.

Notice and Takedown Provisions Limit ISP Liability

The notice and takedown provisions of the DMCA list four requirements that must be met to enable an ISP to take advantage of the safe harbor. First, the ISP may not have actual or constructive knowledge of the infringing content, or it must have expeditiously removed or disabled the infringing content upon becoming aware of its infringing nature.[183] Second, if the ISP had the right and ability to control the infringing activity, it must not have received a direct financial benefit from the infringement.[184] Third, the ISP must take down or disable the infringing content upon receiving notice of the infringement.[185] And fourth, the ISP must have designated an agent to receive "notice" of infringement claims, both by posting the agent's contact information in a visible place on its website and by providing the same to the Copyright Office in Washington, D.C. The statute enumerates certain requirements that must be substantially complied with in order to invoke effective notice compliance.[186]

In the *Wolk* case, the New York federal district court analyzed the artist's claims under the DMCA to determine Photobucket's eligibility for safe harbor. First, the court noted that recent case law in other jurisdictions supported a finding that Photobucket qualified for safe harbor.[187] Other ISPs like YouTube and Veoh.com, which operate video sharing sites, were found to meet the statutory definition of "service providers."[188] As stated earlier, to qualify for safe harbor, "a service provider must (i) adopt a policy that provides for the termination of service access for repeat copyright infringers; (ii) inform users of the service policy; and (iii) implement the policy in a reasonable manner."[189] The court observed that Photobucket's takedown policy was made available on its website; upon receiving takedown notices, infringing material was immediately removed; repeat infringing users were terminated; and the takedown policy contained the address and email of a designated copyright agent.[190]

Next, Wolk argued that the editing software on the photo-sharing site interfered with her image watermarks, which are a form of "standard technical measures" protected from interference by section 512(i)(1)(B) of the DMCA. The court rejected this argument, mainly because Photobucket did not encourage users to circumvent copyright; rather, the users were doing so of their own will.[191] There was also no evidence to show that Photobucket possessed actual knowledge of infringing activities, because most of the takedown notices Wolk submitted to Photobucket were not DMCA-compliant.[192] Moreover, Photobucket did not have the ability to control the infringement as it did not (nor was it able to) prescreen content, or provide extensive advice to users on how to edit content. Nor was there evidence of attracting or losing subscriptions because of infringing activities.[193] Further, Photobucket was not involved with a user's decisions to employ the services of the Gallery and did not receive payment based on the content of the images submitted, but rather for any image printed through the Gallery.[194] Therefore, the court found that Photobucket satisfied the elements for safe harbor, and granted its motion for summary judgment.

Several other cases have addressed what constitutes sufficient notice. Adequate notice has been found when a letter sent to an ISP listed the author of a copyrighted work and was accompanied by printouts of screen shots of the ISP's website pages that contained the infringement but did not include URLs to the infringing material;[195] when a copyright holder identified two websites created for the purpose of publishing its copyrighted works and referred the ISP to the two web addresses that stated its copyright information;[196] and when a copyright holder listed and described the infringing material and its URL.[197] Notice was inadequate, however, when the copyright holder in a motion picture failed to identify the item numbers for the infringing copies of a film being offered on an auction website, which was necessary to distinguish the infringing copies from the copies that were legally purchased and offered for resale;[198] when a takedown letter contained URLs to the infringing material but did not properly cite the copyrighted material that was being infringed;[199] and when a C-level executive of a television conglomerate sent an informal email to an investor of the ISP requesting a takedown of materials, but only listing the copyrighted works that were infringed without anything more.[200]

Once an ISP is adequately notified of a third party using the system to infringe copyright, the takedown provision is triggered. If an ISP prevents users from being able to file an adequate takedown notice, the ISP loses its safe harbor protection.[201] The ISP must act expeditiously to block access to, or to remove, the offending material, but the safe harbor is reached if the ISP substantially complies.[202]

File Sharing and Peer-to-Peer Networks

Although file-sharing litigation to date primarily involves the sharing of music and video files, peer-to-peer file sharing is particularly threatening to art-related copyright holders because it is readily applicable to image-based files and, given the nature of popular file-sharing systems, a direct file exchange between users significantly decreases the possibility of detection.

Because Internet users often maintain anonymity in the transactions they conduct online, especially in the realm of peer-to-peer networks, copyright holders have increasingly turned to theories of contributory and vicarious[203] copyright infringement on the part of peer-to-peer networks as a basis for their claims.[204] Copyright holders may file with the appropriate court a request to identify anonymous users that have allegedly infringed on their copyrighted material.[205] Subpoenas issued for identification purposes are certain to be met with opposition in the form of a motion to quash the subpoenas for procedural and substantive irregularities, though the current trend appears to favor copyright holders over anonymous defendants.[206]

File-sharing protocols work in one of four ways. The first, of which Napster is an example, is a centralized system, which boasts a client-server protocol. Through the use of software downloaded from the service, a user is able to interact with the service's server-side software. Once connected, the service's server reads a list of the MP3 audio files contained on a user's computer and adds them to its directory, making them available to other users to download. At the same time, a user is able to search the directory for files made available by other users on the service's server. This system employs a proprietary centralized indexing software architecture in which a collective index of available files is maintained on servers owned and operated by the service. Search requests for files are transmitted to the service's server. If the search yields results showing another user who is at that time logged into the system and offering to share the file, then the requesting user can connect directly with the offering user and download the file.[207]

In contrast are two decentralized systems: the Gnutella open-source software and the "supernode" model, of which Grokster is an example. These models are decentralized systems in that users do not directly access the service's server. Instead, select user computers on the network are transformed into indexing servers or "supernodes." A searching user then connects to the most easily accessible supernode (instead of a centralized server), and the supernode conducts the search of the index and supplies the searching user with results. Virtually any computer with an adequate processor and sufficient storage space for temporary files could serve as a supernode. The Gnutella protocol may also operate without supernodes, and instead link computers directly to each other.[208]

The fourth decentralized file-sharing architecture, which has spawned a growing number of lawsuits in the music industry and film industry, is torrents, exemplified by the sites in the 2011 case of *Voltage Pictures, LLC v. Doe*.[209] Torrent protocols require the installation of a BitTorrent client software application and concurrent access to torrent websites, which contain the necessary searching indexes of files. A BitTorrent client cannot independently search other computers for files. Torrent files, called "dot-torrent files," do not contain the actual content the user seeks, but rather contain data trackers that work with the client software.[210] Upon opening the dot-torrent file, the software application reads the data trackers and searches the network to locate the different pieces of the file. Each piece contains a "hash" value that the application uses to identify the piece of the file and its location within the network.[211] The BitTorrent client gathers other users who are currently running the application, and that have all or some parts of the desired file into a file-exchanging group called a "swarm."[212] When the downloading process begins, each user in the swarm simultaneously contributes a different piece to the BitTorrent client, which "simultaneously downloads the pieces of the content request, and then reassembles the content file on the requesting computer when the download is complete."[213] Naturally, in comparison to a Napster-type system, the file is downloaded at a considerably quicker rate, because pieces of the file arrive all at once from multiple sources instead of only one source.

The distinctions among filing-sharing architectures are relevant to determine whether a service provider qualifies for safe harbor protection but not, however, to demonstrate a likelihood of contributory and vicarious infringement. For example, both the 2005 Supreme Court decision in *Grokster* and the 2011 New York federal district court decision in *Arista Records LLC v. Lime Group LLC*,[214] each concerning Gnutella architecture, never mention the DMCA, yet do conduct an in-depth discussion about secondary liability for copyright infringement. The district court in *Columbia Pictures Industries, Inc. v. Fung*,[215] in relation to the torrent architecture, found safe harbor provisions of sections 512(a) and (c) inapplicable, because plaintiff's claims were not based on "passive transmission or storage of infringing materials."[216] Even so, the defendant ISP was denied safe harbor under the applicable provision for having awareness that infringing material was available on defendant's torrent sites.[217] While theories of secondary liability were argued, the court only addressed—and later found—inducement of copyright infringement in order to avoid "unnecessar[y] duplicati[on] with respect to the central question at issue."[218]

In the 2001 case of *A&M Records v. Napster*,[219] the Ninth Circuit held that plaintiffs, record companies and music publishers, demonstrated a likelihood of success on the merits for contributory and vicarious infringement of unauthorized distribution of copyrighted digital music files. In support of its holding, the court noted that defendant had actual knowledge of infringing material on its system and failed to purge that material, so it could be held liable for contributory infringement.[220] With respect to liability for vicarious infringement, the court pointed out that Napster exhibited control by reserving the right to terminate user accounts and to police its system for infringing material. Napster could have had a direct financial interest in the infringing material because its future revenue depended upon increasing its user base.[221] In upholding a preliminary injunction, the court also held that Napster was unlikely to succeed on a defense of fair use since some material available on its system was either not copyrighted or in the public domain.[222] The court reserved for trial the issue of whether Napster was entitled to the safe harbor provisions of the DMCA, but held that a balance of the equities strongly favored plaintiffs.[223] On remand, the district court imposed a shutdown order on Napster pending full compliance with the duties placed upon it by the injunction.[224]

At first, the same did not hold true in the case of *Metro-Goldwyn-Mayer Studios v. Grokster*,[225] where plaintiffs claimed that defendant contributed to the distribution of their copyrighted audio and video works. In upholding a Cali-

fornia federal district court's grant of summary judgment in favor of the de-
fendant-distributor, the Ninth Circuit in 2004 distinguished Grokster's systems
from that of Napster and Aimster, which was involved in another peer-to-peer
case decided in the Seventh Circuit.[226] In determining that Grokster was capable
of substantial noninfringing uses based on defendant's evidence,[227] the Ninth
Circuit applied patent law's traditional staple-article-of-commerce doctrine; that
is, that distribution of a component of a patented device will not violate the patent if it is suitable for use in other ways. This doctrine legitimizes the questionable conduct of selling a device having both lawful and unlawful uses and limits
liability to instances of more blatant fault. Here, the Ninth Circuit held that as a
result of the decentralized system, defendant could not have actual knowledge of
copyright infringement because defendant hosted no infringing files or lists of
those files and defendant did not regulate or provide access to such files.[228] Similarly, defendant's inability to supervise or block direct copyright infringers who
used the software was not "turning a blind-eye" like Napster in such a way that
vicarious liability could be imposed.[229]

The decision was appealed to the Supreme Court, and in June 2005, the Court
vacated the grant of summary judgment in favor of Grokster and remanded
the case for reconsideration of summary judgment in favor of MGM, based on
Grokster's actively inducing infringement. In so doing, the Court held that a
party who distributes a device with the objective of promoting its use to infringe
copyright, as demonstrated either by clear expression or by other affirmative
steps going beyond mere distribution with knowledge of third-party action, is
liable for the resultant infringements by third parties—regardless of the lawful
uses of that device.

In so holding, the Court first noted that where "a widely shared service or product is used to commit infringement,"[230] it may be impossible to effectively protect
the work against all direct infringers and therefore "the only practical alternative
[is] to go against the distributor" of that service or product "for secondary liability
on a theory of contributory or vicarious infringement."[231] The Court, then noting
that the Ninth Circuit misapplied the staple-article-of-commerce doctrine, stated
that the doctrine does not require courts to ignore evidence of intent to promote
infringement— nor was the doctrine meant to foreclose common-law rules of
fault-based liability[232] The Court then observed that the evidence indicated that
Grokster induced its users to commit copyright infringements in that

(1) it made efforts to supply services to former Napster users,
(2) it did not attempt to develop filtering mechanisms to diminish infringing
      activity arising from use of its software, and
(3) it derived revenue by selling advertising space and then directing ads to
      the screens of computers using its software.

The more the software is used, the greater the advertising revenue. Taken in
the context of the other evidence, the Court noted, this third factor could indicate
an inference of unlawful intent.[233] Finally, the Court observed that aside from

having both the requisite intent to bring about infringement and the distribution of a device suitable for infringing use, the inducement theory requires evidence of actual infringement. The Court found that there was evidence of such infringement on an enormous scale.[234]

In a 2007 decision, *Metro-Goldwyn-Mayer Studios, Inc. v. Grokster, Ltd.*,[235] the California federal district court limited the scope of an injunction against Grokster, stating that it was improper to issue an injunction that barred the file-sharing platform from violating the Copyright Act in any manner other than inducement of infringement. The court noted an injunction for inducement of infringement was proper, because Grokster could induce more infringement than could ever be adequately redressed to copyright holders.

Hyperlinks

Hyperlinking refers to the practice of providing a click-through point that enables a web user to be referred from one web location to another location for further information. It is similar to a bibliographic footnote.[236] While hyperlinks generally do not provide content, technical differences among certain types of links can form the basis of various theories of liability.

Although hyperlinks transport users from one website to another, the practice does not generally expose the linking website to direct copyright infringement liability.[237] Hyperlinking may, however, result in other theories of liability such as liability for trademark infringement, violations of the DMCA, violations of foreign indecency laws,[238] and contributory infringement if the linking site is aware that the linked-to site contains infringing content.[239]

Hyperlinks may also violate the anticircumvention provision of the DMCA.[240] For example, in the 2001 case of *Universal City Studios v. Corley*,[241] the Second Circuit upheld an injunction that prevented a defendant from providing hyperlinks to other websites that allowed users to download computer software that decrypted digitally encrypted movies— a violation of the DMCA's prohibition on offering and providing access to technologies that defeat copyright protection systems.

Inline Linking and Framing

In contrast to hyperlinking, the practices of inline linking and framing are more likely to involve infringing use of copyrighted digital art within the pages of a website.

> Inline linking allows one to import a graphic from a source website and incorporate it in one's own website, creating the appearance that the in-lined graphic is a seamless part of the second web page. The in-line link instructs the user's browser to retrieve the linked-to image from the source website and display it on the user's screen, but does so without leaving the linking document. Thus, the linking party can incorporate the linked image into its own content . . . [and] the user would not realize that the image actually resided on another web site.[242]

Thus, for example, the inline linking of content from website *B* onto website *A* can cause website *A* to be perceived as reproducing website *B*'s content on website *A*.[243] Framing occurs when a user's browser opens a new window displayed over the original browsing window to display the second web page.

The 2003 case of *Kelly v. Arriba Soft Corp.*[244] is the seminal case on the subject of inline linking and framing. There, plaintiff, a professional photographer, claimed that his reproduction, display, and distribution rights were violated by defendant's Internet search engine. The search engine was unique in that in contrast to typical text-based search engines, its results were displayed as small "thumbnail" images. By clicking on the thumbnails, the user could view a larger version of the same image within the context of the Arriba web page. Thirty-five of plaintiff's images, obtained without authorization from his website, were included in defendant's database.

The defendant conceded it had violated plaintiff's exclusive rights under the Copyright Act, but argued that its use was a fair use under the Supreme Court's guidelines in *Campbell v. Acuff-Rose*.[245] A California federal district court agreed and granted summary judgment in favor of defendant.[246] Specifically, the court found that the purpose and character of defendant's use made it significantly transformative and that the use did not harm the market for, or value of, plaintiff's work. Plaintiff appealed and the Ninth Circuit affirmed in part and reversed in part. There, the court held that defendant's use of plaintiff's images as thumbnails was transformative because they were smaller, were of a lower resolution, and served an entirely different function than plaintiff's original images.[247]

The court, however, refused to find the same with respect to the larger version of the images, because defendant failed to move for summary judgment on the basis of fair use with respect to that activity. Most relevant to the court with respect to the thumbnail images was that the search engine's purpose for using the work was functional (to index) rather than to exploit the artistic work of the various indexed websites.

Fair Use Defense

As seen in *Kelly*, fair use is available as a defense to copyright infringement online.[248] But its application may not be as broad as it is in offline media. One court has refused to acknowledge fair use as a defense where a bulletin board service allowed its members to post, verbatim, the text of news articles from daily newspapers on its website so that other members could add remarks and commentary.[249] Another court has recognized fair use as a defense where a defendant reverse-engineered plaintiff's copyrighted video games to enable the copyright holder's game to be played on a different device.[250] The latter decision appears to be consistent with the circumvention exceptions of the DMCA, but ironically neither those decisions nor *Kelly* makes any reference to the DMCA and its lack of a fair use defense.

Fair Use Defense and Nonprofit Organizations

Is the fair use defense more readily applied to a nonprofit organization than to a for-profit entity? At least one court has held that lack of compensation alone does not preclude imposing liability for the unauthorized use of copyrighted works. In the 1997 case of *Marobie-FL, Inc. v. National Association of Fire Equipment Distributors*,[251] the defendant nonprofit organization was sued for direct and contributory infringement for selling plaintiff's copyrighted clip art (computer line drawings and graphics) on CDs available on the defendant's website. When the defendant asserted a fair use defense, an Illinois federal district court applied the four-factor fair use analysis discussed at length in chapter 11; that is: (1) the purpose and character of the use (including whether the use is commercial), (2) the nature of the copyrighted work, (3) the amount and substantiality of the portion used in relation to the work as a whole, and (4) the effect of the use on the potential market for the copyrighted work. The court ruled against a finding of fair use, determining that the defendant's use was commercial. Although the defendant made the plaintiff's works available to users at no cost, the court noted that defendant's website was used to generate advertising revenue, and that plaintiff's works enhanced the defendant's ability to accomplish this goal.

TRADEMARK PROTECTION

Traditional Trademark Law

Trademark law principles continue to be applied to visual works of art online. However, the nature of the Internet has resulted in more sophisticated types of infringement as well as new theories of consumer confusion. An overview of the basic principles of trademark law including the elements and remedies for trademark infringement and trademark dilution is provided in the trademark section of chapter 10. Therefore, this chapter addresses only these types of infringement that have arisen on the Internet, laws such as the Anticybersquatting Consumer Protection Act and the Uniform Domain Name Dispute Resolution Policy.

Types of Trademark Infringement

TRADITIONAL INFRINGEMENT

Although the bulk of trademark infringement cases on the Internet involve domain name disputes, traditional infringement also occurs. For example, trademark infringement can occur through the use of a hyperlink consisting of a trademark owner's mark, unless the hyperlink is merely the trademark owner's website address. There must be additional action beyond mere registration of a domain name to invoke trademark infringement.[252]

Traditional trademark infringement can also occur if site *A* inlines content from site *B* onto site *A*, giving rise to the implication that site *B*'s content came from site *A*. Even if users are aware that site *B*'s content originates on site *B* by looking at the source code, inlining can imply an endorsement of some kind unless a prominent disclaimer is used. Thus, care should be taken when providing any kind of hyperlink to other sites.

USE OF TRADEMARK IN DOMAIN NAME

The use of registered trademarks in domain names has led to several new theories of trademark liability. In order to understand how domain names may infringe on trademark rights, it is necessary to understand what a domain is and what a domain name does.

Trademark protection can be acquired only for second-level domain names, for example, "sothebys" not "sothebys.com" unless the entire domain name "sothebys.com" is used to indicate the source of goods or services.[253] The level of protection accorded to domain names as trademarks is based on traditional categories of mark protection (generic, descriptive, suggestive, and arbitrary marks) and "use" in commerce,[254] both of which are addressed in the trademark section of chapter 10.

Because companies usually incorporate their company trademarks in their Internet domain names, many consumers have come to rely on Internet domain names to indicate the source of goods or services of a particular company. For example, users seeking a particular company on the Internet often pinpoint the company's domain name by typing in the name of the company followed by the top-level domain ".com."[255] In those instances, domain names are not acting as addresses, but as trademarks and thus are accorded trademark protection.

CYBERSQUATTING[256]

The current method of registering trademarks permits anyone on a first-come-first-served basis to register any name as a domain name as long as that name is not already in use as a domain name. Therefore theoretically, anyone may register the domain name sothebys.com if is not already registered, even if the registrant has no connection to Sotheby's and even though many consumers would assume that Sotheby's website domain name would be sothebys.com. Depending upon the circumstances, including the domain name registrant's intended use in commerce and his communication with the original trademark owner, this practice may be prohibited under the statutory provisions of the federal Anticybersquatting Consumer Protection Act (discussed below on page 1591).

GOOD-FAITH REGISTRATION

Unlike the offline world, where two trademark owners are allowed to coexist with the same trademark, domain names are unique to a single owner. Thus some disputes have arisen because one particular trademark owner registered its offline trademarks in good faith or because a third-party registrant legitimately chose a domain name that happened to incorporate another party's trademark.[257]

INTERNATIONAL DISPUTES

Domain name disputes can also arise from the registration of the same domain name in two different countries, as in the 2001 case of *eToys v. etoy.*[258] Here, a U.S. web-based toy store operating under the name etoys.com filed a claim for trademark infringement and unfair competition against a Swiss-based digital artist's website doing business under the domain name etoy.com.

Despite the fact that the digital artist's use of its domain name predated the plaintiff's use, the court enjoined the artist from using the domain name. The court found that there was too great a likelihood for confusion as the consumers were, in fact, confused by the similar names.

GRIPE SITES[259]

Disputes have also arisen when domain names, including subdomain names, are critical of trademarks. In the 1998 case of *Bally Total Fitness Holding Corp. v. Faber,*[260] the plaintiff company alleged claims of trademark infringement, trademark dilution, and unfair competition. When defendant's website was accessed, the viewer was presented with plaintiff's mark, adorned by the word "sucks" printed across the mark. In granting defendant's motion for summary judgment, the California federal district court noted that the website was far removed from the business of maintaining health clubs. Finding the services unrelated, the court held that there was neither competition nor a likelihood of confusion between the two.[261] In the 2011 case of *Ascentive, LLC v. Opinion Corp.,*[262] defendants hosted a group of consumer review web pages under the main domain name "pissedconsumer," and invited users to post reviews of businesses. Specific company names were listed as subdomains appearing before the defendant's domain name, such as "ascentive.pissedconsumer.com."[263] The court denied plaintiff's motion for a preliminary injunction, reasoning that there was no likelihood of confusion with defendant's use of plaintiff's trademarks as subdomains, and no reason to think that a consumer would believe plaintiff sponsored the use of its trademarks on defendant's pages.[264]

Remedies

UNIFORM DOMAIN NAME DISPUTE RESOLUTION POLICY

The Uniform Domain Name Dispute Resolution Policy (UDRP) provides an expedited way for trademark owners to obtain two types of relief because it requires all registrants to submit to the jurisdiction of the registry that is used to register domain names. The UDRP also provides for in rem jurisdiction over domain names.

The two types of relief available under the UDRP are cancellation of a domain name or transfer of the domain name to the complainant.

PREREQUISITES TO A UDRP PROCEEDING

Three conditions must be met in order to bring a UDRP proceeding. First, the domain name must be identical or confusingly similar to the complainant's trademark or service mark. Second, the domain name registrant must have no legitimate interest in the domain name. Third, the domain name must have been registered and used in bad faith.

A 2007 UDRP proceeding, *SPTC, Inc. v. Juliana*,[265] illustrates how the three conditions may be satisfied. In this dispute, the complainants, related companies SPTC and Sotheby's, filed a proceeding against the respondent, an individual named Juliana, for trading off complainants' famous mark through the registered domain names "sothebyskorea.com" and "sothebykorea.com." The panelists made the following findings. First, respondent's mark was confusingly similar, because complainants' established trademark Sothebys was wholly reproduced within the domain names. (Note that the analysis was not affected by the absence of the "s" in one of the domain names.) Second, complainants showed that respondent (1) was never authorized by complainants to register the domain name using the Sothebys mark, (2) was not commonly known by the domain names, and (3) did not engage in bona fide offerings of goods or services by listing links on the websites that directed users to competitors' goods and services. Third, the list of links on the website, some of which led to complainants' competitors, showed the domain names were registered in bad faith. Since the complainants had proved all three requirements, the panel ordered the transferring of the domain names from the respondent to the complainants.

UNIFORM DISPUTE RESOLUTION SERVICE PROVIDERS

Currently there are four uniform dispute resolution providers approved by the International Committee for the Assignment of Names and Numbers (ICANN), the quasi-governmental body authorized by Congress to oversee the assignment of domain names. The four are the Asian Domain Name Dispute Resolution Centre, the Czech Arbitration Court Arbitration Center for Internet Disputes, the National Arbitration Forum (NAF), and the World Intellectual Property Organization (WIPO).

Each uniform dispute resolution provider must abide by the Uniform Domain-Name Dispute-Resolution Policy adopted by ICANN in August 1999.[266] In addition, each dispute resolution provider has its own supplemental rules requiring compliance.

TRADEMARK DILUTION REVISION ACT

The Trademark Dilution Revision Act of 2006[267] provides infringement remedies for domain name owners. This act permits trademark owners to seek injunctive and monetary relief from those whose infringing activity may dilute the distinctive quality of a famous mark.[268] In order to bring a successful dilution claim, the trademark at issue must be a famous mark, and defendant's use must have begun after the mark became famous. Such use must also have diluted the trademark.

And lastly, defendant's use must occur in commerce. For disputes concerning domain names, courts may also order transference of domain names to the harmed party when the infringer uses his generic domain names to sell counterfeit goods incorporating famous trademarks.[269] Dilution is discussed on pages 851–856.

ANTICYBERSQUATTING CONSUMER PROTECTION ACT

Enacted in 1999 in an effort to protect consumers from cybersquatting, the Anticybersquatting Consumer Protection Act (ACPA)[270] provides recourse to trademark owners against those who register distinctive or famous marks as Internet domain names in bad faith with the intent to profit from the goodwill associated with those marks.[271] The relief provided includes damages[272] and criminal sanctions.[273]

To succeed on an ACPA claim, a plaintiff must establish three elements.[274] First, the plaintiff must demonstrate that his trademark is distinctive or famous.[275] The following factors may be considered by a court in making this determination:

1. mark's inherent/acquired distinctiveness
2. duration and extent of use of mark in commerce
3. duration and extent of advertising/publicity of mark
4. geographical trading area in which mark is used
5. channels of trade in which mark is used
6. degree of recognition of mark in channels of trade
7. nature and extent of third-party use of similar marks

Second, the plaintiff must demonstrate that the defendant's domain name is identical or confusingly similar to the trademark.[276] Strong similarity between the two will satisfy this requirement.

Third, the plaintiff must show that the defendant registered the domain name in bad faith with the intent to profit from the good will associated with the mark.[277] Courts and dispute resolution panels assess "bad faith" based on a variety of factors, including actual ownership of the mark, good-faith prior use in commerce, the registrant's intent to divert or confuse consumers, multiple domain name registrations, and the veracity of registration contact information.[278]

Fair Use Defenses to Trademark Infringement

NOMINATIVE FAIR USE

As with traditional trademark infringement (discussed in chapter 11), the fair use defense is used in cyberspace to permit the unauthorized use of a mark under certain circumstances. Three conditions must be present in order for the defense to apply. First, the user's product or service must be "not readily identifiable without use of the mark." Second, the mark must only be used to the extent necessary to identify the trademark owner's goods or services. Third, the user must not imply sponsorship or endorsement by the trademark owner.

Therefore fair use may permit a virtual gallery owner, for example, to use an artist's trademark in order to describe that artist's paintings for sale in the virtual gallery as long as the gallery makes clear on its website that it is not the artist's website, but rather, a commercial art gallery selling the artist's works.[279]

Toyota Motor Sales, U.S.A., Inc. v. Tabari,[280] a 2010 case, displays another example of fair use. Defendants used the trademark Lexus in their domain name, as well as in metatags, to refer to a genuine Lexus automobile sold by an authorized Lexus dealer. The Ninth Circuit remanded and held that the district court must allow at a minimum for the Lexus mark to be used—as nominative fair use—in some manner in defendant's domain name. As the court stated, "[t]rademarks are part of our common language, and we all have some right to use them to communicate in truthful, non-misleading ways."[281]

PARODY

Parody occurs "when one artist, for comic effect or social commentary, closely imitates the style of another artist and in so doing creates a new artwork that makes ridiculous the style and expression of the original."[282] Applied to the digital medium, courts continue to apply traditional lines of analysis in determining whether a fair use defense exists for those engaged in parody-type artworks. For example, in the 2008 case *Utah Lighthouse Ministry v. Found. for Apologetic Info.& Research*,[283] the Tenth Circuit held that defendant's website—which identically copied the look of plaintiff's online book store—constituted a parody. Importantly, defendant used plaintiff's mark not to support a sale of goods or services, but to support his opinion about plaintiff's books.[284] Courts generally hold that a parody entitles its creator under the fair use doctrine to more extensive use of the copied work than is ordinarily allowed under the substantial similarity test, primarily because this sort of criticism itself fosters the creativity protected by the copyright law.[285]

As a threshold matter, a plaintiff must show that defendant has used the alleged trademark in commerce in order to prevail on a trademark infringement claim.[286] And while use in commerce is a factor militating against a fair use finding, the Second Circuit has stated that the profit element is not controlling per se: A totality of the factors must be considered.[287] Therefore, parody created through the use of digital technology may find protection under a fair use defense, whether used in commerce or not.

FIRST AMENDMENT ISSUES ONLINE

Defamation Law

COMMUNICATIONS DECENCY ACT

Section 230(c)(1)[288] of the Communications Decency Act (CDA) immunizes providers and users of "interactive computer services" from state tort liability for publishing or distributing content provided by third-party users.[289] The statute defines the term "interactive computer services" to mean "any information service, system, or access software provider that provides or enables computer access by multiple users to a computer server, including specifically a service or system that provides access to the Internet. . . ."[290] The definition has been interpreted by the courts to encompasses a broad spectrum of the Internet, including virtually any system or service providing access to the Internet or a website facilitating interaction between different users. The term should be contrasted with that of "information content provider," which means "any person or entity that is responsible, in whole or in part, for the creation or development of information provided through the Internet or any other interactive computer service."[291] An information content provider is not immune from state tort liability. In terms of defamation law, the information content provider is often the user who utilizes the service or system of a service provider to defame a third party.

Citing policy provisions that the statute was enacted to "promote the continued development of the Internet" and "preserve the vibrant and competitive free market that presently exists for the Internet,"[292] courts have interpreted the immunization policy as a choice by Congress to treat ISPs differently from other purveyors of information such as newspapers, television, and radio stations, which have been liable for publishing or distributing content prepared by third parties.[293]

TYPES OF CLAIMS BARRED

In addition to barring claims against ISPs for publication and distribution of defamatory material, section 230 bars claims against ISPs for failure to distribute content, for refusal to deliver content, and for blocking delivery of content. Thus, it has been held that section 230 bars claims against ISPs for failure to protect users from harassment[294] and for distribution of or failure to prevent distribution of defamatory statements,[295] false or inaccurate statements,[296] obscene literature and child pornography,[297] and unauthorized adult nude pictures.[298] Additionally, section 230 bars a plaintiff's claims even if the content that the ISP blocks is constitutionally protected[299] However, a plaintiff may be able to bring a cause of action for content blocked by an ISP if the plaintiff can produce evidence showing that the policy behind the blocking is unconstitutional.[300]

The immunity ISPs enjoy under section 230 from defamation suits was established in large part by the first and most important case to date to interpret the CDA, the 1997 case of *Zeran v. America Online*.[301] In *Zeran*, an unidentified person posted a message on an AOL bulletin board advertising T-shirts for sale with tasteless slogans related to the Oklahoma City bombing, which had taken place a week earlier. Readers of the bulletin board were instructed to call "Ken" (Zeran's first name), and Zeran's home phone number was listed as the contact. The posting prompted voluminous irate phone calls, some with death threats. Zeran contacted AOL and asked that the posting be removed and a retraction posted,[302] but despite his effort, anonymous postings were made over the next several days offering additional merchandise with offensive slogans and asking callers to "please call back if busy." Though the post was eventually removed, Zeran filed suit asserting AOL was negligent because it had a duty upon notice to remove the defamatory postings promptly, notify subscribers of that the messages were not true, and effectively screen future defamatory material.[303] AOL responded that it was immune under section 230, and a Virginia federal district court agreed, awarding summary judgment in favor of AOL.[304]

Zeran appealed the decision with respect to AOL's duty upon notice of defamatory material. On appeal, the Fourth Circuit affirmed, opining that liability upon notice would defeat the dual purposes behind Congress's enactment of section 230, namely to

> encourage service providers to self-regulate the dissemination of offensive material over their services,[305]

and to respond to

> the threat that tort-based lawsuits pose to freedom of speech in the new and burgeoning Internet medium. The imposition of tort liability on service providers for the communications of others represented . . . simply another form of intrusive government regulation of speech. Section 230 was enacted, in part, to maintain the robust nature of Internet communication.[306]

In the court's view, section 230 made no distinction between ISPs that receive notice and do not remove the offending material and those that do not. To hold otherwise, the court said, "would create an impossible burden for service providers, who would be faced with ceaseless choices of suppressing speech or sustaining prohibitive liability."[307]

The court also held that the CDA expressly preempts any state law claim that would be inconsistent with section 230.[308]

The general holding in *Zeran* has been consistently upheld,[309] though one circuit court has attempted to limit the scope of section 230.[310] However, the majority of courts have adopted the broad grant of immunity to ISPs laid out in *Zeran*[311]—and so the lesson is quite clear. Since third-party users who post defamatory content usually are able to maintain anonymity, section 230's grant of immunity, in combination with the broad definition of ISPs and preemption of state law claims, leaves a plaintiff who has been defamed with little legal recourse.

CLAIMS NOT BARRED

Section 230 clearly states that it shall have no effect on existing criminal laws, including those related to obscenity and child pornography, intellectual property claims, state laws consistent with the Act, and communication privacy laws derived from the Electronic Communications Privacy Act of 1986.[312]

The Rights of Privacy and Publicity

PRIVACY

As we noted in chapter 10, the various state laws regarding rights of privacy and publicity are rife with inconsistencies. The rapid evolution of computer technologies and communications compounds the inconsistencies and "has spawned a new area of litigation and legal concerns with regard to the constitutional expectation of privacy in Internet communications."[313] At least one New York state court has, for example, pointed out that because a website is accessible worldwide, the element in New York's statute[314] requiring that the invasion of privacy occur within the state is virtually eliminated.[315]

Presumably, the same exceptions to privacy statutes discussed in chapter 10 (incidental use, newsworthiness, limited artistic dissemination, and opinion) are applicable to invasion of privacy on the Internet. Additionally, reasonable expectations of privacy have generally not been found to exist with regard to information provided by subscribers to their ISPs,[316] records on individuals' Internet usage,[317] or communications made on Internet websites.[318] Nor have courts found reasonable expectations of privacy to exist in emails that have arrived at its recipient or sent and received through an ISP,[319] chat-room communications,[320] or messages to bulletin boards.[321]

More importantly, however, it has been held that section 230 of the CDA entitles interactive computer service providers to statutory immunity for claims of invasion of privacy in the same manner it does for defamation. In the 2003 case of *Carafano v. Metrosplash.com*,[322] the Ninth Circuit held that an Internet dating website could not be liable for invasion of privacy, misappropriation of right of publicity, defamation, or negligence based on a third party's submission of a fake profile of an actress. In what the court characterized as a case of "cruel and sadistic identity theft,"[323] an unknown person posted a personal profile of plaintiff on the website Matchmaker.com. The profile responded to a series of innocuous questions and included photos from plaintiff's film and television credits that were widely available on the Internet. In addition, the profile stated that plaintiff was "looking for a one-night stand" from a "hard and dominant" man with "a strong sexual appetite" and listed plaintiff's home address and email address. A

reply to plaintiff's listed email contact automatically generated a response stating, "You think you are the right one? Prove it!!" and provided plaintiff's home
address and telephone number. After receiving threatening and sexually explicit
contacts, plaintiff contacted the defendant who blocked access to her profile from
the public before plaintiff filed her complaint.

The California federal district court did not grant the defendant immunity
under section 230 but instead rejected plaintiff's invasion of privacy claim on the
grounds that her home address was precluded from protection because it fell under the newsworthiness exception. The court similarly rejected plaintiff's other
claims because she failed to show that defendant acted with actual malice.[324] On
appeal, the court addressed only the issue of whether defendant was immune
under section 230. In holding that defendant was, the court reasoned that the
standardization of defendant's website, which included sixty-two detailed questions with a menu of prepared responses to each, did not transform defendant
into an "information content provider," because without a user to actively create
a profile, no profile existed. In addition, the court noted that the more pertinent
content of the fake profile—the accompanying photographs, essay, and contact
information—were all user-created.[325]

PUBLICITY

With respect to claims for violation of right of publicity, *Carafano* and subsequent California decisions[326] have diverged from several courts across the country, which hold the right of publicity to be a form of intellectual property and
therefore not barred under section 230.[327]

Where states have enacted right of publicity statutes, the same exceptions described in chapter 10 apply to the Internet. This was illustrated by two 2001
cases. In *Gionfriddo v. Major League Baseball*,[328] the California Court of Appeal
held that use of retired baseball players' names, voices, and likenesses on league
websites was noncommercial speech, entitled to full First Amendment protection, and that the use fell within a newsworthy "public affairs" exception.[329]
Similarly, the Ninth Circuit held in *Hoffman v. Capital Cities/ABC*[330] that a
magazine which had taken a still photograph from a motion picture and used it to
create a computer-generated image did not engage in purely commercial speech
and invade an actor's right of publicity by falsely depicting the actor wearing a
designer outfit of women's clothing.

Given the Internet's lack of geographic and jurisdictional boundaries, the
questions put forth in chapter 10 as to how a court determines the situs of an
injury with respect to privacy and publicity rights argue all the more for federal
legislation to govern these rights—although as also noted in chapter 10, differing principal interests in the various jurisdictions render unlikely the enactment
of such federal legislation in the foreseeable future.

Obscenity and Indecency Law

FEDERAL REGULATION OF OBSCENITY

As a mode of communication, the Internet is unique in the anonymity it affords speakers and the speed and breadth with which a message can be communicated. These characteristics gave rise to a perception that without regulation, "indecent" and "obscene" speech could turn the information superhighway into a perilous road for children and families. Accordingly, in 1996, Congress enacted the Communications Decency Act (CDA).[331] One part of the act made it a crime

(1) to transmit obscene material with the intent to annoy, abuse, threaten, or harass another person or to transmit any obscene or indecent communication with knowledge that the recipient of that communication was under the age of eighteen (the indecent transmission provision),[332] or

(2) to transmit to a specific minor a communication that depicts or describes sexual or excretory activities or organs in a manner that is patently offensive according to contemporary community standards or to transmit the communication in such a way that it would be accessible by anyone under eighteen (the patently offensive display provision).[333]

The day the CDA was signed into law, free speech advocacy groups and computer technology corporations filed suit challenging the constitutionality of both provisions. The challengers argued that the legislation restricted the content of the Internet and infringed upon an adult's right to free speech. After plaintiffs obtained a preliminary injunction prohibiting enforcement of the CDA, a three-judge Pennsylvania federal district court held the challenged provisions unconstitutionally overbroad and vague, but reserved the right of the government to investigate and prosecute obscenity and child pornography under the first provision.[334]

In 1997, under a statutory provision for expedited appeal, the U.S. government appealed to the Supreme Court and urged in *Reno v. ACLU*[335] that the CDA was similar to other statutes designed to protect minors from obscene and indecent speech that were upheld by the Court.[336] The Court, however, disagreed, holding that the "indecent transmission" and "patently offensive display" provisions were facially overbroad in violation of the First Amendment and would be stricken from the statute.

As discussed in chapter 10, where a law is challenged as an unconstitutional burden on free speech, courts make a two-part inquiry: first, what level of scrutiny to apply and second, whether the law is a content-neutral or content-based restriction. If a law is determined to be content-based, it is presumed to be unconstitutional. In rare instances, however, such a law can survive a constitutional challenge if the government can show the law has been narrowly tailored to further a compelling government interest and is the least restrictive alternative available.

In *Reno*, the Court determined that unlike the forms of communication at issue in cases cited by the government, the Internet is subject to strict scrutiny because it is not "invasive." The Internet, unlike broadcast television or radio, the court reasoned, "requires the listener to take an affirmative step to receive the communication," has no history of extensive government regulation, and has no scarcity of available frequencies.[337]

The government then argued that the CDA was analogous to constitutionally permitted zoning ordinances prohibiting adult movie theaters in residential neighborhoods. The Court, however, disagreed with the "cyberzoning" analogy. Unlike a zoning ordinance designed to curtail the "secondary effects" of indecent communication such as crime and detriment to property values, the CDA, applying to the entire universe of cyberspace, aimed at the dissemination of "offensive" speech and thus could not be content-neutral. The Court's opinion was further supported in that the CDA contained no limitation as to the time, place, or manner of its application.[338]

Viewing the statute as a content-based restriction on speech, the Court then looked to the wording and application of the CDA to determine whether, in protecting minors from "patently offensive" and "indecent" speech, the statute was sufficiently narrow in scope and provided the least restrictive alternative. In holding the CDA overbroad and vague, the Court pointed to a number of factors in which the CDA differed from other federal obscenity laws.

First, and most importantly, the CDA failed to provide any definition of "indecent" or "patently offensive." As a content-based restriction, its failure to define such terms would have a chilling effect on free speech: Speakers would be uncertain as to where to draw the line between permissible and impermissible material.[339] Further, the statute omitted any requirement that "patently offensive" material lack serious literary, artistic, political, or scientific value—an important prong of the *Miller* test that tempers the uncertain sweep of an obscenity definition.[340] In addition, the *Miller* definition was limited, whereas the sweep of the CDA included "excretory activities," as well as organs of both a sexual and excretory nature. The Court believed that the lack of qualifiers to limit the statute's scope combined with the CDA's expanded definition of indecency would silence some speakers whose messages would otherwise be entitled to constitutional protection, such as discussion of safe sexual practices and artistic images that include nude subjects.[341] To uphold the challenged provisions of the CDA, the Court commented, would be to limit the Internet "to that which would be suitable for a sandbox."[342]

The Court also noted that unlike other obscenity statutes, the CDA imposes criminal penalties, creating a risk of discriminatory enforcement. As the Court observed, even parents who consent to or supervise their child's use of restricted material would fall within the scope of the statute and be subject to criminal prosecution.

Having found the CDA to be unacceptably burdensome on adult speech, the Court then examined whether the protection of minors from indecent speech could be achieved through a less restrictive alternative. At the time of trial, the

Court found, existing technology did not include effective methods for a sender to prevent minors from obtaining access to indecent communications without denying access to adults. Credit card verification systems imposed prohibitive costs on noncommercial websites and also completely barred adults who lacked a credit card or the resources to obtain one.[343] Age verification systems placed similar costs on noncommercial websites. Moreover, though such systems might feasibly block a minor's access to sites containing topics that might elicit potentially "indecent" or "patently offensive" material, it would not be possible to block access to that material and still permit access to the remaining content.[344] In conclusion, the Court noted that soon-to-be-available user-based software enabling parents to block access to sexually explicit material would provide a reasonably effective and less restrictive alternative.[345]

In response to the Court's decision in *Reno*, Congress passed a new law, the Child Online Protection Act (COPA). On its face, COPA is similar to the CDA. It prohibits and criminally penalizes the transmission of certain indecent materials to minors and provides affirmative defenses for those whose websites restrict a minor's access through credit card verification, age verification, or other technologically reasonable measures. But COPA differs from the CDA on a number of important points that led the court in *Reno* to strike down the CDA. First, it imports wholesale the three-prong obscenity test set forth in *Miller* to define "material that is harmful to minors" and thus requires jurors to apply "contemporary community standards." Second, COPA's application is limited to the World Wide Web and therefore does not apply to applications such as email and chat rooms. Third, unlike the CDA, COPA applies only to communications that are made for commercial purposes.

Again, website operators, content providers, and advocacy groups, led by the American Civil Liberties Union, filed suit immediately after COPA's enactment on October 21, 1998, to enjoin its enforcement. A Pennsylvania federal district court granted the preliminary injunction after concluding the government had not satisfied its burden of proof that COPA provided the least restrictive alternative and that COPA, as a content-based regulation of protected speech, was unlikely to survive strict scrutiny.[346] The government appealed, and the Third Circuit affirmed but on the grounds that COPA's use of "contemporary community standards" to identify material harmful to minors as applied to the World Wide Web rendered the statute substantially overbroad.[347] The court specifically emphasized that the web, unlike traditional "bricks-and-mortar" businesses or postal communications, has no geographic boundaries and does not occupy a physical space: Accordingly, this "would essentially require every web communication to abide by the most restrictive community."[348]

The Supreme Court granted certiorari to answer the narrow question of whether COPA's use of "community standards" to identify "material that is harmful to minors" rendered the statute overbroad and in violation of the First Amendment. In the 2002 case of *Ashcroft v. ACLU*,[349] the Court answered that question in the negative, holding in the government's favor. The Court, however, made clear the limit of its holding: It expressed no view as to whether COPA was unconstitutionally vague or overbroad for other reasons, or whether it would not survive strict scrutiny as the district court had opined.[350] Those issues the Court left for further proceedings on remand to the Third Circuit, and the preliminary injunction was stayed.

On remand, the Third Circuit held that the government had not met its burden of proof that COPA provided the least restrictive alternative, and that it was reasonably probable that the plaintiffs would succeed in their claim and that COPA would not survive strict scrutiny.[351] Specifically, the court found three provisions of COPA not to be narrowly tailored.

First, the court found that the concept "taken as a whole" when applied to the definition of "material harmful to minors" was problematic because it would fail to address an image within the context of its web page or website. Similarly, the court took issue with the term "minor" because of the broad age range to which it applied: The court noted that what appeals to the "prurient interest" of a five-year-old differs from what appeals to the prurient interest of a sixteen-year-old.[352]

Second, the court took issue with the definition of "commercial purposes," finding that it would apply not just to commercial pornographers intended by the statute, but also to nonprofit web publishers and those who derive profit indirectly through advertising revenue if such sites included material that could be harmful to minors.[353]

Finally, the court determined that the actual effect of COPA's affirmative defenses would result in economic harm to most website operators as adult users would be deterred from accessing restricted content if required to reveal their identities. Such a requirement would "drive this protected speech from the marketplace of ideas on the Internet."[354]

For many of the same reasons the court also held COPA substantially overbroad.[355]

In 2004, in *Ashcroft v. ACLU II*,[356] the government again appealed to the Supreme Court but without success. The Court, focusing on the possibility of less restrictive alternatives, found that user-employed blocking and filtering software offered a less restrictive alternative without condemning any category of speech. The Court noted that filters, unlike COPA, could prevent a minor's access to harmful material even if purveyors of obscene product moved overseas or a minor circumvented blocking software or evaded verification systems by obtaining a credit card.[357] Filters, the Court went on, could also be applied to a broader number of communications than that which COPA regulated. The Court also noted that since the passage of COPA and the filing of the instant suit, filtering technology had developed rapidly such that it may be a less restrictive alternative, and that two other statutes had already been passed to protect minors on the Internet.[358]

Despite the success in obtaining preliminary injunctions against enforcement of the CDA and COPA, the remaining provision of the CDA and existing obscenity laws remain viable tools in the prosecution of online obscenity. In December 2001, photographer Barbara Nitke[359] and two nonprofit organizations servicing the nontraditional-sex community,[360] failed in their attempt to obtain an injunction against enforcement of the remaining portion of the CDA which allows "local community standards" to define obscenity. In *Nitke v. Ashcroft*,[361] a New York federal district court held that plaintiffs did not establish a showing of irreparable harm necessary to grant the injunction and that the obscenity portion of the CDA was not unconstitutionally vague.

The plaintiffs argued the CDA was overbroad and vague: It prohibited a substantial amount of non-obscene speech and, in failing to define which community standards would be used, chilled the speech of individuals seeking to display Web material that would not be deemed obscene in all localities.[362] Nitke specifically argued that she had delayed in creating a website until 2001, as she feared prosecution and was unsure which of her photographs were safe to display.[363]

Though the court found significant the CDA's failure to limit its application to commercial speech or commercial entities, thus implicating plaintiffs' websites, the court denied the motion for a preliminary injunction for a number of reasons. The court questioned whether the *Miller* test would afford protection to portraits of non-mainstream sexual practice. It also noted the failure of plaintiffs to show that they would face greater inconsistency in the application of community standards than those who can control dissemination of their materials. Furthermore, plaintiffs had not presented evidence that technology could not prevent material from entering particular communities or that the CDA's affirmative defenses were not adequate limitations on the statute's application.[364] But most important was the six-year delay in plaintiffs' filing suit, which, according to the court, suggested that plaintiffs would not be significantly harmed if they did not obtain an injunction.[365] Subsequently, in *Nitke v. Gonzales*,[366] the court abstained from ruling on "whether some of the works that plaintiffs present as examples of chilled speech would be protected by the social value prong of the *Miller* test, whether current technology would enable plaintiffs to control the locations to which their Internet publications are transmitted, or whether the CDA's two affirmative defenses provide an adequate shield from liability," and ruled in favor of the defendant for plaintiff's failure to put forth evidence demonstrating the CDA was overbroad.

It should be noted that prior to the suits challenging the CDA and COPA, courts were willing to apply existing federal restrictions on obscene speech to the Internet. In the 1996 case of *United States v. Thomas*,[367] a Sixth Circuit court upheld prosecution of a California resident under an existing law criminalizing the interstate transportation of obscene material.[368] There, defendant had scanned some 14,000 images from sexually explicit magazines and created an electronic bulletin board to which subscribers could gain access with a password. An undercover U.S. postal inspector obtained access to the site, and defendant was convicted for violating federal obscenity laws in a Tennessee federal district court. On appeal, the Sixth Circuit rejected defendant's argument that the statute, as worded, did not apply to intangible objects like computer files. The court also rejected defendant's argument that the concept of community standards should be refashioned for cyberspace, and instead held to the general principle that the applicable community standard is that of where the material was sent, that is, western Tennessee.[369]

As alluded to in chapter 10, there is currently a circuit split as to whether the contemporary community standard set out in *Miller* calls for a national perspective or local community perspective. The Ninth Circuit addressed this issue in the 2009 decision of *United States v. Kilbride*.[370] A year before *Kilbride*, the same court, in *United States v. Schales*,[371] had found the *Miller* test to apply to obscene speech regulated under federal obscenity statutes.[372] In *Kilbride*, the defendants sent unsolicited spam emails advertising adult websites. Among other things, the lower court found that the defendants had transmitted obscene materials in violation of federal obscenity statutes. On appeal, the defendants argued that the lower court's jury instructions "failed to comply with the prevailing definition of contemporary community standards for purposes of federal obscenity prosecutions outlined in" a 1974 case, *Hamling v. United States*.[373] In particular, the defendants objected to the portion of instructions that encouraged jury members to look to their own experiences and judgment in determining the contemporary community standard.[374] The *Kilbride* court rejected defendants' arguments based on *Hamling*. First, *Hamling* did not mandate that a clear geographical definition be given to the community standard for federal obscenity cases. Second, *Hamling* allowed jurors to consider evidence outside the state. In any event, defendants had not provided any evidence showing that a "global or societal community standard [was] less tolerant than that of the jurors' own sense of contemporary community standards," and thus the jury instructions, even if erroneous, did not affect the case.[375]

Defendants then argued that they had no control over the locations of the recipients of their emails; that those emails might go to many different geographical communities, including the least tolerant; and that therefore, to avoid burdening free speech, a national standard should apply. The court agreed that the district court should have instructed the jury to apply a national community standard to the interstate transportation of images by email over the Internet, but held that the mistake was not plain error.[376]

Piecing together the common threads of agreement from the Supreme Court's fragmented decision in *Ashcroft*, the court reasoned "that a national community standard must be applied in regulating obscene speech on the Internet, including obscenity disseminated via email."[377] Because the jury instructions did not constitute prejudicial error, the appellate court reaffirmed the district court's decision in favor of the government.

One year later, the Eleventh Circuit in *United States v. Little*[378] rejected the Ninth Circuit's application of a national perspective for the contemporary community standard established by *Miller*, stating that the parts of the *Ashcroft* opinion that encouraged a national perspective were dicta and should not be followed.[379]

STATE REGULATION OF OBSCENITY

After the Supreme Court struck down the "indecency" provision of the CDA, the legislatures of several states reacted by amending their state obscenity laws or by enacting new ones in order to shield minors from viewing sexually explicit material. Some of those statutes have been challenged in court, and a number have been held to violate the First Amendment because they imposed a burden on protected adult speech and either were not narrowly tailored to serve a compelling state interest or did not provide the least restrictive means available to do so.[380] Other such statutes have been found unconstitutional as applied to out-of-state actors and in-state actors alike so as to burden interstate commerce in excess of any state interest—in violation of the dormant Commerce Clause.[381] State statutes, however, that have limited their scope by including in their wording "with the intent, or for the purpose, of seducing" a minor have been upheld under both the First Amendment and the Commerce Clause when challenged.[382]

In conclusion, the surviving provisions of the CDA, carefully drafted state laws, and to some extent existing federal obscenity laws remain viable tools for the government to use in prosecuting online obscenity.

CHILD PORNOGRAPHY

Although convictions under preexisting federal child pornography statutes have been upheld with respect to the Internet,[383] the presence of child pornography on the Internet prompted the government in 1996 to enact the Child Pornography Prevention Act (CPPA).[384] The CPPA expanded the federal prohibition on child pornography to include not only pornographic images made using actual children, but also

- any visual depiction generated by conventional or computer-assisted means that "is, or appears to be, of a minor engaged in sexually explicit conduct"[385] and
- any visual depiction that is "advertised, promoted, presented, described, or distributed in such a manner that conveys the impression" it depicts "a minor engaging in sexually explicit conduct."[386]

Those provisions of the statute were quickly challenged by the Free Speech Coalition, an adult-entertainment trade association, as well as by Jim Gingerich, a painter of nudes, and by erotica photographer Ron Raffaelli, among others. They alleged that the "appears to be" and "conveys the impression" provisions were overbroad and vague, casting a chilling effect on protected speech. In 1999, the Ninth Circuit agreed, holding that the statute was a content-based restriction on free speech and that the two provisions were vague and overbroad. Specifically, the court found that the CPPA banned non-obscene material and pornography made without using actual children, such as virtual child pornography and material made with adults who looked like minors.[387] Rehearing was denied over the dissent of three judges who said that virtual child pornography should be treated like real child pornography.[388]

In the 2002 case of *Ashcroft v. Free Speech Coalition*,[389] the Supreme Court affirmed the Ninth Circuit finding that the challenged provisions were substantially overbroad and in violation of the First Amendment. After finding that the CPPA reached beyond obscenity and failed to conform to the three-part *Miller* test, the Court addressed the question of whether the CPPA was constitutional where it proscribed a significant universe of speech that was neither obscene under *Miller* nor child pornography under *Ferber*.[390]

The Court first pointed out that the "appears to be" provision criminalized depictions of sexually explicit conduct that include "virtual child pornography," as well as images from Renaissance paintings and Hollywood movies filmed without child actors, if a jury were to believe a subject or actor "appears to be" a minor engaged in sexually explicit conduct. These images, the Court noted, "do not involve, let alone harm, any children in the production process."[391] The distinction between how an image is produced and what it communicates was the very foundation of the decision in *Ferber*, which supported its holding by distinguishing between actual and virtual child pornography.[392] The government then urged the Court that virtual child pornography should not be distinguished from actual child pornography for two reasons: first, that virtual child pornography encouraged unlawful acts intrinsically related to sexual abuse of children and second, that virtual images were indistinguishable from real ones so that failure to prohibit virtual images would promote the trafficking of works produced with real children.[393] With respect to the first argument, the Court, citing *Stanley*,[394] stated that "the mere tendency of speech to encourage unlawful acts is not a sufficient reason for banning it."[395] The Court found the government's second argument implausible, noting that if "virtual images were identical to illegal [ones], the illegal images would be driven from the market by the indistinguishable substitutes." The Court stated that "few pornographers would risk prosecution by abusing real children if fictional, computerized images would suffice."[396]

The Court then turned to the "conveys the impression" provision. In also finding it unconstitutionally vague and overbroad, the Court noted that the provision stressed the presentation of speech rather than its content. The Court pointed out that a film containing no sexually explicit scenes involving minors would be treated as child pornography merely "if the title and trailers convey the impression that the scenes would be found in the movie" and the provision would apply even if the possessor knew the movie was mislabeled.[397]

As noted earlier, child pornographers may still be prosecuted under existing federal child pornography statutes. In addition, the Supreme Court has ruled that the government can require public libraries to use Internet filters to block access to images that constitute obscenity or child pornography as a condition for receipt of federal subsidies, provided those filters can be easily turned off upon the request of an adult patron.[398] Since that ruling at least nineteen states have enacted laws requiring public libraries and/or public schools to have Internet filtering software.[399]

VISUAL ARTISTS' MORAL RIGHTS
IN A DIGITAL AGE

As discussed in chapter 12, the federal Visual Artists Rights Act (VARA), which grants the creator of a "work of visual art" the rights of attribution and integrity, is exceedingly narrow in scope: It protects solely the work of visual art and not any reproductions of the image. Accordingly, digitally distorted images of a work of visual art do not fall within the protective ambit of VARA.[400] The ease with which an artist's honor or reputation may be prejudiced through the global dissemination of distorted digital images of the artist's work makes a powerful argument for enhanced U.S. federal moral rights legislation.

ART COMMERCE ONLINE

The art market's ever-growing presence online encompasses an array of electronic art resources as well as purchasing venues. For example, there is VIP ("Viewing in Private"), "the world's first and [as of this writing] only online art fair"[401] launched in 2011. Admittance to the annual online fair (the 2012 event was known as VIP 2.0) is free, with over 130 galleries, including some of the world's largest, participating. While VIP is not an e-commerce site (prospective purchasers use a chat function to contact gallery representatives), the online fair does offer curated tours and talks by experts. As to purchasing venues, major auction houses, including Sotheby's, Christie's, and Phillips de Pury & Company, accommodate prospective buyers who wish to bid online during the physical auctions.[402] Among the array of other online art resources are Artnet, which provides for users a database of historical auction results numbering in the millions, as well as operating as an online auction marketplace trading primarily in Modern and Contemporary fine prints for, mostly, dealer-to-dealer transactions;[403] Art*space*, a purchasing venue which offers, primarily, relatively affordable limited edition prints by known artists; Paddle 8, an online exhibition space which, among its offerings, facilitates purchase transactions between its site members and its galleries; and Artlog, which "operates as a contemporary art online travel guide"[404] and provides online newsletters and other promotional material to assist thousands of museums and galleries in marketing their artwork and events to collectors.[405] In addition, the Internet allows any artist to display his works inexpensively to a global market.[406]

Altogether, the growth in online commercial transactions has generated a need for uniform guidelines in their conduct. Accordingly, a variety of uniformity efforts have given rise to federal laws and U.C.C. amendments addressing such transactions, including legal parameters on the use of electronic signatures,[407] privacy rules applicable to certain entities,[408] online contracts, and issues of Internet taxation.[409] While it is beyond the scope of this treatise on art law to delve into these topics, we note that certain significant issues related to online art commerce, such as cyberspace jurisdiction and online fraud, remain unsettled. Accordingly we touch on these latter aspects of online commerce.

Cyberspace Jurisdiction

The Internet as a digital art medium creates unique challenges in determining the amount and quality of contact a defendant must have with a particular jurisdiction so as to fall within its ambit.

The power to assert personal jurisdiction over an out-of-state resident is governed by a state's long-arm statute. This power is constitutionally limited, under the Due Process Clause, by requiring the defendant to have certain minimum contacts with the forum, so that maintenance of a suit does not offend the traditional notions of fair play and substantial justice. These principles were defined in *International Shoe v. Washington*[410] and its progeny.[411] Assertion of jurisdiction is generally appropriate on a showing that

(1) the defendant, through performance of an act or transaction within the forum by which he purposefully availed himself of the privileges (benefits and protections) of the forum, has had fair warning that the particular activity might subject him to jurisdiction;

(2) the claim arises out of or results from the defendant's forum-related activity; and

(3) the court's exercise of jurisdiction is reasonable.

Minimum contacts can be satisfied by a single isolated transaction if it creates a substantial connection to the forum, but it must be more than random, fortuitous, or attenuated.[412]

While the guidelines established by *International Shoe* and subsequent case law apply to cyberspace, technological advances have tested the traditional territorial notions of personal jurisdiction. For example, does a website's posting of information constitute "regularly soliciting business"? Does entrance into an electronic contract over the Internet with a user within the state constitute "transacting business within the state"? If jurisdiction is asserted on the basis of cyber-contact, then what type or types of contact and what volume of contact are sufficient to implicate the application of a state's long-arm statute? Because the Internet is by its nature available in every forum, a defendant who merely maintains a web presence accessible by users from another state or country could potentially purposefully avail himself of the privileges of that forum. In addressing these questions, courts have continued to struggle in assessing when and whether it is reasonable to assert jurisdiction over a defendant.

Courts have uniformly held that a "passive" website is not a sufficient basis upon which to assert personal jurisdiction.[413] But what changes a website from passive to active can be very slight. For example, in the 1996 case of *Inset Systems*,[414] a Connecticut federal district court held that the proximity of defendant's Massachusetts business to plaintiff's Connecticut business combined with use of defendant's trade name in plaintiff's website and the presence of a toll-free telephone number on defendant's website was enough to transform it from a passive to an active website and subject the defendant to the exercise of Connecticut's long-arm statute. Another example is the 2001 case of *Internet Doorway, Inc. v. Parks*,[415] where a Mississippi federal district court exercised the state's long-arm jurisdiction on the basis of a single email.

These decisions to exercise personal jurisdiction can be contrasted with a number of cases where the contacts and purposeful availment appear equal to, if not greater than, those examples, yet the courts declined to find a jurisdictional basis. In particular, the outcome in the 1997 case of *E-Data v. Micropatent*[416] exemplifies the irony. There, a Utah corporation with an office in Connecticut claimed that defendant, a Washington stock photography corporation, infringed its patent by selling photographic images on the Internet. Despite the presence of a toll-free number on defendant's website and no affirmative showing it had not sold images to Connecticut residents, the same Connecticut federal district court that exercised personal jurisdiction in *Inset Systems* declined to exercise it here. The exercise of personal jurisdiction has similarly been declined for sales of copyrighted craft patterns on eBay,[417] for a staged sale of artwork to a private investigator,[418] and for the use of an image of a performance artist, in violation of her copyright in a foreign-language guidebook and its website.[419]

One of the most cited cases (if not *the* most cited case) for determining personal jurisdiction in the Internet age—the 1997 case of *Zippo Mfg. Co. v. Zippo Dot Com, Inc.*[420]—helps shed some light on the confusion of cyberspace jurisdiction. There, a Pennsylvania federal district court determined that Internet activity falls within one of three areas:

(1) proper jurisdiction, where an entity clearly does business with a forum state by entering into contracts that involve knowing and repeated transmission of computer files;

(2) improper jurisdiction, where an entity has a passive website which merely advertises; and

(3) fact-based analysis to determine jurisdiction by assessing the level of interactivity and commercial nature of the information available on a defendant's website.[421]

The defendant in *Zippo* operated a free and a fee-based subscription news service and had obtained various domain names that made use of plaintiff's trademark. The court concluded that the exercise of personal jurisdiction is directly proportionate to the nature and quality of commercial activity that an entity conducts over the Internet and held exercise of personal jurisdiction proper because 3,000 subscribers were residents of the forum state. The *Zippo* test, not without criticism,[422] has been followed in cases involving copyright, trademark, and other types of actions.[423]

Jurisdictional issues are even more complex at the international level. For example, in 2000, a Virginia federal district court refused to grant jurisdiction on plaintiff's claims for trademark infringement and violation of the Anticyber-squatting Consumer Protection Act against a California corporation with its principal place of business in Taiwan.[424] A French court, however, did not find jurisdiction an obstacle in *La Ligue Contre le Racisme et l'Antisémitisme v. Yahoo!* and held defendant in violation of Article R.645-1 of the French Penal Code, which prohibits the exhibition of Nazi memorabilia for sale. Yahoo! was found in violation by virtue of the fact that a French citizen accessing the www.yahoo.fr website could gain access to the auction portion of the www.yahoo.com website and see the public display of Nazi-related objects that were being auctioned by third-party users of Yahoo! The French court imposed a 10,000Fr fine on Yahoo! for each day that the images remained accessible to French users through the yahoo.fr website. The case brings to light another issue, namely enforcing a judgment rendered in a foreign court. Yahoo! refused to comply or pay the judgment and in 2001 filed suit in a California federal district court[425] seeking a declaration that the French court order was unenforceable. The district court held that the French order presented a real and immediate threat to the Yahoo!'s First Amendment rights for purposes of conferring jurisdiction, but that decision was reversed in 2004 by the Ninth Circuit, which determined that the defendants were not subject to personal jurisdiction under California's long-arm statute.[426] In February 2005, the Ninth Circuit ordered the case reheard en banc.[427]

In January 2006, while a majority of the en banc court concluded that the California federal district court did, in fact, have personal jurisdiction over the defendants, the three judges of the en banc court who as a panel had determined that the district court lacked such personal jurisdiction, joining with three other judges of the en banc court who determined that the action should be dismissed for lack of ripeness, together caused the en banc court to reverse the judgment of the district court and to remand with directions to dismiss the action without prejudice.[428]

Given that case law attempts to draw bright-line guidance for personal and long-arm jurisdiction issues, it appears safe to say that current jurisdictional guidelines are overly broad.[429] Accordingly, a party to an online arts transaction should be mindful of the possibility of being hauled into court in a state or even a country other than the one where he intended to conduct business.

Online Art Auctions, Sales, and Fraud

The ease and speed of click-and-purchase transactions have dramatically expanded the sale of artwork online in recent years.[430] Traditional bricks-and-mortar art galleries and auction houses, ecommerce-based start-ups, individual artists, and art dealers have all sought to capitalize on the sale of art over the Internet. Though the Internet has not so far proven especially fruitful for the sale of high-end works of art, there have been a number of individual sales exceeding the million-dollar mark[431] and lower transactional costs are becoming increasing attractive to sellers of mid-range priced works.[432] In any event, the sale of art on-line is a growing market.[433] As noted in chapter 4, online auctions do not always offer consignors and purchasers the same protections and assurances offered by their bricks-and-mortar counterparts. First, with respect to the consignor-auctioneer relationship, an online auctioneer generally has no duty to the consignor to determine whether the work is auctionable, to suggest a reserve price, or to provide expertise with respect to a work's authenticity. One court has in fact held that the sale of art by auction in an online trading forum like eBay is likely to yield a price that is per se fair.[434]

For the purchaser the perils can be even greater. The consignor is the only participant with access to the offered item. Unlike traditional auctions where the auction house serves as agent (and fiduciary) of the seller and the purchaser has a meaningful opportunity to inspect the work, online purchasers must rely exclusively on the consignor's written description of the work and any accompanying digital photographs. Reliance on the consignor's accuracy and veracity in description can be problematic, and because consignors never actually transfer possession of the work to the online auctioneer, the transaction remains a seller-to-buyer transaction, leaving the buyer generally bereft of any recourse vis-à-vis the auctioneer.

With so little protection available to purchasers and the relative anonymity consignors can maintain through fictitious screen names, the potential for abuse is clear. Occurrences of online fraud through false or misleading information are on the rise as evidenced by the creation of units in the FBI and Department of Justice to police such conduct,[435] as well as by a number of recent prosecutions by the government. In addition to false or misleading information, fraud during the bidding process in the form of "bid shielding" (where two or more bidders artificially inflate the auction price and the high bidder withdraws just before the close so that the lower bidder wins) and "shill bidding" (where false bids are entered to artificially drive up the price, usually for the benefit of the seller) has been prevalent in the online forum.

Despite the availability of other Internet venues, eBay has remained one of the preferred hubs for the sale of fraudulent art, and with 110 million items offered for sale at any given minute worldwide, it is not difficult to understand why.[436] The sale of fraudulent fine art on eBay[437] made international headlines yet again in 2008 with the launch of an investigation by the U.S. Department of Justice into an international fraud scheme to sell fine art prints primarily through the discount auction site.[438] Between July 1999 and October 2007, Oswaldo Aulestia-Bach of Barcelona, Spain; Elio Bonfiglioli of Monsummano, Italy; and Patrizia Soliani of Milan, Italy and Miami Beach, Florida distributed counterfeit art prints claiming they were from artists like Picasso, Chagall, Dali, Lichtenstein, and Miro. With knowledge of the counterfeit goods, and even of forged artists' signatures on a number of the works, several indivdiuals—Jerome Bengis of Coral Springs, Florida, principal in the Bengis Fine Art gallery; Michael Zabrin, a Northbrook, Illinois art dealer; Leon Amiel, Jr. of New York City, principal in Glass Inter Corp.; and James Kennedy, a Florida art dealer—resold the prints.

In March 2008, with the aid of the Spanish police, the Department of Justice announced that seven defendants, three of whom were Europeans, were being charged with federal criminal charges for the production and sale of counterfeit, limited edition fine art prints. The fraud ring affected buyers in the United States, Europe, Japan, Australia, and Canada, and resulted in more than $5 million dollars in proceeds.

The scheme was carefully planned, and defendants collectively scammed thousands of innocent buyers. At one point, Amiel distributed 2,500 fake Calder prints and 600 Chagall fake "Exodus" prints to one dealer. On eBay alone, Kennedy executed over sixty-one successful transactions and obtained more than $39,000 from the fraudulent sales, and Zabrin conducted 280 successful transactions through his eBay accounts "Fineartmasters" and "ZFineartmasters." The event that prompted the investigation was the receipt of an email in 2005 about one of the eBay accounts involved in the scheme by a fraud investigator on eBay's in-house Fraud Investigation Team.[439] The investigator sent the email to the FBI in Chicago, and on May 6, 2006, agents from the U.S. Postal Service and the FBI executed a search warrant on Zabrin's house.

Zabrin was often described as "affable" and "able to charm," and even the government was not immune to his deception: During the time the government was obtaining his cooperation to help convict other members of the ring, Zabrin was still committing crimes—for example, he was charged with retail theft in August 2006.

Possibly most disturbing is the fact that Zabrin was a seasoned art fraud criminal who had already served a prison term, nearly a decade earlier, for the same crime of selling fraudulent art to unsuspecting buyers. In 1992, as a result of a federal investigation called "Operation Bogart, Zabrin was found guilty of knowingly selling more than $800,000 in counterfeit fine art prints supplied by Amiel.[440] Though initially set to serve longer, Zabrin served a mere year in prison, a deal provided in exchange for his cooperation in a separate art case also being prosecuted at the time. According to prosecutors, in 1999, a year after he was no longer under supervised release, Zabrin had returned to selling fraudulent artwork.[441] In January 2010, Zabrin admitted to selling more than $1 million in counterfeit prints from 1999 to 2007. Taking Zabrin's history of criminal activity into consideration, the court sentenced him to nine years in prison.[442]

Irrespective of whether an online auction house is deemed a venue or an auctioneer, courts have held that it enjoys the broad immunity of an "interactive computer service provider" under the Communications Decency Act[443] and is thereby immune from liability based on the fraudulent sale of items by its users.[444] Under the CDA, an interactive computer service provider that does not provide information content cannot be held liable for information originating from a third-party user of the service. That immunity preempts any state law claim that would be inconsistent with the CDA, such as defamation claims and the like.[445] The breadth of the immunity is evidenced in the 2000 case of *Stoner v.*

eBay, Inc.,[446] where a California state court held eBay immune from liability for bootleg sales of sound recordings even though eBay had constructive knowledge of the illegal activity. Citing *Zeran*[447] and *Doe,*[448] the court stated that "notice of postings which indicate illegality does not defeat immunity."[449]

The immunity available to interactive service providers with respect to auctions has, however, failed to shield them with respect to violations of laws outside the United States.[450] Buyers must exercise the utmost caution when engaging in a private art auction online, because as previously discussed, the difference between the expectation of purchasing a real work instead of a fake reproduction is an unimaginable division.

NOTES TO CHAPTER 18

1. Paul Crowther, *Ontology and Aesthetics of Digital Art*, J. Aesthetics and Art Criticism, Vol. 66, No. 2 (Spring 2008), 161–70, www.jstor.org/stable/40206323.

2. For a discussion of the history of the digital art movement and its rise in prominence, *see generally* Carly Berwick, *The New New-Media Blitz*, ARTnews (Apr. 2001), *available at* www.artnews.com/2001/04/01/the-new-new-media-blitz/ (last visited Feb. 13, 2012).

3. Royal Collection news, www.royalcollection.org.uk/default.asp?action=article&ID=148 (last visited Feb. 29, 2012).

4. The *Guardian* has a short interview with Levine that can be viewed online. *See* www.guardian.co.uk/artanddesign/video/2010/apr/14/photograph-queen-chris-levine (last visited Feb. 29, 2012). Levine also provides a quick four-minute clip on the documentary about shooting the portrait that shows how the images were processed and edited on the computer. *See* www.chrislevine.com/wd/?page_id=14 (last visited Feb. 29, 2012).

5. *Id.*

6. Charlotte Cripps, *Chris Levine: Light Fantastic*, Independent, Oct. 27, 2011, *available at* www.independent.co.uk/arts-entertainment/art/features/chris-levine-light-fantastic-2376251.html (last visited Feb. 29, 2012).

7. Jorge Colombo's digital prints can be viewed at www.20x200.com/artist/131-jorge-colombo (last visited Feb. 23, 2012).

8. *See*, Sarah Kennedy & Janelle Grace, Digital Finger Drawing at Print Studio with Jorge Colombo. http://www.moma.org/explore/inside_out/2012/02/06/digital-finger-drawing-at-print-studio-with-jorge-colombo/ (last visited Feb. 24, 2012).

9. Recent examples include the Victoria and Albert Museum in London presented in December 2009 the digital art exhibition "Decode: Design Sensations," and La Gaîté lyrique gallery, created by the City of Paris, centers all their programming around digital art and new media art. To visit "Decode: Design Sensations" see: http://www.vam.ac.uk/microsites/decode/ (last visited Feb. 29, 2012). To visit La Gaîté lyrique gallery, see: http://www.gaite-lyrique.net/en/informations-pratiques/who-are-we-0 (last visited Feb. 29, 2012).

10. For more information on "The Space" see: http://www.artscouncil.org.uk/funding/apply-for-funding/strategic-funding/thespace/ (last visited Feb. 23, 2012).

11. Google Art Project, see: http://www.googleartproject.com/ (last visited April. 23, 2012).

12. *Id.*

13. The technology that Google uses in its well-known street-view feature is what makes the virtual tour feature possible.

14. Patricia Cohen, *Art is Long; Copyrights Can Even Be Longer*, N.Y. Times (April 25, 2012).

15. *Id.*

16. Alice Pfeiffer, *Digital Creations Come of Act*, International Herald Tribune (Sept. 5, 2009).

17. *See, e.g.,* Final Report of the National Commission of New Technological Uses of New Technologies (CONTU Report) 44 (1979) (listing numerous ways computers can be used in creating works of art).

18. *See, e.g.,* Eldred v. Ashcroft, 123 S. Ct. 769 (2003); Lawrence Lessig, Free Culture (Penguin Press 2004).

19. For our purposes, "digital art" is defined as artworks produced using digital technology, encompassing fields of activity including computer animation, digital video, interactive media and computer music. *See generally* Christiane Paul, Digital Art (2d ed. 2008). According to Paul, providing a definition for "digital art" is difficult, especially since the definition is constantly subject to revision.

20. Copyright Act of 1976, 17 U.S.C. §§ 106-07.

21. The Statute of Anne (8 Anne, c. 19) was the first copyright law, enacted in England in 1710 and entitled "An Act for the Encouragement of Learning...." *See generally* L. Ray Patterson & Stanley W. Lindberg, The Nature of Copyright, A Law of Users' Rights (1991).

22. U.S. Const. art. I, § 8, cl.8.

23. H.R. Rep. No. 100-609 at 32-34 (1998); *see also* Mazer v. Stein, 347 U.S. 201, 219 (1954) ("The economic philosophy behind the clause empowering Congress to grant patents and copyrights in the conviction that encouragement of individual effort by personal gain is the best way to advance public welfare. . . .").

24. Jeanne English Sullivan, *Copyright for Visual Art in the Digital Age: A Modern Adventure in Wonderland*, 14 Cardozo Arts & Ent. L.J. 563, 586 (1996).

25. David Nimmer, *Access Denied*, 2007 Utah L. Rev. 769 (2007). "An entirely different dynamic now arises in the Internet era. The domain of general publication is no longer limited to those who convince a publishing house of the marketability of their words. Instead, self-publishing has emerged with a vengeance."

26. *Id.* Nimmer uses a hypothetical of a website that provides a paid service of posting any screenplay on its service that makes it automatically accessible to relevant members in the film industry. In this example, Nimmer points out that proving access is reasonable, however, in that same line of reasoning, there may be no claims left for dispute after the plaintiff attempts to prove how the elements of his submission differentiates from the elements of the thousands of other submissions in the service.

27. Am. Civil Liberties Union v. Reno, 929 F. Supp. 824, 830 (E.D. Pa. 1996) (the Internet is "not a physical or tangible entity, but rather a giant network which interconnects innumerable smaller groups of linked computer networks"; it is made up of computers and computer networks owned by governmental and public institutions, nonprofit organizations, and private citizens; "[t]he resulting whole is a . . . global medium of communications—or 'cyberspace'— that links people, institutions, corporations, and governments around the world").

28. *See* Playboy Enters., Inc. v. Sanfilippo, 1998 U.S. Dist. LEXIS 5125 (Mar. 25, 1998) (awarding $500 on each of 7475 incidents of where defendant scanned plaintiff's copyrighted photographs and uploaded them to a website for damages totaling $3,737,500).

29. Motion for summary judgment regarding the right to use the programs and files comprising a website was denied where plaintiff had an oral agreement with defendant web designers to design and maintain plaintiff's website. Holtzbrinck Publ'g Holdings v. Vyne Communications, Inc., 2000 WL 502860, 2000 U.S. Dist. LEXIS 5444 (S.D.N.Y. Apr. 26, 2000). *See also* Conwell v. Gray Loon Outdoor Mktg. Grp., 906 N.E.2d 805 (Ind. 2009); Kirby v. AG of N.M., 2011 U.S. App. LEXIS 19575 (10th Cir. N.M. Sept. 19, 2011).

30. Tiffany Design, Inc. v. Reno-Tahoe Specialty, Inc., 55 F. Supp. 2d 1113, 1124 (D. Nev. 1999) (defendant's creation of a scanned image and loading it into a computer constituted a violation of plaintiffs' exclusive right to reproduce copyrighted works under the Copyright Act). *See also* Greenberg v. Nat'l Geographic Soc'y, 533 F.3d 1244 (11th Cir. 2008) (digitized photographs, as part of an electronic collection of magazines stored and distributed on CD-ROMs, were privileged as original revisions under the Copyright Act).

31. Teter v. Glass Onion, Inc., 723 F. Supp. 2d 1138 (W.D. Mo. 2010).

32. Intellectual Prop. Reserve, Inc. v. Utah Lighthouse Ministry, Inc., 75 F. Supp. 2d 1290, 1295 (D. Utah 1999) ("When a person browses a website . . . a copy . . . is made in the computer's random access memory (RAM), to permit viewing of the material. And in making a copy, even a temporary one, the person who browsed infringed the copyright.").

33. Friedman v. Guetta, 2011 U.S. Dist. LEXIS 66532 (C.D. Cal. May 27, 2011) ("Here, Defendant admits that he obtained the Photograph on the internet and used a digital copy of that image"). The court was referring to downloading the digital image from the Internet. *See* Plaintiff's Opposition to Defendant's Motion in Limine No. 1 to Exclude Evidence of Indirect Profits: "This is a case where Defendant downloaded one of Plaintiff's photographs from the internet, and reproduced it without authorization in works that he sold to the public."

34. *See, e.g.,* Costar Realty Info., Inc. v. Field, 737 F. Supp. 2d 496, 507 (D. Md. 2010).

35. *Id.*

36. *Friedman,* 2011 U.S. Dist. LEXIS 66532, at *3.

37. *Id.* at *1.

38. *Id.* at *15.

39. *Id.* at *19.

40. Grady v. Bremer, 2012 U.S. Dist. LEXIS 13021 (D. Colo. Feb. 2, 2012) (defendant downloaded plaintiff's copyrighted photographs from plaintiff's website, then uploaded the photographs to several other websites that allowed users to download the photographs without compensating the plaintiff; court entered default judgment against defendant for a total of $544,440.00 in damages plus interest.).

41. For example, a common business practice has become to harvest information about users by tracking the websites they view. Companies employ algorithms designed for Internet crawling, such as Google Analytics, that begin tracking and harvesting information about the user from the moment the user views a website. Such trackers can discern the type of hardware device, the company that created the device, the length of time spent on each page of the website, and the location (including the building) of the user accessing the web platform.

42. 1 WILLISTON ON CONTRACTS § 1:5 (4th ed.) ("An express contract is a contract the terms of which are stated by the parties; an implied contract is a contract the terms of which are not explicitly stated. The legal effect of the two types of contracts are [sic] identical[.]").

43. Agence France Presse v. Morel, 769 F. Supp. 2d 295 (S.D.N.Y. 2011).

44. Also known as a "microblogging" site.

45. *Agence France Presse,* 769 F. Supp. 2d at 298.

46. *Id.* at 299 (Twitpic TOS: "By uploading your photos to Twitpic, you give Twitpic permission to use or distribute your photos on Twitpic.com or affiliated sites. All images uploaded are copyright © their respective owners.").

47. To post text, pictures, or videos to Twitter is to "tweet" it.

48. *Agence France Presse,* 769 F. Supp. 2d at 299.

49. *Id.*

50. *Id.* at 300.

51. *Id.* at 303.

52. *Id.*

53. Teter v. Glass Onion, Inc., 723 F. Supp. 2d 1138 (W.D. Mo. 2010).

54. *Id.* at 1144.

55. *Id.*

56. *Id.* at 1145 ("(I) copyright infringement, (II) false designation of origin, (III) unfair competition, (IV) trademark infringement (V) trademark dilution, and (VI) violation of the Visual Arts Rights Act (VARA)").

57. *Id.* at 1146.

58. *Id.* at 1147 (citing Effects Assocs. v. Cohen, 908 F.2d 555, 558-59 (9th Cir. 1990)).

59. *Id.* at 1150.

60. *Id.* at 1149. Defendants sent an email to SFFA asking if digital images of the artwork could be used on their revamped website. Teter's daughter on behalf of SFFA responded: "I wanted to answer your question about your website makeover: Yes, use any images from Summer Field's website."

61. *Id.* at 1150.

62. *Id.* at 1152.

63. Greenberg v. Nat'l Geographic Soc'y, 244 F.3d 1267 (11th Cir.), *cert. denied,* 534 U.S. 951 (2001).

64. N.Y. Times Co. v. Tasini, 533 U.S. 483 (2001).

65. *Id.* at 484.

66. Greenberg v. Nat'l Geographic Soc'y, 533 F.3d 1244 (11th Cir. 2008).

67. *Id.* at 1258.

68. *Id.* at 1257.

69. *Id.* at 1251.

70. *Id.* at 1252.

71. *Id.* at 1253.

72. *Id.*

73. *Id.* at 1255, 1256.
74. *Id.* at 1252.
75. Faulkner v. Nat'l Geographic Enters., 409 F.3d 26 (2d Cir. 2005), *aff'g in part, rev'g in part, and remanding,* 294 F. Supp. 2d 523 (S.D.N.Y. 2003).
76. The Second Circuit affirmed, except for issues relating to seven photographs that were subject to express contractual provisions preserving electronic rights in the copyright owners. As to these, the Second Circuit reversed and remanded.
77. *Faulkner,* 409 F.3d at 30.
78. *Id.*
79. *Id.* at 34 (citing H.R. Rep. No. 94-1476, 94th Cong., 2d Sess. 122-23 (1976)).
80. *Id.* at 35.
81. *Id.*
82. *Id.* at 37.
83. Faulkner v. Nat'l Geographic Soc'y, 576 F. Supp. 2d 609, 611 (S.D.N.Y. 2008).
84. *Id.* at 615-20. ("He concludes, on the basis of various industry sources and unsubstantiated assertions . . . ."; "Indeed, this entire portion of his opinion is constructed on a base of sand. It starts with an unsubstantiated assumption concerning an initial press run limitation and proceeds by nothing more than guesses about multiple renewals or modifications that, in reality, are excuses to increase his $1,350 base fee at a compound rate, each baseless step based on the preceding guess."; "[T]here is nothing in this record to suggest that figures such as these are at all reasonable.")
85. *Id.* at 614, 620.
86. *E.g.,* Voltage Pictures, LLC v. Does 1-5,000, 818 F. Supp. 2d 28 (D.D.C. 2011). A user that seeds files allows other users, normally called peers, to upload those files from him. In *Voltage Pictures,* the court denied motions to dismiss and quash subpoenas seeking disclosure of anonymous putative users who seeded and distributed plaintiff's copyrighted film *The Hurt Locker.*
87. Marobie-FL, Inc. v. National Ass'n of Fire Equipment Distributors, 983 F. Supp. 1167 (plaintiff's motion for summary judgment on copyright infringement granted; issue of damages was sent to trial, and jury returned a verdict finding no damages). A motion for a new trial was denied. 2002 WL 226864 (N.D. Ill 2002). The same result, however, was not reached where licensee of clip-art brought a declaratory action against copyright owner licensor for copyright violation. Xoom, Inc. v. Imageline, Inc., 323 F.3d 279 (4th Cir. 2003) (holding copyright owner's registration of compilations and derivative works was sufficient to permit infringement action on underlying parts.).
88. For an excellent discussion on digital exhaustion and first sale in an increasing digital marketplace, see Aaron Perzanowski & Jason Schultz, *Digital Exhaustion,* 58 UCLA L. Rev. 889, 904 (2011).
89. *E.g.,* Disney Enters., Inc. v. Hotfile Corp., 798 F. Supp. 2d 1303 (S.D. Fla. 2011); Agence France Presse v. Morel, 769 F. Supp. 2d 295 S.D.N.Y. 2011); Wolk v. Kodak Imaging Network, Inc., 2012 WL 11270 (S.D.N.Y. Jan. 3, 2012).
90. *E.g.,* Harvester, Inc. v. Rule Joy Trammell + Rubio, LLC, 716 F. Supp. 2d 428 (E.D. Va. 2010) (defendant hired third party to scan plaintiff's architectural drawings into electronic PDF files then upload them to defendant's website; court denied defendant's motion for summary judgment, declaring that "[t]he fact that Rule Joy commissioned a professional scanning service to perform the electronic copying of Commonwealth's Architectural Drawings, as opposed to physically placing the documents in a scanner on its own, does not cut off exposure to copyright infringement liability"); Corbis Corp. v. Starr, 2009 WL 2901308 (Sept. 2, 2009) (defendant uploaded plaintiff's pictures to its servers and a third-party website; court granted plaintiff's motion for summary judgment on direct copyright infringement); *see also* Playboy Enters. v. Russ Hardenburgh, Inc., 982 F. Supp. 503 (N.D. Ohio 1997) (defendant scanned photographs and uploaded them to his subscription-based site, where they were then available for download by paid users; court found defendant liable for direct copyright infringement, citing defendant's persistent overseeing of the company's operations and control over the site's content).

91. Gershwin Publ'g Corp. v. Columbia Artists Mgmt., Inc., 443 F.2d 1159, 1162 (2d Cir. 1971).

92. Wolk v. Kodak Imaging Network, Inc., 2012 WL 11270, at *24, 840 F. Supp. 2d 724 (S.D.N.Y. Jan. 3, 2012). *See also* MGM Studios Inc. v. Grokster, Ltd., 545 U.S. 913 (2005).

93. *Wolk*, 2012 WL 11270, at *25.

94. *Id.*

95. Metro-Goldwyn-Mayer Studios, Inc. v. Grokster Ltd., 125 S. Ct. 2764, 2776 (2005).

96. Social media sites like Flickr and Facebook expressly permit downloading photographs present on the website via a download button, while sites like Tumblr, Twitter, Instagram, and Pininterest are wholly centered around text, video, and photo sharing.

97. Agence France Presse v. Morel, 769 F. Supp. 2d 295 (S.D.N.Y. 2011).

98. "Photomorel" is Daniel Morel's username, which in Twitter is also known as a "twitter handle."

99. *Agence France Presse*, 769 F. Supp. 2d at 299.

100. *Id.* at 300.

101. *Id.*

102. *Id.* at 301.

103. *Id.*

104. *Id.* at 298.

105. Third-party defendants were Getty Images (US), Inc., CBS Broadcasting, Inc., Turner Broadcasting System, Inc. (for CNN's use of Morel's photographs), and unnamed AFP and Getty licensees. While American Broadcasting Company (ABC) was a named defendant, ABC and Morel reached an agreement prior to this decision.

106. *Agence France Presse*, 769 F. Supp. 2d at 298. The court dismissed the vicarious infringement claim against CBS for failing to show a direct financial interest: "With respect to vicarious infringement, Morel fails to allege facts supporting his claim that CBS had a direct financial interest in their affiliates' exploitation of his images."

107. *Id.* at 304.

108. *See* 17 U.S.C.A. § 1202(a):

> (a) False copyright management information.—No person shall knowingly and with the intent to induce, enable, facilitate, or conceal infringement—
> (1) provide copyright management information that is false, or
> (2) distribute or import for distribution copyright management information that is false.

109. *See* 17 U.S.C.A. § 1202(c):

> (c) Definition.—As used in this section, the term "copyright management information" means any of the following information conveyed in connection with copies or phonorecords of a work or performances or displays of a work, including in digital form, except that such term does not include any personally identifying information about a user of a work or of a copy, phonorecord, performance, or display of a work:
> (1) The title and other information identifying the work, including the information set forth on a notice of copyright.
> (2) The name of, and other identifying information about, the author of a work.
> (3) The name of, and other identifying information about, the copyright owner of the work, including the information set forth in a notice of copyright....

110. *Agence France Presse*, 769 F. Supp. 2d at 305.

111. *Id.* at 305, 306.

112. Dastar Corp. v. Twentieth Century Fox Film Corp., 539 U.S. 23 (2003).

113. *Id.* at 27, 28.

114. *Id.* at 33.

115. *Agence France Presse*, 769 F. Supp. 2d at 307.

116. *Id.*
117. Denny Mfg. Co. v. Drops & Props, Inc., 2011 U.S. Dist. LEXIS 60155 (S.D. Ala. June 1, 2011).
118. *Id.*
119. *Id.* at *1. *See also* Second Amended Complaint at 14.
120. *Denny Mfg. Co.*, 2011 U.S. Dist. LEXIS 60155, at *2.
121. *Id.*
122. *Id.* at *3, *6.
123. *Id* at *3.
124. *Id.* at *4, *6, *10.
125. *Id.* at *7-9.
126. *Id.* at *7, *8.
127. 17 U.S.C. § 106(5).
128. Teter v. Glass Onion, Inc., 723 F. Supp. 2d 1138 (W.D. Mo. 2010); Cohen v. United States, 98 Fed. Cl. 156 (2011) (plaintiff alleged his rights of display, reproduction, and distribution were violated by the U.S. government by displaying plaintiff's copyrighted pictures on an official government website).
129. Perfect 10, Inc. v. Amazon.com, Inc., 508 F.3d 1146 (9th Cir. Cal. 2007).
130. *Id.* at 1156, 1176 ("The process by which the webpage directs a user's browser to incorporate content from different computers into a single window is referred to as 'in-line linking.'"). On remand from this 2007 appellate decision, the district court denied plaintiff's motion for preliminary injunctive relief for alleged copyright infringement through the company's image search and caching, its blog service, and its practice of forwarding takedown notices to the site chillingeffects.org. In 2011, on appeal, the Ninth Circuit reaffirmed the lower court's holding and its 2007 decision. *See* Perfect 10, Inc. v. Google, Inc., 653 F.3d 976 (9th Cir. Cal. 2011), *cert denied*, 132 S. Ct. 1713 (2012).
131. Teter v. Glass Onion, Inc., 723 F. Supp. 2d 1138 (W.D. Mo. 2010).
132. *Id.* at 1146.
133. *Id.* at 1150.
134. *Id.* at 115-1152.
135. *Id.* at 1153.
136. *Id.* at 1153. In direct reference to the decision in *Perfect 10*, the *Teter* court stated: "Unlike the scenario where a general internet search engine "transforms the [thumbnail] image into a pointer directing a user to a source of information," GOI's use of the images is limited to an informative and promotional function on the Gallery's website-to show customers the Teter works available at the Gallery."
137. *Id.*
138. *See* www.AfterSherrieLevine.com and www.AfterWalkerEvans.com (last visited Mar. 26, 2012).
139. Reena Jana, *Is It Art, or Memorex?*, www.wired.com/culture/lifestyle/news/2001/05/43902 (last visited Mar. 26, 2012).
140. While there is not yet a case on point for fine art, courts have addressed originality for other digital creations, including digital wire-frame models of cars. *See* Meshwerks, Inc. v. Toyota Motor Sales U.S.A., Inc., 528 F.3d 1258, 1265 (10th Cir. 2008). (plaintiff's digital car models failed the standard for originality, because "Meshwerks' digital wire-frame computer models depict Toyota's vehicles without any individualizing features: they are untouched by a digital paintbrush; they are not depicted in front of a palm tree, whizzing down the open road, or climbing up a mountainside").
141. N.Y. Times Co. v. Tasini, 533 U.S. 483 (2001); *see also* Lee v. A.R.T. Co., 125 F.3d 580 (7th Cir. 1997).
142. *See, e.g.*, Bridgeman Art Library, Ltd. v. Corel Corp., 36 F. Supp. 2d 191, 196 (S.D.N.Y. 1999) (holding "only a distinguishable variation—something beyond technical skill--will render [a] reproduction original.... [This] distinguishable variation, moreover, is not supplied by a change of medium, as a production of a work of art in a different medium cannot by itself constitute the originality required for copyright protection."); *Lee*, 125 F.3d 580.

143. Pub. L. No. 105-304, 112 Stat. 2860 (Oct. 28, 1998).

144. The Digital Millennium Copyright Act of 1998 U.S. Copyright Office Summary ("DMCA Summary"), *available through links at* www.copyright.gov/laws (last visited Mar. 26, 2012).

145. All of the provisions of the DMCA discussed herein became effective on the date of enactment, October 28, 1998, with the exception of 1201(a)(1)(A) dealing with the circumvention of access control measures (discussed at pages 1951-1954), which became effective October 28, 2000.

146. 17 U.S.C. §§ 1203, 1204.

147. 17 U.S.C. § 1201(a).

148. 17 U.S.C. § 1201(a)(3)(A).

149. 17 U.S.C. § 1201(b).

150. 17 U.S.C. § 1202(a), (b).

151. 17 U.S.C. § 1201(d).

152. 17 U.S.C. § 1201(e).

153. 17 U.S.C. § 1201(f).

154. 17 U.S.C. § 1201(g).

155. *See, e.g.,* Bernard E. Nodzon, *Free Speech in the Digital Economy: An Analysis of How Intellectual Property Rights Have Been Elevated at the Expense of Free Speech,* 36 J. MARSHALL L. REV. 109 (2002); Cassandra Imfeld, *Playing Fair With Fair Use? The Digital Millennium Copyright Act's Impact on Encryption Researchers and Academicians,* 8 COMM. L. & POL'Y 111 (2003); Joseph P. Liu, *The DMCA and the Regulation of Scientific Research,* 18 BERKELEY TECH. L.J. 501 (2003); Thomas A. Mitchell, *Copyright, Congress and Constitutionality: How the Digital Millennium Copyright Act Goes Too Far,* 79 NOTRE DAME L. REV. 2115 (2004). Robert C. Denicola, *Access Controls, Rights Protection, and Circumvention: Interpreting the Digital Millennium Copyright Act to Preserve Noninfringing Use,* 31 COLUM. J.L. & ARTS 209 (2008).

156. 17 U.S.C. § 512(k)(1)(A). Courts may call service providers, either online service providers (OSPs), Internet service providers (ISPs), or both, but the name does not affect the service provider's eligibility for the DMCA's safe harbor provisions (a)-(d) (see e.g., Ellison v. Robertson, 357 F.3d 1072, 1078-1079 (9th Cir. 2004), the company AOL is referred to as both an internet service provider and an online service provider). Traditionally, ISPs referred to Internet access providers like Comcast and Verizon, which are mere conduits to Internet connectivity and qualified for § 512(a), while OSPs referred to providers of online services like YouTube and Twitter, which tended to qualify for § 512(c). As previously stated, courts do not unvaryingly recognize this differentiation anymore. To maintain uniformity throughout the text, we will use the term ISP only.

157. *Id.* Because website owners generally need to use a commercial web server in order to display their site to visitors, if infringing content becomes available on websites that are hosted by those commercial web servers, those servers can be seen as materially contributing to the infringing activity of others because they provide the virtual space for users to infringe.

158. An ISP may also bring suit under the DMCA without being a copyright owner provided it has suffered injury by one of the prohibited measures in Sections 1201 or 1202. This, however, is outside the scope of this chapter and will not be discussed further. [17 U.S.C. § 1203; see e.g., Comcast of Illinois X, LLC. v. Hightech Electronics, Inc., 2004 WL 1718522 (N.D. Ill. July 28, 2004].

159. 17 U.S.C. § 512(a)-(f).

160. The thundering amount of news concerning the DMCA now is undoubtedly the potential copyright-lawsuit storm about to hit the currently fastest growing website Pinterest. The social media sharing site allows users to upload to it any digital picture, image, video, blog and digital artwork a user has access to on the Internet, and by sharing, any user on the website may view, comment, share, and save the post (see e.g., Marie Szaniszlo, *Pinup site poses challenges: Pinterest making changes to address copyright infringement,* available at: http://bostonherald. com/business/technology/general/view/20220325pinup_site_poses_challenges_pinterest_ making_changes_to_address_copyright_infringement (last visited, Mar. 28, 2012).

161. Ellison, *supra* note 156. 357 F.3d 1072.

162. *Id.* at 1077.

163. CoStar Group, Inc. v. LoopNet, Inc., 373 F.3d 544, 553 (4th Cir. 2004).

164. *Id.* at 555.

165. 17 U.S.C. § 512(c).

166. Viacom Int'l, Inc. v. YouTube, Inc., 2012 WL 1130851 (2d Cir. April 5, 2012).

167. *Screen Gems–Columbia Music, Inc. v. Mark–Fi Records, Inc.,* 256 F. Supp. 399, 403 (S.D.N.Y.1966) (Weinfeld, J.).

168. *Id.*

169. Agence France Presse v. Morel, 769 F. Supp. 2d 295, 304 (S.D.N.Y. 2011) (quoting Matthew Bender & Co., Inc. v. West Publ'g Co., 158 F.3d 693, 706 (2d Cir. 1998)).

170. Columbia Pictures Indus. v. Fung, 2009 U.S. Dist. LEXIS 122661 (C.D. Cal. Dec. 21, 2009) (while court expressly refrained from deciding on the contributory and vicarious liability claims, the court found that the overwhelming evidence of inducement and either actual knowledge or willful ignorance of copyright infringement rendered the ISP ineligible for safe harbor). The Ninth Circuit has also held that the amount of impact contributory and vicarious liability claims will have on an ISPs safe harbor eligibility is determined on a case-by-case basis. *See* A&M Records v. Napster, Inc., 239 F.3d 1004, 1025 (9th Cir. Cal. 2001) (contributory and vicarious liability do not per se render an ISP ineligible for safe harbor protection); UMG Recordings, Inc. v. Shelter Capital Partners, LLC, 667 F.3d 1022 (9th Cir. Cal. 2011) ("Although in some cases service providers subject to vicarious liability will be excluded from the § 512(c) safe harbor, in others they will not."). The Second Circuit affirmed a lower court's reasoning that "a finding of safe harbor application necessarily protects a defendant from all affirmative claims for monetary relief." *See* Viacom Int'l, Inc. v. YouTube, Inc., 2012 WL 1130851 (2d Cir. April 5, 2012).

171. Wolk v. Kodak Imaging Network, Inc., 2012 WL 11270, at *24, 840 F. Supp. 2d 724 (S.D.N.Y. Jan. 3, 2012).

172. *Id.*

173. *Id.*, 2012 WL 11270, at *4.

174. *Id.* at *5.

175. *Id.* at *7.

176. *Id.*

177. *Id.*

178. 17 U.S.C. §§ 504(a)(2), (c)(1) and (c)(2).

179. *See* Cartoon Network LP v. CSC Holdings, Inc., 536 F.3d 121, 130–31 (2d Cir. 2008);

180. *See* Twin Peaks Prods., Inc. v. Publications Int'l, Ltd., 996 F.2d 1366, 1382 (2d Cir. 1993).

181. *Wolk,* 2012 WL 11270, at *14, *15.

182. *Id.* at *16. ("Because the Kodak Defendants cannot be held liable for direct infringement, the issues of whether they fall under the DMCA's "safe harbor" provision, whether their alleged infringement was "willful" under the statute and whether Wolk is entitled to damages per work of art infringed need not be reached. Similarly, although the Kodak Defendants dispute whether the Plaintiff has properly asserted a claim of vicarious liability against Eastman Kodak, there is no need to address this issue because the Plaintiff has not established liability on the part of either of the Kodak Defendants.")

183. 17 U.S.C. § 512(c)(1)(A).

184. 17 U.S.C. § 512(c)(1)(B).

185. 17 U.S.C. § 512(c)(1)(C).

186. 17. U.S.C. § 512(c)(3)(A). The notice must: (1) be in writing and signed by the copyright holder or copyright holder's agent, (2) identify the work or provide a representative list of works that are allegedly being infringed, (3) identify the infringing content or provide sufficient information so that the ISP can locate the infringing content, (4) provide the complaining party's contact information, (5) state that the complaining party believes in good faith that the content is infringing, (6) state that the information in the notification is accurate under the penalty of perjury and that the complaining party is authorized to act on behalf of the copyright holder if the complaining party is not the copyright holder himself.

187. 17 U.S.C. § 512(c) & (k)(1)(B); *see* IO Grp., Inc. v. Veoh Networks, Inc., 586 F. Supp. 2d 1132, 1142–43 (N.D. Cal. 2008); Viacom Int'l, Inc. v. YouTube, Inc., 718 F. Supp. 2d 514, 518 (S.D.N.Y.2010).

188. Wolk v. Kodak Imaging Network, Inc., 2012 WL 11270, at *16, 840 F. Supp. 2d 724 (S.D.N.Y. Jan. 3, 2012).

189. *Id.*, 2012 WL 11270, at *17.

190. 17 U.S.C. §512 (i) & (c).

191. *Wolk*, 2012 WL 11270, at *17, *18.

192. *Id.* at *19, *20.

193. *Id.* at *21. The court used the Ninth Circuit's holding in *Perfect 10* that stated absent evidence of subscriptions being affected by infringement, a plaintiff could not infer that a service provider receives direct financial benefit simply by providing access to the infringing material. *See* Perfect 10, Inc. v. CCBill LLC, 488 F.3d 1102 (9th Cir. 2007).

194. *Wolk*, 2012 WL 11270, at *3,*4, *5.

195. Arista Records, Inc. v. MP3Board, Inc., 2002 WL 1997918, 2002 U.S. Dist. LEXIS 16165 (S.D.N.Y. Aug. 29, 2002).

196. ALS Scan, Inc. v. Remarq Cmtys., Inc., 239 F.3d 619 (4th Cir. 2001).

197. Viacom Int'l Inc. v. YouTube, Inc., 718 F. Supp. 2d 514 (S.D.N.Y. 2010); Capitol Records, Inc. v. MP3tunes, LLC, 2011 WL 5104616 (S.D.N.Y. Oct. 25, 2011).

198. Hendrickson v. eBay, Inc., 165 F. Supp. 2d 1082 (C.D. Cal. 2001).

199. Rosen v. Hosting Services, Inc., 771 F. Supp. 2d 1219 (2010).

200. UMG Recordings, Inc. v. Shelter Capital Partners LLC, 667 F.3d 1022 (9th Cir. 2011).

201. *In re* Aimster Copyright Litig., 334 F.3d 643 (7th Cir. 2003), *cert denied*, 540 U.S. 1107 (2004).

202. CoStar Group, Inc. v. LoopNet, Inc., 373 F.3d 544, 553 (4th Cir. 2004).

203. Vicarious infringement differs from contributory infringement in that a vicarious infringer "has the right and ability to supervise the infringing activity and also has a direct financial interest in such activities." A&M Records, Inc. v. Napster, Inc., 239 F.3d 1004 (9th Cir. 2001), *as amended* (Apr. 3, 2001) (citing Fonovisa, Inc. v. Cherry Auction, Inc., 76 F.3d 259 (9th Cir. 1996)); Gershwin Publ'g Corp. v. Columbia Artists Mgmt., Inc., 443 F.2d 1159 (2d Cir. 1971).

204. The DMCA enables copyright holders to subpoena an ISP engaged in storing copyrighted material on its servers, but not against an ISP that is only acting as a conduit for data transferred between two Internet users. Under 17 U.S.C. § 512(A), an ISP serves as a data conduit when it merely transmits, routes, or provides connections for the transmission of online content or when it transiently stores content in the course of performing these functions. As such, a subpoena may not be issued to an ISP acting as a conduit for peer-to-peer file sharing, which does not involve the storage of infringing material on the ISP's server in order to assist copyright holders in gaining access to the identity of the direct infringing user. *See* UMG Recordings, Inc. v. Shelter Capital Partners, LLC, 667 F.3d 1022, 1035 (9th Cir. Cal. 2011).

205. 17 U.S.C. § 512(h).

206. Motion to quash granted: Maximized Living, Inc. v. Google, Inc., 2011 WL 6749017 (N.D. Cal. 2011); London-Sire Records, Inc. v. Doe 1, 542 F. Supp. 2d 153 (D. Mass. 2008); Motion to quash denied: Voltage Pictures, LLC v. Doe, 2011 U.S. Dist. LEXIS 50787 (D.D.C. May 12, 2011); Third Degree Films, Inc. v. Doe, 2011 U.S. Dist. LEXIS 148676 (D. Md. Dec. 28, 2011); Raw Films, Ltd. v. Does, 2012 U.S. Dist. LEXIS 41645 (E.D. Pa. Mar. 23, 2012); K-Beech, Inc. v. Doe, 2011 U.S. Dist. LEXIS 136757 (D. Md. Nov. 29, 2011); Collins v. Doe, 2011 U.S. Dist. LEXIS 129088 (D. Md. Nov. 8, 2011); MGCIP v. Does 1-316, 2011 U.S. Dist. LEXIS 61879 (N.D. Ill. June 9, 2011).

207. Napster, *supra* note 203. 239 F.3d 1004.

208. MGM Studios Inc. v. Grokster, Ltd., 545 U.S. 913 (2005). *See also* Arista Records LLC v. Lime Group LLC, 784 F. Supp. 2d 398 (2011) (court granted plaintiffs' motion for summary judgment for inducement of copyright infringement for defendants' Gnutella architecture program, LimeWire; questions of material fact existed to preclude summary judgment for contributory infringement and vicarious infringement among other claims).

209. Voltage Pictures, LLC v. Doe, 2011 U.S. Dist. LEXIS 50787 (D.D.C. May 12, 2011).

210. Columbia Pictures Indus., Inc. v. Fung, 2009 U.S. Dist. LEXIS 122661 (C.D. Cal. Dec. 21, 2009).

211. *Id.* at *2.

212. *Id.*

213. *Id.*

214. Arista Records LLC v. Lime Group LLC, 784 F. Supp. 2d 398 (S.D.N.Y. 2011).

215. *Fung*, 2009 U.S. Dist. LEXIS 122661, at *7.

216. *Id.* at note 26.

217. 17 U.S.C. § 512(d).

218. *Fung*, 2009 U.S. Dist. LEXIS 122661, at *7.

219. *A&M Records*, 239 F.3d 1004 (9th Cir.), *on remand*, 2001 WL 227083, 2001 U.S. Dist. LEXIS 2186 (N.D. Cal. Mar. 5, 2001), *aff'd*, 284 F.3d 1091 (9th Cir. 2002).

220. *Id.*, 239 F.3d 1004 at 1021.

221. *Id.* at 1023.

222. *Id.* at 1016-20.

223. *Id.* at 1025.

224. *A&M Records*, 2001 WL 227083, 2001 U.S. Dist. LEXIS 2186.

225. Metro-Goldwyn-Mayer Studios, Inc. v. Grokster Ltd., 380 F.3d 1154, 1160 (9th Cir. 2004), *overturned by* 545 U.S. 913, 125 S.Ct. 2764 (2005).

226. *In re* Aimster Copyright Litig., 334 F.3d 643 (7th Cir. 2003), *cert denied*, 540 U.S. 1107 (2004).

227. *Metro-Goldwyn-Mayer Studios*, 380 F.3d at 1162-63 ("even at a 10% level of legitimate use . . ., the volume of use would indicate a minimum of hundreds of thousands of legitimate file exchanges").

228. *Id.* at 1164.

229. *Id.* at 1164-65.

230. 125 S. Ct. at 2776, 2005 U.S. LEXIS 5212, at 29.

231. *Id.*

232. *Id.*, 125 S. Ct. at 2279, 2005 U.S. LEXIS 5212, at 37.

233. *Id.*, 125 S. Ct. at 2279, 2005 U.S. LEXIS 5212, at 47.

234. *Id.*, 125 S. Ct. at 2279, 2005 U.S. LEXIS 5212, at 48. The Graphic Artists Guild submitted an amicus brief on behalf of the plaintiffs in the *Napster* dispute. All defendants settled after the Supreme Court decision except for the corporate distributor. In 2007, the California federal district court affirmed in part plaintiff's motion for a permanent injunction against the distributor for inducement of copyright infringement, clarifying that the distributor must use the most effective means to prevent infringing use and try to preserve its noninfringing use features. *See* MGM Studios, Inc. v. Grokster, Ltd., 518 F. Supp. 2d 1197 (C.D. Cal. 2007).

235. Metro-Goldwyn-Mayer Studios, Inc. v. Grokster, Ltd., 518 F. Supp. 2d 1197 (C. D. Cal. 2007).

236. *See, e.g.,* Dan L. Burk, *Proprietary Rights in Hypertext Linkages*, 2 J. INFO. L. & TECH. 1, 15 (1998) ("Providing a hypertext reference is largely the equivalent of providing a citation in a footnote or bibliography."); Brief of Amici Curiae Open Law Forum at 3, Universal City Studios, Inc. v. Corley, No. 00-277 (S.D.N.Y. 2000) ("A web page with hypertext links does not 'provide' the content offered at the target pages merely by referencing those pages.").

237. MyPlayCity, Inc. v. Conduit Ltd., 2012 WL 1107648, at *12 (S.D.N.Y Mar. 30, 2012) ("Because the actual transfer of a file between computers must occur, merely providing a 'link' to a site containing copyrighted material does not constitute direct infringement of a holder's distribution right."). *See also* Perfect 10, Inc. v. Amazon.com, Inc., 508 F.3d 1146, 1162 (9th Cir. May 16, 2007); Online Policy Grp. v. Diebold, Inc., 337 F. Supp. 2d 1195, 1202 (N.D. Cal.2004).

238. *See* Law of the Internet § 5.02[B] *Linking* (citing Japanese court decision that held that linking to a site that contains pornographic material violated Japanese law that prohibited the distribution of pornography).

239. Intellectual Prop. Reserve, Inc. v. Utah Lighthouse Ministry, Inc., 75 F. Supp. 2d 1290 (D. Utah 1999); Arista Records, Inc. v. Mp3Board, Inc., 2002 WL 1997918 (S.D.N.Y. Aug. 29, 2002).

240. 17 U.S.C § 1201(a)(2). Depending on the nature of the claim, violation of this provision may lead to additional liability under 17 U.S.C. § 1203(a). *See* Comcast of Illinois X, LLC. v. Hightech Elecs., Inc., 2004 WL 1718522, at *6-7 (N.D. Ill. July 29, 2004).

241. Universal City Studios, Inc. v. Corley, 273 F.3d 429 (2d Cir. 2001) (noting that liability was dependent on plaintiff's clear showing that defendant (1) knew that circumvention technology existed on the linked-to site, (2) knew that it was illegal, and (3) created the link for the purpose of distributing illegal technology).

242. Kelly v. Arriba Soft Corp., 336 F.3d 811 (9th Cir. 2003) (citing Mark Sableman, *Link Law Revisited: Internet Linking Law at Five Years*, 16 BERKELEY TECH L.J. 1273, 1297 (2001), and Stacey L. Dogan, *Infringement Once Removed: The Perils of Hyperlinking to Infringing Content*, 87 IOWA L. REV. 829, 839 n.32 (2002)).

243. Futuredontics, Inc. v. Applied Anagramics, Inc., 1997 U.S. Dist. LEXIS 22249 (C.D. Cal.), *aff'd*, 201 F.3d 444 (9th Cir. 1999) (inline framing the entire contents of one website to another does create a copyright infringement but does not constitute a derivative work).

244. *Kelly*, 336 F.3d 811.

245. Campbell v. Acuff-Rose Music, Inc., 510 U.S. 569 (1994). The factors involved in the defense of fair use are discussed in chapter 11, pages 999–1019.

246. Kelly v. Arriba Soft Corp., 77 F. Supp. 2d 1116 (C.D. Cal. 1999).

247. *Kelly*, 336 F.3d at 818.

248. *See also* Field v. Google Inc., 412 F. Supp. 2d 1106 (D. Nev. 2006) (Google's caching copyrighted work was fair use; granting Google safe harbor under the DMCA).

249. L.A. Times v. Free Republic, 1999 WL 33644483, 1999 U.S. Dist. LEXIS 20484 (C.D. Cal. Oct. 29, 1999).

250. Sony Computer Entm't, Inc. v. Connectix Corp., 203 F.3d 596 (9th Cir. 2000).

251. Marobie-FL, Inc. v. National Ass'n of Fire Equipment Distributors, 983 F. Supp. 1167 (N.D. Ill. Nov. 13, 1997).

252. GoPets Ltd. v. Hise, 657 F.3d 1024, 1035 (9th Cir. 2011).

253. Domain names can be registered as trademarks and may be entitled to full protection under trademark laws. *See* USPTO Examination Guide No. 2-99, *available at* www.uspto.gov/web/offices/tac/notices/guide299.html for registration criteria.

254. Cline v. 1-888-PLUMBING Group, Inc., 146 F. Supp. 2d 351 (S.D.N.Y. 2001) (mere registration of trademark does not constitute use in commerce).

255. For more information on the domain name system, visit the Internet Corporation for Assigned Names and Numbers website, www.icann.org.

256. A continued millennial trend among cases brought under the cybersquatting statute and trademark infringement statute has been the use of the terms "typosquatter" and "typosquatter domain name," which is the near replica of an existing trademark in a domain name with a few letters difference. While this terminology is not currently used in any statute and is not a separate a cause of action, it has been used to support claims for cybersquatting and other theories of trademark liability. *E.g.*, Facebook, Inc. v. Banana Ads, LLC, 2012 WL 1038752 (N.D. Cal. 2012); S. Co. v. Dauben Inc., 324 F. App'x 309 (5th Cir. 2009).

257. Nicholas v. Magidson Fine Art, Inc., WIPO Case No. D-2000-0673 (holding respondent gallery was allowed to keep samfrancis.com to sell artist's works as long as it disclaimed affiliation with the artist); Velcro Industries B. V. and Velcro USA Inc. v. allinhosting.com/Andres Chavez, WIPO Case No. D2008-0864 (holding even though respondent art studio's domain name, "velcroart.net," was confusingly similar to complainant's mark, VELCRO, there was no proof bad faith registration of the domain name, and therefore, the panel denied complainant).

258. Reuters, *Etoy Wants Trademark 'Closure'*, WIRED, Jan. 25, 2001, *available at* http://www.wired.com/politics/law/news/2001/01/41438

259. Websites dedicated to primarily negative criticism and commentary, usually about a specific business, are known as "gripe sites."

260. Bally Total Fitness Holding Corp. v. Faber, 29 F. Supp. 2d 1161 (C.D. Cal. 1998).

261. The *Bally* court also found that plaintiff's website and defendant's website had fundamentally different purposes because plaintiff's site was a commercial advertisement and defendant's site was a consumer commentary site. The court further ruled that defendant was exercising his right to publish critical commentary, and made visitors aware that the site was not authorized. The court ruled that because plaintiff could not show that defendant was using plaintiff's mark in commerce, there could be no dilution. *Id*. at 1166-67.

262. Ascentive, LLC v. Opinion Corp., 2011 WL 6181452 (E.D.N.Y. 2011).

263. *Id*. at *2.

264. *Id*. at *21-23. Other courts have heard cases concerning gripe sites. *See* Taubman Co. v. Webfeats, 319 F.3d 770 (6th Cir. 2003); Taylor Bldg. Corp. of Am. v. Benfield, 507 F. Supp. 2d 832 (S.D. Ohio 2007).

265. SPTC, Inc. v. Juliana, Claim Number: FA0706001000082 (July 17, 2007), *available at*: http://domains.adrforum.com/domains/decisions/1000082.htm.

266. The full text of the policy can be found online at http://www.icann.org/en/help/dndr/udrp.

267. 15 U.S.C. § 1125.

268. 15 U.S.C. § 1125(c).

269. *See* Gucci Am., Inc. v. Wang Huoqing, 2011 WL 31191(N.D. Cal. 2011) (infringer sold counterfeit Gucci bags on generic websites, such as bagdo.net).

270. Anticybersquatting Consumer Protection Act, 15 U.S.C. § 1125(d).

271. Marshall v. Marshall, 2012 WL 1079550, at *18 (E.D.N.Y. Mar. 30, 2012).

272. 15 U.S.C. § 1117(d).

273. Violation of the ACPA can result in a class B felony or a class E felony for repeat offenses.

274. K.S.R. X-Ray Supplies, Inc. v. Southeastern X-Ray, Inc., 2010 WL 4317026 (S.D. Fla. Oct. 25, 2010).

275. Shields v. Zuccarini, 254 F.3d 476, 482-83 (3d Cir. 2001). *See* 15 U.S.C. § 1125(d)(1)(A)(ii)(I), (II).

276. *Shields*, 254 F.3d at 483-84. *See* 15 U.S.C. § 1125(d)(1)(A)(ii)(I), (II).

277. *Shields*, 254 F.3d at 484-85. "Bad faith" is enumerated by nine factors in the statute. 15 U.S.C. § 1125(d)(1)(B)(i).

278. 15 U.S.C. § 1125(d)(1)(B)(i).

279. Nicholas v. Magidson Fine Art, Inc., Case No. D2000-0673 (Sept. 27, 2000), *available at* http://www.wipo.int/amc/en/domains/decisions/html/2000/d2000-0673.html

280. Toyota Motor Sales, U.S.A., Inc. v. Tabari, 610 F.3d 1171 (9th Cir. 2010).

281. *Id*. at 1185.

282. Rogers v. Koons, 960 F.2d 301 (2d Cir. 1992).

283. Utah Lighthouse Ministry v. Found. for Apologetic Info.& Research, 527 F.3d 1045 (10th Cir. 2008).

284. *Id*. at 1053.

285. Warner Bros., Inc. v. Am. Broad. Cos., 720 F.2d 231, 242 (2d Cir. 1983); Elsmere Music, Inc. v. Nat'l Broad. Co., 625 F.2d 252, 253, 207 U.S.P.Q. (BNA) 277 (2d Cir. 1980) (per curiam).

286. Utah Lighthouse Ministry, 527 F.3d at 1054; *see also* Charles Atlas Ltd. v. DC Comics, Inc., 112 F. Supp. 2d 330, 336 (S.D.N.Y. 2000) (defendant comic book publisher's use of plaintiff's bodybuilding course advertisement did not constitute unauthorized trademark misappropriation or infringement because (1) defendant's use of the ad was protected expression under the First Amendment; and (2) likelihood of confusion was slim, and was outweighed by public interest in parodic expression).

287. Maxtone-Graham v. Burtchaell, 803 F.2d 1253, 1262, 231 U.S.P.Q. (BNA) 534 (2d Cir. 1986), *cert. denied*, 481 U.S. 1059 (1987).

288. 47 U.S.C. § 230(c)(1) provides that "no provider or user of an interactive computer service shall be treated as the publisher or speaker of any information provided by another information content provider."

289. Ascentive, LLC v. Opinion Corp., 2011 WL 6181452, at *18 (E.D.N.Y. 2011).

290. 47 U.S.C. § 230(f)(2).

291. 47 U.S.C. § 230(f)(3).

292. 47 U.S.C. § 230(b)(1) and (b)(2).

293. Atl. Recording Corp. v. Project Playlist, Inc., 603 F. Supp. 2d 690, 699 (S.D.N.Y. 2009).

294. Noah v. AOL Time Warner, Inc., 261 F. Supp. 2d 532 (E.D. Va. 2003), aff'd, 2004 WL 602711, 2004 U.S. App. LEXIS 5495 (4th Cir. 2004) (unpublished) (ISP immune from claim where user used "chat room" against another in anti-Muslim harassment).

295. Id., see also Doe One v. Oliver, 2000 WL 288357 (Conn. Super. 2000), aff'd, 792 A.2d 911 (Ct. App.), cert. denied, 796 A.2d 556 (2002) (ISP immune from claims for negligence and intentional infliction of emotional distress based on ISP's failure to prevent the distribution of a defamatory email); Shiamili v. Real Estate Group of New York, Inc., 17 N.Y.3d 281 (2011) (ISP immune from defamatory comments posted on website about plaintiff).

296. Carafano v. Metrosplash.com, 339 F.3d 1119 (9th Cir. 2003) (dating service provider immune from claims of negligence, defamation, invasion of privacy, and right of publicity for third-party user's creation of fake profile of actress); see also Ben Ezra, Weinstein & Co. v. Am. Online, 1999 WL 727402, 1999 U.S. Dist. LEXIS 23095 (D.N.M. 1999), aff'd, 206 F.3d 980 (10th Cir.), cert. denied, 531 U.S. 824 (2000) (ISP immune from claim for defamation when value of plaintiff's stock falsely and inaccurately reported by a third party).

297. Doe v. Am. Online, 1997 WL 374223 (Fla. Cir. Ct. 1997), aff'd, 718 So. 2d 385 (Fla. 4th Dist. Ct. App. 1998), approved, 783 So. 2d 1010 (Fla.), cert. denied, 534 U.S. 891 (2001) (ISP from claim where user used ISP chat room to market obscene photographs and pornographic videos of plaintiff's minor son).

298. Doe v. Franco Prods., 2000 WL 816779 (N.D. Ill 2000), aff'd, Doe v. GTE Corp., 347 F.3d 655 (7th Cir. 2003) (website hosting service immune from a third party's use of service to display unauthorized nude photographs).

299. 47 U.S.C. § 230(c)(2).

300. Fair Housing Council of San Fernando Valley v. Roommates.Com, LLC, 521 F.3d 1157 (9th Cir. 2008) (CDA did not immunize ISPs that were designed to force users to divulge personal information in violation of federal law).

301. Zeran v. Am. Online, 129 F.3d 327 (4th Cir. 1997), cert. denied, 524 U.S. 937 (1998).

302. Zeran was told at the time of his call that AOL's policy was not to post retractions. The parties disputed as to when the posting was removed.

303. Zeran, 129 F.3d at 330.

304. Zeran v. Am. Online, 958 F. Supp. 1124 (E.D. Va. 1997).

305. Zeran, 129 F.3d at 331.

306. Id. at 330.

307. Id. at 333. In contrast, the Digital Millennium Copyright Act requires ISPs upon notification of copyright infringement to take certain steps and remove the offending content. 17 U.S.C. § 512(c)(3).

308. Zeran, 129 F.3d at 334 (citing 47 U.S.C. § 230(d)(3)), followed in Doe v. Am. Online, 783 So. 2d 1010 (Fla. 2001); Gentry v. eBay, Inc., 99 Cal. App. 4th 816 (4th Dist. 2002).

309. E.g., Nemet Chevrolet, Ltd. v. Consumeraffairs.com, Inc., 591 F.3d 250 (4th Cir. 2009).

310. Chi. Lawyers' Comm. for Civ. Rights Under the Law, Inc. v. Craigslist, Inc., 519 F.3d 666 (7th Cir. 2008).

311. Shiamili v. Real Estate Group of New York, Inc., 17 N.Y.3d 281, 288 (2011).

312. 47 U.S.C. § 230(e).

313. M. Waldman, Annotation, Expectation of Privacy in Internet Communications, 92 A.L.R.5th 15 (June 2005).

314. N.Y. Civ. Rights Law § 50.

315. Molina v. Phoenix Sound, Inc., 297 A.D.2d 595, 747 N.Y.S.2d 227 (Sup. Ct. App. Div. 1st Dep't 2002) (holding model stated claim against nightclub's website where unauthorized video was used on defendant's website showed her dancing).

316. CineTel Films, Inc. v. Does 1—1,052, 2012 WL 1142272 (D. Md. Apr. 4, 2012); United States v. Christie, 624 F.3d 558, 573–74 (3d Cir. 2010); United States v. Bynum, 604 F.3d 161, 164 (4th Cir. 2010).

317. United States v. Butler, 151 F. Supp. 2d 82 (D. Me. 2001).

318. J.S. *ex rel.* H.S. v. Bethlehem Area Sch. Dist., 757 A.2d 412 (Pa. Commw. Ct. 2000), *aff'd* 794 A.2d 936 (Pa. Commw. Ct. 2002).

319. United States v. Perrine, 518 F.3d 1196, 1204–05 (10th Cir.2008); United States v. Forrester, 512 F.3d 500, 510 (9th Cir.2008).

320. United States v. Charbonneau, 979 F. Supp. 1177 (S.D. Ohio 1997); *Perrine*, 518 F.3d 1196.

321. Guest v. Leis, 255 F.3d 325 (6th Cir. 2001).

322. Carafano v. Metrosplash.com, 339 F.3d 1119 (9th Cir. 2003); *see also* Black v. Google Inc., 2010 WL 3222147 (N.D. Cal. 2010) (ISP was not originator of comments and so was immune from, among other claims, defamation, negligence, misrepresentation, and intentional infliction of emotional distress).

323. *Carafano*, 339 F.3d at 1121.

324. Carafano v. Metrosplash.com, Inc., 207 F. Supp. 2d 1055 (C.D. Cal. 2002).

325. *Carafano*, 339 F.3d at 1124-25.

326. *E.g.*, Fraley v. Facebook, Inc., 830 F. Supp. 2d 785 (N.D. Cal 2011).

327. ETW Corp. v. Jireh Publ'g, Inc., 332 F.3d 915, 928 (6th Cir. 2003); Allison v. Vintage Sports Plaques, 136 F.3d 1443 (11th Cir. 1998).

328. Gionfriddo v. Major League Baseball, 94 Cal. App. 4th 400, 114 Cal. Rptr. 2d 307 (Cal Ct. App. 1st Dist. 2001). *Cf.* Dryer v. Nat'l Football League, 689 F. Supp. 2d 1113, 1120 (D. Minn. 2010) (denying NFL's motion for summary judgment; "Plaintiffs have sufficiently established that the constitutional protection to be afforded the films may not outweigh Plaintiffs' interests in their own identities.").

329. *Major League Baseball*, 94 Cal. App. 4th 400, 114 Cal. Rptr. 2d 307.

330. Hoffman v. Capital Cities/ABC, Inc., 255 F.3d 1180 (9th Cir. 2001). *Cf.* No Doubt v. Activision Publishing, Inc., 192 Cal. App. 4th 1018, 1025 (Cal. App. 2d Dist. 2011) (affirming lower court's denial of motion to strike plaintiff's right of publicity claims based on a First Amendment defense; "Activision's literal reproductions of the images of the No Doubt members did not constitute a 'transformative' use sufficient to bring them within the protection of the First Amendment.").

331. 47 U.S.C.A. § 223

332. 47 U.S.C § 223(a) (superseded).

333. 47 U.S.C. § 223(d) (superseded).

334. Am. Civil Liberties Union v. Reno, 929 F. Supp. 824 (E.D. Pa. 1996).

335. Reno v. Am. Civil Liberties Union, 521 U.S. 844 (1997).

336. Specifically, the government likened the CDA to the statutes challenged in Ginsberg v. New York, 390 U.S. 629 (1968); FCC v. Pacifica Found., 438 U.S. 726 (1978); and Renton v. Playtime Theatres, Inc., 475 U.S. 41 (1986).

337. *Reno*, 521 U.S. at 868-70.

338. *Id.* at 868.

339. *Id.* at 871.

340. *Id.* at 865, 873.

341. *Id.* at 874, 878.

342. *Id.* at 875.

343. *Id.* at 856.

344. *Id.* at 855 [quoting the district court, 929 F. Supp. 824 (E.D. Pa. 1996)].

345. *Id.* at 876.

346. Am. Civil Liberties Union v. Reno, 31 F. Supp. 2d 473 (E.D. Pa. 1999).

347. Am. Civil Liberties Union v. Reno, 217 F.3d 162 (3d Cir. 2000).

348. *Id.* at 175.

349. Ashcroft v. Am. Civil Liberties Union, 535 U.S. 564 (2002).

350. *Id.* at 585-86.

351. Am. Civil Liberties Union v. Ashcroft, 322 F.3d 240, 251 (3d Cir. 2003).

352. *Id.* at 252-55.

353. *Id.* at 256-57.

354. *Id.* at 260.

355. *Id.* at 266.

356. Ashcroft v. Am. Civil Liberties Union, 542 U.S. 656, 124 S. Ct. 2783 (2004) ("Ashcroft v. ACLU II").

357. *Id.*, 124 S. Ct. at 2792.

358. *Id.*, 124 S. Ct. at 2789-90 (*citing* 18 U.S.C. § 2552B, prohibiting the use of misleading domain names, and 47 U.S.C. § 941, creating "Dot Kids" as a second-level Internet domain with content restricted to that fit for minors under thirteen years of age).

359. Barbara Nitke is a photographer and faculty member of the School of Visual Arts in New York City. Her work depicts adults engaged in a variety of sexual practices, including sado-masochism, and behind-the-scenes images of the porn industry.

360. Nitke's co-plaintiffs are the National Coalition for Sexual Freedom, a national advocacy group acting on behalf of individuals who practice alternative sexual expression, and the National Coalition for Sexual Freedom Foundation, an umbrella organization in pursuit of expanded rights for practitioners of nontraditional sex.

361. Nitke v. Ashcroft, 253 F. Supp. 2d 587 (S.D.N.Y. 2003).

362. *Id.* at 595.

363. *Id.* at 597. The court found the argument unavailing to give Nitke standing to file suit, noting that whatever fear she had did not in the end prevent her from displaying her photographs, which contravened the argument her speech had been chilled. In dismissing the complaint with respect to her, the court gave her leave to amend and allege she would prefer to display more explicit photographs.

364. *Id.* at 607.

365. *Id.* at 610-11.

366. Nitke v. Gonzales, 413 F. Supp. 2d 262 (S.D.N.Y. 2005).

367. United States v. Thomas, 74 F.3d 701 (6th Cir.), *cert. denied*, 519 U.S. 820 (1996).

368. 18 U.S.C. § 1465.

369. *Thomas*, 74 F.3d at 711.

370. United States v. Kilbride, 584 F.3d 1240 (9th Cir. 2009).

371. United States v. Schales, 546 F.3d 965, 973 (9th Cir. 2008).

372. 18 U.S.C. §§ 1462, 1465.

373. Hamling v. United States., 418 U.S. 87 (1974).

374. *Kilbride*, 584 F.3d at 1248.

375. *Id.* at 1250.

376. *Id.*

377. *Id.* at 1254.

378. United States v. Little, 365 F. App'x 159 (11th Cir. 2010).

379. *Id.* at 163.

380. *See* Am. Civil Liberties Union v. Johnson, 194 F.3d 1149 (10th Cir. 1999), *aff'g* 4 F. Supp. 2d 1029 (D.N.M. 1998) (preliminary injunction granted against enforcement of N.M. Stat. Ann. § 30-37-3.2[A]); Cyberspace Communications, Inc. v. Engler, 142 F. Supp. 2d 827 (E.D. Mich. 2001) (challenging Mich. Comp. Laws § 722.675[1]; PSINET, Inc. v. Chapman, 167 F. Supp. 2d 878 (W.D. Va. 2001) (challenging Va. Code Ann. § 18.2-391); Am. Booksellers Found. for Free Expression v. Coakley, 2010 WL 4273802 (D. Mass. 2010) (preliminary injunction granted against enforcement of Mass. Gen. Laws ch. 272, §§ 28 & 31).

381. *Id.*; *see also* Am. Libraries Ass'n v. Pataki, 969 F. Supp. 160 (S.D.N.Y. 1997) (challenging N.Y. Penal Law § 235.21(3)); Am. Booksellers Found. for Free Expression v. Dean, 202 F. Supp. 2d 300 (D. Vt. 2002); Southeast Booksellers Ass'n v. McMaster, 282 F. Supp. 2d 389 (D.S.C. 2003) (challenging S.C. Code § 16-15-385).

382. *see* Hatch v. Superior Court, 80 Cal. App. 4th 170 (Cal. App. 4th Dist. 2000) (challenging Cal. Penal Code § 288.2[a]); People v. Hsu, 82 Cal. App. 4th 976 (Cal. App. 1st Dist. 2000) (challenging Cal. Penal Code § 288.2[b]); People v. Foley, 94 N.Y.2d 668 (N.Y. 2000), *cert. denied*, 531 U.S. 875 (challenging N.Y. Penal Law § 235.22); State v. Robbins, 253 Wis. 2d 298 (Wis. 2002), *cert. denied*, 537 U.S. 1003 (2002) (challenging Wis. Stat. Ann. § 948.07); Cashatt v. Florida, 873 So. 2d 430 (Fla. 1st Dist. Ct. App. 2004) (challenging Fla. Stat. Ann. § 847.0135[3]).

383. *See* United States v. Carroll, 105 F.3d 740 (1st Cir. 1997), *cert. denied*, 520 U.S. 1258 (1997) (defendant held to have violated 18 U.S.C. § 2251 for enticing a minor into sexually explicit photographs that were later transported interstate).

384. 18 U.S.C. § 2251.

385. Ashcroft v. Free Speech Coalition, 535 U.S. 234 (2002).

386. *Id.* at 234.

387. Free Speech Coalition v. Reno, 198 F.3d 1083 (9th Cir. 1999).

388. Free Speech Coalition v. Reno, 220 F.3d 1113 (9th Cir. 2000).

389. Ashcroft v. Free Speech Coalition, 535 U.S. 234 (2002).

390. *Id.* at 240 (citing New York v. Ferber, 458 U.S. 747 (1982), which upheld a statute prohibiting the actual use of children in the making of child pornography).

391. *Id.* at 241.

392. *Id.* at 251.

393. *Id.* at 253-54.

394. Stanley v. Georgia, 394 U.S. 557 (1969).

395. Ashcroft, 535 U.S. at 253.

396. *Id.* at 254.

397. *Id.* at 257-58.

398. *See* United States v. Am. Library Ass'n, 539 U.S. 194 (2003) (holding the Children's Internet Protection Act (CIPA) did not violate First Amendment free speech clause and that CIPA did not impose unconstitutional conditions on public libraries), *Cf.* Mainstream Loudoun v. Bd. of Trs. of Loudoun County Library, 2 F. Supp. 2d 783 (E.D. Va. 1998) (holding standard First Amendment principles apply to public library's restriction of access to Internet sites featuring obscenity, child pornography, or material "harmful to juveniles"); Mainstream Loudoun v. Bd. of Trs. of Loudoun County Library, 24 F. Supp. 2d 552 (E.D. Va. 1998) (holding policy was not narrowly tailored to serve compelling government interest and policy was a prior restraint on free speech); Bradburn v. N. Cent. Regional Library Dist., 2012 U.S. Dist. LEXIS 50360 (E.D. Wash. Apr. 10, 2012) (library's policy not to unblock certain constitutionally protected content at the request of an adult did not violate First Amendment).

399. 2012 ARIZ. LEGIS. SERV. Ch. 166 (applies to schools and libraries); ARK. CODE ANN. § 6-21-107, § 13-2-104 (applies to schools and libraries); C.R.S.A. § 24-90-602 (applies to libraries); 29 DEL. C. § 6605C (applies to libraries); GA. CODE ANN., § 39-5-1 to § 39-5-4 (applies to schools and libraries); KY. REV. STAT. ANN. § 156.675 (applies to schools); I.C. § 33-2741 (applies to libraries); MD. CODE, EDUCATION, § 23-506.1 (applies to libraries); MICH. COMP. LAWS § 397.602, § 307.606 (applies to libraries); M.C.L.A. 397.606 (applies to libraries); MINN. STAT. ANN. § 134.50, § 125B.15 (applies to schools and libraries); MO. REV. STAT. § 182.827 (applies to schools and libraries); N.H. REV. STAT. ANN. § 194:3-d (applies to schools); N.Y. EDUC. LAW § 260 (applies to libraries); 24 P.S. § 4605 (applies to libraries); S.D. CODIFIED LAWS §§ 22-24-55 to -59 (applies to schools and libraries); S.C. CODE §§ 10-1-205 to - 206 (applies to schools and libraries); UTAH CODE §§ 9-7-213 to -217, 53A-3-423 to -424 (applies to schools and libraries); VA. CODE ANN. § 22.1-70.2, § 42.1-36.1 (applies to schools and libraries).

400. *See, e.g.*, Teter v. Glass Onion, Inc., 723 F. Supp. 2d 1138 (W.D. Mo. 2010).

401. Andy Wright, *World's Only Online Art Fair Coming to, Well, Everywhere,* BAY CITIZEN, May 2, 2012, *available at* www.baycitizen.org/blogs/culturefeed/vip-20-art-fair-galleries-collectors/print.

402. Joseph F. del Vecchio, *The Art Market's Presence Online: A Curated Survey, available at* www.montagefinance.com/content/news/article/The%20Art%20Market's%20Presence%20Online.pdf (last visited May 2, 2012).

403. *Id.*

404. *Id.*

405. *Id.*

406. *See* Marc E. Wojcik, Lawyers *Who Lie On-Line: How Should the Legal Profession Respond to E-Bay Ethics,* 18 J. MARSHALL J. COMPUTER & INFO. L. 875 (2000). Wojcik notes that art

auctions have been recognized by the Southern District of New York as yielding a price that is "per se fair and the product of good faith and arm's length dealing."

407. Electronic Signatures in Global and National Commerce Act ("E-SIGN"), Pub. L. No. 106-229. Although forty states had already enacted electronic signature laws by fall 2000, Congress passed E-SIGN into law to give legal validity and national uniformity to electronic signatures used in online contracts. Corey Ciocchetti, et al., *Are Online Business Transactions Executed By Electronic Signatures Legally Binding?*, 2001 DUKE L. & TECH. REV. 0005.

408. *See* Fair Credit Reporting Act, 15 U.S.C. § 1681 *et seq.*; Gramm-Leach-Bliley Financial Modernization Act of 1999, Pub. L. No. 106-102, 113 Stat. 1338; Children's Online Privacy Protection Act, 15 U.S.C. § 6501 *et seq.*

409. The Uniform Computer Information Transactions Act (UCITA) has been enacted by the states of Virginia, Maryland, North Carolina, Idaho, Vermont, Iowa, and Oklahoma. *See* Md. Code Ann., Com. Law § 22-101 *et seq.*; Va. Code Ann. § 59.1-501.1 *et seq.*; N.C.G.S.A. § 66-329; I.C. § 29-116; 9 V.S.A. § 2463a; IA ST § 554D.104; 12A Okl. St. Ann. § 2-105;

410. Int'l Shoe Co. v. Washington, 326 U.S. 310 (1945).

411. World-Wide Volkswagen Corp. v. Woodson, 44 U.S. 286 (1980); Helicopteros Nacionales de Columbia, S.A. v. Hall, 466 U.S. 408 (1984); Burger King Corp. v. Rudzewicz, 471 U.S. 462 (1985); Asahi Metal Indus. Co. v. Superior Court of Cal., 480 U.S. 102 (1987).

412. *Id.*

413. Carefirst of Md., Inc. v. Carefirst Pregnancy Ctrs., Inc., 334 F.3d 390 (4th Cir. 2003); Pebble Beach Co. v. Caddy, 453 F.3d 1151 (9th Cir. 2006); See Inc. v. Imago Eyewear Pty, Ltd., 167 F. App'x 518 (6th Cir. 2006); York v. Tropic Air, Ltd., 2012 WL 1077198 (S.D. Tex. Mar. 28, 2012).

414. Inset Sys., Inc. v. Instruction Set, Inc., 937 F. Supp. 161 (D. Conn. 1996).

415. Internet Doorway, Inc. v. Parks, 138 F. Supp. 2d 773 (S.D. Miss. 2001) (plaintiff, ISP, brought suit against defendant, nonresident, for sending a pornographic website advertisement that appeared to be sent from one of provider's accounts.).

416. E-Data Corp. v. Micropatent Corp., 989 F. Supp. 173 (D. Conn. 1997).

417. Winfield Collection, Ltd., v. McCauley, 105 F. Supp. 2d 746 (E.D. Mich. 2000).

418. Figi Graphics, Inc. v. Dollar Gen. Corp., 33 F. Supp. 2d 1263 (S.D. Cal. 1998).

419. Stewart v. Vista Point Verlang & Ringier Publ'g, 2000 WL 145839, 2000 U.S. Dist. LEXIS 14236 (S.D.N.Y. 2000), *aff'd*, 20 F. App'x. 91 (2d Cir. 2001) (unpublished) (on appeal, Second Circuit held that even if New York's long-arm statute applied, exercise of jurisdiction over defendant German firm would offend the Due Process Clause of the Fourteenth Amendment).

420. Zippo Mfg. Co. v. Zippo Dot Com, Inc., 952 F. Supp. 1119 (W.D. Pa. 1997).

421. *Id.* at 1124.

422. Hy Cite Corp. v. Badbusinessbureau.com LLC, 297 F. Supp. 2d 1154 (W.D. Wis. 2004) (citing Panavision Int'l, LP v. Toeppen, 141 F.3d 1316 (9th Cir. 1998) (personal jurisdiction accepted on "passive" website intentionally used to harm plaintiff in forum state); Caiazzo v. Am. Royal Arts Corp., 73 So.3d 245 (Fla. 4th Dist. Ct. App. 2011) ("While a clear majority of federal courts has adopted the *Zippo* analytical framework, Florida never has."); VGM Fin. Servs. v. Singh, 708 F. Supp. 2d 822, 838 (N.D. Iowa 2010) (court echoed Eight Circuit's concern that under *Zippo*, a highly interactive website could still be found to have no "quantity of contacts," which may lead to a finding of continuous but not substantial contacts).

423. *See, e.g.*, Soma Med. Int'l v. Standard Chartered Bank, 196 F.3d 1292 (10th Cir.1999); Sefton v. Jew, 201 F. Supp. 2d 730 (W.D. Tex. 2001); Ty, Inc. v. Baby Me, Inc., 2001 WL 34043540, 2001 U.S. Dist. LEXIS 5761 (N.D. Ill. Apr. 6, 2001); ALS Scan v. Digital Serv. Consultants, Inc., 293 F.3d 707 (4th Cir. 2002); Revell v. Lidov, 317 F.3d 467 (5th Cir. 2002); Neogen Corp. v. Neo Gen Screening, Inc., 282 F.3d 883 (6th Cir. 2002); Toys "R" Us, Inc. v. Step Two, S.A., 318 F.3d 446 (3d Cir. 2003); Fraserside IP L.L.C. v. Gamma Entm't, Inc., 2012 WL 1155682 (N.D. Iowa 2012).

424. Am. Online, Inc. v. Huang, 106 F. Supp. 2d 848 (E.D. Va. 2000) (defendant registered the allegedly infringing domain name in Virginia where plaintiff's principal place of business was located).

425. Yahoo!, Inc. v. La Ligue Contre le Racisme et l'Antisémitisme, 169 F. Supp. 2d 1181 (N.D. Cal. 2001) (overturned).

426. Yahoo!, Inc. v. La Ligue Contre le Racisme et l'Antisémitisme, 379 F.3d 1120 (9th Cir. 2004).

427. Yahoo!, Inc. v. La Ligue Contre le Racisme et l'Antisémitisme, 399 F.3d 1010 (9th Cir. 2005).

428. Yahoo!, Inc. v. La Ligue Contre le Racisme et L'Antisémitisme, 433 F.3d 1199 (9th Cir.), *cert denied*, 547 U.S. 1163 (2006).

429. *See, e.g.*, United States v. Thomas, 74 F.3d 701 (6th Cir.), cert. denied, 519 U.S. 820 (1996); Cal. Software, Inc. v. Reliability Research, Inc., 631 F. Supp. 1356 (C.D. Cal. 1986); Heroes, Inc. v. Heroes Found., 958 F. Supp. 1 (D.D.C. 1996); Europe Committee on Crime Problems Committee of Experts on Crime in Cyber-Space, Draft Convention on Cyber-Crime (Draft No. 24), Article 23 (1)(a)-(b), available at http://www.cyber-rights.org/documents/cybercrime24.htm (statute allows for jurisdiction over a national of a country even if the offense is committed outside the territory of an EU member state, allowing prosecution for computer crimes even if the country where the alleged perpetrator lives does not consider its acts criminal). *See generally* William Crane, *The World-Wide Jurisdiction: An Analysis of Over-Inclusive Internet Jurisdictional Law and an Attempt by Congress to Fix It*, 11 DePaul-LCA J. Art & Ent. L. 267 (Spring 2001).

430. Thane Peterson, *Did You Get that Utrillo on the Web? Collectors Are Flocking Online to Buy Pricey Art*, Bus. Week Investor, July 3, 2000, at E4.

431. *See* Kelly Devine Thomas, *Collecting in Cyberspace*, ARTnews, Jan. 2000. *See also* Kelly Devine Thomas, *The Online Art Market: Hit or Miss*, ARTnews, Jan. 2001 (describing a sale through www.artnet.com by New York's Kennedy Galleries of a painting to a European collector for $3 million and the Internet sale by Sotheby's of a copy of the Declaration of Independence for $8.14 million).

432. Florida-based art dealer Jim Tutwiler sold two Pablo Picasso crayon-on-paper drawings for $35,000 and $40,000 in November 2004 and January 2005 through the discount Internet retailer Costco, whose markup, he said, is one-tenth that of traditional galleries. *Original Picasso Sells on Costco Web Site*, Associated Press (Jan. 20, 2005).

433. *See*, Actusnews English, *Third Part of the exclusive interview of thierry Ehrmann, founder of Artprice.com*, 3/8/12 Actusnews English 14:35:00. The Chairman of Christies predicts the "The future of the middle market (800 to € 10,000) is on the net." *See also* del Vecchio, *supra* note 402.

434. In re AIOC Corp., 1999 WL 1327910 (Bankr. S.D.N.Y. Dec. 20, 1999).

435. *E.g.* www.justice.gov/usncb/programs/cultural_property_loss.php; http://www.fbi.gov/news/news_blog/wyeth-forgery.

436. Liane Hansen, *Online Art Fraud Nets Growing Number of Victims*, NPR Weekend Edition Sunday, May 4, 2008.

437. *E.g.* Judith H. Dobryzynski, *Spitzer Sues Gallery Over Fake Art on eBay*, N.Y. Times, sec. E (May 26, 2000). Judith H. Dobrzynski, *Online Bid Soars to $135,805, Provenance Not Guaranteed*, N.Y. Times, May 9, 2000, at A1; Judith H. Dobrzynski, *Online Seller of Abstract Work Adds a Money-Back Guarantee*, N.Y. Times, May 10, 2000, at A1; Saul Hansell & Judith H. Dobryzynski, *EBay Cancels Art Sale and Suspends Seller*, N.Y. Times, May 11, 2000, at A1; Judith H. Dobrzynski, *In Online Auction World, Hoaxes Aren't Easy to See*, N.Y. Times, June 2, 2000, at A1. Reuters, *Three on eBay Arrested in Fix Over Art Prices*, Houston Chronicle, at 4 (Feb. 10, 2002).

438. Hansen, *supra* note 440; BBC, *Seven Charged in "eBay Art Scam,"* BBC News, March 20, 2008; Becky Schlikerman, *Fraudulent Art Dealer Sentenced in Chicago*, Chicago Tribune, June 8, 2011.

439. Hansen, *supra* note 436.

440. Schlikerman, *supra* note 438.

441. *Id.*

442. Huffington Post, *Michael Zabrin, Fake Art Dealer, Sentenced to Nine Years*, Huff Post Chicago, Aug. 8, 2011. Zabrin's co-ringleader, Amiel, was given two years in prison for his involvement in the art scheme *See* Dominic Trombino, *Man Gets Two Years for Art Fraud*, NBC Chicago, June 16, 2011.

443. 47 U.S.C. § 230(c)(1).

444. Mazur v. eBay Inc., 2008 WL 618988 (N.D. Cal. 2008).

445. *Id.*, 2008 WL 618988, at *9.

446. Stoner v. eBay, Inc., 2000 WL 1705637 (Cal. Super. Ct. Nov. 1, 2000).

447. *See* Zeran v. Am. Online, 129 F.3d 327, 331-34 (4th Cir. 1997).

448. Doe v. Am. Online, 718 So. 2d 385, 388-89 (Fla. 4th Dist. Ct. App. 1998).

449. Stoner, 2000 WL 1705637, at 3.

450. *See* Yahoo!, Inc. v. La Ligue Contre le Racisme et L'Antisémitisme, 433 F.3d 1199, 1203-04 (9th Cir.) (describing a French court decision requiring Yahoo! to remove all Nazi material from its website, including auction items), *cert. denied*, 547 U.S. 1163 (2006).

STATUTORY APPENDIX

FLAG STATUTE (18 U.S.C. § 700)

TITLE 18. CRIMES AND CRIMINAL PROCEDURE
PART I. CRIMES
CHAPTER 33. EMBLEMS, INSIGNIA, AND NAMES

§ 700. DESECRATION OF THE FLAG OF THE UNITED STATES; PENALTIES

(a) (1)   Whoever knowingly mutilates, defaces, physically defiles, burns, maintains on the floor or ground, or tramples upon any flag of the United States shall be fined under this title or imprisoned for not more than one year, or both.

(2)   This subsection does not prohibit any conduct consisting of the disposal of a flag when it has become worn or soiled.

(b)   As used in this section, the term "flag of the United States" means any flag of the United States, or any part thereof, made of any substance, of any size, in a form that is commonly displayed.

(c)   Nothing in this section shall be construed as indicating an intent on the part of Congress to deprive any State, territory, possession, or the Commonwealth of Puerto Rico of jurisdiction over any offense over which it would have jurisdiction in the absence of this section.

(d) (1)   An appeal may be taken directly to the Supreme Court of the United States from any interlocutory or final judgment, decree, or order issued by a United States district court ruling upon the constitutionality of subsection (a).

(2)   The Supreme Court shall, if it has not previously ruled on the question, accept jurisdiction over the appeal and advance on the docket and expedite to the greatest extent possible.

VISUAL ARTISTS RIGHTS ACT OF 1990

(PUBLIC LAW 101-650, TITLE VI)

TITLE VI—VISUAL ARTISTS RIGHTS

SEC. 601. SHORT TITLE.
This title may be cited as the "Visual Artists Rights Act of 1990".

SEC. 602. WORK OF VISUAL ART DEFINED.
Section 101 of title 17, United States Code, is amended by inserting after the paragraph defining "widow" the following:

"A 'work of visual art' is—

"(1) a painting, drawing, print, or sculpture, existing in a single copy, in a limited edition of 200 copies or fewer that are signed and consecutively numbered by the author, or, in the case of a sculpture, in multiple cast, carved, or fabricated sculptures of 200 or fewer that are consecutively numbered by the author and bear the signature or other identifying mark of the author; or

"(2) a still photographic image produced for exhibition purposes only, existing in a single copy that is signed by the author, or in a limited edition of 200 copies or fewer that are signed and consecutively numbered by the author.

"A work of visual art does not include—

"(A)(i) any poster, map, globe, chart, technical drawing, diagram, model, applied art, motion picture or other audiovisual work, book, magazine, newspaper, periodical, data base, electronic information service, electronic publication, or similar publication;

"(ii) any merchandising item or advertising, promotional, descriptive, covering, or packaging material or container;

"(iii) any portion or part of any item described in clause (i) or (ii);

"(B) any work made for hire; or

"(C) any work not subject to copyright protection under this title.".

SEC. 603. RIGHTS OF ATTRIBUTION AND INTEGRITY.

(a) RIGHTS OF ATTRIBUTION AND INTEGRITY.—

Chapter 1 of title 17, United States Code, is amended by inserting after section 106 the following new section:

"§ 106A. Rights of certain authors to attribution and integrity

"(a) RIGHTS OF ATTRIBUTION AND INTEGRITY.— Subject to section 107 and independent of the exclusive rights provided in section 106, the author of a work of visual art—

"(1) shall have the right—

"(A) to claim authorship of that work, and

"(B) to prevent the use of his or her name as the author of any work of visual art which he or she did not create;

"(2) shall have the right to prevent the use of his or her name as the author of the work of visual art in the event of a distortion, mutilation, or other modification of the work which would be prejudicial to his or her honor or reputation; and

"(3) subject to the limitations set forth in section 113(d), shall have the right—

"(A) to prevent any intentional distortion, mutilation, or other modification of that work which would be prejudicial to his or her honor or reputation, and any intentional distortion, mutilation, or modification of that work is a violation of that right, and

"(B) to prevent any destruction of a work of recognized stature, and any intentional or grossly negligent destruction of that work is a violation of that right.

"(b) SCOPE AND EXERCISE OF RIGHTS.—Only the author of a work of visual art has the rights conferred by subsection (a) in that work, whether or not the author is the copyright owner. The authors of a joint work of visual art are coowners of the rights conferred by subsection (a) in that work.

"(c) EXCEPTIONS.—(1) The modification of a work of visual art which is a result of the passage of time or the inherent nature of the materials is not a distortion, mutilation, or other modification described in subsection (a)(3)(A).

"(2) The modification of a work of visual art which is the result of conservation, or of the public presentation, including lighting and placement, of the work is not a destruction, distortion, mutilation, or other modification described in subsection (a)(3) unless the modification is caused by gross negligence.

"(3) The rights described in paragraphs (1) and (2) of subsection (a) shall not apply to any reproduction, depiction, portrayal, or other use of a work in, upon, or in any connection with any item described in subparagraph (A) or (B) of the definition of 'work of visual art' in section 101, and any such reproduction, depiction, portrayal, or other use of a work is not a destruction, distortion, mutilation, or other modification described in paragraph (3) of subsection (a).

"(d) DURATION OF RIGHTS.—(1) With respect to works of visual art created on or after the effective date set forth in section 610(a) of the Visual Artists Rights Act of 1990, the rights conferred by subsection (a) shall endure for a term consisting of the life of the author.

"(2) With respect to works of visual art created before the effective date set forth in section 610(a) of the Visual Artists Rights Act of 1990, but title to which has not, as of such effective date, been transferred from the author, the rights conferred by subsection (a) shall be coextensive with, and shall expire at the same time as, the rights conferred by section 106.

"(3) In the case of a joint work prepared by two or more authors, the rights conferred by subsection (a) shall endure for a term consisting of the life of the last surviving author.

"(4) All terms of the rights conferred by subsection (a) run to the end of the calendar year in which they would otherwise expire.

"(e) TRANSFER AND WAIVER.—(1) The rights conferred by subsection (a) may not be transferred, but those rights may be waived if the author expressly agrees to such waiver in a written instrument signed by the author. Such instrument shall specifically identify the work, and uses of that work, to which the waiver applies, and the waiver shall apply only to the work and uses so identified. In the case of a joint work prepared by two or more authors, a waiver of rights under this paragraph made by one such author waives such rights for all such authors.

"(2) Ownership of the rights conferred by subsection (a) with respect to a work of visual art is distinct from ownership of any copy of that work, or of a copyright or any exclusive right under a copyright in that work. Transfer of ownership of any copy of a work of visual art, or of a copyright or any exclusive right under a copyright, shall not constitute a waiver of the rights conferred by subsection (a). Except as may otherwise be agreed by the author in a written instrument signed by the author, a waiver of the rights conferred by subsection (a) with respect to a work of visual art shall not constitute a transfer of ownership of any copy of that work, or of ownership of a copyright or of any exclusive right under a copyright in that work.".

(b) CONFORMING AMENDMENT.—The table of sections at the beginning of chapter 1 of title 17, United States Code, is amended by inserting after the item relating to section 106 the following new item:

"106A. Rights of certain authors to attribution and integrity.".

SEC. 604. REMOVAL OF WORKS OF VISUAL ART FROM BUILDINGS.
Section 113 of title 17, United States Code, is amended by adding at the end thereof the following:

"(d)(1) In a case in which—

"(A) a work of visual art has been incorporated in or made part of a building in such a way that removing the work from the building will cause the destruction, distortion, mutilation, or other modification of the work as described in section 106A(a)(3), and

"(B) the author consented to the installation of the work in the building either before the effective date set forth in section 610(a) of the Visual Artists Rights Act of 1990, or in a written instrument executed on or after such effective date that is signed by the owner of the building and the author and that specifies that installation of the work may subject the work to destruction, distortion, mutilation, or other modification, by reason of its removal,

"then the rights conferred by paragraphs (2) and (3) of section 106A(a) shall not apply.

"(2) If the owner of a building wishes to remove a work of visual art which is a part of such building and which can be removed from the building without the destruction, distortion, mutilation, or other modification of the work as described in section 106A(a)(3), the author's rights under paragraphs (2) and (3) of section 106A(a) shall apply unless—

"(A) the owner has made a diligent, good faith attempt without success to notify the author of the owner's intended action affecting the work of visual art, or

"(B) the owner did provide such notice in writing and the person so notified failed, within 90 days after receiving such notice, either to remove the work or to pay for its removal.

"For purposes of subparagraph (A), an owner shall be presumed to have made a diligent, good faith attempt to send notice if the owner sent such notice by registered mail to the author at the most recent address of the author that was recorded with the Register of Copyrights pursuant to paragraph (3). If the work is removed at the expense of the author, title to that copy of the work shall be deemed to be in the author.

"(3) The Register of Copyrights shall establish a system of records whereby any author of a work of visual art that has been incorporated in or made part of a building, may record his or her identity and address with the Copyright Office. The Register shall also establish procedures under which any such author may update the information so recorded, and procedures under which owners of buildings may record with the Copyright Office evidence of their efforts to comply with this subsection.".

SEC. 605. PREEMPTION.
Section 301 of title 17, United States Code, is amended by adding at the end the following:

"(f)(1) On or after the effective date set forth in section 610(a) of the Visual Artists Rights Act of 1990, all legal or equitable rights that are equivalent to any of the rights conferred by section 106A with respect to works of visual art to which the rights conferred by section 106A apply are governed exclusively by section 106A and section 113(d) and the provisions of this title relating to such sections. Thereafter, no person is entitled to any such right or equivalent right in any work of visual art under the common law or statutes of any State.

"(2) Nothing in paragraph (1) annuls or limits any rights or remedies under the common law or statutes of any State with respect to—

"(A) any cause of action from undertakings commenced before the effective date set forth in section 610(a) of the Visual Artists Rights Act of 1990;

"(B) activities violating legal or equitable rights that are not equivalent to any of the rights conferred by section 106A with respect to works of visual art; or

"(C) activities violating legal or equitable rights which extend beyond the life of the author.".

SEC. 606. INFRINGEMENT ACTIONS.
(a) IN GENERAL.—Section 501(a) of title 17, United States Code, is amended—

(1) by inserting after "118" the following: "or of the author as provided in section 106A(a)"; and
(2) by striking out "copyright." and inserting in lieu thereof "copyright or right of the author, as the case may be. For purposes of this chapter (other than section 506), any reference to copyright shall be deemed to include the rights conferred by section 106A(a).".

(b) EXCLUSION OF CRIMINAL PENALTIES.—Section 506 of title 17, United States Code, is amended by adding at the end thereof the following:

"(f) RIGHTS OF ATTRIBUTION AND INTEGRITY.— Nothing in this section applies to infringement of the rights conferred by section 106A(a).".

(c) REGISTRATION NOT A PREREQUISITE TO SUIT AND CERTAIN REMEDIES.—(1) Section 411(a) of title 17, United States Code, is amended in the first sentence by inserting after "United States" the following: "and an action brought for a violation of the rights of the author under section 106A(a)".

(2) Section 412 of title 17, United States Code, is amended by inserting "an action brought for a violation of the rights of the author under section 106A(a) or" after "other than".

SEC. 607. FAIR USE.

Section 107 of title 17, United States Code, is amended by striking out "section 106" and inserting in lieu thereof "sections 106 and 106A".

SEC. 608. STUDIES BY COPYRIGHT OFFICE.

(a) STUDY ON WAIVER OF RIGHTS PROVISION.—

(1) STUDY.—The Register of Copyrights shall conduct a study on the extent to which rights conferred by subsection (a) of section 106A of title 17, United States Code, have been waived under subsection (e)(1) of such section.

(2) REPORT TO CONGRESS.—Not later than 2 years after the date of the enactment of this Act, the Register of Copyrights shall submit to the Congress a report on the progress of the study conducted under paragraph (1). Not later than 5 years after such date of enactment, the Register of Copyrights shall submit to the Congress a final report on the results of the study conducted under paragraph (1), and any recommendations that the Register may have as a result of the study.

(b) STUDY ON RESALE ROYALTIES.—

(1) NATURE OF STUDY.—The Register of Copyrights, in consultation with the Chair of the National Endowment for the Arts, shall conduct a study on the feasibility of implementing—

(A) a requirement that, after the first sale of a work of art, a royalty on any resale of the work, consisting of a percentage of the price, be paid to the author of the work; and

(B) other possible requirements that would achieve the objective of allowing an author of a work of art to share monetarily in the enhanced value of that work.

(2) GROUPS TO BE CONSULTED.—The study under paragraph (1) shall be conducted in consultation with other appropriate departments and agencies of the United States, foreign governments, and groups involved in the creation, exhibition, dissemination, and preservation of works of art, including artists, art dealers, collectors of fine art, and curators of art museums.

(3) REPORT TO CONGRESS.—Not later than 18 months after the date of the enactment of this Act, the Register of Copyrights shall submit to the Congress a report containing the results of the study conducted under this subsection.

SEC. 609. FIRST AMENDMENT APPLICATION.

This title does not authorize any governmental entity to take any action or enforce restrictions prohibited by the First Amendment to the United States Constitution.

SEC. 610. EFFECTIVE DATE.

(a) IN GENERAL.—Subject to subsection (b) and except as provided in subsection (c), this title and the amendments made by this title take effect 6 months after the date of the enactment of this Act.

(b) APPLICABILITY.—The rights created by section 106A of title 17, United States Code, shall apply to—

(1) works created before the effective date set forth in subsection (a) but title to which has not, as of such effective date, been transferred from the author, and

(2) works created on or after such effective date, but shall not apply to any destruction, distortion, mutilation, or other modification (as described in section 106A(a)(3) of such title) of any work which occurred before such effective date.

(c) SECTION 608.—Section 608 takes effect on the date of the enactment of this Act.

ARCHITECTURAL WORKS
COPYRIGHT PROTECTION ACT

(PUBLIC LAW 101-650, TITLE VII)

TITLE VII—ARCHITECTURAL WORKS

SEC. 701. SHORT TITLE.
This title may be cited as the "Architectural Works Copyright Protection Act".

SEC. 702. DEFINITIONS.
(a) ARCHITECTURAL WORKS.—Section 101 of title 17, United States Code, is amended by inserting after the definition of "anonymous work" the following:
"An 'architectural work' is the design of a building as embodied in any tangible medium of expression, including a building, architectural plans, or drawings. The work includes the overall form as well as the arrangement and composition of spaces and elements in the design, but does not include individual standard features.".

(b) BERNE CONVENTION WORK.—Section 101 of title 17, United States Code, is amended in the definition of "Berne Convention work"—
(1)   in paragraph (3)(B) by striking "or" after the semicolon;
(2)   in paragraph (4) by striking the period and inserting "; or"; and
(3)   by inserting after paragraph (4) the following:
"(5) in the case of an architectural work embodied in a building, such building is erected in a country adhering to the Berne Convention.".

SEC. 703. SUBJECT MATTER OF COPYRIGHT.
Section 102(a) of title 17, United States Code, is amended—
(1)   in paragraph (6) by striking "and" after the semicolon;
(2)   in paragraph (7) by striking the period and inserting "; and"; and
(3)   by adding after paragraph (7) the following:

"(8) architectural works.".

SEC. 704. SCOPE OF EXCLUSIVE RIGHTS IN ARCHITECTURAL WORKS.
(a) IN GENERAL.—Chapter 1 of title 17, United States Code, is amended by adding at the end the following:
"§ 120. Scope of exclusive rights in architectural works

"(a) PICTORIAL REPRESENTATIONS PERMITTED.— The copyright in an architectural work that has been constructed does not include the right to prevent the making, distributing, or public display of pictures, paintings, photographs, or other pictorial representations of the work, if the building in which the work is embodied is located in or ordinarily visible from a public place.

"(b) ALTERATIONS TO AND DESTRUCTION OF BUILDINGS.—Notwithstanding the provisions of section 106(2), the owners of a building embodying an architectural work may, without the consent of the author or copyright owner of the architectural work, make or authorize the making of alterations to such building, and destroy or authorize the destruction of such building.".

(b) CONFORMING AMENDMENTS.—(1) The table of sections at the beginning of chapter 1 of title 17, United states Code, is amended by adding at the end of the following:
"120. Scope of exclusive rights in architectural works.".

(2) Section 106 of title 17, United States Code, is amended by striking "119" and inserting "120".

SEC. 705. PREEMPTION.
Section 301(b) of title 17, United States Code, is amended—
(1) in paragraph (2) by striking "or" after the semicolon:
(2) in paragraph (3) by striking the period and inserting "; or"; and
(3) by adding after paragraph (3) the following:

"(4) State and local landmarks, historic preservation, zoning, or building codes, relating to architectural works protected under section 102(a)(8).".

SEC. 706. EFFECTIVE DATE.
The amendments made by this title apply to—
(1) any architectural work created on or after the date of the enactment of this Act; and
(2) any architectural work that, on the date of the enactment of this Act, is unconstructed and embodied in unpublished plans or drawings, except that protection for such architectural work under title 17, United States Code, by virtue of the amendments made by this title, shall terminate on December 31, 2002, unless the work is constructed by that date.

ADVANCE VALUATION RULING REQUEST

(REV. PROC. 96-15)

26 CFR 601-201; Rulings and determination letters.

(Also Part I, §§ 170, 2031, 2512; 1.170A-13; 20.2031-6; 25.2512-1.)
1996-1 C.B. 627; 1996 IRB LEXIS 33; 1996-3 I.R.B. 41; Rev. Proc. 96-15
January 16, 1996

SECTION 1. PURPOSE

This revenue procedure informs taxpayers how to request from the Internal Revenue Service a Statement of Value that can be used to substantiate the value of art for income, estate, or gift tax purposes. A taxpayer that complies with the provisions of this revenue procedure may rely on the Statement of Value in completing the taxpayer's federal income tax, estate tax, or gift tax return that reports the transfer of art.

SECTION 2. BACKGROUND
.01 Income Tax Charitable Deduction.

(1) Section 170(a) of the Internal Revenue Code allows as a deduction any charitable contribution (as defined in § 170(c)) payment of which is made during the taxable year.

(2) Section 1.170A-1(c)(1) of the Income Tax Regulations provides that if a charitable contribution is made in property other than money, the amount of the contribution is generally the fair market value of the property at the time of the contribution.

(3) Section 1.170A-1(c)(2) provides that the fair market value is the price at which the property would change hands between a willing buyer and a willing seller, neither being under any compulsion to buy or sell and both having reasonable knowledge of the relevant facts.

(4) Section 1.170A-13 sets forth the recordkeeping and return requirements for deductions for charitable contributions. For a deduction for a charitable contribution of property in excess of $5,000, § 1.170A-13(c) requires a qualified appraisal and an appraisal summary.

(5) Rev. Proc. 66-49, 1966-2 C.B. 1257, provides guidelines for review of appraisals of contributed property for purposes of § 170. Section 4.01 of Rev. Proc. 66-49 states that the Service will not approve valuations or appraisals prior to the actual filing of the tax return to which the appraisal pertains, and will not issue advance rulings approving or disapproving appraisals.

.02 Estate Tax.

(1) Section 2031 provides that the value of the gross estate of a decedent is determined by including the value at the time of death of all property wherever situated.
(2) Section 20.2031-1(b) of the Estate Tax Regulations provides that the value of property includible in a decedent's gross estate is its fair market value at the time of the decedent's death.
(3) Section 2032(a) provides that the executor may elect to determine the value of all the property included in the gross estate as of 6 months after the decedent's death. However, property distributed, sold, exchanged, or otherwise disposed of within 6 months after death must be valued as of the date of distribution, sale, exchange, or other disposition.
(4) Section 20.2031-6(a) provides that the fair market value of a decedent's household and personal effects is the price that a willing buyer would pay to a willing seller, neither being under any compulsion to buy or to sell and both having reasonable knowledge of the relevant facts.
(5) Section 20.2031-6(b) provides that if there are included among the household and personal effects articles having marked artistic or intrinsic value of a total in excess of $3,000, the appraisal of an expert or experts, under oath, must be filed with the estate tax return.
(6) Section 20.2031-6(d) provides that if, pursuant to § 20.2031-6(a) and (b), expert appraisers are employed, care must be taken to see that they are reputable and of recognized competency to appraise the particular class of property involved. In listing paintings having artistic value, the size, subject, and artist's name must be stated.

.03 Gift Tax.

(1) Section 2512(a) provides that if a gift is made in property, the value thereof at the date of the gift is the amount of the gift.
(2) Section 25.2512-1 of the Gift Tax Regulations provides that the value of property is the price at which the property would change hands between a willing buyer and a willing seller, neither being under any compulsion to buy or to sell and both having reasonable knowledge of the relevant facts.

.04 Legislation Authorizing User Fees. Section 10511 of the Revenue Act of 1987, 1987-3 C.B. 1, 166, as amended by § 11319 of the Omnibus Budget Reconciliation Act of 1990, 1991-2 C.B. 481, 511, and by § 743 of the Uruguay Round Agreements Act, 1995-11 I.R.B. 5, 14, requires the Secretary of the Treasury or delegate to establish a program requiring the payment of user fees for requests to the Service for letter rulings, opinion letters, determination letters, and similar requests. The fees apply to requests made on or after February 1, 1988, and before October 1, 2000. The fees charged under the program (1) vary according to categories or subcategories established by the Secretary; (2) are determined after taking into account the average time for, and difficulty of, complying with requests in each category and subcategory; and (3) are payable in advance.

SECTION 3. SCOPE

.01 Except as provided in section 3.02, this revenue procedure applies to an item of art that has been appraised at $50,000 or more, and has been transferred (1) as a "charitable contribution" within the meaning of § 170(c), (2) by reason of a decedent's death, or (3) by intervivos gift.

.02 The Service may issue a Statement of Value for items appraised at less than $50,000 if (1) the request for the Statement of Value includes a request for appraisal review for at least one item appraised at $50,000 or more, and (2) the Service determines that issuance of such a Statement would be in the best interest of efficient tax administration.

.03 The Service may decline to issue a Statement of Value when appropriate in the interest of efficient tax administration. If the Service declines to issue a Statement of Value under this section 3.03, the Service will refund the user fee.

SECTION 4. DEFINITIONS

.01 The term "art" includes paintings, sculpture, watercolors, prints, drawings, ceramics, antique furniture, decorative arts, textiles, carpets, silver, rare manuscripts, historical memorabilia, and other similar objects.

.02 The term "taxpayer" includes an executor or administrator acting on behalf of an estate, and a donor of a gift.

.03 The term "valuation date" refers to the date of death, the alternate valuation date (as established under § 2032(a)), or the date of the gift.

SECTION 5. REQUESTING A STATEMENT OF VALUE FOR INCOME TAX CHARITABLE DEDUCTION PURPOSES

.01 To request a Statement of Value from the Service for an item of art transferred as a charitable contribution within the meaning of § 170(c), a taxpayer must submit to the Service a request for a Statement of Value for the item prior to filing the income tax return that first reports the charitable contribution. The request must include the following:

(1) a copy of an appraisal (as described in section 6 of this revenue procedure) of the item of art;
(2) a check or money order payable to the Internal Revenue Service (user fee) in the amount of $2,500 for a request for a Statement of Value for one, two, or three items of art, plus $250 for each additional item of art for which a Statement of Value is requested;
(3) a completed appraisal summary (Section B of Form 8283, Noncash Charitable Contributions) that meets the requirements of § 1.170A-13(c)(4); and
(4) the location of the District Office that has or will have examination jurisdiction over the return (not the Service Center where the return is filed).

.02 A taxpayer may withdraw the request for a Statement of Value at any time before it is issued by the Service. The user fee will not be refunded for a request that is withdrawn. When a request is withdrawn, the appropriate District Director will be notified.

.03 If a request for a Statement of Value lacks information essential to the issuance of a Statement of Value for an item of art, the Service will notify the taxpayer that the request will not be processed for that item unless the Service receives the missing information within 30 calendar days after the date of such notification.

SECTION 6. APPRAISAL FOR INCOME TAX CHARITABLE DEDUCTION PURPOSES

.01 An appraisal submitted to the Service by a taxpayer under section 5 of this revenue procedure must meet the requirements for a qualified appraisal under § 1.170A-13(c)(3)(i)-(iii), and must also include the following:

(1) a complete description of the item of art, including:
    (a) the name of the artist or culture,
    (b) the title or subject matter,
    (c) the medium, such as oil on canvas, or watercolor on paper,
    (d) the date created,
    (e) the size,
    (f) any marks, signatures, or labels on the item of art, on the back of the item of art, or affixed to the frame,
    (g) the history (provenance) of the item, including proof of authenticity, if that information is available,
    (h) a record of any exhibitions at which the item was displayed,
    (i) any reference source citing the item, and
    (j) the physical condition of the item;
(2) a professional quality photograph of a size and quality fully showing the item, preferably an 8 × 10 inch color photograph or a color transparency not smaller than 4 × 5 inches; and
(3) the specific basis for the valuation.

.02 The appraisal must be made no earlier than 60 days prior to the date of the contribution of the item of art.

.03 Taxpayers are encouraged to include in the request any additional information that may affect the determination of the fair market value of the item of art.

.04 The requirements of section 6 of this revenue procedure must be met by Subchapter C corporations, even though they would otherwise be exempt under § 1.170A-13(c)(2)(ii)(B)(3) from the appraisal requirements.

SECTION 7. REQUESTING A STATEMENT OF VALUE FOR ESTATE TAX OR
GIFT TAX PURPOSES
.01 To request a Statement of Value from the Service for an item of art transferred as part of an estate or as an intervivos gift, a taxpayer must submit to the
Service a request for a Statement of Value for the item prior to filing the federal
estate tax return or the federal gift tax return that first reports the transfer of the
item. The request must include the following:

(1)   a copy of an appraisal (as described in section 8 of this revenue procedure) of the item of art;
(2)   a check or money order payable to the Internal Revenue Service (user
fee) in the amount of $2,500 for a request for a Statement of Value for
one, two, or three items of art, plus $250 for each additional item of art for
which a Statement of Value is requested;
(3)   a description of the item of art;
(4)   the appraised fair market value;
(5)   the cost, date, and manner of acquisition;
(6)   the date of death (or the alternate valuation date, if applicable) or the
date of the gift; and
(7)   the location of the District Office that has or will have examination jurisdiction over the return (not the Service Center where the return is filed).

.02 A taxpayer may withdraw the request for a Statement of Value at any time
before it is issued by the Service. The user fee will not be refunded for a request
that is withdrawn. When a request is withdrawn, the appropriate District Director will be notified.

.03 If a request for a Statement of Value lacks information essential to the issuance of a Statement of Value for an item of art, the Service will notify the
taxpayer that the request will not be processed for that item unless the Service
receives the missing information within 30 calendar days after the date of such
notification.

SECTION 8. APPRAISAL FOR ESTATE TAX OR GIFT TAX PURPOSES
.01 An appraisal submitted to the Service by a taxpayer under section 7
of this revenue procedure must include the following:

(1)   a complete description of the item of art, including:
(a)   the name of the artist or culture,
(b)   the title or subject matter,
(c)   the medium, such as oil on canvas, or watercolor on paper,
(d)   the date created,
(e)   the size,
(f)   any marks, signatures, or labels on the item of art, on the back of
the item of art, or affixed to the frame,
(g)   the history (provenance) of the item, including proof of authenticity, if such information is available,

(h)   a record of any exhibitions at which the item was displayed,
(i)   any reference source citing the item, and
(j)   the physical condition of the item;
(2)   a professional quality photograph of a size and quality fully showing the item, preferably an 8 × 10 inch color photograph or a color transparency not smaller than 4 × 5 inches;
(3)   a statement that the appraisal was prepared for estate tax purposes or gift tax purposes;
(4)   the date (or dates) on which the item of art was appraised;
(5)   the appraised fair market value (within the meaning of § 20.2031-6(a) or 25.2512-1); and
(6)   the specific basis for the valuation.

.02 The appraisal must be made no earlier than 60 days prior to the valuation date.

.03 Taxpayers are encouraged to include in the request any additional information that may affect the determination of the fair market value of the item of art.

.04 An appraisal must:

(1)   be prepared, signed, and dated by an appraiser, and contain a statement by the appraiser that:
(a)   the appraiser either holds himself or herself out to the public as an appraiser or performs appraisals on a regular basis;
(b)   the appraiser is qualified to make appraisals of the item of art;
(c)   the appraiser is not the taxpayer;
(d)   the appraiser was not a party to the transaction in which the decedent or donor of the gift acquired the item of art being appraised, unless the valuation date is within 2 months of the date of acquisition and the appraised value is not less than the acquisition price;
(e)   the appraiser is not the beneficiary or donee receiving the item of art;
(f)   the appraiser is not a person who was employed by the decedent or is employed by the taxpayer;
(g)   the appraiser is not related to any of the foregoing persons under § 267-(b) or married to a person who is in a relationship described in § 267(b) with any of the foregoing persons;
(h)   the appraiser is not an appraiser who was regularly used by the decedent or who is regularly used by the taxpayer or the beneficiary or donee; and
(i)   the appraisal fee is not based on the appraised value of the item of art;
(2)   include the name, address, and taxpayer identification number (if a taxpayer identification number is otherwise required by § 6109 and the regulations thereunder) of the appraiser. If the appraiser is acting in his or her capacity as a partner in a partnership, an employee of any person (whether an individual, corporation, or partnership), or an independent contractor engaged by a person other than the taxpayer, the appraiser must include

the name, address, and taxpayer identification number (if a taxpayer identification number is otherwise required by § 6109 and the regulations
thereunder) of the partnership or the person who employs or engages the
appraiser; and

(3) include the qualifications of the appraiser who signs the appraisal, including the appraiser's background, experience, education, and membership, if
any, in professional appraisal associations.

.05 The appraisal will not satisfy the requirements of this section if the taxpayer
has knowledge of facts that would cause a reasonable person to expect the appraiser to overstate or understate the value of the item of art.

SECTION 9. TAXPAYER'S DECLARATION
.01 A request to obtain a Statement of Value, any factual representations associated with the request, and any amendments to the request must be accompanied
by the following declaration: "UNDER PENALTIES OF PERJURY, I DECLARE THAT I HAVE
EXAMINED THIS REQUEST, INCLUDING THE ACCOMPANYING DOCUMENTS, AND TO THE
BEST OF MY KNOWLEDGE AND BELIEF, THE FACTS PRESENTED IN SUPPORT OF THIS RE-
QUEST ARE TRUE, CORRECT, AND COMPLETE."

.02 The declaration must be signed by the taxpayer, and not the taxpayer's representative. The person signing for an estate must be the executor or administrator
of the estate. The person signing for a trust or partnership must be a trustee or
general partner who has personal knowledge of the facts. The person signing for
a corporate taxpayer must be an officer of the corporate taxpayer who has personal knowledge of the facts. If a corporate taxpayer is a member of an affiliated
group filing consolidated returns, a penalties-of-perjury statement must also be
signed and submitted by an officer of the common parent of the group.

.03 A taxpayer that submits additional factual information on several occasions
may provide one declaration that refers to all submissions.

SECTION 10. WHERE TO SUBMIT REQUESTS
Requests for a Statement of Value should be sent to the Internal Revenue Service,
POB 120, Ben Franklin Station, Washington, DC 20044, Attn: C:AP:AS:ART.

SECTION 11. NATIONAL OFFICE CONSIDERATION OF REQUESTS
.01 For a completed request for a Statement of Value received after July 15, but
on or before January 15, the Service will ordinarily issue a Statement of Value
by the following June 30. For a completed request for a Statement of Value received after January 15, but on or before July 15, the Service will ordinarily issue
a Statement of Value by the following December 31. It is the responsibility of
taxpayers to obtain extensions, as necessary, to file the appropriate tax returns.

.02 If the Service agrees with the value reported on the taxpayer's appraisal, the
Service will issue a Statement of Value approving the appraisal.

.03 If the Service disagrees with the value reported on the taxpayer's appraisal, the Service will issue a Statement of Value with the Service's determination of value, and the basis for its disagreement with the taxpayer's appraisal.

SECTION 12. ATTACHMENT OF STATEMENT OF VALUE TO RETURN

.01 A copy of the Statement of Value, regardless of whether the taxpayer agrees with it, must be attached to and filed with the taxpayer's income, estate, or gift tax return that reports the transfer of the item of art valued in the Statement of Value. However, if, prior to receiving a Statement of Value, the taxpayer files an income, estate, or gift tax return reporting the transfer of an item of art for which a Statement of Value was requested, the taxpayer must indicate on the return that a Statement of Value has been requested and attach a copy of the request to the return. Upon receipt of the Statement of Value, the taxpayer must file an amended income or gift tax return, or a supplemental estate tax return, with the Statement of Value attached.

.02 If a taxpayer disagrees with a Statement of Value issued by the Service, the taxpayer may submit with the tax return additional information in support of a different value.

SECTION 13. EFFECT OF STATEMENT OF VALUE

.01 A taxpayer may rely on a Statement of Value received from the Service for an item of art, except as provided in sections 13.02 and 13.03 of this revenue procedure.

.02 A taxpayer may not rely on a Statement of Value issued to another taxpayer.

.03 A taxpayer may not rely on a Statement of Value if the representations upon which the Statement of Value was based are not accurate statements of the material facts.

SECTION 14. EFFECT ON OTHER DOCUMENTS

Rev. Proc. 66-49 is modified.

SECTION 15. EFFECTIVE DATE

This revenue procedure applies to a request for a Statement of Value for an item of art if the request is submitted after January 15, 1996.

DRAFTING INFORMATION

The principal authors of this revenue procedure are Jefferson K. Fox of the Office of Chief Counsel (Income Tax and Accounting) and Deborah Ryan of the Office of Chief Counsel (Pass-throughs and Special Industries). For further information regarding this revenue procedure, contact Karen Carolan of the Office of Art Appraisal Services at (202) 401-4128 (not a toll-free call).

NEW YORK UNIFORM COMMERCIAL CODE
(SELECTED SECTIONS OF
ARTICLE 2 AND ARTICLE 9)

§ 2-312. WARRANTY OF TITLE AND AGAINST INFRINGEMENT; BUYER'S
OBLIGATION AGAINST INFRINGEMENT

(1) Subject to subsection (2) there is in a contract for sale a warranty by the
     seller that
     (a)   the title conveyed shall be good, and its transfer rightful; and
     (b)   the goods shall be delivered free from any security interest or other
     lien or encumbrance of which the buyer at the time of contracting has no
     knowledge.
(2) A warranty under subsection (1) will be excluded or modified only by spe-
     cific language or by circumstances which give the buyer reason to know
     that the person selling does not claim title in himself or that he is purport-
     ing to sell only such right or title as he or a third person may have.
(3) Unless otherwise agreed a seller who is a merchant regularly dealing in
     goods of the kind warrants that the goods shall be delivered free of the
     rightful claim of any third person by way of infringement or the like but
     a buyer who furnishes specifications to the seller must hold the seller
     harmless against any such claim which arises out of compliance with the
     specifications.

§ 2-313. EXPRESS WARRANTIES BY AFFIRMATION, PROMISE,
DESCRIPTION, SAMPLE

(1) Express warranties by the seller are created as follows:
     (a)   Any affirmation of fact or promise made by the seller to the buyer
     which relates to the goods and becomes part of the basis of the bargain cre-
     ates an express warranty that the goods shall conform to the affirmation or
     promise.
     (b)   Any description of the goods which is made part of the basis of the
     bargain creates an express warranty that the goods shall conform to the
     description.
     (c)   Any sample or model which is made part of the basis of the bargain
     creates an express warranty that the whole of the goods shall conform to
     the sample or model.
(2) It is not necessary to the creation of an express warranty that the seller use
     formal words such as "warrant" or "guarantee" or that he have a specific
     intention to make a warranty, but an affirmation merely of the value of the
     goods or a statement purporting to be merely the seller's opinion or com-
     mendation of the goods does not create a warranty.

§ 2-314. IMPLIED WARRANTY: MERCHANTABILITY; USAGE OF TRADE
(1) Unless excluded or modified (Section 2-316), a warranty that the goods
shall be merchantable is implied in a contract for their sale if the seller is a
merchant with respect to goods of that kind. Under this section the serving
for value of food or drink to be consumed either on the premises or elsewhere is a sale.
(2) Goods to be merchantable must be at least such as
   (a)   pass without objection in the trade under the contract description; and
   (b)   in the case of fungible goods, are of fair average quality within the description; and
   (c)   are fit for the ordinary purposes for which such goods are used; and
   (d)   run, within the variations permitted by the agreement, of even kind,
quality and quantity within each unit and among all units involved; and
   (e)   are adequately contained, packaged, and labeled as the agreement may
require; and
   (f)   conform to the promises or affirmations of fact made on the container
or label if any.
(3) Unless excluded or modified (Section 2-316) other implied warranties may
arise from course of dealing or usage of trade.

§ 2-315. IMPLIED WARRANTY: FITNESS FOR PARTICULAR PURPOSE
Where the seller at the time of contracting has reason to know any particular
purpose for which the goods are required and that the buyer is relying on the
seller's skill or judgment to select or furnish suitable goods, there is unless excluded or modified under the next section an implied warranty that the goods
shall be fit for such purpose.

§ 2-316. EXCLUSION OR MODIFICATION OF WARRANTIES
(1) Words or conduct relevant to the creation of an express warranty and
words or conduct tending to negate or limit warranty shall be construed
wherever reasonable as consistent with each other; but subject to the provisions of this Article on parol or extrinsic evidence (Section 2-202) negation or limitation is inoperative to the extent that such construction is
unreasonable.
(2) Subject to subsection (3), to exclude or modify the implied warranty of
merchantability or any part of it the language must mention merchantability and in case of a writing must be conspicuous, and to exclude or modify
any implied warranty of fitness the exclusion must be by a writing and
conspicuous. Language to exclude all implied warranties of fitness is sufficient if it states, for example, that "There are no warranties which extend
beyond the description on the face hereof."
(3) Notwithstanding subsection (2)
   (a)   unless the circumstances indicate otherwise, all implied warranties
are excluded by expressions like "as is", "with all faults" or other language
which in common understanding calls the buyer's attention to the exclusion of warranties and makes plain that there is no implied warranty; and

(b)   when the buyer before entering into the contract has examined the goods or the sample or model as fully as he desired or has refused to examine the goods there is no implied warranty with regard to defects which an examination ought in the circumstances to have revealed to him; and

(c)   an implied warranty can also be excluded or modified by course of dealing or course of performance or usage of trade.

(4)   Remedies for breach of warranty can be limited in accordance with the provisions of this Article on liquidation or limitation of damages and on contractual modification of remedy (Sections 2-718 and 2-719).

§ 2-326. SALE ON APPROVAL AND SALE OR RETURN; RIGHTS OF CREDITORS

(1)   Unless otherwise agreed, if delivered goods may be returned by the buyer even though they conform to the contract, the transaction is

(a)   a "sale on approval" if the goods are delivered primarily for use, and

(b)   a "sale or return" if the goods are delivered primarily for resale.

(2)   Goods held on approval are not subject to the claims of the buyer's creditors until acceptance; goods held on sale or return are subject to such claims while in the buyer's possession.

(3)   Any "or return" term of a contract for sale is to be treated as a separate contract for sale within the statute of frauds section of this Article (Section 2-201) and as contradicting the sale aspect of the contract within the provisions of this Article on parol or extrinsic evidence (Section 2-202).

§ 2-401. PASSING OF TITLE; RESERVATION FOR SECURITY; LIMITED APPLICATION OF THIS SECTION

Each provision of this Article with regard to the rights, obligations and remedies of the seller, the buyer, purchasers or other third parties applies irrespective of title to the goods except where the provision refers to such title. Insofar as situations are not covered by the other provisions of this Article and matters concerning title become material the following rules apply:

(1)   Title to goods cannot pass under a contract for sale prior to their identification to the contract (Section 2-501), and unless

otherwise explicitly agreed the buyer acquires by their identification a special property as limited by this Act. Any retention or reservation by the seller of the title (property) in goods shipped or delivered to the buyer is limited in effect to a reservation of a security interest. Subject to these provisions and to the provisions of the Article on Secured Transactions (Article 9), title to goods passes from the seller to the buyer in any manner and on any conditions explicitly agreed on by the parties.

(2)   Unless otherwise explicitly agreed title passes to the buyer at the time and place at which the seller completes his performance with reference to the physical delivery of the goods, despite any reservation of a security interest and even though a document of title is to be delivered at a different time or place; and in particular and despite any reservation of a security interest by the bill of lading

(a)   if the contract requires or authorizes the seller to send the goods to the buyer but does not require him to deliver them at destination, title passes to the buyer at the time and place of shipment; but

(b)   if the contract requires delivery at destination, title passes on tender there.

(3)   Unless otherwise explicitly agreed where delivery is to be made without moving the goods,

(a)   if the seller is to deliver a document of title, title passes at the time when and the place where he delivers such documents; or

(b)   if the goods are at the time of contracting already identified and no documents are to be delivered, title passes at the time and place of contracting.

(4)   A rejection or other refusal by the buyer to receive or retain the goods, whether or not justified, or a justified revocation of acceptance revests title to the goods in the seller. Such revesting occurs by operation of law and is not a "sale".

§ 2-403. POWER TO TRANSFER; GOOD FAITH PURCHASE OF GOODS; "ENTRUSTING"

(1)   A purchaser of goods acquires all title which his transferor had or had power to transfer except that a purchaser of a limited interest acquires rights only to the extent of the interest purchased. A person with voidable title has power to transfer a good title to a good faith purchaser for value. When goods have been delivered under a transaction of purchase the purchaser has such power even though

(a)   the transferor was deceived as to the identity of the purchaser, or

(b)   the delivery was in exchange for a check which is later dishonored, or

(c)   it was agreed that the transaction was to be a "cash sale", or

(d)   the delivery was procured through fraud punishable as larcenous under the criminal law.

(2)   Any entrusting of possession of goods to a merchant who deals in goods of that kind gives him power to transfer all rights of the entruster to a buyer in ordinary course of business.

(3)   "Entrusting" includes any delivery and any acquiescence in retention of possession regardless of any condition expressed between the parties to the delivery or acquiescence and regardless of whether the procurement of the entrusting or the possessor's disposition of the goods has been such as to be larcenous under the criminal law.

(4)   The rights of other purchasers of goods and of lien creditors are governed by the Articles on Secured Transactions (Article 9), Bulk Transfers (Article 6) and Documents of Title (Article 7).

§ 2-725. STATUTE OF LIMITATIONS IN CONTRACTS FOR SALE

(1)   An action for breach of any contract for sale must be commenced within four years after the cause of action has accrued. By the original agreement the parties may reduce the period of limitation to not less than one year but may not extend it.

(2)   A cause of action accrues when the breach occurs, regardless of the ag-
      grieved party's lack of knowledge of the breach. A breach of warranty
      occurs when tender of delivery is made, except that where a warranty ex-
      plicitly extends to future performance of the goods and discovery of the
      breach must await the time of such performance the cause of action accrues
      when the breach is or should have been discovered.
(3)   Where an action commenced within the time limited by subsection (1)
      is so terminated as to leave available a remedy by another action for the
      same breach such other action may be commenced after the expiration of
      the time limited and within six months after the termination of the first
      action unless the termination resulted from voluntary discontinuance or
      from dismissal for failure or neglect to prosecute.
(4)   This section does not alter the law on tolling of the statute of limitations
      nor does it apply to causes of action which have accrued before this Act be-
      comes effective.

§ 9-102. DEFINITIONS AND INDEX OF DEFINITIONS
(a)   Article 9 definitions. In this article:
      . . .
(20) "Consignment" means a transaction, regardless of its form, in which a per-
      son delivers goods to a merchant for the purpose of sale and:
      (A) the merchant:
          (i)   deals in goods of that kind under a name other than the name of
                 the person making delivery;
          (ii)   is not an auctioneer; and
          (iii) is not generally known by its creditors to be substantially engaged
                 in selling the goods of others;
      (B) with respect to each delivery, the aggregate value of the goods is $1,000
      or more at the time of delivery;
      (C) the goods are not consumer goods immediately before delivery; and
      (D) the transaction does not create a security interest that secures an
      obligation.

§ 9-315. SECURED PARTY'S RIGHTS ON DISPOSITION OF COLLATERAL
AND IN PROCEEDS
(a)   Disposition of collateral: continuation of security interest or agricultural
      lien; proceeds. Except as otherwise provided in this article and in Section
      2-403(2):
      (1)   a security interest or agricultural lien continues in collateral notwith-
      standing sale, lease, license, exchange, or other disposition thereof unless
      the secured party authorized the disposition free of the security interest or
      agricultural lien; and
      (2)   a security interest attaches to any identifiable proceeds of collateral.

(b) When commingled proceeds identifiable. Proceeds that are commingled with other property are identifiable proceeds:

(1)   if the proceeds are goods, to the extent provided by Section 9-336; and

(2)   if the proceeds are not goods, to the extent that the secured party identifies the proceeds by a method of tracing, including application of equitable principles, that is permitted under law other than this article with respect to commingled property of the type involved.

(c) Perfection of security interest in proceeds. A security interest in proceeds is a perfected security interest if the security interest in the original collateral was perfected.

(d) Continuation of perfection. A perfected security interest in proceeds becomes unperfected on the 21st day after the security interest attaches to the proceeds unless:

(1)   the following conditions are satisfied:

(A)   a filed financing statement covers the original collateral;

(B)   the proceeds are collateral in which a security interest may be perfected by filing in the office in which the financing statement has been filed; and

(C)   the proceeds are not acquired with cash proceeds;

(2)   the proceeds are identifiable cash proceeds; or

(3)   the security interest in the proceeds is perfected other than under subsection (c) when the security interest attaches to the proceeds or within 20 days thereafter.

(e) When perfected security interest in proceeds becomes unperfected. If a filed financing statement covers the original collateral, a security interest in proceeds which remains perfected under subsection (d)(1) becomes unperfected at the later of:

(1)   when the effectiveness of the filed financing statement lapses under Section 9-515 or is terminated under Section 9-513; or

(2)   the 21st day after the security interest attaches to the proceeds.

§ 9-319. RIGHTS AND TITLE OF CONSIGNEE WITH RESPECT TO
CREDITORS AND PURCHASERS

(a) Consignee has consignor's rights. Except as otherwise provided in subsection (b), for purposes of determining the rights of creditors of, and purchasers for value of goods from, a consignee, while the goods are in the possession of the consignee, the consignee is deemed to have rights and title to the goods identical to those the consignor had or had power to transfer.

(b) Applicability of other law. For purposes of determining the rights of a creditor of a consignee, law other than this article determines the rights and title of a consignee while goods are in the consignee's possession if, under this part, a perfected security interest held by the consignor would have priority over the rights of the creditor.

§ 9-320. BUYER OF GOODS

(a) Buyer in ordinary course of business. Except as otherwise provided in subsection (e), a buyer in ordinary course of business, other than a person buying farm products from a person engaged in farming operations, takes free of a security interest created by the buyer's seller, even if the security interest is perfected and the buyer knows of its existence.

(b) Buyer of consumer goods. Except as otherwise provided in subsection (e), a buyer of goods from a person who used or bought the goods for use primarily for personal, family, or household purposes takes free of a security interest, even if perfected, if the buyer buys:
  (1) without knowledge of the security interest;
  (2) for value;
  (3) primarily for the buyer's personal, family, or household purposes; and
  (4) before the filing of a financing statement covering the goods.

(c) Effectiveness of filing for subsection (b). To the extent that it affects the priority of a security interest over a buyer of goods under subsection (b), the period of effectiveness of a filing made in the jurisdiction in which the seller is located is governed by Section 9-316(a) and (b).

(d) Buyer in ordinary course of business at wellhead or minehead. A buyer in ordinary course of business buying oil, gas, or other minerals at the wellhead or minehead or after extraction takes free of an interest arising out of an encumbrance.

(e) Possessory security interest not affected. Subsections (a) and (b) do not affect a security interest in goods in the possession of the secured party under Section 9-313.

NEW YORK ARTS AND
CULTURAL AFFAIRS LAW

§ 11.01. DEFINITIONS

As used in this title:

1. "Artist" means the creator of a work of fine art or, in the case of multiples, the person who conceived or created the image which is contained in or which constitutes the master from which the individual print was made.

2. "Art merchant" means a person who is in the business of dealing, exclusively or non-exclusively, in works of fine art or multiples, or a person who by his occupation holds himself out as having knowledge or skill peculiar to such works, or to whom such knowledge or skill may be attributed by his employment of an agent or other intermediary who by his occupation holds himself out as having such knowledge or skill. The term "art merchant" includes an auctioneer who sells such works at public auction, and except in the case of multiples, includes persons, not otherwise defined or treated as art merchants herein, who are consignors or principals of auctioneers.

3. "Author" or "authorship" refers to the creator of a work of fine art or multiple or to the period, culture, source or origin, as the case may be, with which the creation of such work is identified in the description of the work.

4. "Creditors" means "creditor" as defined in subdivision twelve of section 1-201 of the uniform commercial code.

5. "Counterfeit" means a work of fine art or multiple made, altered or copied, with or without intent to deceive, in such manner that it appears or is claimed to have an authorship which it does not in fact possess.

6. "Certificate of authenticity" means a written statement by an art merchant confirming, approving or attesting to the authorship of a work of fine art or multiple, which is capable of being used to the advantage or disadvantage of some person.

7. "Conservation" means acts taken to correct deterioration and alteration and acts taken to prevent, stop or retard deterioration.

8. "Craft" means a functional or non-functional work individually designed, and crafted by hand, in any medium including but not limited to textile, tile, paper, clay, glass, fiber, wood, metal or plastic; provided, however, that if produced in multiples, craft shall not include works mass produced or produced in other than a limited edition.

9. "Fine art" means a painting, sculpture, drawing, or work of graphic art, and print, but not multiples.

10. "Limited edition" means works of art produced from a master, all of which are the same image and bear numbers or other markings to denote the limited production thereof to a stated maximum number of multiples, or are otherwise held out as limited to a maximum number of multiples.

11. "Master" when used alone is used in lieu of and means the same as such things as printing plate, stone, block, screen, photographic negative or other like material which contains an image used to produce visual art objects in multiples, or in the case of sculptures, a mold, model, cast, form or other prototype, other than from glass, which additional multiples of sculpture are produced, fabricated or carved.

12. "On consignment" means that no title to, estate in, or right to possession of, the work of fine art or multiple that is superior to that of the consignor vests in the consignee, notwithstanding the consignee's power or authority to transfer or convey all the right, title and interest of the consignor, in and to such work, to a third person.

13. "Person" means an individual, partnership, corporation, association or other group, however organized.

14. "Print" in addition to meaning a multiple produced by, but not limited to, such processes as engraving, etching, woodcutting, lithography and serigraphy, also means multiples produced or developed from photographic negatives, or any combination thereof.

15. "Proofs" means multiples which are the same as, and which are produced from the same masters as, the multiples in a limited edition, but which, whether so designated or not, are set aside from and are in addition to the limited edition to which they relate.

16. "Reproduction" means a copy, in any medium, of a work of fine art, that is displayed or published under circumstances that, reasonably construed, evinces an intent that it be taken as a representation of a work of fine art as created by the artist.

17. "Reproduction right" means a right to reproduce, prepare derivative works of, distribute copies of, publicly perform or publicly display a work of fine art.

18. "Sculpture" means a three-dimensional fine art object produced, fabricated or carved in multiple from a mold, model, cast, form or other prototype, other than from glass, sold, offered for sale or consigned in, into or from this state for an amount in excess of fifteen hundred dollars.

19. "Signed" means autographed by the artist's own hand, and not by mechanical means of reproduction, after the multiple was produced, whether or not the master was signed or unsigned.

20. "Visual art multiples" or "multiples" means prints, photographs, positive or negative, sculpture and similar art objects produced in more than one copy and sold, offered for sale or consigned in, into or from this state for an amount in excess of one hundred dollars exclusive of any frame or in the case of sculpture, an amount in excess of fifteen hundred dollars. Pages or sheets taken from books and magazines and offered for sale or sold as visual art objects shall be included, but books and magazines are excluded.

21. "Written instrument" means a written or printed agreement, bill of sale, invoice, certificate of authenticity, catalogue or any other written or printed note or memorandum or label describing the work of fine art or multiple which is to be sold, exchanged or consigned by an art merchant.

§ 12.01. ARTIST-ART MERCHANT RELATIONSHIPS

1. Notwithstanding any custom, practice or usage of the trade, any provision of the uniform commercial code or any other law, statute, requirement or rule, or any agreement, note, memorandum or writing to the contrary:

(a)   Whenever an artist or craftsperson, his heirs or personal representatives, delivers or causes to be delivered a work of fine art, craft or a print of his own creation to an art merchant for the purpose of exhibition and/or sale on a commission, fee or other basis of compensation, the delivery to and acceptance thereof by the art merchant establishes a consignor/consignee relationship as between such artist or craftsperson and such art merchant with respect to the said work, and:

   (i)   such consignee shall thereafter be deemed to be the agent of such consignor with respect to the said work;

   (ii)   such work is trust property in the hands of the consignee for the benefit of the consignor;

   (iii)   any proceeds from the sale of such work are trust funds in the hands of the consignee for the benefit of the consignor;

   (iv)   such work shall remain trust property notwithstanding its purchase by the consignee for his own account until the price is paid in full to the consignor; provided that, if such work is resold to a bona fide third party before the consignor has been paid in full, the resale proceeds are trust funds in the hands of the consignee for the benefit of the consignor to the extent necessary to pay any balance still due to the consignor and such trusteeship shall continue until the fiduciary obligation of the consignee with respect to such transaction is discharged in full; and

   (v)   no such trust property or trust funds shall be subject or subordinate to any claim, liens or security interest of any kind or nature whatsoever.

(b)   Waiver of any provision of this section is absolutely void except that a consignor may lawfully waive the provisions of clause (iii) of paragraph (a) of this subdivision, if such waiver is clear, conspicuous, in writing and subscribed by the consignor, provided:

   (i)   no such waiver shall be valid with respect to the first two thousand five hundred dollars of gross proceeds of sales received in any twelve-month period commencing with the date of the execution of such waiver;

   (ii)   no such waiver shall be valid with respect to the proceeds of work initially received on consignment but subsequently purchased by the consignee directly or indirectly for his own account; and

   (iii)   no such waiver shall inure to the benefit of the consignee's creditors in any manner which might be inconsistent with the consignor's rights under this subdivision.

(c)   proceeds from the sale of consigned works covered by this section shall be deemed to be revenue from the sale of tangible goods and not revenue from the provision of services to the consignor or others, except that the provisions of this paragraph shall not apply to proceeds from the sale of consigned works sold at public auction.

2. Nothing in this section shall be construed to have any effect upon any written or oral contract or arrangement in existence prior to September first, nineteen hundred sixty-nine or to any extensions or renewals thereof except by the mutual written consent of the parties thereto.

§ 12.03. EXEMPTION FROM SEIZURE

No process of attachment, execution, sequestration, replevin, distress or any kind of seizure shall be served or levied upon any work of fine art while the same is en route to or from, or while on exhibition or deposited by a nonresident exhibitor at any exhibition held under the auspices or supervision of any museum, college, university or other nonprofit art gallery, institution or organization within any city or county of this state for any cultural, educational, charitable or other purpose not conducted for profit to the exhibitor, nor shall such work of fine art be subject to attachment, seizure, levy or sale, for any cause whatever in the hands of the authorities of such exhibition or otherwise.

§ 13.01. EXPRESS WARRANTIES

Notwithstanding any provision of any other law to the contrary:

1. Whenever an art merchant, in selling or exchanging a work of fine art, furnishes to a buyer of such work who is not an art merchant a certificate of authenticity or any similar written instrument it:
    (a) Shall be presumed to be part of the basis of the bargain; and
    (b) Shall create an express warranty for the material facts stated as of the date of such sale or exchange.
2. Except as provided in subdivision four of this section, such warranty shall not be negated or limited provided that in construing the degree of warranty, due regard shall be given the terminology used and the meaning accorded such terminology by the customs and usage of the trade at the time and in the locality where the sale or exchange took place.
3. Language used in a certificate of authenticity or similar written instrument, stating that:
    (a) The work is by a named author or has a named authorship, without any limiting words, means uneqivocally, that the work is by such named author or has such named authorship;
    (b) The work is "attributed to a named author" means a work of the period of the author, attributed to him, but not with certainty by him; or
    (c) The work is of the "school of a named author" means a work of the period of the author, by a pupil or close follower of the author, but not by the author.
4. (a) An express warranty and disclaimers intended to negate or limit such warranty shall be construed wherever reasonable as consistent with each other but subject to the provisions of section 2-202 of the uniform commercial code on parol or extrinsic evidence, negation or limitation is inoperative to the extent that such construction is unreasonable.

(b)   Such negation or limitation shall be deemed unreasonable if:
  (i)   the disclaimer is not conspicuous, written and apart from the warranty, in words which clearly and specifically apprise the buyer that the seller assumes no risk, liability or responsibility for the material facts stated concerning such work of fine art. Words of general disclaimer are not sufficient to negate or limit an express warranty; or
  (ii)   the work of fine art is proved to be a counterfeit and this was not clearly indicated in the description of the work; or
  (iii)   the information provided is proved to be, as of the date of sale or exchange, false, mistaken or erroneous.

§ 13.03. FALSIFYING CERTIFICATES OF AUTHENTICITY OR ANY SIMILAR WRITTEN INSTRUMENT

A person who, with intent to defraud, deceive or injure another, makes, utters or issues a certificate of authenticity or any similar written instrument for a work of fine art attesting to material facts which the work does not in fact possess is guilty of a class A misdemeanor.

§ 13.05. EXPRESS WARRANTIES FOR MULTIPLES

1.   When an art merchant furnishes the name of the artist of a multiple, or otherwise furnishes information required by this title for any time period as to transactions including offers, sales or consignments, the provisions of section 13.01 of this article shall apply except that said section shall be deemed to include sales to art merchants. The existence of a reasonable basis in fact for information warranted shall not be a defense in an action to enforce such warranty, except in the case of photographs produced prior to nineteen hundred fifty, and multiples produced prior to nineteen hundred.
2.   The provisions of subdivision four of section 13.01 of this article shall apply when an art merchant disclaims knowledge as to a multiple about which information is required by this title, provided that in addition, such disclaimer shall be ineffective unless clearly, specifically and categorically stated as to each item of information and contained in the physical context of other language setting forth the required information as to a specific multiple.

§ 13.07. CONSTRUCTION

1.   The rights and liabilities created by this article shall be construed to be in addition to and not in substitution, exclusion or displacement of other rights and liabilities provided by law, including the law of principal and agent, except where such construction would, as a matter of law, be unreasonable.
2.   No art merchant who, as buyer, is excluded from obtaining the benefits of an express warranty under this article shall thereby be deprived of the benefits of any other provision of law.

§ 14.01. RIGHT TO REPRODUCE WORKS OF FINE ART

1. Whenever a work of fine art is sold or otherwise transferred by or on be-half of the artist who created it, or his heirs or personal representatives, the reproduction right thereto is reserved to the grantor until it passes into the public domain by act or operation of law unless such right is sooner expressly transferred by an instrument, note or memorandum in writing signed by the owner of the rights conveyed or his duly authorized agent.

2. Whenever an exclusive or non-exclusive conveyance of any reproduction right is made by the holder of such right, or his duly authorized agent, ownership of the physical work of fine art shall be presumed to remain with and be reserved to the grantor unless expressly transferred in writing by an instrument, note or memorandum or by other written means, signed by the grantor or his duly authorized agent.

3. This article shall not apply to the sale, conveyance, donation or other trans-fer of the physical work of fine art which does not include a conveyance of a reproduction right in such work.

4. Nothing herein contained, however, shall be construed to prohibit the fair use of such work of fine art.

5. Nothing in this section shall operate or be construed to conflict with any rights or liabilities under federal copyright law.

§ 14.03. ARTISTS AUTHORSHIP RIGHTS

1. Except as limited by subdivision three of this section, on and after Janu-ary first, nineteen hundred eighty-five, no person other than the artist or a person acting with the artist's consent shall knowingly display in a place accessible to the public or publish a work of fine art or limited edition mul-tiple of not more than three hundred copies by that artist or a reproduction thereof in an altered, defaced, mutilated or modified form if the work is displayed, published or reproduced as being the work of the artist, or under circumstances under which it would reasonably be regarded as being the work of the artist, and damage to the artist's reputation is reasonably likely to result therefrom, except that this section shall not apply to sequential imagery such as that in motion pictures.

2. (a) Except as limited by subdivision three of this section, the artist shall retain at all times the right to claim authorship, or, for just and valid rea-son, to disclaim authorship of such work. The right to claim authorship shall include the right of the artist to have his or her name appear on or in connection with such work as the artist. The right to disclaim authorship shall include the right of the artist to prevent his or her name from appear-ing on or in connection with such work as the artist. Just and valid reason for disclaiming authorship shall include that the work has been altered, defaced, mutilated or modified other than by the artist, without the artist's consent, and damage to the artist's reputation is reasonably likely to result or has resulted therefrom.

    (b) The rights created by this subdivision shall exist in addition to any other rights and duties which may now or in the future be applicable.

3. (a) Alteration, defacement, mutilation or modification of such work resulting from the passage of time or the inherent nature of the materials will not by itself create a violation of subdivision one of this section or a right to disclaim authorship under subdivision two of this section; provided such alteration, defacement, mutilation or modification was not the result of gross negligence in maintaining or protecting the work of fine art.

(b) In the case of a reproduction, a change that is an ordinary result of the medium of reproduction does not by itself create a violation of subdivision one of this section or a right to disclaim authorship under subdivision two of this section.

(c) Conservation shall not constitute an alteration, defacement, mutilation or modification within the meaning of this section, unless the conservation work can be shown to be negligent.

(d) This section shall not apply to work prepared under contract for advertising or trade use unless the contract so provides.

(e) The provisions of this section shall apply only to works of fine art or limited edition multiples of not more than three hundred copies knowingly displayed in a place accessible to the public, published or reproduced in this state.

4. (a) An artist aggrieved under subdivision one or subdivision two of this section shall have a cause of action for legal and injunctive relief.

(b) No action may be maintained to enforce any liability under this section unless brought within three years of the act complained of or one year after the constructive discovery of such act, whichever is longer.

§ 14.05. SCULPTURE; IDENTIFYING MARK

1. Every sculpture produced, fabricated or carved in or from this state after January first, nineteen hundred ninety-one shall contain thereon, in a clear and legible fashion and in an easily accessible location, a distinctive mark which identifies the foundry or other production facility at which such sculpture was made, and the year that such sculpture was made. This section shall also apply to unique works of sculpture produced, fabricated or carved in this state.

2. It shall be unlawful for a foundry or other production facility (a) to fail or refuse to affix an identifying mark and the year or (b) to affix a false identifying mark or incorrect year to any sculpture produced by it. Notwithstanding any other provision of law, violation of this subdivision shall be punishable by a civil penalty not to exceed five thousand dollars for each unlabeled or mislabeled sculpture.

3. It shall be unlawful for any person to deface, mark over or tamper with the identifying mark and date required by this section to be included on a sculpture. Notwithstanding any other provision of law, violation of this subdivision shall be punishable by a civil penalty not to exceed five thousand dollars for each instance of defacing, marking over or tampering with such identifying mark or date. Any violation of this subdivision shall be punishable in accordance with the penal law.

§ 14.06. SCULPTURE; WRITTEN RECORDS

1. Any foundry or person in this state producing one or more sculptures for any person subsequent to the effective date of this article shall prepare, and maintain for a period of not less than twenty-five years from the date of such production, records that shall contain all of the information required to be provided pursuant to subdivisions one and two of section 15.10 of this chapter. Such records shall be open for inspection by the attorney general during ordinary business hours upon notice of no less than three business days.

2. A duplicate of the written instrument provided to a purchaser by an art merchant or art merchant's agent supplying information pursuant to article fifteen of this chapter shall be retained by such art merchant and the art merchant's agent for a period of not less than ten years from the date of sale of the work, and shall be similarly considered a certificate of authenticity subject to the provisions of section 13.03 of this chapter.

§ 14.07. SCULPTURE; UNAUTHORIZED CAST

1. For purposes of this section an "unauthorized sculpture cast" shall mean any sculpture created by an artist which is produced, fabricated, or carved either before or following the death of such artist without the written permission of the artist or the estate, heirs, or other legal representative of the artist.

2. It shall be unlawful to produce, offer for sale, sell or consign an unauthorized sculpture cast, provided, however, that this prohibition shall not apply where the phrase "THIS IS A REPRODUCTION" is imprinted and appears in a clear and legible fashion on each such sculpture in the same location and with the same size lettering as the date and identifying mark as required by section 14.05 of this article.

§ 14.08. VIOLATIONS

Any violation of the provisions of section 14.05, 14.06 or 14.07 of this article may be enforced by the attorney general in accordance with the provisions of section 15.17 of this chapter.

§ 15.01. FULL DISCLOSURE IN THE SALE OF CERTAIN VISUAL ART OBJECTS PRODUCED IN MULTIPLES

1. An art merchant shall not sell or consign a multiple in, into or from this state unless a written instrument is furnished to the purchaser or consignee, at his request, or in any event prior to a sale or consignment, which sets forth as to each multiple the descriptive information required by this article for the appropriate time period. If a prospective purchaser so requests, the information shall be transmitted to him prior to the payment or placing of an order for a multiple. If payment is made by a purchaser prior to delivery of such an art multiple, this information shall be supplied at the time of or prior to delivery. With respect to auctions, this information may be furnished in catalogues or other written materials which are readily available for consultation and purchase prior to sale, provided that a bill of sale, receipt or invoice describing the transaction is then provided which

makes reference to the catalogue and lot number in which such information is supplied. Information supplied pursuant to this subdivision shall be clearly, specifically and distinctly addressed to each item as required by this article for any time period unless the required data is not applicable. This section is applicable to transactions by and between merchants, non-merchants, and others considered art merchants for the purposes of this article.

2. An art merchant shall not cause a catalogue, prospectus, flyer or other written material or advertisement to be distributed in, into or from this state which solicits a direct sale, by inviting transmittal of payment for a specific multiple, unless it clearly sets forth, in close physical proximity to the place in such material where the multiple is described, the descriptive information required by this article for the appropriate time period. In lieu of this required information, such written material or advertising may set forth the material contained in the following quoted passage, or the passage itself, containing terms the nonobservance of which shall constitute a violation of this article, if the art merchant then supplies the required information prior to or with delivery of the multiple:

"Article fifteen of the New York arts and cultural affairs law provides for disclosure in writing of certain information concerning multiples of prints and photographs when sold for more than one hundred dollars ($100) each, exclusive of any frame, and of sculpture when sold for more than fifteen hundred dollars, prior to effecting a sale of them. This law requires disclosure of such matters as the identity of the artist, the artist's signature, the medium, whether the multiple is a reproduction, the time when the multiple was produced, use of the master which produced the multiple, and the number of multiples in a 'limited edition'. If a prospective purchaser so requests, the information shall be transmitted to him prior to payment or the placing of an order for a multiple. If payment is made by a purchaser prior to delivery of such an art multiple, this information will be supplied at the time of or prior to delivery, in which case the purchaser is entitled to a refund if, for reasons related to matter contained in such information, he returns the multiple substantially in the condition in which received, within thirty days of receiving it. In addition, if after payment and delivery, it is ascertained that the information provided is incorrect the purchaser may be entitled to certain remedies."

This requirement is not applicable to general written material or advertising which does not constitute an offer to effect a specific sale.

3. In each place of business in the state where an art merchant is regularly engaged in sales of multiples, the art merchant shall post in a conspicuous place, a sign which, in a legible format, contains the information included in the following passage:

"Article fifteen of the New York arts and cultural affairs law provides for the disclosure in writing of certain information concerning prints, photographs and sculpture. This information is available to you in accordance with that law."

§ 15.03. INFORMATION REQUIRED

The following information shall be supplied, as indicated, as to each multiple produced on or after January first, nineteen hundred eighty-two:

1. Artist. State the name of the artist.
2. Signature. If the artist's name appears on the multiple, state whether the multiple was signed by the artist. If not signed by the artist then state the source of the artist's name on the multiple, such as whether the artist placed his signature on the master, whether his name was stamped or estate stamped on the multiple, or was from some other source or in some other manner placed on the multiple.
3. Medium or process.
   (a)   Describe the medium or process, and where pertinent to photographic processes the material, used in producing the multiple, such as whether the multiple was produced through etching, engraving, lithographic, serigraphic or a particular method and/or material used in the photographic developing processes. If an established term, in accordance with the usage of the trade, cannot be employed accurately to describe the medium or process, a brief, clear description shall be made.
   (b)   If the purported artist was deceased at the time the master was made which produced the multiple, this shall be stated.
   (c)   If the multiple or the image on or in the master constitutes a mechanical, photomechanical, hand-made or photographic type of reproduction, or is a reproduction, of an image produced in a different medium, for a purpose other than the creation of the multiple being described, this information and the respective mediums shall be stated.
   (d)   If paragraph (c) of this subdivision is applicable, and the multiple is not signed, state whether the artist authorized or approved in writing the multiple or the edition of which the multiple being described is one.
4. Use of master.
   (a)   If the multiple is a "posthumous" multiple, that is, if the master was created during the life of the artist but the multiple was produced after the artist's death, this shall be stated.
   (b)   If the multiple was made from a master which produced a prior limited edition, or from a master which constitutes or was made from a reproduction of a prior multiple or of a master which produced prior multiples, this shall be stated.
5. Time produced. As to multiples produced after nineteen hundred forty-nine, state the year or approximate year the multiple was produced. As to multiples produced prior to nineteen hundred fifty, state the year, approximate year or period when the master was made which produced the multiple and/or when the particular multiple being described was produced. The requirements of this subdivision shall be satisfied when the year stated is approximately accurate.
6. Size of the edition.
   (a)   If the multiple being described is offered as one of a limited edition, this shall be so stated, as well as the number of multiples in the edition, and whether and how the multiple is numbered.

(b)   Unless otherwise disclosed, the number of multiples stated pursuant to paragraph (a) of this subdivision shall constitute an express warranty, as defined in section 13.01 of this title, that no additional numbered multiples of the same image, exclusive of proofs, have been produced.

(c)   The number of multiples stated pursuant to paragraph (a) of this subdivision shall also constitute an express warranty, as defined in section 13.01 of this title, that no additional multiples of the same image, whether designated "proofs" other than trial proofs, numbered or otherwise, have been produced in an amount which exceeds the number in the limited edition by twenty or twenty percent, whichever is greater.

(d)   If the number of multiples exceeds the number in the stated limited edition as provided in paragraph (c) of this subdivision, then state the number of proofs other than trial proofs, or other numbered or unnumbered multiples, in the same or other prior editions, produced from the same master as described in paragraph (b) of subdivision four of this section, and whether and how they are signed and numbered.

§ 15.05. INFORMATION REQUIRED; NINETEEN HUNDRED FIFTY TO JANUARY FIRST, NINETEEN HUNDRED EIGHTY-TWO

The information which shall be supplied as to each multiple produced during the period from nineteen hundred fifty to January first, nineteen hundred eighty-two, shall consist of the information required by section 15.03 of this article except for paragraph (d) of subdivision three, paragraph (b) of subdivision four and paragraphs (c) and (d) of subdivision six of such section.

§ 15.07. INFORMATION REQUIRED; NINETEEN HUNDRED TO NINETEEN HUNDRED FORTY-NINE

The information which shall be supplied as to each multiple produced during the period from nineteen hundred through nineteen hundred forty-nine shall consist of the information required by section 15.03 of this article except for paragraphs (b), (c) and (d) of subdivision three and subdivisions four and six of such section.

§ 15.09. INFORMATION REQUIRED; PRE-NINETEEN HUNDRED

The information which shall be supplied as to each multiple produced prior to nineteen hundred shall consist of the information required by section 15.03 of this article except for subdivision two, paragraphs (b), (c) and (d) of subdivision three and subdivisions four and six of such section 15.03.

§ 15.10. INFORMATION REQUIRED FOR SCULPTURES

1.   The following information shall be supplied as indicated in a written instrument as to each multiple produced, fabricated or carved, on or after January first, nineteen hundred ninety-one:

(a)   Artist. State the name of the artist.

(b)   Title. State the title of the sculpture.

(c)   Foundry. State the name, if known, of the foundry which or person who produced, fabricated or carved the sculpture.

(d)   Medium. Describe the medium or process used in producing the multiple. If an established term, in accordance with the usage of the trade, cannot be employed accurately to describe the medium or process, a brief, clear description shall be made.

(e)   Dimensions. State the dimensions of the sculpture.

(f)   Time produced. State the year the sculpture was cast, fabricated or carved.

(g)   Number cast. State the number of sculpture casts, according to the best information available, produced or fabricated or carved as of the date of the sale.

(h)   If the purported artist was deceased at the time the sculpture was produced, this shall be stated.

(i)   Use of master. State whether the sculpture is authorized by the artist or, if produced after the artist's death, whether it was authorized in writing by the artist or by the estate, heirs or other legal representatives of the artist. In the event of a sale after the initial sale, the art merchant may disclose in writing evidence of such reasonable inquiries as have been made pursuant to subdivision two of section 15.15

of this article and any information imparted as may be relevant in fulfilling the intent of this paragraph.

2.   For limited edition sculpture produced on or after January first, nineteen hundred ninety-one, in addition to the information required to be provided pursuant to subdivision one of this section, the following items of information shall also be provided to the purchaser in a written instrument:

(a)   whether and how the sculpture and the edition is numbered;

(b)   the size of the edition or proposed edition and the size of any prior edition or editions of the same sculpture, regardless of the color or material used;

(c)   whether additional sculpture casts have been produced in excess of the stated size of the edition or proposed edition and, if so, the total number of such excess casts produced or proposed to be produced and whether and how they are or will be numbered according to the stated intention of the artist or a statement that the artist has not disclosed his intention about the number of additional casts or their numbering. Additional sculpture casts shall include all casts from the same master regardless of their color, material or size; and

(d)   whether the artist has stated in writing a limitation on the number of additional sculpture casts to be produced in excess of the stated size of the edition or proposed edition and, if so, the total number of such excess casts produced or proposed to be produced and whether and how they are or will be numbered according to the stated intention of the artist or the estate, heirs or other legal representatives of the artist or a statement that the artist has not disclosed his intention about the number of additional casts or their numbering. Additional sculpture casts shall include all casts from the same master regardless of their color, material or size.

3. For copies of sculpture not made from the master and produced after January first, nineteen hundred ninety-one, in addition to the information required to be provided pursuant to subdivisions one and two of this section, the following items of information shall also be provided to the purchaser in a written instrument:
    (a) the means by which the copy was made;
    (b) whether the copy was authorized by the artist or the estate, heirs or other legal representatives of the artist; and
    (c) whether the copy is of the same material and size as the master.

§ 15.11. EXPRESS WARRANTIES

Information provided pursuant to the provisions of this article shall create an express warranty pursuant to section 13.05 of this title. When such information is not supplied because not applicable, this shall constitute an express warranty that such required information is not applicable.

§ 15.13. CONSTRUCTION

1. The rights, liabilities and remedies created by this article shall be construed to be in addition to and not in substitution, exclusion
    or displacement of other rights, liabilities and remedies provided by law, except where such construction would, as a matter of law, be unreasonable.
2. Whenever an artist sells or consigns a multiple of his own creation, the artist shall incur the obligations prescribed by this article for an art merchant, but an artist shall not otherwise be regarded as an art merchant.
3. An artist or merchant who consigns a multiple to a merchant for the purpose of effecting a sale of the multiple shall have no liability to a purchaser under this article if such consignor, as to the consignee, has complied with the provisions of this article.
4. When a merchant has agreed to sell a multiple on behalf of a consignor, who is not an art merchant, or when an artist has not consigned a multiple to a merchant, but the merchant has agreed to act as the agent for an artist for the purpose of supplying the information required by this article, such merchant shall incur liabilities of other merchants prescribed by this article as to a purchaser.
5. When an art merchant or merchant is liable to a purchaser pursuant to the provisions of this article, as a result of providing information in the situations referred to above in this section, as well as when such a merchant purchased such a multiple from another merchant, if the merchant or art merchant can establish that his liability results from incorrect information which was provided by the consignor, artist or merchant to him in writing, the merchant who is liable in good faith relied on such information, the consignor, artist or merchant shall similarly incur such liabilities as to the purchaser and such merchant.

§ 15.15. REMEDIES AND ENFORCEMENT

1.   An art merchant, including a merchant consignee, who offers or sells a
     multiple in, into or from this state without providing the information
     required by this article for the appropriate time period, or who provides
     required information which is mistaken, erroneous or untrue, except for
     harmless errors such as typographical errors, shall be liable to the pur-
     chaser to whom the multiple was sold. The merchant's liability shall con-
     sist of the consideration paid by the purchaser with interest from the time
     of payment at the rate prescribed by section five thousand four of the civil
     practice law and rules or any successor provisions thereto, upon the return
     of the multiple in substantially the same condition in which received by
     the purchaser. This remedy shall not bar or be deemed inconsistent with
     a claim for damages or with the exercise of additional remedies otherwise
     available to the purchaser.

2.   In any proceeding in which an art merchant relies upon a disclaimer of
     knowledge as to any relevant information required by this article for the
     appropriate time period, such disclaimer shall be effective only if it com-
     plies with the provisions of section 13.05 of this title, unless the claimant
     is able to establish that the merchant failed to make reasonable inquiries,
     according to the custom and usage of the trade, to ascertain the relevant
     information or that such relevant information would have been ascertained
     as a result of such reasonable inquiries.

3.   (a)   The purchaser of such a multiple may recover from the art merchant
     an amount equal to three times the amount recoverable under subdivision
     one of this section if an art merchant offers, consigns or sells a multiple
     and:
          (i)   willfully fails to provide the information required by this article
                 for the appropriate time period;
          (ii)   knowingly provides false information; or
          (iii) the purchaser can establish that the merchant willfully and falsely
                 disclaimed knowledge as to any required information.
     (b)   Pursuant to subparagraphs (i) and (iii) of paragraph (a) of this sub-
     division, a merchant may introduce evidence of the relevant usage and
     custom of the trade in any proceeding in which such treble damages are
     sought. This subdivision shall not be deemed to negate the applicability of
     article thirteen of this chapter as to authenticity and article thirteen is ap-
     plicable, as to authenticity, to the multiples covered by the provisions of
     this article.

4.   In any action to enforce any provision of this article, the court may allow
     the prevailing purchaser the costs of the action together with reasonable
     attorneys' and expert witnesses' fees. In the event, however, the court de-
     termines that an action to enforce was brought in bad faith it may allow
     such expenses to the art merchant as it deems appropriate.

5.   An action to enforce any liability under this article shall be brought within
     the period prescribed for such actions by article two of the uniform com-
     mercial code.

§ 15.17. ENJOINING VIOLATIONS

Any violation of this article or of section 14.05, 14.06 or 14.07 of this chapter shall be deemed to be unlawful for the purposes of invoking sections three hundred forty-nine and three hundred fifty of article twenty-two-A of the general business law, and any person who engages in repeated violations of this article shall be deemed to have demonstrated the persistent fraud or illegality necessary to invoke subdivision twelve of section sixty-three of the executive law. The attorney general may bring an action pursuant to article twenty-two-A of the general business law or a proceeding pursuant to subdivision twelve of section sixty-three of the executive law to enjoin violations of this article and seek restitution for any person entitled thereto. In any such action or proceeding, the attorney general may recover, in addition to any other relief provided in those statutes, a civil penalty of not more than five hundred dollars to be forfeited to the state, provided, however, that with respect to actions brought pursuant to this section to which article twenty-two-A of the general business law applies, the foregoing civil penalty shall be in lieu of any penalty set forth therein. In connection with any such proposed action or proceeding, the attorney general is authorized to take proof and make a determination of the relevant facts, and to issue subpoenas in accordance with the civil practice law and rules.

§ 15.19. APPLICATION OF THE ARTICLE

This article shall apply to the visual art objects governed by this article which are sold, offered for sale, consigned or possessed with intent to sell in, into or from this state. With respect to such multiples compliance with this article shall commence six months after January first, nineteen hundred eighty-five.

§ 16.01. SEVERABILITY

Effect of unconstitutionality in part. If any clause, sentence, paragraph, subdivision, section or part of this title shall be adjudged by any court of competent jurisdiction to be invalid, such judgment shall not affect, impair or invalidate the remainder thereof, but shall be confined in its operation to the clause, sentence, paragraph, subdivision, section or part thereof directly involved in the controversy in which such judgment shall have been rendered.

NEW YORK CIVIL RIGHTS LAW

(SELECTED SECTIONS)

§ 50. RIGHT OF PRIVACY

A person, firm or corporation that uses for advertising purposes, or for the purposes of trade, the name, portrait or picture of any living person without having first obtained the written consent of such person, or if a minor of his or her parent or guardian, is guilty of a misdemeanor.

§ 51. ACTION FOR INJUNCTION AND FOR DAMAGES

Any person whose name, portrait, picture or voice is used within this state for advertising purposes or for the purposes of trade without the written consent first obtained as above provided may maintain an equitable action in the supreme court of this state against the person, firm or corporation so using his name, portrait, picture or voice, to prevent and restrain the use thereof; and may also sue and recover damages for any injuries sustained by reason of such use and if the defendant shall have knowingly used such person's name, portrait, picture or voice in such manner as is forbidden or declared to be unlawful by section fifty of this article, the jury, in its discretion, may award exemplary damages. But nothing contained in this article shall be so construed as to prevent any person, firm or corporation from selling or otherwise transferring any material containing such name, portrait, picture or voice in whatever medium to any user of such name, portrait, picture or voice, or to any third party for sale or transfer directly or indirectly to such a user, for use in a manner lawful under this article; nothing contained in this article shall be so construed as to prevent any person, firm or corporation, practicing the profession of photography, from exhibiting in or about his or its establishment specimens of the work of such establishment, unless the same is continued by such person, firm or corporation after written notice objecting thereto has been given by the person portrayed; and nothing contained in this article shall be so construed as to prevent any person, firm or corporation from using the name, portrait, picture or voice of any manufacturer or dealer in connection with the goods, wares and merchandise manufactured, produced or dealt in by him which he has sold or disposed of with such name, portrait, picture or voice used in connection therewith; or from using the name, portrait, picture or voice of any author, composer or artist in connection with his literary, musical or artistic productions which he has sold or disposed of with such name, portrait, picture or voice used in connection therewith. Nothing contained in this section shall be construed to prohibit the copyright owner of a sound recording from disposing of, dealing in, licensing or selling that sound recording to any party, if the right to dispose of, deal in, license or sell such sound recording has been conferred by contract or other written document by such living person or the holder of such right. Nothing contained in the foregoing sentence shall be deemed to abrogate or otherwise limit any rights or remedies otherwise conferred by federal law or state law.

NEW YORK EDUCATION LAW

(SELECTED SECTION)

§ 233-A. PROPERTY OF THE STATE MUSEUM

1. As used in this section:
    (a)   The term "museum" shall mean the New York state museum.
    (b)   The term "deaccession" shall mean the permanent removal or disposal of an object from the collection of the museum by virtue of its sale, exchange, donation or transfer by any means to any person.
    (c)   The term "person" shall mean any natural person, partnership, corporation, company, trust association or other entity, however organized.
    (d)   The term "property" means any inanimate object, document or tangible object under the office's care which has intrinsic historic, artistic, scientific, or cultural value.
    (e)   The term "claimant" means a person who asserts ownership or some other legal right to undocumented property held by the museum.
    (f)   The term "loan" means a deposit of property with the museum not accompanied by a transfer to the museum of title to the property.
    (g)   The term "lender" means a person whose name appears on the records of the museum as the person legally entitled to, or claiming to be legally entitled to, property held by the museum or, if deceased, the legal heirs of such person.
    (h)   The term "lender's address" means the most recent address for the lender shown on the museum's records pertaining to the property on loan, or if the lender is deceased, the last known address of the legal heirs of such lender.
    (i)   The term "permanent loan" means a loan of property to the museum for an unspecified period.
    (j)   The term "undocumented property" means property in the possession of the museum for which the museum cannot determine the owner by reference to its records.
    (k)   The term "conservation measures" means any actions taken to preserve or stabilize a property including, but not limited to, proper storage support, cleaning, proper lighting, and restoration.
2. The deaccessioning of property by the museum must be consistent with the mission of the museum.
3. Prior to the acquisition of property by gift, the museum shall provide the donor with a written copy of its mission statement and collections policy, which shall include policies and procedures of the museum relating to deaccessioning.
4. If the museum has the knowledge of a planned bequest of any property prior to the death of the testator, the museum shall provide the testator with a written copy of its mission statement and collections policy, which shall include policies and procedures of the museum relating to deaccessioning.
5. Repealed by L.2012, c. 59, pt. U, § 18-c, eff. March 30, 2012, deemed eff. April 1, 2012.

6. Notice given by the museum under this section must be mailed to the lender's last known address by certified mail, return receipt requested. Service by mail is complete if the museum receives proof that the notice was received not more than thirty days after it was mailed; provided, however, notice may be given by publication if the museum does not:
    (a)   know the identity of the lender; or
    (b)   know the address of the lender; or
    (c)   receive proof that the notice mailed under this section was received within thirty days of mailing. Notice by publication must be given at least once a week for three consecutive weeks in a newspaper of general circulation in:
        (i)   the county in which the property is held by the museum; and
        (ii) the county of the lender's last address, if known.

    The date of notice under this subdivision shall be the date of the third published notice.

    In addition to any other information that may be required or seem appropriate, any notice given under this section must contain the following:

    (A) The name of the lender or claimant, if known.
    (B) The last address of the lender or claimant, if known.
    (C) A brief description of the property on loan to the museum referenced in the notice.
    (D) The date of the loan, if known or the approximate date of acquisition of the property.
    (E) The name and address of the museum.
    (F) The name, address, and telephone number of the person to be contacted regarding the property.

7. Notwithstanding any other provisions of law regarding abandoned or lost property, the museum may, beginning five years from the date the lender last contacted the museum, clarify title to property on permanent loan or loaned for a specified term that has expired. Proof of such contact shall include previously sent restricted letters or loan forms, returned envelopes, inventories and other documentary evidence. The procedure for clarifying title shall be as follows:
    (a)   The museum must give notice by mail to the lender that it wishes to clarify ownership rights in the property.
    (b)   In addition to the information described in subdivision six of this section, the notice shall be entitled "Notice of Termination" and must include a statement containing substantially the following information: "The records of the New York State Museum indicate that you have property on loan at (name of facility). The museum is seeking to determine whether you wish (i) that the museum return the property to you, (ii) that the property remain on loan to the museum subject to annual renewal (if the museum wishes that the property remain on loan), or (iii) that the museum retain

the property permanently as its owner. Please contact (name of contact) in writing within one hundred twenty days, in order to advise the museum as to which of the above alternatives you wish to follow."

(c)   If, no later than one hundred twenty days following receipt thereof, the lender does not respond to the notice of termination by submitting a written claim to the property on loan with verifying documentation the office shall send a second notice to the lender containing the following information: "On (date of first notice), the New York State Museum sent you a notice concerning property that, according to our records, has been loaned to the office. You have not responded to that notice, a copy of which is enclosed, and the museum will commence proceedings to acquire title to the property if you do not contact (name of contact), in writing within one hundred twenty days of receiving this second notice."

If the lender fails to respond to the second notice within one hundred twenty days of receipt, at the request of the commissioner, the attorney general may make an application to the supreme court pursuant to article thirty of the civil practice law and rules for a declaratory judgment to determine the museum's right to such property. In a case in which there is no evidence that the notices previously sent by the museum were received by the lender, upon application, the supreme court shall specify the method by which service shall be made upon the lender.

8.   Notwithstanding any other provision of law regarding abandoned or lost property the museum may acquire title to undocumented property held by the museum for at least five years as follows:

(a)   The museum must give notice by publication that it is asserting title to the undocumented property.

(b)   In addition to the information described herein, the notice shall be entitled "Notice of Intent to Acquire Title to Property" and must include a statement containing substantially the following information: "The records of the New York State Museum fail to indicate the owner of record of certain property in its possession. The museum hereby asserts its intent to acquire title to the following property: (general description of property). If you claim ownership of this property, you must submit written proof of ownership to the museum and make arrangements to collect the property. If you fail to do so within one hundred eighty days, the museum will commence proceedings to acquire title to the property. If you claim an interest in the property but do not possess written proof of such interest, you should submit your name and address and a written statement of your claim to (name of contact), within one hundred eighty days, in order to receive notice of any legal proceedings concerning the property. If you wish to commence legal proceedings to claim the property, you should consult your attorney."

If after one hundred eighty days following the last date of publication of such notice no claimant has responded thereto by submitting written proof of ownership of the property to the museum, or if there is a dispute between the museum and any claimant as to ownership of the property, upon the request of the commissioner, the attorney general may make an application to the supreme court pursuant to article thirty of the civil practice law and rules for a declaratory judgment to determine the museum's rights in the property.

9.   A copy of all notices required by subdivision seven or eight of this section shall be sent, by certified mail, return receipt requested, to the International Foundation for Art Research, or any successor foundation or agency having similar purposes, on or before the date on which such notices are mailed or first published pursuant to the requirements of this section.

10. Any person who purchases or otherwise acquires property from the museum acquires good title to such property if the museum has acquired title in accordance with this section.

11. The provisions of subdivisions seven and eight of this section shall not apply to any property that has been reported as stolen to a law enforcement agency or to the Art Theft Archives of the International Foundation for Art Research, or any successor foundation or agency having similar purposes, no later than one year following the theft or discovery of the theft.

12. The museum shall have the following duty to lenders:
     (a)   When the museum accepts a loan of property, it shall inform the lender in writing of the provisions of this section.
     (b)   The museum shall give a lender, at the lender's address, prompt written notice by mail of any known injury to, or loss of, property on loan or of the need to apply conservation measures. Such notice shall advise the lender of his right, in lieu of the application of such conservation measures, to terminate the loan and, no later than thirty days after having received such notice, either retrieve the property or arrange for its isolation and retrieval. The museum shall not be required to publish notice of injury or loss to any undocumented property.

13. The owner of property loaned to the museum is responsible for promptly notifying the museum, in writing, of any change of address or change in the ownership of the property.

14. (a)   Unless there is a written loan agreement to the contrary, the museum may apply conservation measures to property on loan to the museum without giving formal notice or first obtaining the lender's permission if immediate action is required to protect the property on loan or other property in the custody of the museum or if the property on loan is a hazard to the health and safety of the public or the museum staff, provided that:
     (i)   the museum is unable to reach the lender at the lender's last known address or telephone number before the time the museum determines action is necessary; or
     (ii)   the lender either (A) does not respond to a request for permission to apply conservation measures made pursuant to subdivision twelve of this section within three days of receiving the request or will not agree to the conservation measures the museum recommends or (B) fails to terminate the loan and either retrieve the property or arrange for its isolation and retrieval within thirty days of receiving the request.

If immediate conservation measures are necessary to protect the property or to protect the health or safety of the public or museum staff, the conditions set forth in subparagraphs (i) and (ii) of this paragraph shall not apply.

(b)   Unless provided otherwise in an agreement with the lender, if the museum applies conservation measures to property under paragraph (a) of this subdivision, and provided that the measures were not required as a result of the museum's own action or inaction, the museum shall acquire a lien on the property in the amount of the costs incurred by the museum, including, but not limited to the cost of labor and materials, and shall not be liable for injury to or loss of the property, provided that the museum:

    (i)   had a reasonable belief at the time the action was taken that the action was necessary to protect the property on loan or other property in the custody of the museum, or that the property on loan was a hazard to the health and safety of the public or the museum staff; and

    (ii)   exercised reasonable care in the choice and application of conservation measures.

15. The museum shall maintain or continue to maintain, as the case may be and to the extent such information is available, a record of acquisition, whether by purchase, bequest, gift, loan or otherwise, of property for display or collection and of deaccessioning or loan of property currently held or thereafter acquired for display or collection. Any such record shall: (a) state the name, address, and telephone number of the person from whom such property was acquired, or to whom such property was transferred by deaccessioning or loan, and a description of such property, its location, if known, and the terms of the acquisition or deaccessioning or loan, including any restrictions as to its use or further disposition, and any other material facts about the terms and conditions of the transaction; (b) include a copy of any document of conveyance relating to the acquisition or deaccessioning or loan of such property and all notices and other documents prepared or received by the museum.

16. Notwithstanding the provisions of the civil practice law and rules or any other law, except for laws governing actions to recover stolen property:

(a)   No action against the museum for damages arising out of injury to or loss of property loaned to the museum shall be commenced more than three years from the date the museum gives the lender or claimant notice of the injury or loss under this section.

(b)   No action against the museum to recover property shall be commenced more than three years from the date the museum gives notice of its intent to terminate the loan or notice of intent to acquire title to undocumented property.

CALIFORNIA CIVIL CODE

(SELECTED ARTS PROVISIONS)

MORAL RIGHTS

§ 987. PROTECTION OF FINE ART AGAINST ALTERATION OR DESTRUCTION; ACTIONS; REMOVAL OF WORK FROM PROPERTY

(a) The Legislature hereby finds and declares that the physical alteration or destruction of fine art, which is an expression of the artist's personality, is detrimental to the artist's reputation, and artists therefore have an interest in protecting their works of fine art against any alteration or destruction; and that there is also a public interest in preserving the integrity of cultural and artistic creations.

(b) As used in this section:

(1) "Artist" means the individual or individuals who create a work of fine art.

(2) "Fine art" means an original painting, sculpture, or drawing, or an original work of art in glass, of recognized quality, but shall not include work prepared under contract for commercial use by its purchaser.

(3) "Person" means an individual, partnership, corporation, limited liability company, association or other group, however organized.

(4) "Frame" means to prepare, or cause to be prepared, a work of fine art for display in a manner customarily considered to be appropriate for a work of fine art in the particular medium.

(5) "Restore" means to return, or cause to be returned, a deteriorated or damaged work of fine art as nearly as is feasible to its original state or condition, in accordance with prevailing standards.

(6) "Conserve" means to preserve, or cause to be preserved, a work of fine art by retarding or preventing deterioration or damage through appropriate treatment in accordance with prevailing standards in order to maintain the structural integrity to the fullest extent possible in an unchanging state.

(7) "Commercial use" means fine art created under a work-for-hire arrangement for use in advertising, magazines, newspapers, or other print and electronic media.

(c) (1) No person, except an artist who owns and possesses a work of fine art which the artist has created, shall intentionally commit, or authorize the intentional commission of, any physical defacement, mutilation, alteration, or destruction of a work of fine art.

(2) In addition to the prohibitions contained in paragraph (1), no person who frames, conserves, or restores a work of fine art shall commit, or authorize the commission of, any physical defacement, mutilation, alteration, or destruction of a work of fine art by any act constituting gross negligence. For purposes of this section, the term "gross negligence" shall mean the exercise of so slight a degree of care as to justify the belief that there was an indifference to the particular work of fine art.

(d) The artist shall retain at all times the right to claim authorship, or, for a just and valid reason, to disclaim authorship of his or her work of fine art.

(e) To effectuate the rights created by this section, the artist may commence an action to recover or obtain any of the following:

(1)   Injunctive relief.

(2)   Actual damages.

(3)   Punitive damages. In the event that punitive damages are awarded, the court shall, in its discretion, select an organization or organizations engaged in charitable or educational activities involving the fine arts in California to receive any punitive damages.

(4)   Reasonable attorneys' and expert witness fees.

(5)   Any other relief which the court deems proper.

(f) In determining whether a work of fine art is of recognized quality, the trier of fact shall rely on the opinions of artists, art dealers, collectors of fine art, curators of art museums, and other persons involved with the creation or marketing of fine art.

(g) The rights and duties created under this section:

(1)   Shall, with respect to the artist, or if any artist is deceased, his or her heir, beneficiary, devisee, or personal representative, exist until the 50th anniversary of the death of the artist.

(2)   Shall exist in addition to any other rights and duties which may now or in the future be applicable.

(3)   Except as provided in paragraph (1) of subdivision (h), may not be waived except by an instrument in writing expressly so providing which is signed by the artist.

(h) (1)   If a work of fine art cannot be removed from a building without substantial physical defacement, mutilation, alteration, or destruction of the work, the rights and duties created under this section, unless expressly reserved by an instrument in writing signed by the owner of the building, containing a legal description of the property and properly recorded, shall be deemed waived. The instrument, if properly recorded, shall be binding on subsequent owners of the building.

(2)   If the owner of a building wishes to remove a work of fine art which is a part of the building but which can be removed from the building without substantial harm to the fine art, and in the course of or after removal, the owner intends to cause or allow the fine art to suffer physical defacement, mutilation, alteration, or destruction, the rights and duties created under this section shall apply unless the owner has diligently attempted without success to notify the artist, or, if the artist is deceased, his or her heir, beneficiary, devisee, or personal representative, in writing of his or her intended action affecting the work of fine art, or unless he or she did provide notice and that person failed within 90 days either to remove the work or to pay for its removal. If the work is removed at the expense of the artist, his or her heir, beneficiary, devisee, or personal representative, title to the fine art shall pass to that person.

(3)   If a work of fine art can be removed from a building scheduled for demolition without substantial physical defacement, mutilation, alteration, or destruction of the work, and the owner of the building has notified the owner of the work of fine art of the scheduled demolition or

the owner of the building is the owner of the work of fine art, and the owner of the work of fine art elects not to remove the work of fine art, the rights and duties created under this section shall apply, unless the owner of the building has diligently attempted without success to notify the artist, or, if the artist is deceased, his or her heir, beneficiary, devisee, or personal representative, in writing of the intended action affecting the work of fine art, or unless he or she did provide notice and that person failed within 90 days either to remove the work or to pay for its removal. If the work is removed at the expense of the artist, his or her heir, beneficiary, devisee, or personal representative, title to the fine art shall pass to that person.

(4)   Nothing in this subdivision shall affect the rights of authorship created in subdivision (d) of this section.

(i)   No action may be maintained to enforce any liability under this section unless brought within three years of the act complained of or one year after discovery of the act, whichever is longer.

(j)   This section shall become operative on January 1, 1980, and shall apply to claims based on proscribed acts occurring on or after that date to works of fine art whenever created.

(k)   If any provision of this section or the application thereof to any person or circumstance is held invalid for any reason, the invalidity shall not affect any other provisions or applications of this section which can be effected without the invalid provision or application, and to this end the provisions of this section are severable.

§ 988. RESIDUAL RIGHTS

(a)   For the purpose of this section:

(1)   The term "artist" means the creator of a work of art.

(2)   The term "work of art" means any work of visual or graphic art of any media including, but not limited to, a painting, print, drawing, sculpture, craft, photograph, or film.

(b)   Whenever an exclusive or nonexclusive conveyance of any right to reproduce, prepare derivative works based on, distribute copies of, publicly perform, or publicly display a work of art is made by or on behalf of the artist who created it or the owner at the time of the conveyance, ownership of the physical work of art shall remain with and be reserved to the artist or owner, as the case may be, unless such right of ownership is expressly transferred by an instrument, note, memorandum, or other writing, signed by the artist, the owner, or their duly authorized agent.

(c)   Whenever an exclusive or nonexclusive conveyance of any right to reproduce, prepare derivative works based on, distribute copies of, publicly perform, or publicly display a work of art is made by or on behalf of the artist who created it or the owner at the time of the conveyance, any ambiguity with respect to the nature or extent of the rights conveyed shall be resolved in favor of the reservation of rights by the artist or owner, unless in any given case the federal copyright law provides to the contrary.

§ 989. PRESERVATION OF INTEGRITY OF CULTURAL AND ARTISTIC
CREATIONS; RIGHT OF ORGANIZATION TO COMMENCE ACTION;
REMOVAL OF ART FROM PROPERTY

(a) The Legislature hereby finds and declares that there is a public interest in preserving the integrity of cultural and artistic creations.

(b) As used in this section:

(1) "Fine art" means an original painting, sculpture, or drawing, or an original work of art in glass, of recognized quality, and of substantial public interest.

(2) "Organization" means a public or private not-for-profit entity or association, in existence at least three years at the time an action is filed pursuant to this section, a major purpose of which is to stage, display, or otherwise present works of art to the public or to promote the interests of the arts or artists.

(3) "Cost of removal" includes reasonable costs, if any, for the repair of damage to the real property caused by the removal of the work of fine art.

(c) An organization acting in the public interest may commence an action for injunctive relief to preserve or restore the integrity of a work of fine art from acts prohibited by subdivision (c) of Section 987.

(d) In determining whether a work of fine art is of recognized quality and of substantial public interest the trier of fact shall rely on the opinions of those described in subdivision (f) of Section 987.

(e) (1) If a work of fine art cannot be removed from real property without substantial physical defacement, mutilation, alteration, or destruction of such work, no action to preserve the integrity of the work of fine art may be brought under this section. However, if an organization offers some evidence giving rise to a reasonable likelihood that a work of art can be removed from the real property without substantial physical defacement, mutilation, alteration, or destruction of the work, and is prepared to pay the cost of removal of the work, it may bring a legal action for a determination of this issue. In that action the organization shall be entitled to injunctive relief to preserve the integrity of the work of fine art, but shall also have the burden of proof. The action shall commence within 30 days after filing. No action may be brought under this paragraph if the organization's interest in preserving the work of art is in conflict with an instrument described in paragraph (1) of subdivision (h) of Section 987.

(2) If the owner of the real property wishes to remove a work of fine art which is part of the real property, but which can be removed from the real property without substantial harm to such fine art, and in the course of or after removal, the owner intends to cause or allow the fine art to suffer physical defacement, mutilation, alteration, or destruction the owner shall do the following:

(A) If the artist or artist's heir, legatee, or personal representative fails to take action to remove the work of fine art after the notice provided by paragraph (2) of subdivision (h) of Section 987, the owner shall provide 30 days' notice of his or her intended action affecting the work of art. The written notice shall be a display advertisement in a newspaper of general circulation in the area where the fine art is located. The notice required by this paragraph may run concurrently with the notice required by subdivision (h) of Section 987.

   (i)   If within the 30-day period an organization agrees to remove the work of fine art and pay the cost of removal of the work, the payment and removal shall occur within 90 days of the first day of the 30-day notice.

   (ii)   If the work is removed at the expense of an organization, title to the fine art shall pass to that organization.

   (B)   If an organization does not agree to remove the work of fine art within the 30-day period or fails to remove and pay the cost of removal of the work of fine art within the 90-day period the owner may take the intended action affecting the work of fine art.

(f)   To effectuate the rights created by this section, the court may do the following:

   (1)   Award reasonable attorney's and expert witness fees to the prevailing party, in an amount as determined by the court.

   (2)   Require the organization to post a bond in a reasonable amount as determined by the court.

(g)   No action may be maintained under this section unless brought within three years of the act complained of or one year after discovery of such act, whichever is longer.

(h)   This section shall become operative on January 1, 1983, and shall apply to claims based on acts occurring on or after that date to works of fine art, whenever created.

(i)   If any provision of this section or the application thereof to any person or circumstances is held invalid, such invalidity shall not affect other provisions or applications of this section which can be given effect without the invalid provision or application, and to this end the provisions of this section are severable.

PRIVACY AND PUBLICITY

§ 3344. UNAUTHORIZED COMMERCIAL USE OF NAME, VOICE, SIGNATURE, PHOTOGRAPH OR LIKENESS

(a)   Any person who knowingly uses another's name, voice, signature, photograph, or likeness, in any manner, on or in products, merchandise, or goods, or for purposes of advertising or selling, or soliciting purchases of, products, merchandise, goods or services, without such person's prior consent, or, in the case of a minor, the prior consent of his parent or legal guardian, shall be liable for any damages sustained by the person or persons injured as a result thereof. In addition, in any action brought under this section, the person who violated the section shall be liable to the injured party or parties in an amount equal to the greater of seven hundred fifty dollars ($750) or the actual damages suffered by him or her as a result of the unauthorized use, and any profits from the unauthorized use that are attributable to the use and are not taken into account in computing the actual damages. In establishing such profits, the injured party or parties are required to present proof only of the gross revenue attributable to such use, and the person who violated this section is required to prove his or her deductible expenses. Punitive damages may also be awarded to the injured party or parties. The prevailing party in any action under this section shall also be entitled to attorney's fees and costs.

(b) As used in this section, "photograph" means any photograph or photographic reproduction, still or moving, or any videotape or live television transmission, of any person, such that the person is readily identifiable.

(1)   A person shall be deemed to be readily identifiable from a photograph when one who views the photograph with the naked eye can reasonably determine that the person depicted in the photograph is the same person who is complaining of its unauthorized use.

(2)   If the photograph includes more than one person so identifiable, then the person or persons complaining of the use shall be represented as individuals rather than solely as members of a definable group represented in the photograph. A definable group includes, but is not limited to, the following examples: a crowd at any sporting event, a crowd in any street or public building, the audience at any theatrical or stage production, a glee club, or a baseball team.

(3)   A person or persons shall be considered to be represented as members of a definable group if they are represented in the photograph solely as a result of being present at the time the photograph was taken and have not been singled out as individuals in any manner.

(c) Where a photograph or likeness of an employee of the person using the photograph or likeness appearing in the advertisement or other publication prepared by or in behalf of the user is only incidental, and not essential, to the purpose of the publication in which it appears, there shall arise a rebuttable presumption affecting the burden of producing evidence that the failure to obtain the consent of the employee was not a knowing use of the employee's photograph or likeness.

(d) For purposes of this section, a use of a name, voice, signature, photograph, or likeness in connection with any news, public affairs, or sports broadcast or account, or any political campaign, shall not constitute a use for which consent is required under subdivision (a).

(e) The use of a name, voice, signature, photograph, or likeness in a commercial medium shall not constitute a use for which consent is required under subdivision (a) solely because the material containing such use is commercially sponsored or contains paid advertising. Rather it shall be a question of fact whether or not the use of the person's name, voice, signature, photograph, or likeness was so directly connected with the commercial sponsorship or with the paid advertising as to constitute a use for which consent is required under subdivision (a).

(f) Nothing in this section shall apply to the owners or employees of any medium used for advertising, including, but not limited to, newspapers, magazines, radio and television networks and stations, cable television systems, billboards, and transit ads, by whom any advertisement or solicitation in violation of this section is published or disseminated, unless it is established that such owners or employees had knowledge of the unauthorized use of the person's name, voice, signature, photograph, or likeness as prohibited by this section.

(g) The remedies provided for in this section are cumulative and shall be in addition to any others provided for by law.

§ 3344.1. DECEASED PERSONALITY'S NAME, VOICE, SIGNATURE, PHOTOGRAPH, OR LIKENESS; UNAUTHORIZED USE; DAMAGES AND PROFITS FROM USE; PROTECTED USES; PERSONS ENTITLED TO EXERCISE RIGHTS; SUCCESSORS IN INTEREST OR LICENSEES; REGISTRATION OF CLAIM

(a) (1) Any person who uses a deceased personality's name, voice, signature, photograph, or likeness, in any manner, on or in products, merchandise, or goods, or for purposes of advertising or selling, or soliciting purchases of, products, merchandise, goods, or services, without prior consent from the person or persons specified in subdivision (c), shall be liable for any damages sustained by the person or persons injured as a result thereof. In addition, in any action brought under this section, the person who violated the section shall be liable to the injured party or parties in an amount equal to the greater of seven hundred fifty dollars ($750) or the actual damages suffered by the injured party or parties, as a result of the unauthorized use, and any profits from the unauthorized use that are attributable to the use and are not taken into account in computing the actual damages. In establishing these profits, the injured party or parties shall be required to present proof only of the gross revenue attributable to the use, and the person who violated the section is required to prove his or her deductible expenses. Punitive damages may also be awarded to the injured party or parties. The prevailing party or parties in any action under this section shall also be entitled to attorney's fees and costs.

(2) For purposes of this subdivision, a play, book, magazine, newspaper, musical composition, audiovisual work, radio or television program, single and original work of art, work of political or newsworthy value, or an advertisement or commercial announcement for any of these works, shall not be considered a product, article of merchandise, good, or service if it is fictional or nonfictional entertainment, or a dramatic, literary, or musical work.

(3) If a work that is protected under paragraph (2) includes within it a use in connection with a product, article of merchandise, good, or service, this use shall not be exempt under this subdivision, notwithstanding the unprotected use's inclusion in a work otherwise exempt under this subdivision, if the claimant proves that this use is so directly connected with a product, article of merchandise, good, or service as to constitute an act of advertising, selling, or soliciting purchases of that product, article of merchandise, good, or service by the deceased personality without prior consent from the person or persons specified in subdivision (c).

(b) The rights recognized under this section are property rights, freely transferable or descendible, in whole or in part, by contract or by means of any trust or any other testamentary instrument, executed before or after January 1, 1985. The rights recognized under this section shall be deemed to have existed at the time of death of any deceased personality who died prior to January 1, 1985, and, except as provided in subdivision (o), shall vest in the persons entitled to these property rights under the testamentary instrument of the deceased personality effective as of the date of his or her death. In the absence of an express transfer in a testamentary instrument of the deceased personality's rights in his or her name, voice, signature, photograph, or likeness, a provision in the testamentary instrument that provides for the disposition of the residue of the deceased personality's assets shall be effective to transfer the rights recognized under this section in accordance with the terms of that provision. The rights established by this section shall also be freely transferable or descendible by contract, trust, or any other testamentary instrument by any subsequent owner of the deceased personality's rights as recognized by this section. Nothing in this section shall be construed to render invalid or unenforceable any contract entered into by a deceased personality during his or her lifetime by which the deceased personality assigned the rights, in whole or in part, to use his or her name, voice, signature, photograph, or likeness, regardless of whether the contract was entered into before or after January 1, 1985.

(c) The consent required by this section shall be exercisable by the person or persons to whom the right of consent, or portion thereof, has been transferred in accordance with subdivision (b), or if no transfer has occurred, then by the person or persons to whom the right of consent, or portion thereof, has passed in accordance with subdivision (d).

(d) Subject to subdivisions (b) and (c), after the death of any person, the rights under this section shall belong to the following person or persons and may be exercised, on behalf of and for the benefit of all of those persons, by those persons who, in the aggregate, are entitled to more than a one-half interest in the rights:

(1) The entire interest in those rights belongs to the surviving spouse of the deceased personality unless there are any surviving children or grandchildren of the deceased personality, in which case one-half of the entire interest in those rights belongs to the surviving spouse.

(2) The entire interest in those rights belongs to the surviving children of the deceased personality and to the surviving children of any dead child of the deceased personality unless the deceased personality has a surviving spouse, in which case the ownership of a one-half interest in rights is divided among the surviving children and grandchildren.

(3) If there is no surviving spouse, and no surviving children or grandchildren, then the entire interest in those rights belongs to the surviving parent or parents of the deceased personality.

(4) The rights of the deceased personality's children and grandchildren are in all cases divided among them and exercisable in the manner provided

in Section 240 of the Probate Code according to the number of the deceased personality's children represented. The share of the children of a dead child of a deceased personality can be exercised only by the action of a majority of them.

(e) If any deceased personality does not transfer his or her rights under this section by contract, or by means of a trust or testamentary instrument, and there are no surviving persons as described in subdivision (d), then the rights set forth in subdivision (a) shall terminate.

(f) (1) A successor in interest to the rights of a deceased personality under this section or a licensee thereof shall not recover damages for a use prohibited by this section that occurs before the successor in interest or licensee registers a claim of the rights under paragraph (2).

(2) Any person claiming to be a successor in interest to the rights of a deceased personality under this section or a licensee thereof may register that claim with the Secretary of State on a form prescribed by the Secretary of State and upon payment of a fee as set forth in subdivision (d) of Section 12195 of the Government Code. The form shall be verified and shall include the name and date of death of the deceased personality, the name and address of the claimant, the basis of the claim, and the rights claimed.

(3) Upon receipt and after filing of any document under this section, the Secretary of State shall post the document along with the entire registry of persons claiming to be a successor in interest to the rights of a deceased personality or a registered licensee under this section upon the Secretary of State's Internet Web site. The Secretary of State may microfilm or reproduce by other techniques any of the filings or documents and destroy the original filing or document. The microfilm or other reproduction of any document under this section shall be admissible in any court of law. The microfilm or other reproduction of any document may be destroyed by the Secretary of State 70 years after the death of the personality named therein.

(4) Claims registered under this subdivision shall be public records.

(g) An action shall not be brought under this section by reason of any use of a deceased personality's name, voice, signature, photograph, or likeness occurring after the expiration of 70 years after the death of the deceased personality.

(h) As used in this section, "deceased personality" means any natural person whose name, voice, signature, photograph, or likeness has commercial value at the time of his or her death, or because of his or her death, whether or not during the lifetime of that natural person the person used his or her name, voice, signature, photograph, or likeness on or in products, merchandise, or goods, or for purposes of advertising or selling, or solicitation of purchase of, products, merchandise, goods, or services. A "deceased personality" shall include, without limitation, any such natural person who has died within 70 years prior to January 1, 1985.

(i) As used in this section, "photograph" means any photograph or photographic reproduction, still or moving, or any videotape or live television transmission, of any person, such that the deceased personality is readily identifiable. A deceased personality shall be deemed to be readily identifiable from a photograph if one who views the photograph with the naked eye can reasonably determine who the person depicted in the photograph is.

(j) For purposes of this section, the use of a name, voice, signature, photograph, or likeness in connection with any news, public affairs, or sports broadcast or account, or any political campaign, shall not constitute a use for which consent is required under subdivision (a).

(k) The use of a name, voice, signature, photograph, or likeness in a commercial medium shall not constitute a use for which consent is required under subdivision (a) solely because the material containing the use is commercially sponsored or contains paid advertising. Rather, it shall be a question of fact whether or not the use of the deceased personality's name, voice, signature, photograph, or likeness was so directly connected with the commercial sponsorship or with the paid advertising as to constitute a use for which consent is required under subdivision (a).

(l) Nothing in this section shall apply to the owners or employees of any medium used for advertising, including, but not limited to, newspapers, magazines, radio and television networks and stations,
cable television systems, billboards, and transit advertisements, by whom any advertisement or solicitation in violation of this section is published or disseminated, unless it is established that the owners or employees had knowledge of the unauthorized use of the deceased personality's name, voice, signature, photograph, or likeness as prohibited by this section.

(m) The remedies provided for in this section are cumulative and shall be in addition to any others provided for by law.

(n) This section shall apply to the adjudication of liability and the imposition of any damages or other remedies in cases in which the liability, damages, and other remedies arise from acts occurring directly in this state. For purposes of this section, acts giving rise to liability shall be limited to the use, on or in products, merchandise, goods, or services, or the advertising or selling, or soliciting purchases of, products, merchandise, goods, or services prohibited by this section.

(o) Notwithstanding any provision of this section to the contrary, if an action was taken prior to May 1, 2007, to exercise rights recognized under this section relating to a deceased personality who died prior to January 1, 1985, by a person described in subdivision (d), other than a person who was disinherited by the deceased personality in a testamentary instrument, and the exercise of those rights was not challenged successfully in a court action by a person described in subdivision (b), that exercise shall not be affected by subdivision (b). In that case, the rights that would otherwise vest in one or more persons described in subdivision (b) shall vest solely in the person or persons described in subdivision (d), other than a person disinherited by the deceased personality in a testamentary instrument, for all future purposes.

(p) The rights recognized by this section are expressly made retroactive, including to those deceased personalities who died before January 1, 1985.

CONSIGNMENT OF FINE ART

§ 1738. DEFINITIONS
As used in this title:

(a)   "Artist" means the person who creates a work of fine art or, if that person is deceased, that person's heir, legatee, or personal representative.

(b)   "Fine art" means a painting, sculpture, drawing, work of graphic art (including an etching, lithograph, offset print, silk screen, or a work of graphic art of like nature), a work of calligraphy, or a work in mixed media (including a collage, assemblage, or any combination of the foregoing art media).

(c)   "Art dealer" means a person engaged in the business of selling works of fine art, other than a person exclusively engaged in the business of selling goods at public auction.

(d)   "Person" means an individual, partnership, corporation, limited liability company, association or other group, however organized.

(e)   "Consignment" means that no title to, estate in, or right to possession of, fine art, superior to that of the consignor shall vest in the consignee, notwithstanding the consignee's power or authority to transfer and convey to a third person all of the right, title and interest of the consignor in and to such fine art.

§ 1738.5. DELIVERY TO AND ACCEPTANCE BY ART DEALER; EFFECT
Notwithstanding any custom, practice or usage of the trade to the contrary, whenever an artist delivers or causes to be delivered a work of fine art of the artist's own creation to an art dealer in this state for the purpose of exhibition or sale, or both, on a commission, fee or other basis of compensation, the delivery to and acceptance of such work of fine art by the art dealer shall constitute a consignment, unless the delivery to the art dealer is pursuant to an outright sale for which the artist receives or has received full compensation for the work of fine art upon delivery.

§ 1738.6. RESULTS OF CONSIGNMENT; AGENCY, PROPERTY IN TRUST, LIABILITY AND PROCEEDS
A consignment of a work of fine art shall result in all of the following:

(a)   The art dealer, after delivery of the work of fine art, shall constitute an agent of the artist for the purpose of sale or exhibition of the consigned work of fine art within the State of California.

(b)   The work of fine art shall constitute property held in trust by the consignee for the benefit of the consignor, and shall not be subject to claim by a creditor of the consignee.

(c)   The consignee shall be responsible for the loss of, or damage to, the work of fine art.

(d)   The proceeds from the sale of the work of fine art shall constitute funds held in trust by the consignee for the benefit of the consignor. Such proceeds shall first be applied to pay any balance due to the consignor, unless the consignor expressly agrees otherwise in writing.

§ 1738.7. TRUST PROPERTY

A work of fine art received as a consignment shall remain trust property, notwithstanding the subsequent purchase thereof by the consignee directly or indirectly for the consignee's own account until the price is paid in full to the consignor. If such work is thereafter resold to a bona fide purchaser before the consignor has been paid in full, the proceeds of the resale received by the consignee shall constitute funds held in trust for the benefit of the consignor to the extent necessary to pay any balance still due to the consignor and such trusteeship shall continue until the fiduciary obligation of the consignee with respect to such transaction is discharged in full.

§ 1738.8. WAIVER BY CONSIGNOR AS VOID

Any provision of a contract or agreement whereby the consignor waives any provision of this title is void.

§ 1738.9. APPLICATION OF TITLE

This title shall not apply to a written contract executed prior to the effective date of this title, unless either the parties agree by mutual written consent that this title shall apply or such contract is extended or renewed after the effective date of this title.

The provisions of this title shall prevail over any conflicting or inconsistent provisions of the Commercial Code affecting the subject matter of this title.

§ 1740. DEFINITIONS

As used in this title:

(a) "Fine art multiple" or "multiple" for the purposes of this title means any fine print, photograph (positive or negative), sculpture cast, collage, or similar art object produced in more than one copy. Pages or sheets taken from books and magazines and offered for sale or sold as art objects shall be included, but books and magazines shall be excluded.

(b) "Fine print" or "print" means a multiple produced by, but not limited to, engraving, etching, woodcutting, lithography, and serigraphy, and means multiples produced or developed from photographic negatives, or any combination thereof.

(c) "Master" is used in lieu of and has the same meaning as a printing plate, stone, block, screen, photographic negative, or mold or other process as to a sculpture, which contains an image used to produce fine art objects in multiples.

(d) "Artist" means the person who created the image which is contained in, or constitutes, the master or conceived of, and approved the image which is contained in, or constitutes, the master.

(e)   Whether a multiple is "signed" or "unsigned" as these terms are used in this title relating to prints and photographs, depends upon whether or not the multiple was autographed by the artist's own hand, and not by mechanical means, after the multiple was produced, irrespective of whether it was signed or unsigned in the plate.

(f)   "Impression" means each individual fine art multiple made by print-ing, stamping, casting, or any other process.

(g)   "Art dealer" means a person who is in the business of dealing, exclu-sively or nonexclusively, in the fine art multiples to which this title is appli-cable, or a person who by his or her occupation holds himself or herself out as having knowledge or skill peculiar to these works, or to whom that knowledge or skill may be attributed by his or her employment of an agent or other inter-mediary who by his or her occupation holds himself or herself out as having that knowledge or skill. The term "art dealer" includes an auctioneer who sells these works at public auction, but excludes persons, not otherwise defined or treated as art dealers herein, who are consignors or principals of auctioneers.

(h)   "Limited edition" means fine art multiples produced from a master, all of which are the same image and bear numbers or other markings to denote the limited production thereof to a stated maximum number of multiples, or are otherwise held out as limited to a maximum number of multiples.

(i)   "Proofs" means multiples which are the same as, and which are pro-duced from the same master as, the multiples in a limited edition, but which, whether so designated or not, are set aside from and are in addition to the limited edition to which they relate.

(j)   "Certificate of authenticity" means a written or printed description of the multiple which is to be sold, exchanged, or consigned by an art dealer. Every certificate shall contain the following statement:

"This is to certify that all information and the statements contained herein are true and correct."

(k)   "Person" means an individual, partnership, corporation, limited liabil-ity company, association, or other entity, however organized.

§ 1741. APPLICATION OF TITLE

This title shall apply to any fine art multiple when offered for sale or sold at wholesale or retail for one hundred dollars ($100) or more, exclusive of any frame.

§ 1742. CERTIFICATE OF AUTHENTICITY TO BE FURNISHED TO BUYER OR CONSIGNEE; AUCTIONS; MATERIALS SOLICITING A DIRECT SALE; DISCLOSURES

(a)   An art dealer shall not sell or consign a multiple into or from this state un-less a certificate of authenticity is furnished to the purchaser or consignee, at his or her request, or in any event prior to a sale or consignment, which sets forth as to each multiple, the descriptive information required by Sec-tion 1744 for any period. If a prospective purchaser so requests, the certificate shall be transmitted to him or her prior to the payment or placing of an order for a multiple. If payment is made by a purchaser prior to delivery of such a multiple, this certificate shall be supplied at the time of or prior to delivery. With respect to auctions, this information may be furnished in catalogues or other written materials which are made readily available for consultation and purchase prior to sale, provided that a bill of sale, receipt, or invoice describing the transaction is then provided which makes reference to the catalogue and lot number in which this information is supplied. Information supplied pursuant to this subdivision shall be clearly, specifically and distinctly addressed to each of the items listed in Section 1744 unless the required data is not applicable. This section is applicable to transactions by and between art dealers and others considered to be art dealers for the purposes of this title.

(b) An art dealer shall not cause a catalogue, prospectus, flyer, or other written material or advertisement to be distributed in, into, or from this state which solicits a direct sale, by inviting transmittal of payment for a specific multiple, unless it clearly sets forth, in close physical proximity to the place in such material where the multiple is described, the descriptive information required by Section 1744 for any time period. In lieu of this required information, the written material or advertising may set forth the material contained in the following quoted passage, or the passage itself, if the art dealer then supplies the required information prior to or with delivery of the multiple. The nonobservance of the terms within the following passage shall constitute a violation of this title:

"California law provides for disclosure in writing of information concerning certain fine prints, photographs, and sculptures prior to effecting a sale of them. This law requires disclosure of such matters as the identity of the artist, the artist's signature, the medium, whether the multiple is a reproduction, the time when the multiple was produced, use of the plate which produced the multiple, and the number of multiples in a "limited edition." If a prospective purchaser so requests, the information shall be transmitted to him or her prior to payment, or the placing of an order for a multiple. If payment is made by a purchaser prior to delivery of the multiple, this information will be supplied at the time of or prior to delivery, in which case the purchaser is entitled to a refund if, for reasons related to matter contained in such information, he or she returns the multiple in the condition in which received, within 30 days of receiving it. In addition, if after payment and delivery, it is ascertained that the information provided is incorrect, the purchaser may be entitled to certain remedies, including refund upon return of the multiple in the condition in which received."

This requirement is not applicable to general written material or advertising which does not constitute an offer to effect a specific sale.

(c) In each place of business in the state where an art dealer is regularly engaged in sales of multiples, the art dealer shall post in a conspicuous place, a sign which, in a legible format, contains the information included in the following passage:

"California law provides for the disclosure in writing of certain information concerning prints, photographs, and sculpture casts. This information is available to you, and you may request to receive it prior to purchase."

(d)   If an art dealer offering multiples by means of a catalogue, prospectus, flyer
      or other written material or advertisement distributed in, into or from this
      state disclaims knowledge as to any relevant detail referred to in Section
      1744, he or she shall so state specifically and categorically with regard to
      each such detail to the end that the purchaser shall be enabled to judge the
      degree of uniqueness or scarcity of each multiple contained in the edition
      so offered. Describing the edition as an edition of "reproductions" elimi-
      nates the need to furnish further informational details unless the edition
      was allegedly published in a signed, numbered, or limited edition, or any
      combination thereof, in which case all of the informational details are re-
      quired to be furnished.
(e)   Whenever an artist sells or consigns a multiple of his or her own creation
      or conception, the artist shall disclose the information required by Section
      1744, but an artist shall not otherwise be regarded as an art dealer.

§ 1742.6. CHARITABLE ORGANIZATIONS; EXEMPTIONS

Any charitable organization which conducts a sale or auction of fine art multiples
shall be exempt from the disclosure requirements of this title if it posts in a conspicuous place, at the site of the sale or auction, a disclaimer of any knowledge of
the information specified in Section 1744, and includes such a disclaimer in a catalogue, if any, distributed by the organization with respect to the sale or auction
of fine art multiples. If a charitable organization uses or employs an art dealer to
conduct a sale or auction of fine art multiples, the art dealer shall be subject to
all disclosure requirements otherwise required of an art dealer under this title.

§ 1744. INFORMATIONAL DETAIL

(a)   Except as provided in subdivisions (c), (d), (e), and otherwise in this title,
      a certificate of authenticity containing the following informational details
      shall be required to be supplied in all transactions covered by subdivisions
      (a), (b), and (e) of Section 1742:
      (1)   The name of the artist.
      (2)   If the artist's name appears on the multiple, a statement whether the
      multiple was signed by the artist.
      If the multiple was not signed by the artist, a statement of the source of the
      artist's name on the multiple, such as whether the artist placed his signa-
      ture on the multiple or on the master, whether his name was stamped or
      estate stamped on the multiple or on the master, or was from some other
      source or in some other manner placed on the multiple or on the master.
      (3)   A description of the medium or process, and where pertinent to pho-
      tographic processes, the material used in producing the multiple, such
      as whether the multiple was produced through the etching, engraving,
      lithographic, serigraphic, or a particular method or material used in photo-
      graphic developing processes. If an established term, in accordance with the
      usage of the trade, cannot be employed accurately to describe the medium
      or process, a brief, clear description shall be made.

(4)   If the multiple or the image on or in the master constitutes, as to prints and photographs, a photomechanical or photographic type of reproduction, or as to sculptures a surmoulage or other form of reproduction of sculpture cases, of an image produced in a different medium, for a purpose other than the creation of the multiple being described, a statement of this information and the respective mediums.

(5)   If paragraph (4) is applicable, and the multiple is not signed, a statement whether the artist authorized or approved in writing the multiple or the edition of which the multiple being described is one.

(6)   If the purported artist was deceased at the time the master was made which produced the multiple, this shall be stated.

(7)   If the multiple is a "posthumous" multiple, that is, if the master was created during the life of the artist but the multiple was produced after the artist's death, this shall be stated.

(8)   If the multiple was made from a master which produced a prior limited edition, or from a master which constitutes or was made from a reproduction or surmoulage of a prior multiple or the master which produced the prior limited edition, this shall be stated as shall the total number of multiples, including proofs, of all other editions produced from that master.

(9)   As to multiples produced after 1949, the year, or approximate year, the multiple was produced shall be stated. As to multiples produced prior to 1950, state the year, approximate year or period when the master was made which produced the multiple and when the particular multiple being described was produced. The requirements of this subdivision shall be satisfied when the year stated is approximately accurate.

(10) Whether the edition is being offered as a limited edition, and if so: (i) the authorized maximum number of signed or numbered impressions, or both, in the edition; (ii) the authorized maximum number of unsigned or unnumbered impressions, or both, in the edition; (iii) the authorized maximum number of artist's, publisher's or other proofs, if any, outside of the regular edition; and (iv) the total size of the edition.

(11) Whether or not the master has been destroyed, effaced, altered, defaced, or canceled after the current edition.

(b) If the multiple is part of a limited edition, and was printed after January 1, 1983, the statement of the size of the limited edition, as stated pursuant to paragraph (10) of subdivision (a) of Section 1744 shall also constitute an express warranty that no additional multiples of the same image, including proofs, have been produced in this or in any other limited edition.

(c) If the multiple was produced in the period from 1950 to the effective date of this section, the information required to be supplied need not include the information required by paragraphs (5) and (8) of subdivision (a).

(d) If the multiple was produced in the period from 1900 to 1949, the information required to be supplied need only consist of the information required by paragraphs (1), (2), (3), and (9) of subdivision (a).

(e) If the multiple was produced before the year 1900, the information to be supplied need only consist of the information required by paragraphs (1), (3), and (9) of subdivision (a).

§ 1744.7. EXPRESS WARRANTIES

Whenever an art dealer furnishes the name of the artist pursuant to Section 1744 for any time period after 1949, and otherwise furnishes information required by any of the subdivisions of Section 1744 for any time period, as to transactions including offers, sales, or consignments made to other than art dealers, and to other art dealers, such information shall be a part of the basis of the bargain and shall create express warranties as to the information provided. Such warranties shall not be negated or limited because the art dealer in the written instrument did not use formal words such as "warrant" or "guarantee" or because the art dealer did not have a specific intention or authorization to make a warranty or because any required statement is, or purports to be, or is capable of being merely the seller's opinion. The existence of a basis in fact for information warranted by virtue of this subdivision shall not be a defense in an action to enforce such warranty. However, with respect to photographs and sculptures produced prior to 1950, and other multiples produced prior to 1900, as to information required by paragraphs (3), (4), (5), and (6) of subdivision (a) of Section 1744, the art dealer shall be deemed to have satisfied this section if a reasonable basis in fact existed for the information provided. When information is not supplied as to any subdivision or paragraph of Section 1744 because not applicable, this shall constitute the express warranty that the paragraph is not applicable.

Whenever an art dealer disclaims knowledge as to a particular item about which information is required, such disclaimer shall be ineffective unless clearly, specifically, and categorically stated as to the particular item and contained in the physical context of other language setting forth the required information as to a specific multiple.

§ 1744.9. LIABILITY; CONSIGNOR TO PURCHASE FROM CONSIGNEE; ART DEALER WHO SELLS FOR CONSIGNOR NOT ART DEALER OR ARTIST AS AGENT

(a) An artist or art dealer who consigns a multiple to an art dealer for the purpose of effecting a sale of the multiple, shall have no liability to a purchaser under this article if the consignor, as to the consignee, has complied with the provisions of this title.

(b) When an art dealer has agreed to sell a multiple on behalf of a consignor, who is not an art dealer, or an artist has not consigned a multiple to an art dealer but the art dealer has agreed to act as the agent for an artist for the purpose of supplying the information required by this title, the art dealer shall incur the liabilities of other art dealers prescribed by this title, as to a purchaser.

§ 1745. VIOLATIONS BY ART DEALER; LIABILITY; LIMITATIONS OF ACTIONS; COSTS, AND ATTORNEYS' AND EXPERT WITNESSES' FEES

(a) An art dealer, including a dealer consignee, who offers or sells a multiple in, into or from this state without providing the certificate of authenticity required in Sections 1742 and 1744 of this title for any time period, or who provides information which is mistaken, erroneous or untrue, except for harmless errors, such as typographical errors, shall be liable to the purchaser of the multiple. The art dealer's liability shall consist of the consideration paid by the purchaser for the multiple, with interest at the legal rate thereon, upon the return of the multiple in the condition in which received by the purchaser.

(b) In any case in which an art dealer, including a dealer consignee, willfully offers or sells a multiple in violation of this title, the person purchasing such multiple may recover from the art dealer, including a dealer consignee, who offers or sells such multiple an amount equal to three times the amount required under subdivision (a).

(c) No action shall be maintained to enforce any liability under this section unless brought within one year after discovery of the violation upon which it is based and in no event more than three years after the multiple was sold.

(d) In any action to enforce any provision of this title, the court may allow the prevailing purchaser the costs of the action together with reasonable attorneys' and expert witnesses' fees. In the event, however, the court determines that an action to enforce was brought in bad faith, it may allow such expenses to the seller as it deems appropriate.

(e) These remedies shall not bar or be deemed inconsistent with a claim for damages or with the exercise of additional remedies otherwise available to the purchaser.

(f) In any proceeding in which an art dealer relies upon a disclaimer of knowledge as to any relevant information set forth in Section 1744 for any time period, such disclaimer shall be effective unless the claimant is able to establish that the art dealer failed to make reasonable inquiries, according to the custom and usage of the trade, to ascertain the relevant information or that such relevant information would have been ascertained as a result of such reasonable inquiries.

§ 1745.5. INJUNCTIONS; CIVIL PENALTY; PENALTY SURCHARGE

(a) Any person performing or proposing to perform an act in violation of this title within this state may be enjoined in any court of competent jurisdiction.

(b) Actions for injunction pursuant to this title may be prosecuted by the following persons:
(1) The Attorney General.
(2) Any district attorney.
(3) Any city attorney.
(4) With the consent of the district attorney, a city prosecutor in any city or city and county having a full-time city prosecutor in the name of the people of the State of California upon their own complaint, or upon the complaint of any board, officer, person, corporation, or association.
(5) Any person acting in his or her own interests, or in the interests of the members of a corporation or association, or in the interests of the general public.

(c) Any person who violates any provision of this title may also be liable for a
     civil penalty not to exceed one thousand dollars ($1,000) for each violation,
     which may be assessed and recovered in a civil action brought in the name
     of the people of the State of California by the Attorney General or by any
     district attorney or any city attorney, and, with the consent of the district
     attorney, by a city prosecutor in any city or city and county having a full-
     time city prosecutor in any court of competent jurisdiction.

     If the action is brought by the Attorney General, one-half of the penalty col-
     lected shall be paid to the treasurer of the county in which the judgment was
     entered, and one-half to the General Fund. If brought by a district attorney,
     the penalty collected shall be paid to the treasurer of the county in which
     the judgment was entered. If brought by a city attorney or city prosecutor,
     one-half of the penalty collected shall be paid to the treasurer of the city in
     which the judgment was entered, and one-half to the treasurer of the county
     in which the judgment was entered.

(d) Any person who violates any provision of this title may also be liable for a
     civil penalty surcharge not to exceed one thousand dollars ($1,000) for each
     violation which shall be assessed and recovered in the manner provided
     in subdivision (c). Any penalty surcharge collected shall be applied to the
     costs of enforcing this title by the prosecuting officer.

TABLE OF AUTHORITIES

CASES

X

Y

Z

STATUTES

Statutes by Name

Public Laws

State Codes

REGULATIONS, RULES, UNIFORM ACTS, RESTATEMENTS

Restatements

TAX MATERIALS

Treasury Regulations

Private Letter Rulings

Revenue Rulings

Revenue Procedures

INDEX

A

AAA *See* Appraisers Association of America, Inc. (AAA)

AAM *See* American Association of Museums (AAM)

AAMD *See* Association of Art Museum Directors (AAMD)

Abrams v. Sotheby Parke Bernet Inc., 312–313

Abstractions test for copyright infringement, 995

Accelerated cost recovery system (ACRS), 1199–1200

Access as element of infringement of copyright test, 1030

Accounting
    artist's right of, 32–33
    merchandising rights, artists', 1451

Accrual, replevin versus conversion, 275–276

ACPA *See* Anticybersquating Consumer Protection Act (ACPA)

ACRS *See* Accelerated cost recovery system (ACRS)

Actionable fraud, 531

ADAA *See* Art Dealers Association of America (ADAA)

Advertising, art as social commentary in, 816

Aesthetic appeal test for copyright infringement, 996–997

Agency, law of
    application of, 5
    entrustment, distinguished from, 125–127

Africa, black market for cultural property in, 608

Agreement for Exchange of Property, 1208

Agreement of sale
    Sale Outside the United States (Cash Escrow) Undisclosed Seller, sample, 672

    samples
        collector-to-collector, 215–219
        dealer-to-collector, 206–210
        with conditions, 239–244

ALR *See* Art Loss Register (ALR)

Alternative minimum tax (AMT), charitable transfers, 1275–1276

American Association of Museums (AAM), 747

American flag
    art, exhibition as, 839–840
    burning of, 833
    flag-desecration statutes *See* Flag-desecration statutes
    Flag Protection Act, 836–837
    nonexpressive conduct and, 837–839

American Indian Religious Freedom Act of 1978, 1485

American Society of Appraisers (ASA), 491

Amsterdam v. Goldreyer, 532–533

AMT *See* Alternative minimum tax (AMT)

Ancient forgeries, 282–283

Andersson, Lennart, 115–116

Annuity trusts, charitable transfers, 1426

Anonymous works, copyright protection for, 947

Anticybersquatting Consumer Protection Act (ACPA), 1591

Antitrust claims, authentication of, 152–153

Antitrust liability, 550–554

Applied art, 1101–1102

Appraisal contracts
    exculpatory language
        limitations of, 559–562
        use of, 558–559
    issues covered by, checklist of, 556–558
    purpose of, 536–538
    sample, 597

O

Q

R

T

X

Z